D1208666

PSYCHOBIOLOGY AND HUMAN DISEASE

PSYCHOBIOLOGY AND HUMAN DISEASE

Herbert Weiner, M.D.
Montefiore Hospital and Medical Center

ELSEVIER

NEW YORK OXFORD AMSTERDAM

ELSEVIER NORTH-HOLLAND, INC.
52 Vanderbilt Avenue, New York, New York 10017

ELSEVIER SCIENTIFIC PUBLISHING COMPANY
335 Jan Van Galenstraat, P.O. Box 211
Amsterdam, The Netherlands

Some sections of chapter 7 are modified and abridged from H.
Weiner and S. Hart, chap. 37, vol. 6 in *American Handbook of
Psychiatry*, edited by S. Arieti. Copyright 1975 by Basic Books; and
H. Weiner, *Psychosomatic Medicine*, 34:355–380. Copyright 1972
by American Psychosomatic Society. Reprinted by permission.

Library of Congress Cataloging in Publication Data

Weiner, Herbert M   1921-
  Psychobiology and human disease.

  Includes bibliographical references and indexes.
  1. Medicine, Psychosomatic. I. Title.
RC49.W39   616.08   77-804
ISBN 0-444-00212-X

Manufactured in the United States of America

This book is for
Dora,
Tim, Richard and Tony

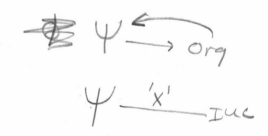

Contents

Foreword

It is an honor to be invited to write this foreword. One senses that there has been a most fortunate pairing of the right man with the timeliness of the state of knowledge in the field about which he reports. Herbert Weiner, if not uniquely, is certainly unusually well-prepared to review critically the work of the past and to present suggestions, in concept as well as in method, for the pursuit of new knowledge in those fields concerned with the relationships between mind and body.

The author's sustained and productive scholarship in neural sciences, endocrinology, psychoanalysis, and clinical psychiatry are clearly evident in his incisive and perceptive reviews. He makes clear that a primary objective of this work has been to present and integrate the data obtained by workers in many fields in order to examine the hypotheses derived from clinical observation, and to assess this information in relation to recent discoveries in the physiology and pathophysiology of the disease conditions he has chosen to report.

Most appropriately, he points out the vagueness of the adjectival use of the word "psychosomatic" and draws attention to its broader connotative meaning, namely, in the maintenance of health, as well as in the predisposition, inception, and maintenance of many diseases. With others, he applauds the coming of age of modern psychiatry in holding that behavior is not exclusively derived from psychological conflict, but that it emerges from a web of complex interactions between genetic endowment and the continuous environments throughout the life cycle.

ix

The book is organized so that each of the seven psychosomatic diseases, chosen because of the amount of information available, is reviewed in depth in order to highlight clearly and separately the issues of predisposing, initiating, and sustaining factors and mechanisms. The book fulfills admirably the assignment of a scholarly, incisive, and perceptive review of the "state of the art," but it goes beyond; as the author states, "Its purpose . . . is to point to promising new areas of investigation which could help to reformulate old questions, to suggest new and alternative hypotheses, and to redress the balance in our understanding of the various roles physical and psychological factors play in the seven diseases."

Readers will learn that the book is a house of many mansions: It will inform the uninformed, generate new ideas and practices in those currently engaged in research, and serve as an excellent stimulus and model to the young in search of a career.

JOHN ROMANO, M.D.
Distinguished University Professor of Psychiatry
University of Rochester School of Medicine and Dentistry

Preface

Medicine may be the only discipline that lacks a comprehensive Theory. Theories of Art, Aesthetics, Biology, Economics, History, Philosophy, Physics, and Psychology exist. In Medicine the only existing Theory derives from Infectious Disease and is generally acknowledged to be unsatisfactory because it is linear, restrictive, and oversimplified. No linear Theory of Disease can advance reasons for paradoxes such as the following. The same virus may cause several diseases: *Treponema pallidum*, in its tertiary phase, may cause aortitis in one person, paretic neurosyphilis in another, or no disease at all in a third. In fact, a patient with asymptomatic tertiary syphilis has a disease without being ill. Conversely, a person may be ill without having a specific disease. A Theory must account for all the factors that predispose to, initiate, or sustain a disease. It should explain the rise or fall in incidence and prevalence over time; the reasons why some diseases occur more frequently in one Society, Culture or group while others do not appear to be culture-bound; the reasons that render some diseases age-dependent and others prevalent in one sex. A Theory of Disease should account for the variable natural history and expression of most diseases. It must also incorporate a Theory of Health and the factors that sustain it.

   Two major impediments stand in the way of the development of a comprehensive Theory of Disease: one conceptual, the other methodological. The conceptual problem may stem from the traditional belief that all disease is a disease of cells as cited by de Duve (*Science* (1975), 189:186), or from the view stated by Dubos that only organisms have diseases (*Man Adapting*, 1965). The methodological problem is due to the fact that we traditionally study diseases after their onset: at that time, predisposing factors tend to be confounded not only with those that initiate the disease but also with those brought into play to adapt to the pathogenetic process itself. For example, arteriolar damage or adrenal cortical hyperplasia (aldosterinoma) may antecede or result from high blood pressure; antibody formation designed to protect the body against antigens may at times culminate in anaphylactic shock and death. Therefore, the first step to be taken in the development of a Theory of Disease is an empirical and methodological one. Persons must be studied before disease onset in order to determine the factors responsible for the maintenance of health and those that are responsible for disease.

Disease is a failure of Adaptation: it is a biological phenomenon. Because it is a biological phenomenon it deals with organisms in interaction with their natural, social, and cultural environments. Disease is not only a matter of a disturbance of the self-regulatory mechanisms within cells, or of any *one* simple factor such as infection, nutritional deprivation, or the psychology of the diseased person.

Most medical explanations of disease are functional in nature. They tell us about the relationship of a low cardiac output to pulmonary edema, but they do not tell us why at a particular point in time the heart failed. In other words, most explanations of the symptoms and signs of a disease (and the functional disturbances that they express) do not explain its antecedents. The disadvantage of an antecedent or historical explanation is that it is descriptive and not predictive: for example, a variety of animal or plant species can, in part, be explained by a genetic mutation, but this theory does not predict when a new mutation will occur. A complete Theory of Disease would allow us to predict who is at risk for a particular disease and when and in what circumstances the predisposed person may develop it. A complete Theory of Disease would need to be functional, historical, and predictive.

The only branch of Medicine that attempts to have a comprehensive view of Disease—in that it tries to provide both functional and historical explanations of Disease—is, awkwardly, named Psychosomatic Medicine. Because Psychosomatic Medicine does not lay claim to any one disease or group of diseases (or to diseases of an organ such as the Brain, or of a system such as the Circulation), it is accorded little status in organized Medicine. Its concerns have always been more with predisposition to and with the initiation of disease than with pathophysiology. Pioneer studies prior to the onset of disease have been carried out under its aegis. These and other studies lead to the belief that social, cultural, psychological, as well as genetic, physiological, biochemical and immunological factors should be accorded roles in the predisposition and inception of disease by those who use the psychosomatic approach. The unstated (and possibly immodest) goal of this approach is the development of a comprehensive Theory of Health and Disease.

The psychosomatic approach is predicated on the axiom that persons (not only cells or organs) have diseases and that diseases occur in persons. If one subscribes to this axiom, one needs to study persons, and the human, social, and cultural environments that they inhabit. The particular aspect of the person and his environment chosen for study will determine the data obtained and their conceptualization: we therefore work with a variety of observations about diseased persons.

This book attempts to review these observations and the multiple predispositions to disease. Persons are not only predisposed to disease by virtue of their genetic endowment, or their physiological experiences in the womb and during birth. Diseases are also a product of the culture, education, nutrition and childhood experiences of organisms. Their physiological and psychological development and maturation may be arrested. They may be exposed to viruses, fast and slow. They may be genetically programmed to have more or less of an enzyme or harbor an enzyme whose structure is altered. They may be predisposed, or exposed to an antigen, so as to develop an immunoglobulin.

All these factors may predispose to disease and determine the "choice" of a particular disease by one person and not another. This book will state that the "choice" is multiple and not singular. Even if a disease is "chosen", no person falls ill until he also encounters circumstances that produce adaptive failure. Such circumstances are multifarious: bereaved persons or those on whom life rings many changes may fall ill; persons who live in societies that change rapidly or those whose occupations make stringent demands may suffer disease. Infection, toxins, drugs, surgery, physical injury or mental conflict have their casualties and these are expressed in many forms of disease.

How these various factors incite disease—the nature of the pathogenetic mechanism—remains unknown, with very few exceptions. The factors that predispose to disease are not only or necessarily the same that initiate it. In a similar vein, those that initiate may or may not be those that sustain a disease.

New questions are raised in the course of this book. We know little about the ontogenesis of many of the predisposing factors because our knowledge of developmental biology is still primitive. The burden of the psychological factors in predisposition and initiation has so far fallen on life experiences, but this generalization may not be universally correct. We need to account for the fact that only some predisposed persons fall ill; others seemingly have a greater adaptive capacity and therefore remain in good health. Events and experiences have an impact on the minds of persons. Some adapt to the experiences, others do not. If they do not and disease ensues, we may ask how the received experience is translated into physiological changes and bodily events: How does psychological distress that may signal adaptive failure become transmuted into disease? We may begin by asking what role the brain, as the organ of mind, plays in the inception of disease.

This book deals with but seven diseases—albeit some are common ones. They were chosen for review not in an attempt to perpetuate the myth that these are the only "psychosomatic" diseases for it may well be that psychological and social factors in combination with genetic, viral, immunological, physiological, and biochemical factors predispose, in some degree, to all disease. These particular diseases were chosen because they are the ones that have been most extensively studied by psychosocial techniques and therefore, more data exists to evaluate the concept that persons have diseases. This review of the extant literature will hopefully aid in the elaboration of a Theory of Health and Disease.

December, 1976   HERBERT WEINER, MD

Acknowledgments

The Center for Advanced Study in the Behavioral Sciences is set on a hillside above Stanford University and San Francisco Bay. It is surrounded by open fields where cattle graze. This combination of a pastoral and littoral setting with a great university provides an ideal location for thought, for the peaceful contemplation of beauty, and for leisure. Through the kindness and the thoughtfulness of its director, O. Meredith Wilson; the associate director, Preston C. Cutler; their assistant, Jane Kielsmeier; and a most gracious staff, the fellows are allowed complete freedom to pursue their scholarly interests, to write, and to engage in discourse with each other. I am indebted to the administration and staff of the Center for their generativity and generosity—were it not for them, this book would not have been written.

Although it is hard to single out anyone from the year spent at the Center, I am particularly grateful to my friends Professor Steven Marcus of Columbia University, Professor Alexander Mitscherlich of the University of Frankfurt, Professor Fritz Redlich of Yale University, Professor Israel Scheffler of Harvard University, and Professor Joseph Weizenbaum of the Massachusetts Institute of Technology.

Formally and informally, I have had the opportunity to discuss some of the content of this book with them; in these discussions, they have steered me away from the shoals where the book may yet founder. By their own extraordinary expertise in fields as diverse as comparative literature and the computer sciences and by their remarkable tolerance of the practical and theoretical problems of other fields, they have once again reaffirmed to me the preeminent importance of concepts and ideas for any field; biomedical scientists, particularly in the United States, often display a preference—perhaps justifiable—for empirical data rather than ideas and concepts. My interest in and knowledge about the brain I owe to my friend and colleague, Dr. Vahé E. Amassian. I owe a deep debt of gratitude to my friend, colleague, and collaborator, Dr. Myron A. Hofer, with whom I have regularly discussed the problems in this field. I am much indebted to my former students—now colleagues and collaborators—Drs. Sigurd Ackerman, Sidney Hart, Jack L. Katz, and Joel Yager for the stimulation of our discussions in recent years.

Financial support during the fellowship year was provided by the Center, by a fellowship from the John Simon Guggenheim Memorial Foundation, an award from the Commonwealth Fund, and by Montefiore Hospital and Medical Center, New York. To their respective presidents and directors, Mr. O. Meredith Wilson, Dr. Gordon Ray, Mr. Quigg Newton, and Dr. Martin Cherkasky, I am deeply grateful.

My debt to my wife, Professor Dora B. Weiner, and my three sons, cannot be measured or estimated. By their understanding, kindness, and love they have provided me with the necessary time and support which this endeavor has required.

I cannot end my acknowledgment without mention of my secretaries, Mesdames Jean Clyde and Nancy Donovan, who over the years have typed and retyped the several drafts of the chapters of this book. The help of my editors, Mr. Michael Connolly and Ms. Margaret Quinlin, is gratefully acknowledged.

HERBERT WEINER, M.D.

Introduction

This book was written with several principal purposes in mind. No in-depth survey of psychosomatic medicine has been made for over 20 years since the works of Alexander (1950) and Weiss and English (1957) were published. During this period, remarkable advances in the biomedical sciences—both empirical and conceptual—have been made. For example, the role of immune mechanisms in bronchial asthma, ulcerative colitis, Graves' disease, and rheumatoid arthritis has been partly clarified. The development of techniques for the estimation of steroid hormones in blood serum and plasma, and of radioimmunoassay for the estimation of pituitary tropic or gastric hormones, has allowed investigators to test certain hypotheses about the pathophysiology and pathogenesis of the diseases that are discussed in this book.

A primary objective in the preparation of this volume has been to present and integrate recent data obtained by epidemiologists, sociologists, psychologists, psychiatrists, psychoanalysts, neurobiologists, and physiologists. In part, this material has been used to examine hypotheses that, in the past, have been central to psychosomatic medicine. Advances in the methodology of research in the behavioral sciences have made it possible not only to test hypotheses derived from clinical observation but also, in combination with physiological or biochemical criterion variables, to carry out predictive studies. The main purposes of this book are to review in depth the accumulation of data and the development of new concepts in the field of psychosomatic medicine, and to assess this information in relation to recent discoveries in the physiology and pathophysiology of the seven disease

1

conditions on which most of the study of psychosocial factors has been concentrated: duodenal ulcer, essential hypertension, bronchial asthma, Graves' disease, rheumatoid arthritis, ulcerative colitis, and regional enteritis.

It is hoped that by reviewing the recent data derived from the use of different techniques, new ways of integrating relevant information from several levels of organization might be discovered and new questions raised.

WHAT THE PSYCHOSOMATIC APPROACH IS

The term "psychosomatic medicine" has itself been a source of much uneasiness over the years. It neither refers to any special techniques or body of knowledge nor does it lay exclusive claim to the investigation of any particular group of diseases. The diseases that have been studied by psychological techniques have little in common with each other, either in terms of the disturbance in function or the anatomical site of the main lesion or symptom; the mechanisms involved in the production of these diseases are also different.

The thrust of psychological investigation has been characterized by the belief that a true biology of health and disease must take into account the fact that human beings are not comprised simply of self-contained organs carrying out specialized metabolic processes in isolation, uninfluenced by external events. Human beings are sentient organisms who, when awake, are usually in continuous interaction with their human and nonhuman environment and are capable of responding to it, modifying it, or choosing to do neither. Events, and changes in the environment acquire meaning for human minds and may have a continuous impact on the mind that is capable of storing experience. In the course of everyday events, human beings—when preparing for or engaging in any activity—respond psychophysiologically; that is, they change from a mental and physiological steady state to one of alertness, attention, and concentration, with accompanying autonomically and hormonally mediated responses.

Human beings also respond in an organismic manner to threat, to danger, or to bereavement. They attach themselves to others, and they help or harm others. They create new environments to which they must adapt. They are capable of self-awareness and self-consciousness—states that are modified rhythmically during every 24-hour period, during sleep and wakefulness. Each of these activities has its behavioral and physiological concomitants; there are responses to changes in state, for instance, when bonds of attachment are broken. The range of the adaptive activities of human beings is very large, yet each activity has its individual past history that has itself been influenced by genetic and experiential factors.

Man does not grow up *pari passu,* but in continuous interaction with his caretakers, siblings, peers, social group, geography, and culture, all of which elicit or impair the development of his individual potentialities. At the same time, every mediating and organ system of his body has its own maturational and developmental sequence, which has been structured by genetic, nutritional, and experiential factors.

It is an historical fact that most of medicine, developing as it has through the study of the structure of diseased organs, and later by a study of altered function and mechanism in disease, has concerned itself largely with those changes in structure and function that occur *after* the onset of disease. Except in the case of hereditary diseases, and of infectious and

2

deficiency diseases, our knowledge of the predisposition to, or initiation of, disease has been obscured by this concentration of investigative effort on the mechanisms of disease *after* it has been established. Even in the case of infectious disease, physicians generally do not ask why a person became ill at a particular time, or why a particular virus or bacterium is the source of challenge. We also know rather little about the natural history of disease and the factors that sustain or cause it to remit.

The psychosomatic approach, then, is predicated on the hypothesis, based on observation, that social and psychological factors play a role in the predisposition, inception, and maintenance of many diseases. It concerns itself with how human beings adapt to changing historical, political, sociocultural, interpersonal, and intrapersonal conditions and forces. It explores, through sociological and psychological tools, the means by which adaptation succeeds or fails and the personal-historical reasons for failures to adapt. It asks, for example, why specific social, cultural, and interpersonal conditions and changes may be perceived as stressful by some persons and not by others—and at a specific point of time in their lives. It explores the antecedent conditions that have produced individual variations in perception at different stages of development. It asks why some people are threatened by experiences and how they deal with these threats, and whether or not they are able psychologically to assimilate them. We explore in man, and test in animals, the nature of the concomitant physiological changes in the body and brain during periods of successful and unsuccessful adaptation. These issues almost immediately raise further questions: How are such changes mediated? And how can the brain translate the perceived threat, expressed in verbal-symbolic terms, into physiological change.

More specific and traditional questions about disease will be explored in this book. Granting that social and psychological factors may play a variable role in the predisposition to and initiation of a disease, psychosomatic medicine has in the past raised the question of the "choice" of a specific disease—why a person is predisposed to and develops one disease and not another. Furthermore, it asks why a predisposed person develops the disease at one particular time in his life and not at another time. These would seem to be legitimate and interesting questions, as indeed is the obverse question: why does another predisposed person not develop the disease, and what are the factors that sustain his health?

This book will emphasize the role of separation or bereavement as an important event in human affairs as a prototype of a social situation that may be correlated both with behavioral and physiological changes and with the onset of disease. Separation may have its most-profound effects on young children and on elderly people. As far as we know, the effects of bereavement transcend social class. Social isolation as a form of separation may be an important variable in the pathogenesis of schizophrenia. Members of the lowest socioeconomic class in cities are most exposed to such isolation; however, only in very large cities is socioeconomic role the critical variable in the pathogenesis of schizophrenia.

Separation may occur when children grow up and move away, or through divorce, or the death of a child, spouse, or parent. It may be caused by political unrest, social disruption, or war. In these situations, separation becomes the intervening variable between the individual and the particular historical era in which he lives. Converse situations—political and economic stability and a stable social structure—may be particularly conducive to the prevention of disease. An interesting study, done over a period of 12 years, demonstrated that in Roseto, Pennsylvania, the death rate from myocardial infarction was less than

3

one-half that in neighboring communities or in the United States as a whole. Obesity, smoking, and other risk factors for myocardial infarction were all present in the population. The relatives of the inhabitants of Roseto who lived elsewhere had as high an incidence of infarction as the rest of the population of the United States. The only variable that could account for the discrepancy in incidence was that Roseto had an unusually cohesive social structure, with no poverty or crime, with great civic pride, and with a tradition of mutual help for neighbors in need. The family structure was patriarchal, and the elderly in the community participated in its affairs.

Studies such as this suggest that the social structure of a community does play a role in averting certain types of disease having strong sociopsychological components. However, one may not casually conclude that a lack of structure can induce disease. For example, even under the most dire sociopsychological stress, such as in the German concentration camps, the incidence of peptic ulcer and bronchial asthma was low (Groen, 1971).

Actual or threatened oppression and discrimination may, however, play an additional and marked role in disease. The incidence of hypertension, and particularly its malignant phase, is much higher in American blacks than it is in whites or in African blacks. Factors other than social ones may play a role in the etiology of essential hypertension. Whereas this form of hypertension is unknown in New Guinea, it is a major cause of death in Japan. Relationships between elevated blood pressure and the dietary content of salt have been sought in order to explain these observations, indicating an interaction of diet, culture, and disease.

Socioeconomic factors may play a role in the pathogenesis of disease; overcrowding, economic hardship, job loss, and poor housing conditions may expose urban dwellers to danger, lead poisoning, insect bites, and rat-borne diseases. The life in the city may prove stressful to those from rural areas, or the reverse may obtain. For some people, success, marriage, or parenthood may prove a hardship and may precipitate disease. An important variable is the rapidity with which political, social, or economic change occurs, even if this change appears to be personally salubrious or desirable. In our particular historical period, there has been a "crisis in leadership" in academic, industrial, and political roles that were previously much sought-after, and which have become increasingly troubled and harassing for their incumbents.

In addition to the objectively stressful aspects of social change or assumption of roles, each individual perceives and reacts to these in his own manner: some adapt constructively to the perception of an event, and some do not. Disease is an adaptive failure, we believe, and no one factor—be it social, political, nutritional, or infectious—is the exclusive cause of a disease itself. Furthermore, the factors themselves may interact with each other to make the adaptive task more difficult.

Most physicians disagree with this view—that disease is a failure to adapt to situations and experiences that are actually adverse or are perceived as adverse and thus constitute a threat. They believe that disease is the *direct* result of these factors themselves.

While no answer will be provided, this book will probe the manner in which earlier hypotheses have been constructed to explain the relationship of a perceived event to subsequent physiological changes, which may or may not lead to disease.

Also implicit in the psychosomatic approach is the belief that although each bodily organ regulates its own function and activities, it is itself controlled and influenced by autonomic neural input, antigens, antibodies, hormones, diet, and blood supply. The viability of some organs and systems is largely dependent on neural input; without it, striated muscle vanishes. The output of the autonomic and volitional nervous system, and of all hormones, is ultimately controlled by the brain. The brain, we believe, is also the seat of all adaptive action and the storehouse of experience and self-awareness. It occupies, therefore, a central position in the mediation of behavior and bodily processes.

Psychosomatic medicine has been characterized by a particular approach to patients and to the problems of illness and disease. This approach is formed by the implicit belief that all physiological processes in the body are ultimately regulated by the brain. Much evidence has accrued to substantiate the belief that the regulatory function of the brain is mediated by the autonomic nervous system, the hypothalamic-pituitary axis, and the neuromuscular (voluntary nervous) system. However, the central nervous system also receives information from the interior of the body; through autonomic afferent inflow and through changing levels of hormones and multifarious other chemical substances, such as glucose, oxygen, and amino acids. Another major source of input is the sensory receptors that are responsive to external stimuli. Not only do the receptors respond selectively to stimuli, but so does the brain. How input and information from all of these sources are integrated in the brain, and how they acquire "meaning," remains one of the great concerns of biology. It is the task of psychosomatic medicine not only to take into complete account all of these processes, but also to understand how these processes are successfully integrated, or disrupted, to produce disease.

Some readers may be somewhat surprised to find so much emphasis placed on the role of the brain. Other readers may note that one major regulatory system has so far not been included in our comments: the immune system. It is, in fact, extraordinarily interesting to postulate that the brain may, in some way, influence either antibody production or antigen-antibody reactions and their consequences. There is some evidence that anaphylaxis may be modified by brain lesions, and results of stress studies have shown that the thymus and lymph nodes of stressed rats are diminished in size.

A major subject of speculation—and, occasionally, of disbelief—is the manner by which the nervous system might influence the complex chemical machinery of the cell. In fact, one of the recurrent criticisms of the psychosomatic approach is that it has failed to provide answers in depth and detail as to how an experience—of bereavement, for example—is "translated" into structural and functional changes in cells. In more general terms, this criticism means that psychosomatic medicine has thus far failed to solve the problem of how an experience is translated into bodily processes. It is also difficult to convince some biomedical scientists that a neurotransmitter substance does more than help the nerve impulse to bridge synaptic gaps—that these transmitter substances also induce intracellular enzymes transsynaptically. Yet it is known that intracellular enzymes may be induced by this means. Intracellular enzymes may be synthesized in response to epinephrine and isoproterenol, which may act directly or indirectly by influencing the intracellular concentration of cyclic adenosine monophosphate (AMP), or, perhaps, the relative concentrations and interactions of cyclic AMP and cyclic guanosine monophosphate (GMP). Concentrations of cyclic GMP in the cell may be increased by the action of acetylcholine, histamine, serotonin, calcium, oxytocin, insulin, or increased activity in cholinergic nerves. Epinephrine, glucagon, the long-acting thyroid stimulator (LATS), and isoproterenol can increase the concentration of intracellular cyclic AMP.

Furthermore, it has now been shown that cyclic AMP can diminish, and cyclic GMP increase, the release of chemical substances by mast cells, which are involved in the immediate form of hypersensitivity reactions (such as anaphylaxis). Clearly, then, links between the nervous system and intracellular mechanisms have been forged.

A BRIEF HISTORY OF PSYCHOSOMATIC MEDICINE IN RECENT TIMES

In the past, the psychosomatic approach to disease addressed itself to a number of questions that are not as yet completely resolved. In this introductory section, these questions will simply be posed and enumerated, while the partial answers now available will be reviewed throughout the remainder of the book.

A primary question, of course, is whether there is any reliable and consistent correlation between specific diseases and particular kinds of personalities (defined in terms of their traits, attitudes, habits, and behaviors). This question was answered in the affirmative by Dunbar (1943) and her co-workers. More recently, Friedman and Rosenman (1959) have also used this framework to describe the personality type at risk for coronary artery disease. Such an individual, they contend, has a high time-urgency, is impatient and irritable, and has an inner sense of being under pressure. This person may also be characterized by certain physiological features (Olewine et al., 1972) such as a higher blood platelet count in whole blood, a lessened decrease in intensity of platelet aggregation to norepinephrine during exercise, an altered lipoprotein pattern (consisting of an elevated β- to α-lipoprotein ratio), and elevated mean serum cholesterol and triglyceride levels. Underlying this attempt at correlation between personality characteristics and disease is the assumption that certain persons are predisposed to a disease by virtue of aspects both of their personality and physiology. However, the postulated associations do not tell us how these features might be related. Do they have a common genetic or experiential root? Do the personality characteristics antecede or follow the physiological changes, or are they independent of each other? In other words, we do not know what "direction" these correlations take, or how they came about. Dunbar's approach to the role of psychological factors in disease did not address itself either to questions about the initiation of a disease or to questions about the mechanisms set into operation at the start of the disease or those that maintained the disease. Thus, the question of when or why a hard-driving (and inwardly driven) executive would develop his attack of angina pectoris or myocardial infarction remains unanswered by this approach.

A number of psychiatrists have found what they believe to be psychological characteristics that are associated with all seven diseases. Ruesch (1948), for example, observed that most patients displayed behavioral and psychological features that were "infantile"—that is, inappropriate to their age. These features included arrested and impaired social learning; a reliance on imitation; a tendency to express themselves in direct physical action or through bodily channels; dependency and passivity; child-like ways of thinking; rigid and self-punishing moral standards and ideals; high and unrealistic aspirations; difficulties in assimilating and integrating life experiences; a reliance on securing love and affection; and

6

an inability to master changes in their lives or to learn new techniques for overcoming frustrations.

Other workers—Deutsch (1953), Grinker (1953), and Schur (1953)—have also been impressed by common features in the personality organization of adult patients suffering from psychosomatic diseases: the persistence of unconscious conflicts appropriate to early periods of maturation and development (in psychoanalytic terms—oral and anal conflicts, and conflicts about aggressive-destructive motives), and by the arrested development or the poor integration of functions involved in adaptation (in psychoanalytic terms—ego functions). These investigators have hypothesized that such persons are poorly equipped to cope with and master life stresses, changes, and crises. They believed, in addition, that the patients they studied were prone to extreme emotional responses of fear, anxiety, and panic, and their physiological concomitants—responses which are, at least in theory, more often seen in children. They concluded that the pathophysiology manifested in their adult patients with this group of diseases resembled the psychophysiology of childhood. They inferred that genetic endowment and early experience had produced arrests in physiological development, which were reinforced by disturbances in the mother-child relationship. In focusing on physiological concomitants, Margolin (1953) and Szasz (1952) have emphasized the arrest at, or return to, earlier forms of physiological functioning in these diseases. All of these hypotheses, however, are massive generalizations and, in view of our ignorance of the maturation of physiological functioning, extremely difficult to test and validate. There is currently no proof either that the same psychophysiological mechanisms are invariant in a disease, or that autonomic mechanisms present in childhood or infancy can be reactivated in adulthood. Neither is there evidence that the regulation of physiological function returns to patterns more appropriate to a prior age of the organism, as Schur and Szasz have proposed.

This group of earlier inferences and hypotheses is mainly concerned with the origin and nature of predispositions to, and the integrated psychobiology of, disease onset. They have been valuable in drawing attention to the possibility of common psychophysiological features in the seven diseases, particularly of a relative adaptive incapacity—an observation that had not been made by Alexander. However, on the basis of other information, alternative hypotheses may be constructed. There is evidence that there is a maturational sequence for certain bodily mechanisms—the regulation of heart rate, for example, and probably for many other functions. It may be that at any given age the maturational sequence of the regulation of hormone release, or of autonomic function, may lag behind other maturational sequences; or that a particular behavior may be subserved by specific neural circuits at one age, and another set of circuits at a later age.

Much of the research during the past 40 years has, in one form or another, been concerned with these central questions about the predisposing factors involved in the initiation and maintenance of disease and of the physiological mechanisms that are set into motion at the time of initiation. The most comprehensive attempt to provide answers is still that of Alexander (1950) and his group of co-workers. It is unfortunate that other contributions of Alexander have been discounted on the basis of his "specificity theory" alone, and that so much effort has been invested in proving or disproving this one aspect of his work. Too often, those engaged in the controversy over the specificity issue lose sight of the fact that Alexander had clearly stated that the specific conflicts he had identified were

7

but one element in an overall predisposition to a disease. He had, in fact, speculated with respect to Graves' disease about the relationship between psychological and physiological predispositions—how physiological predisposition might influence personality development so as to produce the conflict that he had identified in patients. Alexander's central concern was the question of the "choice" of disease—the factors that determine why a person develops one disease and not another. He can hardly be criticized for not having been able to answer this question in 1950, before the development of our detailed understanding of diseases such as sickle cell anemia and glucose-6-phosphate dehydrogenase deficiency. We have been forced to recognize the role of genic factors in disease by extraordinary advances in our knowledge of how the "information" carried by the genes is expressed—in abnormal enzyme or protein structure, in variations in the quantity of normal and abnormal enzymes or proteins in cells—and how this process is regulated. These new data have made it essential to reappraise the issue of "choice" of disease with respect to the role of genic factors. For the particular group of diseases under review in these pages then, the possible contribution of genic factors must be considered in terms of precisely how such factors are expressed, and how that expression interacts with, shapes, or modifies, experience that leads to disease, as well as the disease itself.

As a result, it would seem essential that those using the psychosomatic approach in medicine should recognize and incorporate information from genetics, virology, and immunology in their considerations of the predisposition, initiation, and maintenance of these diseases. Unfortunately, perhaps, the inclusion of these data raises a host of new and unanswered questions about the psychobiology of these disorders.

As the material in the following chapters will indicate, the choice of a disease is an enormously complex matter. Multiple and interrelated predisposing factors operate at the biochemical, immunological, physiological, psychological, and social levels of organization. These factors determine what disease or diseases a person may be predisposed to, but they do not tell us when a person may fall ill or what additional mechanisms, if any, are implicated when the disease is initiated.

It is hard to determine how much of a total predisposing variance is psychological. The psychological contribution to the variance may differ with the age of the subject, at different times within a specified age range, in different subjects and in different forms of the disease. Thus, if we could state with certainty that there are specific predisposing conflicts in one or another of these diseases, we would have to specify in which version of the disease these occur. For it now seems quite likely that each of the diseases reviewed in this book is heterogeneous: no invariant set of predisposing, initiating, and sustaining factors is present as a consistent and universal pathogenetic mechanism. This review of the seven diseases seeks to lay to rest, then, the prospect that "psychogenic" factors *alone* are responsible for the predisposition and initiation of disease. But still central to all the other major issues in the field has been our limited understanding of how the brain translates the emotional meaning of an event, or the emotional concomitants of conflict, into physiological change. Most writers speculating on this issue have assumed that this translation is linear and direct, that an emotional response antecedes and "causes" physiological change. Those who have been more cautious have referred to the "covariance" of emotion and physiological change; covariances that occur in time and are, so to speak, the two sides of the coin—depending on which methods are used to study them. There are, however, several other ways of conceiving the correlation between emotion and physiological changes, and they will be explored in the final chapter of this book.

It was also Alexander's contention that a chronic unconscious emotional conflict over the wish to be fed or cared for would give rise in a linear fashion to high rates of basal secretion of hydrochloric acid by the stomach, even before the development of a duodenal ulcer. Although such high basal secretory rates occur in some patients who already have an ulcer, there is as yet no evidence that the conflict in such a patient "causes" the hypersecretion. The conflict, which may be inferred from an interview, and the hypersecretion of acid, which may be identified by the appropriate test, "covary" or "coexist" in time. The one may not "cause" the other: The unconscious conflict may "coexist" in a patient with an increased parietal cell mass in the stomach giving rise to a high basal secretory rate for hydrochloric acid.

Alexander used the same linear model to account for the initiation of a disease in the predisposed. He strongly implied that the disease-associated conflicts common to certain patients had "sensitized" these individuals to very specific kinds of life events. For example, he stated that the specific disease would ensue when an ulcerative-colitis-prone patient was engaged in a hopeless struggle to achieve, and failed, or when a person potentially at risk for rheumatoid arthritis could no longer dominate or help another. Thus, in Alexander's view, these conflicts were not only predisposing (when dormant, albeit inferable), but initiating (when they were activated). As to why the conflict would not remain dormant, and why it could not be coped with, Alexander did not speculate. The activated conflict was associated with anger, anxiety, or other affects, which were then translated via autonomic, neural, or hormonal outflow channels to bring about the anatomical changes characteristic of the disease.

Some investigators have been particularly concerned with the settings and/or onset conditions of disease. Clearly, changes in life situations—deaths, marriages, divorces births, illness in the family, social and political change, and economic success or failure —have a psychosocial impact on the individual. But, in a psychosomatic context, they must in some manner acquire special meaning or be "interpreted" in such a way as to contribute to disease onset. Some workers have emphasized the importance of the *event* itself (such as bereavement) or its specific character (perceived as threatening) that produces subsequent psychological and behavioral changes. Those who believe that an initiating event must be threatening contend that success or failure in coping with the event is the critical factor that determines whether disease will or will not ensue. Weisman (1956) studying peptic ulcer, Engel studying patients with ulcerative colitis (1954a, b, 1955, 1956, 1958, 1961), and Knapp and Nemetz (1957a, b, 1960) in their observations of bronchial asthma—all using psychoanalytic observational techniques such as Alexander had employed—concluded that there were several conflict issues in their patients. They found it difficult to determine which conflict predominated and was, therefore, specific to the individual diseases.

In his studies of the onset conditions in duodenal ulcer, Weisman (1956) specified many more settings and responses than had Alexander. On the basis of his observations, he concluded that the disease began in a setting in which there was vacillation between active-seeking and passive-yielding behaviors. He postulated that passive-receptive wishes to be loved and admired, or a fear of passivity itself, could be activated either by external events or in episodes that were self-induced. The resulting feelings of conflict, Weisman believed, could take a number of forms—only one of which was the struggle against dependent wishes that Alexander had emphasized. He was also impressed by the absence of depressive affects during periods of exacerbation of the disease.

In contrast with the concept that there are highly specific events that have particularly significant meaning for the (predisposed) person are the observations and hypotheses of Engel (1967) and his co-workers, Greene (1958) and Schmale (1958, 1967). These investigators have emphasized the nonspecific nature of the onset condition of most diseases and have identified a generalized sense of loss (actual, potential, or imaginary) or bereavement as significant factors. Such feelings of loss and bereavement, they assert, lead to a complex emotional response of hopelessness and helplessness that results in "giving up," in functional critical changes in the perception of the self and of relationships to others. In effect, an adaptive psychological failure occurs, during which the person can no longer help himself or "cope" with environmental tasks.

As later sections of this book will detail, an impressive number of physiological concomitants of separation, loss, bereavement, and adaptive failure have been identified. For the moment, however, it should be noted that Engel's and Schmale's observations stand in direct opposition to the onset conditions postulated by Alexander, although adherents of both positions have emphasized that the emotional responses to perceived events are critical intervening variables in disease onset.

The nonspecificity of life events prior to disease is also emphasized by Holmes (1967) and by Rahe (1966). In studies, both retrospective and prospective, they found that life changes (moving from one home to another, the death of others, divorce, and job changes), occurring with increased frequency, often anteceded the onset of disease. In their patients, 80 percent of all disease occurred in a two-year period subsequent to such frequent changes in life situations. There was also a correlation between the subsequent severity of disease and the number of changes and crises during that period. In the studies of Holmes and Rahe, not everyone became ill because of changes; whether or not someone became ill was influenced by age, sex, predisposition, and ways and means of coping with change. The same factors helped determine what disease a person got. Holmes and Rahe did not study the emotional responses to change, or why certain people at certain times are unable to cope with change.

In the development of psychosomatic medicine, the initial hypotheses concerning the interaction of mind and body were formulated some 30 years ago, when much of American psychiatry was of the "dynamic" variety. Building on a framework of psychoanalytic concepts, psychiatrists sought the cause of psychological disease—especially neuroses—in conflictual, unconscious motivations. This model of the pathogenesis of neurotic symptoms was extended to psychosomatic syndromes. But it is difficult to infer reliably, and certainly difficult to verify, the existence of these motivations during a brief scrutiny of research subjects. Understandably, the demonstration of their existence to other—and often skeptical—physicians, was not successful; as a result, much misunderstanding and distortion has been engendered and intensified.

But the emphasis in psychiatry has shifted noticeably with the development of a broader perspective on human behavior and psychological functioning. Man's "intrapsychic self" is no longer seen as primarily the by-product of psychological conflict. His behavior is now viewed in a broader biological context—the web of complex interactions between genetic endowment, genetic expression, and the formative environment in which his early psychological development takes place (Hartmann, 1958). Among these interactions are those primary sociocultural relationships between the growing child and his family, his peers, and the society in which he lives. The broad character and quality of the historical period in which he is raised can also be of determining influence (Erikson, 1950). As a result of the impact and the storage of these experiences, the child is "programmed" to react toward others and toward specific situations in his life in a manner similar to, or identical with, the manner first learned in his childhood. In addition, life experiences and their meanings, and the manner in which the child and parents respond to the child's motives, may sensitize the child to certain categories of life experience and impair his adaptive capacities. When the same or similar experiences recur as the child grows up, they will have highly charged or specific meanings. Childhood conflicts will continue into adulthood if, because of endowment, experience, or the age at which they occurred, they could not be effectively coped with or mastered.

Wolff (1950), in particular, who was not a psychiatrist, first brought to our attention the adaptational framework in psychosomatic research. Influenced by the then current interest in stress, he devised many ingenious experiments to test his hypotheses. One of Wolff's central concepts was that disease was a consequence of the failure to adapt to various life situations and inciting agents, but that it was not a *direct* consequence of these situations or agents themselves. Wolff believed that life situations were stressful because persons perceived them as threats to their life or emotional security. In the face of these threats, the person protected and defended himself with an *organismic* response, which could be studied by both physiological and psychological means. The body's reactions, he contended, were part of a protective response that could either be viewed as "defensive" or "offensive." The organ involved in a defensive response was the one most appropriate to the nature of the stress. These bodily responses, he asserted, were dictated by such factors as natural endowment, past experience, and the specific situations that were perceived as stressful. Both past history and present status determined the relative success or failure of a defensive response to stress and threat.

The protective physiological responses that Wolff observed were related to particular organ functions, such as ejecting and ridding the body of something or taking something in by eating. The psychological responses to stress were immediately apparent, and thus were based on a minimum of inference. The compatibility between Wolff's formulations, based on direct observation, and Alexander's specification of inferred unconscious conflicts is quite remarkable. For example, Wolff's studies showed that persons who feel threatened actually long for emotional support or care, which they repress and "cover" with insistent assertions that they are able to cope, can manage, and are strong. He noted that in this behavioral state the stomach evidences increased blood flow, motility, gastric secretion, and a friable mucous membrane; it functions as if it were readying itself for the arrival of food. Alexander (1950) commented that the "regressive desire to be loved and helped" is expressed in the form of a "wish to ingest food" that is "specifically correlated with increased gastric secretion."

Specific conscious attitudes and responses to threatening life-situations at the time of disease onset were later identified and subjected to predictive tests by Grace and Graham (1952). Although there is no precise correlation between the two descriptions of patient responses, the reported attitudes are also very similar to Alexander's formulations.

11

As would be expected, it has been necessary for investigators working in this area to address the matter of the possible mechanisms that underlie such psychosomatic correlations. In connection with the correlations postulated by Alexander and Wolff, it must be asked whether a secret wish to be supported, cared for, loved, or fed "causes" the physiological change in the stomach in the same manner as the sight of food instigates the "cephalic" phase of gastric secretion, or whether these wishes are covariants, or are independent, of those physiological events.

Alexander was particularly intent on formulating hypotheses about mechanisms that might translate the emotional responses to an activated conflict into bodily changes. He specifically postulated that at the time of inception of Graves' disease, thyroid stimulating hormone (TSH) levels were increased. He was less specific in the case of peptic duodenal ulcer, suggesting that both hormonal and autonomic channels were activated. In the case of the initiation of rheumatoid arthritis, he postulated that musculoskeletal tension was increased through activation of the voluntary nervous system. He did not offer explicit reasons for suggesting these particular channels in each disease.

Alexander also proposed that in some patients with rheumatoid arthritis, conversion mechanisms might obtain—the arthritis might have a specific symbolic meaning that is pathogenetic. This concept has been a recurrent theme in the work of Groddeck (1926), Garma (1958), and Sperling (1957), but it is a hypothesis that is extremely difficult to validate. Clearly, it can only be tested on the basis of predictive studies, since any existing lesion or painful symptom may have secondarily acquired meaning for a patient. Indeed, the patient's "interpretation" of the disease may itself play a role in its maintenance.

Recent developments in psychobiology, such as the study of a broad spectrum of hormonal responses to avoidance conditioning, have raised the whole question of the hormonal concomitants of stress to a new level of complexity. Mason (1971) relates these hormonal patterns in monkeys to their emotional responses to the experimental situation and task. He has also shown that in consequence of the emotional response, the pattern of hormonal changes may long outlast the avoidance task.

One may infer from Mason's work (1968) that there must be neural and neuroendocrine mechanisms to regulate the orderly and sequential release of hormones. When the monkeys in Mason's studies were actively engaged in avoiding shock over a 72-hour period, some hormone levels increased rapidly during and after the avoidance session, while the levels of other hormones declined, and altered levels of still other hormones lasted long after the session had been terminated. Although the monkeys showed some individual variations in production levels and response patterns, we can conclude from Mason's study that avoidance conditioning causes an organized pattern of hormonal release. But these findings do not tell us what regulates such release, or what specific aspect of the experimental situation sets the regulatory mechanisms into motion.

Mason has effectively refuted the argument that any one of the activity or stress variables in his experiments might have induced stress to any significant degree. Rather, he believes that the dominant stressful factor in the avoidance-conditioning experience was the overall emotional disturbance that the avoidance behavior evoked. In short, he contends that the monkey's emotional response to this experience itself, was, in itself, the critical intervening variable in the experimental situation and that this response, in turn, initiated the complex pattern of hormonal release.

Although Mason argues that emotion and physiologic change is correlated in some manner, he would disagree with Alexander (1950) that emotion is narrowly discharged through one output channel such as the release of TSH. Mason has not, however, specifically postulated the possible mechanisms that link emotion to the patterned release of hormones. It is not at all clear at this point how this patterned release is related to the pathogenesis of specific diseases.

Many of the disagreements and ambiguities in data and formulation indicated in this summary could be resolved through new information provided by carefully designed prospective studies. However, such investigations must utilize rather precise criteria on the basis of which persons at risk are selected. A high priority in the preparation of this book was an attempt to determine these criteria. An additional benefit in defining the criteria should, of course, be some refinement of our theoretical conceptualizations.

METHODOLOGICAL PROBLEMS IN PSYCHOSOMATIC RESEARCH

Readers acquainted with the history of psychosomatic medicine will be aware that studies in this field have often been criticized on methodological and conceptual grounds. As we have seen, the early clinical research led to the formulation of hypotheses concerning the role of intrapsychic conflict that were often difficult to test and verify because of inherent methodological inadequacies. More recently, there has been a growing awareness of these common weaknesses in research design, and the focus of research has shifted.

In the years following the elucidation of Alexander's original formulations about the role of intrapsychic conflict in the causation of psychosomatic disease, numerous attempts were made to validate his hypotheses by various techniques. The vast majority of these studies failed to verify Alexander's hypotheses, primarily because of the lack of predictor variables that would have enabled the investigators to select a relevant subject population prior to the onset of disease. Thus, the emphasis shifted at least in part to psychological variables other than intrapsychic conflict, because it was unlikely that scientifically reliable inferences could be drawn about the presence of such conflict. Subsequent research in psychosomatic medicine has focused on the role of situational variables such as bereavement or separation (Engel, 1967; Green, 1958; Schmale, 1958)—as precipitating factors in psychosomatic disease. This line of investigation has also been pursued in studies of the effects of separation on animal behavior (Harlow, 1961; Hinde and Spencer-Booth, 1971; Kaufman and Rosenblum, 1969; Mason et al., 1968); most recently, studies on the concurrent behavioral and physiological responses of animals have been undertaken (Hofer and Weiner, 1971).

The results of this extensive research have now established that behavioral, autonomic, and endocrine responses to separation or other environmental stresses in human beings may be correlated with one important category of intervening psychological variables: "coping" or "defensive" mechanisms.

Observations in man have been tested in animals—in monkeys, for example—by using avoidance conditioning. Of course, it is impossible to determine whether an experimental condition is experienced as stressful by monkeys; the monkey simply performs an operation designed to avoid a painful stimulus. Such an experimental condition is paradigmatic and analogous to the more complex human operation of "coping," or avoiding external situations that are painful or otherwise stressful.

Studies of peptic ulcer disease provide eloquent testimony of the methodological inadequacies in much of the research in psychosomatic medicine—in particular, the lack of care

13

with which subject populations have been selected. In peptic ulcer studies, experimental populations have sometimes included patients with both duodenal and gastric ulcer. Although these syndromes have many features in common, they manifest significant —even crucial—differences other than the anatomical location of the lesion. For one, duodenal ulcer is more prevalent in men (and particularly in younger men), while gastric ulcer occurs with equal frequency in both sexes. Secondly, gastric secretion is markedly increased in some, but not all, forms of duodenal ulcer, while it is characteristically normal or subnormal in gastric ulcer. Finally, psychosocial factors are believed to play a more important role in duodenal ulcer than in gastric ulcer. On the basis of these considerations, most clinicians view these syndromes as separate morbid entities that are brought about by different predisposing and initiating mechanisms (Kirsner, 1968).

A further complicating factor affecting methodology in research design is that a given "disease entity" may exhibit important differences in subtype variants of the primary syndrome. For example, it seems reasonable to assume that the mechanisms which bring about certain forms of gastroduodenal ulceration—"stress," terminal, or drug-induced ulcers—are probably different and distinctive. In the same way, it is possible that duodenal ulceration is not produced by a consistent set of etiological or pathogenetic factors. Certainly, the pathogenetic mechanisms involved in the Zollinger-Ellison syndrome (Cook and French, 1968) or in the carcinoid syndrome can be expected to differ from the more-common forms of duodenal ulceration. In fact, there is some evidence that the perforating, bleeding, and obstructing forms of duodenal ulcer are pathogenetically distinct, and that the presence of fibrosis in ulcers, as reported from southern India (Malhotra, 1967), may indicate the existence of still another variation of the disease. It is possible, then that the term "peptic duodenal ulcer" subsumes a family of disease entities, rather than a single entity with a uniform etiology and pathogenesis.

Another complexity in peptic ulcer research, associated with selection of subjects, has been the difficulty of establishing a definitive diagnosis. The presence of a duodenal ulcer can be verified by X-ray examination in only about two-thirds of all patients. Nor do the various methods of gastric analysis always assure diagnostic accuracy (Littman and Bernstein, 1962).

Thus, the investigator of peptic ulcer disease is immediately faced with two major sources of experimental error: He may not be studying a homogeneous syndrome with a uniform etiology and pathogenesis; and in epidemiologic studies, he cannot be certain that he has identified all cases of the disease in a given population.

The study of each of the seven diseases reviewed in this book entails similar problems of accurately establishing the diagnosis and of ascertaining the homogeneity of the etiology and pathogenesis of each. Because it has become increasingly clear that the diseases with which this book deals may be heterogeneous, much emphasis has been placed on describing the precise criteria that should be used to select an appropriate population for study. Even though patient selection is often difficult, it should be a minimal research requirement to stipulate the criteria used. To illustrate: Crohn's disease may affect virtually any or all parts of the gastrointestinal tract, including the colon. When the colon is involved, great care should be taken to differentiate the disease from ulcerative colitis. It would not be beneficial to progress in research to study a population of patients with "inflammatory bowel disease" of the colon if this term subsumes specific and nonspecific forms of ulcerative colitis as well as the granulomatous colitis of Crohn's disease and postinfectious colitis.

In retrospect, the results of psychosomatic research have been weakened by the lack of precision in the selection of subject population and by the problems of differential diagnosis. These and other methodological weaknesses in clinical psychosomatic research must be avoided in future studies. It should be noted at this point, however, that these methodological problems are hardly unique to psychosomatic research. They are intrinsic to all clinical studies that employ psychological tools. Psychiatry and psychoanalysis do not utilize established, verifiable experimental techniques; at best, they are observational sciences, and the human observer is a difficult instrument to "calibrate." Nevertheless, clinical psychosomatic research has been replete with generalizations formed on the basis of single case studies, interminglings of subjective inference and objective observation, interrater or test-retest reliabilities that have not been assessed, and hypotheses that have not been validated with separate subject populations. Finally, the categories or units of behavior that are under observation have typically either not been defined at all or not operationally defined, resulting in ambiguity as to their character and constituents.

But the major methodological problems that have bedeviled all forms of psychosomatic research—whether clinical interviews, psychological tests, or psychophysiological observations—have stemmed from experimenter and subject bias. In the former case, there is the not-unlikely possibility that an observer's findings will be contaminated, at least to some degree, by his prior knowledge of the nature of his subject's disease. In the other case, bias may be introduced by a subject's awareness that he has been selected for study because his disease is thought to have psychological determinants. Subjects may, therefore, select or withhold relevant historical material—either to please or frustrate the experimenter, because they fear "exposure," or, simply, unknowingly.

To ensure the accuracy of the data that he has accumulated, the experimenter must make sure that all historical material has been verified by family members or by personal records or documents. Studies of hospitalized patients pose particular problems: The fact of hospitalization may assume a psychological significance for patients that can contaminate results, or the disease itself may acquire psychological meaning for the patient in the hospital setting. Proper controls may circumvent some of these problems, but they cannot solve all of them. Only when subjects are selected and studied before the diseases develop (and prior to any hospitalization) do many of these methodological issues fade away.

Psychological findings can also be compromised by other flaws in research design. The importance of taking socioeconomic factors into account was underscored in the evolution of Alexander's original formulations regarding the personality pattern of peptic ulcer patients. And clinical studies have demonstrated the importance of integrating such factors as age, sex, intelligence, and educational background as well. Subjects and controls must be matched with respect to each of these factors, in addition to such variables as the length of the disease, the patient's age at onset, and the patient's medical history —his previous experiences with physicians and various therapeutic regimens. The possible effect of prescribed medication on the psychological functioning of the patient must also be considered.

Finally, it should be standard procedure for appropriate control or comparison groups to be used, depending on the specific research goals. What must be emphasized, above all, is the importance of validating each finding on a new subject and control population.

15

Conceptual Problems

The literature in psychosomatic medicine has been characterized by observations and experiments that focused on the historically major assumptions in the field and were not systematically designed to address and test alternative hypotheses. For example, it is customary to ascribe fixation at an early stage in personality development entirely to early experience in the mother-child relationship or within the family. But this speculation may not be correct because it leaves out the influence that phenotypic variation in the child may have on the mother-child relationship. As Mirsky (1957) has suggested, variations of serum pepsinogen levels in the infant may be expressed in behavior. Specifically, they might result in a child whose need to be fed can rarely or never be satisfied, even by the most solicitous mother. Although Mirsky's alternative hypothesis has never been tested experimentally it provides us with a different way of conceptualizing the role of early experience in predisposing to later disease. In the same vein, many of the main suppositions in psychosomatic research should be tested by designing studies that test alternative hypotheses.

Validation Studies

In view of the substantial lack of verified data, it is not surprising that those of us who subscribe, in principle, to psychosomatic concepts have found it difficult to convince medical and scientific colleagues of the validity of the assertion that psychosocial factors play a part in the etiology and pathogenesis of certain diseases.

Attempts to substantiate Alexander's original formulations concerning the role of intrapsychic conflict in psychosomatic disease have, in the main, been unsuccessful. In only two instances—peptic ulcer and "hyperthyroidism"—where predictor variables were utilized—has the fundamental methodological weaknesses of similar retrospective studies been avoided. Even so, the results obtained in these two predictive studies are not conclusive.

While Alexander's descriptions of subject populations for the two studies were accurate in general, there were important discrepancies in their specific application to his experimental samples. The clinical criteria had to be amended with respect to subjects at risk for peptic ulcer. In the second study, on hyperthyroidism, the psychological profile Alexander had drawn was not specific to subjects with Graves' disease, but could also apply to patients whose hyperthyroidism was due to a toxic adenoma of the gland. Since these two forms of hyperthyroidism are attributed to different pathogenetic mechanisms, Alexander's formulations about the relationship of intrapsychic conflict to the pathogenesis of hyperthyroidism are thrown into doubt.

Further Comments about Predisposition
in Relationship to Validating Studies

It is not an overstatement to say that an "information gap" exists between those concerned with the investigation of psychosocial factors in certain disease conditions and the biomedical scientists working on the immunology or molecular biology of these same diseases.

Recent research has produced important empirical advances and has made substantial contributions to the clarification of the role of the behavioral and hormonal factors that may be involved in psychosomatic disease. As a result of these developments, it has become increasingly apparent that clinical psychosomatic studies have not kept pace with work in related fields on the pathogenesis of those diseases with which psychosomatic research has been primarily concerned. Findings from research in physiology, for example, indicate that the pathogenetic mechanism in Graves' disease may involve a family of antibodies, and not thyrotropin (McKenzie, 1968). There is some evidence implicating viruses in the pathogenesis of some forms of rheumatoid arthritis and excessive gastrin in the pathogenesis of one form of peptic ulcer disease (Kirsner, 1968). It has also become evident that five of the seven diseases (bronchial asthma, Graves's disease, regional enteritis, rheumatoid arthritis, and ulcerative colitis) that have been most intensively studied by investigators in psychosomatic medicine are in some way influenced by immunological processes. Thus, the presence of disturbed immune mechanisms in these diseases may constitute necessary preconditions for some, though not all, forms of each disease.

Only in the regulation of the immediate type of immunological hypersensitivity that is humorally mediated is there any evidence that the brain may play a role. Evidence that the central nervous system influences or regulates cell-mediated immune responses is sparse and indirect. But the relationship of the brain to the biology of the immune systems, responses, and mechanisms is in its infancy; we know virtually nothing about how they influence each other, if at all. Can immune systems and responses be affected by life experience? What is the impact of stress on immune responses, if any? And do immune responses affect brain function and behavior?

One of the major objectives of this book is to bring some of the recent information about the immunology of these diseases to the attention of behavioral scientists working in psychosomatic studies. Many authorities will not agree that autoantibodies predispose to disease. Generally speaking, they are accorded pathogenetic status or are believed to sustain disease. It is, nevertheless, hoped that a review and clarification of the conceptual status of the rheumatoid factors in rheumatoid arthritis, of the LATS and other thyroid antibodies in Graves' disease, of anticolon antibodies in ulcerative colitis and Crohn's disease, and of reaginic antibodies (IgE) in bronchial asthma will encourage predictive studies using the risk strategy previously outlined.

Should such a research effort prove that these various antibodies are, in fact, predictors of future disease, the scientific status of psychosomatic research would be markedly enhanced. Indeed, many of the historically controversial issues would be resolved. However, establishing the value of these immunological agents as predictive factors would only answer some, certainly not all, questions; there is still much to be learned by longitudinal studies of the diseases with which we are primarily concerned.

Longitudinal Studies

It is in the nature of medical practice and investigation to study patients after the inception of disease, when the dominant symptoms and signs are the result of, and not antecedent to or correlated with, its onset.

To unravel antecedent and consequent factors after disease onset is a herculean task. Considering the number of pathogenetic variables involved in, say, rheumatoid arthritis, it is virtually an impossible task to determine the sequence in which they unfold. Certainly, flow diagrams produced by different experts to detail the multiple variables involved in the initiation and the subsequent events in that disease differ a great deal.

Our knowledge of the natural history of disease is often distorted in two basic ways: (1) we generally study only the extreme examples of a disease—as they present themselves in hospitalized patients; and (2) it is in the very nature of the organization of medical care that we do not often study disease in very great detail during periods of partial or complete remission. There is still much to be learned, not only about the mechanisms that result in remission, but about the complex of factors (including drugs) that sustain or terminate a remission. The beneficial action of a drug tells us very little about the predisposing or initiating factors in a disease; for example, the study of the action of a drug such as digitalis is of extraordinary biological interest, but its action reveals nothing about what predisposes to, or initiates, low cardiac output failure. The action of a drug such as propyl thiouracil only discloses that interfering with the rate of binding of iodine into an organic form alleviates Graves' disease in some patients. But this knowledge is tautological, because Graves' disease is, in part, a product of increased synthesis of thyroid hormones.

In the treatment of bronchial asthma, drugs such as epinephrine, aminophylline, and disodium cromoglycate have quite different actions, as is also true for the action of diuretics, reserpine, bretylium, or hexamethonium, methyldopa, hydralazine in essential hypertension. The pharmacokinetics of these different drugs may provide information about the very complex chain of mechanisms that sustain the disease. They may, for example, indicate that this chain can be interrupted at some point, but they tell us nothing about how the series of pathogenetic mechanisms was set into motion.

Although longitudinal studies in clearly defined populations of patients, using behavioral and psychological instruments and relevant measures of hormonal, autonomic, and immune variables (or combinations of these), are much to be desired, their interpretation must be viewed with caution when the subject is being medicated with drugs. Drugs may, occasionally, play an important role in producing exacerbations of a disease. For example, Weisman (1956) has noted that many patients had exacerbations of peptic ulcer when conflict racked them with rage, fear, guilt, and fears of helplessness, which in turn caused them to drink alcohol. There is an increased incidence of peptic ulcer in drinkers, as compared with nondrinkers. This type of observation, which can only be documented in long-term studies, has many implications for our understanding of pathogenesis in these diseases. As I indicate in the last chapter of this book, most investigators in the field of psychosomatic medicine have been guided by a single *pathogenetic* hypothesis. In the case of Weisman's longitudinal studies, for example, it has been assumed that the various feelings engendered by conflict have somehow been translated into unspecified autonomic and/or hormonal discharge, resulting in an exacerbation of the ulcer. But the data do not actually lend themselves to this interpretation. Rather, the conflict is associated not only with feelings, but with the drinking itself—with a specific change in behavior. Thus, it is not the "translated" feeling, but the ingestion of alcohol—with its various effects on gastric secretion, on appetite, and on the liver's capacity to metabolize gastrin—that is the mediating mechanism in some patients. What is, in fact, indicated by Weisman's and similar studies is that the onset or exacerbation of a disease may at times be associated with changes in diet. In the case of gout, it is already known that alcoholic and dietary indiscretions are factors antecedent to attacks of the condition.

Such possible new dimensions in the development of "psychobiology" cannot be meaningfully incorporated without a constant awareness of advances in other areas of research. Unfortunately, clinical biochemists and physiologists have too-often tended to ignore the findings of behavioral scientists and psychophysiologists. At the same time, they have paid little attention to the fact that many of the pathogenetic variables they have discovered may be regulated by, or under the control of, the central nervous system. I believe that it is this lack of interdisciplinary collaboration that accounts, in large measure, for our failure to resolve the empirical and conceptual problems that represent the major barrier to progress in psychosomatic medicine.

FURTHER COMMENTS ON PSYCHOSOMATIC RESEARCH

Throughout this book an attempt is made to identify the major methodological flaws in past research and, at the same time, to suggest future research strategies that may be productive. The emphasis is on a small group of diseases and several closely related disease conditions. The reason for this emphasis is simply that the bulk of the research done on social and psychological factors has been concentrated on six of the seven diseases. This emphasis on these seven diseases should not be misconstrued by the reader; they are not the only diseases to which the psychosomatic approach has been applied. But more information is available about the psychological and social factors of these diseases than others that might be considered, such as the two forms of diabetes mellitus, anorexia nervosa, gout, migraine, or neurodermatitis.

The seven diseases discussed in this book were also chosen because it may now be possible to make statements about the predisposition to them, and about the various factors that initiate and sustain them, which could not have been made 25 years ago. Heuristically, it seemed worthwhile to divide the discussion in this book according to those factors that predispose to each particular disease and those that initiate and sustain it. In the course of this book it will become evident that we know considerably more about predisposing factors of some diseases and more about the initiation and the pathogenetic mechanisms of others. It is also pointed out that due caution must be exercised in formulating general hypotheses about the predisposition to and initiation of these seven diseases. Emphasis will be placed on the probability that even when one confines oneself to patients with diseases that satisfy clearly stated criteria, such as a confirmed duodenal ulcer, the lesions may not always have been brought about by an invariant set of predisposing factors and by the same initiating mechanisms. They may have been brought about by different mechanisms or a different combination of mechanisms. In duodenal ulcer, for example, at least four primary categories of mechanisms may be involved in the initiation of the lesion: the size of the parietal cell mass of the stomach; the degree of neural stimulation (mainly mediated by the vagus nerve); the degree of blood supply and blood flow through the stomach; and the integrity of the mucosal lining of the stomach. Even this list of initiating variables may not be inclusive; there is recent evidence to suggest that sympathetic discharge may alter gastric blood flow and affect gastrin secretion. In addition, the role of other hormones—kinins and prostaglandins—has not yet been worked out for this disease. It is clear then, that many of the hypotheses about the intervening mechanisms by which psychological and social factors may affect bodily function, bringing about a duodenal ulcer, may be premature. When it is known what combination of mechanisms initiate the lesion in specific instances, testable hypotheses may be formulated about the roles of the central nervous system and of behavior in altering, directly or indirectly, the relationships between gastric secretion, gastric blood flow, and mucin production. Even when these hypotheses have been formulated, we will still be faced with the problem of how the perception of a social event, its threatening meaning, and the ways in which the individual copes with that threat can be related to the postulated brain mechanisms that initiate the lesion—if they initiate it at all.

One may well ask whether it will ever be possible to work out the central neural or peripheral mechanisms in live human beings. Ethical and technical considerations militate against our doing so. For this reason, I have, throughout this book, reviewed animal models of these diseases. As a strategy, work on animals allows one to vary genetic strains, to study the effects of experience on later behavior and bodily function, and to analyze predisposing and initiating mechanisms.

The Need for Animal Models

Animal studies have demonstrated that environmental stimuli and a wide range of experimental variables do, in fact, produce physiological or structural changes that are analogous or homologous to clinical psychosomatic disease. The postulate that social stimuli may act via the nervous system to alter bodily functions is strongly supported—if not substantiated—by such work. Through animal studies, much is now known about the behavioral, endocrine, and autonomic changes that may be brought about by conditioning techniques, restraint, or separation, and how these changes may alter target organ structure and function. On the other hand, too little is known as yet about two central matters. First, sufficient data have not yet been accumulated about the neural circuits and the neuronal and neurochemical mechanisms that mediate social stimuli and experimental constraints to produce autonomic and endocrine changes, or how these are modified by "feedback" from the interior of the body. Second, we do not know enough about the genetic, maturational, developmental, and experiential factors that, presumably, make particular molecular and cellular configurations vulnerable, thus inducing disease in one target organ rather than another.

Animal studies of these mechanisms have two distinct advantages over human studies. First, pure genetic strains of animals can be bred—strains that have a particular sensitivity (e.g., to salt ingestion, which produces hypertension, or to restraint, which produces gastric ulceration). Secondly, the early experiences of animals can be programmed to reduce or enhance their susceptibility to later experimental manipulations. Animals can also be used to illuminate three other areas of major concern: (1) predisposing factors in disease, such as genetic strain differences, and the form in which the genotype may be expressed; (2) factors that may initiate the disease, and the mechanisms that mediate these initiating factors to produce the lesion; and (3) rational treatment and/or prevention, which might result from increased knowledge of the predisposing and initiating factors —with therapeutic trials in animals directed at one or all the multiple factors involved in disease production.

Our complete understanding of these complex diseases has been impeded by an inability to understand why some of them, such as bronchial asthma, begin and have their greatest prevalence in childhood, whereas others, such as duodenal ulcer or rheumatoid arthritis, tend to have their highest incidence and prevalence in adulthood. These facts raise complex questions: Do the predisposing and initiating factors in childhood duodenal ulcer, in juvenile rheumatoid arthritis, or in bronchial asthma in the child differ from those in the adult forms of these diseases?

Carefully structured animal studies may provide us with some of the answers. For example, it is well-known that varying the time of weaning of young rats may affect the incidence of restraint-induced erosions in their stomachs. Recently, however, it was demonstrated that gastric erosions can be produced in 95 percent of rats weaned at 15 days and deprived of food at 22 days, without being immobilized by restraint. Rats weaned at 21 days and restrained at 30 days also developed erosions, but with a much lower incidence, and by contrast did not develop ulcers when only deprived of food and not restrained (Ackerman et al., 1975). The production of gastric ulcers, therefore, may depend on the time of weaning and on the age at which the animal is exposed to a specific manipulation (restraint or not feeding). These experiments raise the possibility that the gastric erosions in rats that are prematurely weaned and later not fed are brought about by one group of mechanisms, whereas in rats weaned at the usual age of 21 days, the gastric erosions, which occur only when the rats are immobilized at 30 days, are initiated by another set of mechanisms. Careful analytic experiments incorporating information about the developmental physiology of the rat's stomach might be used to substantiate or refute the speculation that different pathogenetic mechanisms bring about the same gastric erosion at different ages in rats that have been weaned prematurely versus those weaned at the usual age.

These experiments on prematurely weaned rats show that food, and therefore nutritional deprivation, may play a role in the formation of gastric erosions. Nutritional deprivation may have additional effects. Early or prior experiences may be crucial if they occur at specific ("critical") periods of maturation and development. The deprivation of a nutritional substrate may cause a failure of enzyme induction or expression, and thus affect the number, size, and function of cells, both in the body and in the brain. Similar effects may be brought about by social experience alone. Social isolation may lower levels of enzymes and substrates in the brain and body. To complicate the matter further, genetic variation may be expressed in some instances by exactly the same low levels of the same enzymes. All of this information, obtained from animals, casts light on the complexity of the factors that predispose to behavior and to disease.

Epidemiological Information

Despite the considerable body of information that suggests the role of psychological and social factors in illness and disease, these factors alone do not provide a sufficient explanation of disease. The data of medical sociology and of epidemiology have not been adequately integrated into psychosomatic studies through psychological investigations of small groups of patients. Therefore, in this book the epidemiological literature relevant to the diseases under review has been examined in an effort to seek new leads about the nature of the social events that antecede certain diseases and to either confirm or refute other data obtained through the psychological study of subjects and patients. The objective of this appraisal has been to obtain several basic classes of information: (1) does the incidence or prevalence of a disease vary in members of different socioeconomic classes; (2) in different countries and cultural settings; (3) does the incidence change with altered socioeconomic conditions—with social mobility, with migration, in periods of rapid social, political, economic, or cultural changes and events; (4) does the prevalence of a disease vary among different ethnic, majority, or minority groups, or in different subcultures—as we now know it does in the case of sickle cell, Cooley's, and hemolytic anemias. Although extensive epidemiological studies have been carried out on all the diseases reviewed in this volume, and some tantalizing leads have been obtained—especially in patients with essential hypertension and Graves' disease—there are major methodological difficulties that currently limit the utility of this important source of information. Ideally, epidemiological and sociological data, when combined with psychological investigation, should assist us in identifying and verifying the social and psychological setting in which a disease may begin, and the conditions that may alter or sustain its course. For such data to be both reliable and significant, however, populations with a particular disease must be identified on the basis of established and comparable diagnostic criteria. When universally accepted criteria are not utilized, the data obtained can only be crude approximations. In addition to the use of comparable diagnostic criteria, it is necessary to define and enumerate the population—e.g., whether the sample is drawn from hospitalized patients, from clinics, the private offices of physicians, or through health surveys. It should also be standard procedure to identify all the possible and known cases of a disease in a population, and to estimate the ratio of known and undetected cases. Even when reliable figures are obtained, their meaning is subject to different interpretation; statistics on the family aggregation of a disease may underline the role of inheritance or emphasize the social role of the family, depending on the orientation of the investigator.

Epidemiological studies could also be helpful in determining whether certain diseases are likely to occur in combination with others—for instance, peptic duodenal ulcer with rheumatoid arthritis. The cumulative significance of such findings might provide important clues about the predisposition and initiation of these diseases.

ORGANIZATION OF THE BOOK

Each of the diseases reviewed in depth is discussed in an individual chapter. Emphasis is initially placed on its prevalence and on its distribution according to geography, ethnic group, socioeconomic class, sex, age, and family. Diagnostic criteria are discussed. The genetic data are examined for each disease, along with the form in which genetic contributions, if any, are expressed. In addition to genetic contributions, other predisposing factors are explored at several levels of organization, and their origins, when known, are reviewed. Psychological predisposing factors are reviewed in the light of what is known about the prior experience of patients with these diseases, including their family experience.

Initiating factors in the disease are then sought out, and initiating mechanisms of the disease are reviewed. These are compared to what is known about animal models of the diseases. And, finally, the question of the factors that maintain or terminate the disease is explored. Throughout the book, an attempt is made to explore the reliability of the techniques and methods used and the meaning of the data.

The purpose of this organization, as mentioned, is heuristic—to highlight the need to address clearly and separately the issues of predisposing, initiating, and sustaining factors and mechanisms; the failure to do this has seriously confounded both data and concepts in psychosomatic medicine.

NEW MODELS OF PSYCHOSOMATIC RELATIONSHIPS

In the last chapter of this book, I suggest that much of the unproductive controversy concerning the presence and validity of specific psychological factors and conflicts in these diseases will not be resolved until properly designed predictive studies are done. By our definition, this would involve using clearly defined criteria to choose a population at risk, matched for sex, age, and socioeconomic status, and tested by psychological and psychiatric measures that are relevant to the hypothesis being tested.

Predictive studies are predicated on the belief that there are multiple predispositions that determine the "choice" of the disease. The final chapter of this book will discuss in detail these multiple predispositions and their origins and interrelationships. In some instances (e.g., some forms of gout), the predisposition is not only heterogeneous but can be traced back ultimately to a molecular genetic source; in other instances the ultimate origin is much less clear (e.g., of the LATS). We know today that genes may express themselves in either qualitative (structural) and/or quantitative alterations in enzymes. There is some further evidence that these alterations may express themselves, by mechanisms we do not yet understand, as variations in the behavioral reactivity of animals and/or in the perception and storage of experience in the brain.

An issue that flows directly from a discussion of the *origins* of predispositions to disease is the question of specifically what the predisposition involves in terms of *bodily function*. What mechanism is at work where a deficiency or excess of immunoglobulin formation appears to predispose to rheumatoid arthritis? Why do excessive or depressed levels of gastrin appear in different forms of peptic duodenal ulcer? Why do excesses of uric acid in the serum seem to predispose to gout? How does a tendency to bronchoconstriction specifically predispose to bronchial asthmatic attacks?

It is suggested, in the final chapter, that we may regard these factors—if they can in fact be identified as predisposing—as forms of "bias" in important physiological regulatory mechanisms. We now know that several types of regulation exist. There is self-regulation at the cell and the organ level—as in the output of the thyroid hormones, which is remarkably stable, yet clearly dependent on outside supplies of dietary iodine and amino acids for the synthesis of thyroglobulin. There is also the exquisite self-regulation of enzyme synthesis—the induction of enzymes by substrate, and the feedback inhibition of enzyme activity by the end-product of a biosynthetic sequence. But in addition to the self-regulation of cellular activity, the cell is also regulated by *external* influences—neural, hormonal, and immunological. Enzymes may be induced transsynaptically, and also by substances such as epinephrine and the polypeptide pituitary hormones, by corticosteroids and sex hormones, and by antigens and the many products of antigen-antibody reactions.

Thus, cells and the organs they constitute regulate themselves, but they are also ultimately governed by outflow channels from the brain: the autonomic nervous system, the hypothalamic-pituitary axis, and the voluntary nervous system. This superordinate regulation of function may have a dual character. The enzymatic synthesis of epinephrine from norepinephrine in the adrenal medulla is under the control of sympathetic input, mediated by acetylcholine and by ACTH. TSH regulates the synthesis and/or release of thyroid hormones, and its action on the gland is in turn regulated by the level of iodine in the gland, while its release from the pituitary is regulated by free T levels in serum and by hypothalamic thyroid releasing hormone (TRH).

Blood pressure is also maintained by a large variety of processes that involve not only blood volume, heart rate, cardiac output, blood gases, and peripheral resistance, but all the mechanisms that, in turn, regulate these functions. These mechanisms are themselves mediated by hormones from the adrenal medulla and cortex, by enzymes produced in the kidney and liver, as well as by the autonomic nervous system and the pituitary gland. These processes interact and are interrelated. Much is also known about the extraordinary complexity of the regulation of respiration and of gastric function and secretion. Gastric secretion, for example, is under the control of several hormones, including gastrin, which increases with enhanced vagal and probably sympathetic activity, and which, in turn, increases the secretion of pepsin and hydrochloric acid.

Another useful framework for conceptualizing and understanding these diseases is that their manifestations may be more likely to occur at specific times of the day or night. Asthmatic attacks, for example, tend to occur at night in some children. Mice have been shown to have a circadian susceptibility to pneumococcal infection, which is lowest at 4 A.M., when serum corticosterone levels are lowest (Shackleford and Feigin, 1973). Nocturnal attacks of peptic ulcer pain, myocardial infarction, and cardiac arrhythmias have also been documented. A circadian rhythm affecting the regulation of pituitary secretion, with a low secretory rate of ACTH during the night, has been observed (Curtis, 1972). We know today that this rhythm may be disrupted during depressive mood states or other psychological disturbances.

An assumption central to the overall viewpoint of this volume is that these variations in complex regulatory processes are examples of important "bias" in one direction or other. Such biases, we will contend, constitute the essential predispositions to a disease. Bias may take the form of the excessive or inadequate production of regulatory substances. Excessive or inadequate antibody production, which, in turn, may be traced to genetic origins, may lead to a dysfunction in the clearance or disposition of antigen-antibody complexes from the body, which may then be deposited in organs such as the kidney. Or a regulatory substance such as the LATS or its protector, the antibodies that stimulate the thyroid gland to secrete the thyroid hormones, may preempt the role of thyrotropin. In other instances, the secretion of a hormone is stimulated by smaller-than-usual amounts of a regulating substance. In still other cases, the secretion of a hormone may not be checked by the substance that would normally inhibit its secretion. Bias may occur in the self-regulation of the functioning of a cell or an organ, in systems external to the organ that regulate it, or at both levels. These few examples do not exhaust the possibilities; bias can take many forms.

In addition, I suggest that the diseases discussed may be viewed as diseases of regulation. This does not, of course, imply that the regulatory disturbances are of the same nature in each instance. It is, perhaps, an odd and significant fact that in all of medical science —including psychosomatic medicine—no major attempt has been made to conceptualize disease against a background of the highly complex but known regulatory processes that subserve any function.

24

Relationship of Predisposition to Initiation of Disease

Presumably, the specific conflicts described by Alexander had predisposing and initiating significance. He clearly indicated in his work that these conflicts sensitized persons to certain classes of life experiences. They were, so to speak, psychological "markers" for the disease.

Since that time, one has been led to believe, based on the work of many investigators, that a person's predisposition to a disease may be multiple, not just psychological. Among those who are equally predisposed, some do not fall ill, either because they are able to cope with an experience, or because they are not exposed to it. Only when a predisposed person fails to cope, and adaptive failure ensues, does disease occur. The mark of this adaptive failure may well be the helplessness-hopelessness complex described by Engel and Schmale, leading to giving up and the state of having given up. According to the clinical observations of many psychiatrists, the critical antecedents of helplessness and hopelessness is actual, threatened, or imaginary bereavement or separation to which the patients are sensitized by prior experience. Bereavement seems to be a common antecedent of our seven diseases as well as others, but it is not the only one. Other experiences have been identified that cause distress in the lives of these patients. Helplessness, hoplessness, and distress of other kinds represent the emotional state of the patients at the time the disease begins or recurs.

Thus, patients are predisposed to these diseases by prior experience that causes them to react to certain categories of life events. But they are also predisposed to a specific disease genetically, biochemically, immunologically, and physiologically. The reader must judge for himself whether the data that will be reviewed bears out this assertion; if the assertion is borne out, the much-debated question of the exclusive "psychogenicity" of these diseases can be laid to rest. Psychological factors alone would not then account for all of the predisposing and initiating variance of these diseases.

This book reviews in detail the onset conditions in the diseases, and, where observations are available, how persons cope with these conditions. It reviews the success and failure of these coping efforts and the psychological and behavioral concomitants of these coping efforts. The final chapter also reviews the many unsolved problems in the initiation of a disease. It is not clear, as yet, whether there are highly specific initiating, threatening events and experiences that correlate with onset, or if the events are more general, like loss and bereavement. Nor is it clear just how the posed threat of these events, and the emotional responses that are occasioned, are translated into a physiological event. There is some evidence, at least in some patients with a particular disease, that the threat and the responses to it are mediated by changes in behavior that are expressed by the ingestion of alcohol (as in peptic ulcer), and the overeating of meat (as in gout); the predisposing mechanisms may express themselves concomitantly by a preference for the eating of salt *and* by suppressed or repressed hostility (as in essential hypertension).

Learning how emotion is translated into physiological response by the brain would only fill in some gaps in our knowledge of the pathogenetic sequence. We still do not know exactly where the sequence begins, except, possibly, in the case of bronchial asthma. For example, in rheumatoid arthritis we do not know whether the pathogenetic process begins in the synovial or cartilage cells of joints, or in the ground substance of cartilage (Gardner,

1972). We do not know how the pathogenetic process interacts with the predisposing factors, which may be multiple and, as in the case of gout, heterogeneous.

In part, progress is impeded because we really have no idea what proximal and physiological mechanisms produce the structural and functional changes in these diseases. Thus, we cannot say why the LATS and other stimulating immunoglobulins suddenly deprive the thyroid gland of its normal regulatory control. It is not certain, though it is suspected, that the induction of a latent virus may initiate some forms of rheumatoid arthritis. Other forms of rheumatoid arthritis may be systemic diseases: are they also initiated by viruses? Because of our ignorance, in most instances, about the exact, proximal pathogenetic mechanisms of most of these diseases, we are at a loss to know how these mechanisms interact with the physiological changes that accompany the distress brought on by bereavement or other unpleasant life experiences.

Psychosomatic medicine must eventually seek to explain how psychosocial stimuli are translated into acute or chronic changes in structure and in physiological and biochemical function. In spite of all claims to the contrary, the fact is that we have not yet accumulated the empirical data nor the conceptual tools essential to understanding such phenomena. Nor have we been able to formulate a concept about the neural mechanisms by which psychosocial stimuli and the behavioral or psychological responses they evoke are translated into changes in autonomic, endocrine, neuromuscular, and possibly immune functions. Thus, what is traditionally considered to constitute the crucial question in psychosomatic medicine remains unanswered. To put it more succinctly, we simply do not understand how nonmaterial, symbolic events—such as the psychological responses to life experiences or events—are "translated" into material changes—such as the release of pituitary tropic hormones, sustained elevations of blood pressure, alterations in immune processes, autonomic neural discharge, or the induction of enzymes or viruses. There are many unknown links in the chain of events that lead from symbol to physiological change.

If, in addition, these diseases are pathogenetically heterogeneous, the role of social and psychosocial factors may vary in the different forms of each disease. Thus, psychological factors may play no role or only a minimal role in infantile Graves' disease, in which the LATS or its protector is transferred from mother to child. But they may play a role in the predisposition to and initiation of adult Graves' disease. It is also clear that a variety of stimuli to bronchoconstriction may occasion a bronchial asthmatic attack—allergens, cold air, exercise, and emotions—and, with aging, the variance may change. For example, allergic stimuli seem to play much less of a role in middle-aged persons than in the young. Finally, much remains to be learned at every level of biological organization about the highly variable course of these diseases, and about their onset or exacerbation at particular ages and at particular times of the day or night.

This book was not written to provide final answers. Rather, its purpose is to report on the "state of the art" and to point to promising new areas of investigation that could help to reformulate old questions, to suggest new and alternative hypotheses, and to redress the balance in our understanding of the various roles physiological and psychological factors play in the seven diseases.

REFERENCES

Ackerman, S. H., Hofer, M. A., and Weiner, H. 1975. Age at maternal separation and gastric erosion susceptibility in the rat. *Psychosom. Med.* 37:180.

Alexander, F. 1950. *Psychosomatic Medicine*. New York: Norton.

Brady, J. V., Porter, R. W., Conrad, D. G., and Mason, J. W. 1958. Avoidance behavior and the development of gastroduodenal ulcers. *J. Exp. Anal. of Behav.* 1:69.

Cook, H. B., and French, A. B. 1968. Physiologic responses to gastric acid hypersecretion in Zollinger-Ellison syndrome. *Am. J. Dig. Dis.* 13:191.

Curtis, G. C. 1972. Psychosomatics and chronobiology: Possible implications of neuroendocrine rhythms. *Psychosom. Med.* 34:235.

Deutsch, F. 1953. *The Psychosomatic Concept in Psychoanalysis*. New York: International Universities Press.

Dunbar, H. F. 1943. *Psychosomatic Diagnosis*. New York: Hoeber.

Engel, G. L. 1954a. Studies of ulcerative colitis: I. Clinical data bearing on the nature of the somatic processes. *Psychosom. Med.* 16:496.

―――― 1954b. Studies of ulcerative colitis: II. The nature of the somatic processes and the adequacy of psychosomatic hypotheses. *Am. J. Med.* 16:416.

―――― 1955. Studies of ulcerative colitis: III. The nature of the psychologic processes. *Am. J. Med.* 19:231.

―――― 1956. Studies of ulcerative colitis: IV. The significance of headaches. *Psychosom. Med.* 18:334.

―――― 1958. Studies of ulcerative colitis: V. Psychological aspects and their implications for treatment. *Am. J. Dig. Dis.* 3:315.

―――― 1961. Biologic and psychologic features of the ulcerative colitis patient. *Gastroenterology* 40:313.

―――― 1967. A psychological setting of somatic disease: The 'giving up—given up' complex. *Proc. R. Soc. Med.* 60:553.

Erikson, E. 1950. *Childhood and Society*. New York: Norton.

Forsyth, R. P. 1968. Blood pressure and avoidance conditioning. *Psychosom. Med.* 30:125.

―――― 1969. Blood pressure responses to long-term avoidance schedules in the restrained rhesus monkey. *Psychosom. Med.* 31:300.

Friedman, M., and Rosenman, R. H. 1959. Association of specific overt behavior pattern with blood and cardiovascular findings. *J.A.M.A.* 169:1286.

Gardner, D. L. 1972. *The Pathology of Rheumatoid Arthritis*. London: Arnold.

Garma, A. 1958. *Peptic Ulcer and Psychoanalysis*. Baltimore: Williams & Wilkins.

Grace, W. J., and Graham, D. T. 1952. Relationship of specific attitudes and emotions to certain bodily diseases. *Psychosom. Med.* 14:243.

Greene, W. A., Jr. 1958. Role of a vicarious object in the adaptation to object loss. I. Use of a vicarious object as a means of adjustment to separation from a significant person. *Psychosom. Med.* 20:344.

Grinker, R., Sr. 1953. *Psychosomatic Research*. New York: Norton.

Groddeck, G. W. 1926. The book of the it: Psychoanalytic letters to a friend. *Arch. Psa.* 1:174.

Groen, J. J. 1971. Social change and psychosomatic disease. In *Society, Stress and Disease*, Vol. I, edited by L. Levi. London: Oxford University Press.

Harlow, H. F. 1961. The Development of Affectional Patterns in Infant Monkeys. In *Determinants of Infant Behavior*, edited by B. M. Foss. London: Methuen.

Hartmann, H. 1958. *Ego Psychology and the Problem of Adaptation*. New York: International Universities Press.

Hinde, R. A., and Spencer-Booth, Y. 1971. Effects of brief separation from mother on Rhesus monkeys. *Science* 173:111.

Hofer, M. A., and Weiner, H. 1971. The development and mechanisms of cardio-respiratory responses to maternal deprivation in rat pups. *Psychosom. Med.* 33:353.

Holmes, T. H., and Rahe, R. H. 1967. The social readjustment rating scale. *J. Psychosom. Res.* 11:213.

Kaufman, I. C., and Rosenblum, L. 1969. Effects of separation from mother on the emotional behavior of infant monkeys. *Ann. N. Y. Acad. Sci.* 159:681.

Kirsner, J. B. 1968. Peptic ulcer: A review of the current literature on various clinical aspects. *Gastroenterology* 54:610.

Knapp, P. H., and Nemetz, S. J. 1957a. Personality variations in bronchial asthma. *Psychosom. Med.* 19:443.

——— and ——— 1957b. Sources of tension in bronchial asthma. *Psychosom. Med.* 19:466.

——— and ——— 1960. Acute bronchial asthma—concomitant depression with excitement and varied antecedent patterns in 406 attacks. *Psychosom. Med.* 22:1, 42.

Littman, A., and Bernstein, L. L. 1962. Clinical diagnosis in peptic ulcer and esophagitis. *Med. Clin. North Am.* 46:747.

Malhotra, S. L. 1967. Epidemiological study of peptic ulcer in the south of India. *Gut* 8:180.

Margolin, S. 1953. Genetic and dynamic psychophysiological determinants of pathophysiological processes. In *The Psychosomatic Concept in Psychoanalysis,* edited by F. Deutsch. New York: International Universities Press.

Mason, J. W. 1968. Organization of psychoendocrine mechanisms. *Psychosom. Med.* 30:565.

——— 1971. A re-evaluation of the concept of "non-specificity" in stress theory. *J. Psychiatr. Res.* 8:323.

Mason, W. A., Davenport, R. K., Jr., and Menzel, E. W., Jr. 1968. Early experiences and the social development of rhesus monkeys and chimpanzees. In *Early Experience and Behavior,* edited by G. Newton and S. Levine. Springfield: Charles C Thomas.

McKenzie, J. M. 1968. Humoral factors in the pathogenesis of Graves' disease. *Physiol. Rev.* 48:252.

Mirsky, I. A. 1957. The psychosomatic approach to the etiology of clinical disorders. *Psychosom. Med.* 19:424.

Olewine, D., Simpson, M., Jenkins, C. D., Ramsay, F., Zysanski, S., and Hanes, C. G. 1972. Catecholamines, platelet aggregation, and the coronary-prone pattern. *Psychosom. Med.* 34:473.

Rahe, R. H., McKean, J. D., and Arthur, R. J. 1966. A longitudinal study of life change and illness patterns. *J. Psychosom. Res.* 10:355.

Ruesch, J. 1948. The infantile personality: The core problem of psychosomatic medicine. *Psychosom. Med.* 10:134.

Schmale, A. H. 1958. A relationship of separation and depression to disease. *Psychosom. Med.* 20:259.

——— and Engel, G. L. 1967. The "giving up-given up" complex illustrated on film. *Arch. Gen. Psychiatry* 17:135.

Schur, M. 1953. The Ego in Anxiety. In *Drives, Affects, Behavior,* edited by R. M. Loewenstein. New York: International Universities Press.

Shackleford, P. G., and Feigin, R. D. 1973. Periodicity of susceptibility to pneumococcal infection: influence of light and adrenocortical secretions. *Science* 182:285.

Sperling, M. 1957. The psycho-analytic treatment of ulcerative colitis. *Int. J. Psychoanal.* 38:341–349.

Szasz, T. 1952. Psychoanalysis and the autonomic nervous system. *Psychoanal. Rev.* 39:115.

Weisman, A. D. 1956. A study of the psychodynamics of duodenal ulcer exacerbations with special reference to treatment and the problem of specificity. *Psychosom. Med.* 18:2.

Weiss, E., and English, O. S. 1957. *Psychosomatic Medicine.* Philadelphia: Saunders.

Wolff, H. G. 1950. Life Stress and Bodily Disease—A Formulation. In *Life Stress and Bodily Disease,* edited by H. G. Wolff, S. Wolf, Jr., and C. E. Hare. Baltimore: Williams & Wilkins.

1
PEPTIC ULCER

Despite extensive research (Menguy, 1964; Ryss and Ryss, 1968; Susser, 1967) a definitive theory of the etiology and pathogenesis of peptic ulcer disease—one that could satisfactorily explain the complex interrelationship of psychological and physiological factors—has not yet been achieved. On the other hand, we have become increasingly aware of those factors that have impeded our efforts toward this end. First, earlier investigations of the psychological parameters of peptic ulcer, and of the hypotheses derived therefrom, did not reflect current developments in our understanding of the pathological physiology of peptic ulcer disease. Second, although these developments have enabled the accumulation of important new data, our information about the physiological parameters of peptic ulcer disease is still incomplete. Finally, from the outset, our understanding of the etiology and pathogenesis of peptic ulcer disease has been hampered by the methodological problems involved in the study of this syndrome.

An attempt is made in this chapter to provide an overview of the major studies of peptic ulcer disease at the psychosomatic, psychophysiological, and physiological levels. This framework enables us to evaluate psychosomatic hypotheses concerning this disease in the light of newly acquired knowledge of its physiological aspects. Concurrently, the need for further physiological investigations to enhance our understanding of the correla-

This is the edited, updated and expanded version of a chapter, written in collaboration with Joel Yager, M.D., under the title, "Peptic Ulcer: Observations in Man." which was published originally in *Advances in Psychosomatic Medicine*, vol. 6, chap. II. Reprinted here by permission of the publisher. Copyright 1971 by S. Karger AG, Basel.

tion between psychological variables and factors is pointed up. Hopefully, then, this approach may suggest some directions for future research in both these areas. Finally, this review underscores the methodological problems that have diminished the validity of psychosomatic and psychophysiological research findings to date. Some measures are suggested to help solve these problems and thereby implement our future efforts to define more precisely the mechanisms that underly this disease.

PROBLEMS OF DEFINITION

There are specific methodological problems that are inherent in studying the predisposition to and initiation of peptic ulcer disease: the ambiguity of the terminology used in the reports of research on this syndrome further diminishes their validity. A fundamental problem is that the term "peptic ulcer" is not always defined precisely. As a general rule, peptic ulcer is considered to encompass both gastric ulcer and duodenal ulcer. Admittedly, these syndromes have many features in common, but they also present significant differences that extend beyond the anatomical location of the lesion. First, duodenal ulcer is probably more prevalent in men (and particularly in younger men); gastric ulcer occurs in older people, with equal frequency in both sexes. Second, gastric secretion of hydrochloric acid and pepsin is usually increased in the presence of duodenal ulcer, while gastric ulcer is characterized by normal, subnormal or elevated gastric secretion. Last, but not least, it is generally conceded that these syndromes differ significantly in terms of their psychological and emotional correlates, which further justifies their delineation as distinct disorders. Specifically, emotional factors are believed to play a more important role in duodenal ulcer than in gastric ulcer.

The term "peptic ulcer disease" is misleading; it is not one disease but several diseases. Each of the subforms of the disease has a different natural history, anatomical location in the esophagus, stomach, or duodenum, and morphology. In some subforms of the disease the inciting causes and their pathophysiology are known; in other forms they are not. The several forms of the disease also respond differently to medical treatments. A single ulcer may occur in the stomach or the duodenum, or several ulcers may occur in the stomach. The ulcer may be acute or chronic.

The so-called stress ulcer is an acute ulcer that most often occurs in the lower esophagus or the stomach. This ulcer is preceded by major physical trauma—head injuries, brain surgery, burns, sepsis, renal failure, and the ingestion of medications such as the corticosteroids or aspirin. Wangensteen and Golden (1973) have further classified acute gastric ulceration into four distinct forms: stress ulcer, Curling's ulcer, Cushing's ulcer, and steroid ulcer. They distinguish these forms from each other because each form has a different morphology and is elicited by different factors. The stress ulcer is a diffuse, erosive gastritis with hemorrhage that occurs after severe trauma, major surgery with complications, or during a critical medical illness. Curling's ulcers are gastric ulcers that follow extensive burns; they consist of superficial linear gastric erosions occurring first in the fundus and later in the midportion of the corpus of the stomach. Cushing's ulcers occur with central nervous system lesions or brain injury, and often perforate the stomach. The ingestion of corticosteroid medication may produce ulceration in the antrum of the stomach.

34

Chronic gastroduodenal ulcers also differ from each other. Gastric ulcers respond poorly to the usual medical regimen prescribed for duodenal ulcer—anticholinergic agents and antacids. Conversely, gastric ulcers often respond well to carbenoxolone, a triterpene drug extracted from licorice (Doll et al., 1962; Horwich and Galloway, 1965). Duodenal ulcer patients fail to respond to carbenoxolone.

Chronic peptic ulcer patients can also be differentiated by their pathophysiology. In the past, it was assumed that patients with duodenal ulcer were all hypersecretors of acid pepsin and that patients with gastric ulcer were all hyposecretors of these substances. But Johnson (1965) found that some patients with gastric ulcers secreted little hydrochloric acid and some secreted large quantities. In his series about half of the patients had a single ulcer of the lesser curvature of the stomach and were hyposecretors (type 1), another quarter of the patients had both gastric and duodenal ulcers and were hypersecretors (type 2), and the rest had prepyloric ulcers of the stomach and were hypersecretors (type 3). The meaning of these group differences in basal acid secretion remains unclear because Wormsley and Grossman (1965) also showed that some members of each of the three groups responded either with hyposecretion or with hypersecretion when stimulated with histamine.

Nonetheless, there is some genetic evidence in support of Johnson's classification. Type 2 and 3 patients, like duodenal ulcer patients (who also tend to be hypersecretors), are more likely to belong to blood group O and fail to secrete ABH blood group antigens in their saliva, whereas type 1 patients more than normally belong to blood group A (Rhodes, 1972).

Duodenal ulcer patients can also be distinguished according to different patterns of hydrochloric acid secretion. These patients tend to secrete more acid than normal subjects, although, as in the case of gastric ulcer patients, individual patients with duodenal ulcer secrete normal or low quantities of acid (Wormsley and Grossman, 1965). Gundry et al. (1967) were able to divide male duodenal ulcer patients into three groups, according to basal and histamine-stimulated maximal acid output. Their three groups included patients with low basal output (including achlorhydria) and low stimulated output, low basal but high stimulated output, and high basal with high stimulated output. In a recent review, Wormsley (1974) suggests that these differences in basal and stimulated output might be accounted for respectively by a normal parietal cell mass under increased or prolonged stimulation, by an increased parietal cell mass under normal stimulation or by parietal cells abnormally sensitive to normal stimulation.

Based on these considerations, most clinicians conceive of gastric and duodenal ulcer as separate morbid entities, which are brought about by different predisposing and initiating mechanisms (Kirsner, 1968). In addition, different forms of duodenal ulcer exist. However, his crucial distinction between the various forms of peptic ulcer is not always made in investigations of the commonly accepted causative psychological factors. In the psychosomatic literature, the assumption has also been made that all peptic duodenal ulcers have a common predisposition and share the same initiating mechanisms. But this assumption may not be true. Specific initiating mechanisms characterize the duodenal ulceration that occurs in the Zollinger-Ellison syndrome or in carcinoid tumors of the stomach. In the former a pancreatic or duodenal tumor produced gastrin; in the latter the tumor produced histamine (Cook and French, 1968). The remaining instances of duodenal ulcer may neither have a common predisposition nor be initiated by identical mechanisms. Evans et al. (1968) have suggested that there may be different initiating mechanisms in the perforating, bleeding, and obstructing forms of duodenal ulcer. The presence of fibrosis in ulcers as reported from southern India (Malhotra, 1967) may indicate the existence of still another variation of the disease and its initiating mechanisms. It is possible, then, that the term "peptic duodenal ulcer" subsumes a family of disease entities, rather than a single entity with a uniform etiology and pathogenesis.

Research on peptic ulcer is further complicated by the difficulties of establishing the diagnosis. For example, the presence of a duodenal ulcer can be verified by X-ray examination in only about two-thirds of all the patients diagnosed to have one. Nor do the various methods of gastric analysis for peptic ulcer always assure accuracy in diagnosis Cummings, 1967; Kay, 1953; Littman and Bernstein, 1962).

Thus, the investigator in this area is immediately faced with two major sources of experimental error: he may not be studying a homogeneous disease with a uniform etiology and pathogenesis; and he cannot be sure that he is studying all the available cases of peptic ulcer disease in a given population.

One might ask what the relevance of these data is to psychosomatic factors in ulcer disease. The first conclusion is obvious—namely, that peptic ulcer diseases are a group of disorders with rather diverse characteristics. Not only cannot all types be included in a given study without special qualification, but even all patients of a "single" type—such as those with chronic gastric or chronic duodenal ulcer—do not necessarily represent a homogeneous group. Second, when psychosomatic investigators have tried to define a homogeneous population they have tended to do so by excluding patients with gastric ulcer. Alexander, for example, explicitly did so. The wisdom of this exclusion can no longer be taken for granted. On the basis of gastric secretory patterns and genetic markers of these forms of the disease, some patients with chronic duodenal ulcer are similar to other patients with gastric ulcer and vice versa.

Other psychosomatic studies in the past have been too inclusive. Either they did not discriminate between different forms of ulcer disease (e.g., gastric and duodenal), or the authors of the studies assumed that a single subcategory, such as duodenal ulcer disease, was homogeneous. Thus inclusiveness is no longer justified, and much of the past work needs to be reevaluated in the light of new findings.

Psychosomatic studies of ulcer disease in the past 25 years have also tended to focus on the formulations of Alexander (1950), and some have directly or indirectly confirmed them. These formulations remain the most comprehensive statement of the required conditions for a psychosomatic concept of the etiology and pathogenesis of ulcer disease (Fordtran, 1973b), but they, too, need reconsideration in the light of recent data.

On the basis of his psychoanalytic observations of male patients with peptic (duodenal) ulcer, he then formulated the hypothesis that was to provide the foundation for future psychosomatic research on this disease. Stated in simplified form, Alexander postulated that peptic ulcer patients invariably suffer from the same unconscious conflict —dependence versus independence. More precisely, the peptic ulcer patient has a deep-seated wish to be loved and cared for like an infant; however, these motives are repudiated by the adult ego because they give rise to feelings of shame and undermine his sense of pride. To avoid this conflict, the patient employs various mechanisms to defend

36

himself against the emergence into conscious awareness of these oral motives. And these defense mechanisms—repression, overcompensation, and reaction formation—lead, in turn, to the development of certain predictable personality traits: exaggerated self-sufficiency and pseudoindependence, driving ambition, and excessive (and inappropriate) displays of strength.

The exaggerated pseudoindependence of such patients carries with it the seeds for the self-induced frustration of their persistent unconscious motives. Obviously, the patient's unique defense structure will determine his individual reaction to the environmental events which reactivate these cravings. At some point, however, the reactivation of oral-dependent motives in the predisposed individual, and the concomitant excessive frustration of these motives, will lead to the development in the predisposed person of an ulcer via neural and hormonal mechanisms which Alexander did not further specify. (Such frustration would also lead to the mobilization of aggression.) When this wish to be cared for became intensified, further increases in gastric secretion and motility occurred. Alexander postulated that the vagus nerve mediated the increased secretion.

This formulation consisted of three parts: (1) a specific predisposing and chronic psychological conflict; (2) an acute intensification of the conflict that precipitated an ulcer onset or brought about a recurrence; and (3) a mechanism whereby the conflict was associated with gastric hypersecretion.

In any case, one can now say with some assurance that both chronic gastric and chronic duodenal ulcer patients show marked, and to some extent characteristic, within-group differences in acid secretion. Within each group of ulcer patients some are hyposecretors and some are hypersecretors. These findings are at variance with Alexander's hypothesis that chronic hypersecretion forms a major part of the predisposition only to duodenal ulcer disease. Even in those duodenal ulcer patients who are chronic hypersecretors the investigator would have to show whether the abnormal secretory pattern results from psychological influences, from defective peripheral autoregulation of acid secretion, or from an interaction between the two.

EPIDEMIOLOGY OF PEPTIC ULCER DISEASE

Two major authoritative reviews have appeared in recent years on the epidemiology of peptic ulceration in man (Pflanz, 1971; Susser, 1967). Pflanz has cogently emphasized the conceptual and methodological problems that stand in the way of reliably and accurately establishing the incidence and prevalence of this disease in its various forms. He points out that even the classic symptoms of the illness are frequently not verified by the appropriate X-ray examinations. When faced with the same X-rays, interrater agreement between two or more radiologists is never greater than 60 percent. A post-mortem examination often reveals duodenal scarring or ulceration without any history of the illness; pathologists still disagree about the meaning of these findings. We do know whether these are "terminal" lesions whose origin is mysterious in patients who have neither sustained burns nor lesions of the brain. All in all, any conclusions drawn from epidemiological studies must still be viewed with caution.

The prevalence of duodenal ulceration at the time of autopsy varies widely from country to country—the rate was 9 percent among men and women in Germany (Klein, 1951) and Scotland (Thompson, 1954) in the late 1940s. In 1958 the prevalence in Iceland was 0.43 percent in men and 0.35 percent in women (Dungal and Hansen, 1958); in South Africa the prevalence rate in men was 0.7 percent (Higginson and Simpson, 1958). But no conclusion can be drawn from these figures in terms of the impact of an advanced technological society on the prevalence of peptic ulcer. In Uganda during the same period as the South African study (Raper, 1958), peptic ulcer occurred with a remarkable prevalence of 14.5 percent.

Comparative figures on the prevalence of peptic or duodenal ulceration did not completely bear out the contention that men are much more prone to develop the illness. While in Great Britain the prevalence at autopsy of duodenal ulcers was about 3½ times as great in men as in women (Watkinson, 1958, 1960), in Iceland there was an insignificant preponderance of men with duodenal ulcers at autopsy (Dungal and Hansen, 1958).

The morbidity rates of duodenal ulcer have been shown to be equal in all age groups over 20 years of age (Jones, 1955), despite the cherished belief that it is an illness of young men. It may be that a shift has recently occurred away from an increased incidence and prevalence in young people and toward a more random age distribution. There is no way of accounting for this shift in age distribution, although Halliday (1948) has suggested that one age group may be more vulnerable during one historical period than during another.

No firm evidence exists that the incidence or prevalence of duodenal ulcer has changed a great deal in any one country or culture over the past few decades. Therefore, one may not contend that abrupt changes in social and political conditions enhance or depress the incidence of peptic or duodenal ulcer. For instance, there was supposedly an increased rate of perforated peptic ulcers in London during the period of massive air attacks during World War II (Stewart and Winser, 1942). However, a decreased morbidity has also been reported during this war, albeit in soldiers and under different conditions (Pflanz, 1971).

Much has also been written about the relationship of social class to the illness. Implicit in Alexander's formulations (1950) was the concept that the transformation of the unconscious conflict underlying the illness into behavior would lead to psychological independence, achievement, and success. Therefore, one would expect persons with peptic ulcers either to be upwardly socially mobile or to reach the higher ranks of whatever profession they are in (Jantschew et al., 1964; Pflanz, 1971). However, Alexander based his ideas on observations made on patients of higher socioeconomic status. Many patients with peptic duodenal ulcer are poor and do not show the excessive independence originally described by Alexander. From his formulations, one would predict that there would be distinct social class differences in the incidence or prevalence of duodenal ulcer, yet this prediction is not correct; social class differences in incidence or prevalence have not been discerned in broad surveys (Jones, 1956; Rennie and Srole, 1956).

Even though peptic ulcer is a common illness, the critical social and epidemiological variables in its predisposition and onset have not been identified. Further investigation taking into account all the methodological pitfalls of past studies will be necessary to obtain data of real significance to our understanding of this illness.

THE ROLE OF GENETIC FACTORS IN
PEPTIC ULCER DISEASE

Incidence in Families

Certain families have an increased incidence of peptic ulcer. In a study of groups of adult patients (Vesely et al., 1968), approximately 25 percent of all patients with duodenal ulcer disease and about 20 percent of those with gastric ulcer reported that their close relatives had histories of the disease. Among children with duodenal ulcer, a family incidence of 50 percent has been reported (Habbick et al., 1968).

Such reports must be interpreted with caution; for obvious reasons, their reliability is open to question, as the problems of establishing a diagnosis of peptic ulcer disease have been noted. But even with the most accurate diagnostic aids it is difficult to determine reliably the incidence and prevalence of peptic ulcer disease. And it goes without saying that the least reliable sources of data are the reports obtained from patients about their relatives' illnesses. Even if this method yielded accurate figures, the interpretation would pose a serious problem; an increased incidence of the disease in certain families does not tell us whether genetic or environmental factors are prepotent. Thus, we are left with the problem of accurately assessing the contribution of each factor to the etiological variance.

If genetic factors do play a part in the etiology of peptic ulcer disease, they may also be manifested in the stomach's greater secretory capacity. Baron's study (1962) demonstrated that a greater secretory capacity for hydrochloric acid may be a precursor of peptic ulcer disease. Baron attempted to correlate this greater secretory capacity with family histories of peptic ulcer or related diseases. In 1934, 20 subjects in a group of 100 medical students responded to a histamine test with a significantly greater volume both of gastric juice and of higher acidity than the 80 remaining students. One or both parents of each of the 20 students had a medical history of peptic ulcer or severe dyspepsia; the other 80 students had no such family history. In 1961 the same histamine stimulation test was carried out on the same subjects, and additional family histories were obtained; six subjects had first-degree relatives who had developed a proven duodenal ulcer. As a group, these six had secreted more acid than other subjects who had no history of indigestion in the immediate family. In a similar effort, Fodor et al. (1968) studied 160 duodenal ulcer patients, 113 healthy persons with a family history of peptic ulcer disease, and 155 control subjects. These authors used maximal histamine stimulation tests collecting gastric juice for two hours, and typing their subjects for blood groups and secretor status. They found that regardless of blood group and ABH-antigen secretor status, healthy persons with a family history of peptic ulcer had a greater Maximal Acid Output (MAO) in milliequivalents per hour than the control subjects had. Among nonsecretors with blood type O, the MAO of duodenal ulcer patients was not significantly different from the MAO of their healthy relatives, who were also type O and nonsecretors. Among other blood types, duodenal ulcer patients who secreted ABH antigen had significantly higher MAOs than did their healthy relatives, but their relatives had significantly higher MAOs than the controls had. Among the control group there were no significant MAO differences with respect to blood type of secretor status. Thus, within the limitations of the augmented histamine test, the findings are consistent with the hypothesis that the mass of acid secreting cells; ie., the functional secretory capacity of the stomach is an inherited component of duodenal ulcer.

Twin Studies

In Eberhard's study (1968) of 116 pairs of twins of the same sex, the concordance rate for peptic ulcer disease (not further specified as to location of the lesion) was 54 percent for monozygotic twins and 17 percent for dizygotic twins. These concordance figures are probably low. For one thing, only those controls with a history of upper-stomach gastrointestinal distress were X-rayed. Further, the period of follow-up study was not long enough. Some of the twins who did not have an ulcer while the study was in progress may have developed one at some future date, as was the case in the twin pair described by Pilot et al. (1957, 1963).

It can be argued that this evidence does not prove that genetic rather than environmental factors are prepotent: to resolve this issue, twin studies may have to employ a different methodology. The fact remains, however, that both Mirsky et al. (1952) and Pilot et al. (1957) found that the serum pepsinogen levels for identical twins are very similar. These findings suggest that serum pepsinogen levels may be inherited.

Genetic Markers

As is true of all diseases of unknown etiology, the relative roles of genetic and environmental factors in the etiology of peptic ulcer have been debated at length. Those who think that genetic factors play an important role in the etiology of peptic ulcer have identified various genetic markers that either characterize persons who are predisposed to the disease or correlate significantly with the disease itself. For example, body build has been described as one such marker, and it is said that an ectomorphic build is a frequent correlate of peptic ulcer disease (Damon and Polednak, 1967; Niederman et al., 1964; Wretmark, 1953). Blood type is another such marker. Persons who have blood type O, and those who do not secrete the blood group antigens ABH, which are secreted into the saliva and gastric juice, have higher incidences of both gastric and duodenal ulcer (Hanley, 1964; Marcus, 1969; Sievers, 1959; Vesely et al., 1968).

The blood group and nonsecretor factors account for about 2½ percent to 3 percent of the etiological variance of peptic ulcer disease. Stated in other terms, persons of blood type O who do not secrete ABH antigens are 25 to 35 percent more likely to develop peptic ulcer than are individuals of blood type A, B, or AB who do secrete these antigens.

But the mechanisms by which these etiological contributions are made is unclear. It has been suggested (Hanley, 1964; Sievers, 1959) that blood type O may be related to high serum pepsinogen levels. Furthermore, blood group antigens are related to the mucoprotease fraction of gastric mucin (Glass, 1968) whose production may be genetically regulated. But the role of the genes in controlling ABH secretion remains unknown. One possibility is that genes do not play a role in causing the disease; rather, the genes that control blood group O may help determine the severity of duodenal ulcer.

Finally, still another genetic marker has been described for this disease; that is, the ability of a person to taste or not to taste dilute solutions of phenylthiocarbamide (PTC) (Vesely et al., 1968). This ability is determined by simple Mendelian principles of heredity. Interestingly, the PTC taste sensitivity has been found to be more prevalent among patients with duodenal ulcer than among controls. This may, then, be another genetic marker of susceptibility, provided—of course—the presence of duodenal ulcer does not in itself influence the ability to taste PTC.

SOCIAL AND PSYCHOLOGICAL FACTORS IN PEPTIC DUODENAL ULCER

Methodological Problems in Conducting Studies

Very few studies have been published about the social and psychological events that correlate with the onset of peptic duodenal ulcer disease. Implicit in Alexander's formulation were the following assumptions: the onset of the disease correlated in time with the frustration of deep-seated longings to be cared for. In some patients the frustration could be self-induced. The person who is excessively independent carries within himself the seeds of his own frustration; the less he relies on others the less likely are his needs for care and love to be requited. Conversely, the overtly dependent person is prone to frustration of his needs on separation from the person upon whom he depends, unless he seeks and finds another who will satisfy his longings.

But no systematic studies of the onset conditions of peptic duodenal ulcer have addressed themselves to verifying these surmises. Some observations have been made about the events and experiences of patients during exacerbations or recurrences of the disease. Implicit in such studies is that the events surrounding a recurrence are similar or identical with those associated with the initial attack. Such an assumption remains to be proven.

Only one study was carried out before or at the time the disease occurred (Weiner et al., 1957). In this study, which will be discussed later in the chapter, it was impossible to observe in detail the experiences and responses of the subjects to induction into the U.S. Army. The casual assumption cannot be made that induction is stressful to all inductees or that it constitutes a separation. Even if observations on the inductees had been feasible, a major methodological problem in clinical psychiatric research on peptic ulcer disease would not have been surmounted.

Psychiatry and psychoanalysis are restricted to observation of words and behavior and cannot utilize established, verifiable experimental techniques. The fact that, in most instances, the observer is aware of the nature of his subject's illness beforehand is generally regarded as the most pernicious methodological problem in psychosomatic research. The unique characteristics of the peptic ulcer patient present another source of possible bias. To a greater degree than is true of patients who suffer from other so-called psychosomatic diseases, peptic ulcer patients know that their illness is thought to have psychological determinants. They may, therefore, wittingly or not, select or withhold appropriate historical material either to please or frustrate the experimenter or because they fear exposure. This means that all historical material needs to be verified by family members or by personal records or documents.

Studies of hospitalized patients raise additional problems: the patient's dependency needs can be gratified in the hospital setting without inducing shame or guilt. Consequently, hospitalization has psychological significance for this patient population, which may contaminate results, while the illness itself may acquire psychological meaning for the patient. Proper controls may circumvent some of these problems, but they cannot solve them all. Only when subjects are selected and studied before peptic ulcer disease develops and prior to any hospitalization do all these methodological problems fall away.

Psychological findings may be contaminated by other flaws in research design. The evolution of Alexander's original formulations regarding the personality patterns and psychological conflicts of peptic ulcer patients served to underscore the need to take socioeconomic factors into account in clinical studies. Factors such as age, sex, intelligence, and educational background must also be considered. Subjects and controls must be matched with respect to each of these variables. Obviously, it is also important to control variables such as the length of illness—including the age at onset—and the medical history, previous experiences with physicians, and various therapeutic regimens. Finally, in this connection, the possible effect any medication prescribed for the patient may have on his psychological functioning must also be considered.

Different kinds of control or comparison groups may have to be used, depending on specific research goals. But above all, each finding should be validated on a new subject and control population.

The Personality Traits of Male Patients with Peptic Ulcer Disease

On the basis of clinical studies, Alvarez (1943), Draper and Touraine (1932), and Dunbar (1947) concluded that patients with peptic ulcer disease manifested specific personality traits and behaviors. Typically, these patients led active lives, and were ambitious, efficient, and striving. Subsequent clinical experience failed to support this hypothesis: although these psychological characteristics could be identified in patients with peptic ulcer, they also occurred in patients without peptic ulcer disease (e.g., patients with coronary artery disease), as well as healthy individuals.

Alexander (1934, 1947) subsequently extended the findings of his contemporaries and made an effort to correct some conceptual flaws. Thus, he pointed out that the same or similar attitudes and manifest behaviors may derive from various kinds of unconscious conflicts.

Alexander believed that the traits and behaviors that he described stemmed from the transformation of conflictful unconscious dependent longings to be loved, nourished, and cared for. The fact that such transformed longings also characterized patients with other diseases and healthy persons did not, in his opinion, invalidate the observation. Nor did it invalidate the idea that these conflicts could not play an etiological or pathogenetic role in peptic duodenal ulcer disease. These conflicts predisposed a person to the disease, if in addition one assumed a physiological predisposition to it (Alexander, 1950).

Criticism of Alexander's initial formulations centered on his description of the manner in which the unconscious conflict that characterized the peptic ulcer patient manifested itself in behavior or in traits. By 1950, however, on the basis, in part, of a study of 20 patients of low socioeconomic status, he had amended this conceptualization. In this new group the unconscious oral passivity and dependency, instead of being reacted against to produce a mask of exaggerated independence, could also be directly expressed in the behavior and the relationships of patients with peptic duodenal ulcer; the unconscious motives Alexander had uncovered might be expressed more directly in behavior. In fact, Alexander's formulations had been partially revised three years earlier by Kapp et al. (1947). Some of the patients studied by these authors were overtly dependent, "parasitic," disgruntled, and "passive," and the male patients in their sample were frequently effeminate.

In other words, these findings clearly implied that the "oral dependent" motives of patients with peptic ulcer disease did not always conflict with the patient's ego ideal. If the motives were not a source of intrapsychic conflict, they could be expressed more directly. And in that event the frustration of the motives was not self-induced; it occured when the person or persons upon whom the patient depended could no longer satisfy his intense infantile cravings. This "loss" would precipitate the development of an ulcer. But such frustration did not necessarily lead directly to the development of an ulcer. In the "acting out" patient, for example, the frustration of oral cravings and demands might lead to alcoholism or drug addiction, and then, eventually, by a complex chain of physiological processes, to the formation of an ulcer.

De M'uzan and Bonfils (1961) further extended this formulation. On the basis of their study of two groups of male patients (comprising 108 and 85 subjects respectively), they concluded that the unconscious oral motives of peptic ulcer patients may find at least four different modes of expression: 50 percent of the peptic ulcer patients studied by these authors were not particularly competitive, and their professional and home lives were relatively stable. Frequently, the wife was the dominant partner in the marriage; she tended to be quite maternal in her attitude toward her husband; and often she was sexually frigid. For the most part, the patients in this group had been over 30 when they developed an ulcer. It was further noted that onset of the illness had not been accompanied by evidence of serious psychopathology. Another 25 percent of this research sample closely resembled the pseudoindependent patients originally described by Alexander—they were "driven," ambitious, and successful professional men. They characteristically overcompensated in their personal relationships to ward off conscious awareness of their "parasitic" tendencies. Concomitantly, they stressed their need to remain free and independent and their inability to tolerate any frustrations or restraints. The idea of being dependent on their wives in any way was particularly repugnant. Finally—and not surprisingly—for the patients in this subgroup, sexual activity represented still another opportunity to demonstrate their virility (i.e., strength). Fifteen percent of the patients were like the patients studied by Kapp and his co-workers —overtly passive-dependent, disgruntled, and "parasitic." They had usually developed a duodenal ulcer at an older age, and when examined, were overtly anxious and depressed. The remaining 10 percent of the patients in this series vacillated between asserting their independence from, and being very dependent on, other persons. Frequently unmarried, they also drank alcohol in excess.

43

This study clarifies much that had previously been written about these patients. It asserts the fact that oral passivity and dependency may be expressed in several ways—they may be overreacted against, directly expressed all the time or intermittently, or the cravings of a passive and dependent patient may perenially be satisfied.

Subsequent studies have confirmed the variety of ways in which oral passivity and dependency manifests itself in the behavior and personal relationships of peptic ulcer patients (Meeroff and Weitzman, 1963; Sapir, 1962).

Psychological Characteristics of Women with Peptic Ulcer Disease

Studies conducted prior to 1900 clearly demonstrated that peptic ulcer occurred more frequently in women. Since then, there appears to have been a shift in sex incidence, so that today, as noted earlier, peptic (i.e., duodenal) ulcer is generally acknowledged to be more prevalent among men, at least in some countries. As a consequence, the recent literature contains relatively few reports of clinical studies of female patients.

Kezur and his colleagues (1951) in the United States studied a group of women with peptic ulcer and found that, in contrast to a group of male ulcer patients, all the female subjects exhibited rather "severe overt personality disorders." Clinical data revealed that the majority of these women had been rejected by their mothers while they were growing up and had turned to their fathers for emotional support. The disease had its onset when the father could no longer provide this support. Implicit in the description of these women was their dependency on first one parent and then another. The patients described by Cohen et al. (1956) consisted of 200 women with a proven duodenal ulcer, who were classified into one of three groups: the women in the first group were described as "masculine and aggressive," the second group of subjects were "immature and inadequate," the women in the third group accepted their feminine role—they were said to be good mothers, wives, and housekeepers, and to be without demonstrable resentment. Of the 200 women, 69 percent had undergone gynecological surgery or the menopause prior to the onset of peptic ulcer disease. For the third group of women, surgery or the menopause constituted a significant experience anteceding the onset of peptic ulcer disease. Other related precipitating events in this third (and largest) group included the birth of a grandchild or the pregnancy of a younger female relative. In contrast, neither surgery nor the menopause appeared to have played a significant role in the onset of ulcer symptoms in the first group of "masculine and aggressive" women or in the second group of "immature and inadequate" women. The onset of the disease in patients belonging to these two groups was precipitated by the loss of someone upon whom they had depended. Dependency themes appear in two French studies, both of which describe, as in the case of male patients, the different ways in which these themes may be expressed in behavior and personal relationships. The authors of one such study (Hachette et al., 1973) concluded that, in general, the behavior patterns of 20 women with peptic ulcer disease were similar to those observed in male patients. However, as might be expected, so-called "passive-dependent" behavior was more common in women than in men (35 percent versus 15 percent). Another 20 percent of the women patients in this sample were much more difficult to classify by personality pattern than male ulcer patients were. In the other

44

study (Burger and Lambling, 1962) involving 120 women with both gastric and duodenal ulcer, the investigators found that their subjects had assumed more than the usual amount of responsibility at work or in the home and were frequently the titular heads of their families. It is not clear in this study whether the same psychological profiles characterized the patients with one or the other form of ulcer disease.

Explicitly or implicitly, these findings regarding the psychological characteristics of women with peptic ulcer disease conform with Alexander's clinical findings on men with duodenal ulcer disease. Patients of either sex appear to have unconscious motives to be taken care of by others. These motives may be directly expressed in the patients' relationships to others, or they may be reacted against so that the patients become excessively independent, assume excessive responsibility, and appear to rely on no one. Or these patients may appear to be independent at one point in time and dependent at another point, depending upon whether they are cared for or not. However, these formulations do not satisfactorily explain the shift in the sex incidence of peptic ulcer since the first decade of the twentieth century. Current attempts to do so have focused on social and cultural factors. It is said, for instance, that today men are subject to greater social and economic pressures than ever before, and that these pressures contribute to the mobilization of their dependent wishes. On the other hand, in this new social climate, women can be openly dependent without feeling ashamed or guilty, can express their independent impulses, or can express both of these impulses concurrently without the need for repression or reaction formation that is characteristic of men. At first glance, these hypotheses would seem to have a high degree of validity. Obviously, however, at this stage in our knowledge, they can only be applied to certain societies and social groups in certain countries.

Critical Response to the Central Conflict Hypothesis

The criticism that Alexander's formulations have attracted stems from a misunderstanding. Alexander never implied that the unresolved conflict he had identified was the sole cause of peptic duodenal ulceration. He clearly stated that other unknown predisposing factors, besides "oral frustration," were of etiological significance (1950). On the other hand, he postulated a physiological factor in the precipitation of peptic ulcer disease; i.e., he contended that oral frustration was somehow mediated by neuroendocrine mechanisms to produce gastric vasoconstriction and hypersecretion. Furthermore, he later added a constitutional predisposition to his conceptual scheme. Thus, at its present stage of development, Alexander's multifactor theory is both a predisposing or initiating one, which proposes causes in both the psychological and physiological spheres.

Criticism of Alexander's hypothesis has also centered on its "specificity." But Alexander did not state that the core "specific" dependent-independent conflict was unique to patients with duodenal ulcer; rather, he contended that this conflict had a specific configuration in patients with peptic ulcer disease and this configuration was not apparent in individuals who demonstrated other types of oral cravings but suffered from other so-called psychosomatic diseases.

45

Nonspecific Hypotheses

Investigators who oppose Alexander's concept of a "specific" psychological constellation contend that duodenal ulcer is causally related to a state of chronic anxiety in response to a variety of perceived dangers, whether actual or imaginary. This anxiety has no "specific" antecedent such as the danger of one's "oral" wishes, or the anger induced by their frustration; it is "nonspecific."

Mahl (1949, 1950, 1952, 1953) and Mahl and Karpe (1953), the leading proponents of this viewpoint, disputed Alexander's contention that gastric hypersecretion is the physiological concomitant of frustrated oral-dependent wishes, and focused instead on the pathogenetic importance of chronic anxiety—that is, conscious anxiety—in peptic ulcer. Actually, to the extent that anxiety may arise when the psychological defenses of the peptic ulcer patient do not contain the ("specific") conflict, Mahl's theory is not wholly incompatible with Alexander's hypothesis.

The pathogenetic importance of other affective states in peptic ulcer disease has been underscored as well. Mittleman and Wolff (1942) observed that gastric hypersecretion, as well as other physiological changes, occurred in situations where subjects experienced repressed anger, resentment, and guilt. The following efforts to predict variations in gastric secretion on the basis of clinical observations will demonstrate the dimensions of this problem. One study, undertaken by Stein and a group of psychoanalysts (1962), consisted of an attempt to predict measured changes in gastric secretion in a peptic ulcer patient from verbal material obtained in daily psychoanalytic sessions. The analysts were in accord with respect to the patient's manifest behaviors as derivatives of unconscious conflicts. However, they could not agree on such categories as the "adequacy" of his psychological defenses (which had to be based on inference). As a result they were unable to predict changes in gastric secretion from the verbal form or content, or the inferences made about it. Consequently, the hypothesis that one could predict changes in gastric secretion from psychoanalytic material remained untested in this study.

In a similar effort, Mahl and Karpe (1953) reported their psychoanalytic observations of a patient who was seen daily for four weeks. The patient's gastric secretion was measured immediately following each observational session for two of these four weeks. Subsequently, on the basis of their detailed process notes, these investigators attempted to predict which of these ten sessions would be accompanied by high rates of gastric secretion, and which by low. They found that when the patient was believed to be anxious, psysiological tests had shown a high level of gastric secretion; but when the verbal content of a particular session contained expressions of the patient's dependency wishes and their frustration, his rate of secretion was low.

Clearly, these findings are diametrically opposed to Alexander's hypothesis, and support Mahl's theory that psychosomatic symptoms are causally related to "chronic anxiety." However, Alexander's interpretation (1953) of the same verbal content differed drastically from the interpretation advanced by Mahl and Karpe (1953). Based on his understanding of these clinical data, Alexander concluded that high acidity had occurred only in those sessions in which the patient had discussed his oral-dependent motives.

This marked discrepancy in clinical evaluation raises an additional methodological problem. Stein et al. (1962) believe that psychoanalytic observations are compromised when they are made at the same time as physiological tests, to the degree that this combined approach is of very limited value. It is logical to assume that psychological findings may be compromised by obtaining samples of gastric juice. Therefore, Stein's conclusion raises some question about the validity of the interpretations of clinical data set forth in other studies of this type (Fox, 1958; Margolin, 1951).

Validation Studies

In an effort to circumvent the methodological problems enumerated above, investigators in various disciplines have developed a number of techniques and specific methodologies to test Alexander's hypothesis.

PSYCHIATRIC AND PSYCHOANALYTIC STUDIES

The experimental design called "blind analysis" was employed initially by psychoanalytic investigators as a means of minimizing experimenter bias; in recent years, variations of this design have been used with increasing frequency (Graham et al., 1962; Kanter and Hazelton, 1964; Marquis et al., 1952; and Poser and Lee, 1963). In these studies, psychological test data or material elicited in clinical interviews are evaluated by an investigator who has not been informed of the subject's illness; moreover, all "clues" to the medical illness are deleted from the clinical data, since these constitute a major source of bias.

The most ambitious study that has employed this technique was initiated by Alexander et al. (1968). In this project, patients with the seven "classic" psychosomatic illnesses were interviewed by psychoanalysts who did not know the nature of the patients' illnesses. A research group of internists and psychoanalysts were then asked to diagnose the illness of each patient only on the basis of edited interview material and of Alexander's psychodynamic formulations. Finally, a third group of physicians were asked to judge the success with which sources of bias—i.e., clues to the medical illness—had been removed from the clinical data. There were 18 patients (12 men and 6 women) who actually had peptic ulcer disease. The psychoanalysts "blindly" and correctly diagnosed this disease in 49 percent of the men and 16 percent of the women who actually had the disease. The internists' rates of successful diagnosis was 40 percent in men and 10 percent in women patients: because the judges could have assigned these patients to any of the other six disease categories, their diagnostic accuracy by chance alone would have been 14 percent. Therefore, their success in diagnosis exceeded chance only for men patients. The authors concluded that these findings validated the hypothesis that male patients with peptic ulcer disease were characterized by unconscious orally passive and dependent wishes. There is no doubt that this study is a laudable and very elaborate attempt to verify a psychosomatic hypothesis. Nevertheless, it leaves certain questions unanswered. For one, the difference in diagnostic accuracy for male and female patients has not been explained. As noted above, Alexander's original formulations were based on the study of male patients. Clearly, their applicability to female peptic ulcer patients requires further investigation. There is a second major source of conceptual difficulty: we cannot be sure whether the psychological constellation verified by this group of investigators is the patient's psychological response to having the disease, is causally related to that response, or is independent of it. Psychological studies of patients after they have developed peptic ulcer disease cannot in themselves provide a solution to this problem. In fact, some psychological variables observed in patients with peptic ulcer disease (Garma, 1958, 1960) can be interpreted as the patient's symbolic representation of the disease after its onset.

CLINICAL PSYCHOLOGICAL STUDIES

Investigators who have employed clinical psychological methods to validate Alexander's hypothesis have been hampered by special methodological problems beyond those enumerated above.

In 1955, Roth reviewed the body of literature comprising clinical psychological studies of patients with peptic ulcer. He found that all the studies suffered from deficiencies in design. He then suggested that these deficiencies might account for the variety of personality traits with which these patients were supposedly endowed. Other authors had described a number of "typical" personality patterns or traits, but disagreement was rife. Roth felt that Alexander's observations as reported by psychiatrists and psychologists merited further investigation. But at that time clinical psychological methods were clearly inadequate for this purpose, and the validity and significance of any findings in support of Alexander's hypothesis would, therefore, have been open to serious question.

A review of subsequent studies relying solely on psychological test methods would lead one to the same conclusions, based primarily on the methodological problems inherent in such studies (Brown et al., 1950; Friedman and Anderson, 1967; Hoejer-Pederson, 1958; Kanter, 1958; Kanter and Hazelton, 1964; Marquis et al., 1952; Minsky and De Sai, 1955; Poser and Lee, 1963; Streitfeld, 1954; Wretmark, 1953).

For example, many authors have commented on the striking similarity in the test performance of peptic ulcer patients and control subjects (Baugh and Stanford, 1964; Goldberg, 1958; Kanter and Hazelton, 1964; Marshall, 1960; Marquis et al., 1952; Streitfeld, 1954). This may, of course, be due in part to the lack of sensitivity of the instruments employed. It is not surprising that the patients with peptic ulcer disease should demonstrate less variance on tests than control subjects, who are often more heterogeneous (Brown et al., 1950; Minsky and DeSai, 1955).

In light of these findings, the results achieved in two studies were considered "unexpected." In the first study (Streitfeld, 1954), a group of peptic ulcer patients were compared with a group of patients who had other psychosomatic illnesses with no gastric or intestinal symptoms. The patients with peptic ulcer disease demonstrated greater conflict over oral-aggressive wishes, but no greater oral-dependent wishes (as measured by the Rorschach and Blacky tests), than did the control group. In the second study (Lieberman et al., 1959), patterns of self-perception were measured in a group of patients with peptic ulcer disease. Their responses were then compared by experts who were sufficiently familiar with Alexander's theoretical formulations to recognize how the patients might be expected to describe themselves. The ulcer patients saw hostility as a problem both in terms of their object relationships and as a defense against conscious awareness of their need for dependent and intimate relationships. Curiously, the investigators had not expected the peptic ulcer patients to emphasize their hostility as much as they did.

The authors of many psychological studies (Baugh and Stanford, 1964; Silverstone and Kissen, 1968; Thaler et al., 1957) have found that oral fantasy content and passive strivings appear in the test material of peptic ulcer patients, regardless of the test used. On the other hand, Kanter (1958) and Kanter and Hazelton (1964) studied three groups of patients with duodenal ulcer and two control groups by means of the Maudsley Medical Questionnaire and the Maudsley Personality Inventory without finding any differences between the five groups with regard to oral dependent or aggressive content. Yet the ulcer patients scored higher on the Neuroticism category, and lower on the Extraversion category, than did the controls.

In addition, Fisher and Cleveland (1952, 1958, 1960) have developed a technique which has enabled them to investigate the "body image" of patients with peptic ulcer disease. Peptic ulcer patients could be differentiated from patients with rheumatoid arthritis by this method. Specifically, in contrast to the patients with rheumatoid arthritis, the peptic ulcer patients had a much less-certain image of a firm, well-outlined, body boundary. These findings have been replicated by Williams and Krasnoff (1964).

Finally, some psychological test findings indicate that peptic ulcer patients are not very communicative; others emphasize their conventionality, conformity, and lack of creativity (Brown et al., 1950; Eberhard, 1968; Friedman and Anderson, 1967; Marshall 1960).

Taken as a whole, the psychological test data tend to conform to Alexander's formulations. They are, however, flawed by the fact that all of the patients have been tested after the onset of the illness, so that one cannot be certain as to the effect the illness has on psychological functioning.

PREDICTIVE STUDIES

As was noted above, many of the problems that are inherent in psychosomatic studies on peptic ulcer disease could be overcome if there were some way to select a population of subjects who were prone to peptic ulcer disease but had not yet developed it. Such a selection method would eliminate a major source of experimental bias.

Mirsky et al. (1952) took a first major step toward the achievement of this goal by identifying the physiological condition necessary for the development of duodenal ulcer—the hypersecretion of pepsinogen into the blood. He and his co-workers postulated that those individuals with the highest levels of serum pepsinogen were most likely to develop peptic ulcer disease.

Weiner et al. (1957) attempted to test this postulate; at the same time he tested the Alexander hypothesis within a relatively controlled social setting. Serum pepsinogen levels were measured in 2,073 U.S. Army draftees, ranging in age from 17½ to 29. The hypersecretor group that was randomly selected for special study consisted of 63 of the 300 men who were the highest 15 percent in serum pepsinogen values. The hyposecretor group selected for special study consisted of 57 out of the 179 men who were the lowest 9 percent in serum pepsinogen values.

At the start of training, each of the 120 men in this special group completed a battery of psychological tests, including the Rorschach, Blacky Pictures, and Draw-a-Person tests, the Saslow Screening Inventory, and the Cornell Medical Index; and they were also given a gastrointestinal X-ray examination. Between the eighth and sixteenth week of basic training* all but 13 of these 120 men were given a second series of psychological tests and underwent a second X-ray examination.

The psychological data elicited at the start of training were sent to three investigators who were ignorant of the patients' medical status. These investigators then attempted to predict, on the basis of this psychological test material, which individuals were hypersecretors of pepsinogen and which were hyposecretors. Their predictions were based on criteria derived from Mirsky's extension of Alexander's theory, specifically, the hypothesis that the hypersecretor, like the patient with duodenal ulcer, would show intense "oral" cravings and conflicts surrounding these cravings.

On the basis of a majority opinion, the three investigators identified 71 percent of those who were hypersecretors, and 51 percent of the hyposecretors. A further prediction was made: solely on the basis of the psychological test material, ten of the total group of 120 were selected as most likely to have had an ulcer when they began basic training or to have developed one subsequently. These predictions were correct for seven of the ten subjects. Of these seven subjects, three had shown evidence of a chronic ulcer, and one had evidence of an active duodenal ulcer at the time of the initial X-ray examination. Of the three who did not have a duodenal ulcer at the start of training and did not develop one later, two were hypersecretors and one was a hyposecretor.

After this phase of the study was complete, the three "blind" investigators were given the serum pepsinogen values for the group and attempted, in retrospect, to develop more-accurate diagnostic criteria to differentiate hypersecretors from hyposecretors on the basis of psychological test material. They developed a scale of 20 factors by which 85 percent of the men could be assigned to their correct group at a 0.001 level of confidence. No single factor, in itself, permitted assignment into one or the other group with an accuracy greater than 64 percent. Of these 20 criteria, which were equally weighted, 14 were based on Rorschach elements, 2 each on the Saslow and Blacky tests, and 1 each on the Draw-a-Person test and Cornell Medical Index. The psychological configuration of the hypersecretor which emerged from these 20 criteria was expressed as follows:

> [The hypersecretors] show intense needs that were principally "oral" in nature and which are exhibited in terms of wishing to be fed, to lean on others, and to seek close bodily contact with others. Satisfaction of these needs for external support and external sources for satiation is attempted by many means. When such attempts fail, the resultant frustration arouses anger that cannot be expressed lest there ensue a loss of supply for their needs. Consequently these subjects usually do not make complaints or express any feelings of anger.
>
> WEINER ET AL. 1957

Yessler et al. (1959) conducted a two-year follow-up study on the entire group of 2,073 draftees. As noted earlier, Weiner and his co-workers had correctly predicted that seven of the 120 men in the "special group" would have evidence of duodenal ulcer. No further

---

* At the time of this first examination X-ray evidence of duodenal ulcer was found in four subjects, all of whom were hypersecretors of pepsinogen. When the examination was repeated 8–16 weeks later, three additional subjects, all hypersecretors, had X-ray evidence of duodenal ulceration.

cases were detected in this sub-sample of 120 men by Yessler et al. However, six additional cases of peptic ulcer (five duodenal, one gastric) were discovered among the remaining 1,953 subjects. In the total group of 2,073 draftees, 15 had peptic ulcer disease. Of these 15, only 1 had a serum pepsinogen value below the mean for the entire group, and then only slightly. The serum pepsinogen values for the remaining 14 subjects were significantly higher than the mean.

Weiner's and his colleagues' study has been described in some detail. In part, it confirmed the suggestion of Alexander's suggestion (1950) that the predisposition to peptic duodenal ulcer is multiple. The results of this study imply that the predisposition consists minimally of high levels of serum pepsinogen *and* rather specific psychological characteristics. The study also supports, in part, the idea that orally passive motives and fantasies characterize hypersecretors who are at risk for peptic ulcer disease; otherwise the predictions described would not have been possible. However, the limitations of this study are noteworthy.

First, the subjects obviously could not be considered representative, being comprised of young men drawn from a predominantly urban population in the Northeastern United States. Black subjects and those of Italian and Jewish background may have been overrepresented. Ethnic, religious, social, and genetic factors may play an important role —unknown as yet—in determining serum pepsinogen levels. Croog (1957) studied 1,016 recruits (drawn from the same sample of 2,073 studied by Weiner et al.), and found that Irish and Negro inductees had significantly higher serum pepsinogen values than Italian or Jewish inductees. Damon and Bell (1967) could find no relationship between ethnic group and serum pepsinogen levels in a civilian population, so the relationship between ethnicity and serum pepsinogen levels in the inductees must have been a special and unidentified one.

Second, not all of the psychological test criteria that were retrospectively arrived at in the study by Weiner and his colleagues have been verified in other populations. The five test criteria derived from the Blacky, Draw-a-Person, and Saslow tests were used by Cohen et al. (1961) to differentiate duodenal ulcer patients from ten controls in a statistically reliable manner ($p = < 0.05$). On the basis of the several Rorschach items, scored according to the Devos system employed by Weiner et al., Kanter and Hazelton (1964) were unable to differentiate their 21 young male duodenal ulcer patients from a control group. They did not measure serum pepsinogen levels in their study. In other psychiatric studies of duodenal ulcer patients in which serum pepsinogen levels were measured, no psychological tests were administered (Pilot et al., 1967).

Therefore, some of the criteria developed by Weiner et al. may have test-retest reliability, and some may not. In fact, when these authors retested their original subject population, they found that the psychological criteria indicative of anxiety no longer discriminated between the hyposecretor and hypersecretor groups, although the other criteria did.

Because of the apparent instability of some of the test criteria, the study should be validated on a new population, particularly in light of recent developments in our understanding of the pathophysiology of peptic ulcer disease.

Among these developments is recent evidence suggesting that damage to the gastric mucosa may raise levels of serum or plasma pepsinogen. In addition, there is new evidence that individual variations in both plasma and urinary pepsinogen occur from day to day, and possibly from hour to hour. However, some workers believe that despite such variations, individuals maintain their rank order in a population with respect to serum pepsinogen. Levels of serum pepsinogen are distributed in a population in a Gaussian manner. This distribution should permit selection of a group of individuals who are statistically more likely to develop peptic ulcer disease; such a selection was the purpose of Weiner's and his colleagues' study, which was concerned with the etiology of peptic ulcer disease. If the study findings are valid, then a high concentration of serum pepsinogen (as a criterion of gastric hypersecretion), in combination with certain personality characteristics, predisposes some persons to react to a stressful environmental situation by developing a duodenal ulcer. Weiner's and his colleagues' study does not address itself to the problem of the initiation of the disease, and their results do not mean that increased levels of serum pepsinogen play any role in pathogenesis.

Mirsky (1958) believed that variations in the concentration of serum pepsinogen were genetically determined. He postulated that if a high level of serum pepsinogen is present at birth, this inborn trait may influence the mother-child relationship and personality developments, and thereby play a central role in determining the adult psychological characteristics specified by Weiner et al. This hypothesis has not been tested to date, but it is eminently testable by available techniques.

Social and Psychological Factors in the Exacerbation of Peptic Ulcer

In recent years, overall attempts to validate Alexander's hypothesis have given way to studies of one or another aspect of it. For the most part, such studies have attempted to identify the emotional factors that are associated with the exacerbation of duodenal ulcer symptoms. In Weisman's exemplary study (1956), six patients with recurrent exacerbations were interviewed during periods of exacerbation; in addition, each was interviewed for at least 25 hours during periods of remission. The patient's perception of and responses to life events while the illness is in remission were recorded during therapeutic hours and compared to the material elicited during subsequent periods of exacerbation. This comparison may, in turn, uncover certain similarities in these psychological data. Hypotheses about the kind of event that would be expected to precipitate the onset (or exacerbation) of peptic ulcer disease can be derived from Alexander's central conflict hypothesis, and these hypotheses can be evaluated in the light of Weisman's observations.

Weisman's findings with respect to the setting in which exacerbations occurred did not confirm Alexander's formulations. Weisman found that peptic ulcer symptoms invariably recurred in situations in which the patient vacillated between active-seeking and passive-yielding behavior. The symptoms recurred when the patient's passive-receptive wishes were not fulfilled or his unconscious wish to be passively loved and admired with a "singular, non-competitive devotion" were frustrated, or he feared passivity in itself.

These situations, which might be external or self-induced, activated a nuclear conflict between passivity and activity in the patients. This conflict might take a number of different forms—e.g., masculinity versus femininity, self-indulgence versus self-discipline, security versus exposure to danger, or dependence versus independence. The struggle over dependency was considered by Weisman to be a similar but different form of the central conflict described by Alexander in that it did not have the particular "oral" aspects that Alexander postulated.

Weisman also found that when the conflict occurred, it was accompanied by suppressed resentment, angry guilt, guilty fear, and fear of helplessness. The defenses employed by the six patients studied varied considerably and gave rise to thoughts and actions which ranged from fantasy formation to impulsive acting-out behavior, such as alcoholism.

Weisman (1956) concluded that the exacerbation of ulcer symptoms was not associated with any single factor but required "the integrated presence of the nuclear conflict, basic fear, special ego defenses and ambivalent interpersonal relationships." Emotional crises which preceded or accompanied the exacerbation of peptic ulcer symptoms were distinguishable from other emotional crises in which fear was present, because during exacerbations fear was accompanied by an impotent rage. Finally Weisman further commented on the fact that, although some of his patients were acutely depressed at times, depression was not seen during periods of exacerbation: "The inverse relationship between depression and ulcer symptoms was impressive."

Castelnuovo-Tedesco (1962) studied the "perforation prodrome" in 20 patients (17 with duodenal ulcer and 3 with gastric ulcer) who perforated. He contended that perforation had been preceded by "omnipotent" rage which had developed in a situation where personal defeat was imminent but before the patient allowed himself to be aware of the defeat. Stenbäch (1960) studied the "pre-ulcer conflict" and found that, in addition to the long-standing personality conflicts observed in his subjects, the onset of symptoms of the ulcer was associated with chronic anxiety and "fighting fear." The "pre-ulcer conflict" was often brought about by frustration of some "basic" needs. He also noted that his patients were not despondent, although they were afraid that the conflict was insoluble. Finally, Stenbäch found that, in most cases, the "pre-ulcer conflict" had developed less than three months before the diagnosis was established, and Castelnuovo-Tedesco stated that in his patients the "perforation prodrome" had its onset two or three weeks before perforation occurred.

Weisman's observations indicate that no one situation and/or the psychological responses it elicits antecedes exacerbations of the symptoms of the disease. Neither his study nor Castelnuovo-Tedesco's studies of the antecedents of ulcer perforation support an important role for bereavement, in contrast with antecedents of other psychosomatic diseases. Neither author found that their patients were unusually depressed or felt helpless and hopeless when the disease became exacerbated.

THE ROLE OF ALCOHOL

Both Weisman and Castelnuovo-Tedesco found that some patients drank alcohol before suffering relapses or perforations of peptic duodenal ulcer. Both implied that the consumption of alcohol was occasioned by psychological conflict and distress, and that the conflict or distress was not necessarily translated into ulcer disease, but rather that the alcohol might reactivate the duodenal ulcer. This suggestion runs counter to Alexander's hypothesis that the core conflict in these patients is directly translated into increased neuroendocrine discharge to increase gastric secretion and reactivate the ulcer; it affords an alternative inciting cause of the reactivation of a peptic ulcer. In a similar vein, distressed patients may medicate themselves with drugs that may be ulcerogenic.

Alcohol is a known stimulant of acid secretion and has been used to promote acid secretion in clinical tests (Bykov and Kurstin, 1966; Elwin, 1969; Woodward et al., 1957). However, this property in itself cannot account for the role of alcohol in the pathogenesis of peptic ulcer disease.

In all probability, peptic ulcer disease is more prevalent among chronic alcoholics than among nondrinkers (Hagnell and Wretmark, 1957). It is, of course, particularly prevalent among chronic alcoholics who have developed cirrhosis of the liver. In fact, perforation of a gastric or a duodenal ulcer is the immediate cause of death in some patients with cirrhosis of the liver (Eiseman, 1967). Alcohol, liver disease, and peptic ulcer are obviously related in some manner, but the precise nature of this relationship is unknown and probably very complicated. It may be that alcohol impairs the liver's ability to metabolize gastrin.

Many chronic alcoholics eat poorly. Dietary deficiency, such as a deficiency in pantothenic acid, can cause duodenal ulceration in rats (Robert and Stout, 1969), but whether it has the same effect in humans is not known. Of course, it is not absolutely necessary to evoke a specific dietary deficiency; infrequent or irregular food intake alone may be a very potent factor in causing peptic ulceration in predisposed individuals.

On the surface, alcohol would seem to play a proximal role in the pathogenesis of peptic ulcer disease. Yet, in one study of chronic alcoholic patients with peptic ulcers (Hagnell and Wretmark, 1957), the peptic ulcer (gastric and duodenal) anteceded the onset of alcoholic intake. (Parenthetically, it should be stated that the information obtained from such patients is notoriously unreliable.) In other studies, alcoholic intake is considered to be a precipitant rather than a result of peptic ulcer disease, and I am inclined to subscribe to this view. Of Castelnuovo-Tedesco's (1962) 20 consecutive patients with perforated gastric or duodenal ulcers, 12 were chronic alcoholics: the author concluded that in his patients, "emotional stress" had led to an increased consumption of alcohol, which preceded the perforation. In Rubin and Bowman's study (1942) of a series of 100 male outpatients with a verified peptic ulcer (90 duodenal, 10 gastric), 10 percent gave a history of drinking alcohol just before the onset or the recurrence of their gastrointestinal disease. Such information does not, however, resolve the question of whether alcohol intake exacerbates symptoms, reactivates symptoms, or plays a more direct pathogenetic role in peptic ulcer disease.

It has also been suggested that, in some individuals, alcoholism and peptic ulcer have a common etiological root. For instance, Mirsky (1960) reported that 4 percent of a "healthy" population and 20 percent to 30 percent of those with a history of alcoholism had levels of serum pepsinogen beyond the mean of patients with known duodenal ulcer disease. When the alcoholic subjects were followed, 20 percent of them developed duodenal ulcer. The implications of this study are obvious: elevated levels of serum pepsinogen may play a predisposing role in peptic ulcer disease, and also in some forms of alcoholism. However, in the light of other information, Mirsky's study must be viewed with caution. For instance, serum pepsinogen levels may also rise in the presence of gastritis (Pilot and Spiro, 1961), a well-known complication of drinking alcohol.

54

Salicylates may also produce gastritis and erosion of the gastric mucosa, and thereby cause gastrointestinal bleeding. Salicylates directly irritate the mucosa of the stomach, but they also exert an effect after they have been absorbed. When combined with alcohol, the irritating action of salicylates is potentiated (Goulston and Cooke, 1968). Apparently alcohol, by stimulating gastric secretion, lowers the pH of gastric contents.

The irritating action of the salicylates increases as gastric acidity increases. Salicylates may lower the defenses of the gastric mucosa—they are believed to inhibit an enzyme, aminotransferase fructose-6-phosphate, which plays a role in the biosynthesis of mucopolysaccarides by the gastric mucosa (Zwierz et al., 1961).

It would seem, therefore, that salicylates are capable of producing gastrointestinal bleeding by interfering with the production of protective mucus, and there is clinical evidence to support this contention. For instance, Valman and his co-workers (1968) studied 582 consecutive patients admitted to a hospital for upper gastrointestinal bleeding. They found that the great majority—80 percent of those patients with acute gastric lesions, 63 percent of those in whom no lesion was found, 52 percent of those with a chronic duodenal ulcer ($N = 171$), and 40 percent of the patients with a chronic gastric ulcer ($N = 109$)—had taken aspirin in the week prior to admission. In comparison, only 32 percent of the 542 patients admitted consecutively to a hospital for signs other than G.I. bleeding had taken aspirin in the week prior to admission.

Apparently, then, it is safe to assume that salicylates may induce gastrointestinal bleeding. But this does not constitute evidence that they play a role of any kind in peptic ulcer disease. Only one conclusion can be drawn from these data: as compared with other patients, patients with gastric and duodenal ulcer did consume more analgesics (which contained aspirin, phenacetin, and caffeine), and ingested large quantities of coffee, alcohol, phenylbutazone, or steroids, prior to the recurrence of their ulcer symptoms (Bodi and Kazal, 1965; Grant, 1967).

Studies of the Psychological Determinants of Treatment Responses

Reports on the results of surgical treatment of peptic ulcer patients whose symptoms were not alleviated by the usual medical regimen provide additional data on the psychological parameters of this disease entity. Specifically, the authors of such studies have suggested that symptom substitution frequently occurs in such patients. This hypothesis was tested by Browning and Houseworth (1953) in a study of 30 patients who had undergone gastrectomy and a control group that had been placed on a medical regimen. Following gastrectomy, only 43 percent of the patients in the surgically treated group still complained of ulcer symptoms. However, the number of patients who complained of other psychosomatic symptoms rose after surgery from 13 percent to 37 percent and the number who complained of neurotic symptoms rose from 50 percent to 100 percent. In contrast, there were no new symptoms among the medically treated patients.

In another study (Thoroughman et al., 1967), patients with duodenal ulcer who required surgery because of intractable symptoms were compared to patients who required surgery for perforation, hemorrhage, and obstruction. It was found that 60 percent of the patients in the first group and 90 percent of the patients in the second group were relieved of their symptoms by surgery. Those patients whose social adjustment was good and whose personal needs had been met prior to surgery had the best results (Pascal et al., 1966). Conversely, high scores on the Bender-Gestalt test and a history of emotional deprivation in childhood were predictive of poor surgical outcome (Pascal and Thoroughman, 1964). However, we do not know whether these findings are specific to patients who are operated on for peptic ulcer disease, or whether they apply to patients who have undergone surgery for other diseases as well.

Psychological factors may also influence the patient's response to the prescribed medical regimen for peptic ulcer, but little is known about these variables.

Psychophysiological Mechanisms: The Effects of Emotional Responses on Gastric Secretion

Beaumont (1833) observed that stressful environmental events affected the functioning of Alexis St. Martin's fistulous stomach over 100 years ago. And 40 years ago, Cannon (1929) observed depressed gastric secretion in a frightened animal. Since these pioneer investigations, various methods have been devised to influence gastric function artificially by psychological means. For example, patients have been exposed to stressful interviews (Goldman, 1963; Mittleman and Wolf, 1942; Seymour and Weinberg, 1959; Shay et al., 1958; Sun et al., 1958; Szasz et al., 1947; Wolf, 1965), or asked to participate in clinical tests which have not been explained to them in advance; or threatened with an injection (Coddington et al., 1964; Heller et al., 1953; Jungmann and Venning, 1955; Sternbach, 1962; Wolff and Levine, 1955). The patient's emotional and verbal behavior were then observed and recorded while the volume and acidity of his gastric juice were measured. When they are anxious, such patients usually show both an increase in the volume of gastric secretion and a fall in the pH for brief or prolonged periods (Hoelzel, 1942). Other affects—such as resentment, anger, guilt, and feelings of humiliation—are accompanied by similar changes.

Any of these affects may also produce changes in the motility of the stomach as measured by kymography (Mittleman and Wolff, 1942), fluoroscopy (Seymour and Weinberg, 1959), and electrogastrogram (Coddington et al., 1968; Sternbach, 1962). However, the changes in motility observed in these studies were bidirectional; emptying time was both increased and decreased.

The changes in acid secretion and in volume of fluid which were correlated with a stressful interview disappeared with vagotomy (Wolf, 1965): presumably, then, these changes are mediated by the intact vagus nerve. On the other hand, while increases in acid secretion during a stressful interview have been observed both in "healthy" individuals and in patients with gastric and duodenal ulcers, these changes do not always occur. In fact, some individuals are relatively immune to every type of affective arousal, in that such arousal produced little change in acid secretion (Mittleman and Wolff, 1942; Wolf, 1965).

Another interesting method of inducing stress was patterned after Brady's experiment with the "executive" monkey (Brady, 1964). Surface electrodes measured the stomach movements of pairs of college students who were given an electric shock after the presentation of an auditory signal. One of the partners could prevent the shock by pressing a button. Nevertheless, both members of the pair received the same number of shocks. Only the subject who could prevent the shock manifested an increase in gastric motility both during the experiment and after it was over (Davis and Berry, 1963).

THE EFFECTS OF HYPNOSIS ON GASTRIC SECRETION

Hypnosis has been used to verify the impression that specific affects or moods are correlated with changes in gastric function. In these studies, affects were suggested while the subject was in a hypnotic trance. First, the induction of the trance, in itself, may alter gastric functioning. Second, even when no suggestions are given during a hypnotic trance, changes in the physiology of the stomach also occur. Finally, suggestions given to an unhypnotized subject may produce changes in gastric functioning that are similar to those seen during a hypnotic trance (Kehoe and Ironside, 1964). It cannot, therefore, be assumed that a hypnotically induced affect produces changes in gastric function if commands or suggestions that do not produce an emotional reaction in the conscious subject can also do so.

Despite these methodological difficulties, studies using hypnotic suggestion clearly demonstrate that affects are important correlates of gastric function (Hall et al., 1967). Kehoe and Ironside (1963, 1964) correlated the gastric secretion of acid with the predominant affect of their subjects during 5-minute segments of a 2½-hour hypnotic trance. These authors found that the hypnotically induced mental experiences of their subjects (e.g., hunger, dizziness, or olfactory hallucinations), as well as their associated affective states (i.e., pleasure or unpleasure), were reliably correlated with changes in the mean gastric secretory rate. In general, anger was associated with the highest mean secretory rates, anxiety and contentment were associated with moderate rates of secretion, and feelings of depression, helplessness, and hopelessness with the lowest rate of acid secretion. Ikemi et al. (1959) reported similar findings—for instance, that sadness decreased the acid secretion and motility of the stomach. On the other hand, in contrast to Kehoe and Ironside (1964), Eichorn and Tractir (1955a, b, c) found that in hypnotized subjects, fear, rather than anger, was also associated with the greatest increase in the rate of gastric acid secretion.

In any event, these studies offer conclusive evidence that certain induced or spontaneously occurring effects can raise mean rates of acid secretion in the stomach.

PSYCHOPHYSIOLOGICAL STUDIES ON PATIENTS WITH GASTRIC FISTULAE

Concurrent, relatively long-term psychological and physiological observations of patients with gastric fistulae have been recorded (Coddington, 1968; Engel, 1967; Engel et al., 1956; Fox, 1958; Mahl and Karpe, 1953; Margolin, 1951; Stein et al., 1962; Sun et al., 1958; Wolf, 1965). And, once again, these studies point up the complexity of such efforts. First, it is generally recognized that the relationship between the investigator and subject has a significant effect on the rate of gastric secretion; this variable is obviously difficult to control and must be studied in its own right (Engel et al., 1956; Thaler et al.,

1957). Second, although the presence of a gastric fistula facilitates the collection of gastric secretion and eliminates the need for intubation, the fistula will have an inevitable psychological effect on the patient. Moreover, it may also alter the patterning of physiological responses of the stomach to various psychological stimuli (Margolin, 1951).

The subjects used in these studies of gastric fistulae have ranged widely in age: Monica, an infant who had a gastric fistula from the fourth day of life, was first studied by Engel et al. (1956) when she was 15 months old. They found that the infant's acid secretion was related to her total behavioral activity; acid secretion was elevated during manifest unpleasurable states ("irritation, rage") and pleasurable states ("joy, contentment"), and it was reduced during periods of withdrawal from the environment. Monica's relationship to her nurse and doctor also affected secretion. When the relationship was active, secretion was high; when she had no contact with them, secretion fell. When Monica was depressed and withdrawn, the injection of histamine produced no increase in acid secretion; but when she was interacting with others and her emotional behavior indicated pleasure, histamine produced its expected effect—the stimulation of acid secretion.

Engel and his associates (1956, 1967) predicted that the close correlation between gastric secretion, affects, and interpersonal interactions would diminish with the child's increased mental development. And, to some extent, this prediction has been borne out by the observations of Coddington (1968), who studied a 17-month-old girl with a gastric fistula and her normal twin, both of whom were more advanced developmentally than was Monica at the time he studied them. It has also been verified by Engel's subsequent study (1967) of Doris, a 4½-year-old girl who also had a gastric fistula. In contrast to Monica, Doris had low acid secretion for a wide range of behaviors when she was effectively interacting with the experimenter. Acid secretion rose when she was exerting a determined effort to establish, maintain, or reestablish a human relationship. Gastric acid secretion fell in the adult patient studied by Stein and his co-workers (1962) when she became aware of and verbalized certain psychological conflicts about dependency, which led, in turn, to feelings of depression. The study by Mahl and Karpe (1953) of an adult fistulous patient, using psychoanalytic techniques, produced similar conclusions.

Unfortunately, as noted earlier, the psychoanalytic method provides such a wealth of overdetermined data that it is very difficult to isolate with any degree of validity the psychological data with which changes in gastric function are to be correlated. Margolin's study (1951) clearly demonstrated the complexity of this problem. Acid and pepsin secretion, gastric motility, and the color of the subject's mucosa were studied; concurrently, data were collected on the subject's manifest behavior and conscious mental content, from which inferences were drawn about unconscious content and meaning. Margolin stressed that the essential determinant of changes in the function of the stomach was unconscious mental content rather than conscious mental content. However, Wolf (1965), after observing their patient Tom for an entire year, concluded that although the patient was more likely to suppress and repress important conflicts than trivial ones, the comparative importance of the conflict to the subject, rather than whether it was conscious or unconscious, was the critical determinant of changes in gastric function. They also observed that during prolonged periods of psychological turmoil, the acid secretion in Tom's stomach would be consistently high for days in a row; at times, peptic erosions of the gastric mucosa with bleeding could be seen during such periods.

The findings derived from this group of studies can be summarized as follows: in some subjects, certain dominant affects, such as anxiety and anger, are associated with elevations in the gastric secretion of acid; and if these affects persist, these elevations may continue for several days. Other psychological states, such as conflicts and their concomitant feelings and ideas, and pleasure or unpleasure, may modify secretion. However, the complex patterns of gastric functioning are not limited to the secretion of acid; the secretion of pepsin and mucus, as well as changes in mucosal blood flow (which may be of central importance in ulcer formation), have not yet been properly correlated with psychological events. Furthermore, it has not been directly demonstrated in man that changes in acid secretion really have anything to do with duodenal or gastric ulceration; that is, with the initiation of peptic ulcer disease.

I have pointed out that the psychophysiological studies reviewed above have methodological problems in the psychological sphere. Perhaps this is one reason why investigators of the physiological aspects of peptic ulcer disease tend to overlook important psychological factors that may influence particular aspects of gastric secretion.

It is well-known, for example, that sham feeding, which is a potent psychogenic stimulant of gastric secretion in animals, is also a powerful stimulant in man (Janowitz et al., 1950; Wolf, 1965). In a subject with gastric fistula, a self-selected meal stimulated higher levels of acid and pepsin secretion than did a routine hospital meal of gruel. Presumably, then, appetite plays an important role as a stimulus of the secretory response.

Another important aspect of gastric functioning—one which must be taken into account in psychophysiological studies—is the phasing and timing of events in the stomach. Certain complex psychophysiological interactions, which occur both in nature and in experimental situations, contribute to hypersecretion, to variations in mucuos production, and to ulcer formation. Brady (1964) has pointed out the importance of the relative duration and timing of work-rest conditioning cycles in the experimental production of ulcers in monkeys. And Ader (1970) has demonstrated the differential susceptibility of rats to "stress" ulcers, depending on when during their daily activity cycle they were exposed to stress. Changes in light-dark cycles are also reported to be capable of leading to ulcer formation in animals (Lunedei, 1961).

On the cellular level, it is known that there are diurnal rhythms to cell division of the gastric mucosa (Teir, 1967). In the two "decorticate" men studied by Wolf (1965), there were endogenous rhythms of spontaneous secretory activity. It seems apparent that the reaction of gastric physiological processes to any stimulus will depend, in part, on the ongoing state of the organism and the stomach.

Dissociation of the various gastric functions may, in itself, be an important element in the pathogenesis of peptic ulcer disease. Margolin (1951) observed dissociation of functions in his patient, and Bykov and Kurstin (1966) have commented on the dissociation of various secretory functions of the stomach during classical conditioning experiments on animals. The impact at dissociation underscores the need to measure several different parameters of gastric function in determining the pathogenesis of peptic ulcers.

PSYCHOPHYSIOLOGICAL STUDIES OF NOCTURNAL GASTRIC SECRETION

In some patients with peptic ulcer disease, the gastric secretion of acid remains high at night, regardless of whether the ulcer is active. The advent of the era of sleep research and the discovery that sleep can be divided into four states, which can be electrophysiologically and behaviorally defined, has had important repercussions for investigators of nocturnal gastric secretion. Specifically, these workers have asked whether increased secretion occurs primarily or exclusively during any single one of the four sleep stages.

Armstrong et al. (1965) studied the patterns of nocturnal gastric acid secretion and correlated these with the stage of sleep, as monitored by electroencephalography and by electromyography of the eye and submental muscles, in seven acutely ill duodenal ulcer patients and three healthy control subjects. Ulcer patients were found to have higher secretion rates than the control group for all periods of the night. The ulcer patients also had much higher secretion rates during periods of rapid eye movement (REM) sleep then during non-REM sleep; while healthy subjects did not show any consistent correlation between an increased rate of secretion and REM periods. On the other hand, during some REM periods the peptic ulcer patients did not show increases in gastric secretion; it would seem, therefore, that it is not the REM period (or the dream) that is associated with increased gastric secretion. But this problem can only be resolved if the study is repeated and extended to include observations of dream content. Reichsman et al. (1960), in their study of healthy subjects, found no correlation between the stages of sleep and gastric acid secretion; however, they did not specifically look for the correlates of REM periods.

The relationship between gastric acid secretion and the stages of sleep is by no means settled. Specific questions remain to be answered. For example, one might ask whether healthy individuals secrete acid (and pepsin, mucus, or gastrin) at every stage of sleep, while patients with peptic ulcer not only have elevated baseline levels of acid secretion, but show further elevations during one stage of sleep.

CONCLUSION

The main aim of psychophysiological studies has been to determine whether gastric secretion is changed in concert with changes in the emotional state of patient, with thoughts derivative of the conflict that Alexander described, or with changes in the relationship of the subject to the experimenter. As we have seen, the literature in this area of investigation is confusing. Taken as a whole it would seem that feelings of anger and anxiety may increase both the volume and the acidity of gastric juice, and a depressive feeling or mood state tends to suppress both basal and maximal secretion (Gundry et al., 1967). Most studies have been done on patients with gastric fistulae, and the meaning of the fistula to the patient and its effects on the functioning of the stomach are hard to evaluate and control. In any case, these studies have yielded few consistent results.

However, most tests of gastric acid, pepsin, mucus, and gastric motility require the intubation of the patient, and intubation is an unpleasant procedure. Only in the case of the estimation of serum gastrin and pepsinogen levels can the psychological effect on the patient of intubation be avoided. Psychophysiological studies that assess the role of changes in the psychological state on serum gastrin levels have not yet been carried out. The techniques for estimating gastric function could, however, be used in the selection and characterization of subgroups of patients with gastric or duodenal ulcer, who could then also be studied socially and psychologically.

60

Two main groups of tests are available to the diagnostician and investigator: tests of basal acid secretion over a specific period of time, such as 1 hour or 12 hours, and tests of peak secretion in response to a test meal, histamine (or its anlogues), insulin, or gastrin.

Tests of basal acid output provide information about the total amount of acid secreted. Despite extensive investigation, the upper limit of the normal range of the distribution of basal acid secretion is still not known (Ivy et al., 1950; Wormsley and Grossman, 1965). Therefore, a single test of basal acid secretion cannot easily establish whether a subject is a hypersecretor or not. In addition, basal acid output is very variable in any one person from day to day and from hour to hour. Hence, basal acid secretion for one hour does not provide reliable information about the hypersecretor status of a subject prone to or having peptic ulcer disease (Bradlow, 1967). The reasons for this variability are not understood. Variability may in part be a function of a circadian rhythm. Short-term changes may or may not be correlated with changes in the psychological state of the patient; only carefully designed studies will elucidate the reasons for the variability in basal acid secretion.

The overnight collection of gastric acid for a period of 12 hours produces two kinds of information. Patients with peptic duodenal ulcer secrete large amounts of gastric acid at night, and the highest rates of secretion occur at 1:00 A.M. (Dragstedt, 1967; Moor and Englert, 1970). When collections are made over a 24-hour period and hourly samples are taken, rates of gastric secretion show a circadian rhythm in ulcer patients and control subjects (Moore and Englert, 1970). However, we do not know by what mechanisms this circadian rhythm is controlled, or how the rhythm can be influenced experimentally, for instance, by having a subject awake at night and asleep during the day.

Although the 12-hour test has yielded much information, it has its disadvantages. The prolonged discomfort of intubation is one of these. Today, intubation has been replaced by the sampling of basal secretion over a period of one or two hours after a 12-hour, overnight fast. The results of this method of collecting acid correlate well with the 12-hour test (Ivy et al., 1950). The 12-hour test has given different results in the hands of different investigators when applied to patients with duodenal ulcer and to normal subjects. Dragstedt (1967), for example, claimed that the nocturnal gastric acid secretion rate was from 3 to 20 times greater in patients with duodenal ulcer than in normal subjects. Sandweiss and his colleagues (1946) and Wormsley and Grossman (1965) have been unable to confirm this finding. Such discrepancies are presumed to be a function of the selection of patients for study, but may also depend on whether or not the disease is active, and on the presence or absence of gastritis.

Taken as a whole, the results of the 12-hour secretion test tend to indicate that average gastric secretion rates are somewhat higher in patients with duodenal ulcer than in normal control subjects (Baron, 1970; Dragstedt, 1951; Levin et al., 1948, 1950). Those patients with high levels of acid output may, however, constitute a special group with a poorer prognosis. It would, of course, be of interest to see whether the profile of their psychological state or traits differs from that of those who have 12-hour secretory rates within the normal range.

The second group of tests provides a measure of the parietal cell mass of the stomach by measuring its maximum or peak secretory output, without regard to the amount that the stomach secretes spontaneously. Included among this group of tests are various stimulation tests that are designed to measure the stomach's secretory response to particular meals, caffeine, alcohol, histamine, insulin, and gastrin. Technical difficulties in obtaining completely uncontaminated specimens may influence the results of those tests (Kirsner, 1968).

In patients with dudenal ulcer, average peak secretory responses are higher than in control subjects. This result forms the basis for the inference that these patients have an increased parietal cell mass (Cannon, 1929; Cooke and Cooke, 1968; Marks et al., 1960; Mirsky, 1958). It is unknown what causes the increased parietal cell mass. Some authorities regard the increase to be an inherited characteristic, and others have shown experimentally that the parietal cell mass in animals can increase by repeated injections of histamine or by hypercalcemia (Marks, 1957; Neely and Goldman, 1962). In any case, the peak secretory response to histamine stimulation is not a stable characteristic of the individual (Glen, 1968; Kay, 1953; Norgaard et al., 1970; Sun et al., 1967).

Among the factors causing intra-individual and interindividual variation in the response to histamine stimulation is the psychological state of the patient. In a group of duodenal ulcer patients whose psychological and peak secretory response were independently assessed, Gundry et al. (1967) were able to correlate low basal secretion and low peak acid output with a depressive affect, and high basal secretion and high maximal acid output with anxiety.

One could, therefore, conclude that the peak secretory response is a measure of the number of parietal cells that are functioning in a particular person at a given time. However, it seems that even large doses of histamine stimulate only about 65 to 80 percent of the parietal cells at a particular time (Bradlow, 1967). Therefore, the investigator cannot obtain a complete picture of the extent of the parietal cell mass by this test. However, there is a good correlation between the secretory response to histamine or gastrin and the response to a test meal (Rune, 1966, 1967). By this method an estimate is obtained of how much acid patients with duodenal ulcer and normal persons secrete when they eat food. From this response a peak secretion rate (12mEq/hr) can be determined below which no duodenal ulcer will develop (Baron, 1963a, b, 1970; Wormsley and Grossman, 1965). Patients with duodenal ulcer are also more sensitive to gastrin stimulation. They respond in a brisker manner and with a greater maximal acid output than control subjects (Isenberg et al., 1972).

A more interesting measure, perhaps, than either basal or peak secretory rates is the ratio of basal to peak acid secretion rates in response to histamine or gastrin. This ratio indicates how much the stomach can change when it is stimulated to secrete. Results of studies to date are quite surprising; they show that as basal secretion increases, the ratio of basal to peak secretion increases, for reasons that are still unclear. Fordtran (1973) has interpreted this finding to mean that the basal secretion rate is not always determined by the parietal cell mass alone. Yet, the ratio is higher in some, but not in most, patients with duodenal ulcer than in normal controls. The fact that most patients with duodenal ulcer have high basal secretion rates, but a ratio that does not differ from normal control subjects, can be explained by their having a larger parietal cell mass and not by increased vagal tonic discharge.

To those readers familiar with Alexander's writings, this finding may come as a surprise. For Alexander postulated that the long-standing dependency conflicts enhanced tonic vagal discharge to produce hypersecretion. The facts just mentioned do not support

Alexander's contention and can be explained on the basis of the increased parietal cell mass alone. In fact, attempts to prove indirectly chronic increases in tonic vagal discharge have failed (Fordtran, 1973; Grossman, 1967).

Apart from the question of whether tonic vagal discharge is elevated in patients with duodenal ulcer, an evaluation of the ratio of basal to peak acid secretion may be of importance in characterizing such patients. Fordtran (1973) has reported that patients in whom the ratio was high required a much smaller dose of histamine to elicit a half secretory response of acid than subjects with low ratios. They also responded with brisker secretory responses to food; their sensitivity primed them to respond in a brisker manner to several stimuli to secretion.

THE ROLE OF PHYSIOLOGICAL FACTORS IN PEPTIC ULCER

The Normal Physiology of the Stomach

A discussion of gastric secretory tests in duodenal ulcer must be based on understanding of gastric physiology, specifically, the regulation of blood supply and mucus production, and the secretion of gastrin, pepsin, and hydrochloric acid. Mucus in the stomach is produced by the cardiac and pyloric glands which are located, respectively, at the junction of the esophagus and stomach and in the gastric antrum. The pyloric glands of the gastric antrum secrete gastrin. The parietal cells produce hydrochloric acid, and the chief cells produce pepsinogen; these cells are located in the rest of the stomach, which also contains other mucus-producing cells, namely the surface and neck mucuos cells. The stomach also contains argentaffine cells, which may produce serotonin.

Hydrochloric acid is continually being secreted into the stomach, even during sleep. This basal secretory rate is elevated in about 50 percent of patients both during and after active duodenal ulcer disease. The mean rate of basal secretion of acid apparently depends on tonic vagal discharge (Brooks, 1973; Gillespie et al., 1960; Hollander and Weinstein, 1956).

Marked increases in gastric secretion above the basal rate occur at the thought, smell, taste, or sight of food (Walsh and Grossman, 1975), such increases mediated by the vagus nerve and gastrin (Brooks, 1973; Fyrö, 1967; Pethein and Schofield, 1959). Whether other psychological processes can be translated by these mediating mechanisms remains unknown. However, gastric secretion is also powerfully stimulated by mechanical distension of the stomach, by an increase in blood flow in the stomach (which causes the release of gastrin), and by chemical substances, particularly glycine, acetylcholine, epinephrine, and ethyl alcohol. The intestinal phase of gastric secretion of acid may be mediated by several hormones, collectively called enterogastrones (Grossman, 1967; Grossman et al., 1974; Sircus, 1953), whose release is stimulated by mechanical distension of the intestine and by hydrogen ions and chyme in the intestine.

Although most of the experimental work on gastric secretion has concentrated on its activation, the factors that inhibit secretion may be more important to our ultimate understanding of peptic ulcer disease. For it has become increasingly clear that in peptic duodenal ulcer disease there may be a failure of the normal regulatory processes that control acid secretion in the stomach. Inhibition of gastric acid secretion is usually

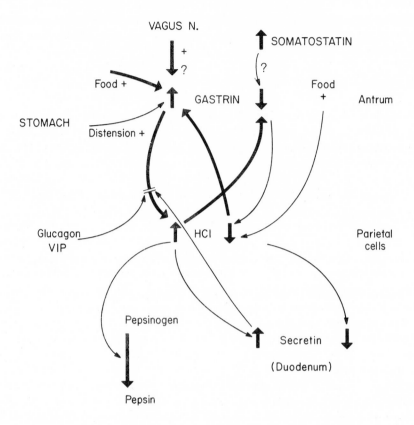

VAGUS N.

SOMATOSTATIN

STOMACH

Food +

Distension +

GASTRIN

Food +

Antrum

Glucagon
VIP

HCl

Parietal
cells

Pepsinogen

Secretin

(Duodenum)

Pepsin

FIGURE 1 The Gastrin-Hydrochloric Acid Negative Feedback System That Normally Controls Gastric Acid Secretion. Gastrin is probably released (↑) by increased vagal discharge (+), and by food (especially protein), gastric distension, and by a diminished gastric acidity (↓). Increased gastrin levels stimulate the secretion of hydrochloric acid by the gastric parietal cells (↑). In this acid medium, pepsinogen is converted into pepsin. Food in the stomach neutralizes hydrochloric acid (↓). Increased acidification of the gastric antrum inhibits gastrin secretion (↓). As the duodenal contents become acid, secretin is released which inhibits the simulating effect of gastrin on the parietal cells (=). Glucagon and the vasoactive intestinal peptide (VIP) act like secretin.

brought about by several regulatory mechanisms, both self-regulatory and extraneous. Gastrin release increases acid and pepsin secretion (Hirschowitz, 1967a, b). As the pH of the stomach falls, gastrin release is inhibited. As food intake stops, acid secretion falls. Acid is also rendered more neutral by food and saliva, by the mucus of the stomach, and by refluxing alkaline duodenal contents. Acid contents entering the first portion of the duodenum inhibit gastric acid secretion by neural, reflex, and hormonal mechanisms. As the duodenal contents become more acid, a hormone, secretin, is secreted. Secretin stimulates the secretion of pancreatic bicarbonate, salt, and water. It also inhibits hydrochloric acid secretion by the stomach that has been stimulated by gastrin (Hubel, 1972; Johnson and Grossman, 1968). Glucagon, calcitonin, and several putative gastrointestinal hormones also inhibit gastrin-stimulated hydrochloric acid secretion (Grossman et al., 1974; Hubel, 1972). [See Figure 1.]

Physiological Factors in Peptic Ulcer

It is a basic premise of this volume that progress in psychosomatic research has been impeded not only by the methodological weaknesses of the studies, but also by the failure of researchers to keep abreast of developments in other areas of biomedical research. In this subsection, an attempt is made to delineate those recent advances in physiological research that are pertinent to the understanding of peptic ulcer disease. Of particular significance are those physiological studies that have cast serious doubt on the role of gastric acid in ulcer formation. We know little about the etiology and pathogenesis of peptic ulcer disease, and most psychosomatic research on the illness has focused on the role of hydrochloric acid and pepsin in ulcer formation. There are other possible initiating pathogenetic agents. The factors enumerated below have been given little if any attention in the psychosomatic research to date. However, we believe that psychophysiologists may find some of these factors, such as gastrin and various other hormones, interesting dependent variables that merit further study.

NEURAL MECHANISMS

The studies on the etiology and pathogenesis of peptic ulcer reviewed earlier in this chapter do not satisfactorily explain the mechanisms that mediate psychological factors to produce changes in the physiology of the stomach. These mechanisms, Alexander believed, must reside in the central nervous system and its principal neural and humoral outflows.

There is evidence to suggest that intracerebral stimulation and lesions of various parts of the nervous system may stimulate or inhibit the secretion of acid and pepsin or may change the production and quality of gastric mucus (Brooks, 1967; French et al., 1957).

For example, low-intensity (but long-term) stimulation of the anterior hypothalamus in cats produces hyperplasia of the gastric mucosa. In dogs, a lesion of the anterior hypothalamus increases the basal acidity of the gastric contents, but does not change the response to maximal histamine stimulation (Davis et al., 1968). Gastric ulceration and duodenal ulceration in guinea pigs have been brought about by stimulation of either the anterior or posterior hypothalamus (Luparello, 1967). In monkeys, peptic erosion of the duodenum and stomach has been produced by chronic posterior hypothalamic stimulation (French et al., 1957). It may be that the cerebral cortex tonically inhibits gastric secretion: both in dogs (Brooks, 1967) and in man (Wolf, 1965), decortication raises the basal secretion of acid in the stomach. These findings are hard to reconcile. Obviously, species differ in their responses to brain stimulation. In addition, the effects of electrical stimulation on the nervous system are always difficult to interpret, partly because different stimulus strengths and frequencies produce different results.

Presumably, the excitatory effects of brain stimulation are mediated by the vagus nerve. But we do not know how brain stimulation can both increase and decrease vagal discharge (Jansson et al., 1969). An increase in neural activity in the vagus nerve causes an increase in gastric motility and secretion. But the vagus is not purely excitatory; it also inhibits the physiological activities of the stomach (Christensen, 1968). And we still do not know how these two opposing influences affect the stomach: for example, we do not know how increased vagal discharge can cause a dissociation of acid from pepsin secretion (Hirschowitz, 1967; Lambert et al., 1968). The kind of information that is needed to resolve this problem is exemplified by the work of Iggo and Leek (1967), who have recorded the action potential from single axons of the vagus nerve of sheep and related the pattern of discharge to contractile movements of the stomach.

THE VAGUS NERVE

We still do not know how the vagus nerve regulates the various phases of acid secretion. One might ask whether there is vagal regulation, or some other mode of neural regula-tion, of the two phases of acid secretion—interprandial and postprandial. If so, which specific mechanisms perform this regulatory function? And do such mechanisms interact with the hormonal regulation of secretion?

The vagus nerve regulates the release of acid, pepsin, and gastrin. Vagal discharge also seems to act in synergism with gastrin and histamine to stimulate acid secretion by the stomach (Glass, 1968; Hirschowitz, 1967). After vagotomy, the stomach's secretory response to these two substances is diminished. Conversely, the direct stimulation of the vagus nerve has been shown not only to increase gastric secretion (Shaw and Urguhart, 1972) but also to produce experimental gastric and duodenal ulceration in dogs (Jeffer-son, 1963), and to increase gastrin secretion in the dog (Lanciault et al., 1975). Yet, there is almost no direct evidence that abnormalities of vagal activity play a role in the pathogenesis of any peptic ulcer disease. The only such evidence comes from Graväard (1968). In Graväard's study (1968), examinations at autopsy of the cross-sectional area and diameter of the vagus nerve at the level of the first gastric branch revealed differences between a group of patients with acute and chronic gastroduodenal ulceration and a comparison group without such lesions. The diameters and cross-sectional transverse areas of the vagus nerve, which were measured from the inside and outside of the perineural membranes, were significantly greater in the two groups with ulcer lesions than they were in the comparison group. But the patients with acute gastroduodenal ulceration did not differ significantly in nerve size from the group of chronic patients.

Graväard's efforts constitute a new approach to the study of peptic ulcer disease. First, the validity of the methods must be determined. Specifically, it must be shown that the observed differences preceded the appearance of peptic ulcer disease. If this work can be validated—i.e., if it can be shown that the vagus nerve contained more, or larger, fibers before the inception of the disease—then the size of the vagus nerve, may, in fact, be an etiological factor in peptic ulcer disease.

Another possible factor in the etiology of peptic ulcer disease is the overall size of the stomach, which may be the anatomical basis for the known increase in the secretory capacity of the stomach in some patients. Cox (1953) demonstrated, at autopsy, marked variations in the size of the human stomach. Specifically, patients with duodenal ulcer had larger stomachs and an increased parietal cell mass than the comparison group. This variation was not related to the size of other body organs. (For example, obese persons did not have unusually larger stomachs.) Rather, this difference was in part due to variations in mass of the part of the stomach that contains the parietal cells. Cox further noted that the stomach of human infants did not show the pronounced variations in size seen in the adult. And he concluded from this observation that variation in stomach size was an acquired characteristic.

The finding of an increased stomach size and a greater parietal cell mass in this disease has not been explained. Genetic variation is one possible explanation. Like Alexander (1950), State (1971) believes that the increased size of the stomach and mass of parietal cells results from excessive and persistent stimulation of the stomach by increased vagal discharge. An alternative view might be that the enhancement of stomach size is caused by human growth hormone or gastrin.

These interesting findings require further elucidation: is the increase in stomach size a cause or an effect of the peptic ulcer? Or is the increase in size seen only in patients with pyloric obstruction? In rats, for example, pyloric or duodenal ligation and administration of pentagastrin lead to increases in the size of the stomach (Crean, 1967; Crean et al., 1969). Finally, Cox's findings also raise the question of the correlation of stomach size with the production of acid and pepsin in peptic ulcer disease; I do not know of any studies that have correlated the structure and function of the stomach in this manner.

HORMONAL MECHANISMS

One of the principal mechanisms by which the nervous system regulates bodily function is the release of the several trophic hormones of the pituitary gland. The release of adrenocorticotrophic hormone and, therefore, of adrenocortical and other hormones, is sensitive to psychological stress and distress (see chapter 8).

The adrenocortical hormones. The role of the adrenocortical hormones in the production of peptic ulcer and in the regulation of gastric secretion remains enigmatic (Cooke, 1967). The effects of chronic administration of steroids on other aspects of gastric physiology are equally obscure. At one time, it was thought that prolonged administration of steroids to patients with rheumatoid arthritis increased the incidence of peptic ulcer disease among these patients. However, the current consensus is that, in all probability, the increased incidence of peptic ulcer disease in this group cannot be attributed to the steroids; rather, patients with rheumatoid arthritis develop peptic ulcer disease, in part, because salicylates, indomethacin, and phenylbutazone are used in the clinical treatment of the disease (Cooke, 1967). In addition, the fact that patients with Cushing's syndrome (who produce copious quantities of endogenous cortisol) do not have an unusually high incidence of peptic ulcer disease argues against a pathogenetic role for corticosteroids in peptic ulcer disease.

On the other hand, there is evidence that the chronic administration of steroids causes peptic ulceration in rats. It is possible, however, that this effect is not mediated by an increase in the secretion of gastric acid or pepsin. Ragins and Wincze (1969) found that the administration of cortisone to rats led to a decrease in the formation of parietal cells. These findings are consistent with Teir's report (1967) that stress decreases the mitotic count, and that cortisol inhibits DNA synthesis in the rat's stomach.

In brief, the role of both the endogenous and exogenous adrenocortical steroids in the pathogenesis of peptic ulcer remains unsettled, and their action on various phases of the function of the stomach is not fully understood.

Formerly, most investigators believed that the adrenocortical hormones stimulated gastric secretion: there was thought to be a late "adrenal" phase in the gastric hypersecretion produced by insulin hypoglycemia (Shay, 1959) or by stimulation of the posterior hypothalamus (Porter et al., 1953). But these results have not been confirmed by subsequent investigations (Bachrach, 1963; Smith, 1967). In fact, it is doubtful that there is a late phase in the gastric secretion either of normal persons or of patients with duodenal ulcer (Bachrach, 1963; Williams et al., 1967). Williams et al. (1967) attempted to assess the gastric stimulatory effects of constant infusions of intravenous cortisol on healthy men with plasma levels maintained at 20–30 mg/100 ml (which is in the normal distribution of values); the infusions produced no increase in gastric secretion, even when continued for five hours. Similar experiments in dogs did elicit a gastric secretory response (Cooke, 1967). In monkeys, however, it has not been possible to demonstrate a correlation between a rise in endogenous corticosteroids and a rise in gastric acid secretion over a three-day period (Brady, 1964; Smith, 1967).

The available evidence seems to indicate that adrenocortical hormones per se do not increase gastric secretion in man, although they do cause gastric ulcers in rats. It has been suggested that adrenal hormones may act in synergy with other hormones and neural influences, in addition to having "trophic" influences on the gastric cells (Ryss and Ryss, 1968). Horowitz (1967) and Menguy (1967) have demonstrated the effects of adrenocortical hormones on the production of protective mucus; for example, the treatment of rats with high doses of corticosteroids resulted in a decreased secretion of mucus and changes in its chemical composition.

The specific relevance of these studies to the clinical problem of peptic ulcer disease has yet to be determined: as reported by Ryss and Ryss (1968), Mosin (1967) showed increased responsiveness of the adrenal gland to injections of ACTH in patients whose peptic ulcer was clinically active. He further noted that when improvement in the illness occurred there was a decreased adrenal response to ACTH injections. Tarquini et al. (1967) studied the diurnal rhythm of adrenocortical excretion in a group of 8 hospitalized peptic ulcer patients, and compared it to a control group of 15 patients admitted for minor surgery. All of the patients studied were kept on the same activity schedule during the day and the same sleep schedule at night. In only one of the eight peptic ulcer patients were the hormone levels within the 95 percent probability range of the control group: the patients with peptic ulcer disease had higher peak levels of the adrenocortical hormones.

Before we attempt to assess the meaning of these studies, their limiting features should be pointed out. First, the change in adrenal function, if any, was studied only after the onset of illness. Consequently, we cannot know with any degree of certainty whether the change in adrenal function preceded the illness, or whether the change was due to the physical and emotional reactions to specific aspects of the illness (e.g., pain). Secondly, neither of these reports refer to the age, height, or weight of the patients studied, nor do we know whether the patients were using any medications. Yet, these variables obviously need to be controlled (Sachar, 1967).

In summary, then, there is no good evidence that adrenocortical hormones play an initiating role in peptic ulcer disease, perhaps by altering the composition of gastric mucus or by acting synergistically with other secretory stimulants. The respective roles of these hormones might be elucidated by studies of the gastric and steroid secretions of animals subjected to psychological stresses.

Insulin. Insulin has been used for many years to stimulate vagal activity. When the blood sugar level is lowered by the administration of insulin, gastric secretion increases. Presumably, certain neurons in the brain are activated by the fall in blood sugar, and this activation is mediated by the vagus nerve to the stomach (Hirschowitz, 1967). If glucose is administered in combination with insulin, the gastric secretory response does not occur. However, once the gastric secretory response has been set into motion, the administration of glucose will not bring it to a halt.

The most recent evidence on the mechanism by which a fall in blood sugar level stimulates gastric secretion suggests that increased vagal activity does not play an exclusive role. Bilateral vagotomy did not abolish an elevation of gastrin levels in response to hypoglycemia (Stadil, 1972). Catecholamines also released gastrin (Hayes et al., 1972; Stadil and Rehfeld, 1973), and β-adrenergic blockade with propranolol decreased the rise in gastric acid secretion in response to hypoglycemia in vagotomized patients (Read et al., 1972). Catecholamines also inhibit the release of insulin, but they stimulate the production of glucagon (Leclerq-Meyer et al., 1971).

The roles of insulin and glucagon in peptic ulcer disease are therefore still enigmatic. Their roles in the regulation of gastrin and acid secretion require further elucidation. Changes in blood sugar levels influence other gastric functions: the quality of gastric mucus depends in part on the blood sugar level (Menguy, 1967). In animals with denervated gastric pouches, the administration of insulin in sufficient amounts to produce hypoglycemia results in a decreased rate of mucus secretion and a lower concentration of hexose in the mucus. In addition, insulin may directly inhibit gastric secretion by virtue of its influence on potassium uptake by the parietal cells.

Growth hormone and somatostatin. The role of growth hormone and its regulating hormone, somatostatin, in gastric function is still not fully understood. However, we do know that both of these hormones influence the pancreatic hormones (Williams, 1968), and may therefore indirectly affect gastric secretion. And somatostatin directly inhibits gastrin release (Bloom et al., 1974). In addition, Crean (1968a, b) found that hypophysectomized rats showed a reduction in the weight and surface area of the stomach, as well as a reduction in the mucosal volume of the fundus and in the total parietal-cell population. Since appropriate control groups were used, these reductions could not simply be ascribed to the adverse effects of the operation or to starvation. Removal of the adrenal glands, in contrast to hypophysectomy, caused a reduction of the stomach weight and surface area of the stomach, but did not affect the volume of fundic mucosa or the parietal-cell population.

Cox's findings (1953) that patients with duodenal ulcer typically show an increased stomach size and parietal cell mass were discussed above. In the past, these variations have been attributed to excessive vagal stimulation. But the effects of growth hormone on the structure of the stomach might provide an alternative hypothesis to account for his data.

Parathyroid hormone and calcium. Of those who suffer from hyperparathyroidism, 15 to 20 percent also suffer from peptic ulcer disease. In some hyperparathyroid patients serum pepsinogen levels are raised (Anscombe, 1964). Hypersecretion of hydrochloric acid occurs in some hyperparathyroid patients, presumably as a result of elevations of serum calcium (Barreras and Donaldson, 1967). The increases in serum pepsinogen and acid are believed to account for the increased incidence of peptic ulcer disease in some hyperparathyroid patients.

Some patients with the Zollinger-Ellison syndrome not only have a pancreatic gastrinoma but also have a functional parathyroid tumor (and tumors of other endocrine glands). When their hyperparathyroidism is corrected, the symptoms of peptic ulcer disease abate and gastric acid hypersecretion decreases despite the continuing presence of the gastrinoma (Turbey and Passaro, 1972). In such patients, in whom the hypercalcemia has been corrected, the infusion of calcium raises the secretion of acid and serum gastrin levels (Trudeau and McGuigan, 1969). Presumably, elevated calcium levels stimulate acid secretion in these patients.

Even in patients with peptic duodenal ulcer who are not hyperparathyroid, the infusion of 12 to 15 mg of calcium per kg of body weight for a period of three hours causes an increase of gastric acid secretion. The increase in acid secretion produced by the infusion of calcium is about 30 to 60 percent of that produced by histamine (Reeder et al., 1970). But patients with the Zollinger-Ellison syndrome respond to the same dose of calcium with a secretory response of hydrochloric acid that equals the response brought about by histamine. Presumably, calcium releases gastrin from gastrin-producing tumors more than it does from the gastrin-producing cells in the gastric antrum (Isenberg et al., 1973; Passaro et al., 1970; Trudeau and McGuigan, 1969). Alternatively, calcium may have a more intense effect on the parietal cells of the stomach in patients with the Zollinger-Ellison syndrome than in patients with a peptic duodenal ulcer and normal gastrin levels (Passaro et al., 1972). However, patients with sarcoidosis, who also have increased serum calcium levels, are not usually prone to peptic ulcer disease (Winnacker et al., 1968). Nonetheless, the data suggest that the calcium ion does play a role in the regulation of hydrochloric acid secretion.

Other hormones. A number of other hormones and naturally occurring substances have been implicated, either directly in peptic ulcer disease or indirectly in the regulation of the secretory functions of the stomach. These include the male and female sex hormones (Eisenberg et al., 1964), the thyroid hormone (Baron, 1962; Williams and Blair, 1964), vasopressin (Baron, 1962; Lawson and Dragstedt, 1964), serotonin (Menguy, 1967; Pincus and Horowitz, 1967), the prostaglandins (Davies, 1967; Horton, 1969; Nezamis and Phillips, 1968), and various gastroduodenal hormones (Glass, 1968; Johnson and Grossman, 1968; Menguy, 1967). Unfortunately, no definitive statement can yet be made as to just what part these hormones play in the pathogenesis of peptic ulcer.

THE AUTOREGULATION OF GASTRIC SECRETION

On the other hand, it is well-known that hypersecretion of acid and pepsin is correlated with peptic ulcer disease in up to one-half of all patients. As noted above, in view of the fact that the secretion of these substances is under the influence of the vagus and gastrin, one would be inclined to believe that the ultimate regulator of their secretion must be the central nervous system. But, as Mirsky et al. (1952) have pointed out, the fact that the hypersecretion of pepsin and hydrochloric acid is a concomitant of peptic ulcer disease does not prove either that the hypersecretion causes the ulcer or that the ulcer causes the hypersecretion.

Hydrochloric acid. Although there is some experimental evidence that acid secretion may increase following injury to the gastric mucosa or duodenum (Bykov and Kurstin, 1966; Crean, 1967; Wolf, 1965), most authors feel that hypersecretion precedes the appearance of the ulcer. Admittedly, there is no direct evidence to support this position; however, there are several suggestive studies, both in man and animals. Brady (1964) had shown that in monkeys, hypersecretion of acid may precede the appearance of duodenal ulcer. And human subjects studied by Baron (1962) showed an increase in acid secretion, in response to an evocative histamine test, before an ulcer developed. More precisely, Baron administered the histamine test to 100 doctors while they were medical students, and then followed them for a period of 27 years. The nine subjects who had originally secreted a larger volume of gastric juice, of greater acidity, in response to the test than the other subjects subsequently developed a proven duodenal ulcer. Thus this study indicates, once again, that a greater secretory capacity for hydrochloric acid is precursor of peptic ulcer disease in this group of subjects.

Yet the hypersecretion of acid cannot, in itself, account for the appearance or the exacerbations of peptic ulcer disease, because acid secretion remains high in some patients with a healed peptic ulcer (Levin et al., 1948b). Even the very marked hypersecretion of acid which occurs in the Zollinger-Ellison syndrome (Cook and French, 1968; Isenberg et al., 1973; Stempien et al., 1964) is not invariably associated with the development of a peptic ulcer.

In patients with the Zollinger-Ellison syndrome, gastrin or gastrin-like substances have been extracted from the pancreatic adenoma. In this syndrome the hypersecretion of acid does not reduce gastrin production because the source of the gastrin is outside the stomach.

Other factors also seem to play a part in the regulation of acid production by the stomach. It is possible that once production occurs, neural and hormonal regulatory mechanisms are brought into play. It is also known that as the contents of the duodenum become more acid, the gastric secretion of acid diminishes (Johnston and Duthie, 1964, 1965). The inhibition of gastric secretion of acid by acid duodenal contents depends in part on the integrity of the vagus nerve. In some patients with duodenal ulcer, the regulation of acid secretion by duodenal mechanisms may be disturbed (Harvey, 1969; Love, 1970; Rhodes and Prestwich, 1966).

Pepsinogen and pepsin. So much clinical research on peptic ulcer disease has revolved about the role of acid, that we tend to forget that the chief proteolytic enzyme of the stomach is pepsin. Its precursor, pepsinogen, is released by the chief cells. The optimum pH for pepsin is 1.8, although its proteolytic activity can occur at a pH as high as 4.5.

Pepsinogen is secreted under the influences of the vagus nerve, gastrin, histamine, insuline, and acetylcholine. A certain small percentage (1–2 percent) of pepsinogen appears in the bloodstream and then in the urine, regardless of the amounts secreted into the stomach. High serum pepsinogen levels may be of value in predicting populations that will develop duodenal ulcer at a later time (Mirsky, 1958; Mirsky et al., 1952; Weiner et al., 1957). But the fact that high serum pepsinogen levels constitute a predictor of future ulcer disease in some people does not mean that there is an increase in the secretion of pepsin into the stomach lumen in such individuals. In fact, the relationship of serum levels of pepsinogen and the content of pepsin in the stomach is not linear. Certainly, there is no proof that increased amounts of pepsin in the stomach "causes" the ulcer.

Mirsky's data (1952, 1958, 1960) indicate that differences in levels of plasma or serum pepsinogen permit some discrimination between populations of subjects with duodenal ulcer and healthy subjects. Despite some overlap on values for the two groups, only 4 percent of the normal subjects in his study has serum pepsinogen values higher than the mean value for patients with duodenal ulcer. Mirsky's follow-up study of this sample demonstrated that normal persons with high serum pepsinogen values may develop duodenal ulcer. He also concluded that intra-individual variance and diurnal changes in pepsinogen are minor. Changes in blood pepsinogen do not correlate with changes in gastric secretion (Pilot and Spiro, 1961), and in general the blood pepsinogen level is only roughly correlated with the parietal cell mass (Hirschowitz, 1967a, b). Behavioral manipulations lead to relatively insignificant changes in blood pepsinogen level in animals (Ader, 1963; Shapiro and Horn, 1955), so one may conclude that serum pepsinogen levels may, in animals at least, be a stable characteristic. In man, on the other hand, elevations of serum pepsinogen are seen in gastritis and in renal disease. The elevations seen with hyperparathyroidism and the diminution seen with hyperthyroidism and pernicious anemia may reflect changes in the total mass of chief cells. And changes in the release and excretion of pepsinogen from the chief cells may, in turn, account for the increased levels found in gastritis and renal disease (Anscombe, 1964), Therefore, in estimating serum levels in man as a means of selecting persons predisposed to peptic ulcer, the presence of other diseases must be considered.

Another complicating factor is that seven electorphoretically distinct pepsinogens can be extracted from human gastroduodenal mucosa (Samloff, 1969; Samloff and Townes, 1969). Pepsinogens (Pg) 1–5 occur in the gastric body and fundus; three of these (Pg 2–4) are invariably excreted in the urine. Two additional pepsinogens (Pg 6, 7) are found in the antrum and proximal duodenum and are rarely excreted. Pg 1–4 occur in all human beings but Pg 5 does not. Its presence or absence appears to be genetically determined; its presence may be related to the etiology of peptic ulcer (Samloff and Townes, 1970).

On the other hand, Taylor (1970) has published data that suggest a significant increase in frequency of occurrence of Pepsin 1 in the gastric juice of patients with gastric ulcer and a less-significant increase in those with duodenal ulcer. Whether this relationship is causal remains to be determined. These findings suggest that the relationship of pepsinogens to peptic ulcer is considerably more complex than was originally believed and that the pepsin isoenzymes relevant to peptic ulcer do not appear in the urine. Only further work can resolve this puzzle.

Gastrins. (Silen, 1967; Classen, 1968) The crucial role of gastrin in the regulation of acid secretion, described above, clearly merits more detailed discussion. Gastrin is a peptide: two heptadecapeptide amides (gastrin I and II) represent the antral hormone, gastrin, which is isolated from the human stomach (Gregory et al., 1966).

All of the physiological actions of the gastrins reside in a C-terminal tetrapeptide amide. Curiously enough, this amino acid sequence also occurs in the hormone cholecystokinin, which is a weak stimulator of gastric secretion. A synthetic pentapeptide containing the four amino acids that are the active moiety of gastrin is available, and is being used in clinical tests of gastric secretion.

Gastrin is probably excreted by the gut and the kidney (Brooks, 1973). Laster and Walsh (1968) have uncovered evidence, based on *in vitro* studies, that the kidney contains an enzyme system capable of degrading gastrin.

Gastrin is apparently formed in enterochromaffin-like cells of the antral mucosa (McGuigan, 1968). Its release from these cells is under the control of the vagus nerve (Fyrö, 1967): gastrin can, for example, be released by sham feeding and by a protein meal. Its release can also be caused by the presence of food in the stomach, or by distention of the antrum of the stomach, even when denervated. In the intact stomach, the release of gastrin by vagal stimulation is blocked by atropine, which apparently also blocks the action of gastrin itself.

Gastrin strongly stimulates the secretion of HCl and pancreatic enzymes and weakly stimulates the secretion of pepsinogen and of pancreatic and biliary bicarbonate. As mentioned previously, gastrin, the vagus nerve, and histamine appear to act synergistically with regard to parietal cell stimulation and the concomitant secretion of hydrochloric acid.

Methods sufficiently sensitive to measure circulating levels of gastrin have been developed recently (Colin-Jones et al., 1969; McGuigan and Trudeau, 1968, 1969; Uvnäs and Emås, 1961). McGuigan and Trudeau (1969) have used these new methods to demonstrate that patients with Zollinger-Ellison syndrome have 10 to 40 times more circulating gastrin than do normal individuals. These findings, combined with the data cited above, would certainly be considered conclusive evidence that gastrin may play an important mediating role in the Zollinger-Ellison syndrome.

It was pointed out earlier in this chapter that the Zollinger-Ellison syndrome must be differentiated from other forms of duodenal ulcer. In the syndrome, serum gastrin levels are usually and significantly above the upper limits of normal. However, this is not always the case; some patients with this syndrome have only mildly elevated levels of serum gastrin, moderate basal increases in acid secretion, and a stimulated acid output that is twice the basal output. Therefore, they may be misdiagnosed, and great care must be taken in psychosomatic studies to select patients who do not have this syndrome. In patients with duodenal ulcer, gastrin levels are usually within normal range. When the values are elevated, gastric ulcer, gastrinoma, achlorhydria, or hypochlorhydria should be suspected (Ganguli and Hunter, 1972; Hansky and Cain, 1969; Trudeau and McGuigan, 1971). The evidence that gastrin plays a pathogenetic role in the Zollinger-Ellison syndrome is strong. However, we have not yet accumulated evidence of equal weight to attest to the mediating role of gastrin in peptic ulcer disease in man. We know that the chronic administration of gastrin produced *duodenal* ulceration in cats (Emås and Grossman, 1968), guinea pigs (Gobbel and Adkins, 1967), and rats (Robert and Stout, 1969; Robert et al., 1970). But the mucus of the gastric antrum in human patients with duodenal ulcer does not seem to contain increased amounts of gastrin (Lythgoe et al., 1962).

Trudeau and McGuigan (1970, 1971) demonstrated that there was an inverse relationship between fasting serum gastrin concentraions and basal gastric acid concentrations or maximum-stimulated gastric acid secretion in man. In patients with duodenal ulcer they again found that the mean unstimulated and maximum-stimulated rates of gastric acid secretion were elevated. In patients with gastric ulcer, both rates of gastric acid secretion were within the normal range. Whereas the mean fasting serum gastrin concentration was elevated in patients with gastric ulcer, it was within the normal range in patients with duodenal ulcer. As Berson and Yalow (1971) pointed out (based in part on their finding that plasma gastrin concentrations both in the basal state and after feeding may be *higher* in patients with duodenal ulcer than in normal subjects) these findings suggest that in patients with duodenal ulcer the normal feedback inhibition of gastrin secretion in the face of higher levels of hydrochloric acid secretion may be defective. At the present time, there is no explanation for the finding that the normal feedback is not functioning. As mentioned above, it was believed until recently that one important regulator of gastrin release was vagal activity. Recently, Stadil and Rehfeld (1973) found that the infusion of 25 to 75 ng per kg per minute of epinephrine in eight normal subjects transiently and significantly increased serum gastrin concentrations and gastric acid concentrations. Marked individual differences in these responses occurred, and the increases were blocked by the prior administration of β-adrenergic blocking agents. Doses of 125 to 150 ng per kg per minute of epinephrine lowered serum gastrin concentration. In dogs, similar observations have been made (Hayes et al., 1972), and it was also found that α-adrenergic blockade inhibited the release of gastrin by epinephrine. These data combined with data to be reviewed later suggest that the regulation of gastrin release is more complicated than was originally thought.

Other duodenal ulcer patients show a gastrin response to a protein meal that is more elevated and prolonged than that of control subjects, suggesting an increased sensitivity of gastrin cells to this stimulus or a failure of inhibition of gastrin release by the subsequent acid secretion (Forrester and Ganguli, 1970; Ganguli and Hunter, 1972; Korman et al., 1971; McGuigan and Trudeau, 1973). Still other duodenal ulcer patients secrete more acid per unit of exogenous pentagastrin suggesting an increased sensitivity of parietal cell receptors to gastrin in these patients (Isenberg et al., 1972). [See Figure 2.]

What may one conclude from these data on the peripheral hormonal regulation of gastric secretion? They suggest that several different variations in gastric and duodenal autoregulation may occur in patients with duodenal ulcers. Some chronic duodenal ulcers may result from increased gastrin production, as in the Zollinger-Ellison syndrome; other forms may be associated with increased parietal cell sensitivity to gastrin; and still others may result from decreased gastrin cell sensitivity to hydrogen ion. The problem, of course, is that because one still lacks an adequate understanding of the pathogenesis of any of these lesions, one cannot distinguish physiological and endocrinological abnormalities which merely correlate statistically with the presence of the lesion from those which contribute to its inception. Given the variety of these abnormalities among patients with peptic ulcer disease, it seems likely that there are several different regulatory abnormalities related to ulcer pathogenesis and that specific combinations of these are required for the occurrence of specific forms of peptic ulcer disease. No single factor is alone pathogenetic. In trying to produce acute gastric erosions in the dog, Ritchie (1975)

74

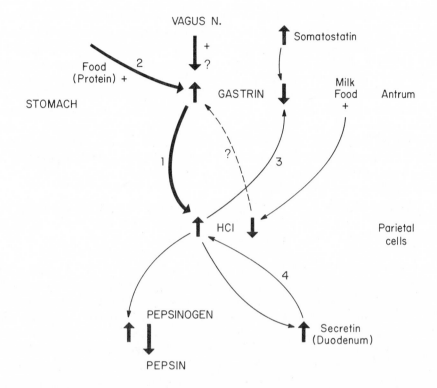

FIGURE 2 **Several Types of Regulatory Disturbances Described in Patients with Peptic Duodenal Ulcer.** (1) In some patients administered gastrin has an excessive (↑) stimulating effect on the secretion of hydrochloric acid by gastric parietal cells. (2) In other patients a protein meal excessively stimulates gastrin and hydrochloric acid secretion. (3) In another group of patients the inhibition of gastrin secretion by hydrochloric acid is diminished. In the presence of high levels of acidity in the stomach, gastrin levels remain normal, not low. (4) In some patients with gastrinoma, secretin may further stimulate hydrochloric acid secretion, rather than inhibiting the stimulating effects of gastrin on hydrochloric acid secretion (*see* Figure 1).

found that mucosal ischemia, topically applied acid, and topically applied bile salts separately produced no lesions. But he found that significant lesions were formed when all three of these factors were combined.

The relevance of these data to a psychosomatic theory of the pathogenesis of duodenal ulcer is that psychological factors may interact in different ways with the several different autoregulatory disturbances described to date. It may be that developmental and emotional factors contribute to the various disturbances in endocrine or neural organization of gastric and duodenal physiology that culminate in duodenal ulceration. But the manner in which such factors might do so are unknown.

Histamine. As is well known, histamine powerfully stimulates the secretion of acid by the stomach and weakly stimulates the secretion of pepsinogen. Thus, in the carcinoid tumors of the stomach and in mastocytosis, both of which are characterized by the release of large amounts of histamine, peptic ulceration is common (Melmon, 1968). This does not mean that histamine plays a key role in the pathogenesis of peptic ulcer disease. Its natural role in the regulation of acid secretion by the stomach has not been determined (Glass, 1968; Hirschowitz, 1967). However, enzymes for histamine synthesis do reside in the mucosa of the human stomach, and repeated injections of histamine have produced duodenal ulceration of the stomachs of guinea pigs (Gobbel and Adkins, 1967) and rats (Robert and Stout, 1969), especially when both histamine and gastrin were administered together (Robert et al., 1970).

Yet a role for histamine in peptic duodenal ulcer disease is suggested by the observation that drugs that block one (H_2) of the two histamine receptors are therapeutic in the disease (Pounder et al., 1975).

ANIMAL MODELS OF PEPTIC ULCER AND GASTRIC EROSIONS

Spontaneous Peptic Ulcer and Gastric Erosions

Our knowledge of a human illness is enhanced by the animal model of the disease. The search for an animal analogue of duodenal ulcer disease in man has been a long one and is still not complete. First, erosions, whether spontaneous or experimentally produced in animals, are usually located in the stomach. Therefore, the lesion may have more relevance to human gastric ulcers, or stress ulcers, then to duodenal ulcer disease (Grosz and Wu, 1967). Or, as Ackerman (1975) has pointed out, restraint- or cold-induced gastric erosions in young rats may tell us more about the conditions that produce duodenal ulceration in children than in adults. Second, many different experimental conditions can produce gastric erosions in rats, which are the preferred experimental animal. Despite the importance of studying the conditions that promote gastric erosions in a controlled setting, there are advantages to knowing whether gastric or duodenal ulcers occur naturally in animals. Pigs and mice have been reported to develop "spontaneous" ulcers. Pigs brought to slaughter may develop perforating ulcers of the gastroesophageal region (Perry et al., 1966). Attempts to explain this frequent occurrence have concentrated on a search for specific dietary factors, but without success. The incidence of these ulcers may be connected with the manner in which the animals are housed prior to slaughter. Each animal is housed in a small pen, in a condition of virtual restraint which may be "stressful" in the same way as restraint-stress may be to rats in the laboratory.

Williams et al. (1967) reported spontaneous ulcers in mice of the NZB strain. In these mice, erosions began to appear at about 9 months of age; by the age of 26 months, from 80 to 100 percent of the animals are affected. We do not know the mechanism by which gastric erosions occur in these animals or why the erosions develop at a particular age.

Duodenal Ulceration in Animals

As has been mentioned, most of the experimental techniques produce not duodenal ulcers but gastric erosions. Occasionally, drugs—either singly or in combination—may produce duodenal ulceration. Each of the drugs used is a powerful stimulus to gastric acid secretion, and has also been shown to increase the parietal cell mass in some species of animals. Both histamine and gastrin produce duodenal ulcers in animals. Carbachol, a powerful parasympathetic agent, potentiates the effects of histamine and of gastrin in producing duodenal ulcers (Robert et al., 1970). Duodenal ulcers occurred in rats fed a diet deficient in pantothenic acid. Even those rats that did not develop ulcers developed hypersecretion of gastric acid when fed a diet deficient in this vitamin (Berg, et al., 1949; Seronde, 1963; Zucker, 1958). Finally, chronic ulcers have occasionally been produced in monkeys by avoidance-conditioning techniques. The pathogenetic mechanisms involved in producing these ulcers remain unknown (Brady, 1964; Porter, et al., 1958).

The Experimental Production of Gastric Erosions in Animals

Gastric erosions can be produced in animals by a wide variety of experimental manipulations—burns, intense sensory stimulation, the administration of a large variety of drugs, tying off the pylorus, brain stimulation, diet, starvation, restraint, immobilization, and conditioning techniques (Brodie, 1968; Ader, 1970)—used singly or in combination.

The technique most frequently used to induce ulcers in animals is restraint-immobilization; it was pioneered by Selye (1950), and further explored by Ader (1963), Lamberg (1968) and Bonfils and his colleagues (1959, 1960). It is a simple technique that has produced a variety of interesting results, demonstrating that a number of variables are involved in causing ulceration in the glandular portion of the animal's stomach. Only recently, however, has it become evident that this technique confounds the effects of food deprivation and restraint. Ackerman et al. (1975) demonstrated that gastric ulceration could be produced without restraint in rats that were weaned at 15 days and were not fed for 24 hours at 22 days. The same result could not be obtained with rats weaned at 21 days; they had to be restrained before gastric ulcers could be produced.

When restraint is used in the usual manner, the important variables in producing gastric erosions are the species and age of the experimental animal, the length of time and the number of times he is immobilized, and the availability of food and water (Brodie and Hanson, 1960). The experimenter must also bear in mind that different experimental manipulations may produce gastric erosions in different parts of the stomach and may, therefore, be mediated by different physiological mechanisms, which are still unidentified.

Another important experimental variable is that some animals of a defined strain are more susceptible to a particular manipulation than others. The individual susceptibilities to gastric erosions are due to individual variations in serum pepsinogen levels. Ader (1963) bred rats for their susceptibility to gastric lesions on restraint. These animals had higher levels of serum pepsinogen prior to restraint; high serum pepsinogen levels were not, therefore, a response to restraint. However, not every animal that had higher levels of serum pepsinogen developed gastric lesions. Ader (1964, 1967) later explored the reason for the individual differences in susceptibility to ulceration, which were found even in predisposed animals. He found that animals restrained at the peak of their circadian activity were much more likely to develop ulceration than those restrained at the least-active period of their cycle. A high level of serum pepsinogen may be assumed, therefore, to constitute one physiological indicator of an increased susceptibility to erosion in the glandular portion of the stomach in one species of rats (Ader, 1963; Ader et al. 1960).

The prior experience of rats constitutes another variable that affects their individual susceptibility to ulceration. Rats that were individually housed after weaning and restrained at about 80 days were less likely to develop gastric ulcers than comparable animals who were housed together (Ader, 1965; Sines, 1965; Stern et al., 1960). The handling of animals also seems to play a role in determining later responses to restraint. Rats that were handled daily for the first 21 days of life were less likely to develop gastric lesions on immobilization-restraint than rats that were not handled (Weininger, 1956; Winokur et al., 1959). Premature weaning at age 16 days predisposed male rats to gastric erosions when they were immobilized at various ages before and after sexual maturity. The prematurely weaned rats were more susceptible to erosions before sexual maturity, but not after, when compared to rats weaned at the usual age of 21 days (Erdösóva et al., 1967). These experiments have pointed up the importance of prior experience in the later production of gastric erosions. This variable is usually overlooked in experiments using classical- and avoidance-conditioning techniques, which have proved to be very productive in demonstrating that gastric secretory responses can be brought under environmental control; these techniques are also associated with duodenal and gastric ulceration.

Increased gastric secretion of acid can be brought about by classical and avoidance-conditioning in animals and in man (Brady, 1964; Brooks, 1967; Bykov and Kurstin, 1966; Smith, 1967; Sun et al., 1958; Wolf, 1965). Human subjects may, however, respond to the meaning that these techniques have acquired for them rather than the actual conditioning technique itself. Generally speaking, chronic elevations of gastric acid secretion are not produced until an animal (monkey or dog) has had prolonged exposure to the conditioning schedule (Mahl, 1949, 1952; Polish et al., 1962). However, these secretory changes do not occur in every animal, and animals in which they do occur differ in their responses. It has been suggested that temperamental differences between "nervous" and "aggressive" dogs may account for their differences in gastric secretory responses to conditioning techniques. Species differences may also explain why monkeys of some species, and not others, develop duodenal ulcers when exposed to operant avoidance schedules (Brady et al., 1958; Polish et al., 1962; Porter et al., 1958). But this technique is not always successful; Foltz and Millet (1964), who duplicated the experimental design and conditions that Brady and his co-workers (1958) had used successfully, claimed that no duodenal ulceration occurred. On the other hand, Foltz's and Millet's criterion of a lack of ulceration was the absence of blood in the animal's stool; no post-mortem examination of the animal's stomach was made. Moreover, Brady (1967) has suggested that the "red-faced" monkeys (Macaca iris) used in his experiments differ significantly from the Macaca mulatta monkeys used by Foltz and Millet (1964). He has also recommended that important individual differences be taken into account when monkeys are used in research on chronic elevations of acid secretion and the production of peptic ulcer by behavioral means. Thus, Brady (1964) found that in a series of nine monkeys, the two animals who developed peptic ulceration at the end of a 28-period had the highest initial-free-acid concentration, showed a progressive increase in the level of secretion during the first two weeks of the experiment, and maintained these levels for the duration of the experiment. The monkeys who did not develop ulcers had lower levels of acid secretion initially, and some showed a decline in the level of secretion after the first two weeks of the experiment. Mason et al. (1961) reported changes in urinary pepsinogen with these operant conditioning techniques in the monkey, but it has been suggested that these changes may have been due to inflammation of the gastric mucosa, rather than to emotional stimuli (Pilot and Spiro, 1961).

Another offshoot of the work of Porter et al. (1958) and Brady and his colleagues (1958) was the demonstration that if two animals who had initially been trained to avoid shock were put in situations where only one of them (the "executive") could turn off the shock for both of them after a warning signal had been given, the "executive" monkey died. At autopsy it was found to have ulceration of the gastric and duodenal mucosa. This dramatic demonstration is not easy to conceptualize; supposedly, the avoidance of shock is "stressful" in some undefined way, because the "executive" monkey did avoid the pain of electric shock both for itself and its partner.

On the surface it would seem that the "executive" monkey "coped" well in avoiding shock, but nevertheless developed gastric and duodenal ulcers. That "coping" to avoid shock may be important in *preventing* the development of gastric erosions was first demonstrated by Weiss in 1968. Rats that were prevented from avoiding a shock developed more and larger gastric erosions than animals who either received no shock at all or who could avoid it by turning it off when a light signal was given. In a similar vein, Weiss et al. (1974) showed that when pairs of rats were shocked, each fought or bit its companion tethered nearby. When they were prevented from biting or fighting each other they were more likely to develop gastric erosions. Presumably, biting or fighting a companion attenuates the effects of painful shock in producing gastric erosions; they may be the animal's way of "coping" with painful shock. In any case, the concept of "coping" in an animal is a tenuous one. What may be of more scientific interest is a careful analysis of the changes in brain and gastric chemistry and physiology under these two different conditions.

Another frequently used experimental situation is the production of "conflict" in animals. A conflict situation is one in which an animal is forced to make behavioral responses that are opposite to or are in competition with one another. There are many ways to set up a conflict situation. Sawrey and Weiss (1956) employed an approach-avoidance situation, in which the animal had to cross an electrically charged grid in order to obtain food and water for 47 out of 48 horus. During 1 hour out of the 48 the electric current was turned off so that the animal was not prevented from eating. Six out of nine animals developed erosions in the nonglandular rumen of the stomach. None of the control animals did. In a later study, Sawrey and his colleagues (1956) established that the conflict situation was more likely to produce gastric erosions than was a combination of electric shock, hunger, and thirst without conflict. Other methods of producing conflict produced erosions in the glandular portion of rats' stomachs, not in the rumen. Lower (1967) produced conflict by irregularly and unpredictably shocking animals with an electric current when they had been trained to press a lever for a food reward. These animals developed ulcers in the glandular portion of the stomach. The reasons for the different locations of the erosions in these two different conflict situations are still unknown.

However, food deprivation and some form of (painful) sensory stimulation are potent factors in producing gastric erosions (Paré, 1964, 1972). The sensory stimulus does not have to be an electric shock. Continuous stimulation by light or sounds can produce gastric erosions. When exposed to light or sound stimulation, rats fed a normal diet are less likely to develop erosions than those on a diet deficient in methionine.

We do not as yet know why various forms of sensory stimulation should produce gastric erosions. However, it is well-known that the mere sight of food acts as a potent stimulus to the secretion of hydrochloric acid and gastrin by the stomach in dogs and in man (Pavlov, 1927; Perthein and Schofield, 1959). Various forms of sensory stimulation and immobilization-restraint stimulate the secretion of acid by the stomach (Brodie, 1962). Conversely, depriving a dog of its senses of smell, vision, or hearing, or of vestibular stimulation not only lowers its basal rate but also its histamine—or insulin—induced peak rate of gastric acid secretion (Schapiro et al., 1970a, b, 1971).

Some advances in our understanding of the mechanisms that produce gastric erosions has come from studying the manner in whch cold (5–8° C) enhances the capacity of electric shock or immobilization-restraint (Rosenberg, 1967). Senay and Levine (1967) found that when rats were restrained in a cold climate, intragastric pH fell and ulcers were produced; an antacid protected against the production of ulcers under these conditions. Interestingly, Levine and Senay (1970) also demonstrated that restraint and cold increase the activity of the enzyme histidine decarboxylase; this increase is positively correlated with the incidence and severity of stress ulcers. The inhibition of diamine oxidase (the enzyme that catabolizes histamine) has the same effect. One may infer that restraint in a cold climate induces the synthesis of histamine and inhibits its disposition in the cells of the rat's stomach. In turn, histamine stimulates gastric acid production and secretion, which in turn produces gastric erosion.

Although histamine synthesis may be induced by cold, histamine given to rats housed at room temperature also produced gastric erosions. But it is still not clear whether histamine is the only or the main humoral mediator of the effects of restraint-immobilization. That these effects are humorally mediated is suggested by experiments on parabiotic rats. One of a pair of parabiotic rats was restrained on a moveable cart, and the other rat was allowed to pull the cart about.All of the restrained rats and 15 of the 17 pulling rats developed gastric ulcers after an initial 24 hours of food deprivation and an additional 28 to 30 hours in the experiment. Most variables were well controlled. The results suggest the transmission of a humoral substance from the restrained to the unrestrained member of the pair, and the authors proposed that this substance might be either histamine or serotonin (Tran and Gregg, 1974).

There is indirect evidence that serotonin, rather than histamine, mediates the effects of immobolization. Administration of 5-hydroxytryptophan, the precursor of the biosynthesis of serotonin, produces erosions in the glandular portion of the stomach and ulceration of the proximal duodenum of rats. When cholinergic transmission is blocked by atropine sulphate, lesion formation is prevented (Haverback and Bogdanski, 1957). The administration of 5-hydroxytryptophan increases the number of mast cells in the serosa and the muscular and submucosal layers of a rat's stomach. In turn, these particular mast cells contain more 5-hydroxytryptophan (Muryobayashi et al., 1968). It is, therefore, possible that the biosynthesis and release of serotonin is enhanced by these experimental procedures, and that serotonin mediates the effects of immobilization-restraint and cold in the production of erosions. But the experimental conditions may also be mediated by increased sympathetic activity in adrenergic nerves. This contention is based on the work of Djahanguiri et al. (1973), who found that the turnover rates of catecholamines (especially norepinephrine) in the glandular portions of the stomach of rats was increased by restraint immobilization, with and without cold exposure. The increase in turnover rates was ascribed specifically to an increase in α-adrenergic neuronal activity, because α-adrenergic blocking agents prevented the effect; β-adrenergic blocking agents or adrenalectomy did not. It was the contention of these authors, on the basis of work by Delaney and Grime (1965) in the dog, that the increased turnover of norepinephrine might reduce blood flow through the stomach. The reduction in turn might be conducive to gastric erosion. Whether ischemia of the gastric mucosa actually does produce gastric erosions in rats is, however, still a matter of controversy (Davenport and Barr, 1973; Hase and Moss, 1973).

Up to this point, gastric erosions brought about by immobilizing or cooling animals have been ascribed to local biochemical changes in the stomach. In all likelihood, gastric erosions brought about by conditioning procedures and sensory stimulation are mediated by the brain, which may also participate in the effects of immobilization and exposure to cold. Restraint and cold change the levels and turnover rates of various biogenic amines in the brain. As in the case of the production of gastrin erosions, it is essential in such experiments to take into account the prior experience of the animal. Welch and Welch (1968) showed that immobilization produced greater elevations of brain catecholamine and serotinin levels in mice that had been reared in isolation for 8 to 12 weeks than in those animals reared in groups. Prior to immobilization, the isolated animals had lower baseline turnover rates in the brain than the mice who had been reared together. The Welches concluded that immobilization produced an increased demand for biogenic amines in the brain, and that the mechanisms to conserve them are activated to different degrees in animals with different prior experiences. Decreases in the concentration and increases in turnover of brain serotonin after restraint have been fairly well-established (Bliss and Zwanziger, 1966; Curzon and Green, 1971 and 1972), especially for the pons, medulla, and cortex of rats. One to two hours of restraint and cold (4 °C), separately or together, reduce histamine levels in various parts of the rat brain (specifically in the hypothalamus, thalamus-midbrain, and cerebral cortex), but also increase its synthesis in the hypothalamus. Therefore, the two "stresses" increase the disposition of histamine more than its synthesis, with the net effect of lowering histamine levels in the hypothalamus (Taylor and Snyder, 1971). These changes in biogenic amines do not necessarily have a bearing on the production of gastric erosions. Only Paré and Livingston (1970) have studied the production of gastric erosions in rats placed in an experimental conflict situation for three days, while also estimating norepinephrine levels (not turnover rates) in the brains of their animals. Sixty-one percent developed gastric erosions and had elevated brain norepinephrine levels. The reported changes in brain biogenic amines may or may not have anything to do with the development of gastric erosions. In the state of our present knowledge, it is very difficult to divine the connection between the correlated effects on the brain and the stomach.

SUMMARY AND CONCLUSIONS

This chapter comprises an overview of research on peptic duodenal ulcer relevant to psychosomatic medicine. On the basis of this review, certain tentative conclusions can be reached. It seems that at the present time we know somewhat more about the factors that predispose to this disease than about the factors that initiate or sustain it. One of these predisposing factors is genetic because duodenal ulcer runs in families. Of course, a familial tendency to a disease does not necessarily mean that it is inherited. But Eberhard's twin study (1968) indicates that genetic factors do play a role in duodenal ulcer disease. Eberhard shows that the concordance rate for duodenal ulcer is about 50 percent for monozygotic twins and 14 percent for dizygotic ones. But other evidence suggests that the propensities for duodenal and gastric ulcer are independently inherited.

We do not know, however, how the genetic tendency to duodenal ulcer manifests itself. It may be expressed by increased acid-pepsin secretion in some patients, or by a decreased resistance of the mucosa to acid and pepsin, or both. The greater parietal cell-mass may be an inherited characteristic in other patients. The increased incidence of O blood group in patients with duodenal ulcer and the fact that nonsecretors of ABH antigens have a significantly higher incidence of duodenal ulcer than secretors may reflect a genetic predisposition to duodenal ulcer. In turn, the absence of these mucoprotein antigens may mean that there is also an inherited defect in the mucoprotein composition of the protective mucus of the duodenum.

Another possibility was suggested by Mirsky. He believed that at birth there were genetic variations in the secretory capacity of the stomach—as reflected in an increased production of pepsinogen—and that the psychological predisposition to peptic duodenal ulcer, which consists of a fixation at an infantile level, might be brought about by this increased secretory capacity of the stomach. In some unexplained way, this increase in secretory capacity might lead to a disturbance in the early mother-child relationship, consisting of a failure of the child to feel satisfied despite adequate mothering. In this way, a physiological variation might lead to oral fixation and the persistence of the oral conflicts that many have identified in ulcer patients. But this attractive speculation has not been tested.

Mirsky's speculation sought to explain the childhood origins of the psychological characteristics of the adult patient with peptic duodenal ulcer. Yet duodenal ulcer in children and adolescents does occur, albeit rarely. About two patients per year are seen in major pediatric centers in the United States (Tudor, 1972). Peptic ulcer disease may occur acutely in infants and is associated with a large parietal cell mass and high levels of gastric acidity (Polacek and Ellison, 1966). This discovery suggests that an increased size of the parietal cell mass is an inborn trait, as I have previously suggested. In other children, acute peptic ulcers occur both in the stomach and duodenum, secondary to infection, the ingestion of drugs such as corticosteroids, or in a variety of hepatic and chronic pulmonary diseases (Avery et al., 1966). Chronic duodenal ulcer, often beginning in adolescence, shows many of the characteristics of the same disease in adults. In

82

adolescence it occurs much more frequently than chronic gastric ulcers. Yet there have been virtually no psychological studies of chronic peptic duodenal ulcer in children and adolescents. Such studies should exclude patients whose disease is secondary to the other chronic diseases mentioned above.

If the psychosomatic theory of peptic duodenal ulcer is correct, the psychological profile in children and adolescents should not differ significantly from that described by Alexander in adults. From the evidence reviewed in this chapter it can be concluded that many male adult patients are indeed predisposed to peptic duodenal ulcer by long-standing and unconscious wishes to be loved, cared for, and fed, given that they also have the anatomical and physiological predispositions to the illness. Therefore, one part of Alexander's original hypothesis does seem to have considerable validity for male patients. But it may not be valid for female patients, as Alexander's own later study (Alexander et al., 1968) seems to indicate. Nor does Alexander's hypothesis allow the fact that men are more frequently vulnerable to the disease, or that there is an apparent shift in the ratio of men to women patients over the course of the last decades. Unidentified social, economic, or cultural factors may account for these observations.

Suffice it to say that the first part of Alexander's formulation has received substantial confirmation by a predictive study. This study tended to support the notion that some men were both psychologically and physiologically predisposed to peptic duodenal ulcer. The psychological predisposition consisted of the wish to be cared for, nourished, and loved; and the physiological predisposition consisted of increased levels of serum pepsinogen. More recently it has been shown that patients with peptic ulcer have elevated levels of a pepsin isoenzyme—pepsin I—in their gastric juice.

Alexander also suggested that the chronic persistent, intrapsychic conflict over dependency in the overly independent person continually stimulates gastric secretion, presumably by heightening tonic vagal discharge. The evidence reviewed does not fully bear out his speculation. Only one-third to one-half of all patients are hypersecretors of gastric acid. Second, the positive evidence for increased vagal tone has been difficult, if not impossible, to accumulate (Fordtran, 1973a,b). Finally, the evidence presented in support of the role of emotional states in heightening gastric secretion has not been consistent. Mahl (1950) did find that examination anxiety enhanced acid secretion, but many other studies have produced contradictory results or have been made in patients with a gastrostomy. The results of studies on mucus production and mucosal blood flow using psychophysiological techniques have also been inconsistent.

Be that as it may, Alexander's supposition may not be necessary to demonstrate the role of psychological factors in the etiology and pathogenesis of peptic duodenal ulcer. The conflicts he described and the manner in which they express themselves may not "cause gastric acid hypersecretion;" they may simply "live side by side" with an increased parietal cell mass and, therefore, an increased basal secretion of acid. There is considerable evidence that increased acid and pepsin secretion is neither a necessary nor sufficient cause of duodenal ulcer formation. Hypersecretion is not unique to duodenal ulcer: it also occurs in some forms of gastric ulcer. And hypersecretion frequently persists even when the duodenal ulcer is inactive or healed. And as mentioned, less than half of all patients with duodenal ulcer are hypersecretors. Because not all patients with duodenal ulcer have an excessive secretory capacity for pepsin and hydrochloric acid, and not all persons with this excessive capacity develop the disease, additional factors to explain the initiation of the disease have to be considered; these include changes in the local blood supply to the duodenum, which is under automatic neural control; the protective role of mucus; the permeability of duodenal cells to hydrogen ion; and the roles of glucagon, histamine, and the calcium ion. Various combinations of these factors may account for the initiation of the disease. For example, ischemia may lower mucus production in some patients and make the duodenal mucosa vulnerable in the presence of excess acid. Excessive acid and pepsin secretion in the presence of increased autonomic discharge, but with normal mucus production, may initiate ulceration in other forms, especially if duodenal inhibition of acid secretion by secretin has failed (Harkins and Nyhus, 1962; Love, 1970; Shay et al., 1942; State, 1971). Still other patients with duodenal ulcer are more sensitive on injection to the naturally-occurring hormone, gastrin. They respond with a maximal acid output on one-half the dose of gastrin required by control subjects. The reasons for this heightened sensitivity have not been elucidated. Another group of patients show a very high maximal acid output even with high basal, unstimulated acid output. In these patients increases in output are exaggerated in response to the eating of food and to a smaller-than-usual dose of histamine stimulation.

These data suggest that in some patients with duodenal ulcer disease there is a heightened reactivity of the parietal cells to stimulation, so that the same stimulus (food, gastrin, etc.) produces an exaggerated acid secretory response when compared with normal persons. In still other patients, the autoregulation of gastrin by hydrochloric acid is altered, a defect in regulation that would tend to promote continuous acid secretion. How this heightened sensitivity of the parietal cell mass or the disturbance in feedback regulation of gastrin interact either with changes in vagal or sympathetic discharge or with the action of secretin and other enterogastrone inhibitors of acid secretion is not known.

Finally, psychosomatic theory and research has overlooked the role of the protective mucous layer. Because many patients secrete more acid even when in remission, it has been suggested that ischemia of the circulation of the stomach and a diminished protective mucus may play an important proximal role in initiating ulceration. By what means psychological factors could cause variations in the circulation or in mucus production is unknown, with one exception. Distressed predisposed persons may ingest more drugs such as aspirin and alcohol. Aspirin seems to interfere with the synthesis of the mucoproteins of the protective mucous layer.

Therefore, there is no evidence to substantiate Alexander's hypothesis that the chronic psychological conflict promotes gastric hypersecretion before an ulcer is formed, or that hypersecretion is enhanced at the same time the duodenal lesion appears. Since the time he formulated these hypotheses it has become apparent that no single or invariant set of pathogenetic factors can incite a duodenal ulcer. The ulcer can be caused by a gastrinoma and a carcinoid tumor of the stomach—that is, by different mechanisms. Therefore it is logical to assume that still others could also cause duodenal ulcer. These other mechanisms consist of: (1) various kinds of variations and disturbances in the autoregulation of gastric secretion by gastrin and secretin, (2) an enlarged parietal cell mass, (3) changes in gastric blood flow and motility, (4) altered mucin production or mucosal integrity. Different forms of peptic ulcer disease may result from different (local) pathogenetic causes.

Perhaps emotional distress in the predisposed person may be mediated by brain mechanisms, but these may modify the various local pathogenetic mechanisms in different ways. More than one neural and hormonal mechanism exists that can alter the physiology of the stomach and duodenum in man and in animals. In future psychosomatic studies of duodenal ulcer, the investigator will need to describe the psychological or social characteristics of his patient population. He will also need to describe his subjects accurately according to such characteristics as the pattern of their basal and stimulated gastric acid secretion (and the ratio between them), the pattern of gastrin release and the presence or absence of other regulatory abnormalities, as they become more clearly defined and technically more accessible to routine investigation.

Alexander's final assumption that the psychological conflict was mediated by the vagus nerve is probably also not entirely correct. The role of vagal efferent activity in ulcer pathogenesis may be an important one, but it has probably been overemphasized in the past. Interestingly, the role of vagal afferents has probably been underestimated—and certainly inadequately investigated—by many researchers, despite the fact that approximately 90 percent of vagal fibers are afferent. One cannot, for instance, assume that the effect of vagotomy in the treatment of peptic ulcer disease results primarily from the beneficial effects of disconnecting the stomach from the efferent stimuli it receives from the brain. The effect of interrupting afferent vagal impulses in vagotomized patients remains to be investigated.

Aside from the neural regulation of gastroduodenal function, the recent evidence of its hormonal regulation (including hormones released from the hypothalamus and pituitary) open new vistas on the pathogenesis of peptic ulcer disease. One would like to know more about the effects of development, behavior, psychological experience, and conflict on the release of these hormones and more about the effect of their release in the pathogenesis of duodenal ulcer.

The elucidation of the mechanisms whereby psychological stress and distress leads to ulcer formation has also been advanced by studies on animals. The studies that have been reviewed attest to the complexity of the physiological changes and the multiplicity of factors that can incite ulcers. But considering the importance of the concept of predisposing factors in psychosomatic formulations about human ulcer disease, little supporting data exists in animals that elucidates the role of genetic, developmental, or behavioral factors in predisposing them to ulcer formation. Rats have been selectively bred for predisposition to experimental gastric erosions, and several studies have demonstrated that early separation from the mother increases the vulnerability of rats to gastric erosions later in life. But the neural or gastric processes mediating these effects need to be elucidated by future research; and the applicability of the animal model to the human peptic ulcer disease needs also to be clarified.

REFERENCES

Ackerman, S. H. 1975. Restraint ulceration as an experimental disease model. *Psychosom. Med.* 37:4.

———, Hofer, M. A., and Weiner, H. 1975. Age at maternal separation and gastric erosion susceptibility in the rat. *Psychosom. Med.* 37:180.

Ader, R. 1963. Plasma pepsinogen level as a predictor of susceptibility to gastric erosions in the rat. *Psychosom. Med.* 25:221.

———— 1964. Gastric erosions in the rat. Effects of immobilization at different points in the activity cycle. *Science* 145:406.

———— 1965. Effects of early experience and differential housing on behavior and susceptibility to gastric erosions in the rat. *J. Comp. Physiol. Psychol.* 60:233.

———— 1967. Behavioral and physiological rhythms and the development of gastric erosions in the rat. *Psychosom. Med.* 29:345.

———— 1970. Peptic Ulcer: Results and implications of studies in animals. *Adv. Psychosom. Med.* 6:1.

————, Beels, C. C., and Tatum, R. 1960. Blood pepsinogen and gastric erosions in the rat. *Psychosom. Med.* 22:1.

Alexander, F. 1934. The influence of psychologic factors upon gastrointestinal disturbances: General principles, objectives and preliminary results. *Psychoanal. Q.* 3:501.

———— 1947. A case of peptic ulcer and personality disorder. *Psychosom. Med.* 9:320.

———— 1950. *Psychosomatic Medicine.* New York: Norton.

———— 1953. Discussion of paper by Mahl and Karpe. *Psychosom. Med.* 15:327.

————, French, T. M., and Pollack, G. H. 1968. *Psychosomatic Specificity: Experimental Study and Results.* Chicago: University of Chicago Press.

Alvarez, W. C. 1943. *Nervous Indigestion and Pain.* New York: Hoeber.

Anscombe, A. R. 1964. Plasma pepsinogen: Normal and abnormal secretion. *Ann. R. Coll. Surg. Engl.* 35:34.

Armstrong, R. H., Burnap, D., Jacobson, A., Kales, A., Ward, S., and Golden, J. 1965. Dreams and gastric secretion in duodenal ulcer patients. *The New Physician* 14:241.

Artz, C. P., and Fitts, C. T. 1966. Gastrointestinal ulcerations associated with central nervous system lesions and burns. *Surg. Clin. North Am.* 46:309.

Avery, G. B., Randolph, J. G., and Weaver, T. 1966. Gastric response to specific disease in infants. *Pediatrics* 38:874.

Bachrach, W. H. 1963. On the question of a pituitary-adrenal component in the gastric secretory response to insulin hypoglycemia. *Gastroenterology* 44:178.

Bacon, C. L. 1934. Typical personality trends and conflicts in cases of gastric disturbances. *Psychoanal. Q.* 3:558.

Baron, J. H. 1962. Gastric secretion in relation to subsequent duodenal ulcer and family history. *Gut* 3:158.

———— 1963a. An assessment of the augmented histamine test in the diagnosis of peptic ulcer. *Gut* 4:243.

———— 1963b. The relationship between basal and maximum acid output in normal subjects and patients with duodenal ulcer. *Clin. Sci. Mol. Med.* 24:357.

———— 1970. The clinical use of gastric function tests. *Scand. J. Gastroenterol.* [Suppl.] 6:9.

Barreras, R. F., and Donaldson, R. M. 1967. Role of calcium in gastric hypersecretion, parathyroid adenoma and peptic ulcer. *N. Engl. J. Med.* 276:1122.

Baugh, V. S., and Stanford, G. A. 1964. Psychological factors in ulcer patients. *Dis. Nerv. Syst.* 25:553.

Beaumont, W. 1959. (1833) *Experiments and Observations on the Gastric Juice and the Physiology of Digestion.* New York: Dover.

Berg, B. N., Zucker, T. F., and Zucker, L. M. 1949. Duodenal ulcers produced on a diet deficient in panthothenic acid. *Proc. Soc. Exp. Biol. Med.* 71:374.

Berson, S. A., and Yalow, R. S. 1971. Gastrin in duodenal ulcer. *N. Engl. J. Med.* 284:445.

Bliss, E., and Zwanziger, J. 1966. Brain amines and emotional stress. *J. Psychiatr. Res.* 4:189.

Bloom, S. R., Mortimer, C. H., Thorner, M. O., Besser, G. M., Hall, R., Gomez-Pan, A., Roy,

V. M., Russell, R. C. G., Coy, D. H., Kastin, A. J., and Schally, A. V. 1974. Inhibition of gastrin and gastric acid secretion by growth-hormone release-inhibiting hormone. *Lancet* 2:1106.

Bodi, T., and Kazal, L. A. 1965. Some aspects of the pathophysiology and the multiple contributing factors in hemorrhage from the upper gastrointestinal tract. *Am. J. Gastroenterol.* 44:202.

Bonfils, S., Liefooghe, G., Rossi, G., and Lambling, A. 1957. L'ulcère de contrainte du rat blanc. Modifications de la fréquence lésionnelle par différents procédés opératoires et pharmacodynamiques. *C. R. Soc. Biol.* (Paris) 151:1149.

———, Gellé, X., Dubrasquet, M., et Lambling, A. 1960 'Ulcère' expérimental de contrainte du rat blanc. III. Mise en évidence et analyse du rôle de certains facteurs psychologiques. *Rev. franç. Et. clin. biol.* 4:888.

———, Richir, C., Potet, F., Liefooghe, G., et Lambling, A. 1959. Ulcère expérimental de contrainte du rat blanc. II. Anatomopathologie des lésions gastriques et de différentes lésions viscérales. *Rev. franç. Et. clin. biol.* 4:888.

Bradlow, S. P. 1967. Parietal cell mass and gastric secretion. In *The Stomach*, edited by C. M. Thompson. New York: Grune & Stratton.

Brady, J. V. 1958. Ulcers in "executive" monkeys. *Sci. Am.* 199:95.

——— 1964. Experimental studies of psychophysiologic responses to stressful situations. In *Symposium on Medical Aspects of Stress in the Military Climate*. Washington, D. C.: Walter Reed Army Institute of Research.

——— 1967. Quoted by Smith, G. P. 1967.

———, Porter, R. W., Conrad, D. G., and Mason, J. W. 1958. Avoidance behavior and the development of gastroduodenal ulcers. *J. Exp. Anal. Behav.* 1:69.

Brodie, D. A. 1962. Ulceration of the stomach produced by restraint in rats. *Gastroenterology* 43:107.

——— 1968. Experimental peptic ulcer. *Prog. Gastroenterol.* 55:125.

——— and Hanson, H. M. 1960. A study of the factors involved in the production of gastric ulcers by the restraint technique. *Gastroenterology* 38:353.

Brooks, F. P. 1967. Central neural control of acid secretion. In *Handbook of Physiology, Section VI, Alimentary Canal*, vol. 2. Baltimore: Williams & Wilkins.

——— 1973. Hormones and peptic ulcer. *Am. J. Gastroenterol.* 60:250.

Brown, M., Bresnahan, T. J., Chalke, F. C. R., Peters, B., Poser, E. G., and Tougas, R. V. 1950. Personality factors in duodenal ulcer: A Rorschach study. *Psychosom. Med.* 12:1.

Browning, J. S., and Houseworth, J. H. 1953. Development of new symptoms following medical and surgical treatment for duodenal ulcer. *Psychosom. Med.* 15:328.

Burger, A. J., and Lambling, A. 1962. Formes cliniques psychosomatiques de la maladie ulcéreuse. In *Psychosomatique et Gastroentérologie*, edited by P. Aboulker, L. Chertok, and M. Sapir. Paris: Masson.

Bykov, K. M., and Kurstin, I. T. 1966. *The Corticovisceral Theory of the Pathogenesis of Peptic Ulcer*, trans. by S. A. Korson. New York: Pergamon.

Cannon, W. 1929. *Bodily Changes in Pain, Hunger, Fear and Rage*. New York: Appleton-Century-Crofts.

Card, W. I., and Marks, I. N. 1960. The relationship between the acid output of the stomach following "maximal" histamine stimulation and the parietal cell mass. *Clin. Sci. Mol. Med.* 19:147.

Castelnuovo-Tedesco, P. 1962. Emotional antecedents of perforation of ulcers of the stomach and duodenum. *Psychosom. Med.* 24:398.

Christensen, J. 1968. The adrenergic nerves and gastrointestinal smooth muscle function. *Gastroenterology* 55:135.

Classen, M. 1968. Gastrin and its significance. *Digestion* 1:120.

87

Cleveland, S., and Fisher, S. 1960. A comparison of psychological characteristics and physiological reactivity in ulcer and rheumatoid arthritis groups. I. Psychological measures. *Psychosom. Med.* 22:283.

Coddington, R. D. 1968. Study of an infant with a gastric fistula and her normal twin. *Psychosom. Med.* 30:172.

———, Sours, J. A., and Bruch, H. 1964. Electrogastrographic findings associated with affective changes. *Am. J. Psychiatr.* 121:41.

Cohen, S. I., Silverman, A. J., and Magnusson, F. 1956. New psychophysiologic correlates in women with peptic ulcer. *Am. J. Psychiatry* 112:1025.

———, ———, Waddell, W., and Zuidema, G. D. 1961. Urinary catecholamine levels, gastric secretion and specific psychological factors in ulcer and non-ulcer patients. *J. Psychosom. Res.* 5:90.

Colin-Jones, D. G., Gibbs, D. D., Copping, R. M. L., and Scharr, M. M. 1969. Malignant Zollinger-Ellison syndrome with gastrin-containing skin metastases. *Lancet* 1:492.

Cook, H. B., and French, A. B. 1968. Physiologic responses to gastric acid hypersecretion in Zollinger-Ellison syndrome. *Am. J. Dig. Dis.* 13:191.

Cooke, A. J. 1967. Corticosteroids and peptic ulcer: Is there a relationship? *Am. J. Dig. Dis.* 12:323.

Cooke, A. R. 1967. Role of adrenocortical steroids in the regulation of gastric secretion. *Gastroenterology* 52:272.

Cooke, H. J., and Cooke, A. R. 1968. Correlation between the weight of gastric mucosa and maximal acid secretion. *Digestion* 1:209.

Cox, A. J. 1953. Stomach size and its relation to chronic peptic ulcer. *Arch. Path.* 54:407.

Crean, G. P. 1967. Observations on the regulation of growth of the gastric mucosa. In *Gastric Secretion: Mechanisms and Control,* edited by T. K. Shnitka, J. A. L. Gilbert, and R. C. Harrison. New York: Pergamon.

——— 1968a. Effect of hypophysectomy on the gastric mucosa of the rat. *Gut* 9:332.

——— 1968b. A comparison between the effect of hypophysectomy and adrenalectomy on the gastric mucosa of the rat. *Gut* 9:343.

———, Marshall, M. W., and Rumsey, R. D. E. 1969. Parietal cell hyperplasia induced by the administration of pentagastrin to rats. *Gastroenterology* 57:147.

———, Hogg, D. F., and Rumsey, R. D. E. 1969. Hyperplasia of the gastric mucosa produced by duodenal obstruction. *Gastroenterology* 56:193.

Croog, S. H. 1957. Relation of plasma pepsinogen to ethnic origins. *U. S. Armed Forces Med. J.* 8:795.

Csalay, L., Frenkl, R., and Hegyváry, C. 1962. Ulcerogenic action of chronic neurogenic stimulation in the rat. *Acta Physiol. Scand.* 22:81.

Cummings, A. J. 1967. Gastric analysis: Methods and interpretations. In *The Stomach,* edited by C. M. Thompson et al. New York: Grune & Stratton.

Curzon, G., and Green, A. R. 1971. Regional and subcellular changes in the concentration of 5-hydroxytryptamine and 5-hydroxyindoleacetic acid in the rat brain caused by hydrocortisone, DL-methyltryptophan, L-kynurenine and immobilization. *Br. J. Pharmacol.* 43:39.

———, Joseph, M. H., and Knott, P. J. 1972. Effects of immobilization and food deprivation on rat brain tryptophan metabolism. *J. Neurochem.* 19:1967.

Damon, A., and Bell, B. 1967. Ethnic group and serum pepsinogen. *J. Chronic Dis.* 20:803.

———, and Polednak, A. P. 1967. Constitution, genetics and body form in peptic ulcer: A review. *J. Chronic Dis.* 20:787.

Davenport, H. W., and Barr, L. L. 1973. Failure of ischemia to break the dog's gastric mucosal barrier. *Gastroenterology* 65:619.

Davies, R. E. 1967. The metabolism of gastric mucosa during the secretion of hydrochloric acid. In

Gastric Secretion: Mechanisms and Control, edited by T. K. Shnitka, J. A. Gilbert, and R. C. Harrison. New York: Pergamon.

Davis, R. A., Brooks, F. P., and Steckel, D. C. 1968. Gastric secretory changes after anterior hypothalamic lesions. *Amer. J. Physiol.* 215:600.

Davis, R. C., and Berry, F. 1963. Gastrointestinal reactions during a noise avoidance task. *Psychol. Rep.* 12:135.

Delaney, J. P., and Grime, E. 1965. Experimentally induced variations in canine gastric blood flow and its distribution. *Am. J. Physiol.* 208:353.

De M'Uzan, M., and Bonfils, S. 1961. Étude et classification des aspects psychosomatiques de l'ulcére gastro-duodénal en milieu hospitalier. *Rev. Franc. Et Clin. Biol.* 6:46.

Djahanguiri, B., Taubin, H. L., and Landsberg, L. 1973. Increased sympathetic activity in the pathogenesis of restraint ulcer in the rat. *J. Pharmacol. Exp. Ther.* 184:163.

Doll, R., Hill, I. D., Hutton, C., and Underwood, D. J. 1962. Clinical trial of a triterpenoid liquorice compound in gastric and duodenal ulcer. *Lancet* 2:793.

Dragstedt, L. R. 1951. Gastric vagotomy in the treatment of peptic ulcer. *Postgrad. Med.* 10:482.

———— 1967. Gastric secretion and duodenal ulcer. In *Gastric Secretion: Mechanisms and Control*, edited by T. K. Shnitka, J. A. Gilbert and R. C. Harrison. New York: Pergamon.

————, Lulu, D. J., Riley, W. J., and Lawson, L. G. 1971. Cephalic hypersecreting primary gastric ulcer patients. *Arch. Surg.* 102:462.

Draper, G., and Touraine, G. A. 1932. The man-environment unit and peptic ulcers. *Arch. Intern. Med.* 49:615.

Dunbar, F. 1947. *Emotions and Bodily Change*, 3rd ed. New York: Columbia University Press.

Dungal, N., and Hansen, H. 1958. Peptic ulcers in Iceland. *Schweiz. Z. Allg. Pathol.* 21:225.

Eberhard, G. 1968. Personality and peptic ulcer: Preliminary report of a twin study. *Acta Psychiatr. Scand.* 203:131.

Eichhorn, R., and Tractir, J. 1955a. The effect of hypnosis upon gastric secretion. *Gastroenterology* 29:417.

————, and ———— 1955b. The relationship between anxiety, hypnotically induced emotions and gastric secretion. *Gastroenterology* 29:422.

————, and ———— 1955c. The effects of hypnotically induced emotions upon gastric secretion. *Gastroenterology* 29:432.

Eiseman, B. 1967. Relationship between liver disease and intestinal phase of gastric secretion. In *The Stomach*, edited by C. M. Thompson et al. New York: Grune & Stratton.

Eisenberg, M. M., Owens, J. E., and Woodward, E. R. 1964. Androgenic effect on gastric secretion. *Surg. Forum* 15:321.

Elivin, C. E., and Uvnäs, B. 1966. Distribution and local release of gastrin. In *Gastrin*, edited by M. I. Grossman. Proceedings of a Conference. Los Angeles: University of California Press.

Elliot, D. W. 1967. The endocrines and peptic ulcer. In *The Stomach*, edited by C. M. Thompson et al. New York: Grune & Stratton.

Elwin, C. W. 1969. Some factors influencing the stimulatory effect of ethanol on gastric acid secretion during antrum application. *Acta Physiol. Scand.* 75:12.

Ely, N. E., and Johnson, M. H. 1966. Emotional responses to peptic ulcer management. *Amer. J. Psychiat.* 122:1362.

Emås, S., and Grossman, M. I. 1968. Production of duodenal ulcer in cats by infusion of porcine gastrin. *Gastroenterology* 52:959.

Engel, G. L. 1962. *Psychological Development in Health and Disease*. Philadelphia: Saunders.

———— 1967. The concept of psychosomatic disease. *J. Psychosom. Res.* 11:1.

————, Reichsman, F., and Segal, H. L. 1956. Study of an infant with a gastric fistula. I. Behavior and the rate of total hydrochloric acid secretion. *Psychosom. Med.* 18:374.

Erdösová, R., Flandera, V., Křeček, J., and Wiener, P. 1967. The effect of premature weaning on the sensitivity of rats to experimental erosions of the gastric mucosa. *Physiol. Bohemosl.* 16:400.

Evans, D. A. P., Horwich, L., and McConnell, R. B. 1968. Influence of the ABO blood groups and secretor status on bleeding and on performation of duodenal ulcer. *Gut* 9:319.

Evans, D. H. L., and Murray, J. G. 1954. Histological and functional studies on the fibre composition of the vagus nerve of the rabbit. *J. Anat.* 88:320.

Feldman, S., Wajsbort, J., and Birnbaum, D. 1967. Effect of combined brain stimulation on gastric secretion, acidity and potassium concentration in cats. *Brain Res.* 4:103.

Fisher, S., and Cleveland, S. E. 1952. A comparison of psychological characteristics and physiological reactivity in ulcer and rheumatoid arthritis groups. I. Differences in physiological reactivity. *Psychosom. Med.* 14:243.

————, and ——— 1958. *Body Image and Personality.* New York: Van Nostrand.

————, and ——— 1960. A comparison of psychological characteristics and physiological reactivity in ulcer and rheumatoid arthritis groups. II. Differences in physiological reactivity. *Psychosom. Med.* 22:290.

Fodor, O., Vestea, S., and Urcan, S. 1968. Hydrochloric acid secretion capacity of the stomach as an inherited factor in the pathogenesis of duodenal ulcer. *Am. J. Dig. Dis.* 13:260.

Foltz, E. L., and Millet, F. E., Jr. 1964. Experimental psychosomatic disease states in monkeys. I. Peptic ulcer—"executive monkeys." *J. Surg. Res.* 4:445.

Fordtran, J. S. 1973a. Acid secretion in peptic ulcer. In *Gastrointestinal Disease,* edited by M. H. Sleisenger and J. S. Fordtran. Philadelphia: Saunders.

——— 1973b. The psychosomatic theory of peptic ulcer. In *Gastrointestinal Disease,* edited by M. H. Sleisinger and J. S. Fordtran. Philadelphia: Saunders.

Forrester, J. M., and Ganguli, P. C. 1970. The effect of meat extract (Oxo) on plasma gastrin concentration in human subjects. *J. Physiol.* (Lond.) 211:33.

Fox, H. M. 1958. Effect of psychophysiological research on the transference. *J. Am. Psychoanal. Assoc.* 6:413.

French, J. D., Porter, R. W., Cavanaugh, E. B., and Longmire, R. L. 1957. Experimental gastroduodenal lesions induced by stimulation of the brain. *Psychosom. Med.* 19:209.

Friedman, J. H., and Anderson, J. 1967. Body image variability in peptic ulcer: A perceptual experiment with identical twins. *Arch. Gen. Psychiatry* 16:334.

Fyrö, B. 1967. Reduction of antral and duodenal gastrin activity by electrical vagal stimulation. *Acta Physiol. Scand.* 71:334.

Ganguli, P. C., and Hunter, W. M. 1972. Radio-immunoassay of gastrin in human plasma. *J. Physiol.* (Lond.), 220:499.

Garma, A. 1958. *Peptic Ulcer and Psychoanalysis.* Baltimore: Williams & Wilkins.

——— 1960. The unconscious images in the genesis of peptic ulcer. *Int. J. Psychoanal.* 41:444.

Gillespie, I. E., Clark, D. H., Kay, A. W., and Tankel, H. I. 1960. Effects of antrectomy, vagotomy with gastrojejunostomy and antrectomy with vagotomy on the spontaneous and maximal gastric acid output in men. *Gastroenterology* 38:361.

Glass, G. B. J. 1967. Current status of the "glandular mucoprotein" and "mucoproteose" fractions of the gastric mucin: A review of 15 years' progress in this area. *Ann. N.Y. Acad. Sci.* 140:804.

——— 1968. *Introduction to Gastrointestinal Physiology.* Englewood Cliffs, N.J.: Prentice-Hall.

Glen, A. I. M. 1968. Psychotherapy and medical treatment for duodenal ulcer compared using the augmented histamine test. *J. Psychosom. Res.* 12:163.

Gobbel, W. G., Jr., and Adkins, R. B. 1967. Production of duodenal ulcers by exogenous gastrin: An experimental model. *Am. J. Surg.* 113:183.

Goidsenhoven, G. V., Wilkoff, L., and Kirsner, J. B. 1958. Serum and urine pepsinogen and gastric secretion. *Gastroenterology* 34:421.

Goldberg, E. M. 1958. *Family Influences and Psychosomatic Illness: An Inquiry into the Social and Psychological Background of Duodenal Ulcer.* London: Tavistock.

Goldman, M. C. 1963. Gastric secretion during a medical interview. *Psychosom. Med.* 25:351.

Goulston, K., and Cooke, A. R. 1968. Alcohol, aspirin and gastrointestinal bleeding. *Brit. Med. J.* 4:664.

Grace, W. J., and Graham, D. T. 1952. Relationship of specific attitudes and emotions to certain bodily diseases. *Psychosom. Med.* 14:243.

Graham, D. T., Lundy, R. M., Benjamin, L. S., Kabler, J. D., Lewis, W. C., Kunish, N. O., and Graham, F. K. 1962. Specific attitudes in initial interviews with patients having different "psychosomatic" diseases. *Psychosom. Med.* 24:257.

Grant, G. 1967. Quoted by D. Elliot. In *The Stomach*, edited by C. M. Thompson et al. New York: Grune & Stratton.

Graväard, E. 1968. A study of the vagus nerves at the lower end of the esophagus, with special reference to duodenal ulcer and acute gastroduodenal ulcerations. *Scand. J. Gastroenterol.* 3:327.

Gregory, R. A. 1968. Recent advances in the physiology of gastrin. *Proc. Roy. Soc. Lond.* [*Biol.*] B 170:81.

———, Tracy, H. J., and Grossman, M. I. 1966. Human gastrin: Isolation, structure and synthesis. *Nature* 209:583.

Grossman, M. I. 1967. Neural and hormonal stimulation of acid secretion. In *Handbook of Physiology, section 6, Alimentary Canal*, vol. 2, edited by American Physiological Society. Baltimore: Williams & Wilkins.

——— et al. 1974. Candidate hormones of the gut. *Gastroenterology* 67:730.

Grosz, C. R., and Wu, K. 1967. Stress ulcers—a survey of the experience in a large general hospital. *Surgery* 61:853.

Gundry, R. K., Donaldson, R. K., Pinderhughes, C. A., and Barrabee, E. 1967. Patterns of gastric acid secretion in patients with duodenal ulcer: Correlations with clinical and personality features. *Gastroenterology* 52:176.

Habbick, B. F., Melrose, A. G., and Grant, J. C. 1968. Duodenal ulcer in childhood: A study of predisposing factors. *Arch. Dis. Child.* 43:23.

Hachette, J.-C., Bordry, M., de M'Uzan, M., and Bonfils, S. 1973. Étude psychosomatique de 20 cas d'ulcères duodénaux chez la femme. *Arch. Fr. Mal. App. Dig.* 62:217.

Hagnell, O., and Wretmark, G. 1957. Peptic ulcer and alcoholism. *J. Psychosom. Res.* 2:35.

Hall, W. H., Herb, R. W., and Brady, J. P. 1967. Gastric function during hypnosis and hypnotically induced gastrointestinal symptoms. *J. Psychosom. Res.* 11:263.

Halliday, J. L. 1948. *Psychosocial Medicine: A Study of the Sick Society.* New York: Norton.

Hanley, W. B. 1964. Hereditary aspects of duodenal ulceration: Serum pepsinogen level in relation to ABO blood group and salivary ABH secretor status. *Br. J. Med.* 1:936.

Hansky, J., and Cain, M. D. 1969. Radioimmunoassay of gastrin in human serum. *Lancet* 2:1388.

Harkins, H. H., and Nyhus, L. M. 1962. *Surgery of the Stomach and Duodenum*, 1st ed. Boston: Little, Brown.

Harvey, N. A. 1969. The cybernetics of peptic ulcer. *N. Y. State J. Med.* 69:430.

Hase, T., and Moss, B. J. 1973. Microvascular changes of gastric mucosa in the development of stress ulcers in rats. *Gastroenterology* 65:224.

Haverback, B. J., and Bogdanski, D. F. 1957. Gastric mucosal erosion in the rat following administration of the serotonin precursor, 5-hydroxytryptophane. *Proc. Soc. Exp. Biol. Med.* 95:392.

Hayes, J. R., Ardill, J., Kennedy, T. L., Shanks, R. G., and Buchanan, K. D. 1972. Stimulation of gastrin release by catecholamines. *Lancet* 1:819.

Heller, M. H., Levine, J., and Sohler, T. P. 1953. Gastric acidity and normally produced anxiety. *Psychosom. Med.* 15:509.

Higginson, J., and Simson, I. 1958. Lesions of the gastrointestinal tract in the non-white population of South Africa. *Schweiz. Z. Allg. Path.* 21:577.

Hirschowitz, B. I. 1967a. Secretion of pepsinogen. In *Handbook of Physiology, Section 6, Alimentary Canal*, vol. 2. Baltimore: Williams & Wilkins.

——— 1967b. The control of pepsinogen secretion. *Ann. N. Y. Acad. Sci.* 140:709.

———, Streeton, D. H. P., London, J. A., and Pollard, H. M. 1957. Effects of 8-hour intravenous infusions of ACTH and adrenocortical steroids in normal men. *J. Clin. Invest.* 36:1171.

Hoejer-Pederson, W. 1958. On the significance of psychic factors in the development of peptic ulcer. *Acta Psychiatr. et Neurol. Scand.* 33 [Suppl.]:119.

Hoelzel, F. 1942. Fear and gastric acidity. *Am. J. Dig. Dis.* 9:188.

Hollander, F., and Weinstein, V. A. 1956. Cause of basal secretion of HCl in the dog. *Fed. Proc.* 15:95.

Horowitz, M. I. 1967. Chemistry of the secretion layer. *Ann. N. Y. Acad. Sci.* 140:784.

Horton, E. W. 1969. Hypotheses on physiological roles of prostaglandins. *Physiol. Rev.* 49:112.

Horwich, L., and Galloway, R. 1965. Treatment of gastric ulcer with carbenoxolone sodium: A clinical and radiologic evaluation. *Brit. Med. J.* 2:1274.

Hubel, K. A. 1972. Secretin: A long progress note. *Gastroenterology* 62:318.

Iggo, A., and Leek, B. F. 1967. An electrophysiological study of single vagal efferent units associated with gastric movements in sheep. *J. Physiol. (Lond.)* 191:177.

Ikemi, Y., Akagi, M., Maeda, J., Fukumoto, T., Kawate, K., Kirakawa, K., Gondo, S., Nakagawa, T., Honda, T., Sakamoto, A., and Kumagai, M. 1959. Experimental studies on the psychosomatic disorders of the digestive system. In *Proceedings of the World Congress of Gastroenterology*, vol. 1. Baltimore: Williams & Wilkins.

Isenberg, J. I., Walsh, J. H., and Best, W. R. 1972. Effect of graded doses of pentagastrin on gastric acid secretion in duodenal ulcer and non-duodenal ulcer subjects. *Gastroenterology* 62:764.

———, Walsh, J. H., and Grossman, M. I. 1973. Zollinger-Ellison Syndrome. *Gastroenterology* 65:140.

Ivy, A. C. 1950. Cited in Grossman, M. I. Gastrointestinal hormones. *Physiol. Rev.* 30:33.

———, Grossman, M. I., and Bachrach, W. H. 1950. Psychosomatic etiology of peptic ulcer. In *Peptic Ulcer*, edited by A. C. Ivy. Philadelphia: Blakiston.

Janowitz, H. D., Hollander, F., Orringer, D., Levy, M. H., Winkelstein, A., Kaufman, M. R., and Margolin, S. G. 1950. A quantitative study of the gastric secretory response to sham feeding in a human subject. *Gastroenterology* 16:104.

Jansson, G. 1969. Extrinsic control of gastric motility: An experimental study in the cat. *Acta Physiol. Scand.* [Suppl.] 326:1.

———, Lisander, B., and Martinson, J. 1969. Hypothalamic control of adrenergic outflow to the stomach in the cat. *Acta Physiol. Scand.* 75:176.

Jantschew, W., Jordanow, E., and Kuntschew, I. 1964. Das Duodenalgeschwür im Zusammenhang mit dem Beruf, Z. *Gesamte Inn. Med.* 19:629.

Jefferson, N. C. 1963. Neurogenic production of peptic ulcer lesions and associated phenomena. *Am. J. Gastroenterol.* 40:264.

Johnson, H. D. 1965. Gastric ulcer: Classification, blood group characteristics, secretion patterns and pathogenesis. *Ann. Surg.* 162:996.

Johnson, L. R., and Grossman, M. I. 1968. The enterogastrone released by acid in the duodenum. *Am. J. Physiol.* 215:885.

———, and ——— 1968. Secretin: The enterogastrone released by acid in the duodenum. *Am. J. Physiol.* 215:885.

Johnston, D., and Duthie, H. L. 1964. Effect of acid in the duodenum on histamine stimulated gastric secretion in man. *Gut* 5:573.

———, and ——— 1965. Inhibition of gastrin secretion in the human stomach. *Lancet* 2:1032.

Jones, F. A. 1955. Social aspects of peptic ulcer. *J. R. Inst. Publ. Hlth.* 18:64.

——— 1956. The problem of peptic ulcer. *Ann. Intern. Med.* 44:63.

Jungmann, H., and Venning, P. 1955. Radiological observations of stomach changes accompanying threat of injection in a sample of peptic ulcer patients. *Psychosom. Med.* 17:57.

Kanter, V. B. 1958. A comparison by means of psychological tests. Young men with duodenal ulcer and controls. In *Family Influences and Psychosomatic Illness: An Inquiry into the Social and Psychological Background of Duodenal Ulcer*, edited by E. M. Goldberg. London: Tavistock.

———, and Hazelton, J. E. 1964. An attempt to measure some aspects of personality in young men with duodenal ulcer by means of questionnaires and a projective test. *J. Psychosom. Res.* 8:297.

Kaplan, H. I. 1956. The psychosomatic concept of peptic ulcer. *J. Nerv. Ment. Dis.* 123:93.

Kapp, F. T., Rosenbaum, M., and Romano, J. 1947. Psychological factors in men with peptic ulcers. *Am. J. Psychiatry* 103:700.

Kay, A. W. 1953. Effect of large doses of histamine on gastric secretion of HCl: An augmented histamine test. *Brit. Med. J.* 2:77.

Kehoe, M., and Ironside, W. 1963. Studies on the experimental evocation of depressive responses using hypnosis. II. The influence of depressive responses upon the secretion of gastric acid. *Psychosom. Med.* 25:403.

———, and ——— 1964. Studies of the experimental evocation of depressive responses using hypnosis. III. The secretory rate of total gastric acid with respect to various spontaneous experiences such as nausea, disgust, crying and dyspnea. *Psychosom. Med.* 26:224.

Kezur, E., Kapp, F. T., and Rosenbaum, M. 1951. Psychological factors in women with peptic ulcer. *Am. J. Psychiatry* 108:368.

Kirsner, J. B. 1968. Peptic ulcer: A review of the current literature on various clinical aspects. *Gastroenterology* 54:610.

Klein, G. 1951. Über das Magen- und Duodenalgeschwür am Sektionsmaterial. *Dtsch. Z. Verdau. Stoffwechselkr.* 11:153.

Korman, M. G., Soveny, C., and Hansky, J. 1971. Serum gastrin in duodenal ulcer. *Gut* 12:899.

Kosake, T., Lim, R. K. S., Long, S. M., and Liu, A. C. 1932. On the mechanism of the inhibition of gastric secretion by fat. *Clin. J. Physiol.* 6:107.

Lambert, R. 1968. Use of the rat in the exploration of experimental peptic ulcer in sequelae of gastrectomy. *Prog. Gastroenterol.* 1:40.

———, Martin, F., and Vagne, M. 1968. Relationship between hydrogen ion and pepsin in human gastric secretion. *Digestion* 1:65.

Lanciault, G., Shaw, J. E., Urquhart, J., Adair, L. S., and Brooks, F. P. 1975. Response of the isolated perfused stomach of the dog to electrical vagal stimulation. *Gastroenterology* 68:294.

Laster, L., and Walsh, J. H. 1968. Enzymatic degradation of C-terminal tetrapeptide amide of gastrin by mammalian tissue extracts. *Fed. Proc.* 27:1328.

Lawson, L. J., and Dragstedt, L. R. 1964. Vasopressin and gastric secretion. *Surg. Forum* 15:118.

Leclerq-Meyer, L., Brisson, G. R., and Malaisse, W. J. 1971. Effect of adrenaline and glucose on release of glucagon and insulin *in vitro*. *Nature* [*New Biol.*] 231:248.

Leonard, A. S., Long, D., French, L. A., Peter, E. T., and Wangensteen, O. H. 1964. Pendular pattern in gastric secretion and blood flow following hypothalamic stimulation—origin of stress ulcer? *Surgery* 56:109.

———, Gilsdorf, R. B., Pearl, J. M., Peter, E. T., and Ritchie, W. P. 1967. Hypothalamic influence on gastric blood flow, cell counts, acid and mucus secretion—factors in ulcer provocation. In *Gastric Secretion: Mechanisms and Control*, edited by T. K. Shnitka, J. A. L. Gilbert, and R. C. Harrison. New York: Pergamon.

Levey, H. B. 1934. Oral trends and oral conflicts in a case of duodenal ulcer. *Psychoanal. Q.* 3:574.

Levin, E., Kirsner, J. B., Palmer, W. L., and Butler, C. 1948a. Nocturnal gastric secretion. *Arch. Surg.* 56:345.

———, ———, and ——— 1948b. Twelve-hour nocturnal gastric secretion in uncomplicated duodenal ulcer patients: Before and after healing. *Proc. Soc. Exp. Biol. Med.* 69:153.

————, ————, and ———— 1950. The continuous twelve-hour nocturnal gastric secretion in normal individuals and in patients with duodenal ulcer after a 24-hour fast. *Gastroenterology* 15:454.

Levine, R. J., and Senay, E. C. 1970. Studies on the role of acid in the pathogenesis of experimental stress ulcers. *Psychosom. Med.* 32:61.

Lidz, T., and Rubenstein, R. 1959. Psychology of gastrointestinal disorders. In *American Handbook of Psychiatry,* vol. 1, edited by S. Arieti. New York: Basic Books.

Lieberman, M. A., Stock, D., and Whitman, R. M. 1959. Self-perceptual patterns among ulcer patients. *Arch. Gen. Psychiatry* 1:167.

Littman, A., and Bernstein, L. L. 1962. Clinical diagnosis in peptic ulcer and esophagitis. *Med. Clin. North Am.* 46:747.

Love, J. W. 1970. Secretin: A neglected key? *Gastroenterology* 59:147.

Lower, J. S. 1967. Approach-avoidance conflict as a determinant of peptic ulceration in the rat. Ph.D. Dissertation, Western Reserve University.

Lunedei, A. 1961. Quoted by Teir (1967).

Luparello, T. J. 1967. Neurogenic gastroduodenal erosions in the guinea pig. *J. Psychosom. Res.* 11:299.

Lythgoe, J. P., Dickinson, J. C., and Waddell, W. R. 1962. Gastrin content of human stomachs in patients with gastric and duodenal ulcer. *Surgery* 51:705.

Mahl, G. F. 1949. Effect of chronic fear on the gastric secretion of HCl in dogs. *Psychosom. Med.* 11:30.

———— 1950. Anxiety, HCl secretion and peptic ulcer etiology. *Psychosom. Med.* 12:158.

———— 1952. Relationship between acute and chronic fear and the gastric acidity and blood sugar levels in *Macaca mulatta* monkeys. *Psychosom. Med.* 14:182.

———— 1953. Physiological changes during chronic fear. *Ann. N.Y. Acad. Sci.* 56:240.

————, and Karpe, R. 1953. Emotions and hydrochloric acid secretion during psychoanalytic hours. *Psychosom. Med.* 15:312.

Malhotra, S. L. 1967. Epidemiological study of peptic ulcer in the south of India. *Gut* 8:180.

Marcus, D. M. 1969. The ABO and Lewis blood-group system. *N. Engl. J. Med.* 280:994.

Margolin, S. G. 1951. The behavior of the stomach during psychoanalysis: A contribution to a method of verifying psychoanalytic data. *Psychoanal. Quart.* 20:349.

Marks, I. N. 1957. The effect of prolonged histamine stimulation on the parietal cell population and the secretory function of the guinea-pig stomach. *Q. J. Exp. Physiol.* 42:180.

————, Komorov, S. A., and Shay, H. 1960. Maximal acid secretory response to histamine and its relation to parietal mass in the dog. *Am. J. Physiol.* 199:579.

Marquis, D. P., Sinnett, E. R., and Winter, W. D. 1952. A psychological study of peptic ulcer patients. *J. Clin. Psychol.* 8:266.

Marshall, S. 1960. Personality correlates of peptic ulcer patients. *J. Consult. Psychol.* 24:218.

Mason, J. W. 1968. Organization of psychoendocrine mechanisms. *Psychosom. Med.* 30:565.

————, Brady, J. V., Polish, E., Bauer, J. A., Robinson, J. A., Rose, R. M., and Taylor, E. D. 1961. Patterns of corticosteroid and pepsinogen change related to emotional stress in the monkey. *Science* 133:1596.

McGuigan, J. E. 1968. Gastric mucosal intracellular localization of gastrin by immunofluorescence. *Gastroenterology* 55:315.

————, and Trudeau, W. L. 1968. Immunochemical measurement of elevated levels of gastrin in the serum of patients with pancreatic tumors of the Zollinger-Ellison variety. *N. Engl. J. Med.* 278:1308.

————, and ———— 1969. Little gastrin in normal serum. *N. Engl. J. Med.* 280:509.

94

————, and ———— 1973. Differences in rates of gastrin release in normal persons and patients with duodenal ulcer disease. *N. Engl. J. Med.* 288:64.

Mednick, S. A., Garner, A. M., and Stone, H. K. 1959. A test of some behavioral hypotheses drawn from Alexander's specificity theory. *Am. J. Orthopsychiatry* 29:592.

Meeroff, M., and Weitzman, S. 1963. Psychic elements of the patient with gastroduodenal ulcer. *Sem. Med. (Buenos Aires)* 123:678.

Melmon, K. L. 1968. The endocrinologic manifestations of the carcinoid tumor. In *Textbook of Endocrinology*, edited by R. H. Williams. Philadelphia: Saunders.

Menguy, R. 1964. Current concepts of the etiology of duodenal ulcer. *Am. J. Dig. Dis.* 9:199.

———— 1967. Gastric inhibitory substance. In *The Stomach,* edited by C. M. Thompson. New York: Grune & Stratton.

————, and Thompson, A. E. 1967. Regulation of secretion of mucus from the gastric antrum. *Ann. N.Y. Acad. Sci.* 140:797.

Minsky, L., and DeSai, M. M. 1955. Aspects of personality in peptic ulcer patients. *Br. J. Med. Psychol.* 28:113.

Mirsky, I. A. 1958. Physiologic, psychologic and social determinants in etiology of duodenal ulcer. *Am. J. Dig. Dis.* 3:285.

———— 1960. Physiologic, psychologic and social determinants of psychosomatic disorders. *Dis. Nerv. Syst.* 21:50.

————, Futterman, P., and Kaplan, S. 1952. Blood plasma pepsinogen. II. The activity of the plasma from "normal" subjects, patients with duodenal ulcer and patients with pernicious anemia. *J. Lab. Clin. Med.* 40:188.

Mittleman, B., and Wolff, H. G. 1942. Emotions and gastroduodenal function: Experimental studies on patients with gastritis, duodenitis and peptic ulcer. *Psychosom. Med.* 4:5.

Modell, A. H., and Potter, H. M. 1949. Human figure drawings of patients with arterial hypertension, peptic ulcer and bronchial asthma. *Psychosom. Med.* 11:282.

Moore, J. G., and Englert, E. 1970. Circadian rhythm of gastric acid secretion in man. *Nature* 226:1261.

Mosin, V. M. 1967. The state of the hypophysis-adrenal cortex system in peptic ulcer of the stomach. *Vrachebnoye Delo* 2:123.

Muryobayashi, T., Fujiwara, M., and Shimamoto, K. 1968. Fluorescence histochemical findings of the stomach walls in response to ulcerogenic stimuli in rats. *Jpn. J. Pharmacol.* 18:299.

Neely, J. C., and Goldman, L. 1962. Effect of calciferol-induced chronic hypercalcemia on the gastric secretion from a Heidenhain pouch. *Ann. Surg.* 155:406.

Nezamis, R. A., and Phillips, J. P. 1968. Effect of prostaglandin E1 on gastric secretion and ulcer formation in the rat. *Gastroenterology* 55:481.

Niederman, J. C., Spiro, H. M., and Sheldon, W. H. 1964. Blood pepsin as a marker of susceptibility to duodenal ulcer disease. *Arch. Environ. Health* 8:540.

Norgaard, R. P., Polter, D. E., Wheeler, J. W., Jr., and Fordtran, J. S. 1970. Effect of long term anticholinergic therapy on gastric acid secretion, with observations on the serial measurement of peak Histalog response. *Gastroenterology* 58:750.

Nyhus, L. M., Chapman, N. D., DeVito, R. V., and Harkins, H. N. 1960. The control of gastrin release. An experimental study illustrating a new concept. *Gastroenterology* 39:582.

Odell, W. D., Charters, A. C., Davidson, W. D., and Thompson, J. C. 1968. Radioimmunoassay for human gastrin using unconjugated gastrin as antigen. *J. Clin. Endocrinol.* 28:1840.

Ontanenda, M. 1968. Biological—psychological—social factors in genesis of peptic ulcer. *Am. J. Proctol.* 19:55.

Paré, W. P. 1964. The effect of chronic environmental stress on stomach ulceration, adrenal function, and consummatory behavior in the rat. *J. Psychol.* 57:143.

————— 1972. Gastric ulcers in the rat as a function of the temporal relationship between punishment and reward. *Psychosom. Med.* 34:9.

—————, and Livingston, A., Jr. 1970. Brain norepinephrine and stomach ulcers in rats exposed to chronic conflict. *Physiol. Behav.* 5:215.

Pascal, G. R., and Thoroughman, J. C. 1964. Relationship between Bender-Gestalt test scores and the response of patients with intractable duodenal ulcer to surgery. *Psychosom. Med.* 26:625.

—————, —————, Jarvis, J. R., and Jenkins, W. O. 1966. Early history variables in predicting surgical success for intractable duodenal ulcer patients. *Psychosom. Med.* 78:207.

Passaro, E., Jr., Basso, N., and Walsh, J. H. 1972. Calcium challenge in the Zollinger-Ellison syndrome. *Surgery* 72:60.

—————, —————, Sanchez, R. E., and Gordon, H. E. 1970. Newer studies in the Zollinger-Ellison syndrome. *Am. J. Surg.* 120:138.

Pavlov, I. P. 1927. *Conditioned Reflexes.* An Investigation of the Physiological Activity of the Cerebral Cortex, translated by G. V. Anrep. London: Oxford.

Pearl, J. M., Ritchie, W. P., Jr., Gilsdorf, R. B., Delaney, J. P., and Leonard, A. P. 1966. Hypothalamic stimulation and feline gastric mucosal cellular populations. *J.A.M.A.* 195:281.

Peñaloza-Rojas, J. H., Barrera-Mera, B., and Kubli-Garfias, C. 1969. Behavioral and brain electrical changes after vagal stimulation. *Exper. Neurol.* 23:378.

Perry, T. W., Pickett, R. A., Curtin, T. M., Beeson, W. M., and Numer, A. J. 1966 Studies on esophagogastric ulcers in swine. In *Swine in Biomedical Research,* edited by L. K Bustad and R. D. McClellan. Richland, Wash.: Battelle Memorial Institute.

Perthein, M., and Schofield, B. 1959. Release of gastrin from the gastric antrum following vagal stimulation by sham feedings in dogs. *J. Physiol. (Lond.)* 148:291.

Pflanz, M. 1971. Epidemiological and sociocultural factors in the etiology of duodenal ulcer. *Adv. Psychosom. Med.* 6:121.

Pilot, M. L., and Spiro, H. M. 1961. Comments on the use of blood pepsin (pepsinogen) as a research technique. *Psychosom. Med.* 23:420.

—————, Lenkoski, L. D., Spiro, H. M., and Schafer, R. 1957. Duodenal ulcer in one of identical twins. *Psychosom. Med.* 19:221.

—————, Rubin, J., Schafer, R., and Spiro, H. M. 1963. Duodenal ulcer in one of identical twins: A follow-up study. *Psychosom. Med.* 25:285.

—————, Muggia, A., and Spiro, H. M. 1967. Duodenal ulcer in women. *Psychosom. Med.* 29:586.

Pincus, I. J., and Horowitz, R. E. 1967. The acute stress ulcer. In *The Stomach,* edited by C. M. Thompson et al. New York: Grune & Stratton.

Polacek, M. A., and Ellison, E. H. 1966. Gastric acid secretion and parietal cell mass in the stomach of a newborn infant. *Am. J. Surg.* 111:777.

Polish, E., Brady, J. V., Mason, J. W., Thach, J. S., and Niemeck, W. 1962. Gastric contents and the occurrence of duodenal lesions in the rhesus monkey during avoidance behavior. *Gastroenterology* 43:193.

Porter, R. W., Movius, H. J., and French, J. D. 1953. Hypothalamic influences on hydrochloric acid secretion of the stomach. *Surgery* 33:875.

—————, Brady, J. V., Conrad, D., Mason, J. W., Galambos, R., and Rioch, D. M. 1958. Some experimental observations of gastroduodenal lesions in behaviorally conditioned monkeys. *Psychosom. Med.* 20:379.

Poser, E. G., and Lee, S. G. 1963. Thematic content associated with two gastrointestinal disorders. *Psychosom. Med.* 25:162.

Pounder, R. E., Williams, J. G., Milton-Thompson, G. J., and Misiewicz, J. J. 1975. Relief of duodenal ulcer symptoms by oral metiamide. *Brit. Med. J.* 2:307.

96

Puiggari, J. M., and Fennegan, F. M. 1966. Cerebral electrical activity recorded during sleep and gastric distension in the dog. *J. Nerv. Ment. Dis.* 142:540.

Ragins, H., and Wincze, F. 1969. Effects of cortisone on the turnover of gastric parietal cells in the mouse. *Endocrinology* 84:83.

Raper, A. B. 1958. The incidence of peptic ulceration in some African tribal groups. *Trans. R. Soc. Trop. Med. Hyg.* 52:535.

Read, R. C., Thompson, B. W., and Hall, W. H. 1972. Conversion of Hollander tests in man from positive to negative. *Arch. Surg.* 104:573.

Reeder, D. D., Jackson, B. M., Ban, J., Clendinnen, B. G., Davidson, W. D., and Thompson, J. C. 1970. Influence of hypercalcemia on gastric secretion and serum gastrin concentrations in man. *Ann. Surg.* 172:540.

Reichsman, F., Cohen, J., Colwill, J., Davis, N., Kessler, W., Sheppardson, C. R., and Engel, G. L. 1960. Natural and histamine-induced gastric secretion during waking and sleeping states. *Psychosom. Med.* 22:14.

Rennie, T. A. C., and Srole, L. 1956. Social class prevalence and distribution of psychosomatic conditions in an urban population. *Psychosom. Med.* 18:449.

Retterstoll, N., and Sund, A. 1962. Psychosomatic aspects of ulcer disease illustrated by material from a psychiatric clinic. *J. Neuropsychiatry* 3:345.

Rhodes, J. 1972. Etiology of gastric ulcer. *Gastroenterology* 63:171.

———, and Prestwich, C. J. 1966. Acidity at different sites in the proximal duodenum of normal subjects and patients with duodenal ulcer. *Gut* 7:509.

Ritchie, W. P. 1975. Acute gastric mucosal damage induced by bile salts, acid and ischemia. *Gastroenterology* 68:699.

Robert, A., and Stout, T. J. 1969. Production of duodenal ulcers in rats. *Fed. Proc.* 28:323.

———, ———, and Dale, J. E. 1970. Production by secretagogues of duodenal ulcers in the rat. *Gastroenterology* 59:95.

Rosenbaum, M. 1967. Peptic Ulcer. In *Comprehensive Textbook of Psychiatry*, edited by A. M. Freedman and H. I. Kaplan. Baltimore: Williams & Wilkins.

Rosenberg, A. 1967. Production of gastric lesions in rats by combined cold and electrostress. *Am. J. Dig. Dis.* 12:1140.

Rossi, G., Bonfils, S., Liefooghe, F., and Lambling, A. 1956. Technique nouvelle pour produire des ulcérations gastriques chez le rat blanc. L'ulcére de contrainte. *C. R. Soc. Biol.* (Paris) 150:2124.

Roth, H. P. 1955. The peptic ulcer personality. *Arch. Intern. Med.* 96:32.

Rubenson, A. 1969. Alterations in noradrenaline turnover in the peripheral sympathetic neurons induced by stress. *J. Pharm. Pharmacol.* 21:278.

Rubin, S., and Bowman, K. M. 1942. Electroencephalographic and personality correlates in peptic ulcer. *Psychosom. Med.* 4:309.

Rune, S. J. 1966. Comparison of the rates of gastric acid secretion in man after ingestion of food and after maximal stimulation with histamine. *Gut* 7:344.

——— 1967. Individual variation in secretory capacity of gastric acid stimulation with solid food and with histamine. *Clin. Sci.* 32:443.

Ryss, S., and Ryss, E. 1968. Modern concepts of etiology and pathogenesis of peptic ulcer: Disorders of the regulating mechanisms. *Scand. J. Gastroenterol.* 3:513.

Sachar, E. J. 1967. Corticosteroids in depressive illness. I. A re-evaluation of control issues and the literature. *Arch. Gen. Psychiatry* 17:544.

Samloff, I. M. 1969. Multiple molecular forms of pepsinogen and their distribution in gastric and duodenal mucosa. *Clin. Res.* 17:310.

————, and Townes, P. L. 1969. Heterogeneity and genetic polymorphism of human pepsinogen. *Gastroenterology* 56:1194.

————, and ———— 1970. Pepsinogens—genetic polymorphism in man. *Science* 168:144.

Sandweiss, D. J., Friedman, M. H. F., Sugarman, M. H.,and Podolsky, H. M. 1946. Nocturnal gastric secretion: Studies on normal subjects and patients with duodenal ulcer. *Gastroenterology* 7:38.

Sapir, M. 1962. L'étiopathogénie psychosomatique de l'ulcèrs existe-t-elle? In *Psychosomatique et Gastroentérologie*, edited by P. Aboulker, L. Chertok, and M. Sapir. Paris: Masson.

Sawrey, W. L., and Long, D. H. 1962. Strain and sex differences in ulceration in the rat. *J. Comp. Physiol. Psychol.* 55:603.

————, and Weiss, J. D. 1956. An experimental method of producing gastric ulcers. *J. Comp. Physiol. Psychol.* 49:269.

————, Conger, J. J., and Turrell, E. S. 1956. An experimental investigation of the role of psychological factors in the production of gastric ulcers in rats. *J. Comp. Physiol. Psychol.* 49:457.

Schapiro, H., Wruble, L. D., Britt, L. G., and Bell, T. A. 1970a. Sensory deprivation on visceral activity. I. The effect of visual deprivation on canine gastric secretion. *Psychosom. Med.* 32:379.

————, Gross, C. W., Nakamura, T., Wruble, L. D., and Britt, L. G. 1970b. Sensory deprivation on visceral activity. II. The effect of auditory and vestibular deprivation on canine gastric secretion. *Psychosom. Med.* 32:515.

————, Britt, L. G., Gross, C. W., and Gaines, K. J. 1971. Sensory deprivation on visceral activity. III. The effect of olfactory deprivation on canine gastric secretion. *Psychosom. Med.* 33:429.

Segal, H. L., Miller, L. L., Reichsman, F., Plumb, E. J., and Glaser, G. L. 1957. Urinary proteolytic activity at pH 1.5 in adults. *Gastroenterology* 33:557.

Selye, H. 1950. *Stress*. Montreal: Acta.

Senay, E. C., and Levine, R. J. 1967. Synergism between cold and restraint for rapid production of stress ulcers in rats. *Proc. Soc. Exp. Biol. Med.* 124:1221.

Seronde, J. 1963. The pathogenesis of duodenal ulcer disease in the pantothenate-deficient rat. *Yale J. Biol. Med.* 36:141.

Seymour, C. T., and Weinberg, J. A. 1959. Emotions and gastric activity. *J.A.M.A.* 171:1193.

Shapiro, A. P., and Horn, P. W. 1955. Blood pressure, plasma pepsinogen and behavior in cats subjected to experimental production of anxiety. *J. Nerv. Ment. Dis.* 122:222.

Shay, H. 1959. Emotional stress and parietal cell mass: Their role in the etiology of peptic ulcer. *Am. J. Dig. Dis.* 4:846.

————, Gershon-Cohen, J., and Fels, S. S. 1942. A self-regulatory duodenal mechanism for gastric acid control and an explanation for the pathologic gastric physiology in uncomplicated duodenal ulcer. *Am. J. Dig. Dis.* 9:124.

————, Sun, D. C. H., Dlin, B., and Weiss, E. 1958. Gastric secretory response to emotional stress in a case of duodenal ulcer: A consideration of a possible mechanism involved. *J. Appl. Physiol.* 12:461.

Shaw, J. E., and Urquhart, J. 1972. Parameters of the control of acid secretion in the isolated blood perfused stomach. *J. Physiol. (London).* 226:107.

Sievers, M. L. 1959. Hereditary aspects of gastric secretory function: Race and ABO blood groups in relationship to acid and pepsin production. *Am. J. Med.* 27:246.

Silen, W. 1967. Advances in gastric physiology. *N. Engl. J. Med.* 277:864.

Silverstone, S., and Kissen, B. 1968. Field dependence in essential hypertension and peptic ulcer. *J. Psychosom. Res.* 12:157.

Sines, J. O. 1965. Pre-stress sensory input as a non-pharmacologic method for controlling restraint-ulcer susceptibility. *J. Psychosom. Res.* 8:399.

Singh, H., Goyal, R. K., Ahluwaila, D. S., and Chuttani, H. K. 1968. Vagal influence on gastric acid secretion in normals and in duodenal ulcer patients. *Gut* 9:604.

Sircus, W. 1953. The intestinal phase of gastric secretion. *Q. J. Exp. Physiol.* 38:91.

Smith, G. P. 1967. Experimental ulcer and the limbic system. In *The Stomach,* edited by C. M. Thompson et al. New York: Grune & Stratton.

Spira, J. J. 1956. The incidence of peptic ulcer in animals. In *Gastroduodenal Ulcer.* London: Butterworth.

Spiro, H. M., Ryan, A. E., and Jones, C. M. 1955. The utility of the blood pepsin assay in clinical medicine. *N. Engl. J. Med.* 253:261.

Stadil, F. 1972. Effect of vagotomy on gastrin release during insulin hypoglycemia in ulcer patients. *Scand. J. Gastroenterol.* 7:225.

———, and Rehfeld, J. F. 1973. Release of gastrin by epinephrine. *Gastroenterology* 65:210.

State, D. 1971. Peptic ulceration: Physiologic considerations. *Adv. Psychosom. Med.* 6:104.

Stein, A., Kaufman, M. R., Janowitz, H. D., Levy, M. H., Hollander, F., and Winkelstein, A. 1962. Changes in hydrochloric acid secretion in a patient with a gastric fistula during intensive psychotherapy. *Psychosom. Med.* 24:427.

Stempien, S. J., Dagradi, A. E., and Reingold, I. M. 1964. Hypertrophic hypersecretory gastritis. *Am. J. Dig. Dis.* 9:471.

Stenbäch, A. 1960. Gastric neurosis, pre-ulcer conflict and personality in duodenal ulcer. *J. Psychosom. Res.* 4:282.

Stern, J. A., Winokur, G., Eisenstein, A., Taylor, R., and Sly, M. 1960. The effect of group vs. individual housing on behaviour and physiological responses to stress in the albino rat. *J. Psychosom. Res.* 4:185.

Sternbach, R. A. 1962. Assessing differential autonomic patterns in emotions. *J. Psychosom. Res.* 6:87.

Stewart, D. N., and Winser, D. M. R. de. 1942. Incidence of perforated peptic ulcer. Effect of heavy air-raids. *Lancet* 1:259.

Streitfeld, H. S. 1954. Specificity of peptic ulcer to intense oral conflicts. *Psychosom. Med.* 16:315.

Sun, D. C. H., Shay, H., Dlin, B., and Weiss, E. 1958. Conditioned secretory response of the stomach following repeated emotional stress in a case of duodenal ulcer. *Gastroenterology* 35:155.

——— Chang, P. L., Ryan, M. L., and Keogh, R. 1967. *Augmented histamine test.* Ann. N.Y. Acad. Sci. 140:875.

Susser, M. 1967. Causes of peptic ulcer: A selective epidemiological review. *J. Chronic Dis.* 20:435.

Szasz, T. S., Levin, E., Kirsner, J. B., and Palmer, W. L. 1947. The role of hostility in the pathogenesis of peptic ulcer: Theoretical considerations with the report of a case. *Psychosom. Med.* 9:331.

Tarquini, B., Della Corte, M., and Orzalesi, R. 1967. Circadian studies on plasma cortisol in subjects with peptic ulcer. *J. Endocrinol.* 38:475.

Taylor, K. M., and Snyder, S. H. 1971. Brain histamine—rapid apparent turnover altered by restraint and cold stress. *Science* 172:1037.

Taylor, W. H. 1970. Pepsins of patients with peptic ulcer. *Nature* 227:76.

Teir, H. 1967. Mitotic homeostatis and physiological control of cell renewal in healthy and diseased gastric mucosa. In *Gastric Secretion: Mechanisms and Control,* edited by T. K. Shnitka, J. A. L. Gilbert, and R. C. Harrison. New York: Pergamon.

Thaler, M., Weiner, H., and Reiser, M. F. 1957. Exploration of the doctor-patient relationship through projective techniques: Their use in psychosomatic illness. *Psychosom. Med.* 19:228.

Thompson, H. 1954. An investigation into the *post mortem* incidence of peptic ulcers and erosions. *Glasg. Med. J.* 35:326.

Thoroughman, J. C., Pascal, G. R., Jenkins, W. O., Crutcher, J. C., and Peoples, L. C. 1964. Psychological factors predictive of surgical success in patients with intractable duodenal ulcer: A study of male veterans. *Psychosom. Med.* 26:618.

————, ————, Jarvis, J. R., and Crutcher, J. C. 1967. A study of psychological factors in patients with surgically intractable duodenal ulcer and those with other intractable disorders. *Psychosom. Med.* 29:273.

Tran, T., and Gregg, R. V. 1974. Transmittal of restraint-induced gastric ulcers by parabiosis in rats. *Gastroenterology* 66:63.

Trudeau, W. L.,and McGuigan, J. E. 1969. Effects of calcium on serum gastrin levels in the Zollinger-Ellison syndrome. *N. Engl. J. Med.* 281:862.

————, and ———— 1970. Serum gastrin levels in patients with peptic ulcer disease. *Gastroenterology* 59:6.

————, and ———— 1971. Relations between serum gastrin levels and rates of gastric hydrochloric acid secretion. *N. Engl. J. Med.* 284:408.

Tudor, R. V. 1972. Gastric and duodenal ulcers in children. *Gastroenterology* 62:823.

Turbey, W. J., and Passaro, E., Jr. 1972. Hyperparathyroidism in the Zollinger-Ellison syndrome. *Arch. Surg.* 105.

Uvnäs, B., and Emås, S. 1961. A method for biological assay of gastrin. *Gastroenterology* 40:644.

Valman, H. B., Parry, D. J., and Coghill, N. F. 1968. Lesions associated with gastroduodenal hemorrhage, in relation to aspirin uptake. *Brit. Med. J.* 4:661.

Van Der Heide, C. 1940. A study of mechanisms in 2 cases of peptic ulcer. *Psychosom. Med.* 2:398.

Vesely, K. T., Kubickova, K. T., and Dvorakova, M. 1968. Clinical data and characteristics differentiating types of peptic ulcer. *Gut* 9:57.

Walsh, J. H., and Grossman, M. I. 1975. Gastrin (Part I). *N. Engl. J. Med.* 26:1324.

Wangensteen, S. L., and Golden, G. T. 1973. Acute "stress" ulcers of the stomach: A review. *Am. Surg.* 39:562.

Watkinson, G. 1958. The autopsy incidence of chronic peptic ulceration, a national and regional survey of 20,000 examinations performed in Leeds, England, between 1930 and 1940, and in 9 towns in England and Scotland in 1956. *Schweiz. Z. Allg. Path.* 21:405.

———— 1960. The incidence of chronic peptic ulcer found at necropsy. A study of 20,000 examinations performed in Leeds in 1930–1949 and in England and Scotland in 1956. *Gut* 1:14.

Weiner, H., Thaler, M., Reiser, M. F., and Mirsky, I. A. 1957. Etiology of duodenal ulcer. I. Relation of specific psychological characteristics to rate of gastric secretion (serum pepsinogen). *Psychosom. Med.* 19:1.

Weininger, O. 1956. The effects of early experience on behavior and growth characteristics. *J. Comp. Physiol. Psychol.* 49:1.

Weisman, A. D. 1956. A study of the psychodynamics of duodenal ulcer exacerbations with special reference to treatment and the problem of specificity. *Psychosom. Med.* 18:2.

Weiss, J. M. 1968. Effects of coping responses on stress. *J. Comp. Physiol. Psychol.* 65:251.

————, Pohorecky, L., Salman, S., and Gruenthal, M. 1974. Attenuation of gastric lesions by psychological aspects of aggression. *Psychosom. Med.* 36:463.

Welch, B. S., and Welch, A. S. 1968. Differential activation by restraint stress of a mechanism to conserve brain catecholamines and serotonin in mice differing in excitability. *Nature* 218:575.

Williams, A. W., Howie, J. B., Helyer, B. J., and Simpson, L. O. 1967. Spontaneous peptic ulcers in mice. *Aust. J. Exp. Biol. Med. Sci.* 45:105.

Williams, E. J., DeCastella, H. C., Lawson, J. O. N., Hopkins, J. D. P., and Irvine, W. T. 1967. The late acid response to insulin induced hypoglycemia and its relation to vagal stimulated gastrin release. In *Gastric Secretion: Mechanisms and Control,* edited by T. K. Shnitka, J. A. Gilbert and R. C. Harrison. New York: Pergamon.

Williams, M. J., and Blair, D. W. 1964. Gastric secretion in hyperthyroidism. *Brit. Med. J.* 1:940.

Williams, R. H. 1968. The Pancreas. In *Textbook of Endocrinology,* edited by R. H. Williams. Philadelphia: Saunders.

Williams, R. L., and Krasnoff, A. C. 1964. Body image and physiological patterns in patients with peptic ulcer and rheumatoid arthritis. *Psychosom. Med.* 26:701.

Winnacker, J. L., Becker, K. L., and Katz, S. 1968. Endocrine aspects of sarcoidosis. *N. Engl. J. Med.* 278:427.

Winokur, G., Stern, J. A., and Taylor, R. 1959. Early handling and group housing. Effect on development and response to stress in the rat. *J. Psychosom. Res.* 4:1.

Winter, W. D. 1955. Two personality patterns in peptic ulcer patients. *J. Proj. Techniques* 19:332.

Wolf, S. 1965. *The Stomach.* New York: Oxford.

———, and Wolff, H. G. 1947. *Human Gastric Function.* New York: Oxford.

Wolff, P., and Levine, J. 1955. Nocturnal gastric secretions of ulcer and non-ulcer patients under stress. *Psychosom. Med.* 17:218.

Wolowitz, H. M., and Wagonfeld, S. 1968. Oral derivatives in the food preferences of ulcer patients: An experimental test of Alexander's hypothesis. *J. Nerv. Ment. Dis.* 146:18.

Woodward, E. R., Robertson, C., Ruttenberg, H. D., and Schapiro, H. 1957. Alcohol as a gastric secretory stimulant. *Gastroenterology* 32:727.

Wormsley, K. G. 1974. The pathophysiology of duodenal ulceration. *Gut* 15:59.

——— and Grossman, M. I. 1965. Maximal Histalog test in control subjects and patients with peptic ulcer. *Gut* 6:427.

Wretmark, G. 1953. The peptic ulcer individual: A study in heredity, physique and personality. *Acta Psychiatr. Neurol. Scandinav.* [Suppl. 84].

Yager, J., and Weiner, H. 1970. Observations in Man. *Adv. Psychosom. Med.* 6:40.

Yessler, P. G., Reiser, M F., and Rioch, D. McK. 1959. Etiology of duodenal ulcer. II. Serum pepsinogen and peptic ulcer in inductees. *J.A.M.A.* 169:451.

Zawoiski, E. J. 1967. Gastric secretory response of the unrestrained cat following electrical stimulation of the hypothalamus, amygdala and basal ganglia. *Exp. Neurol.* 17:128.

Zucker, T. F. 1958. Panthothenic acid deficiency and its effect on the integrity and functions of the intestines. *Am. J. Clin. Nutr.* 6:65.

Zwierz, K., Gindzienski, A., Badurski, J., and Popowicz, J. 1961. Aminosugars in cases of gastric ulcers. II: The activity of *L*-Glutamine *D*-Fructose-6-Phosphate aminotransferase (E.C. 2.6.1.16) in human gastric mucous membrane. *Digestion* 1:183.

2

ESSENTIAL HYPERTENSION

Essential hypertension and the complications it produces constitute the major hazard to the health of the members of most Western societies. Because it ravages health, and because its pathophysiology is complex and interesting, it has received more investigative attention than any other disease. Despite the vast variety of studies on the factors that control blood pressure and the multiple variables that regulate the circulation and the excretion of salt and water, no agreement has been reached as to which factors elevate blood pressure levels. The regulation of blood pressure and of the circulation, of salt, water and extracellular fluid volume constitutes one of the marvels of Nature. Innumerable processes in intimate interaction regulate them; some processes are self-regulatory, others are influenced by multiple and complex inputs at several levels of organization. Although much is known about these processes both in health and in essential hypertension, no definitive data or theory satisfactorily accounting for the disease has been presented.

Many regulatory processes maintain blood pressure levels within a remarkably narrow range in human beings at rest. Admittedly, blood pressure levels vary a great deal within this range with changes in posture and salt intake, with exercise, heat, cold, noise, pain, emotional and sexual excitement, mental concentration, novel situations, and during

Some sections of this chapter originally appeared in a different version in *Psychosomatics in Essential Hypertension*, eds. M. Koster, H. Musaph, and P. Visser under the title, "Psychosomatic Research in Essential Hypertension: Retrospect and Prospect." Reprinted here with permission of the publisher. Copyright 1970 by S. Karger AG, Basel.

107

talking. Blood pressure levels also tend to rise with age in most human beings. Blood pressure levels vary within a certain range not only with changes in the environment or with age, but with changes in the behavioral state of human beings: blood pressure levels may either be highly variable or be at very low levels (60/40 mm Hg) in sleeping adults. On awakening, the blood pressure rises to levels within the normal range.

Once resting blood pressure levels rise above some arbitrary level—140/90 mm Hg, for example—the physician suspects essential hypertension, especially if the levels remain above this level on repeated measurement. Presumably, one or other of the many mechanisms that maintain the blood pressure within the usual range have failed.

The problem of essential hypertension is so complex that we may well be at the very limits of our capacity to account for and conceptualize the multiple processes involved in its etiology. Our capacity to solve the problem of its etiology is diminished by the fact that there is no established way of discovering who is at risk for this disease. By the time we study patients after the onset of high blood pressure, a set of compensatory physiological processes have set in. It becomes impossible then to differentiate the antecedent initiating factors from the consequent sustaining factors of elevated blood pressure.

In the past 25 years we have also learned that high blood pressure and essential hypertension are not synonymous. Elevations of blood pressure occur in a wide variety of conditions and diseases. They may occur with increased intracranial pressure, various kidney diseases, coarctation of the aorta, renal artery stenosis, aldosterinomas, reninomas, pheochromocytomas, in women taking contraceptive pills, and in Cushing's and Graves' Disease. Although this list is not all-inclusive, it suggests that high blood pressure levels can occur for a variety of reasons, and that high blood pressure should not be used as a synonym for essential hypertension. As our knowledge of this disease increases, new forms of high blood pressure are continually being discovered in patients who are now diagnosed as having "essential" hypertension. At the present time, essential hypertension is probably a heterogeneous disease made up of several unspecified subgroups.

BASIC METHODOLOGICAL AND CONCEPTUAL ISSUES

Problems of Definition

There is general agreement about only three aspects of essential hypertension. The disease consists of an elevation of blood pressure; an increase in peripheral resistance occurs at some time during the course of the disease; and genetic factors play an etiological role in most instances of the disease. There is disagreement about every other aspect of its etiology and pathogenesis. The main, if not the only, reason for this disagreement is that we have no recognized way of predicting who will develop essential hypertension and cannot determine the sequence of events that lead up to it. Several attempts to study patients at risk for the disease have been made. Some adolescents and young adults with a verified family history of hypertension or high blood pressure may be predisposed to develop hypertension later in life (Remington et al., 1960). Other young people have high casual blood pressure levels. Harris et al. (1953), Kalis et al. (1961), and Sokolow and Harris (1961a) showed that college students with high casual pressures differed in

108

psychological functioning from people with lower pressures. Also, in the former, stressful life events produced larger sympathetically mediated vasopressor responses, which lasted longer than in the latter.

Doyle and Fraser (1961) infused norepinephrine into the brachial arteries of the normotensive adult sons of patients with documented essential hypertension and compared them with medical students and house officers of similar ages whose parents did not have elevated blood pressure levels. Norepinephrine was infused into one brachial artery at two different dosage levels—0.2 and 0.4μg per min. The response to infusion was measured in terms of the percent fall in forearm blood flow. At both dose levels the mean responses of the sons of hypertensive parents were significantly greater than those of the sons of normotensive parents. An inherently greater vascular reactivity to norepinephrine infusion is present in the sons of hypertensive parents. This vascular hyperreactivity resides in the smooth muscle of the arteriolar or arterial wall, and may be an inherited trait.

But we do not know whether young people with a high casual blood pressure level or hyperreactive arterioles develop essential hypertension. Essential hypertension is usually diagnosed by chance. The early stage of the disease is asymptomatic. Therefore the task of identifying a population of subjects with essential hypertension remains extremely difficult, as the physician cannot tell when the blood pressure becomes elevated.

The upper limits of normal blood pressure levels are defined arbitrarily; no consensus has been achieved. Pickering (1961) has drawn attention to the lack of agreement about the dividing line between a normal and elevated blood pressure. The dividing line is 120/80 mm Hg in some studies (Robinson and Brucer, 1939) and 180/110 mm Hg in others (Evans, 1920). Most clinicians would consider a blood pressure of 180/110 mm Hg high. Some do not. The dividing line between a normal and high blood pressure is arbitrary and fixed. But blood pressure levels vary continually and markedly throughout the day and night in both hypertensive and normal subjects. Daily measurements of blood pressure may vary by 25 percent or more in patients with initial arterial pressure readings of 140/90 mm Hg (Glock et al., 1957; Koster, 1970). At one time a marked variability in blood pressure levels in normotensive persons was thought to be predictive of future essential hypertension. This method of selecting a population of normotensive patients at risk for essential hypertension has been discredited (Page, 1960). Provocative tests, such as the cold pressor test, or the administration of tetraethylammonium chloride, epinephrine, or norepinephrine (designed to bring out the excessive blood pressure reactivity of the future hypertensive), produce different results in the hands of different investigators. Blood pressure lability by itself cannot be considered to be a reliable predictor of the tendency to develop essential hypertension.

Problems of Diagnosis

It is difficult to establish that the patients who comprise a research sample actually suffer from essential hypertension, and not from one of the gamut of diseases in which high blood pressure is a symptom. This problem can be illustrated by the attempts that have been made to discriminate between primary (Conn's syndrome) and secondary aldosteronism, which are both accompanied by high blood pressure.

109

Primary aldosteronism may or may not be a very rare cause of symptomatic hypertension. If rare, it does not constitute a problem in the selection of hypertensive subjects for study. But it may be common. In a series of 33 patients with a diagnosis of essential hypertension (Conn et al., 1966), five were found to be normokalemic and to have suppressed plasma renin levels and increased aldosterone production levels. In this series of patients initially diagnosed as having essential hypertension the incidence of Conn's syndrome was 15 percent. Laragh and his co-workers (1966) and Ledingham et al. (1967) concluded from a study of 113 patients with essential hypertension that Conn's syndrome is rare. The lack of agreement about the incidence of Conn's syndrome is due to the difficulty in applying consistent criteria in the diagnosis of primary aldosteronism (Conn et al., 1966; Dollery et al., 1959; Ledingham et al., 1967; Page and McCubbin, 1965).

If primary aldosteronism is as common as Conn and co-workers (1966) believe, differentiating primary aldosteronism from the secondary form poses a major problem in subject selection. When Conn's syndrome (1955) is fully developed— with tetany, weakness, paralysis, high blood pressure, hypokalemia, an excess production of aldosterone, and an adrenal adenoma—it can be distinguished from essential hypertension. In less-blatant or asymptomatic forms of primary aldosteronism, hypokalemia might be variable and mild (Conn et al., 1964). Secondary aldosteronism occurs in malignant and renovascular hypertension and consists of a syndrome of hypokalemia, increased aldosterone production (secondary to increased angiotensin activity) and a high blood pressure (Conn, 1961; Dollery et al., 1959; Laidlaw et al., 1960).

When hypertensive disease is advanced, severe, or long-standing, carbohydrate intolerance may also occur (Biglieri et al., 1967; Christiansen et al., 1964; Kirkendall et al., 1964), presumably as a result of secondary aldosteronism. Aberrations of carbohydrate metabolism are also seen in primary aldosteronism (Conn, 1955; Conn et al., 1966). Many patients with benign essential hypertension have low serum or plasma renin levels (Brunner et al., 1972; Creditor and Loschky, 1967; Gunnels et al., 1967; Ledingham et al., 1967) and their aldosterone secretion is normal.

Primary and secondary aldosteronism can be differentiated, but care is needed. In the secondary form, plasma renin levels are very high (Genest et al., 1964; Morris, 1962). In primary aldosteronism renin levels are either normal or very low (Conn, 1955; Conn et al., 1964; Genest et al., 1964; Meyer, 1967). Many hypertensive patients restrict the amount of salt in their food. A low intake of salt and an upright posture stimulate plasma renin activity (Conn et al., 1964). Care must, therefore, be taken when measurements of renin activity are made in hypertensive patients not to stimulate renin production and simulate primary aldosteronism. Primary and secondary aldosteronism need to be differentiated if an investigator wishes to study some aspect of essential hypertension. Diagnostic difficulties also face the investigator in differentiating between patients with essential and renovascular hypertension.

Conceptual Issues

Conceptual disagreements about a variety of issues characterize hypertension research. To begin with, it is not clear whether an elevated level of blood pressure is but the outward sign of some more basic disturbance, a central feature of the disease, or a normal variation and not a manifestation of disease.

Platt (1967) has argued that blood pressure readings are discontinuously (bimodally) distributed in populations of human beings. Those with high levels of blood pressure are set apart from those with normal levels. High blood pressure levels are, therefore, a manifestation of the disease essential hypertension. Pickering (1967) asserts that blood pressure levels are continuously (unimodally) distributed in the population. At one end of a unimodal or Gaussian distribution of blood pressure, high levels would occur. Therefore, the high blood pressure levels of essential hypertension are due to normal variation, and do not constitute a disease per se.

Pickering's argument disturbs our traditional concepts of disease, for the following reasons. Although essential hypertension is frequently a symptomless disease, persons with essential hypertension are at risk for a number of serious complications from which they die (Bechgaard, 1967). One serious and direct complication of essential hypertension is arterial and arteriolar disease. Since the introduction of arterial surgery for relief of a coarctation of the aorta, it has been found that the sudden impact of elevated blood pressure on the arterial bed distal to the former constriction leads to swelling and necrosis of arterial walls to the point of gangrene (Benson and Sealy, 1956). When blood pressure levels are kept low after surgery the damage is averted (Groves and Effler, 1960). In essential hypertension, arterial lesions often occur after many years of elevated blood pressure levels. Any part of the arterial bed can be affected. In view of the fact that the high blood pressure levels of essential hypertension predispose to arterial damage, it would be hard to argue that it is not a disease.

Patients with "high normal" pressure or "borderline hypertension" are more likely to develop elevated blood pressure levels than are normotensive persons and are, therefore, at risk for arterial disease (Evans, 1957; Hines, 1940; Julius et al., 1964; Julius and Shork, 1970; Palmer, 1930). Twelve percent of persons whose blood pressure readings were initially normal had blood pressure levels of 150/90 mm Hg or more 20 years later. By comparison, 26 percent of those whose blood pressure was more than 140/90 at 20 years of age later had a blood pressure above 150/90 mm Hg (Julius et al., 1964). Therefore, the risk of essential hypertension is doubled in those with borderline high blood pressure at 20 years of age. The risk of dying of the complications of high blood pressure is greater in those with borderline hypertension than in people with normal blood pressure readings (Heyden et al., 1969; Kannel et al., 1969; Levy et al., 1945; Lew, 1967; McKenzie and Shepherd, 1937; Thomson, 1950). And the eventual morbidity for coronary artery disease (Kannel et al., 1969) and other kinds of cardiovascular disease is enhanced on borderline hypertension (Heyden et al., 1969; Thomson, 1950). It is, therefore, difficult to argue that essential hypertension is not a disease, because it does cause death and disability.

The concept that hypertension is "essential," may also be seriously misleading. This label is intended to set essential hypertension apart from kidney diseases or diseases of the endocrine system in which the etiology and pathogenesis of the blood pressure elevations are better known. The term "essential" implies that we do not know what produces the high blood pressure in essential hypertension (Shapiro, 1973). Actually, more is known than is conceded. The problem is that there is no agreement about what is known. The lack of agreement stems from the need to find a single "cause" for the etiology and pathogenesis of essential hypertension. Single pathogenetic hypotheses are advocated. Some advocate specific defects within the kidney. Others advocate a disturbance in salt intake and metabolism. Still others believe that the adrenal gland is at fault; among

111

them, some point a finger at the adrenocortical hormones, others at the adrenomedullary hormones (norepinephrine). Environmental stresses and the emotional responses that they elicit in physiologically and psychologically predisposed persons have also been blamed for the pathogenesis of essential hypertension. For many years increases in the peripheral resistance were considered to be the antecedent and central "cause" of essential hypertension. And indeed the peripheral resistance is usually elevated in patients with essential hypertension.

Recently, the role of the circulation in the pathogenesis of essential hypertension has been reassessed. It appears that early in the course of essential hypertension in some patients, the cardiac output is elevated, and this in turn later increases the peripheral resistance (Guyton and Coleman, 1969). Therefore, in some patients increases in peripheral resistance are secondary and probably help to sustain, but do not initiate, the development of high blood pressure levels.

These disagreements about the pathogenesis of essential hypertension could be resolved if it could be demonstrated that there is no single invariant "cause" or combination of antecedent causes of this disease. Given the number of variables that control and regulate the arterial pressure, it should not be surprising that elevated levels of blood pressure are produced by a variety of factors that either alter the relationship between these variables or alter the level of one of the variables to bias the entire system. It is now fairly clear that essential hypertension occurs with high, normal, or low renin levels (Brunner et al., 1972). Different mechanisms may, therefore, initiate the disease. No one cause or mechanism does so. Also, it may be important to separate out the mechanisms that initiate the disease from those that sustain it (later in this chapter the reasons for this statement will be described). The disagreements about its pathogenesis could be resolved with studies of subjects at risk for essential hypertension, because once hypertension has begun, it is impossible to determine which devices are involved in initiating the illness and which in sustaining it.

THE CURRENT STATUS OF PSYCHOSOMATIC RESEARCH ON
ESSENTIAL HYPERTENSION

The problem of defining essential hypertension and the conceptual issue of attempting to infer its etiology and pathogenesis after onset have also plagued the behavioral scientist. Some behavioral scientists have found that hypertensive patients struggle against unconscious feelings of rage, hatred, and anger. Other behavioral scientists have described the way hypertensive patients perceive other people as dangerous, derisive, unsympathetic, and untrustworthy. Some hypertensive patients, therefore, avoid other people, provoke others to behave in the very manner in which they perceive them, or deny derisive or unsympathetic behavior on the part of others.

Originally, some behavioral scientists believed that the origin of the anger and rage that colors the hypertensive's perceptions could be traced back to frustrated dependency wishes in childhood. More recently, medical sociologists have pointed out that the incidence and prevalence of essential hypertension is highest in the male black population living in the poorest parts of American cities. In that setting, people are particularly liable to experience violence and prejudice, police brutality, economic hardship, family discord, and divorce. The rage that these attitudes and events engender and the alertness to derision and danger are real. Other hypertensive patients struggle against their anger and are afraid to express it. They are often unassertive. Still other patients are assertive, combative, bitter, and rebellious. Most behavioral scientists would agree that many, but not all, hypertensive patients have conflicts about anger and rage that are expressed in different traits, styles, and ways of relating. Probably not all such patients are constituted psychologically in a uniform way.

Even if the psychological characteristics of these patients were uniform, it might not have etiological or pathogenetic significance. Because these characteristics are observed after the onset of the disease, they might be a product of high blood pressure levels or high serum renin and angiotensin activity. Or they might covary with changes in blood pressure levels, sustain them, or influence the course of the disease. Normal or high blood pressure levels do indeed vary markedly throughout the day and night, with everyday events, and with changes in the behavioral state of human beings (Sokolow et al., 1970).

Behavioral and physiological studies on animals strongly suggest that social isolation early in life that is followed by a return to communal life is not only marked by aggressive behavior but results in high blood pressure. On the other hand, genetic factors play a major role in some strains of rats that can be bred for salt sensitivity or the "spontaneous" development of hypertension.

Even if anger and aggression play a role in essential hypertension in man, not all angry people develop it. Anger must be combined with physiological predisposition to the disease. Although the predisposing physiological factors are not known, they seem to consist of a variety of different disturbances in the regulation of blood pressure. Recent studies in animals also point to the fact that the brain participates either in the initiation or in the mediation of the initial phases of experimental hypertension, and it may also be involved in sustaining some other forms of hypertension—a generalization that has always been implicit in the psychosomatic theory of essential hypertension (Alexander, 1950; Charvat et al., 1964; Folkow, 1971; Henry and Cassel, 1969; Weiner, 1970).

THE ROLE OF GENETIC FACTORS IN ESSENTIAL HYPERTENSION

Introduction

Even though no consensus has been reached about the pathogenesis of essential hypertension, genetic factors are believed to play an etiological role in the disease. Essential hypertension is believed to be an inherited disease (Hamilton et al., 1954, 1963; Hoobler, 1961; Pickering, 1955). This belief is based on family and twin studies (Ayman, 1934; Bøe et al., 1957; Hines et al., 1957; Mathers et al., 1961) and the stable incidence of essential hypertension in white persons from Norway to Nassau (Bøe et al., 1957; Johnson and Remington; 1961). The best evidence that genetic factors play a role in high blood pressure comes from animal studies. At least in one strain of rats, the inheritance of high blood pressure is polygenic. It is easier to determine the mode of inheritance by breeding rats than by population studies. Population studies, with few exceptions, do not reveal the mode of inheritance of a trait (McKusick, 1960). Nonetheless, Pickering (1961, 1967) believes that the mode of inheritance of essential hypertension is polygenic. He bases his inference on the fact that he and others (Bøe et al., 1957; Comstock, 1957; Ostfeld and Paul, 1963) have found that the frequency distribution of blood pressure in a population is unimodal. He believes that a particular level of blood pressure is polygenically inherited. In his opinion each of the multiple genetic factors operate through different mechanisms to determine blood pressure levels.

Platt (1947; 1963; 1967) has disagreed with Pickering. He points out that systolic blood pressure is not continuously, but is bimodally (or multimodally) distributed in the population. This distribution speaks for the existence of two or more different populations. The bimodal distribution is also evidence of the existence of a single dominant genetic factor in the etiology of essential hypertension. Platt argues that the two populations might behave differently in regard to increases in blood pressure. In one population a rise in diastolic blood pressure would be expected to occur in middle life. In the other population, very little change in blood pressure would occur at this age. Platt believes that the rise in blood pressure is an inherited trait and not merely a function of age. However, the evidence in support of this thesis (Cruz-Coke, 1959, 1960; Thomson, 1950) is not conclusive.

Pickering (1967) does not consider the rate with which blood pressure levels increase with age to be an inherited trait. Rather he ascribes the increase in blood pressure with age to environmental factors. Pickering's view is indirectly supported by Harris' and Singer's (1968) prospective study of 500 persons working in an insurance company, who were observed for 30 years. The blood pressure of some did not increase at all with age. In some others a steep increase occurred. The increases were continuously distributed throughout this population. If Platt's hypothesis were correct, a majority of subjects would have shown no increase in blood pressure with age, and a few would have developed elevated levels rapidly.

Different populations of both sexes at different ages differ greatly in regard to the rate of change in blood pressure with age (Henry and Cassel, 1969). In some groups (e.g., Navajo Indians on reservations, U.S. Navy aviators, and some rural Africans and Asians) no increase in blood pressure with age occurs. In other groups, such as black persons living in the Southern United States, the rise is steep and begins early in life. The data support Pickering's position that increases in blood pressure are not inherited but indicate the operation of various environmental factors. The data are consistent enough to indicate that genetic factors alone do not account for elevated levels in blood pressure. They also suggest that blood pressure levels are randomly distributed in a population in the same manner as height and weight. In some persons in the population, a tendency to high blood pressure is probably polygenically inherited. This unspecified tendency accounts for about 30 percent of the etiological variance. The tendency is elicited by environmental factors. Some persons with this tendency respond to environmental factors either with high blood pressure levels or essential hypertension. At least in some animals the level of the blood pressure is not inherited; it can be "set" by external factors such as salt or "stress."

114

Evidence Derived from Studies on Human Twins

Hines et al. (1957) studied the blood pressure levels of 17 monozygotic (Mz) and 3 dizygotic (Dz) twins. Zygosity was determined in 13 twin pairs. Eight pairs of Mz twins were condordant for hypertension. In two of these the hypertension was due to polycystic disease of the kidney. The blood pressure levels in the female twin pairs were concordant. Male Mz twins were concordant for blood pressure levels but discordant for the presence of hypertensive vascular changes. Three Mz twin pairs were discordant for hypertension. Six other Mz pairs were normotensive. There were 200 additional pairs of twins studied. Exact zygosity determinations on these twins were not carried out. Of these pairs, 87 were assumed to be Mz. Of the 200 twin pairs, 97 percent were less than 25 years of age: none had hypertension. The blood pressure levels of the Mz twins were more alike in the Dz twins with respect to resting levels and to pressor responses to the cold pressor test. Hines concludes that a "genetic" factor is responsible for the mechanisms that control blood pressure in normotensive and hypertensive persons.

In normotensive male Mz twins the blood pressure variance is greater than in Dz male twins. In female twins the reverse is true in regard to systolic and mean blood pressure. When intrapair variance of blood pressure in male and female Mz twins is compared, the variance in men is consistently larger for systolic blood pressure. Therefore, the basal blood pressure in men is subject to greater environmental influences than in women (Mathers et al., 1961).

Much can be learned from studying Mz twins discordant for blood pressure levels or for essential hypertension in order to determine the factors that are responsible for the different phenotypes. Among these factors may be the psychological state of each of the twins at the time the blood pressure is determined. Instances of essential hypertension developing in the more emotionally disturbed member of four twin pairs have been described (Flynn et al., 1950; Friedman and Kasanin, 1943; Jones et al., 1948; Sheldon and Ball, 1950). Torgersen and Kringlen (1971) studied the blood pressure levels of 48 adult Mz twins. They found that the more obedient, quiet, reserved, submissive, insecure, depressed, and withdrawn of each pair of twins had higher systolic blood pressure levels than his brother or sister. The systolic blood pressure levels in some instances ranged from 97 to 227 mm Hg.

Evidence for Genetic Factors from Studies of Families

The oral contraceptive pills produce elevations of blood pressure only in women with a family history of high blood pressure (Shapiro, 1973). "The pill" presumably elicits a genetically determined tendency to high blood pressure. But this tendency does not account for the finding that spouses, who are not related to each other except by marriage, tend to share similar blood pressure levels the longer they remain married to each other (Winkelstein et al., 1966).[*] Other family members besides spouses share common blood pressure levels. The family incidence of hypertension is frequent. O'Hare et al. (1924) found a positive family history in almost three-quarters of 300 persons with hypertension. If one parent is hypertensive, 12 to 28 percent of the children also are.

[*] This finding has not been confirmed by Gearing et al. (1962) and Johnson et al. (1965).

With two hypertensive parents 16 to 41 percent of the children are hypertensive. Of the adult siblings of hypertensive patients, 20 to 65 percent are also hypertensive (Thomas and Cohen, 1955). By comparison, the incidence of hypertension in the siblings of normotensive people is between 6.5 and 20 percent and the incidence is 6 percent in the children of normotensive parents (Johnson et al., 1965; Miall et al., 1962, 1967; Speransky et al., 1959). Zinner and his co-workers (1971) found that the variation of systolic and diastolic blood pressure levels in children of the same families was less than in unrelated people. Systolic and diastolic blood pressure levels cluster in siblings and their mothers. A family tendency to similar blood pressure levels is established early in life.

The family aggregation of hypertensive and normotensive blood pressure levels is a well-established fact (Perera et al., 1961; Pickering, 1961; Schweitzer et al., 1967) but its interpretation is not, because either genetic or familial factors could acount for the similarity of the blood pressure that occurs in relatives. The similarity of blood pressure levels in families and Mz twins suggests that the level is an inherited trait. Some would disagree with this interpretation. They would consider that a predisposition to high blood pressure is inherited, but the level is not. Another possibility is that dietary factors, such as a sensitivity to salt, are inherited. Studies in hypertensive rats suggest that different physiological mechanisms, including salt sensitivity, may be inherited and may produce high blood pressure levels. Therefore, different genetic factors can be assumed to control different mechanisms that produce high blood pressure levels in rats. And, the search for an invariant set of genetic factors may be fruitless.

The discussions about the inheritance of high blood pressure or of essential hypertension tend to overlook the possibility that it is a heterogeneous illness with different predispositions and initiating factors that are under different genetic control. Support for this suggestion derives from the fact that essential hypertension may occur with low, normal, or high renin levels. And low-renin hypertension can result from different disturbances in the regulation of the renin-angiotensin-aldosterone system that may be inherited (Brunner et al., 1971, 1972).

EPIDEMIOLOGICAL STUDIES OF ESSENTIAL HYPERTENSION

About 70 percent of the etiology of essential hypertension can be accounted for by environmental factors. But environmental factors can be specified only when accurate incidence and prevalence figures for the disease are available—a goal that has not yet been achieved.

Prevalence figures for essential hypertension should be separately gathered for the borderline or early, and the established forms of essential hypertension. Borderline systolic blood pressure elevations occur in about 10 percent of a population of 20 years of age or more. The prevalence of essential hypertension usually increases with age. By the age of 60, its prevalence is 40 percent. Below the age of 50 years it occurs with less prevalence in women than in men. All prevalence figures should, therefore, take into account the sex and age of patients and the specific stage of their disease. Because many studies have failed adequately to classify their subjects along these lines, the large literature on the epidemiology of essential hypertension and high blood pressure is confusing. The incidence and prevalence figures vary from patient series to patient series, according to their age, sex, geographic location and ethnic group. Prevalence figures for the disease vary from 5 to 25 percent or more of a population. Scotch (1961) found an even larger prevalence in South Africa, where it was 20 percent under the age of 45 years and 58 percent in older Zulu men.

There is sound evidence that geographic and cultural factors, in addition to the age and the sex, significantly influence the prevalence of essential hypertension. Natives of New Guinea who live in very "primitive" conditions have higher blood pressure levels (Whyte, 1958) than some Brazilian Indians who live under similar conditions (Loewenstein, 1961). The blood pressures of Indian workers living and working in the tea plantations of Assam (Wilson, 1958) rise with age much more rapidly than in three other Indian populations (Padmavati and Gupta, 1959). Marked differences in the prevalence and the increase of blood pressure levels with age have been observed in various Micronesian societies, whose members live under similar climactic conditions (Lovell, 1967).

In the United States, people who live in towns have higher blood pressure levels (Berkson et al., 1960; Stamler et al., 1967a, b) or mortality rates (Stamler et al., 1967b) than those who live in the country. In black American women an opposite trend is found: in Mississippi, black rural women have higher mean systolic and diastolic blood pressures than black urban women (Langford et al., 1968). Stamler et al. (1967a) reports that the age-corrected prevalence rates per 1,000 men of diastolic blood pressure levels over 95 mm Hg were 209, 108, and 67 in black, native-born white, and foreign-born white blue-collar men in Illinois respectively.

Consistent trends in the prevalence rates of high blood pressure levels are found when black and white Americans are compared. Throughout the United States, black Americans have higher levels (Stamler et al., 1967b). In Detroit, higher blood pressure levels occur in black men living in areas of the city marked by low socioeconomic status, high crime rates, police brutality and high rates of separation and divorce. The blood pressure levels were higher than in the poor blacks than in black or white persons living in areas of the city that were not marked by such social and economic conditions (Harburg et al., 1973). However, differences in blood pressure levels between black and white American women matched for socioeconomic status may be less apparent than in men (Langford et al., 1968).

This section will not attempt exhaustively to review the very rich epidemiological literature. Recent reviews on this topic have been carried out by Guttmann and Benson (1971); Henry and Cassel (1969) and Stamler et al. (1967b). It will try to summarize some of the explanations that may account for the puzzling and often discrepant results obtained in prevalence studies of essential hypertension. These discrepancies have given rise to much discussion about the relative roles of genetic and environmental factors in essential hypertension. Epidemiologists of essential hypertension emphasize the roles of various environmental factors and discount genetic factors.

Because the coefficient of resemblance for blood pressure levels is greater in family members and in spouses, environmental factors must play a major role in the etiology of essential hypertension. But the specific nature of these factors has not been identified. For example, we do not know why blood pressure levels rise with age. If we did know, we might be able to identify the environmental factors that produce the rise. Perhaps, the

117

increase in blood pressure levels with age may be more related to changes in the elasticity of blood vessels.

In any case, and in most populations throughout the world, levels of blood pressure rise with age (Henry and Cassel, 1969; Sokolow and Harris, 1961). Systolic blood pressure levels tend to rise faster with age than diastolic ones. The blood pressure of young persons with blood pressure levels at the upper end of the distribution curve rise faster with age than those with levels in the median range (Harris and Singer, 1968; Julius and Schorck, 1971). In women, the rate of increase of both systolic and diastolic blood pressure is greater than in men in Norway (Bøe et al.; 1957), England (Pickering, 1955, 1961), and the United States (Kagan et al., 1958). In women the increase in blood pressure with age begins earlier (35–40 years) than in men (Platt, 1959; Robinson and Brucer, 1939; Winckelstein and Kantor, 1967). Elevated diastolic levels are less-prevalent in young women and more prevalent in middle-aged ones than in men (Aleksandrow, 1967).

Although the distribution of blood pressure progressively moves toward higher levels and greater variability in levels occurs as people get older, exceptions to these generalizations occur; in some individuals the blood pressure levels remain the same throughout adulthood, whereas in other people they actually decrease with age (Bassett et al., 1966; Stamler et al.; 1958). Increased blood pressure levels in the hypertensive range occur most often in middle life, but they can already be seen in children 5 to 7 years of age (Sokolow and Harris, 1961; Stamler et al., 1958).

The differences in the prevalence of essential hypertension, especially its malignant phase, in black and white Americans remains unexplained. The differences in the course of the disease in men and women have not been accounted for (Perera, 1955; Simpson and Gilchrist, 1958; Smirk, 1957; Sokolow and Perloff, 1961).

THE ROLE OF SOCIOCULTURAL FACTORS
IN ESSENTIAL HYPERTENSION AND HIGH BLOOD PRESSURE

Epidemiological studies have not accounted for the difference in the prevalence of essential hypertension in various social and cultural groups. Sociocultural and psychological studies have tentatively identified some of the environmental factors that may play a role in the predisposition and initiation of the disease. These factors may interact with the genetic tendency to the disease. Henry and Cassell (1969) in their exhaustive review have critically examined the evidence for and against the roles of exercise, salt intake, tobacco smoking, malnutrition, illness, obesity, and heredity in essential hypertension. They have concluded that physical exertion, labor, or exercise may be associated with either high or low blood pressure levels. Persons who do not exert themselves may have either high or low levels. Presumably, exertion is associated with high blood pressure only in the predisposed.

Much has been written about the role of salt in essential hypertension. A high salt intake has been associated with very high blood pressure levels in farmers living on the northern isalnd of Japan (Takahashi et al., 1957). Actually, the role of salt in essential hypertension is likely to be an additive one; salt may elevate blood pressure levels only in the presence of preexisting renal damage, caused, for instance, by pyelonephritis (Shapiro, 1963).

A high salt intake may be associated with low blood pressure levels in some cultures and high levels in others. In the United States no relationship has been found between blood pressure levels and the amount of sodium excreted in the urine—an index of salt intake (Dawber et al., 1967). A diet rich in fat is eaten by people with normal blood pressure levels; other people on a lean diet have high blood pressure levels. Other habits, such as smoking tobacco are not associated with high blood pressure levels (Dawber et al., 1967). Malnutrition does not per se reduce the blood pressure or prevent the increase in blood pressure levels with age. Even the traditional view that a strong positive correlation exists between obesity and high blood pressure has been weakened by a careful analysis of the data: Aleksandrow (1967) found that the systolic blood pressure of the obese is 10 to 15 mm Hg higher on the average than that of the underweight. The increased blood pressure in the obese is in part accounted for by the greater volume of the upper arm in the obese. Obese people also have increasing levels of blood pressure with age, but the increase is no faster than in the lean and can, therefore, not be explained on the basis of obesity alone.

Sociocultural factors, other than diet, salt, or obesity play a predisposing or initiating role in essential hypertension (Charvat et al., 1964; Gutmann and Benson, 1971; Henry and Cassel, 1969; Scotch and Geiger, 1963). They are mediated by brain mechanisms (Folkow and Rubinstein, 1966; Henry and Cassel, 1969; Weiner, 1970). When a society is stable, and when its customs, traditions and institutions are well-established and well-structured and its members respond to a predictable sociocultural environment with integrated patterns of psychological adaptation, then blood pressure levels do not become elevated with age. Those who live in a social milieu that is rapidly changing, is unpredictable, dangerous, or unfamiliar—so that psychological adaptation to it is difficult or impossible—tend to develop increasing blood pressure levels with age. Not everyone who lives in such a social milieu develops high blood pressure levels or essential hypertension—probably, only the predisposed do.

Culture change or social chaos may impose adaptive psychological burdens that become intolerable if they also disrupt a person's habitual patterns of psychological adaptation or coping. Patterns of coping are usually established in childhood: if successful, they become habitual. If they become disrupted and are no longer effective, especially during early middle life, blood pressure levels may rise. Some participants in rapid social change and migrants to an urban environment or to another culture are likely to develop high blood pressure levels (Cruz-Coke, 1960; Stamler et al., 1967a; Syme et al., 1964). New roles that have to be assumed in a new setting may be stressful (Scotch, 1961). A change in social or professional status may impose strains on psychological adaptation (Christenson and Hinkle, 1961). Not all persons develop essential hypertension in new settings. Additional factors must play a pathogenetic role. Not everyone is the same in the way he meets and overcomes the challenge of change, migration, a new job, or new relationships in a different setting.

Support for this contention is found in studies on hypertensive women. The relationships of these women to other people are often hostile, combative, and "abrasive." The hypertensive women are less attractive physically. They cannot accept and are resentful of their feminine role. They are careful not to express their angry feelings. They bear secret grudges longer than others. Their marriages are frequently unhappy. Their capacity to be anything but truculent is limited (Harris and Singer, 1968). These women do not adapt well in new social environments. Their truculence only makes it more difficult for them to gain the help and support of others in new settings or when social change occurs. When exposed to danger they fight, or when they are divorced they savor their misfortune.

These psychological and sociocultural factors may play a role in the etiology of essential hypertension but they do not explain in any specific way why black Americans are particularly prone to essential hypertension. Blacks are exposed to similar social changes to those of white Americans. But black Americans have higher blood pressure levels and a higher morbidity and mortality due to hypertensive disease and strokes than their white compatriots. Some blacks are also exposed to more prejudice and violence, especially if poor. In fact, the prevalence of high blood pressure is greater in poor than in middle-class black Americans. Poor black Americans also live in more crowded conditions, have higher rates of divorce, and move more frequently than middle class blacks. They are deeply resentful of police brutality but feel they must keep a rein on expressing their resentments (Harburg et al., 1973).

The correlations between socioeconomic conditions and status and blood pressure levels in black Americans support the hypothesis that sociocultural factors play an etiological role in essential hypertension and hypertensive disease. The data partly elucidate how social and socioeconomic factors may elicit unexpressible or unexpressed anger and resentment in hypertensive parients. In this case the anger is a response to real danger, external prejudice, and violence.

Sociocultural studies are, however, correlational in nature: socioeconomic status, living conditions, and the marital status of patients with different levels of blood pressure are validly related to each other. But the exact nature of the relationships is not clear. The correlations between sociocultural or socioeconomic conditions may or may not be causal to the etiology and pathogenesis of essential hypertension. Such studies should be combined with studies of the social conditons and changes in the lives of patients before or at the time blood pressure levels begin to increase.

THE ROLE OF PSYCHOLOGICAL AND PSYCHOPHYSIOLOGICAL VARIABLES IN ESSENTIAL HYPERTENSION

Relatively few psychiatric studies of the onset conditions of essential hypertension have been carried out. Many obstacles stand in the way of such studies. Very often essential hypertension is discovered on routine examination and it is then impossible to determine when the blood pressure became elevated. Because the level of blood pressure rises with age in many people, individual blood pressure levels should be age-adjusted before they are judged to be normal or not. Generally speaking, this is not done in most studies.

Usually no symptoms accompany early hypertension (Pickering, 1961), although some patients complain of headache, fatigue, weakness, palpitations, loss of appetite, dizziness, true vertigo, and insomnia. They are then found to have elevated blood pressures on routine examination (Ayman, 1930; Ayman and Pratt, 1931; Benedict, 1956; Tucker, 1949, 1950). These symptoms should not be causally ascribed to high blood pressure levels because they are frequently relieved by reassurance, suggestion, or placebos

(Ayman, 1930; Goldring et al., 1956). The symptoms can usually be related to the patient's knowing and being concerned about an elevated blood pressure rather than to the direct effect of the hypertension (Stewart, 1953). In any case, the appearance of these symptoms is not a reliable indication of the onset of essential hypertension. The onset may antedate the symptoms that often occur after the unexpected discovery of the hypertension.

Antecedent and Concomitant Life Events

Relatively prolonged elevations of blood pressure have been reported after man-made disasters (Ruskin et al., 1948) or after prolonged engagement in military combat (Gelshteyn, 1943; Ehrstrom, 1945; Graham, 1945). Not all persons developed high blood pressure under these circumstances, but in those who did, the elevations lasted a maximum of two months and then returned to "normal" levels. The incidence of hypertension in Russia is greater in persons chronically exposed to high levels of noise (Simonson and Brožek, 1959).

The onset of hypertension may occur in the course of everyday events and situations. Similar events may also suddenly alter the course of essential hypertension, so that the disease changes from its benign to its malignant form. Weiss (1942) found that the symptoms of hypertension begin in stressful situations. And Fischer (1961) reported that the onset of hypertension could be correlated in time with the anniversary of an important relative's death. The personal relationship of the patient to the dead relative was "primitive," close, dependent, and ambivalent.

Such formulations about the personal relationships of patients appear and reappear in the psychosomatic literature, not only with respect to patients with hypertension but also with respect to persons who have other diseases or no diseases at all. Despite the lack of apparent specificity of these life events for hypertension, they play a "necessary," if not "sufficient," role in the onset of essential hypertension. Other predisposing factors, including genetic ones, may play additional roles. However, these assertions need be verified with much greater rigor and validated on more than one patient. Reiser and co-workers (1950, 1951a) did so. They found that in 50 percent of 80 patients significant and palpable life events could be identified that preceded or corresponded in time with the known onset of hypertension. Because of the psychological make-up of these patients, the events had particular meanings for their patients.

The psychosocial factors that modify the course of the disease have also been studied by Reiser et al. (1951b). The onset of the malignant phase of primary and secondary hypertension in 12 patients in whom the disease had previously had a benign course was precipitated by interpersonal conflicts about dependency and hostility expressed in sadomasochistic fears. Moreover, these conflicts were very much like those with which the onset of the disease had been correlated. In 76 percent of the patients studied by Chambers and Reiser (1953), the occurrence of cardiac failure in patients with limited cardiac reserve was correlated in time with events that were emotionally significant to the individual patient. Two classes of interpersonal events were identified; those leading to feelings of frustration and rage, and those leading to a feeling of rejection in which the threat of loss of security predominated.

121

The course of the disease can be improved by the ministrations of a benign and supportive physician combined with the use of drugs (Shapiro and Teng, 1957; Shapiro et al., 1954) or by a thoughtful physician upon whom the patient can depend (Moses et al., 1956; Reiser et al., 1951a; Weiss, 1957).

Such studies—and there are still too few—raise a number of questions about the specific physiological event or events that change the course of the illness. Or is the critical variable that produces the change the "quantity" of the stress rather than any specific event? Or is the change in course a product of the interaction of physiological and psychological factors?

Other Factors: The Role of Salt Intake

The foregoing studies have been repeatedly criticized for being "subjective" and "anecdotal." Pejorative criticism of this kind is easily leveled at clinical studies even when serious attempts are made to verify the reliability of the observation. However, the relative lack of progress in psychosomatic studies of essential hypertension mainly stems from two sources—the impossibility of carrying out predictive studies and a failure to test alternative hypotheses. It may very well be true that inhibited hostility and anger in response to frustration, external danger, and violence may, in some instances, be a necessary condition in the predisposed individual; but it is also possible that this anger does not directly lead to raised blood pressure, but rather leads to changes in diet or in the carrying out of the doctor's instructions once the illness is established, which either further promote hypertension or affect the course of the disease.

One alternative hypothesis to the exclusive etiological role of psychosocial factors is that the individual predisposed to essential hypertension ingests more salt and water than normal people do. Dahl (1958), 1960) and Dahl and Love (1957) have pointed out that there is a linear correlation between the quantity of salt intake and the incidence of essential hypertension. In a cultural group where the intake of salt is low, the probability of some percentage of that group developing essential hypertension is lower than in another group in which there is a greater intake of salt. Cultural factors do seem to play a role in the incidence of hypertension: for example, the illness is unknown in New Guinea, but it is a major cause of death in Japan, where the dietary content of salt is very high. The amount of dietary salt is partly a function of the cultural setting. However, an individual's appetite for salt may be independent of his requirement for it. We are just beginning to learn what accounts for individual variations in salt appetite. For instance, they could be due to altered thresholds in the taste for salt (Fallis et al., 1962; Wotman et al., 1967); however, this has not been confirmed. When 10 patients with essential hypertension were compared with 12 normotensive volunteers, no differences in the detection and recognition thresholds for salt could be discerned. However, when placed on a constant dry diet containing 9 mEq of sodium, the hypertensive patients much preferred to drink water containing 0.15 M sodium chloride than distilled water. They consumed a significantly greater proportion of their total fluid intake as saline and drank more fluids per day. They consumed more than four times as much salt per day as did the volunteers (Schechter et al., 1973). The meaning of this correlation is uncertain. The increased consumption of salt may be related to some aspect of the disease, such as increased serum levels of angiotensin II. However, the preference for salt in some hypertensives may cause high blood pressure levels to be perpetuated. Predictive studies are needed to determine whether individuals predisposed to hypertension show the same salt preference as those who already suffer from it.

Many more studies of this kind will have to be done before conclusions can be reached about the role of a preference for salt in the pathogenesis of essential hypertension. The relationships of feelings and attitudes to salt intake might also be studied, because angry hypertensives may not follow their low-salt diets, may consume more fluids (including alcohol), or may discard their antihypertensive medication when they are disappointed in either their physician or the effectiveness of treatment or are bothered by the side effects of their medications.

Conceptual and Methodological Problems

Psychological studies of patients after the onset of essential hypertension have the implied purpose of uncovering those features of the personality that may play a role in the etiology, pathogenesis, or maintenance of the disease. Since it has not been established that features of the personality studied after disease onset play an etiological or pathogenetic role in essential hypertension (Glock and Lennard, 1957), the logic of this implied research goal is open to question. In order to circumvent this problem, a more careful assertion should be made—that personality factors that characterize hypertensive patients covary with elevated blood pressure levels. Indeed they may; for in the absence of established fact, the hypothesis could be put forward that both the personality features and the elevated blood pressure levels are but the expression of a third variable—for instance, a genetic one or the effect on the brain of some pathophysiological disturbance, such as raised angiotensin levels.

Clinical psychiatric studies of hypertension have suffered from methodological flaws. Many subject variables—such as socioeconomic status, age, and sex—or disease variables—such as the duration and stage of the illness, or whether essential hypertension or some other form is being studied—have often been disregarded. In some studies, blood pressure readings were only taken once. Control subjects have not always been chosen with sufficient care, and in some studies control groups have not been used at all (Crisp, 1963). All findings on one patient population need to be validated on a new population. Most studies are biased because the investigator knows that his patients are hypertensive. Attempts to circumvent this problem have been made. Subjects have been selected for study before they had developed hypertension (Harris et al., 1953; Kalis et al., 1961). Subjects have been chosen because they had a verified family history of hypertension, or because they had a vascular hyperreactivity. As noted previously, not everyone would agree that these subjects are at risk for the development of hypertension. New research strategies are needed: it might be possible to study hypertensive patients before and after they had been rendered normotensive by sinus nerve stimulation (Griffith and Schwartz, 1963; 1964; Schwartz and Griffith, 1967). This method would control for the effects of high blood pressure levels on psychological functioning; and it is preferred because antihypertensive drugs, such as reserpine, have powerful pharmacological effects on the central nervous system and at times produce profound depression. New techniques for

123

studying the personal behavioral and psychological characteristics of hypertensive patients are needed to verify the observations made in the past.

The Central Conflict in Essential Hypertension and Concomitant Personality Patterns

The particular facets of the personality chosen for study at any given time parallel the conceptual trends in vogue at that time in psychiatry. The authors of the early studies of patients with essential hypertension tended to focus on the psychological conflicts of their patients. They concluded that patients with essential hypertension had lifelong and largely unconscious conflicts about the expression of hostility, aggression, resentment, rage, rebellion, ambition or dependency (Alexander, 1939, 1950; Ayman, 1933; Barach, 1928; Binger et al., 1945; Dunbar, 1943; Hambling, 1951, 1952; Harris et al., 1953; Hill, 1935; Miller, 1939; Moschowitz, 1919, Moses et al., 1956; O'Hare, 1920; Palmer, 1950; Saslow et al., 1950; Saul, 1939; Thomas, 1964; Van Der Valk, 1957; Weiss, 1942). The psychological mechanisms used to defend against the emergence of these conflicts led to the development of various personality traits: many patients covered up their anger by an outer friendliness or by exercising self-control (Alexander, 1939; Saul, 1939). Other patients were perfectionistic or had difficulties with those in authority, especially if they rebelled against them (Saslow et al., 1950). The conflicts in some of these patients made them anxious; other patients were depressed.

Binger et al. (1945) agreed that hypertensive patients were angry but stressed that these patients lacked the psychological capacity adequately to integrate, handle, or resolve their conflicts about aggression. Patients were made insecure because they could not be certain that they could handle their anger, external danger, or the fear of separation. Fifty percent of their subjects had lost a parent during childhood; they were sensitized by early experience to separation. In fact, 23 of 24 subjects developed hypertension in a setting of actual or threatened bereavement. It is not particularly surprising then that an important variable in *stabilizing* the course of the disease is a sustained, therapeutic, well-managed relationship with a doctor that undoes the fear of separation (Reiser et al., 1951).

Wolf and Wolff and their associates (1948, 1951, 1953, 1955) studied 103 hypertensive patients and concluded that their latent hostility alerted and prepared them to take offensive action against other people. In contrast with members of a hospital staff, normotensive patients, and patients who suffered from bronchial asthma and vasomotor rhinitis, many of the hypertensive patients preferred offensive action to thoughtful reflection. They were tense, suspicious, and wary. Others tried to please and placate those that they feared, rather than take offensive action against them. Hypertensive patients who were prepared to fight were often outwardly calm, easy-going, and restrained.

All of these studies have been criticized because they are based on subjective impression (Davies, 1971): many critics are dissatisfied with the methods of clinical observation and inference. Yet it is remarkable how consistent the clinical descriptions of hypertensive patients are. Nonetheless, they should be verified by psychological tests, such as those of Saslow and his co-workers (1950). They confirmed the fact that hypertensive patients had certain traits; they were less overtly assertive and manifested compul-

124

sive character traits more often than normotensive patients who had personality disorders. Wolf and Wolff's studies emphasized that the latent hostility of hypertensive patients was directed at other people, but it was hidden from them by various traits. Thaler and her co-workers (1957) and Weiner and his (1962) further attempted to specify the nature of the hypertensive patient's interpersonal relationships by studying how these patients perceive and interact with their physicians. The implicit aim of these studies was to identify how hypertensive patients perceive other people and how that perception affects their relationships to them. These studies made no explicit or implicit assumption that either the patient's perception of or relationships with others had etiologic or pathogenetic significance for the disease. They found that hypertensive subjects perceive other people as dangerous, derisive, and untrustworthy. Because of this perception, patients attempt to maintain a distant relationship. Paradoxically, they provoke others and are alert to anger and hostility—the very reactions they most fear.

When hypertensive patients successively maintained their distance and avoided relationships, the blood pressure levels remain unchanged, but when this habitual defensive style fails, *critical* elevations of blood pressure occur.

This interpersonal style in the manner with which hypertensive subjects defend against personal involvements was also described by Grace and Graham (1952) who verified their findings in a later study (Graham et al., 1962b). The characteristic attitude of hypertensive patients consists of an "awareness of threat of bodily harm, without any possibility of running away or fighting back." Implicit in this description was an inhibited desire to fight danger.

The observations of Thaler and co-workers (1957) were put to the test by Sapira and co-workers (1971) by a different method: 19 hypertensive and 15 normotensive patients were shown two movies, one depicted a rude and disinterested physician and the other a physician who was at ease and related with patients in a warm and kindly manner. The hypertensive patients had significantly greater blood pressure and heart rate responses while viewing the two films and during a later interview. The hypertensive patients denied perceiving any differences between the actions and attitudes of the two physicians. The normotensive group could tell the difference in the behavior of the two physicians. The interviewer evoked greater blood pressure response in hypertensive patients when he played the roles of the physician in the movies than when he did not (Sapira et al., 1971). The authors postulate that the hypertensive patients screen out the perception of the differences between the "good" and "bad" doctor while still showing blood pressure responses in order to defend against their cardiovascular hyperreactivity. The patients in this study did not state that they could tell the difference between a "good" and "bad" doctor because to admit that they saw one would be tantamount to seeing the other.

If hypertensive patients avoid the perception of potentially hostile and dangerous relationships they should differ from patients in whom high blood pressure levels are the consequence of kidney disease; but they do not. Ostfeld and Lebovitz (1959) studied 50 patients with essential hypertension and compared them to 50 with renovascular hypertension. They concluded on the basis of MMPI and Rorschach test findings that no psychological differences existed between the two groups. Patients in both groups reacted similarly to anxiety by equivalent elevations of blood pressure. The authors concluded, therefore, that no particular psychological factors play any etiological role in essential hypertension. Their observations suggest that once high blood pressure is established, anxiety may further raise it. Anxiety, regardless of its source, may sustain or further elevate preexisting blood pressure levels, regardless of etiology. Because of this study, the contribution of psychological factors to the etiology and pathogenesis is questionable. In particular, the role that anger, rage, or hostility plays in inciting the disease remains enigmatic.

In an attempt to verify the role of anger or hostility in the production of high blood pressure levels, psychotic persons have been studied. Psychotic persons are often either overtly angry, hostile, and suspicious, or they struggle against the direct expression of such feelings. Miller (1939) tested this hypothesis. He found much higher blood pressure levels in patients who had hostile, paranoid delusions or who were agitated and depressed than in patients who had grandiose delusions or who were depressed and apathetic. But Monroe and co-workers (1961) could not verify Miller's findings on 766 hospitalized psychotic patients.

This research strategy is probably not a good one. Neither study takes into account the expected prevalence of high blood pressure in a population of this age group. Psychotic people also vary a great deal, and psychiatrists cannot agree among themselves about their diagnoses. Therefore, two populations of psychotic persons are not comparable if different psychiatrists make the diagnoses. Finally, these studies are based on the belief that overt or unexpressed anger alone produces high blood pressure.

Because no agreement has been reached about the role of hostility in the etiology or pathogenesis of essential hypertension, it might be worthwhile to review the attempts to verify clinical impressions by predictive psychiatric and psychological studies. Notable among these are studies carried out by Alexander and his colleagues (1968). The psychological criteria used to diagnose hypertensive patients in this study were that they were

> struggling against aggressive feelings and had difficulties in asserting them. The patients were afraid to lose the affection of others and had to control the expression of their hostility. In childhood the patients were prone to outbursts of rage and aggression. As they matured and developed the angry attacks came under control. Consequently they became overtly compliant and unassertive. As adults they perservered doggedly, often against insuperable obstacles. When promoted to executive positions they encountered difficulties because they could not assert themselves or make others follow their orders. They were overconscientious and too responsible. Their conscientiousness only increased their feelings of resentment at self-imposed tasks.
>
> ALEXANDER, 1968

The onset of hypertension was brought about by events that mobilized hostility and the urge for self-assertion but at the same time prohibited their free expression.

About 40 percent of the hypertensive patients were correctly diagnosed by nine judges. Male hypertensive patients were more-often correctly diagnosed than female ones. This study attests to the fact that these criteria may not be correct in all patients, especially not women. It suggests that patients with essential hypertension are psychologically heterogeneous. The psychological heterogeneity of hypertensive patients may reflect the

126

physiological heterogeneity and stage of the disease. Alexander's study was an attempt to validate his formulations about aggressive conflicts and how they are expressed. A better research strategy is to predict before onset who will develop essential hypertension. But, as has been noted, no criteria for predicting who is at risk for the disease have been developed, except that it occurs more frequently in the children of parents with hypertension.

Thomas (1957, 1958, 1961, 1964a, 1967) and her co-workers (Bruce and Thomas, 1953; Thomas et al., 1964a, b; Thomas and Ross, 1963) carried out such a prospective study. They administered psychological tests to 1,200 medical students and their parents in 1953. By 1967, 400 parents had died. Of these, 100 had died of the complications of hypertensive or coronary artery disease. No striking definitive psychological differences were found between the offspring of parents dying of hypertension and heart disease and the offspring of parents dead of other diseases, or those still alive and well. However, the children of hypertensive parents tended to be more aggressive and hostile and to feel more inadequate. They had compulsive character traits. Although no huge differences were uncovered between the offspring of hypertensive parents and the offspring of those who were not hypertensive, these studies tend to confirm the observations obtained by retrospective studies.

Clinical psychiatric impressions have also partly been verified by the use of psychological tests after the onset of hypertension. Many of these studies are hard to compare, as the tests employed differ and the medical data on the patients are not described. Often it is not clear how frequently blood pressure was taken, whether the level had been elevated for days, months, or years, or whether it was affected by the manner in which it was taken (Ostfeld and Shekelle, 1967). The question of whether the patient had essential or some other form of hypertension is usually left unanswered. In fact, patients at risk for related diseases are similar psychologically to patients with essential hypertension.

Patients at risk for or with coronary heart disease are like patients with essential hypertension (Friedman and Rosenman, 1959; Jenkins et al., 1967; Rosenman, 1969; Rosenman and Friedman, 1963; Rosenman et al., 1964, 1966). Many factors predispose to coronary artery disease but high blood pressure is certainly one of them. In studies that were both retrospective and predictive, a behavior pattern has been described that is prognostic of coronary artery disease. The patients are "driven," ambitious, and aggressive, and pressure themselves to be productive and to meet deadlines. They are competitive, restless in manner, and staccato in speech; they hurry constantly and have an enhanced sense of the urgency of time. The risk of coronary artery disease is heightened when this style is associated with elevated blood pressure and serum lipoprotein levels (Rosenman and Friedman, 1963). In the hands of other investigators the results have not been as clear-cut (Friedman et al., 1968), perhaps because socioeconomic, cultural, and other environmental variables also influence the behavior pattern (Keith et al., 1965). The description of this behavior pattern is reminiscent of the behavior pattern of women with borderline hypertension (Harris et al., 1953; Kalis et al., 1961; Harris and Singer, 1968).

Male patients with borderline blood pressure elevations seem more "nervous and excitable" than matched comparison subjects. They are submissive, lethargic, introverted, lacking in self-confidence, sensitive and suspicious, and derive no pleasure from sexual relationships (Hamilton, 1942; Harburg et al., 1964). Patients with borderline hypertension do not constitute a uniform subgroup. Some young men with this stage or form of essential hypertension have a high cardiac output; other borderline hypertensives have a normal cardiac output.

Attempts to relate blood pressure levels to various features of the personality have also been made. Brower (1947a, b) discovered a negative correlation between diastolic blood pressure levels and good social adjustment, and a positive correlation with depressive, psychopathic, and hypochondriacal scores on the MMPI.

Cattell and Scheier (1959) demonstrated a positive relationship between systolic blood pressure levels, exuberance, and optimism about attaining long-range goals. But the hypertensive patients also lacked confidence in their ability to perform in novel situations.

A number of other psychological studies have found no differences between patients with other diseases or with different forms of high blood pressure: when four groups, each consisting of 15 patients with duodenal ulcer, essential hypertension, neuromuscular tension, and control subjects were compared, the patients in the three clinical groups scored higher than the control group on scales of depression, hysteria, psychopathy, and hypochrondriasis (Innes et al., 1959; Lewinsohn, 1956; Robinson, 1962; Storment, 1951).

Patients who do not have borderline hypertension but who do have higher blood pressure levels have been described as insecure and submissive, yet sensitive to criticism about their anger. A test of this observation was made by criticizing hypertensive patients and normotensive subjects while they responded to the Thematic Apperception Test. Twelve normotensive and only one hypertensive refused to continue with the test. Both groups became less verbally aggressive when criticized (Matarazzo, 1954). Neiberg (1957) concluded that neither patients nor control subjects inhibited their anger when criticized.

Ostfeld and Lebovitz (1959, 1960) found no significant psychological differences between patients with essential or renovascular hypertension and normotensive subjects. The patients did show increases in blood pressure greater than those of normotensive subjects during a discussion of distressing life experiences or interviews. The patients and subjects who were most emotionally labile were also likely to show the greatest changes in blood pressure levels.

Psychological tests can reveal whether patients are anxious or more emotionally labile. Some psychoneurotic patients are both. A number of studies have compared hypertensive and psychoneurotic patients with each other and with supposedly normal subjects. There are many psychological similarities between patients, but they differ equally from normals. On the other hand, the most neurotic patients do not have the highest blood pressure levels (Robinson, 1962, 1964; Sainsbury, 1960, 1964).

The most sophisticated study to date related the psychological features of patients to various measures of the circulation. By the use of the proper controls, hypertensive patients were found to be more emotional, tense, unstable and excitable, guilt-ridden, timid, insecure and sexually inhibited than normotensive patients. They were deferential to others and abased themselves. The more deferential they were, the greater the peripheral resistance and resting blood pressure levels. The more they abased themselves, the higher the resting blood pressure levels. The more they were emotionally stimulated, the greater were the changes in diastolic and systolic blood pressure levels. Those hypertensive patients who expressed interest in members of the opposite sex had high heart rates and diastolic blood pressure levels. The more anxious and tense they were, the higher the basal peripheral resistance, and the more it increased on stimulation (Pilowsky et al., 1973).

The tentative conclusion can be reached that the clinical psychiatric traits and psychological states occur in some, but not in all, hypertensive patients. There is psychological heterogeneity. On the other hand, a relationship exists between emotionality, excessive vascular hyperreactivity, and blood pressure variability in patients with essential and renovascular hypertension.

Essential hypertension runs in families—a fact that is not well-understood, but that is quoted in support of genetic factors in the disease. The family aggregation of essential hypertension could also be understood in terms of altered family relationships. If hypertensive parents perceive the human environment, including their children, as hostile and dangerous, they could intimidate their children.

Few studies of the families of hypertensive patients have been conducted. Harburg and co-workers (1965) found that patients with the most labile blood pressure did not like their fathers because they were domineering, stern, and socially ambitious for their families. Davies (1970) found that blood pressure variability and levels had to be treated separately when they were correlated with parental attitudes. Subjects with high basal blood pressure levels reported that their fathers were tolerant. Patients with lower levels were more critical of their fathers. In this connection it should be recalled that hypertensive patients when they are compensated psychologically tend to eschew criticizing other people (Sapira et al., 1971). Saul (1939) was one of the few ever to study the mothers of hypertensive patients. He ascribed the patients' repressed feelings of hostility to the domineering behavior of their mothers.

We still lack the kinds of detailed studies of families of hypertensive patients that have been done on the families of patients with bronchial asthma, ulcerative colitis, or rheumatoid arthritis. We also know rather little about the psychological make-up of patients in childhood, or how they are treated by their parents to predispose them to essential hypertension.

Reiser (1970) postulated that in infancy these children may cry a lot. During crying, the child expires against a partially closed glottis and increases intrathoracic pressure, diminishing the venous return to the heart and the cardiac output. The peripheral resistance and heart rate rise as a consequence. The Valsalva maneuver, carried out in adulthood, mimics the changes brought about by crying. In hypertensive patients the maneuver produces more than the usual increase in blood pressure. Reiser's suggestion has not been put to the test. He implies that the crying is the child's response to inadequate or inappropriate mothering. As a result of repeated bouts of crying the circulation becomes "conditioned" to respond with excessive blood pressure responses. It becomes hyperreactive to stimuli, including emotional ones. But we do not know whether babies who cry excessively or repeatedly are at risk for essential hypertension. Perhaps some are, because they are born with a hyperreactive cardiovascular system. The hyperreactivity may be genotypic, but the crying is provoked by the mother who does not satisfy the child, eliciting the hypertensive phenotype. To complicate the matter further, children vary temperamentally at birth. Some are easily satisfied, others are not: the mother should not receive the blame for being the only cause of the child's unhappiness.

Studies should be done of the families of hypertensive patients and of the psychological development of children of hypertensive patients as well as of children with elevated blood pressure levels.

Studies of the Psychophysiological Correlates of Blood Pressure and of Essential Hypertension in Man

Psychophysiological studies on patients with essential hypertension have been carried out with several purposes in mind: (1) to determine whether persons who later develop essential hypertension can be identified in advance; (2) to assess the role of simple and complex psychological stimuli and the emotions they elicit in changing blood pressure; and (3) to determine whether there are differences in cardiovascular dynamics between hypertensive and normotensive subjects. For example, hypnotic trances have been induced to study changes in blood pressure, and meditative states and biofeedback techniques have been used to lower the blood pressure of hypertensive patients and normal subjects.

Psychophysiological studies are fraught with technical, methodological, and conceptual problems. The fact that elevations of blood pressure occur in hypertensive patients in response to psychological stimuli does not constitute prima facie evidence that psychological stimuli have etiologic or pathogenetic relevance to the disease. Short-term changes in blood pressure produced in the laboratory do not necessarily provide us with important insights into the nature of sustained high blood pressure, diastolic and systolic. A major methodological problem in such studies is the fact that—with the exception of Brod's important studies—there has been a tendency to study one or two cardiovascular variables, such as the heart rate and blood pressure. Studies that use only two parameters of cardiovascular function may be misleading, because profound hemodynamic changes (for example, in regional blood flow) may occur without a discernible change in blood pressure. Several cardiovascular variables must be studied simultaneously in psychophysiological studies.

Because of the repeated clinical observation that patients with essential hypertension harbor strong feelings of anger, there have been attempts to correlate anger with cardiovascular responses (Moses et al., 1956; Schachter, 1957) and to contrast these responses to those obtained when fear, pain or anxiety are elicited. Pain can be produced by immersion of the patient's hand in ice water at 3° C for one minute, anger is stimulated by insulting and abusing the subject, and fear can be produced by a mild electric shock (Ax, 1953).

In the hypertensive patients greater increments in blood pressure occurred in the three situations designed to produce, respectively, fear, pain, and anger (Schachter, 1957). In both the pain and anger conditions, diastolic blood pressure rose significantly because of an increased peripheral resistance, whereas fear produced increases in systolic blood pressure as the cardiac output increased.

In Schachter's (1957) experiment, the situation designed to produce pain is also conducive to vasoconstriction; immersion of a limb in ice water has often been used to measure blood pressure reactivity in normal and hypertensive subjects. The effects of mild pain and vasoconstriction are confounded in this experiment. Pain and other feelings interact with vasoconstriction; blood pressure reactivity is greater if the cold immersion test is given to anxious patients (White and Gildea, 1937). The blood pressure reactivity is also greater in neurotic (Malmo and Shagass, 1952) and angry patients than in calm ones (Cranston et al., 1949). Heart rate and blood pressure changes have been used to infer (Schachter, 1957) or measure the associated humoral changes that correlate with specific affects. When aggression and active emotional states are elicited in subjects, norepinephrine secretion occurs. Whereas when anger is handled intrapunitively, urinary epinephrine levels are increased in normal subjects (Cohen et al., 1957; Cohen and Silverman, 1959; Elmadjian et al., 1957). The relationship between the blood pressure, catecholamine excretion, and mental stress depends in part on the state and stage of hypertension. It may be that borderline cases or young male hypertensive patients have different cardiovascular dynamics with different excretion levels of the catecholamines than do patients with well-established hypertension or normals. Nestel (1969) has reexamined this problem by studying 17 normotensive subjects and 20 hypertensive patients with a mean resting blood pressure of 147/95 mm Hg. Basal urinary excretion levels of norepinephrine and epinephrine were the same in both groups of subjects. The subjects were asked to solve visual puzzles—the Raven's matrix test—for 40 minutes. Much greater increments in systolic (Δ = 35 mm Hg) and diastolic (Δ = 25 mm Hg) blood pressure occurred in the labile hypertensive group than in the normotensive group. The urinary output of norepinephrine and epinephrine rose in all subjects but the increases were significantly greater in the hypertensive patients, rising in 17 of the 20. By comparison, the urinary output of the neurotransmitters rose in only 7 of the 17 normotensive subjects. Mean postexperimental levels of both catecholamines were also higher in the former group. The changes in urinary catecholamine levels correlated significantly with changes in blood pressure levels, particularly in the labile hypertensive group.

Apparently patients with labile hypertension respond to a complex psychological task by increased sympathetic nervous activity and greater blood pressure responses. More direct approaches to the evaluation of sympathetic activity in this group of patients have also been made. Attempts to evaluate overall sympathetic activity in patients with labile hypertension by estimating dopamine β-hydroxylase (DBH) levels have not been successful. No individual differences in levels occur and there is no relationship between DBH levels, the blood pressure levels, or the age of subjects. DBH levels are lower in black than in white persons and in men than in women. The reduction of the blood pressure by drugs in borderline or labile hypertensive patients does not reduce serum DBH activity (Horwitz et al., 1973).

Whether discernible differences in physiological responses occur in different affective states continues to be a moot point (Buss, 1961). Harris and his co-workers (1965) do not believe in such differences. They performed cardiac catheterization and serial blood-chemical studies while intense, lifelike fear and anger were induced under hypnosis. Similar physiological responses accompanied fear and anger. Fear and angry responses were both associated with a 33 percent increase in cardiac index, with a 50 percent rise in the heart rate, a 20 percent fall in stroke volume, a 10 mm Hg increase in blood pressure, and a 13 percent fall in peripheral resistance. The respiratory rate doubled and six subjects developed a respiratory alkalosis. Mean levels of plasma hydrocortisone and plasma nonesterified fatty acids doubled. A β-adrenergic blocking agent reduced the cardioaccelerator response due to fear but not due to anger. The agent failed to block the increases of cardiac output, plasma hydrocortisone, and free fatty acids. In three subjects the entire experiment was repeated several weeks later and the results were replicated. Therefore, under hypnosis it is impossible to discriminate between the physiological correlates of fear and anger in normal subjects. In other experiments, anger produces qualitatively similar but quantitatively greater cardiovascular responses. Hokanson (1961a, b) harassed subjects while they were counting. He found that the more hostile subjects had brisker increases in systolic and diastolic blood pressure. Those who expressed their anger and hostility openly had a great fall in systolic blood pressure when the experiment was over, which suggested, Hokanson argued, that the failure to express these feelings, due to guilt or anxiety, delayed the fall in blood pressure to preexperimental levels. Graham et al. (1960, 1962a) hypnotized two groups of normal subjects. A psychological attitude correlated with hives was suggested to one group, and an attitude of unexpressible rage to another group. Significant skin temperature changes occurred when hives were suggested, and increases in diastolic blood pressure when rage was suggested. Inhibited or partially expressed hostile verbal content in awake subjects can be evaluated by the method of Gottschalk and Hambidge (1955) while blood pressure is measured. Using this technique, Kaplan et al. (1960) found that while hypertensive subjects spoke, their blood pressures rose. In contrast, while normotensive subjects spoke, their blood pressures fell. In hypertensive subjects a significant relationship was found between the intensity of the hostile content of speech and the diastolic blood pressure levels.

In normal subjects the evidence that differen feelings, such as fear or anger, are correlated with specific cardiovascular or humoral responses is by no means established. In some studies specific physiological responses to specific feelings have been demonstrated in normal subjects. In other studies, the degree but not the specific kind of physiological response is related to anger that is partially inhibited in its expression. Psychophysiological studies in normal subjects may be relevant to the etiology of high blood pressure, but they do not prove that anger or hostility specifically raise the blood pressure any more than fear does. Responses to feelings in normal subjects are often different in degree, duration, or kind than in hypertensive subjects.

Many studies have been designed to show that psychological stimuli of various kinds in the laboratory do elicit changes in blood pressure in hypertensive subjects, and that these changes were greater or longer-lasting than in normal subjects (Jost et al., 1952).

Wolf and Wolff (1951) interviewed 203 normotiensive subjects and 103 subjects with blood pressure levels of 160/95 mm Hg or more. Although the hypertensive subjects were usually affable and friendly to the experimenter, their blood pressure rose more during the interview. It did not do so consistently, however, because different changes in cardiovascular dynamics occurred with different feelings. When the predominant feeling in the interview was restrained hostility or anxiety, the cardiac output did not change, but the peripheral resistance rose. With overt anxiety, the cardiac output increased and the peripheral resistance fell. With feelings of despair and of being overwhelmed, both

132

cardiac output and peripheral resistance fell. An association between specific feelings and specific changes in the circulation has not always been observed. Changes in blood pressure do occur during interviews; but the changes may have more to do with the speed with which the subject talks than with the feelings he expresses. Nonetheless, hypertensive patients differ from normotensive ones—even when they talk with the same speed, their blood pressure responses last longer, even after they fall silent (Innes et al., 1959). Innes also found that some neurotic and some hypertensive patients share a common psychological characteristic that he called "emotional lability" (Davies, 1971).

Whether specific emotions produce specific alterations of cardiovascular function has not been settled. Studies in animals support the view that specific emotions are associated with specific cardiovascular responses; studies in humans tend not to (Cannon, 1929). Both Lacey and his co-workers (1952, 1953, 1958) and Wenger and his (1961) have pointed out that changes in cardiovascular function occur against a background of different and individual resting levels and fluctuations in the baseline of heart rate, blood pressure, and peripheral resistance. Although intraindividual autonomically mediated response patterns to psychological stimuli, feelings, and emotional states may be fairly consistent, marked differences between patterns occur when two subjects are compared. Some individuals respond with a particular pattern of cardiovascular responses regardless of the stimulus used. The individual response specificity to various stimuli has also been observed in hypertensive patients (Engel and Bickford, 1961): they responded to various stimuli (such as lights, sounds, mental arithmetic, exercise, and the cold-pressor test by increases in systolic blood pressure and not by other cardiovascular responses. Their systolic blood pressure responses were greater than in normal subjects and did not depend on the stimulus used. The magnitude of these responses was always greater than in normal subjects. Larger responses are elicited by psychological stimuli as well as physical stimuli such as sounds and immersing the hand in cold water (Reiser et al., 1951a). The blood pressure responses to cold may last for several days.

Pfeiffer and Wolf (1950) used the stress interview to study the renal circulation in 23 hypertensive and 13 normotensive subjects. The renal blood flow fell and the filtration fraction increased in both groups. Presumably, these changes were due to constriction of the renal glomerular arterioles, and they could be conducive to the release of renin. It may well be that such renal changes with psychological stimuli are important in hypertensive subjects; but some additional factors must be involved in the pathogenesis of hypertension, because both groups showed the same changes in renal function. Stressful interviews that had personal significance to hypertensive patients reduced renal flood flow (Wolf et al., 1948) and elicited brisk pressor responses—a rise of 14 mm Hg (Wolf et al., 1955)—and even greater mean blood pressure responses (26.5 mm Hg) in another study (Hardyck and Singer, 1962).

But blood pressure changes in normotensive subjects and hypertensive patients are not only produced by feelings; intellectual tasks and pain also elicit brisk responses. Brod et al. (1959, 1960, 1962, 1970) used mental arithmetic performed under duress to produce increases in arterial blood pressure, muscle blood flow, splanchnic vasoconstriction, and cardiac output in normotensive and hypertensive subjects. More renal vasoconstriction and less vasodilation in muscle was found in hypertensive subjects. The hemodynamic changes and elevations of blood pressure persisted longer in the hypertensive subjects than in the normotensive group. These results must be evaluated bearing in mind that six of the eight normotensive subjects, but only two of the ten hypertensive subjects, were women. Sex differences in cardiovascular reactivity are known to occur. The *patterns* of physiological change Brod has demonstrated in human subjects have also been produced in animals by brain stimulation. The pathways in the brain that regulate this pattern of change are known (Folkow and Rubinstein, 1966; Löfving, 1961; Uvnäs, 1960).

With simple painful stimuli, hypertensive and normotensive subjects with a family history of hypertension have more-rapid and brisker blood pressure responses than normal subjects have. No significant changes in peripheral resistance occur in hypertensive patients with pain. Subjects with a family history of hypertension increase their cardiac output and, therefore, their blood pressure (Shapiro, 1960a, b). The degree and duration of the blood pressure responses to various stimuli and tasks are greater in hypertensive patients than in normal subjects. This increased responsivity occurs both in essential and renovascular hypertension (Ostfeld and Lebovitz, 1959, 1960). In patients with essential hypertension and renovascular hypertension, anxiety produces similar elevations of blood pressure that last equally long. The similar blood pressure responses in different forms of hypertension have been interpreted to mean that psychological factors played no etiological role in essential hypertension. Alternative interpretations are possible: anxiety may interact with some mechanism common to both forms of hypertension to raise the blood pressure. Although anxiety may not play an etiological role, it may help to sustain both forms of hypertension by repeatedly raising blood pressure further. Psychophysiological studies must compare patients with different forms of hypertension like Ostfeld and Lebovitz (1959) did, and take into account the stage and state of the different forms of the disease. It has been suggested that although renal factors may play a prepotent role early in essential hypertension, they are later supplanted by sustaining neurogenic mechanisms. The reverse sequence has also been suggested.

Whatever the sequence may be, psychological factors may be mediated by one set of physiological mechanisms at one stage of the disease and by another set at another stage to raise the blood pressure.

Psychophysiological studies have shown that each person responds physiologically to many different stimuli in his own manner; hypertensive persons also have larger blood pressure responses. Subjects in the psychophysiological laboratory also respond psychologically in their own particular ways. In most studies, the experimenter has attempted to provoke a particular feeling in his subject. In more recent studies, feelings were not provoked. Instead, the experimenter or an observer of the interaction of the experimenter and the subject observed the individual psychological style of the subject. Innes and his colleagues (1959) showed that the speed with which a subject talks is individual and is related to his blood pressure responses.

In other experiments, observations were focused on the style in which the subject and experimenter related to each other, while the blood pressure and other hemodynamic changes were measured. Weiner et al. (1962) found that hypertensive subjects were more unreactive physiologically than normotensive ones, because they interacted little with the experimenter. One hypertensive subject who had previously been unresponsive physiologically was persuaded against his will to undergo the laboratory procedure on a second occasion. He equated the second experiment with a threat to his life, his distant style crumbled, and a very brisk, long-lasting blood pressure response occurred. These experiments demonstrate that the nature of the experimenter-subject relationship, and the effectiveness of a habitual style of relating to the experimenter may be the critical determinants in producing cardiovascular changes in the laboratory. As long as a style "works" no changes occur in normotensive or hypertensive subjects. The detailed findings of this study have been verified (McKegney and Williams, 1967; Williams and McKegney, 1965; Williams et al., 1972a). The findings shed some light on the complex interactions between the nature of the subject-experimenter relationship, the manner in and success with which subjects cope with a task and an experimenter, and changes in cardiovascular function.

Hypertensive patients have individual styles of relating to physicians and experimenters in the laboratory. They keep their distance from them and avoid close personal involvements. They eschew relationships because they perceive the physician as hostile, dangerous, coercive, or ungiving. If they cannot avoid the relationship, their blood pressure responses are brisker and more prolonged than those of normotensive patients (Shapiro, 1973; Thaler et al., 1957; Weiner et al., 1962).

"Coping" and "defensive" styles in man may be the critical intervening variables between the perception of a psychosocial stimulus, the psychological response (including the emotional one) to that perception, and the individual physiological response to the stimulus. If these styles are successful, little physiological change occurs. If not successful, changes do occur. The changes are greater and last longer in hypertensive patients than in normotensive ones. The specific feelings that a stimulus provokes are not associated with specific physiological changes. Anger does not uniquely raise the blood pressure. Other feelings, such as fear and pain, also do. Rather each person responds physiologically in his own manner to a variety of feelings and stimuli. Hypertensive patients respond with brisker blood pressure responses that last longer to a variety of psychological tasks and feelings, as well as to cold and pain. Their cardiovascular responses are predetermined, individual, and hyperreactive for unknown reasons. Their responses may reflect an intrinsic defect in the regulation of blood pressure that may antedate the disease. Hypertensive patients also have individual psychological responses to the experimenter and laboratory and cope differently with pain, cold, and cognitive tasks.

Studies on the Conditioning of Cardiovascular Responses in Man

Psychophysiological experiments on hypertensive patients in the laboratory are complex and difficult to control. Multiple variables such as the nature of the subject-experimenter interaction, the psychological responses to pain or various tasks, and the effect of medication are not easily quantified or controllable. Therefore, a number of investigators have preferred to use various forms of conditioning procedures that are much more easily controlled to elicit blood pressure and other cardiovascular responses.

Human subjects have been conditioned by classical and operant techniques while direct or indirect measurements of blood flow in the extremities, heart rate, or blood pressure are made (Zeaman and Smith, 1965). Classical conditioning stimuli produce vasoconstriction in the extremities. Once a conditioned response (CR) in man has been established, the conditioning stimulus may generalize to the experimenter or the whole laboratory and the CR is set off (Bykov, 1947). The CRs are associated with changes in the caliber of blood vessels in the skin of the extremities. But because blood flow in the splanchnic bed is much more difficult to measure in intact human beings, we do not know directly whether changes in splanchnic flow that are directly relevant to increases in blood pressure can also be conditioned. We can only infer changes in splanchnic blood flow from other studies that show that vascular changes in the skin are usually the reciprocal of those occurring in the splanchnic bed.

Nonetheless, studies on conditioned vasoconstriction in the extremities and increases in blood pressure have heuristic values for hypertension research. Conditioned vasoconstriction in human subjects can be produced not only by simple conditioning stimuli, such as a tone, but also by tasks, such as mental arithmetic (Abramson, 1944: Abramson and Ferris, 1940; Figar, 1965; Petyelina, 1952; Tomaszewski, 1937), or by words. Words related to simple conditioning stimuli tend to produce even brisker skin and blood pressure responses than the simple stimuli themselves (Bykov, 1947). When conflicting stimuli are used, the largest blood pressure responses occur. Sleep abolishes conditioned vasoconstriction. When the patient is awake, awareness of, and attention to the stimulus determine the speed of the establishment of a conditioned vasoconstrictor response (Lacey, 1950; Lacey and Smith, 1954).

Conditioned cardiovascular responses have been established and compared in normotensive and hypertensive subjects. In human subjects in the early stages of essential hypertension, peripheral vasoconstrictor responses are brisker and extinguish less readily than in normotensive subjects (Figar, 1965; Kaminskiy, 1951; Miasnikov, 1954). As the disease progresses, the conditioned responses decrease progressively, presumably because vasoconstriction is already intense. It is difficult, however, to assess these studies because the patients used in these studies were not well-classified: they may have had essential or some other form of hypertension. These studies suggest, nonetheless, that early in the disease vascular hyperreactivity is greater and lasts longer (Page, 1960).

Small but statistically significant and reliable *decreases* in systolic and diastolic blood pressure have been obtained by operant conditioning techniques in normotensive (e.g., Shapiro et al., 1969, 1970) and in hypertensive subjects. The changes in systolic blood pressure obtained by operant means in five of seven hypertensive subjects is of the order of 16 to 34 mm Hg (Benson et al., 1971). The fall in blood pressure is probably not permanent, so that one cannot as yet ascertain whether operant procedures have a role in the treatment of human hypertension.

The studies have been met with some criticism (Blanchard and Young, 1973). As in all psychophysiological experiments, a number of uncontrollable variables occur: they include the subjett's knowledge of the experimenter's intentions to lower blood pressure, the effect instructions have on the subject, and the subject's relationship to the experimenter—all of which influence the results. Unless these variables are controlled, the assertion cannot be made that operant or biofeedback procedures lower the blood pressure. In fact, the blood pressure of hypertensive patients can be made to rise and fall when subjects are forcefully instructed to raise or lower their blood pressure. Significant changes in blood pressure also occur with progressive muscular relaxation, but only when the physician encourages the patient to relax. The direction and degree of change in blood pressure equal those obtained by biofeedback techniques that include both instruction and relaxation (Redmond et al., 1974).

136

Psychophysiological Studies of Blood Pressure in a Naturalistic Setting

Much has been learned about the correlations between psychological and physiological variables from laboratory and conditioning studies. Variations in blood pressure could not be studied over the long term and in everyday settings until a method had been developed that would continuously measure the blood pressure. With this nonintrusive method, it becomes possible to relate changes in blood pressure to daily events and the psychological responses that they occasion. Sokolow and his co-workers (1970) studied 124 hypertensive patients in this manner. Marked variations in blood pressure occurred depending on the changing events of the day. For example, one middle-aged student had a blood pressure of 160/95 mm Hg while anticipating a campus interview, and 100/82 mm Hg while at home talking to her son.

An analysis of the changes in 50 hypertensive patients lead to the conclusion that the highest systolic blood pressure levels and pulse rates occur when patients are alert, anxious, or under pressure. The highest diastolic blood pressure levels occur when the patients are anxious or pressured. Contentment lowers levels. Sokolow and his co-workers (1970) also found that the most anxious, hostile, and depressed patients were the ones most likely to develop hypertensive disease and all its complications. This finding should not be surprising, as these patients also had the highest blood pressure levels.

These studies relate high blood pressure levels to the emotional state of patients. They should be viewed with caution. Blood pressure levels vary with behavioral as well as emotional states. They are low in sleep and increase markedly on awakening. Acute increases occur with pain or during coitus. Blood pressure levels are not a stable function—they are subject to circadian rhythms upon which pain, excitement, mental work, anxiety, and anger are superimposed.

ANIMAL MODELS OF ESSENTIAL HYPERTENSION

High Blood Pressure Produced by Conditioning Techniques

The study of animals with high blood pressure has alerted us to the complexity of the various factors that predispose, initiate, and sustain high blood pressure. They have significantly contributed to the elucidation of the mechanisms involved. The techniques used to produce blood pressure elevations in animals vary from constricting the renal artery to exposing animals to "white" noise. In this section, particular attention will be paid to the results obtained by the use of conditioning techniques.

The conditioning procedures take many different forms: unconditioned stimuli (Us), classical and avoidance procedures, and the production of an experimental neurosis have been used to produce elevations of blood pressure (Anderson and Brady, 1971, 1973; Beier, 1940; Bykov, 1947; Forsyth, 1968; 1969; Gantt, 1935, 1958; Napalkov and Karas, 1957; Simonson and Brožek, 1959). Once the animal is conditioned, generalization of the conditioned stimulus (Cs) readily occurs; blood pressure elevations occur when the experimenter enters the laboratory, when the animal anticipates the conditioning procedure, or when the animal is strapped in the laboratory chair in which it sat before or during the training procedure. Based on such observations, Miasnikov (1954) has formulated the hypothesis that essential hypertension is a "conditioned neurosis" that has become generalized to many environmental stimuli. Once developed, the conditioned elevations are retained for many months (Dykman and Gantt, 1960).

Conditioning experiments are successful in monkeys and dogs but are less successful in cats (Shapiro and Horn, 1955). Mararychev and Kuritsa (1951) used injections of epinephrine as the Us, and a tone as the Cs to produce elevations in dogs. Renin has also been used as the Us (Andreev et al., 1952).

In some animals species, but not in others, both simple and complex unconditioned stimuli produce elevated levels of blood pressure. "Audiogenic" hypertension has been produced in rats by daily exposure to air blasts (Aceto et al., 1963; Farris et al., 1945; Rothlin et al., 1953). "Audiogenic" seizures produced by air blast may be accompanied by elevations of blood pressure in some rat strains and not in others: the predisposition to seizures is an inherited trait (Morgan and Galambos, 1942).

Pickering (1961) quoted a Russian experiment carried out by Miminoshvili (1960) in which a male monkey developed elevated arterial pressure and died after he was separated from his mate, who was put into an adjacent cage with another male monkey. Lapin (1965) and Miasnikov (1962) have confirmed this observation.

Not all animals develop high blood pressure when separated or exposed to simple stimuli, such as electric shock or loud noises. A combination of stimuli may have to be used. Shapiro and his co-workers (1955, 1957a) found that in rats, a combination of the experimental production of "anxiety" and the restriction of renal blood flow on one side after the removal of the other kidney caused hypertension to appear sooner and produced more-severe renal lesions than when rats were not made "anxious."

When rats are exposed to a light that warned of an impending electric shock to produce "conditioned emotional responses (CER)," transient pressor responses occur. Elevated blood pressure levels produced by injecting animals with angiotensin II could be further increased by producing a CER (Sapira et al., 1966).

Other types of conditioning procedures besides the CER elicit circulatory responses and also affect the animal's behavior in general (Figar, 1965; Gavlichek, 1952). Experimentally conditioned emotional responses, such as fear, alter the behavior of an animal even when it is not exposed to the conditioning procedure (Asafov, 1958; Gantt, 1958; Reese and Dykman, 1960). These unconditioned responses gradually disappear. Conditioned cardiovascular responses, such as elevations of blood pressure, can still be elicited experimentally for many years, even after the emotional, motor, or salivary responses that originally accompanied the circulatory responses can no longer be elicited (Froňková et al., 1957; Gantt, 1958).

Direct brain stimulation has also been used either as the Cs or the Us. Motor cortical area stimulation (as a Us) that does not produce muscular movements leads to vasoconstriction or vasodilation; parietal lobe stimulation leads only to vasoconstriction. When the Us is applied to one cortical site and the Cs to another, only vasoconstriction is produced in dogs (Orlov, 1959). These dogs develop hypertension that progressively becomes more severe over a period of months; the blood pressure remains elevated despite the fact that the conditioning procedures had previously been stopped (Froňková et al., 1959; Gantt, 1960). The hypertension is associated with pathological changes in the kidney. But not every animal subjected to conditioned brain stimulation develops high blood pressure or renal lesions—individual differences in blood pressure elevations are observed (Gantt, 1960).

Operant or conditioned avoidance procedures, not only classical conditioning, cause the blood pressure of monkeys to increase. Avoidance training carried out for a period of 15 days causes an initial acute rise and then a fall in both blood pressure and pulse rate. After the initial period of training, a continuous avoidance schedule is eventually associated with sustained increases in blood pressure. The level of blood pressure attained depends on the duration and complexity of the training schedule. When monkeys are placed on complex schedules, high blood pressure levels are sustained even when the monkey does not press a lever to avoid a shock (Forsyth, 1968). Systolic and diastolic blood pressures are raised continually after 7 to 12 months of daily avoidance conditioning lasting 12 hours a day. After months of avoidance conditioning, the animals also became more excitable and active. Pressor responses occur in response to many different stimuli, such as noises that had been "neutral" before training. In these experiments, there appeared to be no consistent relationship between the number of electric shocks the animal received, the animal's bar-pressing to avoid them, and the level of blood pressure attained.

It seems hard to understand why the acute elevations of blood pressure that had occurred in the first 15 days of this experiment then subsided, and that it took another 7 to 12 months for permanent hypertension to become established. It is possible that two separate mechanisms are responsible for the initial and the later increase in blood pressure levels. But we do not know what the nature of these two mechanisms is.

Forsyth's results in Rhesus monkeys have been verified in other laboratories and with other species of monkeys (Anderson and Brady, 1971, 1973; Benson et al., 1969, 1970; Herd et al., 1969). Benson and co-workers (1969) trained squirrel monkeys on a fixed-ratio schedule to turn off a light signaling painful shock. In four of six monkeys, elevations of mean arterial blood pressure ensued before, during, and after the experimental periods. Sustained blood pressure elevations were also obtained by changing the method, so that increases in the blood pressure would turn off the light and avert delivery of the shock. When a fall in blood pressure was used to control the signal and the electric shock, sustained decreases in blood pressure were obtained. Anderson and Brady (1973) reported on the cardiovascular effects of free-operant shock-avoidance in dogs. During the period before the experimental session, the blood pressure rose and the heart rate fell. During the session, both increased.

Until recently, studies on the conditioning of autonomic—and more specifically of cardiovascular—responses, were fraught with uncertainties. It has been argued that autonomic components of a conditioned response might result from an increase in muscular activity (Smith, 1954). Since no attempt had been made to put this issue to a test, this criticism lingered on until Miller and his co-workers (1969) disposed of it by paralyzing rats with curare and then conditioning them. They produced exquisite differential autonomic vasomotor responses, including increases and decreases in systolic blood pressure. These investigators also showed that glomerular filtration rate, renal blood flow, and urine formation can be altered by conditioning. These experiments have opened up a new area of investigation which has direct relevance for our understanding of hypertension (Folkow, 1971).

The use of conditioning procedures is not the only method of producing elevation of blood pressure. Immobilizing animals repeatedly for two weeks does so also. (This technique also produces gastric ulceration in the rat.) After a fortnight of daily restraint-immobilization, blood pressure levels are significantly elevated (50 mm Hg). Because serum levels of the enzyme DBH also rise after immobilization, the blood pressure increase is probably due to enhanced peripheral sympathetic activity. Two additional weeks of daily immobilization for two hours increases blood pressure and enzyme levels further. When the procedure is stopped, the blood pressure takes three weeks to fall to baseline levels, but serum levels of the enzyme become normal after five days, suggesting that blood pressure levels are sustained by some mechanism besides increased sympathetic activity (Lamprecht et al., 1973).

The evidence derived from studies on the conditioning of high blood pressure in animals is quite convincing. Blood pressure increases, changes in vasomotor tone, and other physiological variables that have been implicated in the pathogenesis of essential hypertension in man can be brought about by a variety of experimental techniques in the controlled setting of the laboratory. The recent studies by Mason (1968) and by Miller (1969) raise the exciting possibility that we may be on the verge of a major increase in knowledge about the factors and mechanisms that initiate essential hypertension and sustain high blood pressure. The experimental, in contrast to the clinical, evidence is much more convincing that environmental and "psychological" factors do influence blood pressure regulation by their impact on the brain. However, some may argue that these experimental studies, despite their elegance, are laboratory artifacts. They are not natural experiments because avoiding painful shock or being restrained is not the customary experience of animals. These studies need therefore to be supplemented by more naturalistic ones.

Hypertension Produced by Social Manipulation

THE ROLE OF PRIOR EXPERIENCE AND OF FIGHTING

The most convincing and systematic study of the role of natural and social experiences that produce prolonged systolic hypertension has been carried out in mice by Henry et al. (1967). Mixing male mice from different boxes, aggregating them in small boxes, exposing mice to a cat for 6 to 12 months, and producing territorial conflict in colonies of mixed males and females results in sustained elevations of systolic blood pressure, which are higher in male than in female mice. Henry and his co-workers (1967) also found that castrated male mice show minimal elevations in blood pressure when crowded into small boxes. Reserpine, but not anesthesia, also lowers sustained blood pressure elevations. When young mice are raised together, rather than apart, and are later crowded together or made to fight for territory, food, and females, their blood pressure does not show the increases seen in those brought up in isolation from weaning to maturity. Previously isolated mice with high levels of blood pressure were also found to have an interstitial nephritis after they died.

Henry (1971a, b) and his co-workers later worked out the mechanisms of the hypertension and interstitial nephritis in their mice. Socially isolated mice first show a decreased activity of tyrosine hydroxylase (TH) and phenylethanolamine N-methylatransferase (PNMT) activity in the adrenal gland. But the activity of both enzymes and of monoamine oxidase, and the levels of norepinephrine and epinephrine become elevated in animals that are subsequently stimulated by contact with other animals. The mechanisms of these increases was worked out by Thoenen and co-workers (1969). A reflex increase of sympathetic nerve activity on stimulation transsynaptically induces enzyme activity in the adrenal gland after a period of one to three days. Adrenal TH activity decreases after the splanchnic (sympathetic) nerve to the adrenal gland is cut. Therefore, the increase in TH activity in the adrenal gland is due to increased sympathetic activity and not increased pituitary or adrenocortical steroid activity.

Other experiments show that social stimulation (such as fighting) may increase the levels of adrenocortical steroids (Bronson, 1967; Christian et al., 1965), constrict renal vessels (Bing and Vinthen-Paulsen, 1952), and raise levels of epinephrine, norepinephrine, and serotonin in the brain (Welch and Welch, 1965, 1971). In mice, daily fighting that is sustained for 14 days induces elevations of brain catecholamine levels, and levels of epinephrine (but not norepinephrine) in the adrenal glands, causes the kidneys to be "shrunken and contracted," and the adrenals, hearts, and spleens to be enlarged.

Although there is much controversy among behavioral scientists about what constitutes aggression, an aggressive act in animals, and hostility in man, a considerable body of information has recently been accumulated by behavioral biologists about the physiology of fighting among animals, about fighting among animals for their territorial rights, the effects of crowding, the establishment of dominance and submission patterns, and the results of rearing animals alone and then later bringing them together. Ethological techniques are used to study the effects on the behavior of animals subjected to these procedures. By using these techniques, Henry's and his co-workers' studies have thrown light on the development of high blood pressure and renal disease in mice. They and others have also elucidated some of the biochemical mechanisms in the adrenal gland and brain that may bring about elevated blood pressure levels and renal disease.

In these studies the effect of prior experience on the neurochemistry of the brain has been studied. Socially isolating young animals alters the mean levels of various catecholamines, indoleamines, and amino acids as well as their biosynthetic and degradative enzymes in the brain (Welch and Welch, 1968b, 1971). Rearing young rodents in social isolation also alters the animals' reaction to various changes in their environment, their dominance and submission patterns in their social group, and their aggressive behavior. During the change from previous isolation to group living, marked changes occur in levels and turnover rates of both substrate and the enzyme levels in the brain.

Not all members of an animal genus or species are temperamentally aggressive: strain differences occur. Bourgault and co-workers (1963), and Karczmar and Scudder (1967) contrasted one aggressive strain of mice with a more peaceful strain. The brains of the aggressive mice contained lower levels of brain serotonin and norepinephrine. Subsequently, it was found that the content of biogenic amines in the brains of mice of different aggressive strains was not the same. In some aggressive strains, Maas (1962) found low levels of serotonin in the brain stem. In other strains, brain stem levels of serotonin are normal, but forebrain levels are low (Lagerspetz et al., 1967). When serotonin synthesis is inhibited by parachlorphenylalanine, nonaggressive mice kill members of their own species (Karli, 1969). Other mice of the same strain become killers when norepinephrine biosynthesis is inhibited by α-methylparatyrosine (Leaf, 1969). Therefore, the depletion of serotonin and of norepinephrine may cause some strains of mice to become killers. However, this effect cannot be the final answer to the problem of muricide because reserpine, which also depletes the brain of serotonin and norepinephrine, sedates animals. Sedated mice do not kill members of their species. The effects of inhibiting the synthesis of serotonin and norepinephrine by parachlorphenalanine and α-methylparatyrosine also produces exploratory behavior in addition to muricide. So far, we have no explanation for observations of this kind because a change in the level of a single neurotransmitter produces changes in a number of complex behaviors such as muricide or exploration.

It is easier to understand that early experience may lower the levels of an enzyme in the brain. Low levels of neuronal discharge in turn produce low levels of neurotransmitter biosynthesis and their biosynthetic products. Henry's (1967, 1969, 1971a, b) and the Welches' work (1971) can be understood in this context. When placed in a new and unfamiliar environment that provides excessive and unfamiliar stimulation, both aggressive behavior and increases in blood pressure occur because sensory stimulation is suddenly increased. As a consequence, a precipitous increase in the biosynthesis of neurotransmitter substances occurs.

Some support for this statement lies in the observation that male mice that had previously been isolated fought when they were individually paired with another mouse in an unfamiliar environment. The speed with which the fighting occurred and the duration and intensity of the fight was directly related to the length of prior isolation (Welch and Welch, 1971). Mice brought up together in groups took a much longer time to start a fight; the latent period before the onset of fighting depended on the number of peers in the group in which they had been raised (Welch and Welch, 1966, 1971). Both Henry and his co-workers (1967, 1969, 1971a, b) and Welch and Welch (1971) have found that prior isolation not only led to increased fighting when such animals are exposed to other animals, but also led them to assume a dominant role in the social hierarchy to which they have been introduced. Previously isolated animals even defeat a dominant animal that had been raised in a group (Welch and Welch, 1971).

Fighting produces peripheral sympathetic activation when the fight is intense. A reduction of epinephrine stores in the adrenal galnd and of levels of norepinephrine and dopamine in the brain stems of fighting rats and mice occurs (Vogt, 1954; Welch and Welch, 1971). A direct manner of measuring the level of peripheral sympathetic activation is to determine levels of DBH, the enzyme that converts dopamine into norepinephrine. The enzyme levels can be determined in different strains of rats, including those predisposed to hypertension, before and after a fight. In nonhypertensive strains of rats, the end of a fight is associated with a fall in blood pressure. But in spontaneously hypertensive rats and in salt-sensitive hypertensive and salt-resistant rats a fall in blood pressure levels does not occur after a fight. Animals in which a fall in blood pressure occurs after a fight have high initial levels of the enzyme: the higher the level of enzyme before the fight, the greater the fall in blood pressure after the fight. Therefore, a *decreased* peripheral sympathetic activity is associated with a failure of blood pressure to fall after fighting and characterizes strains of rats prone to hypertension (Lamprecht et al., 1974). These studies suggest that hypertensive strains of rats have a decreased peripheral sympathetic activity during and after a fight. Fighting does not change the blood pressure levels of hypertensive rats, because peripheral sympathetic activity remains unchanged during the fight. These results can be understood in only one way. During the inception of high blood pressure levels, peripheral sympathetic activity may be increased, but as soon as high blood pressure levels are established the activity may decrease and be unresponsive to fighting. In normal animals, by comparison, fighting causes a considerable fluctuation of sympathetic activity.

The observations suggest that marked individual differences in behavior and blood pressure levels occur in different strains of rodents when made to fight. In addition, the prior experience of a rodent determines its behavioral response. Rodents that are isolated when young fight more and assume the dominant role when they rejoin their group. They pay the price for their aggressive and assertive behavior by developing high blood pressure and interstitial nephritis. Their aggressive behavior is in some way functionally related to marked changes in the levels of enzymes involved in the biosynthesis of catecholamines in the brain. Levels of the enzymes in the brain are initially lower in animals isolated from the time of weaning but increase dramatically and excessively when the animals rejoin their group. Even when the animals have not previously been isolated, fighting changes levels of brain catecholamines. Furthermore, animals who are mere spectators to a fight and not participants in it, show changes in norepinephrine levels in the brain stem (Welch and Welch, 1968b, c, 1969).

Much has been learned about the complex interaction of strain differences, early experience, aggressive behavior, and high blood pressure from these studies. These experiments establish a relationship between aggressive or assertive behavior and high blood pressure in certain strains of animals. The relationship of aggression and high blood pressure has also been described in human beings. In animals this relationship seems to be mediated by changes in biogenic amine levels in the brain. Biogenic amines in the brain are organized in finite systems that also have an integral place in the regulation of arterial blood pressure (Chalmers, 1975). Indeed, strains of animals prone to hypertension differ from normotensive strains in the manner in which central monoaminergic systems are organized. These differences manifest themselves in the manner in which monoaminergic metabolism is organized in hypertensive and normotensive animals.

Genetic Factors and Experimental Hypertension in Animals

Early and later social experiences in mice not only cause high blood pressure but also influence behavior. The results of these experiments support the idea that social experiences can play a role in the initiation of high blood pressure. But the role of genetic factors in the establishment of hypertension in these mice was not determined. Other experiments clearly indicate that rodents vary in their predisposition to high blood pressure. Some strains develop high blood pressure spontaneously, other strains only do so when fed salt. Even in the former, the exact level of the blood pressure can be set by varying the amount of salt in the diet; in these animals, dietary salt does not initiate high blood pressure but determines its level. No experiment has been done to date in order to determine whether social experiences accelerate or retard the "spontaneous" develop-

143

ment of high blood pressure in either strain, although we do know that different strains of rats develop high blood pressure in different ways. For example, Smirk and Hall (1958) bred Wistar rats selectively for high blood pressure. The male rats in the group had higher resting blood pressure levels than the female rats. Both sexes responded with brisker blood pressure responses to the administration of drugs that produce pressor responses than did the normotensive rats. Their hearts weighed more and were frequently hypertrophic. Their heart rates under light anesthesia were higher, and some were found to have arteriolar necrosis. In young "hypertensive" rats, no arteriolar lesions occurred in the kidney. The peripheral resistance was increased in the hind-leg blood vessels of these hypertensive animals by neurogenic mechanisms. Both adrenalectomy and hyophysectomy reduced blood pressure levels. Therefore, adrenal or pituitary hormones may have contributed to the hypertension. Many of the hormones could have done so, but vasopressin was not one of them (Laverty and Smirk, 1961). Another strain of rats was bred by Okamoto and Aoki (1963) and Okamoto (1969). These rats developed hypertension "spontaneously" by a polygenic mechanism at about the age of 10 to 12 weeks. Although hypertension does develop when the rats are fed a salt-free diet (170 mm Hg), the amount of salt intake determines the level of the mean arterial pressure attained (to 230 mm Hg on 4% NaCl). Increasing the amount of potassium in the diet, which promotes sodium excretion, reduces the blood pressure levels (Louis et al., 1971). The spontaneously hypertensive strain of rats differs from the strain described by Dahl (see below) in that the former develop hypertension despite the absence of salt, as well as renal, cardiac, and cerebrovascular lesions that are akin to those in human hypertensive disease.

Spontaneously hypertensive rats show physiological variations from the norm even before hypertension begins. In spontaneously hypertensive rats of 8 weeks of age, plasma renin levels are similar to those in normotensive controls. Between 12 and 35 weeks of age, these rats have elevated plasma renin activity (DeJong et al., 1972; Sen et al., 1972). And Sinaiko and Mirkin (1974) have shown that kidney renin activity progressively increases in spontaneously hypertensive and control normotensive rats from the eighteenth day of fetal life until the first day of neonatal life. But in one-day old spontaneously hypertensive animals renin activity is significantly higher than in the control animals of the same age; the activity continues to be higher until the rats are 2¹ days old. By then the kidney renin activity in the normotensive animals has also increased, but now a fall in renin activity occurs only in the spontaneously hypertensive rat, only to increase again later.

A variety of other disturbances occur in these rats. Folkow and his co-workers (1973) subjected a pair of rats, one belonging to the spontaneously hypertensive strain and the other to a normotensive strain, to flashes of light, intermittent sound and vibration and measured their blood pressures and heart rates. Young (prehypertensive) and old (hypertensive) rats of the spontaneously hypertensive strain responded with greater and longer-lasting increases of blood pressure and heart rates, due to an increase in β-adrenergic activity, with sensory stimulation than did normotensive rats. Therefore, prehypertensive rats of the spontaneously hypertensive strain are predisposed to react to sensory stimuli by an increased β-adrenergic sympathetic activity that these investigators ascribe to a greater readiness for the mobilization of the defense alarm reaction. Pfeffer and Frohlich (1973) have also demonstrated that the heart rate, cardiac output, and

144

arterior flow rates are increased during the inception of hypertension (at 10–12 weeks of age) in spontaneously hypertensive rats. The cardiac activity is significantly greater in 10- to 12-week old hypertensive rats than in normotensive rats of the same age. But both groups of rats of this age have a normal peripheral resistance. Later, in those rats in whom hypertension is established, the cardiac output is normal and the peripheral resistance is heightened. (The analogy of this form of spontaneous rat hypertension to some instances of human labile and later stable hypertension is striking because both initially have elevated heart rates and cardiac outputs but a normal peripheral resistance.)

Other physiological studies carried out on spontaneously hypertensive rats describe the sequence of events that accompany the development of high blood pressure. Folkow and co-workers (1970) found that despite complete relaxation of the arterioles, the resistance to blood flow in the systemic vascular bed relative to the perfusion pressure was higher in spontaneously hypertensive than in normotensive rats. But the resistance to flow in the renal vessels was *lower* in the spontaneously hypertensive rats, though the renal vessels themselves were less distensible. Because the resistance to flow in the kidney is lower than is usual, the high blood pressure in these animals is probably not initiated by the kidney. Rather, the increased resistance to flow in the rest of the circulation may produce the elevated blood pressure levels (Folkow, 1971). Folkow (1971) believes that the changes in resistance to flow in the systemic blood vessels in these animals is due to increased sympathetic nervous system activity. The increased activity may be produced by increased angiotensin II levels in the central nervous system. But Folkow's suggestion may not be correct because Williams and co-workers (1972b) found that the spontaneously hypertensive rats had significantly lower serum levels of DBH than normotensive, age-matched controls of the N.I.H.-Wistar strain, both before and after the development of the elevated blood pressures. As DBH levels reflect overall peripheral sympathetic activity, the lower levels in hypertensive rats suggest decreased, not increased, sympathetic activity.

Folkow has also suggested that the central nervous system participates in the pathogenesis of the high blood pressure in spontaneously hypertensive rats. Norepinephrine and aromatic L-amino acid decarboxylase levels are significantly reduced in the lower brain stem and hypothalamus of spontaneously hypertensive rats, when compared with a control group of normal animals (Yamori et al., 1970). But these determinations were made after the experimental group of animals had become hypertensive; therefore, the reduced levels might be the consequence of the high blood pressure levels. In fact, more recent studies did not confirm this finding (Nakamura et al., 1971).

The failure to reproduce these findings highlights the scientific problem that has repeatedly been mentioned throughout this chapter: the pathophysiological changes produced by high blood pressure levels must be separated from the antecedent physiological causes of hypertension. The best illustration of this thesis is that injections of 6-hydroxydopamine into the lateral ventricles of young rats of the spontaneously hypertensive strain prevents the development of elevated blood pressure levels (Finch et al., 1972). The intraventricular injection of 6-hydroxydopamine, which causes degeneration of catecholaminergic (noradrenergic and dopaminergic) nerve endings in the brain and depletion of their transmitter stores, does not lower high blood pressure levels once they are established in this strain of rats (Haeusler et al., 1972). Therefore, noradrenergic and dopaminergic neurons in the brain may play a role in the initiation of, but do not seem to play a role in the maintenance of, high blood pressure. Once established, the high levels may be maintained by serotonergic neurons in the brain. Parachlorphenylalanine, which reduces serotonin synthesis, also reduces high systolic blood pressure in this strain of rats (Jarrot et al., 1975).

Brain stem levels of the catecholamines may also be affected by stress that changes levels or turnover rates of brain monoamines. Although the manner in which stress alters levels and turnover rates of these putative neurotransmitters is unknown, recent experiments suggest that changed levels of brain monoamines are due to the complex interaction of stress, genetic endowment, and the previous experience of an animal. Welch and Welch (1968a) found that restraint stress—which can cause some rats to become hypertensive—of various durations raises the brain levels of norepinephrine, dopamine, and serotonin. The release of these substances from neurons is accelerated by sensory stimulation (Glowinski and Baldessarini, 1966; Norberg, 1967). Their decline in levels after pharmacological inhibition of their biosynthesis depends on the nature of the stimulus (Andén et al., 1966; Gordon, et al., 1966; Hillarp et al., 1966). In some circumstances and rat strains, monoamine concentrations in the brain are actually lowered by stress (Andén et al., 1966; Bliss and Zwanziger, 1966; Gordon et al., 1966; Maynert and Levi, 1964; Paulsen and Hess, 1963; Toh, 1960; Welch and Welch, 1968b). In other strains of rats, salt has been found to play a role in the pathogenesis of hypertension. Salt-sensitive strains of rats regularly develop hypertension on eating small amounts of salt, but it takes time (Meneely et al., 1954). Dahl et al. (1962, 1968), and Jaffe et al. (1969) reported that two genetic strains of rats exist; one strain is resistant to salt ingestion, and the other is sensitive to salt ingestion. Even a diet containing only 0.38 percent of salt causes salt-sensitive rats to have higher blood pressure levels (134 mm Hg, mean) than the salt-resistant ones (112 mm Hg, mean). Salt-resistant rats on a diet of 8 percent sodium chloride have no blood pressure increases, but the blood pressure of the salt-sensitive ones rises to 210 mm Hg on this excess of dietary salt, and they develop moderate to severe lesions of the kidneys. Moreover, even the sensitive rats on a low-salt diet showed changes in the musculoelastic arteriolar pads of the kidney. This anatomical lesion is thought to be inherited and not to be due to salt ingestion. The hypertensive tendency of the salt-sensitive strain can be transmitted to members of the salt-resistant strain by parabiosis (Dahl et al., 1969); presumably a humoral factor is responsible for transmission of the tendency to salt-sensitivity. Recent evidence suggests that transplanting a kidney from a salt-sensitive animal into a salt-resistant animal raises the latter's blood pressure—a result that suggests that the kidney produces a hypertensive substance (Dahl et al., 1972).

Salt-sensitive animals have low aldosterone output on a diet of salt (Rapp and Dahl, 1972). The reduction in aldosterone output may be one of several inherited tendencies that determine salt sensitivity for which a multigenic mode of inheritance has been demonstrated. One genetic locus with two alleles inherited by codominance accounts for 16 percent of the blood pressure differences between salt-sensitive and salt-resistant strains; it also accounts for an increased secretion of 18-OH desoxycorticosterone (Rapp and Dahl, 1971, 1972; Rapp et al., 1973). Other factors must account for the rest of the etiological variance. Williams and co-workers (1972b) reported lower serum levels of

146

DBH in the salt-sensitive strain than in salt-resistant animals. Animals made hypertensive by feeding salt and injecting desoxycorticosterone acetate also have low levels of DBH. And Iwai and co-workers (1973) found that the salt-sensitive strain of rats had low serum-renin activity and that the kidney contained low levels of renin. The amount of salt in the diet modifies the amount of serum renin activity, but serum-renin-activity level in blood remains lower on a high-salt diet in salt-sensitive rats when compared to members of the salt-resistant strain. Serum renin levels do not increase as much as expected when the renal artery is compressed on one side in salt-sensitive rats. Therefore, low renin levels in salt-sensitive rats may be an inherited characteristic.

Apparently, high blood pressure in salt-sensitive rats is not the product of any one factor. In fact, the level of blood pressure attained in these rats is not only determined by the amount of salt in the diet. Friedman and Dahl (1975) have shown that the blood pressure level attained can also be determined by a conflict situation that combines food deprivation and the application of electric shocks. Salt-sensitive rats exposed to this conflict develop a higher level of systolic blood pressure than rats of the same strain merely food deprived, or shocked without food deprivation. In some rats, the high levels of blood pressure after exposure to conflict persisted for three to four months. These experiments suggest that this strain of rats is as sensitive to psychological stress as it is to the amounts of salt in the diet and that high levels of blood pressure can be produced by both stress and salt.

Summary

High blood pressure may be initiated in the rat by a wide variety of techniques and experimental procedures and is not the product of any one "cause." There are many pathways by which the rat can develop high blood pressure. Different strains of rats may develop hypertension by different means: the salt-sensitive rat develops hypertension even when it ingests little salt, but the spontaneously hypertensive rat develops high blood pressure without salt, although the amounts of salt ingested determine the level of the high blood pressure. Environmental factors, stress, or salt ingestion determine the blood pressure level, and genetic factors determine the predisposition to hypertension. The genetic predisposition to hypertension is different in different strains of rats. The predisposition is multigenic and is expressed in different physiological disturbances. The work on genetic strains of rats that become hypertensive suggests that genetic heterogeneity exists. Hypertension can be produced by environmental manipulation in rats and mice without regard to inheritance. Henry's and the Welches' work highlights the importance of prior experience, of changing the ecological conditions, and of the roles of fighting and dominance patterns in the development of high blood pressure and renal disease in rodents. In addition, many different behavioral manipulations raise an animal's blood pressure. These manipulations consist of restraint-immobilization, excessive stimulation by noise, and conditioning techniques.

To summarize the results of investigations with animals: many different methods of inducing hypertension in animals have been successful. Experiments with the Goldblatt technique of producing hypertension suggest that the kidney has a self-regulating function in controlling the blood pressure—compression of one renal artery produces hypertension; when the other kidney is later removed, the blood pressure rises further, suggesting that prior to removal the second kidney suppressed the blood pressure.

Salt-feeding can produce sustained hypertension in some strains of rats. In part, this effect is mediated by increased mineralocorticoid (18-hydroxydesoxycorticosterone) production. In other rats, desoxycorticosterone acetate and aldosterone given with salt also produce experimental hypertension. Once hypertension is produced in this way and combined treatment is stopped, the blood pressure falls, only to increase again when only salt is fed. Presumably, different mechanisms are involved in initiating hypertension and producing its recurrence.

The spontaneously hypertensive rat is the best analog of human hypertension. Although differences between this animal model and the human disease exist (Okamoto, 1969), the similarities are striking. The elevation of blood pressure in the spontaneously hypertensive rat are age-related, for reasons that are still not understood, just as in human beings. Spontaneously hypertensive subjects could be studied serially in order to determine the physiological changes that precede the development of hypertension. The sequential changes could be compared with those that occur in other forms of hypertension in animals. Comparative studies of this kind could teach us that in different animal species, hypertension can develop by different mechanisms. In borderline or labile hypertension in man, or early in experimental hypertension in the dog, the cardiac output is raised, but the peripheral resistance is not (Coleman and Guyton, 1969). In dogs, an initial increase in cardiac output occurs followed sequentially by vasoconstriction and an increased peripheral resistance. In other forms of human hypertension, the cardiac output is normal initially, but the peripheral resistance is increased. It is probably premature to generalize too much from these findings to other species. Although in the dog an initial increase in cardiac output occurs, in other species the cardiac output may be normal at the beginning of experimental hypertension.

The physiological changes that occur early in experimental hypertension seem to differ in different species or in different members of the same species. Certainly different species have different physiological responses to the same experimental procedure. The same experimental procedure responded to differently may initiate hypertension by one set of mechanisms and sustain it by another set.

Experiments in rats seemed to have clarified a number of controversies. Different strains of rats develop hypertension by different mechanisms. In some strains, the tendency to high blood pressure is polygenically determined. In one strain, even small amounts of salt interact with multiple genetically determined variations to elicit the hypertensive tendency. But the level of the blood pressure attained is determined by the amount of salt in the diet or by stressful manipulations. In still other strains of rats, hypertension develops inevitably at a particular age, but the blood pressure levels can be manipulated by varying the amount of dietary salt. The development of hypertension in the spontaneously hypertensive strain can be prevented by injections of 6-hydroxydopamine into the brain. But once hypertension is established, injecting 6-hydroxydopamine into the brain does not lower the blood pressure. Therefore, different physiological mechanisms seem to be involved in the establishment and in the maintenance of hypertension in these rats.

THE PATHOPHYSIOLOGY OF ESSENTIAL HYPERTENSION

The psychological heterogeneity of patients with essential hypertension may reflect the physiological heterogeneity of the disease. The probable heterogeneity of the pathogenetic mechanisms of the disease is present in its very early phases (Eich et al., 1966; Freis, 1960; Julius and Schork, 1971). Behavioral scientists have generally not kept abreast of this fact. For many years they have been guided by a single concept—that all patients with essential hypertension have an unusual cardiovascular reactivity and that essential hypertension is a product of an increased peripheral resistance. They have tried to correlate emotional and other psychological states with the excessive vascular reactivity or with the increase in peripheral resistance. They have asked how inhibited anger or rage raises blood levels by raising the peripheral resistance. But the cardiac output and not the peripheral resistance is elevated in the early phases of some forms of disease.

Behavioral scientists have proceeded on the assumption that anger or rage must raise blood pressure levels (choleric people do get red in the face!). They have not considered that in essential hypertension, the anger might be the product of the increased blood pressure levels or reflect some underlying physiological change that is also expressed in high blood pressure. Until we have a way of predicting people who will develop essential hypertension, these alternative possibilities will continue to plague the behavioral scientist.

Progress in understanding essential hypertension occurs daily. One major advance has been made in specifying the physiology of the early phases of the disease.

The Role of the Cardiovascular System and the Circulation in Essential Hypertension

Early in the course of essential hypertension, a high cardiac output occurs in some young patients with borderline essential hypertension (Eich et al., 1966; Folkow, 1971; Tobian, 1972). The increased cardiac output is accompanied by a slight increase in peripheral resistance. After a time, the peripheral resistance rises further, and the cardiac output returns to normal levels (Freis, 1960; Guyton and Coleman, 1969). In these patients, the increases in peripheral resistance are secondary—the consequence of the increase in cardiac output. The reasons for the elevation of the cardiac output are not known. An initial increase in cardiac output may be due to an increase in extracellular fluid volume (Coleman and Guyton, 1969). On the other hand it may be due to increased β-adrenergic sympathetic stimulation of the heart.

The increase in cardiac output does not occur in all patients (Widimsky et al., 1957). It may depend on the patient's age (Julius and Conway, 1968; Lund-Johansen, 1967). In young patients the increased cardiac output at rest is of the order of 14 percent. An increased heart rate and oxygen consumption may also occur with an increased cardiac output. Later, when the peripheral resistance is increased and there is visible evidence of retinal arteriolar spasm, the cardiac output, heart rate, and oxygen consumption become normal. Once the peripheral resistance is increased, exercise causes the arterial blood pressure to rise. Cardiac output and stroke volume do not rise in borderline hypertensive

149

patients or hypertensive patients with an increased peripheral resistance as much as in a normal group of subjects during exercise. But in both groups of hypertensive patients, exercise is associated with greater increases in peripheral resistance than in normal subjects (Sannerstedt, 1969). Some borderline hypertensive patients with an increased cardiac output have and some do not have an increased heart rate at rest (Bello et al., 1967; Finkielman et al., 1965). Propranolol does not reduce the elevated heart rate (Julius et al., 1968), but it does lower the cardiac output in borderline hypertensive patients (Julius et al., 1968; Ulrych et al., 1968). Therefore, the increased cardiac output is probably due to β-adrenergic stimulation of the heart.

In some animals, the constriction of one renal artery may at first produce an increase in cardiac output and blood pressure that are later followed by an increase in peripheral resistance (Bianchi et al., 1970; Ferrario et al., 1970; Frohlich et al., 1969; Ledingham, 1971). After a period of several weeks and further increases in blood pressure and peripheral resistance, the cardiac output settles back to normal levels. When the clamp on the renal artery is removed, a further temporary increase in peripheral resistance occurs, in the face of a prompt decrease in cardiac output and blood pressure. These hemodynamic responses, following the relief of renal artery constriction, can only, in part, be explained by changes in blood volume (Floyer, 1955).

The secondary increases in peripheral resistance seem to be the regulatory consequence of an increased cardiac output. When the output exceeds the metabolic requirements of local tissue, local vasoconstriction occurs, raising the peripheral resistance to lower the blood flow in that region of the body (Patterson et al., 1957). If the increase in peripheral resistance occurs throughout the body, the blood pressure increases and the cardiac output is reduced to normal. Regional differences in resistance to blood flow do occur in essential hypertension and in the experimental forms of hypertension produced by clamping a renal artery (Brod, 1970; Folkow, 1971; Rushmer, 1958). The causes of an increased cardiac output, experimentally produced in animals, are understood somewhat better than the causes of an increased cardiac output in some young male borderline hypertensives. (It is possible that the increased β-adrenergic stimulation of the heart can be related to emotional states that are mediated by the brain.)

Early in essential hypertension, physiological heterogeneity exists. In some patients both cardiac output and heart rate are increased; in others, only the cardiac output is elevated; in a third group the cardiac output is normal but the peripheral resistance is increased. In other hypertensive patients with established high blood pressure levels, the cardiac output may be lower than normal, even when no congestive heart failure is present. In these patients the high blood pressure and the low cardiac output do not respond to the stimulus of exercise.

FACTORS AFFECTING THE INCREASED PERIPHERAL RESISTANCE
IN ESSENTIAL HYPERTENSION

At some stage in essential hypertension the increased peripheral resistance is increased. It is not clear whether the increase precedes or follows the disease process in every form of essential hypertension. The enhanced peripheral resistance is due to constriction of the small arteries and veins—the so-called resistance vessels. The increase is not due to changes in blood viscosity, blood flow, or velocity profiles. The changes in the diameter of resistance vessels account for virtually all the changes in regional blood flow. Their reduced diameter is caused by local metabolic products and by adjustments in the tonic and phasic activity of sympathetic vasoconstrictor (or vasodilator) neurons, rather than by the action of the catecholamines (Celander, 1954). Adjustments in the ratio of resistance between the pre- and post-capillary bed affects the balance between the intravascular and extravascular body-water compartments that in turn affect the kidney (Rankin and Pappenheimer, 1957; Mellander, 1960). Regional blood volume and flow can change relatively independently of each other, by virtue of the design of resistance vessels. Major changes in blood flow in a region of the body can occur with only trivial changes in blood volume. Moderate increases in the tone of the smooth muscle in the vessel wall can occasion very large increments in the resistance to flow. Intrinsic myogenic activity in part determines such shifts that need not be produced by changes in vasomotor tone.

Peterson (1961) has suggested that in essential hypertension, excessive contraction of the smooth muscle wall of the resistance vessels causes increasd moduli of elasticity and viscosity. The increased stiffness of the resistance vessels is due to an increase in their water and electrolyte content. As they swell, their radius is reduced. The increased peripheral resistance may be due to local or systemic factors that account for the increase in peripheral resistance in essential hypertension.

Discharge in sympathetic vasodilator neurons may contribute to the increased peripheral resistance. These neurons are distributed to the arteriolar section of resistance vessels (Folkow et al., 1961; Uvnäs, 1960). They could account for the contraction of the vessels. But local tissue needs determine their own blood supply and the patency of vessels. No method has been developed for determining whether the increased vasoconstrictor tone in essential hypertension is due to changes in the chemical composition or structure of the arteriolar wall (Tobian and Binion, 1952; Tobian and Chesley, 1966; Tobian et al., 1961, 1969a), to the increased responsiveness of arteriolar muscle cells and their myogenic activity, to local tissue needs or to increased sympathetic discharge. In the rat the increase of peripheral resistance is caused by a change in the chemical composition of the arteriolar wall—a consequence of persistent hypertension. In man, the wall of the renal artery in hypertensive patients also contains an excess of sodium and water (Tobian and Binion, 1952).

We do not know which of these several possible causes of increased resistance comes first. It cannot be assumed, therefore, that the increased peripheral resistance in essential hypertension is only produced by increased sympathetic discharge. This assumption is based on the idea that incréased sympathetic discharge mediates emotional changes in hypertensive persons.

Once changes in the arteriolar wall occur, the peripheral resistance may be affected in different ways. The narrowed arteriolar lumen may impede flow. The increased salt and water content of the wall may reduce the elasticity of the arteriole (Feigl et al., 1963). The increased sodium content of the arteriolar cell may diminish the intracellular content of potassium and lower its membrane potential to produce partial depolarization and contraction of the arteriolar smooth muscle (Emanuel et al., 1959). The increased intracellular content of free calcium may directly cause smooth muscle proteins to contract. These proteins are sensitized to calcium by the presence of sodium, whose content is increased within the arteriolar cell wall.

The increased content of water, sodium, and calcium may cause the wall to swell and produce mechanically and functionally an increased resistance to the flow of blood. The hypertrophy of muscle in the arteriolar wall also augments the resistance. The resistance changes must be viewed in dynamic terms of dilation or contraction that occur in the arteriolar vascular bed. In essential hypertension, the arterioles resist flow even under conditions of maximal dilatation (Folkow, 1971) presumably because they are thickened (Short, 1966) or "waterlogged."

When these arterioles are made to contract by the interarterial injection of norepinephrine, the resistance increases in hypertensive but not in normotensive humans (Doyle and Fraser, 1961) and in hypertensive rats. This effect is not only due to the drug but is also the product of the preexisting state of the arteriolar wall. Norepinephrine augments the resistance to flow because it causes further contraction of an already narrowed arteriole. On further contraction the slope of increase of resistance is much steeper for a thickened, contracted arteriole (Redleaf and Tobian, 1958b; Mendlowitz et al., 1959, 1961; Sivertsson, 1970; Folkow, 1971).

Therefore the reactivity of the arterioles to norepinephrine may be no different in hypertensive patients than in normals, but the state of the arterioles differs. Neurogenic vasoconstriction has been indirectly implicated as the cause of the increased peripheral resistance in essential hypertension because of the effects of sympathectomy and of antihypertensive drugs. The same dose of a drug has a greater depressor effect in hypertensive than in normotensive subjects (Arnold and Rosenheim, 1949). A drug like chlorothiazide increases the caliber of blood vessels (Hollander and Wilkins, 1957; Freis et al., 1958) and, therefore, reduces the effects of norepinephrine (Beavers and Blackmore, 1958). But the effects of drugs cannot be used to support the neurogenic vasoconstrictor hypothesis of essential hypertension because drugs that block ganglionic transmission also decrease cardiac output and lower the blood pressure.

Increased neurogenic vasoconstriction in essential hypertension has been more directly inferred from studies of the circulation of the fingers after injection of norepinephrine (Folkow, 1971; Mendlowitz et al., 1958; Mendlowitz and Naftchi, 1958). But the evidence for an increased sensitivity of the arterioles in the fingers of hypertensive patients is not clearcut.

Norepinephrine acts directly on the vessel wall of hypertensive animals and increases its stiffness tenfold (Peterson et al., 1961; Holloway et al., 1973). But the action of norepinephrine may be secondary to the presence of other factors in the disease, and may not be the initial reason for vasoconstriction. Sympathetic denervation or blockade of an area enhances the sensitivity of its blood vessels to norepinephrine. Infusion of angiotensin potentiates the effects of norepinephrine on blood vessels. Cortisone increases the sensitivity of blood vessels to norepinephrine (Mendlowitz et al, 1958, 1961), possibly by interfering with its enzymatic degradation (Mendlowitz et al., 1959). Norepinephrine may play a role in enhancing the peripheral resistance during the course of the disease by interacting with other factors, but may not initiate the original increase in peripheral resistance. The increased blood pressure in essential hypertension was formerly thought to be secondary to an increase in peripheral resistance. Actually the

152

reverse may be correct. Thickening of blood vessel walls can be produced by experimentally raising the blood pressure in animals (Silvertsson, 1970; Folkow, 1971). The arteriolar wall thins out when the blood pressure is reduced to normal levels. Damage to large vessels such as the renal artery may result from high blood pressure (Shapiro et al., 1969). Once a renal artery is damaged, a vicious cycle is set up: essential hypertension may produce renovascular hypertension that sustains or augments preexisting high blood pressure levels. However, Tobian (1972) believes that thickened or damaged renal arterioles do not maintain high blood pressure levels by themselves. Recent evidence suggests that both the increased peripheral resistance and vascular damage are respectively the consequences of an increase in cardiac output and of high blood pressure levels in some patients with essential hypertension. They may help to sustain but not to initiate the disease.

The Role of the Kidney in Essential Hypertension

Because the kidney plays major roles in raising and lowering the blood pressure, it has also figured prominently in theories about the pathogenesis of essential hypertension. Constriction of the renal artery by various lesions and acute and chronic kidney diseases all elevate blood pressure. Some of the reasons for a narrowed renal artery may, however, stem from preexisting hypertension.

Ever since Goldblatt (1947) demonstrated that narrowing of one renal artery experimentally produces hypertension in animals, an enormous amount of investigative effort has been expended on the role of the kidney in the pathogenesis of essential hypertension and in maintaining normal blood pressure levels. When one renal artery is partly occluded, removal of the other kidney further enhances blood pressure levels (Goldblatt, 1947). Therefore, the normal kidney lowers the blood pressure possibly by regulating the extracellular fluid volume. In the rat, even when the salt intake is restricted, clamping the renal artery on one side and removing the other kidney still produces further elevations of blood pressure levels (Redleaf and Tobian, 1958). Therefore, the blood pressure increases despite a stable extracellular fluid volume and without further increases of already elevated renin levels (Brown et al., 1966).

In sheep, extracellular fluid volume actually falls following constriction of one renal artery, but the blood pressure rises so that the increase in fluid volume cannot account for the hypertension. When both renal arteries are constricted, sodium is not conserved, so extracellular fluid volume is not increased, and the hypertension is due to the release of renin and the mobilization of the angiotensin-aldosterone system. Therefore, different mechanisms can make the blood pressure increase when different experimental techniques are used. Furthermore, different species respond in different ways to the same experimental procedure. In dogs, unilateral constriction of the renal artery is associated almost immediately by renin release and an increase in blood pressure that can be prevented by an enzyme inhibitor that is injected at the time the artery is clamped. But once high blood levels are established for a week by clamping the artery, the enzyme inhibitor no longer reduces the blood pressure—a result suggesting that two different mechanisms are sequentially involved in initiating and in sustaining elevations of the blood pressure (Gutmann et al., 1973; Miller et al., 1972).

153

After both the rat's kidneys are removed, the intake of large amounts of sodium and water—that increase the extracellular fluid volume—raises the blood pressure even further (Tobian, 1950). The antihypertensive function of the kidney is, therefore, only in part due to the excretion of excess salt and water.

In man, the normal kidney also has an antihypertensive function (Merrill et al., 1956). In the rat, a normal kidney implanted after renal artery constriction lowers the blood pressure, providing that the perfusion pressure of the new kidney is at high levels (Tobian et al., 1964). When the perfusion pressure is in the normal range the blood pressure remains high. The high perfusion pressure causes the normal kidney to release antihypertensive substances, possibly the prostaglandins.

When a renal artery is constricted experimentally or by disease, a fall in pressure occurs distal to the constriction. As a result of this pressure drop renin is released by the kidney and serum renin activity increases. The hypertensive effects of the kidney may be mediated by the renin-angiotensin mechanism (Tobian, 1960), but this hypothesis has been questioned, because a fall in blood pressure can be produced in rats and sheep even when their blood angiotensin and plasma renin levels remain unchanged (Blair-West et al., 1968a, b; Byrom and Dodson, 1949; Floyer, 1955). The acute fall in blood pressure after unclipping a renal artery may be due to reflex sympathetic discharge that raises the heart rate and maintains cardiac output to compensate for the fall in blood pressure. Because renin and angiotensin levels remain the same despite a fall in blood pressure they may not be essential to the maintenance of renovascular hypertension (Funder et al., 1970).

When antibodies to renin or angiotensin are administered to dogs or rats with a constricted renal artery, the increase in blood pressure levels is averted or the blood pressure, if already elevated, falls (Christlieb et al., 1969; Carretero et al., 1971). Other species, such as the rabbit, may respond differently. When the contralateral kidney is removed from a rabbit whose other renal artery was constricted, the antibodies to renin and angiotensin have no antihypertensive effect (Bing and Poulsen, 1970; Brunner et al., 1971; Christlieb et al., 1969). Presumably, a new mechanism, other than renin release, sustains blood pressure levels in the rabbit. Therefore, the conclusion can be reached that different mechanisms sustain high blood pressure in different species. And different species of animals respond to the same experimental techniques in a different manner.

THE CONTROL OF THE RENIN AND ANGIOTENSIN MECHANISMS

One of the major advances our understanding of the pathophysiology of essential hypertension has been the elucidation of the physiological mechanism by which the kidney and the enzyme renin are related to the adrenocortical mineralocorticoid, aldosterone, and to the formation of the polypeptides, angiotensin I and II. Renin release is controlled by interrelated regulatory mechanisms that influence the level of arterial pressure and, therefore, the pressure within the renal artery. A fall in renal artery perfusion pressure causes the increased production and secretion of renin by the granular, juxtaglomerular cells that lie within the walls of the afferent arterioles of the kidney (Tobian, 1960, 1962).

The exact mechanism by which a fall in perfusion pressure produces renin release is unknown. Vander and Miller (1964) do not believe that renin release is stimulated by the mechanical effect of a fall in renal artery pressure. Renin release can be ascribed to a reduction in the delivery of sodium to the macula densa portion of the distal renal tubules when the pressure falls. Eide and co-workers (1973), on the other hand, believe that renin release depends on the state of dilatation of the renal arterioles. Renin release would then be stimulated by the active dilatation of the renal arterioles in response to a fall in blood pressure—an autoregulatory process—rather than by reduced distension of the arteriolar wall. Once released, renin may act locally within the kidney to raise the blood pressure. It also enters the circulation directly or indirectly by way of the lymphatic system (Skinner et al., 1963). Renin converts the plasma globulin angiotensinogen into a decapeptide, angiotensin I, which further loses two amino acids, through the agency of an enzyme in the kidney, lung, and blood, to form the potent pressor substance angiotensin II. Angiotensin II acts on brain-stem pressor mechanisms and directly on arterioles to raise the blood pressure. As angiotensin II levels increase, the adrenocortical mineralocorticoid aldosterone is released. Angiotensin II is an important but not the only regulator of aldosterone secretion.

Renin may not be the only enzyme in the body to produce angiotensin I from the globulin substrate. An enzyme called tonin, found in the submaxillary gland, also converts angiotensin I into angiotensin II, but, unlike renin, it may produce the latter directly from globulin and from a 14-amino-acid polypeptide derived from the substrate (Boucher et al., 1974).

Although a fall in renal artery perfusion pressure is the main stimulus to renin release, a fall in plasma volume also causes its release. Conversely, increases in plasma volume or renal artery pressure inhibit renin release from the kidney (Tobian et al., 1964).

Adrenergic stimulation of the kidney also releases renin (Gordon et al., 1967). The effect is mediated by the β-adrenergic receptors (Ganong, 1972). In the isolated rat kidney, isoproterenol stimulates renin release without changing renal artery perfusion pressure. The effect of isoproterenol is blocked by dipropananol. Norepinephrine also releases renin while causing renal artery vasoconstriction. When the vasoconstriction is averted by the appropriate blocking agent, renin release still occurs (Vandongen et al., 1973).

The sympathetic nervous system not only releases renin; it also exerts a resting, tonic effect on the juxaglomerular cells of the kidney. Renal sympathectomy decreases plasma renin activity (Mogil et al., 1969). Stimulation of the medulla oblongata increases it (Passo et al., 1971). Stimulation of the hypothalamus of the dog at various points —rostral to the preoptic area and ventral to the anterior commissure, at the level of the premammillary nucleus, and in the tuberal region—lowers plasma renin activity. Renal denervation prevents the fall in renin activity when the hypothalamus is stimulated. The pathways that mediate the effect of hypothalamic stimulation are not known. Hypothalamic stimulation at the same site also lowers the blood pressure, but not by altering renal blood flow (Zehr and Feigl, 1973). Therefore, the central nervous system may exert direct control on renin release and may be implicated in the pathogensis of essential hypertension.

The control of renin release after renal artery constriction may be more complicated and more individual than was once believed. After renal artery constriction some dogs develop elevated blood pressure levels, increased renin and aldosterone blood levels, and convulsions. In other dogs the levels of renin and aldosterone rise initially, then they fall, despite a permanent elevation of blood pressure (Brown et al., 1966; Carpenter et al., 1961b). The mechanisms whereby renin levels return to normal values in the second group of dogs have not been elucidated as yet.

In the second group of dogs, blood pressure levels are maintained in the face of normal serum renin activity. The lack of a correlation between blood pressure and renin levels occurs both in man and in dogs. Patients with essential hypertension may have low, normal, or high serum renin levels (Brunner et al., 1972). In dogs, arterial pressure levels do not correlate with serum renin levels; marked discrepancies and changes in renin levels occur (Ayers et al., 1969). In man, no linear relationship between blood pressure and renin levels occurs either, even in patients with essential or renovascular hypertension (Kaneko et al., 1967, 1968). The release of renin and the production of angiotensin II may occur at the inception of experimental hypertension in some animals, but high blood pressure levels are probably not sustained by increased renin or angiotensin II activity.

The role the renin-angiotensin-aldosterone system in the etiology and pathogenesis of essential hypertension remains enigmatic. In this disease, plasma renin levels may be low, normal, or high (Helmer, 1964; Creditor and Loschky, 1967; Ledingham et al., 1967; Jose et al., 1970; Brunner et al., 1972). High levels of renin and aldosterone activity in blood serum occur mainly in the malignant phase of the disease, when the kidney is damaged (Laragh, 1960, 1961; Laragh et al., 1972) or in Goldblatt hypertension and its natural analogues. The vascular lesions during the malignant phase of hypertensive disease may be directly due to the damaging effects of excessive renin and angiotensin activity on the walls of blood vessels (Carpenter et al., 1961b; Masson et al., 1962; Giese, 1964).

Of 219 patients with essential hypertension, 27 percent had reduced plasma renin activity when compared to normal volunteers. Of these patients, 16 percent had elevated levels of plasma renin, and 57 percent had normal levels. The amounts of aldosterone excreted by hypertensive patients vary more than in normal volunteers (Brunner et al., 1972). Black hypertensive patients are unusually likely to have a low serum renin activity despite the fact that they are more likely to develop malignant hypertension than white hypertensive patients. Patients with high serum renin activity have significantly higher mean diastolic blood pressures and blood urea nitrogen levels and lower plasma potassium levels, but suprisingly, their aldosterone levels are normal. Some (13–21 percent) of the patients with low serum renin activity had normal urinary aldosterone levels, which was unexpected. Only about 50 percent of all 219 patients with essential hypertension had preserved the usual linear relationshps between renin and aldosterone levels (Brunner et al., 1972).

These findings suggest that essential hypertension is a heterogeneous disease. In 50 percent of the patients, a disturbance in the regulation of aldosterone by angiotensin occurs. In other patients, the relationship between the two is retained. Heterogeneity is also suggested by the fact that essential hypertension can occur with every kind of serum renin activity—low, normal, and high. It remains to be shown whether variations in renin levels antecede the development of essential hypertension, are a correlate, or a result from it. Brunner et al. (1972) have found that renin levels remain the same in hypertensive patients over a period of months or years, suggesting that they are an abiding characteristic of these patients and do not result from some other variable, such as the disease process or elevated blood pressure levels. Renin levels may rise only when the malignant phase of the disease is ushered in.

THE PHYSIOLOGICAL ACTIONS OF ANGIOTENSIN

In normal subjects, angiotensin II infusion diminishes diuresis and produces sodium retention and an increased secretion rate of aldosterone and cortisol. Antigiotensin II also stimulates ACTH secretion to increase cortisol production (Ames et al., 1965). The retention of sodium is brought about by direct stimulation of aldosterone secretion. Changes in cortisol production are also produced by mechanisms besides ACTH secretion. Fluctuations in levels of the glucocorticoids (such as cortisol) covary with changes in intravascular pressure, or an effective plasma volume (Ehrlich et al., 1966, 1967; Ehrlich, 1968; Kuchel et al., 1967). Patients with essential hypertension show no alterations in total exchangeable sodium, extracellular fluid, or plasma volume unless they are in congestive heart failure (Chobanian et al., 1961; Hollander and Wilkins, 1957). They paradoxically eliminate a greater proportion of a salt and water load after saline, water, or angiotensin infusion than normotensive subjects do (Baldwin et al., 1958; Cottier, 1960; Farnsworth, 1946; Green and Ellis, 1954; Hollander and Wilkins, 1957). The increased natriuresis and diuresis may be the result of the elevated blood pressure (Cottier, 1960) or of an increased tubular rejection of sodium that in turn depends on elevations of intrarenal pressure (Cottier, 1960). With a fall in blood pressure, regardless of what occasions it, the increased natriuresis and diuresis brought about by saline or water infusion diminishes.

The infusion of 5 mg of angiotensin II into patients with hypertension, regardless of pathogenesis, regularly produces an osmotic diuresis.[*] Increased amounts of electrolyte and water are excreted, even when no increases in blood pressure are produced by angiotensin. By contrast, 5 mg of angiotensin II produces an antidiuresis and a fall in electrolyte excretion in normal individuals (Bock and Krecke, 1958; Peart, 1959). When a renal artery stenosis is relieved and the blood pressure reverts to normal levels, the normal antidiuretic response to angiotensin infusion is reestablished (Peart, 1959).

The effect of angiotensin II on the excretion of salt and water depends on the level of the blood pressure. The paradoxical effect of angiotensin II on salt excretion may be an

---

[*] Osmotic diuresis also occurs with the "emotional effects" of passing a urethral catheter into women, when catheterization is followed by a discussion of their illness. Miles and De Wardener (1953) found that an increase in urine flow, chloride, and osmolar excretion rates occured in both hypertensive and normotensive patients. But the increases were considerably greater in the hypertensive than in the normotensive subjects. These authors also found that the increases mentioned often began before the catheter was actually inserted, but the specific emotional states of their subjects are not described in detail. They concluded that the mechanism of this osmotic diuresis was a diminished tubular reabsorption of salt. This experiment is important because it may account for the results obtained when mannitol, salt, or water are infused into hypertensive subjects.

adaptation to high blood pressure levels. If hypertensive patients eliminate more salt and water when angiotensin II or salt is infused, the blood pressure would be reduced.

The effects of angiotensin II can be understood in terms of physiological adaptation because the effect of any stimulus—in this instance angiotensin II—depends on the preexisting state, specifically whether blood pressure levels are elevated or not.

THE ROLE OF ANGIOTENSIN IN PRODUCING ELEVATED BLOOD PRESSURE

Angiotensin II has effects on the functions of the kidney, and it also has powerful pressor effects. Angiotensin II constricts arterioles directly, and also reflexly produces vasoconstriction by its effects on the pressor mechanisms in the brain stem. It stimulates aldosterone secretion thereby producing salt retention, which elevates the blood pressure (Carpenter et al., 1961b). Angiotensin II indirectly produces an increase in the sodium content of the arteriolar wall. It stimulates the release of norepinephrine from sympathetic postganglionic neurons and the adrenal medulla, and it potentiates the vasoconstrictor action of norepinephrine. Hypertensive patients may be sensitized by angiotensin II to overreact physiologically to psychological stimuli once the disease process has begun. Psychological stimuli may, therefore, aggravate the disease. In support of this hypothesis McCubbin (1967) has found that after very small doses of angiotensin II, which had no immediate effect on blood pressure levels, had been infused for several days into dogs, the arterial blood pressure became elevated and labile. When the dogs were surrounded by everyday activity in the laboratory, the arterial pressures were labile and high. If the laboratory was quiet, minor distractions caused marked further increases in arterial pressure. After the injection of angiotensin II the dogs became sensitized to the administration of tyramine, which releases endogenous stores of norepinephrine. Tyramine injection produced further elevations of the dogs' arterial pressures. The results of McCubbin's experiments strongly suggest that angiotensin II plays a role in the initiation of high blood pressure levels and alters the reactivity of the animal to environmental stimuli. Once these changes have occurred, the animal overreacts even to trivial stimuli. Environmental stimuli or drugs, such as tyramine, produce excessive responses that did not occur before treatment with angiotensin II. Therefore, one may conclude that psychological stimuli do not necessarily initiate high blood pressure levels. Angiotensin II alters the reactivity of dogs to environmental stimuli by mechanisms that may include the effects of angiotensin II on the brain. It may alter the function of the brain so that it responds in new ways to environmental stimuli by changing levels or turnover rates of brain catecholamines (Chalmers, 1975).

Angiotensin II amide in very small amounts acts directly on certain regions of the brain. It increases water drinking in rats who are in normal fluid balance without raising the blood pressure. Repetitive brain injections continue to produce the effect on drinking. Injections also wake up the sleeping rat. They interrupt eating in hungry rats and cause them to drink. Angiotensin II acts on the anterior hypothalamus and the preoptic and septal areas of the brain to produce drinking. Injections of angiotensin elsewhere in the brain do not produce drinking. The effect of angiotensin II on drinking behavior can also be produced by renin and carbachol (Booth, 1968; Epstein et al., 1970), but the effects of angiotensin II are more potent. Lehr and his co-workers (1973) believe that

158

angiotensin I is as potent as angiotensin II in producing drinking in the rat. Drinking water is also usually accompanied by salt intake. If excessive amounts of water are drunk or salt is eaten, the extracellular fluid volume of the organism would increase and the blood pressure would rise.

The fact that injecting renin into the hypothalamus also produces drinking suggests that renin substrate is present in the brain. In fact, renin isoenzymes have been isolated from the brain, so that it is possible that the brain is itself capable of manufacturing angiotensin I or II. Angiotensin II levels are elevated in the cerebrospinal fluid (CSF) of the spontaneously hypertensive rat—the best animal model of essential hypertension in man. Antibodies against angiotensin II administered to these rats lowers their blood pressure (Ganten et al., 1974). But we do not know whether the angiotensin II in the CSF of these rats comes from brain or kidney renin activity.

THE PROSTAGLANDINS AS NATURALLY OCCURRING ANTIHYPERTENSIVE AGENTS

The kidney not only produces substances, such as renin, that are indirectly involved in raising blood pressure, but it also produces substances that lower it. In short, the kidney contains an autoregulatory mechanism for the control of blood pressure. The antihypertensive substances are produced by cells in the renal medulla (Muirhead et al., 1970). Removal of these cells causes the blood pressure to increase. The renal medullary cells of the rabbit contain prostaglandin E_2 (PGE2) (Hickler et al., 1964; Lee et al., 1966; Muirhead et al., 1967; Strong et al., 1966). Injections of PGE2 lower the blood pressure in normal and hypertensive rats. Other antihypertensive lipids have also been isolated from the renal medulla. They, too, lower the blood pressure of animals after constriction of one renal artery (Muirhead et al., 1967).

A third substance, polypeptide in nature, has been isolated from the aorta of dogs and from human and canine plasma. It also rapidly reduces blood pressure levels when injected into rats. Plasma levels of the polypeptide are increased in human beings and dogs with low blood pressure levels caused by surgical or experimental shock (Rosenthal et al., 1973). Still other hypotensive substances are released by shock and may account for the reduced blood pressure levels in shock (Lefer, 1973).

Antihypertensive substances such as PGE2 play a role in experimental hypertension in animals. It is as yet too early to say what the role of these substances is in human essential hypertension or in its treatment; little is known about the mechanisms regulating their synthesis, release, or secretion, or how they may interact with the various other regulators of blood pressure.

The Role of Salt and Water Metabolism in Essential Hypertension

INTRODUCTION

The maintenance of normal blood pressure levels in man depends in part on the volume of circulating blood. If hemorrhage occurs, the blood volume diminishes and the blood pressure falls. As the blood pressure falls a large number of mechanisms are brought

159

into action to maintain the normal or raise the fallen blood pressure levels. Physiological readjustments occur to restore the blood volume. The fluid contained in the blood vessels constitutes only one part of all the fluid in the tissue spaces between cells. The extracellular fluid volume of the body is made up of all the fluid within blood vessels and outside cells in tissue spaces. The fluids in tissue spaces and in the blood vessels are in dynamic equilibrium with each other. As hemorrhage occurs, the fluid shifts out of tissue spaces into blood vessels to increase the blood volume. As the blood volume diminishes with hemorrhage, thirst promotes the drinking of water and intake of salt.

If the extracellular fluid volume is too large, or the osmotic pressure of the fluid is increased by salt, the body rids itself of water and salt respectively to maintain a relatively constant fluid volume and osmotic pressure. A number of interrelated mechanisms are involved in maintaining the equilibrium between fluid volume and salt content. The kidney, the mineralocorticoid and antidiuretic hormones, and the baroreceptors of the carotid sinus and aortic arch are involved in maintaining this equilibrium. Increases or decreases in extracellular fluid volume are directly related to increases or decreases in salt intake and content of the fluid and to increases and decreases in blood pressure levels.

Several lines of evidence suggest that salt may play a role in the initiation or maintenace of hypertension. In man the hypotensive effect of chlorothiazide—which lowers extracellular fluid volume—are undone by a high-salt diet. The addition of salt to the diet of untreated hypertensive patients raises their blood pressure to even higher levels (McDonough and Wilhelmj, 1954). The ingestion of salt by hypertensive persons who previously responded to its dietary restriction by a lowering of blood pressure levels reestablishes their previous high levels (Dole et al., 1951). Salt and water ingestion may cause an increase in the extracellular fluid volume. Hypertensive patients are particularly sensitive to such an increase and respond by a further increase in blood pressure.

The riddle of the pathogenesis of essential hypertension would easily be solved if salt intake were the only causative factor. Actually, salt may contribute to the initiation of, may sustain or enhance preexisting high blood pressure levels, but does not alone seem to cause them, except in certain strains of rats who are sensitive to salt (Ball and Meneely, 1957; Dahl et al., 1960; Meneely et al., 1953, 1954). In other strains of rats, salt must be combined with desoxycorticosterone acetate to produce high blood pressure (Fukuda, 1951; Grollman et al., 1960; Knowlton et al., 1947; Lenel et al., 1948; Sapirstein et al., 1950; Selye et al., 1943). Once the combination of desoxycorticosterone acetate and salt have produced high blood pressure levels, stopping their administration will cause the blood pressure to become normal again. Later, salt by itself will raise the levels. The combined regimen sensitizes some rats to respond only to salt. Therefore, the factors that initiate high blood pressure levels in these rats may be different than those that cause rats later to respond with hypertension to salt alone.

Some epidemiological studies of the incidence and prevalance of essential hypertension implicate salt. In some human populations a linear correlation exists between salt intake and the incidence of hypertension. If the intake of salt is low in a social group, the incidence of hypertension is lower than in another group whose members consume large amounts of salt (Dahl, 1957, 1958, 1960). The amount of salt in a diet is also partly a function of cultural habits. Yet in some individuals, an appetite for salt, independent of cultural habits or the body's requirement for it, seems to exist. Little is known about the variables responsible for the individual craving for salt (Dahl, 1960).

160

The amount of dietary salt, specifically the amount of sodium ion (Gross, 1960), usually determines the amount of renin extractable from the kidney (Gross and Sulser, 1956; Gross and Lichtlen, 1958). In some hypertensive patients, however, plasma renin activity or aldosterone secretion rates are not responsive to salt intake (Luetscher et al., 1969; Streeten et al., 1969; Williams et al., 1970).

The more salt there is in a diet, the greater is the extracellular fluid volume. As the extracellular fluid volume increases, the more renin activity can be detected in serum and the less renin is contained in the kidney. However, the increase in levels of blood sodium do not parallel the increase in blood pressure (Gross, 1960). A variety of regulatory adjustments occur to the increases in serum sodium and renin activity. The arterial pressure at first increases due to an increased cardiac output and stroke volume. Initially there is a fall in peripheral resistance that is then followed by a sustained increase (Coleman and Guyton, 1969).

Any increase of salt in the body increases the extracellular fluid volume to which the circulation adjusts. These adjustments are carried out not only by increases in cardiac output, but by the kidney, by changes in the levels of the mineralocorticoids of the adrenal cortex, and by inhibition of antidiuretic hormone secretion. The kidney responds to an increase in the extracellular fluid volume by increasing urine output in order to reduce the excess of salt and water. In nephrectomized, dialyzed patients, who cannot excrete urine, the blood pressure level fluctuates with changes in the extracellular fluid volume. When the fluid volume increases, the peripheral resistance also does, especially in nephrectomized patients who were previously hypertensive (Muirhead et al., 1966, 1970).

When increases in extracellular fluid volume occur, the level of the blood pressure is determined by a number of additional factors. Epinephrine and angiotensin II are more effective in raising the blood pressure when the blood volume is increased than when it is not. In women with a family history of essential hypertension, the blood pressure is raised by the oral contraceptive pill, which raises levels of plasma angiotensinogen, angiotensin II, and the extracellular fluid volume.

These observations are relevant to an understanding of the nature of the basic physiological defect in essential hypertension. Tobian (1960, 1961, 1972) has suggested that the circulation behaves *as if* there were an excess of extracellular fluid volume (Tobian, 1961) even though the average volume in hypertension may be 10 to 12 percent less than in normotensive persons (Rochlin et al., 1959). He suggests that all the compensatory mechanisms that have been described when the extracellular fluid volume is increased operate upon a normal or below-normal extracellular fluid volume. His suggestion touches upon a central thesis in this chapter that essential hypertension is a "disease of regulation," and that the regulatory disturbances are multiple.

Tobian (1961) has also suggested that an elevated renal arterial pressure in essential hypertension could distend the stretch receptors in the arterial wall and stimulate the juxtaglomerular cells in the wall of the afferent glomerular arteriole. The cells react as if there were an overabundance of extracellular fluid. A further increase in extracellular fluid volume produces an exaggerated sodium diuresis that occurs when sodium, water, or angiotensin are infused into hypertensive patients.

A somewhat different regulatory disturbance in essential hypertension has been suggested by Wilson (1961). According to his view the relationship between the tone of

161

blood vessels and extracellular fluid volume is altered in essential hypertension. The blood-vessel tone in the hypertensive patient is exaggerated for a given fluid volume. Even when the fluid volume is normal, the tone acts as if the fluid volume were increased.

High blood pressure levels can, however, be produced experimentally in animals even when the amount of salt in their diets is low. Presumably the extracellular fluid volume is also low in salt-restricted animals with a high blood pressure produced by renal artery constriction (Redleaf and Tobian, 1958b).

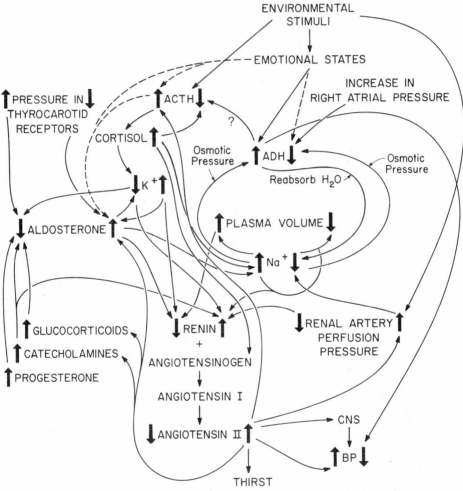

FIGURE 1 Feedback Regulatory System of the Renin-Angiotensin-Aldosterone System and Its Relationship to Variations in Sodium and Potassium Levels. The arrows on the left indicate other influences (e.g., dilatation of the renal artery and sympathetic tonic and phasic influences which increase renin secretion and activity). Modified with permission from Laragh et al. in *American J. of Medicine.* Copyright 1972 by Dun-Donnelley.

The regulatory disturbances in essential hypertension suggested by Tobian and Wilson may follow rather than precede the development of high blood pressure. The sodium ion may not initially exert its effect by increasing the extracellular fluid. Large amounts of dietary sodium may also deplete the kidney of its antihypertensive substances such as the prostaglandins.

Large amounts of salt fed to weanling rats for seven weeks, followed by a normal amount of salt in the diet, produces hypertension and reduces the cytoplasmic granules in the renal papilla (Tobian et al., 1969b). The blood pressure of these rats can be reduced by implanting the renal papilla that contains prostaglandins from normotensive rats. In severe human hypertension the papillary granules are also much fewer (Tobian, 1972).

The hypertensive patient paradoxically excretes more salt and water when he partakes of them. The amount of sodium in the body is not only determined by the amount ingested in the diet and the amount excreted in the urine. It is also regulated by the renin-angiotensin-aldosterone system. The serum levels of these hormones fluctuate in concert with the state of sodium balance (Brunner et al., 1972). The complex relationships between sodium and these hormones may be disturbed in some forms of essential hypertension. Some patients with a form of hypertension characterized by low levels of plasma renin activity cannot maintain their blood pressure levels and develop postural hypotension on a low-salt diet. They are unable to conserve their fluid volume on a low-salt diet (Weinberger et al., 1968). In other patients, eating salt does not suppress aldosterone secretion rates as it does in normal persons (Leutscher et al., 1969), nor is the rate of renin secretion responsive to salt deprivation (Streeten et al., 1969; Williams et al., 1970). In normotensive persons, renin, angiotensin II, aldosterone levels, and secretory rates rise as sodium levels in the blood fall, and they decline with rising or excessive sodium levels.

In some forms of essential hypertension the regulation of sodium excretion and reabsorption by the kidney under the influence of aldosterone is disturbed. In other forms, renin and, therefore, aldosterone levels are not responsive to changes in sodium—and its reciprocal ion, potassium—levels in the blood. The regulation of sodium and potassium blood levels is carried out by a number of hormones and organ systems (Figure 1).

THE ROLE OF THE ANTIDIURETIC HORMONE (ADH) IN ESSENTIAL HYPERTENSION

Patients with essential hypertension are sensitive to any increase in extracellular fluid volume. Such increases are produced by eating salt and drinking water. Paradoxically, infusions of salt solution or angiotensin, or increasing the extracellular fluid volume by other methods, produce an exaggerated diuresis in patients. The extracellular fluid volume can also be increased by angiotensin I and II because they are powerful stimuli to drinking water. Another regulator of water metabolism is the antidiuretic hormone (ADH) released by the posterior portion of the pituitary gland, which is under the control of the hypothalamus. Despite reports that the rate of excretion of ADH by the kidney is increased in human and experimental hypertension (Ellis and Grollman, 1949), the role of this important hormone in the disease remains enigmatic. The increased excretion may occur in response to changes in extracellular fluid volume (Sapirstein, 1957) and is, therefore, a secondary phenomenon that would help to sustain high blood

163

pressure levels. ADH and aldosterone are the main but not the only hormones that regulate water and salt metabolism. ADH and aldosterone produce an expansion of the body fluid compartments and increase the glomerular filtration rate. The reabsorption of sodium and chloride is mainly under the influence of aldosterone through a cation exchange mechanism. ADH increases the permeability of the distal convoluted tubules and collecting ducts of the kidney so that water is reabsorbed.

The secretion of ADH is stimulated by an increase in the osmotic pressure of extracellular fluid. ADH, by increasing the reabsorption of water by the kidney, dilutes the extracellular fluid and reduces its osmotic pressure. When the osmolality of extracellular fluid is decreased, ADH secretion is inhibited, and more water is excreted by the kidney. The release of ADH and its inhibition are mediated through the paraventricular nucleus of the hypothalamus, the supraopticohypophyseal tract, and the posterior pituitary gland. When the osmotic pressure of the blood increases, neurons in the supraoptic nucleus of the hypothalamus are excited, and ADH is released from the gland (Brooks et al., 1962; Cross and Green, 1959; Kandel, 1964; Verney, 1947). Stimulating the supraopticohypophyseal tract in rabbits causes ADH secretion and inhibts the excretion of water by the kidney. Water intake is increased by electrical stimulation or the injection of very small volumes of hypertonic saline into the hypothalamus of goats (Andersson and McCann, 1955).

In addition to changes in the osmolality of the blood, various physiological, pharmacological, and psychological factors influence the rate with which ADH is secreted (Rydin and Verney, 1938). Painful stimuli (Mirsky et al., 1954), avoidance conditioning (Mason et al., 1968), and hemorrhage reduce urine excretion, presumably by stimulating ADH secretion. Emotional inhibition of water excretion is also mediated by ADH (Abrahams and Pickford, 1956; Mirsky et al., 1954; O'Connor and Verney, 1945; Verney, 1947). "Stressful" stimuli also release both ACTH and ADH, probably by separate mechanisms (Guillemin et al., 1957; McDonald et al., 1957; Nagareda and Gaunt, 1951; Saffran et al., 1955). The release of ADH is also controlled by the mechanoreceptors in the aorta, carotid arteries, and atrium of the heart. Negative-pressure breathing in the presence of the intact vagus nerve produces a diuresis, presumably through the participation and decreased stimulation of the mechanoreceptors in the left atrium of the heart and the inhibition of ADH secretion (Gauer and Henry, 1963). ADH release is produced by lowering the pressure in the carotid sinus. As the pressure falls, blood volume would be maintained by inhibiting the excretion of water (Perlmutt, 1963; Share and Levy, 1962; Usami et al., 1962). The pathway from the carotid sinus mediating this effect is through the brain.

Some of the central nervous system pathways mediating painful or stressful stimuli and producing ADH release have been mapped by brain-stimulation experiments. ADH release is produced by stimulating the medial midbrain reticular formulation and the interpeduncular nucleus (Hayward and Smith, 1962; Kogel and Rothballer, 1962; Mills and Wang, 1963; Rothballer, 1966). These midbrain sites are capable of phasically increasing neuronal activity in the supraopticohypophyseal system. The release of ADH is brought about by stimulation of midbrain structures and is inhibited by raising the pressure within the carotid sinus, which increases baroreceptor discharge (Rothballer, 1966). Therefore, midbrain structures may integrate ascending neuronal activity from the

164

medulla with activity in the midbrain. Painful peripheral stimuli release ADH. They are mediated by the spinothalamic and spinoreticular tracts and the lateral reticular formation of the medulla oblongata to release ADH. Painful, emotional, and stressful stimuli and changes in blood pressure all effect ADH release and the extracellular fluid volume. Therefore, stressful stimuli may play a role in affecting blood pressure levels in essential hypertension through this mechanism.

The Role of the Adrenal Gland in Essential Hypertension and High Blood Pressure: The Role of Adrenocortical Steroids

ADRENOCORTICAL DISEASE AND HIGH BLOOD PRESSURE

The source of aldosterone is the adrenal cortex. Knowledge of the adrenal gland is central to the understanding of the pathophysiology of essential hypertension. Its weight increases as hypertensive disease progresses (Cooper et al., 1958). In patients with severe hypertension, nodular hyperplasia of the adrenal cortex occurs (Russi et al., 1945; Shamma et al., 1958). The hyperplasia is a compensatory response to the disease and is not due to a primary hyperplasia seen in Conn's syndrome. The secondary form of hyperplasia may be the result of long-standing essential hypertension (Baer et al., 1970). Secondary hyperplasia may be associated with secondary aldosteronism, which can be difficult to distinguish clinically from Conn's syndrome (Conn, 1955, 1961). The relationship of high blood pressure levels to diseases of the adrenal cortex is complex. In Cushing's syndrome due to hyperplasia or adenomata of the adrenal cortex, the increased levels of blood pressure are ascribed to an increased production of hydrocortisone (Christy and Laragh, 1961) or of desoxycorticosterone by the gland (Crane and Harris, 1966). Therefore, high blood pressure levels can occur when one of several adrenocortical hormones are produced in excess.

ACTION OF ALDOSTERONE

Aldosterone, a mineralocorticoid, acts upon the distal tubules of the kidney and causes them to retain sodium and chloride ions and to excrete potassium ions. Aldosterone production and secretion is enhanced in Conn's syndrome, in the malignant phase of essential hypertension, in advanced unilateral renal disease with hypertension, in states in which chronic potassium loss with alkalosis occurs, and in the nephrotic or cirrhotic syndromes with edema. In these pathological states, salt administration does not lower aldosterone secretion as it normally does.

CONTROL OF ALDOSTERONE SECRETION

Angiotensin II is the main, but not the only, regulator of aldosterone production and secretion (Conn et al., 1965; Davis et al., 1962; Mulrow et al., 1962). Its secretion is also influenced by changes in sodium and potassium levels in the blood. Elevated potassium levels and low sodium levels increase aldosterone production but decrease renin secretion

165

(Cannon et al., 1966; Laragh and Stoerk, 1957; Ledingham et al., 1967). Conversely, reduced postassium levels in the serum correlate with reduced aldosterone blood levels (Cannon et al., 1966). Even very small changes in potassium levels produce changes in aldosterone secretion (Boyd and Mulrow, 1972). These changes are independent of the amount of angiotensin II in the blood. In fact, increased levels of serum potassium suppress plasma renin activity but they stimulate aldosterone secretion (Brunner et al., 1970). The effects of potassium on aldosterone secretion are independent of serum sodium levels. The sodium ion also indirectly affects aldosterone production and secretion. Sodium deprivation increases the secretion and renal disposition of aldosterone without measurably changing the concentration of sodium in blood plasma (Luetscher and Axelrad, 1954; Ulick et al., 1958). Changes in the fluid volume of the blood are inversely related to aldosterone excretion (Bartter et al., 1959, 1960). Aldosterone production and changes in the activity of the renin-angiotensin system are brought about by changes in the effective plasma volume (Jose et al., 1970)—and indirectly rather than directly by changes in levels of serum sodium (Bartter et al., 1959; Conn et al., 1965; Cope et al, 1961; Farrell, 1958; Muller et al., 1958; Murlow et al., 1962).

Aldosterone production is also regulated by the nervous system. Stimulation by an increased pulse pressure acting upon the mechanoreceptors at the junction of the thyroid and carotid arteries of the dog, reflexly inhibits aldersterone secretion. A fall in pulse pressure stimulates aldosterone secretion (Bartter et al., 1960). Afferent fibers of the vagus nerve mediate the effect on aldosterone secretion. (The efferent arc of the reflex control of aldosterone secretion is not known.) Increases in venous or right atrial pressure may also reflexly increase aldosterone secretion. The reflex is abolished by nephrectomy but not by denervation of the adrenal glands (Carpenter et al., 1961; Davis et al., 1960).

ACTH also has a transient stimulating effect on aldosterone secretion (Davis et al., 1970; Laragh, 1961), although aldosterone secretion is not altered very much by hypophysectomy. Therefore, the pituitary control of aldosterone secretion has not been firmly established, but is actively being investigated at the moment. The pineal gland has also been implicated in the regulation of aldosterone secretion (Yankopolous et al., 1959). Farrell (1959a, b) claimed that the pineal gland secretes a hormone that enhances aldosterone secretion. Later he claimed that another pineal factor inhibits the secretion of ACTH. He believed that the pineal gland produced two factors that could alter aldosterone secretion. This was confirmed by Wurtman et al. (1959) who found that pinealectomy was followed by adrenal hypertrophy. Juan (1963) showed that ACTH secretion increases after removal of the pineal gland. Pineal extracts, by inhibiting β-hydroxylation in the adrenal cortex, could reduce the production of aldosterone, cortisol, corticosterone, and cortisone (Mess, 1967). The concept that the pineal gland is involved in the regulation of aldosterone production has been challenged (Barbour et al., 1965; Davis, 1961; Denton, 1961; Wurtman et al., 1960).

In summary, aldosterone is regulated by angiotensin, the content of the potassium ion in blood serum, the extracellular fluid volume, and probably by increased blood pressure levels acting through mechanoreceptors in the arteries of the neck. It may also be under the control of the pituitary and pineal glands. Because aldosterone is intimately concerned with regulating the sodium and potassium content of body fluids, it is central to our understanding of blood pressure control. Excessive aldosterone secretion raises the blood pressure. Although increases of aldosterone secretion usually only occur in the advanced or malignant phases of hypertensive vascular disease, several lines of evidence suggest that in some subgroups of patients with essential hypertension the regulation of aldosterone secretion is disturbed. In other subgroups the rate of its metabolic disposition is retarded.

THE ROLE OF ALDOSTERONE IN ESSENTIAL HYPERTENSION

Angiotensin II consistently stimulates the secretion of aldosterone and, therefore, the retention in the body of salt and water. The renin-angiotensin-aldosterone mechanism is believed to play a part in initiating essential hypertension. Two lines of evidence argue against this hypothesis because increases in aldosterone secretion and excretion probably only occur in malignant or advanced cases of hypertension (Garst et al., 1960; Genest, 1961; Laragh et al., 1960), and are secondary to increased levels of renin and angiotensin II (Biron et al., 1961). In normal persons or patients with the normal or high-renin forms of hypertension, urinary aldosterone excretion is highly correlated with plasma renin levels (Laragh et al., 1972). However, there are instances of low-renin hypertension that are associated with deviations in the normal mechanisms regulating the interactions between renin, angiotensin II, and aldosterone. In the presence of low-plasma-renin (and presumably of low-angiotensin-II) activity, urinary aldosterone excretion can be low, normal, or high.

In low-renin hypertension considerable variation in the responses of renin and aldosterone levels to changes in sodium balance occur. In some instances renin levels vary with changes in sodium balance, but aldosterone excretion levels do not change; they remain high and fixed. In other instances, changes in sodium balance do not affect low-plasma-renin levels but do alter aldosterone excretion. In a fourth group of low-renin hypertensive patients, renin and aldosterone levels increase with a fall in sodium levels (Laragh et al., 1972). It has been suggested that the variations from the normal in low-renin hypertension are due to different disturbances in the usual feedback regulation of renin, aldosterone, and fluid volume (see Figure 1). When aldosterone levels are high and fixed, idiopathic bilateral adrenal hyperplasia may occur, despite normal potassium levels (Baer et al., 1970). Patients with a baseline of low renin levels and normal-to-high aldosterone excretion, which both respond to changes in sodium balance, have an increased sensitivity or responsiveness of the adrenal cortex to angiotensin II (Laragh et al., 1972). When low renin and low aldosterone levels occur in hypertensive patients, both responsive to shifts in sodium balance and fluid volume, the vasoconstrictive properties of angiotensin II (acting either on the brain stem or directly on blood vessels) may be enhanced. Alternatively, such patients may have a renal defect that produces an excessive reabsorption of salt in the presence of low aldosterone levels (Lowenstein et al., 1970). As a consequence, an abnormal expansion of plasma and extracellular fluid volume occurs (Jose et al., 1970).

Another explanation for the role of aldosterone in the pathophysiology of essential hypertension has been put forward by Genest (1974). Circulating levels of plasma aldosterone fall into the high-normal range in about one-third of patients with benign essential hypertension. They are somewhat raised, not because the production or secretion rates of aldosterone are high but because its metabolic clearance rates are lower than normal. These investigators suggest that a hepatic defect occurs in patients who have normal or low plasma renin levels and, therefore, should have normal or undetectable aldosterone levels. The abnormally low clearance rate of the mineralocorticoid may be due to a decreased hepatic blood flow that, in turn, may either reduce the chemical inactivation of aldosterone in the liver or increase its globulin-binding in plasma.

No one has proven that disturbances in aldosterone metabolism or its regulating mechanisms antecede the development of essential hypertension. But these new data suggest that patients with essential hypertension fall into several subgroups. Therefore, no single mechanism could account for the pathophysiology of all the subgroups of essential hypertension.

The Adrenal Corticoids: Cortisol and Desoxycorticosterone

The several glucocorticoids of the adrenal cortex play an enigmatic role in the pathogenesis of essential hypertension. One of the adrenal glucocorticoids that can produce elevated levels of blood pressure in animals is desoxycorticosterone. The mode of action of the glucocorticoids in essential hypertension is complex; they interact with and modify the action of aldosterone. They prevent prostaglandin release (Lewis and Piper, 1975). Aldosterone produces elevated blood pressure in patients treated for adrenal cortical insufficiency with glucocorticoids. In these patients the elevated blood pressure produced by aldosterone is associated with sodium retention, which is attenuated by cortisol and corticosterone (Leutscher et al., 1954, 1969, 1973; Ross et al., 1960). The production and secretion of the glucocorticoids is regulated by ACTH, which also produces acute increases in aldosterone secretion (Davis et al., 1970). If ACTH is administered for a prolonged time, aldosterone secretion either returns to normal or to subnormal levels (Newton and Laragh, 1968a) probably because of the associated increase of glucocorticoid secretion that reduces aldosterone production and secretion (Newton and Laragh, 1968b). Normally, the glucocorticoids appear to maintain vascular reactivity and the pressor response to norepinephrine (Fritz and Levine, 1951; Ramey et al., 1951). But in hypertensive patients glucocorticoids do not increase vascular reactivity to vasoconstrictors such as norepinephrine. Aldosterone and salt alter vascular reactivity instead (Mendlowitz, 1967) by increasing the water and salt content of the arteriolar wall and, hence, its elasticity (Knowlton, 1960; Laramore and Grollman, 1950; Tobian et al., 1961, 1969). The changes in vascular reactivity to norepinephrine in essential hypertension help to sustain elevated blood pressure levels but do not initiate them (Grollmam, 1960). Changes in serum levels of the glucocorticoids are the consequences of the advanced stages of hypertensive disease. In less-advanced hypertension, the *in vitro* synthesis of corticosterone in the adrenal glands is enhanced. In severe hypertensive disease, cortisol synthesis is depressed. Cortisol output in the adrenal vein, measured at the time of operation, is lower when diastolic blood pressure is higher (Cooper et al., 1958). Increases in plasma or urinary cortisol, cortisone, tetrahydrocortisone, or 17-hydroxycorticosteroids in essential hypertension occur in some patients or some forms of the disease (Genest et al., 1960; Vermeulen and Van der Straeten, 1963). Urinary

168

pregnanetriol, or the ratio of pregnanetriol to aldosterone, is depressed in essential, renal, or malignant hypertension (Genest et al., 1960; Vermeulen and Van der Straeten, 1963). Progesterone inhibits the sodium-retaining effect of aldosterone (Genest et al., 1960), as do other glucocorticoids, and both Genest et al. (1960) and Armstong (1959) have found that progesterone lowers the blood pressure of hypertensive patients, possibly by its effect on aldosterone levels.

In a series of patients with labile essential hypertension who were on a controlled diet of salt, 45 percent had progesterone levels three times higher than normal (Genest, 1974). When sodium intake is restricted, progesterone levels usually rise in normal subjects. In patients with high progesterone levels the increase is much less. Thus, there may be an inability to increase progesterone levels in these patients when their aldosterone levels are increased on a low-sodium diet. Therefore, in some patients with labile essential hypertension, another regulatory disturbance exists consisting of a diminished progesterone response to a low-salt diet. In the presence of this regulatory disturbance, the blood pressure would not fall as completely on a low-salt diet as it should.

A complete account of all the hormonal factors involved in blood pressure regulation and in essential hypertension has not yet been rendered: but the interactions of the hormones in the normal and diseased state are multiple and complex.

The mineralocorticoid desoxycorticosterone has potent hypertensive properties only in the presence of salt. On a diet poor in salt, large doses of desoxycorticosterone acetate produce modest elevations of blood pressure in the rat (Grollman et al., 1940; Knowlton et al., 1947; Selye et al., 1943). When rats drink a 1 percent salt solution the same dose of desoxycorticosterone acetate produces much greater elevations of blood pressure. The blood pressure remains high as long as the rats continue to drink saline. If the rat drinks ordinary drinking water instead of saline, the blood pressure falls. Gross (1956, 1960) and Gross and Lichtlen (1958) showed that the renin content of the kidney is directly proportional to the amounts of salt and water the rat ingests. If the salt intake is high, renin is released from the kidney in these rats.

Once excessive salt and desoxycorticosterone acetate have produced an elevated blood pressure and they are discountinued, the blood pressure falls to normal. But these rats remain permanently sensitive to excessive salt intake. They develop a high blood pressure when they again eat salt in excess. The rat is the only animal that develops high blood pressure when fed excessive amounts of salt after desoxycorticosterone acetate injections. The rabbit and the dog do not.

Desoxycorticosterone-salt hypertension in rats is associated with an increase in the activity of peripheral sympathetic nerves and of the adrenal medulla (De Champlain, 1972; De Champlain and Van Amerigen, 1973). While peripheral sympathetic activity increases, a decrease in norepinephrine turnover rates in the medulla oblongata occurs (De Champlain and van Amerigen, 1973; Nakamura et al., 1971). Sympathetic ganglionic blocking agents lower the blood pressure of pretreated rats but do not increase norepinephrine turnover rates in the medulla oblongata. The lowered turnover rates in the medulla are related to the increased peripheral sympathetic activity. If noradrenergic neurons in the medulla oblongata are destroyed by the prior intraventicular installation of 6-hydroxydopamine, high blood pressure levels and the increased peripheral sympathetic activity are prevented from occurring in treated rats (Finch et al., 1972). Once high blood pressure levels are established in these rats, 6-hydroxydopamine treatment does not lower them (Finch et al., 1972; Haeusler et al., 1972b).

Desoxycorticosterone-salt hypertension in rats is, therefore, mediated through the brain stem. The treatment with salt and desoxycorticosterone acetate lowers norepinephrine turnover rates. As noradrenergic activity in the medulla oblongata diminishes, peripheral sympathetic activity increases. Presumably, there are noradrenergic neurons in the brain stem that usually inhibit vasoconstrictor discharge down the spinal cord. In this form of experimental hypertension, the neurons are less-active and disinhibition occurs. Once high blood pressure levels are installed, some other mechanisms sustain them, because destruction of noradrenergic neurons in the medulla oblongata only prevents its development but does not "cure it."

The increased peripheral sympathetic activity is well-documented in this form of experimental hypertension. The increase should be accompanied by increases of blood levels of the enzyme DBH. But it is not. The elevated blood-pressure levels produced in rats by treatment with desoxycorticosterone acetate and salt actually results in a fall of serum DBH levels (Williams et al., 1972b). The repeated immobilization of rats also produces high blood pressure levels. In restrained rats the catecholamine synthesizing enzyme DBH is increased. Therefore, the conclusion is justified that different experimental techniques produce high blood pressure levels in rats by different mechanisms. Yet the same techniques may produce high blood pressure levels in one animal genus but not in another.

OTHER MINERALCORTICOIDS: THE ROLE OF 18-HYDROXY-DESOXYCORTICOSTERONE

Low-renin essential hypertension in man may be produced by the excessive production of another corticosteroid, 18-hydroxy-desoxycorticosterone (18-OH desoxycorticosterone) (Gross, 1971); 18-OH desoxycorticosterone is a mineralocoricoid that suppresses renin, aldosterone, and serum potassium levels, thereby causing salt and water retention. It is regulated by ACTH in man and in rat.

The administration of 18-OH desoxycorticosterone to unilaterally nephrectomized rats significantly increases the blood pressure to high levels (Oliver et al., 1973). Usually, it takes 16 days of the administration of 18-OH desoxycorticosterone for the blood pressure to increase in nephrectomized rats. But in the salt-sensitive strain of rats, no nephrectomy is required and 18-OH desoxycorticosterone plays a significant and etiologic role in elevating the blood pressure. In human hypertension the role of 18-OH desoxycorticosterone needs further clarification. It may play a pathogenetic but not an etiologic role in some forms of human essential hypertension. In other patients it may sustain high blood pressure levels.

THE ROLE OF THE CATECHOLAMINES IN ESSENTIAL HYPERTENSION

The central and peripheral sympathetic nervous system and the catecholamines have a wide variety of actions on the heart, the kidney, and the arterioles. Increased peripheral sympathetic activity may increase the heart rate, the force of the heart beat, and cardiac

170

output, contract arterioles to raise the peripheral resistance, and release renin (Davis, 1974). Central catecholaminergic and serotonergic neurons are involved in the control of the circulation and blood pressure (Chalmers, 1975). Central catecholaminergic mechanisms have been implicated in the initiation of several different forms of experimental high blood pressure in animals.

Nonetheless the role of the sympathetic nervous system and its neurotransmitters in the etiology and pathogenesis of essential hypertension are not fully understood. Several competing hypotheses that could account for the increase in peripheral resistance exist. One hypothesis proposes that increased tonic sympathetic vasoconstrictor activity leads to the increased release of norepinephrine within the arteriolar wall. Normally, norepinephrine produces only vasoconstriction in the skin, muscle, and intestinal blood vessels (Folkow and Uvnäs, 1948; Folkow et al., 1965; Youmans et al., 1955). The walls of these blood vessels contain only norepinephrine (Schmiterlow, 1948).

Another hypothesis states that there is a heightened sensitivity of the arterioles to normal tonic sympathetic activity. A third hypothesis holds that once hypertrophy of the arteriolar wall encroaches on its lumen, regular changes in sympathetic discharge produce an unusual increase in the resistance to blood flow (Folkow, 1952, 1971; Folkow et al., 1956). According to the last two hypotheses, sympathetic discharge and the release of neurotransmitter substances, either from the adrenal medulla or from the site of innervation of the arterioles, is normal, but the response of the arteriole is altered. The test of this alternative hypothesis is difficult and cannot be carried out merely by studying increased blood or urinary excretion levels of catecholamines.

Some investigators have found increase of catecholamine levels in essential hypertension early in its course (Engelman et al., 1970; Goodall and Bogdonoff, 1961; Holtz et al., 1947; von Euler et al., 1954) or only in the malignant phase of the disease (Goldenberg et al., 1948). Most investigators have found normal levels in every phase of the disease.

These contradictory results can partly be explained by the presence or absence of impaired kidney function. In hypertensive patients with normal kidney function, catecholamine excretion is increased. Impaired kidney function reduces catecholamine excretion (Ikoma, 1965).

That the catecholamines play a partial role either in etiology, pathogensis, or pathophysiology of essential hypertension is attested to by the fact that reserpine, monoamine oxidase inhibitors and a number of other drugs that affect catecholamine metabolism reduce the blood pressure in hypertensive patients (DiPalma, 1961). Reserpine is believed to produce its hypotensive effect mainly by depleting peripheral neuroeffector sites and sympathetic ganglia of their stores of catecholamines (Costa, 1961; Holzbauer and Vogt, 1956). Drugs that do not deplete peripheral norepinephrine stores do not lower the blood pressure. Guanethidine causes a fall in blood pressure by reducing the stores of norepinephrine at peripheral synapses. But reserpine also depletes the brain of serotonin and of the catecholamines. The hypotensive action of reserpine is probably partly mediated through its central, not only its peripheral, actions. Reserpine also lowers epinephrine and norepinephrine levels in the adrenal medulla (Kroneberg and Schümann, 1959). Reserpine given to cats and dogs causes a slow and progressive decline in efferent splanchnic nerve activity and a fall in blood pressure. The effect of reserpine

171

on blood pressure is different from that produced by tetraethylammonium chloride and mecamylamine, which act peripherally, (McCubbin and Page, 1958). Some drugs that are effective in the treatment of human essential hypertension may act only peripherally, while others act both centrally and peripherally to reduce sympathetic activity.

Much remains to be learned: in animals the same drugs may increase or have no effects on blood pressure levels (Brodie and Costa, 1961; Franco-Browder et al., 1958). The fact that these drugs lower the blood pressure in humans suggests that the sympathetic nervous system plays some role—perhaps only a sustaining one—in essential hypertension.

Conversely, a genetic and predisposing defect may be present in the form of the altered synthesis, storage or disposition of the catecholamines. De Champlain et al. (1969) have suggested that this defect consists of a reduced capacity of the storage granules in sympathetic nerve endings to bind and store norepinephrine. In rats made hypertensive by pretreatment with desoxycorticosterone acetate and salt, an inverse relationship exists between the systolic blood pressure and the capacity of the heart to store norepinephrine. As a result of a failure to store it, larger amounts of free norepinephrine are physiologically active in these animals. The increased liberation of norepinephrine precedes the increase in blood pressure in these animals.

The increased turnover of norepinephrine has been described in experimental neurogenic hypertension in various species of animals, in rats of the spontaneously hypertensive strain (Louis et al., 1968), and in rats made hypertensive by encapsulating one kidney and removing the other (Volicer et al., 1968). Impaired storage of the catecholamines in hypertensive human subjects has also been described (Gitlow et al., 1964) and may explain the reports of increased excretion of the catecholamines if the kidney functions normally (Stott and Robinson, 1967).

Once released, the catecholamines may play another role in essential hypertension by their effects on electrolyte metabolism and the kidney. Small or intermediate doses of injected norepinephrine increase urine flow, presumably by reducing ADH secretion (Pickford, 1952). When norepinephrine is given in larger doses, glomerular filtration rate and urine volume are diminished (Handley and Moyer, 1954; King and Baldwin, 1956). The reduction of filtration rate is always accompanied by a reduction in the excretion of sodium and potassium (King and Baldwin, 1956; McSmythe et al., 1952; Mills et al., 1953). In normal subjects infusion of a saline solution after sympathetic transmission is blocked with guanethidine increases the excretion of sodium and usually enhances the glomerular filtration rate. If, in addition to sodium and guanethidine, a mineralocorticoid is injected, the excretion of sodium is still increased (Gill et al., 1964). Therefore, the catecholamines play a complex role in the regulation of electrolyte metabolism and modify the effects of corticosteroids.

In patients with labile, borderline hypertension, an increased β-adrenergic drive on the heart raises the cardiac output. When lying down, these patients excrete more than the usual amounts of epinephrine and norepinephrine in the urine. When these patients sit up their norepinephrine levels rise further and excessively, their epinephrine levels fall slightly, their dopamine levels fall less than expected, and their plasma renin activity increase more than in normotensive persons. On a low-sodium diet the differences between borderline hypertensive patients and normotensive subjects disappear.

Therefore, in labile, borderline essential hypertension there seems to be excessive adrenergic activity and mildly increased plasma renin levels (Frohlich et al., 1970), in contrast with normal and other forms of essential hypertension, which have stable, elevated blood pressure levels and normal cardiac output. In patients with borderline hypertension isoproterenol produces a greater and more persistent increase in renin activity (Genest, 1974) that is blocked by propranolol (Hamet et al., 1973a, b).

In labile, borderline hypertension the sympathetic nervous system exerts its effects by increasing renin activity, cardiac output and heart rate, sodium retention, and a positive sodium balance. In these patients, increases in peripheral vascular resistance eventually occur, and other and sustaining mechanisms take over to produce more-stable elevated blood pressure levels with a normal cardiac output.

The cause of the increased sympathetic nervous system activity early in borderline hypertension is unknown. In this form of hypertension the sympathetic nervous system probably plays a primary, initiating role. But we do not know whether the increased sympathetic activity is central or peripheral in origin. If it could be shown that the increased sympathetic nervous system is central in origin, the neurogenic theory of some, if not all forms of essential hypertension would receive some support. In the meantime, patients with borderline and labile essential hypertension should be studied socially and psychologically in order to try to account for their increased sympathetic activity.

The Role of the Central Nervous System in the Control of Blood Pressure and in Essential Hypertension

MULTIFACTOR AND NEUROGENIC THEORIES OF ESSENTIAL HYPERTENSION

The neurogenic theory of the etiology and pathogenesis of essential hypertension is currently not popular. In its original form it placed the entire burden for the etiology of the disease on the central nervous system and its autonomic and neuroendocrine outflow tracts. The neurogenic theory has been replaced by multifactor theories of etiology, the best known of which is Page's mosaic theory (1960). Multifactor hypotheses are favored by many besides Page (Peterson, 1963; Pickering, 1961; Shapiro, 1973). These theorists contend that linear, single-cause, explanatory theories do not adequately cover the clinical facts. They contend that there are many regulatory mechanisms in equilibrium that control tissue perfusion and blood pressure. Some of these mechanisms are chemical; others are neural and cardiovascular: they regulate cardiac output, blood volume and viscosity, electrolyte and water balance, and the caliber, elasticity, and reactivity of blood vessels. Each mechanism in turn influences the other (See Figure 2).

The mosaic or other multifactor theories lack parsimony, but they do account for most of the known facts about the disease. Multifactor theories imply the operation of complex feedback regulatory devices in normal blood pressure control and in essential hypertension. Any one of these regulatory devices may be biased, or may deviate from the norm, in essential hypertension to alter their interrelationships. The multifactor theories do not tell us how these relationships are altered to produce essential hypertension or the exact nature of these alterations: hereditary and congenital factors may produce structural alterations to effect the function of the kidney. For example, these alterations may lie

173

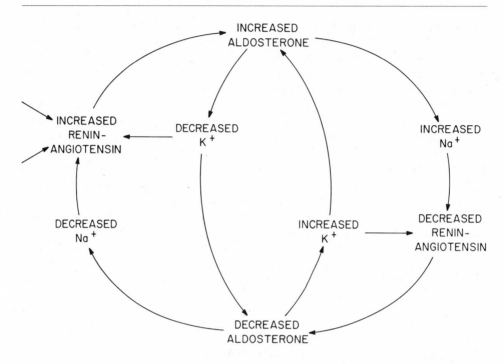

FIGURE 2 The relationships, including feedback regulatory mechanisms, of some of the main mechanisms involved in the maintenance of blood pressure, which have also been implicated in the pathogenesis of essential hypertension. The vertical arrows indicate increases (↑) or decreases (↓) of levels: for example, an increase (↑) of angiotensin II levels in the blood is reflected in increased secretion of aldosterone (↑) and vice versa. The other arrows (→) depict both the positive (as in the foregoing example) and negative feedback regulatory mechanisms involved in the control of blood pressure: other mechanisms are not displayed.

dormant and blood pressure levels may be normal, until a drug, such as the oral contraceptive pill, elicits the latent tendency.

In women who develop hypertension when taking oral contraceptives, some have family histories of hypertension, or they have congenital fibromuscular hyperplasia of the renal artery that has been "dormant" and only reveals itself in hypertension after the oral contraceptive is taken (Shapiro, 1973). The family history or the congenital renal artery lesion constitute latent tendencies to high blood pressure that are activated by the oral contraceptives. Each one of these factors by itself is insufficient to raise the blood pressure. Not every woman taking the pill develops hypertension.

Most multifactor theories about the nature of essential hypertension emphasize the etiological role of disturbances in autoregulatory mechanisms in the arterioles, in the kidney, or in the regulatory relationship between the kidney and the adrenal gland. Changes in the regulation of these organ systems by the brain are not currently emphasized in etiological or pathogenetic theories of essential or other forms of hypertension. It was once argued that the nervous system could not be involved in the pathogenesis of renal hypertension because renal denervation does not prevent the de-

174

velopment of renal hypertension (Page, 1935). The pathogenetic role of the sympathetic nervous system in essential hypertension was also dismissed, because prolonged stimulation of the splanchnic nerves fails to produce self-perpetuating, chronic hypertension in dogs (Kubicek et al., 1953). Until recently no clear-cut evidence existed that excesses or aberrations in pressor catecholamine levels or metabolism contribute to the etiology of any form of essential hypertension (Wilson, 1961; Page and McCubbin, 1965). With the development of new techniques, it has been shown that, at least in some hospitalized patients with essential hypertension, plasma or urinary catecholamine levels are elevated (Engelman et al., 1970; Frohlich et al., 1970).

The most telling argument against the neurogenic hypothesis is the evidence that the kidney is the primary initiating agent of essential hypertension. A normal kidney transplanted into a hypertensive patient will develop the vascular lesions of malignant hypertension unless the diseased kidney is removed (Merrill et al., 1956; Murray et al., 1958). Either the high blood pressure levels or the diseased kidney in some way turns the normal kidney into a diseased one.

In animals, hypertension occurs when both kidneys are removed (Braun-Menendez and von Euler, 1947; Grollman et al., 1949). When a normal kidney is then transplanted into a dog without kidneys, the blood pressure returns to normal levels (Kolff et al., 1954). The high blood pressure in an animal without kidneys seems to depend, in part, on the amounts of sodium and protein in the diet (Orbison et al., 1952; Kolff and Page, 1954) or on increased hydration that presumably causes an increased effective plasma volume (Merrill et al., 1961).

These examples are powerful arguments for the role of the kidney in the pathogenesis of essential hypertension. In the first example, a normal kidney becomes diseased. The inference can be drawn from the second example that the kidney regulates the blood pressure by virtue of its role in maintaining the extracellular fluid volume in an equilibrium condition.

The kidney also contains the antihypertensive prostaglandins; therefore, removing it would deprive the body of these substances. Small wonder that the kidney is often considered to be the main initiator of essential hypertension.

The disease is considered by many to be due to an autoregulatory disturbance within the kidney, specifically an imbalance between its hypertensive and antihypertensive mechanisms. Alternatively, Floyer (1955) has suggested that the kidney maintains a normal blood pressure by inhibiting extrarenal pressor mechanisms. This inhibitory mechanism is impaired either by constriction of a renal artery or a fall in renal artery pressure and the subsequent release of renin. Once impaired, a disinhibition of the extrarenal pressor mechanisms occurs and blood pressure levels rise. The pressor mechanisms are sustained by the brain.

Certainly, congenital and acquired kidney disease produces secondary hypertension. Essential hypertension can also eventuate in kidney disease that sustains high blood pressure levels. The evidence is certainly very strong that the kidney can initiate and sustain high blood pressure levels. Therefore, multifactor theories are unnecessary to explain the pathogensis of essential hypertension.

Nonetheless, strong evidence exists that even when the kidney initiates high blood pressure levels, it does so through the mediation of the brain. The development of high

175

blood pressure in animals, produced by renal artery constriction, can be averted by pretreatment with intraventricular 6-hydroxydopamine that destroys catecholaminergic neurons (Chalmers, 1975). But once high blood pressure levels are established in these animals, 6-hydroxydopamine treatment does not lower the blood pressure (Finch et al., 1972; Lewis et al., 1973). The sequence of events is probably as follows: constricting the renal artery releases renin and angiotensin II is produced. Angiotensin II enters the brain via the area postrema (Joy and Lowe, 1970; Lewis et al., 1973) to produce powerful pressor effects that are in turn mediated by sympathetic discharge (Ferrario et al., 1969, 1972; Fukyama et al., 1973; Gildenberg, 1971; Scroop and Lowe, 1968; Sweet and Brody, 1970). Angiotensin II, when infused in very small amounts intervertebrally, significantly increases the blood pressure. Its effect can be blocked by pretreatment with reserpine (Sweet and Brody, 1971) and by destruction of central catecholaminergic neurons. The sympathetic discharge not only produces vasoconstriction but may release more renin from the kidney (Bunag et al., 1966).

The brain, therefore, appears to participate in the initial rise in blood pressure produced by experimental renal artery constriction. Hypertension can be produced experimentally by many other methods. In these other forms of experimental hypertension, the brain seems to pay a primary initiating, not only a mediating, role.

Hypertension can also be produced by denervation of the baroreceptors (Kezdi, 1967), by conditioning techniques, and by social manipulation. The development of spontaneous hypertension in selected strains of rats can be prevented by the intraventricular injection of 6-hydroxydopamine (Finch et al., 1972). The brain also participates in the development of desoxycorticosterone-salt hypertension in rats. Therefore, the brain is either involved in the initiation or the mediation of the initial phases of experimental hypertension. Because destruction of central catecholaminergic neurons prevents the development of some forms of experimental hypertension but does not "cure" it, one may conclude that a different chain of mechanisms are involved in initiating than in sustaining high blood pressure levels. If this conclusion is correct, the multifactor theory is alos correct.

THE ROLE OF THE CENTRAL NERVOUS SYSTEM
IN THE INITIATION OF HYPERTENSION

Central to current psychosomatic theories is that is that social and psychological factors predispose to initiate, sustain, or alter the course of essential hypertension. Some experiments in animals support the idea that social and psychological factors may initiate hypertension, presumably through the brain. Other experiments suggest that the primary initiating role of the kidney is mediated through the brain. Conversely, there is also evidence that the brain can alter the function of the kidney and many other systems that regulate blood pressure levels.

The brain also participates in the regulation of the autonomic nervous system, renal artery flow, ADH output, adrenal corticosteroid, and renin release. It ultimately regulates plasma volume, salt and water metabolism, and the peripheral resistance. The central nervous system is sometimes thought to have no influence in essential hypertension because a direct neural effect on the kidney has not been demonstrated. Yet the nervous system can modify renal function in other ways (Hoff and Green, 1936; Lund, 1943). Psychological stimuli decrease diodrast clearance, increase insulin clearance, and diminish renal plasma flow (Meehan, 1960; Smith, 1939, 1940). Stimulation of the supraorbital gyrus diminishes renal blood flow (Cort, 1953). Hoff et al (1951) produced renocortical ischemia sufficient to produce tubular necrosis by stimulation of the anterior sigmoid gyrus of cats. Stimulation of the dorsal medulla lateral to the midline increases blood pressure and urine volume and diminishes the glomerular filtration rate. Stimulation at the level of the obex increases glomerular filtration rate and urine volume (Wise and Ganong, 1960).

Therefore, the initial impetus to high blood pressure may be imparted by the brain to the kidney, because the brain can lower renal artery blood flow and release renin. Alternatively, the brain may initially act to disinhibit the inhibitory action of the kidney on extrarenal pressor mechanisms. Once the function of the kidney is altered, reflex sympathetic activity may increase (Chalmers, 1975; Reed et al., 1944). In fact, in experimental renal hypertension, there is a decreased hypotensive response to agents blocking the sympathetic ganglia and to attempts to reduce the increased sympathetic vasoconstriction and stimulation of the heart (Henning, 1969; Kezdi, 1962; Kezdi and Wennemark, 1958; Page and McCubbin, 1951; Volicer et al., 1969). Chemical or immunosympathectomy of peripheral sympathetic nerves prevents the development of renal hypertension, especially if chemical sympathectomy is combined with adrenalectomy (Ayitey-Smith and Varma, 1970; De Champlain and van Amerigen, 1973; Finch et al., 1972; Haeusler et al., 1972b). In rabbits, the longer experimental renal hypertension lasts, the less likely is nephrectomy to lower the blood pressure (Pickering, 1945), a result suggesting that renal hypertension is eventually sustained by an extrarenal mechanism.

Destruction of the nervous system by pithing reduces the elevated arterial pressure in experimental renal hypertension, however long-standing. If pithing is carried out while angiotensin is infused, the blood pressure is not reduced, which suggests that angiotensin in sufficient dosage acts directly on the circulation (Dock, 1940; Taquini et al., 1961).

Other experiments have also suggested that a tandem mechanism is involved in the experimental renal hypertension that is produced by interfering with the renal circulation (Drury and Schapiro, 1956; Gomez et al., 1960; Reed et al., 1944). The experiments have indicated that at first a pressor substance is released by the kidney and later an additional (perhaps neural) mechanism is involved in sustaining elevated blood pressure levels.

SOME GENERAL PRINCIPLES: THE DIFFERENTIAL REGULATION OF CARDIOVASCULAR MECHANISMS BY THE BRAIN

Conclusions drawn from studies on the neurogenic control of blood pressure are limited. Much of our knowlege about the regulation of the circulation and the control of blood pressure by the nervous system is derived from observations made on excised organs and anesthetized animals. Only with the development of new recording methods has it become feasible to make observations on intact unanesthetized animals. These new techniques eliminate the various artifacts caused by exposing the heart and lungs in acute experiments and by anesthesia. Behavioral observations can also be made in intact,

177

unanesthetized animals. Behavior and cardiovascular function can be studied together during exercise, while the animal is interacting with its environment, or while brain stimulation is being carried out. Chronic brain stimulation may be used to induce elevations of blood pressure while an animal's behavior is observed.

The rapid cardiovascular adjustments that precede and accompany exercise demonstrate the participation of the brain in the regulation of the circulation. These adjustments were once thought to be instigated solely by peripheral mechanisms. The onset of vasodilation, increased blood flow in muscle, increased heart rate and cardiac output in anticipation and at the start of exercise are produced by the nervous system. They are the autonomic concomitants of the muscular activity of exercise. The cardiovascular changes at the start of exercise can be abolished by lesions in the fields of Forel. They can be reproduced by stimulation in this area in resting animals (Rushmer, 1958). Therefore, integrated patterns of cardiovascular and motor activity on exercise are orchestrated by the brain.

Different cardiovascular changes may be quite specific to a given behavioral state, or activity. In man, integrated patterns of cardiovascular changes occur in emotional states and during mental effort or physical exercise (Barcroft et al., 1960; Blair et al., 1959; Brod, 1959, 1970). In animals, too, quite specific cardiovascular changes occur during different behavioral states, including during states with strong emotional overtones. In preparing to fight another cat, a cat shows bradycardia, a decreased cardiac output, and vasoconstriction in the iliac and mesenteric vessels. When he strikes the other cat, the heart rate and cardiac output increase, the iliac bed dilates, and the mesenteric bed constricts. In neither case does the blood pressure rise very much (Adams et al., 1968).

Theoretically, stimulation at different brain sites should also produce different patterns of changes in the circulation. This occurs in practice. Stimulation of the cerebral cortex facilitates vasomotor discharge and increases the blood pressure. The stimulus is mediated by the pyramidal tract that begins in the sigmoid gyrus and the pericruciate cortex. The pyramidal tract regulates vasomotor activity through collaterals to the pons and medulla (Landau, 1953; Rossi and Brodal, 1956; Wall and Davis, 1951). Stimulating the pyramidal tract electrically raises the blood pressure and produces movements. Other cortical areas may produce their pressor effects by pathways to the hypothalamus, because lesions of the hypothalamus abolish vasomotor responses to stimulation of the surfaces of the posterior orbital gyrus.

On stimulation of frontal and temporal cortex, the blood pressure can be both raised and lowered in many mammals, including man (Anand and Dua, 1956a, b; Kaada et al., 1949; Sachs et al., 1949). Several rhinencephalic areas (the anterior limbic cortex, anterior insula, and the hippocampal gyrus) produce significant changes in blood pressure when stimulated electrically (Kaada, 1951). The cingulate gyrus and the amygdala are also involved in blood pressure regulation (Anand and Dua, 1956a; Kaada, 1951; Pool and Ransohoff, 1949; Ward, 1948). When a number of midline structures—the non-specific thalamic nuclei and the midbrain reticular system—are subjected to high-frequency electrical stimulation, marked elevations of blood pressure occur. The effects of such stimulation persist after stimulation ceases. Stimulation of the vermis of the cerebellum modifies ongoing activity in bulbopontine, vasomotor, and hypothalamic centers, and can produce either elevation or depression of blood pressure levels (Moruzzi, 1940, 1950; Zanchetti and Zoccolini, 1954).

178

High-frequency stimulation of the hypothalamus produces acute phasic increases in blood pressure (Hess, 1949). The rate of hypothalamic stimulation is linearly related to the discharge frequency in single fibers of the inferior-cardiac and cervical-sympathetic nerves: the higher the rate of hypothalamic stimulation, the greater is the discharge frequency. Hypothalamic stimulation also increases the blood pressure increments produced by stimulation of a peripheral sensory nerve (Pitts et al., 1941, 1941/2). After hypothalamic stimulation is ended, the blood pressure remains elevated for several minutes due to the release of vasopressin or of catecholamines (Berry et al., 1942; Bronk et al., 1939). Local vasoconstriction in blood vessels has been observed when the hypothalamus is stimulated (Eliasson et al., 1952, 1954). These responses to stimulation are mediated by the brain-stem pressor mechanisms (Alexander, 1946; Lindgren, 1955; McQueen et al., 1954; Wang and Ranson, 1939).

When the hypothalamus is stimulated, adrenergic (vasoconstrictor) discharge is distributed to the entire vascular bed with the exception of skeletal muscle, in which vasodilatation occurs (Eichna and McQuarrie, 1960; Eliasson et al., 1952, 1954; Lindgren, 1955; Lindgren and Uvnäs, 1954; Uvnäs, 1960). The same effects on the vascular bed occur when vasoconstrictor fibers are activated by cerebral cortical stimulation (Löfving, 1961).

Hypothalamic stimulation also elicits a behavioral response called the "defense" reaction, first described by Hess (1949) in the cat. During this reaction sympathetically mediated vasodilation occurs in muscle, accompanied by an increased heart rate, vasoconstriction in vascular beds other than muscle, and the increased secretion of catecholamines (Abrahams et al., 1960) and ACTH (Folkow et al., 1965). When the defense reaction is elicited, the cat growls, hisses, runs, and its pupils are dilated and its fur stands up (Hess, 1949; Hunsperger, 1956). The reaction is brought about by stimulation of the hypothalamus near the entrance of the fornix, the dorsomedial amygdala, and the striae terminalis (Fernandez de Molina and Hunsperger, 1959, 1962). The cerebral cortex in turn attenuates the violence of the defense reaction produced by stimulation of the hypothalamic sites. Repetitive stimulation of the same site permanently increases blood pressure levels in some animals. Folkow and Rubinstein (1966) produced sustained hypertension in rats by mild and intermittent daily stimulation, for several months, of the perifornical area of the hypothalamus. The implications of this study are manifold. Folkow (1971) has pointed out that activation of this area of the brain leads to dilatation of the blood vessels in muscle and constriction of the renal circulation to produce the release of renin and angiotensin, which, in turn, may act directly on the brain stem to raise the blood pressure.

The Regulation of Blood Pressure and Peripheral Resistance by the Central Nervous System

Central to our current notions about the regulation of blood pressure by the brain is that changes in vasomotor tone are brought about by variations in vasoconstrictor activity: decreased vasoconstrictor discharge leads to vasodilation and a fall in blood pressure, increased discharge to vasoconstriction and an increase in the blood pressure (Folkow and Uvnäs, 1950; Lindgren and Uvnäs, 1954). Vasoconstrictor tone is partly controlled by afferent impulses passing from the carotid sinus baroreceptors and aortic arch

179

mechanoreceptors that respond to increased in arterial pCO_2. Stimulation of the baroreceptors leads to vasoconstriction (Heymans and Neil, 1958). The mechanoreceptors respond to their pulsatile distension (Ead et al., 1952) and to the rate with which changes in arterial pressure occur (Peterson, 1961). From the carotid mechanoreceptors, afferent impulses pass via the sinus nerve to the medullary vasomotor centers. The mechanreceptors usually discharge in rhythmic bursts, beginning with the start of systole and ending as the pulse wave passes (Douglas et al., 1956; Douglas and Ritchie, 1956; Landgren, 1952). When the arterial pressure is high, neural discharge is sustained not phasic (Bronk and Stella, 1932). Adaptation to the high pressures occurs eventually so that neural discharge diminishes in rate. As a result of this adaptation the high blood pressure is not reflexly reduced.

Tonic neuronal activity in the sinus nerve is always present; cutting the sinus nerve immediately raises the blood pressure. Therefore, afferent tonic activity in the sinus nerve reflexly inhibits vasoconstrictor tone and continually prevents the blood pressure from rising.

Other afferent impulses also arise from receptors in the atrial walls of the heart and ventricles and from the walls of the great veins. All afferent neuronal activity from the various receptors in the heart and great vessels pass to the vasomotor centers in the medulla oblongata. The vasomotor centers also receive neuronal input from other parts of the body through sympathetic afferent fibers that first enter the spinal cord. The fibers travel up an ipsilateral pathway in the fasciculus gracilis and a bilateral one in the anterolateral portion of the cord. These pathways reach the posterior hypothalamus, the thalamus, and the cerebral cortex and act as the afferent arm of circuits that eventually feed back into the vasomotor center (Amassian, 1951; Downman, 1955). Afferent baroreceptor and mechanoreceptor impulses first pass to the nucleus of the tractus solitarius (NTS) in the medulla. From this nucleus, inhibitory neurons pass to the pressor vasomotor center, and excitatory neurons pass to the depressor center. Inhibitory catecholaminergic neurons also enter the depressor center. These catecholaminergic neurons probably originate from the higher parts of the brain stem and hypothalamus. Other catecholaminergic neurons from higher centers pass to the NTS (Fuxe, 1965) and to the pressor center. Their exact function is not known. Destruction of the NTS releases the pressor center from inhibition, and high blood pressure levels occur (Doba and Reis, 1973, 1974). The pressor center lies in the lateral reticular formation of the rostral two-thirds of the medulla oblongata. The depressor center lies medially and caudally in the reticular formation of the medulla (Alexander, 1946; Korner, 1971; Ranson and Billingsley, 1916). Tonic inhibitory impulses to spinal vasomotor mechanisms emanate from the depressor zone (Wang and Ranson, 1939). These inhibitory neurons may be serotonergic (Neumayr et al., 1974). The neurons of both centers are constantly active (Alexander, 1946). Tonic excitatory influences mediated by noradrenergic neurons from the pressor area impinge on spinal vasomotor neurons (Chalmers and Wurtman, 1971). The synaptic events at spinal vasomotor neurons causing increased or decreased discharge are not known (Humphrey, 1967).

The intensity of the discharge in preganglionic vasoconstrictor neurons is the resultant of the excitatory and inhibitory tonic impulses that flow from the brain stem (Alexander, 1945). The frequency of tonic discharge in vasoconstrictor nerves is low (Bronk et al., 1936; Celander and Folkow, 1953; Folkow, 1952); the discharge occurs in rhythmic

180

bursts, in concert with the pulse beat and the respiratory rhythm (Dontas, 1955). The fall in arterial blood pressure on activation of the baroreceptor reflex causes a decrease in spinal sympathetic neuronal discharge, diminished activity in noradrenergic postganglionic nerves, vasodilation in muscle, the splanchnic bed, and the skin (von Euler, 1956; Folkow et al, 1950; Uvnäs, 1960).

Acute and chronic elevations in arterial pressure—neurogenic hypertension—results from denervation of the baroreceptors and mechanoreceptors (Hering, 1923; Koch, 1931). In experimental neurogenic hypertension blood pressure levels fluctuate wildly and tachycardia occurs. Destruction of central noradrenergic and dopaminergic neurons by 6-hydroxydopamine both prevents the development and "cures" established neurogenic hypertension (Chalmers and Wurtman, 1971). Destruction of central serotonergic neurons also prevents neurogenic hypertension (Wing and Chalmers, 1974).

Denervating the baroreceptors and producing neurogenic hypertension is an instructive experiment that does not necessarily prove that the baroreceptors play a role in the pathogenesis of essential hypertension. In human hypertension the carotid sinus (baroreceptor) reflex remains active and functioning, but the baroreceptors gradually adapt to high blood pressure levels and no longer act maximally to reduce them. The adaptation occurs in dogs within one to two days after a renal artery is clamped to produce high blood pressure (McCubbin, 1958), and it is characterized by an increase both in the threshold and a decrease in the range of response to stimulation. The sinus nerve shows a decrease in hypertensive animals (McCubbin et al., 1956). The adaptation to high blood pressure levels may be due to the direct effect of the high systemic arterial pressures rather than to some chemical substance that is liberated (Kezdi, 1962). The adaptation of the baroreceptors to an elevated mean blood pressure would act to sustain it; the decrease in afferent discharge would lead to a decreased inhibition of vasomotor tone and, therefore, to vasoconstriction. Therapeutic measures have been devised to counteract baroreceptor adaptation in human hypertension. Electrical stimulation of the sinus nerve (to restore neural activity after adaptation) lowers blood pressure in hypertensive patients (Bilgutay and Lillehei, 1965; Schwartz and Griffith, 1967).

In addition to lowering the blood pressure, stimulating the baroreceptors by stretching has effects on the brain. Bonvallet et al. (1956) distended the carotid sinus while keeping the blood pressure at a constant level. They produced synchronization of the electroencephalogram (EEG). They believe that an increase in afferent activity occludes the tonic, corticopetal, desynchronizing influences of the midbrain reticular-activating formation. Therefore, it is possible that when baroreceptor adaptation occurs in human hypertension, cortical desynchronization and behavioral arousal might be produced.

Elevated blood pressure levels affect the brain directly, in addition to those effects mediated by mechanoreceptors. Thus, Baust et al. (1963) have reported that raising the blood pressure directly causes desynchronization of the EEG in the *encephale isolé* cat, by virtue of its effect on the mesencephalic reticular formation. The mechanical effect of a rise in blood pressure may cause the firing rate of single posterior hypothalamic and mesencephalic reticular neurons to increase (Baust and Katz, 1961; Baust et al., 1962). This mechanical stimulus to the brain may also cause the release of humoral substances, such as vasopressin.

This brief review of the brain mechanisms involved in cardiovascular regulation suggests that medullary and spinal vasomotor neurons are reflexly controlled by afferent input from mechanoreceptors, but are also powerfully influenced by sensory inputs, by motor mechanisms, and by numerous circuits from diverse areas of the brain. In addition to the classical vasomotor mechanisms, a separate sympathetic vasodilator system has been described (Eliasson et al., 1952, 1954; Lindgren, 1955; Löfving, 1961; Uvnäs, 1960). This second system may be responsible for the integrated motor and circulatory changes seen with exercise and difficult intellectual tasks. Activation of this system produces phasic constriction of the splanchnic bed and increases in blood pressure. It is not yet known whether such changes are related to the onset of hypertension. Perhaps the only certainty is that the central nervous system is involved in sustaining high levels of blood pressure due to adaptation of the baroreceptors, and that a lowering of blood pressure occurs when the sinus nerve is stimulated electrically.

The increased appetite for salt in patients with hypertension, the confirmed evidence of the action of angiotensin II on the brain stem, and the regulation of the adrenal cortex and medulla by the hypothalmic-pituitary axis all point to the participation of the central nervous system in some phase of essential hypertension.

SUMMARY AND CONCLUSIONS

Anyone attempting to assess the current status of this field must hesitate in making any definitive statement about the predisposition to, initiation of, and sustaining factors in high blood pressure. Such a hesitation is occasioned by the realization that many of the most hallowed ideas about essential hypertension have undergone drastic revision in the past 20 years. It was once believed that cardiac output was normal in patients with essential hypertension who were not in cardiac failure. This belief has been shattered by the observation of an enhanced cardiac output in some patients with an early, "labile" form of the illness, who have borderline elevations of blood pressure.

The implication of this finding is that the initial phase of the disease is different in different patients. Presumably, different physiological mechanisms underlie different forms of the initial phase of the disease. In borderline, labile hypertension, the increased cardiac output seems to be due to increased β-adrenergic sympathetic stimulation of the heart. In other forms of early high blood pressure, plasma renin levels may be elevated. Still other hypertensive patients have a low plasma renin activity. Essential hypertension can also occur in association with normal plasma renin activity. But the interesting aspect of the relationship of plasma renin activity to essential hypertension is not the level of this enzyme's activity, but the fact that in many patients there are a variety of disturbances in the regulation of aldosterone by renin and its product, angiotensin II.

Shapiro (1973) has pointed out that with the exception of reninomas, pheochromocytomas, and aldosterinomas, no single physiological disturbance will fully account for the elevated blood pressure of essential hypertension in all its forms. The conclusion that does emerge at the present time is that essential hypertension comes about by a variety of disturbances in the relationship between the various systems involved in the regulation of blood pressure. Essential hypertension is a heterogeneous condition brought about by various mechanisms. No single cause, or single change in the level of a hormone or enzyme, will explain the etiology, pathogenesis, or pathophysiology of all forms of essential hypertension. The disturbances in the mechanisms of blood pressure regulation are different at different stages of the disease, and in different stages in its subgroups. These general conclusions are supported by work on animals. High blood pressure can be produced by many different experimental manipulations—from altering the early social experiences of the animal to constricting one renal artery. Not all strains of one species of animals respond with high blood pressure to the same experimental manipulation. The same experimental procedure also produces high blood pressure in one animal genus and not another. And when members of different animal genera are subjected to the same procedure the mechanisms that produce high blood pressure differ.

In animals high blood pressure can be produced by varying their early and later social experiences. These experiences also affect the neurochemistry of the brain and the later behavior of these animals. The brain mediates the effects of social experiences. It also mediates the effect of desoxycorticosterone acetate and salt treatment of rats, the hypertensive effects of carotid sinus denervation, and the initiation of high blood pressure in the spontaneously hypertensive rat. The brain, through its regulation of vasomotor tone participates in the initiation of these various forms of high blood pressure in different ways. Once high blood pressure levels are instituted, other mechanisms in the body may sustain them.

These conclusions are relevant to the discussion of psychological factors in essential hypertension. In a general way, animal experiments support the notion that social and psychological factors in human beings may play an etiological and pathogenetic role in essential hypertension. These experiments underline the importance of prior experience and of social conflict in producing high blood pressure, renal disease, and changes in brain and adrenal neurotransmitter substances and their biosynthetic enzymes. They support the idea that these physiological changes are the consequences of changes in social conditions and behavior. A note of caution must be introduced at this point. Social and psychological factors may play a role in some but not all subgroups of the disease. Alternatively, these factors may play more of a role in some but not all forms of the disease, or at some stage of the disease and not at other stages. For example, the inception of the malignant phase of essential hypertension has been correlated with changes in the personal life of hypertensive patients or in the doctor-patient relationship.

Psychosocial factors do not by themselves "cause" essential hypertension. Genetic factors also predispose to the disease. Even the high blood pressure of renovascular disease is usually associated with a family history of high blood pressure (Shapiro, 1973; Shapiro et al., 1969). The exact nature of these family factors is unknown. They may or may not be genetic.

The social environment seems to play a major role in preventing or facilitating the development of high blood pressure in genetically predisposed human beings. Social injustice, dislocation and disruption, physical danger, violence, marital discord, separation, and poverty promote high blood pressure, fear, and rage. Social stability is conducive to blood pressure levels that remain even throughout a person's life.

Some patients with high blood pressure levels are particularly sensitive and alert to danger, violence, lack of tact, scorn, and malevolence in others. Some patients may be able to cope with tactlessness or danger by not being aware of or disregarding them. When this method of coping no longer works, the patients become afraid and angry.

183

Many hypertensives do seem to be vigilant to danger, unwilling to engage in close personal interaction, and particularly sensitive to potentially hostile interactions with others. They may superficially appear to be submissive, inhibited in expressing aggressive or hostile thoughts, or in engaging in hostile deeds. In any case, no one personality type is predisposed to essential hypertension. Some hypertensive patients are submissive, and some are provocative, challenging, and combative.

Anger is frequently present in patients with high blood pressure levels. But we cannot assume that anger "causes" high blood pressure. Anger might result from the high blood pressure or the physiological changes that accompany it. Future experiments could test these alternative views. The hypothesis that conflicts about anger antecede the development of essential hypertension should also be tested before the high blood pressure levels develop or in patients with borderline, labile hypertension. But predictive studies cannot be carried out without knowing the nature of the risk factors of this disease. In patients with labile hypertension, studies to determine the psychological, social, and dietary factors in producing an increase in β-adrenergic sympathetic stimulus to the heart should be carried out. The everyday events that produce increases in blood pressure, cardiac output, and heart rate in these patients should be recorded. Everyday events and the psychological responses to them do correspond to profound blood pressure changes in patients with established hypertension. Even banal events in the lives of these patients can correspond to excessive blood pressure changes.

We cannot as yet be certain that in man social and psychological factors are the antecedents, and not the consequences, of the altered physiological changes in essential hypertension. Experiments in animals that later develop high blood pressure point up the important role of prior experience, but in some animals, stressful experiences do not initiate high blood pressure, but determine its level. Two conclusions can be drawn from these experiments.

First, early experiences of the future hypertensive patient may be etiologically relevant. Much more needs to be known about the childhood experiences and the families of persons who later develop essential hypertension. For example, the reasons for the family aggregation of essential hypertension are unknown. We might ask whether parents of the future patient do not also display the same perceptual and interpersonal styles and sensitivities that have been described in hypertensive patients themselves. If so, how do such parents affect their children?

Second, psychological factors are known to play a role in altering the course of the disease. Separation may antecede the malignant phase. Other factors such as excessive renin activity, a renal infection, and excessive salt and water intake in the presence of long-standing changes in the kidney may also antecede the accelerated, malignant phase. Therefore, the course of the disease may be altered not by any particular factor but by one of many, or by a combination of factors.

This chapter has attempted to bring to the attention of behavioral scientists the complex factors that are involved in elevating blood pressure levels. Essential hypertension seems to be a multifactoral and heterogeneous disease. Bias in, or disturbance of any of the mechanisms regulating blood pressure levels may set off a chain of events that end in high blood pressure. The disturbance may begin with changes in cardiac output, peripheral resistance, the kidney, adrenal cortex or medulla, or the brain. Once the disturbance starts, the other mechanisms regulating blood pressure are altered.

It would have been desirable, if possible, to have made a definitive statement about the role of psychological factors in essential hypertension: however, no such statement can be made. Psychological factors clearly do not by themselves "cause" the syndrome. These factors interact with the other predispositions to high blood pressure. In some persons, the social factors and the psychological responses they provoke may interact with a biased system, such as an altered regulation of aldosterone by renin and angiotensin. In other persons these psychosocial factors may increase β-adrenergic discharge to the heart, cardiac output, and, finally, the peripheral resistance, to produce high blood pressure.

In still other patients, social conditions, separation, anxiety, and anger may potentiate and aggravate an already increased blood pressure level and vascular hyperreactivity. The inferences can be drawn from the accumulated knowledge about essential hypertension that it is a disease that can be brought about by many different mechanisms, and that social and psychological factors may play a different etiological, pathogenetic, and sustaining role in its different forms.

REFERENCES

Abrahams, V. C., and Pickford, M. 1956. Observations on a central antagonism between adrenaline and acetylcholine. *J. Physiol.* (Lond.) 131:712.

———, Hilton, S. M., and Zbrozyna, A. 1960. Active muscle vasodilation produced by stimulation of the brain stem: Its significance in the defence reaction. *J. Physiol.* (Lond.) 154:491.

Abramson, D. I. 1944. *Vascular responses in the extremities of man in health and disease.* Chicago: University of Chicago Press.

——— and Ferris, E. B., Jr. 1940. Responses of blood vessels in the resting hand and forearm to various stimuli. *Am. Heart J.* 19:541.

Aceto, M. D. G., Kinnard, W. J., and Buckley, J. P. 1963. Effect of compounds on blood pressure and behavioural response of rats chronically subjected to an avoidance escape situation. *Arch. Int. Pharmacodyn. Ther.* 144:214.

Acheson, R. M., and Fowler, G. B. 1967. On the inheritance of stature and blood pressure. *J. Chronic Dis.* 20:731.

Adams, D. B., Baccelli, G., Mancia, G., and Zanchetti, A. 1968. Cardiovascular changes during preparation for fighting behavior in the cat. *Nature* 220:1239.

Aleksandrow, D. 1967. Studies on the epidemiology of hypertension in Poland. In *The Epidemiology of Hypertension*, edited by J. Stamler, R. Stamler, and T. N. Pullman. New York: Grune & Stratton.

Alexander, F. 1939. Psychoanalytic study of a case of essential hypertension. *Psychosom. Med.* 1:139.

——— 1950. *Psychosomatic Medicine.* New York: Norton.

———, French, T. M., and Pollock, G. H. 1968. *Psychosomatic Specificity.* Chicago: University of Chicago Press.

Alexander, R. S. 1945. The effects of blood flow and anoxia on spinal cardiovascular centers. *Am. J. Physiol.* 143:698.

——— 1946. Tonic and reflex functions of medullary sympathetic cardiovascular centers. *J. Neurophysiol.* 9:205.

Amassian, V. E. 1951. Fiber groups and spinal pathways of cortically represented visceral afferents. *J. Neurophysiol.* 14:445.

Ames, R. P.; Borkowski, A. W., Sicinski, A. M., and Laragh, J. H. 1965. Prolonged infusions of angiotensin II and norepinephrine and blood pressure, electrolyte balance, and aldosterone and cortisol secretion in normal man and in cirrhosis with ascites. *J. Clin. Invest.* **44**:1171.

Anand, B. K., and Dua, S. 1956a. Circulatory and respiratory changes induced by electrical stimulation of limbic system (visceral brain). *J. Neurophysiol.* **19**:393.

——— and ——— 1956b. Electrical stimulation of the limbic system of brain (visceral brain) in the waking animals. *Indian J. Med. Res.* **44**:107.

Andén, N. E., Carrodi, H., Dahlström, A., Fuxe, K., and Hökfelt, J. 1966. Effects of tyrosine hydroxylase inhibition on the amine levels of central monamine levels. *Life Sci.* **5**:561.

Anderson, D. E., and Brady, J. V. 1971. Pre-avoidance blood pressure elevations accompanied by heart rate decreases in the dog. *Science* **172**:595.

——— and ——— 1973. Prolonged pre-avoidance effects upon blood pressure and heart rate in the dog. *Psychosom. Med.* **35**:4.

Andersson, B., and McCann, S. M. 1955. A further study of polydipsia evoked by hypothalamic stimulation in the goat. *Acta Physiol. Scand.* **33**:333.

Andreev, S. V., Vadkovskaia, I. D., and Glebova, M. S. 1952. Effect of renin preparations on the blood pressure. *Tr. Akad. Med. Nauk. Gipertonicheskaia Bolezn.* **2**:56.

Armstrong, J. G. 1959. Hypotensive action of progesterone in experimental and human hypertension. *Proc. Soc. Exp. Biol. Med.* **102**:452.

Arnold, P., and Rosenheim, M. I. 1949. Effect of pentamethonium iodide on normal and hypertensive persons. *Lancet* **257**:321.

Asafov, B. D. 1958. *The Orienting Reflex and Exploratory Behavior.* Moscow: Akad. Ped. Nauk RSFSR.

August, J. T., Nelson, D. H., and Thorn, G. W. 1958. Response of normal subjects to large amounts of aldosterone. *J. Clin. Invest.* **37**:1549.

Ax, A. F. 1953. The physiological differentiation between fear and anger in humans. *Psychosom. Med.* **15**:433.

Ayers, C. B., Harris, R. H., Jr., and Lefer, L. G. 1969. Control of renin release in experimental hypertension. *Circ. Res.* **34** (Suppl. I): I–103.

Ayitey-Smith, E., and Varma, D. R. 1970. Assessment of the role of the sympathetic nervous system in experimental hypertension using normal and immunosympathectomised rats. *Br. J. Pharmacol.* **40**:175.

Ayman, D. 1930. An evaluation of therapeutic results in essential hypertension. *J.A.M.A.* **95**:246.

——— 1933. The personality type of patients with arteriolar essential hypertension. *Am. J. Med. Sci.* **186**:213.

——— 1934. Heredity in arteriolar (essential) hypertension: a clinical study of the blood pressure of 1,524 members of 277 families. *Arch. Intern. Med.* **53**:792.

——— and Pratt, J. H. 1931. Nature of the symptoms associated with essential hypertension. *Arch. Intern. Med.* **47**:675.

Baer, L., Sommers, S. C., Krakoff, L. R., Newton, M. A., and Laragh, J. H. 1970. Pseudo-primary aldosteronism: an entity distinct from true primary aldosteronism. *Circ. Res.* **26–27** (Suppl. I):203.

Baldwin, D. S., Biggs, A. W., Goldring, W., Hulet, W. M., and Chasis, H. 1958. Exaggerated natriuresis in essential hypertension. *Am. J. Med.* **24**:893.

Ball, C. O. T., and Meneely, G. R. 1957. Observations on dietary sodium chloride. *J. Am. Diet. Assoc.* **33**:366.

Barach, J. H. 1928. The constitutional factors in hypertensive disease. *J.A.M.A.* **91**:1511.

Barbour, B. H., Slater, J. D. H., Casper, A. G. I., and Bartter, F. C. 1965. On the role of the central nervous system in control of aldosterone secretion. *Life Sci.* **4**:1161.

Barcroft, H., Brod, J., Hejl, Z., Hirsjarvi, E. A., and Kitchin, A. H. 1960. The mechanism of the vasodilatation in the forearm muscle during stress (mental arithmetic). *Clin. Sci.* **19**:577.

186

Bartter, F. C., Mills, I. H., Biglieri, E. G., and Delia, C. 1959. Studies on the control and physiologic action of aldosterone. *Recent Prog. Horm. Res.* 15:311.

——, ——, and Gann, D. S. 1960. Increase in aldosterone secretion by carotid artery constriction in the dog and its prevention by thyrocarotid arterial function denervation. *J. Clin. Invest.* 39:1330.

Bassett, D. R., Rosenblatt, G., Moellerung, R. D., and Hartwell, A. S. 1966. Cardiovascular disease, diabetes mellitus and anthropometric evaluation of Polynesian males on the Island of Niihau—1963. *Circulation* 34:1088.

Baust, W., and Katz, P. 1961. Untersuchung zur Tonisierung einzelner Neurone im hinteren Hypothalamus. *Pflügers Arch.* 272:575.

——, Niemczyk, H., Schaeffer, H., and Vieth, J. 1962. On a pressor sensitive area in the posterior hypothalamus of cats. *Pflügers Arch.* 274:374.

——, ——, and Vieth, J. 1963. The action of blood pressure on the ascending reticular activating system with special reference to adrenaline-induced EEG arousal. *Electroencephogr. Clin. Neurophysiol.* 15:63.

Bays, R. P., and Scrimshaw, N. S. 1953. Facts and fallacies regarding the blood pressure of different regional and racial groups. *Circulation* 8:655.

Beavers, W. R., and Blackmore, W. P. 1958. Effect of chlorothiazide on vascular reactivity. *Proc. Soc. Exp. Biol. Med.* 98:133.

Bechgaard, P. 1967. The natural history of benign hypertension: one thousand hypertensive patients followed from 26 to 32 years. In *The Epidemiology of Essential Hypertension*, edited by J. Stamler, R. Stamler, and T. N. Pullman. New York: Grune & Stratton.

Beier, D. C. 1940. Conditioned cardiovascular responses and suggestions for treatment of cardiac neuroses. *J. Exp. Psychol.* 26:311.

Bello, C. T., Sevy, R. W., Harakal, C., and Hillyer, P. N. 1967. Relationship between clinical severity of disease and hemodynamic patterns in essential hypertension. *Am. J. Med. Sci.* 253:194.

Benedict, R. 1956. Onset and early course of essential hypertension. *J. Chron. Dis.* 4:221.

Benson, H., Herd, J. A., Morse, W. H., and Kelleher, R. T. 1969. Behavioral induction of arterial hypertension and its reversal. *Am. J. Physiol.* 217:30.

——, ——, ——, and —— 1970. Behaviorally induced hypertension in the squirrel monkey. *Circ. Res.* 26–27 (Suppl. I):I–21.

——, Shapiro, D., Tursky, B., and Schwartz, G. E. 1971. Decreased systolic blood pressure through operant conditioning techniques in patients with essential hypertension. *Science* 173:740.

Benson, W. R., and Sealy, W. C. 1956. Arterial necrosis following resection of coarctation of the aorta. *Lab. Invest.* 5:359.

Berkson, D. M., Stamler, J., Lindberg, H. A., Miller, W., Mathias, H., Lasky, H., and Hall, Y. 1960. Socioeconomic correlates of atherosclerotic and hypertensive heart disease. *Ann. N.Y. Acad. Sci.* 84:835.

Berry, C., McKinley, W., and Hodes, R. 1942. Reversals of blood pressure responses caused by changes in frequency of brain stem stimulation. *Am. J. Physiol.* 135:338.

Bianchi, G., Tenconi, L. T., and Lucca, R. 1970. Effect in the conscious dog of constriction of the renal artery to a sole remaining kidney on haemodynamics, sodium balance, body fluid volumes, plasma renin concentration and pressor responsiveness to angiotensin. *Clin. Sci. Mol. Med.* 38:741.

Biglieri, E. G., Slaton, P. E., Jr., Kronefield, S. J., and Deck, J. B. 1967. Primary aldosteronism with unusual secretory pattern. *J. Clin. Endocrinol. Metab.* 27:715.

Bilgutay, A. M., and Lillehei, C. W. 1965. Treatment of hypertension with an implantable electronic device. *J.A.M.A.* 191:649.

Bing, J., and Poulsen, K. 1970. Effect of anti-angiotensin II on blood pressure and sensitivity to angiotensin and renin. *Acta Path. Microbiol. Scand.* [A] 78:6.

────── and Vinthen-Paulsen, N. 1952. Effects of severe anoxia on the kidneys of normal and dehydrated mice. *Acta Physiol. Scand.* 27:337.

Binger, C. A., Ackerman, N. W., Cohn, A. E., Schroeder, H. A., and Steele, J. M. 1945. *Personality in Arterial Hypertension*. New York: Brunner.

Biron, P., Koiw, E., Nowaczynski, W., Brouillet, J., and Genest, J. 1961. The effects of intravenous infusions of valine-5 angiotensin II and other pressor agents on urinary electrolytes and corticosteroids, including aldosterone. *J. Clin. Invest.* 40:338.

Blair, D. A., Glover, W. E., Greenfield, A. D. M., and Roddie, I. C. 1959. Excitation of cholinergic vasodilator nerves to human skeletal muscles during emotional states. *J. Physiol.* (Lond.) 148:633.

Blair-West, J. R., Coghlan, J. P., Denton, D. A., Orchard, E., Scoggins, B. A., and Wright, R. D. 1968a. Renin-angiotensin-aldosterone system and sodium balance in experimental renal hypertension. *Endocrinology* 83:119.

──────, ──────, ──────, Funder, J. W., Scoggins, B. A., and Wright, R. D. 1968b. Effects of adrenal steroid withdrawal on chronic renovascular hypertension in adrenalectomized sheep. *Circ. Res.* 23:803.

Blanchard, E. B., and Young, L. D. 1973. Self-control of cardiac functioning: A promise as yet unfulfilled. *Psychol. Bull.* 79:145.

Bliss, E. L., and Zwanziger, J. 1966. Brain amines and emotional stress. *J. Psychiat. Res.* 4:189.

Bøe, J., Humerfelt, S., and Wedervang, F. 1957. Blood pressure in a population. *Acta Med. Scand.* 157 (Suppl. 321):1.

Bock, K. D., and Krecke, H. J. 1958. Die Wirkung von syntetischem Hypertensin II auf die PAH—und Inulin—clearance, die renale Hemodynamik und die Diurese beim Menschen. *Klin. Wschr.* 36:69.

Bonvallet, M., Hugelin, A., and Dell, P. 1956. The interior environment and automatic activities of the reticular cells of the mesencephalon. *J. Physiol.* (Paris) 48:403.

Booth, D. A. 1968. Mechanism of action of norepinephrine in eliciting an eating response on injection into the rat hypothalamus. *J. Pharmacol. Exp. Ther.* 160:336.

Boucher, R., Asselin, J., and Genest, J. 1974. A new enzyme leading to the direct formation of angiotensin II. *Circ. Res.* 34 (Suppl. I):I–203.

Bourgault, P. C., Karczmar, A. G., and Scudder, C. L. 1963. Contrasting behavioral, pharmacological, neurophysiological, and biochemical profiles of C57BL/6 and SC-I strains of mice. *Life Sci.* 8:533.

Boyd, J. E., and Mulrow, P. J. 1972. Intracellular potassium: the regulator of aldosterone production. *J. Clin. Invest.* 51:13a.

Braun-Menendez, E., and von Euler, U. S. 1947. Hypertension after bilateral nephrectomy in the rat. *Nature* 160:905.

Brod, J. 1960. Essential hypertension—hemodynamic observations with bearing on its pathogenesis. *Lancet* ii:773.

────── 1970. Hemodynamics and emotional stress. *Bibl. Psychiatr.* 144:13.

──────, Fenčl, V., Hejl, Z., and Jirka, J. 1959. Circulatory changes underlying blood pressure elevation during acute emotional stress (mental arithmetic) in normotensive and hypertensive subjects. *Clin. Sci.* 18:269.

──────, ──────, ──────, ──────, and Ulrych, M. 1962. General and regional hemodynamic pattern underlying essential hypertension. *Clin. Sci.* 23:339.

Brodie, B. B., and Costa, E. 1961. Role of norepinephrine in peripheral ganglia on blood pressure.

188

In *Hypertension–Recent Advances: The Second Hahnemann Symposium on Hypertensive Disease*, edited by A. N. Brest and J. H. Moyer. Philadelphia: Lea & Febiger.

Bronk, D. W., and Stella, G. 1932. Afferent impulses in the carotid sinus nerve. *J. Cell Physiol.* 1:113.

———, Pitts, R. F., and Larrabee, M. G. 1939. Role of hypothalamus in cardiovascular regulation. *Res. Publ. Assoc. Nerv. Ment. Dis.* 20:323.

Bronson, F. H. 1967. Effects of social stimulation on adrenal and reproductive physiology of rodents. In *Husbandry of Laboratory Animals*, edited by M. L. Conalty. New York: Academic.

Brooks, C. McC., Ushiyama, J., and Lange, G. 1962. Reactions of neurons in or near the supraoptic nuclei. *Am. J. Physiol.* 202:487.

Brower, D. 1947a. The relation between certain Rorschach factors and cardiovascular activity before and after visuo-motor conflict. *J. Gen. Psychol.* 37:93.

——— 1947b. The relations between Minnesota Multiphasic Personality Inventory scores and cardiovascular measures before and after experimentally induced visuo-motor conflict. *J. Soc. Psychol.* 26:55.

Brown, T. C., Davis, J. O., Olichney, M. J., and Johnston, C. I. 1966. Relation of plasma renin to sodium balance and arterial pressure in experimental renal hypertension. *Circ. Res.* 18:475.

Bruce, J. M., Jr., and Thomas, C. B. 1953. A method of rating certain personality factors as determined by the Rorschach test for use in a study of the precursors of hypertension and coronary artery disease. *Psychiatr. Q.* 27(Suppl.):207.

Brunner, H. R., Baer, L., Sealey, J. E., Ledingham, J. G. G., and Laragh, J. H. 1970. The influence of potassium administration and of potassium deprivation on plasma renin in normal and hypertensive subjects. *J. Clin. Invest.* 49:2128.

———, Kirshman, J. D., Sealey, J. E., and Laragh, J. H. 1971. Hypertension of renal origin. Evidence for two different mechanisms. *Science* 174:1344.

———, Laragh, J. H., Baer, L., Newton, M. A., Goodwin, F. T., Krakoff, L. R., Bard, R. H., and Buhler, F. R. 1972. Essential hypertension: renin and aldosterone, heart attack and stroke. *N. Engl. J. Med.* 286:441.

Bunag, R. D., Page, I. H., and McCubbin, J. W. 1966. Neural stimulation of release of renin. *Circ. Res.* 19:851.

Buss, A. H. 1961. *The Psychology of Aggression.* New York: Wiley.

Bykov, K. M. 1947. *The Cerebral Cortex and the Internal Organs.* Moscow: Medgiz.

Byrom, F. B., and Dodson, L. F. 1949. Mechanism of the vicious cycle in chronic hypertension. *Clin. Sci.* 8:1.

Cannon, P. J., Ames, R. P., and Laragh, J. H. 1966. Relation between potassium balance and aldosterone secretion in normal subjects and in patients with hypertensive or renal tubular disease. *J. Clin. Invest.* 45:865.

Cannon, W. B. 1929. *Bodily Changes in Pain, Hunger, Fear and Rage.* New York: Appleton-Century-Crofts.

Carpenter, C. C. J., Davis, J. O., and Ayers, C. R. 1961a, Concerning the role of arterial baroreceptors in the control of aldosterone secretion. *J. Clin. Invest.* 40:1160.

———, ———, and ——— 1961b. Relation of renin, angiotensin II, and experimental renal hypertension to aldosterone secretion. *J. Clin. Invest.* 40:2026.

Carretero, O. A., Kuk, P., Bujak, B., and Houle, J. 1971. Effect of antibodies against angiotensin II on the blood pressure of rats with severe experimental hypertension. *Fed. Proc.* 30:432.

Catt, K. J., Kimmet, P. Z., Cain, M. D., Cran, E., Best, J. B., and Coghlan, J. P. 1971. Angiotensin II blood levels in human hypertension. *Lancet* i:459.

Cattell, R. B., and Scheier, I. H. 1959. Extension of meaning of objective test personality factors:

Especially into anxiety, neuroticism, questionnaire, and physical factors. *J. Gen. Psychol.* 61:287.

Celander, O. 1954. The range of control exercised by the sympathico-adrenal system: a quantive study on blood vessels and other smooth muscle effectors in the cat. *Acta Physiol. Scand.* (Suppl. 32):116:1.

———— and Folkow, B. 1953. A comparison of the sympathetic vasomotor fibre control of the vessels within the skin and the muscles. *Acta Physiol. Scand.* 29:241.

Chalmers, J. P. 1975. Brain amines and models of experimental hypertension. *Circ. Res.* 36:469.

Chalmers, J. P., and Wurtman, R. J. 1971. Participation of central noradrenergic neurons in arterial baroreceptor reflexes in the rabbit. *Circ. Res.* 28:480.

Chambers, W. W., and Reiser, M. F. 1953. Emotional stress in the precipitation of congestive heart failure. *Psychosom. Med.* 15:38.

Charvat, J., Dell, P., and Folkow, B. 1964. Mental factors and cardiovascular diseases. *Cardiologia* 44:124.

Chobanian, A. V., Burrows, B. A., and Hollander, W. 1961. Body fluid and electrolyte composition in arterial hypertension. II. Studies in mineralocorticoid hypertension. *J. Clin. Invest.* 40:416.

Christenson, W. N., and Hinkle, L. E. 1961. Differences in illness and prognostic signs in two groups of young men. *J.A.M.A.* 177:247.

Christian, J. J., Lloyd, J. A., and Davis, D. 1965. The role of endocrines in the self-regulation of mammalian populations. *Recent Prog. Horm. Res.* 22:501.

Christiansen, J., Hagerup, L., and Nielsen, B. 1964. Hypokalemia and hypertension. *Acta Med. Scand.* 176:665.

Christlieb, A. R., Biber, T. U. L., and Hickler, R. B. 1969. Studies on the role of angiotensin in experimental renovascular hypertension: an immunologic approach. *J. Clin. Invest.* 48:1506.

Christy, N. P., and Laragh, J. H. 1961. Pathogenesis of hypokalemic alkalosis in Cushing's syndrome. *N. Engl. J. Med.* 265:1083.

Cohen, S. I., and Silverman, A. J. 1959. Psychophysiological investigations of vascular response variability. *J. Psychosom. Res.* 3:185.

————, ————, Zuidema, G., and Lazar, C. 1957. Psychotherapeutic alteration of a physiologic stress response. *J. Nerv. Ment. Dis.* 125:112.

Coleman, T. G., and Guyton, A. C. 1969. Hypertension caused by salt loading in the dog. III. Onset transients of cardiac output and other variables. *Circ. Res.* 25:153.

Comstock, G. W. 1957. An epidemiologic study of blood pressure levels in a biracial community in the Southern United States. *Am. J. Hyg.* 65:271.

Conn, J. W. 1955. Part II. Primary aldosteronism, a new clinical syndrome. *J. Lab. Clin. Med.* 45:6.

———— 1961. Aldosteronism and hypertension. *Arch. Int. Med.* 107:813.

————, Cohen, E. L., and Rovner, D. R. 1964. Suppression of plasma renin activity in primary aldosteronism. *J.A.M.A.* 190:213.

————, Rovner, D. R., and Cohen, E. L. 1965. Normal and altered function of the renin-angiotensin-aldosterone system in man. *Ann. Intern. Med.* 63:266.

————, ————, ————, and Nesbit, R. M. 1966. Normokalemic primary aldosteronism: Its masquerade as essential hypertension. *J.A.M.A.* 195:21.

Cooper, D. Y., Touchstone, J. C., Roberts, J. M., Blakemore, W. S., and Rosenthal, O. 1958. Steroid formation by adrenal tissue from hypertensives. *J. Clin. Invest.* 37:1524.

Cope, C. L., Nicolis, G., and Fraser, B. 1961. Measurement of aldosterone secretion rate in man by the use of a metabolite. *Clin. Sci.* 21:367.

190

Cort, J. H. 1953. Effect of nervous stimulation of the arterio-venous oxygen and carbon dioxide differences across the kidney. *Nature* 171:784.

Costa, E. 1961. Renal concepts of the role of peripheral vs. central action of catecholamines in blood pressure regulation. In *Hypertension–Recent Advances: The Second Hahnemann Symposium on Hypertensive Disease*, edited by A. N. Brest and J. H. Moyer. Philadelphia: Lea & Febiger.

Cottier, P. T. 1960. Renal hemodynamics, water and electrolyte excretion in essential hypertension. In *Essential Hypertension*, edited by K. D. Bock and P. T. Cottier. Berlin: Springer.

Crane, M. G., and Harris, J. J. 1966. Desoxycorticosterone secretion rates in hyperadrenocorticism. *J. Clin. Endocrinol. Metab.* 26:1135.

Cranston, R. W., Chalmers, J. H., Taylor, H. L., Henschel, A., and Keys, A. 1949. Effect of a psychiatric interview on the blood pressure response to cold stimuli. *Fed. Proc.* 8:30.

Creditor, M. C., and Loschky, U. K. 1967. Plasma renin activity in hypertension. *Am. J. Med.* 43:371.

Crisp, A. H. 1963. Some current aspects of psychosomatic research. *Postgrad. Med. J.* 39:5.

Cross, B. A., and Green, J. D. 1959. Activity of single neurones in the hypothalamus: effect of osmotic and other stimuli. *J. Physiol.* (Lond.) 148:554.

Cruz-Coke, R. 1959. The hereditary factor in hypertension. *Acta Genet* (Basel) 9:207.

——— 1960. Environmental influences and arterial blood pressure. *Lancet* 2:885.

Dahl, L. K. 1959. Salt intake and salt need. *N. Engl. J. Med.* 258:1152.

——— 1960. Possible role of salt intake in the development of essential hypertension. In *Essential Hypertension*, edited by K. D. Bock and P. T. Cottier. Berlin: Springer.

——— and Love, R. A. 1957. Etiological role of sodium choloride in essential hypertension in humans. *J.A.M.A.* 164:397.

———, Heine, M., and Tassinari, L. 1962. Role of genetic factors in susceptibility to experimental hypertension due to chronic excess salt ingestion. *Nature* 194:480.

———, Knudsen, K. D., Heine, M., and Leitl, G. 1968. Effects of chronic excess salt ingestion: Modification of experimental hypertension in the rat by variations in the diet. *Circ. Res.* 22:11.

———, ———, and Iwai, J. 1969. Humoral transmission of hypertension: evidence from parabiosis. *Circ. Res.* Suppl. I, ad. 34/35:21.

———, Heine, M., and Thompson, K. 1972. Genetic influence of renal homografts on the blood pressure of rats from different strains. *Proc. Soc. Exp. Biol. Med.* 140:852.

Davies, M. H. 1970. Blood pressure and personality. *J. Psychosom. Res.* 14:89.

——— 1971. Is high blood pressure a psychosomatic disorder? *J. Chron. Dis.* 24:239.

Davis, J. O. 1961. A critical evaluation of the role of receptors in the control of aldosterone secretion and sodium excretion. *Prog. Cardiovasc. Dis.* 4:27.

——— 1974. Control of renin release. *Hosp. Pract.* 9:55.

———, Yankopoulos, N. A., Lieberman, F., Holman, J., and Bahn, R. C. 1960. The role of the anterior pituitary in the control of aldosterone secretion in experimental secondary hyperaldosteronism. *J. Clin. Invest.* 39:765.

———, Hartoft, P. M., Titus, E. O., and Carpenter, C. C. J. 1962. The role of the renin-angiotensin system in the control of aldosterone secretion. *J. Clin. Invest.* 41:378.

———, Urquhart, J., and Higgins, J. T., Jr. 1963. The effects of alterations of plasma sodium and potassium concentration on aldosterone secretion. *J. Clin. Invest.* 42:597.

———, Yankopoulos, N. A., Lieberman, F., Holman, J., and Bahn, R. C. 1970. The role of the anterior pituitary in the control of aldosterone secretion in experimental secondary hyperaldosteronism. *J. Clin. Invest.* 39:765.

Dawber, T. R., Kannel, W. B., Kagan, A., Donabedian, R. K., McNamara, P. M., and Pearson, G. 1967. Environmental factors in hypertension. In *The Epidemiology of Hypertension*, edited by J. Stamler, R. Stamler, and T. N. Pullman, New York: Grune & Stratton.

De Champlain, J. 1972. Hypertension and the sympathetic nervous system. In *Perspectives in Neuropharmacology*, edited by S. Snyder. Oxford: Oxford University Press.

De Champlain, J., Mueller, R. A., and Axelrod, J. 1969. Turnover and synthesis of norepinephrine in experimental hypertension in rats. *Circ. Res.* 25:285.

De Champlain, J., and van Amerigen, M. R. 1973. Role of sympathetic fibers and of adrenal medulla in the maintenance of cardiovascular homeostasis in normotensive and hypertensive rats. In *Frontiers in Catecholamine Research*, edited by E. Usdin and S. Snyder. Oxford: Pergamon.

DeJong, W. Lovenberg, W., and Sjoerdsma, A. 1972. Increased plasma renin activity in spontaneously hypertensive rats. *Proc. Soc. Exp. Biol. Med.* 139:1213.

Denton, D. 1961. Discussion of the lecture of J. O. Davis. *Recent Progr. Hormone Res.* 17:331.

DiPalma, J. R. 1961. Antihypertensive agents which affect catecholamine release. *Hypertension—Recent Advances: The Second Hahnemann Symposium on Hypertensive Disease*, edited by A. N. Brest and J. H. Moyer. Philadelphia: Lea & Febiger.

Doba, N., and Reis, D. J. 1974. Role of central and peripheral adrenergic mechanisms in neurogenic hypertension produced by brain stem lesion in rats. *Circ. Res.* 34:293.

————, and ————. 1973. Acute fulminating neurogenic hypertension produced by brain stem lesions in the rat. *Circ. Res*, 32:584.

Dock, W. 1940. Vasoconstriction in renal hypertension abolished by pithing. *Am. J. Physiol.* 130:1.

Dole, V. P., Dahl, L. K., Cotzias, G. C., Eder, H. A., and Krebs, M. E. 1951. Dietary treatment of hypertension. Clinical and metabolic studies of patients on the rice-fruit diet. *J. Clin. Invest.* 29:1189.

Dollery, C. T., Shakman, R., and Shillingford, J. 1959. Malignant hypertension and hypokalaemia cured by nephrectomy. *Brit. Med. J.* ii:1367.

Dontas, A. S. 1955. Effects of protoveratrine, serotonin and ATP on afferent and splanchnic nerve activity. *Circ. Res.* 3:363.

Douglas, W. W., and Ritchie, J. M. 1956. Cardiovascular reflexes produced by electrical excitation of non-medullated afferents in the vagus, carotid sinus and aortic nerves. *J. Physiol.* (Lond.) 134:167.

————, ————, and Schaumann, W. 1956. Depressor reflexes from medullated and nonmedullated fibers in the rabbit's aortic nerve. *J. Physiol.* (Lond.) 132:187.

Downman, C. B. B. 1955. Skeletal muscle reflexes of splanchnic and intercostal nerve origin in acute spinal and decerebrate cats. *J. Neurophysiol.* 18:217.

Doyle, A. E., and Fraser, J. R. E. 1961. Essential hypertension and inheritance of vascular reactivity. *Lancet* ii:509.

Drury, D. R., and Schapiro, S. 1956. Renin tachyphylaxis and renal ischemia in the cat. *Am. J. Physiol.* 187:520.

Dunbar, H. F. 1943. *Psychosomatic Diagnosis*. New York: Hoeber.

Dykman, R. A., and Gantt, W. H. 1960. Experimental psychogenic hypertension: blood pressure changes conditioned to painful stimuli (Schizokinesis). *Bull. Johns Hopkins Hosp.* 107:72.

Ead, H. W., Green, J. H., and Neil, E. 1952. A comparison of the effects of pulsatile and non-pulsatile flow through the carotid sinus on the reflexogenic activity of the sinus baroreceptors in the cat. *J. Physiol.* (Lond.) 119:509.

Ehrlich, E. N. 1968. Aldosterone, the adrenal cortex, and hypertension. *Annu. Rev. Med.* 19:373.

192

————, Lugibihl, K., Laves, M., and Janulis, M. 1966. Reciprocal variations in urinary cortisol and aldosterone in response to increased salt intake in humans. *J. Clin. Endocrinol. Metab.* 26:1160.

————, ————, Taylor, C., and Janulis, M. 1967. Reciprocal variations in urinary cortisol and aldosterone in response to the sodium-depleting influence of hydrochlorothiazide and ethacrynic acid in humans. *J. Clin. Endocrinol. Metab.* 27:836.

Ehrstrom, M. D. 1945. Psychogene Blutdruckssteigerung in Kriegshypertonien. *Acta Med. Scand.* 122:546.

Eich, R. H., Cuddy, R. P. Smulyan, H., and Lyons, R. H. 1966. Haemodynamics in labile hypertension. *Circulation* 34:299.

Eichna, L. W., and McQuarrie, D. G. 1960. Proceedings of a Symposium on Central Nervous System Control of Circulation. *Physiol. Rev.* Suppl. 4, 40.

Eide, I., Løyning, E., and Kiil, F. 1973. Evidence for hemodynamic autoregulation of renin release. *Circ. Res.* 32:237.

Eisenstein, A. B., and Hartroft, P. M. 1956. Sodium deficiency and adrenocortical hormone secretion. *J. Lab. Clin. Med.* 48:802.

Eliasson, S., Lindgren, P., and Uvnäs, B. 1952. Representation in the hypothalamus and the motor cortex in the dog of the sympathetic vasodilator outflow to the skeletal muscles. *Acta Physiol. Scand.* 27:18.

————, ————, and ———— 1954. The hypothalamus, a relay station of the sympathetic vasodilator tract. *Acta Physiol. Scand.* 31:290.

Ellis, M. E., and Grollman, A. 1949. The antidiuretic hormone in the urine in experimental and clinical hypertension. *Endocrinology* 44:415.

Elmadjian, F., Hope, J. M., and Lamson, E. T. 1957. Excretion of epinephrine and norepinephrine in various emotional states. *J. Clin. Endocrinol. Metab.* 17:608.

Emanuel, D., Scott, J. B., and Haddy, F. J. 1959. Effect of potassium upon small and large blood vessels of the dog forelimb. *Am. J. Physiol.* 197:637.

Engel, B. T., and Bickford, A. F. 1961. Response specificity. *Arch. Gen. Psychiatry* 5:82.

Engelman, K., Portnoy, B., and Sjoerdsma, A. 1970. Plasma catecholamine concentrations in patients with hypertension. *Circ. Res.* 26–27(Suppl. 1):141.

Epstein, A. N., Fitzimmons, J. T., and Rolls, B. J. 1970. Drinking induced by injection of angiotensin into the brain of the rat. *J. Physiol.* (Lond.) 210:457.

Evans, G. 1920. A contribution to the study of arterial-sclerosis with special reference to its relation to chronic renal disease. *Q. J. Med.* 14:215.

Evans, W. 1957. Hypertonia or uneventful high blood pressure. *Lancet* ii:53.

Fallis, N., Lasagna, L., and Tetreault, L. 1962. Gustatory thresholds in patients with hypertension. *Nature* 196:74.

Farnsworth, E. B. 1946. Renal reabsorption of chloride and phosphate in normal subjects and in patients with essential hypertension. *J. Clin. Invest.* 25:897.

Farrell, G. 1958. Regulation of aldosterone secretion. *Physiol. Rev.* 38:709.

———— 1959a. Glomerulotropic activity of an acetone extract of pineal tissue. *Endocrinology* 65:239.

———— 1959b. The physiological factors which influence the secretion of aldosterone. *Recent Progr. Hormone Res.* 15:275.

———— 1963. Discussion of the lecture by J. R. Blair-West. *Recent Prog. Horm. Res.* 19:367.

Farris, E. J., Yeakel, E. H., and Medoff, H. S. 1945. Development of hypertension in emotional gray Norwegian rats after airblasting. *Am. J. Physiol.* 144:331.

Feigl, E. O., Peterson, L. H., and Jones, A. W. 1963. Mechanical and chemical properties of arteries in experimental hypertension. *J. Clin. Invest.* 42:1640.

193

Fernandez De Molina, A., and Hunsperger, R. W. 1959. Central representation of affective reactions in forebrain and brain stem: Electrical stimulation of amygdala, stria terminalis, and adjacent structures. *J. Physiol.* (Lond.) 145:251.

────── and ────── 1962. Organization of the subcortical system governing defence and flight reactions in the cat. *J. Physiol.* (Lond.) 160:200.

Ferrario, C. M., Dickinson, C. J., Gildenberg, P. L., and McCubbin, J. W. 1969. Central vasomotor stimulation by angiotensin. *Fed. Proc.* 28:394.

──────, Gildenberg, P. L., and McCubbin, J. W. 1972. Cardiovascular effects of angiotensin mediated by the central nervous system. *Circ. Res.* 30:257.

──────, Page, I. H., and McCubbin, J. W. 1970. Increased cardiac output as a contributing factor in experimental renal hypertension in dogs. *Circ. Res.* 27:799.

Figar, S. 1965. Conditional circulatory responses in man and animals. In *Handbook of Physiology*, sect. 2, vol. 3, Washington, D.C.: American Physiological Society.

Finch, L., Haeusler, G., and Thoenen, H. 1972. Failure to induce experimental hypertension in rats after intraventricular injection of 6-hydroxydopamine. *Br. J. Pharmacol.* 44:356.

Finkielman, S., Worcel, M., and Agrest, A. 1965. Hemodynamic patterns in essential hypertension. *Circulation* 31:356.

Finnerty, F. A., Jr., Davidov, M., and Kakaviatos, N. 1968. Relation of sodium balance to arterial pressure during drug-induced saluresis. *Circulation* 37:175.

Fischer, H. K. 1961. Hypertension and the psyche. In *Hypertension—Recent Advances: The Second Hahnemann Symposium on Hypertensive Disease*, edited by A. N. Brest and J. H. Moyer. Philadelphia: Lea & Febiger.

Floyer, M. A. 1955. Further studies on the mechanism of experimental hypertension in the rat. *Clin. Sci.* 14:163.

Flynn, J. T., Kennedy, M. A. K., and Wolf, S. 1950. Essential hypertension in one of identical twins. An experimental study of cardiovascular reactions in the Y twins. *Res. Publ. Assoc. Nerv. Ment. Dis.* 29:954.

Folkow, B. 1952. Impulse frequency in sympathetic vasomotor fibres correlated to release and elimination of transmitter. *Acta Physiol. Scand.* 25:49.

────── 1971. The haemodynamic consequences of adaptive structural changes of the resistance vessels in hypertension. *Clin. Sci.* 41:1.

──────, Strom, G., and Uvnäs, B. 1950. Do dorsal root fibres convey centrally induced vasodilator impulses? *Acta Physiol. Scand.* 21:145.

────── and Uvnäs, B. 1948. The chemical tramission of vasoconstrictor impulses to the hind limbs and the splanchnic region of the cat. *Acta Physiol. Scand.* 15:365.

────── and ────── 1950. Do adrenergic vasodilator nerves exist? *Acta Physiol. Scand.* 20:329.

────── and Rubinstein, E. H. 1966. Cardiovascular effects of acute and chronic stimulations of the hypothalamic defence area in the rat. *Acta Physiol. Scand.* 68:48.

──────, Löfving, B., and Mellander, S. 1956. Quantitative aspects of sympathetic neurohormonal control of heart rate. *Acta Physiol. Scand.* 37:363.

──────, Mellander, S., and Öberg, B. 1961. The range of effect of the sympathetic vasodilator fibres with regard to consecutive sections of the muscle vessels. *Acta Physiol. Scand.* 53:7.

──────, Hedner, P., Lisander, B., and Rubinstein, E. H. 1965. Release of cortisol upon stimulation of the hypothalamic defence area in cats. A symposium on stress. *Försvarsmed. Tidskrift.*

──────, Hallbäck, M., Lundren, Y., and Weiss, L. 1970. Structurally based increase of flow resistance in spontaneously hypertensive rats. *Acta Physiol. Scand.* 79:373.

──────, ──────, ──────, Sivertsson, R., and Weiss, L. 1973. Importance of adaptive changes in vascular design for establishment of primary hypertension, studied in man and in spontaneously hypertensive rats. *Circ. Res.* 32(Suppl. I):I-2.

Forsyth, R. P. 1968. Blood pressure and avoidance conditioning. *Psychosom. Med.* 30:125.

194

————— 1969. Blood pressure responses to long-term avoidance schedules in the restrained rhesus monkey. *Psychosom. Med.* 31:300.

Franco-Browder, S., Masson, G. M. C., and Corcoran, A. C. 1958. Pharmacologic characterization of reserpine responses in rats pretreated with iproniazid. *Proc. Soc. Exp. Biol. Med.* 97:778.

Freis, E. D. 1960. Hemodynamics of hypertension. *Physiol. Rev.* 40:27.

—————, Wanko, A., Wilson, I. M., and Parrish, A. E. 1958. Treatment of essential hypertension with chlorothiazide (diuril). *J.A.M.A.* 166:137.

Friedman, E. H., Hellerstein, H. K., Eastwood, G. L., and Jones, S. E. 1968. Behavior patterns and serum cholesterol in two groups of normal males. *Am. J. Med. Sci.* 255:237.

Friedman, M., and Kasanin, J. S. 1943. Hypertension in only one of identical twins: report of a case with consideration of psychosomatic factors. *Arch. Intern. Med.* 72:767.

————— and Rosenman, R. H. 1959. Association of specific overt behavior pattern with blood and cardiovascular findings. *J.A.M.A.* 169:1286.

Friedman, R., and Dahl, L. K. 1975. The effect of chronic conflict on the blood pressure of rats with a genetic susceptibility to experimental hypertension. *Psychosom. Med.* 37:402.

Fritz, I., and Levine, R. 1951. Action of adrenal cortical steroids and norepinephrine on vascular responses of stress in adrenalectomized rats. *Am. J. Physiol.* 165:456.

Frohlich, E. D., Tarazi, R. C., and Dustan, H. P. 1969. Re-examination of the hemodynamics of hypertension. *Am. J. Med. Sci.* 257:9.

—————, Kozul, V. J., Tarazi, K. C., and Dustan, H. P. 1970. Physiological comparison of labile and essential hypertension. *Circ. Res.* 26–27:1.

Froňková, K., Ehrlich, V., and Šlégr, L. 1957. Die Kreislaufänderung beim Hunde während des bedingten und unbedingten Nährungsreflexes und seiner Hemmung. *Pflügers Arch.* 236:704.

—————, —————, and ————— 1959. Changes in resting blood pressure values during elaboration of conditioned reflexes and their active inhibition. *Physiol. Bohemoslov.* 8:40.

Fukuda, T. 1951. L'hypertension par le sel chez les lapins et ses relations avec la glande surrénale. *Union Méd. Can.* 80:1278.

Fukyama, K. 1973. Central modulation of baroreceptor reflex by angiotensin. *Japon. Heart J.* 14:135.

Funder, J. W., Blair-West, J. R., Cain, M. C., Catt, K. J., Coghlan, J. P., Denton, D. A., Nelson, J. F., Scoggins, B. A., and Wright, R. D. 1970. Circulatory and humoral changes in the reversal of renovascular hypertension in sheep by unclipping the renal artery. *Circ. Res.* 27:249.

Funkenstein, D. H., King, S. H., and Drolette, M. E. 1957. *The Mastery of Stress.* Cambridge, Mass.: Harvard University Press.

Fuxe, K. 1965. Distribution of monoamine terminals in the central nervous system. *Acta Physiol. Scand.* 64(Suppl. 247):38.

Gampel, M. B., Slome, C., Scotch, N., and Abramson, J. H. 1962. Urbanization and hypertension among Zulu adults. *J. Chronic Dis.* 15:67.

Ganong, W. F. 1972. Effects of sympathetic activity and ACTH on renin and aldosterone secretion. In *Hypertension 1972*, edited by J. Genest and E. Koiw. Berlin: Springer.

Ganten, D., Hutchinson, J. S., Hackenthal, E., Schelling, P., Rosas, B. P., and Genest, J. 1974. Intrinsic brain iso-renin-angiotensin system. (ISO-RAS) and hypertension in rats. *Clin. Sci.* (Suppl.)

Ganten, D., Marquez-Julio, A., Granger, P., Hayduk, K., Karsunsky, K. P., Boucher, R., and Genest, J. 1971. Renin in dog brain. *Am. J. Physiol.* 221:1733.

Gantt, W. H. 1935. Effect of alcohol on cortical and subcortical activity measured by conditioned reflex method. *Bull. Johns Hopkins Hosp.* 56:61.

————— 1958. *Physiological Basis of Psychiatry.* Springfield, Ill.: Charles C Thomas.

195

———— 1960. Cardiovascular component of the conditioned reflex to pain, food and other stimuli. *Physiol. Rev.* 40(Suppl. 4):266.

Garst, J. B., Shumway, N. P., Schwartz, H., and Farrel, G. L. 1960. Aldosterone excretion in essential hypertension. *J. Clin. Endocrinol. Metab.* 20:1351.

Gauer, O. H., and Henry, J. P. 1963. Circulatory basis of fluid volume control. *Physiol. Rev.* 43:423.

Gavlichek, V. A. 1952. Changes of the blood pressure level during various functional states of the cortex in dogs. *Vyschey Nervnoy Dejatelmosty* 2:742.

Gearing, F. R., Clark, E. G., Perera, G. A., and Schweitzer, M. D. 1962. Hypertension among relatives of hypertensives. *Am. J. Public Health* 52:2058.

Gelshteyn, E. M. 1943. Clinical characteristics of hypertensive disease under wartime conditions. *Klin. Med.* (Mosk.) 21:10.

Genest, J. 1961. Angiotensin, aldosterone and human arterial hypertension. *Can. Med. Assoc. J.* 84:403.

———— 1974. Basic mechanisms in benign essential hypertension. *Hosp. Pract.* 9:97.

————, Koiw, E., Nowaczynski, W., and Sandor, T. 1960. Study of a large steroid spectrum in normal subjects and hypertensive patients. *Acta Endocrinol.* (Kbh.) 35:413.

————, Boucher, R., De Champlain, J., Veyrat, R., Chretien, M., Birow, P., Tremblay, G., Roy, P., and Cartier, P. 1964. Studies on the renin-angiotensin system in hypertensive patients. *Can. Med. Assoc. J.* 90:263.

————, ————, Kuchel, O., and Nowaczynski, W. 1973. Renin in hypertension: how important as a risk factor? *Can. Med. Assoc. J.* 109:475.

Giese, J. 1964. Acute hypertensive vascular disease: I. Relation between blood pressure changes and vascular lesions in different forms of actue hypertension. *Acta Pathol. Microbiol. Scand.* 62:481.

Gildenberg, P. L. 1971. Site of angiotensin vasopressor activity in the brain stem. *Fed. Proc.* 30:432.

Gill, J. R., Jr., Mason, D. T., and Bartter, F. C. 1964. Adrenergic nervous system in sodium metabolism: Effects of guanethidine and sodium-retaining steroids in normal man. *J. Clin. Invest.* 43:177.

Girling, F. 1952. Vasomotor effects of electrical stimulation. *Am. J. Physiol.* 170:131.

Gitlow, S. E., Mendlowitz, M., Kruk-Wilk, E., Wilk, S., Wolf, R. L., and Naftchi, N. E. 1964. Plasma clearance of dl-H^3-norepinephrine in normal human subjects and patients with essential hypertension. *J. Clin. Invest.* 43:2009.

Glock, C. Y., and Lennard, H. L. 1957. Studies in hypertension. V. Psychologic factors in hypertension: An interpretative review. *J. Chronic Dis.* 5:174.

————, Vought, R. L., Clark, E. G., and Schweitzer, M. D. 1957. Studies in hypertension. II. Variability of daily blood pressure measurements in the same individuals over a three-week period. *J. Chronic Dis.* 4:469.

Glowinski, J., and Baldessarini, R. J. 1966. Metabolism of norepinephrine in the central nervous system. *Pharmacol. Rev.* 18:1201.

Goldblatt, H. 1947. Renal origin of hypertension. *Physiol. Rev.* 27:120.

Goldenberg, M., Pines, K. L., Baldwin, E. F., Greene, D. G., and Roh, C. E. 1948. Hemodynamic response of man to norepinephrine and epinephrine and its relation to the problem of hypertension. *Am. J. Med.* 5:792.

Goldring, E., Chasis, H., Schneiner, G. E., and Smith, H. W. 1956. Reassurance in the management of benign hypertensive disease. *Circulation* 14:260.

Gomez, A., Hoobler, S. W., and Blaquier, P. 1960. Effect of addition and removal of a kidney transplant in renal and adrenocortical hypertensive rats. *Circ. Res.* 8:464.

Goodall, M., and Bogdonoff, M. 1961. Essential hypertension with elevated noradrenaline excretion. *Am. Heart J.* 61:640.

Gordon, R. D., Spector, S., Sjoerdsma, A., and Udenfriend, S. 1966. Increased synthesis of norepinephrine and epinephrine in the intact rat during exercise and exposure to cold. *J. Pharmacol. Exp. Ther.* 153:440.

————, Küchel, O., Liddle, G. W., and Island, D. W. 1967. Role of the sympathetic nervous system in regulating renin and aldosterone production in man. *J. Clin. Invest.* 46:599.

Gottschalk, L., and Hambidge, G. 1955. Verbal behavior analysis: A systematic approach to the problem of quantifying psychologic processes. *J. Project. Techn.* 19:387.

Grace, W. J., and Graham, D. T. 1952. Relationship of specific attitudes and emotions to certain bodily diseases. *Psychosom. Med.* 14:243.

Graham, D. T., Kabler, J. D., and Graham, F. K. 1960. Experimental production of predicted physiological differences by suggestion of attitude. *Psychosom. Med.* 22:321.

————, ————, and ———— 1962a. Physiological response to the suggestion of attitudes specific for hives and hypertension. *Psychosom. Med.* 24:159.

————, Lundy, R. M., Benjamin, L. S., Kabler, J. D., Lewis, W. C., Kunish, N. O., and Graham, F. K. 1962b. Specific attitudes in initial interviews with patients having different "psychosomatic" diseases. *Psychosom. Med.* 24:257.

Graham, J. D. P. 1945. High blood pressure after battle. *Lancet* i:239.

Green, D. M., and Ellis, E. J. 1954. Sodium-output-blood pressure relationships and their modification by treatment. *Circulation* 10:536.

Griffith, L. S. C., and Schwartz, S. I. 1963. Electrical stimulation of the carotid sinus nerve in normotensive and renal hypertensive dogs. *Circulation* 28:730.

———— and ———— 1964. Reversal of renal hypertension by electrical stimulation of the carotid sinus nerve. *Surgery* 56:232.

Grollman, A. 1960. Therapeutic aspects of salt restriction. In *Essential Hypertension,* edited by K. D. Bock and P. T. Cottier. Berlin: Springer.

————, Harrison, T. R., and Williams, J. R., Jr. 1940. The effect of various steroid derivatives on the blood pressure of the rat. *J. Pharmacol. Exp. Ther.* 69:149.

————, Muirhead, E. E., and Vanatta, J. 1949. Role of the kidney in the pathogenesis of hypertension as determined by a study of the effects of bilateral nephrectomy and other experimental procedures on the blood pressure of the dog. *Am. J. Physiol.* 157:21.

Gross, F. 1960. Adrenocortical function and renal pressor mechanisms in experimental hypertension. In *Essential Hypertension,* edited by K. D. Bock and P. T. Cottier. Berlin: Springer.

———— 1971. The renin-angiotensin system and hypertension. *Ann. Intern. Med.* 75:777.

———— and Lichtlen, P. 1958. Pressor substances in kidneys of renal hypertensive rats with and without adrenals. *Proc. Soc. Exp. Biol. Med.* 98:341.

———— and Sulser, F. 1956. Wirkungsverstärkerung von Renin und Nierenextrakt an der nierenlosen Ratte. *Naunyn-Schmiederbergs Arch. Pharmacol.* 229:338.

Groves, L. K., and Effler, D. B. 1960. Problems in surgical management of coarctation of the aorta. *J. Thorac. Cardiovasc. Surg.* 39:60.

Guillemin, R., Hearn, W. R., Cheek, W. R., and Householder, D. E. 1957. Control of corticotrophin release: further studies with *in vitro* methods. *Endocrinology* 60:488.

Gunnels, J. C., Jr., Grim, C. E., Robinson, R. R., Wildemann, N. M. 1967. Plasma renin activity in healthy subjects and patients with hypertension. Preliminary experience with a quantitative bioassay. *Arch. Int. Med.* 119:232.

Gutmann, F. D., Tagawa, H., Haber, E., and Barger, A. C. 1973. Renal arterial pressure, renin secretion, and blood pressure control in trained dogs. *Am. J. Physiol.* 224:66.

197

Gutmann, M. C., and Benson, H. 1971. Interaction of environmental factors and systemic arterial pressure. *Medicine* 50:543.

Guyton, A. C., and Coleman, T. G. 1969. Quantitative analysis of the pathophysiology of hypertension. *Circ. Res.* 24 (Suppl.):I–1.

Haeusler, G., Finch, L., and Thoenen, H. 1972a. Central adrenergic neurons and the initiation and development of experimental hypertension. *Experientia* 28:1200.

———, Gerold, J., and Thoenen, T. 1972b. Cardiovascular effects of 6-hydroxydopamine injected into a lateral brain ventricle of the rat. *Naunyn-Schmiedebergs Arch. Pharmacol.* 274:211.

Hambling, J. 1951. Emotions and symptoms of essential hypertension. *Br. J. Med. Psychol.* 24:242.

——— 1952. Psychosomatic aspects of essential hypertension. *Br. J. Med. Psychol.* 25:39.

Hamet, P., Kuchel, O., Cuche, J. L., Boucher, R., and Genest, J. 1973a. Effects of propranolol on cyclic AMP excretion and plasma renin activity in labile essential hypertension. *Can. Med. Assoc. J.* 109:1099.

———, ———, and Genest, J. 1973b. Effect of upright posture and isoproterenol infusion on cyclic adenosine monophosphate excretion in control subjects and patients with labile hypertension. *J. Clin. Endocrinol.* 36:218.

Hamilton, J. A. 1942. Psychophysiology of blood pressure—I. Personality and behavior ratings. *Psychosom. Med.* 4·125.

Hamilton, M., Pickering, G. W., Roberts, J. A. F., and Sowry, G. S. C. 1954. The etiology of essential hypertension. *Clin. Sci. Mol. Med.* 13:273.

———, ———, ———, and ——— 1963. Arterial pressures of relatives of patients with secondary and malignant hypertension. *Clin. Sci. Mol. Med.* 24:91.

Handley, C. A., and Moyer, J. H. 1954. Changes in sodium and water excretion by vaso-active and by ganglionic and adrenergic blocking agents. *Am. J. Physiol.* 178:309.

Harburg, E., Julius, S., McGinn, N. F., McLeod, J., and Hoobler, S. W. 1964. Personality traits and behavioral patterns associated with systolic blood pressure levels in college males. *J. Chronic Dis.* 17:405.

———, McGinn, N. F., and Wigle, J. B. 1965. Recalled treatment by parents among college males and blood pressure levels vs. variability. *J. Psychosom. Res.* 9:173.

———, Erfurt, J. C., Hauenstein, L. S., Chape, C., Schull, W. J., and Schork, M. A. 1973. Socio-ecological stress, suppressed hostility, skin color, and black-white male blood pressure: Detroit. *Psychosom. Med.* 35:276.

Hardyck, C., and Singer, M. T. 1962. Transient changes in affect and blood pressure. *Arch. Gen. Psychiatry* 7:15.

Harris, G. W. 1947. The innervation and actions of the neurohypophysis; an investigation using the method of remote-control stimulation. *Philos. Trans. R. Soc. Lond.* [*Biol.*] 232b:385.

Harris, R. E., and Singer, M. T. 1968. Interaction of personality and stress in the pathogenesis of essential hypertension. In *Hypertension. Neural Control of Arterial Pressure.* Volume 16 in *Proceedings of the Council for High Blood Pressure Research.* New York: American Heart Association.

———, Sokolow, M., Carpenter, L. G., Freedman, M., and Hunt, S. P. 1953. Response to psychologic stress in persons who are potentially hypertensive. *Circulation* 7:874.

Harris, W. S., Schoenfeld, C. D., Gwynne, P. H., Weissler, A. M., and Warren, J. V. 1965. Circulatory and humoral responses to fear and anger. *J. Lab. Clin. Med.* 64:867.

Hayward, J. N., and Smith, W. K. 1962. The role of mesencephalic tegmental structures in the regulation of neurohypophysial function. *Fed. Proc.* 21:354.

Helmer, O. M. 1964. Renin activity in blood from patients with hypertension. *Can. Med. Assoc. J.* 90:221.

Henning, M. 1969. Noradrenaline turnover in renal hypertensive rats. *J. Pharm. Pharmacol.* 21:1969.

198

Henry, J. P., and Cassel, J. C. 1969. Psychosocial factors in essential hypertension. Recent epidemiologic and animal experimental evidence. *Am. J. Epidemiol.* 90:171.

———, Meehan, J. P., and Stephens, P. M. 1967. The use of psychosocial stimuli to induce prolonged systolic hypertension in mice. *Psychosom. Med.* 29:408.

———, Stephens, P. M., Axelrod, J., and Mueller, R. A. 1971a. Effect of psychosocial stimulation on the enzymes involved in the biosynthesis and metabolism of noradrenaline and adrenaline. *Psychosom. Med.* 33:227.

———, Ely, D. L., and Stephens, P. M. 1971b. Role of the autonomic system in social adaptation and stress. *Proc. Int. Union Physiol. Sci.* 8:50.

Herd, J. A., Morse, W. H., Kelleher, R. T., and Jones, J. G. 1969. Arterial hypertension in the squirrel monkey during behavioral experiments. *Am. J. Physiol.* 217:24.

Hering, H. E. 1923. Das Carotisdruckversuch. *Münch. Med. Wochenschr.* 42:1

Hess, W. 1949. *Das Zwischenhirn.* Basel: Schwabe.

Heyden, S., Bartel, A. G., Hames, C. G., and McDonough, J. R. 1969. Elevated blood pressure levels in adolescents, Evans County, Georgia: 7-year follow-up of 30 patients and 30 controls. *J.A.M.A.* 209:1683.

Heymans, C., and Neil, E. 1958. *Reflexogenic Areas of the Cardiovascular System.* Boston: Little, Brown.

Hickler, R. B., Lauler, D. P., Saravis, C. A., and Thorn, G. W. 1964. Characterization of a vasodepressor lipid of the renal medulla. *Trans. Assoc. Am. Physicians* 77:196.

Hill, L. B. 1935. A psychoanalytic observation on essential hypertension. *Psychoanal. Rev.* 22:60.

Hillarp, N.-A., Fuxe, K., and Dahlstrom, A. 1966. Demonstration and mapping of central neurons containing dopamine, noradrenaline, and 5-hydroxytryptamine and their reactions to psychopharmacological agents. *Pharmacol. Rev.* 18:727.

Hines, E. A., Jr. 1940. Range of normal blood pressure and subsequent development of hypertension: A follow-up study of 1522 patients. *J.A.M.A.* 115:271.

———, McIlhaney, M. L., and Gage, R. P. 1957. A study of twins with normal blood pressures and with hypertension. *Trans. Assoc. Am. Physicians* 70:282.

Hoff, E. C., and Green, H. D. 1936. Cardiovascular reactions induced by electrical stimulation of cerebral cortex. *Am. J. Physiol.* 117:411.

———, Kell, J. F., Jr., Hastings, N., Gray, E. N., and Scholes, D. M. 1951. Vasomotor, cellular and functional changes produced in kidney by brain stimulation. *J. Neurophysiol.* 14:317.

Hoff, H. E., Breckenridge, C. G., and Spencer, W. A. 1952. Suprasegmental integration of cardiac innervation. *Am. J. Physiol.* 171:178.

Hokanson, J. E. 1961a. The effects of frustration and anxiety on overt aggression. *J. Abnorm. Psychol.* 62:346.

——— 1961b. Vascular and psychogalvanic effects of experimentally aroused anger. *J. Pers.* 29:30.

Hollander, W., and Wilkins, R. W. 1957. Chlorothiazide: A new type of drug for the treatment of arterial hypertension. *Boston Med. Q.* 8:69.

Holloway, E. T., Seidel, C. L., and Bohr, D. F. 1973. Altered dependence on calcium of vascular smooth muscle from animals with experimental hypertension. *Hypertension, 1972. Second International Symposium on the Renin-Angiotensin-Aldosterone-Sodium System in Hypertension,* Mont Gabriel, Quebec. Berlin: Springer.

Holtz, P., Credner, K., and Kroneberg, G. 1947. Über das sympathicomimetische pressorische des Harns ("Urosympathin"). *Naunyn-Schmiedebergs Arch. Pharmacol.* 204:228.

Holzbauer, M., and Vogt, M. 1956. Depression by reserpine of the noradrenaline concentration in the hypothalamus of the cat. *J. Neurochem.* 1:8.

Hoobler, S. W. 1961. Current concepts of the mechanism of essential hypertension. In *Hypertension—Recent Advances: The Second Hahnemann Symposium on Hypertensive Disease,* edited by A. N. Brest and J. H. Moyer. Philadelphia: Lea & Febiger.

Horwitz, D., Alexander, R. W., Lovenberg, W., and Keiser, H. R. 1973. Human serum dopamine—β-hydroxylase: relationship to hypertension and sympathetic activity. *Circ. Res.* 32:594.

Humphrey, D. R. 1967. Neuronal activity in the medulla oblongata of cat evoked by stimulation of the carotid sinus nerve. In *Baroreceptors and Hypertension,* edited by P. Kezdi. New York: Pergamon.

Hunsperger, R. W. 1956. Affectreaktione auf elektrische Reizung im Hirnstamm der Katze. *Helv. Physiol. Acta* 14:7.

Ikoma, T. 1965. Studies on catechols with reference to hypertension (chap. I). *Jpn. Circ. J.* 29:1269.

Innes, G., Miller, W. M., and Valentine, M. 1959. Emotion and blood pressure. *J. Ment. Sci.* 105:840.

Iwai, J., Dahl, L. K., and Knudsen, K. D. 1973. Genetic influence on the renin-angiotensin system. Low renin activities in hypertension-prone rats. *Circ. Res.* 32:678.

Jaffe, D., Dahl, L. K., Sutherland, L., and Barker, D. 1969. Effects of chronic excess salt ingestion: Morphological findings in kidneys of rats with differing genetic susceptibility to hypertension. *Fed. Proc.* 28:422.

Jarrot, B., McQueen, A., and Louis, W. J. 1975. Serotonin levels in vascular tissue and the effects of a serotonin synthesis inhibitor on blood pressure in rats. *Clin. Exp. Pharmacol. Physiol.* 2:201.

Jenkins, C. D., Rosenman, R. H., and Friedman, M. 1967. Development of an objective psychological test for the determination of the coronary-prone behavior pattern in employed men. *J. Chronic Dis.* 20:371.

Johnson, B. C., and Remington, R. D. 1961. A sampling study of blood pressure levels in white and Negro residents of Nassau, Bahamas. *J. Chronic Dis.* 13:39.

———, Epstein, F. H., and Kjelsberg, M. O. 1965. Distributions and familial studies of blood pressure and serum cholesterol levels in a rural community—Tecumseh, Michigan. *J. Chronic Dis.* 18:147.

Jones, S. H., Younghusband, O. Z., and Evans, J. A. 1948. Human parabiotic pygopagus twins with essential hypertension. *J.A.M.A.* 138:642.

Jose, A., Crout, J. R., and Kaplan, N. M. 1970. Suppressed plasma renin activity in essential hypertension: roles of plasma volume, blood pressure and sympathetic nervous system. *Ann. Intern. Med.* 72:9.

Jost, H., Ruilmann, C. J., Hill, T. S., and Gulo, M. J. 1952. Studies in hypertension II: central and autonomic nervous system reactions of hypertensive individuals to simple physical and psychologic stress situations. *J. Nerv. Ment. Dis.* 115:152.

Joy, M. D., and Lowe, R. D. 1970. The site of cardiovascular action of angiotensin II in the brain. *Clin. Sci. Mol. Med.* 39:327.

Juan, P. 1963. Epiphyse, 5-hydroxytryptamine et corticoidogenese in vitro. *Ann. Endocrinol.* (Paris) 24:365.

Julius, S., and Conway, J. 1968. Hemodynamic studies in patients with borderline blood pressure elevation. *Circulation* 38:282.

——— and Schork, M. A. 1971. Borderline hypertension—a critical review. *J. Chronic Dis.* 23:723.

———, Harburg, E., McGinn, N. F., Keyes, J., and Hoobler, S. W. 1964. Relation between casual blood pressure readings in youth and at age 40: A retrospective study. *J. Chronic Dis.* 17:397.

———, Sannerstedt, R., and Conway, J. 1968. Hemodynamic effects of propranolol in borderline hypertension. *Circulation* 37 (Suppl. 6):109.

Kaada, B. R. 1951. Somatomotor, autonomic and electrocorticographic responses to electrical stimulation of "rhinencephalic" and other structures in primate, cat and dog. *Acta Physiol. Scand.* 83 (Suppl. 24):1.

———, Pribram, K. H., and Epstein, J. A. 1949. Respiratory and vascular responses in monkeys from temporal pole, insula, oribal surface and angulate gyrus. *J. Neurophysiol.* 12:347.

Kagan, A., Gordon, T., Kannel, W. B., and Dawber, T. R. 1958. Blood pressure and its relation to coronary heart disease in the Framingham study. *Hypertension* 7:53.

Kalis, B. L., Harris, R. E., Bennett, L. F., and Sokolow, M. 1961. Personality and life history factors in persons who are potentially hypertensive. *J. Nerv. Ment. Dis.* 132:457.

Kaminskiy, S. D. 1951. Role of central mechanisms in development of hypertension. *Klin. Med. (Mosk.)* 29:22.

Kandel, E. R. 1964. Electrical properties of hypothalamic neuroendocrine cells. *J. Gen. Physiol.* 47:691.

Kaneko, Y., Ikeda, T., Takeda, T., and Ueda, H. 1967. Renin release during acute reduction of arterial pressure in normotensive subjects and patients with renovascular hypertension. *J. Clin. Invest.* 46:705.

———, ———, ———, Inoue, G., Tagawa, H., and Ueda, H. 1968. Renin release in patients with benign essential hypertension. *Circulation* 38:353.

Kannel, W. B., Schwartz, M. J., and McNamara, P. M. 1969. Blood pressure and risk of coronary heart disease: The Framingham study. *Dis. Chest* 56:43.

Kaplan, S. M., Gottschalk, L. A., Magliocco, B., Rohovit, D., and Ross, W. D. 1960. Hostility in verbal productions and hypnotic "dreams" of hypertensive patients (comparisons between hypertensive and normotensive groups and within hypertensive individuals). *Psychosom. Med.* 22:320.

Karczmar, A. G., and Scudder, C. L. 1967. Behavioral responses to drugs and brain catecholamine levels in mice of different strains and genera. *Fed. Proc.* 26:1186.

Karli, P. 1969. Rat-mouse interspecific aggressive behavior and its manipulation by brain ablations and by brain stimulation. In *Biology of Aggressive Behavior*, edited by S. Garattini and E. B. Sigg. Amsterdam: Excerpta Medica.

Keith, R. L., Lown, B., and Stare, F. J. 1965. Coronary heart disease and behavior patterns. *Psychosom. Med.* 27:424.

Kezdi, P. 1962. Mechanism of the carotid sinus in experimental hypertension. *Circ. Res.* 11:145.

——— (ed.) 1967. *Baroreceptors and Hypertension.* New York: Pergamon.

——— and Wennemark, J. R. 1958. Baroreceptor and sympathetic activity in experimental renal hypertension in the dog. *Circulation* 17:785.

King, S. E., and Baldwin, D. S. 1956. Production of renal ischemia and proteinuria in man by the adrenal medullary hormones. *Am. J. Med.* 20:217.

Kirkendall, W. M., Fitz, A., and Armstrong, M. L. 1964. Hypokalemia and the diagnosis of hypertension. *Dis. Chest* 45:337.

Knowlton, A. I. 1960. Comparison of effect of desoxycorticosterone acetate and cortisone acetate on rat skeletal muscle electrolytes. *Proc. Soc. Exp. Biol. Med.* 104:13.

———, Loeb, E. N., Stoerk, H. C., and Seegal, B. C. 1947. Desoxycorticosterone acetate. The potentiation of its activity by sodium chloride. *J. Exp. Med.* 85:187.

Koch, E. 1931. *Die reflektorische Selbsteuerung des Kreislaufes.* Leipzig: Steinkopf.

Kogel, J. E., and Rothballer, A. B. 1962. Brainstem localization of a neurohypophysial activating system in the cat. *Fed. Proc.* 21:353.

Kolff, W. J., and Page, I. H. 1954. Blood pressure reducing function of the kidney: reduction of renoprival hypertension by kidney perfusion. *Am. J. Physiol.* 178:75.

———, ———, and Corcoran, A. C. 1954. Pathogenesis of renoprival cardiovascular disease in dogs. *Am. J. Physiol.* 178:237.

Korner, P. I. 1971. Integrative neural cardiovascular control. *Physiol. Rev.* 51:312.

201

Koster, M. 1970. Patterns of hypertension. *Bibl. Psychiatr.* 144:1.

Kroneberg, G., and Shümann, H. J. 1959. Über die Bedeutung der Innervation für die Adrenalin-synthese in Nebennierenmark. *Experientia* 15:234.

Kubicek, W. G., Kottke, F. J., Laker, D. J., and Visscher, M. B. 1953. Adaptation in the pressor receptor reflex mechanisms in experimental neurogenic hypertension. *Am. J. Physiol.* 175:380.

Kuchel, O., Fishman, L. M., Liddle, G. W., and Michelakis, A. 1967. Effect of diazoxide on plasma renin activity in hypertensive patients. *Ann. Intern. Med.* 67:791.

Kurland, G. S., and Freedberg, A. S. 1951. The potentiating effect of ACTH and of cortisone on pressor response to intravenous infusion of L-norepinephrine. *Proc. Soc. Exp. Biol. Med.* 78:28.

Lacey, J. I. 1950. Individual differences in somatic response patterns. *J. Comp. Physiol. Psychol.* 43:338.

———— and Lacey, B. E. 1958. Verification and extension of the principle of autonomic response sterotypy. *Am. J. Psychol.* 71:50.

———— and Smith, R. L. 1954. Conditioning and generalization of unconscious anxiety. *Science* 120:1045.

———— and Van Lehn, R. 1952. Differential emphasis in somatic response to stress. An experimental study. *Psychosom. Med.* 14:71.

————, Bateman, D. E., and Van Lehn, R. 1953. Autonomic response specificity. An experimental study. *Psychosom. Med.* 15:8.

Lagerspetz, K. Y. H., Tirri, R., and Lagerspetz, K. M. J. 1967. Neurochemical and endocrinological studies of mice selectively bred for aggressiveness. *Rep. Inst. Psychol.* (Turku) 29:1.

Laidlaw, J. C., Yendt, E. R., and Gornall, A. G. 1963. Hypertension caused by renal artery occlusion simulating primary aldosteronism. *Metabolism* 9:612.

Lamprecht, F., Williams, R. B., and Kopin, I. J. 1973. Serum dopamine-beta-hydroxylase during development of immobilization-induced hypertension. *Endocrinology* 92:953.

————, Eichelman, B. S., Williams, R. B., Wooten, G. F., and Kopin, I. J. 1974. Serum dopamine-beta-hydroxylase (DBH) activity and blood pressure response of rat strains to shock-induced fighting. *Psychosom. Med.* 36:298.

Landau, W. M. 1953. Autonomic responses mediated via the corticospinal tract. *J. Neurophysiol.* 16:299.

Landgren, S. 1952. On the excitation mechanism of the carotid baroreceptors. *Acta Physiol. Scand.* 26:1.

Langford, H. G., Watson, R. L., and Douglas, B. H. 1968. Factors affecting blood pressure in population groups. *Trans. Assoc. Am. Physicians* 81:135.

Lapin, B. A. 1965. Response of the cardiovascular system of monkeys to stress. *Acta Cardiol.* (Brux.) 11:276.

Laragh, J. H. 1960. The role of aldosterone in man: evidence for regulation of electrolyte balance and arterial pressure by a renal-adrenal system which may be involved in malignant hypertension. *J.A.M.A.* 174:293.

———— 1961. Oversecretion of aldosterone in man and its relation to hypertensive vascular disease: Factors which control secretion of the hormone. In *Hypertension—Recent Advances: The Second Hahnemann Symposium on Hypertensive Disease,* edited by A. N. Brest and J. H. Moyer. Philadelphia: Lea & Febiger.

———— and Stoerk, H. C. 1957. A study of the mechanism of secretion of the sodium-retaining hormone (aldosterone). *J. Clin. Invest.* 36:383.

————, Angers, M., Kelly, W. G., and Lieberman, S. 1960. Hypotensive agents and pressor

202

substances. The effect of epinephrine, norepinephrine, angiotensin II and others on the secretory rate of aldosterone in man. *J.A.M.A.* 174:234.

———, Sealey, J. E., and Sommers, S. C. 1966. Patterns of adrenal secretion and urinary excretion of aldosterone on plasma renin activity in normal and hypertensive subjects. *Circ. Res.* 18–19(Suppl. I):158.

———, ———, and Brunner, H. R. 1972. The control of aldosterone secretion in normal and hypertensive man: abnormal renin-aldosterone patterns in low renin hypertension. *Am. J. Med.* 53:549.

Laramore, D. C., and Grollman, A. 1950. Water and electrolyte content of tissues in normal and hypertensive rats. *Am. J. Physiol.* 161:278.

Laverty, R., and Smirk, F. H. 1961. Observations on the pathogenesis of spontaneous inherited hypertension and constricted renal-artery hypertension. *Circ. Res.* 9:455.

Leaf, R. C., Lerner, L., and Horovitz, Z. P. 1969. The role of the amygdala in the pharmacological and endocrinological manipulation of aggression. In *The Biology of Aggressive Behavior*, edited by S. Garattini and E. B. Sigg. Amsterdam: Excerpta Medica.

Ledingham, J. G. G., Bull, M. B., and Laragh, J. H. 1967. The meaning of aldosteronism in hypertensive disease. *Circ. Res.* 21 (Suppl. II):177.

Ledingham, J. M. 1971. Mechanisms in renal hypertension. *Proc. Roy. Soc. Med.* 64:409.

Ledsome, J. R., Linden, R. J., and O'Connor, W. J. 1961. The mechanisms by which distension of the left atrium produces diuresis in anesthetized dogs. *J. Physiol.* (Lond.) 159:87.

Lee, J. B., Gougoutos, J. Z., Takman, B. H., Daniels, E. G., Grostic, M. F., Pike, J. E., Hinman, J. W., and Muirhead, E. E. 1966. Vasodepressor and antihypertensive prostaglandins of PGE type with emphasis on the identification of medullin as PGE_2. *J. Clin. Invest.* 45:1036.

Lefer, A. M. 1973. Blood-borne humoral factors in the pathophysiology of circulatory shock. *Circ. Res.* 32:129.

Lehr, D., Goldman, H. W., and Casner, P. 1973. Renin-angiotensin role in thirst: paradoxical enhancement of drinking by angiotensin converting inhibitor. *Science* 182:1031.

Lenel, R., Katz, L. N., and Rodbard, S. 1948. Arterial hypertension in the chicken. *Am. J. Physiol.* 152:557.

Levy, R. L., White, P. D., Stroud, W. D., and Hillman, C. C. 1945. Transient hypertension: The relative prognostic importance of various systolic and diastolic levels. *J.A.M.A.* 128:1059.

Lew, E. A. 1967. Blood pressure and mortality—Life insurance experience. In *The Epidemiology of Hypertension: Proceedings of an Internatioal Symposium*, edited by J. Stamler, R. Stamler, and T. N. Pullman. New York: Grune & Stratton.

Lewinsohn, P. M. 1956. Personality correlates of duodenal ulcer and other psychosomatic reactions. *J. Clin. Psychol.* 12:296.

Lewis, G. P., and Piper, P. J. 1975. Inhibition of release of prostaglandins as an explanation of some of the actions of anti-inflammatory corticosteroids. *Nature* 254:308.

Lewis, P. J., Reid, J. L., Chalmers, J. P., and Dollery, C. T. 1973. Importance of central catecholaminergic neurons in the development of renal hypertension. *Clin. Sci. Mol. Med.* 45:115S.

Lindgren, P. 1955. The mesencephalon and the vasomotor system. *Acta Physiol. Scand.* 35 (Suppl.):121.

——— and Uvnäs, B. 1954. Photo-electric recording of the venous and arterial blood flow. *Acta Physiol. Scand.* 32:259.

Loewenstein, F. W. 1961. Blood pressure in relation to age and sex in the tropics and subtropics. A review of the literature and an investigation in two tribes of Brazil Indians. *Lancet* i:389.

203

Löfving, B. 1961. Cardiovascular adjustments induced from the rostral cingulate gyrus with special reference to sympatho-inhibitory mechanisms. *Acta Physiol. Scand.* 53 (Suppl. 184):1.

Louis, W. J. Spector, S., Tabei, R., and Sjoerdsma, A. 1968. Noradrenaline in the heart of the spontaneously hypertensive rats. *Lancet* i:1013.

———, Tabei, R., and Spector, S. 1971. Effects of sodium intake on inherited hypertension in the rat. *Lancet* ii:1283

Lovell, R. R. H. 1967. Race and blood pressure with special reference to Oceania. In *The Epidemiology of Essential Hypertension,* edited by J. Stamler, R. Stamler, and T. N. Pullman. New York: Grune & Stratton.

Lowenstein, J., Beranbaum, E. R., Chasis, H., and Baldwin, D. S. 1970. Intrarenal pressure and exaggerated natriuresis in essential hypertension. *Clin. Sci. Mol. Med.* 38:359.

Luetscher, J. A., Jr., and Axelrad, B. J. 1954. Increased aldosterone output during sodium deprivation in normal men. *Proc. Soc. Exp. Biol. Med.* 87:650.

———, Weinberger, M. H., Dowdy, A. J., Nokes, G. W., Balikian, H., Brodie, A., and Willoughby, S. 1969. Effects of sodium loading, sodium depletion and posture on plasma aldosterone concentration and renin activity in hypertensive patients. *J. Clin. Endocrinol.* 29:1310.

———, Boyers, D. G., Cuthbertson, J. G., and McMahon, D. F. 1973. A model of the human circulation. *Circ. Res.* 32, Suppl. I:I–84.

Lund, A. 1943. *Cortex Cerebris Betydning for Extemiteternes Vasomotoric.* Copenhagen: Munksgaard.

Lund-Johansen, P. 1967. Hemodynamics in early essential hypertension. *Acta Med. Scand.* Suppl. 482, 1.

Maas, J. W. 1962. Neurochemical differences between two strains of mice. *Science* 137:621.

McConnell, S. D., and Henkin, R. L. 1973. Increased preference for Na^+ and K^+ salts in spontaneously hypertensive (SH) rats. *Proc. Soc. Exp. Biol. Med.* 143:185.

McCubbin, J. W. 1958. Carotid sinus participation in experimental renal hypertension. *Circulation* 17:791.

——— and Page, I. H. 1958. Do ganglion-blocking agents and reserpine affect central vasomotor activity? *Circ. Res.* 6:816.

———, Green, J. H., and Page, I. H. 1956. Baroreceptor function in chronic renal hypertension. *Circ. Res.* 4:205.

McCubbin, J. W. 1967. Interrelationships between the sympathetic nervous system and the renin-angiotensin system. In *Baroreceptors and Hypertension,* edited by P. Kezdi. New York: Pergamon.

McDonald, R. K., Wagner, E. N., Jr., and Weise, V. K. 1957. Relationship between endogenous antidiuretic hormone activity and ACTH release in man. *Proc. Soc. Exp. Biol. Med.* 96:652.

McDonough, J., and Wilhelmj, C. M. 1954. The effect of excess salt intake on human blood pressure. *Am. J. Dig. Dis.* 21:180.

McGinn, N. F., Harburg, E., Julius, S., and MacLeod, J. M. 1964. Psychological correlates of blood pressure. *Psych. Bull.* 61:209.

McKegney, F. P., and Williams, R. B., Jr. 1967. Psychological aspects of hypertension: II. The differential influence of interview variables on blood pressure. *Am. J. Psychiatry* 123:1539.

McKenzie, J. K., and Phelan, E. L. 1969. Plasma and renin in the New Zealand strain of genetic hypertensive and random-bred control rats. *Proc. Univ. Otago Med. Sch.* 47:23.

MacKenzie, L. F., and Shepherd, P. 1937. The significance of past hypertension in applicants later presenting normal average blood pressures. *Proc. Med. Sect. Life Insur. Assoc.* 24:157.

McKusick, V. 1960. Genetics and the nature of essential hypertension. *Circulation* 22:857.

McQueen, J. D., Brown, K. M., and Walker, A. E. 1954. Role of the brainstem in blood pressure regulation in the dog. *Neurology* 4:1.

204

McSmythe, C., Nickel, J. F., and Bradley, S. E. 1952. The effect of epinephrine (USP), 1-epinephrine, and 1-norepinephrine on glomerular filtration rate, renal plasma flow, and the urinary excretion of sodium, potassium, and water in normal man. *J. Clin. Invest.* 31:499.

Maddocks, I. 1961. The influence of standard of living on blood pressure in Fiji. *Circulation* 24:1220.

Makarychev, A. I., and Kuritsa, A. I. 1951. Experimental hypertension of cortical origin. *Zh. Vyssh. Nerv. Deiat.* 1:199.

Malmo, R. B., and Shagass, C. 1952. Studies of blood pressure in psychiatric patients under stress. *Psychosom. Med.* 14:82.

Mason, J. W. 1968. The scope of psychoendocrine research. *Psychosom. Med.* Part 2, 30:565.

Masson, G. M. C., Mikasa, A., and Yasuda, H. 1962. Experimental vascular disease elicited by aldosterone and renin. *Endocrinology* 71:505.

Matarazzo, G. 1954. An experimental study of aggression in the hypertensive patient. *J. Pers.* 22:423.

Mathers, J. A. L., Osborne, R. H., and DeGeorge, F. V. 1961. Studies of blood pressure, heart rate, and the electrocardiogram in adult twins. *Am. Heart J.* 63:634.

Maynert, E. W., and Levi, R. 1964. Stress-induced release of brain norepinephrine and its inhibition by drugs. *J. Pharmacol. Exp. Ther.* 143:90.

Meehan, J. P. 1960. Central nervous control of the renal circulation. *Am. Heart J.* 6:318.

Mellander, S. 1960. Comparative studies on the adrenergic neuro-hormonal control of resistance and capacitance blood vessels in the cat. *Acta Physiol. Scand.* 176 Suppl.:1.

Mendlowitz, M. 1967. Vascular reactivity in essential and renal hypertension in man. *Am. Heart J.* 73:121.

—— and Naftchi, N. 1958. Work of digital vasoconstriction produced by infused norepinephrine in primary hypertension. *J. Appl. Physiol.* 13:247.

——, Gitlow, S., and Naftchi, N. 1958. Work of digital vasoconstriction produced by infused norepinephrine in Cushing's syndrome. *J. Appl. Physiol.* 13:252.

——, ——, and —— 1959. The cause of essential hypertension. *Perspect. Biol. Med.* 2:354.

——, Naftchi, N., Weinreb, H. L., and Gitlow, S. E. 1961. Effect of prednisone on digital vascular reactivity in normotensive and hypertensive subjects. *J. Appl. Physiol.* 16:89.

Meneely, G. R., Tucker, R. G., Darby, W. J., and Auerbach, S. H. 1953. Chronic sodium chloride toxicity in the albino rat. II. Occurrence of hypertension and of a syndrome of edema and renal failure. *J. Exp. Med.* 98:71.

——, ——, ——, Ball, C. O. T., Kory, R. C., and Auerbach, S. H. 1954. Electrocardiographic changes, disturbed lipid metabolism and decreased survival rates observed in rats chronically eating increased sodium chloride. *Am. J. Med.* 16:599.

Merrill, J. P., Murray, J. E., Harrison, J. H., and Guild, W. R. 1956. Successful homotransplantation of the human kidney between identical twins. *J.A.M.A.* 160:277.

——, Giordano, C., and Heetderks, D. R. 1961. The role of the kidney in human hypertension. I. Failure of hypertension to develop in the renoprival subject. *Am. J. Med.* 31:931.

Mess, B. 1967. Endocrine and neurochemical aspects of pineal function. *Int. Rev. Neurobiol.* 11:171.

Meyer, P. H. (Discussant). 1967. The meaning of aldosteronism in hypertensive disease. *Circ. Res.* 21 (Suppl. II):186.

Miall, W. E., and Oldham, P. D. 1958. Factors influencing arterial blood pressure in the general population. *Clin. Sci.* 17:409.

——, Kass, E. H., Ling, J., and Stuart, K. L. 1962. Factors influencing arterial pressure in the general population in Jamaica. *Br. Med. J.* 2:497.

——, Heneage, P., Khosla, T., Lovell, H. G., and Moore, F. 1967. Factors influencing the degree of resemblance in arterial pressure of close relatives. *Clin. Sci.* 33:271.

205

Miasnikov, A. L. 1954. *Hypertensive Disease.* Moscow: Medgiz.

———— 1962. Significance of disturbances of higher nervous activity in the pathogenesis of hypertensive disease. In *Symposium on the Pathogenesis of Essential Hypertension,* edited by J. H. Cort, V. Fencl, Z. Hejl, and J. Jirka. New York: Pergamon.

Miles, B. E., and De Wardener, H. E. 1953. Effect of emotion on renal function in normotensive and hypertensive women. *Lancet* ii:539.

Miller, E. D., Jr., Samuels, A. I., Haber, E., and Barger, A. C. 1972. Inhibition of angiotensin conversion in experimental renovascular hypertension. *Science* 177:1108.

Miller, M. L. 1939. Blood pressure and inhibited aggression in psychotics. *Psychosom. Med.* 1:162.

Miller, N. E. 1969. Learning of visceral and glandular responses. *Science* 163:434.

Mills, E., and Wang, S. C. 1963. Localization of ascending pathways in the rostral brainstem of the dog for ADH liberation. *Fed. Proc.* 22:572.

Mills, L. C., Moyer, J. H., and Skelton, J. M. 1953. The effect of norepinephrine and epinephrine on renal hemodynamics. *Am. J. Med. Sci.* 226:653.

Miminoshvili, D. I. 1960. Experimental neurosis in monkeys. In *Theoretical and Practical Problems of Medicine in Biology in Experiments on Monkeys,* edited by I. A. Utkin. New York: Pergamon.

Mirsky, I. A., Stein, M., and Paulisch, G. 1954. The secretion of an antidiuretic substance into the circulation of rats exposed to noxious stimuli. *Endocrinology* 54:491.

Mogil, R. A., Irskovitz, H., Russell, J. H., and Murphy, J. J. 1969. Renal innervation and renin activity in salt metabolism and hypertension. *Am. J. Physiol.* 216:693.

Monroe, R. R., Heath, R. G., Head, R. G., Stone, R. L., and Ritter, K. A. 1961. A comparison of hypertensive and hypotensive schizophrenics. *Psychosom. Med.* 23:508.

Morgan, C. T., and Galambos, R. 1942. Production of audiogenic seizures by tones of low frequency. *Am. J. Psychol.* 55:555.

Morris, R. E., Jr., Ranson, P. A., and Howard, J. E. 1962. Studies on the relationship of angiotensin to hypertension of renal origin. *J. Clin. Invest.* 41:1386.

Moruzzi, G. 1940. Paleocerebellar inhibition of vasomotor and respiratory carotid sinus reflexes. *J. Neurophysiol.* 3:20.

———— 1950. *Problems in Cerebellar Physiology.* Springfield, Ill.: Charles C Thomas.

Moschowitz, E. 1919. Hypertension: its significance, relation to arteriosclerosis and nephritis, and etiology. *Am. J. Med. Sci.* 158:668.

Moses, L., Daniels, G. E., and Nickerson, J. L. 1956. Psychogenic factors in essential hypertension: Methodology and preliminary report. *Psychosom. Med.* 18:471.

Muirhead, E. E., Brooks, B., Kosinski, M., Daniels, E. E., and Hinman, J. W. 1966. Renomedullary antihypertensive principle in renal hypertension. *J. Lab. Clin. Med.* 67:778.

————, Leach, B. E., Brown, G. B., Daniels, E. G., and Hinman, J. W. 1967. Antihypertensive effect of prostaglandin E2 (PGE2) in renovascular hypertension. *J. Lab. Clin. Med.* 70:986.

————, Brown, G. B., Germain, G. S., and Leach, B. E. 1970. The renal medulla as an antihypertensive organ. *J. Lab. Clin. Med.* 76:641.

Muller, A. F., Manning, E. L., and Riondel, A. M. 1958. Influence of position and activity on the secretion of aldosterone. *Lancet* i:711.

Mulrow, P. J., Ganong, W. F., Cera, G., and Kulgian, A. 1962. The nature of the aldosterone-stimulating factor in dog kidneys. *J. Clin. Invest.* 41:505.

Murray, J. E., Merrill, J. P., and Harrison, J. H. 1958. Kidney transplantation between seven pairs of identical twins. *Ann. Surg.* 148:343.

Nagareda, C. S., and Gaunt, R. 1951. Functional relationship between the adrenal cortex and posterior pituitary. *Endocrinology* 48:560.

Nakamura, K., Gerold, M., and Thoenen, H. 1971. Experimental hypertension of the rat: Reciprocal changes of norepinephrine turnover in heart and brainstem. *Naunyn-Schmiedebergs Arch. Pharmacol.* 268:125.

206

——, ——, and ——. 1971. Genetically hypertensive rats: Relationship between the development of hypertension and the changes in norepinephrine turnover of peripheral and central adrenergic neurons. *Naunyn-Schmiedebergs Arch. Pharmacol.* 271:157.

Napalkov, A. V., and Karas, I. 1957. Abolishment of pathologic conditioned associations in experimental hypertension. *Zh. Vysshei Nerv. Deiat.* 7:402.

Neiberg, N. A. 1957. The effects of induced stress on the management of hostility in essential hypertension. *Dissert. Abstr.* 17:1597.

Nestel, P. J. 1969. Blood pressure and catecholamine excretion after mental stress in labile hypertension. *Lancet* i:692.

Neumayr, R. J., Hare, B. D., and Franz, D. N. 1974. Evidence for bulbospinal control of sympathetic preganglionic neurons by monoaminergic pathways. *Life Sci.* 14:793.

Newton, M. A., and Laragh, J. H. 1968a. Effect of corticotropin on aldosterone excretion and plasma renin in normal subjects, in essental hypertension and in primary aldosteronism. *J. Clin. Endocrinol. Metab.* 28:1006.

—— and —— 1968b. Effects of glucocorticoid administration on aldosterone excretion and plasma renin in normal subjects, in essential hypertension and in primary aldosteronism. *J. Clin. Endocrinol. Metab.* 28:1014.

Nicotero, J. A., Beamer, V., Moutsos, S. E., and Shapiro, A. P. 1968. Effects of propranolol on the pressor response to noxious stimuli in hypertensive patients. *Am. J. Cardiol.* 22:657.

Norberg, K.-A. 1967. Transmitter histochemistry of the sympathetic adrenergic nervous system. *Brain Res.* 5:125.

O'Connor, W. J., and Verney, E. B. 1945. The effect of increased activity of the sympathetic system in the inhibition of water diuresis by emotional stress. *Q. J. Exp. Physiol.* 33:77.

O'Hare, J. P. 1920. Vascular reactions in vascular hypertension. *Am. J. Med. Sci.* 159:371.

——, Walker, W. G., and Vickers, M. C. 1924. Heredity and hypertension. *J.A.M.A.* 83:27.

Okamoto, K. 1969. Spontaneous hypertension in rats. *Int. Rev. Exp. Pathol.* 7:227.

—— and Aoki, K. 1963. Development of a strain of spontaneously hypertensive rats. *Jpn. Circ. J.* 27:282.

Oliver, J. T., Birmingham, M. K., Bartova, A., Li, M. P., and Chan, T. H. 1973. Hypertensive action of 18-hydroxydeoxycorticosterone. *Science* 182:1249.

Orbison, J. L., Christian, C. L., and Peters, E. 1952. Studies on experimental hypertension and cardiovascular disease. *Arch. Pathol.* 54:185.

Orlov, V. V. 1959. On mechanics of influence of cerebral cortex on reaction of peripheral vessels. *Zh. Vysshei Nerv. Deiat.* 9:712.

Ostfeld, A. M. 1973. Editorial: What's the payoff in hypertension research? *Psychosom. Med.* 35:1.

—— and Lebovitz, B. Z. 1959. Personality factors and pressor mechanisms in renal and essential hypertension. *Arch. Intern. Med.* 104:497.

—— and —— 1960. Blood pressure lability: a correlative study. *J. Chronic Dis.* 12:428.

—— and Paul, O. 1963. The inheritance of hypertension. *Lancet* i:575.

—— and Shekelle, R. B. 1967. Psychological variables and blood pressure. In *The Epidemiology of Essential Hypertension*, edited by J. Stamler, R. Stamler, and T. N. Pullman. New York: Grune & Stratton.

Padmavati, S., and Gupta, S. 1959. Blood pressure studies in rural and urban groups in Delhi. *Circulation* 19:395.

Page, I. H. 1935. Relationship of extrinsic venal nerves to origin of experimental hypertension. *Am. J. Physiol.* 112:166.

—— 1960. The mosaic theory of hypertension. In *Essential Hypertension*, edited by K. D. Bock and P. T. Cottier. Berlin: Springer.

—— and McCubbin, J. W. 1951. The pattern of vascular reactivity in experimental hypertension of varied origin. *Circulation* 4:70.

———— and ———— 1965. The physiology of hypertension. In *Handbook of Physiology*, Sect. 2: Circulation. American Physiological Society.

Palmer, R. S. 1930. The significance of essential hypertension in young male adults. *J.A.M.A.* 94:694.

———— 1950. Psyche and blood pressure. *J.A.M.A.* 144:295.

Papez, J. W. 1926. Reticulo-spinal tracts in the cat. Marchi method. *J. Comp. Neurol.* 41:365.

Passo, S. S., Assaykeen, T. A., Orsuka, K., Wise, B. L., Goldfien, A., and Ganong, W. F. 1971. Effect of stimulation of the medulla oblongata on renin secretion in dogs. *Neuroendocrinology* 7:1.

Patterson, G. C., Shepard, J. T., and Whelan, R. F. 1957. Resistance to flow in the upper and lower limb vessels in patients with coarctation of the aorta. *Clin. Sci.* 16:627.

Paulsen, E. C., and Hess, S. M. 1963. The rate of synthesis of catecholamines following depletion in guinea pig brain and heart. *J. Neurochem.* 10:453.

Peart, W. S. 1959. Hypertension and the kidney. I. Clinical, pathological, and functional disorders, especially in man. II. Experimental basis of renal hypertension. *Br. Med. J.* ii:1353; 1421.

Perera, G. W. 1955. Hypertensive vascular disease: description and natural history. *J. Chronic Dis.* 1:33.

————, Clark, E. G., Gearing. F. R., and Schweitzer, M. D. 1961. The family of hypertensive man. *Am. J. Med. Sci.* 241:18.

Perlmutt, J. H. 1963. Reflex diuresis after occlusion of common carotid arteries in hydrated dogs. *Am. J. Physiol.* 204:197.

Peterson, L. H. 1961. Hemodynamic alterations in essential hypertension. In *Hypertension-Recent Advances. The Second Hahnemann Symposium on Hypertensive Disease*, edited by A. N. Brest and J. H. Moyer. Philadelphia: Lea & Febiger.

———— 1963. Systems behavior, feed-back loops and high blood pressure research. *Circ. Res.* 12:585.

Petyelina, V. V. 1952. Conditional reflexive influences on blood vessels and respiration during strenuous mental activity. *Fiziol. Zh. SSSR* 38:566.

Pfeffer, M. A., and Frohlich, E. D. 1973. Hemodynamic and myocardial function in young and old normotensive and spontaneously hypertensive rats. *Circ. Res.* 32(Suppl. I):28.

Pfeiffer, J. B., Jr., and Wolff, H. G. 1950. Studies in renal circulation during periods of life stress and accompanying emotional reactions in subjects with and without essential hypertension: Observations on the role of neural activity in the regulation of renal blood flow. *Res. Publ. Assoc. Res. Nerv. Ment. Dis.* 29:929.

Pickering, G. W. 1945. Role of kidney in acute and chronic hypertension following renal artery constriction in rabbit. *Clin. Sci.* 5:229.

———— 1955. *High Blood Pressure.* London: Churchill.

———— 1961. *The Nature of Essential Hypertension.* New York: Grune & Stratton.

———— 1967. The inheritance of arterial pressure. In *The Epidemiology of Hypertension*, edited by J. Stamler, R. Stamler, and T. N. Pullman. New York: Grune & Stratton.

Pickford, M. 1952. Antidiuretic substances. *Pharmacol. Rev.* 4:255.

Pilowsky, I., Spalding, D., Shaw, J., and Korner, P. I. 1973. Hypertension and personality. *Psychosom. Med.* 35:50.

Pitts, R. F., and Bronk, D. W. 1941/1942. Excitability cycle of the hypothalamus-sympathetic neurone system. *Am. J. Physiol.* 135:504.

————, Larrabee, M. G., and Bronk, D. W. 1941. An analysis of hypothalamic cardiovascular control. *Am. J. Physiol.* 134:359.

Platt, R. 1947. Heredity in hypertension. *Q. J. Med.* 16:111.

———— 1959. The nature of essential hypertension. *Lancet* ii:55.

208

————— 1963. Heredity in hypertension. *Lancet* i:899.

————— 1967. The influence of heredity. In *The Epidemiology of Essential Hypertension,* edited by J. Stamler, R. Stamler, and T. N. Pullman. New York: Grune & Stratton.

Pool, J. L., and Ransohoff, J. 1949. Autonomic effects on stimulating rostral portion of cingulate gyri in man. *J. Neurophysiol.* 12:385.

Ramey, E. R., Goldstein, M. S., and Levine, R. 1951. Action of nor-epinephrine and adrenal cortical steroids on blood pressure and work performance of adrenalectomized dogs. *Am. J. Physiol.* 165:450.

Rankin, E. M., and Pappenheimer, J. R. 1957. Wasserdurchlässigkeit und Permeabilitet der Kapillarwande. *Ergeb. Physiol.* 49:59.

Ranson, S. W., and Billingsley, P. R. 1916. Vasomotor reactions from stimulation of the floor of the fourth ventricle. *Am. J. Physiol.* 41:85.

Rapp, J. P., and Dahl, L. K. 1971. Adrenal steroidogenesis in rats bred for susceptibility and resistance to the hypertensive effect of salt. *Endocrinology* 88:52.

————— and ————— 1972. Possible role of 18-hydroxycorticosterone in hypertension. *Nature* 237:338.

—————, Knudsen, K. D., Iwai, J., and Dahl, L. K. 1973. Genetic control of blood pressure and corticosteroid production in rats. *Circ. Res.* 32(Suppl. I):139.

Redleaf, P., and Tobian, L. 1958a. The question of vascular hyperresponsiveness in hypertension. *Circ. Res.* 6:185.

————— and ————— 1958b. Sodium restriction and reserpine administration in experimental renal hypertension. A correlation of arterial blood pressure responses with the ionic composition of the arterial wall. *Circ. Res.* 6:343.

Redmond, D. P., Gaylor, M. S., McDonald, R. H., Jr., and Shapiro, A. P. 1974. Blood pressure and heart-rate response to verbal instruction and relaxation in hypertension. *Psychosom. Med.* 36:285.

Reed, R. K., Sapirstein, L. A., Southard, F. D., Jr., and Ogden, E. 1944. The effects of nembutal and yohimbine on chronic renal hypertension in the rat. *Am. J. Physiol.* 141:707.

Reese, W. G., and Dykman, R. A. 1960. Conditional cardiovascular reflexes in dogs and men. *Physiol. Rev.* 40(Suppl. 4):250.

Reiser, M. F. 1970. Theoretical considerations of the role of psychological factors in pathogenesis and etiology of essential hypertension. *Bibl. Psychiatr.* 144:117.

—————, Brust, A. A., Shapiro, A. P., Baker, H. M., Ranschoff, W., and Ferris, E. B. 1950. Life situations, emotions and the course of patients with arterial hypertension. *Res. Publ. Assoc. Res. Nerv. Ment. Dis.* 29:870.

—————, —————, and Ferris, E. B. 1951a. Life situations, emotions and the course of patients with arterial hypertension. *Psychosom. Med.* 13:133.

—————, Rosenbaum, M., and Ferris, E. B. 1951b. Psychologic mechanisms in malignant hypertension. *Psychosom. Med.* 13:147.

Remington, R. D., Lambarth, B., Moser, M., and Hoobler, S. W., 1960. Circulatory reactions of normotensive and hypertensive subjects and of the children of normal and hypertensive parents. *Am. Heart J.* 59:58.

Robinson, J. O. 1962. A study of neuroticism and casual arterial blood pressure. *Br. J. Clin. Psychol.* 2:56.

————— 1964. A possible effect of selection on the test scores of a group of hypertensives. *J. Psychosom. Res.* 8:239.

————— 1969. Symptoms and the discovery of high blood pressure. *J. Psychosom. Res.* 13:157.

Robinson, S. C., and Brucer, M. 1939. Range of normal blood pressure, statistical study of 11,383 persons. *Arch. Intern. Med.* 6:409.

Rochlin, D. B., Shohl, T. E., and Cary, A. L. 1959. A comparison of (Cr 51) blood volumes in hypertensive and normal patients. *Fed. Proc.* 18:129.

Rosenman, R. H. 1969. The possible general causes of coronary artery disease. In *Pathogenesis of Coronary Artery Disease*, edited by M. Friedman. New York: McGraw-Hill.

—— and Friedman, M. 1963. Behavior patterns, blood lipids, and coronary heart disease. *J.A.M.A.* 184:934.

——, ——, Straus, R., Wurm, M., Kositechek, R., Hahn, W., and Werthessen, N. T. 1964. A predictive study of coronary heart disease. *J.A.M.A.* 189:15.

——, ——, ——, ——, Jenkins, D., and Messinger, H. 1966. Coronary heart disease in the Western Collaborative Group Study. *J.A.M.A.* 195:86.

Rosenthal, J., Paddock, J., and Hollander, W. 1973. Identification of a new vasodepressor factor (VDF) in arterial tissue and plasma of dogs and humans. *Circ. Res.* 32(Suppl. I):I–169.

Ross, E. J. 1960. Modification of the effects of aldosterone on electrolyte excretion in man by simultaneous administration of corticosterone and hydrocortisone. Relevance to Conn's syndrome. *J. Clin. Endocrinol.* 20:229.

Rossi, G. F., and Brodal, A. 1956. Corticofugal fibres to brain-stem reticular formation; experimental study in cat. *J. Anat.* (Lond.) 90:42.

Rothballer, A. 1966. Pathways of secretion and regulation of posterior pituitary factors. *Res. Publ. Assoc. Res. Nerv. Ment. Dis.* 43:86.

Rothlin, E., Emmenger, H., and Cerletti, A. 1953. Experiments to produce essential hypertension in rats. *Helv. Physiol. Pharmacol. Acta* 11:C25.

——, Cerletti, A., and Emmenger, H. 1956. Experimental psychoneurogenic hypertension and its treatment with hydrogenated ergotalkaloids (Hydrergine). *Acta Med. Scand.* 312(Suppl.):27.

Rovner, D. R., Conn, J. W., Knopf, R. F., Cohen, E. L., and Hsueh, M. T.-Y. 1965. Nature of renal escape from the sodium-retaining effects of aldosterone in primary aldosteronism and in normal subjects. *J. Clin. Endocrinol. Metab.* 25:53.

Rushmer, R. F. 1958. Heart adaptation to environment. Neural and humoral control of the heart. *Abstracts of the Symposium, World Congress of Cardiology.* Brussels.

Ruskin, A., Beard, O. W., and Schaffer, R. L. 1948. "Blast hypertension": Elevated arterial pressure in victims of the Texas City disaster. *Am. J. Med.* 4:228.

Russi, S., Blumenthal, H. T., and Gray, S. H. 1945. Small adenomas of the adrenal cortex in hypertension and diabetes. *Arch. Intern. Med.* 76:284.

Rydin, H., and Verney, E. B. 1938. The inhibition of water-diuresis by emotional stress and by muscular exercise. *Q. J. Exp. Physiol.* 27:343.

Ryvkin, I. A. 1960. The role of heredity in the etiology of hypertensive vascular disease. *Klin. Med.* (Moskva) 38:24.

Sachs, E., Jr., Brendler, S. J., and Fulton, J. F. 1949. The orbital gyri. *Brain* 72:227.

Saffran, M., Schally, A. V., and Benfey, B. G. 1955. Stimulation of the release of corticotropin from the adenohypophysis by a neurohypophysial factor. *Endocrinology* 57:439.

Sainsbury, P. 1960. Psychosomatic disorders and neurosis in out-patients attending a general hospital. *J. Psychosom. Res.* 4:261.

—— 1964. Neuroticism and hypertension in an out-patient population. *J. Psychosom. Res.* 8:235.

Sannerstedt, R. 1969. Hemodynamic findings at rest and during exercise in mild arterial hypertension. *Am. J. Med. Sci.* 258:70.

Sapira, J. D., Lipman, R. L., and Shapiro, A. P. 1966. Hyperresponsivity to angiotensin induced in rats by behavioral stimulation. *Proc. Soc. Exp. Biol. Med.* 123:52.

——, Scheib, E. T., Moriarty, R., and Shapiro, A. P. 1971. Differences in perception between hypertensive and normotensive populations. *Psychosom. Med.* 33:239.

210

Sapirstein, L. A. 1957. Sodium and water ratios in the pathogenesis of hypertension. *Proc. Coun. High Blood Press. Res.* 6:28.

————, Brandt, W. L., and Drury, D. R. 1950. Production of hypertension in rat by substituting hypertonic sodium chloride solutions for drinking water. *Proc. Soc. Exp. Biol. Med.* 73:82.

Saslow, G., Gressel, G. C., Shobe, F. O., Dubois, P. H., and Schroeder, H. A. 1950. Possible etiological relevance of personality factors in hypertension. *Psychosom. Med.* 12:292.

Saul, L. J. 1939. Hostility in cases of essential hypertension. *Psychosom. Med.* 1:153.

Schachter, J. 1957. Pain, fear and anger in hypertensives and normotensives: A psychophysiologic study. *Psychosom. Med.* 19:17.

Schechter, P. J., Horwitz, D., and Henkin, R. I. 1973. Sodium chloride preference in essential hypertension. *J.A.M.A.* 225:1311.

Schlager, G. 1966. Systolic blood pressure in eight inbred strains of mice. *Nature* 212:519.

Schmiterlow, C. G. 1948. Nature and occurrence of pressor and depressor substances in extracts from blood vessels. *Acta Physiol. Scand.* (Suppl.)56:1.

Schwartz, S. I., and Griffith, L. S. C. 1967. Reduction of hypertension by electrical stimulation of the carotid sinus nerve. In *Baroreceptors and Hypertension*, edited by P. Kezdi. New York: Pergamon.

Schweitzer, M. D., Gearing, F. R., and Perera, G. A. 1967. Family studies of primary hypertension: their contribution to the understanding of genetic factors. In *The Epidemiology of Essential Hypertension*, edited by J. Stamler, R. Stamler, and T. N. Pullman. New York: Grune & Stratton.

Scotch, N. A. 1961. Blood pressure measurements of urban Zulu adults. *Am. Heart J.* 61:173.

———— and Geiger, J. H. 1963. Epidemiology of essential hypertension: psychologic and sociocultural factors in etiology. *J. Chronic Dis.* 16:1183.

Scroop, G. C., and Lowe, R. D. 1968. Central pressor effect of angiotensin mediated by the parasympathetic nervous system. *Nature* 220:331.

Selye, H., Hall, C. E., and Rowley, E. M. 1943. Malignant hypertension produced by treatment with desoxycorticosterone acetate and sodium chloride. *Can. Med. Assoc. J.* 49:88.

Sen, S., Smeby, R. R., and Bumpus, F. M. 1972. Renin in rats with spontaneous hypertension. *Circ. Res.* 31:876.

Shamma, A. H., Goodard, J. W., and Sommers, S. C. 1958. A study of the adrenal states in hypertension. *J. Chron. Dis.* 8:587.

Shapiro, A. P. 1960a. Comparative studies of the blood pressure response to different noxious stimuli. *Psychosom. Med.* 22:320.

———— 1960b. Psychophysiologic mechanisms in hypertensive vascular disease. *Ann. Intern. Med.* 53:64.

———— 1963. Experimental pyelonephritis and hypertension. *Ann. Intern. Med.* 59:37.

———— 1973. Essential hypertension—Why idiopathic? *Am. J. Med.* 54:1.

———— and Grollman, A. 1953. A critical evaluation of the hypotensive action of hydrallazine, hexamethonium, tetraethylammonium and dibenzyline salts in human and experimental hypertension. *Circulation* 8:188.

———— and Horn, P. W. 1955. Blood pressure, plasma pepsinogen, and behavior in cats subjected to experimental production of anxiety. *J. Nerv. Ment. Dis.* 122:222.

———— and Melhado, J. 1957. Factors affecting development of hypertensive vascular disease after renal injury in rats. *Proc. Soc. Exp. Biol. Med.* 96:619.

———— and Teng, H. C. 1957. Technic of controlled drug assay illustrated by a comparative study of rauwolfia serpentina, phenobarbital and placebo in the hypertensive patient. *N. Engl. J. Med.* 256:970.

————, Rosenbaum, M., and Ferris, E. B. 1954. Comparison of blood pressure response to veriloid and to the doctor. *Psychosom. Med.* 16:478.

————, Perez-Stable, E., Scheib, E. T., Broń, K., Moutsos, S. E., Berg, G., Misage, J. R., Bahnson, H., Fisher, B., and Drapanas, T. 1969. Renal artery stenosis and hypertension: Observations on current status of therapy from a study of 115 patients. *Am. J. Med.* 47:175.

Shapiro, D., Tursky, B., Gershon, E., and Stern, M. 1969. Effects of feedback and reinforcement on the control of human systolic blood pressure. *Science* 163:588.

————, Schwartz, G. E., and Tursky, B. 1970. Control of diastolic blood pressure in man by feedback and reinforcement. *Psychophysiology* 8:262.

Share, L., and Levy, M. N. 1962. Cardiovascular receptors and blood titer of antidiuretic hormone. *Am. J. Physiol.* 203:425.

Shekelle, R. B., Ostfeld, A. M., Lebovitz, B. Z., and Paul, O. 1970. Personality traits and coronary heart disease: a re-examination of Ibrahim's hypothesis using longitudinal data. *J. Chronic. Dis.* 23:33.

Sheldon, S. H., and Ball, R. 1950. Physiological characteristics of the Y twins and their relation to hypertension. *Res. Publ. Assoc. Res. Nerv. Ment. Dis.* 29:962.

Short, D. 1966. Morphology of the intestinal arterioles in chronic human hypertension. *Br. Heart J.* 28:184.

Simonson, E., and Brožek, J. 1959. Russian research on arterial hypertension. *Ann. Intern. Med.* 50:129.

Simpson, F. O., and Gilchrist, A. R. 1958. Prognosis in untreated hypertensive vascular disease. *Scott. Med. J.* 3:1.

Sinaiko, A., and Mirkin, B. L. 1974. Ontogenesis of the renin-angiotensin system in spontaneously hypertensive and normal Wistar rats. *Circ. Res.* 34:693.

Sivertsson, R. 1970. The hemodynamic importance of structural vascular changes in essential hypertension. *Acta Physiol. Scand.* Suppl. 343, 1.

Skinner, S. L., McCubbin, J. W., and Page, I. H. 1963. Route of renin release. *Fed. Proc.* 22:181.

Smirk, F. A. 1957. *High Arterial Pressure.* Springfield, Ill.: Charles C Thomas.

Smirk, F. H., and Hall, W. H. 1958. Inherited hypertension in rats. *Nature* 182:727.

Smith, H. W. 1939/1940. Physiology of the renal circulation. *Harvey Lect.* 35:166.

Smith, K. 1954. Conditioning as an artifact. *Psychol. Rev.* 61:217.

Sokolow, M., and Harris, R. E. 1961. The natural history of hypertensive disease. In *Hypertension—Recent Advances: The Second Hahnemann Symposium on Hypertensive Disease,* edited by A. N. Brest and J. H. Moyer. Philadelphia: Lea & Febiger.

———— and Perloff, D. B. 1961. The prognosis of essential hypertension treated conservatively. *Circulation* 23:697.

————, Werdegar, D., Perloff, D. B., Cowan, R. M., and Brenenstuhl, H. 1970. Preliminary studies relating portably recorded blood pressures to daily life events in patients with essential hypertension. *Bibl. Psychiatr.* 144:164.

Speransky, I. I., Soulie, E. U., and Bitkova, S. I. 1959. Hereditary-familial data on patients with hypertension. *Ter. Arkh.* 31:7.

Stamler, J., Lindberg, N. A., Berkson, D. M., Schaffer, A., Miller, W., and Poindexter, A. 1958. Epidemiological analysis of hypertension and hypertensive disease in the labor force of a Chicago utility company. *Hypertension* 7:23.

————, Berkson, D. M., Lindberg, H. A., Miller, W. A., Stamler, R., and Collette, R. 1967a. Socioeconomic factors in the epidemiology of hypertensive disease. In *The Epidemiology of Hypertension,* edited by J. Stamler, R. Stamler, and T. N. Pullman. New York: Grune & Stratton.

————, Stamler, R., and Pullman, T. 1967b. *The Epidemiology of Essential Hypertension.* New York: Grune & Stratton.

Stewart, I. McD. G. 1953. Headache and hypertension. *Lancet* i:1261.

Stone, E. A. 1970. Swim-stress-induced inactivity: relation to brain norepinephrine and body temperature, and effects of d-amphetamine. *Psychosom. Med.* 32:51.

Storment, C. T. 1951. Personality and heart disease. *Psychosom. Med.* 13:304.

Stott, A. W., and Robinson, R. 1967. Urinary normetadrenaline excretion in essential hypertension. *Clin. Chim. Acta* 16:249.

Streeten, D. H. P., Schletter, F. E., Clift, G. V., Stevenson, C. T., and Dalakos, T. G. 1969. Studies of the renin-angiotensin-aldosterone system in patients with hypertension and in normal subjects. *Am. J. Med.* 46:844.

Strong, C. G., Boucher, R., Nowaczynski, W., and Genest, J. 1966. Renal vasodepressor lipid. *Mayo Clin. Proc.* 41:433.

Suda, I., Koizumi, K., and Brooks, C. McC. 1963. Study of unitary activity in the supraoptic nucleus of the hypothalamus. *Jpn. J. Physiol.* 13:374.

Sweet, C. S., and Brody, M. J. 1971. Arterial hypertension elicited by prolonged intravertebral infusion of angiotensin in the conscious dog. *Fed. Proc.* 30:432.

————, and ———— 1970. Central inhibition of reflex vasodilation by angiotensin and reduced renal pressure. *Am. J. Physiol.* 219:1751.

Syme, S. L., Hyman, M. M., and Enterline, P. E. 1964. Some social and cultural factors associated with the occurrence of coronary heart disease. *J. Chronic Dis.* 17:277.

Takahashi, E., Sasaki, N., Takeda, J., and Ito, H. 1957. Geographic distribution of cerebral hemorrhage and hypertension in Japan. *Hum. Biol.* 29:139.

Taquini, A. C., Jr., Blaquier, P., and Bohr, D. F. 1961. Neurogenic factors and angiotensin in the etiology of hypertension. *Am. J. Physiol.* 201:1173.

Thaler, M., Weiner, H., and Reiser, M. F. 1957. Exploration of the doctor-patient relationship through projective techniques. *Psychosom. Med.* 19:228.

Thoenen, H., Mueller, R. A., and Axelrod, J. 1969. Trans-synaptic induction of adrenal tyrosine hydroxylase. *J. Pharmacol. Exp.* 169:249.

Thomas, C. B. 1957. Characteristics of the individual as guideposts to the prevention of heart disease. *Ann. Intern. Med.* 47:389.

———— 1958. Familial and epidemiologic aspects of coronary disease and hypertension. *J. Chronic Dis.* 7:198.

———— 1961. Pathogenetic interrelations in hypertension and coronary artery disease. *Dis. Nerv. Syst.* 22(Suppl.):39.

———— 1964a. Psychophysiologic aspects of blood pressure regulation: A clinician's view. *J. Chronic Dis.* 17:599.

———— 1964b. Psychophysiological aspects of blood pressure regulation: the clinician's view. *Psychosom. Med.* 26:454.

———— 1967. The psychological dimensions of hypertension. In *The Epidemiology of Essential Hypertension,* edited by J. Stamler, R. Stamler, and T. N. Pullman. New York: Grune & Stratton.

———— and Cohen, B. H. 1955. The familial occurrence of hypertension and coronary artery disease, with observations concerning obesity and diabetes. *Ann. Intern. Med.* 42:90.

———— and Ross, D. C. 1963. A new approach to the Rorschach test as a research tool. *Bull. Johns Hopkins Hosp.* 112:312.

————, Ross, D. C., and Higinbotham. C. Q. 1964a. Precursors of hypertension and coronary disease among healthy medical students; discriminant function analysis. II. Using parental history as the criterion. *Bull. Johns Hopkins Hosp.* 115:245.

————, Ross, D. C., and Freed, E. S. 1964b. *An Index of Rorschach Responses: Studies on the Psychological Characteristics of Medical Students.* Baltimore: Johns Hopkins University Press.

Thomson, K. J. 1950. Some observations on the development and course of hypertensive vascular disease. *Proc. Sect. Am. Life Insur. Assoc.*

Tobian, L. 1950. Hypertension following bilateral nephrectomy. *J. Clin. Invest.* 29:849.

——— 1960. Interrelationship of electrolytes, juxtaglomerular cells and hypertension. *Physiol. Rev.* 40:280.

——— 1961. The relationship of sodium to hypertension (clinical observations). In *Hypertension—Recent Advances. The Second Hahnemann Symposium on Hypertensive Disease,* edited by A. N. Brest, and J. H. Moyer. Philadelphia: Lea & Febiger.

——— 1962. Relationship of the juxtaglomerular apparatus to renin and angiotensin. *Circulation* 25:189.

——— 1972. A viewpoint concerning the enigma of hypertension. *Am. J. Med.* 52:595.

——— 1974. Experimental models for the study of hypertension. *Hosp. Pract.* 9:99.

——— and Azar, S. 1971. Antihypertensive and other functions of the renal papilla. *Trans. Assoc. Am. Physicians* 84:281.

——— and Binion, J. T. 1952. Tissue cations and water in arterial hypertension. *Circulation* 5:754.

——— and Chesley, G. 1966. Calcium content of arteriolar walls in normotensive and hypertensive rats. *Proc. Soc. Exp. Biol. Med.* 121:340.

———, Janecek, J., Tomboulian, A., and Ferreira, D. 1961. Sodium and potassium in the walls of arterioles in experimental renal hypertension. *J. Clin. Invest.* 40:1922.

———, Schonning, S., and Seefeldt, C. 1964. The influence of arterial pressure on the antihypertensive action of a normal kidney, a biological servo mechanism. *Ann. Intern. Med.* 60:378.

———, Olson, R., and Chesley, G. 1969a. Water content of arteriolar wall in renovascular hypertension. *Am. J. Physiol.* 216:22.

———, Ishii, M., and Duke, M. 1969b. Relationship of cytoplasmic granules in renal papillary interstitial cells to "post-salt" hypertension. *J. Lab. Clin. Med.* 73:309.

Toh, C. C. 1960. Effects of temperature on the 5-hydroxytryptamine content of tissues. *J. Physiol.* (Lond.) 151:410.

Tomaszewski, W. 1937. Puls- und Atmungsfrequenz unter psychischer Beeinflussung. *Z. Kreislaufforsch.* 29:745.

Torgersen, S., and Kringlen, E. 1971. Blood pressure and personality. A study of the relationship between intrapair differences in systolic blood pressure and personality in monozygotic twins. *J. Psychosom. Res.* 15:183.

Tucker, W. I. 1949. Psychiatric factors in essential hypertension. *Dis. Nerv. Syst.* 10:273.

——— 1950. Psychiatric factors in essential hypertension. *N. Engl. J. Med.* 243:211.

Ulick, S., Laragh, J. H., and Lieberman, S. 1958. The isolation of a urinary metabolite of aldosterone and its use to measure the rate of secretion of aldosterone by the adrenal cortex of man. *Trans. Assoc. Am. Physicians* 71:225.

Ulrych, M., Frohlich, E. D., Dustan, H. P., and Page, I. H. 1968. Immediate hemodynamic effects of beta-adrenergic blockade with propranolol in normotensive and hypertensive man. *Circulation* 37:411.

Usami, S., Peric, B., and Chien, S. 1962. Release of antidiuretic hormone due to common carotid occlusion and its relation with vagus nerve. *Proc. Soc. Exp. Biol. Med.* 111:189.

Uvnäs, B. 1960. Central cardiovascular control: In *Handbook of Physiology,* Sect. 1: Neurophysiology, vol. 2, chapt. 44. American Physiological Society.

Vander, A. J., and Miller, R. 1964. Control of renin secretion in the dog. *Am. J. Physiol.* 207:537.

Van Der Valk, J. M. 1957. Blood pressure changes under emotional influences in patients with essential hypertension and control subjects. *J. Psychosom. Res.* 2:134.

Vandongen, R., Peart, W. S., and Boyd, G. W. 1973. Adrenergic stimulation of renin secretion in the isolated perfused rat kidney. *Circ. Res.* 32:290.

Vermeulen, A., and Van der Straeten, M. 1963. Adrenal cortical function in benign essential hypertension. *J. Clin. Endocrinol. Metab.* 23:574.

Verney, E. B. 1947. Croonian lecture: The antidiuretic hormone and the factors which determine its release. *Proc. R. Soc. Lond.* [Biol.] 135:25.

Vogt, M. 1954. The concentration of sympathin in different parts of the central nervous systems under normal conditions and after the administration of drugs. *J. Physiol.* (Lond.) 123:451.

Volicer, L., Scheer, E., Hilse, H., and Visweswaram, D. 1968. Turnover of norepinephrine in the heart during experimental hypertension in rats. *Life Sci.* 7:525.

von Euler, U. S. 1956. *Noradrenaline.* Springfield, Ill.: Charles C Thomas.

————, Hellner, S., and Burkhold, A. 1954. Excretion of noradrenaline in urine in hypertension. *Scand. J. Clin. Lab. Invest.* 6:54.

Wall, P. D., and Davis, G. D. 1951. Three cerebral cortical systems affecting autonomic function. *J. Neurophysiol.* 14:507.

Wang, S. C., and Ranson, S. W. 1939. Autonomic responses to electrical stimulation of the lower brain stem. *J. Comp. Neurol.* 71:437.

Ward, A. A., Jr. 1948. The cingular gyrus: Area 24. *J. Neurophysiol.* 11:13.

Weinberger, M. H., Dowdy, A. J., Nokes, G. W., and Leutscher, J. A. 1968. Plasma renin activity and aldosterone secretion in hypertensive patients during high and low sodium intake and administration of diuretic. *J. Clin. Endocrinol. Metab.* 28:359.

Weiner, H. 1970. Psychosomatic research in essential hypertension: retrospect and prospect. *Bibl. Psychiatr.* 144:58.

————, Singer, M. T., and Reiser, M. F. 1962. Cardiovascular responses and their psychological correlates. A study in healthy young adults and patients with peptic ulcer and hypertension. *Psychosom. Med.* 24:477.

Weiss, E. 1942. Psychosomatic aspects of hypertension. *J.A.M.A.* 120:1081.

———— 1957. *Psychosomatic Medicine,* 3rd ed., edited by E. Weiss and O. S. English. Philadelphia: Saunders.

Welch, A. S., and Welch, B. L. 1968a. Effect of stress and p-chlorophenylalanine upon brain serotonin, 5-hydroxyindoleacetic acid and catecholamines in grouped and isolated mice. *Biochem. Pharmacol.* 17:699.

———— and ———— 1968b. Reduction of norepinephrine in the lower brainstem by psychological stimulus. *Proc. Nat. Acad. Sci. USA* 60:478.

Welch, B. L. 1967. Aggression and defense: Neural mechanisms and social patterns. In *Brain Function,* edited by C. D. Clemente and D. B. Lindsley. Los Angeles: University of California Press.

———— and Welch, A. S. 1965. Effect of grouping on the level of brain norepinephrine in white swiss mice. *Life Sci.* 4:1011.

———— and ———— 1966. Graded effect of social stimulation upon d-amphetamine toxicity, aggressiveness and heart and adrenal weight. *J. Pharmacol. Exp. Ther.* 151:331.

———— and ———— 1968c. Differential activation by restraint stress of a mechanism to conserve brain catecholamines and serotonin in mice differing in excitability. *Nature* 218:575.

———— and ———— 1969. Aggression and the biogenic amines. In *Biology of Aggressive Behavior,* edited by S. Garattini and E. B. Sigg. Amsterdam: Excerpta Medica.

———— and ———— 1971. Isolation, reactivity and aggression: evidence for an involvement of brain catecholamines and serotonin. In *The Physiology of Aggression and Defeat,* edited by B. E. Eleftheriou and J. P. Scott. New York: Plenum.

Wenger, M. A., Clemens, T. L., and Coleman, D. R. 1961. Autonomic response specificity. *Psychosom. Med.* 23:185.

White, B. V., Jr., and Gildea, E. F. 1937. "Cold pressor test" in tension and anxiety: A cardiochronographic study. *Arch. Neurol. Psychiatry* 38:914.

Whyte, H. M. 1958. Body fat and blood pressure of natives in New Guinea: reflections on essential hypertension. *Aust. Ann. Med.* 7:36.

Widimsky, J., Fejfarová, M. H., and Fejfar, Z. 1957. Changes of cardiac output in hypertensive disease. *Cardiology* 31:381.

Williams, G. H., Rose, L. I., Dluhy, R. G., McCaughin, D., Jagger, P. I., Hickler, R. B., and Lauler, D. P. 1970. Abnormal responsiveness of the renin aldosterone system to acute stimulation in patients with essential hypertension. *Ann. Intern. Med.* 72:317.

Williams, R. B., Jr., and McKegney, F. P. 1965. Psychological aspects of hypertension: I. The influence of experimental variables on blood pressure. *Yale J. Biol. Med.* 38:265.

———, Kimball, C. P., and Williard, H. N. 1972a. The influence of interpersonal interaction on diastolic blood pressure. *Psychosom. Med.* 34:194.

———, Lamprecht, F., and Lopin, I. J. 1972b. Serum dopamine-β-hydroxylase levels during development of various forms of hypertension in rats. *J. Clin. Invest.* 51:104a.

Wilson, C. 1961. Etiological considerations in essential hypertension. In *Hypertension—Recent Advances: The Second Hahnemann Symposium on Hypertensive Disease*, edited by A. N. Brest and J. H. Moyer. Philadelphia: Lea & Febiger.

Wilson, J. M. G. 1958. Arterial blood pressure in plantation workers in North East India. *Br. J. Prev. Soc. Med.* 12:204.

Wing, L. M. H., and Chalmers, J. P. 1974. Effects of p-chlorophenylalanine on blood pressure and heart rate in normal rabbits and rabbits with neurogenic hypertension. *Clin. Exp. Pharmacol. Physiol.* 1:219.

Winkelstein, W., Jr., and Kantor, S. 1967. Some observations on the relationships between age, sex, and blood pressure. In *The Epidemiology of Essential Hypertension*, edited by J. Stamler, R. Stamler, and T. N. Pullman. New York: Grune & Stratton.

———, ———, Ibrahim, M., and Sackett, D. L. 1966. Familial aggregation of blood pressure: preliminary report. *J.A.M.A.* 195:848.

Wise, B. L., and Ganong, W. F. 1960. Effect of brain-stem stimulation on renal function. *Am. J. Physiol.* 198:1291.

Wolf, S., and Wolff, H. G. 1951. A summary of experimental evidence relating life stress to the pathogenesis of essential hypertension in man. In *Essential Hypertension*, edited by E. T. Bell. Minneapolis: University of Minnesota Press.

———, Pfeiffer, J. B., Ripley, H. S., Winter, O. S., and Wolff, H. G. 1948. Hypertension as reaction pattern to stress: Summary of experimental data on variations in blood pressure and renal blood flow. *Ann. Intern. Med.* 29:1056.

———, Cardon, P. V., Jr., Shephard, E. M., and Wolff, H. G. 1955. *Life Stress and Essential Hypertension*. Baltimore: Williams and Wilkins.

Wolff, H. G. 1953. *Stress and Disease*. Springfield, Ill.: Charles C Thomas.

Wotman, S., Mandel, I. D., Thompson, R. H., Jr., and Laragh, J. H. 1967. Salivary electrolytes and salt taste thresholds in hypertension. *J. Chronic Dis.* 20:833.

Wurtman, R. J., Altschule, M. D., and Holmgren, U. 1959. Effects of pinealectomy and of a bovine pineal extract in rats. *Am. J. Physiol.* 197:108.

———, ———, Greep, R. O., Falk, J. L., and Grave, G. 1960. The pineal gland and aldosterone. *Am. J. Physiol.* 199:1109.

Yamori, Y., Lovenberg, W., and Sjoerdsma, A. 1970. Norepinephrine metabolism in brainstem of spontaneously hypertensive rats. *Science* 170:544.

Yankopolous, N. A., Davis, J. O., Kliman, B., and Peterson, R. E. 1959. Evidence that a humoral agent stimulates the adrenal cortex to secrete aldosterone in experimental secondary hyperaldosteronism. *J. Clin. Invest.* 38:1278.

Youmans, P. L., Green, H. D., and Denison, A. B., Jr. 1955. Nature of the vasodilator and vasoconstrictor receptors in skeletal muscle of the dog. *Circ. Res.* 3:171.

Zanchetti, A., and Zoccolini, A. 1954. Autonomic hypothalamic outbursts elicited by cerebellar stimulation. *J. Neurophysiol.* 17:475.

Zeaman, D., and Smith, R. W. 1965. Review of some recent findings in human cardiac conditioning. In *Classical Conditioning: A Symposium,* edited by W. F. Prokasy. New York: Appleton-Century-Crofts.

Zehr, J. E., and Feigl, E. O. 1973. Suppression of renin activity by hypothalamic stimulation. *Circ. Res.* 32(Suppl. I):I–17.

Zinner, S. H., Levy, P. S., and Kass, E. H. 1971. Familial aggregation of blood pressure in childhood. *N. Engl. J. Med.* 284:401.

3
BRONCHIAL ASTHMA

THE CURRENT STATUS OF RESEARCH

Much has been written about bronchial asthma; indeed, it has probably received more attention from behavioral scientists than any other "psychosomatic" disease. In their 1964 review of the psychosomatic literature on allergic disorders, Freeman et al. cited 195 papers on bronchial asthma; and many additional studies have appeared in journals and symposia in the years since. Yet, despite these extensive and varied efforts, certain problems that are central to the formulation of a comprehensive explanation of the etiology, pathogenesis, pathophysiology, and variable course of bronchial asthma remain unsolved.

It is presently conceded that psychological factors constitute one of the three major influences that initiate attacks of bronchial asthma, the other two being antigenic and infectious agents. But a consensus has not yet been reached on what percentage of the variance is contributed by psychological and social factors. The failure to do so can be attributed, at least in part, to the continuing controversy about whether bronchial asthma is a homogeneous or heterogeneous illness. If subsequent investigations provide definitive evidence that it is a heterogeneous illness (Cooke, 1947; Pearson, 1968; Pinkerton and Weaver, 1970; Swineford, 1962), then the etiological and pathogenetic variance played by psychological and social factors may be different in each subgroup.

Bronchial asthma is an obstructive disease of the bronchial airways characterized by a tendency of the bronchial tree to respond by bronchoconstriction, edema, and excessive secretion to a variety of stimuli (Gold, 1976; Holman and Muschenheim, 1972; Parish and Pepys, 1968; Scadding, 1963). Wheezing results from bronchoconstriction. The wheezing may be temporary or mild, episodic or paroxysmal, or chronic and severe. Two distinct forms of asthma are generally recognized: an extrinsic and an intrinsic form (Hampton, 1968; Rackemann, 1947, 1950). About 30 to 50 percent of all cases are extrinsic (Holman and Muschenheim, 1972).

In recent years, the extrinsic form has become synonymous with allergic asthma (Gold, 1976; Sherman, 1967; Unger, 1945). Patients with extrinsic asthma usually have a strong family history of allergy. Specific immune mechanisms have been identified in the patients with extrinsic asthma, which are characterized by a tendency of antigens —particularly, inhaled (pollen) antigens—to combine with immunoglobulin-E (IgE) antibodies to release mediators of the antigen-antibody reaction which lead to bronchoconstriction (Austen, 1974). This form of asthma begins before the age of 40 and is associated with allergic rhinitis and eczema. Skin tests for antigens are often positive. Patients often have a history of allergy to foods in childhood. The asthmatic attacks are frequently seasonal. The influence of hereditary factors is less-apparent in patients with intrinsic asthma, who are usually middle-aged (Pearson, 1968). In contrast with extrinsic asthma, intrinsic asthma is less-frequently associated with allergic rhinitis and eczema. Nasal polyps containing eosinophils, an eosinophilia of blood (Archer, 1963), and aspirin- and indomethacin-sensitivity are common features of intrinsic asthma (Aas, 1961). Skin tests for specific allergens are usually negative. The asthmatic attacks tend to be perennial. The intrinsic disease frequently follows a viral infection of the lung (Frazier, 1961; Gold, 1976). The asthmatic attacks may become refractory to drugs such as steroids, in which case intractable asthma may result. Death occurs more frequently in patients in the intrinsic than in the extrinsic group.

The pathophysiology of asthma consists of an increased resistance to airflow at all lung volumes (Samter, 1959). The increased resistance is reflected in prolonged expiration and decreased rates of airflow that can be measured by estimating the forced expiratory volume (FEV) in one second, midmaximal and peak-expiratory flow rates. In asthma, the vital capacity of the lung is decreased, and the residual volume of air is increased. The lung is overinflated because the time for expelling air is reduced due to premature closure of the airways. Air is also unevenly distributed throughout the lung because some airways are obstructed and others are not (Lecks et al., 1966). Blood does not uniformly perfuse the lung (Mishkin and Wagner, 1967).

The minute volume of ventilation and respiratory rate may be increased in an asthmatic attack. The severe asthmatic attack may be associated with markedly increased ventilation due to hypoxemia and acidosis. Eventually, late in the attack, when the FEV is reduced by 75 percent, CO_2 is retained (Austen and Lichenstein, 1973; Gold, 1976).

Whereas the pathogenetic mechanisms caused by allergy in extrinsic asthma are being rapidly elucidated, the pathogenesis of intrinsic asthma is shrouded in mystery. Significant advances have been made in our understanding of immunological mechanisms, the mechanisms of the release of mediators of the immune response that stimulate bronchoconstriction by direct and reflex mechanisms in extrinsic asthma (Austen, 1974;

Gold, 1976; Nadel, 1973). But no consensus has been reached as to whether these mechanisms are sufficient to account for bronchoconstriction (Gold, 1976). The same immunological mechanisms that release mediators of the antigen-antibody response occur in other diseases not characterized by asthma (Connell, 1970; Stanworth, 1971). Other people are skin sensitive, their serum contains IgE antibodies but they never develop bronchial asthma or any other allergic disease. For asthma to occur, an additional factor—an inherent tendency to bronchoconstriction—may have to be present (Hurst, 1943; Scadding, 1963; Swineford, 1962; Widdicombe, 1963). Many stimuli, such as cold air, chemical irritants, odors, exercise, nasal polyps, or psychological factors can provoke asthma. The tendency to bronchoconstriction would also account for the fact that allergic factors alone do not account for repeated attacks of bronchial asthma.

After the first attack of bronchial asthma, neither viral, allergic nor psychological factors individually precipitate every attack. One of these factors may predominate and the others are subsidiary. The predominant factor may interact with the subsidiary ones. In addition, the predominant factor is different in different age groups (Cooke, 1947; Fagerberg, 1958; Pearson, 1968; Sherman, 1967; Swineford et al., 1962).

In their study of 487 asthmatic clinic patients of all ages, Williams et al. (1958) found that extrinsic allergenic factors played a *predominant* precipitating role in 29 percent, respiratory infections in 40 percent, and psychological factors in 30 percent. But even in this last group—those in whom psychological factors played a predominant role—attacks were precipitated, in addition, by allergic factors in 50 percent of the patients. And in the group in whom infection played the primary role, allergic precipitants were present in 22 percent.

In other words, no one factor bears the sole responsibility for the precipitation of bronchial asthmatic attacks. The central finding that emerged from the study by Williams and his co-workers, and from subsequent studies by Pearson (1968) and by Rees (1956b, 1964), was that allergic, infectious, and psychological factors interact (Table 1). In the series investigated by Williams et al., more than one factor was present in 60 to 77 percent of the 487 patients studied; the exact figure depended on which was considered the predominant factor. Psychological factors played some role in 70 percent of all the patients in this sample, but were the sole precipitants in only 1.2 percent.

Reports of the interaction of psychological, infectious, and allergic factors in the precipitation of bronchial asthma, as well as studies of the relative role of psychological factors in the initiation and recurrence of the illness (Table 1), must be evaluated in light of the methodological problems inherent in such studies.

For one, it is well-known that patients with asthma may not consult a physician for months, or even years, after the disease has had its onset. Consequently, the factors that produced the first attack, and the factors that precipitated subsequent attacks (which may or may not be the same as the initiating factors), must be determined in retrospect. It is of interest in this connection that Sclare (1959), who was able to study 58 patients very soon after their illness had its onset, found that a psychologically threatening situation had preceded the asthmatic attack in 36 cases.

Efforts to assess the relative role of psychological, infectious, and allergic factors in the initiation and recurrence of bronchial asthma may be impeded by conceptual problems as well. As noted earlier, the proportion of the variance played by each of these factors may

225

TABLE 1

Percentage of the Variance Played by Psychological, Infectious, and Allergic Factors in the Initiation and Recurrence of Bronchial Asthma

AGE		PSYCHOLOGICAL		INFECTIOUS		ALLERGIC	
		S	D	S	D	S	D
1011 Children[a]		30	19				
388 Children [b]							
262 Boys		30	42	31	40	13	17
126 Girls		30	41	29	42	13	17
56 Children [c]			35				
441 Patients[d]							
16–25	M	33	8	18	18	0	54
	F	35	22	39	22	39	32
26–35	M	30	4	35	21	6	47
	F	48	31	63	26	34	23
36–45	M	42	19	11	46	4	23
	F	53	35	35	20	42	4
46–55	M	37	6	31	43	26	12
	F	56	44	48	4	20	20
56–65	M	54	27	18	31	10	9
	F	50	40	41	18	18	9
65+ both sexes		34	44	20	46	20	10
487 Patients							
both sexes, all ages [e]		26	30	47	41	72	29[f]
0–4			46		38		15
5–14			40		36		24
15–24			10		18		72
25–34			23		30		48
35–45			20		52		25
45+			18		71		10
233 Patients [g]							
0–9	M		64				
	F		52				
10–19	M		60				
	F		70				
20+	M		29				
	F		66				
611 Patients [h]							
3–14			54		26		74
15–29					45		55
30–44					56		44
45+			61		68		32

[a] Munro Ford, 1963
[b] Rees, 1964
[c] Graham et al., 1967
[d] Rees, 1956b
[e] Williams et al., 1958

[f] Sole-precipitant-12
[g] Wright, 1965
[h] Pearson, 1968

S = Subsidiary Role
D = Dominant Role
M = Male
F = Female

change over time and with the age at onset, and according to the sex of patients (Rees, 1956a; Williams, 1959a; Wright, 1965). For example, the problem of determining the predominant initiating factor in childhood asthma is compounded by the fact that while the onset of the disease usually follows a (viral) infection, allergens later play the primary role (Rees, 1964).

The reliability of the information provided in a given study must be judged in light of its source. Questions as to whether such information was provided by an epidemiologist, an allergist, or a psychiatrist, who, in turn, obtained his research data from the patient, the parents of an asthmatic child, or from other sources, such as hospital charts or a physician's clinical records, are of critical importance in evaluating study findings. Data provided by disparate sources have yielded divergent findings. Thus, according to Graham et al. (1967), the parents of 35.1 percent of the 56 school-aged children in his series reported that in some instances, their children's asthmatic attacks were precipitated by emotional factors. These antecedent emotional states were variously identified as fear, anticipatory excitement, and anger, often in combination with "other factors." Dawson et al. (1969) obtained information from asthmatic children, their parents, and physicians about these other factors. They listed cold and frost, hot weather, dampness, mist, fog, heating, nervous tension, and cut grass as precipitants. Exercise brought on wheezing in severe cases, but not in mild ones. In other instances, study findings may reflect the investigator's particular orientation: a psychiatrist, Munro Ford (1963) found that a "significant" psychological factor was present in 50 percent of the 1,010 asthmatic children in his series and that this factor played a predominant role in 19 percent.

Mention has already been made of Rees's conclusion (1956b, 1964), from his studies of both adults and children (Table 1), that allergic, infectious, and psychological factors interact in initiating and producing recurrences of bronchial asthma. Infectious and psychological factors interacted to produce bronchial asthma in 70 percent of his series of 388 children. This study is of particular interest because Rees was careful to distinguish between the role of psychological factors in the onset of the disease and their role in subsequent attacks. He found that in the children in his sample, the onset of the first attack coincided with psychosocial "stresses" in 12 percent, with infection in 35 percent, and with allergy in 3 percent. The main causes of psychosocial "stress" were the death of a parent, relative, or friend; accidents and other frightening experiences; and school problems. In all of these patients, psychological factors also played a predominant role in the precipitation of recurrent attacks.

In older or in elderly patients a variety of adjustment problems of old age culminated not only in asthmatic attacks but in anxiety and depression, which, in addition to anger, resentment, and feelings of humiliation, immediately anteceded asthmatic attacks in the middle-aged and elderly (Leigh and Rawnsley, 1956). Rees (1956b) commented, as Knapp (1960) did later, that predisposed persons who suppressed or did not adequately express their emotions were more likely to have asthmatic attacks than those who fully expressed their feelings.

It may be critical to differentiate between patients, not only on the basis of the nature of the initiating event, but also in terms of the relationship of events, and of the psychological reactions elicited by them, to the course of the disease. For example, it would be important to know whether a particular life event is acute and leads to short-term responses, or whether it sets off a chain of psychological reactions that are not resolved over the long term, in which case one might expect the progressive exacerbation of asthmatic attacks. Interestingly, Wright (1965) found that, although life events and the emotional responses they evoke may increase the severity and frequency of attacks, they do not alter the fundamental nature of the disease; that is, they do not transform an intermittent form of bronchial asthma into a chronic form.

Unfortunately, the facts that have emerged from the various studies reviewed in this section have not fully penetrated the thinking of those workers who have addressed themselves to the psychosocial aspects of asthma. Discussions continue to revolve around "either/or" arguments for and against a specific initiating factor. It seems obvious that these arguments would be much more productive if they centered on the relative contribution of each of these three factors at a specific stage of the disease in a particular individual, the relative contribution of each in different forms of the disease, and the mechanisms of interaction of these factors. Efforts to specify the nature of the interrelationship between the immunological and physiological mechanisms and the psychological ones have been impeded by our primitive knowledge of the brain and by our continually changing understanding of the role of the autonomic nervous system, its neurotransmitters, and various hormones in the pathogensis and pathophysiology of the disease.

THE CURRENT STATUS OF PSYCHOSOMATIC RESEARCH

Three-quarters of the etiological variance in bronchial asthma is accounted for by environmental factors that are allergic, infectious, and psychological. A comprehensive account of this disease will need to specify the mechanisms whereby psychological changes alone or in interaction with allergy and infection, produce bronchoconstriction and thus the symptoms of the disease. This aim has not been achieved. A survey of recently published research on bronchial asthma consists of controlled clinical and laboratory studies directed toward an understanding of the way in which psychosocial stimuli interact with physiological and immunological ones to promote bronchoconstriction. It was not always so. Forty years ago, the search was directed to understanding of the kinds of people who were asthmatic (Dunbar, 1938; Wittkower and Petow, 1932). The hope implicit in this quest was that some unique feature of the personality of asthmatic persons would emerge. That hope was dashed: no one personality type is prone to asthmatic attacks. The next phase of this quest consisted of a search for those deep structures of the personality that produced psychological conflict and were regularly associated with bronchial asthmatic attacks.

Patients with bronchial asthma have unconscious conflicts about dependency that are expressed in a variety of traits and habits. Some patients are ambitious, aggressive, or daring; some are sensitive and poetic; some can be classified as hysterical or compulsive character types. The unconscious conflict about dependency takes the form of a wish to be protected, enveloped, or encompassed by the mother (French and Alexander, 1941). The threat or actuality of losing the protecting mother may precipitate attacks. But the conflict may by itself be frightening to some patients, so that closeness to the mother is perceived as dangerous. In frightened patients, separation from the mother may produce rapid remission. The threat or actuality of separation or a closeness is associated with

228

intense emotions. In fact, the quest for the deep structures of the personality resulted in the realization that the asthmatic attack was associated with intensive emotional arousal or change, an observation already made by Hippocrates. Logically, the next question that was raised was how the physiological correlates of emotional arousal would be expressed in bronchoconstriction. We have no answer to this question. But we do know more about the situations that produce emotional arousal or strong emotions in asthmatic patients than we did 30 years ago. The review that follows will trace out the progress made in these years.

The environmental situations that produce emotional arousal in asthmatic children have been also ascribed to the attitudes of parents, especially mothers (Alexander, 1950; Miller and Baruch, 1948a). Their attitudes have been blamed for creating situations that emotionally exercise the child with asthma. The subsequent review will document the fact that this formulation is an oversimplification. Parental attitudes of various kinds do not alone incite attacks of asthma. The child must be predisposed to respond psychologically and physiologically to the attitudes with an attack of asthma. A comprehensive account of this disease must include all of the factors—the attitude of the parent (in childhood asthma), the relationships between the parent and child and between the adult asthmatic with his relatives and friends, the changes in relationships that may occur that antecede the attack, and the patient's allergic potential and tendency to bronchoconstricition.

THE ROLE OF GENETIC FACTORS IN BRONCHIAL ASTHMA AND OTHER ALLERGIC DISEASES

Allergic, infectious, psychological, and social factors in various combinations play a role in inciting and precipitating asthmatic attacks. Experienced students of bronchial asthma have suspected for a long time that these factors cannot exert their influence unless the lung responds to them by bronchoconstriction. Other students have suggested that this response tendency is inherited. Hereditary factors play a role in the extrinsic, and not in the intrinsic, form of bronchial asthma. The following review of the genetic factors in bronchial asthma does not answer questions of the heritability of the bronchoconstrictor and the allergic tendencies, but it does show that genetic factors do play a minor role in the etiology of bronchial asthma.

This conclusion is based on evidence derived from family aggregations of bronchial asthma and other allergic diseases, from twin studies, and from demonstrations of the increased incidence of positive skin tests in patients, their siblings, and parents (Schwartz, 1952). The mode of inheritance of these diseases has been discussed at length and is probably polygenic. But, in fact, the evidence that they are inherited is by no means irrefutable (Frankland, 1968; Ratner and Silberman, 1953). A familial tendency cannot be considered proof positive of an inherited predisposition (Morrison Smith, 1961).

Studies of Families

A positive family history of allergic illness was found in 30 to 80 percent of asthmatic children in various studies (Kantor and Speer, 1963; Leigh and Marley, 1967; McKee,

1966; Ratner and Silberman, 1953; Rees, 1956a; Schnyder, 1960). Of the children studied by Ratner and Silberman (1953), 22 percent had one parent with a history of bronchial asthma. In asthmatic patients of various ages, the incidence of a family history of allergic illness ranged from 23 to 83 percent in 19 different series studied by Schwartz (1952). And the reported incidence of a history of asthma in the families of asthma patients has ranged from 23 percent (Baagoe, 1936) to 56 (Gram, 1931).

When Pearson (1968) studied a group of patients under 30 with either extrinsic or intrinsic asthmatic illness, he found that 25 percent had a positive family history of bronchial asthma in near relatives. After that age, the proportion of patients with intrinsic or extrinsic asthma who had a family history of asthma was 26 percent and 30 percent, respectively—a difference that is not statistically significant. Dawson and his co-workers (1969) found that the incidence of bronchial asthma in the first-degree relatives of 121 asthmatic children they studied was 53 percent. They also found that 12 percent of these children had a family history of eczema "of some kind," and 17 percent had a family history of allergic rhinitis.

The variations in family incidences are due, in part, to variations in the diagnostic criteria used in selection, to variations in geographical distribution, and to biases with regard to the age of patients and sample size. Indeed, in the past 20 years only three major studies (Leigh and Marley, 1967; Schnyder, 1960; Schwartz, 1952) addressed specifically to the problem of heredity in clearly defined bronchial asthma and other allergic diseases have used asthmatic probands, their families, and a matched control series.

Schwartz (1952), who conducted the first of these controlled investigations, studied 191 (117 extrinsic and 74 intrinsic) asthmatic probands who were outpatients, 50 probands with asthma due to an allergy to flour (baker's asthma), 200 control probands, and the first- and second-degree relatives of all the probands. The control population, which consisted of 50 inpatients, 128 outpatients, 20 medical students, and 2 masseurs, were selected so as to exclude any person with a history of allergic disease. A total of 3,815 first- and second-degree relatives were studied: of these, 1,634 were related to the asthmatic patients, 391 to the probands with baker's asthma, and 1,790 to the control group. Bronchial asthma was six times more prevalent in the male, and seven times more prevalent in the female relatives of probands with bronchial or baker's asthma than it was in relatives of the control population. These figures hold for both extrinsic and intrinsic bronchial asthma; in fact, Schwartz concluded that these were genetically identical. He also found that an impressive number of aunts and uncles of the asthmatic probands suffered from bronchial asthma. In addition, in contrast to the relatives of probands in other groups, there was a significant increase in the prevalence of vasomotor rhinitis in the relatives (especially the male relatives) of the asthmatic probands, and of eczema in the first-degree female relatives of patients with extrinsic asthma. There was a trend in the same direction for allergic rhinitis.

Having concluded that asthma is inherited, Schwartz further concluded that it was genetically related to allergic rhinitis. He also suggested that atopic eczema and allergic rhinitis might be genetically related to bronchial asthma, but the figures he provided in support of this contention are not convincing. Finally, based on his finding that probands with asthma due to an allergy to flour and those with extrinsic and intrinsic bronchial asthma had approximately the same number of relatives with bronchial asthma, Schwartz concluded that these illnesses are related. Specifically, he postulated that an interaction between a specific allergen and an inherited predisposition occurred in each, and that about 40 percent of the etiological variance could be accounted for by genetic factors.

Schwartz's study was criticized, first by Ratner and Silberman (1953) and later by Leigh and Marley (1967). In both instances, his critics pointed out that serious problems in defining and diagnosing the disorders under investigation greatly diminished the validity of the findings. Clearly, however, the most serious criticism leveled at Schwartz's study is that he excluded from his comparison group any person with a history of allergic disease. Only persons with bronchial asthma should have been excluded from the control group. Probands with vasomotor and allergic rhinitis, various eczemas, urticaria, etc. should have been included. Not to do so, as Leigh and Marley (1967) have pointed out, is to assume that the hypothesis that asthma is inherited is valid before proving it.

Schwartz's study has other serious limitations as well: first, clinic outpatients with bronchial asthma are less incapacitated, and therefore may not be representative of all cases of the disease. Second, clinic patients may differ from hospitalized patients without asthma (who were included in Schwartz's comparison group) in the degree of their illness. However, despite these weaknesses, one significant finding does emerge from Schwartz's investigation—the fact that the aunts and uncles of the asthmatic probands, not just their first-degree relatives, had histories of bronchial asthma is important evidence of an hereditary predisposition.

Schnyder (1960) carried out a somewhat similar study on the families of 361 patients with various allergic diseases, but he used a very large population (8,246) of control probands, selected at random, from whom he obtained data by means of a survey questionnaire. As compared to the families of the control probands, there was a significant increase in the prevalence of bronchial asthma in the families of patients with bronchial asthma, various forms of rhinitis, and neurodermatitis. Schnyder concluded, on the basis of this finding, that these illnesses were genetically related to each other, but not to contact dermatitis, urticaria, and drug reactions. A major limitation of Schnyder's study is that his experimental and control groups were not matched for age. In an earlier study, Rees (1956b) had found that 32 percent of the parents and siblings of 50 asthmatic patients over the age of 60 had a history of asthma, vasomotor rhinitis, and flexural eczema, as compared to a 10 percent prevalence rate in a control population. Also, asthmatic probands should be matched with control probands for sex. The prevalance of other allergic illnesses in the relatives of older female asthmatic patients may be greater than in the relatives of older male patients (Leigh and Marley, 1956).

In the most recent of the major investigations, Leigh and Marley (1967) capitalized on some of the limitations of the two previous studies. Fifty-five patients (25 men and 30 women) with bronchial asthma and their 250 first-degree relatives and 289 second-degree relatives were matched for age, age distribution, and—quite successfully—for sex and socioeconomic variables with the same number of control patients attending the same two general practices, one in London and the other in a small town south of London. Patients in both groups were either interviewed by the authors or asked to fill out questionnaires. Diagnostic criteria were carefully defined for the illnesses under study:

bronchial asthma, acute and chronic pulmonary diseases, allergic and vasomotor rhinitis, urticaria, eczema, psoriasis, herpes zoster, epilepsy, migraine, peptic ulcer, rheumatoid arthritis, delayed drug reactions, and psychiatric illnesses.

Forty-four (17.6 percent) relatives of the asthmatic probands had a history of bronchial asthma; in the comparison group only 15 relatives had such a history. Of the 44 asthmatic relatives in the experimental group, 33 were first-degree, and 11 were second-degree relatives; in the comparison group there were 3 first-degree and 12 second-degree relatives with bronchial asthma. (These reported differences for first-degree relatives have statistic reliability at the 0.1 percent level.) Members of 26 of the 55 families of asthmatic probands were afflicted with bronchial asthma; of these 26 families, 10 families contributed 29 of the 44 asthmatic relatives.

In addition, chronic (but not acute) respiratory diseases occurred more frequently in the first-degree relatives of asthmatic probands than in the comparison population. In fact, chronic respiratory illness was found only in first-degree relatives, and in the parents of the asthmatic probands in particular.

Twice as many (23 percent) patients in the asthmatic population as those in the comparison group suffered from either allergic or vasomotor rhinitis or both. The prevalence of one or both of these illnesses was significantly greater in the asthmatic probands (both men and women) and in those second-degree relatives who suffered from bronchial asthma. Childhood eczema and urticaria were significantly more common in asthmatic probands than in comparison probands, and eczema occurred much more frequently in the first-degree relatives of asthmatic probands. Finally, for relatives in both the experimental and comparison groups, the likelihood of developing bronchial asthma increased with age: by the age of 55, it reached 30 percent and 11 percent, respectively.

These findings appear at fist glance to be fairly conclusive. However, the family studies that have been reported to date all have one major weakness: even when control probands are used, there is a tendency to assume that chance plays no part in determining family aggregations of bronchial asthma or allergic illness. But this assumption is not valid unless a number of important variables are controlled (Kallio et al., 1966). Allergic illnesses are common in the general population. On the basis of estimates that the frequency of allergy in the population is 16.7 percent (Ratner and Silberman, 1953), and that the extended family includes ten relatives, Van Arsdel and Motulsky (1949) calculated that, by chance alone, 84 percent of all individuals, allergic or not, would have a positive family history of allergy. Studies of the family incidence or prevalence of bronchial asthma and allergic illness, which frequently conclude that these diseases are inherited, must be interpreted in light of these chance probabilities. These diseases are not generally thought to be inherited directly; rather, a predisposition to allergic illness or to asthma is inherited. This predisposition may take the form of a tendency to form reaginic antibodies (Kallio et al., 1966; Rapaport, 1958) but the exact mode of inheritance has not been established.

It would be easy to conclude that the family data attest to a hereditary component. In fact, many writers on this subject have concluded that a positive family history of 45 to 75 percent constitutes proof of a hereditary component in bronchial asthma (Adkinson, 1920; Hansel, 1953; Ratner and Silberman, 1952; Schwartz, 1952; Spaich and Ostertag, 1936; Spain and Cook, 1924). But such family studies do not prove an hereditary component, nor do they help to clarify the relative roles of heredity and environment. Families share a common human and physical environment. They are exposed to the same pollens, bacteria, irritants, fumes, or animals. Children may be exposed to the sight of asthmatic attacks in their parents or other relatives. Therefore, even if conclusive data were obtained by family studies, their interpretation would have to be made with care.

The relative importance of heredity and environment in the etiology of bronchial asthma is no trivial question: a better understanding of their relative roles would permit an estimate of those at risk for the disease and would, therefore, be clinically important. Should environmental factors play a major role in etiology, they could be identified and removed. Similarly, a predominant genetic factor could be eliminated by genetic counseling. The best mode of determining the relative roles of nature and nurture is by studying twins, provided that the twin sample is large, random, and unbiased in its selection.

Twin Studies of Bronchial Asthma and Allergic Diseases

The most extensive studies of twins with bronchial asthma has been done by Harvald and Hauge (1965) and by Edfors-Lubs (1971), though the methodological problems inherent in the former study have diminished its validity. The findings are worth reporting: 30 of 64 pairs of monozygotic (Mz) twins were found to be concordant for bronchial asthma, compared to 24 of 101 pairs of dizygotic (Dz), same-sexed twins and 22 of 91 pairs of Dz twins of opposite sexes.

Bowen's report (1953) on 59 pairs of Mz twins should be briefly mentioned. Seven pairs had two allergies: three of these pairs had infantile eczema—and in two of these both twins later developed bronchial asthma; two pairs were concordant for allergic rhinitis that was both perennial and due to ragweed pollen; and the remaining two pairs were concordant for bronchial asthma and allergic rhinitis.

The author went on to say that "the remaining 52 pairs all had bronchial asthma with coexisting nasal blockage in some patients but in this group only one in each set of twins was affected to such a degree that medical help was sought." Bowen concluded from these findings that these 52 pairs were discordant for bronchial asthma "since only one twin in each of 52 sets was affected by allergy." If, in fact, 52 of 59 pairs of Mz twins were really discordant for bronchial asthma and other allergic illnesses, the genetic basis for bronchial asthma would, of course, be questionable. It should be noted, however, that the author assumed that the twins were Mz, but he did not employ modern methods to determine zygosity. Furthermore, he failed to set down the criteria used for diagnosis. Edfors-Lubs (1971) studied 7,000 twin pairs of all ages with various allergic diseases. Of the sample, 3.8 percent had bronchial asthma. The concordance rates for the Mz twins was 19 percent and for the Dz twin pairs was 4.8 percent. The concordance rates in Mz twin pairs was 21 percent for allergic rhinitis and 15 percent for allergic eczema, signifying a low heritability for any one of the three diseases. Her conclusions are at a variance with the conclusions of most writers in this field and attest to the fact that unidentified environmental influences play a major role in every one of these diseases. Because the concordance rate for asthma (as well as for eczema and rhinitis) is significantly greater in Mz than in Dz twins, genetic factors also play a role: in asthma they account for about a quarter of the etiological variance.

233

Edfors-Lubs also concluded that even if both parents had various allergic diseases the risk of the child developing asthma, eczema, or hay fever was 1 in 3. The majority of allergic children were born into families where only one or neither parent was allergic.

Despite the large numbers of twins studied in Sweden, Edfors-Lubs could come to no conclusion as to the mode of inheritance, although she favored a multigenic one. As in other studies, her observations fit a variety of interpretations and suggestions. It has been suggested that allergic diseases (including bronchial asthma) are inherited by means of multiple additive genes (Van Arsdel and Motulsky, 1949). Others have postulated an autosomal locus, which would account for the late onset of allergy in 18 percent of the heterozygotes, and the early onset of allergy in those homozygous for one allele (Wiener et al., 1936); an autosomal dominant gene (Spain and Cook, 1924) with reduced penetrance (Leigh and Marley, 1967; Schnyder, 1960; Schwartz, 1952); an autosomal recessive gene (Adkinson, 1920; Viswanathan and Bharadway, 1962); a recessive locus for each of the main allergic diseases (Tips, 1954); or a multifactoral mode of inheritance (Leigh and Marley, 1967).

Despite the fact that no conclusion has been reached about the mode of inheritance by these studies, it has become possible to assign a figure for the relative role of heredity in bronchial asthma and other allergic diseases on the basis of Edfors-Lubs' study. She concludes that environmental factors play a predominant role in the disease but does not specify them. They may be social, familial, psychological, infectious, allergic, occupational, or industrial. They must in some manner interact with genetic factors. But we do know how the genetic factor expresses itself in patients: it could do so by the formation of specific IgE antibodies, by an inherited defect in pulmonary functioning expressed as a bias towards bronchoconstriction, or by both. Specific genes have been identified that control IgE antibody responses to ragweed antigen, which permit the development of ragweed hayfever and asthma in humans (Levine et al., 1972). In experimental animals, different steps in the immune response are under specific genetic control. Separate genes control basal levels of IgE, the degree of IgE response to an antigen, the concentration and secretion of the chemical mediators of the immune response, and the ease with which antigen passes through bronchial mucosa to reach sensitized cells (Gold, 1976).

THE ROLE OF THE ENVIRONMENT: EPIDEMIOLOGICAL STUDIES

One of the intentions of epidemiological studies is to seek out those environmental factors that play a role in predisposing to or initiating bronchial asthma. It would be important to know if the disease favors any one age, national, regional, occupational, socioeconomic, or ethnic group, or if it occurs with a greater prevalence in boys than in girls or vice versa. Once such differences were found more analytic studies would allow one to identify the factors that account for these group differences. Unfortunately, these aims have not been achieved.

The Incidence of the Illness

In this country, 31 million people suffer from one or more allergic disorders. Of these, 13 million have allergic rhinitis, and the remaining 18 million suffer from bronchial asthma and other allergic diseases (Malkiel, 1971; National Center for Health Statistics, 1971). Approximately 10 percent of all children under the age of 15 suffer from some form of allergic illness, and about one-half of these children have bronchial asthma and/or allergic rhinitis. It is well-known, of course, that many children outgrow their allergic illnesses. Yet, in England, the prevalence rate of bronchial asthma doubles in those over 65, as compared to those between 16 and 44 years of age (Logan and Brooke, 1957).

The predisposition to bronchial asthma may, therefore, be expressed in clinical attacks at any age, particularly in childhood and in the elderly. Conversely, children with a history of clinical asthma outgrow their disease, and many patients first develop attacks when old.

Epidemiological Studies

The figures obtained from epidemiological studies of children—a major preoccupation of investigators in recent years—vary widely from country to country, ranging from 0.7 percent to 4.9 percent (see Table 2). Bronchial asthma appears to be less prevalent in Scandinavia than it is in the United Kingdom or the United States. To a large extent, however, these differences can be attributed to the different methods used by individual investigators. For example, some workers (Kraepelien, 1954) report on whole populations; others (Broder et al., 1962a, b; Dawson et al., 1969; Graham et al., 1967) select a random sample for study. The discrepancies can also be ascribed, at least in part, to the concentration in some studies on school-age children, when the peak age of onset occurs in preschool children.

But these methodological defects cannot satisfactorily account for the wide differences in prevalence rates obtained in three studies that originated in the United Kingdom——two in England (Graham et al., 1967; Morrison Smith, 1961) and one in Scotland (Dawson et al., 1969) (see Table 2). No attempt has been made to explain these variations. Nor did Kraepelien (1954) attempt to explain his interesting finding that bronchial asthma was twice as prevalent among children in Stockholm as in the Swedish population at large. It can be speculated, however, that, to some degree, Kraepelien's finding reflects still another methodological weakness intrinsic to epidemiological studies on bronchial asthma, which may further explain the differences in the prevalence rates reported in such investigations. Specifically, Kraepelien obtained his data directly from physicians in a series of personal interviews. The criteria for diagnosis were not stated, which means, of course, that one cannot be certain that all the subjects in Kraepelien's sample were actually suffering from bronchial asthma. There is another side to this coin, however: although studies of hospitalized patients or hospital records may ensure diagnostic accuracy, it is important to study representative sample populations when carrying out prevalence studies. Less than half of all asthmatic children are so severely incapacitated by their illness that they must be hospitalized; the rest are treated in the private offices of physicians or at home (Dawson et al., 1969).

The efforts of Dawson and his co-workers (1969) to circumvent this methodological problem, i.e., to ensure diagnostic accuracy in a representative sample population, are relevant in this context: they used a sampling technique in which every fifth child in the

235

TABLE 2

Prevalance Rates

Childhood Asthma

STUDY	COUNTRY	PREVALENCE RARES (%)
Schwartz (1952)	Denmark	1.0
Kraepelien (1954)	Sweden	0.7
	Sweden (Stockholm)	1.4
Peltonen et al. (1955)	Finland	0.85
Frandsen (1958)	Denmark	0.8
Solomon (1958)	Australia	2.7
Morrison Smith (1961)	England (Birmingham)	1.8
Broder et al. (1962a, b)	USA (Michigan)	4.0 (Cumulative)
Graham et al. (1967)	England (Isle of Wight)	2.3
Arbeiter (1967)	USA (Indiana)	4.9
Dawson et al. (1969)	Scotland (Aberdeen)	4.8

Adult Asthma

STUDY	COUNTRY	MEN (%)	AGES	WOMEN (%)
Catsch (1943)	Germany	1.4		0.8
Baltimore (National Center, 1971)		1.24[a]		
Logan and Brooke (1957)	U.K.	0.6	16–44	0.6[b]
		0.9	45–64	1.1
		1.3	65+	1.5
Van Arsdel (1959)	USA (U. Wash.)	4.7 (Both)[c]		
Broder et al. (1962a, b)	USA (Mich.)	4.0 (Cumulative)[d]		
Maternowski and Mathews (1962)	USA (U. Mich.)	5.7		

[a] Rates same in black and white persons
[b] Monthly prevalence rates
[c] College students
[d] All ages

236

Aberdeen primary school system was interviewed by a specially trained interviewer. The children were then given thorough physical examinations, which included X-rays of the chest and sinuses and pulmonary function studies. Diagnosis was based on the definition of asthma as "recurrent dyspnea of an obstructive type without other demonstrable cause." Only those children with confirmed diagnoses were included in the sample.

The importance of diagnostic accuracy, and, concomitantly, of the methodological weakness that may have contaminated Kraepelien's findings, emerged clearly in a subsequent study conducted in Michigan by Broder et al. (1962a). These workers studied an entire population of 9,823 persons 6 years of age and older and were able to examine 88 percent of their subjects personally. The figures for the *cumulative* prevalence of the disease depended upon whether patients were diagnosed as probably or only possibly having the disease, being 4.1 percent and 6.3 percent respectively.

Epidemiologists have also focused on the prevalence of other allergic diseases in comparison to bronchial asthma. In the study described above, Broder et al. found that the cumulative prevalence rate of hay fever in their research population was about 2½ times greater than that of asthma. In a second study (1962b) they showed that hay fever does not necessarily lead to bronchial asthma; in fact, 75 percent of the individuals in their sample who had a history of both had either suffered only from asthma initially or reported that the two illnesses had appeared within the same year. And in the study referred to earlier in this subsection, Dawson et al. (1969) found that 74 (61 percent) of the 121 asthmatic children in their sample had a history of other allergic diseases: 45 (37 percent) had a history of infantile eczema, as opposed to 5 percent of the rest of their population; 35 (29 percent) had suffered from allergic rhinitis, which had its onset after the age of 6 in most cases; 8 percent had urticaria.

Finally, although it does not deal directly with epidemiological issues, the study reported by Gutmann (1958) includes some very suggestive epidemiological and psychosocial data that clearly merit description in this context. According to Gutmann, surviving Jewish inmates of concentration camps who had previously suffered from asthma were frequently free of wheezing during their confinement, thus confirming observations that had also been made by workers in Holland (Bastiaans and Groen, 1954; Groen, 1950). Gutmann also found that on their arrival in Israel some emigrants from Iraq who had settled in a well-defined area near Tel Aviv developed bronchial asthma for the first time. These individuals had a negligible family history for asthma and other allergies. With rare exception, they were between the ages of 20 and 40; interestingly, children were largely exempt (although asthma is common among Israeli children). Skin tests incriminated bacteria and molds, but the symptoms of the illness disappeared after the new immigrants became integrated into the community.

Age at Onset

Bronchial asthma may begin at any age, but in about half of all patients it begins before adolescence (Broder et al., 1962a). Rackemann and Edwards (1952) reported the onset of the illness in a 4-week-old infant. However, studies of children who have required hospitalization indicate that the peak age at onset occurs prior to or at about age 3 (Frazier, 1961; Morrison Smith, 1961; Peshkin and Abramson, 1958). Nor are these findings unique to this patient population. Studies of school-aged children (Dawson et al., 1969; Rees, 1964) and of whole populations (Broder et al., 1962a) have yielded similar figures as to the peak age at onset. In fact, the disease had its onset before the age of 5 in 38 percent of the 25,000 patients surveyed by Williams et al. (1958), and it began before the age of 15 in 63 percent of the sample population studied by Rees (1956b).

Distribution According to Sex

In childhood, boys with the illness outnumber girls by 2:1 to 3:1 (Arbeiter, 1967; Dawson et al., 1969; Frandsen, 1958; Morrison Smith, 1961; National Center for Health Statistics, 1971; Peshkin and Abramson, 1958; Rackemann and Edwards, 1952). If asthmatic children are further classified according to the presumed nature of their asthma, the distribution according to sex is the same in the extrinsic and intrinsic groups. In adolescence, however, the ratio of boys to girls falls to 1:1 to 3:1 (Dawson et al., 1969). Prevalence rates increase with age in both sexes: after the age of 45, the proportion of men in the intrinsic group increases. And in the study conducted by Williams (1959a) and his co-workers (1958) older women (over 45) had the illness more frequently (two to three times more) than did younger women. On the whole, these trends have been borne out by large-scale studies.

The Significance of Socioeconomic Variables

Investigators have not yet reached a consensus about the relationship of socioeconomic variables to the prevalence of bronchial asthma. Logan (1960) concluded, on the basis of data he obtained by sampling a number of general practices in the United Kingdom, that the consultation rate for asthma was higher for children whose fathers held white-collar jobs, a conclusion also reached independently by Freeman and Johnson (1964) in the United States and Peltonen et al. (1955) in Finland. In fact, Peltonen and his co-workers found that bronchial asthma was almost twice as prevalent in Finnish children from urban areas (where, presumably, most men hold white-collar jobs), as it was in those children who came from rural areas (where men are more apt to be engaged in manual work, and where, in Finland at least, families are less-affluent). And Graham et al. (1967) found that a significant preponderance of the asthmatic children in their series had fathers who performed nonmanual jobs and that children whose fathers belonged to the lowest socioeconomic groups (as defined by occupation) were underrepresented.

However, contradictory data have been gathered in other studies: using the same criterion—father's occupation—as the basis for socioeconomic classification, Dawson et al. (1969) studied the relationship of socioeconomic status to the severity of asthma in children. Although the size of the sample studied was small, these authors found that the severely asthmatic children in their series tended to come from families at a lower socioeconomic level in which the father was a semiskilled or unskilled manual worker and in which there were more than four children. Mild cases occurred mainly in small families, although no specific trend was apparent with respect to the socioeconomic status of such families. Dawson and his co-workers also found that 54 of the 121 asthmatic children who comprised their sample were second children.

238

The Relationship between Intelligence and Bronchial Asthma

Just as no definitive statement can be made as yet about the significance of socioeconomic variables in prevalence studies, so there is difference of opinion regarding the relationship of intelligence to bronchial asthma. Some workers (Knapp, 1963) maintain that asthmatic children are neither more- nor less-intelligent than nonasthmatic children. However, Dawson et al. (1969) found that regardless of social class, at the age of 7, children with bronchial asthma tended to have higher IQs than the general population. This slight but consistent tendency on the part of asthmatic children to excel in the performance of such tests, especially nonverbal tests, had also been described by Graham et al. (1967) in an earlier study. However, the validity of their findings was diminished somewhat because these authors did not attempt to relate test performance to social class.

No clearcut group differences emerge from these socioeconomic and psychosocial data, although Gutmann's report suggests that immigration may play a role in initiating asthmatic attacks in the predisposed. This conclusion is supported by the impression that Puerto Rican immigrants (especially children) who have relocated in the large Northern cities of the United States are unusually likely to develop bronchial asthma. Accurate figures to support this impression do not exist, and no studies assessing the relative roles of pollens, dusts, air pollutants, infection, climate, occupation, or the psychological roles of moving and relocating have been carried out.

PSYCHOLOGICAL FACTORS

The individual and social psychology of asthmatic patients has been studied for many years. Every aspect of the personal and family lives of patients has been examined. The conclusions reached to date must, however, be tempered in light of the fact that no consensus has been reached about the definition and diagnosis of bronchial asthma. No universally accepted definition of the disease exists: a number of closely related syndromes—asthmatic and chronic bronchitis, for example—are recognized. Bronchial asthma can be divided into two main subforms—the extrinsic and intrinsic. There is no reason to suspect that the same psychological profiles or constellation of psychological conflicts are present in the two forms of bronchial asthma. In fact, there is some evidence to suggest that patients suffering from one of these forms differ psychologically from those with the other form.

Nonetheless, research on psychological factors has been guided for many years by four main principles: (1) There is no such thing as an asthmatic personality. (2) Asthmatic patients—especially children—have unconscious wishes for dependency: specifically, they wish to be encompassed and protected. The wish sensitizes them to imagined or actual bereavement. But the wish may produce such conflict that children improve clinically when separated from their parents. (3) The wishes for dependency are brought about by the attitudes of the parents. (4) The asthmatic attack occurs when the wish is frustrated or the conflict is activated. In both instances strong emotions are aroused. (We do not know by what mechanisms the aroused emotions could incite bronchoconstriction, or interact with the allergic mechanisms.)

All of the foregoing assertions must be evaluated in the light of the methodological problems inherent in clinical research on bronchial asthma. First and foremost, it is essential to distinguish between the psychological antecedents, both proximal and distal, of asthmatic attacks and the psychological effects of such attacks on the person who has the illness. Obviously, a similar distinction must be made in evaluating the role of psychological factors in all the diseases reviewed in this book. But it would be expected to have special relevance for a disease as subtle, complex, seasonal, and variable as bronchial asthma—one in which attacks may occur with little warning; and which is particularly apt to affect young children who are less able to cope with fear and anxiety (Purcell, 1965).

Some authors have concluded from their studies of asthmatic patients that unsatisfactory parental attitudes, and the conflicts and emotional and behavioral disturbances engendered by them, significantly antedated the onset of bronchial asthma (Rees, 1963, 1964). But the findings derived from such retrospective studies cannot be regarded as conclusive evidence that these variables predispose to the illness by determining the child's future responses to a particular kind of stressful event, thereby playing a role in the initiation and recurrence of asthmatic attacks. The question of whether psychological factors preceded the onset of bronchial asthma will be definitively resolved only when predictive studies of individuals at risk for this disease are done.

Similar problems have impeded our understanding of the role of psychological factors in the pathogenesis of bronchial asthma. Workers in this field must also be able to identify the factors with which social and psychological variables correlate after the disease has had its inception. It is assumed in most studies that emotional responses to specific situations, or the conflicts induced by such situations, produce bronchoconstriction in some way (Alexander, 1950; Knapp, 1969; Knapp et al., 1966a, b; 1970; Stein, 1962). However, one must also consider the possibility that long-term "maladjustment" may affect the individual's responses to his illness (Dubo et al., 1961; Wright, 1965) and its course, in the sense that it may lead to the exacerbation of symptoms or invalidism, as well as more frequent visits to the doctor, absenteeism from school or work, etc. In other words, psychological factors do not necessarily interact primarily with allergy, infection, or the disposition to bronchoconstriction.

Many other methodological problems have impeded our understanding of the role of psychological and social factors in the etiology and pathogenesis of bronchial asthma. These problems (and recommendations for their solution) have been discussed at length in the literature (Feingold et al., 1962, 1966; Freeman et al., 1964; Leigh, 1953; Lipton et al., 1966; Maurer, 1965; Pinkerton and Weaver, 1970; Purcell, 1965), and will not be reviewed here. In many ways they closely resemble the methodological problems described in this book; indeed, they are intrinsic to all psychosomatic research. Among those problems which have received least attention and have particular relevance in this context, is the failure of some workers to take the effects of medication on psychological function into account in studies of chronic illness. All the medications used in the treatment of bronchial asthma—e.g., epinephrine, ephedrine, antihistamines, aminophylline, ACTH, the corticosteroids, and some antibiotics, may profoundly alter the patient's psychological functioning and behavior. It follows, then, that this methodological defect would further detract from the validity of retrospective studies of the roles of social, environmental, and psychological factors in the etiology and pathogenesis of bronchial asthma.

The Personality Traits of Patients with Bronchial Asthma

Viewed from a historical perspective it is clear that no single or unique personality type characterizes asthmatic children, adolescents, or adults. They differ widely in their habitual moods, traits, attitudes, and personal relationships (Baraff and Cunningham, 1965; Billings, 1947; Brown and Goitein, 1943; Dubo et al., 1961; French and Alexander, 1941; Kiell, 1963; Knapp, 1969; Knapp and Nemetz, 1957a; Rees, 1956a, b; 1963, 1964; Rogerson, 1937, 1943; Rogerson et al., 1935; Sperling, 1963).

Children with bronchial asthma have been described as immature, lacking in self-confidence, insecure, overanxious, restless, tense, high-strung, potentially aggressive, egocentric, and rebellious; as intelligent underachievers (Block et al., 1964; Fine, 1963; Gerard, 1946; Rogerson, 1937; Wittkower and White, 1959); as irritable, aggressive, and bossy (Rogerson, 1937); and as polite, imaginative, and timid (Lamont, 1963). These clinical descriptions, partly at odds with each other, have been confirmed by psychological test data (Chobat et al., 1939; Dees, 1945; Schatia, 1941; Wilken-Jensen et al., 1951).

But these studies did not use control groups and they did not pay attention to differences between boys and girls. A more scientific approach was used by Fine (1963). He administered a battery of psychological tests—the Rorschach, Despert Fables, Maps, TAT, and Wolff tests—to 30 asthmatic children selected at random from a clinic population, and compared the test performance of each child with that of the sibling closest to his age who did not suffer from asthma. Twelve of the 30 pairs of children in the sample were black, and eight were Mexican-American. On the basis of the test results, Fine concluded that, in general, the asthmatic children were more dependent, introverted, explosive, and uncontrolled than their siblings. However, certain differences emerged between the boys and girls in the asthmatic group. The boys depended on their mothers, the girls on their fathers. The girls strove to achieve independence; the boys were content to remain passively dependent, babyish, and immature. And, compared to the girls, the boys were more sensitive to maternal rejection than their siblings. All the asthmatic children in Fine's series were prone to mood swings, but the boys found it particularly difficult to control their feelings; in general, they were irritable and hypersensitive. In addition, the boys tended to avoid relationships with others; the girls, on the other hand, sought to establish such relationships. The girls with asthma tended to become depressed, but they did not cry when they were sad. in fact, the asthmatic children of both sexes tended to inhibit their crying to a greater extent than their siblings did, especially at times of conflict with their parents. The asthmatic children had a low frustration tolerance. And, when frustrated, strong feelings of anger, often explosive and uncontrolled, occurred. This was especially true of the boys, and, not surprisingly, the frustrating person was often the mother. Some test results also indicated that the boys did not express affection. The boys had oral conflicts, the girls had sexual ones. All the children in Fine's study were hospitalized. Studies on hospitalized asthmatic children should employ a matched control group of hospitalized children with a chronic illness.

In the series reported by Vles and Groen (1951) and Neuhaus (1958), employing standard projective tests, comparisons between hospitalized asthmatic and other chronically ill, as well as nonhospitalized healthy children were made. Neuhaus found that the asthmatic children in his sample did not differ essentially from those with cardiac disease. He suggested that anxiety and traits of dependency and insecurity are common to all children who suffer from protracted illness and that these traits are the consequences of the illness. Other psychological traits elicited by the tests were the same in the hospitalized asthmatic and the chronically ill children as in healthy children. This study has been quoted on a number of occasions as evidence that any "atypical" personality traits found in asthmatic children are the consequences, rather than the antecedents, of the illness (Feingold et al., 1966; Freeman et al., 1964; Harris, 1955; Harris and Schure, 1956).

To circumvent the problem of studying children after the onset of the disease in order to determine its psychological antecedents, children at risk for bronchial asthma could be evaluated. Since approximately 25 percent of all children with infantile (atopic) eczema subsequently develop bronchial asthma, studies of such children before the onset of the asthmatic illness would permit one to distinguish between antecedent psychological conditions and the psychological consequences of having an illness as frightening as asthma. Mohr et al. (1963b) carried out such a study. They compared five asthmatic children, four of whom had a history of eczema, with five eczematous children, two of whom later became asthmatic. The eczematous children were passive, submissive, and dependent, presumably because they had been infantilized by their parents. (The seemingly excessive bodily contact between these children and their mothers was considered evidence of such infantilization.) However, they struggled actively to become independent, even in the face of their parents' threat to withdraw their support if they did. The asthmatic children were also dominated by a fear of losing parental support. They attempted to defend against this fear by a show of independence, maturity, and "masculinity." The mothers of some of the children were seductive; others overemphasized achievement and self-control. But regardless of the quality of parental attitudes, whenever separation from their parents (and particularly the mother) was threatened or actually occurred, the asthmatic children became anxious, lost control, became dependent, or had an asthmatic attack.

The personality characteristics of asthmatic children have been determined, not only by direct observation, but also from the descriptions of these children by their parents. Parents of asthmatic children tend to emphasize that their children are not affectionate, and do not seem to welcome gestures of affection from others; in short they do not enjoy being the center of attention (Graham et al., 1967).

Purcell studied asthmatic children from another vantage point: in two collaborative studies (1961, 1962), and a third independent effort (1963), he attempted to differentiate psychologically children with intractable asthma on the basis of their favorable response to hospitalization or, alternatively, to steroid medication. In one such study, which involved the use of various projective tests and the Porteus Maze Test, Purcell and his co-workers (1962) found no differences between rapidly remitting-hospitalized children and steroid-dependent children. However, some differences emerged between the boys and girls in these series: the girls were less outgoing, more anxious and depressed, and more conscientious. The authors concluded that global tests for neuroticism or maladjustment are not discriminating enough to be helpful in investigations of bronchial asthma.

Some children with bronchial asthma outgrow their symptomatic attacks in adolescence as they develop to become increasingly independent of their parents. Others continue to be asthmatic, and a third group develops the disease during adolescence. Asthmatic adolescents share many of the same personality characteristics of asthmatic children. Eighteen hospitalized adolescents, albeit with serious psychopathology (nine were psychotic), were socially withdrawn, externally passive, immature, and had tenuous relationships with others, except with their mothers, to whom they clung and were extremely demanding.

Asthmatic attacks in these adolescents were frequently precipitated by physical activity, such as fighting or dancing, which excited the patients sexually, or by situations that evoked outbursts of anger or feelings of disappointment, fear, frustration, or jealousy (particularly of siblings). In seven patients, the initial attack or exacerbation of asthma in childhood coincided with the death of a relative or the birth of a sibling. Of the 18 patients in this group, 17 had been separated from close relatives during childhood; at the time of the study, 10 of these 18 patients were depressed; 6 had phobias of animals, of being out alone, or of riding on subways or in cars. Both observation and projective tests bore out the authors' impression that these adolescents had fantasies of violence and death (Fink and Schneer, 1963).

Studies of Adults

In early personality studies on adult patients, hysterical and compulsive character traits (orderliness, neatness, meticulousness) were predominant or very common in up to 40 percent of a population of asthmatic adults of various ages (Brown and Goitein, 1943; Dunbar, 1938; Fenichel, 1945; Israel, 1954; Leigh and Rawnsley, 1956; McDermott and Cobb, 1939; Rees, 1956b; Schatia, 1941); such patients were also said to have dependent relationships. Elsewhere in the literature asthmatic patients have been described as seclusive, moody (with frequent depressive moods), or egocentric (Groen, 1950, 1951; Kerman, 1946; Treuting and Ripley, 1948). In addition, their tendency toward mood swings, suspiciousness, self-punishment, and strong hostile wishes and impulses were cited by Stokes and Beerman (1940) and Brown and Goitein (1943). The presence of hostile wishes and impulses was also noted by Groen (1950, 1951) and Bastiaans and Groen (1954), who further noted that asthmatic patients typically experienced feelings of oppression, or constriction, which they tried to ward off by behaving impulsively. According to McDermott and Cobb (1939), asthmatic patients were irritable, plaintive people who wept easily. At other times, they were described as shy (Knapp and Nemetz, 1957b) and oversensitive.

The results of these clinical studies indicate that no invariant set of personal traits characterize asthmatic patients. Also, a large number of asthmatic patients would have to be compared to healthy subjects to determine whether any particular set of traits occurred more- or less-frequently in patients than in subjects. It remained for Rees (1956a, b) to study 441 clinic patients of all ages with bronchial asthma and 321 control patients who had been hospitalized for hernia operations or appendectomies. Anxiety reactions were the most common form of reaction found in asthmatic patients, who had a significantly higher incidence of anxiety, timidity, hypersensitivity, and depression. Obsessional traits were also more common in the experimental population, except for the adult male patients. In addition, an increased incidence of mood swings occurred in the asthmatic group, especially in the adult female patients, and hysterical personality features were present more frequently in asthmatic patients of both sexes. In fact, Rees concluded that the asthmatic patients, except for prepubertal boys, were unstable and maladjusted.

Knapp and Nemetz (1957a) studied 40 hospitalized patients either with intrinsic or extrinsic asthma. They were also careful to take into account the effects of medication on their subject's psychological functioning. The failure of some other investigators to take into account the effects of drugs constitutes a major methodological weakness of their studies.

The personalities of these patients ranged from normal (with evidence of anxiety) to paranoid. Nine patients were described as hysterical, and fifteen had personality characteristics in which impulsive or compulsive behavior, depressive moods, or conversion symptoms were evident. An additional five patients had transient psychotic episodes, which, in some instances, coincided with the use of ACTH. The authors concluded from their findings that the more severe the clinical asthma, the more severe was the subject's personality disturbance. In a second study, Knapp and Nemetz (1957b) found that 80 percent of the adult patients in their experimental group felt depressed at times, and that such feelings were not necessarily associated with their asthmatic attacks. In addition, they expressed chronic feelings of longing, emptiness, feelings of sadness, guilt, anger, and rage (which they inhibited), wishes to die, not knowing whether to weep or not, and concerns about becoming addicted to the medication they were receiving. It is clear from these clinical studies that no single personality type is typical of the asthmatic patient. The descriptions provided by Knapp and Nemetz cover the entire spectrum of personality types described previously by other authors.

Psychological tests, particularly the Rorschach test in the hands of Barendregt (1957), Israel (1954), and Schatia (1941) have confirmed the clinical psychiatric descriptions that some asthmatic patients are inhibited and compulsive and harbor within themselves hostile impulses to anyone who oppresses or constrains them.

The Nature of the Conflict

Alexander (1950) and French and Alexander (1941) pointed out that an excessive dependency on the mother lay behind the bewildering array of personal traits, hostile impulses, behaviors, and inhibitions, and the instability of mood and feeling states, of asthmatic patients. They found that asthmatic patients had the unconscious dependent longing to be protected and engulfed by the mother. Actual or threatened separation or an interference with the relationship between child and mother increases the wish to be protected and engulfed and may, in the predisposed child or adult, activate the wish.

Even though the "specificity" of Alexander's hypothesis has been criticized, the psychosomatic "orientation" to bronchial asthma has, until recently, been based largely

244

on his hypothesis (1950) of the role of conflict and its emotional concomitants in patients with this disease.

Alexander also emphasized that the dependency conflict in bronchial asthma was different from the oral dependency conflict he had hypothesized in peptic ulcer disease. In peptic ulcer, the content of the conflict was the wish to be fed by the mother. In bronchial asthma, the conflict had its roots in the patient's exaggerated unconscious wish to be protected and encompassed by the mother. The symbolic expression of this wish in dreams and fantasies about water was prominent among bronchial asthma patients.*

Given this psychological configuration, any situation that revived the patient's fear of separation would precipitate an asthmatic attack. Alexander mentioned that in children the onset of the disease was frequently associated with the birth of a sibling, who was perceived as a rival for the mother's love and attention. The expression by the child of hostile feelings directed toward the mother could provoke an attack, if the child believed that the integrity of the dependent relationship would be compromised as a result. In adults, sexual temptation or an impending marriage might bring forth the conflict between the fear of separation from the mother and the patient's desire for freedom and independence, thus precipitating an asthmatic attack.

The situation that is most likely to precipitate asthmatic attacks in children is one that engenders a fear of separation from the mother, or the loss of her love (Fine, 1963; French, 1939; Harris et al., 1950; Jessner et al., 1955; Lamont, 1963; Mohr et al., 1963a, b; Sperling, 1963). Many specific situations in addition to those mentioned by Alexander can evoke this response: fears of separation may be revived when the child starts school (Rees, 1964), or if the mother becomes ill or dies. Even comparatively innocuous events may give rise to fears of separation. The mother might express a legitimate, but transient, anger with the child or punish the child, or the child might witness a quarrel between his parents and anticipate the dissolution of their marriage and his abandonment by the mother (Mohr et al., 1963a). Related fears of the loss of her love may arise in situations where the mother's love is given conditionally and depends on the child's ability to live up to her expectations. The mother's controlling attitudes may elicit predictable responses from the child: he may rebel or express his anger with his mother, but such behavior will produce the concomitant fear that the mother will withdraw her approval and recognition as a result (Greenfield, 1958; Mansmann, 1952).

---

* The prominence for asthmatic patients of specific fantasies about water were a central feature of Alexander's formulations. For Deutsch (1953), such fantasies were the symbolic expression of birth, impregnation, or rebirth. For Alexander (1950), and Saul and Lyons (1954), they symbolized the wish to be encompassed or sheltered by the mother. The introjection of the mother by respiration, in order to be permanently protected, is fantasied as an accomplished fact, and conflicts arise between the patient's ego and his respiratory apparatus, which represents the introjected object. Thus, conscious imaginary preoccupation with, or aversion to, water (which was associated with a fear of drowning) was noted in about half the patients in two series (Knapp and Nemetz, 1957b; McDermott and Cobb, 1939). But Wittkower and White (1959) subsequently pointed out that this aversion to water was not necessarily an expression of conflict. Some of the patients in the series they studied had actually had a frightening experience in the water before the onset of bronchial asthma. Parenthetically, one might ask whether the initial episode of asthma might not "reinforce" the fear of drowning, for during an asthmatic attack, some patients must feel as though they are drowning in their bronchial secretions.

On the surface, these findings would seem to support Alexander's hypothesis that dependency conflicts, which center on the wish to be protected by the mother, play a central role in the predisposition to and initiation of asthmatic attacks. However, it is a basic thesis of this presentation that inasmuch as asthma is a heterogeneous disease, the role of psychological factors in the pathogenesis of bronchial asthma probably cannot be understood in terms of any one set of personal conflicts that psychologically sensitizes the asthmatic to any one kind of initiating event.

Concrete evidence in refutation of Alexander's observations that fears of separation initiate asthmatic attacks consists in the finding that actual separation of the child from his family may result in an alleviation of his symptoms. In fact, in light of Alexander's early influence on psychosomatic research, it is an interesting paradox that, despite the methodological weaknesses inherent in retrospective clinical studies, the finding that separation of the severely ill asthmatic child from his family resulted in a marked improvement in the condition of about one-half of the children studied (Bastiaans and Groen, 1954; Hallowitz, 1954; Jessner et al., 1955; Peshkin, 1930, 1959; Purcell, 1965; Rogerson, 1937; Rogerson et al., 1935; Steen, 1959; Tuft, 1957) constitutes one of the most powerful pieces of evidence obtained to date in support of the proposition that psychosocial factors play a role in the initiation and recurrence of this illness. Furthermore, the observation reported by Lamont (1963) that a child who is sensitive to a specific and proven allergen may have an attack at home when he is exposed to the allergen, but that such exposure will not provoke an attack if he is away from home, provided he is not accompanied by his parents (Rogerson, 1937), is additional evidence of the manner in which psychological and allergenic factors in the initiation of some attacks interact.

Some authors have argued that the removal of a child from his family to a hospital, for example, is effective because the child has been removed thereby from the specific allergens to which he would normally be exposed at home. Two studies have demonstrated (Lamont, 1963; Long et al., 1958) the fallacy of this argument: when dust collected from an asthmatic child's home was sprayed in his hospital room while he was recovering from an attack, no new attack occurred. In other words, the removal of the child from his home, rather than his exposure to the allergen, seemed to be the critical precipitating factor in this case (Lamont, 1963; Long et al., 1958).

Lamont (1963) has suggested that hospitalization may also serve an important psychological function in such cases: the child is relieved of the anxiety inherent in the close, mutually ambivalent tie to his mother, and reassured simultaneously that his need for protection and care will be gratified by the hospital personnel. And Knapp (1960) ascribed the dramatic improvement in some children once they are separated from their mothers to the fact that, although they want to maintain their dependent relationships in the hospital, they feel threatened by too much closeness to the mother. In other words, wishing to be protected and encompassed by the mother may, in itself, be a source of conflict; for a boy to do so may have specific, conflict-laden sexual (incestuous) implications (Alexander, 1950; Knapp, 1960). Greenacre (1953) has also commented on the coexistence of strong wishes for and conscious fears of fusion with the mother in some patients with bronchial asthma, and Jessner et al. (1955) have reported a tendency among patients to avoid their mothers. It should be noted, however, that these formulations may apply only to those children and adults with severe (intractable) asthma, and could have little relevance for patients suffering from mild forms that are conspicuously seasonal in character.

Not all children improve when separated from their parents and hospitalized, even if they do not require hospitalization. Some do and some do not. In the ones that do improve, emotional factors seem to play the predominant, inciting role of an asthmatic attack. Purcell and his co-workers (1969b) classified 25 children with chronic asthma into two groups. They predicted that the 13 children whose attacks were precipitated by emotional factors to a significant degree would improve on separation, but that separation would not effect an improvement in the status of a second group of 12 children whose illness was unrelated to emotional factors. Once they had been so classified, the children were hospitalized, and repeated measurements of pulmonary function, the daily history of attacks, the degree of wheezing, and the amount of medication required were recorded for each child in each group. In fact, the children in the first group did show significant functional improvement on pulmonary tests (especially of airway obstruction), wheezed less, required significantly less medication, and had fewer asthmatic attacks. Once these children had been reunited with their families these trends were reversed. However, not all of the children in the first group improved on all of these measures. Fewer attacks also occurred in the second group of children, who the authors had predicted would not improve on separation—a finding that suggested that emotional factors also played a role in precipitating attacks.

To summarize, two kinds of situations—those that stimulate fears of separation or, conversely, fears of closeness, both of which are transformation of the same unresolved dependency conflicts—play a role in the precipitation of asthmatic attacks in children. More precisely, attacks occur when the child is unable to cope with these situations, when, in short, the defenses he has erected against the emergence of these fears fail.

Based on the foregoing, the conclusion might be reached that in children the same interpersonal events characterize the first and all subsequent asthmatic attacks, and that the incidence with which these events can be identified at the time of the first attack is the same as subsequently. Therefore, the study by McDermott and Cobb (1939) is noteworthy, particularly because these authors were careful to distinguish between the role of emotional factors in initiating the first attack and the role of such factors in initiating attacks in 40 percent of the patients of various ages in their series, and a preeminent role in the later attacks of 60 percent.

VALIDATION OF ALEXANDER'S CONCEPT OF THE CONFLICT

If the asthmatic attack is precipitated by the fear of separation in some patients, the attack itself could be understood as a "repressed cry" calling the mother to return (Alcock, 1960; Alexander, 1950; Löfgren, 1961; Weiss, 1922). In 1968, Alexander et al. reiterated these formulations but added that the child's cry for help was inhibited initially by the fear that the mother would repudiate it. In later life, however, this conflict was replaced by another conflict—the wish to confide in the mother, on the one hand, and the fear of confiding in her, on the other. The wish to confide was motivated by the desire to propitiate the mother; the fear of doing so was generated by the thought that confession would alienate her.

A study was designed by Alexander and co-workers (1968) to test and validate Alexander's hypothesis regarding these conflicts operative in "psychosomatic" disease. Nine psychoanalysts listened to taped interviews of patients chosen because they had been medically diagnosed as having one of the eight "psychosomatic" diseases. There were ten men and women patients, each with one of the diseases. The nine psychoanalysts correctly assigned the correct diagnosis to one-half of the patients with bronchial asthma.

Although they were not so interpreted by Alexander and his co-workers, the results of this validating study indicate that Alexander's formulation only applied to about one-half of the patients in the sample studied. One might also conclude from these findings that, from a psychological point of view, patients with bronchial asthma are psychologically heterogeneous. A number of investigations have attested to the validity of this conclusion and have underscored other conceptual flaws inherent in Alexander's hypothesis. For one, Alexander made no attempt to relate the psychological conflict purportedly predisposing to bronchial asthma to the age of the patients he studied. The fact that approximately one-half of all asthmatic attacks begin before the age of 5—and are particularly likely to have their onset when the child is about 3 years old, at which time conflicts surrounding autonomy and socialization are prominent—lends credence to Alexander's hypothesis that such attacks are precipitated by the fear of separation. But the meaning of separation may be quite different for a 6-year-old (Selesnick, 1963) or 11-year-old child.

RESPONSE TO ALEXANDER'S FORMULATION OF A SPECIFIC CONFLICT

Alexander's contention that the specific conflict configuration is operative in bronchial asthma has been the target of growing criticism in recent years because it is too restrictive. Studies later indicate that any attempt to define a characteristic conflict in bronchial asthma is futile. No single set of personal conflicts could psychologically sensitize all individuals who are biologically predisposed to bronchial asthma to a single kind of initiating event.

Thus, Knapp and his co-workers (1957b, 1970) concluded, on the basis of their systematic clinical study of 40 adult patients with bronchial asthma, that the conflicts Alexander had hypothesized were not always present in their patients; there were other sources of conflict as well. Moreover, in some cases, conflict and tension arose, in part, in response to the disease. Specifically, the authors noted the presence of passive-dependent social attitudes, which had also been described by Dunbar in 1943, and were subsequently observed by other workers (Fine, 1963; Giovacchini, 1959; Glasberg et al., 1969; Jessner et al., 1955; Stokvis, 1959; Treuting and Ripley, 1948; Wolf et al., 1950). In the series studied by Knapp et al. (1970) and Knapp and Nemetz (1960) conflicts surrounding such attitudes, as exemplified by helplessness in relation to the mother or some other person, occurred in 33 patients. Psychological states observed in these patients were similarly interpreted as expressions of conflict. For example, Knapp and Bahnson (1963) and Knapp et al. (1966a, b) and others (Alcock, 1960; Gillespie, 1936; Saul and Lyons,

248

1954; Treuting and Ripley, 1948) commented on the fact that depressive and sorrowful states, both chronic and episodic, which were related only in part to feelings about being ill, frequently occurred in these patients. Of the patients studied by Knapp et al. 83 percent suffered intermittently from depression, which was profound at times (Knapp et al., 1966b). Additionally, shame and guilt about their overt dependent demands and about the symptoms of their asthmatic illness were observed in 63 percent of the patients in this series. And 78 percent evidenced a preoccupation with food, hunger, eating, and weight gain and loss. This oral preoccupation extended to medication as well. Thus, some patients responded to real or imagined deprivation with impatience, anger, and anxiety. In other patients, however, primitive reaction patterns were evoked to defend against the threatened emergence of oral wishes. Food and medication tasted "bad," and had to be expelled from the mouth. Finally, the conflict between wanting to conceal some personal matter and wanting to confess it, which Alexander had observed in his adult patients, was prominent in 75 percent of the patients in this series. However, Knapp and Nemetz (1957b) pointed out that this conflict is frequently inherent in the patient's relationship to his psychiatrist, and can therefore not be unique to patients with bronchial asthma. Other authors have suggested, on the basis of their clinical observations, that conflicts surrounding elimination, aggression, and rebellion—which are rooted, in turn, in deep-seated, pregenital dependency conflicts—may be a major source of tension in bronchial asthma patients (Abramson, 1963; Bacon, 1956; Brown and Goitein, 1943; Deutsch, 1953; Dunbar, 1938; Fenichel, 1945; Giovacchini, 1959; Gunnarson, 1950; Knapp, 1960, 1969; Sperling, 1963; Wright, 1965). Sexual conflicts also occur, especially in girls (Fine, 1963; Knapp, 1960; Treuting and Ripley, 1948). And, in some instances, the conflicts described were identical to those postulated by Alexander (1950). For example, as noted previously, Alexander stated that in the presence of the nuclear dependency conflict he hypothesized, impending marriage might bring to the fore the conflict between the fear of leaving home (i.e., mother) and the desire to enter into a mature sexual relationship, and thus bring about the onset of the illness. Conflicts of this nature anteceded asthmatic attacks in the patients studied by Knapp and Nemetz (1957b) and Treuting and Ripley (1948). In the sample studied by Treuting and Ripley (1948), masturbation was conflictful and correlated with the onset and recurrence of asthmatic attacks, especially when it was associated with threats of, or actual, punishment by the patient's parents. And homosexual attachments have also been cited as a possible source of tension and conflict. In addition, Rees's finding (1956a) that in one-third of the 81 women in his series, asthmatic attacks were likely to occur premenstrually—at a time when more primitive, i.e., pregenital, conflicts are likely to emerge—can be interpreted as further evidence of the role of nonspecific conflicts in the etiology and pathogenesis of bronchial asthma. While the nature of these pregenital patterns may vary, they are invariably associated with residual intrapsychic sexual conflicts that originated in early childhood. By the same token, the finding that a frigid woman's asthmatic attacks disappeared when she was able to experience sexual pleasure would seem to indicate that this patient was able to resolve the sexual conflicts that played a role in precipitating her illness.

Thus, a variety of conflicts, in addition to the specific conflict hypothesized by Alexander, are, therefore, operative in bronchial asthma. It is important to distinguish bet-

249

ween those conflicts that precede the illness from those that arise in response to it. From the studies cited above, certain general propositions can be formulated about the role of conflict in bronchial asthma. Alexander's specificity hypothesis in all asthma patients has not been confirmed in more than about one-half of the patients. In them, dependency conflicts of the kind described by him do seem to play a role. In other patients, sexual and aggressive conflicts do also. Therefore, it is not the nature of the conflict that plays the critical role, but rather some factor other than the conflict. The factor may be a failure to contain the conflict or the intense feeling the conflict engenders. The conflicts are currently considered to represent necessary (but not sufficient) conditions in the functional explanation of some forms of the illness (Knapp, 1963, 1969; Stein, 1962). Clearly, then, the mechanisms that are employed to defend against the emergence of these conflicts, their emotional concomitants, and, finally, their ontogenesis, merit detailed discussion.

Defense Mechanisms

It is axiomatic that it is not the conflict per se that plays a critical role in the onset and recurrence of bronchial asthma. The significance of the conflict depends on how it is coped with psychologically. Thus, it can be speculated that children are more vulnerable to asthmatic attacks because their defenses are not yet properly integrated or are less effective, so they are less able to cope successfully with the conflicts that may precipitate the attacks. The balance of three variables—the nature and strength of the conflict, the defensive and coping mechanisms available to the patient, and the extent to which these enable concurrent gratification of certain basic human needs—may determine whether bronchial asthma or some other illness will occur in an individual with the appropriate psychological predispositions.

Implicit in Alexander's initial formulation was the contention, elucidated by French (1939), that asthmatic patients employed several defense mechanisms to ward off conscious awareness of their fears of separation and the conflict that surrounded such fears (Leigh, 1953). By confessing something for which he felt guilty, the adult patient hoped to effect a reconciliation with the person on whom he depended. In the child, the attack itself might serve a similar purpose: it would help him to gain the mother's attention and forgiveness. Some patients developed a variety of personality traits as defenses against their infantile fixation. For example, a child might attempt to achieve mastery of his dependency conflict by affecting a pseudo-independence vis-à-vis the mother. He might attempt to convince her (and himself) that he was not afraid of her rejection by testing her responses to his overt expressions of hostility.

Personality traits may serve as a defense against persistent dependency motives in adults. However, women are less likely than men to develop such traits. A study by Glasberg et al. (1969) of male and female asthmatic patients and comparison groups showed that the men in their experimental group had independent traits, whereas the women had dependent ones. The female asthmatic patients studied by these workers lacked emotional independence and individuation, were sexually prudish, and had expressed oral-dependent needs. Although the male asthmatic patients also harbored fears of separation and wishes to be mothered, warmed, and comforted, they attempted to defend against the emergence of their desire for passive gratification and the conflict surrounding their dependency motives.

The asthmatic attack occurs when these various defenses in part fail (Giovacchini, 1959; Lidz, 1969), and the patient is overwhelmed by the anticipation or actuality of rejection by the object (Sclare, 1959); or when he experiences a profound sense of depletion (Knapp, 1960, 1969; Knapp and Nemetz, 1960), occasioned by the rejection, withdrawal, or the actual or anticipated loss of the loved object. Identification with the mother as a defense against such loss was inferred by Dunbar (1938).

The formulations set forth by Giovacchini (1959) and by Knapp and Nemetz (1960) and Knapp et al. (1970) differ from the propositions advanced by Alexander. Knapp (1960, 1969) emphasized the importance of regression as a major defense during periods of active conflict. Under conditions of severe stress, the patient may regress from action to fantasy, "the refuge for wishes that cannot be fulfilled," or to earlier levels of adaptation.

Thus, Knapp and his co-workers hypothesized that asthmatic attacks would occur in response to actual separation or the threat thereof, the failure of the defenses that could have enabled the patient to cope with the situation, and the anxiety and guilt that were mobilized by a series of related, childlike, destructive fantasies. At the same time, other fantasies of incorporating and thereby retaining the loved object, or of eliminating the object if incorporation was perceived as dangerous, were also present. The manner in which these conflictive fantasies were managed psychologically differed from individual to individual. if the patient's destructive urge was predominant, it might, in fantasy, endanger the person to whom it was directed. In that event, the patient would be expected to distance himself from the object, which might lead to abatement of the conflict. If, on the other hand, the desire for closeness was predominant, separation would enhance it, and closeness would cause the conflict's abatement.

Knapp's ideas begin to explain the paradox that some asthmatic children cannot do with their mothers and others cannot do without them. The observation that some children lose their symptoms when away from their mothers suggests that despite their wish to be enveloped by their mothers they are fearful of being enveloped. Other children give in to the wish because the prospect of separation arouses destructive and incorporative fantasies that subside when the relationship is preserved. The intense ambivalence in some of these patients is expressed in terms of the fear of closeness versus the fear of separation. In each instance, these fears, the anticipation of the frightening feelings, or the expectation of their resolution are accompanied by the intense arousal of feelings.

Another body of observations attests to the fact that defenses may play another role at the time of the asthmatic attack. By preventing the free expression of feelings, they appear to contribute to the attack. Rogerson (1937) and Rees (1956a) have added considerably to our knowledge along this line. Rees (1956a), who studied a group of children selected at random, found, as did Knapp and Nemetz (1957b, 1960) and Knapp et al. (1966b) in subsequent studies of adults, that the immediate precipitation of attacks was associated with sudden changes in emotions. More precisely, he noted that at times, pent-up emotions gave rise to mounting inner tension, which led directly to an asthmatic attack. Thus, the discharge of emotions and impulses in disobedient behavior resulted in

251

a decrease in the frequency of attacks, whereas controlled, obedient, and well-mannered behavior was correlated with an increase in the frequency of attacks. Therefore, asthmatic attacks do not always occur because "defenses fail," as French (1939) had suggested. On the contrary, in some instances attacks occur because the patient's well-integrated "defenses" preclude the complete or adequate development and discharge of conscious feeling. If they are not fully discharged, strong feelings of many kinds (e.g., anger, fear, anxiety, longing, guilt, etc.) may be correlated with the onset of an attack in some children (Hurst, 1943). If, on the other hand, these feelings are completely discharged, the attack does not occur.

Rogerson (1937) pointed out that a latency period, ranging from a few minutes to 4 to 12 hours, occurred between the patient's exposure to a frightening situation, his reaction to that situation in the form of an anxiety attack and a temper tantrum, and his asthmatic attack. But he also noted that the fright the patient suffered might be associated with breathlessness, followed after some time had elapsed by an asthmatic attack.

The idea that unexpressed or unexpressible emotion, or rather, emotional behavior—a suppressed cry for the mother—triggered asthmatic attacks had already been put forward by Weiss (1922). His observation became a central feature of Alexander's formulation (1950) about the emotional correlate of the asthmatic attack. Both authors implied that the conscious psychological defense of suppression prevented the cry from being expressed. The attack occurs because the wish to be protected by the mother and fantasies of being encompassed by her cannot be consciously expressed or acknowledged. According to Alexander, this theory was substantiated by two findings: first, that most of the asthmatic patients in his sample spontaneously reported that it was difficult for them to cry, and second, that asthmatic attacks were observed to terminate once the patient was able to "give vent to his feelings by crying" (Alexander, 1950).

The conflict over crying—whether or not to cry—occurred in 43 percent of a series of patients studied by Knapp and Nemetz (1957b). However, the second finding noted by Alexander—that once the suppressed cry was expressed, the asthmatic attack ceased —which was based on observations reported by a number of authors (Doust and Leigh, 1953; French, 1939; Gerard, 1946; Scheflen, 1953; Selinsky, 1960) was not confirmed by Knapp and Nemetz. Purcell (1963, 1965) reported that only 5 of the 38 children in his series ascribed the onset of an attack to crying, and that laughing could also initiate attacks in some patients. Purcell (1963) suggested that both crying and laughing caused gross alterations in respiratory patterns. The asthmatic child voluntarily inhibits tears and laughter out of the fear that were he to give vent to them, their expression might induce an attack.

The suppression of anger (lest it endanger the dependent relationship) might also induce an asthmatic attack: for example, Metcalfe (1956) found that the probability that his 21-year-old female patient would have an asthmatic attack was significantly increased in the 24 hours immediately following a visit with her mother, to whom she could not openly express her angry feelings.

Aroused Emotions as Precipitants

Many conflictful fantasies occur in patients with bronchial asthma (Löfgren, 1961). But, more important, Knapp (1960, 1963, 1969) has addressed himself to the question of whether the diverse fantasies that find their plastic expression in alterations of respiratory function might have a common denominator, because each of these fantasies has the capacity markedly to arouse the person emotionally. In turn, such intense emotional arousal may alter respiratory function and promote bronchoconstriction, to which the patient is predisposed.

The direct observation of the behavior of children has confirmed the impression that a variety of aroused emotions correlate with the onset of the attack. In addition, various actions—excitement translated into motor activity, physical exercise, or dancing and singing—initiate attacks. These conclusions derive from Rees's study (1956a), subsequently elaborated on by Purcell in a series of studies conducted independently (1965) and in collaboration with his co-workers (1961, 1962). Asthmatic children were divided into two subgroups, comprising, respectively, rapidly remitting and steroid-dependent children who had to be hospitalized. The studies showed that attacks might be precipitated by a variety of psychological and behavioral states but that these interacted with exposure to allergens and upper respiratory infections. In about one-half of the patients in both groups, asthma attacks often occurred at night. During the day, attacks were induced by pleasant, as well as unpleasant, feeling states; exertion and pleasurable excitement, laughing, crying, coughing, exposure to allergens, and the presence of infection were equally prevalent as precipitating conditions in both the rapidly remitting and steroid-dependent patients. Attacks were more likely to be associated with feeling states such as anger, anxiety, depression, in the rapidly remitting than in the steroid-dependent patients. It was the authors' impression that in the steroid-dependent group, attacks were more-commonly triggered by changes in the weather.

Although it does not deal with the emotional antecedents but concomitants of asthmatic attacks, Weiss (1966) studied 32 children of both sexes by means of the Nowlis mood adjective checklist during attacks and in intervening periods. Weiss reported that significant increases in anxiety, inability to concentrate, and fatigue occurred during attacks, but measures of depression and anxiety were unchanged. Girls scored higher than boys on measures of pleasant moods, both during attacks and in the intervals between attacks. These results would support the contention that both pleasant and unpleasant mood and feeling states may antecede attacks in childhood.

Most of the conclusions about the role of emotional arousal were done in children and are either based on self-reports (that in children are often hard to elicit) or direct observation. Adults are often more-reliable reporters of their own conscious feelings and moods. In adults, too, the conclusion has been reached that intense emotional arousal may also precipitate or accompany an asthmatic attack, particularly since many asthmatics tend to have little control over their emotions. However, adult patients with bronchial asthma are frequently, and sometimes severely, depressed and moody, and this complex mood state commonly occurs in the intervals between (Knapp and Nemetz, 1957b; Sclare, 1959; Treuting and Ripley, 1948) or during attacks (Knapp and Nemetz, 1957a, b, 1960; Knapp et al., 1966b). Yet, the meaning of, and reasons for this depression have only infrequently connected to antecedent loss, longing, and disappointment (Knapp and Nemetz, 1957a, b). Other authors have variously noted that adult patients are frequently anxious, fearful, or enraged before the attack (Sclare, 1959); that guilt and sorrow may be present (Treuting and Ripley, 1948); that excitement (McDermott and

Cobb, 1939), laughing (McDermott and Cobb, 1939), and crying (Treuting and Ripley, 1948) may occur; or the attack may be preceded by a reactive elation (Brown and Goitein, 1943; Knapp, 1960). The most-comprehensive study of moods and feelings was conducted by Knapp and Nemetz (1960). The emotional responses surrounding 406 attacks (most of which were verified by pulmonary function studies) were observed in nine patients with asthma. They found that 34 percent of these 406 attacks were preceded by an admixture of anger, general irritability and arousal, restlessness, and sweating; 10 percent were preceded by elation and erotic arousal, often with increased motor activity; and 5 percent were preceded by depression. During the attack, 45 to 60 percent of the patients studied felt depressed, helpless, and hopeless, and 6 percent were preoccupied with conscious fantasies that poisonous substances had entered their bodies and desired to get rid of these substances. Some crying occurred in 5 percent of the patients in this series, but the urge to weep, rather than weeping, per se, was more common.

Knapp (1960), Knapp and Nemetz (1960), and Löfgren, (1961) have postulated that emotional arousal occurs in response to a given situation, that the emotions aroused are discharged only in part as a concomitant of the attack, and that the fact that complete discharge has not occurred gives rise to depression and urges to cry, but an apparent inability or only limited ability to do so.

In summary, then, the studies reviewed indicate that actual or anticipated separation or loss does play an important role in initiating attacks in about 50 percent of all asthmatic patients, regardless of age. Subsequent attacks may be triggered by a wide variety of situations in which emotions, both pleasant and unpleasant, are aroused. In addition, it may very well be that the failure to fully express these emotions may be an important element in triggering attacks (Knapp, 1960, 1963, 1969; Knapp and Bahnson, 1963; Knapp et al., 1970; Miller and Baruch, 1948b; Rees, 1964). By the same token the complete discharge of a strong emotion, such as anger, may relieve the attack (Lamont, 1963). But physical exertion also triggers attacks. Exercise or exertion can produce bronchoconstriction in some asthmatic persons (Jones, 1966; Pinkerton, 1967; Pinkerton and Weaver, 1970; Swineford, 1962).

Psychological Characteristics of Patients Sensitive and Not Sensitive to Skin Tests

Behavioral scientists have used skin tests to verify the clinical diagnosis of bronchial asthma and to compare children with positive and negative skin tests in an attempt to determine whether the two groups differ psychologically. The aim of carrying out such studies was to find out whether children with extrinsic asthma (those with positive tests) differed from those with intrinsic asthma. However, skin tests are not sufficiently reliable in determining such a differentiation. They may be positive when the child does not have asthma. They may be negative in extrinsic asthma; an asthmatic child may have a negative skin test to an allergen, but the same allergen may produce a positive pulmonary provocation test, and a false-positive skin test occurs and may be misleading. Therefore, the pulmonary provocation test may be more reliable for the purpose of diagnosing and classifying asthmatic patients.

The relationship between bronchial asthma and evidence of skin hypersensitivity is complex (see Table 3). A child who has asthmatic attacks initiated by pollen may show no reaction to skin testing with pollen for a period of months, but may then become increasingly sensitive to intradermal injection of pollen or scratch tests for pollen. Consequently, skin tests can only be regarded as evidence of a latent tendency toward allergic sensitivity and the formation of IgE antibodies.

A negative skin test does not preclude the diagnosis of bronchial asthma (Pearson, 1968). Test results depend, in part, on the nature of the provocative antigen used (Aas, 1965). It is important, too, to evaluate the results in light of previous desensitization procedures and medication—specifically, antihistamines, epinephrine, other sympathomimetic drugs, and methylxanthines—which decrease skin reactivity. The clinical significance of skin tests varies greatly with age (Kallio et al., 1966; Pearson, 1968) and with the care with which the tests are administered. In addition, the local circulation of the skin may influence test results, for the erythema and heat produced depends, to some extent, on local arteriolar, capillary, and lymphatic flow. Moreover, the arteriolar flow is influenced, in turn, by environmental temperature and psychological factors (such as fear and mood states), as well as hormonal and other variables.

Because of the variable correlation between positive skin tests and a clinical history of bronchial asthma, these tests cannot be used as the sole basis for diagnosis in asthma; diagnostic error may be of the order of 30 to 35 percent (Aas, 1969). A growing number of workers have come to recognize the need to achieve further validation of the diagnosis of extrinsic asthma by bronchial provocation tests. The provocation of impaired pulmonary function by the inhalation of atomized extracts of allergens and control substances has become regular practice (Aas, 1966, 1969; Colldahl, 1967; Kim, 1965; Vanselow, 1967). The disease, asthma, and patients with asthma fall into subgroups at every level of organization. In children, asthma may take different courses. Some children remit rapidly on being taken out of their homes and require no further drugs, and others who are also sent away from home continue to require steroids for the relief of symptoms. Children with

TABLE 3

Clinical History (Asthma, Allergic Rhinitis)		
	No	Yes
Positive Skin Test (Adults)	17%	64% (Hagy and Settipane, 1966)
Positive Scratch Test	5%	3–10% (Spoujitch, 1960; Curran and Goldman, 1961)
Positive Intracutaneous Test	40%	
Positive Skin Test (Children)		65%[a] (Pinkerton, 1967)

Family History of Allergy. No Clinical History		
	No	Yes
Positive Skin Test	4%	30% (Pearson, 1937)

[a] 25% clinically relevant.

asthma differ in their behavior and in their capacity to express feelings. The unconscious conflicts of children and adults are not uniform. Mothers vary in their attitudes toward their asthmatic children even before the onset of the first attack of the disease. There are several types of mother-child interactions (Block et al., 1964).

It is, therefore, entirely legitimate to ask what accounts for these differences—whether children or adults with extrinsic asthma, for instance, differ in terms of psychological characteristics from those with intrinsic asthma. The attitudes of mothers toward the children with these two forms of the disease may differ. Behind such questions lies the idea that there might be an inverse relationship between the extrinsic form of asthma and the contribution that the mother's attitude makes to inciting the asthmatic attacks in the child. The more liable the child is to the immediate form of hypersensitivity the less likely a disturbance in the mother-child relationship could be found. The obverse situation would occur in the intrinsic form. In theory, asthma could be seen either as a disease in which allergic and other physiological factors, or in which psychosocial ones, played the predominant roles. This line of inquiry was pursued by Block et al. (1964) and Freeman et al. (1967). In the first study, 62 children were differentiated on the basis of an allergic potential scale (APS) consisting of five items: a weighted score for a family history of allergies, blood eosinophile count, skin reactivity to allergens, total number of allergies, and ease of diagnosability of the allergy. Children who scored high (i.e., were more allergic) were assigned to one group, and those who scored low to another. The asthmatic children with low scores had other characteristics of intrinsic asthma. Independent assessments were made of the child's and parents' personalities. Descriptions of the children were obtained from their parents.

Children who scored low on the APS, as compared to those who scored high, were more pessimistic that their needs would be met, were less able to tolerate frustration, were more conforming (at times), and evidenced a greater preoccupation with themes of "orality" and aggression. They were described by their mothers as intelligent, rebellious, clinging, jealous, nervous, and whiny; and their fathers used additional terms, such as awkward, fussy, greedy, shy, and quarrelsome. Obviously, these terms have unpleasant implications, and tell much about the relationship between the parents and the child. The children who scored high on the APS were more adaptable and had more-positive relationships, but they also had more anxiety about their illness. The mothers of the children in this group described their children as self-confident, reasonable, and as playing their sex roles appropriately. They were described by their fathers as adventurous, eager to please, "showy," and impulsive.

The mothers of the children in the low-scoring group were more conservative than the mothers of the high scorers, but they were fearful and unsure of themselves and tended to arouse the "protective instincts" of others, had unconventional thought processes, were apt to procrastinate, and harbored feelings of guilt and self-pity. In addition, they felt "cheated" and victimized; they tended to ruminate, engage in self-defeating behavior, and to give up in the face of adversity. In their relationships with their children, these mothers were condescending, easily disappointed in the children's performance, and alternately ignored the children's difficult behavior or became angry, depriving, rejecting, and excessively authoritarian. In contrast, the mothers of the high-scoring group were more casual and helpful, and less intrusive in their relationship to their children;

256

moreover, they were able to grant their children a greater degree of autonomy. Finally, the marital relationships of the parents of the low-scoring group were fraught with friction. Typically, the wife was domineering, demanding, and angry; she belittled herself or her husband, and also tended to exclude her husband from participating in the child's care. The husband's hostility and frustration found expression in his efforts to embarrass and belittle others. In view of the fact mentioned above, that the symptomatology of the illness was essentially the same in both groups, these descriptions cannot be ascribed solely to the effects of the illness on the child or his family.

It is not clear, however, just how the two subgroups defined by Block's allergic potential scale relate to the subgroups of asthmatic children defined by Purcell et al. (1961, 1962, 1969b)—that is, the rapidly remitting and steroid-dependent groups. It is difficult to reconcile the results obtained in studies of subgroups because of differences in research design: the children in the series studied by Purcell had intractable asthma and required hospitalization, whereas the children in Block's study were ambulatory patients. Each of these authors had used different instruments for the psychological assessment of their research populations.

In an effort to resolve some of these discrepancies, Purcell et al. (1969b) studied 347 hospitalized asthmatic children by means of the APS, the same scale used by Block and Freeman. The results of the study indicated that the severity of the asthma and the response to hospitalization are independent of the predisposition to allergy, and, therefore, seem to relate more to psychological factors and perhaps to the development of structural changes in the bronchial mucosa.

The children who scored low on the APS were significantly more tense than the high scorers. And the mothers of the low scorers exerted harsher control over the child (especially over his sexual behavior) than the mothers of the high scorers; specifically, they were stricter with their children, and made excessive demands on them. But in contrast to the earlier studies by Purcell et al., these categories of attitudes did not discriminate between the steroid-dependent and rapidly remitting children. On the other hand, discriminations could be made on the basis of Cattell scales between subgroups of rapidly remitting children with high and low allergic potential. As compared to the rapidly remitting children with high allergic potential, those with low allergic potential were more timid, depressed, prone to guilt feelings, anxious, and introverted; and their mothers were more restrictive, authoritarian, and apt to suppress sexual behavior in their children. In addition, these mothers were more remote, demanding, martyr-like, and overpossessive. Thus, one might conclude from these findings that removal from their home would prove especially beneficial to the rapidly remitting children with low allergic potential.

Purcell's study, therefore, partially confirms Block's and Freeman's conclusions that patients with a high allergic potential seem healthier psychologically and have more-benign mothers.

On the basis of a number of other studies, the conclusion has been reached that rather than a reciprocal relationship between an allergic potential and psychological factors, there is an additive one in ways and by mechanisms that are not yet understood. This conclusion was reached by Treuting and Ripley (1948), who studied 51 patients, 28 of whom had positive skin tests to one or several allergens. When the patient was exposed to these allergens without his knowledge, no attack occurred. An attack could be induced, however, when such exposure coincided with the discussion of significant life events. Similarly, in patients with allergic rhinitis, exposure to an allergen brought on symptoms only when the patient was depressed, worried, and overwhelmed by feelings of hopelessness; symptoms did not appear when the patient felt cheerful and optimistic. Thus, these findings provide further confirmation of the hypothesis that allergic and emotional states are additive in asthma. The interaction of the psychological states and the response to parasympathomimetic bronchoconstrictor agents has also been demonstrated by Funkenstein (1950a, b, 1953). He found that an inverse relationship existed in six patients between psychosis (both paranoid and depressive), severe neurosis, and clinical asthmatic attacks. When the patients were psychotic, methacholine chloride induced mild asthmatic attacks. Naturally occurring stresses (such as exams) produced in other subjects patterns of increased sympathetic activity (inferred from measures of cardiovascular responses and altered response to methacholine chloride). However, when these subjects were apprehensive, no asthmatic attacks, or only mild ones, were induced by methacholine chloride. The subjects' physiological responses to methacholine chloride also depended on whether an epinephrine- or norepinephrine-like response to stress preceded the injection of the drug.

The conclusion that emotional states, allergens, or the effects of drugs such as methacholine chloride and histamine are additive was also reached by Dekker et al. (1961) and Jacobs et al. (1967). Combinations of psychological factors (particularly dependency in the child and rejection or control by the mother) plus sensitivity to allergens and histamine were used to study 41 college students with a history of allergic rhinitis or mild asthma and 24 healthy subjects. On the basis of either the psychological characteristics or the allergic diathesis, correct assignments of the 65 men could blindly be made to the allergic or healthy group. If the two factors did not occur together, such a correct, blind classification could not have been made. As it was, the two factors were combined in 75 percent of the allergic group.

The manner in which they are combined in extrinsic asthma remains unknown. We do not know whether in all "extrinsic" patients every single attack is the result of a combination of the two factors or if some attacks are entirely psychologically induced and others are wholly initiated by an allergen.

The skin tests or an increased histamine sensitivity in these studies are of dubious validity as criteria of bronchial asthma. Future studies might use the presence or absence of IgE antibodies in blood serum specific for the allergen that induces asthmatic attacks, as a criterion for the comparing asthmatic patients. In this way, subjects with and without IgE antibodies in serum could be selected and studied psychologically and socially.

The Role of Odors in Asthma

Behavioral scientists studying asthmatic children understandably focus their observations on changes occurring in the human relationship between child and parent, or adult and his family members or other people important in his life. But nonhuman factors, specifically odors, also appear to play a role in triggering asthmatic attacks.

Approximately 50 percent of all asthmatics are unusually sensitive to smells (Knapp

258

and Nemetz, 1957b). In fact, it has been known for many years that asthmatic attacks may be triggered, if not initiated, by odors (Brown and Colombo, 1954; Dunbar, 1938; Feinberg and Aries, 1932; Hansen, 1930). As a general rule, such attacks occur either because the source of these odors is allergenic, or because their particular nature is irritating to the nose and bronchial tree. Unpleasant odors may induce coughing, sneezing, and dyspnea, which precipitate wheezing. However, the possibility that odors may have psychological significance must also be considered (Dunbar, 1938; Löfgren, 1961; Ottenberg and Stein, 1958a, b). In the study by Kepecs et al. (1958) of the responses of psychosomatic patients to olfactory and other sensory stimulation, odors aroused a much more intense reaction in asthmatic patients than did stimulation of other sensory receptor sites (such as the skin or muscle). Only in the asthmatic patients studied was a smell the preferred and most emotionally arousing stimulus. Patients with neurodermatitis were most aroused by skin stimulation, and muscle stimulation was most arousing for patients with arthritis. Furthermore, evidence indicates that stimulation of the nasal mucosa or the olfactory bulb may lead to bronchconstriction (Rall et al., 1945). Thus, once again, if these two mediating mechanisms are confirmed, the data would suggest that the nervous system is involved in the mediation of asthma attacks.

Twenty-two of the 25 patients studied in the laboratory by Ottenberg and Stein (1958a) admitted that odors precipitated their attacks in everyday life. Accordingly, these patients were exposed to 19 different odors, and their associations to each were collected after inhalation. The associations, which were categorized as relating to food, cleanliness, and uncleanliness were then rated independently by three judges. Seventy-four percent of the substances were assigned to the cleanliness or uncleanliness categories. The patients with bronchial asthma did not differ significantly from a comparison group without bronchial asthma with respect to the number of substances assigned to each of the three categories. However, the asthmatic group did differ significantly from the control group in that they "blocked" associations to the odors more often: they either claimed that they had not perceived the smell or that they had no associations to it. The authors concluded from their findings that odors, and especially those odors that signify uncleanliness and unpleasantness, may activate psychological conflict, which, combined with stimulating the olfactory system, precipitates asthmatic attacks.

This interesting study has certain obvious implications. It indicates that the role of odors may not have received sufficient attention in asthma research, and it is an interesting example of the usefulness of clinical observation as a tool in such research. Apart from such considerations, the findings reported by Ottenberg and Stein, and their conclusions, require further comment. The fact that the role of odors in bronchial asthma consists not only in their physiological effects (via a nasobronchoconstrictor reflex), but also in their psychological significance, does not necessarily mean that the psychological response the odor elicits is an antecedent of the asthmatic attack; it may be a concomitant of the attack. What needs to be emphasized is that the stimulation of the nose and nasal sinuses by dust and other inert substances may elicit bronchoconstriction by a vagal reflex (Nadel and Widdicombe, 1963) even in normal persons, because atropine can block the stimulus.

Some further attempts to determine whether odors were psychological precipitants or concomitants of asthmatic attacks was made by Herbert et al. (1967). They found that odors precipitated attacks in the great majority of cases they investigated. Eighty percent of their patients were psychologically affected by them. The sources of the odors responsible for inducing attacks were specified as fresh paint, tobacco and wood smoke, paraffin, household odors, cosmetics, gasoline, tar, and oil. Moreover, Herbert and his co-workers noted that individual patients might be acutely sensitive to one odor and not to another that might be equally acrid. It seemed likely to them that the role of odors in the initiation of asthmatic attacks is determined by a reflex mechanism *alone*. They could not confirm that the specific meaning of the odor was an additional factor in the onset of attacks; rather they found that in those patients in whom allergenic and infectious factors played a predominant initiating role, odors were especially likely to incite attacks. Although the evidence that odors may play a crucial role in the precipitation of asthmatic attacks appears to be irresistible, the importance of this variable has not been fully acknowledged and the literature emphasizes psychological ones.

Based on their studies of adult (rather than child) asthmatic patients, French (1939), and later Knapp (1960) and Knapp and Nemetz (1960) summarized the nature of the major events surrounding the onset of asthmatic attacks as follows: (1) a disturbing change in the (dependent) relationship of two people, generating fears of separation or loss, which may arise if the life of a close relative is endangered (e.g., by illness), or if such separation or loss will deprive the patient of his source of medication. Going away to school or the army, or losing one's home (Alexander and Visotsky, 1955) may engender similar fears of separation from the object on whom the patient is excessively dependent. Conversely, the change in the dependent relationship may generate fears of closeness which, as noted above, may also be a source of conflict, in which event their reactivation may precipitate an asthmatic attack; (2) crying, which may either precipitate or relieve an attack; (3) intense emotional arousal, of guilt, anger, anxiety, humiliation (Rees, 1964), fear in response to danger, or of pleasurable feelings, such as sexual feelings (which conflict with the patient's desire for approval); (4) identification with the asthmatic or dyspneic attacks of someone in the family (French, 1939; Kleeman, 1967; Knapp and Nemetz, 1957a; Wittkower, 1935); (5) utilization of the attack for secondary psychological gain, e.g., avoidance of an unpleasant situation; (6) the premenstrual period, at which time there is likely to be a resurgence of unresolved, residual psychological conflicts; (7) odors.

Thus, we can see from this summary that the events that are currently considered to play a preeminent role in the onset of asthmatic attacks represent an admixture of actual or threatened situations, their meanings for the patient, and the emotional responses these meanings occasion. For heuristic reasons, it may be important to separate these three (interrelated) categories of events. Yet such an attempt requires the further refinement of the initiating events themselves. French's delineation of these subcategories in 1939 has not been improved upon in later studies (Rees, 1956a, b; Treuting and Ripley, 1948). Some progress toward this end has been made, however, by Grace and Graham (1952), and Graham et al. (1962), who suggested that the meaning the actual or threatened situation held for the patient was reflected in his attitude. Characteristically, the attitude of the patient with asthma conveys his sense of being left out in the cold and of wanting to shut out the person or situation responsible for his predicament. Implicit in this attitude, as Graham (1972) pointed out, is the patient's emotional response to separation and his defense against that response. It goes without saying, of course, that marked individual differences may occur both in terms of how the feeling is expressed and how it is defended against.

In general, specification of the interrelationship between these three categories of events poses major problems. One of the problems that confronts the investigator who addresses himself to the study of the psychological antecedents and concomitants of bronchial asthmatic attacks stems from the fact that each attack is likely to be associated with fears (or even terror) of choking, drowning, asphyxiation, and even dying. Admittedly, these reactions would not be likely to occur before the first attack, unless the future patient had been exposed to someone with asthmatic attacks. But in subsequent attacks he may be preoccupied with such fears and with unique breathing sensations as well as perceptual distortions.

With specific reference to the events that are purported to play a preeminent role in the onset of asthmatic attacks, one important (and well-studied) variable has been omitted from the summary provided above; the attitudes of key figures toward the child or adult may play an important role in the initiation of the first attack, and their subsequent responses to that attack may influence the frequency with which attacks recur (Rees, 1963; Tuft, 1957).

The Origins of the Dependency Conflicts in Asthmatic Patients

A comprehensive explanation of the psychology of bronchial asthma would have to account for the ontogeny of the persistant dependency and other conflicts that predispose to the ambivalent relationship between mother and asthmatic child and adult: the child can neither bear to be with her nor away from her. In an attempt to account for the persistence of these conflicts, clinical investigators began to study the attitudes of mothers to the child only to discover that after the start of the disease, these maternal attitudes were not as they should be. Some students of asthma have also suggested that inadequate mothering might cause undue crying in the newborn infant. Crying is accompanied by bronchoconstriction in the infant (Karlberg, 1957). In this account, the tendency to bronchoconstriction is thought to be the result of early experience rather than genetic variation (Stein, 1962).

The suggestion that the tendency to bronchoconstriction in asthmatic patients is brought about by early childhood experience is not backed by empirical fact. Should this suggestion be borne out in the future, we would still have to account for the fact that 25 percent of the etiological variance is genetic, because then all the known etiological factors (the bronchoconstrictor tendency; the allergic, infectious, and psychological factors) would be environmental. Environmental hypotheses are particularly popular in the psychological area of investigation; they have even led to the suggestion that bronchial asthma is a learned response that comes about from the exposure of children to their asthmatic progenitors and relatives. Indeed, asthma does occur in families, but this fact can variously be interpreted. To some it is proof of a genetic factor at work; to others it is an example of social learning; and to still others it represents an example of unconscious identification. The exposure of children to their asthmatic relatives might account for asthmatic attacks. It would not account for the dependency conflicts except that exposure to asthma in the adult, and the subsequent asthmatic attack could cause arrest in psychological development. Alternatively, some believe that bodily illness in childhood, such as eczema, rhinitis, and pulmonary infection, may also produce fixations in personality development.

These various ideas, therefore, fall into three categories. The first attempts to account for the etiology of the psychological conflicts in asthmatic patients and for how early experience might be conducive to bronchoconstriction. The second attempts to account for the disease itself. The third suggests that childhood illness may arrest personality development in the oral-dependent stage of personality development.

Dependent relationships were consistently observed as a prominent characteristic of asthmatic patients in the earlier literature, and, recently, attempts have been made to assess and define more precisely the family relationships of asthmatic children and the parental attitudes to which they were exposed, with the purpose of accounting for the child's dependency.

THE MOTHER-CHILD RELATIONSHIP

French and Alexander (1941) stated, on the basis of their clinical observations, that a history of maternal rejection was a recurrent theme in the lives of asthmatic patients. A combination of covert maternal seduction and overt rejection was a common finding. In some instances, the mother had manifested her rejection by attempting to foster a premature independence in the child. Both behaviors elicited the same response in the child—increased feelings of insecurity and an increased desire to cling to the mother.

In the years since, however, it has become increasingly apparent that French's and Alexander's formulation was an oversimplification. A wide spectrum of maternal (and paternal) attitudes towards asthmatic children have been described, ranging from realistic concern, acceptance, affectionate feelings, and a wish to help the child—especially during his frightening attacks—to being oversolicitous (Shands, 1963), overconcerned (Knapp, 1969; Peshkin, 1959), overprotective (Rees, 1963), overly fussy (Pinkerton, 1967), and tending to "smother" the child (Abramson, 1963), and thereby perhaps increasing the child's fearfulness during an attack.

In defense of French and Alexander, it should be noted that Miller and Baruch (1948a, 1951) had pointed out that the mother of an asthmatic patient might assume an overprotective attitude (Creak and Stephen, 1958) in an effort to compensate for her unconscious rejection of or, hostility toward, the child (Shands, 1963). Or overprotective attitudes, at one end of the continuum, might alternate with overt rejection, at the other extreme (Mitchell et al., 1953). French and Alexander had been further vindicated by the findings by Miller and Baruch (1948a) that rejecting attitudes occurred in 98 percent of mothers of the 55 asthmatic children in their series, and these attitudes anteceded the illness. We might ask, however, how frequently these attitudes, which have also been emphasized by Gerard (1946), Mohr et al. (1963a), and Rogerson et al. (1935), obtain in other series. These findings were not, in fact, substantiated in later studies. Rather, three main categories of maternal attitudes have emerged (Rees, 1963, 1964):

1. Overt overprotective maternal attitudes have been observed by various authors (Bostock, 1956; Miller and Baruch, 1948a; Mitchell et al., 1953; Rees, 1963, 1964;

Rogerson, 1937). Such attitudes tend to leave the child immature and dependent (Pinkerton, 1967), and may limit his development and thwart him from carrying out various activities (Rogerson, 1937).

2. A second category of mothers was described as perfectionistic. At times, their attitude seemed to incorporate elements of understanding and acceptance of their child; but at other times they were overly ambitious for the child (Morris, 1959), or expected too much of him (Little and Cohen, 1951; Mohr et al., 1963a; Rees, 1963). When the child could not fulfill these expectations, he was either disparaged or pressured to attain them. In many instances, the mother's high and unrealistic expectations of the child are transmitted nonverbally. Thus, the mother may be loving, but only on condition that the child meet her "demands"; if he is unable to do so, she may not only withdraw her love, but tyrannize him by her recriminations and by increased pressure on him to attain the goals she has defined (Bastiaans and Groen, 1954; Groen et al., 1965; Pinkerton, 1967). Pinkerton (1967) has pointed out that this kind of maternal attitude contains unpredictable features that are disquieting to, and create tension in, the child. In the face of the unpredictable and challenging behavior of the mother, the child becomes overcontrolled, conforming, and emotionally inarticulate. The child may respond to the mother's escalating expectations by striving for independence and achievement in order to please her (Long et al., 1958). This striving necessarily conflicts with his dependency wishes (Little and Cohen, 1951; Morris, 1959; Wittkower and White, 1959). In any event, children who are exposed to such perfectionistic attitudes have strong needs for recognition and may develop ambivalent feelings toward their mothers (Greenfield, 1958).

3. The third category of mothers was overtly rejecting, hostile, cruel, domineering, punitive, intolerant, and critical of the child, as depicted by Miller and Baruch (1948a) and Rogerson (1937). This form of maternal attitude has probably been studied most intensively (Pinkerton, 1967). It is the cause of the anxiety, invalidism, and stoicism, or the hostile, defiant, rebellious, jealous, frustrated, or withdrawing behavior of the child vis-à-vis the mother, which, according to Miller and Baruch (1948a), occurred significantly more frequently in asthmatic children than in a comparison population of children with psychiatric illnesses. What needs to be emphasized, however, is that the asthmatic child is not necessarily rejected more than his healthy sibling; he may simply be more sensitive to rejection (Fine, 1963) for reasons that are not yet understood.

Rees (1963) has clearly demonstrated the validity of this three-part schema for the categorization of maternal attitudes. The attitudes of the mothers of 170 asthmatic children and a control group of 160 children who were under treatment in the accident unit of a general hospital were rated "blindly" as satisfactory or unsatisfactory (i.e., as overtly rejecting, overprotective, or overpermissive). Maternal attitudes were rated satisfactory in 44 percent of the experimental group and 82 percent of the comparison group. With regard to those mothers in the experimental group whose attitudes were considered unsatisfactory, 44.5 percent were described as overprotective, 7 percent as perfectionistic, and 4.5 percent as overtly rejecting. On the whole, these figures are in accord with the figures obtained in less-well-controlled studies (Bastiaans and Groen, 1954; Jacoby and Bostock, 1960; Rogerson et al., 1935).

Rees (1963) went on to show that even in those cases where maternal attitudes were satisfactory, the asthmatic children tended to be meeker, more sensitive, anxious, and meticulous, and, in general, more unstable emotionally than the children in the comparison group. But when maternal attitudes were unsatisfactory, even greater differences occurred in these psychological variables. In this study, rejecting maternal attitudes antedated the child's illness in only one-half of the instances in which they occurred. On the other hand, all of the perfectionistic maternal attitudes detected antedated the illness. Finally, Rees found that one-quarter of the mothers who were rated as overprotective had become so after the onset of the child's illness, and that in most of these cases, this overprotective attitude was directed only to the patient (and not to his healthy siblings). Thus, this attitude probably reflected the concern and solicitude any parent might have for a sick child. However, in these mothers, this concern and solicitude were exaggerated. Consequently, this attitude, however well-meant, caused increased anxiety and tension in the asthmatic child. The overprotective or rejecting maternal attitudes seem to be the response of some mothers but not of others to the child's illness and symptoms, and they may sustain the illness. They, therefore, do not in all instances seem to contribute to the dependency conflict and, therefore, to the etiology or the pathogenesis of asthma.

Correlations between maternal attitudes and the pulmonary function of asthmatic children have also been made. The pulmonary function was assessed by a bronchial provocation test. A common form of bronchial provocation test uses the FEV in one second as the criterion of bronchial reactivity. In the normal person, FEV is usually increased by exercise and by isoproterenol. Jones et al. (1962), Jones (1966), and Pinkerton (1967) have shown that childhood patients can be defined in terms of the resting FEV, the percentage reduction of FEV with exercise, and its restoration by isoproterenol. They have used these criteria to differentiate hospitalized asthmatic children into four groups, one of which can, be further subdivided.

1. *Group I* is comprised of asthmatic children who have normal resting FEV levels. On exercise, there is a drop of FEV in the 15 to 30 percent range, and it is restored to normal by inhaled isoproterenol.

2. *Group II.A.* children have normal resting FEV; a fall in FEV of from 30 to 85 percent on exercise; and a return to normal FEV values with isoproterenol. The asthmatic children in this group constitute about one-half of all children who are hospitalized with this illness (Pinkerton and Weaver, 1970).

Group II.B. children resemble those in Group II.A. in that they show a similar fall in FEV on exercise. The difference between these subgroups is that the children in Group II.B. the resting FEV is below normal, and inhalation of the drug after exercise restores the FEV to this subnormal level.

3. *Group III* children have reduced resting FEV levels. Exercise reduces it even further, but only by 20 to 40 percent, since the baseline level is so low. This reduced lability can be reversed by corticosteroids, but not by isoproterenol. Clinically, these children are rarely free of symptoms. The asthmatic children in these four groups differed psychologically, as well as in their physiological responses to exercise. Pinkerton (1967) and Pinkerton and Weaver (1970) also studied the parents of the children in each group; an independent assessment of the parental attitudes toward their children was made. The parents of Group I children were predominantly overprotective. They were either concerned or overconcerned, and "fussed" over their child, who was "dependent," imma-

ture, sensitive. Despite their excessive concern, these parents were able to respond to the child's illness appropriately.

A second group of parents accepted their children and their illness, but they had high aspirations for their children, pressured them to fulfill their aspirations, and disparaged them when they failed. Not surprisingly, the parent-child relationship tended to be "tense." As a consequence of these parental attitudes, the child was often overcontrolled and conforming in his behavior. By the physiological criteria used in these studies, the children fell into Group II.

The parents of the third group of patients were dissatisfied with and critical and intolerant of their children. Moreover, they were overtly rejecting—an attitude that antedated the onset of the asthma. The asthmatic child responded to these attitudes with invalidism, stoicism, or rebellious protest. These children, who were assigned to Group III, evidenced the most marked bronchoconstriction, even at rest, which tended not to respond to bronchodilator drugs. The children in Group III depended on steroid drugs for relief of symptoms. The authors concluded from these findings that a threatening or hostile family atmosphere correlates with persistent bronchoconstriction.

The psychophysiologic studies that form the basis of Pinkerton's classification were done on hospitalized children. A greater number of children, who do not require hospitalization, may be less-severely impaired physiologically when exercised. When the FEV was measured in ambulatory, asthmatic children 45 percent showed a mild impairment of function, as evidenced by reduced FEV resting levels; 40 percent showed moderate impairment; and 15 percent presented evidence of severe impairment (Dawson et al., 1969).

Pinkerton's studies are fraught nonetheless with a number of methodological weaknesses. Ideally, findings obtained from pulmonary function studies should be correlated at the time of the test with descriptions of the subject's allergic and psychological state, although this variable is difficult to control. The tests require the volitional effort and full attention of the subject; he must keep his mind on the task before him, and any attempt to investigate conscious mental content concurrently should reveal that he is attending fully to the task. A second variable, equally difficult to control, is the subject's exposure to an allergen on any particular day. If exposed on that day, he might show marked impairment of pulmonary function. Yet on other days pulmonary function might show minimal impairment.

Implicit in these studies was the fact that the various degrees of functional pulmonary impairment were not only an abiding (and rather arbitrary) characteristic of patients, but were also a measure of the severity of the disease. But such a conclusion cannot be reached, as the impairment of function at any one point in time does not necessarily correlate with the duration or frequency of asthmatic attacks—bad pulmonary function at any one point in time does not equal bad asthma.

THE ROLE OF THE FATHER

With the exception of Fine's study (1963), less attention has been paid to fathers than to mothers of asthmatic children. Fine found that asthmatic children of both sexes perceived their fathers as "disagreeable"; in other studies (Jacobs et al., 1967; Mohr et al., 1963a; Wittkower and White, 1959), they were described as passive, dependent, and unsupportive. In short, although more readily apparent in the mother, the same attitudes of rejection, overprotection, or overpermissiveness occurred in the fathers of asthmatic children.

Clearly, the history of these parental attitudes needs to be studied in relation to the stage and phase of the child's personality development, and the onset of asthma. The psychological consequences of punitiveness and rejection when the child is 3 years old may be quite different from what they would be when he is aged 5 or 6 (Abramson, 1963 and Selesnick, 1963).

Another set of observations suggest that the various parental attitudes to the child reflect ongoing relationships within the family.

FAMILY RELATIONSHIPS

Studies of families indicate that the attitudes of some parents toward their asthmatic children are themselves the product of marital unhappiness (Block et al., 1964; Rees, 1964). The mothers have been described as cold and unloving, and many of the women studied by Fine (1963) were sexually frustrated. The fathers resented their wives' lack of affection. The couple tended to handle their negative feelings toward each other, especially their anger and disappointment, by fighting openly (Mohr et al., 1963a).

It has also been suggested that these disturbed family relationships may be the product of psychopathology in individual family members (McDermott and Cobb, 1939; Rees, 1964). Leigh and Marley (1967) found a significantly increased prevalence of psychiatric illness (other than psychosis) in the first-degree relatives (especially the female relatives) of asthmatic children, as compared with their second-degree relatives or with the relatives of patients with other medical illnesses. Anxieties and fears were the symptoms most frequently observed in the relatives of asthmatic patients. Many of the mothers studied had doubts about their capacity for motherhood and strong fears of separation from their children.

On the other hand, specific parental attitudes may be related not only to specific features of a family, but to specific personality traits of the father or mother (Rees, 1963). For example, the mother's overprotective attitude may be a reaction to her unhappy marriage; but it may also be due to her being a fearful person (Mitchell et al., 1953), or to her overconcern about her child, either because he is an only child, or is the product of a difficult pregnancy or labor, or had feeding problems. The child's illness might then reinforce the mother's tendency to be overprotective. Similarly, rejecting attitudes may stem from the child's not being wanted, or from marital difficulties, sexual frustration (Margolis, 1961), or the mother's dissatisfaction with her role as a woman (Rees, 1963, 1964). The child's asthma would mean an added burden or disappointment to an already disappointed woman. The mother's attitude may also stem from a wish to keep her child childishly dependent and close (Coolidge, 1956; Dubo et al., 1961; Jessner et al., 1955; Mohr et al., 1963a; Sperling, 1963).

It is unfortunate that we are rarely told which parents were themselves suffering from bronchial asthma. In view of the increased prevalence of the illness in the relatives of asthmatics, it seems likely that many of the families studied included mothers and fathers

266

with bronchial asthma. It would be of considerable interest to know which of the predominant attitudes occur in parents with the illness and which occur in parents without the illness, and how these data correlate with the behavior and psychological characteristics of the children, if at all. Another possible link between parental asthma or chronic pulmonary disease was first suggested by Wittkower (1935): the child exposed to such attacks could become frightened that he, too, might have an attack, or could fear the loss of his parent. Knapp and Nemetz (1957b) found that 7 of the 40 patients in their series had one or more relatives with asthma, and 15 others were in frequent contact with a relative who suffered from chronic bronchitis, "catarrh," or some symptom or other disease referrable to the lung.

Similarly, Kleeman (1967) found that 35 percent of the 26 hospitalized patients she studied (who were selected at random) had been exposed to asthma attacks in their near relatives. At the time their illness had its onset these patients were emotionally involved in meaningful changes in their lives (such as marriage or bereavement). This unverified finding suggests that patients with a family history of asthma are in some way more sensitive to meaningful life events. The interpretation of this finding is enigmatic. As mentioned in the introduction to this section, it is difficult to understand how bronchoconstriction is learned by a child when exposed to an adult having an asthmatic attack. It is much easier to understand that a wheezing, choking, gasping, and dyspneic parent is a frightening spectacle to a child, who may imagine his parent's imminent death or disability.

The child's exposure to asthmatic attacks in parents has not been ruled out as a sensitizing factor either to dependency conflicts, fears of bereavement, or the disease. It is one form of early life experience that may be significant; another may be crying behavior in the early months of life, at a time when the cry is an important signal to adults who responded to it inadequately. Either the cry evoked undue attention at this preverbal stage of development, or excessive attempts were made to suppress it (Bostock, 1956; Gerard, 1946; Lipton et al., 1966; Stein, 1962), or the responses to it were inconsistent. On the other hand, the mother may also have failed to respond adequately to upper respiratory infection in the infant. Or it may be that, given a labile bronchiolar tree, crying behavior may be associated with repeated bronchoconstriction, which may be the *anlage* for later asthmatic attacks. Much more needs to be known not only about individual differences in maternal behavior during crying and how these affect later personality development, but also about the physiology of crying in infants.

For the most part, however, investigative interest has centered on the role of the family, and particularly of the mother, in the ontogenesis of the various dependency conflicts. In fact, more energy has been expended on investigations of the family relationships of asthmatic children than on family relationships of children with the other diseases reviewed in this book (Treuting and Ripley, 1948).

The attitudes of some mothers are in response to the child's asthmatic bouts and follow the onset of the disease. Therefore, the maternal attitudes could reinforce the child's dependency conflicts but do not cause them. One must look for other reasons for the arrested psychological development of these children, including antecedent disease —respiratory infection, infantile atopic eczema, and hay fever (Greenacre, 1953; Langner et al., 1974). Deutsch (1953) suggested, on the basis of his extensive clinical experience, that respiratory infection, when it occurs at a critical, early period in personality development, might produce arrests of personality development. He did not mention that the parents' attitudes toward the ill child might be another important variable. Dependency motives and relationships, and the conflicts they engender, may arise as a response to the fear and anxiety occasioned by illness in childhood (Harris, 1955; Harris and Schure, 1956).

The studies on parental attitudes and on the families of patients with bronchial asthma leave many questions unanswered. They are based on the concept that either the arrests of personality development or the disease stem from the behavior and attitudes of parents. Without adequate comparison groups we cannot conclude that these attitudes are unique to the parents of asthmatic children. They have been described in the parents of children with psychiatric or psychosomatic illness or no illness at all. Some added etiological factor(s) must operate, such as the predisposition to IgE antibody formation or bronchoconstriction. The exact nature and origin of these biological predispositions are not yet understood. Given these predispositions, parental attitudes and family relationships may contribute either to the etiology, initiation, or maintenance of bronchial asthma, or to all three together. But it is doubtful that the entire etiological variance of the psychological make-up of asthmatic children and adults can be ascribed to them. That does not mean that parents and families contribute nothing to some aspect of the disease. Some have argued that the failure to identify some unique psychological features in the asthmatic child or his parents which could account for bronchial asthma vitiated the validity of the role of psychological factors in the disease. They have argued that the apparent absence of such characteristics cast doubt on the role of psychosocial and family factors as a contributing factor in the illness. In fact, however, these investigators did not always take the precautions necessary to ensure that the comparing and contrasting instrument used was sensitive enough to detect such characteristics. Other workers reached the same conclusion—that psychosocial and family factors play a minimal role (if any) in bronchial asthma—on the basis of their finding that, in terms of the psychological characteristics, asthmatic children did not differ from other chronically ill children, and that parents of asthmatic children did not differ psychologically from the parents of children with other diverse chronic ailments. The fallacy in this reasoning is self-evident: such findings do not preclude the inference that the same psychological factors play a role in both (or several) patient populations. Fitzelle (1959), who studied the parents of asthmatic children and the parents of children with other chronic diseases by the use of the MMPI, personal interview, and a parent attitude survey obtained such results—that in terms of personality factors and attitudes toward childrearing, the parents of the asthmatic children did not differ significantly from the parents in the other group. But Fitzelle also found that the MPPI scores were consistently higher in both these groups of parents than the mean scores in the general population. Therefore, while this study may contravene the proposition that the attitudes and behaviors of parents of asthmatic children are unique to this population, it does not invalidate the idea that these attitudes play a role in predisposing children to this disease. Nor does it negate the correlation between parental attitudes and the intitiation and recurrence of asthmatic episodes in children who have been exposed to such attitudes. The value of studies of families and parental attitudes is that they help us to understand how personal traits and habits evolve

268

to produce the personality characteristics of some asthmatic patients. Granted that genetic and temperamental factors play a role, as yet unknown, in determining individual traits, habits, and personal relationships, personality is also the result of life experience. Thus, the mother who has high expectations of her child and makes premature demands on him to "grow up" may produce strivings for independence in the child, or provoke assertions of masculine behavior, but her efforts may not diminish his unconscious longings for a dependent relationship. Furthermore, since these unconscious longings conflict with his more conscious strivings, they are likely to produce shame and guilt feelings and to sensitize him to frustration and reactive aggressive impulses. The overprotective mother, on the other hand, exacerbates the child's persistent longings for protection and prepares the child poorly for her absence and for adult life. For boys, in particular, disturbances in the mother-child interaction often produce feminine identification, which may conflict with masculine strivings to produce shame and guilt.

Obviously, the conflicts and problems outlined are not characteristic of all patients with bronchial asthma. Some workers subscribe to the more specific view that crying in infancy may elicit certain kinds of maternal behavior and create strong bonds between mother and child (Stein, 1962), which, in the metaphor of certain psychiatric formulations, are described as "symbiotic" (Coolidge, 1956; Knapp, 1969).

Psychological and Other Factors that Influence or Alter the Course of Bronchial Asthma

Some children and adolescents outgrow their asthmatic attacks. Some do not. Those who remit in adolescence may have a recurrence of attacks in middle-age. The variable course of the disease has so far defied full explanation. The factors that sustain the occurrence of recurrent attacks include changes in the structure and function of the lung[*] (Cardell and Pearson, 1959; Gold, 1976; Naylor, 1962; Takizawa and Thurlbeck, 1971). Social and psychological factors also influence the course of the disease. And having asthma may alter the person's adaptation to school and work, and his relationships with other people. Bronchial asthmatic attacks cause school absences. The child may not be allowed to participate in athletic activities. He may have to be hospitalized. He may fall behind in his studies. His peer relationships may be impaired by his attacks, which frighten away his schoolmates. He may or may not follow a treatment program. Later he may eschew marriage because of his chronic illness. Some asthmatic children fall behind in their physical maturation. The drugs used in the treatment of asthma may have adverse side effects that affect the child in diverse ways. Some asthmatic patients have frank neurotic or psychotic illnesses.

Any or all of these complications may depend on the response of parents, siblings, teachers, and peers and lead to various forms of psychological maladaptation. Two studies

---

[*] Changes in the structure of the lung are not evenly distributed throughout its airways. Pathological changes also occur with time. At first only bronchospasm occurs. Later the bronchial wall is edematous and infiltrated with inflammatory cells especially eosinophils. Excessive mucous is secreted. After more time, the amount of bronchial smooth muscle increases, the basement membrane thickens, and many small airways contain mucous plugs. These changes may even be found in asymptomatic patients.

bear on this matter. Dubo et al. (1961) observed 71 nonhospitalized children and their families by interview techniques. No relationship could be found between the degree of disturbance in the family and the clinical course of the child's asthma, its symptomatology, or the child's response to medical treatment. However, the degree of disturbance in the family was meaningfully related to indices of social maladjustment in the child. A second study, by Pinkerton and Weaver (1970), of 206 children yielded the same conclusions. These findings underscore the importance of differentiating between the effects of parental attitudes on the child's behavior and adjustment and the effects of such attitudes on his disease and its symptoms.

The complex interactions between bronchial asthma, the child, his caretakers, behavior pathology, and symptoms are further attested to in children with rapidly remitting asthma. When sent away from home to a hospital, they become free of asthmatic symptoms and no longer need medication. A second group of hospitalized children continue to require steroids to treat their asthmatic symptomatology.

Purcell and Merz (1962) and Purcell and his colleagues (1961, 1962) were interested in differentiating the children in these groups in terms of the age at which their illness had had its onset and the number of neurotic and asthmatic symptoms they manifested. The children who remitted rapidly without medication had more "neurotic" symptoms, such as headaches, constipation, and nightmares, than did the steroid-dependent children. They had developed asthma at a later age. When the authors compared the mothers of the children in the two groups by the Parental Attitude Research Instrument, they found that the attitudes of the mothers of the rapidly remitting group were more authoritarian and controlling, or hostile and rejecting, than the mothers of the steroid-dependent children. The fathers of the rapidly remitting children scored higher on variables that clearly designated them as psychologically "unhealthy"—that is, they were the agents of marital conflict, and were neither understanding nor tolerant of their children.

This study was an important attempt to discriminate between asthmatic *children*, rather than specific aspects of their illness. It is difficult, however, to reconcile the findings obtained in these studies by Purcell and his co-workers with those obtained by Dubo et al. (1961) and by Pinkerton (1967).

This inconsistency can be attributed to two factors. First, the children studied in Denver by Purcell and his co-workers had been hospitalized for many months. Second, different criteria were used—Pinkerton used pulmonary function test, Purcell et al. used the responses to environmental change and to drugs and the findings derived from various psychological tests. Therefore, these studies are not truly comparable. The studies shed some light on the reasons why some children with bronchial asthma lose their asthmatic symptoms while at the same time their functioning as human beings may be affected not only by having asthma but also by the attitudes of their parents towards them or their disease.

Between 30 and 45 percent of all children with extrinsic (allergic) asthma outgrow their clinical symptoms (Flensborg, 1945; Pearson, 1958, 1968; Rackmann and Edwards, 1952; Ryssing, 1959; Von Harnack and Panten, 1957). Moreover, 50 percent of all children with asthma that is intractable to drug treatment remit on removal from their homes. Other children lose their symptoms without leaving home. Very few of these children have been studied. In fact, Lamont (1963) is one of the few authors to have

270

done so. He studied two children who outgrew their asthma by mastering their dependency conflicts. It would have been interesting to know more about these children who outgrow their symptoms and to learn about the nature of the changes that occurred in their family relationships, whether they became more competent in coping with adaptive tasks, needed less medication, or did better clinically than those children who were less able to cope with situations that evoked fears of separation and loss.

Of importance is the fact that patients who outgrow clinical asthma remain at risk for the disease. Former patients were tested by measuring the FEV. The test has demonstrated its usefulness in demonstrating that some asymptomatic patients remain at risk for clinical asthma by virtue of their persistent tendency to reduce the FEV with excercise. Young adults who have outgrown clinical attacks of bronchial asthma show an increased lability of their bronchial tree; that is, the fall in their FEV with exercise exceeds the normal reduction of 15 percent (Hemlich et al., 1966; Jones and Jones, 1966; Jones et al., 1962). This finding suggests that increased lability is a characteristic of those predisposed to bronchial asthma and is not limited to children with the disease.

Very little information is currently available as to why some patients with either form of asthma remit, why the disease follows an intermittent or continuous course in others, or why still others repeatedly develop *status asthmaticus*, or why others die (Ogilvie, 1962). Clearly, longitudinal studies, such as those done by Knapp and Nemetz (1960) and Knapp et al. (1966a, b), in which social, psychological, and physiological variables are measured over a period of many months, or even years, are needed to shed further light on this issue. The social conditions in which exacerbations and remissions occur should be assessed.

De Araujo et al. (1972) used the Berle Index to measure the psychosocial "coping" ability of 36 asthmatic patients who ranged in age from 19 to 74. They found that those who scored low on coping ability on this measure required higher steroid doses than those who scored high. In this study, responses to medication in asthmatic patients were related to their coping ability. It would also be of interest to relate coping ability to other indicators of the course of the disease. If psychopathology is also an index of the inability to cope, the findings obtained by de Araujo and his co-workers tend to confirm the impression reported by Knapp and Nemetz (1957a) that in adult patients there is a direct correlation between the severity of the patient's impaired coping ability, psychopathology, and the severity of his symptoms.

ASTHMA AND NEUROTIC ILLNESS

The psychopathology may take the form of a neurosis or a functional or drug-induced psychosis. Many studies on the prevalance of neurosis in asthmatic patients and on the relationship between neurosis and asthma have been published in the last 50 years (Dekker, 1934; Knapp, 1963; McDermott and Cobb, 1939; Wittkower and Petow, 1932). Yet, these issues remain a source of controversy, due to the methodological and conceptual problems that abound in this area of investigation.

A number of authors (Fink and Schneer, 1963; Sperling, 1963) have reported on individual asthmatic patients who present clear-cut neurotic symptoms—specifically, phobias (e.g., phobias of leaving the mother or of death) (Monsour, 1960). Sperling, who has had extensive clinical experience with asthmatic children who have a phobia of going out (and leaving their mother) are, in fact, afraid that she will die during their absence. Such single-case studies are of interest; however, they do not permit generalizations with respect to the prevalence of phobias in asthmatic persons or tell us whether these symptoms are more common in this population than in others.

Studies of groups of asthmatic patients present another set of conceptual and methodological weaknesses. The problem of defining neurosis is particularly conspicuous in such investigations. Some workers use neurotic symptoms as a criterion of neurosis; others use broader categories of psychopathology, such as personality traits or behaviors. Some workers use projective test results as evidence of the presence of neurosis; others rely on personality inventories, such as various neuroticism scales. In some studies, medical patients are used as comparison groups; in others, psychiatric patients are used as controls. Finally, it is not quite clear what these studies are really supposed to mean. For example, if it were shown that during a symptom-free period, asthmatic patients had neither more nor less anxiety than ambulatory neurotic patients attending a psychiatric clinic, could such a finding really be used to refute the hypothesis that social and psychological factors may play a variable role in the onset and recurrence of asthma in groups of patients with this disease? The findings derived from these studies must be evaluated in light of these considerations.

The experimental population studied by Leigh and Marley (1956) by means of the Cornell Medical Index actually comprised two distinct subgroups: the first subgroup comprised asthmatic patients who were being seen at a general hospital; the second consisted of asthmatic patients who were being seen by psychiatrists on an outpatient basis at a psychiatric clinic. Both subgroups were compared with ambulatory "neurotic" patients who were being seen at the same psychiatric clinic and with a randomly selected group of department store employees. Feelings of inadequacy, depression, anxiety, sensitivity, anger, and inner tension were equally common in the asthmatic and neurotic men patients and more common than in the comparison group. But women asthmatic patients had fewer of these feelings than neurotic patients, and more than the employees with whom they were compared. Other studies have confirmed the observation that asthmatic and neurotic adult patients, perhaps men in particular, suffer from a variety of unpleasant feelings that in Europe are called neurotic (Dekker et al., 1961; Franks and Leigh, 1959; Rees, 1956a, b). In most studies of children, similar findings have been obtained. Rees (1964) compared 388 asthmatic children of both sexes who were being treated in an outpatient clinic with a group of children who were being treated in the same setting for injuries sustained in accidents. Mild to severe anxiety was present in 39 percent of the experimental group, versus 6 percent of the comparison group, and an "anxiety state" occurred in 4.5 percent of the experimental group versus 0 percent of the comparison group. Tension was observed in 36 percent of the asthmatic patients, versus 5 percent of the accident victims; and depressive symptoms were present in 10 percent of the experimental subjects, versus 0 percent of the comparison group. In addition, palpitations, sweating, dizziness, trembling, dyspepsia, and diarrhea were more prevalent in the asthmatic children. Other symptoms may also occur in children, as evidenced by Leigh's and Marley's (1967) study comparing a group of asthmatic children under 12 years of age with a control group of ambulatory nonasthmatic children with other medical problems;

they found that more asthmatic patients suffered from disturbances of eating, elimination, or sleeping; or they sucked their thumbs, rocked, bit their nails, scratched, pulled their hair, were overactive; or they had tics, temper tantrums, breathholding attacks, or otherwise engaged in attention-seeking behavior. Also, when these symptoms were present in both the asthmatic patients and the controls, they were more severe in the asthmatic children. In addition, Leigh and Marley found that the number of adult asthmatic patients in their series who had a history of similar behavioral manifestations exceeded the number of medical patients in their control group who had such a history. These findings appear to constitute conclusive evidence of the higher incidence of neurotic symptoms in asthmatics. In fact, however, it is difficult to assess the reliability of the data: first, these data derive from medical records, rather than the authors' independent evaluation of the patients who comprised their experimental and control groups. Second, the number of children and adults in the series studied was not large enough to permit generalizations as to the greater prevalence of neurotic symptoms in asthmatic patients. Third, the effects of drugs in producing symptoms was not evaluated.

Zealley et al. (1971) studied 48 adult asthmatic outpatients, selected at random, and compared them with 22 matched psychiatric outpatients who had "mood disturbances" and 22 normal persons by means of the Taylor manifest anxiety scale, the Eysenck Personality Inventory, and a "hostility and direction of hostility" questionnaire. The asthmatic patients had a marked spread of scores that would be considered indicative of a heterogeneous group, with some scoring very high and others very low on criteria of neurosis; the mean score for the asthmatic patients ranked between the mean score for normal persons and the mean for psychiatric ("neurotic") outpatients. Zealley and his co-workers found that in their series there was no relationship between the presence of neurotic personality disorders, or the apparent tendency to manifest such disorders, and the clinical severity of the asthma. But they also found that the more overtly anxious patients in their sample were significantly more likely to acknowledge the presence of emotional factors which, presumably, precipitated their attacks.

ASTHMA AND PSYCHOSIS

Over the years, a number of workers have addressed themselves to the question of the relationship of bronchial asthma to psychosis. The nature of this relationship has been variously conceptualized in such studies. Some workers have attempted to demonstrate that patients with bronchial asthma are psychotic or that psychosis may in itself predispose to bronchial asthma, given the proper biological predisposition. Others have suggested that psychosis and bronchial asthma may alternate in the same patients; and some contend that the coincidence of psychosis and bronchial asthma is indirect evidence of the validity of the assertion that profound personal conflicts occur in such patients. Other studies, which are of great potential interest and may help to unravel these relationships, have provided data on the prevalence of positive skin tests in a large population of carefully diagnosed patients with serious psychopathology. However, there is also some contradictory evidence that psychotic patients in various diagnostic categories do not respond to the intracutaneous injection of allergens or histimine (Zeller and Edlin, 1943). And Freedman, et al. (1956) found that although schizophrenic patients did not react less positively in skin tests to allergens, they reacted less vigorously to the intracutaneous injection of histamine. It is possible, of course, that the immediate type of hypersensitivity manifested by such patients is, in some mysterious manner, influenced by an altered central neural state.

It is the current consensus of opinion that severe psychiatric illnesses do not occur more frequently in patients with bronchial asthma than they do in comparable groups of medical patients (Leigh and Marley, 1967). However, there have been a number of reports of the high incidence of bronchial asthma in patients with a psychotic illness characterized by mood disturbances (Appel and Rosen, 1951; Brown and Goitein, 1943; Leavitt, 1943; Prout, 1951), perverse behavior (Knapp et al., 1966a, b), and addiction to drugs (Chessick et al., 1960). But the validity of such findings is open to question: obviously, gathering anamnestic data either from psychotic patients or their charts presents serious difficulties. One must conclude, therefore, that there is no real evidence that bronchial asthma is more prevalent in hospitalized psychiatric patients. Granted that prevalence studies show wide variations, it would still appear that bronchial asthma occurs only as frequently (Zeller and Edlin, 1943), or even less frequently, in hospitalized psychotic patients than it does in the general population (Leavitt, 1943; Leigh, 1953; Leigh and Doust, 1953; McAllister and Hecker, 1949; MacInnis, 1936; Ross, 1954; Ross et al., 1950; Swartz and Semrad, 1951).

Yet the findings derived from one study of the coincidence of bronchial asthma and psychopathology have interesting implications that clearly merit further investigation. Specifically, Chessick et al. (1960) reported that in their series, 5 to 6 percent of the narcotic addicts who were newly admitted to a hospital for drug withdrawal had a history of bronchial asthma, whereas the incidence of asthma was 12.5 percent of the addicts who had been hospitalized for two months. A large number (80 percent) of patients developed asthmatic attacks in the hospital, during the period of withdrawal. In other words the attacks of wheezing were not due to fresh emboli (that can cause wheezing) brought about by injecting narcotics intravenously.

There are no systematic data suggesting that serious psychopathology per se predisposes to bronchial asthma. The fact that the psychiatric diagnoses of those psychotic patients who develop bronchial asthma are representative of all the major categories of psychopathology (Leigh and Doust, 1953; Ross et al., 1950; Sabbath and Luce, 1952), argues against the possibility that any one form of psychopathology predisposes to bronchial asthma.

The proposition that bronchial asthma alternates with frank psychosis, or with severe personality discorganization that could be diagnosed as psychosis, has been asserted by some workers (Appel and Rosen, 1951; Funkenstein, 1950a; Gillespie, 1936; Kerman, 1946; Mandell and Younger, 1962; Sabbath and Luce, 1952; Swartz and Semrad, 1951; Vaughan and Black, 1948), and denied by others (Leavitt, 1943; Leigh and Doust, 1953; Prout, 1951). Actually, however, this proposition has been studied from two different perspectives: some authors have focused on the alternation of asthmatic attacks with psychotic episodes; others have investigated the coincidence of bronchial asthma attacks during various stages of a psychotic illness (Funkenstein, 1950b; Sabbath and Luce, 1952). The study reported by Sabbath and Luce (1952) is of considerable interest because it deals with both of these alternatives. These authors studied 32 hospitalized adult

274

psychiatric patients drawn from various diagnostic categories, who had histories of bronchial asthma. But during the phase of psychotic disorganization, when systematized delusions did not occur, the patients were free of asthmatic attacks. In the patients, asthmatic symptoms did alternate with various stages of the psychosis, but not with the psychotic illness. The psychotic state may alter the asthmatic patient's reactivity to drugs such as histamine and methacholine chloride. Funkenstein (1950a, 1950b, 1953) found that variations in physiological response occurred in his sample of asthmatic patients during, as well as in the absence of, psychotic episodes. When these patients were actively psychotic, injections of methacholine chloride led to transient increases in systolic blood pressure and minimal wheezing; when they were not psychotic, asthmatic attacks occurred and wheezing was marked.

PSYCHOLOGICAL FACTORS IN THE DEATH OF ASTHMATIC PATIENTS

One other topic about the relationship of psychological factors, affecting the course of patients with bronchial asthma should be mentioned. The disease may terminate in death when the patient in *status asthmaticus* no longer responds to any form of treatment. The steps leading to *status asthmaticus* are not clearly understood. Once this state occurs, central respiratory or right heart failure may supervene and terminate the patient's life.

A number of explanations have been sought for the increasing number of deaths of patients with bronchial asthma, either because they go into *status asthmaticus*, or not. The use of certain drugs have been blamed for this increase (Pinkerton and Weaver, 1970; Rackemann, 1944; Rackemann and Edwards, 1952; Richards and Patrick, 1965; Speizer and Heaf, 1968; Tulou, 1961; Walton and Elliot, 1952; Walton et al., 1951). Granting that drugs and the relentless changes in the structure and function of the lung may be critical factors in causing sudden death in asthma or in *status asthmaticus*, they would not explain the sudden appearance of these states at one time and not another. In fact, the events leading up to death may be precipitated by changes in the psychological state of the patient. Schneer (1963) reported on a 9-year-old girl who died suddenly while in treatment at a time when anger at her mother was being expressed. And several authors have commented on the fact that in adults, psychological states reminiscent of the "giving up/given up" pattern described by Engel (1967) precede death (Jores, 1956; Knapp et al., 1966a, b). In his report on nine patients whose illness began after the age of 35 years, Maxwell (1955) observed that in seven instances death was preceded by feelings of defeat and of impending death, loss of confidence, and feelings hopelessness. Leigh's (1955) patient who had had asthma for 30 years died suddenly after four hours of treatment, when she was awakened by an asthmatic attack that followed a tearful, powerful abreaction of her personal problems. Another author (Knick, 1954) maintains that the feeling of overwhelming anxiety antecedes death.

PSYCHOPHYSIOLOGICAL STUDIES

In recent years, psychosomatic research has consisted more and more of controlled studies in the laboratory whose aim was to demonstrate that psychological stimuli could produce bronchoconstriction and the symptoms of asthma in patients, but not in a control population. Because wheezing, cough and dyspnea can occur in other diseases —asthmatic and chronic bronchitis, and various forms of obstructive lung diseases—it is incumbent on the investigator to ascertain unequivocally that he is studying bronchial asthma and not another disease. He is aided in his diagnosis by the history of the disease. To further ascertain the diagnosis, he may use a number of measures of pulmonary function to study changes in vital capacity, peak expiratory flow, and FEV. Clinical laboratory tests are combined with the inhalation of allergens, catecholamines, parasympathomimetic amines, histamine and the various mediators of the antigen-antibody reaction, or exercise in order to reduce or alter these measures of bronchial patency (Aas, 1965; Makino, 1966; Ten Cate, 1961; Tiffeneau, 1959). The lung of the asthmatic is unusually likely to bronchoconstrict and produce wheezes. The purpose of these tests is not only to aid in diagnosis but to demonstrate the influence of psychological factors on pulmonary function (Dudley, 1969). It is, however, difficult in the controlled situation to produce strong feelings in conscious patients in anything but a contrived way. Therefore, strong feelings have been induced during hypnotic trances during which pulmonary function has been measured. Another less-direct approach has been to alter pulmonary function by suggestion, relaxation, and conditioning techniques. In these studies the emphasis has been placed on controlling the psychological conditions in a reliable and verifiable manner. The studies indicate that bronchial constriction or dilatation may be brought about by psychological manipulations. The results of these experiments only indirectly attest to the role of mental factors in bronchial asthma, but they tell us nothing about the mechanisms that mediate the phenomena observed in the laboratory.

Psychophysiological Relationship
between Bronchial Asthma and Suggestion

In order to affirm the role of psychological factors in bronchial asthma, it would be necessary to show that bronchoconstriction, dyspnea, and wheezing, can be brought about by one or another of a variety of psychological means. The experimental bronchoconstriction produced should have the same psychological results that characterize an asthmatic attack. The psychological stimuli used in experiments should verify the clinical observation that emotional arousal or symbolic stimuli can bring about bronchoconstriction. Ideally, the mechanism by which these stimuli antecede bronchoconstriction should be worked out in the laboratory. These investigative aims have only partly been attained in a variety of psychophysiological studies, some of which have used hypnotic suggestion and conditioning techniques to bring about bronchoconstriction in some subjects.

Bronchoconstriction occurs not only in response to allergens and parasympathomimetic agents, but, also in response to the suggestion of personal topics of an unpleasant nature that evoke feelings of insecurity. And when Faulkner (1941) studied a nonasthmatic patient who also had esophageal spasm by means of direct bronchoscopy, he found that bronchodilatation occurred in response to the suggestion of pleasant and desirable subjects.

Bronchoconstriction may also occur in response to the suggestion of an allergen. The series studied by Luparello et al. (1968, 1970, 1971) and McFadden et al. (1969) comprised 40 adult asthmatic patients, who were compared with 10 normal patients, 10 patients with chronic bronchitis, and 11 with sarcoidosis and tuberculosis of the lungs. Each subject was told that he would be inhaling five different concentrations of an irritant or allergen (actually a pharmacological saline solution) that he had previously associated with his attacks; airway resistance and thoracic gas volume were measured concurrently in a whole-body plethysmograph. Only in the patients with bronchial asthma was there a significant rise in airway resistance together with a slight rise in thoracic gas volume so that the ratio between them was significantly lowered. This reaction was particularly apparent in 19 of the 40 asthmatic patients, 12 of whom went on to develop wheezing and dyspnea. Furthermore, the inhalation of a saline placebo (which the patient was led to believe was isoproterenol) cleared up these "asthmatic" attacks, and the physiological evidence of bronchoconstriction disappeared. In one of their more recent studies, Luparello et al. (1970) further demonstrated the interaction of psychological stimuli and pharmacological agents on airway reactivity. Thus, if the subject was led to believe that inhaled carbachol was a bronchodilator, it produced less of an increase in airway resistance than it did if he believed it to be a bronchoconstrictor. Similar effects, albeit in an opposite direction, occurred if the subject believed that the inhaled bronchodilator was isoproterenol. In 13 of 15 of the original reactors, changes in airway resistance could be reproduced a second time.

The conclusion to be drawn from this work—that both increases and decreases in airway resistance can be induced by suggestion in some asthmatic patients—has been confirmed in other studies. The additional finding that these changes can be blocked by atropine suggests that the induction of asthmatic attacks is mediated by parasympathetic mechanisms (McFadden et al., 1969).

In 1970, Weiss et al. attempted to replicate in children the work Luparello and his group had done in adults. Accordingly, the 16 asthmatic children in their series were told they were inhaling allergen when they were actually inhaling saline solution. However, only one of the children responded to this suggestion with a decreased expiratory flow rate and wheezing, and then only after the fifth exposure to the saline inhalant. The discrepancy in the findings obtained by these workers and those obtained by Luparello is puzzling. However, it may be ascribed, in part, to the different methods used to test pulmonary function: Weiss and his co-workers did not use the whole body plethysmograph. In addition, the children studied by Weiss had intractable asthma; 9 of the 16 were receiving steroid medication. In contrast, the subjects studied by Luparello and his co-workers were outpatients who suffered from relatively mild forms of the disease.

The Effects of Hypnosis on Bronchial Asthma

A number of authors have studied the effects of hypnosis on patients with bronchial asthma (Magonet, 1955; Meares, 1960; Stewart, 1957). Most of them have sought to demonstrate the therapeutic efficacy of hypnosis in this illness (Sinclair-Gieben, 1960), and their claims of therapeutic benefit are not without foundation. Indeed, Maher-Loughnan et al. (1962) found that in 27 adult patients, ten sessions of hypnotic suggestion reduced the frequency of wheezing over a six-month period, and these patients showed significantly greater improvement than a carefully matched control group who were treated with bronchodilator drugs. On the other hand, Morrison Smith and Burns (1960) carried out a controlled study of 25 children who were treated by weekly hypnotic sessions for a month and found that no demonstrable symptomatic improvement or changes in pulmonary function tests occurred in their experimental group.

Mason and Black (1958) reported a single case study of a woman with extrinsic asthma and allergic rhinitis, who was treated by weekly post-hypnotic suggestions for 2½ months. Her symptoms were relieved, and weekly skin tests showed a decreasing sensitivity to allergens to which she had been known to be sensitive. Yet at the end of treatment when her serum was injected into a nonsensitive volunteer, it produced a Prausnitz-Kustner reaction (i.e., passive transfer of skin sensitivity was effected).

An interesting aspect of some of these studies has been underscored by White (1961). He found that posthypnotic suggestion produced dissociated symptoms, such as wheezing, in ten adult asthmatic patients who also presented physiological evidence of the persistance of bronchial constriction. Thus, White concluded that while hypnosis can enable clinical relief of depression and anxiety and of asthmatic symptoms in adult patients, the vital capacity may continue to be reduced in most patients. Yet, others have found that pulmonary function itself can be altered by hypnosis: Edwards (1960), who studied the changes in symptoms and in pulmonary function that occurred in six adult asthmatic patients who had been hypnotized, found that their FEVs increased within several days. Furthermore, four of these six patients continued to show improvement on follow-up a year after treatment had been terminated.

It is difficult, of course, to reconcile these findings. Once again these discrepancies can be ascribed to the methodological weaknesses inherent in such studies. In view of the strong possibility that bronchial asthma is a heterogeneous disease, any attempt to determine whether asthmatic patients respond to hypnosis would necessarily require the specific characterization of the subject population both with regard to pulmonary function and from a behavioral and clinical point of view.

If it could be shown definitively that posthypnotic suggestion can directly alter pulmonary function by relieving bronchial constriction, this would constitute a powerful piece of evidence in support of the belief that psychological factors do play a role in some forms of bronchial asthma. Alternatively, hypnotic suggestion may not produce bronchodilatation but may alleviate the anxiety and fears associated with the anticipation of another attack or the awareness of difficulty in breathing.

In any event, much of the research reviewed above seems to indicate that emotional factors and pulmonary function interact. It should also be noted, however, that the patients studied by many of these authors were referred for psychiatric treatment and may constitute a special group.

The Effects of Relaxation Training on Bronchial Patency

Another approach that may help to substantiate the contention that psychological variables influence measures of bronchial patency has focused on the role of psychophysiological relationships in the termination rather than the inception of asthmatic attacks. It is well-known that instructions to asthmatic patients to sit quietly at the

278

onset or during an asthmatic attack may expedite its alleviation. But there has been some dispute as to whether this effect can be attributed to lack of exertion (or exercise) or to relaxation. The recent study done by A. B. Alexander and his co-workers (1972) would seem to indicate that relaxation is the critical variable. Specifically, they reported on the effects of three sessions of modified systematic relaxation training in 20 asthmatic children. They found that each session induced self-reported feelings of relaxation and a significant mean increase in peak expiratory flow rate in the children in their experimental group. Instructions to "just sit quietly" did not induce similar effects in a matched control group of 16 asthmatic children. Prior to the sessions, all the subjects had shown airflow impairment. Consequently, the effects noted could be accounted for by the benefits of relaxation training.

Data Derived from Sleep Studies

Many asthmatic attacks (up to 40 percent) have their onset during sleep. To understand this phenomenon we need to know at what time of night and during what stage of sleep the attacks occur. Preliminary evidence suggests that nocturnal asthmatic attacks occur during the rapid-eye-movement phase of sleep (Hartmann, 1967). Ideally, further efforts to relate asthmatic attacks to a particular sleep stage should also include data pertaining to body and respiratory movements, cortisol production rates, and other physiological measures. For instance, it might be interesting to know whether nocturnal attacks occur early in sleep, when corisol production is low, or toward morning when it is rising rapidly (Reinberg et al., 1963).

The Effects of Emotional Responses to Stressful Situations on Respiration in Bronchial Asthma

Clinical observations suggest that in many awake patients the asthmatic attack is preceded by mounting emotional tension—including anger, fear, or excitement—and may be accompanied by depression. Our understanding of the interrelationship between psychological and physiological factors in this illness would be greatly enhanced by studies of the relationship of different emotional states to respiration in bronchial asthma. Furthermore, such studies would also have a bearing on the suggestion that exercise may produce bronchodilation in normal subjects and bronchoconstriction in at least some asthmatic subjects (Finesinger and Mazick, 1940; Itkin and Anand, 1968; Jones et al., 1962; Pinkerton, 1967; Schiavi et al., 1961; Sly et al., 1967; Zaid et al., 1968), and that hyperventilation may cause wheezing (Graham, 1972; Swineford, 1962).

Excitement may antecede athletic exercise; therefore, it would be important to know whether bronchoconstriction begins with the excitement or after the exercise has begun. Excitement may lead to an increased rate of respiration: at what point in this sequence does bronchoconstriction or wheezing start? These are not idle questions, as in animals the cardiorespiratory changes observed on exercise actually start before muscular activity occurs. In other words, there is a centrally mediated, anticipatory phase of exercise, and some of the neural correlates of this phase are known. Concomitantly, some of the hormonal correlates of exercise have also been identified (Von Euler, 1969). Analytic studies of these sequences might provide leads as to the central neural mechanisms involved in exercise-induced wheezing and bronchoconstriction, and the role of hormones in these phenomena.

Several authors have demonstrated that changes in respiration occur in normal and neurotic patients even when they are not talking. Others have shown that anxiety and anger may, at times, be associated with increases in the frequency, amplitude, and irregularity of respiration in patients with cardiovascular disease (Stevenson and Duncan, 1952), and that neurotic patients (Clausen, 1951) and "excited" individuals (Christiansen, 1965) have higher respiratory rates.

For obvious reasons, it is very difficult to induce emotional states in the laboratory reliably and reproducibly. One such attempt, by Dudley et al. (1964b), relied on the use of hypnosis to induce specific behavioral and emotional states. When hypnosis was used to induce relaxation or sleep and a feeling of depression in ten normal young men and one patient with pulmonary tuberculosis, a decrease in alveolar ventilation and oxygen consumption and elevations of alveolar carbon dioxide concentration occurred. Dudley and his co-workers (1964a, b) also found that the hypnotic induction of pain, anger, anxiety, and a hypnotic state in which the subject reexperienced the physical and psychological sensations evoked by active exercise produced changes that were the exact opposite of those evoked by the hypnotic suggestion of relaxation, sleep, or depression. The hypnotic induction of unpleasant emotional states produced increases in alveolar ventilation and oxygen consumption and reductions of alveolar carbon dioxide concentration, as did the production of actual head pain. These physiological changes also occurred when a psychologically meaningful and personally painful subject was suggested to the hypnotized patient. In the unhypnotized state, a discussion of topics personally painful to the subject brought about the same physiological changes, a prolonged expiratory phase, or wheezing (Dudley et al., 1964a; Masuda et al., 1966; Stevenson and Ripley, 1952). And Stein (1962) correlated increased airway resistance with both anxiety and elation in two patients with bronchial asthma.

Longitudinal studies using whole-body plethysmography have yielded the observation that bronchial asthma may be characterized not only by lowered airway conductance, but also by greater variability in conductance. In the asthmatic patients studied by Heim et al. (1967, 1968), attacks were preceded by the usual clinical manifestations, e.g., wheezing and dyspnea. But the patients' subjective distress during the attack did not correlate highly with airway conductance measures. On the other hand, although, as a group, these patients were highly sensitive to carbachol, the degree of sensitivity varied in individual patients, and in two of the four patients studied it could be positively correlated with emotional factors—the presence of guilt feelings and the adequacy or "failure" of psychological "defenses."

Owen (1963) compared 20 chronically ill, hospitalized asthmatic children with 20 children with a past history of bronchial asthma. Owen's investigative efforts centered on the respiratory responses of asthmatic children when they listened to the tape recordings of the voice of their mother and the voice of an unfamiliar person. The research design additionally provided for the proper distribution of a "threatening" and a "neutral" story read by both among the tapes listened to by each child. The hospitalized asthmatic children showed greater variability in the amplitude and pattern of respiration on listening to their mothers' voices than did the other children. Furthermore, variations in the amplitude of respiration occurred in the hospitalized asthmatic children in response to "neutral" as well as "threatening" stories, indicating that they mainly discriminated different voices, rather than voice tones. A variety of psychological procedures —suggestion, unpleasant topics, and various emotional states—do seem to produce changes in various parameters of respiratory function, especially in the asthmatic. The results of such correlative studies are interpreted to mean that psychological factors may change respiratory function, in a direct manner. The experiments of Doust and Leigh (1953) on 25 asthmatic patients were directed to test this idea. Psychiatric interviews and discontinuous spectroscopic oximetry to measure blood oxygen saturation levels were carried out concurrently. The authors proceeded on the premise that the asthmatic attack is a response to rage or depression. Heightened tension ensues when these emotions are denied free expression; they can be overcome by the asthmatic attack, or by crying, laughing, or the expression of anger and confession. When no asthmatic attack occurred, the patient's blood pressure was low, his pulse rate increased, and perspiration and skin pallor were observed.

Doust and Leigh note that not infrequently, patients were either enraged, unhappy, or depressed before the experiment, and that these feeling states alternated with asthmatic attacks or were released in the manner outlined.

The study by Doust and Leigh deals with the relationship of asthmatic attacks to emotional states and their discharge. It is unfortunate that they did not measure airflow resistance during their experiments to ascertain whether bronchoconstriction had occurred.

Autonomic Responses

Autonomic responses to induced laboratory stress have also been studied in normal children and children with intractable bronchial asthma by Hahn (1966) and Hahn and Clark (1967). Hahn's first study (1966) yielded evidence that the resting heart rates as a measure of increased sympathetic activity and skin temperatures of asthmatic children were higher than those of normal children and were also significantly more responsive to two problem-solving tasks. Anticipation of an electric shock evoked no significant change in heart rate or skin temperature. Moreover, no difference in respiratory response occurred under these experimental conditions. In Hahn's second study, conducted in collaboration with Clark (1967), his earlier findings of an increase in resting heart rate were confirmed. Hahn and Clark had the children in this series perform mental arithmetic while they criticized each child's performance. To determine the emotional effects of this procedure, they assessed mood changes by means of the Mood Adjective Check List and interviews. The subjects' responses were defined as negative (tension, bewilderment, depression, and anger), neutral, or positive. The asthmatic patients showed a significantly greater increment in negative effects and a greater decrease of positive ones. Nevertheless, despite very high prestimulus levels, the asthmatic children still showed increased heart rates in response to the arithmetic task. However, respiratory rates under these stressful conditions tended not to increase progressively in the asthmatic children as they did in normal children.

281

These studies suggest that in asthmatic children there is either an increase in β-adrenergic sympathetic drive on the heart, or diminished parasympathetic discharge on cardiac receptors. Arithmetic tasks combined with criticism further increased cardiac acceleration, while also producing more negative affects in the asthmatic than in the normal children. Hahn's results show that cardioaccelerator and emotional responses are exaggerated in asthmatic children. He believes that the exaggerated cardiac responses are due to an inherent autonomic imbalance in asthmatic children.

In summary, results of psychophysiological experiments are difficult to interpret. A true understanding of the meaning of the correlations between emotional responses and physiological changes—to put it crudely, whether the response antecedes or "causes" the change, or vice versa, or whether both are the product of some other variable—has not been achieved. Therefore, many investigators prefer to control rigorously their independent variable; for instance, by producing a conditioned response and measuring a subsequent physiological change (Turnbull, 1962).

Conditioned Asthmatic Attacks in Man and in Animals

The studies of Dekker and Groen (1956), Dekker et al. (1957), and Herxheimer (1953) are cited most frequently in the literature as demonstrating that asthmatic subjects can develop conditioned asthmatic attacks when exposed to pictures of the objects that normally induce attacks. In these experiments generalization from the conditioned stimulus to the experimental situation also occurs. In their earlier experiments, however, Dekker and Groen (1956) found that the pictures of objects that normally induced attacks had to produce profound and specific feelings in the laboratory, as an expression of the emotional significance of the picture for the patient.

In the second experiment by Dekker et al. (1957), the unconditioned stimulus was the allergen to which their subjects were sensitive. The conditioned stimulus was some aspect of the laboratory situation. Thus, when the same nebulizer through which the allergen was inhaled was used for the inhalation of oxygen alone, the inhalation of oxygen reproduced an attack. This study has been criticized on two grounds: first, if the authors had not shown that the mouthpiece of the nebulizer also precipitated an attack, the results of inhaling oxygen only would have to be viewed with caution, for oxygen can act as an irritant. Second, the physiological criterion of attacks was a reduction in vital capacity, which is considered a rather unreliable and insensitive measure of changes in airway resistance (D'Silva and Lewis, 1961). These studies were not well-controlled. As Purcell (1965) has pointed out, they do not provide compelling evidence that conditioned asthmatic attacks can occur in humans. Nor has the fact that conditioned asthmatic attacks can occur in animals been definitively established.

Animal Models of Bronchial Asthma

A full explanation of the etiology, pathogenesis, and course of a disease depends in part on the development of an animal model. This model could be used to study the roles of early experience and psychological stress in interaction with allergic and infectious factors.

282

Once it is clear that they do play a role, the brain mechanisms that mediate these interactions can be studied. The brain does seem to influence the extreme form —anaphylaxis—of the immediate form of hypersensitivity, which also characterizes the less-violent allergic response in bronchial asthma. A basic requirement of work with an animal model is to be certain that the allergenic challenge, or the drug used to induce wheezing, also reproduces edema, bronchoconstriction, mucous production, and eosinophilia, and not just signs of bronchoconstriction or laryngeal spasm. The studies reviewed below need to be evaluated from this perspective.

Various methods have been used to induce experimental asthmatic attacks in animals. Guinea pigs, in particular, can be sensitized by antigenic injection, and the antigen can then be reinjected or inhaled. Or dry dusts with antigenic properties can be introduced repeatedly into the bronchi and lungs for a period of about six hours, after which reexposure to this aerosol leads to asthmatic attacks that may be quite prolonged. However, these attacks do not always occur. Moreover, individual animals exhibit marked individual differences in reactivity (Ottenberg et al., 1958; Ratner, 1953a, b; Stein et al., 1961). When the animal dies after an attack lasting 24 hours and consisting of wheezing and rales, the bronchiolar mucosa is thickened and infiltrated with cells, mucous plugs are seen in the bronchioles, eosinophiles occur in the mucosa and mucous secretions, and the lungs are emphysematous (Kallós and Pagel, 1937). Noelpp-Eschenhagen and Noelpp (1954) and Stein et al. (1961) were able to show that when experimental asthma was induced in guinea pigs, an increase in airway resistance and a decrease in the elastic distensibility of the lungs occurred. These anatomical and physiological changes are analogous, if not homologous, to those seen in human bronchial asthma, and may be reproduced by vagal stimulation using the same criteria of increased airway resistance and decreased pulmonary compliance (Chia-mo Wan and Stein, 1968).

In their experiments with guinea pugs, Noelpp and Noelpp-Eschenhagen (1951, 1952) combined exposure to allergenic aerosols with a conditioning stimulus (a tone) to induce an asthmatic attack. After ten trials, the conditioning stimulus alone led to a partial asthmatic attack. Similar attacks occurred when histamine aerosol was combined with a conditioning stimulus. In the experiments in which allergenic aerosols were combined with a tone, positive results were obtained only if the tone was presented on the day following the conditioning trial and not later; in other words, the conditioned response was rapidly extinguished. When a conditioned "asthmatic" response was obtained, recordings of the changes in respiration were made: they consisted of an increase in the depth and speed of breathing and prolongation and irregularity of the expiratory phase. The tone —the conditioning stimulus—could be primed. Guinea pigs who had been exposed to a flashing light for some weeks before and during the conditioning procedure were more likely to develop the conditioned response than guinea pigs which were not primed in this manner.

The authors also noted that generalization occurred: animals who were returned to the laboratory where they had previously participated in experiments, or placed in the chamber in which they had previously been exposed to aerosol, developed "asthma-like" breathing (Noelpp and Noelpp-Eschenhagen 1951, 1952; Noelpp-Eschenhagen and Noelpp, 1954; Ottenberg et al., 1958). Extinction of this response occurred after 12 trials (Ottenberg et al., 1958).

Histamine aerosol, in suitable dilution (1:100), tends to produce anaphylactic shock is followed by physiological signs of asthmatic breathing; rapid recovery occurs after withdrawal of the aerosol. Acetylcholine aerosol tends to produce convulsions, coughing, and deeper breathing, which cease when application of the drug is discontinued. Thus the experimental attacks that occur when these two drugs are introduced into the bronchial tree of guinea pigs differ from those produced by allergenic challenge in that they are less persistent (Ratner, 1953a), and possibly largely dependent on bronchoconstriction and bronchospasm without eosinophilia.

Respiratory changes can be conditioned in animals without the use of allergens or drugs as the unconditioned stimulus. Thus, when "experimental neuroses" are induced in animals (dogs, monkeys, cats), conditioned changes in the rate, rhythm, and pattern of breathing occur (Liddell, 1951; Masserman and Pechtel, 1953; Seitz, 1959); "loud breathing" and wheezing with labored expiration was observed by Gantt (1941) in a dog, which, however, showed no bronchoconstriction. And when Schiavi et al. (1961) exposed guinea pigs to a pain-fear stimulus, such as electric shock, shortened inspiration, prolonged expiration, and increases in tidal and minute volume occurred, which were related to the animal's screeching and disappeared with tracheotomy. Once again, no evidence of bronchoconstriction was seen.

The animal most often used in asthma experiments is the guinea pig. Although the experimental production of asthma in these animals by allergenic aerosols results in pulmonary changes that simulate those seen in man, there is considerable evidence to suggest that the dog is more akin immunologically to man than is the guinea pig. Allergic rhinitis, sneezing and wheezing, and eczema occurred naturally in dogs studied by Noelpp-Eschenhagen and Noelpp (1954). Allergic dogs have positive skin tests to dust, foods (Moreno and Bentolila, 1945), and pollen. When an attack was caused by exposure to pollen, it was reproducible. Furthermore, skin sensitivity could be passively transferred to a normal dog by a serum factor that is heat-labile (Patterson and Sparks, 1962), a characteristic of reaginic antibodies (Stanworth, 1963, 1971). The normal dog also develops asthmatic breathing when given large doses of an asthmatic human's serum. IgE antibodies from humans can also be passively transferred to monkeys (Patterson et al., 1965, 1967; Layton, 1966), but not to other mammals. Once the passive transfer has occurred, bronchial asthma can be provoked by letting the animals inhale the allergen to which the human donor was sensitive. Dogs sensitized passively have not been used in conditioning or other psychological experiments. In summary, bronchial asthma attacks in animals mimic those that occur in humans, in that spirography indicates a reduced vital capacity, dyspnea occurs, and epinephrine injection brings relief from the attack. In addition, when bronchial tissue is removed from asthmatic animals, the smooth muscle contracts when exposed to the allergen (Patterson et al., 1967).

ALLERGIC MECHANISMS IN THE PATHOGENESIS
OF BRONCHIAL ASTHMA

IgE Antibodies

The extrinsic form of bronchial asthma is an example of an immunological disorder, characterized by the immediate form of hypersensitivity to various allergens. The extrinsic

284

form of bronchial asthma, is preceded by or associated with other allergic diseases, such as allergic rhinitis, eczema, and urticaria in about 60 percent of patients (Pearson, 1968). About one-quarter to one-half of all children suffering from atopic eczema later develop bronchial asthma (Bono and Levitt, 1964; Dawson et al., 1969; Edgren, 1943; Leigh and Marley, 1967; Pearson, 1968; Rackemann and Edwards, 1952; Rajka, 1960; Ratner and Silberman, 1953; Schwartz, 1952; Wright, 1965). Patients whose extrinsic asthma begins after the age of 30 years, or those with the intrinsic form of the disease, are not nearly as likely to have a history of allergic rhinitis or atopic eczema (Pearson, 1968). The fact that other immunological disorders precede or accompany bronchial asthma is explained in the following way: IgE antibodies formed in response to allergens are fixed by cells either in the skin to produce atopic eczema, in the nose to cause allergic rhinitis, or in the bronchi to lay the groundwork for bronchial asthma.

Commonly occuring allergens—found in house dusts, feathers, animal hair, pollens, molds, and foods—induce the production of IgE antibodies in predisposed persons Stanworth (1963). Fifty years ago Prausnitz and Küstner (1921) discovered that these antibodies could be transferred passively to sensitize a previously nonallergic recipient.

Not every person exposed to common allergens develops IgE antibodies. Some persons may be predisposed to do so (Humphrey and White, 1970; Rajka, 1960). IgE antibody formation may merely depend on how long and how thoroughly a person is exposed to the allergen: some allergens are more antigenic than others (Aas, 1966; Diedrichs and Lübbers, 1955; Linko, 1947; Pearson, 1968; Schwartz, 1952; Spoujitch, 1960). Yet only 40 percent of people heavily and continually exposed to allergens such as animal hair or flour develop evidence of a hypersensitivity to them, and less than half of those who are hypersensitive develop bronchial asthma (Spoujitch, 1960). Most people in certain regions of the world are seasonally and heavily exposed to the pollen of the plane tree, but only 1 in 500 become hypersensitive to this allergen (Aas, 1969).

Following the identification of reaginic antibodies as a new (IgE) class of antibodies by Ishizaka and various coworkers (1966 a,b,c, 1967, 1968, 1970), Johansson (1967) and Johansson and colleagues (1967, 1968a) found that patients with allergic rhinitis, asthma, and hay fever had elevated serum levels of IgE. Johansson (1967) also found that serum levels of IgE were six times higher in patients with allergic asthma than those with intrinsic asthma or in normal controls.

IgE levels vary in children with bronchial asthma, ranging from normal to six or seven times normal. The higher levels are particularly apt to occur in children with perennial asthma who are hypersensitive to animal dandruff and dust. Children who suffer only from allergic rhinitis tend to have lower mean IgE levels, but the levels rise when the pollen season begins. IgE concentrations also rise in most children undergoing specific desensitization procedures (Berg and Johansson, 1969). Not all children who are sensitive to several allergens have increased IgE levels; conversely, high values occur in some children who are hypersensitive to only a few allergens (Berg and Johansson, 1969).

Berg and Johansson (1969), Johansson et al. (1968b) and Wide et al. (1967) have also demonstrated that elevations of IgE levels may occur in the absence of any symptoms of asthma or other allergic illnesses, and have estimated that this phenomenon may occur in about 25 percent of any clinical population. In other words, the tendency to form IgE antibodies may be a necessary, but not a sufficient, predisposing factor in some forms of bronchial asthma, allergic rhinitis, and atopic eczema.

Immunological Mechanisms in Allergic Asthma

When the specific allergen is inhaled or ingested it is first recognized by B-lymphocytes that reside in the nasopharyngeal, bronchial, and gastrointestinal lymphoid tissue. The B-lymphocytes divide and mature into plasma cells that form the specific IgE. IgEs are glycoproteins with a molecular weight of 198,000 daltons. The IgE molecules attach themselves for many weeks to mast cells and basophils (Riley, 1959; Stanworth, 1963) that reside either in the ground substance of the connective tissue of the bronchi and bronchioles (Berdal, 1952; Warren and Dixon, 1948), or to the epithelial cells of the bronchi and bronchioles (Gold, 1976; McCarter and Vasquez, 1966; Richardson et al., 1973). When the subject is next exposed, the allergen combines with and binds together two adjacent molecules of the IgE antibody fixed on the surface of mast cells (Litt, 1964; Stanworth, 1971), basophils or epithelial cells to produce the release of several mediators[*] (Austen, 1974; Stechschulte et al., 1966)—histamine (Ishizaka et al., 1969; Katz and Cohen, 1941; Kay and Austen, 1971), the slow-reactive substance of anaphylaxis (SRS-A) of Brocklehurst (1956, 1968), the eosinophil chemotactic factor of anaphylaxis (ECF-A), the platelet activating factor (PAF), and probably other active substances such as heparin (Osler et al., 1968), serotonin, the prostaglandins, and bradykinin (see Figure 1) (Austen, 1974).

Mechanism of the Release of the Mediators

When the allergen and the IgE antibodies react, the mediators are released from the mast and the other cells through a series of biochemical steps that require calcium ions, the activation of an esterase enzyme and glucose (Austen, 1974; Brocklehurst, 1968; Kaliner et al., 1972; Kaliner and Austen, 1973, 1974a,b; Wasserman et al., 1974). Finally the granules that contain the mediators are released under the influence of more calcium ions (see Figure 2).

HISTAMINE

Histamine causes contraction of smooth muscles of the bronchial airways, increases the permeability of small blood vessels, and promotes the secretion of mucus (Dale, 1920; Nadel, 1973). It also releases catecholamines.

Bronchial tissue contains a large number of mast cells, and even under normal conditions the lungs have the highest concentration of histamine of any tissue in the body (Austen, 1965, 1974; Stone et al., 1955). Isolated nasal polyps and even pieces of lung of patients with bronchial asthma release larger amounts of histamine on contact with the allergen in vitro (Austen, 1974). Histamine levels rise in blood and urine during asthmatic attacks (Rose et al., 1950), and pharmacological agents that release tissue stores of histamine can provoke anaphylactic responses and asthmatic attacks. However, this is true of parasympathomimetic agents as well (Curry, 1947; Townley et al., 1967). Persons with bronchial

---

[*] This allergen-antibody interaction and the concomitant release of histamine can be blocked by a disodium cromoglycate, now being used successfully in the treatment of some patients with bronchial asthma (Altounyan, 1967; Cox, 1967; Jones and Blackhall, 1970; Kennedy, 1967; Orr et al., 1970).

286

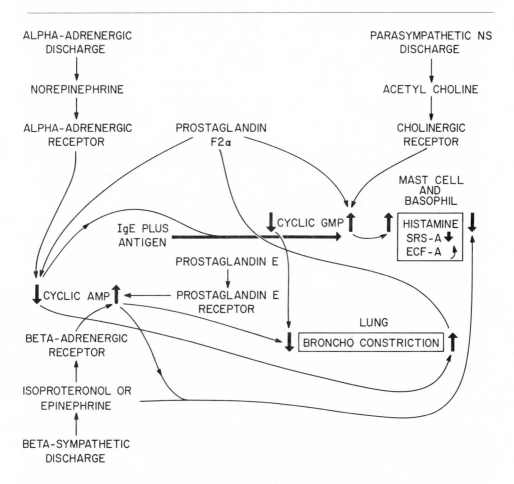

FIGURE 1 The mechanism of action by which antigen in combination with the IgE antibody acts on the surface of mast cells and basophils to release the chemical mediators of anaphylaxis. In addition the antigen-induced, IgE-dependent reaction acts upon bronchial musculature to produce bronchoconstriction. The reaction is in turn modulated by sympathetic and parasympathetic discharge, and by the prostaglandins. The antigen-antibody reaction and its modulation proceed through the medium of intracellular increases (↑) or decreases (↓) of the cyclic nucleotides to promote (↑) or inhibit (↓) bronchonconstriction and the release of the chemical mediators of anaphylaxis. Modified with permission from Kaliner and Austen (1974).

asthma seem to be abnormally reactive to nontoxic concentrations of histamine: asthmatic wheezing is regularly produced by small doses insufficient to produce hives.

Schild et al. (1951) demonstrated that a chain of isolated bronchial rings, taken during surgery from the lung of an asthmatic patient who was sensitive to pollen and dust, showed strong contractions when first exposed to pollen allergens; but on second exposure, they became desensitized to the pollen. Specimens of bronchial rings taken from patients with no history of asthma did not respond to antigen (however, normal tissue of the kind studied by Schild et al. could be induced to react to allergens following exposure to reaginic

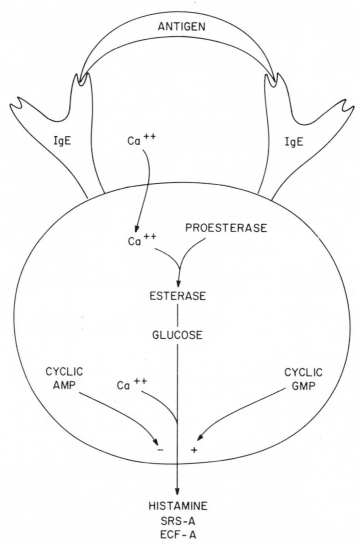

FIGURE 2 The sequence of biochemical events occasioned by the binding of two adjacent molecules of the IgE antibody by the antigen on the surface of a target cell in lung tissue. The secretion of histamine, the SRS-A and the ECF-A depends on a series of intracellular events that depend on increases of cyclic-GMP. The secretion of the chemical mediators of anaphylaxis is inhibited by increases of cyclic-AMP. Modified with permission from Kaliner and Austen (1974).

antibodies) (Goodfriend et al., 1966; Tollackson and Frick, 1966); but they did respond to the application of histamine, as did the rings taken from asthmatic patients. Pollen and dust released histamine, not only from bronchial rings but also from the lung tissue obtained from the asthmatic patient. Thus, the experiments reported by Schild and his co-workers constitute a potent argument for the proposition that bronchial constriction can occur independent of neural connections. But this does not mean that the neural control of the lung is not implicated in bronchial asthma.

Histamine is not only released from cells by antigen-IgE antibody reactions. It can also be released by neural discharge. Histamine is formed from histidine through the agency of the enzyme histidine decarboxylase. Increases in the level of the enzyme are induced by cold and other stresses, such as restraint (Levine and Senay, 1970; Schayer, 1960). Moreover, these high levels of histidine decarboxylase, and therefore of histamine, are sustained for some time following stress.

THE SRS-A

The SRS-A was first described by Kellaway and Trethewie (1940) and Brocklehurst (1956, 1970); its chemical nature is still not completely known. SRS-A is believed to be an acidic, sulfer-containing lipid (Orange et al., 1969, 1973, 1974). It causes profound long-lasting contraction of smooth muscle, including bronchial muscle. SRS-A is destroyed by an enzyme, arylsulfatase, contained in eosinophils that are attracted to the site of antigen-IgE reactions (Parish and Coombs, 1968) by the ECF-A (Kay and Austen, 1971; Kay et al., 1973). ECF-A, a peptide, is also released by the antigen-IgE reaction (Kay and Austen, 1973; Kay et al., 1971; Orange et al., 1971).

THE PAF

The PAF is released from passively sensitized human and animal lung tissue in vitro. PAF causes blood platelets to aggregate and to release serotonin. Serotonin is known to cause contraction of bronchial smooth muscle, both by its direct stimulating effects and by reflex mechanisms (Gold, 1976).

BRADYKININ

This nonapeptide causes contraction of airway smooth muscle after its release in antigen-IgE antibody reactions (Herxheimer and Streseman, 1961). It also lowers blood pressure, increases the permeability of blood vessels, and induces sweating and salivation (Rocha and Silva, 1963; Schachter, 1959). It is liberated during anaphylactic reactions in animals (Brocklehurst and Lahiri, 1961; Jonasson and Becker, 1966; Piper and Vane, 1969) and produces bronchoconstriction in man when inhaled in the form of an aerosol.

THE PROSTAGLANDINS

Other substances are released from sensitized animal or human lung tissue by allergens (Swineford, 1971). Some of these mediators have been identified and some have not. The prostaglandins (PGs) are to be found among the identified mediators. (Tauber et al., 1973).

Normal constituents of pulmonary tissue, they are released from lung preparations sensitized by allergens (Änggård, 1965; Fereira and Vane, 1967; Karim et al., 1967; Mathé

289

and Levine, 1973). A number of prostaglandins exist, but PGF2 seems to have the most relevance to a discussion of bronchial asthma. Normally it acts as a potent stimulus to bronchoconstriction and vasoconstriction (Gold, 1976; Mathé et al., 1973). Asthmatic bronchial tissue is unusually sensitive to PGF2 (Hedqvist et al., 1971). The effects of PGF2 are potentiated by parasympathetic discharge and by parasympathomimetic drugs (Hedqvist, 1973). Conversely, the catecholamines (especially epinephrine) inhibit the release of the prostaglandins and their metabolites from the lungs of guinea pigs in anaphylactic shock (Mathé and Levine, 1973). Another class of the prostaglandins (PGE1 and PGE2) in turn inhibit the release of catecholamines from a number of tissue (Brundin, 1968; Hedqvist, 1970; Kadowitz et al., 1973). The PGEs have the opposite effect of the PGFs: they dilate bronchial airways and blood vessels. Both classes of PGs are released by antigens and other stimuli, such as bradykinin and acetylcholine (Stoner et al., 1973).

The Role of the Cyclic Nucleotides in the Allergic Response and in Bronchoconstriction

The secretion of the mediators of antigen-IgE antibody reactions by mast cells and basophils is modulated by the cyclic nucleotides (Austen, 1974). The PGs, catecholamines, methylxanthines and acetylcholine—acting by separate mechanisms —alter intracellular levels of the cyclic nucleotides, thereby inhibiting or promoting secretion of the mediators by mast and other cells, and producing bronchodilation or bronchoconstriction by their actions on bronchial smooth muscle.

Increased levels of adenosine 3, 5-monophosphate (cyclic AMP) within the mast cell and basophil inhibit secretion of the mediators (Orange et al., 1971). Epinephrine and the methylxanthines prevent histamine release (Assem and Schild, 1971; Lichtenstein and Margolis, 1968) by this mechanism. Decreased levels of cyclic AMP promote secretion. Increased levels of cyclic guanosyl monophosphate (cyclic GMP) enhance the secretion of mediators brought about by antigen-antibody (IgE) interaction and by acetylcholine (Kaliner et al., 1972). Increases in the levels of cyclic GMP and decreased intracellular levels of cyclic AMP additively enhance the release of mediators from human lung tissue that is stimulated by the immune response (Gold, 1976).

The β-catecholamines and and PGE1 activate adenylate cyclase to raise cyclic AMP levels (Kaliner and Austen, 1974). Isoproterenol—the β-catecholamine—is much more potent than epinephrine in doing so, and norepinephrine is the least potent (Murad et al., 1962). Once activated, the enzyme converts adenosine triphosphate into cyclic AMP, which in turn is inactivated by means of the enzyme phosphodiesterase (Butcher and Sutherland, 1962). Theophylline inhibits the action and phosphodiesterase, so that the inactivation of cyclic AMP is retarded and its tissue concentration rises.

Increased levels of cyclic AMP promote bronchial relaxation. Epinephrine stimulates both α- and β-receptors (Furchgott, 1955). When both receptors are intact, epinephrine produces bronchial relaxation by raising intracellular levels of cyclic AMP. But when the β-receptors that customarily cause bronchial relaxation are blocked by dichlorisoproterenol, epinephrine causes bronchoconstriction (Castro de la Mata et al., 1962). In many animals, β-adrenergic receptor blockade also markedly enhances sensitivity to acetycholine, histamine, serotonin and SRS-A (Fishel et al., 1962; Innes, 1962; Townley et al., 1967).

290

Acetylcholine, bradykinin and PGF_2 produce bronchoconstriction by increasing levels of cyclic GMP (Stoner et al., 1973). But bronchoconstriction is also brought about by decreasing levels of cyclic AMP—a mechanism that is stimulated by α-catecholamines through their own receptors. (The role of α-receptors and the α-catecholamines in regulating bronchial tone in the human lung or in bronchial asthma remains uncertain.)

In summary, the secretion of the mediators of antigen-antibody reaction and the regulation of airway smooth muscle tone are modulated by a common mechanism. Increased levels of cyclic AMP or decreased levels of cyclic GMP inhibit secretion and promote bronchial relaxation. Augmented levels of cyclic GMP or decreased levels of cyclic AMP produce bronchoconstriction. Once the mediators of the immune response are secreted outside the mast cells and basophils, they act upon their individual membrane receptors on airway smooth muscle cells to activate the cyclic nucleotides and bring about bronchoconstriction.

The mechanisms of the release of the mediators of the immediate form of hypersensitivity and of bronchoconstriction have been elucidated by means of tissue culture, by challenging the passively sensitized lung tissue of animals and man, or by testing excised lung tissue of asthmatic patients. But we still do not really know the nature of the actual chemical mediators released by patients or the causes of bronchoconstriction during an asthmatic atack.

The data is seductively elegant. The conclusion is that an inhaled or ingested allergen or irritant can produce bronchoconstriction by a local process. The mediators released can produce bronchoconstriction by their direct effect on airway smooth muscle. But the matter may not be that simple.

Neural Mechanisms

In the immediate form of hypersensitivity and in experimental asthma in animals, bronchospasm and hyperventilation is mediated by vagal reflexes (Karczewski, 1962). First, Karczewski and Widdicombe (1969) showed that the intravenous injection of antigen into passively sensitized rabbits produced bronchoconstriction and hyperventilation. Cooling the cervical vagus inhibited these effects. Cutting the nerves averted them.

Then Gold and his colleagues (1972) demonstrated that the exposure of dogs to allergens to which they were sensitive raised airway resistance that could be blocked either by afferent or efferent vagal blockade. When the allergen was instilled into one lung only, bilateral bronchoconstriction was produced. Vagal blockade on the challenged side eliminated the bronchoconstriction on both sides. This work implies that allergens, by stimulating sensory receptors in the lung, increase reflex vagal activity to cause bronchoconstriction.

Anaphylactic shock is also accompanied by increases in vagal afferent and efferent activity in the guinea pig. Karczewski (1962) found that the afferent activity was caused by stimulation of the pulmonary stretch receptors brought about by bronchoconstriction. The afferent activity gave rise, in turn, to an increase in efferent activity, thus causing further bronchoconstriction. It is therefore possible that histamine or other mediators may stimulate receptors in the lung to increase vagal afferent activity.

Gold's observations imply the participation of a reflex mechanism mediated by the brain stem. Efferent vagal discharge contributes to bronchoconstriction presumably after receptors in the lung are stimulated by the allergen. The results of these experiments strongly suggest that bronchoconstriction in bronchial asthma cannot only be explained by the local effect of histamine and other mediators on the antigen-antibody reaction on bronchiolar smooth muscle. Reflex mechanisms are probably also responsible for bronchoconstriction in asthma induced by exercise, or when the nose or nasal sinuses are stimulated by odors, nonallergenic dusts, irritants, or polyp formation (Wells et al., 1960). In the latter situation, the first and fifth nerve are the afferent arc of the reflex, and the vagus nerve is the efferent arc.

Increased vagal efferent activity can in turn interact with the local release of the mediators of the immune response to produce mucous secretion, cough, and hyperventilation, so characteristic of the acute asthmatic attack (Gold, 1976; Goodman and Gilman, 1965). Chronic asthmatic attacks may by sustained by histamine release, abnormal patterns of breathing, and sustained irritation of the bronchial mucosa and other stimuli to bronchoconstriction (Gold, 1976).

At the present time, the pathogenesis of extrinsic asthma is explained on the basis of the local release of the mediators of the immune response that directly cause bronchoconstriction and also stimulate rapidly adapting receptors in the lung to produce reflex bronchoconstriction.

The modern explanation of extrinsic asthma omits to mention that the asthmatic patient may need to be predisposed to bronchoconstriction. Only the predisposed person responds to the release of the mediators of the immune response in the lung by further bronchoconstriction. In addition, the modern explanation does not make room for the observation that psychological factors interact with allergic and infectious ones: in short, we still do not understand how psychological factors could bring about bronchoconstriction.

In the recent past, the suggestion was made that the predisposition to bronchoconstriction was due to a relative imbalance between those forces that produce bronchodilation—the β-adrenergic mechanisms—and bronchoconstriction—the α-adrenergic and parasympathetic mechanisms. A relative deficiency of β-adrenergic discharge would bias the bronchi to constriction. The deficiency might be caused by diminished tonic discharge, neurotransmitter release, by a deficiency at the β-receptor or at the biochemical level (Szentivanyi, 1968). Specifically, the cyclic AMP response to transmitter release might be deficient, or the balance between cyclic AMP and cyclic GMP might be altered.

Although it is known that tendency to bronchoconstriction is enhanced by a variety of factors that include the chemical mediators of the allergic response, chemicals, infections, irritants, increased sympathetic or parasympathetic discharge, and psychological ones, there is ample evidence that in patients with allergic rhinitis, β-adrenergic blockade enhances bronchial reactivity to inhaled antigens (Ouellette and Reed, 1967), to histamine (Fishel et al., 1962), and to methacholine (McGready et al., 1968). Blockade markedly aggravates clinical asthma (McNeill, 1964; Meier et al., 1953), and produces bronchoconstriction, as measured by pulmonary function tests (McNeill and Ingram, 1966; Sly et al., 1967). However, in two other studies, Zaid and his co-workers (1966,

1968) found that β-adrenergic blockade by propranolol, before and after challenge with histamine and methacholine chloride, or with exercise, did not significantly increase bronchoconstriction (as measured by changes in FEV in one second) in normal adults or in patients with allergic rhinitis. This procedure did enhance bronchoconstriction in patients with bronchial asthma. The authors concluded from these findings that, although the consequences of the blockade are demonstrable in patients with bronchial asthma, β-adrenergic blockade is not the "cause" of the illness, because it does not produce asthmatic attacks in normal persons.

The results of Zaid's studies—specifically the failure to produce wheezing and other signs of asthma in normal persons—constitute a strong argument against the hypothesis that β-adrenergic deficiency or blockade is a necessary condition for asthmatic attacks to occur.

Other suggestions about the predisposition to bronchoconstriction in asthma have been made: a deficiency in available epinephrine concentration at pulmonary receptors may be due to increased turnover or reuptake of the neurotransmitter (Mathé and Levine, 1971; Mathé et al., 1974a, b; Mathé and Knapp, 1969, 1971; Mathé and Levine, 1974). The decreased availability of epinephrine would lead to increased bronchoconstriction and to increased antibody formation (Benner et al., 1968; Hadden et al., 1970; Watson et al., 1973).

An explanation is also needed for the interaction of psychological factors with immunological and reflex vagal mechanisms in initiating asthmatic attacks.

The Brain and Anaphylaxis

Throughout this chapter the question of the interaction of psychological and allergic and physiological factors in bronchial asthma has been posed. No final answer to this question can be given. Yet it is an interesting question: briefly stated, it asks whether the brain, as the regulator of many bodily systems, also regulates the specific allergic response that characterizes bronchial asthma.

In recent years, a beginning has been made to answer this question. Lesions of various hypothalamic or brain-stem sites can protect against anaphylaxis produced by histamine in animals (Freedman and Fenichel, 1958). Lesions of the tuber cinereum and of the anterior hypothalamus protect the rat or the guinea pig against anaphylactic shock. Posterior hypothalamic lesions in guinea pigs enhance shock induced by histamine. Circulating antibodies are also reduced by anterior hypothalamic lesions (Stein et al., 1976; Szentivanyi, 1968).

These findings suggest that the most-extreme form of the immediate form of hypersensitivity, anaphylaxis, may be attenuated or enhanced by lesions of certain brain areas. Only future investigation will determine the mechanisms that are responsible for these phenomena. The unraveling of these mechanisms should provide profound insights to our understanding of bronchial asthma.

THE PATHOGENESIS OF INTRINSIC ASTHMA

Major progress has been made in elucidating the pathogenetic mechanisms of extrinsic asthma. The same statement cannot be made for intrinsic asthma in which skin reactivity to injected antigens cannot be demonstrated and the pathogenetic immunological mechanisms described for extrinsic asthma do not take place. Patients with the intrinsic form of bronchial asthma have no family history of allergy. They are usually older. Their symptoms are often perennial. The first attack of asthma occurs in some patients after a virus infection (Prigal, 1960), such as measles (Peshkin, 1963), influenza (Hajos, 1961), and primary atypical pneumonia (Fagerberg, 1958). In other patients—especially middle-aged ones—an abnormal sensitivity to drugs such as aspirin and indomethacin, occurs. These drugs may precipitate attacks of wheezing. They probably do not do so by immunological mechanisms but rather by inhibiting prostaglandin synthesis. Aspirin inhibits PGE synthesis (Stoner et al., 1973; Weissman et al., 1971).

Many middle-aged patients with intrinsic asthma have a chronic bronchitis with intermittent spasms of wheezing. They might better be labeled as having "asthmatic bronchitis" (Gold, 1976; Meneely et al., 1962). The pathogenetic mechanisms of asthmatic bronchitis are still not known, although many have been proposed.

The smooth muscle of the airways of some patients with bronchitis and healthy individuals who have had viral infections of the respiratory tree respond to a variety of nonantigenic stimuli, irritants, parasympathomimetic drugs and bradykinin with bronchoconstriction. The patients wheeze, cough, have an increased respiratory rate and dyspnea when their bronchi are stimulated. The smooth muscle of airways of patients with chronic bronchitis may be sensitized to respond to acetylcholine, methacholine chloride or by virus, bacteria or bacterial endotoxins (Gold, 1976; Ouellette and Reed, 1965; Szentivanyi and Fishel, 1968).

Gold (1976) has suggested that in intrinsic asthma the threshold of sensory receptors in the airways may be lowered, or they may be partially depolarized to produce reflex bronchoconstriction. Infection, immune mechanisms and their products, inflammation, or damage may alter the function of the receptors. As a result, the various stimuli that may incite asthmatic attacks in patients with intrinsic asthma or bronchitis, or after a viral disease trigger bronchoconstriction. The bronchoconstriction can be prevented by atropine, implying that it is mediated by the vagus nerve, or by hexamethonium.

SUMMARY AND CONCLUSIONS

Although the data are not yet complete, the evidence reviewed in this chapter would lead one to conclude that bronchial asthma is a heterogeneous disease (Aas, 1969). For this reason alone, any unified statement about the predisposing, initiating, and sustaining factors in bronchial asthma can only be tentative.

Within the limits imposed by this injuction, a tentative conclusion can be reached that without a tendency to bronchoconstriction there can be no asthma. Sherman (1967) subscribes to this idea. He believes that bronchoconstriction is "conditioned" by extrinsic allergens or respiratory infection; others maintain that the tendency to bronchoconstriction is fundamental and that infection, allergenic-reaginic antibody interactions, and psychosocial events, as well as many other factors (cold, smoke, odors, exercise, etc.) elicit bronchoconstriction (Prigal, 1960; Wright, 1965). Proponents of the first hypothesis believe that allergy and infection initiate bronchial asthma and, in conjunction with psychological factors, bring about its recurrences once bronchoconstriction has been "conditioned."

The evidence accumulated in recent years seems to indicate that, essentially, the second hypothesis is correct, but it has been further refined. Specifically, the data suggest that although emotional factors are rarely sufficient in themselves, they may initiate bronchial asthma in persons who are biologically predisposed to the disease (Rees, 1964; Wright, 1965). Once the disease has been initiated, recurrent attacks may also be triggered by allergens or infections. Or, if allergens or infections initiate the disease, psychological factors may antecede recurrences.

Three main categories of predisposing and initiating factors (i.e., allergenic, infectious, and psychological) interact in bronchial asthma (Prigal, 1960). Sherman's contention (1967) that there are only two such categories—allergenic and infectious—is not supported by the findings reviewed in this chapter. For example, the interesting question of why some persons known to be hypersensitive to an allergen do not have an attack of 20 to 30 years or even longer, has not yet been solved, and would not be amenable to solution on the basis of Sherman's hypothesis. It is likely that in such predisposd persons an attack could be precipitated by a personal crisis. Clearly, then, as Rees (1964), Williams (1959a, b), and Williams et al. (1958) have concluded in the majority of people (70 percent), attacks are precipitated by interactions between the allergic predisposition and psychological events, or between infection and allergy. It looks as if exposure to an allergen per se does not necessarily lead to disease. "Candidates" for bronchial asthma must have the capacity to form IgE antibodies on exposure to the allergen, but not all individuals who have that capacity develop the disease.

Although bronchial asthma probably cannot occur without the tendency to bronchoconstriction, the extrinsic form of the disease cannot be explained without also postulating that the IgE antibodies are fixed in the lung. In those related diseases—atopic eczema and allergic rhinitis—the antibodies are fixed in the skin and nose, respectively. When the three diseases occur together, the antibodies presumably are fixed in all three locations. If the three diseases occur in sequence, as so often occurs in children, the antibodies are first fixed in the skin, later in the nose, and finally in the lung. The reasons for their location in one part of the body at one time and another part at some other time, remain unknown.

No IgE antibodies can be detected in the blood serum in many patients with bronchial asthma. Either the methods for their detection are too insensitive, or the antibodies are fixed to mast cells and basophils in tissue and do not appear in the serum, or they are not formed at all. In many patients, the tendency to bronchoconstriction persists throughout their lives, and the recurrence of asthma after a variable period of years is brought about by a pulmonary infection with a virus, often in combination with some change, or personal crisis, in their lives.

There are two major reasons why so much remains in the study of bronchial asthma. First, the data published to date have been based on retrospective clinical studies. Second, much of the work presented is "correlation-oriented." Correlations are sought, for example, between skin tests and the disease, or between various indicators of increased airway resistance and parental attitudes. Although such correlations are of obvious interest, we also need to know the direction of the correlations. We need to know not only whether early childhood experience is related to bronchial lability, but how it is related, if, in fact, a relationship exists. Is the lability an inherited characteristic that, due to the fact that it is continually induced by crying, subsequently becomes a conditioned response to all kinds of other stimuli, such as the release of chemical mediators by allergenic antibody interactions? Or is the lability an acquired characteristic caused by infection, immune responses, or life experience? Or, conversely, does bronchial lability influence the child's life experience in some way?

The tendency to bronchoconstriction is relative and is not present to the same degree in all patients. Actually, patients with bronchial asthma manifest wide variations in bronchoconstriction in response to exercise (Jones, 1966; Pinkerton, 1967) and to inhaled substances such as histamine and acetylcholine (Felanca and Itkin, 1966; Makino, 1966). Moreover, this distribution may not be due to one intrinsic defect, such as adrenergic receptor blockade. Rather, the tendency to bronchoconstriction may reflect variations in the balance between bronchoconstriction and bronchodilation, due to interactions between sympathetic and parasympathetic effectors, which may be more or less biased to produce a spectrum of bronchoconstrictor tendencies.

This summary merely underlines the fact that much about bronchial asthma remains unanswered, despite the progress that has been made. Without the tendency to bronchoconstriction, bronchial asthmatic attacks probably will not occur. We do not know how this tendency comes about—whether in fact it is due to a genetic defect in the regulation of the tone of the bronchiolar muscles or due to an acquired defect. The mechanism of the bronchoconstrictor tendency has not been conclusively worked out (the several alternative suggestions were reviewed in this chapter). In the meantime, the mechanism of the immediate form of hypersensitivity has been worked out with elegance and in detail. The chemical nature of the reaginic antibodies has been determined. The mechanism of the interaction between these IgE antibodies and the allergen on the cell membrane of mast cells and basophils has been described. Specific mediators of their interaction have been identified. Specific chemical substances are now being used therapeutically, either because they prevent the attachment of the IgE antibody to mast cells, or they prevent the interaction between the IgE and allergen and, therefore, the release of the mediators. The chemical mediators released by the interaction of the IgE and allergen can excite bronchoconstriction and mucus production. They may also stimulate a vagal reflex that further promotes bronchoconstriction, and may inhibit catecholamine release in the lung. Catecholamine release may also be diminished by some prostaglandins, one of which is an extremely potent bronchoconstrictor. Conversely, epinephrine inhibits the release of histamine and the prostaglandins.

Once the asthmatic attack has started, a number of neural reflexes are set into motion which tend to prolong bronchoconstriction. Other reflexes are probably responsible for starting an asthmatic attack when the predisposed person exercises or his nasal passages are irritated by odors, smoke or nonallergenic dusts.

But, we still do not know the mechanisms whereby virus infection of the lung or psychological arousal bring about asthmatic attacks. Yet, it is clear that various combinations of psychological arousal, infection, and allergy interact to initiate asthmatic attacks. In some patients, infection or allergy may play a predominant role, and emotional factors a subsidiary one; in others the roles are reversed. In any event, it is evident that the term "psychogenic asthma" has no validity. Psychological factors may initiate or produce recurrences of asthmatic attacks only in persons who are biologically predisposed to the disease (Rackemann, 1958). As Pinkerton and Weaver (1970) have pointed out, it is entirely legitimate to study patients with bronchial asthma by psychological and social tools, but it is not legitimate to claim sufficiency for psychological and social factors. The factors are necessary for the development of the illness in many persons, in the same way that it is necessary for some to have a tendency to form reaginic antibodies or all persons to be predisposed to bronchoconstriction. This does not mean that the influence of psychological factors rests on the presence of a specific psychological conflict. Many conflicts may be mediated through emotional states, which, in the presence of immune mechanisms and the disposition to bronchoconstriction, produce the attack. When the role of psychological and social factors is thus conceptualized, bronchial asthma can be truly defined as a psychosomatic disorder. The biological predisposition is the necessity; the life crisis is the chance event.

Patients prone to asthma are psychologically predisposed to life crises, not by virtue of their personalities but by virtue of their conflicts, which reflect an arrest in their psychological development. In general, conflicts stemming from exaggerated dependency needs are central to current formulations concerning the role of psychological factors in the predisposition to bronchial asthma. However, we lack definitive knowledge of the role of these conflicts and their emotional concomitants in the etiology and pathogenesis of the disease. In the absence of predictive studies of persons at risk for this disease, one cannot lightly assume that the identified psychological conflicts always precede the onset of disease. Conflict, and consequent arrests in development or regression, may occur as a result of the disease, or such conflicts may even occur independent of the disease.

In about one-half of asthmatic patients the dependency conflicts take the form of the unconscious wish to be engulfed and protected. The threat or actuality of separation may then mobilize the cry for the mother which may not be fully expressed, and which is associated with the asthmatic attack. In other patients the fear of separation is heightened by fears of destructive or cruel impulses toward the person who threatens the separation. These impulses produce profound conflict and are deeply buried, and often defended against by passive-dependent and masochistic traits.

In other asthmatic patients the wish to be engulfed and protected may cause conflict and be expressed as a fear of fusion with another person. Such patients, therefore, avoid the relationship with the person upon whom they would depend. Other conflicts also occur in these patients and express themselves as concerns about drowning, over water, and with odors. The frightening symptoms of asthma may color these psychological features, which nonetheless often seem to be determined by experiences antedating the onset of the disease.

The conflicts described seem to be aroused in many patients by the threat of separation. In other patients the symptoms of the disease rapidly abate on separation, probably because the fear of closeness is greater than the fear of separation, or the human interaction between the asthmatic child and his parent is marked by animosity, rejection, or cruelty.

When the conflict is activated, various forms of emotional arousal occur—anger, depression, excitement, or crying. In some, these emotions are fully expressed; in others they are partly inhibited. The brain mechanisms that mediate the emotional arousal and lead to bronchoconstriction are completely unknown.

Actually, it has not yet been determined whether changes in emotional states, ranging from arousal to depression, are linearly related to bronchoconstriction, or whether they are concomitants of bronchoconstriction or independent of it. There is a strong possibility that such changes are only concomitant events related to central neural states.

It is not necessary in all instances to postulate that brain mechanisms translate emotional arousal into bronchoconstriction. Crying may cause nasal congestion and activate the nasobronchial reflex to produce bronchoconstriction. The unhappy child may sob or sigh; the change in rate and rhythm of breathing may activate pulmonary reflexes ending in bronchiolar narrowing. The aroused or excited child may dance or run and incite bronchoconstriction and the asthmatic attack.

Alternative ways of conceptualizing the psychophysiological relationship between emotional arousal and asthmatic attacks, therefore, exist. Arousal often occurs when personal relationships change or are fraught with conflict, to which the asthmatic patient is sensitive. The sensitivity stems from arrests in personality development that have largely been ascribed to the attitudes of the child's parents. These parental attitudes are not uniform ones. Some mothers are benign with their children, whereas others are rejecting, cruel, unsympathetic, or overprotective. These attitudes often but not invariably antedate the child's asthma. They are, therefore, neither necessary nor sufficient to explain the arrests in the child's psychological development. The attitudes toward the child may in some instances have more to do with the child's social maladjustment to schoolwork and peers than with the illness itself.

Therefore, we do not really know the causes leading to arrest in the child's psychological development. Alternative explanations should be sought. One might ask whether both the psychological and physiological characteristics of asthmatic patients have a common origin (Prigal, 1960). Is there a parallel or a common disposition in the areas of immune responses and personality development, which is reflected, on the one hand, in the tendency to form reaginic antibodies and, on the other, the tendency to manifest arrests in development, or are these related in some other way (Wright, 1965)? The solutions to these questions must await further research.

Current formulations regarding the role of psychological factors in bronchial asthma leave other questions unanswered as well. The finding that more boys than girls develop this disease in childhood (the ratio being 2:1 to 3:1) has not been explained (Purcell, 1965) on the basis of personality development; nor can it yet be ascribed to endocrine, allergic, or other maturational factors. Nor has the fact that the ratio falls to one in adulthood been explained.

We might also ask why from 30 to 45 percent of those asthmatic patients who develop the disease in childhood outgrow it. Perhaps these children are able to resolve their dependency conflicts; or the disease may abate if the child or adolescent leaves home (Lamont, 1963). Clearly, further studies of such patients would enhance our understanding of the interrelationship of social, psychological, immunological, infectious, and other variables—which is the overriding goal of psychosomatic research on this disease.

298

REFERENCES

Aas, K. 1961. Nasal eosinophilia in so-called bacterial hypersensitivity in asthmatic children: a preliminary report. *Acta Paediatr. Scand.* 50:1.

——— 1965. Modern concepts of allergology. *Acta Paediatr. Scand* 54:474.

——— 1966. Studies of hypersensitivity to fish: a clinical study. *Int. Arch. Allergy Appl. Immunol.* 29:346.

——— 1969. Allergic asthma in childhood. *Arch. Dis. Child.* 44:1.

Abramson, H. A. 1963. Some aspects of the psychodynamics of intractable asthma in children. In *The Asthmatic Child,* edited by H. I. Schneer. New York: Hoeber.

Adkinson, J. 1920. The behavior of bronchial asthma as an inherited character. *Genetics* 1:363.

Alcock, T. 1960. Some personality characteristics of asthmatic children. *B. J. Med. Psychol.* 33:133.

Alexander, A. B., Miklich, D. R., and Hershkoff, H. 1972. The immediate effects of systematic relaxation training on peak expiratory flow rates in asthmatic children. *Psychosom. Med.* 34:388.

Alexander, F. 1950. *Psychomatic Medicine.* New York: Norton.

——— and Visotsky, H. 1955. Psychosomatic study of a case of asthma. *Psychosom. Med.* 17:470.

———, French, T. M., and Pollock, G. H. 1968. *Psychosomatic Specificity.* Chicago: University of Chicago Press.

Altounyan, R. E. C. 1967. Inhibition of experimental asthma by a new compound—disodium cromoglycate Intal. *Acta Allergol.* (Kbh.) 22:487.

Änggård, E. 1965. The isolation and determination of prostaglandin in lungs of sheep, guinea-pig, monkey and man. *Biochem. Pharmacol.* 14:1507.

Appel, J., and Rosen, S. R. 1951. Psychosomatic disorders in psychoses. *Psychosom. Med.* 13:314.

Arbeiter, H. I. 1967. How prevalent is allergy among United States school children? *Clin. Pediatr.* (Phila.) 6:140.

Archer, R. K. 1963. *The Eosinophil Leukocyte.* Oxford: Blackwell.

Assem, E. S. K., and Schild, H. O. 1971. Inhibition of the anaphylactic mechanism by sympathomimetic amines. *Int. Arch. Allergy Appl. Immunol.* 40:567.

Austen, K. F. 1965. Histamine and other mediators of allergic reactions. In *Immunological Diseases,* edited by M. Samter. Boston: Little, Brown.

Austen, K. F., and Lichtenstein, L. M. 1973. *Asthma: Physiology, Immuno-pharmacology, and Treatment.* New York: Academic.

Austen, K. F. 1974. Reaction mechanisms in the release of mediators of immediate hypersensitivity from human lung tissue. *Fed. Proc.* 33:2256.

Baagoe, K. H. 1936. On the occurrence of allergic illnesses. *Hospitalstid.* 79:888.

Bacon, C. L. 1956. The role of aggression in the asthmatic attack. *Psychoanal. Q.* 25:309.

Baraff, A. S., and Cunningham, A. P. 1965. Asthmatic and normal children. *J.A.M.A.* 192:13.

Barendreght, J. T. 1957. A cross-validation study of the hypothesis of psychosomatic specificity. *J. Psychosom. Res.* 2:109.

Bartosch, R., Feldberg, W., and Nagel, E. 1932. Das Freiwerden eines histaminähnlichen Stoffes bei der Anaphylaxie des Meerschweinchens. *Arch. Physiol.* (Frankf.) 230:129.

Bastiaans, J., and Groen, J., 1954. Psychogenesis and Psychotherapy of Bronchial Asthma. In *Modern Trends in Psychosomatic Medicine,* edited by D. O'Neill. London: Butterworth.

Bates, D. V. 1952. Impairment of respiratory function in bronchial asthma. *Clin. Sci. Mol. Med.* 11:203.

Benner, M. H., Enta, T., Lockey, S., Jr., Makino, S., and Reed, C. E. 1968. Immunosuppressive effect of epinephrine and adjuvant effect of beta-adrenergic blockade. *J. Allergy Clin. Immunol.* 41:110.

Berdal, P. 1952. Serologic investigations on the edema fluid from nasal polyps. *J. Allergy Clin. Immunol.* 23:11.

Berg, T., and Johansson, S. G. O. 1969. IgE concentrations in children with atopic disease. *Int. Arch. Allergy Appl. Immunol.* 36:219.

Billings, E. G. 1947. Dynamic and therapeutic features of 17 cases of so-called psychogenic asthma. *J. Nerv. Ment. Dis.* 105:81.

Block, J., Jennings, P. H., Harvey, E., and Simpson, E. 1964. Interaction between allergic potential and psychopathology in childhood asthma. *Psychosom. Med.* 26:307.

Bono, J., and Levitt, P. 1964. Relationship of infantile atopic dermatitis to asthma and other respiratory allergies. *Ann. Allergy* 22:72.

Bostock, J. 1956. Asthma: a synthesis involving primitive speech, organism, and insecurity. *J. Ment. Sci.* 102:559.

Bowen, R. 1953. Allergy in identical twins. *J. Allergy Clin. Immunol.* 24:236.

Brocklehurst, W. E. 1960. The release of histamine and formation of a slow reacting substance (SRS-A) during anaphylactic shock. *J. Physiol.* (Lond.) 151:416.

Brocklehurst, W. E. 1956. A slow reacting substance in anaphylaxis, SRS-A. In *Ciba Foundation Symposium on Histamine,* edited by C. E. W. Wolstenholme and C. M. O'Connor. London: Churchill.

———— 1968. Pharmacological mediators of hypersensitivity reactions. In *Clinical Aspects of Immunology,* 2nd ed., edited by P. G. H. Gell and R. R. A. Coombs. Oxford: Blackwell.

———— 1970. The role of slow reacting substance in asthma. *Adv. Drug Res.* 5:109.

———— and Lahiri, S. C. 1961. The production of bradykinin in anaphylaxis. *J. Physiol.* (Lond.) 160:15P.

Broder, I., Barlow, P. P., and Horton, R. J. M. 1962a. The epidemiology of asthma and hay fever in a total community, Techumseh, Michigan. I. Description of study and general findings. *J. Allergy Clin. Immunol.* 33:513.

————, ————, and ———— 1962b. The epidemiology of asthma and hay fever in a total community, Tecumseh, Michigan. II. The relationship between asthma and hay fever. *J. Allergy Clin. Immunol.* 33:524.

Brown, E. A., and Colombo, N. J. 1954. The asthmagenic effect of odors, smells and fumes. *Ann. Allergy* 12:14.

———— and Goitein, E. L. 1943. Aspects of mind in asthma and allergy, comparative personality studies. *J. Nerv. Ment. Dis.* 98:638.

Brundin, J. 1968. The effect of prostaglandin E1 on the response of the rabbit oviduct to hypograstric nerve stimulation. *Acta Physiol. Scand.* 73:54.

Butcher, R. W., and Sutherland, E. W. 1962. Adenosine 3',5'-phosphate in biological materials. *J. Biol. Chem.* 237:1244.

Cardell, B. S., and Pearson, R. S. B. 1959. Death in asthmatics. *Thorax* 14:341.

Castro de la Mata, R., Penna, M., and Aviado, D. M. 1962. Reversal of sympathomimetic bronchodilatation by dichlorisoproterenol. *J. Pharmacol. Exp. Ther.* 135:197.

Catsch, A. 1943. Konstitution und Allergische Diathese. *Ztschr. f. Mensch. Vererb. u. Konstitutionslehre* 26:218.

Chessick, R. D., Kurland, M. L., Husted, R. M., and Diamond, M. A. 1960. The asthmatic narcotic addict. *Psychosomatics* 1:36.

Chia-mo Wan, W., and Stein, M. 1968. Effects of vagal stimulation on the mechanical properties of the lungs of guinea pigs. *Psychosom. Med.* 30:846.

300

Chobat, R., Spadavecchia, R., and DeSanctis, R. M. 1939. Intelligence rating and emotional pattern of allergic children. *Am. J. Dis. Child.* 57:831.

Christiansen, B. 1965 *Studies in Respiration and Personality.* Oslo: Institute of Social Research.

Clausen, J. 1951. Respiration movement in normal, neurotic and psychotic subjects. *Acta Psychiatr. Scand.* [Suppl. 68], p. 1.

Colldahl, H. 1967. The importance of inhalation tests in the etiological diagnosis of allergic diseases of the bronchi and in the evaluation of the effects of specific hyposensitization treatment. *Acta allergol.* (Kbh.) 22[Suppl. 8], 7.

Connell, J. T. 1970. Allergic rhinitis—human experimental model. *N. Y. State J. Med.* 70:1751.

Cooke, R. A. (editor). 1947. *Allergy in Theory and Practice.* Philadelphia: Saunders.

Coolidge, J. C. 1956. Asthma in mother and child as a special form of intercommunication. *Am. J. Orthopsychiatr.* 26:165.

Cox. J. S. G. 1967. Disodium cromoglycate (FPL 670) (Intal); a specific inhibitor of reaginic antibody-antigen mechanisms. *Nature* 216:1328.

Creak, M., and Stephen, J. M. 1958. The psychological aspects of asthma in children. *Pediatr. Clin. N. Am.* 5:731.

Curran, W. S., and Goldman, G. 1961. The incidence of immediately reacting allergy skin tests in a "normal" adult population. *Ann. Intern. Med.* 55:777.

Curry, J. J. 1947. Comparative action of acetyl-beta-methylcholine and histamine on the respiratory tract in normals, patients with hay fever, and subjects with bronchial asthma. *J. Clin. Invest.* 26:430.

Dale, J. H. 1920. Conditions which are conducive to the production of shock by histamine. *Br. J. Exp. Pathol.* 1:103.

Dawson, B., Horobin, G., Illsley, R., and Mitchell, R. 1969. A survey of childhood asthma in Aberdeen. *Lancet* 1:827.

de Araujo, G., Dudley, D. L., and Van Asdel, P. P., Jr. 1972. Psychosocial assets and severity of chronic asthma. *J. Allergy Clin. Immunol.* 50:257.

Dees, S. 1945. Interrelationships of allergic and psychiatric factors in allergic children. *Proc. Inst. Child. Res. Clin., Woods Schls.* 12:59.

Dekker, E., and Groen, J. 1956. Reproducible psychogenic attacks of asthma: a laboratory study. *J. Psychosom. Res.* 1:58.

———, Pelser, H. E., and Groen, J. 1957. Conditioning as a cause of asthmatic attacks. *J. Psychosom. Res.* 2:97.

———, Barendreght, J. T., and De Vries, K. 1961. Allergy and neurosis in asthma. *J. Psychosom. Res.* 5:83.

Dekker, H. 1934. Gibt es ein "asthma nervosum"? *Münch. Med. Wochenschr.* 81:323.

Deutsch, F. 1953. Basic psychoanalytic principles in psychosomatic disorders. *Acta Psychotherapeutica* I:102.

Diedrichs, W., and Lübbers, P. 1955. Das Mehlasthma als Berufskrankheit. *Zbl. Arbeitsmed.* 5:189.

Doust, J. W. L., and Leigh, D. 1953. Studies on the physiology of awareness: interrelationships of emotions, life situations and anoxemia in patients with bronchial asthma. *Psychosom. Med.* 15:292.

D'Silva, S. L., and Lewis, A. F. 1961. The measurement of bronchoconstriction *in vivo. J. Physiol.* (Lond.) 157:611.

Dubo, S., McLean, J. R., Ching, A. Y. T., Wright, H. L., Kauffman, P. E., and Sheldon, J. M. 1961. A study of relations between family situation, bronchial asthma, and personal adjustment in children. *J. Pediatr.* 59:402.

Dudley, D. L., Martin, C. J., and Holmes, T. H. 1964a. Psychophysiologic studies of pulmonary ventilation. *Psychosom. Med.* 26:645.

———, Holmes, T. H., Martin, C. J., and Ripely, H. S. 1964b. Changes in respiration associated with hypnotically induced emotion, pain, and exercise. *Psychosom. Med.* 26:46.

Dudley, D. L. 1969. *Psychophysiology of Respiration in Health and Disease.* New York: Appleton-Century-Crofts.

Dunbar, H. F. 1938. Psychoanalytic notes relating to syndromes of asthma and hay fever. *Psychoanal. Q.* 7:25.

——— 1943. *Psychosomatic Diagnosis.* New York: Hoeber.

Edfors-Lubs, M.-L. 1971. Allergy in 7000 twin pairs. *Acta Allergol. (Kbh).* 26:249.

Edgren, G. 1943. Prognose und Erblichkeitsmomente bei Ekzema infantum. *Acta Paediatr. Scand.* 30:Suppl. 2.

Edwards, G. 1960. Hypnotic treatment of asthma. *Br. Med. J.* 2:492.

Engel, G. L. 1967. A psychological setting of somatic disease: The 'Giving Up—Given Up' Complex. *Proc. R. Soc. Med.* 60:553.

Fagerberg, E. 1958. Studies in bronchial asthma: IV: A comparative examination between patients with endogenous and exogenous bronchial asthma respectively with regard to the part played by infection for the first onset of the complaint. *Açta Allergol.* (Kbh.). 12:17.

Faulkner, W. B. 1941. Influence of suggestion on size of bronchial lumen; bronchoscopic study and report of one case. *Northwest. Med.* 40:367.

Feinberg, S. M., and Aries, P. L. 1932. Asthma from food odors. *J.A.M.A.* 98:2280.

Feingold, B. F., Gorman, F. J., Singer, M. T., and Schlesinger, K. 1962. Psychological studies of allergic women. *Psychosom. Med.* 24:195.

———, Singer, M. T., Freeman, E. H., and Deskins, A. 1966. Psychological variables in allergic disease: a critical appraisal of methodology. *J. Allergy Clin. Immunol.* 38:143.

Felanca, A. B., and Itkin, I. H. 1966. Studies with quantitative challenge technique. I: Curve of dose response to acetyl-beta-methylcholine in patients with asthma of known and unknown origin, hay fever subjects and non-atopic volunteers. *J. Allergy Clin. Immunol.* 37:223.

Fenichel, O. 1945. *The Psychoanalytic Theory of Neurosis.* New York: Norton.

Fereira, S. H., and Vane, J. B. 1967. Prostaglandins: Their disappearance from and release into the circulation. *Nature* 216:868.

Fine, R. 1963. The personality of the asthmatic child. In *The Asthmatic Child,* edited by H. I. Schneer. New York: Hoeber.

Finesinger, J. E., and Mazick, S. G. 1940. The respiratory response of psychoneurotic patients to ideational and sensory stimuli. *Am. J. Psychiatry.* 97:27.

Fink, G., and Schneer, H. I. 1963. Psychiatric evaluation of adolescent asthmatics. In *The Asthmatic Child,* edited by H. I. Schneer. New York: Hoeber.

Fishbein, G. M. 1963. Perceptual modes and asthmatic symptoms. *J. Consult. Clin. Psychol.* 27:54.

Fishel, C. W., Szentivanyi, A., and Talmage, D. W. 1962. Sensitization and desensitization of mice to histamine and serotonin by neurohumors. *J. Immunol.* 88:8.

Fitzelle, G. T. 1959. Personality factors and certain attitudes toward child rearing among parents of asthmatic children. *Psychosom. Med.* 21:208.

Flensborg, E. W. 1945. Prognosis for bronchial asthma arisen in infancy after nonspecific treatment hitherto applied. *Acta Paediatr.* 33:4.

Frandsen, S. 1958. Bronchial asthma among school children in Copenhagen. *Acta Allergol.* (Kbh.) 12:341.

Frankland, A. W. 1968. The pathogenesis of asthma, hay fever and atopic diseases. In *Clinical Aspects of Immunology,* 2nd ed., edited by P. G. H. Gell and R. R. A. Coombs. Oxford: Blackwell.

302

Franks, C. M., and Leigh, D. 1959. The theoretical and experimental applications of a conditioning model to a consideration of bronchial asthma in man. *J. Psychosom. Res.* 4:88.

Frazier, C. A. 1961. Asthma in patients whose syptoms began before six years of age. *Ann. Allergy* 19:1146.

Freedman, D. X., and Fenichel, G. 1958. Effect of midbrain lesions in experimental allergy. *Arch. Neurol. Psych.* 79:164.

Freedman, D. X., Redlich, F. C., and Igersheimer, W. W. 1956. Psychosis and allergy: experimental approach. *Am. J. Psychiatry* 112:873.

Freeman, E. H., Feingold, B. F., Schlesinger, K., and Gorman, F. J. 1964. Psychologic variables in allergic disorders: a review. *Psychosom. Med.* 26:543.

————, Gorman, F. J., Singer, M. T., Affelder, J. T., and Feingold, B. F. 1967. Personality variables and allergic skin reactivity: a cross-validation study. *Psychosom. Med.* 29:313.

Freeman, G. L., and Johnson, S. 1964. Allergic diseases in adolescents. *Am. J. Dis. Child.* 107:549.

French, T. M. 1939. Psychogenic factors in Asthma. *Am. J. Psychiatry* 96:1,87.

———— and Alexander, F. 1941. *Psychogenic Factors in Bronchial Asthma.* Psychosomatic Medicine Monograph 4. Washington, D.C.: National Research Council.

Fry, J. 1961. *The Catarrhal Child.* London: Butterworth.

Funkenstein, D. H. 1950a. Psychophysiologic relationship to asthma and urticaria to mental illness. *Psychosom. Med.* 12:377.

———— 1950b. Variations in response to standard amounts of chemical agents during alterations in feeling states in relation to occurrence of asthma. *Res. Publ. Assoc. Res. Nerv. Ment. Dis.* 29:566.

———— 1953. The relationship of experimentally produced asthmatic attacks to certain acute life stresses. *J. Allergy Clin. Immunol.* 24:11.

Furchgott, R. F. 1955. The pharmacology of vascular smooth muscle. *Pharmacol. Rev.* 7:183.

Gantt, W. H. 1941. *Experimental Basis for Neurotic Behavior.* Psychosomatic Medicine Monograph 3. Washington, D.C.: National Research Council.

Gerard, M. W. 1946. Bronchial asthma in children. *Nervous Child* 5:327.

Gillespie, R. D. 1936. Psychological factors in asthma. *Br. Med. J.* 1:1285.

Giovacchini, P. 1959. The ego and the psychosomatic state: a report of 2 cases. *Psychosom. Med.* 21:218.

Glasberg, H. M., Bromberg, P. M., Stein, M., and Luparello, T. J. 1969. A personality study of asthmatic patients. *J. Psychosom. Res.* 13:197.

Gold, W. M., Kessler, G. R., and Yu, D. Y. C. 1972. Role of vagus nerves in experimental asthma in allergic dogs. *J. Appl. Physiol.* 33(6):719.

Gold, W. M. 1976. Asthma. *Am. Thoracic Soc. News* 1:12.

Goodfriend, L., Kovacs, B. A., and Rose, B. 1966. *In vitro* sensitization of monkey lung fragments with human ragweed atopic serum. *Int. Arch. Allergy Appl. Immunol.* 30:511.

Goodman, L. S., and Gilman, A. 1965. *The Pharmacological Basis of Therapeutics,* 3rd ed. New York: Macmillan.

Grace, W. J., and Graham, D. T. 1952. Relationship of specific attitudes and emotions to certain bodily diseases. *Psychosom. Med.* 14:243.

Graham, D. T. 1972. Psychosomatic medicine. In *Handbook of Psychophysiology,* edited by N. S. Greenfield and R. A. Sternbach. New York: Holt, Rinehart, and Winston.

————, Lundy, R. M., Benjamin, L. S., Kabler, J. D., Lewis, W. C., Kunish, N. O., and Graham, F. K. 1962. Specific attitudes in intial interviews with patients having different "psychosomatic diseases." *Psychosom. Med.* 24:257.

Graham, P. J., Rutter, M. L., Yule, W., and Pless, I. B. 1967. Childhood asthma: a psychosomatic disorder? Some epidemiological considerations. *Br. J. Prev. Soc. Med.* 21:78.

Gram, H. C. 1931. Bronchial asthma. *Nord. Med. Tidskr.* 3:616, 625.

Greenacre, P. 1953. *Trauma, Growth and Personality.* New York: Norton.

Greenfield, J. G. 1958. Allergy and the need for recognition. *J. Consult. Clin. Psychol.* 22:230.

Groen, J. 1950. *Asthma Bronchiale seu Nervosum.* Amsterdam: Scheltema & Holkema.

——— 1951. Emotional factors in the etiology of internal diseases. *Mt. Sinai J. Med. N.Y.* 18:71.

———, Van Der Valk, J. M., Bastiaans, J., Dekker, E., Ledeboer, R. C., Defares, J., Heemstra, H., Barendreght, J. T., and de Vries, K. 1965. *Psychosomatic Research.* Oxford: Pergamon.

Gunnarson, S. 1950. Asthma in children as a psychosomatic disease. *Int. Arch. Allergy Appl. Immunol.* 1:103.

Gutmann, M. J. 1958. An investigation into environmental influences in bronchial asthma. *Ann. Allergy* 16:536.

Hadden, J. W., Hadden, E. M., and Middleton, E. Jr., 1970. Lymphocyte blast transformation. I. Demonstration of adrenergic receptors in human peripheral lymphocytes. *Cell. Immunol.* 1:583.

Hagy, G. W., and Settipane, G. A. 1966. The frequency of allergens and positive skin tests among college students. *J. Allergy Clin. Immunol.* 37:107.

Hahn, W. W. 1966. Autonomic responses of asthmatic children. *Psychosom. Med.* 28:323.

——— and Clark, J. A. 1967. Psychophysiological reactivity of asthmatic children. *Psychosom. Med.* 29:526.

Hajos, M. K. 1961. Influenza virus sensitization in bronchial asthma. *Acta Allergol. (Kbh.)* 16:347.

Hallowitz, D. 1954. Residential treatment of chronic asthmatic children. *Am. J. Orthopsychiatry* 24:576.

Hampton, S. F. 1968. Infection in bronchial asthma. In *Immunological Diseases*, 2nd ed., edited by M. Samter. Boston: Little, Brown.

Hansel, F. K. 1953. *Clinical Allergy.* St. Louis, Mo.: Mosby.

Hansen, K. 1930. Zur Frage der Psycho–oder Organo–genese beim allergischen Bronchial Asthma und der verwandten Krankheiten. *Nervenarzt* 3:313.

Harris, I. D., Rapaport, L., Rynerson, M. A., and Samter, M. 1950. Observations on asthmatic children. *Am. J. Orthopsychiatry* 20:490.

Harris, M. C. 1955. Is there a specific emotional pattern in allergic disease? *Ann. Allergy* 13:654.

——— and Schure, N. 1956. A study of behavior patterns in asthmatic children. *J. Allergy Clin. Immunol.* 4:312.

Hartmann, E. 1967. *The Biology of Dreaming.* Springfield, Ill.: Charles C Thomas.

Harvald, B., and Hauge, M. 1965. Hereditary factors elucidated by twin studies. In *Genetics and Epidemiology of Chronic Diseases*, edited by J. V. Neel, M. W. Shaw, and W. J. Shull. Washington, D.C.: U.S. Dept. of Health, Education and Welfare.

Hedqvist, P. 1970. Studies on the effect of prostaglandins E_1 and E_2 on the sympathetic neuromuscular transmission in some animal tissues. *Acta Physiol. Scand. (Suppl. 345).*

——— 1973. *Autonomic neurotransmission.* In *The Prostaglandins*, edited by P. W. Ramwell. New York: Plenum.

Hedqvist, P., Holmgren, A., and Mathé, A. A. 1971. Effect of prostaglandin F_2 on airway resistance in man. *Acta Physiol. Scand.* 82:29A.

Heim, E., Constantine, H., Knapp, P. H., Graham, W. G. B., Globus, G. G., Vachon, L., and Nemetz, S. J. 1967. Airway resistance and emotional state in bronchial asthma. *Psychosom. Med.* 29:450.

———, Knapp, P. H., Vachon, L., Globus, G. G., and Nemetz, S. J. 1968. Emotion, breathing and speech. *J. Psychosom. Res.* 12:261.

304

Heimlich, E. M., Strick, L., and Busser, R. J. 1966. An exercise response test in childhood asthma. *J. Allergy Clin. Immunol.* 37:103.

Herbert, M., Glick, R., and Black, H. 1967. Olfactory precipitants of bronchial asthma. *J. Psychosom. Res.* 11:195.

Herxheimer, H. 1953. Induced asthma in humans. *Int. Arch. Allergy Appl. Immunol.* 3:192.

———— and Streseman, E. 1961. The effect of bradykinin aerosol in guinea pigs and in man. *J. Physiol.* (Lond.) 158:38P.

Holman, C. W., and Muschenheim, C. 1972. *Bronchopulmonary Diseases and Related Disorders*, Vol. 2. New York: Harper & Row.

Humphrey, J. H., and White, R. G. 1970. *Immunology for Students of Medicine*, 3rd ed. Philadelphia: Davis.

Hurst, A. 1943. Asthma in childhood. *Br. Med. J.* 1:403.

Innes, I. R. 1962. An action of 5-hydroxytryptamine on adrenaline receptors. *Br. J. Pharmacol.* 19:427.

Ishizaka, K., and Ishizaka, T. 1966. Physicochemical properties of reaginic antibody. Ill. Further studies on the reaginic antibody in γA-globulin preparation. *J. Allergy Clin. Immunol.* 38:108.

———— and ———— 1967. Identification of γE-antibodies as a carrier of reaginic activity. *J. Immunol.* 99:1187.

———— and ———— 1968. Human reaginic antibodies and immunoglobulin E. *J. Allergy Clin. Immunol.* 42:330.

———— and ———— 1970. Biological function of γE antibodies and mechanisms of reaginic hypersensitivity. *Clin. Exp. Immunol.* 6:25.

————, ————, and Lee, C. H. 1966a. Physicochemical properties of reaginic antibodies. II. Characteristic properties of reaginic antibody different from human γ-isohemagglutinin and γD-globulin. *J. Allergy Clin. Immunol.* 37:336.

————, ————, and Hornbrook, M. M. 1966b. Physicochemical properties of human reaginic antibody. V. *J. Immunol.* 97:840.

Ishizaka, T., Ishizaka, K., Orange, R., and Austen, K. F. 1969. Release of histamine and slow reacting substance of anaphylaxis (SRS-A) by γE system from sensitized monkey lung. *J. Allergy Clin. Immunol.* 43:168.

Israel, M. 1954. Rorschach responses of a group of adult asthmatics. *J. Ment. Science* 100:735.

Itkin, I. H., and Anand, S. C. 1968. The role of atropine as a mediator blocker of induced bronchial obstruction. *J. Allergy Clin. Immunol.* 41:88.

Jacobs, M. A., Anderson, L. S., Eisman, H. D., Muller, J. J., and Friedman, S. 1967. Interaction of psychologic and biologic predisposing factors in allergic disorders. *Psychosom. Med.* 29:572.

Jacoby, M. G., and Bostock, J. 1960. Does asthma originate in childhood? *Med. J. Aust.* 2:858.

Jessner, L., Lamont, J., Long, R., Rollins, N., Whipple, B., and Prentice, N. 1955. Emotional impact of nearness and separation for the asthmatic child and his mother. *Psychoanal. Study Child* 10:353.

Johansson, S. G. O. 1967. Raised levels of a new immunoglobulin class (IgND) in asthma. *Lancet* 2:951.

———— and Bennich, H. 1967. Immunological studies of an atypical (myeloma) immunoglobulin. *Immunology* 13:381.

————, Bennich, H., and Wide, L. 1968a. A new class of immunoglobulins in human serum. *Immunology* 14:265.

————, Mellbin, T., and Vahlquist, B. 1968b. Immunoglobulin levels in Ethiopian preschool children with special reference to high concentrations of immunoglobulin E (IgND). *Lancet* 1:1118.

305

Jonasson, O., and Becker, E. L. 1966. Release of kallikrein from guinea-pig lung during anaphylaxis. *J. Exp. Med.* 123:509.

Jones, R. H. T., and Jones, R. S. 1966. Ventilatory capacity in young adults with a history of asthma in childhood. *Br. Med. J.* 2:976.

Jones, R. S. 1966. Assessment of respiratory function in the asthmatic child. *Br. Med. J.* 2:972.

—— and Blackhall, M. I. 1970. Role of disodium cromoglycate (Intal) in treatment of childhood asthma. *Arch. Dis. Child.* 45:49.

——, Buston, M. H., and Wharton, M. J. 1962. The effect of exercise on ventilatory function in the child with asthma. *Br. J. Dis. Chest* 56:78.

Jores, A. 1956. *Der Mensch und Seine Krankheit.* Stuttgart: Klett.

Kadowitz, P. M., Sweet, C. S., and Brody, M. J. 1973. Influence of prostaglandins on adrenergic transmission to vascular smooth muscle. *Cir. Res.* 31(Suppl. 2):1136.

Kaliner, M., and Austen, K. F. 1973. A sequence of biochemical events in the antigen-induced release of chemical mediators from sensitized human lung tissue. *J. Exp. Med.* 138:1077.

——, and ——. 1974. Cyclic AMP, ATP and reversed anaphylactic histamine release from rat mast cells. *J. Immunol.* 112:664.

——, and ——. 1974. The hormonal control of the immunologic release of histamine and slow reacting substance of anaphylaxis from human lung. In *Cyclic AMP, Cell Growth, and the Immune Response,* edited by W. Braun, L. Lichtenstein and C. Parker. New York: Springer.

Kaliner, M., Orange, R. P., and Austen, K. F. 1972. Immunological release of histamine and slow reacting substance of anaphylaxis from human lung. IV. Enhancement by cholinergic and alpha adrenergic stimulation. *J. Exp. Med.* 136:546.

Kallio, E. I. S., Bacall, H. L., Eisen, A., and Fraser, F. C. 1966. A familial tendency towards skin sensitivity to ragweed pollen. *J. Allergy Clin. Immunol.* 38:241.

Kallós, P., and Pagel, W. 1937. Experimentelle Untersuchungen über Asthma bronchiale. *Acta Med. Scand.* 91:292.

Kantor, J. M., and Speer, F. 1963. Characteristics of the allergic child. In *The Allergic Child,* edited by F. Speer. New York: Hoeber.

Karczewski, W. 1962. The electrical activity of the vagus nerve in anaphylactic shock. *Acta Alergol.* (Kbh.) 17:334.

Karczewski, W., and Widdicombe, J. G. 1969. The role of the vagus nerves in the respiratory and circulatory reactions to anaphylaxis in rabbits. *J. Physiol.* (Lond.) 201:293.

Karim, S. M. M., Sandler, M., and Williams, E. D. 1967. Distribution of prostaglandins in human tissue. *Br. J. Pharmcacol.* 31:340.

Karlberg, P. J. E. 1957. Breathing and its control in premature infants. In *Physiology of Prematurity.* Transactions of the Second Conference. New York: Josiah Macy Jr. Foundation.

Katz, G., and Cohen, S. 1941. Experimental evidence of histamine release in allergy. *J.A.M.A.* 117:1782.

Kay, A. B., and Austen, K. F. 1971. The IgE-mediated release of an eosinophil leukocyte chemotactic factor from human lung. *J. Immunol.* 107:899.

Kay, A. B., Shin, H., and Austen, K. F. 1973. Selective attraction of eosinophils and synergism between eosinophil chemotactic factor of anaphylaxis and a fragment cleaved from the fifth component of complement. *Immunology* 24:969.

Kellaway, C. H., and Trethewie, E. R. 1940. The liberation of a slow reacting smooth muscle stimulating substance in anaphylaxis. *Q. J. Exp. Physiol.* 30:121.

Kennedy, M. C. S. 1967. Preliminary results of a double-blind crossover trial on the value of FPL670 in the treatment of asthma. *Acta Allergol.* 22:487.

Kepecs, J. G., Robin, M., and Munro, C. 1958. Response to sensory stimulation in certain psychosomatic disorders. *Psychosom. Med.* 20:351.

Kerman, E. F. 1946. Bronchial asthma and affective psychoses. *Psychosom. Med.* 8:53.

Kiell, N. 1963. Effects of asthma on the character of Theodore Roosevelt. In *The Asthmatic Child*, edited by H. I. Schneer. New York: Hoeber.

Kim, C. J. 1965. The bronchial provocation test: its clinical evaluation and the course of induced asthma. *J. Allergy Clin. Immunol.* 36:353.

Kleeman, S. T. 1967. Psychiatric contributions in the treatment of asthma. *Ann. Allergy* 25:719.

Knapp, P. H. 1960. Acute bronchial asthma. Psychoanalytic observations on fantasy, emotional arousal and partial discharge. *Psychosom. Med.* 22:88.

——— 1963. The psychosomatic problem of asthma. In *The Asthmatic Child*, edited by H. I. Schneer, New York: Hoeber.

——— 1969. The asthmatic and his environment. *J. Nerv. Ment. Dis.* 149:133.

——— and Bahnson, C. B. 1963. The emotional field: a sequential study of mood and fantasy in 2 asthmatic patients. *Psychosom. Med.* 25:460.

——— and Nemetz, S. J. 1957a. Personality variations in bronchial asthma. *Psychosom. Med.* 19:443.

——— and ——— 1957b. Sources of tension in bronchial asthma. *Psychosom. Med.* 19:466.

——— and ——— 1960. Acute bronchial asthma—concomitant depression with excitement and varied antecedent patterns in 406 attacks. *Psychosom. Med.* 22:1,42.

———, Carr, H. E., Jr., Mushatt, C., and Nemetz, S. J. 1966a. Asthma, melancholia and death. II. Psychosomatic considerations. *Psychosom. Med.* 28:134.

———, ———, Nemetz, S. J., Constantine, H., and Friedman, S. 1970. The context of reported asthma during psychoanalysis. *Psychosom. Med.* 32:167.

Knick, B. 1954. Der Psychogene Tod des Asthmatikers. *Z. Gesamte Inn. Med.* 9:17.

Kraepelien, S. 1954. The frequency of bronchial asthma in Swedish school children. *Acta Paediatr. Scand.* 43(Suppl. 100):149.

Lamont, J. H. 1963. Which children outgrow asthma and which do not? In *The Asthmatic Child*, edited by H. I. Schneer, New York: Hoeber.

Langner, T. S., Gersten, J. C., Greene, E. L., Eisenberg, J. G., Herson, J. H. and McCarthy, E. D. 1974. Treatment of Psychological Disorders Among Urban Children. *J. Consult. Clin. Psychol.* 42:170.

Layton, L. L. 1966. Human allergic serum transfer tests in marmosets. *Int. Arch. Allergy Appl. Immunol.* 30:360.

Leavitt, H. C. 1943. Bronchial asthma in functional psychoses. *Psychosom. Med.* 5:39.

Lecks, H. I., Whitney, T., Wood, D., and Kravis, L. P. 1966. Newer concepts in the occurrence of segmental atelectasis in acute bronchial asthma and status asthmaticus in children. *J. Asthma Res.* 4:65.

Leigh, D. 1953. Asthma and the psychiatrist—a critical review. *Int. Arch. Allergy Appl. Immunol.* 4:227.

——— 1955. Sudden death in asthma. *Psychosom. Med.* 17:232.

——— and Doust, J. W. L. 1953. Asthma and psychosis. *J. Ment. Sci.* 99:489.

——— and Marley, E. 1956. A psychiatric assessment of adult asthmatics, a statistical study. *J. Psychosom. Res.* 1:109.

——— and ——— 1967. *Bronchial Asthma.* Oxford: Pergamon.

——— and Pond, D. A. 1956. The electroencephalogram in cases of bronchial asthma. *J. Psychosom. Res.* 1:120.

——— and Rawnsley, K. 1956. Bronchial asthma of late onset. *Int. Arch. Allergy Appl. Immunol.* 9:6,305.

Levine, B. B., Stember, R. H., and Fotino, M. 1972. Ragweed hay fever: genetic control and linkage to HL-A haplotypes. *Science* 178:1201.

Levine, R. J., and Senay, E. C. 1970. Studies on the role of acid in the pathogenesis of experimental stress ulcers. *Psychosom. Med.* 32:61.

Lichtenstein, L. M., and Margolis, S. 1968. Histamine release in vitro: Inhibition by catecholamines and methylxanthines. *Science* 161:902.

Liddell, H. S. 1951. The influence of experimental neuroses on respiratory function. In *Treatment of Asthma*, edited by H. A. Abramson, Baltimore: Williams & Wilkins.

Lidz, T. 1969. Disruptions of defensive life patterns and psychosomatic disorders. *Johns Hopkins Med. J.* 125:233.

Linko, E. 1947. Allergic rhinitis and bronchial asthma in bakers. *Ann. Clin. Res.* 36:98.

Lipton, E. L., Steinschneider, A., and Richmond, J. B. 1966. Psychophysiologic disorders in children. In *Review of Child Development Research*, vol. 2, edited by L. W. Hoffman and M. L. Hoffman. New York: Russell Sage Foundation.

Litt, M. 1964. Studies in experimental eosinophilia. VI. Uptake of immune complexes by eosinophils. *J. Cell. Biol.* 23:355.

Little, S. W., and Cohen, L. D. 1951. Goal-setting behavior of asthmatic children and of their mothers for them. *J. Pers.* 19:377.

Löfgren, L. B. 1961. A case of bronchial asthma with unusual dynamic factors, treated by psychotherapy and psychoanalysis. *Int. J. Psychoanal.* 42:414.

Logan, W. P. D. 1960. Morbidity statistics from General Practice (occupation). In *Studies on Medical and Population Subjects*, vol. 2, no. 14. London: Her Majesty's Stationery Office.

——— and Brooke, E. M. 1957. The survey of sickness, 1943–1952. In *Studies on Medical and Population Subjects*, vol. 2, no. 12. London: Her Majesty's Stationery Office.

Long, R. T., Lamont, J. H., Whipple, B., Bandler, L., Blom, G., Burgin, L., and Jessner, L. 1958. A psychosomatic study of allergic and emotional factors in children with asthma. *Am. J. Psychiatry* 114:890.

Luparello, T. J., Lyons, H. A., Bleecker, E. R., and McFadden, E. R., Jr. 1968. Influences of suggestion on airway reactivity in asthmatic subjects. *Psychosom. Med.* 30:819.

———, Leist, N., Lourie, C. N., and Sweet, P. 1970. The interaction of psychologic stimuli and pharmacologic agents on airway reactivity in asthmatic subjects. *Psychosom. Med.* 32:509.

———, McFadden, E. R., Jr., Lyons, H. A., and Bleecker, E. R. 1971. Psychologic factors and bronchial asthma. *N.Y. State J. Med.* 71:2161.

MacInnis, K. B. 1936. Allergic symptoms in the psychiatric patient. *J. Allergy Clin. Immunol.* 8:73.

Magonet, A. P. 1955. *Hypnosis in Asthma.* London: Heinemann.

Maher-Loughnan, G. P., MacDonald, N., Mason, A. A., and Fry, L. 1962. Controlled trial of hypnosis in the symptomatic treatment of asthma. *Br. Med. J.* 2:371.

Makino, S. 1966. Clinical significance of bronchial sensitivity to acetylcholine and histamine in bronchial asthma. *J. Allergy Clin. Immunol.* 38:127.

Malkiel, S. 1971. Presidential address. *J. Allergy Clin. Immunol.* 48:1.

Mandell, A. J., and Younger, C. B. 1962. Asthma alternating with psychiatric symptomatology. *Calif. Med.* 96:251.

Mansmann, J. A. 1952. Projective psychological tests applied to the study of bronchial asthma. *Ann. Allergy* 10:583.

Margolis, M. 1961. The mother-child relationship in bronchial asthma. *J. Abnorm. Psychol.* 63:360.

Mason, A. A., and Black, S. 1958. Allergic skin responses abolished under treatment of asthma and hay fever by hypnosis. *Lancet* i:877.

Masserman, J. H., and Pechtel, C. 1953. Neurosis in monkeys: a preliminary report of experimental observations. *Ann. N.Y. Acad. Sci.* 56:253.

Masuda, M., Notske, R. N., and Holmes, T. H. 1966. Catecholamine excretion and asthmatic behavior. *J Psychosom. Res.* 10:255.

Maternowski, C. J., and Mathews, K. P. 1962. The prevalence of ragweed pollinosis in foreign and native students at a midwestern university and its implications concerning methods for determining the inheritance of atopy. *J. Allergy Clin. Immunol.* 33:130.

Mathé, A. A. 1971. Decreased circulating epinephrine possibly secondary to decreased hypothalamic adrenomedullary discharge: A supplementary hypothesis of bronchial asthma pathogenesis. *J. Psychosom. Res.* 15:349.

———— and Knapp, P. H. 1969. Decreased plasma free fatty acids and urinary epinephrine in bronchial asthma. *N. Engl. J. Med.* 281:234.

———— and ———— 1971. Emotional and adrenal reactions to stress in bronchial asthma. *Psychosom. Med.* 33:323.

———— and Levine, L. 1973. Release of prostaglandins and metabolites from guinea-pig lung: Inhibition of catecholamines. *Prostaglandins* 4:877.

————, and Levine, B. 1974. Uptake of catecholamines in guinea-pig lungs: Influence of cortisol and anaphylaxis. *J. Allergy Clin. Immunol.* 53:106.

————, Birke, G. and Stjarne, L. 1974a. Altered patterns of excretion of catecholamines during acute asthma after infusion of H^3-epinephrine and H^3-norepinephrine to asthmatic patients and healthy subjects (in press).

————, Hedqvist, P., Holmgren, A., and Svanborn, N. 1973. Bronchial hyperreactivity to prostaglandin F_2 and histamine in patients with asthma. *Br. Med. J.* 1:193.

————, Levine, B., and Antonucci, J. M. 1974b. Uptake of catecholamines in guinea-pig lungs: Influence of cortisol and anaphylaxis. *J. Allergy Clin. Immunol.* (in press).

Maurer, E. 1965. The child with asthma: an assessment of the relative importance of emotional factors in asthma. *J. Asthma Res.* 3:25.

Maxwell, J. 1955. Unexpected death in asthma. *Chest* (Chicago). 27:208.

McAllister, R. M., and Hecker, A. O. 1949. The incidence of allergy in psychotic reactions. *Am. J. Psychiatry* 105:843.

McCarter, J. H., and Vasquez, J. J. 1966. The bronchial basement membrane in asthma. Immunohistochemical and ultrastructural observations. *Arch. Pathol.* 82:328.

McDermott, N. T., and Cobb, S. 1939. A psychiatric survey of fifty cases of bronchial asthma. *Psychosom. Med.* 1:203.

McFadden, E. R., Jr., Luparello, T., Lyons, H. A., and Bleecker, E. 1969. The mechanism of action of suggestion in the induction of acute asthma attacks. *Psychosom. Med.* 31:134.

McGready, S., Conboy, K., and Townley, R. 1968. The effect of beta-adrenergic blockade on bronchial activity to methacholine in normal and allergic rhinitis subjects. *J. Allergy Clin. Immunol.* 41:108.

McKee, W. D. 1966. The incidence and familial occurrence of allergy. *J. Allergy Clin. Immunol.* 38:226.

McNeill, R. S. 1964. Effect of a beta-adrenergic blocking agent, propranolol, on asthmatics. *Lancet* ii:1101.

———— and Ingram, C. G. 1966. Effect of propanolol on ventilatory function. *Am. J. Cardiol.* 18:473.

Meares, A. 1960. *A System of Medical Hypnosis.* Philadelphia: Saunders.

Meier, J., Lydtin, H., and Zollner, H. 1953. Über die Wirkung von adrenergen β-Rezeptorenblockern auf ventilatorische Funktionen bei obstruktiven Lungen-Krankheiten. *Dtsch. Med. Wochenscher.* 65:620.

Meneely, G. R., Renzetti, A. D., Jr., Steele, J. D., Wyatt, J. P., and Harris, H. W. 1962. Chronic bronchitis, asthma, and pulmonary emphysema. Definitions and classification, *Am. Rev. Respir. Dis.* 85:762.

Metcalfe, M. 1956. Demonstration of a psychosomatic relationship. *Br. J. Med. Psychol.* 29:63.

Meyers, J. L., Dain, D., Gold, W. M., Miller, R. L., and Bourne, H. R., 1973. Bronchial mast cells and histamine in experimental canine asthma. *Physiologist* 16:396.

Miller, H., and Baruch, D. W. 1948a. Psychosomatic studies in children. Maternal rejection and allergic manifestations. *Psychosom. Med.* 10:275.

———— and ———— 1948b. Psychological dynamics in allergic patients as shown in group and individual psychotherapy. *J. Consult. Psychol.* 12:110.

———— and ———— 1951. *Somatic and Psychiatric Treatment of Asthma.* Baltimore: Williams & Wilkins.

Mishkin, F., and Wagner, N. H., Jr. 1967. Regional abnormalities in pulmonary arterial blood flow during acute asthmatic attacks. *Radiology* 88:142.

Mitchell, A. J., Frost, L., and Marx, J. R. 1953. Emotional aspects of pediatric allergy—the role of the mother-child relationship. *Ann. Allergy* 4:744.

Mitchell, J. H., Curran, C. A., and Myers, R. N. 1947. Some psychosomatic aspects of allergic diseases. *Psychosom. Med.* 9:184.

Mohr, G. J., Selesnick, S., and Augenbraun, B. 1963a. Family dynamics in early childhood asthma: some mental health considerations. In *The Asthmatic Child,* edited by H. I. Schneer. New York: Hoeber.

————, Tausend, H., Selesnick, S., and Augenbraun, B. 1963b. Studies of eczema and asthma in the preschool child. *J. Am. Acad. Child Psychiatry* 2:271.

Monsour, K. J. 1960. Asthma and the fear of death. *Psychoanal. Q.* 29:56.

Moreno, G. D., and Bentolila, L. 1945. Report of a case of spontaneous animal allergy. *Ann. Allergy* 1:61.

Morris, R. P. 1959. Effect of the mother on goal–setting behavior of the asthmatic child. *Dissertation Abst.* 20:1440.

Morrison Smith, J. 1961. Prevalence and natural history of asthma in school children. *Br. Med. J.* 1:711.

———— and Burns, C. L. C. 1960. The treatment of asthmatic children by hypnotic suggestion. *Br. J. Dis. Chest.* 54:78.

Munro Ford, R. 1963. The causes of childhood asthma. *Med. J. Aust.* 2:128.

Murad, F., Chi, Y. M., Rall, T. W., and Sutherland, E. W. 1962. Adenylcyclase. III: The effect of catecholamines and choline esters on the formation of adenosine 3',5'-phosphate by preparations of cardiac muscle and liver. *J. Biol. Chem.* 237:1233.

Nadel, J. A., and Widdicombe, J. G. 1963. Reflex control of airway size. *Ann. N.Y. Acad. Sci.* 109:712.

Nadel, J. A. 1973. Neurophysiologic aspects of asthma. In *Asthma: Physiology, Immunopharmacology and Treatment,* edited by K. F. Austen and L. Lichenstein. New York: Academic.

National Center for Health Statistics. 1971. Chronic conditions and limitations of activity and morbidity in the United States. July 1965–June 1967. Vital and Health Statistics, Publication No. 1000, Series 10, No. 61.

Naylor, B. 1962. The shedding of the mucosa of the bronchial tree in asthma. *Thorax* 17:69.

Neuhaus, E. C. 1958. A personality study of asthmatic and cardiac children. *Psychosom. Med.* 20:2,181.

Noelpp, B., and Noelpp-Eschenhagen, I. 1951. Das experimentalle Asthma bronchiale des Meerschweinchens. *Int. Arch. Allergy Appl. Immunol.* 2:321.

———— and ———— 1952. Das experimentalle Asthma bronchiale des Meerschweinchens. *Int. Arch. Allergy Appl. Immunol.* 3:108.

310

Noelpp-Eschenhagen, I., and Noelpp, B. 1954. New contributions to experimental asthma. In *Progress in Allergy*, edited by P. Kallós. Basel: Karger, 4:361.

Ogilvie, A. G. 1962. Asthma: a study in prognosis in 1,000 patients. *Thorax* 17:183.

Orange, R. P., Stechschulte, D. J., and Austen, K. F. 1969. Cellular mechanisms involved in the release of slow reacting substance of anaphylaxis. *Fed. Proc.* 28:1710.

Orange, R. P., Austen, W. G., and Austen, K. F. 1971. Immunological release of histamine and slow reacting substance of anaphylaxis from human lung. I. Modulation by agents influencing cellular levels of cyclic 3',5'-adenosine monophosphate. *J. Exp. Med.* 134:136s.

Orange, R. P., Murphy, R. C., Karnovsky, M. L., and Austen, K. F. 1973. The physicochemical characteristics and purification of slow reacting substance of anaphylaxis. *J. Immunol.* 110:760.

Orange, R. P., Murphy, R. C., and Austen, K. F. 1974. Inactivation of slow reacting substance of anaphylaxis (SRS-A) by arylsulphatases. *J. Immunol.* 133:316.

Orr, T. S. C., Pollard, M. C., Gwilliam, J., and Cox, J. S. G. 1970. Mode of action of disodium cromoglycate; studies on immediate type hypersensitivity reactions using "double sensitization" with two antigenically distinct rat reagins. *Clin. Exp. Immunol.* 7:745.

Osler, A. G., Lichtenstein, L. M., and Levy, D. A. 1968. *In vitro* studies of human reaginic allergy. *Adv. Immunol.* 8:183

Ottenberg, P., and Stein, M. 1958a. Role of odors in asthma. *Psychosom. Med.* 20:60.

———— and ———— 1958b. Psychological determinants in asthma. *Transactions of the 5th Annual Meeting of the Academy of Psychosomatic Medicine.*

————, ————, Lewis J., and Hamilton, C. 1958. Learned asthma in the guinea-pig. *Psychosom. Med.* 20:395.

Ouellette, J. J., and Reed, C. E. 1967. The effect of partial beta adrenergic blockade on the bronchial response of hay fever subjects to ragweed aerosol. *J. Allergy Clin. Immunol.* 39:160.

Ouellette, J. J., and Reed, C. E. 1965. Increased response of asthmatic subjects to methacholine after influenza vaccine. *J. Allergy Clin. Immunol.* 36:558.

Owen, F. W. 1963. Patterns of respiratory disturbance in asthmatic children, evoked by the stimulus of the mother's voice. *Acta Psychotherapeutica* 2:228.

Parish, W. E., and Coombs, R. R. A. 1968. Peripheral blood eosinophilia in guinea pigs following implantation of anaphylactic guinea-pig and human lung. *Br. J. Haematol.* 14:421.

———— and Pepys, J. 1968. The lung in allergic disease. In *Clinical Aspects of Immunology*, 2nd ed., edited by P. G. H. Gell and R. R. A. Coombs. Oxford: Butterworth.

Patterson, R., and Sparks, D. B. 1962. The passive transfer to normal dogs of skin reactivity, asthma and anaphylaxis from a dog with spontaneous ragweed pollen hypersensitivity. *J. Immunol.* 88:262.

————, Fink, J. N., Nichimura, E. T., and Pruzansky, J. J. 1965. The passive transfer of immediate type hypersensitivity from man to other primates. *J. Clin. Invest.* 44:140.

————, Miyamato, T., Reynolds, L., and Pruzansky, J. 1967. Comparative studies of two models of allergic respiratory disease. *Int. Arch. Allergy Appl. Immunol.* 32:31.

Pearson, R. S. B. 1937. Observations on skin sensitivity in asthmatic and control subjects. *Q. J. Med.* 30:165.

———— 1958. Natural history of asthma. *Acta Allergol.* 12:277.

———— 1968. Asthma-allergy and prognosis. *Proc. R. Soc. Med.* 61:467.

Peltonen, M., Kasanen, A., and Peltonen, T. E. 1955. Occurrence of allergic conditions in school children. *Ann. Pediat. Fenn.* 1:119.

Peshkin, M. M. 1930. Asthma in children refractory to treatment—a plea for a "Home" as a restorative measure. *Am. J. Dis. Child.* 39:774.

———— 1959. Intractable asthma of childhood, rehabilitation at the institutional level with a follow-up of 150 cases. *Int. Arch. Allergy Appl. Immunol.* 15:91.

──── 1963. Diagnosis of asthma in children: past and present. In *The Asthmatic Child*, edited by H. I. Schneer. New York: Hoeber.

──── and Abramson, H. A. 1958. First national seminar of regional medical consultants. *Ann. Allergy* 16:473.

Pinkerton, P. 1967. Correlating physiologic with psychodynamic data in the study and management of childhood asthma. *J. Psychosom. Res.* 11:11.

──── and Weaver, C. M. 1970. Childhood asthma. In *Modern Trends in Psychosomatic Medicine-2*, edited by O. W. Hill. New York: Appleton-Century-Crofts.

Piper, P. J., and Vane, J. R. 1960. Release of additional factors in anaphylaxis and its antagonism by anti-inflammatory drugs. *Nature* 223:29.

Pollnow, H., Wittkower, E. D., and Petow, H. 1929. Beitrage zur Klinik des Asthma Bronchiale und Verwandter Zustände. *Z. Klin. Med.* 110:701.

Prausnitz, C., and Küstner, H. 1921. Studien über die Überempfindlichkeit. *Zentralbl. Bakteriol.* [Naturwiss.] 86:160.

Prigal, S. J. 1960. The interrelationships of allergy, infection, and the psyche: a "unified field theory" for the allergist. *Rev. of Allergy* 14:190.

Prout, C. 1951. Psychiatric aspects of asthma. *Psychiatr. Q.* 25:237.

Purcell, K. 1963. Distinctions between subgroups of asthmatic children. Children's perceptions of events associated with asthma. *Pediatrics* 31:486.

──── 1965. Critical appraisal of psychosomatic studies of asthma. *N.Y. State J. Med.* 65:2103.

──── and Metz, J. R. 1962. Distinctions between subgroups of asthmatic children: some parent attitude variables related to age of onset of asthma. *J. Psychosom. Res.* 6:251.

────, Bernstein, L., and Bukantz, S. C. 1961. A preliminary comparison of rapidly remitting and persistently "steroid dependent" asthmatic children. *Psychosom. Med.* 23:305.

────, Turnbull, J. W., and Bernstein, L. 1962. Distinctions between subgroups of asthmatic children; psychological tests and behavioral rating comparisons. *J. Psychosom. Res.* 6:283.

────, Brady, K., Chai, K., Muser, J., Molk, L., Gordon, N., and Means, J. 1969a. The effect of asthma in children of experimental separation from the family. *Psychosom. Med.* 31:144.

────, Muser, J., Miklich, D., and Kietiker, K. E. 1969b. A comparison of psychologic findings in variously defined asthmatic subgroups. *J. Psychosom. Res.* 13:67.

Rackemann, F. M. 1944. Deaths from asthma. *J. Allergy Clin. Immunol.* 15:249.

──── 1947. A working classification of asthma. *Am. J. Med.* 3:601.

──── 1950. Other factors besides allergy in asthma. *J.A.M.A.* 142:534.

──── 1958. Asthma is a constitutional disease. *J. Allergy Clin. Immunol.* 29:535.

──── and Edwards, M. C. 1952. Asthma in children. *N. Engl. J. Med.* 246:815.

Rajka, G. 1960. Prurigo Besner (atopic dermatitis) with special reference to the role of allergic factors. *Acta Derm. Venereol.* (Stockh.) 40:285.

Rall, J. E., Bilbert, N. C., and Trump, R. 1945. Certain aspects of bronchial reflexes obtained by stimulation of the nasopharynx. *J. Lab. Clin. Med.* 30:953.

Rapaport, H. G. 1958. Heredity and allergy. *N.Y. State J. Med.* 58:393.

Ratner, B. 1953a. Individual differences in guinea pigs in the development of experimental asthma. *Trans. N.Y. Acad. Sci.* 15:77.

──── 1953b. Temporal and quantitative factors influencing development of experimental asthma in the guinea pig. *J. Allergy Clin. Immunol.* 24:316.

──── and Silberman, D. E. 1952. Allergy—its distribution and the hereditary concept. *Ann. Allergy* 9:1.

──── and ──── 1953. A critical analysis of the hereditary concept of allergy. *J. Allergy Clin. Immunol.* 24:371.

Rees, L. 1956a. Physical and emotional factors in bronchial asthma. *J. Psychosom. Res.* 1:98.

312

———— 1956b. Psychosomatic aspects of asthma in elderly patients. *J. Psychosom. Res.* 1:212.

———— 1963. The significance of parental attitudes in childhood asthma. *J. Psychosom. Res.* 7:181.

———— 1964. The importance of psychological, allergic and infective factors in childhood asthma. *J. Psychosom. Res.* 7:253.

Reinberg, A., Chata, D., and Sidi, E. 1963. Nocturnal asthma attacks and their relationship to the circadian adrenal cycle. *J. Allergy Clin. Immunol.* 34:323.

Richards, W., and Patrick, J. R. 1965. Death from asthma in children. *Am. J. Dis. Child.* 110:4.

Richardson, J. B., Hogg, J. C., Bouchard, T., and Hall, D. 1973. Localization of antigen in experimental bronchoconstriction in guinea pigs. *J. Allergy Clin. Immunol.* 52:172.

Riley, J. F. 1959. *The Mast Cells.* Edinburgh: Livingstone.

Rocha e Silva, M. 1963. The physiological significance of bradykinin. *Ann. N.Y. Acad. Sci.* 104:190.

Rogerson, C. H. 1937. The psychological factors in asthma-prurigo. *Q. J. Med.* 30:367.

———— 1943. Psychological factors in asthma. *Br. Med. J.* 1:406.

————, Hardcastle, D. H., and Duguid, K. 1935. Psychological approach to the problem of asthma. *Guy's Hosp. Rep.* 85:289.

Rose, B., Rusted, I., and Fownes, A. 1950. Intravascular catheterization studies of bronchial asthma: I. Histamine levels in arterial and mixed venous blood of asthmatic patients before and during induced attacks. *J. Clin. Invest.* 29:1113.

Ross, W. D. 1954. Psychosomatic disorders and psychosis. In *Recent Developments in Psychosomatic Medicine,* edited by E. Wittkower and R. A. Cleghorn. London: Pitman.

————, Hay, J., and McDowall, M. F. 1950. The incidence of certain vegetative disturbances in relation to psychosis. *Psychosom. Med.* 12:179.

Ryssing, E. 1959. Continued follow-up investigation concerning the fact of 298 asthmatic children. *Acta Paediatr. Scand.* 48:255.

Sabbath, M. C., and Luce, R. A. 1952. Psychosis and bronchial asthma. *Psychiatr. Q.* 26:562.

Samter, M. 1959. Pathophysiology of bronchial asthma. In *International Textbook of Allergy,* edited by J. M. Jamar. Oxford: Blackwell.

Saul, L. J., and Lyons, J. W. 1954. Motivation and respiratory disorders. In *Recent Developments in Psychosomatic Medicine,* edited by E. D. Wittkower and R. A. Cleghorn. London: Pitman.

Scadding, J. G. 1963. Meaning of diagnostic terms in broncho-pulmonary disease. *Br. Med. J.* 2:1425.

Schachter, M. 1959. *Polypeptides Which Affect Smooth Muscles and Blood Vessels.* London: Pergamon.

Schatia, V. 1941. The incidence of neurosis in cases of bronchial asthma. *Psychosom. Med.* 3:157.

Schayer, R. W. 1960. Relationship of induced histidine decarboxylase activity and histamine synthesis to shock from stress and from endotoxin. *Am. J. Physiol.* 198:1187.

Scheflen, A. E. 1953. On bronchial asthma: a case report. *Psychiatr. Q.* 27:650.

Schiavi, R. C.: Stein, M., and Sethi, B. B. 1961. Respiratory variables in response to a pain-fear stimulus in experimental asthma. *Psychosom. Med.* 23:485.

Schild, H. O. 1937. Histamine release and anaphylactic shock in isolated lung of guinea pigs. *Q. J. Exp. Physiol.* 26:165.

Schild, H. O., Hawkins, D. F., Mongar, J. L., and Herxheimer, H. 1951. Reactions of isolated human asthmatic lung and bronchial tissue to a specific antigen: histamine release and muscular contraction. *Lancet* ii:376.

Schneer, H. I. 1963. The death of an asthmatic child. In *The Asthmatic Child,* edited by H. I. Schneer. New York: Hoeber.

Schnyder, U. W. 1960. Neurodermatitis-asthma-rhinitis: a genetic-allergic study. *Hum. Hered.* 10:(Suppl.).

Schwartz, M. 1952. *Heredity in Bronchial Asthma.* Copenhagen: Munksgaard.

Sclare, A. B. 1959. Psychological aspects of bronchial asthma. In *Bronchial Asthma: A Symposium.* London: The Chest and Heart Association.

——— and Crocket, J. A. 1957. Group psychotherapy in bronchial asthma. *J. Psychosom. Res.* 2:157.

Seitz, P. F. 1959. Infantile experience and adult behavior in animal subjects. *Psychosom. Med.* 21:353.

Selesnick, S. 1963. Separation anxiety and asthmatic attacks related to shifts in object cathexes. In *The Asthmatic Child,* edited by H. I. Schneer. New York: Hoeber.

Selinsky, H. 1960. Emotional factors related to perennial allergy. *Ann. Allergy* 18:886.

Shands, H. C. 1963. Change in a mother-child relationship in asthma. In *The Asthmatic Child,* edited by H. I. Schneer. New York: Hoeber

Sherman, W. B. 1967. Asthma. In *Textbook of Medicine,* 12th ed., edited by P. B. Beeson and W. McDermott. Philadelphia: Saunders.

Sinclair-Gieben, A. H. C. 1960. Treatment of status asthmaticus by hypnosis. *Br. Med. J.* 2:1651.

Sly, R. M., Heimlich, E. M., Busser, R. J., and Strick, L. 1967. Exercise induced bronchospasm: effect of adrenergic or cholinergic blockade. *J. Allergy Clin. Immunol.* 40:93.

Solomon, N. S. 1958. A study of results obtained at the asthma clinic, School Medical Service, N.S.W. Dept. of Public Health. *Med. J. Aust.* 45:592.

Spaich, D., and Ostertag, M. 1936. Untersuchungen über allergische Erkrankungen bei Zwillingen. *Z. f. Menschl. Vererb. u. Konstitutionslehre.* 19:731.

Spain, W. C., and Cook, R. A. 1924. Studies in specific hypersensitiveness. XI. The familial occurrence of hay fever and bronchial asthma. *J. Immunol.* 9:521.

Speizer, F. E., and Heaf, P. 1968. Observations on recent increase in mortality from asthma. *Br. Med. J.* 1:335.

Sperling, M. 1963. A psychoanalytic study of bronchial asthma in children. In *The Asthmatic Child,* edited by H. I. Schneer. New York: Hoeber.

Spoujitch, V. 1960. The complexity of allergic reactions. *Acta Allergol. (Kbh.)* 15(Suppl. 7):112.

Stanworth, D. R. 1963. Reaginic antibodies. In *Advances in Immunology,* vol. 3, edited by F. J. Dixon and J. H. Humphrey. New York: Academic.

——— 1971. The experimental inhibitor of reagin mediated reactions. *Clin. Allergy* 1:25.

Stechschulte, D. J., Bloch, K. J., and Austen, K. F. 1966. The antigen-induced release of slow-reacting substance (SRS-A) from passively sensitized guinea pig and rat tissue. *Fed. Proc.* 25:681.

Steen, W. B. 1959. Rehabilitation of children with intractable asthma. *Ann. Allergy* 17:864.

Stein, M. 1962. Etiology and mechanisms in the development of asthma. In *Psychosomatic Medicine, The Hahnemann Symposium* edited by J. H. Nodine and J. H. Moyer. Philadelphia: Lea and Febiger.

———, Schiavi, R. C., Ottenberg, P., and Hamilton, C. L. 1961. The mechanical properties of the lungs in experimental asthma in the guinea pig. *J. Allergy Clin. Immunol.* 32:8.

Stein, M., Schiavi, R. C., and Camerino, M. 1976. Influence of brain and behavior on the immune system. *Science* 191:435.

Stevenson, I., and Duncan, C. H. 1952. Alterations in cardiac function and circulatory efficiency during periods of life stress as shown by changes in the rate, rhythm, electrocardiographic pattern and output of the heart in those with cardiovascular disease. *Res. Publ. Assoc. Res. Nerv. Ment. Dis.* 29:476.

——— and Ripley, H. S. 1952. Variations in respiration and in respiratory systems during changes in emotion. *Psychosom. Med.* 14:476.

Stewart, A. 1957. Some uses of hypnosis in general practice. *Br. Med. J.* 1:1320.

314

Stokes, J. H., and Beerman, H. 1940. Psychosomatic correlations in allergic conditions. *Psychosom. Med.* 2:438.

Stokvis, B. 1959. Psychosomatic aspects in allergic diseases. In *International Textbook of Allergy*, edited by J. M. Jamar. Oxford: Blackwell.

Stone, J. L., Merrill, J. M. and Meneely, G. R. 1955. Distribution of histamine in human tissues. *Fed. Proc.* 14:147.

Stoner, J., Manganiello, V. C., and Vaughan, M. 1973. Effects of bradykinin and indomethacin on cyclic GMP and cyclic AMP in lung slices. *Proc. Natl. Acad. Sci. U.S.A.* 70:3830.

Swartz, J., and Semrad, E. V. 1951. Psychosomatic disorders in psychoses. *Psychosom. Med.* 13:314.

Swineford, O., Jr. 1962. The asthma problem: a critical analysis. *Ann. Intern. Med.* 57:144.

———— 1971. *Asthma and Hay Fever.* Springfield, Ill.: Charles C Thomas.

————, Johnson, E. R., Jr., Cook, H. M., Jr., and Ochota, L. 1962. Infectious asthma: an analysis of the asthmagrams of 100 cases and a critical review. *Ann. Allergy* 20:155.

Szentivanyi, A. 1968. Beta adrenergic theory of atopic abnormality in bronchial asthma. *J. Allergy Clin. Immunol.* 42:203.

———— and Fishel, C. W. 1968. Effects of bacterial products on responses to the allergic mediators. In *Immunological Diseases*, 2nd ed., edited by M. Samter. Boston: Little, Brown.

Takizawa, T., and Thurlbeck, W. M. 1971. Muscle and mucous gland size in the major bronchi of patients with chronic bronchitis, asthma and asthmatic bronchitis. *Am. Rev. Respir. Dis.* 104:331.

Tauber, A. I., Kaliner, M., Stechschulte, D. J., and Austen, K. F. 1973. Immunological release of histamine and slow reacting substance of anaphylaxis from human lung. V. Effects of prostaglandins on release of histamine. *J. Immunol.* 111:27.

Ten Cate, H. J. 1961. Provocation tests with inhalants and exposure tests with foods. In *Test Procedures Used in the Examination of the Allergic Patient: Proceedings of the European Academy of Allergy.* Leiden: Kroese.

Tiffeneau, R. 1959. Recherches quantitatives sur les médiateurs bronchosconstrictifs produits par l'inhalation continuée d'allergènes. *Pathol. Biol.* (Paris) 7:2293.

Tips, R. L. 1954. A study of the inheritance of atopic hypersensitivity in man. *Am. J. Hum. Genet.* 6:328.

Tollackson, K. A., and Frick, O. L. 1966. Response of human smooth muscle in Schultz-Dale experiments. *J. Allergy Clin. Immunol.* 37:195.

Townley, R. G., Trapani, I. L., and Szentivanyi, A. 1967. Sensitization to anaphylaxis and to some of its pharmacological mediators by blockade of beta adrenergic receptors. *J. Allergy Clin. Immunol.* 39:177.

Treuting, T. F., and Ripley, H. S. 1948. Life situations, emotion and bronchial asthma. *J. Nerv. Ment. Dis.* 108:380.

Tuft, H. S. 1957. The development and management of intractable asthma. *Am. J. Dis. Child.* 93:251.

Tulou, P. 1961. Influence du calibre de la trachée et des grosses bronches sur la ventilation pulmonaire: rapports des méthodes d'évaluation fonctionnelle et en particulier de la mesure de l'éspace mort anatomique. *Bronches* 11:55.

Turnbull, J. W. 1962. Asthma conceived as a learned response. *J. Psychosom. Res.* 6:59.

Unger, L. 1945. *Bronchial Asthma.* Springfield, Ill.: Charles C Thomas.

Van Arsdel, P. P., Jr. 1959. Blood groups and secretion of blood group substances. Comparison of allergic and non-allergic persons in a Pacific Northwest college population. *J. Allergy Clin. Immunol.* 30:460.

———— and Motulsky, A. 1949. Frequency and heritability of asthma and allergic rhinitis in college students. *Hum. Hered.* 9:101.

Vanselow, N. A. 1967. Skin testing and other diagnostic procedures. In *A Manual of Clinical Allergy*, 2nd ed., edited by J. M. Sheldon, R. G. Lovell, and K. P. Mathews. Philadelphia: Saunders.

Vaughan, W. T., and Black, J. H. 1948. *Practice of Allergy*, 2nd ed. St. Louis: Mosby.

———— and ———— 1954. *Practice of Allergy*, 3rd ed. St. Louis: Mosby.

Viswanathan, R., and Bharadway, H. 1962. The mode of inheritance of bronchial asthma. *Int. Arch. Allergy Appl. Immunol.* 20:174.

Vles, S. J., and Groen, J. 1951. An investigation into the personality structure of a group of juvenile asthmatic patients by the use of the Behn-Rohrschach test. *Ned. Tijdschr. Psychol.* 6:23.

Von Euler, U. S. 1969. Sympatho-adrenal activity and physical exercise. *Med. Sport* 3:170.

Von Harnack, G. A., and Panten, B. 1957. Bronchial asthma in childhood. Results of a follow-up study of 500 patients. *Monatsscher. Kinderheilkd.* 105:255.

Walton, C. H. A., and Elliot, G. B. 1952. Sudden death from bronchial asthma following injection of Pyromen. *J. Allergy Clin. Immunol.* 15:249.

————, Penner, D. W., and Wilt, D. C. 1951. Sudden death from asthma. *Can. Med. Assoc. J.* 64:295.

Warren, S., and Dixon, F. J. 1948. Antigen tracer studies and histologic observations in anaphylactic shock in the guinea pig. *Am. J. Med. Sci.* 216:136.

Wasserman, S. I., Goetzi, E. J., Kaliner, M., and Austen, K. F. 1974. Modulation of the immunologic release of the eosinophil chemotactic factor of anaphylaxis from human lung. *Immunology* 26:677.

Watson, J., Epstein, R., and Cohn, M. 1973. Cyclic nucleotides as intracellular mediators of the expression of antigen-sensitive cells. *Nature* 246:405.

Weiss, E. 1922. Psychoanalyse eines Falles von Nervosen Asthma. *Z. Psychosom. Med. Psychoanal.* 8:440.

Weiss, J. H., Martin, C., and Riley, J. 1970. Effects of suggestion on respiration in asthmatic children. *Psychosom. Med.* 32:409.

Weiss, J. M. 1966. Mood states associated with asthma in children. *J. Psychosom. Res.* 10:267.

Weissman, P., Duker, P., and Zurier, R. B. 1971. Effect of cyclic AMP on release of lysosomal enzymes from phagocytes. *Nature* [*New Biol.*] 231:131.

Wells, R. E., Walker, J. E. C., and Hickler, R. B. 1960. Effects of cold air on respiratory air flow resistance in patients with respiratory-tract disease. *N. Engl. J. Med.* 263:268.

White, H. C. 1961. Hypnosis in bronchial asthma. *J. Psychosom. Res.* 5:272.

Widdicombe, J. G. 1963. Regulation of tracheobronchial smooth muscle. *Physiol. Rev.* 43:1.

———— 1964. Respiratory reflexes. In *Handbook of Physiology, Sec. III, Respiration*, vol. I, edited by W. O. Fenn and H. Rahn. Washington: American Physiological Society.

Wide, L., Bennich, H., and Johansson, S. G. O. 1967. Diagnosis of allergy by an *in vitro* test for allergen antibodies. *Lancet* 2:1105.

Wiener, A. S., Zieve, I., and Fries, J. H. 1936. The inheritance of allergic disease. *Ann. Eugenics* 7:141.

Wilken-Jensen, K., Waal, N., Farup, B. and Bülow, K. 1951. Psychosomatic investigations of asthmatic children. *Acta Paediatr. Scand.* 40(Suppl. 83):52.

Williams, D. A. 1959a. Allergy-definition-prevalence-predisposing and contributing factors. In *International Textbook of Allergy*, edited by J. M. Jamar. Oxford: Blackwell.

———— 1959b. Allergy in asthma. *Br. Med. J.* 2:880.

————, Lewis-Faning, E., Rees, L., Jacobs, J., and Thomas, A. 1958. Assessment of the relative

316

importance of the allergic, infective and psychological factors in asthma. *Acta Allergol. (Kbh.)* 12:376.

Wittkower, E. D. 1935. Studies on the influence of emotions on the functions of organs. *Ment. Science* 81:533.

———— and Petow, H. 1932. Beiträge zur Klinik der Asthma bronchiale und verwandten Zuständen. *Z. Klin. Med.* 119:293.

———— and White, K. L. 1959. Psychophysiologic aspects of respiratory disorders. In *American Handbook of Psychiatry*, vol. 1, edited by S. Arieti. New York: Basic Books.

Wolf, S., Holmes, T. H., Trueting, T., Goodell, H., and Wolff, H. G. 1950. An experimental approach to psychosomatic phenomena in rhinitis and asthma. *J. Allergy Clin. Immunol.* 1:21.

Wright, G. L. T. 1965. Asthma and the emotions. *Med. J. Aust.* 1:961.

Zaid, G., and Beall, G. N. 1966. Bronchial response to beta-adrenergic blockade. *N. Engl. J. Med.* 275:580.

————, ————, and Heimlich, E. M. 1968. Bronchial response to exercise following beta-adrenergic blockade. *J. Allergy Clin. Immunol.* 42:177.

Zealley, A. K., Aitken, R. C. B., and Rosenthal, S. V. 1971. Asthma: a psychophysiological investigation. *Proc. R. Soc. Med.* 64:825.

Zeller, M., and Edlin, J. V. 1943. Allergy in the insane. *J. Allergy Clin. Immunol.* 14:564.

4
GRAVES' DISEASE

CURRENT STATUS OF PSYCHOSOMATIC RESEARCH

Many major advances have been made in our understanding of the normal physiology of the thyroid gland and of the pathophysiology of Graves' disease in the past 20 years. Much information has been accumulated about the self-regulation of the gland in its work of synthesizing, storing, and discharging its two hormones, triiodothyronine (T_3) and tetraiodothyronine (T_4) (Ingbar, 1972). We now know that T_3 is the more important of these two hormones, both in the normal economy of the body and in Graves' disease. The thyroid gland is remarkably stable in its self-regulatory processes, but it is also externally regulated by thyrotropin (TSH), a pituitary polypeptide. The release of TSH is directly regulated by T_3. As T_3 levels increase in the blood, TSH release is inhibited. T_3 may also act on the hypothalamus. The hypothalamus secretes a tripeptide, the thyrotropin-releasing hormone (TRH) that stimulates the release of TSH.

One of the unsolved mysteries is why the thyroid gland is capable of regulating its own function in a stable manner, even in the absence of the pituitary gland. (Ingbar, 1972). The gland's capacity for self-regulation continues after hypophysectomy despite the double-negative feedback system between it and the pituitary gland that usually regulates how much T_3 and T_4 are secreted by the thyroid gland.

In Graves' disease these regulatory processes are disrupted. The gland is no longer regulated by TSH—it becomes autonomous (Ingbar, 1972). The puzzle of Graves' disease has also been heightened by major advances in immunology. It has long been known that in Graves' disease the thyroid gland is infiltrated by lymphocytes and plasma cells. In the last 20 years, the general roles of two kinds of lymphocytes (B- and T-lymphocytes) in humoral and cellular immune reactions have become clearer, but their specific roles in Graves' disease remains unknown (Volpé et al., 1974). B-lymphocytes produce immunoglobulins that are antibodies. A variety of immunoglobulins have been implicated in Graves' disease. Antithyroglobulin and antimicrosomal antibodies occur in most, if not all, patients with Graves' disease. Immunoglobulins of the IgG, IgM, and IgE class are also deposited in the thyroid gland (Solomon and Chopra, 1972; Werner et al., 1972). The IgG antibody that has received the most attention in Graves' disease has been the long-acting thyroid stimulator (LATS). The LATS has assumed prominence in many current hypotheses about the pathogenesis of Graves' disease (McKenzie, 1968a). Other immunoglobulins, the human thyroid stimulator and the LATS-protector vie with the LATS as the pathogenetic agents of Graves' disease (Adams et al., 1974). The LATS and the LATS-protector have the properties of TSH in that they stimulate the release of T_3 and T_4 but are not in turn regulated by them. The LATS is present in the serum of 60 to 70% of all patients with Graves' disease. Its presence accounts for many but not all the phenomena of Graves' disease (Silverstein and Burke, 1970; Solomon and Chopra, 1972). The presence of the LATS in some, but not all, patients would account for the disturbance in regulation of the thyroid gland, characterized by the fact that the gland in Graves' disease is no longer regulated by TSH.

No consensus has been reached about the physiological and immunological factors that predispose to and initiate Graves' disease. The evidence at the present time is overwhelming that immunological disturbances occur in the disease, but their precise role in the disease has not been clarified. Nonetheless, they cannot be disregarded in any comprehensive understanding or explanation of the disease. In the past, explanations of the etiology and pathogenesis of the disease have been endocrinological and psychosomatic, and not immunological.

Since the first description of Graves' disease, clinicians have suspected that psychological and social factors play a role in the predisposition to and initiation of Graves' disease, and especially in those patients in whom the disease begins abruptly. A careful reading of the psychosomatic literature on this topic raises serious doubts, because most behavioral scientists have failed to define clearly their patient population. Specifically, they have made observations on patients who were "hyperthyroid" or "thyrotoxic." But the thyrotoxic state that reflects an overproduction or excess of the free thyroid hormones in the blood are not unique to Graves' disease. They occur in toxic nodular and multinodular goiter. They can come about by the transplacental transfer of the LATS from the mother to her infant or by the ingestion of T_3 and T_4 in the adult. Graves' disease is not synonymous with thyrotoxicosis. Thyrotoxicosis can exist without Graves' disease, and Graves' disease without thyrotoxicosis. Thyrotoxicosis may occur rarely when TSH is produced by neoplastic tissue. Choriocarcinomas and hydatiform moles produce a circulating thyrotropin that, despite being different from the usual TSH, produces thyrotoxicosis (Galton et al., 1971). An adenoma of the pituitary gland occasionally releases TSH in excess to produce thyrotoxicosis (Hamilton et al., 1970). Thyrotoxicosis has also been reported in conjunction with Cushing's syndrome (Lamberg, 1964), Addison's disease (Burke and Feldman,

1965), diabetes mellitus and insipidus (Del Castillo et al., 1964), polyostotic fibrous dysplasia (Zangeneb et al., 1966), pheochromocytoma (Braverman and Sullivan, 1969), and parathyroid adenomas (Jackson et al., 1961). It occurs in conjunction with collagen diseases (Librick et al., 1970), and with a combination of glomerulonephritis and absent frontal sinuses (Wochner et al., 1969).

Thyrotoxicosis can occur in conjunction with a specific deficiency of thyroid-binding globulin (TBG). As a result of this deficiency, a greater amount of the thyroid hormones are unbound in the bloodstream; the resulting change is the equivalent of excessive production of T_3 and T_4. Not all patients with a TBG deficiency develop thyrotoxicosis (Cavalieri, 1961; Inada and Sterling, 1967; Lemarchand-Béraud et al., 1964).

Thyrotoxicosis is a generic term for a state of hypermetabolism; it is not a disease. Before concluding that psychological factors play a role in predisposing to and initiating Graves' disease, the behavioral scientist must be certain that he is studying patients with this disease and not patients with a gamut of other diseases in which thyrotoxicosis occurs. In the past experimenters have not exercised sufficient care in defining their patient populations.

The conclusion that some thyrotoxic patients are afraid of dying before the onset of the disease can be drawn from past observations. But not every thyrotoxic patient has Graves' disease. Depending on the observer's frame of reference, the symptoms of Graves' disease can interpreted differently. The most common symptom of thyrotoxicosis is "nervousness." Because thyrotoxic patients report that nervousness begins when they experience life-threatening danger, such as in a car accident or in wartime, some interpret the "nervousness" as a fearful response to danger, and others interpret it as the correlate of an altered metabolic state. Both groups of observers may be right. Yet, in the past, psychiatrists and psychologists have been biased when studying nervous thyrotoxic patients to look for psychological, not other, reasons for the "nervousness."

The extensive information about environmental and psychological factors in Graves' disease must, therefore, be reevaluated because observations were made on a heterogeneous group of thyrotoxic patients, and not exclusively on patients with Graves' disease, and their nervousness may have been misinterpreted.

These egregious errors should be avoided in future studies on environmental factors (including psychosocial ones) in Graves' disease. The disease must be defined rigorously by clinical and laboratory procedures (Appendix 1 and 2 at the end of this chapter). It is a disease of many body systems whose pathogenesis still remains unknown. It is characterized by thyrotoxicosis, diffuse hyperplasia of the thyroid gland, a variety of eye signs due to diffuse infiltrative ophthalmopathy, and pretibial edema (Solomon and Chopra, 1972). The thyrotoxicosis, eye signs, pretibial edema, or goiter need not be present in order to reach the diagnosis of Graves' disease. The eye signs may precede, accompany, or follow the onset of the hyperthyroid, hypermetabolic state (Bartels and Irie, 1961). Not all patients with Graves' disease are thyrotoxic (Appendix 2).

Many of the symptoms and signs of Graves' disease may not be present in individual cases; for example, atrial fibrillation or congestive heart failure may be the only signs of the disease. In 3 percent of all cases, goiter may not be present. About 30 percent of all patients have no eye symptoms. In patients who are not thyrotoxic, the diagnosis of Graves' disease is made solely on the basis of eye signs and a variety of disturbances of thyroid function on special laboratory tests (Appendix 1). Localized edema (usually pretibial) occurs in only about 5 percent of all patients with Graves' disease (Gimlette, 1960). Despite the usual occurrence of nervousness, irritability, emotional lability, a shortened attention span, increased restlessness, insomnia, and memory difficulties, some patients with Graves' disease are listless, apathetic, and slowed in motor behavior.

INCIDENCE

The incidence of Graves' disease is between 1 (Bartels, 1941) and 2.3 (Logan and Cushion, 1958) per 1,000 of population. In women, it occurs from 4.4 to 9 times more frequently than in men (Bartels, 1941; Joll, 1951). The lifetime risk is between 2 and 3 percent of a population. About 1 to 5 percent of all cases of thyrotoxicosis occur in children (McClintock et al., 1956; Nilsonn, 1961; Saxena et al., 1964). In children the thyrotoxicosis is believed by some to be more-often a result of a toxic nodular goiter; but not all would agree. Thyrotoxicosis is four to five times more frequent in girls than in boys (Mäenpää et al., 1966).

Thyrotoxicosis can also occur in neonates. In some neonates, thyrotoxicosis is due to the transplacental transfer of the LATS. But in 60 percent of all children, thyrotoxicosis begins after the age of 10 years (Mäenpää et al., 1966). In older children the disease is not due to the transplacental transfer of the LATS. As in adult thyrotoxicosis its pathogenesis is not known. The peak age of onset of adult Graves' disease is at the start of the fifth decade of life (Joll, 1951). The fact that the onset of Graves' disease is greatest early in middle life remains unexplained, especially as Graves' disease runs in families, and is, therefore, believed to be hereditary (Bartels, 1941; Jayson et al., 1967; Volpé et al., 1972). Presumably, the phenotypic expression of the hereditary tendency to Graves' disease is usually delayed until the fourth or fifth decade.

THE ROLE OF GENETIC FACTORS IN GRAVES' DISEASE AND IN OTHER DISEASES OF THE THYROID GLAND

Genetic factors play a role in Graves' disease and in other diseases of the thyroid gland. Evidence for these assertions comes from studies showing that Graves' disease runs in families. But the relatives of patients with Graves' disease may not only have Graves' disease, they may have other diseases of the thyroid gland.

Studies of Families

The figures on the family incidence of Graves' disease vary considerably. From 10 to 47 percent of the family members of patients with Graves' disease also suffer from the same disease. In a systematic study of families of propositi with toxic diffuse goiter, Lewit et al. (1930) found that 25 percent of the 32 mothers of patients, 15 percent of 80 sisters, and 27 percent of 26 daughters were afflicted with Graves' disease. The authors were led to the conclusion that an autosomal dominant gene was responsible for the disease. Bartels

(1941) published a study of 204 propositi (16 men and 178 women) with Graves' disease and 21 patients who had been diagnosed as having toxic nodular goiter. They were compared with 498 normal subjects. Both clinic and hospitalized thyrotoxic patients were studied. The family members of 47 percent of the patients had thyroid disease. The mothers, sisters, and aunts of the patients either had Graves' disease and nontoxic nodular goiter more frequently than the family members of normal subjects did. The fact that aunts are afflicted with the disease strongly suggests that heredity plays a role in the etiology of Graves' disease. Or, at least, hereditary factors play a role in various diseases of the thyroid gland, because more mothers and sisters of patients with Graves' disease had a nontoxic goiter or other thyroid disease than Graves' disease (Bartels, 1941; Martin and Fisher, 1945).

Sisters of patients with Graves' disease are the most frequently affected relatives. In several reports, the number of siblings (especially sisters) of patients who have Graves' disease exceeds the number of affected parents. But not all homozygotes in a family manifest the trait; although several, if not all, siblings may be thyrotoxic (Boas and Ober, 1946; Garrett, 1961; Librik et al., 1970; Staub, 1966).

Although the sisters of women patients are most likely to develop Graves' disease, the brothers of men patients also do so. The sons of a thyrotoxic father may develop thyrotox-icosis; male-to-male transmission has been observed more than once (Boas and Ober, 1946; Mason et al., 1970; Sorensen, 1958). Fraser (1963) studied the relatives of 17 male patients with Graves' disease and found 1 brother and 1 daughter to have this disease, while 9 relatives (2 mothers, 3 aunts, and 4 sisters) had a nontoxic goiter. These family studies do not allow one to determine a mode of inheritance, but they do show that the relatives of patients with Graves' disease may be predisposed not only to this disease but to a variety of diseases of the thyroid gland. The total overall risk for several diseases of the thyroid gland in the families of patients with one of the diseases of the gland may be 60 percent. For example, Hashimoto's disease and myxedema occur more often in family members of patients with Graves' disease. Conversely, an increased incidence of Graves' disease occurs in the relatives of patients with Hashimoto's thyroiditis. Thirty-two percent of patients with Hashimoto's thyroiditis had relatives with a variety of thyroid diseases, not only Graves' disease or thyroiditis (Hall et al., 1964; Heimann, 1966; Hoffman, 1966; Thier et al., 1965).

The family aggregation of Hashimoto's disease has been described several times, and this disease has also been reported to occur in monozygotic (Mz) twins (Diamond and Joffe, 1966; Hall and Stanbury, 1967; Hoffman, 1966; Jayson et al., 1967). Therefore, it seems very likely that what is inherited genetically is not a predisposition to Graves' disease, but a predisposition to diseases of the thyroid gland, of which Graves' disease is but one.

The family risk studies are flawed by methodological errors. For one, the families are not chosen at random. Furthermore, the figures for the incidence of thyroid disease in families are probably low, because of the likelihood that some of the younger members of the families under study might have developed Graves' disease or some other thyroid disease after the completion of the study, and as they approached 30 to 50 years of age.

The family studies on patients with Graves' disease have also not proven a particular mode of inheritance. Several different modes of inheritance have been suggested. Fraser (1963) and Mason et al. (1970) inferred a polygenic one; Bartels (1941) and Martin and

Fisher (1945) inferred a recessive one; and other investigators have inferred a dominant mode of inheritance (Boas and Ober, 1946; Lewit et al., 1930; Sorensen, 1958).

The fact that relatives of patients with Graves' disease are prone to Hashimoto's thyroiditis (an autoimmune disease), and vice versa, suggests, but does not prove, that both groups inherit an altered or an increased reactivity or defect of the immunological system.

Twin Studies of Graves' Disease and Other Diseases of the Thyroid Gland

Twin, and not family, studies are more likely to prove the inheritance of a disease. In twin studies on thyrotoxicosis, in which zygosity was assumed and not determined, the concordance rate for thyrotoxicosis in Mz twins was 60 percent, compared with 9 percent for Dz twins of the same sex (Vogel, 1959). But most twin studies are suspect if zygosity determinations are not made. In most twin studies zygosity was not determined (Bartels, 1941; Boas and Ober, 1946; Carmena, 1949; Cunningham and Kral, 1959; Hassan et al., 1966; Jayson et al., 1967; Loewenstein, 1961; McCormack and Sheline, 1961; Priest, 1970; Robinson and Orr, 1955). There has also been a tendency to report Mz twins with Graves' disease, rather than Dz ones. In the past 30 years or so, 27 pairs of presumably Mz twins have been studied. The zygosity was only established in 8 of these 27 pairs. Seven of the eight pairs of twins were monozygous. Seven of eight pairs consisted of twin girls. Five of the eight pairs were concordant for Graves' disease. The remaining three twin pairs were discordant for Graves' disease, but concordant for diseases of the thyroid gland. One of a pair of Mz twins suffered from Hashimoto's thyroiditis, rheumatoid arthritis, and bronchial asthma, and the other had Graves' disease (Jayson et al., 1967); in the remaining two Mz pairs, the discordant twins had toxic nodular goiters (Cunningham and Kral, 1959). The studies suggest that there is a strong concordance in Mz twins not only for Graves' disease, but also for other diseases of the thyroid gland. However, the reports are not frequent enough to establish differential concordance rates in Mz and Dz twins. Therefore, no statement based on twin studies can be made about the inheritance of Graves' disease.

No twin studies on Graves' disease have involved surveys of all twins in a total population. The twin studies have so far been flawed because they have reported only twins concordant for Graves' disease. And the reports have not included data about thyroid disease in other siblings and in the parents of the twin index cases. Matching data on Dz twins of the same and opposite sexes and on twins raised together or apart have not been obtained. Based on these and other methodological flaws, it is impossible at this date to conclude anything from the results of twin studies on Graves' disease.

What is Inherited—Antibodies against Thyroid Gland Components

Genes might express themselves in various ways in thyroid disease. The most-likely expression is in the form of an altered immunological reactivity that occurs in Graves' disease and other thyroid diseases. Antibodies against various components of the thyroid gland, for example against microsomes, thyroglobulin, and thyroid colloid occur in the serum of patients with Graves' disease and their family members. The serum of 85 percent of all patients with Graves' disease contains low to moderate titers of antithyroid antibodies (Doniach and Roitt, 1966). The incidence of these antibodies in the general population is about eight times less (Doniach and Roitt, 1966). Antithyroid antibodies also occur in the serum of the euthyroid (female) relatives of patients with juvenile and adult forms of Graves' disease much more often than in the general population (Hall et al., 1960).

Saxena (1965) studied 12 patients with juvenile Graves' disease: the sera of 11 contained antithyroglobulin antibodies either in low or very high titers. The serum of either one or the other parent of 10 of the 12 children contained the same antibody. Yet only one father and one mother of the 12 children had a history of Graves' disease. The serum of the euthyroid mother of the only child from whose serum no antibody could be recovered, contained antithyroglobulin antibody.

Antithyroid (antithyroglobulin and antimicrosomal) and also antigastric parietal cell antibodies are present in over 70 percent of the mothers and 60 to 85 percent of the patients with Graves' disease—an incidence that is significantly greater than in the general population, especially in the patients' mothers and sisters who are 40 years of age or older. The serum of the male relatives of patients does not contain these antibodies more frequently than would be expected in the general population. Six of the 57 mothers, 6 of the 101 sisters, and 1 of the 76 brothers of these patients had had a history of, or were discovered to have, thyrotoxicosis in the course of study to determine the incidence of antithyroid antibodies in relatives. Four other relatives were myxedematous and 2 had nontoxic goiter (Howel Evans et al., 1967).

The LATS is present in the sera of the euthyroid relatives of Graves' disease patients (Wall et al., 1969; Zakrzewskea-Henisz et al., 1967). In Walls' series of the concentrated serum of 9 of 43 euthyroid relatives of 16 patients with thyrotoxicosis contained the LATS. In these relatives the incidence of elevated immunoglobulin levels and of antithyroid antibodies was higher than in a control population whose members were matched for sex and age, but lower than in matched series with thyrotoxicosis. None of the relatives were clinically thyrotoxic; but two had elevated PBI levels and the serum of one of these two contained the LATS.

Evidence for an inherited alteration of immunological reactivity in Graves' disease has also been sought in twins. Hassan and his co-workers (1966) reported four sets of twins concordant for proven Graves' disease. The serum of all four twin pairs was concordant for antibodies against thyroid microsomal antigens. Three of the four pairs were concordant for antibodies against gastric parietal cells. None of the sera of the four twin pairs contained antibody to thyroglobulin.

Jayson and his co-workers (1967) reported that one of a pair of 39-year-old Mz twins had Graves' disease and bronchial asthma, and the other twin had Hashimoto's disease, bronchial asthma, and rheumatoid arthritis. The serum of *both* patients contained the LATS. The serum of the twin with Graves' disease contained antibodies against thyroid colloid cytoplasm and thyroglobulin and gastric parietal cells. The serum of the twin with Hashimoto's disease contained antibodies to thyroglobulin, to the microsomal and colloid component of thyroid cells, and to gastric parietal cells. During a seven-year period of observation, the latter twin developed symptoms of Graves' disease.

These studies are far too few to conclude that antithyroid antibodies are an expression of an inherited tendency to an altered immunological reactivity. The antibodies have also

329

been studied in healthy twins. In 105 Mz and Dz pairs of such twins (mean ages about 22 years), the concordance rates for antithyroglobulin and antithyroid microsomal antibodies were only slightly higher than in Dz twin pairs. The authors concluded on the basis of their calculations that the presence of these antibodies in the serum of the twins can only partly be explained by heredity (Buchanan et al., 1967).

Antithyroid antibodies cannot by themselves be pathogenetic of Graves' disease because they occur in the serum of the euthyroid relatives of patients, of healthy twins, and of other adults. They may, however, predispose to Graves' disease and to other diseases of the thyroid gland. They are present in Hashimoto's thyroiditis, myxedema, and other forms of thyroid disease (Hall, 1965). The common factor in all these diseases may consist of an inherited tendency to thyroid disease, whose specific form is determined by environmental or other factors. The inherited factor may consist of altered genetic mechanisms that normally control immunological tolerance, reactivity, or surveillance (Cole et al., 1968; Solomon and Chopra, 1972). The tendency to produce autoimmune antibodies in the various thyroid diseases may also be set into motion by the vertical (genetic) transmission of a virus that exists in latent form but alters the antigenicity of various cell components of the gland.

Other Familial Defects

Additional defects in function of the thyroid gland are found in the relatives of patients with Graves' disease. Ingbar and Woebar (1968) reported that the uptake of ^{131}I is increased in about 20 percent of the euthyroid relatives (particularly in sisters and daughters) of patients with Graves' disease. In addition, an increased peripheral turnover rate of T_4 has also been observed in these relatives—a variation that is observed in clinical Graves' disease both before and after treatment.

EPIDEMIOLOGICAL STUDIES RELEVANT TO THE ONSET CONDITIONS AND PATHOGENESIS

In contrast to some of the other diseases reviewed in this book, genetic studies on Graves' disease do not allow one to calculate the genetic contribution to the etiological variance. Obviously, genetic factors play a role in Graves' disease, just as in most other diseases. The environmental elicits the genetic tendency. The environmental factors that do so in Graves' disease are dietary, infectious, surgical, psychological, cultural, and social.

Comparative epidemiological studies, especially those that are carried out under changing social and political conditions, have helped to identify some factors in the etiology and pathogenesis of Graves' disease. Before this conclusion is fully accepted as established fact, the studies on Graves' disease under changing political conditions must be evaluated further. These epidemiological studies have been made on both toxic diffuse and nodular goiter. But they did not maintain separate categories for the incidence and prevalence of the two different diseases.

330

Changes in Incidence during Wartime and Thereafter

An increase in the incidence of "thyrotoxicosis" was first reported during the Boer War, and from France in World War I (Bérard, 1916; Firgau, 1926; Maranon, 1921). During World War I a decreased incidence was reported from Scandinavia and the German-speaking countries of Europe (Curschmann, 1922; Klose, 1928; Pulay, 1919; Tallquist, 1922). The onset of Graves' disease can follow an infection. During wartime, infectious epidemics occur. Therefore, one cannot conclude that wartime conditions other than infection increase the incidence of thyrotoxicosis. In fact an epidemic of "influenza" coincided both with the Boer War and the last years of World War I. One of the complications of "influenza" is an encephalitis, and cases of Graves' disease have been described in conjunction with von Economo's encephalitis (Werner and Ingbar, 1971).

Epidemics of thyroid disease also occur in times of peace. Plummer (1931) described an "epidemic" of toxic nodular and diffuse goiter in Minnesota between 1923 and 1931. He did not try to explain the three- to fourfold increase in incidence of these disorders. During World War II, marked changes in the incidence of thyrotoxicosis due to Graves' disease and toxic nodular goiter occurred in some but not other countries. These changes in incidence strongly suggest that political and social change produce changes in the incidence of Graves' disease. But so do changes in diet.

Between 1941 and 1947 an increase of thyrotoxicosis occurred in every part of Denmark. In one hospital in Copenhagen, the incidence of toxic diffuse and nodular goiter increased five to seven times (Iversen, 1948, 1949; Meulengracht, 1949). Iversen (1948, 1949) reported that four times as many patients with true Graves' disease and exophthalmos were seen during this period. The number of thyrotoxic patients began to fall in 1945. The increase was not due to an increase in the size of the population. The incidence of thyrotoxicosis increased more in men than in women. The incidence increased more for toxic nodular goiter than the diffuse variety. Recurrences of both forms of goiter doubled during this period. A tenfold increase in the number of patients with Graves' disease was observed in the public hospitals of Paris between 1938 and 1944. In Norway, the incidence of thyrotoxicosis increased four to five times between 1934 and 1943; one-half of this increase occurred between 1941 and 1943. Of 200 Norwegian patients with thyrotoxicosis, 140 had a toxic diffuse goiter (Grelland, 1946).

But no increases in the incidence of thyrotoxicosis occurred in the United States, Great Britain, Russia, Belgium, and Finland during World War II, or in noncombatant countries such as Sweden, Switzerland, and Argentina. In wartime Holland there was a fourfold *decrease* in thyrotoxicosis (Schweitzer, 1944). Concentration camp victims developed thyrotoxicosis four times more frequently than those who had never been incarcerated, but only *after* they had been liberated (Weisman, 1958). The discrepant reports from various European countries during World War II are hard to account for. Particularly striking is the increased incidence in Norway and Denmark and the decreased incidence in Holland. Bacterial and viral infections did occur with increased frequency in Denmark and may have played a role in precipitating thyrotoxicosis (Iversen, 1948, 1949). The authors of the Scandinavian reports reject the idea that the political and social conditions created by the German occupation may have played a role in increasing the incidence of toxic goiters.

Rather, they believe that variations in the pool of predisposed individuals may have played a role in these increases. But the causes of these variations are unknown. One of the causes may be that more food and calories were available to the Danes than to the Dutch. A small drop in the individual daily caloric intake to 2,687 calories occurred in Denmark during World War II (Iversen, 1949), whereas in Holland the population was virtually starved by the Germans (Schweitzer, 1944). In Norway, the increase in the incidence in thyrotoxicosis stopped, coincident with a decrease in food intake to 1,570 calories per day (Grelland, 1946). The number of calories may have played a role in determining the increased incidence of thyrotoxicosis in the population of one country and the decrease in incidence in another.

Thyrotoxicosis may also be precipitated by an increase in dietary iodine in a region where endemic goiter occurs. Stewart and his co-workers (1971) reported that the urinary iodine excretion levels in a population of Tasmanian children were low. In 1965, in order to correct the iodine deficiency the bread was iodinated. Within four months after this campaign was instituted a threefold increase in reported cases of thyrotoxicosis occurred throughout Tasmania.

Actually, an increase in the number of reported cases had begun two years before the bread was iodinated. The increase in patients occurred in the older age groups. Forty-four percent of the patients had a long-standing history of goiter. The threefold increase in incidence of thyrotoxicosis was mainly due to an increase in toxic multinodular goiters. An increase in thyrotoxicosis without exophthalmos had also been reported in the Netherlands after the institution of bread iodination for the purpose of preventing goiter (Van Leeuwen, 1954).

In the light of the absence of microscopic confirmation of the nature of the goiter, the known unreliability of the clinical examination in the determination of the exact nature of the goiter, and the fact that only about 70 percent of all Graves' disease patients show exophthalmos, these reports do not settle the question whether Graves' disease can be precipitated by an increase in dietary iodine. These two reports suggest that the appearance of toxic multinodular goiter may be occasioned by the ingestion of iodine in patients who have a preexisting goiter, most likely of the nontoxic nodular variety. In the Tasmanian study, the increased incidence was a function of an increase, but not an excessive one, in iodine intake in a population in which there was a long-standing iodine deficiency.

Some inhabitants, especially some children, of regions of endemic goiter have raised serum levels of TSH in response to the iodine deficiency. In these children, the increase in TSH levels is independent of an enlarged thyroid gland (Delange et al., 1971). But we do not know whether those with increased TSH levels are the ones who become thyrotoxic when fed iodine. Nor do we know whether Graves' disease may be brought on by the increased ingestion of iodine in patients with a preexisting nonendemic goiter. However, an increase in iodine intake in those without a goiter may "uncover" Graves' disease that had been latent by virtue of a low level of iodine in the diet. We also know that *nontoxic* diffuse and multinodular goiters are both associated with increased TSH secretion (Ingbar, 1971), and that nontoxic multinodular goiters may become toxic in older persons whether or not an increase in iodine intake occurs.

The increased incidence of thyrotoxicosis during the enemy occupation of some countries seems to occur only when caloric intake is sufficient. In Norway a decrease in thyrotoxicosis occurred when food supplies became low. The thyrotoxicosis was due to both toxic diffuse and nodular goiters. In countries where goiter is endemic, an increased iodine intake may be associated with an increase in toxic multinodular goiters in some persons, but not in all. The toxic diffuse goiter of Graves' disease may occur when iodine intake is increased in patients who probably do not have a preexisting nontoxic goiter.

FACTORS WHICH INITIATE AND PRODUCE RECURRENCES

Problems in Determining the Time of Onset

The mystery of Graves' disease is deepened by the many difficulties that face the clinician in determining its onset. Controversy has surrounded the roles of pregnancy, parturition, surgery, infection, frightening personal experiences, bereavements, and separations as precipitants of Graves' disease. Its onset and course are highly variable. It may begin abruptly or slowly. It may remit spontaneously. The symptoms and signs at onset vary widely from patient to patient.

Especially when the disease begins slowly, the timing of the onset of its symptoms and signs can be very difficult. If its onset cannot be determined with precision the role that the various precipating events play in inciting the disease remains uncertain.

Some consider that various life events play a permissive, rather than an inciting, role. They suggest that the earliest physiological changes of the disease produce an exaggerated psychophysiological response to the precipitating event. Alternatively, some circumstance, such as surgery, and the onset of the disease coincide by chance, and does not cause the disease (Gibson, 1962; Mandelbrote and Wittkower, 1955; Wilson et al., 1961).

Evidence exists that physiological changes do occur before the symptoms and signs of thyrotoxicosis begin. T_3 levels may be raised five weeks to ten months before the onset of the usual gamut of symptoms of thyrotoxicosis, and before increased T_4 levels occur. Nervousness may be the only symptom that brings these patients to the doctor, who discovers that the patient has raised T_3 levels. Only later do the other symptoms of thyrotoxicosis appear in these patients (Hollander et al., 1971). Therefore, it is possible that abnormally high circulating T_3 levels may precede the development of frank thyrotoxicosis, and may sensitize the patient to respond to the so-called precipitating event that acts permissively to develop thyrotoxic symptoms. There is no real way of deciding between these alternatives. In other patients many of the symptoms and signs of the disease, such as nervousness, fear, and insomnia, may have been present for many years before the disease develops.

Because Graves' disease is so variable and complex, its onset is difficult to determine retrospectively. The clinician may misinterpret some of its signs. Characteristic signs of the disease, such as exophthalmos, a stare, or a lid lag, may occur in *normal* persons and in the *euthyroid* relatives of patients with Graves' disease (Wall et al., 1969). These eye signs also may be the only manifestations of Graves' disease diagnosed by laboratory criteria (Liddle et al., 1965; Werner, 1955). In addition, subclinical or latent forms of Graves' disease have been described. Therefore, it is difficult to determine whether the disease is active or inactive in these forms. Perhaps surgery, an acute infection, pregnancy, or distressing

333

situations interact with the subclinical or latent forms of the disease to elicit symptoms, but not the disease itself.

In the face of all these unknowns, the cause of the onset of Graves' disease is uncertain. When the disease begins abruptly, it is often associated in a clearcut manner with a pregnancy, delivery, surgery, a painful life event, or an accident. In still other instances "latent" or "subclinical" disease may become overt, or certain symptoms and signs may be brought into the open in response to distressing experience. On a few occasions it has been possible to demonstrate that surgery, bereavement, or infection is closely correlated in time with an abrupt change in the functioning of the thyroid gland and the onset of a recurrence of the thyrotoxicosis of Graves' disease. Cushman (1967) reported a patient who had a recurrence of Graves' disease following surgical biopsy of a benign breast tumor. Prior to surgery, the T_3 suppression test had been normal. The recurrence was associated with rapid elevations of PBI, T_3 levels, and ^{131}I uptake. Another woman patient had successfully been treated for Graves' disease. Within two months after the death of two young members of her family, the illness recurred and was associated with increases in PBI levels, the free T_4 index, T_3 levels, and the development of an abnormal T_3 suppression test. Another patient became thyrotoxic with Graves' disease after a severe throat infection, at which time the gland's function could no longer be supressed with T_3 (Alexander et al., 1968). The mechanism by which bereavement or infection can cause the gland's function not to be suppressed by T_3 is unknown. But the abnormal T_3 suppression is an excellent indicator (Appendix 1).

In these instances surgery, bereavement, or infection did seem to "cause" a physiological change in the thyroid gland. In other instances, the physiological change may anticipate the stressful precipitating event and in some undisclosed manner interact with it or make it more difficult for the patient to cope with it.

The Incidence and Nature of the Precipitating Events

THE ROLES OF PSYCHOLOGICAL AND OTHER STRESSES

The tantalizing data on changes in the incidence of thyrotoxicosis, including toxic diffuse goiter, in Denmark, Norway, and Holland during the German occupation in World War II remain unexplained. No studies critical to this question were, or could have been, carried out. A sudden change in incidence of this kind could have provided valuable clues about the onset conditions of the disease. It would have been helpful to know whether infection or danger, the personal fears engendered by terror, or other factors, such as changes in diet and caloric intake, played crucial roles in causing the increased incidence or in maintaining or diminishing the incidence in other countries. The data do seem to show that a low caloric intake protects against thyrotoxicosis.

Other studies on thyrotoxic patients suggest that personal and psychological factors play a role in predisposing to and initiating diseases of the thyroid gland, including Graves' disease. Alexander (1950), Bennett and Cambor (1961), and Brown and Gildea (1937) found that future patients are sensitive to three kinds of precipitating situations or events: (1) situations in which their strivings for self-sufficiency failed or were frustrated; (2) situations that prevented patients from taking care of others; (3) actual or threatened harm or danger that breached the counterphobic defenses of patients. A more general set of situations was identified by Lidz (1949). They consisted of actual or imaginary bereavement, separation, and abandonment. Most observers agree with Lidz that an actual or threatened break in an emotionally significant relationship acts as a precipitant in the predisposed person (Bennett and Cambor, 1961; Brown and Gildea, 1937; Conrad, 1934a, b; Ferguson-Rayport, 1956; Lidz, 1949; Lidz and Whitehorn, 1950; Mittelman, 1933; Wilson et al., 1961).

These observations confirmed those of Bram, who had carried out the most extensive clinical study ever carried out on the onset conditions of Graves' disease—defined in this case as exophthalmic goiter. In 3,343 adult patients, the onset conditions were:

1. Worry, grief, disappointment, sexual incompatibility, etc. 61%
2. Involvement in an accident, or injury, imminent personal danger 13%
3. Minor surgery 7%
4. No exciting cause found 6%
5. Infections—general and local 5%
6. Parturition 4%
7. Ingestion of iodine 3%
8. Ingestion of thyroxine 1%

In children, on the other hand, the disease seemed to be most frequently preceded by an infectious illness and not by psychologically significant events (Bram, 1933).

The brief, personal vignettes that Bram wrote indicate that a combination of situations involving both fear *and* impending loss or separation anteceded the onset of exophthalmic goiter.

Psychiatrically or psychoanalytically trained observers have studied patients with "thyrotoxicosis" or Graves' disease. They have neither been able to agree on the number of patients who experienced some stressful life event that was related in time to the onset of the disease nor about the nature and meaning of the event. They have found that the incidence of meaningful life events antecede or coincide with the onset of Graves' disease or thyrotoxicosis in 28 percent (Maranon, 1921) to 94 percent of patients (Conrad, 1934a, b; Hetzel, 1960).

Clinical endocrinologists cannot agree either as to the role or frequency of social and personal factors in initiating Graves' disease. Some endocrinologists have stated that significant personal events were correlated in time with the onset of Graves' disease in 50 percent of their patients (Astwood, 1967; Grelland, 1946; Means, 1948). Other endocrinologists have put the figure at 100 percent (Goodall and Rogers, 1944). Still others have refuted the assertion altogether (Iversen, 1948; Wilson, 1967). One investigator described its onset in four wives of U.S. Air Force personnel within two months of their being told that their husbands were to be sent to Vietnam (Werner, 1967).

When the onset of the disease is *sudden,* the patient has more often experienced danger than separation or marital discord (Mandelbrote and Wittkower, 1955). The disease begins suddenly in about one-fifth of patients with Graves' disease. In others, the onset is so gradual and insidious that it is impossible to specify just when it started (Fitz, 1944).

The meaning of these observations can be interpreted in different ways. One interpretation is that changes or separation cannot be coped with and is followed by disease onset. Another interpretation of the observations was made by Gibson (1962). He believes that the stressful live events could not be coped with because the disease had already started and the metabolic changes of the disease impaired the patients' capacity to cope. At least in some patients, Gibson's contention is not borne out. Kaplan and Hetrick (1962) documented the onset of the symptoms of Graves' disease in a 28-year-old man. The symptoms began two weeks after a traffic accident in which the patient lost consciousness. The accident frightened the patient and resulted in the symptoms of a traumatic neurosis—fears of cars, avoidance of buses, and repetitive dreams of the accident. In this patient, Graves' disease had begun two weeks after a period of fearfulness that did not seem to be the result of an already existing thyrotoxic condition, but was due to the accident. As a child, this patient had lived in constant fear of a violent mother. In response to his earlier experiences with his mother, he attempted to protect himself constantly against actual or assumed danger in his environment, while at the same time feeling powerless and helpless to do so. The automobile accident had occurred during a period of mounting marital discord.

Gibson's interpretation of the observations about the role of significant life events that antecede recurrences of thyrotoxicosis is not borne out by Ferguson-Rayport's study (1956). She observed patients after clinical recurrences had already begun. The study provides us with a longitudinal picture of the manner in which patients cope with lifelong problems of a dependent nature. Recurrences happened only when these problems were not adequately handled. These patients were not able to cope with bereavement, loss, or separation, caused by the death of parents, emigration, or the loss of financial security. The patients were all taking antithyroid medication. The onset of recurrences happened when the patients could not manage loss or bereavement. As coping improved and equanimity was restored, the recurrence subsided; when not, the course of the disease was prolonged.

These longitudinal observations could also explain the highly variable natural history of Graves' disease. It is known that before the institution of modern methods of treatment, the "spontaneous" remission rate of thyrotoxicosis was almost 50 percent (Sattler, 1952). Continued remission for a four-year period is only imparted by antithyroid drugs in 57 percent of all patients (Solomon, 1971).

At least in some of Ferguson-Rayport's patients the ability to cope with personal problems was not impaired by the metabolic changes of thyrotoxicosis. Nonetheless, Gibson may be right. Increased levels of T_3 in the serum may antedate the onset of frank thyrotoxicosis for several weeks or months. Many thyrotoxic patients manifest mild symptoms some time before the full-blown syndrome develops. Raised levels of T_3 correlate in time with symptoms of nervousness (Hollander et al., 1971). Therefore, a tentative conclusion may be reached that in some patients Graves' disease may be a response to psychological stress. In other patients, stress occurs at a time when T_3 levels are already increased. Because they are increased, they may impair psychological adaptation to everyday events that would otherwise have been adequately coped with.

One way of settling the controversy between those who believe that psychological stress antedates the initiation of Graves' disease and those who believe that Graves' disease alters the capacity of the patient to cope with stress, is to study the T_3 suppression test before and after the stress. To do so, longitudinal studies may have to be carried out. Indeed, a few

336

instances have been reported in which the T_3 suppression test became abnormal after bereavement or infection (Alexander et al., 1968; Cushman, 1967).

PREGNANCY AS A CAUSATIVE FACTOR

Graves' disease may start during or after a pregnancy. Preexisting Graves' disease may also improve or remit during a pregnancy (Astwood, 1951; Lidz, 1955; Sattler, 1952). A woman may go through several pregnancies and not develop Graves' disease until a subsequent one.

Thyrotoxicosis, not necessarily caused by Graves' disease, occurs in about 3 out of 1,000 pregnancies (Bram, 1922; Lidz, 1955). This figure may be too low by a factor of 10 or more (Gardiner Hill, 1929). Pregnant women who develop thyrotoxicosis have psychological conflicts about marriage and pregnancy. They may have married with reluctance, having been torn between their devotion to their parents and the prospect of marriage. Some of the women were considering separation from their spouses to return to their parents when they became pregnant. Their conflicts of loyalty are compounded by jealousy of her husband's attachment to his own parents and siblings. Some pregnant thyrotoxic patients are separated from their husbands. Some multiparous mothers whose previous pregnancies had been complicated by toxemia were fearful of being pregnant again and becoming toxemic (Lidz, 1955). Pregnant women who develop thyrotoxicosis have multiple conflicts (Conrad, 1934a, b; Ham et al., 1951). These conflicts are not unique to women who develop thyrotoxicosis during pregnancy; therefore, additional, unknown factors must play a part in bringing about thyrotoxicosis in pregnancy. Some of the physiological changes that *normally* occur in pregnancy also occur in Graves' disease. The thyroid gland is enlarged, possibly due to an increase in its blood flow. The basal metabolic rate (BMR) is increased; the ^{131}I uptake or clearance by the gland is elevated; the urinary excretion of ^{131}I, the plasma inorganic iodine concentration, serum levels of T_4 and of ^{127}I are decreased. Total T_3 levels are increased both in Graves' disease and in pregnancy (Hotelling and Sherwood, 1971). The absolute iodine uptake and $PB^{131}I$ levels are elevated only during the disease. Increases in PBI and butanol-extractable iodine (BEI) levels occur early in pregnancy and may be due to increased TBG levels (Hotelling and Sherwood, 1971) that depress free T_4 levels (Oppenheimer et al., 1963). Levels of the prealbumin that binds T_4 are decreased. The absolute rate of disposal of T_4 is unchanged in pregnancy (Dowling et al., 1967). The increased binding capacity of T_4 by TBG is probably due to increased levels of estrogen in pregnancy—similar changes are produced by oral contraceptive agents (Hollander et al., 1963). The female sex hormones alter levels of TSH in serum. The administration of ethinyl estradiol to human subjects suppresses the circulating level of TSH, a change that is not mediated by altered levels of serum cortisol, TBG, or total or free T_4 (Gross et al., 1971). Whether the effect of estradiol is mediated by the pituitary or the hypothalamus remains to be shown.

The net effect of all these changes in pregnancy is to increase total T_3 and T_4 levels. In the pregnant woman with Graves' disease the T_3 suppression test is usually abnormal. PBI levels and the BMR are increased beyond the usual levels that occur in an uncomplicated pregnancy. The LATS is recovered from the serum at term in pregnant women with Graves' disease.

337

Why some pregnant women develop Graves' disease and others do not is not known. Obviously, some may be suffering from a mild or latent form of the disease when they become pregnant. The pregnancy may make the symptoms worse, or exaggerate the physiological changes of the disease.

THE ROLE OF SURGICAL STRESS

The onset of Graves' disease has often been reported in association with major or minor surgery. It has been assumed that the surgical operation was a direct "stress" of a physiological nature, an assumption that disregards the anticipatory concerns of patients awaiting surgery (Price et al., 1956). These anticipatory psychological responses have been shown to have a variety of autonomic and hormonal concomitants. The pain after surgery and the effects of anesthesia must also be considered.

The mechanisms by which surgical stress precipitates Graves' disease are unknown. $PB^{131}I$ transiently increases after surgery (Engstrom and Markhardt, 1955; Fore et al., 1966; Hanbury, 1959). Changes in T_4 turnover rate due to a shift of T_4 from tissues to blood, are the result of ether anesthesia (Fore et al., 1966; Bernstein et al., 1967), and are not caused by increased secretion of T_4 by the thyroid gland, or increased clearance of T_4 by the kidney (Brockis, 1962). Increases in the radioactive iodine conversion ratios (Blount and Hardy, 1952) or the $PB^{131}I$ (Shipley and MacIntyre, 1954) have occurred in some patients, and decreases (Blount and Hardy, 1952) have been reported in others. Perry and Gemmell (1949) and Volpé et al. (1960) were unable to confirm any of these findings. In nonanesthetized rats, amputation of the tail decreased 24-hour ^{131}I uptake (Skebelskaya and Bagramyan, 1962).

At the present time, and in the face of such contradictory evidence, no conclusion can be reached about the relationship of surgical stress to changes in thyroid function that lead to Graves' disease.

THE ROLE OF INFECTIOUS ILLNESS

Graves' disease may start during or after various acute infections. During infectious illness there are three- or fourfold increases in the peripheral turnover of T_3 and T_4. The increased turnover is especially likely with acute infections of the lung. The increase in T_4 may last for two weeks after the start of the infection (Gregerman and Solomon, 1967; Sterling and Chodos, 1956). An increased T_3 and T_4 turnover occurs only with some febrile infectious diseases and not with others. The T_3 suppression test may become abnormal after a throat infection in patients who are in remission with Graves' disease (Alexander et al., 1968).

In mice infected with coccidioides a reduced ^{131}I uptake occurs (Sternberg et al., 1955). In rats, experimental streptococcus infection produces a diminished output of thyroidal iodine (Reichlen and Glaser, 1958). A pneumococcus infection in rats diminishes ^{131}I uptake and release, in the face of unchanged TSH levels (Shambaugh and Beisel, 1966). Diphtheria toxin decreases thyroid activity in guinea pigs (Brown-Grant and Pettes, 1960). Gerwin and his co-workers (1958) found that the single administration of a bacterial exotoxin depresses the release of ^{131}I from the thyroid gland of small mammals (mice, rats, rabbits) and increases it in larger ones (guinea pigs and rhesus monkeys).

The findings in human beings with infections are at variance with the findings in experimental animals. Fever and infections may cause a loss of appetite, and decrease food intake. Starvation in man inhibits thyroid activity (Van Middlesworth and Berry, 1951). The mechanism whereby infection precipitates Graves' disease is, therefore, unknown.

Psychological Responses to the Disease

Many thyrotoxic patients are depressed after Graves' disease begins (Artunkal and Togrol, 1964; Brown and Hetzel, 1963; Clower et al., 1969; Lidz, 1955; Mandelbrote and Wittkower, 1955; Wilson et al., 1961). The interpretation of this observation is not simple. It could readily be ascribed to the reaction to bereavement or loss. But when normal subjects are given T_3 they become more "jittery," depressed, and less friendly (Wilson et al., 1961). The depressed mood in thyrotoxic patients may be the result of the metabolic effect of T_3. They cannot only be ascribed to the emotional reaction to the separation that occurred prior to the onset of thyrotoxicosis.

The Psychological Conflict and Its Basis in Life Experience

Central to most psychological formulations about patients with Graves' disease is that they have been predisposed to respond to danger or separation by previous experiences. Patients with Graves' disease are sensitized by life experience to be fearful of danger or separation. Alexander (1950) went further. He believed that patients prone to Graves' disease strive after premature self-sufficiency. He also stated that the striving after self-sufficiency is not only determined by life experience but is promoted by the excessive production of thyroid hormone in childhood. The patients demonstrated their self-sufficiency by needing to care for other people at the expense of their own needs. They are especially sensitive to any disruption of their caretaking role.

Thyrotoxic patients are inordinately anxious and insecure. They also overcompensate for their extreme dependent attachment to their mothers by prematurely assuming a caretaking role and domestic responsibilities, and by acting mature and self-sufficient (Alexander, 1950; Brown and Gildea, 1937; Delay et al., 1949; Ham et al., 1950, 1951; Mittleman, 1933). Alexander (1950), Conrad (1934a, b), and Ham et al. (1950, 1951) ascribed the persistent, unconscious dependency of thyrotoxic patients to the experience of loss in childhood. Many of these patients when children had lost their mothers or a relative other than the mother. The patients frequently had long-standing fears of death and various phobias. Later they dreamed about dead persons, death, and funerals.

Other thyrotoxic patients had many siblings. The marriage of their parents was frequently unhappy and unstable. The families were economically insecure. The future thyrotoxic patients felt neglected and rejected as children. In childhood they had helped their parents to raise the other children. Adult responsibilities or work were prematurely thrust upon them when a parent died or because of the family's financial needs. When grown up, they had many children of their own (Ruesch et al., 1947).

339

Psychological Defenses

The patients express their unconscious dependency longings in various symptoms and traits. Patients identify with their absent, unavailable, and preoccupied mother; patients of both sexes tend to identify with their mothers (Lewis, 1923, 1925). The patients exercise strict control over the expression of their feelings (Brown and Gildea, 1937). They also overcompensate for their own longings for being taken care of by looking for more responsibility and by wanting to be helpful to others. When the strivings for self-sufficiency fail, or when the patient can no longer take care of others, thyrotoxicosis begins in the predisposed person.

Some patients with thyrotoxicosis are, however, more openly dependent upon the affection and the slavish devotion of other people (Conrad, 1934a, b; Lidz, 1949; Lidz and Whitehorn, 1949, 1950; Mandelbrote and Wittkower, 1955; Ruesch, 1948). When their wishes for affection and the devotion of others are required, they are in a state of "emotional equilibrium." If their wishes are not fulfilled or they are separated from the people upon whom they depend, the equilibrium is disturbed and they become thyrotoxic. In childhood, and later as adults, these patients are closely attached to one or the other parent, usually the mother. They successfully compete with their siblings for the attention, devotion, and affection of their mothers. As adults they care for their mothers in order to preserve the close relationship. Their mothers' death is followed by prolonged periods of grief or depression. Many of the patients have a previous history of a frank depressive illness. As adults they give to other people and demand little in return for fear that their demands would be spurned. They lavish affection on their children in order to preserve the bonds of mutual attachment. But in comparison to other thyrotoxic patients, these patients are not excessively or prematurely self-sufficient. The descriptions of these patients were made without using comparison groups and without verification by means of psychological tests.

Mandelbrote and Wittkower (1955) validated their clinical descriptions of thyrotoxic patients by observing a matched comparison group of patients, and by the use of psychological tests. They studied 20 women and 5 men while acutely thyrotoxic with Graves' disease, with the euthyroid form of the disease, and during a remission. They interviewed the patients' relatives. They followed the patients for a period of three months after they had become euthyroid. The comparison group consisted of outpatients with a wide variety of benign and serious diseases. The patients with Graves' disease differed significantly from those in the comparison group in three ways. Of the thyroid patients, 28 percent had a family history of Graves' disease (versus 4 percent in the controls). The thyrotoxic patients complained of an unhappy childhood. They were judged to have a poor sexual adjustment in comparison to patients with other diseases.

Mandelbrote and Wittkower could not confirm Ham's observation that women with Graves' disease were prolific bearers and caretakers of children, but they did confirm the fact that patients with Graves' disease are more anxious, depressed and unassertive than other patients. The patients with Graves' disease were confused about their sexual roles and anxious about their sexual fantasies. They harbored strong feelings of having been rejected. They were insecure in their relationships to others. They yearned to remain dependent on their mothers and other people. They had a frustrated but intense need for bearing

340

children. In contrast to patients with other diseases, patients with Graves' disease felt that they had been rejected by their mothers as children. The rejection generated an unquenchable desire for love and had produced reactive anger, anxiety, and guilt. When they were older, any situation in which love was unrequited revived the memories of previous experiences of rejection by the mother and was accompanied by a vicious cycle of frustration, longings for love and care, and anger, anxiety, and guilt. Throughout their lives they felt the need to placate the mother and other people in order to assure constant supplies of affection. At the same time, they lavished affection on their own children, presumably to make certain that their children would repay them. These patients harbored strong fears of being left alone, unloved, unattended, and deserted. They were apprehensive of and sensitive to the death of their parents and desertion by their spouses. They feared the day that their children would grow up and leave home. They reacted with fear, anger, and depression to actual separation and bereavement.

This study is noteworthy because the patients not only had Graves' disease but some were also euthyroid after treatment. Therefore, the effects of thyrotoxicosis on mental functioning and mood was controlled for. The effect of being treated for an illness was also controlled for. The study strongly supports Lidz's rather than Alexander's and Ham's observations on thyrotoxic patients, some of whom may, and others may not, have been thyrotoxic with Graves' disease. But the study did not control for the persistence of symptoms of the disease after treatment, nor the possible effects of surgery and medication. In more than one-half of all patients, thyrotoxic symptoms persist for a long time after treatment even though the physiological disturbances of the disease have returned to normal (Ruesch et al., 1947). To be specific, many patients treated for Graves' disease continue to be nervous, apprehensive, irritable, insomniac, easily startled, frightened, angered, and moved to tears. They have numerous fears.

Some patients not only continue to have symptoms, but actually become depressed after treatment. Some patients following treatment become hypothyroid. Yet studies of treated euthyroid patients can be used to test the validity of observations made during the thyrotoxic phase (Kleinschmidt et al., 1956; Ruesch et al., 1947).

The conflicts and the symptoms of untreated and treated thyrotoxic patients may be so severe that they have identifiable psychiatric disease. In 84 patients treated with ^{131}I and 2 with thiouracil and methimazole the incidence of diagnosable psychiatric illness was 44 percent: 9 percent were schizophrenic, 10 percent "borderline" schizophrenic, and 25 percent had various character disorders. The patients were observed for as long as two years, and the prevalence of psychiatric illness did not change with continuing treatment. The patients without clinical psychiatric illness were also anxious, depressed, full of destructive rage, and had sexual problems (Kleinschmidt et al., 1956).

Invalided patients with (treated) thyrotoxicosis differ socially, psychologically, and symptomatically from other chronically invalided patients, including patients who had thyroid surgery for nontoxic goiters. They are older, are more often still married, tend to be of foreign parentage, and have conventional and conservative values, interests, and hobbies. Most of the patients treated for thyrotoxicosis belong to a low socioeconomic group. Married, previously thyrotoxic patients recovered faster with treatment than unmarried ones.

Patients, after they recover from thyrotoxicosis, harbor secret wishes for success, wealth, and power that conflict with their wishes for care and guidance by others. They are often the first or the last children born into families that were larger than those found in the other invalided patients. More than one-half of the parents of the ex-thyrotoxic patients had been separated, divorced, or had died when the patients were growing up (Ruesch et al., 1947).

Marked fluctuations in mood and behavior occur in treated patients. The mood changes occur in response to the same or similar life experiences that before treatment were associated with the onset of thyrotoxicosis, but the antithyroid drugs avert recurrence of the disease. The mood changes because the patient's psychological capacity to adapt to these disturbing life experiences seems to be even less than before the onset of the disease (Kleinschmidt et al., 1956).

Psychological adaptation is impaired with altered brain function due to metabolic disturbances. Hypothyroidism is a known cause of cerebral metabolic disturbances and is a frequent complication of thyroid surgery and antithyroid medication. ^{131}I treatment destroys the thyroid gland: 25 percent of thyrotoxic patients who have received radioiodine treatment for two years become clinically hypothyroid (Dunn and Chapman, 1964). After radioiodine treatment, the gland becomes defective in its capacity to bind thyroidal iodine organically. Treatment may limit its capacity to respond to changes in the environment such as a cold climate. Thiouracil and methimazole reduce the synthesis of T_3 and T_4 by inhibiting the coupling of iodotyrosines to produce iodothyronines, the transformation of monoiodotyrosine to diiodotyrosine, and the formation of monoiodotyrosine in the gland. The inhibition of hormone synthesis by these drugs occasionally produces hypothyroidism.

In conclusion, all the clinical observations attest to the dependency of thyrotoxic patients on other people for love and attention. Patients are apprehensive and fearful about separation and danger. Some patients overcompensate for their dependency and are prematurely and excessively self-sufficient. Other patients adapt to their dependency by making their children and others depend on them. But these studies are flawed because thyrotoxicosis is a heterogeneous condition brought about by a number of quite separate factors, including Graves' disease and the ingestion of thyroid hormone (see, for example, Case #5 of Kleinschmidt et al., 1956).

These flaws cast a shadow over all studies of the psychological preconditions in Graves' disease. Most of the studies of personalities, traits, conflicts, and defenses of patients with thyroid disorders have been done in those with hyperthyroidism or thyrotoxicosis. These functional states are heterogeneous in etiology, and are not specific to Graves' disease (Appendixes 1 and 2). Even when behavioral scientists have studied patients with identified Graves' disease they have not taken sufficient care to identify and take account of the known effects of the thyrotoxic state on brain function and the faculties of the mind. Even the most experienced clinician may have difficulty in discriminating between clinical thyrotoxicosis and an anxiety state when thyrotoxic patients with Graves' disease complain of "nervousness," apprehension, increased perspiration, palpitations, fatigue, weakness, difficulties in concentration and in remembering, tremulousness, and insomnia. Further, physicians have often not specified the nature of the "nervousness"—whether it is fear, anxiety, fearfulness about the future, frank phobic anxiety, or insecurity.

Therefore, the insecurity and anxiety so often retrospectively ascribed to patients with Graves' disease as an essential and permanent feature of their personalities may be a symptom of the disease. It may also be a psychological response to being ill, or even a response to some of the symptoms, such as the exophthalmos or the rapid heartbeat.

Thyrotoxic patients frequently complain of memory difficulties, which have been confirmed by appropriate psychological tests. Frank deliria occur in severe Graves' disease, especially during thyrotoxic "storm." The incidence of delirium in thyrotoxic Graves' disease without storm may be 20 percent (Lidz and Whitehorn, 1949). Delirium impairs attention, cognition, and memory. Memory impairment makes the reliability of personal data difficult to establish. The accounts that patients provide should be confirmed, either by the patient when the memory difficulties have faded away, or by the patient's relatives. Observations about the psychology of Graves' disease should be checked against patients with euthyroid Graves' disease, in which the symptoms and signs of the thyrotoxic state are absent, or in patients during remission of the thyrotoxic state.

Because of these possible sources of error, efforts to validate clinical observations have been made by means of clinical psychiatric, psychological studies and predictive studies of patients at risk for Graves' disease or other thyrotoxic conditions. Hermann and Quarton (1965) designed a study specifically to test Ham's and Alexander's observations. The study dealt explicitly with many of the methodological difficulties that bedevil clinical psychiatric research; in particular, it addressed the problems of experimenter and response bias, of inferences from data, and of not having a comparison group.

The problem of picking a meaningful control group was overcome in this study by choosing 50 consecutive admissions to a thyroid clinic of a general hospital. The experimental and control groups consisted of 24 with Graves' disease, 11 with primary hypothyroidism and 15 euthyroid patients who had either nontoxic nodular or "colloid" goiters. Some in the last group of patients had no disease of the thyroid gland but were having its function evaluated by the usual tests. The 26 euthyroid and hypothyroid patients constituted the comparison groups.

The patients with Graves' disease complained much more frequently of shakiness, insomnia, distractability, heat intolerance, shortness of breath, or change in menstrual flow than the patients in the comparison group did. The distractability in patients with Graves' disease was due to a disturbance of memory function.

The outcome of this inquiry was disappointing. The only significant finding was that patients with Graves' disease had brought more children into the world, just as Alexander (1950) had found. But Alexander's finding that these patients are excessively self-sufficient and had strong unconscious wishes to be dependent on other people were not confirmed. The fear, anxiety, and shakiness are the symptoms of thyrotoxicosis, and are neither abiding characteristics of the patient or responses to life events before the onset of thyrotoxicosis (Hermann and Quarton, 1965).

The results of this study could also be interpreted in another way: that patients with different diseases of the thyroid gland psychologically resemble each other more than they differ. When patients become thyrotoxic they become sleepless, nervous, shaky, and distractable. But many different diseases of the thyroid gland may become toxic (Appendix 2).

Nontoxic solitary and multinodular goiters may both become toxic (Sheline and McCormack, 1960). A simple goiter may antecede either a toxic diffuse or a toxic multinodular goiter—especially if the simple form is present in the patient at the time of puberty (Taylor, 1953, 1960). Studies of patients *predisposed* to toxic diffuse goiter and single toxic adenomata of the thyroid gland have revealed their social and psychological similarities (Voth et al., 1970; Wallerstein et al., 1965). Therefore patients with different diseases causing thyrotoxicosis resemble each other, and patients with thyrotoxic Graves' disease do not differ from patients who have other diseases that produce thyrotoxicosis. This conclusion is borne out by a validating study done by Alexander and his co-workers (1968). Patients with active thyrotoxicosis were studied without further specification as to whether the patients' toxic state was due to a diffuse, multinodular, or single nodular goiter. A test was made of the formulation that patients with thyrotoxicosis struggle against the fear of physical damage to their bodies and against the fear of death. The patients attempt to master these fears by denying them and seek dangerous situations in order to overcome them alone.

In his original formulation Alexander (1950) had placed the pathogenetic burden on premature maturation and psychological development, self-sufficiency, and the wish to "help others." When "strivings for self-sufficiency and taking care of others" failed, thyrotoxicosis ensued. In 1968, he stated that "the precipitating situation is often some kind of threat to survival, in which the counterphobic defense breaks down"; the "counterphobic defense" had been erected against dangerous situations, such as an accident.

The study carried out by Alexander in 1968 used new criteria for the "blind" selection of 10 patients (5 men and 5 women) with thyrotoxicosis from a group of 83 patients with seven psychosomatic diseases. A group of eight internists and nine psychoanalysts were asked "blindly" to diagnose each patient's disease on the basis of psychological criteria. The nine psychoanalysts correctly diagnosed thyrotoxicosis in almost half the patients who actually had the disease, thereby confirming the formulation in those patients correctly diagnosed. The diagnostic accuracy achieved by the nine psychoanalysts significantly exceeded the likelihood of being correct by chance.

Some of the results of this study are of further interest; bronchial asthma was the disease most easily confounded with thyrotoxicosis, suggesting that the fear of survival is great in both groups of patients. Despite the diagnostic success achieved in this study, the study does not prove that the psychological factors play a predisposing or initiating role in thyrotoxicosis.

Validating Psychological Studies

Compared to the large number of studies employing clinical psychological tests on patients with peptic duodenal ulcer or bronchial asthma, relatively few studies of this kind have been published on patients with Graves' disease. Psychiatrists like Kleinschmidt, Mandelbrote and Wittkower, and Ruesch et al. used clinical psychological tests to extend, modify, quantify, and validate their psychiatric observations. The most relevant, other psychological study was done by Artunkal and Togrol (1964). It documented the specific cognitive defects in thyrotoxicosis. A number of clinical and laboratory tests (including T_3 suppression test) were used to select 23 middle-class Turkish women with thyrotoxicosis; some were illiterate, others had finished 6 to 12 grades of high school. Matching euthyroid women were also tested. Ten thyrotoxic patients were retested after treatment with radioiodine, antithyroid drugs, or surgery.

344

During the active phase of the disease, the patients performed more slowly on reaction-time experiments to visual stimuli but they were not slower after treatment. Treatment failed to alter defects in auditory reaction times between patients and control subjects. On tests of visual-motor coordination, untreated thyrotoxic patients were less accurate, unsteadier, and slower, and they became fatigued more rapidly than normal subjects. They made more mistakes on mirror-drawing tests. They perseverated on other tests. They were also more depressed than normal subjects, both during the active phase and phase of remission of the disease.

A depressed mood certainly occurs in many thyrotoxic patients for reasons that are still not understood. The occurrence of this mood state has been confirmed repeatedly (Brown and Hetzel, 1963; Ruesch et al., 1947; Wilson et al., 1961). The main lesson that can be learned from the results of these studies is that patients with thyrotoxicosis are both depressed and have cognitive defects because of a metabolic disturbance of the brain that disappears with treatment.

Many English investigators prefer to use the Maudsley Personality Inventory and its precursor, the Maudsley Medical Questionnaire, because of their objectivity and validity, rather than tests of cognition or mood. Inconsistent results have been obtained. Thyrotoxic patients treated in an outpatient department (Sainsbury, 1960), or with a past history of thyrotoxicosis (Eysenck, 1963), have higher than average "neuroticism" scores. Robbins and Vinson (1960) obtained the same results by the use of this inventory, but Brown and Hetzel (1963) and Paykel (1966) found no differences in "neuroticism" scores between untreated or treated patients who were thyrotoxic and patients with nontoxic goiters or myxedema. The neuroticism items of the Maudsley Personality Inventory has been used to compare patients having a history of thyrotoxicosis with patients having other psychosomatic diseases. After carrying out this comparison, Sainsbury (1960) and Eysenck (1963) came to diametrically opposite conclusions.

It is very hard to ascertain the basis of these conflicting results. The inability of psychologists to verify each other's findings has brought about a nihilistic attitude on the part of their medical colleagues, who are always prepared to accept negative findings as confirmation of their belief that psychosocial factors play no role in thyrotoxicosis or in Graves' disease. They have, for example, made much of the study carried out by Robbins and Vinson (1960), who concluded that their ten untreated thyrotoxic patients (nine of whom probably had Graves' disease) differed from normal subjects or other patients with psychiatric symptoms or illnesses ("somatization" reactions, compulsive neurosis, schizophrenia), when tested by means of the Maudsley Medical Questionnaire, the Crown Word Connection Test, and the Stroop color-naming test. The thyrotoxic patients performed on these tests like patients with impaired brain function. After treatment of these patients for thyrotoxicosis, significant changes in performance on the tests occurred. But the changes in their responses to this questionnaire cannot only be ascribed to changes brought about by treatment with antithyroid medication. The changes in performance might be due to a practice effect which was not ruled out. This study demonstrates that untreated thyrotoxic patients have cognitive deficits when tested by the Stroop test. But such tests cannot be used to infer the presence of mood states, psychological conflict, defenses, or traits.

The basis for the cognitive deficits in thyrotoxicosis have also been investigated (Wilson et al., 1961). Thyrotoxic patients and normal subjects given T_3 to ingest, show an

345

increased voltage when the EEG is photically driven. The increased voltage is associated with the formation of visual illusions. And Kopell et al. (1970) showed that T_3 impairs selective attention and simultaneously reduces the latencies of the early negative and positive waves of the visual evoked potential in normal subjects. The impaired selective attention by T_3 may form the basis of the distractability that is a prominent symptom in thyrotoxic patients.

On balance, psychological tests, when appropriately used, tend to confirm the impression that thyrotoxic patients have impaired cerebral function brought about in part by increased T_3. The exact nature of this impairment is not known.

Predictive Studies: The Risk Strategy

When patients with Graves' disease are studied after they become ill, clinical psychiatric observations are influenced by the patients' cognitive disturbances and the effects of hospitalization on the patients. Patients react individually to being thyrotoxic; and the thyrotoxicosis of Graves' disease may also be life-threatening. For these reasons, all social and psychological observations should, in theory, be verified by predictive studies. Two such predictive studies have been carried out in the past. The subjects in the first study were selected on the basis of physiological criteria that consisted of the duration of the biological half-life of administered ^{131}I and psychological criteria derived from the previous psychiatric observations of other patients. Subjects were selected if they had premature strivings for independence, denied their hostility, "undid" hostile impulses by an overconcern for relatives and friends, sought affection by service to others, and had a desire for bearing children that was associated with fears of pregnancy and parturition. In addition, if women identified with men, and their psychological defenses were poorly integrated, making them prone to fear and anxiety, they were also chosen for the study. Twenty-seven subjects were assigned to one of two groups—one group had and the other did not have the psychological characteristics. The subjects who satisfied the correct psychological criteria were found to have a shorter half-life of ^{131}I in their sera. In a separate group of 44 subjects these findings were confirmed by predictions about which subjects would have a longer or shorter biological half-life of ^{131}I on the basis of the psychological profile (Dongier et al., 1956).

If the validity of the physiological criterion, as a measure of being prone to thyrotoxicosis, is accepted, this study provides impressive validation of retrospective, psychiatric observations made on patients; and Dongier and his co-workers (1956), who carried out this study, stated that the physiological criterion was valid "provided that the rapidity of disappearance of ^{131}I from the thyroid gland can be regarded as a reliable index of its function." In the light of more-recent research, we now know that biological half-life of ^{131}I is a product of a number of processes that do and do not directly reflect the gland's functioning. Therefore, its validity as a measure of predispostion to, or of, Graves' disease is only partial.

The thyroidal uptake of ^{131}I by the thyroid gland—and by inference its release into the blood by the gland—reveals: (1) the gland's efficiency over time in removing iodide from plasma, relative to the efficiency of the kidney in excreting it; (2) the efficiency by which iodide is excreted by the gut; (3) the metabolic disposition of a part of ^{131}I as $^{131}T_4$—a disposition that has been shown to be more rapid in periods of thyrotoxicosis in Graves' disease, in the latent phase of the disease, and in relatives of patients with Graves' disease; (4) the intracellular accumulation of bound ^{131}I; and (5) the normal flux of labeled iodide into and out of extracellular fluid.

In order for the biological half-life of ^{131}I to be a valid criterion of a predisposition to Graves' disease, it must be shown that ^{131}I is being used to form and release the relevant biologically active products (such as radioactive T_3 and T_4), and/or that it is not being used to replenish depleted stores of thyroid hormone produced, for example, by an inadequate intake of iodine, suppression of the gland, subacute thyroiditis, or withdrawal of antithyroid drugs.

Both the methodology of this study and its results are impressive. The physiological criterion was the best available 20 years ago, and the results confirm the findings made by clinical, retrospective observation of thyrotoxic patients.

More recently, another validating study was carried out by Wallerstein and his co-workers (1965) and Voth et al. (1970). The localized avidity ("hot-spots") of the thyroid gland for radioactive iodine was used as a criterion to select candidates for future disease. Such "hot-spots", in otherwise euthyroid patients, represent a transition state from the nontoxic state to the toxic functioning ("hot") thyroid adenoma (Perlmutter and Slater, 1955). This later study involved 195 subjects referred for diagnosis to the radiologist for symptoms of irritability, apprehensiveness, crying spells, weight loss, palpitations, and excessive sweating. They were given radioiodine. Thirty-three subjects were found to have "hot-spots." Their ^{131}I uptake by the gland over a 32-hour period, PB^{131}I, and levels of radioiodine in the urine were otherwise normal. Some of the 33 subjects had a palpable nodule in the thyroid gland. The exact number with a nodule is not stated in the report. One woman was said to have a diffusely enlarged gland, and three women a small nodule.

Fifteen women with "hot-spots" were interviewed. They gave a history of being lonely, shy, timid, submissive, and fearful children. As adults they had many physical complaints, were fearfully preoccupied with malfunctioning of their thyroid gland and reproductive system. They were afraid of other diseases and of physicians. Eight of the 15 women had had surgical operations. They were frightened, emotionally inhibited, and "constricted" people with great difficulties in expressing sad, depressed, and hostile feelings. They over-idealized their parents and spouses. They were long-suffering, unhappy, guilt-ridden and cheerless women. They were excessively altruistic, to the point of being martyrs. Based on these observations and on psychological tests a 25 item personality inventory was drawn up that formed the basis for predicting who among a new group of 363 subjects would have "hot-spots." Two investigators rated the interview protocols in order to predict which subjects did and which did not have a normal uptake of radioiodine by the gland. Their predictions were accurate in a subgroup of 107 symptom-free women. Nine of the 13 women with "hot-spots" and two women whose gland took up ^{131}I in a diffuse and mildly increased manner were correctly identified by the psychological criteria. In the remaining 256 women identification of "hot-spots" was not possible. Nine frankly thyrotoxic patients were also assessed by the same inventory. In eight of nine patients, 20 or more of the 25 items were checked as salient.

The main aim was to determine whether the psychiatric descriptions of subjects who are at risk for thyrotoxicosis (presumably of Graves' disease) are the same as descriptions of frankly thyrotoxic patients. The answer to this question is in the affirmative.

The study yielded another striking finding. Subjects with "hot-spots" had psychological profiles that were similar, if not identical, to the profiles of those with diffuse increases of ^{131}I uptake but not thyrotoxic and patients who were frankly thyrotoxic. It follows, then, that the same psychological characteristics occurred in subjects who were prone to or who had two or more diseases of the thyroid gland.

It is usually assumed that in the normally functioning thyroid gland the uptake of radioiodine is symmetrical. Yet Thomas (1966) found that in 10 of 25 persons an asymmetrical uptake occurred, despite the absence of any other detectable abnormality in the function or structure of the gland. A "hot-spot" was defined in Wallerstein's study as a localized area of the gland emitting twice the number of counts per minute after the ingestion of ^{131}I as the contralateral area or the entire remainder of the gland. A local "hot-spot" in the presence of the less-intense collection of radio-iodine in the surrounding tissue makes it unlikely that the nodule is causing thyrotoxicosis. A similar scanning picture—local avidity and reduced function in surrounding tissue—also occurs with thyroiditis. An additional test, such as the injection of a test-dose of TSH in order to stimulate the less-avid tissue to accumulate ^{131}I more intensively must be carried out before the "hot-spot" is designated an adenoma or not. This test is based upon the knowledge that the autonomous adenoma puts out increased amounts of thyroid hormones, which lower levels of TSH by feedback inhibition. The rest of the gland is thus laggard in its uptake of iodine when it is not being stimulated to do so by TSH. In Wallerstein's study, the assumption was made that the "hot-spot" was an adenoma that could become toxic.

Actually, the matter is even more complicated: in all probability, there are two kinds of "hot" nodules or "spots" that take up iodine more avidly than the surrounding thyroid tissue does. One kind represents the solitary "autonomous" adenoma of the thyroid gland in that it takes up iodine independently of TSH (Sheline and McCormack, 1960). The second kind probably consists of a single, or one of several, nodules whose uptake of iodine and size are regulated by TSH; they diminish their uptake and shrink in size when TSH levels fall upon administration of T_4 (Greene and Farran, 1965). Neither of these kinds of "hot-spots" antecede or accompany Graves' disease (Weiner, 1970a).

Despite the local avidity of the gland for iodine, patients with "hot-spots" in their thyroid glands are not necessarily at risk for thyrotoxicosis—the underlying assumption of the study done by Wallerstein. This assumption is not necessarily correct, as the investigations of Silverstein and his co-workers (1967) attest. They carried out observations for two to seven years on 9 patients selected from a group of 47 with solitary hyperfunctioning nodules. In 22 of these 47 patients the nodule was "autonomous" (i.e., independent of the control by TSH). Nineteen of these 22 patients were euthyroid by the usual laboratory criteria; in only 1 patient was the diagnosis of a *toxic* adenoma of the gland clearly established. A long-term follow-up was carried out on 9 of these 19 patients. Four of these 9 patients remained clinically euthyroid and the adenoma did not change in size or alter the amount of ^{131}I it accumulated. In one patient, the nodule was partly dependent on TSH; in a six-year period it became less avid, with the surrounding thyroid tissue accumulating iodine. The "autonomous" nodule in three other patients became dependent on TSH in time. In the ninth patient, an autonomous nodule underwent cystic degeneration and calcification with reversion of the gland to control by TSH. None of the nine patients became thyrotoxic during the years of investigation. Thus, the natural history of "hot-spots" is not only very variable, as Voth et al. (1970) also discovered, but "hot-spots" do not necessarily lead to thyrotoxicosis. Actually the association of a "hot-spot," discovered on a single survey of the gland with ^{131}I, with thyrotoxicosis is as low as 33 percent in some series and as high as 100 percent in others (Gilbert-Dreyfus, 1963; Lobo et al., 1965; Savoie, 1961; Sheline and McCormack, 1960).

Additional tests of thyroid function (e.g., T_3 and T_4 content of serum, the T_3 suppression, and TSH-stimulation test) should have been carried out by Wallerstein and his colleagues in order to ascertain whether the subjects with "hot-spots" were euthyroid, had thyroiditis, were at risk for or in the early stages of thyrotoxicosis due to Graves' disease or a toxic adenoma of the thyroid. It is also possible that some of their subjects may have had the "hot-spots" that signify an autonomous *nontoxic* adenoma of the gland and were never at risk for thyrotoxicosis.

Wallerstein's study presents a new and intriguing conclusion. The authors state that their predictions were as correct for nine subjects with "hot-spots" as they were for two subjects with diffusely increased ^{131}I uptake and for nine thyrotoxic patients. Therefore, the psychological criteria apply, with equal validity, to the small number of subjects at risk for or with incipient or actual Graves' disease, but also to subjects who may have had nontoxic adenomata of the gland.

It is possible that these results are due to (1) the inability of psychological techniques to discriminate between subtle differences in the psychological characteristics of persons predisposed to or suffering from several distinct thyroid diseases; or (2) the absence of distinctive psychological features of patients with different diseases of the thyroid gland; what is more, there may be no characteristics distinguishing patients who never will be thyrotoxic and those who will.

In summary, Wallerstein's work was designed to validate, by using a risk strategy, the characteristic psychological patterns of thyrotoxicosis described by Ham and Alexander. But it failed to do so. Rather, it uncovered the interesting finding that "hot-spots" are not uncommon in women. The "hot-spots" occurred in women who were either predisposed to, in the process of developing, or who had thyrotoxicosis due to an adenoma of the gland. The women have the same personal conflicts, ways of handling them, symptoms, and traits as patients who were predisposed to or were in the incipient phase of Graves' disease. Because of questions about the validity of the physiological measures used by Dongier et al., and the questions that Wallerstein's study raises, the formulations arrived at by clinically interviewing patients with Graves' disease have not been fully validated. Rather, one may conclude that certain psychological features characterize persons who are predisposed to thyrotoxicosis, later associated with more than one disease of the thyroid gland.

Studies on the Causes of the Psychological Predisposition

Patients are psychologically and physiologically predisposed to Graves' disease. These predispositions probably long antedate the disease. But we have no real idea if the various predispositions to the disease are in some way related to each other. Alexander (1950) thought they were. He postulated that thyroid hormone stimulated the physical and psychological maturation of the child more than is usual to produce premature self-sufficiency. He

349

also implied that life experiences were responsible for stimulating thyroid hormone secretion, the premature self-sufficiency and the early assumption of a caretaking role: growing up in a large family or the death of a parent thrust the mothering role on the child prematurely. These hypotheses about the psychological characteristics of patients are probably correct in some patients only. All patients do have strong needs for love, affection, and reassurance. Some patients are also fearful of separation, injury, and death because of parent died when they were children.

But thyrotoxic patients with Graves' disease also have a family history of the disease. Ham et al. (1951) and Mandelbrote and Wittkower (1955) found a family history of thyrotoxicosis or Graves' disease in 21 percent and 24 percent, respectively, of their patients. In other series, the figure is even higher (Aschner, 1936; Heimann, 1966). Alexander deserves much credit because he attempted to relate the life experiences and the psychological conflicts they produced in patients with Graves' disease to physiological variation. He ventured the hypothesis that premature responsibility, forced upon patients by circumstance, produced an accelerated rate of maturation and personality development and left specific conflicts and traits in its wake.

He stated that "in view of the known stimulating function of the thyroid gland in the growth of the infant, it becomes tempting to relate the hyperactivity of this gland with the apparent need of the hyperthyroid patient to become mature in an accelerated tempo." He felt that the "patient's constant effort to maintain a pseudomaturity must be quite stressful and may serve to activate the secretion of thyrotropic hormone." Alexander further speculated that the premature self-sufficiency and the facade of maturity and of nurturance had etiological and pathogenetic significance. But these traits and the conflicts they engendered were the product of increased production of thyroid hormone, which then caused an accelerated rate of maturation. In current terminology, a double positive feedback loop existed between the thyroid gland and the mind.

Alexander's hypothesis was tentatively reiterated by Wallerstein and his co-workers (1965). They suggested that a partial state of thyroid hyperactivity begins early in life and induces accelerated activity and physical and psychological maturation that outstrips the ability of the child to cope with it. Premature maturation leaves unrequited dependency needs behind that continue throughout the patient's life behind a facade of pseudomaturity.

Alexander's hypothesis was based on the known stimulating effect of thyroid hormone on the maturation and metamorphosis of amphibia and on the physical growth rate of hypothyroid mammals. In cretinism and in infantile and juvenile hypothyroidism, treatment with T_4 partly or wholly reverses the impairment of physical, sexual, and intellectual growth and maturation. The thyroid hormones do play a role in bone growth and sexual maturation, and in the development of intelligence and the capacity to learn. But there is no evidence that excessive levels of the hormones accelerate these processes in normal children. In fact, patients with juvenile Graves' disease or thyrotoxicosis are characterized by normal physical development and accelerated skeletal growth (Mäenpää et al., 1966) but *delayed* sexual maturation. It is believed that sexual maturation is delayed because increases in thyroid hormone output alter the metabolism of the sex hormones. Specifically, the transformations of estradiol to estriol (Fishman et al., 1965) and of testosterone and dehydroepiandrosterone to etiocholanolone are reduced (Gallagher et al., 1960).

350

Patients with juvenile thyrotoxicosis or Graves' disease show no spurt in intellectual growth before treatment. Unfortunately, the personality development or the conflicts of juvenile patients has not been studied, so that we do not know whether an increased thyroid hormone output produces an accelerated progression of personality development. Actually, physical and psychological growth and development are influenced by a number of genes, hormones, and nutritional and environmental factors, many of which remain to be specified. This general assertion is based on negative evidence: in deficiency states, growth, development, and adaptive behavior are impaired (Eayrs, 1960).

The hormones that are believed to affect all areas of development are the pituitary growth hormone (hGH), the sex hormones, the thyroid hormones, and the glucocorticosteroids. Complex interactions between the thyroid hormones and hGH occur: specifically, low levels of T_3 and T_4 in the bloodstream are associated with a reduced content of hGH in the pituitary gland of rats. In both hypothyroid and hyperthyroid patients, the maximum response of hGH to insulin-induced hypoglycemia is reduced in extent and delayed in time (Burgess et al., 1966). Normal physical growth is dependent on hGH. In excess hGH increases the amount of growth but does not control growth *rate*. But nothing is known about the effect of hGH on brain and psychological development. Alexander contended that the *rate* of psychological growth and development in predisposed patients is accelerated in childhood. One must conclude, then, that at least this part of Alexander's hypothesis has not as yet been borne out by direct or indirect evidence.

The hypothesis that the production and secretion of T_3 and T_4 (supposedly under the influence of TSH) is increased prior to the development of Graves' disease is tenuous. In any normal adult population (Lowrey and Starr, 1959) protein bound iodine (PBI) levels in serum are normally distributed with a range in men of 2.5 to 8.5 μg percent (mean: 5.33 μg $\pm$ 1.19) and in women of 3.5 to 8.5 μg percent (mean: 5.67 μg $\pm$ 1.22). The distribution in children is unknown. It should be investigated experimentally whether those persons whose PBI levels fall within the lowest and highest segments of the distribution curve under steady state conditions differ physically, intellectually, or psychologically, and whether those in the highest segment of the curve are prone to Graves' disease. Nonetheless, Alexander addressed an important question: can certain life experiences alter bodily function, which in turn alters the maturation and development of the brain, psychological functioning, and the processing of experience? Only future research can answer this question. In the case of Graves' disease this question remains unanswered. The psychological features of adults with Graves' disease have also been ascribed to exposure to loss, death, many siblings, parental divorce and financial hardship in childhood (Alexander, 1950; Conrad, 1934 a,b; Ham et al., 1950, 1951). Curiously enough psychiatrists have paid little attention to the fact that Graves' disease or other forms of thyrotoxicosis runs in families. Graves' disease frequently occurs in a mother and in her daughter when she grows up. If the mother is a self-sufficient caretaker of her children, upon whom she lavishes affection, why should the daughter suffer from unrequited affection and dependency needs and feel rejected? How does the mother's personal style, attitude and behavior predispose her daughter psychologically to Graves' disease? This question could be answered by studies of mothers with a history of Graves' disease and their offspring. In fact, the families of Graves' disease patients have not been studied psychologically in the ways families of patients with bronchial asthma have been.

PSYCHOENDOCRINE STUDIES IN MAN RELEVANT TO THE ONSET OF GRAVES' DISEASE AND THYROTOXICOSIS

A comprehensive explanation of the pathogenesis of Graves' disease should include a precise description of all the mechanisms that link the psychological events with the altered physiology and anatomy of the thyroid gland. Such links have not been forged. Alexander (1950) suggested that in the face of fright or loss, TSH secretion is enhanced, and Graves' disease begins. This hypothesis has never been tested because it has not yet been possible to select patients at risk prior to the onset of the disease. After the inception of Graves' disease, TSH levels appear to be normal, low, or markedly depressed, and even this finding is somewhat suspect because of the limited sensitivity of radioimmunoassay as a technique for estimating TSH levels; only elevated levels of TSH can be reliably detected. Thus, it cannot be concluded that at the time of inception of the disease, TSH levels are not acutely elevated. Nevertheless, TSH plays no part in most current hypotheses about the pathogenesis of Graves' disease. The disease is currently considered to be an autoimmune disease due to the presence of a number of antibodies and autoantibodies, some of which have hormonal properties.

Alexander's hypothesis has not be tested by psychophysiological techniques, either. In fact, psychophysiological investigations of the pathogenetic mechanisms in Graves' disease have seldom been investigated. When they have, recurrences of the disease have usually been studied with psychological and physiological techniques used in parallel. Voth et al. (1970) studied 475 women by giving them ^{131}I to determine the incidence of localized increase in ^{131}I uptake in the thyroid gland. Forty-one women had localized ("hot-spots") increases of radioiodine uptake, 41 were at risk for toxic adenoma, and 10 had an increase in uptake. The physiological status of the thyroid gland of 239 of the 475 women was reassessed by the use of the ^{131}I method one to four times during a period of 12 years. Sixty-three of these 239 women were also retested psychologically and interviewed on several different occasions in order to determine the occurrence of chronic emotional strain in their lives. Emotional strain and changes in the presence of appearance of thyroid "hot-spots" and diffuse increases in ^{131}I uptake coincided with significantly greater frequency than in a control group of women who had no local or diffuse increase in uptake. When no strain was experienced, diffuse or local increases in uptake remained unchanged. Therefore, "hot-spots" wax and wane in concert with life stresses and emotional strains. The research strategy of this study has much to commend it, and the conclusions clarify the fact that the function of the gland changes with stress and strain. Because TSH levels were not measured, it is impossible to determine the mechanism mediating stress and strain.

It is, of course, possible that frightening situations and losses may be mediated by different physiological mechanisms. In animals the *duration* of certain "stressful" events may be the critical factor in determining which mechanism is brought into play (Weiner, 1972). Actually, stressful situations mobilize a wide range of physiological changes beside changes in TSH levels. The situations are mediated by autonomic, hormonal, and neuromuscular mechanisms (Mason, 1968b; Weiner and Hart, 1975).

At the present time, changes in TSH levels cannot be assumed to be the mechanism by which fright or bereavement are mediated to precipitate the disease. Bereavement produces a wide variety of behavioral and psychological responses besides anxiety, anger, depression, or grief. The appetite may diminish or increase, and insomnia may occur (Wilson et al., 1961). The influence of increased or reduced food intake or sleeplessness on thyroid function should not be overlooked in trying to understand the pathogenesis of Graves' disease.

Psychoendocrine Correlations between Stress and the Function of the Thyroid Gland

One of the remarkable features of the thyroid gland is its functional stability in the face of many environmental stresses. A cold climate is the only change that regularly produces an increased output of thyroid hormones. But as Voth's study shows psychological "stress" also alters the uptake of iodine in women. And if it could be demonstrated that psychological stress regularly changes the output of T_3 and T_4, it would still be necessary to show that such changes in output are related to the pathogenesis or course of Graves' disease. The pathogenetic effect of psychological stress remains unexplored.

In most studies on the psychophysiology of stress and thyroid function changes in PBI, not TSH, levels have been measured in euthyroid and thyrotoxic subjects. Stress was induced in many different ways: some investigators used the interview technique to elicit unpleasant experiences in their subjects; others used film or studied subjects during hypnotic trances or during naturally occurring events, such as school examinations or during simulated military exercises.

In 1925, Ziegler and Levin reported that the BMR of veterans rose when they recalled their wartime experiences. In another study, mean blood iodine levels increased by 32 to 200 percent in 13 of 15 presumably euthyroid volunteers during hypnotically induced feeling states. During the recovery period the levels returned to baseline in 90 to 360 minutes (Wittkower et al., 1932).

PBI levels are responsive to stressful interviews. In some subjects they rise at first; in others, a biphasic response occurs that is preceded by an initial fall (Hetzel et al., 1952). Biphasic response patterns occur in euthyroid subjects and in thyrotoxic patients. The response patterns and the amounts of response are individual both in patients and in subjects. In hypothyroid patients the low PBI levels either remain unchanged or fall further (Hetzel et al., 1956; Wolff, 1953).

Another author reported that during an examination period the PBI levels of 11 medical students were elevated for four hours (Tingley et al., 1958). A wide variety of stressful or painful conditions—examinations, athletic contests, surgery, and myocardial infarction—no more affect group mean serum PBI levels than do everyday events (Volpé et al., 1960). It may take extreme stress to do so. Johansson et al. (1970) subjected 32 Swedish army personnel to 72 hours of experimental "stress" consisting of 24 consecutive three-hour periods of simulated battle conditions without rest or sleep. PBI levels were measured initially, 24 hours after the onset, and at the end of the experimental period. The levels rose from 5.5 ± 0.2 μg percent to 6.0 ± 0.3 μg percent during the first 24 hours and to 6.5 ± 0.2 μg percent by the end of the experiment. Another group of 31 younger army officers (age 20–44 years) were asked to spend 72 hours in a shooting range in semidark conditions without sleep or rest. PBI levels rose from control values of 6.1 ± 0.2 μg percent to 7.9 ± 0.2 μg percent by the end of the experiment.

The situation to which these army personnel were subjected produced not only boredom and fatigue, but also lack of sleep. It demanded intense attention and mental concentration and it may have irritated and angered the participants. (The authors reported that two subjects in the second series of experiments became manifestly paranoid.)

Obviously a complex study of this kind must be evaluated in the light of daily fluctuations of PBI levels. It is believed that individual PBI levels do not change appreciably over short (Danowski et al., 1949) or long (Gaffney et al., 1960) periods of time. Circadian fluctuations in plasma PBI levels are, however, believed to occur in animals and man (Schatz and Volpé, 1959; Tingley et al., 1958). Neither the duration of the circadian cycle nor the times of the day when the highest and lowest PBI levels occur have been established. Margolese and Golub (1957) reported that the complete cycle in two men and three women lasted 36 hours. Normal fluctuations in the level of PBI amount to about 10 percent (Auerbach, 1963; Bushler et al., 1968). Peak mean values have been obtained at 11 P.M. and 12:30 P.M. (Auerbach, 1963); the lowest levels seem to occur at 7:30 A.M. Reversal of the sleep-wake cycle inverts the phases of the PBI cycle (Bushler et al., 1968).

The rate of disappearance of thyroid hormones from the blood is maximal when subjects are physically active or are eating, as these soldiers were (Walfish et al., 1961). During the day, PBI levels are also influenced by changes in posture, which affect shifts of fluids from body compartments that influence levels of PBI (Bushler et al., 1968; Reichlin and O'Neal, 1962; Wilson, 1966). Any psychophysiological study that employs PBI levels must take into account a number of variables, including the time of day of the study and the previous activity and the posture of the subject.

The meaning of changes in PBI levels must also be carefully scrutinized because the PBI contains T_4, small amounts of T_3, iodine bound to protein (not to tyrosine), iodinated dyes, and thyroglobulin. Therefore, the PBI is only an approximate measure of the concentration of the thyroid hormones in the blood, and then only of that fraction bound to prealbumin (TBA) and globulin (TBG). The bound fraction of the thyroid hormones is not interesting physiologically: the physiologically active form is the nonprotein-bound or free T_3 or T_4 fraction.

Elevated PBI levels can occur when thyroid function is otherwise normal (Rosenbaum et al., 1968); when they are elevated, the thyroxine binding capacity of TBG and TBA has probably increased. Increases in PBI do not necessarily reflect the increased release of T_3 or T_4 by the gland, but may represent shifts in the distribution of iodide in the body or a decrease in the disposition of T_3 and T_4 by excretion, tissue binding, or utilization. In order to obtain a true picture of a physiologically relevant increase of output of the thyroid gland, free T_3 and T_4 levels should be measured. Failing this, it is preferable to assess BEI not PBI, levels (Appendix 1). Mason (1968a) reported that BEI levels rose 1 to 1.5 μg percent in the plasma of five college students selected on the basis of having had the greatest increases in 17-hydroxycorticosteroid levels coincident to taking examinations. Presumably these students were the most responsive to stress.

Radioactive iodine uptake or release by the thyroid gland as another measure of its activity has also been used as a dependent variable in psychoendocrine studies of stress. Dongier et al. (1956) studied 28 anxious and calm subjects to assess the impact of stressful interviews on the 24-hour uptake and release of [131]I. No significant changes occurred.

The four-hour [132]I uptake as an index of thyroid function, can be raised when subjects

354

take an examination, but not by exercise or being exposed to heat or cold. The rates of release of ^{127}I and ^{131}I (measured at $PB^{131}I$) and PBI levels in the blood were studied in five euthyroid, seven untreated, and seven treated thyrotoxic patients before, during, and 24 hours after viewing a film designed to induce strong emotional responses. The emotional responses to this "horror" film were compared with those obtained by watching a travelog. All patients had 1 to 2 μg percent elevations of unlabeled PBI levels after viewing the "horror" film. The PBI levels of the untreated thyrotoxic patients changed the most and continued to remain elevated for another hour after the end of the film. In the euthyroid patients changes in $PB^{131}I$ levels were biphasic, with an initial fall in levels. In the patients treated for thyrotoxicosis the highest $PB^{131}I$ counts occurred immediately after the film was over, and then fell. In untreated thyrotoxic patients, radioiodine counts increased significantly during the showing of the film, with a further twofold increase for two hours after the film ended—an increase that lasted for 24 hours. Very rapid and acute changes in radioactive counting rates occurred in response to dramatic incidents in the "horror" film, but did not change at all during the travelog. The overall count fell during the "horror" film and then rose after it was over (Alexander et al., 1961; Flagg et al., 1965). These findings were confirmed in a much larger group of untreated thyrotoxic patients (43) and in control subjects. Release rates were again enhanced in untreated patients, both during and after seeing the "horror" film as compared to viewing the travelog. It was concluded that the responses of patients who are thyrotoxic are more intense, extensive, and prolonged than those of treated patients or control subjects. In addition, untreated thyrotoxic patients showed more-significant skin-conductance changes and increases in heart rate during the "horror" film than during the travelog (Flagg et al., 1965). In these studies significant correlations between "psychological defenses," the patient's ability to cope with the disturbing content of the film and physiological variables were found. The untreated thyrotoxic patients who were most disturbed by the film and least-"defended" psychologically had the largest fall in radioactive "neck" counts during the film and the greatest increases in $PB^{131}I$ levels after it.

The findings of this study indicate that there are differences between euthyroid and thyrotoxic patients in the rate of accumulation and disposal of radioactive iodine by the thyroid gland when watching a distressing, but not a bland film. Significant correlations were obtained between the changes in the hormonal variables, distressing emotions, and the effectiveness of "defenses" that prevented the emotion from being experienced.

Throughout this section, the validity of the various indicators, such as PBI levels, in studying changes in the functioning of the gland during periods of naturally occurring or experimentally induced stresses have been discussed. In all these studies perceived stress was not studied while TSH levels were measured in order to assess the state of the hypothalamic-pituitary axis. Two such studies have recently appeared in which TSH levels were measured. Zuckerman and his co-workers (1966) used eight hours of sensory deprivation to produce increases in TSH levels. Mean TSH levels rose 21 percent in 10 or 11 subjects who became anxious and depressed when deprived of sensory stimulation, and Kotchen and his co-workers (1972) studied eight army recruits in the 20-minute period *before* they were asked to do exhaustive exercise on a bicycle ergometer. Using radioimmunoassay methods, plasma TSH concentrations rose significantly ($p < .01$) in all subjects, from 3.1 μU/cc (± 0.4, SE) to 4.0 μU/cc (± 0.3 SE). Total T_4, but not free T_4,

355

levels, plasma cortisol, and norepinephrine concentrations were also significantly increased during the period of anticipation. During the stress of sensory deprivation and the anticipation of exercise changes in the release of iodine by the thyroid gland is produced by TSH. The pituitary-thyroid axis is, therefore, responsive to changes in the environment or to anticipation. Unfortunately, these observations neither prove nor refute the role of social and psychological factors and TSH in the pathogenesis of Graves' disease.

The Function of the Thyroid Gland in Relation to Mood

The emotional distress elicited by experimental constraints such as a "horror" film is not the same as the distress that occurs in patients with Graves' disease. As has been noted, patients with Graves' disease are often depressed, anxious, or nervous (Brown and Hetzel, 1963; Wilson et al., 1961). Therefore, it seems reasonable to ask whether any correlation exists between depressive affect and evidence of changes in thyroid function. Both decreased and normal values of serum iodide levels have been found in depressed patients (Man and Kahn, 1945; Neustadt and Howard, 1942–43). PBI levels have been low (Bowman et al., 1950), normal (Brody and Man, 1950; Starr et al., 1950; Stevens and Dunn, 1958), and elevated (Board et al., 1956, 1957; Kleinsorge et al., 1962). When the 24-hour uptake of ^{131}I by the gland was measured, normal values were obtained by Gibbons et al. (1960) and Lingjaerde et al. (1960). These discrepant results are not easy to reconcile, except to say that these studies were really not comparable. There are too many uncontrolled variables that are not constant from study to study. For example, Board et al. (1956) were careful to show that the initial impact of hospitalization on psychiatric patients of various diagnostic labels was an important variable in raising PBI levels by 20 percent. Both Board et al. (1956) and Dewhurst et al. (1968) found that the highest levels of PBI occurred during the first hospital day in psychotically depressed and other distressed patients who had recently become ill. The most distressed, regardless of their diagnostic category, had the highest mean PBI levels. Retarded depressed patients had higher PBI levels than agitated patients. Depressed patients do not comprise a homogeneous group, and PBI levels have to be related to behavior, psychological state, and the duration of the illness of patients, and not to a particular diagnosis.

These complex correlations were confirmed by Libow and Durrell (1965) who carried out serial ^{131}I thyroidal uptake studies on a 47-year-old chronic schizophrenic subject. When the patient became mute and lapsed into stupor, the 24-hour thyroidal ^{131}I uptake was twice as great as when he was excited. During the transition from the excited to the mute phase highly significant increases in ^{131}I uptake took place ($p < .001$). The increases in ^{131}I uptake was not a function of diminshed renal clearance of iodine.

Therefore, the behavioral and emotional states of psychotic patients correlate with changes in some measures of thyroid function. Surprisingly enough, the behavioral and mood states do not correlate with TSH levels in psychiatric patients, 20 of whom were schizophrenic, 42 depressed, and 2 hypomanic (Dewhurst et al., 1968). Sixteen of the 44 patients with affective disorders had raised blood TSH levels at some time during their illness; in eight of them high levels were sustained throughout the illness. Seventeen of these patients had high PB[127]I levels. But in only two of 174 blood samples obtained from these 44 patients was there a correlated increase in both TSH and PB[127]I levels. The lack of relationship between changes in TSH and PB^{127}I levels may have been because the free T_4 (or T_3) levels were raised while PBI levels remained normal, or because the peripheral turnover rate of T_4 was increased while serum PBI levels remained constant. Nonetheless, the hope that a clearcut relationship would be found between thyroidal activity and depressive illness, or other kinds of affective variations, has not been realized in this and other studies because it is crucial to ascertain the amount of iodine in the diets of psychotic patients. High values for ^{131}I have occurred when the dietary supply of iodine is low (Kelsey et al., 1957; Simpson et al., 1963, 1964). Also, studies that measure ^{131}I uptake after 24 hours should be suspect, because in some circumstances the uptake of ^{131}I and the release of accumulated ^{131}I (either as the true hormone or some hormonally inactive product) may be so rapid that a return to normal levels occurs before the end of 24 hours.

A number of other physiological processes are responsive to fear or bereavement. Stressful experiences may affect a wide variety of hormones such as ACTH and cortisol, the sex hormones, the catecholamines, vasopressin, and hGH (Brown and Reichlin, 1972; Mason, 1968a), and may also affect autonomically mediated responses (Hofer, 1975; Weiner and Hart, 1975). The interactions of the hormones with TSH and the thyroid hormones are by no means fully worked out.

Evidence against the Role of TSH in Graves' Disease

Alexander (1950) contended that the onset of Graves' disease is initiated by excessive TSH production. He quoted the findings of Soffer et al. (1947) and DeRobertis (1948) to support his hypothesis. Since that time, this hypothesis has been completely discarded. With the development of the technique of radioimmunoassay for measuring TSH levels in the blood of patients with the disease, it was found that levels of TSH are either normal (Pimstone et al., 1963) or undetectably low (Adams, 1969; Lemarchand-Béraud et al., 1966; Odell et al., 1967; Utiger, 1965) after the onset of the disease. Therefore, it is assumed that TSH plays no role in initiating or maintaining the disease, and it left those interested in the role of psychosocial factors bereft of an hypothesis about the mediating psychophysiological mechanism involved.

The fact that TSH may not maintain the disease does not mean that it could not initiate it because the factors that sustain a disease do not necessarily initiate it. The principle that the mechanisms that initiate a disease are different than the ones that sustain it is best illustrated by the data on various forms of experimental hypertension in animals.

Therefore, Alexander's hypothesis remains unproven. If he was wrong, the psychosomatic theory of the role of psychosocial factors in the pathogenesis of Graves' disease is also wrong. It will have failed to explain how fear or feelings of bereavement could alter thyroid function. But if Alexander is proved correct, the theory will still have to take into account the role of immunological factors in the etiology and pathogenesis of Graves' disease. Admittedly, no agreement has been reached about the presence of autoantibodies in Graves' disease and other diseases of the thyroid gland. In fact, a primary pathogenetic role for the autoantibodies in Graves' disease has been questioned. They may be the consequence of the disease—for example, they could be a response to a change in the antigenic properties of the TSH receptors on the surface of thyroid cells (Solomon and Chopra, 1972). Should they play a primary role in the disease, an interesting question is raised:

could psychological, social, and experiential factors affect immunological reactivity or surveillance, the production of antibodies or antigen-antibody reactions to promote Graves' disease?

There is no answer to this question. And there is no answer to the question of the pathogenetic mechanism in Graves' disease despite the very large body of information about the pathophysiology and immunopathology of the disease. There are a number of competing hypotheses about the mechanisms that produce Graves' disease following infection, surgery, fright, and bereavement (Gibson, 1962; Hetzel, 1960; Solomon and Chopra, 1972).

These hypotheses generally assume that fright and bereavement produce increased TSH levels. But the evidence suggests that, in animals at least, TSH levels may initially be depressed by stress. That TSH levels are appropriately depressed after the onset of Graves' disease is to be expected (Reichlin and Utiger, 1967). They rise as thyrotoxicosis is treated and the patient become euthyroid or hypothyroid (Adams and Kennedy, 1965; Chopra et al., 1970b). In other words, changes in TSH levels parallel changes in blood levels of T_3. As T_3 levels increase TSH levels fall, and vice versa. The usual negative feedback system is intact in Graves' disease.

However, the regulation of TSH by TRH may be disturbed. Some patients with definite or probable Graves' disease, while still euthyroid, have a blunted or absent response of TSH to TRH (Hershman and Pittnam, 1970; Lawton et al., 1971; Ormston et al., 1971). This lack of response may be due to the blocking action of T_3 on the secretion of TSH by the pituitary gland (Schadlow et al., 1972). In other instances the abnormal TSH response to TRH occurs with normal T_3 levels (Ormston et al., 1971; Solomon and Chopra, 1972). Therefore, in Graves' disease the hypothalamic-pituitary feedback relationship may be altered in some unknown manner so that TSH is less responsive to TRH. In fact, in Graves' disease, TRH levels may be higher than normal because TSH levels are low (Bakke and Lawrence, 1966). Alternatively, high T_4 levels in Graves' disease may stimulate TRH production and secretion (Reichlin and Utiger, 1967).

High levels of TRH in the hypothalamus may not have any pathogenetic significance in Graves' disease, although they may produce some symptoms of the disease by their effects on other areas of the brain. TRH is known to increase catecholamine turnover in the brain, in addition to regulating TSH secretion (Keller et al., 1974).

Although TSH may not play a pathogenetic role in Graves' disease, two regulatory disturbances in the hypothalmic-pituitary axis have recently been described. Another regulatory disturbance exists in the relationship of the pituitary and the thyroid gland. This disturbance is manifested in the abnormal T_3 suppression test (Bayliss, 1967; Greer and Smith, 1954; Werner et al., 1955) (Appendix 1).

A number of disturbances in regulation occur in Graves' disease. They may be the consequence of the disease. But their occurrence still does not substantiate the idea that TSH is involved in the pathogenesis of the disease.

Actually, the most powerful argument against the role of TSH in initiating Graves' disease is that the disease can develop in patients after the destruction by disease or the surgical removal of the pituitary gland (Christensen and Binder, 1962; Fajans, 1958; Grinberg et al., 1966; Gurling et al., 1959; Pazianos et al., 1960). Some of these patients become thyrotoxic because they develop a toxic adenoma (Pazianos, 1960). Other patients

358

remain euthyroid despite hypophysectomy (Becker, 1959; Becker and Furth, 1965). Therefore, the thyroid gland seems not to depend on the hypophysis (Ingbar, 1972).

One hypophysectomized patient was receiving 2.5 mg prednisolone and 60 mg of desiccated thyroid daily before she developed Graves' disease. She had no goiter. An elevated PBI and ^{131}I uptake was found. Later, T_3 levels became elevated, and the T_3 suppression test became abnormal (Christensen and Binder, 1962). Another patient, who suffered a postpartum necrosis of the pituitary gland, was receiving 128 to 192 mg of desiccated thyroid because she was hypothyroid (Fajans, 1958). In both patients the thyrotoxic state persisted after the medication was stopped.

The thyroid gland of patients with Graves' disease can still incorporate ^{131}I into T_3 and T_4 in the normal manner despite hypophysectomy possibly because the LATS is present (Becker and Furth, 1965; Werner et al., 1959). Instances of Graves' disease after hypophysectomy and the finding that the thyroid in hypophysectomized patients can still incorporate iodine and manufacture T_3 and T_4 has biased current thinking against the idea that TSH plays a role in the pathogenesis and maintenance of Graves' disease. However, the possibility that TSH may play a role in the inception of Graves' disease has not been excluded, because no one has been able to study patients prior to, and at the time of the inception of, the disease. In the absence of predictive studies of persons at risk for the disease, no definitive conclusion can be reached about the role of TSH in the pathogenesis of Graves' disease. Obviously, once the disease has begun and the thyroid gland is releasing high levels of T_3, TSH output is diminished (Patel et al., 1971). But from data about TSH levels during the disease, it is not possible to determine what has occurred just prior to or at the moment of inception.

The Role of the Catecholamines in Graves' Disease:
Stress and Symptom Formation

Threatening life events are associated with marked elevations of urinary and blood catecholamine levels in normal human beings (Carlson et al., 1967; Fröberg et al., 1971). In animals, the enzymes responsible for the biosynthesis of catecholamines in the adrenal gland are progressively elevated by stresses such as restraint (Kvetnansky and Mikulaj, 1970; Kvetnansky et al., 1970a, b), or crowding and fighting (Henry et al., 1971a, b). Both kinds of stress also alter brain catecholamines (Welch and Welch, 1968).

The hypothalamus of the rat (Glowinski and Iversen, 1966), the dog and the cat is rich in norepinephrine-containing neurons (Vogt, 1954), that probably affect TRH release. TRH is released by dopamine and norepinephrine and its release is inhibited by serotonin (Grimm and Reichlin, 1973; McCann and Porter, 1969; Wurtman, 1971). In turn, TRH and T_3 increase the turnover rate of norepinephrine in the brain (Keller et al., 1974). The neurohypophysis produces vasopressin in response to cholinergic or adrenergic discharge in the supraoptic and paraventricular nuclei of the hypothalamus (Scharrer and Scharrer, 1963).

Epinephrine or norepinephrine also affect the blood flow and blood supply (Worthington, 1960) and cause the release of tropic hormones from the pituitary gland. The gonadotropins (Sawyer et al., 1950) and ACTH (McDermott et al., 1950) are directly

359

released from the pituitary gland of the rabbit by epinephrine. Epinephrine may produce the release of TSH indirectly; epinephrine increases the peripheral utilization of free T_4 by lowering the level of it in the blood (Botkin and Jensen, 1952). T_3 levels fall with T_4 levels and TSH is released.

Sympathetic discharge and epinephrine may act directly upon the thyroid gland in some species. In man neither ^{131}I uptake nor discharge by the gland is affected by epinephrine (Mowbray and Peart, 1960). However, the effect of epinephrine in man is complicated, and it depends in part on how long after injection the measurements are made. A single injection of epinephrine has to precede the measurement of radioiodine uptake by 30 to 60 minutes to increase ^{131}I uptake. Continuous infusion of epinephrine produces a biphasic change in ^{131}I uptake, consisting of an initial fall in the rate of accumulation, followed by a rise (Hays, 1965). In animals, epinephrine inhibits ^{131}I uptake by the thyroid gland because the thyroid arteries become constricted (Brown-Grant and Gibson, 1956; D'Angelo, 1956; Soffer et al., 1949).

There is as yet no explanation for these species differences. The actions of norepinephrine, epinephrine, acetylcholine, and serotonin on the thyroid gland in the cat, rabbit, and dog depend on the presence of TSH levels in the blood at the time of injection (Földes et al., 1963; Söderberg, 1958). In the dog, electrical stimulation of the cervical sympathetic nerves after hypophysectomy, or the injection of epinephrine or norepinephrine (Ackerman and Arons, 1958; Iino, 1959), markedly increases the release of PB[131]I into the thyroidal vein. Therefore, in the dog the effects of these neurotransmitters on the thyroid gland are not mediated by the adenohypophysis, and do not depend on the presence of TSH.

It is not yet known how the sympathetic nervous system and its neurotransmitters exert their effects on the regulation and function of the thyroid gland. It is very likely that the discrepancies in results are a function of a number of uncontrolled variables: differences in species, whether the animal was anesthetized or not, the route of administration of the drugs, the behavioral state of the animal, and ongoing levels of hormones, such as TSH. How the catecholamines interact with the active products produced by the thyroid gland is not known. The catecholamines and T_3 and T_4 seem to act in synergism (Ramey, 1966). In fact, the symptoms and signs of thyrotoxicosis resemble excessive sympathetic discharge. Propranolol, a β-adrenergic blocking agent, attenuates thyrotoxic "storm" (Das and Krieger, 1969). In thyrotoxic storm, reserpine and guanethidine stop auricular fibrillation, and the heart rate and cardiac output fall. The symptoms of thyrotoxicosis without storm (nervousness, tremor, excessive sweating, heat intolerance, and palpitations) can also be reduced by propranolol (Shanks et al., 1969). But direct evidence of excessive catecholamine production does not exist; urinary levels of catecholamines and their principal metabolites, vanillyl mandelic acid and the metanephrines, are normal in thyrotoxicosis (Wiswell et al., 1963).

Actually, catecholamine production does not need to be increased in Graves' disease. T_3 and T_4 may potentiate the effects of normal circulating catecholamine levels because the thyroid hormones have very subtle effects on epinephrine uptake and disposal by the tissues. Special techniques are needed to demonstrate these effects. The delivery of epinephrine to the heart depends on how much blood flows through the coronary arteries. In rats after administration of T_4, the heart receives a greater share of epinephrine but is also less capable of binding it. As a result, more free epinephrine acts upon cardiac receptors. T_4 decreases the binding of epinephrine by the tissues so that inactivation of epinephrine by deamination is less (Wurtman and Axelrod, 1966). T_4, norepinephrine, and epinephrine potentiate each other's action on the heart. In dogs, the elevated heart rate produced by T_4 is abolished by sympathetic blockade (Brewster et al., 1956). Increases in heart rate, pulse pressure, cardiac output, stroke work and speed of ventricular contraction occur when epinephrine is infused into thyrotoxic patients, indicating that the thyroid hormones sensitize the β-adrenergic receptors of the heart (Bruccino et al., 1967; Harrison, 1964; Zsoter et al., 1964).

The thyroid hormones and catecholamines also combine to increase hyperglycemia (Lamberg, 1965), augment oxygen consumption (Strubelt, 1968), and BMR (Brewster et al., 1956), and enhance free-fatty-acid mobilization (Harlan et al., 1963).

The mechanism of the synergism between the thyroid hormones and epinephrine is under active investigation. Epinephrine stimulates adenylcyclase, and T_4 retards the disposition of cyclic-AMP. The overall results would be to raise the level of cyclic-AMP to heights that each alone does not achieve, thereby enhancing β-adrenergic receptor activity (Robison et al., 1968).

Progress has been made in our understanding of the manner in which the thyroid hormones and the catecholamines potentiate each other's actions and produce some of the signs and symptoms of thyrotoxicosis that has been likened to an "epinephrine-like state." But this state probably does not alone account for the nervousness, irritability, labile emotional behavior, motor restlessness, insomnia, and memory difficulties of thyrotoxicosis. Conrad (1934a, b) was probably the first to point out that these symptoms and signs resemble those observed in patients with an agitated depression. This observation would suggest that the metabolism of the central nervous system is altered in thyrotoxicosis and that the symptoms cannot be explained by the peripheral interaction of the catecholamines and T_3 and T_4.

The other symptoms of thyrotoxicosis—the cutaneous vasodilatation, increased respiratory ventilation, tachycardia, increased appetite, tremulousness and altered menses—have been ascribed to regional changes in blood flow and to enhanced calorigenesis. Little attention has been paid to the possibility that the various regulatory systems in the brain that control heat loss, the respiratory and heart rates, appetite, motor activity and tone, and the menstrual cycle might be implicated in Graves' disease. In some women with Graves' disease the menstrual cycle is anovulatory, probably because of a decreased production of luteinizing hormone by the pituitary gland (Steinbeck, 1963).

We know very little about the effect of the thyroid hormones on the hypothalamic centers that control body temperature. In goats, hyperthermia results from cooling the preoptic area of the hypothalamus, which normally regulates heat loss from the body. The hyperthermia is accompanied by the release of epinephrine, norepinephrine, TSH, and the thyroid hormones. The response of the thyroid gland to cooling of the preoptic area is blocked by T_4 or by lesions of the median eminence of the hypothalamus. Warming of the preoptic region has the opposite effect (Andersson, 1964).

The Role of Vasopressin

Vasopressin release by the neurohypophysis is acutely responsive to environmental and emotional stimuli (Harris, 1960; Mason, 1968a; Verney, 1947). Avoidance conditioning is associated with a fall or a biphasic response in urine volume, and this is presumably due to vasopressin release (Mason et al., 1968a). Emotionally significant life events may be mediated by the release of vasopressin. What, then, is the effect, if any, of vasopressin on thyroid function?

Purified or synthetic vasopressin injected into rabbits and dogs who have been prepared by the administration of ^{131}I after suppression of TSH release by T_4, causes increased ^{131}I levels in the blood. The increased levels of ^{131}I are due to the increased release of T_4 (and possibly T_3) by the thyroid gland. Because ^{131}I levels also increase with vasopressin in hypophysectomized animals, vasopressin probably exerts its effect directly upon the thyroid gland (Garcia et al., 1964; Lipscomb et al., 1961). But in the rat, vasopressin does not release TSH (D'Angelo, 1963) nor does it produce the release of T_3 or T_4 from the thyroid gland (Harris, 1963).

In man the effect of administered pitressin or vasopressin is to increase ^{131}I uptake after vasopressin administration (Mertz, 1962), a finding which Moses et al. (1961) did not obtain. When given to patients with pituitary insufficiency, pitressin increases ^{131}I uptake and elevates PBI levels (Gilbert-Dreyfus et al., 1959; Reichlin, 1966b; Rosner et al., 1962).

Interactions between the Pituitary Hormones

The hypothalamic releasing factors and hormones that regulate the pituitary polypeptides interact in the hypothalamus. The hypothalamic areas that harbor the releasing and inhibiting hormones lie in close anatomical relationship to each other. The factors and hormones that release hGH, luteinizing hormone, follicle stimulating hormone, TSH, and ACTH by the pituitary gland may interact with each other. For example, the release of ACTH inhibits the release of TSH and the usual release of hGH by insulin-induced hypoglycemia is inhibited in thyrotoxic patients. Normal subjects given T_3 respond in the usual manner with increased blood levels of hGH to hypoglycemia (Burgess et al., 1966).

THE ROLE OF ACTH

The hypothalamic-pituitary-adrenocortical axis is rapidly responsive to novel or frightening experiences and to bereavement (Hamburg, 1966; Mason, 1968a; Weiner and Hart, 1975). A reciprocal interaction occurs at the hypothalamic level between the releasing factors for ACTH and TSH (Sakiz and Guillemin, 1965).

In rats, when the release of TSH by the pituitary is promoted by treatment with TRH, significantly less ACTH is secreted in response to the stresses of ether anesthesia or surgery. On the other hand, when release of ACTH is inhibited by prior treatment with pentobarbital or dexamethasone, thyroid releasing factor causes the pituitary to secrete more TSH (Sakiz and Guillemin, 1965). Further evidence of this mutual interaction has been obtained by the work of D'Angelo and Young (1966). When T_4 is systematically injected into rats with anterior hypothalamic lesions, plasma corticosterone levels rise, suggesting that T_4 releases ACTH.

The glucocorticoids of the adrenal gland may also affect the regulation of thyroid gland.

362

For example, plasma TSH levels are reduced by the administration of glucocorticoids (Wilbur and Utiger, 1969). The glucocorticoids probably act directly on the thyroid gland to slow the release of radioiodine, to diminish the turnover of iodine within the gland, and to increase the excretion of iodine by the kidney (Scherer and Siefring, 1956). Glucocorticoids also reduce levels of TBG while increasing the amount of TBA, the net effect being to reduce PBI levels (Oppenheimer and Werner, 1966). They enhance levels of free T_3 while keeping levels of T_4 constant (Blomstedt and Einhorn, 1967). The net effect of all of these changes produced by the glucocorticoids is to reduce the release of iodine from the thyroid gland and PBI levels.

Increased thyroid function in Graves' disease alters the output of the pituitary-adrenocortical axis. The thyrotoxic state is associated with increases in ACTH blood levels (Eartly and Lebond, 1954; Hilton et al., 1962). The characteristic circadian variation in corticosteroid levels is enhanced in Graves' disease (Martin et al., 1963). An increase in the rate of catabolism of the glucocorticoids (Peterson, 1958) and the rate of urinary excretion of the metabolites of 17-hydroxycorticosteroids (17-OHCS) occurs in thyrotoxic Graves' disease (Kenney et al., 1967; Peterson, 1959). The overall effect of administering ACTH to thyrotoxic patients is to increase plasma levels of 17-OHCS. But the levels attained are significantly less than in normal patients because their catabolism is increased (Felber et al., 1959; Martin and Mintz, 1965).

Although much is known about the interrelationships between ACTH, TSH and the thyroid hormones, the role of ACTH and the glucocorticoids in the etiology, pathogenesis, and maintenance of Graves' disease is unsolved. In normal biological functioning, the organization and patterning of hormones may be more important than their interrelationships. Some hormones—the corticosteroids, hGH, aldosterone, epinephrine, norepinephrine, and possibly the antidiuretic hormone—show circadian variations. The male and female hormones, insulin, and thyroid hormones also vary over time. If the usual circadian patterns of the hormones are disorganized and their phase relationships are altered, disease may be incited or be maintained (Curtis, 1972).

ANIMAL MODELS OF GRAVES' DISEASE AND THYROTOXICOSIS

Naturally Occurring and Experimentally Induced Thyrotoxicosis

Investigations to study the relationship of thyroid function in humans to stressful experiences are difficult to execute, and the results are difficult to interpret. They do suggest that various measures of thyroid function change, at times quite acutely, with changes in the behavioral and emotional state of patients. But too few studies have been done in human beings to permit broad generalizations about the role of stress and distress in normal subjects and thyrotoxic patients. Nor can any definitive statement be made about the mechanisms that mediate distress to precipitate Graves' disease. Therefore, the literature on the role of stress and thyroid function and on thyrotoxic states in animals is worth reviewing, in order to learn how stress may alter the function of the thyroid gland.

Unfortunately, not everyone agrees that thyrotoxicosis can occur naturally in animals. Sattler (1952) reviewed reports of the spontaneous occurrence of thyrotoxicosis in many dogs, cows, and horses. Despite the excellence of the "clinical" descriptions, these reports

363

are usually considered mere curiosities. All these animals had a goiter, exophthalmos, and evidence of thyrotoxicosis. When the sex of the animal was identified, most of them were female. It is a pity that these observations are not taken seriously because the inquiry into the etiology and pathogenesis of Graves' disease in man would be furthered if an animal model of the disease existed. Attempts to develop an animal model have been made. Eickhoff (1949, 1950) "frightened" mice. Kracht and Kracht (1952; Kracht, 1954) used ferrets to trap wild rabbits. They then compared the histology of the thyroid gland and adenohypophysis in trapped animals with wild animals who had been shot. Shortly after capture, trapped animals were immobile, had an increased heart and respiratory rate, a tremor, and exophthalmos, which gradually subsided. The fearful, immobile animals soon tried to escape. When the trapped rabbits were later repeatedly exposed to dogs or to man, they lost weight, despite an adequate food intake, and died. The weight loss and death could be prevented by thyroidectomy or the administration of antithyroid drugs. On the basis of the histological findings on the thyroid and pituitary glands of the rabbits, and the fact that ^{131}I uptake by the thyroid gland was doubled, the Krachts (1952) concluded that "fright-thyrotoxicosis" was mediated by TSH. They also suggested that some animals responded to the stressful conditions by an increased TSH output, and other animals responded with the release of ACTH. In mice, at least, TSH and ACTH release occur in a reciprocal manner (Sakiz and Guillemin, 1965). The reports that frightening rabbits can produce thyrotoxicosis are suggestive but need to be confirmed before any conclusion can be reached about their relevance to our understanding of the pathogenesis of Graves' disease in man.

The Relationship of Emotional Behavior to Thyroid Function in Animals

Attempts have also been made to relate differences in emotional behavior in purebred strains of animals to the weight of the thyroid gland, but no consistent results have been obtained (Anderson and Anderson, 1938; Donaldson and King, 1929; Freudenberger, 1932; Hatai, 1914; Yeakel and Rhoades, 1941). One reason for the lack of consensus is that it is difficult to determine reliably the "emotionality" of or "nervousness" in animals. Equal difficulties stand in the way of establishing norms for the weight of the thyroid gland in wild and domesticated animals. Dietary factors also influence the weight of the gland, and they cannot be evaluated with any degree of accuracy in wild animals. Such norms need to be established before the effects of stress on thyroid function can be studied in animals.

When animals are subjected to "stresses," consistent findings are not obtained. Some investigators have found an increase in the weight of the gland with stress (Yeakel and Rhoades, 1941), and some have not (Uno, 1922). Rats exposed to a variety of stimuli such as sound, electric shock, light, and changes in atmospheric pressure show an initial increase in PBI levels that last ten days and is followed by a decrease (LaRoche and Johnson, 1967; Ramey, 1966). Frequent changes in housing conditions produce histological evidence of decreased thyroid activity in mice (Carriere and Isler, 1959). Mice isolated for a period of four months show an initial increase and then a decrease in thyroid activity (Weltman et al., 1962). Mice kept in continuous darkness for a month have shown evidence of increased thyroid activity (Puntriano and Meites, 1951).

After the introduction of radioisotope techniques for estimating thyroid function, not its

364

weight, a number of studies were carried out to determine the effect of "stresses" such as electric shock, variations in sound or light stimulation, restraint, and changes in housing conditions on different animal species or different strains of animals. In the rat, "stressful" stimuli decrease the accumulation of ^{131}I by the gland (Bogoroch and Timiras, 1951; Pasckis et al., 1950; Soffer et al., 1949; Williams et al., 1949), its rate of uptake (Badrick et al., 1954; Reiss, 1956), or release (Evans and Barnett, 1966). When mice are exposed to cats, increased ^{131}I uptake by the gland occurred (Rantanen et al., 1965).

TSH levels increase when guinea pigs are given electric shocks, and the secretion of thyroid hormones also increases (Del Conte et al., 1955). In other experiments an inhibition of the release of ^{131}I was found in stressed guinea pigs (Brown-Grant and Pettes, 1960). In rabbits, the rate of release of ^{131}I by the gland and levels of ^{131}PBI are decreased by restraint, electric shock, or changes in the intensity of light (Brown-Grant, 1957; Brown-Grant et al., 1954). In rabbits, contradictory findings about the effect of stress on the uptake and accumulation of ^{131}I by the thyroid gland have been obtained (Kracht, 1954). The reasons for the contradiction may lie in the fact that the response of the thyroid gland after acute, stressful conditions is biphasic. Therefore, the time at which measurements of ^{131}I uptake or release during the biphasic response may determine whether the levels are increased or decreased (Badrick et al., 1954; Ducommun et al., 1967; Reiss, 1956).

The mechanisms that cause the decrease in ^{131}I uptake are poorly understood. The decrease is not mediated by the release of the catecholamines, the adrenal steroids, or the pituitary hormones (Badrick et al., 1954; Brown-Grant et al., 1954; Reiss, 1956). The fact that a decrease in ^{131}I uptake by the thyroid gland is not mediated by the pituitary gland is puzzling, because the decrease can be prevented by reserpinizing rats that are then stressed. In such rats plasma TSH levels increase. Therefore, the increase in radioiodine uptake is mediated by TSH when reserpinized rats are stressed. One would presume, therefore, that the decrease in rats that have not been given reserpine would also be mediated by TSH.

In other experiments on rats, handling, sham subcutaneous injections, and ether anesthesia on each of 30 consecutive days, produces a fall in plasma TSH that reserpine prevents. After two weeks of these stresses elevated basal TSH levels occur despite reserpine (Ducommun et al., 1967). Reserpine has both peripheral or central actions, either of which could produce changes in TSH levels that could be due to changes in the secretory output of the pituitary gland or variations in the metabolic clearance or peripheral distribution of TSH.

Because the effects of stress on rodents may be different than on larger animals, attempts to study thyroid activity in larger stressed mammals have been made. Blood was obtained from the thyroid vein in conscious sheep who were exposed to a barking dog or to loud noises. Marked increases in venous plasma PBI and ^{127}PBI and ^{131}PBI levels were observed 15 to 30 minutes after the end of stimulation, due to an increased rate of release of iodine from the glandular iodine pool. Such increases could be due to an enhanced rate of venous flow, or to a true increase in rate of I_2 release from the gland under the influence of TSH (Falconer, 1963, 1965; Falconer and Hetzel, 1964).

Stressful stimuli can produce changes in thyroid function that initially consist of a decrease in some species of animals and not in others. Mason (1968) has suggested that the discrepancies in results can be understood in terms of differences in the genus and the size of the experimental animals. When Rhesus monkeys are subjected either to 72 hours of avoidance conditioning, or to an unconditioned emotional stimulus, prolonged elevations in the levels of plasma occurred. Similar results were obtained when pairs of monkeys were subjected to the "executive" paradigm of avoiding shock. Avoidance shock also produces elevated serum PBI and BEI levels and a decreased urinary excretion of ^{131}I, which are not affected by removal of the adrenal medulla. The implication of their work was that the changes in thyroid activity are mediated by the hypothalamic-pituitary axis and not the catecholamines (Harrison et al., 1966; Mason, 1968a, b; Mason and Mougey, 1972).

Two other reports have been made from Mason's laboratory: both conditioned avoidance (Mason et al., 1968a) and an unconditioned emotional stimulus in the form of chair restraint for six days produce prolonged elevations of BEI levels (Mason and Mougey, 1972). The details of the pattern of the changes in BEI levels with stress are worth examining. Mean BEI levels rise gradually and significantly during an entire 72-hour period of avoidance conditioning and continue after the experiment is stopped. They only return to mean baseline levels on the ninth day of the recovery period. Peak BEI values may not be reached until after the experiment is over. With repeated sessions of 72-hour avoidance conditioning, the changes in BEI levels are less dramatic, only to become large again when trained monkeys are given unexpected and undeserved electric shocks. ^{125}PBI responses also occur in conditioned avoidance experiments. The level may double during the first 30 minutes of the experiment and remain elevated for 6 hours; in the other monkeys the increase in ^{125}I and BEI is slower. Each monkey responds in a different way. And the rate of turnover and release of the glandular iodine pool is increased by avoidance conditioning and is not due to changes in ^{125}I excretion by the kidney.

Several of these results are worth commenting upon. Elevations of BEI levels in monkeys continue well after the experiment is over. The element of novelty also seems to play an important role in determining the degree and duration of changes in BEI levels. Animals that are merely restrained have marked hormonal responses. The results of these experiments may be conceptualized in the following way: animals trained to avoid shock by pressing a lever "cope" actively with a potentially painful stimulus. The restrained animal has no way actively of dealing with restraint—it cannot escape, it has to adapt passively (Weiss, 1971). In either case, BEI levels increase and decrease slowly. In order to analyze the mechanisms entailed in these hormonal responses, the physiologically active fraction of T_3 and T_4 in serum and levels of TSH should be determined in such experiments. Otherwise, the changes in BEI levels cannot unequivocally be ascribed to the stress-induced release of TSH. The changes in BEI levels must also be related to increases in the production of T_3 and T_4 by the gland. Increases in BEI levels could otherwise be due to enhanced binding of T_3 and T_4 by the binding proteins, to hemoconcentration, or to decreased utilization and turnover of the bound thyroid hormones.

It is very difficult to compare all these experiments on stress. Exposing animals to their predators is a more "natural" and complex stimulus than keeping mice in the dark or training monkeys. In laboratory experiments a number of uncontrolled variables may be present and should be considered: for example, how the dark affects sleep and other rhythmic phenomena, their food intake, and the weight of the animal.

When small animals are acutely stressed they first show decreases in thyroid activity, while larger ones show increase. Nana et al. (1961) found that these responses have a uniform pattern and are independent of the size of the animal. Their studies with mice, rats, and dogs have demonstrated biphasic changes in activity of the thyroid gland, which begin with an intense increase followed by a decrease.

Considerably more direct evidence must be obtained in this area of research before any conclusion can be reached that naturally occurring or experimentally induced stresses either directly mobilize the hypothalamic-pituitary axis to increase the release of TSH, or in some other manner increase the production of the biologically active thyroid hormones from the gland. With our present knowledge, one may only surmise that the thyroid gland of animals is responsive to psychological and other stresses. Such a conclusion would be an important first step in understanding how stress can initiate Graves' disease in man.

NEURAL AND NEUROENDOCRINE MECHANISMS MEDIATING STRESSFUL RESPONSES

Increases and decreases in the activity of the thyroid gland and the release of TSH occur under stressful conditions in some animals and in man. Presumably the effects of stress are mediated by the brain in some manner that is incompletely understood. The release of TSH is controlled by a number of neural regulatory processes and by T_3 and the hypothalamic thyrotropin releasing hormone (TRH). A number of neural pathways to the anterior hypothalamus may also mediate TSH responses to stress.

Hypothalamic Regulation of the Release of TSH by the Pituitary Gland

The release of thyrotropin (TSH), a glycoprotein, by the adenohypophysis is regulated by: (1) the concentration of the nonprotein-bound (free) fraction of T_3 in the blood (Reichlin and Utiger, 1967). When the concentration of T_3 rises above a certain level, TSH release is inhibited by mechanisms that are not yet fully understood. The only effective thyroid hormone in the regulation of TSH release is T_3 not T_4 (Schadlow et al., 1972). T_4 is probably converted into T_3 in the blood or in the pituitary gland by the loss of one iodide atom (Braverman et al., 1970; Grinberg et al., 1963; Reichlin et al., 1966; Schwartz et al., 1971). T_3 acts directly on the cells in the pituitary gland to prevent TSH secretion (Patel et al., 1971; Schadlow et al., 1972). If blood levels of T_3 fall, TSH secretion occurs. (2) The rate of inactivation of TSH in blood that may determine its rate of secretion by the pituitary gland. (3) The release of thyrotropin releasing hormone (TRH) from the anterior hypothalamus.

TRH has now been identified in a number of species, including man, as a tripeptide amide–(pyro)Glu-His-Pro(NH2) (Bowers et al., 1970; Burgus et al., 1970a, b; Schally et al., 1970). Once released, TRH passes into the blood of the capillary plexus of the median eminence that perfuses the pituitary gland, to promote TSH secretion. Interactions of TRH and T_4 have been demonstrated (Schally and Redding, 1967; Vale et al., 1967; Wilbur and Utiger, 1968). The release of TRH is probably controlled by blood levels of T_3 and (probably) T_4 when they reach the hypothalamus. As levels of the hormones increase, the release of TRH by the hypothalamus is sequentially inhibited (Reichlin, 1971). T_4 (or T_3) apparently reduces the synthesis and the release of TRH by the hypothalamus. But controversy exists on this point. T_3 may determine the set-point above which TRH is released and below which release is inhibited, or T_3 may not control TRH at all.

Normally, the release of TRH from the hypothalamus is tightly controlled (Mason, 1968a). However, this control may be overcome by environmental stresses of various kinds that increase the tonic stimulation exerted by the hypothalamus on the pituitary gland, so that TSH is released. The release of TRH is also controlled by neural inputs from regions in the brain that lie above the hypothalamus and from other hypothalamic nuclei.

The thyroid gland is unique among the endocrine glands in being regulated by a dual negative feedback system—one to the pituitary gland and the other to the hypothalamus. (See Figure 1.) Both in vitro and in vivo, the response of the putuitary gland to TRH is blocked when circulating levels of the thyroid hormones are high. Thus, in some euthyroid patients with Graves' disease the pituitary responds less, or not at all, to TRH, the response being measured by changes in levels of TSH in the blood (D'Amour et al., 1973; Haigler et al., 1971). In other patients of this kind, the response of TSH to TRH is excessive (Chopra et al., 1973). The intrahypothalamic injection of the thyroid hormones inhibits TSH secretion (Kendall et al., 1967). TSH secretion is also inhibited by electrical stimulation of the anterior hypothalamic nucleus in various animal species (Averill and Slaman, 1967; D'Angelo et al., 1964; Harris and Woods, 1958). Thyroidectomy markedly increases levels of TRH in the hypothalamus (Sinha and Meites, 1966). Injection of chemically identified TRH causes release of TSH in man that can be blocked by another hypothalamic hormone, somatostatin (Fleischer et al., 1970; Haigler et al., 1971). Lesions of the paraventricular region or the area ventral to it in the anterior hypothalamic nucleus of rats (Reichlin, 1966a, b; Martin et al., 1969) lower TSH levels in plasma. Following the placement of lesions and thyroidectomy, TSH levels slowly rise in the blood, suggesting that the pituitary gland still responds to low levels of thyroid hormone in the absence of paraventricular neurons. However, the rise of TSH is much slower in lesioned animals than in the presence of an intact hypothalamus (Van Rees and Moll, 1968).

Rats with anterior hypothalamic lesions also have lower T_4 levels in plasma and are more sensitive to inhibition of TSH by administered thyroid hormone (Martin et al., 1969).

When TRH is released, it is relayed into the portal plexus of the pituitary gland by cells in the median eminence and the pituitary stalk. The neurons of the anterior hypothalamic and basal portion of the paraventricular nucleus seem to exert tonic excitatory control on both the arcuate nucleus and the median eminence in an unknown manner (Halasz et al., 1967). The axons of the arcuate neurons end in the median eminence. Lesions of the suprachiasmatic, paraventricular, ventromedial, and arcuate nuclei of the hypothalamus reduce the amount of TRH present at the level of the median eminence (Mess et al., 1967).

In other words, a rather large area of the hypothalamus extending from and including the anterior and ventral hypothalamus, perhaps reaching as far back as the mammillary bodies, is believed to be the site of TRH synthesis or storage (Averill et al., 1961; Kovács et al., 1959; Shibusawa et al., 1959).

Rather than only maintaining a "set point" (von Euler and Holmgren, 1956), the anterior hypothalamus also tonically maintains a basal secretory rate of TSH under normal conditions. From this basal rate, the rate of TSH secretion accelerates to a new secretory level when blood levels of T_3 (or T_4) fall or are low. When the concentrations of T_3 (or T_4) in serum rise or are high, the inhibition of TSH release from the gland is regulated entirely by T_3 at the level of the pituitary gland, because high levels of T_4 do not reduce TRH levels in the hypothalamus (Sinha and Meites, 1966).

368

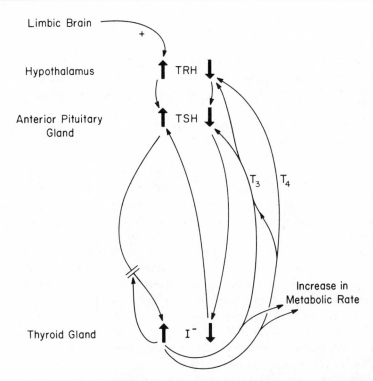

FIGURE 1. **The Hypothalamo-Pituitary Thyroid Negative Feedback System That Normally Controls Levels of the Two Thyroid Hormones (T_3 and T_4) in the Euthyroid Patient.** Increases ($\uparrow$) in thyrotropin releasing hormone (TRH) stimulate the release ($\uparrow$) of thyrotropin (TSH) from the anterior pituitary gland that in turn causes an enhanced uptake ($\uparrow$) of iodine by the thyroid gland. As a result more thyroglobulin is produced, and the two thyroid hormones are released. The increase in iodide (I^-) within the gland may blunt the stimulating effect of TSH ($\uparrow$). T_4 is largely converted in the blood stream into T_3. T_3 and T_4 stimulate the metabolic rate. T_3 diminishes the secretion of TSH ($\downarrow$) by the pituitary gland (normal T_3 suppression). Both T_3 and T_4 probably inhibit either the production or secretion of hypothalamic TRH.

The output of TSH is also influenced by the rate of synthesis by and the amounts stored in the pituitary gland. In addition, TSH plays a role in the function of the median eminence, possibly by inhibiting TRH transmission, because the concentration of TSH in the median eminence is inversely proportional to the levels in the pituitary gland (Bakke and Lawrence, 1966).

Regulation of the Anterior Hypothalamus by Other Neural Structures

Stressful influences appear to affect thyroid function. The receptor areas in the hypothalamus from which TRH is released may also be controlled by circuits that mediate, transmit, or are activated by stressful stimuli. Neural inputs to the anterior and ventral hypothalamus have been identified. Thus, the experimental manipulation of these axons, or of their nuclei of origin, should influence pituitary or thyroid function.

369

The main inputs to the relevant hypothalamic regions come from the hippocampus via the precommissural fornix, from the amygdala via the diagonal band and striae terminalis, from the habenular nucleus via the striae medullaris, from the midbrain via collaterals from the median forebrain bundle, and from the periventricular system, lateral hypothalamus, and mammillary peduncle (DeGroot, 1966). Hippocampal, but not amygdaloid, stimulation in the dog increases the output of thyroid hormone (Shizume et al., 1962). Although bilateral lesions of the amygdala in rats do not seem to disturb thyroid function (Yamada and Greer, 1960), Kovács and co-workers (1965a, 1966) found that the effects of electrical stimulation of the amygdala and of the habenula on thyroid function depend on the rate of stimulation. Stimuli of low frequency increase, and stimuli of high frequency reduce the uptake of ^{131}I by the thyroid gland in the rat. Lesions of the globus pallidum and septal area increase the activity of the thyroid gland, presumably the release of TSH (Lupelescu et al., 1962). Lesions of the midbrain reticular area apparently increase the uptake of radioactive iodine by the thyroid gland of the rat, whereas electrical stimulation of the same area has the opposite effect on uptake and release of radioiodine (Kovács et al., 1965b).

A reciprocal relationship exists between the habenular nucleus and the thyroid gland. Thyroidectomy causes the cells of the medial habenular nucleus to shrink. Lesions of the habenula not only affect body weight and the histology of the adenohypophysis and thyroid gland, but also decrease the response of the thyroid gland to cold. When the habenular nuclei are lesioned, the release of TSH from the pituitary after thyroidectomy and the effect of T_4 in depressing the production of TSH by the pituitary are inhibited (Bogdanove, 1962; Mess, 1958a, b, 1959). Lesioned rats also have an increased ^{131}I uptake by the thyroid gland despite the fact that TSH secretion is reduced (Knigge, 1964; Yasamura and Knigge, 1962). The increased uptake of ^{131}I is also observed in heat-adapted rats with habenular lesions when they are exposed to cold. The rats have a greater increase in body temperature and ^{131}I uptake than rats without habenular lesions (Beattie and Chambers, 1953; Mess, 1967). Following lesions of the habenula, these effects on the uptake of ^{131}I and on regulation of body temperature are transient; apparently, other structures in the brain assume the normal role of the habenula (Knigge, 1964; Mess, 1964).

These data suggest that limbic and habenular circuits are involved in the regulation of the hypothalamic-pituitary axis controlling TSH release. Limbic structures and circuits are also involved in the mediation of emotional and appetitive behavior. They may, therefore, mediate the effects of stress-induced emotional behavior in animals. These structures also seem to mediate the animal's response to cold to which the thyroid gland is sensitive. But much more information of the effects of brain lesions on responses to physical and emotional stress, and to cold and conditioned avoidance, is required while changes in levels of TSH are estimated and measurements of thyroid function are made.

THE PATHOPHYSIOLOGY AND IMMUNOPATHOLOGY
OF GRAVES' DISEASE

Stress alters blood levels of TSH and thyroid hormones. But in Graves' disease, the increased output of thyroid hormones by the thyroid gland occurs in the face of normal or depressed TSH levels. Therefore, TSH plays no part in maintaining the high levels of thyroid hormone secretion in Graves' disease. The high output of T_3 and T_4 in the disease

370

is produced by other factors. Presumably, these factors are the human thyroid stimulator (HTS), the LATS and the LATS protector; they are antibodies with hormonal properties that mimic the action of TSH (Adams et al., 1974; Onaya et al., 1973). The HTS, the LATS and the LATS protector stimulate thyroid hormone production. When present in the serum of Graves' disease they may account for the continued high production of T_3 and T_4 in a high proportion of Graves' disease patients. But the factors that maintain a disease are not necessarily the same ones that predispose or initiate it. The hypothesis that the LATS or related substances are the pathogenetic agents of Graves' disease is a more tenuous one than the hypothesis that they maintain it. In Graves' disease, the HTS, the LATS or the LATS protector are believed to increase and sustain the excessive production of T_3 and T_4. The secretion of T_3 and T_4 remains high because the thyroid gland has escaped the regulatory control of TSH (Adams, 1965; Adams et al., 1974). That the gland has escaped from the control of the pituitary gland is indicated by the fact that administering T_3 and T_4 to patients with Graves' disease does not suppress ^{131}I uptake or release (Bayliss, 1967; Greer, 1951b; Greer and Smith, 1954; Werner, 1962; Werner et al., 1955). In Graves' disease, the usual feedback regulation of TSH output by the pituitary has been disrupted. But it is quite unclear at what stage of the disease this disruption occurs and by what mechanism the disruption actually is brought about.

Immunological Mechanisms

The LATS is an immunoglobulin-G (IgG) with hormonal properties that closely mimic the actions of TSH (McKenzie, 1968a). The inception of Graves' disease was, until recently, explained by the fact that usual regulation of the function of the thyroid gland by TSH is taken over by the LATS. The thyroid gland escapes regulation by the pituitary gland when the LATS is present. (See Figure 2.)

THE NATURE OF THE LATS

In 1956 Adams and Purves discovered the presence of the LATS in the serum of patients with Graves' disease that stimulated the release of ^{125}I or ^{131}I from the thyroid gland of guinea pigs and mice after suppressive treatment with T_3 or T_4. TSH given to treated animals causes the maximum release of radioiodine after 2 to 3 hours. When the LATS is injected intravenously, the peak release of radioiodine occurs after 9 to 12 hours. Because of the delayed response, the substance has been called the LATS.

The LATS had a direct effect on the thyroid gland of the mouse and man. It causes an increase in the uptake of ^{131}I, it releases radioiodinated protein, T_3 and T_4 from the gland, and increases the height of its acinar cells (Major and Munro, 1960; McKenzie, 1960; Pinchera et al., 1965a). Removal of the pituitary gland does not abolish the effect of the LATS on the thyroid gland (Adams et al., 1961). Therefore, the LATS stimulates the thyroid gland directly and not through the release of TSH. The action of the LATS and TSH is to stimulate the thyroid gland to take up iodine so as to produce thyroglobulin and increase glucose oxidation. These effects are mediated by the adenylate cyclase cyclic-AMP system (Bastomsky and McKenzie, 1967; Field et al., 1967; Kriss et al., 1964; McKenzie, 1967; 1968a; Pastan, 1966; Schneider and Goldberg, 1965; Taurog and Thio,

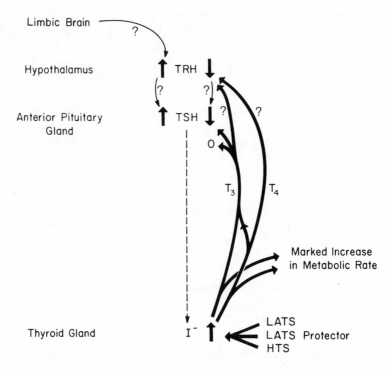

Limbic Brain

Hypothalamus — TRH

Anterior Pituitary
Gland — TSH

T_3 T_4

Marked Increase
in Metabolic Rate

Thyroid Gland I^-

LATS
LATS Protector
HTS

FIGURE 2. **Postulated Effect of the Long Acting Thyroid Stimulating Hormone (LATS), Its Protector, and the Human Thyroid Stimulating Hormone (HTS) in Producing a Markedly Raised Level (↑) of the Thyroid Hormones (T_3 and T_4) in the Hyperthyroidism of Graves' Disease.** The usual regulating, feedback system between thyrotropin (TSH) and the thyroid gland is broken (↓). TSH levels are normal or low because of the continuous inhibition (↓) of TSH release by T_3. Additional TRH production or release is inhibited by raised T_3 and T_4 levels. Yet additional T_3 does not suppress and may actually increase I^{131} uptake, suggesting that T_3 rather than inhibiting TSH release may actually stimulate it or leave it unaffected (0) (abnormal T_3 suppression).

1966). The release by the cyclic-AMP systems of iodine and iodinated products by the thyroid gland is not only raised by TSH and the LATS. ACTH, vasopressin, and serotonin also release thyroidal iodine through their action on the cyclic-AMP system (Rall and Sutherland, 1961; Werner et al., 1964).

Although the physiological actions of the LATS and TSH on the thyroid gland are very similar, their chemical structure is different (Adams, 1965). The LATS is a component of the 7S γ-G (IgG) moiety of serum proteins (Meek et al., 1964; Kriss et al., 1964; McKenzie, 1965; Miyai and Werner, 1966). It is both a hormone and an antibody. TSH is found in the 4S protein fraction. Antisera to TSH and the LATS are effective only against their homologous antigens (Dorrington and Munro, 1965). Therefore, they have separate chemical identities, because they do not cross-react with each other.

The LATS is an antibody to an unidentified antigen. The antigen is not TSH, but some other protein antigen (Dorrington and Munro, 1965; Kriss et al., 1965; Meek et al., 1964; Ochi and DeGroot, 1968).

372

The LATS may be an antibody to an antigen that resides in one of the cellular components of the thyroid gland (Burke, 1967b; Ochi and DeGroot, 1968). Homogenates of thyroid tissue bind the LATS (Beall and Solomon, 1966; Kriss et al., 1964), particularly microsomes from thyroid tissue (Beall and Solomon, 1966; Dorrington et al., 1966; El Kabir et al., 1966). On the other hand, Berumen et al. (1967) and Beall et al. (1969) believe that the LATS is an antibody to thyroglobulin (Schleusener et al., 1971). When thyroglobulin is digested by enzymes, it no longer binds and inhibits the action of the LATS—digestion has destroyed its antigenic properties. Therefore, the LATS may be an antibody either against several thyroid components or against thyroglobulin (Chopra et al., 1971; Fagraeus et al., 1970; Mahaux and Chamla-Soumenkoff, 1968). Antibodies to thyroid tissue, including the LATS, may be the product of damage to the thyroid cell by radioiodine or other forms of radiation (Mori and Kriss, 1971b). A patient with Graves' disease, whose serum does not contain autoimmune antibodies, does not produce them after cellular damage to cells of the thyroid gland caused by therapeutic irradiation with [131]I.

The antigen that stimulates the production of the LATS has not been conclusively identified (Dorrington and Munro, 1966; Mori and Kriss, 1971a; Pinchera et al., 1965a). The antigen to the LATS may not be identifiable because the LATS may be a product or derivative of another IgG, that is present in the serum of patients with Graves' disease and protects the LATS against neutralization by the microsomal fraction of the thyroid cell (Beall and Solomon, 1966; Beall et al., 1969; Dorrington et al., 1966; El Kabir et al., 1966; Volpé et al., 1974). The neutralization of the LATS can be prevented by an IgG (the LATS protector) present only in the serum of patients with Graves' disease that does not contain the LATS; the LATS protector is not present in the sera of euthyroid or myxedematous subjects (Adams and Kennedy, 1967, 1971). The LATS protector stimulates the human thyroid gland to produce thyroid hormones; it is more likely to be the pathogenetic agent in Graves' disease than the LATS (Adams and Kennedy, 1971).

If the LATS is an antibody, it should be present in the lymphocytes of patients with Graves' disease. But the lymphocytes do not seem to contain or produce the LATS (Werner and Ingbar, 1971). The lymphocytes of some, but not all patients with Graves' disease produce the LATS only when stimulated by phytohemagglutinin. Unstimulated lymphocytes do not produce the LATS (McKenzie, 1968b).

Because the LATS is an antibody, it should be possible to produce it experimentally in animals. McKenzie (1967) prepared an antiserum in rabbits by using homogenates of the whole thyroid gland and thyroid microsomes as antigens. The antiserum to the whole thyroid gland produced the greatest nine-hour assay response in mice that simulated the action of the LATS. The rabbits who were injected with the antigens did not become thyrotoxic but did develop elevated PBI levels that lasted for several weeks. They also developed antibodies against TSH (Solomon and Beall, 1968), a fact which could have explained why the rabbits failed to become hyperthyroid. The antibody that simulates the action of the LATS could be an anti-TSH antibody rather than an antibody against thyroglobulin or thyroid microsomes.

The experimental production of LATS in animals does not always take place (McKenzie, 1968b; Solomon and Beall, 1968). WHen the LATS is used as an antigen and is injected into animals it neither produces lymphoid infiltration of the thyroid gland nor the expected antigen-antibody responses (Burke, 1967b). If the LATS were an antibody against compo-

373

nents of thyroid cells, removal of the antigen by thyroidectomy should lower the titer of the LATS titer. Actually, the titer remains the same after thyroidectomy (Volpé et al., 1969; Werner et al., 1967).

In summary, therefore, the nature of the antigen that stimulates LATS production has not been identified. The failure to identify the antigen may be due to the fact that the LATS is a derivative of another antibody, the LATS protector.

Patients with Graves' disease and their relatives are predisposed in some manner to develop a number of antibodies to components of thyroid cells. The LATS is only one of a family of antibodies produced in Graves' disease. The LATS is, of course, of interest because it has the properties of a hormone stimulating the uptake of iodine and the release of radioiodinated protein. Two other members of the family of antibodies, the HTS and LATS protector, have similar hormonal properties.

The Possible Role of Autoantibodies

The presence of thyroid autoantibodies in the majority of patients with Graves' disease and the infiltration of their thyroid glands with immunocompetent and T-lymphocytes have caused a revision of the concepts about the predisposition to and the pathogenesis of the disease (Anderson et al., 1964; Doniach and Roitt, 1966; Fialkow et al., 1964; Lamki et al., 1972; Volpé et al., 1974).

Antibodies against thyroglobulin were at first only found, in low to medium titers, in about 60 percent of 181 patients with thyrotoxicosis (Doniach et al., 1960). Antibodies against thyroid gland microsomes are also present in patients with thyrotoxicosis, in low to moderate titers. The serum of 63 percent of all patients with thyrotoxicosis contains both of these autoantibodies, which are specific to components of the thyroid gland. The serum of their relatives who are not thyrotoxic may also contain both antibodies. The highest incidence and titers of these autoantibodies occur in Hashimoto's disease. That Graves' and Hashimoto's disease share common properties is also attested to by the fact that an enhanced incidence of Graves' disease and of Hashimoto's disease occurs in the near relatives of patients with Hashimoto's disease (Fialkow, 1969; Hall et al., 1964). The sera of 11 of 12 children with juvenile Graves' disease also contains antithyroid antibodies, which were also present in the sera of either one or the other parent of 10 of these 11 children (Saxena, 1965).

With the development of more refined techniques for antibody detection, even higher figures than 63 percent have been obtained for the incidence of antibodies to various elements in the thyroid gland. In 55 untreated patients with Graves' disease, the incidence of antibodies against thyroid microsomes was 98 percent and of antibodies against thyroglobulin, 89 percent. In a control series, the sera of 20 percent and 23 percent of 111 patients with various other diseases contained antimicrosomal and antithyroglobulin antibodies respectively. Thyroid autoimmunity is, therefore, a manifestation of untreated Graves' disease and several other diseases of the gland, as antimicrosomal antibodies are also to be found in 95 percent of patients with Hashimoto's disease, in 75 percent of patients with hypothyroidism and myxedema. Treatment of Graves' disease with ^{131}I enhances antimicrosomal antibody titer levels only, and not the titers of the other autoantibodies. Measurable antimicrosomal antibody titers persist after patients become euthyroid (Mori and Kriss, 1971b).

These various autoantibodies are not specific to Graves' disease. Their presence in healthy relatives of patients and their persistence in serum after treatment imply that they cannot be the pathogenetic agents of Graves' disease. Their source and their role in this disease remain unexplained. It is not known whether the predisposition to form these antibodies is genetically inherited, is due to a mutation or the vertical transmission of a virus from one generation to another, or is an expression of autoimmunity. The presence of thyroid-specific antibodies in the serum of relatives of patients suggests that they may play a predisposing but not initiating role in Graves' disease. Autoantibodies do not necessarily cause a disease: they may be present in the serum without being pathogenetic. For instance, the serum of many patients with chronic gastritis and that of their relatives who do not have gastritis contains antithyroid antibodies, but they do not have discernible thyroid disease.

In Graves' disease, the autoantibodies to thyroid tissue are usually only present when the thyroid gland is infiltrated with lymphoid cells. Hypothyroidism after the disease has been treated by partial thyroidectomy or with ^{131}I is more likely to develop when the autoantibodies are present in the serum (Green and Wilson, 1964). In other words, the presence of autoantibodies is related more to treatment outcome, or to injury to the gland by ^{131}I than to the pathogenesis of Graves' disease.

OTHER CLASSES OF ANTIBODIES

The LATS and the antithyroid autoantibodies belong to the IgG class of antibodies. Other classes of immunoglobulins have been discovered in Graves' disease. This discovery supports the idea that disturbances in immune mechanisms play an etiological role in Graves' disease. The manner in which these disturbances come about is a matter of active debate and investigation at the present time (Volpé et al., 1974).

In 1969, Mahaux et al. reported that increased amounts of IgM could be found in the sera of patients with Graves' disease. Since then, other studies have revealed that a variety of immunoglobulims are present in the connective tissue stroma and basement membrane of cells of the thyroid gland and at other sites in the body. By the use of immunofluorescent techniques, Werner et al. (1972) found that the stroma of thyroid tissue taken at operation from patients with Graves' disease contained IgG, IgM, and IgE.* Six of eight samples were also stained with antisera to specific complement. The subpapillary layer of the skin and subepithelial layer of the conjunctiva of patients with Graves' disease also contains the three classes of immunoglobulins. Localization of immune responses in connective tissue and in the basement membrane of cells also occurs in rheumatoid arthritis, chronic glomerulonephritis, and systemic lupus erythematosus, which are characterized by disturbances in immune mechanisms. Similar disturbances may occur in Graves' disease. Graves' disease, therefore, has an immunopathology, but not necessarily an autoimmune one. The pathology may reside in lymphoid tissue or the thymus, both of which are known to be involved in Graves' disease (Gunn et al., 1964; Michie et al., 1967), but its origins remain

---

* Because IgE is present in the thyroid gland of Graves' disease patients, the immediate form of hypersensitivity that is mediated by vasoactive substances may play a role in the pathogenesis of Graves' disease.

unknown. Some ascribe the immunopathology to autoimmunity, others do not (Volpé et al., 1974).

Some immunologists classify autoimmune diseases into two categories: (1) organ-specified diseases such as Graves' disease, Hashimoto's thyroiditis, and hypothyroidism characterized by the presence of antibodies directed only against components of one specific organ, such as a gland, and (2) nonorgan-specific diseases such as systemic lupus erythematosus, in which many different organ systems are affected by autoantibodies.

Specific criteria for organ-specific autoimmune diseases have been developed. Graves' disease meets these criteria, which are: (1) a familial tendency to form organ-specific antibodies; (2) the presence of antibodies directed at cell components in other organs (such as gastric parietal cells); (3) the presence of organ-specific antibodies; (4) lymph cell invasion of the specific organ; (5) the elicitation of antibodies by specific antigen (e.g., thyroglobulin) when injected into experimental animals.

However, Graves' disease can also occur during the course of non-organ-specific autoimmune diseases, such as a collagen disease (Librick et al., 1970). The characteristics of nonorgan-specific diseases are: (1) a much greater incidence in women; (2) an increase in immunoglobulins that react with normal cellular constituents; (3) the occurrence of remissions and excerbations during the course of the illness (Roitt and Doniach, 1965). These three criteria also characterize Graves' disease, so that Graves' disease is both an organ-specific and nonorganic-specific autoimmune disease. Graves' disease may be an autoimmune disease, but autoimmunity need not necessarily cause disease. Those who believe that autoimmunity is pathogenetic have put forward the hypothesis that a TSH receptor on the surface of, or within, the thyroid cell becomes antigenic as immune tolerance breaks down for unknown reasons (Solomon and Chopra, 1972). An antibody, the LATS, to the antigen is formed. It stimulates the release of T_3 and T_4. The thyroid gland then escapes the control of the pituitary-hypothalamic axis.

The hypothesis does not explain the presence of the LATS in the euthyroid relatives of patients with Graves' disease. It does not explain the origin or the action of other antibodies in the disease. It does not account for the presence of the same autoantibodies in other diseases of the thyroid gland. Finally, the evidence that in Graves' disease the thyroid gland has become independent of TSH is tenuous (Volpé et al., 1974). Because of these reasons, the autoimmune hypothesis of the pathogenesis of Graves' disease is unproven.

The hypothesis of the pathogenetic role of the LATS has been shaken by the fact that infantile Graves' disease is not always caused by the transplacental transfer of the LATS from mother to child (Hollingworth and Mabry, 1972). Instances of infantile thyrotoxicosis have been reported, in which the mother did not have the LATS in her serum, but the thyrotoxic child did (McKenzie, 1964; Sunshine et al., 1965). When this phenomenon was reassessed, the discovery was made that the serum of the mother contained the LATS protector, and the child's serum contained the LATS (Scott, 1976; Thomson et al., 1975). Therefore, the presence of the LATS may simply be an indicator of the presence of the LATS protector in the serum of patients predisposed to or having clinical thyrotoxicosis (Adams, 1975; Shishiba et al., 1973).

The LATS can be recovered from the serum of patients with Graves' disease. In Graves' disease unaccompanied by exophthalmos or pretibial edema, the LATS is recovered from the serum of 6 to 76 percent of patients (McKenzie, 1961; Werner, 1963). In patients with exophthalmos, the incidents of the LATS in serum is 38 to 39 percent (McKenzie, 1961; Sellers et al., 1970). When thyrotoxicosis, exophthalmos, and pretibial edema is present in Graves' disease, the LATS can be recovered in 80 percent (Chopra et al., 1970b; Major and Munro, 1962; Mori and Kriss, 1971b). The more of the classical triad of signs of Graves' disease a patient has, the more likely is his serum to contain the LATS.

The inability to detect the LATS in the serum of every patient with Graves' disease has been explained by the insensitivity of the bioassay method, or the dilution of the LATS in the serum. In some patients, the LATS can only be detected when the serum is concentrated, otherwise the assay is negative (Carneiro et al., 1966a). The LATS is more-often discovered in concentrated than in unconcentrated serum; although the LATS is not present in the serum of all patients, even when the serum is concentrated (Carneiro et al., 1966a; Chopra et al., 1970a). The incidence of the LATS in the sera of patients with Graves' disease varies with the number of the major clinical features of the disease but not with the severity of the thyrotoxicosis (Bonnyns et al., 1968; Chopra et al., 1970a, b, c; Lipman et al., 1967; Pinchera et al., 1965a; Sellers et al., 1970; Solomon and Chopra, 1972).

As Graves' disease remits spontaneously or with treatment, the LATS gradually disappears and its titer diminishes; but it does not disappear altogether in all patients (Lipman et al., 1967; Pinchera et al., 1969; Solomon and Chopra, 1972). In fact, the LATS can persist in the serum of patients from two to ten years after clinical Graves' disease has subsided (Lipman et al., 1967). Because it has also been found in the serum of the euthyroid relatives of patients with Graves' disease and in individuals without a history of Graves' disease (Adams, 1965; Lipman et al., 1967; McKenzie, 1968a; Wall et al., 1969; Zakrzewskea-Henisz et al., 1967), serious doubt is cast on its role in the pathogenesis of Graves' disease despite the fact that it stimulates the thyroid gland to secrete T_3 and T_4 (Burke, 1967b, 1971; Pastan et al., 1966).

The Relationship of the LATS to the Production
of the Physiological Changes

The infusion of serum containing the LATS stimulates thyroid function in both animals and man. In one study of humans, serum containing the LATS taken from patients with a history of Graves' disease increased the organic metabolism of iodine when it was infused into volunteer subjects in five of seven instances. The peak response to infusion occurred after two days and lasted six days. When the serum of myxedematous patients was infused into volunteers the peak response occurred on one-half to one day and lasted about three days. Presumably the myxedematous serum contained high levels of TSH (Arnaud et al., 1965).

Similar but somewhat less-convincing findings were obtained by Bjorkman et al. (1961). The PBI content of the blood of four of eight recipients increased when the serum of patients with euthyroid or thryotoxic Graves' disease was infused. But the peak levels of PBI were reached between 30 to 40 hours after infusion; in contrast to Arnaud and co-workers' findings, the same latency of the peak response was obtained with the injection of TSH. The findings suggest that there is an unidentified substance in the blood of patients with Graves' disease that stimulates the release of thyroidal iodine and increases PBI levels.

But one may not conclude that the LATS was the only stimulus to increase PBI levels in these experiments. Nonspecific factors (such as the experiment itself) were not controlled. No attempt was made to identify other substances in the patients' blood that could have increased PBI levels. In addition, neither of the two studies proved that the LATS (presumed to have been present in the serum of the donors) produces Graves' disease. They only demonstrate that release of thyroidal iodine and the increase of PBI levels in normal subjects is stimulated by some substance that is present in the blood of patients with Graves' disease.

Some authors (Carneiro et al., 1966b; Major and Munro, 1962) have claimed that there is a correlation in Graves' disease between the presence of the LATS in serum and the ^{131}I turnover rate in the thyroid gland. This claim has been denied by others. No correlation between the level of the LATS in unconcentrated or concentrated serum and the levels of serum cholesterol, T_3 and T_4, $PB^{127}I$, the ^{131}I uptake test, or the 24-hour $PB^{131}I$ level were found (Bonnyns et al., 1968; Chopra et al., 1970b; Sellers et al., 1970).

If the LATS were responsible for stimulating the thyroid gland, then it should be present in the serum of all patients who evidenced an increased release of thyroidal iodine or elevated T_3 T_4 blood levels. One might also expect that if the LATS increases blood levels of T_3 and T_4, TSH secretion should be completely suppressed. Yet no correlation can be found between TSH levels and the presence or absence of the LATS. TSH is undetectable in a greater percentage (30 percent) of patients *without* than *with* (18 percent) detectable LATS activity in unconcentrated or concentrated serum (Chopra et al., 1970b; Sellers et al., 1970). These results could be a function of the assay methods used to detect TSH or of the failure to concentrate the LATS in serum, yet similar results were obtained by Chopra et al., (1970b) with *concentrated* serum.

TSH levels are suppressed by the administration of T_3, whether or not the LATS is present in the serum. The fall of TSH levels and the failure of ^{131}I uptake levels to be suppressed when T_3 is administered occur independently of the presence or absence of the LATS in Graves' disease. Therefore, an abnormal T_3 suppression test cannot depend on the presence, or the titer of the LATS in serum (Chopra et al., 1970b,c; McKenzie, 1967, 1968a; Sellers et al., 1970; Wong and Doe, 1969).

The work just cited raises serious questions about the hypothetical role of the LATS in the pathogenesis and pathophysiology of Graves' disease and thyrotoxicosis. Central to this hypothesis is the assumption that T_3 or T_4 administration does not suppress the function of the gland either in the euthyroid or the thyrotoxic forms of Graves' disease, because the LATS is continually stimulating the gland (Adams, 1965; McKenzie, 1967, 1968a). If the mechanism for the uptake and/or release of iodine by the thyroid gland is not suppressed, the gland must be functioning independently of pituitary control, which must have been preempted by the LATS. But this hypothesis must be rejected in the light of the work just cited.

THE ROLE OF THE LATS IN THE PRODUCTION
OF THE THYROTOXICOSIS

Thyrotoxicosis can occur in the absence of the LATS. Thyrotoxicosis has been described in a single toxic adenomata of the thyroid (Ingbar and Woeber, 1968; McKenzie and Solomon, 1967; Pinchera et al., 1965b) without the presence of the LATS in serum.

In this disease thyroid function continues to be regulated by the interaction of the thyroid hormones and TSH. The adenoma produces enough thyroid hormones to lower TSH levels, so that the functions of the nonnodular portions of the gland are suppressed. The suppressed areas of the gland continue to be reactive to TSH. Thyrotoxicosis has also been described in patients who medicate themselves with T_3 or T_4, in patients with choriocarcinoma, which secretes a substance analogous, if not homologous, to TSH (Odell et al., 1963; Steigbigel et al., 1964). The LATS does not occur in any of these disease states that produce thyrotoxicosis. Therefore, the LATS cannot exclusively cause thyrotoxicosis.

In fact, the LATS is present in the serum of patients with euthyroid Graves' disease and exophthalmos (Adams, 1965; Adams et al., 1969; Chopra and Solomon, 1970a; Liddle et al., 1965; Lipman et al., 1967; Pinchera et al., 1965a, b; Pimstone et al., 1963). In a patient with euthyroid Graves' disease the eventual onset of thyrotoxicosis was accompanied by a fall in the titer of the LATS (Chopra and Solomon, 1970a).

If the LATS were the sole cause of the thyrotoxicosis, it should only be present if the patient were thyrotoxic and not in euthyroid Graves' disease. The LATS is also not the cause of the eye signs of Graves' disease, despite the fact that the LATS is present in the serum of more patients who have exophthalmos than in patients who do not. In some series, the LATS is present in the serum of only a few untreated or insufficiently treated patients without eye signs, but it is present in the serum of all thyrotoxic patients with eye signs (Bonnyns et al., 1968; Kriss et al., 1967; Liddle et al., 1965; Lipman et al., 1967; Pinchera et al., 1969). In other series, this was not the case (Bowden and Rose, 1969; Sellers et al., 1970).

The occurrence of exophthalmos in Graves' disease could be due to very high concentrations of the LATS in serum. Actually, some patients with very high serum titers of the LATS are not exophthalmic. Therefore, no direct relationship of high titers of the LATS to eye signs exists (Major and Munro, 1962; McKenzie, 1962).

Longitudinal studies of the relationship of the eye signs to the presence of the LATS in serum have been equally controversial. Eye signs may become worse, or only partly improve, with treatment while the LATS becomes undetectable in the serum (Werner, 1971); or the eye signs and the LATS may spontaneously disappear at the same time (Lipman et al., 1967). Therefore, the action of LATS cannot account for the eye signs of patients with the euthyroid or thyrotoxic forms of Graves' disease. In fact, the mechanism responsible for the appearance of eye signs is still not understood (Dobyns, 1966; Dobyns and Wilson, 1954; Dobyns et al., 1965; McGill, 1960). The eye signs may be due to a substance that has been extracted from the serum of patients with exophthalmic opthalmoplegia and that may originate from the pituitary gland, but is chemically different from the LATS (Pimstone et al., 1963).

Localized myxedema is an uncommon manifestation of Graves' disease whose presence in some patients is closely related to high titers of the LATS in the serum (Bonnyns et al., 1968). The deposition of the LATS in tissue may produce localized myxedema in some but not in all patients (Pimstone et al., 1964; Pinchera et al., 1965a; Solomon et al., 1964). But not all patients with Graves' disease with high serum levels of the LATS develop localized myxedema. Localized myxedema is a relatively rare phenomenon in Graves' disease and is, therefore, difficult to study. The evidence that the LATS is deposited in tissues to produce localized myxedema is tenuous.

379

If it is true that the LATS is responsible only for the thyrotoxicosis of Graves' disease and not for the disease itself, the activity of the LATS in serum should be reduced with treatment, or with the remission of the illness. Actually, a number of authors have reported that the LATS can be more-frequently detected in the serum of patients after treatment for Graves' disease than before (Bonnyns et al., 1968; Kriss et al., 1967; Pinchera et al., 1969). Therefore, the presence of the LATS in the serum of patients with Graves' disease may be a product of damage to the cells of the thyroid gland by drug treatment or by surgery. Such damage would release cell constituents or products, which, acting as antigens, would stimulate the production of the LATS.

But Lipman et al. (1967) and Sellers et al. (1970) found that the detectability of the LATS in the serum of treated patients was independent of the treatment method used. Therefore, the presence of the LATS in the serum cannot depend on cell damage because some treatment methods are much more-likely to damage or destroy cells than other methods (Burke, 1967; Lipman et al., 1967; McKenzie, 1965; McKenzie and Solomon, 1967; Meek and Vanderlaan, 1964; Pinchera et al., 1969; Sellers et al., 1970; Volpé et al., 1969).

The presence of the LATS is not merely a result of treatment. Furthermore, the LATS has been found in the serum of patients in variable amounts before treatment, and it may vary in level or disappear from the serum without any treatment (Lipman et al., 1967; Werner, 1971).

If the LATS plays a pathogenetic role, it would have had to be present in the serum of patients just *prior* to the development of the disease, and not for months or years earlier. It should disappear from serum in concert with recovery, but it does not always do so.

Therefore, the role of the LATS in Graves' disease has recently been downgraded. Its original discovery led to a very major change in the focus of research on Graves' disease and stimulated a great deal of research on the immunological mechanisms in all diseases of the thyroid gland, not only in Graves' disease (Adams, 1965; Bastémie et al., 1967; Jayson et al., 1967; Wyse et al., 1968).

To summarize: the evidence that the LATS is the pathogenetic agent of Graves' disease, thyrotoxicosis or its other clinical and physiological manifestations remains unconvincing. However, its presence in serum and its ability to stimulate thyroid iodine uptake and release poses a serious problem to anyone who would propose an alternative hypothesis of pathogenesis or pathophysiology. Such alternative theories have been put forward: for example, that Graves' disease is either an autoimmune or immune disease and that LATS is a marker for a tendency to form autoantibodies. The fact that the antigen for LATS production has not been identified militates against the autoantibody hypothesis. However, the antigen may be an unidentified, exogenous one such as a virus.

SUMMARY AND CONCLUSIONS

For 25 years, Alexander's hypothesis has guided psychosomatic research on Graves' disease. His hypothesis was divided into three parts. He believed that patients are physiologically and psychologically predisposed to Graves' disease. Although, at that time, he could not have known the nature of the physiological predisposition, he suggested that in patients predisposed to Graves' disease life experiences stimulated premature self-sufficiency and caretaking. He believed that the future patient was burdened as a child by excessive demands and expectations that in turn stimulated the production of the thyroid hormones. Excessive production of thyroid hormones in turn accelerated psychological maturation and development.

The second part of Alexander's hypothesis stated that patients with Graves' disease overcompensate for their extreme insecurity and dependent attachment to their mothers: they take care of others, assume more than their share of domestic responsibilities, and display excessive maturity and self-sufficiency. Some patients develop thyrotoxic Graves' disease in situations that prevent them from being self-sufficient or from taking care of other people. A third group of patients are afraid of bodily harm and physical danger, which, paradoxically, they may court. When their counterphobic defiance of harm and danger no longer functions, or they are injured, they become frightened or afraid of dying.

Alexander went on to suggest that in situations where the patient could no longer be self-sufficient, care for others, or counterphobically cope with danger or injury, excessive TSH production occurs to initiate Graves' disease.

The review carried out in this chapter attests to the fact that the second part of Alexander's hypothesis is partly correct but that we still have no evidence for the first or third part of his hypothesis.

Some patients with thyrotoxicosis are prematurely self-sufficient and ardent care-takers. Other patients are afraid of dying, and some are openly dependent upon the affection and the slavish devotion of other people. The latter group is especially sensitive to separation from the persons upon whom they depend.

But we have no real idea how adult patients with Graves' disease become the way they are. The burden of explanation for the childhood origins of their traits, relationships, and fears has been assigned to the experience of loss, excessive demands, and economic hardship. Alexander's ideas that increased thyroid hormone secretion promoted premature developmental progression has not been proven.

Graves' disease runs in families. Yet little is known about the impact on her children of a mother who is predisposed to, or develops the disease. Theoretically, it is hard to understand how excessive dependency could be engendered in a child by a mother who is slavishly devoted to and expertly takes care of her child, unless the mother's excessive devotion overindulges the child, who then has no incentive to grow up. But there is no data to support this suggestion, which could be confirmed or refuted by the study of the families of patients with Graves' disease.

Another tentative conclusion arises from this review. The psychological characteristics of patients with Graves' disease are also found in patients with other diseases of the thyroid gland, especially in patients with toxic multinodular and single adenoma of the goiter. Unfortunately, behavioral scientists have not studied the traits and conflicts of patients with other diseases of the thyroid gland such as Hashimoto's thyroiditis or myxedema. (They have studied the organic mental syndrome of myxedema and hypothyroidism). They should study other forms of thyroid disease, and also compare patients with different forms of thyrotoxicosis (Appendix 2). In fact, we really do not know whether excessive self-sufficiency or fears of dying only characterize patients with Graves' disease, or all thyrotoxic patients.

It would be interesting to know whether the same psychological characteristics occur in several thyroid diseases, because these diseases also share many common immunopathological features. Antithyroid autoantibodies occur in the serum of patients with Graves' disease and of their relatives, in Hashimoto's disease and in hypothyroidism and myxedema. The cause and sources of these autoimmune antibodies are under active investigation at the present time (Chopra and Solomon, 1972; Volpé et al., 1974).

Patients with Graves' disease and their relatives also share other immunopathological features. The LATS appears in the serum of 60 to 80 percent of all patients with Graves' disease and in about 20 to 25 percent of their relatives.

In the period between 1956 and 1970, the hypothesis that most closely fitted the facts was that the LATS was the pathogenetic agent of Graves' disease. But a number of observations have mitigated against this hypothesis (Scott, 1976; Solomon and Chopra, 1972). At present the reigning hypotheses are equally divided between those who believe that the LATS protector or the HTS are the pathogenetic agent (Adams, 1975; Adams et al., 1974; Volpé et al., 1974), and those who believe that Graves' disease is a response to a family of immunoglobulins to which the LATS, the LATS protector, and the HTS belong (Volpé et al., 1974).

TSH plays no role in the pathogenesis of Graves' disease in this hypothesis. In Graves' disease the relationship between TSH and the thyroid gland is intact, and the low or normal levels of TSH found in patients are ascribed to the high levels of T_3 that suppress TSH production. However, Alexander did not state that TSH sustains the disease; rather, he said that it initiates it. He may still be correct because there is no agreement about the pathogenetic mechanisms of Graves' disease. At the present time, it is believed that, once the disease starts, the high levels of thyroid hormone production are maintained by one or another of the immunoglobulins—the LATS, its protector, or the HTS—that have hormonal properties. In this way the thyroid gland escapes regulation by the pituitary gland.

However, two new pieces of information may lead to a reassessment of the role of TSH in Graves' disease, because in some euthyroid patients with Graves' disease TSH is either unresponsive or excessively responsive to TRH. These findings suggest that at the level of the hypothalamus or the pituitary gland two kinds of regulatory disturbances exist in some forms of Graves' disease. It remains to be shown whether these regulatory disturbances antecede the onset of the disease. We do in fact know that the function of the hypothalamic-pituitary axis can be altered by early experience, including the experimental production of thyrotoxicosis in young animals by the injection of T_3.

Although much is known about the predisposition to Graves' disease and its immunopathology and pathophysiology, a comprehensive account of the disease cannot be rendered because the mechanisms of its pathogenesis are not known. We do not know how stressful events, pregnancy, surgery, or infection incite the disease. And we do not know why it can begin abruptly in some and slowly in others. In some patients, a fright does seem to antedate disease onset. In other patients, T_3 levels may be elevated before the full panoply of symptoms of the disease unfolds. This metabolic change may, in some manner, make it more difficult for the patient to cope with fear, bereavement, surgery, or infection.

Studies on some animals suggest that fright or stressful experimental procedures do produce a biphasic response in the release of the thyroid hormones that initially consists of a fall. Therefore, it is possible that stressful events could depress TSH production in man

382

and the HTS or LATS and its protector could then take over its role as the regulators of excessive thyroid hormone production. Or, infection and stress could produce an immune response of the anaphylactic type—IgE antibodies are present in the thyroid gland of patients with Graves' disease. These IgE antibodies could combine with a specific antigen to release vasoactive amines that cause the release of the thyroid hormones and initiate the disease.

These suggestions must be tentative. They can only be studied in patients at risk for the disease, or before its recurrences. Both risk and longitudinal studies are called for. Risk studies could be done on euthyroid subjects in the general population whose serum contains the LATS or antithyroid autoantibodies. Such subjects could be studied socially, psychologically, immunologically, and physiologically; when they face stressful events, when they become pregnant or undergo surgery, they should be restudied. Particular attention might be paid to the events that coincide with a change in the T_3 suppression test from normal to abnormal.

Once the disease has begun and has been treated, longitudinal studies of its remissions and exacerbations should be carried out. They could be most instructive if exact observations on the psychological and physiological changes were carried out during a remission and exacerbation.

Finally, one might well ask how psychological events, surgery, infection or pregnancy could influence immune mechanisms, alter immune surveillance or antigen-antibody reactions, or even induce a virus that may underlie the immumopathological changes in Graves' disease.

APPENDIX 1
LABORATORY CRITERIA FOR DIAGNOSIS

Disturbances of thyroid function, assessed by special tests, do not only occur when Graves' disease is active. They may be present before, or long after, the clinical symptoms and signs of the disease are over. The disease may continue to exist in a subclinical form for the rest of the patient's life. Treatment is not directed at the (unknown) pathogenetic mechanisms in Graves' disease, but at reducing or limiting the output of T_3 and T_4 by the gland. After thyroidectomy, the remnant of the gland continues to function as it did before the operation, but the output of thyroid hormones is decreased because the amount of functioning overactive tissue has been reduced.

The changes in thyroid function in Graves' disease are not specific to it. They consist of an increased metabolism (as measured by the BMR), an overproduction and increased release of thyroxine (T_4) and/or triiodothyronine (T_3) (measured by increases in protein bound iodine [PBI], butanol extractable iodine [BEI], and T_4 and T_3 concentrations in plasma). Normal or slight depression of inorganic iodine levels in the plasma do occur. The rate of clearance of iodine by the thyroid is elevated, producing an enhanced absolute uptake of iodine that is best demonstrated by the increased uptake of radioiodine by the gland. Iodide transport and binding within the gland are accelerated, the rate of coupling of T_3 and T_4 by protein to produce thyroglobulin within the gland is also increased. The high rate of turnover of iodide, and its increased release from the glandular iodine pool, is evidenced by high values of serum $PB^{131}I$, which may persist for years after successful symptomatic treatment (Eckert et al., 1961). Recently it has been shown that although the major product of the gland is T_4, peripheral deiodinization of T_4 occurs to produce T_3. In Graves' disease the ratio of T_3 to T_4 is increased. Even before thyrotoxicosis develops in Graves' disease, T_3 levels may be high, and T_4 levels normal (Hollander et al., 1971). Later in its course an absolute and proportionate increase occurs in the ratio of free T_4 in serum to T_4 bound to the carrier proteins. In Graves' disease the absolute amounts of T_4 produced by the gland are greater, and its binding by the specific carrier albumin and globulin is increased (Harvey et al., 1970). The body also disposes of T_4 more rapidly during the active disease and thereafter. A defect in the peripheral metabolism of T_4, which persists after the thyrotoxicosis of Graves' disease is relieved, may also be present in some euthyroid relatives of patients with Graves' disease. The defect takes the form of an accelerated fractional turnover of T_4 during the late phase of its disposition. T_4 labeled with radioactive iodine disappears more rapidly from the body during the 20- to 50-minute period after it is injected, even if the patient is in remission from the illness (Ingbar and Woeber, 1968). The uptake of iodine by the thyroid gland is partly regulated by thyrotropin (thyroid-stimulating hormone [TSH]) in the normal state (Tong, 1971): TSH accelerates the accumulation of iodine by the thyroid gland and the synthesis and secretion of the thyroid hormones; it increases the synthesis of protein and nucleoprotein, and the levels of cyclic 3', 5'-AMP (Gilman and Rall, 1966) in the cells of the thyroid gland. The release of TSH by the adenohypophysis is, in part, regulated by levels of unbound T_3 in the blood.

In Graves' disease thyrotropin levels are either normal or low, presumably because free T_3 levels are increased. Normally, when T_3 is administered to normal subjects, the rate of uptake of ^{131}I by the gland is reduced—a normal T_3-suppression test. In Graves' disease the rate of uptake of ^{131}I is either unaffected or is actually enhanced by T_3. The failure to suppress ^{131}I uptake by T_3 in Graves' disease is called an abnormal suppression test (Eckert et al., 1961; Werner, 1956). Failure of T_3 to suppress the gland's uptake of ^{131}I also occurs in about 70 percent of patients with euthyroid Graves' disease who, despite being euthyroid, have active eye changes (Bayliss, 1967; Bowden and Rose, 1969; Burke, 1967a; Hall and Stanbury, 1967; Werner, 1955). An abnormal T_3 suppression test in the *absence* of thyrotoxicosis always indicates that Graves' disease is present. An abnormal T_3 suppression test may persist for as long as 20 years in some patients otherwise successfully treated for euthyroid or thyrotoxic Graves' disease (Bowden and Rose, 1969). In other patients, test results may revert to normal, but may become abnormal again when the disease recurs. When TSH is given to patients with Graves' disease, the 24-hour ^{131}I uptake is not increased[*](Werner et al., 1955), or it is increased much less than one would expect it to be after successful treatment with ^{131}I or surgery (Eckert et al., 1961).

T_3 and T_4 may markedly enhance ^{131}I uptake in patients with Graves' disease despite normal or low levels of TSH (Bayliss, 1967). This abnormal effect suggests that the expected negative-feedback system between T_3 and TSH is not in operation. No one has ascertained why the negative feedback system has become a positive one. One explanation is that a positive feedback effect is caused by the release of TSH by high levels of T_3.

Alternative hypotheses have been proposed to explain the failure of T_3 or T_4 to suppress

---

[*] Generally the TSH test is not given to patients who are thyrotoxic with Graves' disease, because it is not considered safe to carry it out.

the function of the thyroid gland. In the first, they fail to suppress ^{131}I release because the gland is constantly being stimulated by the LATS or other thyroid stimulators. The second accounts for the "escape" of the thyroid gland from the control of TSH by another mechanism: the gland is now somehow regulating its own activity (Ingbar, 1972). This hypothesis has been discarded by some authors (Ingar and Woeber, 1968; McKenzie, 1968a), largely because the gland continues to be responsive to TSH (Charkes, 1969; Goolden, 1959; Greer and Shull, 1957) and is therefore not "autonomous." Greer and Shull (1957) had to use larger doses in thyrotoxic patients than in normal subjects to produce a comparable increase in labeled T_4 secretion rates. Charkes (1969), however, observed a normal increase in 24-hour ^{131}I uptake when TSH was given to patients who satisfied the usual criteria for mild Graves' disease and who had normal *baseline* uptake rates of the radioisotope.

It is generally conceded that in Graves' disease, TSH augments the clearance rate for thyroidal iodide (Goolden, 1959), the ten-minute accumulation gradient (Einhorn, 1958), the short-term (up to six-hours) uptake of radioiodine (Goolden, 1959), and the secretion rates of labeled (Becker et al., 1953; Greer and Shull, 1957) and unlabeled (Werner et al., 1952) thyroid hormone. In those instances in which the 24-hour uptake of ^{131}I is unaffected by TSH (Einhorn, 1958; Goolden, 1959; Werner et al., 1952), the baseline rate of uptake has already increased markedly before TSH is administered. It is, therefore, erroneous to conclude that TSH has no effect on the uptake of radioiodine, and that the gland is completely autonomous of it, when in actuality the gland is already taking up the labeled isotope at a maximum rate.

What is more, the adenohypophysis remains responsive to exogenous T_3 (Adams and Kennedy, 1965; Chopra et al., 1970b), suggesting that the usual negative feedback mechanism is operative in some cases of Graves' disease, especially in patients in whom TSH is still detectable in serum. Chopra et al. (1970b) found that the 20-minute ^{131}I uptake by the gland fell to lower levels after the administration of T_3 when TSH was detectable in their sera than when it was not. Therefore, the apparent absolute autonomy of the gland has not been proven.

Other physiological changes also help in diagnosis. Tyrosine is the amino acid precursor of T_3 and T_4. The estimation of tyrosine levels in blood, and the measurement of the tolerance for administered tyrosine may be useful in tests in Graves' disease. Fasting tyrosine levels in blood are elevated. The circadian rhythm in tyrosine levels persists in Graves' disease (Levine et al., 1962; Melmon et al., 1964). When tyrosine is given orally the plasma concentration rises to twice the levels obtained in euthyroid patients (Belanger and Rivlin, 1971; Besser, 1968; Rivlin et al., 1965). To determine the meaning of these test results, it would be necessary first to ascertain that the elevated levels of tyrosine in Graves' disease do not result from an increase in monoiodo- and di-iodotyrosine levels released into the blood stream by the gland.

The recovery of various antibodies in serum aids in the diagnosis of Graves' disease. The LATS is present in 30 to 80 percent of all patients. Another immunoglobulin, the LATS protector, is also present in serum, even when the LATS is not (Adams and Kennedy, 1971). The serum of many patients also contains (antithyroid) antibodies against thyroglobulin, the microsomes of thyroid cells, and other components of the gland.

Antithyroid antibodies occur in the serum of 52 percent of all women patients with

Graves' disease and thyrotoxicosis. The serum of 37 percent of such patients contain microsomal antibodies; 28 percent contain antibodies against thyroid colloid (other than thyroglobulin) and 47 percent antibodies against thyroid microsomes (Roitt and Doniach, 1965, 1967). Antithyroid antibodies are present in other thyroid diseases; they are present in high titers in almost all cases of Hashimoto's disease, and in about 80 percent of patients with primary myxedema (Doniach et al., 1960). The LATS may be recovered from the serum of patients with Hashimoto's disease, and it has also been found in the euthyroid relatives of patients with Graves' disease.

The absence of a palpable goiter, or a normal BMR, does not preclude the diagnosis of Graves' disease. When the BMR is normal, the levels of PBI in serum and the 24-hour uptake of ^{131}I may be enhanced (Werner and Hamilton, 1961). Atypical forms of Graves' disease occur: only eye signs may occur without thyrotoxicosis. In the atypical form an abnormal T_3 suppression test occurs, and patients may show a failure to respond with an increase in TSH when TRH is administered (Lawton et al., 1971). Patients who are euthyroid with eye signs may not have Graves' disease but may have Hashimoto's thyroiditis, or they have both diseases simultaneously (Liddle et al., 1965; Wyse et al., 1968).

APPENDIX 2
DIFFERENTIAL DIAGNOSIS

In the study of any illness, the investigator must be sure that he is dealing with a homogeneous process. But the clinical picture of Graves' disease is variable, and the validating laboratory tests are not specific to the disease.

Another major source of potential error in psychosomatic studies is that thyrotoxicosis is not unique to Graves' disease. As a first step to avoid repeating past errors in selecting patients, it may be necessary also to study patients with Graves' disease with or without thyrotoxicosis. The thyrotoxic state alters brain and mental functioning. Theoretically, the psychological conflicts should be present in all forms of Graves' disease, whether thyrotoxic or not. But the observation and description of these conflicts may be altered by the effect of thyrotoxicosis on mental functioning.

Thyrotoxicosis occurs in toxic multinodular goiters that must be differentiated from Graves' disease. Two types of multinodular goiter have been described (Fraser, 1963; Ingbar and Woeber, 1968). In the first type, ^{131}I is diffusely and unevenly localized in the gland, as evidenced by scintillation scanning. Its uneven localization remains unaltered after the administration of TSH. Anatomically, the gland consists of small, actively functioning follicles interspersed with local accretions of large follicles that are physiologically inactive and do not respond to TSH.

In the second type of toxic multinodular goiter the adenomatous nodules accumulate iodine actively and "suppress" the remainder of the gland into functional inactivity. The inactive parts of the gland can be stimulated into activity by TSH. Multinodular toxic goiters usually occur in older people. Women are much more prone than men to toxic multinodular goiter, but the ratio of women to men is less than in Graves' disease. Thyrotoxic symptoms are usually milder than in Graves' disease. Eye symptoms and apathy occur less frequently in toxic multinodular goiter than in Graves' disease. In toxic nodular goiter, the physiological indicators of thyroid overactivity are slight. Thus the BMR, PBI, and ^{131}I uptake may be normal or only mildly elevated. The T_3 suppression test is usually abnormal. Toxic diffuse and multinodular goiter are different diseases and should be treated as such in studies on the social and psychological factors in their origins.

Thyrotoxicosis also occurs when T_3 production and release are excessive. In this form of thyrotoxicosis T_3 levels and secretion rates are elevated, while the secretory rate and concentration of T_4 in the serum are either normal or low. The T_3 suppression test is abnormal. The BMR and the ^{131}I uptake are elevated by the PBI and the TBG levels are within the normal range. This disease is called T_3 thyrotoxicosis; it is associated with single and multiple nodules in the gland as well as with a diffuse goiter (Czerniak and Chairchik, 1964; Hollander, 1968; Mack et al., 1961; Rupp et al., 1959; Shimaoka, 1963; Werner, 1971; Werner et al., 1960).

Thyrotoxicosis has been reported in patients with a genetic deficiency in TBG (Cavalieri, 1961; Inada and Sterling, 1967; Lemarchand-Béraud et al., 1964). Most patients with this deficiency are euthyroid (Nicoloff et al., 1964); it is, of course, possible that they might have become thyrotoxic later in their lives. Thyrotoxicosis due to a proven solitary adenoma of the thyroid has also been described as a consequence of TBG deficiency (Wahner et al., 1971). In the euthyroid state in the presence of this deficiency, total T_4 levels remain low because T_4 is bound mainly to TBG. As T_3 is usually only weakly bound to the carrier protein, the main influence of the deficiency is on total T_4 levels, and not on levels of T_3. In fact, when the patient is euthyroid in the face of this deficiency, serum T_3 levels are normal. When thyrotosic, serum T_3 levels are elevated, and free T_4 levels are in the upper range of normal (Wahner et al., 1971). The mode of inheritance of this thyroxine-binding deficiency (Marshall et al., 1964; Nikolai and Seal, 1966a, b; Refetoff and Selenkow, 1968) is believed to be through a dominant trait inherited by linkage to an X-chromosome.

A familial *increase* in TBG levels has also been described. The members of these families are usually euthyroid with elevated levels of TBG binding capacity and PBI (Beierwaltes and Robbins, 1959; Beierwaltes et al., 1961; Florsheim et al., 1962; Tanaka and Starr, 1959). The mode of inheritance of increases in TBG levels has not been determined. Opinion is divided between those who infer that the defect is inherited as an autosomal dominant trait (Beierwaltes et al., 1961; Florsheim et al., 1962) and those who believe it to be a dominant trait that is linked to an X-chromosome (Fialkow et al., 1970; Jones and Seal, 1967; Nikolai and Seal, 1966a, b; Shane et al., 1971). Thyrotoxicosis with increases in TBG levels has been described in two sisters. Both of them had toxic adenomatous goiters. Thirteen of 15 of their consanguineous family members with high TBG levels also had a goiter (presumably a simple one). In 16 of 17 other relatives with normal TBG levels, no goiter was found. Altogether in this family, there were 19 members with elevated levels of TBG, all of whom had elevation of T_4 levels, but normal T_3 levels. Twenty-one other members showed none of these changes.

Another form of thyrotoxic illness is recognized. It occurs in geographic areas where goiter is endemic. In some patients endemic and sporadic goiter may not be the sole product of iodine deficiency; genetic factors also play a role in their etiology. Persons prone to react to iodine deficiency with thyrotoxicosis may have inherited a subthreshold enzymatic defect that causes them to respond with goiter formation, either to dietary iodine deficiency, or to a goitrogen in the diet that prevents the uptake of iodine by the gland. In such patients, the uptake of ^{131}I by the thyroid is increased due to an increase of TSH production and before they receive iodine. Their urinary excretion of iodine is decreased. The PBI and BMR are normal or low. When the patients are given T_3, the uptake of ^{131}I is appropriately suppressed to normal values. When iodine is then given, thyrotoxicosis may develop (Stanbury et al., 1954; Stewart et al., 1971). The incidence of thyrotoxicosis is 7 percent in 100 patients with endemic goiter who later receive dietary iodine. The BMR and PBI then increase and the uptake of ^{131}I continue at high levels (Ek et al., 1963) after the onset of the illness.

REFERENCES

Ackerman, N.B., and Arons, W.H. 1958. The effect of epinephrine and norepinephrine on the acute thyroid release of thyroid hormones. *Endocrinology.* 62:723.

Adams, D.D. 1965. Pathogenesis of the hyperthyroidism of Graves' disease. *Br. Med. J.* 1:1015.

———. 1975. LATS protector, the human thyroid stimulator. *N. Z. Med. J.* 81:22.

——— and Kennedy, T. H. 1965. Evidence of a normally functioning pituitary TSH secretion mechanism in a patient with a high blood level of long-acting thyroid stimulator. *J. Clin. Endocrinol. Metab.* 25:571.

——— and ———. 1967. Occurrence in thyrotoxicosis of a gamma globulin which protects LATS from neutralization by an extract of thyroid gland. *J. Clin. Endocrinol. Metab.* 27:173.

———, and ———. 1971. Evidence to suggest that LATS protector stimulates the human thyroid gland. *J. Clin. Endocrinol. Metab.* 33:47.

———, Fastier, F. N., Howie, J. B., Kennedy, T. H., Kilpatrick, J. A., and Stewart, R. D. H. 1974. Stimulation of the human thyroid by infusions of plasma containing LATS protector. *J. Clin. Endocrinol. Metab.* 39:826.

——— and Purves, H. D. 1956. Abnormal responses in the assay of thyrotrophin. *Proc. Univ. Otago Med. School.* 34:11.

———, ———, and Sirett, N. E. 1961. The response of hypophysectomized mice to injections of human serum containing long-acting thyroid stimulator. *Endocrinology.* 68:154.

———, Kennedy, T. H., and Purves, H. D. 1969. Comparison of the thyroid-stimulating hormone content of serum from thyrotoxic and euthyroid people. *J. Clin. Endocrinol. Metab.* 29:900.

Alexander, F. 1950. *Psychosomatic Medicine.* New York: Norton.

———, Flagg, G. W., Foster, S., Clemens, T., and Blahd, W. 1961. Experimental studies of emotional stress: I. Hyperthyroidism. *Psychosom. Med.* 23:104.

———, French, T. M., and Pollock, G. H. 1968. *Psychosomatic Specificity.* Chicago: University of Chicago Press.

Alexander, W. D., Harden, R. McG., and Shimmins, J. 1968. Emotion and non-specific infection as possible aetiological factors in Graves' disease. *Lancet* ii:196.

Anderson, E. E., and Anderson, S. F. 1938. The relation between the weight of the endocrine glands and measures of sexual, emotional and exploratory behavior in the male albino rat. *J. Comp. Physiol. Psychol.* 26:459.

Anderson, J. R., Gray, K. G., Middleton, D. G., and Young, J. A. 1964. Autoimmunity and thyrotoxicosis. *Br. Med. J.* (2):1630.

Andersson, B. 1964. Hypothalamic temperature and thyroid activity. CIBA Fdtn. Study Group No. 18. *Brain-Thyroid Relationships,* edited by M. P. Cameron and M. O'Connor. Boston: Little, Brown..

388

Arnaud, D. C., Kneubuhler, H. A., Seiling, V. L., Wightman, B. K., and Engbring, N. H. 1965. Response of the normal human to infusions of plasma from patients with Graves' disease. *J. Clin. Invest.* 44:1287.

Artunkal, S., and Togrol, B. 1964. Psychological studies in hyperthyroidism. CIBA Fdtn. Study Group No. 8. *Brain-Thyroid Relationships*, edited by M. P. Cameron and M. O'Connor. Boston: Little, Brown.

Aschner, B. 1936. Zur Vererbung Endokriner Stoerungen. *Wien. Arch. Inn. Med.* 28:69.

Astwood, E. B., Jr. 1951. The use of antithyroid drugs during pregnancy. *J. Clin. Endocrinol. Metab.* 11:1045.

———. 1967. Use of antithyroid drugs. In *Thyrotoxicosis*, edited by W. J. Irvine. Edinburgh: Livingstone.

Auerbach, N. 1963: Diurnal variation in the level of serum protein-bound iodine in humans. *Hartford Hosp. Bull.* 18:168.

Averill, R. L. W., and Slaman, D. F. 1967. Elevation of plasma thyrotropin (TSH) during electrical stimulation of the rabbit hypothalamus. *Endocrinology.* 81:173.

———, Purves, H. D., and Sirett, N. E. 1961. Relation of the hypothalamus to anterior pituitary thyrotropin secretion. *Endocrinology.* 69:735.

Azizi, F., Vagenakis, A. G., Vollinger, J., Reichlin, D., Braverman, L. E. and Ingbar S. H., 1974. Persistent Abnormalities in pituitary function following neonatal thyrotoxicosis in the rate. *Endocrinology.* 94:1581.

Badrick, F. E., Brimblecombe, R. W., Reiss, J. M., and Reiss, M. 1954. The influence of stress conditions on the uptake of ^{131}I by the rat thyroid. *J. Endocrinol.* 11:305.

Bakke, J. L., and Lawrence, N. 1966. Thyrotropin (TSH) in the rat hypothalamus. *Program of the Forty-Eighth Meeting of the Endocrine Society, p. 89.*

Bartels, E. D. 1941. *Heredity in Graves' Disease.* Copenhagen: Munksgaard.

———, and Iri, M. 1961. Thyroid function in patients with progressive exophthalmos: Study of 117 cases requiring orbital decompression. In *Advances in Thyroid Research*, edited by R. Pitt-Rivers, pp. 163–170. New York: Pergamon Press, Inc.

Bastémie, P. A., Neue, P., Bonnyns, M., Van-Haelst, L., and Chailly, M. 1967. Clinical and pathological significance of asymptomatic atropic thyroiditis: A condition of latent hypothyroidism. *Lancet.* i:915.

Bastomsky, C. H., and McKenzie, J. M. 1967. Cyclic AMP: a mediator of thyroid stimulation by thyrotropin. *Am. J. Physiol.* 213:753.

Bayliss, R. S. 1967. Stimulation and suppression test of thyroid function. *Proc. R. Soc. Med.* 60:303.

Beall, G. N., and Solomon, D. H. 1966. Inhibition of long-acting thyroid stimulator by thyroid particulate fractions. *J. Clin. Invest.* 45:552.

———, Doniach, D., Roitt, I., and El Kabir, D. 1969. LATS inhibitor in thyroid microsomal fragments. *Clin. Res.* 17:141.

Beattie, J., and Chambers, R. D. 1953. Changes in oxygen consumption, radioiodine uptake and body temperature following exposure to cold in albino rats with hypothalamic lesions. *J. Exp. Physiol.* 38:193.

Becker, D. V. 1959. The effects of hypophysectomy on certain parameters of thyroid function in two patients with Graves' disease. *J. Clin. Endocrinol. Metab.* 19:840.

——— and Furth, E. D. 1965. Total surgical hypophysectomy in nine patients with Graves' disease: evidence for the extra-pituitary maintenance of this disorder. In *Current Topics in Thyroid Research, Proc. Intern. Thyroid Conf., 5th, Rome, 1965*, edited by C. Cassano and M. Andreoli. New York: Academic.

———, Rall, J. E., Peacock, W., and Rawson, R. W. 1953. The effect of thyrotropic hormone preparation on the metabolism of radioiodine in euthyroid, hyperthyroid and acromegalic individuals. *J. Clin. Invest.* 32:149.

Beierwaltes, W. H., and Robbins, J. 1959. Familial increase in thyroxine-binding sites in serum globulins. *J. Clin. Invest.* 38:1683.

———, Carr, E. A., Jr., and Hunter, R. L. 1961. Hereditary increase in thyroxine-binding in the serum alpha globulin. *Trans. Assoc. Am. Physicians.* 74:170.

Belanger, R., and Rivlin, R. S. 1971. Daily variations in plasma concentration of tyrosine in thyrotoxicosis and myxedema. *Metabolism.* 20:384.

Bennet, A. W., and Cambor, C. G. 1961. Clinical study of hyperthyroidism. *Arch. Gen. Psychiatry.* 4:160.

Bérard, L. 1916. La maladie de Basedow et la guerre. *Bull. Acad. Nat. Méd.* 76:428.

Bernstein, G., Hasen, J., and Oppenheimer, J. H. 1967. Turnover of ^{131}I-thyroxine in patients subjected to surgical trauma. *J. Clin. Endocrinol.* 27:741.

Berumen, F. O., Lobsenz, I. L., and Uttiger, R. D. 1967. Neutralization of the long-lasting thyroid stimulator by thyroid subcellular fractions. *J. Lab. Clin. Med.* 70:640.

Besser, G. M. 1968. Tyrosine tolerance in thyroid disease. *Clin. Sci.* 35:171.

Beugen, Van L., and Werff Ten Bosch, Van Der J. J. 1961. Rat thyroid activity and cold response after removal of frontal parts of the brain. *Acta Endocrinol. (Kbh.).* 37:470.

Bjorkman, S. E., Denneberg, T., and Hedenskog, I. 1961. Clinical evaluation of the thyroid stimulating hormone activity in exophthalmos. *Acta Endocrinol. (Kbh.).* 38:577.

Blomstedt, B., and Einhorn, J. 1967. Effect of cortisone on the PBI and the resin uptake of ^{131}I-triiodothyronine. *Metabolism.* 16:319.

Blount, H. C., and Hardy, J. D. 1952. Thyroid function and surgical trauma as evaluated by iodine conversion ratio. *Am. J. Med. Sci.* 224:112.

Board, F., Persky, H., and Hamburg, D. A. 1956. Psychological stress and endocrine functions. *Psychosom. Med.* 18:324.

———, Wadeson, R., and Persky, H. 1957. Depressive affect and endocrine functions. *Arch. Neurol. Psychiatry.* 78:612.

Boas, N. F., and Ober, W. B. 1946. Hereditary exophthalmic goiter-report of 11 cases in one family. *J. Clin. Endocrinol.* 6:575.

Bogdanove, E. M. 1962. Regulation of TSH secretion. *Fed. Proc.* 21:623.

Bogoroch, R., and Timiras, P. 1951. The response of the thyroid gland of the rat to severe stress. *Endocrinology.* 49:548.

Bonnyns, M., Demeester-Mirkine, N., Calay, R., and Bastémie, P. 1968. Evaluation of the relationship between long-acting thyroid stimulator, clinical and biological thyrotoxicosis and exophthalmos. *Acta Endocrinol. (Kbh.).* 58:581.

Botkin, A. L., and Jensen, H. 1952. The effect of epinephrine and thyrotropin on thyroid function in rats. *Endocrinology.* 50:68.

Bourne, P. G., Rose, R. M., and Mason, J. W. 1967. Urinary 17-OHCS levels: Data on seven helicopter ambulance medics in combat. *Arch. Gen. Psychiatry.* 17:104.

Bowden, A. N., and Rose, F. D. 1969. Dysthyroid exophthalmos. *Proc. R. Soc. Med.* 62:13.

Bowers, C. Y., Schally, A. V., Enzmann, F., Bøler, J., and Folkers, K. 1970. Porcine thyrotropin releasing factor is (pyro) Glu-His-Pro(NH2). *Endocrinology.* 86:1143.

Bowman, K. M., Miller, E. R., Dailey, M. E., Simon, A., and Mayer, B. F. 1950. Thyroid function in mental disease. *J. Nerv. Ment. Dis.* 112:404.

Bram, I. 1927. Psychic trauma in pathogenesis of exophthalmic goiter. *Endocrinology.* 11:106.

———. 1933. Exophthalmic goiter in children ten and under. *Pa. Med.* 37:45.

Braverman, L. E., and Sullivan, R. M. 1969. Another polyendocrine disorder: pheochromocytoma and diffuse toxic goiter. *Johns Hopkins Med. J.* 125:331.

———, Ingbar, S. H., and Sterling, K. 1970. Conversion of thyroxine (T_4) to triiodothyronine (T_3) in athyreotic subjects. *J. Clin. Invest.* 49:855.

Brewster, W. R., Isaacs, J. P., Osgood, P. F., and King, T. L. 1956. The hemodynamic and metabolic interrelationships in the activity of epinephrine, norepinephrine and the thyroid hormones. *Circulation.* 13:1.

Brockis, J. G. 1962. Some observations on the function of the thyroid gland following surgical operations. *Aust. N.Z. J. Surg.* 31:171.

Brody, E. B., and Man, E. B. 1950. Thyroid function in schizophrenia. *Am. J. Psychiatry.* 107:357.

Brody, J. L., and Greenberg, S. 1971. Thyrotoxicosis: A disease of defective thymic-dependent lymphocytes (abstract). *J. Clin. Invest.* 50:13a.

Brown, G. M., and Reichlin, S. 1972. Psychologic and neural regulation of growth hormone secretion. *Psychosom. Med.* 34:45.

Brown, L. B., and Hetzel, B. S. 1963. Stress, personality and thyroid disease. *J. Psychosom. Res.* 7:223.

Brown, W. T., and Gildea, E. A. 1937. Hyperthyroidism and personality. *Am. J. Psychiatry.* 94:59.

Brown-Grant, K. 1957. The "feed-back" hypothesis of the control of thyroid function. In *CIBA Foundation Colloquia on Endocrinology, Regulation and Mode of Action of Thyroid Hormones,* vol. 10, edited by G. Wolstenholme and E. Millar. Boston: Little, Brown.

——— and Gibson, J. G. 1956. The effect of exogenous and endogenous adrenaline on the uptake of radioiodine by the thyroid gland of the rabbit. *J. Physiol.* (Lond.). 131:85.

——— and Pettes, G. 1960. The response of the thyroid gland of the guinea pig to stress. *J. Physiol.* (Lond.). 151:40.

———, Harris, G. W., and Reichlin, S. 1954. The effect of emotional and physical stress on thyroid activity in the rabbit. *J. Physiol.* (Lond.). 126:29.

Bruccino, R. A., Spann, J. F., Jr., Pool, P. E., Sonnenblick, E. H., and Braunwald, E. 1967. Influence of the thyroid state on the intrinsic contractile properties and energy stores of the myocardium. *J. Clin. Invest.* 46:1669.

Buchanan, W. W., Boyle, J. A., Greig, W. R., McAndrew, R., Barr, M., Gray, K. C., Anderson, J. R., and Goudie, R. B. 1967. Occurrence of autoantibodies in healthy twins. *Clin. Exp. Immunol.* 2:803.

Burgess, J. A., Smith, B.R., and Merimee, T. J. 1966. Growth hormone in thyrotoxicosis: effect of insulin-induced hypoglycemia. *J. Clin. Endocrinol. Metab.* 26:1257.

Burgus, R., Dunn, T. F., Desiderio, D., Ward, D. N., Vale, W., and Guillemin, R. 1970a. Characterization of ovine hypothalamic hypophysiotropic TSH-releasing factor. *Nature.* 226:321.

———, ———, ———, ———, ———, ———, Felix, A. M., Gillessen, D., and Studer, R. O. 1970b. Biological activity of synthetic polypeptide derivatives related to the structure of hypothalamic TRF. *Endocrinology.* 86:573.

Burke, G. 1967a. The triiodothyronine suppression test. *Am. J. Med.* 42:600.

———, 1967b. Failure of the immunologic reaction of long-acting thyroid stimulator (LATS) to thyroid components and the demonstration of a plasma inhibitor of LATS. *J. Lab. Clin. Med.* 69:713.

———. 1971. Thyroid stimulators and thyroid stimulation. *Acta Endocrinol.* (Kbh.). 66:558.

——— and Feldman, J. M. 1965. Addison's disease and hyperthyroidism. *Am. J. Med.* 38:470.

Bushler, U., DeCostre, P., Refetoff, S., et al. 1968. Diurnal variations of plasma thyroxine concentration. *Proceedings of the Annual Meeting of the American Thyroid Association, Washington, D.C., Oct. 9–12, 1968.*

Campbell, H. J., George, R., and Harris, G. W. 1960. The acute effects of injection of thyrotrophic hormone or of electrical stimulation of the hypothalamus on thyroid activity. *J. Physiol* (Lond.). 152:527.

Carlson, L. A., Levi, L., and Orö, L. 1967. Plasma lipids and urinary excretion of catecholamines during acute emotional stress in man and their modification by nicotinic acid. *Forsvars Med.* 3(2):129.

Carmena, M. 1949. Hyperthyroidismus bei eineiigen Zwillingen. *Z. Menschl. Vererb.-u. Konstitutionslehre.* 29:386.

Carneiro, L., Dorrington, K. J., and Munro, D. S. 1966a. Recovery of the long-acting thyroid stimulator from serum of patients with thyrotoxicosis by concentration of immunoglobulin G. *Clin. Sci.* 31:215.

———, ———, and ———. 1966b. Relation between long-acting thyroid stimulator and thyroid function in thyrotoxicosis. *Lancet.* ii:878.

Carriere, R., and Isler, H. 1959. Effect of frequent housing changes and of muscular exercise on the thyroid gland of mice. *Endocrinology.* 64:414.

Cavalieri, R. R. 1961. Hyperthyroidism and decreased thyroxine binding by serum proteins. *J. Clin. Endocrinol. Metab.* 21:1455.

Charkes, N. D. 1969. Effect of TSH on the 24-hour ^{131}I uptake in Graves' disease. *J. Nucl. Med.* 10:246.

Chopra, I. J., and Solomon, D. H. 1970. Graves' disease with delayed hyperthyroidism. *Ann. Intern. Med.* 73:985.

———, ———, and Limberg, N. P. 1970a. Specific and non-specific responses in the bioassay of long-acting thyroid stimulator (LATS). *J. Clin. Endocrinol. Metab.* 31:382.

———, ———, Johnson, D. E., and Chopra, U. 1970b. Thyroid gland in Graves' disease: victim or culprit. *Metabolism.* 19:760.

———, ———, ———, ———, and Fisher, D. A. 1970c. Dissociation of serum LATS content and thyroid suppressibility during treatment of hyperthyroidism. *J. Clin. Endocrinol. Metab.* 30:524.

———, Beall, G. N., and Solomon, D. H. 1971. LATS inhibition by a soluble lipoprotein from human thyroid. *J. Clin. Endocrinol. Metab.* 32:772.

———, Chopra, U., and Orgiazzi, J. 1973. Abnormalities of hypothalamo-hypophyseal thyroid axis in patients with Graves' ophthalmopathy. *Proc. 49th Mtg. Amer. Thyroid Assoc.*, Seattle, Sept. 12–15, p.T-9.

Christensen, L. K., and Binder, V. 1962. A case of hyperthyroidism developed in spite of previous hypophysectomy. *Acta Med. Scand.* 172:285.

Clower, C. G., Young, A. J., and Kepas, D. 1969. Psychotic states from disorders of thyroid function. *Johns Hopkins Med. J.* 124:305.

Cole, R. K., Kite, J. H., Jr., and Witebsky, E. 1968. Hereditary autoimmune thyroiditis in the fowl *Science.* 160:1357.

Conrad, A. 1934a. The psychiatric study of hyperthyroid patients. *J. Nerv. Ment. Dis.* 79:505.

———. 1934b. The psychiatric study of hyperthyroid patients. *J. Nerv. Ment. Dis.* 79:656.

Cunningham, J. A., and Kral. F. 1959. Thyrotoxicosis in identical twins. *N. Z. Med. J.* 58:600.

Curschmann, H. 1922. Über die Einwirkung der Kriegskost auf die Basedowsche Krankheit. *Klin. Wochenschr.* 1:1296.

Curtis, G. C. 1972. Psychosomatics and chronobiology: possible implications of neuroendocrine rhythms. *Psychosom. Med.* 34:235.

Cushman, P. 1967. Recurrent hyperthyroidism after normal response to triiodothyronine. *J.A.M.A.* 199:588.

Czerniak, P., and Chaitchik, S. 1964. Hypertri-iodothyronism, clinical and laboratory findings. *Harefuah.* 66:218.

D'Amour, P., Banovac, K., Salisbury Murphy, S., Friesen, H., and McKenzie, J. M. 1973. TRH tests, T_3 suppression tests and serum T_3 concentrations in euthyroid Graves' disease. *Proceedings of the 49th Meeting of the American Thyroid Association*, Seattle, Sept. 12–15, p.T-9.

D'Angelo, S. A. 1956. Pituitary-thyroid function in the epinephrine treated rat. *Fed. Proc.* 15:137.

———. 1963. Central nervous regulation of the secretion and release of thyroid stimulating hormone. In *Advances in Neuroendocrinology*, edited by A. V. Nalbandov. Urbana: U. of Illinois Press.

——— and Synder, J. 1963. Electrical stimulation of the hypothalamus and TSH secretion in the rat. *Endocrinology.* 73:75.

——— and Young, R. 1966. Chronic lesions and ACTH: effects of thyroid hormones and electrical stimulation. *Am. J. Physiol.* 210:795.

———, Snyder, J., and Grodin, J. M. 1964. Electrical stimulation of the hypothalamus: simultaneous effects on the pituitary-adrenal and thyroid systems of the rat. *Endocrinology.* 75:417.

Danowski, T. S., Hedenburg, S., and Greenman, J. H. 1949. The constancy of the serum precipitable or protein-bound iodine in healthy adults. *J. Clin. Endocrinol. Metab.* 9:768.

Das, G., and Krieger, M. 1969. Treatment of thyrotoxic storm with intravenous administration of propanolol. *Ann. Intern. Med.* 70:985.

DeGroot, L. J. 1966. Limbic and other neural pathways that regulate endocrine function. In *Neuroendocrinology*, vol. 1, edited by L. Martini and W. F. Ganong. New York: Academic.

Delange, F., Hershman, J. M., and Ermans, A. M. 1971. Relationship between the serum thyrotropin level, the prevalence of goiter and the pattern of iodine metabolism in Idjwi island. *J. Clin. Endocrinol. Metab.* 33:261.

Delay, J., Boittelle, G., and Boittelle-Lentulo, C. 1949. Rôle de l'émotion dans la genèse de l'hyperthyroidie. *Sem. Hôp. Paris.* 25:327.

Del Castillo, E. B., Trucco, E., and Radzyminski, D. 1964. Diabetes insipidus associated with exophthalmic goiter. *Acta Endocrinol. (Kbh.).* 45:237.

Del Conte, E., Ravello, J. J., and Stux, M. 1955. The increase of circulating thyrotrophin and the activation of the thyroid by means of electroshock in guinea pigs. *Acta Endocrinol. (Kbh.)* 18:8.

DeRobertis, E. 1948. Assay of thyrotropic hormone in human blood. *J. Clin. Endocrinol. Metab.* 8:956.

Dewhurst, K. E., El Kabir, D. J., Harris, G. W., and Mandelbrote, B. M. 1968. A review of the effect of stress on the activity of the central nervous-pituitary-thyroid axis in animals and man. *Confin. Neurol.* 30:161.

———, ———, Exley, D., Harris, G. W., and Mandelbrote, B. M. 1968. Blood levels of thyrotrophic hormone, protein-bound iodine, and cortisol in schizophrenia and affective states. *Lancet*, ii:1160.

Diamond, M. T., and Joffe, B. 1966. Monozygotic twins with chronic lymphocytic thyroiditis. (Hashimoto's disease). *J.A.M.A.* 198:182.

Dobyns, B. M. 1966. The physiology and chemistry of the exophthalmos producing substance (EPS) of the pituitary. In *The Pituitary Gland*, vol. 1, edited by G. W. Harris and B. T. Donovan. London: Butterworths.

——— and Wilson, L. A. 1954. An exophthalmos-producing substance in the serum of patients suffering from progressive exophthalmos. *J. Clin. Endocrinol. Metab.* 14:1393.

———, Rudd, A., and Liebe, D. 1965. The assay of the exophthalmos-producing substance (EPS) and the long-acting thyroid stimulator (LATS) in whole and fractionated serum of patients with progressive exophthalmos. In *Current Topics in Thyroid Research, Proceedings of the Fifth International Thyroid Conference, Rome*, edited by C. Cassano and M. Andreoli. New York: Academic.

Donaldson, H. H., and King, H. D. 1929. Life processes and size of the body and organs of the gray Norway rat during ten generations in captivity. *Am. Anat. Mem.* No. 14.

Dongier, M., Wittkower, E. D., Stephens-Newsham, L., and Hoffman, M. M. 1956.

Psychophysiological studies in thyroid function. *Psychosom. Med.* 18:310.

Doniach, D., and Roitt, I. M. 1966. Family studies on gastric autoimmunity. *Proc. R. Soc. Med.* 59:691.

————, Hudson, R. V., and Roitt, I. M. 1960. Human auto-immune thyroiditis: clinical studies. *Br. Med. J.* 1:365.

Dorrington, K. J., and Munro, D. S. 1965. Immunological studies on the long-acting thyroid stimulator. *Clin. Sci. Mol. Med.* 28:165.

———— and ————. 1966. The long-acting thyroid stimulator. *Clin. Pharmacol. Ther.* 7:788.

————, Carneiro, L., and Munro, D. S. 1966. Absorption of the long-acting thyroid stimulator by human thyroid microsomes. *J. Endocrinol.* 34:133.

Dowling, J. T., Appleton, W. G., and Nicoloff, J. T. 1967. Thyroxine turnover during human pregnancy. *J. Clin. Endocrinol. Metab.* 27:1749.

Ducommun, P., Vale, W., Sakiz, E., and Guillemin, R. 1967. Reversal of the inhibition of TSH secretion due to acute stress. *Endocrinology.* 80:953.

Dunn, J. T., and Chapman, E. M. 1964. Rising incidence of hypothyroidism after radioactive iodine therapy in thyrotoxicosis. *N. Eng. J. Med.* 271:1037.

Eartly, H., and Lebond, C. P. 1954. Identification of the effects of thyroxine mediated by the hypophysis. *Endocrinology.* 54:249.

Eayrs, J. T. 1960. Influence of the thyroid on the central nervous system. *Br. Med. Bull.* 16:122.

Eckert, H., Green, M., Kilpatrick, R., and Wilson, G. M. 1961. Thyroid function after the treatment of thyrotoxicosis by partial thyroidectomy or ^{131}iodine. *Clin. Sci. Mol. Med.* 20:87.

Edmonds, M. W., Row, V. V., and Volpé, R. 1970. Action of globulin and lymphocytes from peripheral blood of patients with Graves' disease on isolated bovine thyroid cells. *J. Clin. Endocrinol. Metab.* 31:480.

Eickhoff, W. 1949. Über den experimentellen nervösen Vollbasedow. *Zbl. allg. Path. Anat.* 85:112.

————. 1950. Über den experimentellen nervösen Vollbasedow. *Verh. dtsch. Ges. Pathol.* 32:295.

Einhorn, J. 1958. Studies on the effect of thyrotropic hormone on thyroid function in man. *Acta Radiol. (Stockh.).* 160 Suppl.:1.

Ek, B., Johnsson, S., and von Porat, B. 1963. Iodine repletion test in an endemic goitre area: risk of iodine induced hyperthyroidism. *Acta Med. Scand.* 173:34.

El Kabir, D. J., Benhamou-Glynn, N., Doniach, D., and Roitt, I. M. 1966. Absorption of thyroid-stimulating globulin from thyrotoxic sera by organ homogenates. *Nature.* 210:319.

Engstrom, W. W., and Markhardt, B. 1955. The effects of serious illness and surgical stress on the circulating thyroid hormones. *J. Clin. Endocrinol. Metab.* 15:953.

von Euler, C., and Holmgren, B. 1956. The role of hypothalamo-hypophysial connexions in thyroid secretion. *J. Physiol. (Lond.).* 131:137.

Evans, C. S., and Barnett, S. A. 1966. Physiological effects of "social stress" in wild rats: 3. Thyroid. *Neuroendocrinology.* 1:113.

Eysenck, H. J. 1963. Smoking, personality and psychosomatic disorders. *J. Psychosom. Res.* 7:107.

Fagraeus, A., Jonsson, J., and El Kabir, D. J. 1970. What is the antibody specificity of LATS? *J. Clin. Endocrinol. Metab.* 31:445.

Faird, N. R., Munro, R. E., Row, V. V., and Volpé, R. 1973a. Peripheral thymus-dependent T-lymphocytes in Graves' disease and Hashimoto's thyroiditis. *N. Engl. J. Med.* 288:1313.

————, von Westarp, C., Row, V. V., and Volpé, R. 1973b. Increase of T cells in Graves' disease. *Lancet.* ii:204.

————, Munro, R. E., Row, V. V., and Volpé, R. 1973c. The use of a rosette inhibition test for the demonstration of sensitization of thymus-dependent (T) lymphocytes in Graves' disease and Hashimoto's thyroiditis. *N. Engl. J. Med.* 289:1111.

394

————, Row, V. V., and Volpé, R. 1973d. The characterization of lymphocytes in the thyroid gland of patients with Graves' and Hashimoto's diseases. *Clin. Res.* 21:1025.

————, Munro, R., Row, V. V., and Volpé, R. 1974. The use of the E-rosette as a test for remission in Graves' disease treated with anti-thyroid drugs. *Clin. Endocr.* 3:55.

Fajans, S. S. 1958. Hyperthyroidism in a patient with postpartum necrosis of the pituitary: case report and implications. *J. Clin. Endocrinol. Metab.* 18:271.

Falconer, I. R. 1963. The exteriorization of the thyroid gland and measurement of its function. *J. Endocrinol.* 26:241.

————. 1965. Effects of fear and adrenaline on blood flow from the thyroid vein in sheep with exteriorized thyroids. *J. Physiol.* (Lond.). 177:215.

———— and Hetzel, B. S. 1964. Effect of emotional stress and TSH on thyroid vein hormone level in sheep with exteriorized thyroids. *Endocrinology.* 75:42.

Felber, J. P., Reddy, W. J., Selenkow, H. A., and Thorn, G. W. 1959. Adrenocortical response to the 48-hour ACTH test in myxedema and hypothyroidism. *J. Clin. Endocrinol. Metab.* 19:895.

Ferguson-Rayport, S. M. 1956. The relation of emotional factors to recurrence of thyrotoxicosis. *Can. Med. Assoc. J.* 15:993.

Fialkow, P. J. 1969. Genetical aspects of autoimmunity. *Prog. Med. Genet.* 6:117.

————, Fudenberg, H., and Epstein, W. V. 1964. "Acquired" antibody hemolytic anemia and familial aberrations in gamma globulin. *Am. J. Med.* 36:188.

————, Giblett, E. R., and Musa, B. 1970. Increased serum thyroxine-binding globulin capacity: inheritance and linkage relationships. *J. Clin. Endocrinol. Metab.* 30:66.

Field, J. B., Remer, A., Bloom, G., and Kriss, J. P. 1967. In vitro stimulation by LATS of thyroid glucose oxidation and ^{32}P incorporation into phospholipids (abstr.). In *Program of the 59th Annual Meeting of the American Society for Clinical Investigation, Inc., Atlantic City, N.J., May, 1967.*

Firgau, F. 1926. Über das läufige Auftreten des basedowschen Krankheitsbildes beim weiblichen Geschlecht in der Nachkriegszeit und seine Erklärung. *Dtsch. Med. Wochenscher.* 52:511.

Fishman, J., Hellman, L., Zumoff, B., and Gallagher, T. F. 1965. Effect of thyroid on hydroxylation of estrogen in man. *J. Clin. Endocrinol. Metab.* 25:365.

Fitz, R. 1944. A panoramic view of thyrotoxicosis. *J.A.M.A.* 125:943.

Flagg, G. W., Clemens, T. L., Michael, E. A., Alexander, F., and Wark, J. 1965. A psychophysiological investigation of hyperthyroidism. *Psychosom. Med.* 27:497.

Fleischer, N., Burgus, R., Vale, W., Dunn, T., and Guillemin, R. 1970. Preliminary observations on the effect of synthetic thyrotropin releasing factor on plasma thyrotropin levels in man. *J. Clin. Endocrinol. Metab.* 31:109.

Florsheim, W. H., Dowling, J. T., Meister, L., and Bodfish, R. E. 1962. Familial elevation of serum thyroxine-binding capacity. *J. Clin. Endocrinol. Metab.* 22:735.

Földes, J., Krasnai, I., and Megyesi, K. 1963. Effect of nor-adrenaline on the response of the thyroid to thyrotropic hormone. *Acta Endocrinol.* (Kbh.). 43:280.

Fore, W., Kohler, P., and Wynn, J. 1966. Rapid redistribution of serum thyroxine during ether anesthesia. *J. Clin. Endocrinol. Metab.* 26:821.

Frantz, V. K., Quimby, E. H., and Evans, T. C. 1948. Radioactive iodine studies of functional thyroid carcinoma. *Radiology.* 51:532.

Fraser, G. R. 1963. A genetical study of goiter. *Ann. Hum. Genet.* 26:335.

Fröberg, J., Karlsson, C-G., Levi, L., and Lidberg, L. 1971. Physiological and biochemical stress reactions induced by psychosocial stimuli. In *Society, Stress and Disease,* edited by L. Levi. London: Oxford.

Freudenberger, C. B. 1932. A comparison of the Wistar albino and the Long-Evans hybrid strain of the Norway rat. *Am. J. Anat.* 50:293.

Furth, E. D., Becker, D. V., Ray, B. S., and Kane, J. W. 1962. Appearance of unilateral infiltrative exophthalmos of Graves' disease after the successful treatment of the same process in the contralateral eye by apparently total surgical hypophysectomy. *J. Clin. Endocrinol. Metab.* 22:518.

Gaffney, G. W., Gregerman, R. I., Yiengst, M. J., and Shock, N. W. 1960. Serum protein bound iodine concentration in blood of euthyroid men aged 18 to 94 years. *J. Gerontol.* 15:234.

Gallagher, T. F., Hellman, L., Bradlow, H. L., Zumoff, B., and Fukushima, D. K. 1960. The effects of thyroid hormones on the metabolism of steroids. *Ann. N.Y. Acad. Sci.* 86:605.

Galton, V. A., Ingbar, S. H., Jimenez-Fonseca, J., and Hershman, J. M. 1971. Alterations in thyroid hormone economy in patients with hydatidiform mole. *J. Clin. Invest.* 50:1345–1354.

Garcia, J., Harris, G. W., and Schindler, W. J. 1964. Vasopressin and thyroid function in the rabbit. *J. Physiol.* (Lond.). 170:487.

Gardiner Hill, H. 1929. Pregnangy complicating simple goiter and Graves' disease. *Lancet.* 216:120.

Garrett, N. H., Jr. 1961. Hereditary thyroid disease. A report of hyperthyroidism in five of six siblings. *N.C. Med. J.* 22:305.

Gerwin, J., Long, D. A., and Pitt-Rivers, R. 1958. The influence of bacterial exotoxins on the activity of the thyroid gland in different species. *J. Physiol.* (Lond.). 144:229.

Gibbons, J. L., Gibson, J. G., Maxwell, A. E., and Willcox, D. R. C. 1960. An endocrine study of depressive illness. *J. Psychosom. Res.* 5:32.

Gibson, J. G. 1962. Emotions and the thyroid gland: a critical appraisal. *J. Psychosom. Res.* 6:93.

Gilbert-Dreyfus, J. C., and Gali, P. 1963. Les critères de guérison des adénomes toxiques traités par l'iode radio-actif. *Rev. Fr. Endocr. Clin.* 4:27.

———, Savoie, J., Sebaoun, E., Bernard-Weil, E., and Delzant, G. 1959. Modification de la fixation thyroïdienne de l'I^{131} après perfusion intraveineuse d'extrait post-hypophysaire. *Ann. Endocrinol.* (Paris). 20:450.

Gilman, A. G., and Rall, T. W. 1966. Studies on the relation of cyclic 3′,5′-AMP (CA) to TSH action in beef thyroid slices. *Fed. Proc.* 25:617.

Gimlette, T. M. D. 1960. Pretibial myxedema. *Br. Med. J.* 2:348.

Glowinski, J., and Iversen, L. L. 1966. Regional studies of catecholamines in the rat brain. I. The disposition of [3H] norepinephrine, [3H] dopamine and [3H] dopa in various regions of the brain. *J. Neurochem.* 13:655.

Goodall, J. S., and Rogers, L. 1944. The effects of the emotions in the production of thyrotoxicosis. *Med. J. and Rec.* 138:411.

Goolden, A. W. G. 1959. Effect of thyrotropic hormone on the accumulation of radioactive iodine in thyrotoxicosis. *J. Clin. Endocrinol. Metab.* 19:1252.

Green, M., and Wilson, G. M. 1964. Thyrotoxicosis treated by surgery or iodine-131. With special reference to development of hypothyroidism. *Br. Med. J.* 1:1005.

Greene, R., and Farran, H. E. A. 1965. On single "hot" nodules of the thyroid gland. *J. Endocrinol.* 33:537.

Greer, M. A. 1951a. The effect on endogenous thyroid activity of feeding desiccated thyroid to normal human subjects. *N. Engl. J. Med.* 244:385.

———. 1951b. The results of feeding desiccated thyroid to thyrotoxic subjects (abstr.). *J. Clin. Invest.* 30:644.

——— and De Groot, L. J. 1956. The effect of stable iodide on thyroid secretion in man. In *Symposium on the Thyroid,* edited by E. B. Astwood. *Metabolism.* 5:682.

——— and Shull, H. F. 1957. A quantitative study of the effect of thyrotropin upon the thyroidal secretion rate in euthyroid and thyrotoxic subjects. *J. Clin. Endocrinol. Metab.* 17:1030.

——— and Smith, G. E. 1954. Method for increasing the accuracy of radioiodine uptake as a test for thyroid function by the use of desiccated thyroid. *J. Clin. Endocrinol. Metab.* 14:1374.

Gregerman, R. I., and Solomon, N. 1967. Acceleration of thyroxine and triiodothyronine turnover during bacterial pulmonary infections and fever: implications for the functional state of the thyroid during stress and in senescence. *J. Clin. Endocrinol. Metab.* 27:93.

Grelland, R. 1946. Thyrotoxicosis at Ullevål Hospital in the years 1934–1944 with a special view to frequency of the disease. *Acta Med. Scand.* 125:108.

Grimm, Y., and Reichlin, S. 1973. Thyrotropin-releasing hormone (TRH): Neurotransmitter regulation of secretion by mouse hypothalamic tissue *in vitro*. *Endocrinology.* 93:626.

Grinberg, R., Volpert, E. M., and Werner, S. C. 1963. In vivo deiodination of labeled L-thyroxine to L-3,5,3'-triiodothyronine in mouse and human pituitaries. *J. Clin. Endocrinol. Metab.* 23:140.

———, Cavanzo, F., and Owens, G. 1966. Studies in a hyperthyroid subject after hypophysectomy. *J.A.M.A.* 197:327.

Gross, H. A., Appleman, M. D., Jr., and Nicoloff, J. T. 1971. Effect of biologically active steroids on thyroid function in man. *J. Clin. Endocrinol. Metab.* 33:242.

Gunn, A., Michie, W., and Irvine, W. J. 1964. The thymus in thyroid disease. *Lancet.* ii:776.

Gurling, K. J., Baron, D. N., and Smith, E. J. R. 1959. Thyroid adenomas and thyrotoxicosis in patients with hypopituitarism following hypophysectomy. *J. Clin. Endocrinol. Metab.* 19:717.

Haigler, E. D., Jr., Pittman, J. A., Jr., Hershman, J. E., and Baugh, C. M. 1971. Direct evaluation of pituitary thyrotropin reserve utilizing synthetic thyrotropin releasing hormone. *J. Clin. Endocrinol. Metab.* 33:573.

Hales, I., Stiel, J., Reeve, T., Heap, T., and Myhill, J. 1969. Prediction of long-term results of antithyroid drug therapy for thyrotoxicosis. *J. Clin. Endocrinol. Metab.* 29:998.

Hall, P. F. 1965. Familial occurrence of myxedema. *J. Med. Genet.* 2:173.

Hall, R., and Stanbury, J. B. 1967. Familial studies of autoimmune thyroiditis. *Clin. Exp. Immunol.* 2:719.

———, Owen, S. G., and Smart, G. A. 1960. Evidence for genetic predisposition to formation of thyroid autoantibodies. *Lancet.* ii:187.

———, Saxena, K. M., and Owen, S. G. 1962. A study of the parents of patients with Hashimoto's disease. *Lancet.* ii:1291.

———, Owen, S. G., and Smart, G. A. 1964. Paternal transmission of thyroid autoimmunity. *Lancet.* ii:115.

Ham, G. C., Alexander, F., and Carmichael, H. T. 1950. Dynamic aspects of the personality features and reactions characteristic of patients with Graves' disease. *Res. Publ. Assoc. Res. Nerv. Ment. Dis.* 29:451.

———, ———, and ———. 1951. A psychosomatic theory of thyrotoxicosis. *Psychosom. Med.* 13:18.

Hamburg, D. A. 1966. Genetics of adrenocortical hormone metabolism in relation to psychological stress. In *Behavior-Genetic Analysis*, edited by J. Hirsch. New York: McGraw-Hill.

——— and Lunde, D. T. 1967. Relation of behavioral, genetic, and neuroendocrine factors to thyroid function. In *Genetic Diversity and Human Behavior*, edited by J. N. Spuhler. Chicago: Aldine.

Hamilton, C. R., Jr., Adams, L. C., and Maloof, F. 1970. Hyperthyroidism due to thyrotropin-producing pituitary chromophobe adenoma. *N. Engl. J. Med.* 283:1077.

Hanbury, E. M. 1959. Thyroid function after trauma in man. *Metabolism.* 8:904.

Harlan, W. R., Laszio, J., Bogdonoff, M. D., and Estes, E. H., Jr. 1963. Alternatives in free fatty acid metabolism in endocrine disorders. *J. Clin. Endocrinol. Metab.* 23:33.

Harris, G. W. 1960. Central control of pituitary secretion. In *Handbook of Physiology: Neurophysiology 2*, edited by J. Field, H. W. Magoun, and V. E. Hall. Washington, D.C.: American Physiological Society.

————. 1963. Discussion. In *Advances in Neuroendocrinology*, edited by A. V. Nalbandov. Urbana: University of Illinois Press.

———— and Woods, J. W. 1958. The effect of electrical stimulation of the hypothalamus or pituitary gland on thyroid activity. *J. Physiol.* (Lond.). 143:246.

Harrison, T. S. 1964. Adrenal medullary and thyroid relationships. *Physiol. Rev.* 44:161.

————, Silver, D. M., and Zuidema, G. D. 1966. Thyroid and adrenal medullary function in chronic "executive" monkeys. *Endocrinology.* 78:685.

Harvald, B., and Hauge, M. 1956. A catamnestic investigation of Danish twins: a preliminary report. *Dan. Med. Bull.* 3:150.

Harvey, R. F., Williams, E. S., Ellis, S., and Ekins, R. F. 1970. Changes in thyroxine-binding globulin levels in thyrotoxicosis and in healthy subjects after triiodothyronine administration. *Acta Endocrinol. (Kbh.).* 63:527.

Hassan, T. H. A., Greig, W. R., Boyle, J. A., Boyle, I. T., and Wallace, T. J. 1966. Toxic diffuse goiter in monozygotic twins. *Lancet.* ii:306.

Hatai, S. 1914. On the weight of some of the ductless glands of the Norway and of the albino rat according to sex and variety. *Anat. Rec.* 8:511.

Hays, M. T. 1965. Effect of epinephrine on radioiodide uptake by the normal human thyroid. *J. Clin. Endocrinol. Metab.* 25:465.

Heimann, P. 1966. Familial incidence of thyroid disease and anamnestic incidence of pubertal struma in 449 consecutive struma patients. *Acta Med. Scand.* 179:113.

Hennen, G. 1966. Thyrotropin-like factor in a nonendocrine cancer tissue. *Arch. Int. Physiol. Bioch.* 74:701.

Henry, J. P., Ely, D. L., Stephens, P. M. 1971a. Role of the autonomic system in social adaptation and stress. *Proc. Int. Union Physiol. Sci.* 8:50.

————, Stephens, P. M., Axelrod, J., and Meuller, R. A. 1971b. Effect of psychosocial stimulation on the enzymes involved in the biosynthesis and metabolism of noradrenaline and adrenaline. *Psychosom. Med.* 33:227.

Hermann, H. T., and Quarton. G. C. 1965. Psychological changes and psychogenesis in thyroid hormone disorders. *J. Clin. Endocrinol. Metab.* 25:327.

Hershman, J. M., and Pittman, J. A. 1970. Response to synthetic thyrotropin-releasing hormone in man. *J. Clin. Endocrinol. Metab.* 31:457.

Hetzel, B. S. 1960. Cannon revisited: emotions and bodily changes: their relevance to disease. *Med. J. Aust.* 1:193.

————, de la Haba, D. S., and Hinkle, L. E. 1952. Rapid changes in plasma PBI in euthyroid and hyperthyroid subjects. *Trans. Am. Goiter Ass.* Springfield, Ill.: Charles C Thomas.

————, Schottstaedt, W. W., Grace, W. J., and Wolff, H. G. 1956. Changes in urinary nitrogen and electrolyte excretion during stressful life experiences and their relation to thyroid function. *J. Psychosom. Res.* 1:177.

Hilton, J. C., Black, W. C., Athos, W., McHugh, B., and Westermann, C. D. 1962. Incresed ACTH-like activity in plasma of patients with thyrotoxicosis. *J. Clin. Endocrinol. Metab.* 22:900.

Hofer, M. A. 1975. The principles of autonomic function in the life of animals and man. In *American Handbook of Psychiatry*, vol. 4, edited by M. F. Reiser. New York: Basic Books.

———— and Weiner, H. 1971. The development and mechanisms of cardiorespiratory responses to maternal deprivation in rat pups. *Psychosom. Med.* 33:353.

Hoffman, E. 1966. Hashimoto's thyroiditis (struma lymphomatosa). Case report of a mother and three daughters, two of whom are monovular twins. *Arch. Surg.* 92:865.

Hollander, C.S. 1968. On the nature of the circulating thyroid hormone. *Trans. Assoc: Am. Physicians.* 81:76.

———, Mitsuma, T., Kastin, A. J. Shenkman, L., Blum, M., and Anderson, D. G. 1971. Hypertriiodothyroninaemia as a premonitory manifestation of thyrotoxicosis. *Lancet* ii:731.

———, Garcia, A. M., Sturgis, S. H., and Selenkow, H. A. 1963. Effect of an ovulatory suppressant on the serum protein-bound iodine and the red-cell uptake of radioactive triiodothyronine. *N. Engl. J. Med.* 269:501.

Hollingsworth, D. R., Mabry, C. C., and Eckerd, J. M. 1972. Hereditary aspects of Graves' disease in infancy and childhood. *J. Pediatr.* 81:446.

Hotelling, D. R., and Sherwood, L. M. 1971. The effects of pregnancy on circulating triiodothyronine. *J. Clin. Endocrinol. Metab.* 33:783.

Howel Evans, A. W., Woodrow, J. C., McDougall, C. D. M., Chew, A. R., and Winston Evans, R. 1967. Antibodies in the families of thyrotoxic patients. *Lancet* i:636.

Iino, S. 1959. Influence of the stimulation of the cervical sympathetic nerve on the mechanism of the hormonal secretion of the thyroid gland. *Endocrinol. Jpn.* 6:148.

Inada, M., and Sterling, K. 1967. Thyroxine transport in thyrotoxicosis and hypothyroidism. *J. Clin. Invest.* 46:1442.

Ingbar, S. H. 1971. Autoregulation of thyroid function. In *The Thyroid,* edited by S. C. Werner and S. H. Ingbar. New York: Harper & Row.

——— 1972. Autoregulation of the thyroid. Response to iodide excess and depletion. *Mayo Clin. Proc.* 47:814.

——— and Woeber, K. A. 1968. The thyroid gland, *Textbook of Endocrinology,* edited by R. H. Williams. 4th ed. Philadelphia: Saunders.

Iversen, K. 1948. *Temporary Rise in the Frequency of Thyrotoxicosis in Denmark 1941–1945.* Copenhagen: Rosenkilde and Bagger.

———. 1949. An epidemic wave of thyrotoxicosis in Denmark during World War II. *Am. J. Med. Sci.* 217:121.

Jackson, C. E., Webster, J. S., Talbert, P. C., and Caylor, J. S. 1961. Concomitant hyperparathyroidism as a cause of the hypercalcemia associated with hyperthyroidism. *Ann. Intern. Med.* 54:992.

Jayson, M. I. V., Doniach, D., Benhamou-Glynn, N., Roitt, I. M., and El Kabir, D. J., 1967. Thyrotoxicosis and Hashimoto Goiter in a pair of monozygotic twins with serum long-acting thyroid stimulator. *Lancet.* ii:15.

Johansson, S., Levi, L., and Lindstedt, S. 1970. Stress and the thyroid gland. *Rep. Lab. Clin. Stress Res. No. 17.*

Joll, A. C. 1951. *Disease of the Thyroid Gland.* 2nd ed. New York: Grune & Stratton.

Jones, J. E., and Seal, U. S. 1967. X-chromosome linked inheritance of elevated thyroxine-binding globulin. *J. Clin. Endocrinol. Metab.* 27:1521.

Kaplan, S. M., and Hetrick, E. S. 1962. Thyrotoxicosis, traumatic neurosis, and the dangerous environment. *Psychosom. Med.* 24:240.

Katz, J. E., and Weiner, H. 1972. Psychosomatic considerations in hyperuricemia and gout. *Psychosom. Med.* 34:165.

———, ———, Gallagher, T. F., and Hellman, L. 1970. Stress, distress and ego defenses. *Arch. Gen. Psychiatry.* 23:131.

Keller, H. H., Bartholini, G., and Pletscher, A. 1974. Enhancement of cerebral noradrenaline turnover by thyrotropin-releasing hormone. *Nature.* 248:528.

Kelsey, F. O., Gullock, A. H., and Kelsey, F. E. 1957. Thyroid activity in hospitalized psychiatric patients. *Arch. Neurol. Psychiatry.* 77:543.

Kendall, J. W., Shimoda, S.-I., and Greer, M. A. 1967. Brain dependent TSH secretion from heterotopic pituitaries. *Neuroendocrinology.* 2:76.

Kenny, M. F., Iturzaeta, N., Preeyasombat, C., Taylor, F. H., and Migeon, C. J. 1967. Cortisol production rate. VII. Hypothyroidism and hyperthyroidism in infants and children. *J. Clin. Endocrinol. Metab.* 27:1616.

Kleinschmidt, H. J., Waxenberg, S. E., and Cuker, R. 1956. Psychophysiology and psychiatric management of thyrotoxicosis: a two year follow-up study. *Mt. Sinai J. Med. N.Y.* 23:131.

Kleinsorge, G., Klumbies, H.-J., Bauer, C. B., Dressler, E., Finck, W., and Völkner, E. 1962. *Angina Pectoris, Fear and Thyroid Function.* Jena: Fischer.

Klose, H. 1928. Die Chirurgie der Basedowschen Krankheit. *Neue deutsche Chirurgie.* 44:657.

Knigge, K. M. 1964. Neural regulation of TSH secretion: effect of diencephalic lesions and intracerebral injection of thyroxin and thyrotropin upon thyroid activity in the rat. In *Major Problems in Neuroendocrinology,* edited by E. Bajusz and G. Jasmin. Basel: Karger.

Kopell, B. S., Wittner, W. K., Lunde, D., Warrick, G., and Edwards, D. 1970. Influence of triiodothyronine on selective attention in man as measured by the visual averaged evoked potential. *Psychosom. Med.* 32:495.

Kotchen, T. A., Mason, J. W., Hartley, L. H., Jones, L. G., Wherry, F. E., Pennington, L. L., and Mougey, E. H. 1972. Thyroid responses to the anticipation of exhaustive muscular exercise. *Psychosom. Med.* 34:473.

Kovács, S., Lissák, K., and Endröczi, E. 1959. Effect of the lesion of paraventricular nucleus on the function of the pituitary, thyroid, adrenal cortex and gonadal systems. *Acta Physiol. Acad. Sci. Hung.* 15:137.

———, Sándor, A., Vértes, A., and Vértes, M. 1965a. The effect of lesions and stimulation of the amygdala on pituitary-thyroid function. *Acta Physiol. Acad. Sci. Hung.* 27:221.

———, Vértes, A., Sándor, A., and Vértes, M. 1965b. The effect of mesencephalic lesions and stimulation on pituitary-thyroid function. *Acta Physiol. Acad. Sci. Hung.* 26:227.

———, Sándor, A., Vértes, Z., and Vértes, M. 1966. The effect of stimulation of the habenular nucleus on pituitary-thyroid function. *Acta Physiol. Acad. Sci. Hung.* 30:39.

Kracht, J. 1954. Fright-thyrotoxicosis in the wild rabbit, a model of thyrotrophic alarm-reaction. *Acta Endocrinol. (Kbh.).* 15:355.

——— and Kracht, U. 1952. Zur Histopathologie und Therapie der Schreckthyreotoxikose des Wildkaninchens. *Virchows Arch.* [*Zellpathol.*]. 321:238.

Kriss, J. P., Peshakov, V., and Chein, J. R. 1964. Isolation and identification of the long-acting thyroid stimulator and its relation to hyperthyroidism and circumscribed pretibial myxedema. *J. Clin. Endocrinol. Metab.* 24:1005.

———, ———, Rosenblum, A. L., and Chien, J. R. 1965. Studies on the formation of long-acting thyroid stimulator globulin (LATS) and the alteration of its biological activity by enzymatic digestion and partial chemical degradation. In *Current Topics in Thyroid Research, Proceedings of the Fifth International Thyroid Conference, Rome,* edited by C. Cassano and M. Andreoli. New York; Academic.

———, ———, ———, Holderness, M. Sharp, G., and Utiger, R. 1967. Studies on the pathogenesis of the opthalmopathy of Graves' disease. *J. Clin. Endocrinol. Metab.* 27:582.

Kvetnansky, R., and Mikulaj, L. 1970. Adrenal and urinary catecholamines in rats during adaptation to repeated immobilization stress. *Endocrinology.* 87:738.

———, Weise, V. K., Kopin, I. J. 1970a. Elevation of adrenal tyrosine hydroxylase and phenylethanolamine-N-methyl transferase by repeated immobilization of rats. *Endocrinology.* 87:738.

———, Gerwirtz, G. P., Weiss, V. R., et al. 1970b. Effect of hypophysectomy on immobilization-induced elevation of tyrosine hydroxylase and phenylethanolamine-N-methyl transferase in the rat adrenal. *Endocrinology.* 87:1323.

Lamberg, B. A. 1964. Cushing's syndrome coexisting with hyperthyroidism. Report of a case and some metabolic observations. *Acta Med. Scand.* 412:159.

————. 1965. Glucose metabolism in thyroid disease. *Acta Med. Scand.* 178:351.

————, Gordin, A., Viheroski, M., and Kirst, G. 1969. Long-acting thyroid stimulator (LATS) in toxic nodular goiter, toxic adenoma and Graves' disease. *Acta Endocrinol. (Kbh.)*. 62:119.

Lamki, L., Row, V. V., and Volpé, R. 1972. Cellular immunity in Graves' disease and Hashimoto's thyroiditis shown by migration inhibition factor. *Clin. Res.* 20:431.

————, ————, and ————. 1973. Cell-mediated immunity in Graves' disease and Hashimoto's thyroiditis as shown by the demonstration of migration inhibition factor (MIF). *J. Clin. Endocrinol. Metab.* 36:358.

LaRoche, G., and Johnson, C. H. 1967. Simulated altitude and iodine metabolism in rats: I. Acute effects on serum and thyroid components. *Aerosp. Med.* 38:499.

Larsen, P. R. 1971. Technical aspects of the estimation of triiodothyronine in human serum: evidence of conversion of thyroxine to triiodothyronine during assay. *Metabolism.* 20:609.

Lawton, N. F., Ekins, R. P., Nabarro, J. D. N. 1971. Failure of pituitary response to thyrotrophin-releasing hormone in euthyroid Graves' disease. *Lancet.* ii:14.

Lamarchand-Béraud, B., Assayah, M.-R., and Vannotti, A. 1964. Alterations of thyroxine-binding protein in clinically hypo- and hyperthyroid patients with normal PBI level. *Acta Endocrinol. (Kbh).* 45:99.

Lemarchand-Béraud, T., Scazziga, B. R., and Vannotti, A. 1966. Étude de la thyréostimuline plasmatique dans les affections thyroïdiennes. *Schweiz. Med. Wochenschr.* 96:718.

Levine, R. J., Oates, J. A., Vendsalu, A., and Sjoerdsma, A. 1962. Studies on the metabolism of aromatic amines in relation to altered thyroid function in man. *J. Clin. Endocrinol. Metab.* 22:1242.

Lewis, N. D. C. 1923. Psychoanalytic study of hyperthyroidism. *Psychoanal. Rev.* 10:140.

————. 1925. Psychological factors in hyperthyroidism. *M. J. Rec.* 122:121.

Lewit, S. G., Rywkin, L. A. Serejsky, M. J., Fogelson, L. J., Dorfman, I. A., and Lichzieher, I. B. 1930. Über die Genetik der Basedowschen Krankheit und der ihr nachstehenden pathologischen Formen. *Zh. Mediko-Biol.* 6:368.

Libow, S. L., and Durrell, J. 1965. Clinical studies on the relationship between psychosis and the regulation of thyroid gland activity. *Psychosom. Med.* 27:369.

Librik, L. Susman, L., Bejar, R., and Clayton, G. W. 1970. Thyrotoxicosis and collagen-like disease in three sisters of American Indian extraction. *J. Pediatr.* 76:64.

Liddle, G. W., Heyssel, R. M., and McKenzie, J. M. 1965. Graves' disease without hyperthyroidism. *Am. J. Med.* 39:845.

Lidz, T. 1949. Emotional factors in the etiology of hyperthyroidism. *Psychosom. Med.* 11:2.

————. 1955. Emotional factors in the etiology of hyperthyroidism occurring in relation to pregnancy. *Psychosom. Med.* 17:420.

———— and Whitehorn, J. C. 1949. Psychiatric problems in a thyroid clinic. *J.A.M.A.* 139:698.

———— and ————. 1950. Life situations, emotions and Graves' disease. *Psychosom. Med.* 12:184.

Lingjaerde, O. 1929. Psykoser behandlet med thyreoideatabletter og lever. *Nord. Med.* 1:523.

Lingjaerde, P., Skaug, O. E., and Lingjaerde, O. 1960. The determination of thyroid function with radioiodine (I-131) in mental patients. *Acta Psychiat. Neurol.* 35:498.

Lipman, L. M., Green, D. E., Snyder, N. J., Nelson, J. C., and Solomon, D. H. 1967. Relationship of long-acting thyroid stimulator to the clinical features and course of Graves' disease. *Am. J. Med.* 43:486.

Lipscomb, H., Pathway, D., and Gard, D. 1961. Direct effect of vasopressin on thyroid. *Clin. Res.* 9:29.

Lloyd, C. W. 1963. Central nervous system regulation of endocrine function in the human. In *Advances in Neuroendocrinology*, edited by A. V. Nalbandov. Urbana: University of Illinois Press.

Lobo, L. C. G., Rosenthal, D., and Friedman, J. 1965. Evolution of autonomous thyroid nodules. In *Current Topics in Thyroid Research*, edited by C. Cassano and M. Andreoli, New York: Academic.

Loewenstein, J. H. 1961. Hyperthyroidism in identical twins. Report of cases, one treated by surgery, the other by I^{131}. *J.A.M.A.* 176:377.

Logan, W.P. D., and Cushion, A. A. 1958. *Morbidity Statistics from General Practice*, vol. 1. London: Her Majesty's Stationery Office.

Lowrey, R., and Starr, P. 1959. Chemical evidence of incidence for hypothyroidism. *J.A.M.A.* 171:2045.

Lubart, J. M. 1964. Implicit personality disorder in patients with toxic and nontoxic goiter. *J. Nerv. Ment. Dis.* 138:255.

Lupulescu, A., Nicolescu, A. L., Gheorghiescu, B., Merculieu, E. L., and Lungu, M. 1962. Neural control of the thyroid gland: studies on the role of extrapyramidal and rhinencephalon areas in the development of the goiter. *Endocrinology.* 70:517.

Mack, R. E., Hart, K. T., Druet, D., Bauer, M. A. 1961. An abnormality of thyroid hormone secretion. *Am. J. Med.* 30:323.

Mäenpää, J., Hiekkala, H., and Lamberg, A. A. 1966. Childhood hyperthyroidism. *Acta Endocrinol, (Kbh.).* 51:321.

Mahaux, J. E., and Chamia-Soumenkoff, J. 1968. Évolution de la captation iodée du PBI 131, du PBI 127 et des symptomes cliniques lors de l'administration de triiodothyronine à des hyperthyroidiens par hyperplasie thyroidienne diffuse—Rôle de l'appareil lymphoide er du LATS dans l'effect de stimulation basedowienne. *Ann. Endocrinol.* (Paris). 29:483.

————, ————, Delcourt, R., Nagel, N., and Levin, S. 1969. The effect of triiodothyronine on cervical lymphoid structure, thyroid activity, IgG, IgM immunoglobulin level, and exophthalmos in Graves' disease. *Acta Endocrinol. (Kbh.).* 61:400.

Major, P. W., and Munro, D. S. 1960. Thyroid stimulating activity in human sera (abstr.). *J. Endocrinol.* 20:xix.

———— and ————. 1962. Observations on the stimulation of thyroid function in mice by the injection of serum from normal subjects and from patients with thyroid disorders. *Clin. Sci. Mol. Med.* 23:463.

Man, E. B., and Kahn, E. 1945. Thyroid function of manic-depressive patients evaluated by determinations of the serum iodine. *Arch. Neurol. Psychiat.* 54:51.

Mandelbrote, B. M., and Wittkower, E. D. 1955. Emotional factors in Graves' disease. *Psychosom. Med.* 17:109.

Mantley, H. G., and Droste, D. 1957. Thyreotoxikosen in Psycho-somatischer Betrachtung. *Z. Psychosom. Med. Psychoanal.* 3:5.

Maranon, G. 1921. Le facteur émotionnel dans la pathogénie des états d'hyperthyroidisme. *Ann. Med.* 60:81.

Margolese, M. S., and Golub, O. J. 1957. Daily fluctuation of the serum protein-bound iodine level. *J. Clin. Endocrinol. Metab.* 17:849.

Marshall, J. S., Levy, R. P., and Steinberg, A. G. 1964. Human thyroxine-binding globulin deficiency. A genetic study. *N. Engl. J. Med.* 274:1469.

Martin, J. B., Reichlin, S., and Boshans, R. L. 1969. Feedback regulation of TSH secretion in rats with hypothalamic lesions. *Fed. Proc.* 28:437.

Martin, L., and Fisher, R. A. 1945. The hereditary and familial aspects of exophthalmic goiter and nodular goiter. *Q. J. Med.* 14:207.

Martin, M. M., and Mintz, D. H. 1965. Effect of altered thyroid function upon adrenocortical ACTH and methopyrapone (SU-4885) responsiveness in man. *J. Clin. Endocrinol. Metab.* 25:20.

————, ————, and Tamagaki, H. 1963. Effect of altered thyroid function upon steroid circadian rhythms in man. *J. Clin. Endocrinol. Metab.* 23:242.

Mason, A. M. S., Raper, C. G., and Lloyd, R. 1970. Thyrotoxicosis in a father and two sons. *Lancet.* i:81.

Mason, J. W. 1968a. Organization of Psychoendocrine Mechanisms. *Psychosom. Med.* 30:565.

————. 1968b. A review of psychoendocrine research on the pituitary-thyroid system. *Psychosom. Med.* 30:666.

———— and Mougey, E. H. 1972. Thyroid (plasma BEI) response to chair restraint in the monkey. *Psychosom. Med.* 34:441.

————, ————, Brady, J. V., and Tolliver, G. A. 1968a. Thyroid (plasma butanol-extractable iodine) responses to 72-hr. avoidance sessions in the monkey. *Psychosom. Med.* 30:682.

————, Jones, J. A., Ricketts, P. T., Brady, J. V., and Tolliver, G. A. 1968b. Urinary aldosterone and urine volume responses to 72-hr. avoidance sessions in monkeys. *Psychosom. Med.* 30:733.

McCann, S. M., and Porter, J. C. 1969. Hypothalamic pituitary stimulating and inhibiting hormones. *Physiol. Rev.* 49:240.

McClintock, J. C., Frawley. T. F., and Holden, J. H. P. 1956. Hyperthyroidism in children: observations in 50 treated cases, including an evaluation of endocrine factors. *J. Clin. Endocrinol. Metab.* 16:62.

McCormack, K. R., and Sheline, G. E. 1961. Hyperthyroidism in young female twins. *Acta Genet. Med. Gemellol.* (Roma). 10:70.

McDermott, W. V., Fry, E. G., Brobeck, J. R., and Long, C. N. H. 1950. Release of adrenocorticotrophic hormone by direct application of epinephrine to pituitary grafts. *Proc. Soc. Exp. Biol. Med.* 73:609.

McGill, D. A. 1960. Some investigations into endocrine exophthalmos. *Q. J. Med. N. S.* 24:423.

McKenzie, J. M. 1959. The thyroid activator of hyperthyroidism. *Trans. Assoc. Am. Physicians.* 72:122.

————. 1960. Further evidence for a thyroid activator of hyperthyroidism. *J. Clin. Endocrinol. Metab.* 20:380.

————. 1961. Studies on the thyroid activator of hyperthyroidism. *J. Clin. Endocrinol. Metab.* 21:635.

————. 1962. The pituitary and Graves' disease. *Proc. R. Soc. Med.* 55:539.

————. 1964. Neonatal Graves' disease. *J. Clin. Endocrinol. Metab.* 24:660.

————. 1965. Review: pathogenesis of Graves' disease: role of the long-acting thyroid stimulator. *J. Clin. Endocrinol. Metab.* 25:424.

————. 1965. The gammaglobulin of Graves' disease: thyroid stimulation by fraction and fragment. *Trans. Assoc. Am. Physicians.* 78:174.

————. 1967. The long-acting thyroid stimulator: its role in Graves' disease. *Recent Prog. Horm. Res.* 23:1.

————. 1968a. Humoral factors in the pathogenesis of Graves' disease. *Physiol. Rev.* 48:252.

————. 1968b. Experimental production of a thyroid-stimulating antithyroid antibody. *J. Clin. Endocrinol. Metab.* 28:596.

————, and Gordon, J. 1965. The origin of the long-acting thyroid stimulator. In *Current Topics in Thyroid Research,* edited by C. Cassano, M. Andreoli. New York: Academic.

———— and Solomon, D. H. 1967. Neuroendocrine factors in thyroid disease. In *An Introduction to Clinical Neuroendocrinolgy,* edited by E. Bajusz, New York: Karger.

Means, J. H. 1948. *The Thyroid and Its Diseases.* 2nd ed. Philadelphia: Lippincott.

Meek, J. C., and Vanderlaan, W. P. 1964. Disappearance of the long-acting thyroid stimulator with treatment of hyperthyroidism (abstr.). *Clin. Res.* 12:92.

————, Jones, A. E., Lewis, U. J., and Vanderlan, W. P. 1964. Characterization of the long-acting thyroid stimulator of Graves' disease. *Proc. Natl. Acad. Sci. U.S.A.* 52:342.

Melmon, K. L., Rivlin, R., Oates, J. A., and Sjoerdsma, A. 1964. Further studies of plasma tyrosine in patients with altered thyroid function. *J. Clin. Endocrinol. Metab.* 24:691.

Mertz, D. P. 1962. Über die Wirkung von endogenem antidiuretischem Hormon (ADH) auf die Schilddrüsenfunktion. *Acta Endocrinol. (Kbh.).* 40:290.

Mess, B. 1958a. Verhinderung des Thiouracileffektes und der 'Jodmangelstrume' durch experimentelle Zerstörung der Nuclei habenulae. *Endokrinologie.* (Leipzig) 35:196.

————, 1958b. Veränderungen des Gehaltes der Hypophyse an thyreotropem Hormon nach Thyroidektomie und gleichzeitiger Laesion der Nuclei habenulae. *Endokrinologie. (Leipzig).* 35:296.

————. 1959. Die Rolle der Nuclei habenulae bei der auf erhöhtem Thyroxin Blutspiegel eintretenden zentralnervösen Hemmung der thyreotrophen Aktivität des Hypophysenvorderlappens. *Endokrinologie.* (Lepizig). 37:104.

————. 1964. Changes in thyroidal cold response of heat adapted rats following bilateral lesions of the habenular nuclei. *Acta Physiol. Acad. Sci. Hung.* 24:299.

————. 1967. The thyroid regulating habenular mechanism and the thyrotrophic area of the anterior hypothalamus. *Acta Biol. Acad. Sci. Hung.* 18:129.

————, Fraschini, F., Motta, M., and Martini, L. 1967. The topography of the neurons synthesizing the hypothalamic releasing factors. *Proceedings of the Second International Congress on Hormonal Steroids, Milan, 1966. International Congress Series No. 132,* edited by L. Martini, F. Fraschini and M. Motta. Amsterdam: Excerpta Medica Foundation.

Metuzals, J. 1956. The innervation of the adenohypophysis in the duck. *J. Endocrinol.* 14:87.

Meulengracht, E. 1949. Epidemiologic aspects of thyrotoxicosis. *Arch. Intern. Med.* 83:119.

Michael, R. P., and Gibbons, J. L. 1963. Interrelationship between the endocrine system and neuropsychiatry. *Int. Rev. Neurobiol.* 5:243.

Michie, W., Beck, J. S., Mafaffy, R. G., Honein, E. F., and Fowler, G. 1967. Quantitative radiological and histological studies of the thymus in thyroid disease. *Lancet.* i:691.

Mittleman, B. 1933. Psychogenic factors and psychotherapy in hyperthyreosis and rapid heart imbalance. *J. Nerv. Ment. Dis.* 77:465.

Miyai, K., Fukuchi, M., and Kumahara, Y. 1967. LATS production by lymphocyte culture in patients with Graves' disease. *J. Clin. Endocrinol. Metab.* 27:855.

————, and Werner, S. C. 1966. Concentration of long-acting thyroid stimulator (LATS) by subfractionation of γ–globulin from Graves' disease serum. *J. Clin. Endocrinol. Metab.* 26:504.

Mori, T., and Kriss, J. P. 1971a. Measurements by competitive binding radioassay of serum anti-microsomal and anti-thyroglobulin antibodies in Graves' disease and other thyroid diseases. *J. Clin. Endocrinol. Metab.* 33:688.

———— and ————. 1971b. Preparation and binding of anti-microsomal antibody-free LATS, and the effect of iodination on LATS biological activity. *J. Clin. Endocrinol. Metab.* 33:813.

Moses, A. M., Lobovsky, F., Chodos, R. B., and Lloyd, C. W. 1961. Failure of vasopressin or oxytocin to stimulate thyroid function in the normal male. *J. Clin. Endocrinol. Metab.* 21:1543.

Mougey, E. H., and Mason, J. W. 1962. The measurement of butanol extractable iodide in the rhesus monkey. *J. Lab. Clin. Med.* 59:672.

Mowbray, J. F., and Peart, W. L. 1960. Effects of nor-adrenaline and adrenaline on the thyroid. *J. Physiol. (Lond.).* 151:261.

Nana, A., Mircioiu, C., Neumann, E., Strolla, C., and Rusu, J. 1961. Les corrélations thyro-surréaliennes au cours du choc experimental. *Bull. Soc. Int. Chir.* 20:614.

Neustadt, R., and Howard, L. G. 1942-43. Fluctuations of blood iodine in cyclic psychoses. *Am. J. Psychiatry.* 99:130.

Nicoloff, J. T., Dowling, J. T., and Patton, D. D. 1964. Inheritance of decreased thyroxine-binding by the thyroxine-binding globulin. *J. Clin. Invest.* 24:294.

Nikolai, T. F., and Seal, U. S. 1966a. X-chromosome linked familial decrease in thyroxine-binding globulin activity. *J. Clin. Endocrinol. Metab.* 26:835.

——— and ———. 1966b. X-chromosome linked inheritance of thyroxine-binding globulin deficiency. *J. Clin. Endocrinol. Metab.* 26:1515.

Nilsson, L. R. 1961. Thyrotoxicosis in children. *Nord. Med.* 67:667.

Ochi, Y., and DeGroot, L. J. 1968. Studies on the immunological properties of LATS. *Endocrinology.* 83:845.

Odell, W. D., Bates, R. W., Silvin, R. S., Lipsett, M. B., and Hertz, R. 1963. Increased thyroid function without clinical hyperthyroidism in patients with choriocarcinoma. *J. Clin. Endocrinol. Metab.* 23:658.

———, Utiger, R. D., and Wilber, J. 1967. Studies of thyrotropin physiology by means of radioimmunoassay. *Recent Prog. Horm. Res.* 23:47.

Onaya, T., Kotania, M., Yamada, T., and Ochi, Y. 1973. New in vitro tests to detect the thyroid stimulator in sera from hyperthyroid patients by measuring colloid droplet formation and cyclic AMP in human thyroid slices. *J. Clin. Endocrinol. Metab.* 26:859.

Oppenheimer, J. H. 1968. Role of plasma proteins in the binding, distribution and metabolism of thyroid hormones. *N. Engl. J. Med.* 277:995.

——— and Werner, S. C. 1966. Effect of prednisone on thyroxine-binding proteins. *J. Clin. Endocrinol. Metab.* 26:715.

———, Squef, R., Surks, M. I., and Hauer, H. 1963. Binding of thyroxine by serum proteins evaluated by equilibrium dialysis and electrophoretic techniques. Alterations in non-thyroidal illness. *J. Clin. Invest.* 42:1769.

Ormston, B. J., Cryer, R. J., Garry, R., Besser, G. M., and Hall, R. 1971. Thyrotropin-releasing hormone as a thyroid-function-test. *Lancet* ii:10.

Parry, C. H. 1825. *Collected Works*, vol. 2. Unpublished.

Pasckis, K. E., Cantarow, A., Eberhard, T., and Boyle, D. 1950. Thyroid function in the alarm reaction. *Proc. Soc. Exp. Biol. Med.* 73:117.

Pastan, L. 1966. The effect of dibutyl cyclic 3′,5′-AMP on the thyroid. *Biochem. Biophys. Res. Commun.* 25:14.

Patel, Y. C., Burger, H. G., and Hudson, B. 1971. Radioimmunoassay of serum thyrotropin: sensitivity and specificity. *J. Clin. Endocrinol. Metab.* 33:768.

Paykel, E. S. 1966. Abnormal personality and thyrotoxicosis: a follow-up study. *J. Psychosom. Res.* 10:143.

Pazianos, A. G., Benua, R., Ray, B. S., and Pearson, O. H. 1960. Persistent thyroid function following hypophysectomy. *J. Clin. Endocrinol. Metab.* 20:1051.

Perlmutter, M., and Slater, S. 1955. Use of thyroid hormone to differentiate between hyperthyroidism and euthyroidism. *J.A.M.A.* 158:718.

Perry, W. F., and Gemmell, J. P. 1949. The effect of surgical operations on the excretion of iodine, corticosteroids and uric acid. *Can. J. Res.* 27:320.

Peterson, R. E. 1958. The influence of the thyroid on adrenal cortical function. *J. Clin. Invest.* 37:736.

———. 1959. The miscible pool and turnover rate of adrenocortical steroids in man. *Recent Prog. Horm. Res.* 15:231.

Pimstone, B. L., Hoffenberg, R., and Black, E. 1963. Parallel assays of thyrotrophin, long-acting thyroid stimulator and exophthalmos-producing substance in some endocrine disorders. *J. Clin. Endocrinol. Metab.* 23:336.

———, ———, and ———. 1964. Parallel assays of thyrotrophin, long-acting thyroid stimulator and exophthalmos-producing substance in endocrine exophthalmos and pretibial myxedema. *J. Clin. Endocrinol. Metab.* 24:976.

Pinchera, A., Liberti, P., and Badalamenti, G. 1965a. Long-acting thyroid stimulator assays of thyroid disease. *J. Clin. Endocrinol. Metab.* 25:189.

————, Pinchera, M. G., and Stanbury, J. B. 1965b. Thyrotropin and the long-acting thyroid stimulator assays of thyroid disease. *J. Clin. Endocrinol. Metab.* 25:189.

————, Liberti, P., Martino, E., Fenzi, G. F., Grasso, L., Rovis, L., Baschieri, L., and Doria, G. 1969. Effects of antithyroid therapy on the long-acting thyroid stimulator and the antithyroglobulin antibodies. *J. Clin. Endocrinol. Metab.* 29:231.

Plummer, H. S. 1931. Exophthalmic goiter in Olmstead County, Minnesota. *Trans. Assoc. Am. Physicians.* 46:171.

Price, D. B., Thaler, M., and Mason, J. W. 1956. Preoperative emotional states and adrenal cortical activity. *Arch. Neurol. Psychiat.* 77:646.

Priest, W. M. 1970. Long-acting thyroid stimulator in thyrotoxic monozygous twins. *Br. Med. J.* ii:205.

Pulay, E. 1919. Thyreoidismus und Morbus Basedowii als eine Form der traumatischen Neurose. *Z. Klin. Med.* 88:87.

Puntriano, G., and Meites, J. 1951. The effects of continuous light or darkness on thyroid function in mice. *Endocrinology.* 48:217.

Rall, T. W., and Sutherland, E. W. 1961. The regulatory role of adenosine 3',5'-phosphate. *Cold Spring Harbor Symp. Quant. Biol.* 25:347.

Ramey, E. R. 1966. Relation of the thyroid to the autonomic nervous system. *Res. Publ. Assoc. Res. Nerv. Ment. Dis.* 43:309.

Rantanen, P., Fagerström, K., and Pekkarinen, A. 1965. The neurogenic influence of cats on the uptake and release of ^{131}I of the thyroid gland of mice. *Acta Endocrinol. (Kbh.).* Suppl. 100:150.

Rasmussen, A. F., Jr. 1969. Emotions and immunity. *Ann. N.Y. Acad. Sci.* 164:458.

Rees, G. P. van, and Moll, J. 1968. Influence of thyroidectomy with and without thyroxine treatment on thyrotropin secretion in gonadectomized rat with anterior hypothalamic lesion. *Neuroendocrinology.* 3:115.

Refetoff, S., and Selenkow, H. A. 1968. Familial thyroxine-binding globulin deficiency in a patient with Turner's syndrome (XO). *N. Engl. J. Med.* 278:1081.

Reichlin, S. 1966a. Functions of the median eminence gland. *N. Engl. J. Med.* 275:600.

————. 1966b. Control of thyrotropic hormone secretion. In *Neuroendocrinolgy*, vol. 1, edited by L. Martini and W. F. Ganong. London: Academic.

————. 1971. Neuroendocrine-pituitary control. In *The Thyroid*, edited by S. C. Werner and S. H. Ingbar. New York: Harper & Row.

———— and Glaser, R. I. 1958. Thyroid function in experimental streptococcal pneumonia in the rat. *J. Exp. Med.* 107:219.

———— and O'Neal, L. W. 1962. Thyroid hormone levels of the blood after electroshock induced convulsions in man. *J. Clin. Endocrinol. Metab.* 22:385.

———— and Utiger, R. D. 1967. Regulation of pituitary-thyroid axis in man: relationship of TSH concentration to concentration of free and total thyroxine in plasma. *J. Clin. Endocrinol. Metab.* 27:251.

————, Volpert, E. M., and Werner, S. C. 1966. Hypothalamic influence on thyroxine monodeiodination by rat anterior pituitary gland. *Endocrinology.* 78:302.

Reiss, M. 1956. Endocrine concomitants of certain physical psychiatric treatments. *Internat. Record Med.* 169:431.

Rivlin, R. S., Melmon, K. L., and Sjoerdsma, A. 1965. An oral tyrosine tolerance test in thyrotoxicosis and myxedema. *N. Engl. J. Med.* 272:1143.

Robbins, L. R., and Vinson, D. B. 1960. Objective psychologic assessment of the thyrotoxic patient and the response to treatment: preliminary report. *J. Clin. Endocrinol. Metab.* 20:120.

Robinson, D. W., and Orr, T. G. 1955. Carcinoma of the thyroid and other diseases of the thyroid in identical twins. *Arch. Surg.* 70:923.

406

Robison, G. A., Butcher, R. W., and Sutherland, E. W. 1968. Cyclic AMP. *Annu. Rev. Biochem.* 37:149.

Roitt, I. M., and Doniach, D. 1965. Autoimmunity and disease. Chapter VII. *The Scientific Basis of Medicine.* London: Athlone Press.

——— and ———. 1967. A reassessment of studies on the aggregation of thyroid autoimmunity in families of thyroiditis patients. *Clin. Exp. Immunol.* 2:727.

Rosenbaum, J. M., Krieg, A. F., Henry, J. B., Mozley, J. M., and McAfee, J. G. 1968. Thyroid function evaluation in patients with increased or decreased thyroxine-binding protein. *Am. J. Clin. Pathol.* 50:336.

Rosner, J. M., Houssay, B. A., and Rotmistrovsky, J. H. 1962. Diabetes insipidus and pituitary myxedema-effect of pitressin on thyroid function. *J. Clin. Endocrinol. Metab.* 22:449.

Ruesch, J. 1948. The infantile personality: The core problem of psychosomatic medicine. *Psychosom. Med.* 10:134.

———, Christiansen, C., Patterson, L. C., Dewees, S., and Jacobson, A. 1947. Psychological invalidism in thyroidectomized patients. *Psychosom. Med.* 9:77.

Rundle, F. E. 1941. A study of the pathogenesis of thyrotoxicosis. *Lancet.* ii:149.

Rupp, J. J., Chavarria, C., Paschkis, K. E., and Chublabian, E. 1959. The occurrence of triiodothyronine as the only circulating thyroid hormone. *Ann. Intern. Med.* 51:359.

Sachar, E. J., Mason, J. W., Kolmer, H. S., and Artiss, K. L. 1963. Psychoendocrine aspects of acute schizophrenic reactions. *Psychosom. Med.* 25:510.

Sackler, A. M., and Weltman, A. D. 1963. Endocrine and behavioral aspects of intense auditory stress. *Colloques Internationaux du Centre National de la Recherche Scientifique.* 112:255.

Sainsbury, P. 1960. Psychosomatic disorders and neuroses in outpatients attending a general hospital. *J. Psychosom. Res.* 4:261.

Sakiz, E., and Guillemin, R. 1965. Inverse effects of purified hypothalamic TRF on the acute secretion of TSH and ACTH. *Endocrinology.* 77:797.

Sattler, H. 1952. *Basedow's Disease.* New York: Grune & Stratton.

Savoie, J. C. 1961. Étude clinique et biologique de quarante-trois cas d'adénome toxique thyroïden. *Rev. Franc. Étude. Clin. Biol.* 6:263.

Sawyer, C. H., Markee, J. E., and Everett, J. W. 1950. Activation of the adenohypophysis by intravenous injections of epinephrine in the atropinized rabbit. *Endocrinology.* 46:536.

Saxena, K. M. 1965. Inheritance of thyroglobulin antibody in thyrotoxic children. *Lancet.* i:583.

———, Crawford, J. D., and Talbot, N. B. 1964. Childhood thyrotoxicosis: a long term perspective. *Br. Med. J.* 2:1153.

Schadlow, A. R., Surks, M. I., Schwartz, H. L., and Oppenheimer, J. H. 1972. Specific triiodothyronine binding sites in the anterior pituitary of the rat. *Science.* 176:1252.

Schally, A. V., and Redding, T. W. 1967. In vitro studies with thyrotropin releasing factor. *Proc. Soc. Exp. Biol. Med.* 126:320.

———, Arimura, A., Bowers, C. Y., Wakabayashi, I., Kastin, A. J., Redding, T. W., Mittler, J. C., Nair, R. M. G., Pizzolato, P., and Segal, A. J. 1970. Purification of hypothalamic releasing hormones of human origin. *J. Clin. Endocrinol. Metab.* 31:291.

Scharrer, E., and Scharrer, B. 1963. *Neuroendocrinology.* New York: Columbia University Press.

Schatz, D. L., and Volpé, R. 1959. Lack of diurnal variation in the level of serum protein-bound iodine. *J. Clin. Endocrinol. Metab.* 19:1495.

Scherer, M. G., and Siefring, B. N. 1956. Effect of prednisone and prednisolone on thyroid function. *J. Clin. Endocrinol. Metab.* 16:643.

Schleusener, J., Murthy, P. V. N., and McKenzie, J. M. 1971. Studies on thyroid gland component inhibiting LATS. *Metabolism.* 20:299.

Schneider, A. B., and Goldberg, I. H. 1965. Effect of actinomycin on TSH-induced activities of hypophysectomized rat thyroid (abstr.). *Fed. Proc.* 24:383.

Schwartz, H. L., Surks, M. I., and Oppenheimer, J. H. 1971. Quantization of extra thyroidal conversion of L-thyroxine to 3,5,3′-triiodo-L-thyronine in the rat. *J. Clin. Invest.* 50:1124.

Schweitzer, P. M. J. 1944. Calorie supply and basal metabolism. *Acta Med. Scand.* 119:306.

Scott, J. S. 1976. Pregnancy: Nature's experimental system. *Lancet.* i:78.

Seldon, W. A. 1958. The role of psychic stress in the etiology of non-toxic goitre. *Med. J. Aust.* 2:443.

Sellers, E. A., Awad, A. G., and Schönbaum, E. 1970. Long-acting thyroid stimulator in Graves' disease. *Lancet.* ii:335.

Shambaugh, G. E., and Beisel, W.R. 1966. Alterations in thyroid physiology during pneumococcal septicemia in the rat. *Endocrinology.* 79:511.

Shane, S. R., Seal, U. S., and Jones, J. E. 1971. X-chromosome linked inheritance of elevated thyroxine-binding globulin in association with goiter. *J. Clin. Endocrinol. Metab.* 32:587.

Shanks, R. G., Hadden, D. R., Lowe, D. C., McDevitt, D. G., and Montgomery, D. A. D. 1969. Controlled trial of propanolol in thyrotoxicosis. *Lancet.* i:993.

Sheline, G. E., and McCormack, K. 1960. Solitary hyperfunctioning thyroid nodules. *J. Clin. Endocrinol. Metab.* 20:1401.

Shibusawa, K., Yamamoto, T., Nishi, K., Abe, C., Tomie, S., and Shirota, K. 1959. TRF concentrations in various tissues following anterior hypothalamic lesions. *Endocrinol. (Jpn.).* 6:149.

Shimaoka, K. 1963. Toxic adenoma of the thyroid with triiodothyronine as the principal circulating thyroid hormone. *Acta Endocrinol. (Kbh.)* 43:285.

Shipley, R. A., and MacIntyre, F. H. 1954. The effect of stress, TSH and ACTH on the level of hormonal I^{131} of serum. *J. Clin. Endocrinol. Metab.* 14:309.

Shishiba, Y., Shimizu, T., Yoshimura, S., and Shizume, K. 1973. Direct evidence for human thyroidal stimulation by LATS protector. *J. Clin. Endocrinol. Metab.* 36:517.

——, Solomon, D. H., and Beall, G. N. 1967. Comparison of the early effects of thyrotropin (TSH) and long acting thyroid stimulator (LATS) on thyroidal secretion (abstr.). *Clin. Res.* 15:99.

Shizume, K., Matsuzaki, K., Iino, S., Matsuda, K., Nagataki, S., and Okinaka, S. 1962. Effect of electrical stimulation of the limbic system on pituitary-thyroid function. *Endocrinology.* 71:456.

Silverstein, G. E., and Burke, G. 1970. Thyroid suppressibility and long-acting thyroid stimulator in thyrotoxicosis. *Arch. Intern. Med.* 126:615.

——, ——, and Cogan, R. 1967. The natural history of the autonomous hyperfunctioning thyroid nodule. *Ann. Intern. Med.* 67:539.

Simpson, G. M., Cranswick, E. H., and Blair, J. H. 1963. Thyroid indices in chronic schizophrenia. I. *J. Nerv. Ment. Dis.* 137:582.

——, ——, and ——. 1964. Thyroid indices in chronic schizophrenia. II. *J. Nerv. Ment. Dis.* 138:581.

Sinha, D., and Meites, J. 1966. Effects of thyroidectomy and thyroxine on hypothalamic concentration of thyrotropin releasing factor and pituitary content of thyrotropin in rats. *Neuroendocrinology.* 1:4.

Skebelskaya, Yu., and Bagramyan, E. R. 1962. Reaction of the thyroid gland of hypophysectomized rats to stress. *Probl. Endokrinol. (Mosk.).* 8:6.

Smith, B. R., Dorrington, K. J., and Munro, D. S. 1969. The thyroid-stimulating properties of long-acting thyroid stimulator-globulin subunits. *Biochem. Biophys. Acta.* 192:277.

Smitheman, T. C., and Pittman, J. A., Jr. 1966. Non-toxic Graves' disease. *Clin. Res.* 14:101.

Söderberg, U. 1958. Short term reactions in the thyroid gland. *Acta Physiol. Scand.* 42 (Suppl. 147):5.

408

Soffer, L. J., Volterra, M., Gabrilove, J. L., Pollack, A., and Jacobs, M. 1947. Effect of iodine and adrenaline on thyrotropin in Graves' disease and in normal and thyroidectomized dogs. *Proc. Soc. Exp. Biol. Med.* 64:446.

———, Gabrilove, J. L., and Jailer, J. W. 1949. Role of adrenal in uptake of I^{131} by the thyroid following parenteral administration of epinephrine. *Proc. Soc. Exp. Biol. Med.* 71:117.

Solomon, D. H. 1971. Antithyroid drugs. In *The Thyroid*, edited by S. C. Werner and S. H. Ingbar. New York: Harper & Row.

——— and Beall, G. N. 1968. Thyroid-stimulating activity in the serum of immunized rabbits. II. Nature of the thyroid-stimulating activity. *J. Clin. Endocrinol. Metab.* 28:1496.

———, and Chopra, I. J. 1972. Graves' disease—1972. *Mayo Clinic Proc.* 47:803.

———, Green, D. E., Snyder, N. J., and Nelson, J. C. 1964. Clinical significance of the long-acting thyroid stimulator of Graves' disease (abstr.). *Clin. Res.* 12:119.

Solomon, G. F. 1969. Stress and antibody response in rats. *Int. Arch. Allergy. Appl. Immunol.* 35:97.

Sorensen, E. W. 1958. Thyroid disease in a family. *Acta Med. Scand.* 162:123.

Stanbury, J. B., Brownell, G. L., Riggs, D. S., Perinetti, H., Itoiz, J., and del Castillo, E. B. 1954. *Endemic Goiter: The Adaptation of Man to Iodine Deficiency.* Cambridge: Harvard University Press.

Starr, P., Petit, D. W., Chaney, A. L., Rollman, H., Aiken, J. B., Jamieson, B., and Kling, I., 1950. Clinical experience with the blood protein-bound iodine determination as a routine procedure. *J. Clin. Endocrinol. Metab.* 10:1237.

Staub, M. C. 1966. Familial hyperthyroidism. *Schweiz. Med. Wochenschr.* 96:727.

Steigbigel, N. H., Oppenheim, J. J., Fishman, L. M., and Carbone, P. P. 1964. Metastatic embryonal carcinoma of the testes associated with elevated plasma TSH-like activity and hyperthyroidism. *N. Engl. J. Med.* 271:345.

Steinbeck, A. W. 1963. The thyroid gland in human reproduction. *Modern Trends in Human Reproductive Physiology*, edited by H. M. Carey. Washington: Butterworths.

Sterling, K., and Chodos, R. B. 1956. Radiothyroxine turnover studies in myxedema, thyrotoxicosis, and hypermetabolism without endocrine disease. *J. Clin. Invest.* 35:806.

Sternberg, T. H., Newcomer, V. D., Steffen, C. G., Fields, M., and Libby, R. L. 1955. Distribution of radioactive iodine (I^{131}) in experimental coccidioidomycosis and sporotrichosis. *J. Invest. Dermatol.* 24:397.

Stevens, J. D., and Dunn, A. L. 1958. Thyroid function in mental diseases. *Dis. Nerv. Syst.* 19:338.

Stewart, J. C., Vidor, G. I., Buttfield, I. H., and Hetzel, B. S. 1971. Epidemic thyrotoxicosis in Northern Tasmania: studies of clinical features and iodine nutrition. *Aust. N.Z. J. Med.* 3:203.

Stokvis, B. 1953–54. Structure-analytical approach to the problem of "specificity" in psychosomatic medicine. *Acta Psychotherapeut.* 1:30.

Strubelt, O. 1968. Der Einfluss der Schilddrüsenfunktion auf die pharmakologischen Wirkungen von propanolol, adrenalin, noradrenalin und dinitrophenol. *Arch. Int. Pharmacodyn. Ther.* 176:263.

Sunshine, P., Kusumoto, H., and Kriss, J. P. 1965. Survival time of circulating long-acting thyroid stimulator in neonatal thyrotoxicosis: implications for diagnosis and therapy of the disorder. *Pediatrics.* 36:869.

Surko, M. I., Beckwitt, H. J., and Chidsey, C. A. 1967. Changes in plasma thyroxine concentration and metabolism, catecholamine excretion and basal oxygen consumption in man during acute exposure to high altitudes. *J. Clin. Endocrinol. Metab.* 27:789.

Svedmyr, M. 1968. Studies on the relationships between some metabolic effects of thyroid hormones and catecholamines in animals and man. *Acta Physiol. Scand.* 68 (Suppl. 274):1.

Tallquist, T. W. 1922. Unterernährung und innere Sekretion. *Acta Med. Scand.* 56:640.

Tanaka, S., and Starr, P. 1959. Clinical observations on serum globulin thyroxine-binding capacity, using a simplified technique. *J. Clin. Endocrinol. Metab.* 19:84.

409

Taurog, A., and Thio, D. T. 1966. TSH-induced thyroxine release from puromycin-blocked thyroid glands of intact rabbits. *Endocrinology.* 78:103.

Taylor, S. 1953. The evolution of nodular goiter. *J. Clin. Endocrinol. Metab.* 13:1232.

———. 1960. Genesis of the thyroid nodule. *Br. Med. Bull.* 16:102.

Thier, S. O., Black, P., and Williams, H. E. 1965. Chronic lymphocytic thyroiditis: Report of a kindred with viral, immunological and chemical studies. *J. Clin. Endocrinol. Metab.* 25:65.

Thomson, J. A. 1966. The normal thyroid scan. *Lancet.* ii:308.

———, and Mukhtar, E. D. 1975. Neonatal hyperthyroidism and long-acting thyroid stimulator protector. *Br. Med. J.* 2:36.

———, and Riley, I. A. 1966. Neonatal thyrotoxicosis associated with maternal hypothyroidism. *Lancet.* i:635.

Thomson, J. A., Dirmikis, S. M., Munro, D. S., Smith, B. R., Hall, R., and Mukhtar, E. D. 1975. Neonatal hyperthyroidism and long-acting thyroid stimulator protector. *Br. Med. J.* 2:36.

Tingley, J. O., Morris, A. W., and Hill, S. R. 1958. Studies on the diurnal variation and response to emotional stress of the thyroid gland. *Clin. Res.* 6:134.

Tong, W. 1971. Thyroid hormone synthesis and release. In *The Thyroid,* edited by S. C. Werner and S. H. Ingbar. New York: Harper & Row.

Uno, T. 1922. Effect of general excitement and of fighting on some ductless glands of male albino rats. *Am. J. Physiol.* 61:203.

Utiger, R. D. 1965. Radioimmunoassay of human plasma thyrotropin. *J. Clin. Invest.* 44:1277.

Vale, W., Burgus, R., and Guillemin, R. 1967. Competition between thyroxine and TRF at the pituitary level in the release of TSH. *Proc. Soc. Exp. Biol. Med.* 125:210.

Van Leeuwen, E. 1954. Form of true hyperthyroidism (Basedow's disease without exophthalmos) following use of bread made with iodized salt for goiter prophylaxis in endemic region. *Ned. Tijdschr. Geneeskd.* 98:81.

Van Middlesworth, C., and Berry, M. M. 1951. Iodine metabolism during anoxia, nephrectomy, trauma, avitaminoses and starvation in the rat. *Am. J. Physiol.* 167:576.

Van Rees, G. P., and Moll, J. 1968. Influence of thyroidectomy with and without thyroxine treatment on thyrotropin secretion in gonadectomized rats with anterior hypothalamic lesions. *Neuroendocrinology.* 3:115.

Verney, E. B. 1947. The antidiuretic hormone and the factors which determine its release. *Proc. R. Soc. Lond.* [B] 135:25.

Vogel, F. 1959. Modern problems of human genetics. *Ergeb. Inn. Med. Kinderheilkd.* 12:52.

Vogt, M. 1954. The concentration of sympathin in different parts of the central nervous system under normal conditions and after the administration of drugs. *J. Physiol.* (Lond.). 123:451.

Volpé, R., Edmonds, M., Lamki, L., Clarke, P. V., and Row, V. V. 1972. The pathogenesis of Graves' disease. *Mayo Clin. Proc.* 47:824.

———, Farid, N. R., von Westarp, C., and Row, V. V. 1974. The pathogenesis of Graves' disease and Hashimoto's thyroiditis. *Clin. Endocr.* 3:239.

———, Vale, J., and Johnston, M. W. 1960. The effects of certain physical and emotional tensions and strains on fluctuations on the level of serum protein bound iodine. *J. Clin. Endocrinol. Metab.* 20:415.

———, Desbarats-Schönbaum, M. L., Schönbaum, E., Row, V. V., and Ezrin, C. 1969. The effect of radioablation of the thyroid gland in Graves' disease with high levels of long-acting thyroid stimulator (LATS). *Am. J. Med.* 46:217.

Voth, H. M., Holzman, P. S., Katz, J. B., and Wallerstein, R. S. 1970. Thyroid "hot spots": Their relationship to life stress. *Psychosom. Med.* 32:561.

Wahner, H. W., Emslander, R. F., and Gorman, C. A. 1971. Thyroid overactivity and TBG

410

deficiency stimulating "T_3 hyperthyroidism." *J. Clin. Endocrinol. Metab.* 33:93.

Waldstein, S. S. 1966. Thyroid-catecholamine interrelations. *Annu. Rev. Med.* 17:123.

Walfish, P. G., Britton, A., Melville, P. H., and Ezrin, C. 1961. A diurnal pattern in the rate of disappearance of I^{131}-labeled L-thyroxine from the serum. *J. Clin. Endocrinol. Metab.* 21:582.

Wall, J. R., Good, B. F., and Hetzel, B. S. 1969. Long-acting thyroid stimulator in euthyroid relatives of thyrotoxic patients. *Lancet.* ii:1024.

Wallace, H. L. 1931. Hyperthyroidism: a statistical presentation of its symptomatology. *Edinburgh Med. J.* 38:578.

Wallerstein, R. S., Holzman, P. S., Voth, H. M., and Uhr, N. 1965. Thyroid "hot spots": a psychophysiological study. *Psychosom. Med.* 27:508.

Weltman, A. S., Sackler, A. M., Sparber, S. B., and Opert, S. 1962. Endocrine aspects of isolation stress of female mice. *Fed. Proc.* 21:1.

Weiner, H. 1970a. The specificity hypothesis revisited. *Psychosom. Med.* 32:543.

———. 1970b. Psychosomatic research in essential hypertension: retrospect and prospect. In *Psychosomatics in Essential Hypertension*, edited by M. Koster, H. Musaph, and P. Visser. *Bibl. Psychiatr.* 144:58.

———. 1972. Some comments on the transduction of experience by the brain. *Psychosom. Med.* 34:355.

———, 1975. Autonomic psychophysiology: peripheral autonomic mechanisms and their central control. In *American Handbook of Psychiatry*, vol. 4, edited by M. F. Reiser. New York: Basic Books.

——— and Hart, S. 1975. Promising interactions between psychiatry and medicine. In *American handbook of Psychiatry*, vol. 6, edited by D. A. Hamburg and H. K. H. Brodie. New York: Basic Books.

Weisman, S. A. 1958. Incidence of thyrotoxicosis among refugees from Nazi prison camps. *Ann. Intern Med.* 48:747.

Weiss, J. M. 1971. Effects of coping behavior with and without a feedback signal on stress pathology in rats. *J. Comp. Physiol. Psychol.* 77:22.

Welch, B. L., and Welch, A. S. 1968. Differential activation by restraint stress of a mechanism to conserve brain catecholamines and serotonin in mice differing in excitability. *Nature.* 218:575.

Werner, S. C. 1955. Euthyroid Graves' disease with early eye signs of Graves' disease; their responses to L-triiodothyronine and thyrotropin. *Am. J. Med.* 18:608.

———. 1956. Response to triiodothyronine as index of persistence of disease in the thyroid remnant of patients in remission from hyperthyroidism. *J. Clin. Invest.* 35:57.

———. 1962. Clinical use of triiodothyronine in suppressing thyrotropin secretion by the anterior pituitary: a survey. *Proc. R. Soc. Med.* 55:1000.

———. 1963. Discussion of S. C. Werner, Immune method of thyrotropin assay. In *Thyrotropin*, edited by S. C. Werner. Springfield, Ill.: Charles C Thomas.

———. 1967. In *Thyrotoxicosis*, edited by W. J. Irvine. Edinburgh: Livingstone.

———. 1971. Hyperthyroidism. In *The Thyroid*, edited by S. C. Werner and S. H. Ingbar. 3rd ed. New York: Harper & Row.

——— and Hamilton, H. 1961. Hyperthyroidism without apparent hypermetabolism. *J.A.M.A.* 146:450.

——— and Ingbar, S. H., eds. 1971. *The Thyroid*. New York: Harper & Row.

——— and Tierney, J. 1961. Neutralization of "long-acting thyroid stimulator" of Graves' disease by antisera to bovine pituitary thyrotropin. *Proc. Soc. Exp. Biol. Med.* 108:780.

———, Hamilton, H., and Nemeth, M. 1952. Graves' disease: hyperthyroidism or hyper-pituitarism? *J. Clin. Endocrinll. Metab.* 12:1561.

————, Spooner, M., and Hamilton, H. 1955. Further evidence that hyperthyroidism (Graves' disease) is not hyperpituitarism: effects of triiodothyronine and sodium iodide. *J. Clin. Endocrinol. Metab.* 15:715.

————, Becker, D. V., and Row, V. V. 1959. Distribution of serum radioiodinated compounds in euthyroid and hyperthyroid patients following hypophysectomy. *J. Clin. Endocrinol. Metab.* 19:953.

————, Row, V. V., and Radichevich, I. 1960. Non-toxic nodular goiter with formation and release of a compound with the chromatographic mobility characteristics of triiodothyronine. *J. Clin. Endocrinol. Metab.* 20:1373.

————, Tierney, J., and Tallberg, T. 1964. Thyrotropic and "long-acting thyroid stimulator" effects from certain polypeptides. *J. Clin. Endocrinol. Metab.* 24:339.

————, Feind, C. R., and Aida, M. 1967. Graves' disease and total thyroidectomy. *N. Engl. J. Med.* 276:132.

————, Wegelius, O., and Fierer, J. A. 1972. Immunoglobulins (E, M, G) and complement in the connective tissues of the thyroid in Graves' disease. *N. Engl. J. Med.* 287:241.

————, ————, and Hsu, K. C. 1971. Immune responses in stroma and basement membranes of the Graves' disease thyroid (IgM, IgE, IgG and complement). *Trans. Asoc. Am. Physicians.* 84:139.

Wilbur, J. F., and Utiger, R. D. 1968. *In vitro* studies on mechanism of action of thyrotropin releasing factor. *Proc. Soc. Exp. Biol. Med.* 127:488.

———— and ————. 1969. The effect of glucocorticoids on thyrotropin secretion. *J. Clin. Invest.* 48:2096.

Williams, R. H., Jaffe, H., and Kemp, C. 1949. Effect of severe stress upon thyroid function. *Am. J. Physiol.* 159:291.

Wilson, G. M. 1967. *The Treatment of Thyrotoxicosis.* Edinburgh: Royal College of Physicians.

Wilson, O. 1966. Field study of the effect of cold exposure and increased muscular activity upon metabolic rate and thyroid function in man. *Fed. Proc.* 25:1357.

Wilson, W. P., and Johnson, J. E. 1960. Clinical laboratory and electroencephalographic correlations in hyperthyroidism. *South. Med. J.* 53:606.

————, ————, and Smith, R. B. 1961. Affective change in thyrotoxicosis and experimental hypermetabolism. In *Recent Advances in Biological Psychiatry.* 4:234.

Winkelstein, W., Jr., Kantor, S., and Ibrahim, M. 1966. Familial aggregation of blood pressure: preliminary report. *J.A.M.A.* 195:848.

Wiswell, J. G., Hurwitz, G. E., Coronho, V., Bing, O. H. L., and Child, D. L. 1963. Urinary catecholamines and their metabolites in hyperthyroidism and hypothyroidism. *J. Clin. Endocrinol. Metab.* 23:1102.

Wittkower, E., Schringer, W., and Bay, E. 1932. Zur affektiven Beeinflussbarkeit des Blutjodspiegels. *Klin. Wochenschr.* 2:1186.

Wochner, R. D., Silverman, D., Germuth, F., Kaufman, R., Kechijian, P., and Perkoff, G. T. 1969. An apparently hereditary syndrome of thyrotoxicosis, renal disease and absent frontal sinuses. *Clin. Res.* 17:530.

Wolff, C. T., Friedman, S. B., Hofer, M. A., and Mason, J. W. 1964a. Relationship between psychological defenses and mean urinary 17-hydroxycorticosteroid excretion rates. I. *Psychosom. Med.* 26:576.

————, Hofer, M. A., and Mason, J. W. 1964b. Relationship between psychological defenses and mean urinary 17-hydroxycorticosteroid excretion rates. *Psychosom. Med.* 26:592.

Wolff, H. G. 1953. *Stress and Disease.* Springfield: Thomas.

Wong, E. T., and Doe, R. P. 1969. Suppressibility of thyroid function despite high levels of long-acting thyroid stimulator (LATS). *Program. 45th Meeting, American Thyroid Asociation,* Chicago.

412

Worthington, C. W. 1960. Vascular responses of the pituitary stalk. *Endocrinology.* 66:19.

Wurtman, R. J. 1971. Brain monoamines and endocrine function. *Neurosci. Res. Program Bull.* 9(2):182.

———— and Axelrod, J. 1966. Control of enzymatic synthesis of adrenaline in the adrenal medulla by adrenal cortical steroids. *J. Biol. Chem.* 241:2301.

———— and ————. 1966. The effect of thyroid and estrogen on the fate of catecholamines. *Res. Publ. Assoc. Res. Nerv. Ment. Dis.* 43:354.

Wyse, E. P., McConahey, W. M., Wollner, L. B., Scholz, D. A., and Kearns, T. P. 1968. Ophthalmopathy without hyperthyroidism in patients with histologic Hashimoto's thyroiditis. *J. Clin. Endocrinol. Metab.* 28:1623.

Yager, J., and Weiner, H. 1971. Observations in man. *Adv. Psychosom. Med.* 6:40.

Yamada, T., and Greer, M. A. 1960. The effect of bilateral ablation of the amygdala on endocrine function in the rat. *Endocrinology.* 66:565.

Yasumura, S., and Knigge, K. M. 1962. The habenula: effect of lesions and thyroid grafts on thyroid function in the rat. *Abstracts of the XXII International Congress of Physiological Sciences. International Congress Series, No. 48*, edited by J. W. Duyff. Amsterdam: Excerpta Medica Foundation.

Yeakel, E. H., and Rhoades, R. P. 1941. A comparison of the body and endocrine gland (adrenal, thyroid and pituitary) weights of emotional and non-emotional rats. *Endocrinology.* 28:337.

Zakrzewskea-Henisz, A., Szpilmanowa, H., and Kopée, M. 1967. Familial incidence of long-acting thyroid stimulator. *Pathol. Eur.* 2:81.

Zangeneb, F., Lulejian, G. A., and Steiner, M. 1966. McCune-Albright syndrome with hyperthyroidism. *Am. J. Dis. Child.* 111:644.

Ziegler, L. H., and Levin, B. S. 1925. The influence of emotional reactions on basal metabolism. *Am. J. Med. Sci.* 169:68.

Zsoter, T., Tom, H., and Chappel, C. 1964. Effect of thyroid hormones on vascular response. *J. Clin. Lab. Med.* 64:433.

Zuckerman, M., Persky, H., Hopkins, T. R., Murtaugh, T., Basu, G. K., and Schilling, M. 1966. Comparison of stress effects of perceptual and social isolation. *Arch. Gen. Psychiatry.* 14:348.

5
RHEUMATOID ARTHRITIS

Of all the chronic illnesses that afflict mankind, none is more disabling and widespread than arthritis. It has been estimated that 20 million Americans suffer from one kind of arthritis or another. About 85 percent of those with arthritis are 45 years of age or older; 60 percent of the patients in this age group suffer from osteoarthritis. However, the majority of arthritis patients under 45 years of age are afflicted with rheumatoid arthritis; approximately 200,000 children and 2 million adolescents and young adults are victims of this disease, and about half of those affected will be permanently crippled by it. In all, about 5 million adults in the United States have rheumatoid arthritis.

It is particularly unfortunate, in view of the prevalence and potentially destructive nature of this disease, that our understanding of its etiology and pathogenesis is very limited. This limitation in our understanding continues to exist despite major advances in the elucidation of the complex pathophysiology—specifically the immunopathology—of the disease. The causes of this immunopathology are not known. The immunopathology does not occur in some patients with rheumatoid arthritis, but in most patients it does.

The existence of this immunopathology has largely escaped most behavioral scientists, who have studied the sociology and psychology of rheumatoid arthritis. They have so far been guided by a hypothesis that these patients are predisposed to the disease by virtue of having been strictly disciplined as children. In adolescence they rebelled against their parents' discipline; the girls, particularly, expressed their rebellion and resentment by being tomboys and actively participating in sports. As adults they turned into tyrants,

419

disciplining other people, while complaining of their own unhappy lives. The disease has its onset when the object of their tyranny parts with them. Incapable of coping with the separation, they fall ill. When ill, they are often depressed, stoical, or embittered. In the process of falling ill, the resentment at the departing object of their tyranny is translated into increased musculoskeletal tension to produce the joint disease.

We owe this three-part formulation to Alexander (1950) who attempted to explain the psychological predisposition to, and the initiation and pathogenesis of rheumatoid arthritis, especially in women patients. Much evidence has been accumulated to support some parts of Alexander's formulation, while other evidence refutes it. One source of disagreement is that rheumatoid arthritis is a highly variable disease. It can occur in a mild remitting form, yet it can also cause severe progressive destruction of joints. The definite and classical forms (Bennett and Burch, 1967) represent a systemic disease (Bevans et al., 1954; Gardner, 1972; Hart, 1969; Pearson, 1966), not only a disease of joints. Mild and "possible" forms of the disease also exist.

Thus one source of disagreement among behavioral scientists may be that they are studying different forms or stages of the disease. And different behavioral scientists have used different methods. Some base their observations on clinical interviews; others use questionnaires or projective tests. In any case, no consistent set of psychological observations exists that would account for the etiology and pathogenesis of the disease. It is also clear that social and psychological factors alone do not account for the disease. There are other predisposing factors that in most adult patients[*] partly consist of a tendency to form rheumatoid factors that are antibodies directed against the patients' own gamma-globulins (IgG).

In juvenile rheumatoid arthritis, the tendency to form rheumatoid factors is less-apparent. The juvenile form is now considered to be distinct from the adult disease. On the basis of clinical criteria, juvenile rheumatoid arthritis has been divided into three subforms (Brewer et al., 1972; Calabro et al., 1970). The problems in the diagnosis—especially the early diagnosis—of rheumatoid arthritis are underscored for a number of reasons. So far, no prospective studies have been done to validate the social and psychological observations and descriptions of patients with the established disease, although at this time such studies are probably feasible. Should they prove infeasible, the investigator should still attempt to study patients as soon as possible after the onset of the disease, in order to obtain the most-reliable possible data on the circumstances surrounding the onset of the disease. At onset, however, the symptoms and signs of the disease are often vague and nonspecific. The criteria for the diagnosis of rheumatoid arthritis at its inception are not universally agreed upon; other forms of arthritis may begin in a similar or the identical manner. Should

---

[*] Rheumoid arthritis in adults is usually defined in a multifactoral manner as a chronic destructive arthritis characterized: (1) clinically, by pain, inflammation, and deformity in one or several joints; (2) anatomically, by inflammation with progressive deformity of joints, subcutaneous nodules (especially over pressure points and sites of friction), and necrotizing and obliterative vascular lesions in a number of different organs of the body; (3) immunologically, by the presence in the blood serum, in many but not all patients, of rheumatoid factors. But these criteria do not always ensure diagnostic accuracy. For example, questions concerning the reliability of rheumatoid factors as major diagnostic criteria are raised by the following findings: (1) patients whose sera do not include rheumatoid factors may nonetheless manifest the clinical symptoms of rheumatoid arthritis (Dixon, 1960), (2) the presence of rheumatoid factors in the serum is not specific to rheumatoid arthritis.

420

the investigator wait until the diagnosis of rheumatoid arthritis can be established une-quivocally by clinical, X-ray, and laboratory criteria, his data may be "contaminated" by the patient's psychological response to having a painful, debilitating, and deforming disease for which there is no certain or established treatment and cure.

Furthermore, information reviewed in this chapter will clearly establish that social and psychological factors do not uniquely predispose, initiate, or sustain rheumatoid arthritis. Immunological (autoimmune) factors play an important etiologic and pathogenetic role, although the causes of these rheumoid factors are not yet certain. The disease is variable in the form it takes and in its course and outcome. The implications of this variability are evident; whether the investigator addresses himself to the epidemiology, pathogenesis, or psychosomatic aspects of rheumatoid arthriois, his efforts will necessarily be impeded by the lack of criteria that would enable him to establish an unequivocal diagnosis of rheumatoid arthritis at its inception or early in its course, as well as by the difficulties of selecting a homogeneous population for study.

THE ROLE OF GENETIC FACTORS

The etiology of rheumatoid arthritis is not known. There is no reason for not believing that genetic factors might not play an etiological role in the disease. In the ensuing sections the evidence for the role of genetic factors will be reviewed by scrutinizing data from studies employing population genetical methods and the strategy of comparing concordance rates for the disease in monozygotic (Mz) and dizygotic (Dz) twins.

Studies of Families

A number of authors have sought to establish whether rheumatoid arthritis and rheumatoid factors[*] occur with increased frequency in the relatives of patients with rheumatoid arthritis (Lawrence, 1967; Lawrence and Wood, 1968; O'Brien, 1967; Short et al., 1957). The wide discrepancies in their results have been attributed to various methodological problems that are inherent in such research (O'Brien, 1967). In addition, a review of the literature to date reveals that some of these studies contain certain conceptual flaws. For example, the fact that rheumatoid arthritis apparently occurs in a higher proportion of relatives than would be expected by chance does not necessarily mean that genetic factors are at play (Cobb, 1965; O'Brien, 1967). In fact, in two studies—by Schmid and Slatis (1962) and Schull and Cobb (1969)—serum and clinical abnormalities seemed to occur with increased incidence (16 percent) in spouses of patients with rheumatoid arthritis, when compared to a control group. This finding was not confirmed in

---

[*] Rheumatoid factors are detected in serum by the sheep cell agglutination test (SCAT), the latex fixation test (LFT), and the bentonite flocculation test (BFT). The three tests for rheumatoid factors (SCAT, LFT, BFT) primarily detect IgM rheumatoid factors. However, IgA and IgG rheumatoid factors are also of importance for rheumatoid arthritis; different and special tests must be used for their detection.

The SCAT is somewhat more specific for rheumatoid factors, but less sensitive than the LFT. The LFT may be falsely positive, unless special precautions are taken. Without these precautions it may detect various substances besides IgM rheumatoid factors (Cheng and Persellin, 1971; Dequeker et al., 1969; Stage and Mannik, 1972; Vaughan, 1969; Waller, 1969).

421

later studies (Bennett and Burch, 1968; Hellgren, 1969; Lawrence and Wood, 1968). If it had been, it would, of course, have constituted powerful evidence against the proposition that genetic factors alone play a role in the disease, since the chance of two spouses both being genetically predisposed is small.

In 19 studies, the prevalence of rheumatoid arthritis in relatives of patients varied from 3.0 percent (Masiero and Toso, 1961) through 15 percent (Lewis-Faning, 1950) to 32 percent (Rimón, 1969), and the percentage in controls ranged from 0 (Siegel et al., 1965) to 9 percent (Lewis-Faning, 1950). In the study conducted by the Empire Rheumatism Council (1950), 7 percent of the fathers of patients having rheumatoid arthritis, 15 percent of the mothers, and 3.8 percent of the siblings also had arthritis. These figures were significantly higher than those found in a control population. The families of some patients may contain several members with rheumatoid arthritis; usually, these are siblings (Rimón, 1969; Short et al., 1957).

Much of the disagreement about the prevalence of rheumatoid arthritis in families stems from the fact that the criteria employed to diagnose the disease differ in different series. A study that employed only the most rigorous clinical criteria has demonstrated that the prevalence of the disease among direct relatives of patients exceeded chance by a factor of 1,000. However, these results should not be construed in simplistic terms: the age of onset of the disease was an important variable. The patients who developed the disease earlier in life had a higher prevalence among their relatives than those who developed the disease later in life. This result would seem to suggest a strong genetic factor, were it not for the fact that the prevalence of the disease in the spouses of patients was significantly greater than the prevalence among the spouses of first- and second-degree relatives of patients (Wasmuth et al., 1972). Clearly then, both genetic and environmental factors play a role in the disease, and both require specification.

In addition to a family aggregation of rheumatoid arthrits, some authors have found an increased prevalence of rheumatic fever in the families of patients with rheumatoid arthritis: in the series studied by Short and his co-workers (1957), 11.6 percent of 293 patients had such a history, in comparison to 3.4 percent of the controls. An increased prevalence of asthma, hay fever, and urticaria did not occur in family members.

Kellgren (1966), who conducted the most rigorous study reported to date, using clinical, X-ray, and serological diagnostic criteria, found that the family prevalence of rheumatoid arthritis was 6.3 percent—which is 4.5 times the expected rate, and statistically significant. Yet, in three other studies, the prevalence of rheumatoid arthirits (Burch et al., 1965), and of rheumatoid factors was no greater in the families of patients with rheumatoid arthritis than it was in a control population (Burch et al., 1965; Maseiro and Toso, 1961).

The methodological pitfalls inherent in such research have been enumerated, specifically by O'Brien (1967). One of the major reasons for the wide variations is that different methods have been used to gather data and establish a diagnosis. For instance, in some studies the diagnosis of rheumatoid arthritis was made solely on the basis of the relatives' history (Neri Serneri and Bartoli, 1956). In Miall's study (1955) only the patient's male relatives were examined, and, once again, diagnosis of the disease was based on the relatives' history. In the study by Burch and his co-workers (1965), diagnosis was based on the Ropes criteria, and the author's figures included relatives with a probable diagnosis of the disease, although their symptoms may well have been due to causes other than rheumatoid arthritis. Yet, contrary to all expectations, given these methodological "flaws," this study failed to show any family aggregation of rheumatoid arthritis.

FAMILY AGGREGATION OF RHEUMATOID FACTORS

In the years since Ziff (1961, 1968) assessed the percentage of relatives whose sera contained rheumatoid factors, a number of similar studies have been carried out. In six of these, the figures varied from 32 to 40 percent (Goldenberg et al., 1960; Robecchi and Daneo, 1959) to 4.5 percent (Siegel et al., 1965) in relatives, and from 8 percent to 1.3 percent in controls. In some series, the apparent presence of a family aggregation of rheumatoid factors depended on which test was used to detect such factors (Goldenberg et al., 1960).

Neither Ansell et al. (1962), Bremner et al., (1959), nor Burch et al., (1965) found evidence of family aggregation of rheumatoid factors. It is possible, however, that these negative findings can be explained, in part, on methodological grounds. It is generally recognized that the prevalence of rheumatoid factors increases with age. Therefore, an important variable to control in these studies is the age of the subjects. The fact that Ansell's series was limited to young patients and their young families may account for his failure to show a family aggregation of rheumatoid factors. On the other hand, Bremner, who studied both younger and older families, found that those families with positive serological tests were somewhat younger than those whose tests were negative.

COMBINED STUDIES

It has been suggested that one reason for the wide diversity in the results obtained on the family aggregation of rheumatoid arthritis is that it is not a homogeneous disease: patients with polyarthritis, systemic manifestations of the disease, and rheumatoid factors in their sera have one form of the disease; those whose sera do not contain rheumatoid factors may have another form (O'Brien, 1967). Yet, rheumatoid factors may appear in the sera of some patients after the disease begins (Hill, 1968).

Lawrence and Ball (1958) found that the relatives of patients without detectable rheumatoid factors in their sera showed no more extensive erosive arthritis (by X-ray) than control subjects. But the relatives of patients whose blood contained rheumatoid factors had five times as much X-ray evidence of arthritis. These findings were subsequently confirmed by Lawrence and Wood (1968) and by De Blécourt et al. (1961), but not by Bremner et al. (1959) or Veenhoff-Garman et al. (1968). Bremner and his co-workers found no difference in the clinical evidence and X-ray evidence of rheumatoid arthirtis between the relatives of patients who had and those who did not have positive tests for rheumatoid arthritis. However, this view is not shared by the majority of investigators.

As further evidence of their validity, Lawrence and Wood (1968) have demonstrated that the findings reported by Lawrence and Ball hold true for the relatives of both hospitalized patients and random samples of patients, and that they apply regardless of whether the dependent variable is clinical rheumatoid arthritis or erosive arthritis as evidenced on X-ray. In the series studied by Lawrence and Wood (1968), among patients with a positive sheep cell agglutination test (SCAT) for rheumatoid factors, the observed rate of severe erosive arthritis in first-degree relatives was 6.8 times the expected rate, and 5.5 times the rate in the relatives of patients with a negative SCAT.

Mode of Inheritance and What Is Inherited

Obviously, no firm conclusions can be drawn from the data reviewed above. The family studies conducted to date do not prove that rheumatoid arthritis is inherited. Concomitantly, no clear mode of inheritance can be identified, if, indeed, one exists (Lawrence and Wood, 1968; O'Brien, 1967). Nor is it clear whether the production of rheumatoid factors is partly an inheritied trait. In view of their presence in the general population, it is safe to assume that while some of the factors may be inherited, others may be the consequence of the disease (Hill, 1968; Kaplan, 1963), and still others may be related to nutritional factors (Valkenburg, 1963).

It seems fairly certain, then, that the family aggregation of rheumatoid arthritis is not dependent on the aggregation of rheumatoid factors alone (Lawrence, 1963). However, aggregation does seem to be limited to the families of patients whose sera contain rheumatoid factors (Lawrence, 1967), and the relatives of such patients show the most-severe forms of joint damage, according to X-rays. Rheumatoid factors seem to be related to the severity and prognosis of rheumatoid arthritis, and not only to the pathogenesis of the disease (Lawrence, 1967; Stage and Mannik, 1972).

It is also possible that the family aggregation of rheumatoid arthritis and of rheumatoid factors (which appear to be independent of each other) may be present in some ethnic groups and not in others. For example, Burch et al. (1965) found no family aggregation in a population of American Indians (Blackfeet), although others found such an aggregation (Kellgren, 1966; 1968). One characteristic that may possibly be inherited in some patients is a disinhibition of autoimmune antibody formation because of the presence of rheumatoid factors.

One rare form of rheumatoid arthritis (Barnett et al., 1970) is associated with a genetically determined (X-linked) agammaglobulinemia (Bruton-type). The result of the lack of immunoglobulin production is that humoral antibody response are deficient, but cellular immune responses are not (Rose and Janeway, 1966; Strober et al., 1971). The incidence of the rheumatoid arthritis in these patients is about 35 percent, presumably because they are less able to form antibodies against infectious agents.

All the main classes of antibodies are deficiently formed in this hereditary form of agammaglobulinemia. But in other forms, only one class of immunoglobulin may be deficient. Selective IgA deficiency occurs as a familial trait in normal people and with congenital or specific chromosomal abnormalities. Selective IgA deficiency occurs with high frequency in patients with rheumatoid arthritis—especially the juvenile form (Cassidy et al., 1968; Strober et al., 1971; Wolf, 1962). Whether this selective form of deficiency is inherited or acquired is still not known. In any case, specific genetic defects in immunoglobulin production seems to place patients at risk for rheumatoid arthritis.

Twin Studies

In twin studies, the diagnostic problems that surround rheumatoid arthritis present major impediments to ascertaining concordance figures. In addition, many earlier studies

424

did not use the rigorous criteria for zygosity determinations that are presently employed. And the value of the findings derived from other studies has been diminished by problems of sampling bias; for example, in some instances only the hospitalized member of a pair of twins was studied. What follows must be evaluated in the light of these methodological defects.

The most extensive study published to date was done by Harvald and Hauge (1965). These authors reviewed all twins born between 1870 and 1910 in Denmark; of the total population of 37,914 twins born during this period, 6,893 were available for study. For the most part, zygosity was determined by questionnaire and on the basis of physical similarity. (Relatives of the twins were used to establish the reliability of the authors' judgment of similarity in appearance.) In only 165 pairs was zygosity determined by blood- and serum-examination. Medical diagnosis was established by questionnaires and interviews, although, wherever possible, the diagnosis obtained by these means was verified by hospital and physicians' records, death certificates, and autopsy records. In 188 pairs, at least one twin was diagnosed as having rheumatoid arthritis. Of the 141 pairs of dizygotic (Dz) twins included in this experimental population, 71 pairs were of the same sex, and 70 were of opposite sexes. Concordance for rheumatoid arthritis was found in 16 of the 47 pairs of monozygotic (Mz) twins, 2 of the 71 pairs of Dz twins of the same sex, and 8 of the 70 pairs of Dz twins of the opposite sex. In contrast, Lawrence (1967) found no difference in concordance rates between Mz and Dz twins.

After extensive zygosity determinations, Meyerowitz et al. (1968) selected nine pairs of Mz female twins for study, three of which were under 16 years of age. The criteria used to diagnose rheumatoid arthritis were those enumerated by Ropes et al. in 1958, plus the LFT, preparations for lupus erythemosus (LE) cells, and X-ray evidence of joint erosion. The diagnosis could not be established for one pair of twins. All of the remaining eight pairs of twins, in whom the disease had been definitely diagnosed, were discordant for rheumatoid arthritis. They were also discordant for rheumatoid factors. The presence of the factors was associated with the disease. In six of the eight pairs, the LFT was positive in the twin who had rheumatoid arthritis, but negative in her healthy sister. In the other two pairs (girls aged 8 and 14) the LFT was negative in both the arthritic and the nonarthritic twin.

Meyerowitz et al. (1968) also critically reviewed previous studies (including Thymann, 1957, but excluding the report by Harvald and Hauge) and concluded that of the Mz twins described in the literature, only 28 pairs could be said to satisfy the criteria both for zygosity and for rheumatoid arthritis. Of these 28 pairs of Mz twins, 25 were discordant for rheumatoid arthritis. Thus, if we add these figures to those reported by Harvald and Hauge, we find that 19 of 75 pairs of Mz twins were concordant for rheumatoid arthritis—a rate of 25 percent—as opposed to a concordance rate of about 10 percent for fraternal twins.

In 1970, Lawrence reported on a new sample of 19 Mz twin pairs and 67 Dz pairs (37 same-sexed and 30 not), all with positive tests for rheumatoid factors; an additional 58 pairs in whom the tests were negative; and 217 control siblings. He found that the concordance rate for definite rheumatoid arthritis in the Dz twins with positive tests did not differ from the rate in siblings with positive tests. However, the concordance rate in Mz twins was five times greater than the rate for Dz twins. Of the 19 pairs of Mz twins included in his sample, 6 were concordant for the disease, whereas only 4 of the 67 pairs of Dz twins were concordant. None of the 58 twin pairs in whom tests for rheumatoid factors were negative were concordant for rheumatoid arthritis. Lawrence drew several conclusions from his

425

data; the similarity of the environment was not a factor in the incidence of concordance because the concordance rates for seropositve disease was no greater in Dz like-sexed twins than for other siblings. He also concluded that genetic predisposition was important for the development of seropositive rheumatoid arthritis but cannot exclusively account for the entire etiologic variance of the disease.

Although the Harvald-Hauge data show that the difference in concordance for Mz twins, as compared to Dz twins, is statistically significant ($p < .001$), these data cannot be considered definitive proof that genetic factors alone play a primary, direct role in the etiology of rheumatoid arthrits. Nor, as Harvald and Hauge have pointed out, can the difference necessarily be ascribed to a hereditary tendency to immunological responses; it may be due, at least, in part, to common environmental influences. Lawrence and Wood (1968) and Lawrence (1970) feel that the findings reported in the literature raise questions about the small samples studied and the inclusion in such samples of young patients. Nevertheless, they believe that a polygenic inheritance is suggested by their own data and those published by Harvald and Hauge. This interpretation of the data has been disputed by O'Brien (1967). He has pointed out that the concordance rates for Mz twins are low: more specifically, in view of the bias toward reporting on Mz rather than Dz twins, the difference in corcordance rates (25 percent versus about 10 percent) is not impressive. Moesmann (1959) had come to the same conclusion earlier.

The consensus of opinion, therefore, seems to be that hereditary factors, as judged by twin studies (and studies of families), play only a small role, but a numerically undetermined one, in the etiology of rheumatoid arthritis (Lawrence, 1970; Schull and Cobb, 1969).

Although genetic factors do play a role in the disease, they do not alone account for its etiology. Therefore, many investigators have searched for the environmental factors that, taken with the genetic ones, would account for the phenotype of rheumatoid arthritis. They have done so by extensive epidemiological, sociological, psychological, and bacteriological investigations.

EPIDEMIOLOGICAL AND SOCIOECONOMIC FACTORS

Methodological Problems

It is a basic premise of this chapter that the conflicting results of epidemiological and psychosocial research on rheumatoid arthritis can be properly evaluated only if the study findings reported in the literature to date are viewed in light of the diagnostic problems that presently confront epidemiologists, not only behavioral scientists. It is axiomatic that the validity of any research findings depends first and foremost on the homogeneity of the population on which the findings are based. Broadly stated, the chief impediment to an epidemiologist's efforts to select a homogeneous population for the study of rheumatoid arthritis is the lack of criteria to ensure accurate diagnosis of the disease, to differentiate it from other forms of chronic arthritic diseases, and, possibly, to differentiate forms of rheumatoid arthritis of different etiology (Kellgren, 1966; Scotch and Geiger, 1962). Within this frame of reference, attempts to study the epidemiology of rheumatoid arthritis have been hampered, in particular, by the fact that criteria have not yet been constructed that would enable definitive diagnosis of the disease during its early stages or during periods of remission. However, this does not mean that diagnosis presents no problem once the disease has entered its active phase. Kellgren's statement to that effect (1968) can be challenged on several counts.

It is Kellgren's contention that when the disease is far advanced, and major evidence of a destructive arthritis is clinically at hand, with X-ray evidence of the erosion of joints, positive tests for rheumatoid factors, rheumatoid nodules, and associated lesions, the diagnosis should present no difficulty. Some of the holes in this statement are self-evident. For one, the presence of these variables does not obviate problems of differential diagnosis. Even under these conditions, the destructive arthritis of some forms of gout can closely mimic that of rheumatoid arthritis. Secondly, as Kellgren, himself, has pointed out (1956), interrater reliability with regard to erosions of joints, as seen on X-ray, is low. And finally, as we have seen, positive tests for rheumatoid factors are not specific to rheumatoid arthrits. They occur in persons with a wide variety of other diseases, and in healthy persons as well (Bartfeld, 1960, 1969; Hill, 1968; Kellgren, 1968).

The selection of experimental populations for epidemiological study is currently based on three categories of diagnostic criteria: clinical symptoms and signs, the presence of rheumatoid factors in the sera, and X-ray signs of joint erosion. Obviously, the questions raised in the preceding paragraph regarding the reliability of two of these critera—i.e., X-ray evidence of joint erosion, and positive tests for rheumatoid factors—apply in this context as well. However, their validity can also be challenged on other grounds. To begin with, the intercorrelation of these three categories of diagnostic criteria (clinical, immunological, and X-ray) is quite low (Kellgren, 1968). Secondly, the usefulness of some of the clinical diagnostic criteria is open to debate. For example, prominent among the clinical symptoms used as criteria in early diagnosis is painful swelling and stiffness of one or more joints, particularly on arising. The problem, of course, is that all investigators do not agree that this symptom is specific to rheumatoid arthritis. Epidemiological studies have also been criticized on the grounds that active and inactive cases of rheumatoid arthritis are intermingled in some series. According to Kellgren (1968) they can be distingushed on the basis of clinical symptoms: specifically, pain on motion, tenderness or swelling in at least one joint, swelling of at least one other joint within three months of the first, and symmetrical swelling of joints other than the terminal interphalangeal joint (Ropes et al., 1958) clearly constitute criteria of the active disease.

Kellgren has also pointed out that it is evident from longitudinal studies that the frequency with which episodes of joint swelling occur increases over time. But it cannot be said with certainty that all or even some such episodes are actually related to the development of rheumatoid arthritis.

In addition to the diagnostic problems that impede the study of rheumatoid arthritis, the epidemiologist is confronted with some other very special problems: for one, criteria for diagnoses have differed since 1958, when Ropes and her co-workers (1958) were authorized by the American Rheumatism Association to set up clearly defined criteria for diagnosis. As opposed to the three categories of criteria (clinical, immunological, and X-ray) that are currently used for diagnosis, these workers divided the criteria they identified into four categories. Each of these categories consisted of 11 criteria. However, only 4 of these 11 criteria required a physician's evaluation; the remaining 7 might depend on the patient's

427

estimate of his symptoms or the judgment of an observer. Thus, epidemiological studies done prior to 1958 can hardly be compared with those done thereafter. And, by the same token, epidemiological studies that do not use the American criteria cannot be compared with those that do. To further confound the issue, nine years after Ropes et al. had delineated their criteria, quite different, stricter diagnostic criteria were constructed in New York by Bennett and Burch (1967). Specifically, these include a history of an episode of three joints, not one; swelling, limitation, subluxation, or ankylosis of three limb joints—which must include hand, wrist, and foot—on each of which one joint must be symmetrically impaired. In addition, certain joints are excluded, X-ray evidence of erosions must be present, and the serum must be positive for rheumatoid factors. As a result, even within the United States, studies that use the Ropes criteria cannot be compared with those that rely on the New York criteria (Kellgren, 1966, 1968; Lawrence, 1961).

Furthermore, the main clinical criteria used are concerned exclusively with symptoms and signs involving the joints. But these are only the most conspicuous manifestations of what, in all probability, is a systemic disease.

Another methodological defect, described by Cobb and his co-workers (Beall and Cobb, 1961; Cobb and Kasl, 1966), is that in most epidemiological studies the investigator estimates the prevalence of the disease at a particular point in time. As a result, the only cases of rheumatoid arthritis recorded are those that are giving active trouble at that time; those that are in temporary remission are ignored. Thus, Cobb and his co-workers found that if a population that had initially been examined at a given time was subsequently screened at monthly intervals over a 28-month period, the figure for probable arthritis rose from 2 percent to 15 percent, and for definite arthritis from just over 1 percent to 5 percent.

The Prevalence of Rheumatoid Arthritis by Clinical Criteria

Perhaps the study done by Cathcart and O'Sullivan (1970) demonstrates most clearly the dependence of epidemiological figures on reliable diagnostic criteria. Seventy-seven percent ($N = 4,626$) of the adult population of a New England town responded for testing. When the authors used the Ropes' criteria as the basis for a diagnosis of rheumatoid arthritis, they found that 3.8 percent of the women and 1.3 percent of the men probably or definitely had the disease. But when the stricter New York criteria were used, these figures fell to 1.55 percent and 0.14 percent respectively. Yet, some authorities who consider the New York criteria unrealistically strict argue that when diagnosis is based on clinical criteria alone, the prevalence of definite rheumatoid arthritis may range from 0.5 to 5 percent of a population, but that it increases with age (Cobb and Lawrence, 1957; Kellgren, 1966, 1968; Mikkelsen et al., 1967; O'Brien, 1967; Wolfe, 1968). Thus, the significant symptom of morning stiffness of a joint—which occurred in 11.6 percent of the men and 18.0 percent of the women under age 45 in the series studied by Cathcart and O'Sullivan—was more than doubled in those from 45 to 75 years of age. Similarly, joint pain or tenderness occurred in 7.6 percent of the men, and 11.1 percent of the women in the younger group, but rose to 16.9 percent and 33.2 percent in the older men and women. And the least common of the clinical signs and symptoms was soft-tissue swelling, which rose in prevalence from 2.1 percent in the younger women to 15.4 percent in those over 45.

The prevalence of rheumatoid arthritis appears to range from 0.5 to 5.0 percent in certain populations studied in the United States and Great Britain. The prevalence has been reported to be as high as 9.0 percent in Jamaica (Lawrence et al., 1966) and 7.5 percent in Finland (Laine, 1962), and as low as 0.5 percent in Japan (Schichikawa et al., 1966), and 0.4 percent in Michigan (Mikkelsen et al., 1967). All of these studies used the Ropes' criteria; and thus one would expect the figures to be comparable and reliable. Unfortunately, however, it is apparent on closer examination of these reports that the clinical criteria used and the populations studied were not fully comparable in all these series. For example, only severe cases were included in the Japanese series, and these series also included younger patients.

In summary, current estimates of the prevalence of definite cases of rheumatoid arthritis range from 0.34 percent (Mendez-Bryan et al., 1964) to 3.0 percent (Laine, 1962). If probable cases are included, prevalence figures range from 0.7 percent (DeGraaff, 1959) to 9.0 percent (Lawrence et al., 1966). In most studies, however, the concordance rate between clinical and radiological evidence falls progressively as the clinical diagnosis becomes less definite (Lawrence, 1970).

It is clear, then, that one can only really compare studies in which the same criteria are used by the same investigators. This proposition was tested in a study of three English populations by Lawrence (1961) and by Ansel and Lawrence (1966). The prevalence of rheumatoid arthritis by clinical criteria was the same in both sexes in two of these populations, but the prevalence of a positive SCAT was much greater in one population than in the other. In the third English population, the prevalence of the disease was only one-sixth of that found in the other two, and the prevalence of a positive SCAT was also low (Kellgren, 1966).

These data suggest that rheumatoid arthritis is a heterogeneous disease, and that certain populations harbor different proportions of the various forms of the disease, and, therefore, different proportions of positive SCATs.

The Prevalence of Rheumatoid Arthritis by X-ray Criteria

The prevalence of definite X-ray evidence of joint erosion has been reported as 0.9 percent and 1.3 percent in two populations of 1,283 and 904 subjects, respectively (Lawrence, 1961). The frequency was approximately equal in men and women (Mikkelsen, 1966), but X-ray evidence of severe damage to the joints was found more frequently in women.

The Prevalence of Rheumatoid Factors in the General Population

Mention must be made, once again, of the relatively low correlation between the three tests commonly used for rheumatoid factors—the SCAT, the LFT, and the BFT (Ball et al., 1962; Goldenberg et al., 1960). Incidence figures also depend on the titer at which the test is considered significant. The best figures on the incidence of rheumatoid factors in the sera of the general population have been provided by Aho (1961), based on his study of 539 Finnish subjects. Three percent were SCAT-positive, 5.4 percent LFT-positive, and 2.4 percent BFT-positive. Obviously, some of these subjects had definite or probable rhematoid arthritis; when they were taken out of the series, the figures reported for the remaining nonarthritic population were 1.6 percent SCAT-positive, 4.1 percent LFT-positive, and 1.4 percent BFT-positive. If a positive result on any one of these tests was used as the criterion, the incidence of rheumatoid factors in this nonarthritic population rose to 7.2 percent. Figures as high as 12 percent have also been reported for th SCAT (Scotch and Geiger, 1962). In Cathcart's and O'Sullivan's study (1970), the SCAT was positive in 0.8 percent of the men under 44 and in 0.9 percent of those between 45 and 74 years of age. It was positive in 0.7 percent of their group of younger women, and 1.8 percent of the women over 45. The BFT was positive in 1.3 percent of the younger men and 0.8 percent of the younger women, and in 2.4 percent of the older men and 2.7 percent of the older women.

Much higher age-related figures for the SCAT were obtained on an English population by Ball and Lawrence (1961), Lawrence (1961), and Laine (1962). These workers also found that the prevalence was twice as high in urban as in rural inhabitants (5.1 percent versus 2.4 percent), which led them to conclude that infection might play a role in the disease (Lawrence, 1963). Mikkelsen and his co-workers (1967), who used only the LFT in their Michigan study, found that positive tests at comparable titers occurred with equal frequency in men and women (3.4 percent versus 3.3 percent). However, their prevalence increased progressively with age to 14 percent in men and 9.2 percent in women over 70 years old. Similar findings were obtained by Hooper et al. (1972) in their Australian study: the prevalence of rheumatoid factors was evenly distributed in men and women, and rose serially with age, being present in 1.6 percent of the subjects in the 21 to 30 age group, 2.1 to 2.5 percent of those between ages 31 and 60, 4.1 percent between ages 71 and 80, and 5.9 percent between ages 81 and 85.

What needs to be emphasized once again is that one cannot automatically assume that all the individuals with positive serological tests suffer from rheumatoid arthritis. One would expect such a group to include persons with a wide variety of disease, as well as healthy individuals. Since there are several rheumatoid factors it is necessary to know whether the three that are generally considered to be important in this disease are present in those individuals with positive serological test.

There is a correlation, however, between the concentration of the factor and the likelihood of the disease occurring. Lawrence (1967) found that 20 percent of the individuals in his series who had a positive SCAT and 26 percent of those whose LFT was positive had clinical rheumatoid arthritis (Mikkelsen et al., 1967), and that the higher the titer, the greater the likelihood that the clinical disease was present. He also concluded from his study findings that the presence of rheumatoid factors in blood constitutes a "marker" of those in a population who are at risk for the disease.

GEOGRAPHIC DISTRIBUTION

It is increasingly clear from population studies, several of which were reviewed above that rheumatoid arthritis has a worldwide distribution (Blumberg et al., 1961; Kellgren, 1968; Valkenburg, 1963). Contrary to popular belief, the disease is not limited to people living in cold climates; the highest prevalence rate for rheumatoid arthritis has been reported in Jamaica. As might be expected, however, given the methodological problems outlined earlier in this section, precise figures for the incidence and prevalence of the disease are very difficult to obtain. The need for comparative studies, based on the same clearly defined criteria and using the same observers has already been mentioned; in addition, these studies must, of course, use populations matched for age and sex. Moreover, apart from his obligation to fulfill these basic methodological prerequisites, the epidemiologist must take still another potential source of research error into consideration: it may be that the tendency to complain of symptoms such as morning stiffness or pain in the joints (and to seek medical help) differs in different populations, in men and women, at different ages, and perhaps in different cultures, with the result that the prevalence of rheumatoid arthritis by clinical criteria may vary accordingly, whereas the prevalence of X-ray changes or positive serological tests may remain unaltered by these variables. This may account for the fact that in both of the studies described below the investigators assessed the prevalence of rheumatoid arthritis by only two of the three categories of diagnostic criteria used in epidemiological studies—X-ray evidence of joint erosion and positive tests for rheumatoid factors.

Kellgren (1966, 1968) published figures on the prevalence of these criteria in nine series from the United States, Canada, England, Jamaica, and Germany. The populations studied included men and women from 35 to 64. Positive X-ray evidence of erosive arthritis ranged from 1.5 percent (Watford, England) to 12.1 percent (Jamaica) of the populations studied. The prevalence of positive SCATs ranged from 1.1 percent (Watford, England) to 9.2 percent (Pima, Arizona), and the prevalence of positive LFTs or BFTs ranged from about 5 percent (Tecumseh, Michigan) to 20.3 percent (Pima, Arizona). Interestingly, the prevalence of positive tests for rheumatoid factors in a series of Blackfoot Indians studies was 5.6 percent.

Reference has been made to the findings, by Ball and Lawrence (1961), Laine (1962), and Lawrence (1961), that the prevalence of positive SCATs was higher in an urban than in a rural population in England. Some similar evidence has been accumulated by Miall and his co-workers (1958), who used X-ray, as well as positive tests for rheumatoid factors, as diagnostic criteria. Specifically, these authors concluded that rheumatoid arthritis was more prevalent in a mining town in Wales than in a rural area in that country. However, in the rural area the prevalence rose sharply after the age of 50 from about 0.5 percent to 4 percent in both men and women. In the town, the prevalence began to rise in women at that age, but only to about 2 percent. In men, it rose slowly to about 1.2 percent at age 50, and then began to decline. These findings could not be confirmed in the United States.

Comment

Unfortunately, it is clear that because of the methodological problems commented on in this subsection, valid comparisons cannot be made between populations in different regions of the same country, in different countries, and in different ethnic groups. Consequently, it is impossible as yet to investigate with any accuracy why this disease might be more prevalent in one region or culture than another, or in one country than another. No attempt can be made at this stage in our knowledge to investigate the relationship between specific sociocultural, geographic, or other environmental factors

431

and the predisposition to or initiation and recurrence of rheumatoid arthritis. And data on this relationship are crucial to our understanding of the disease, for genetic factors alone seem to account for only a small proportion of the etiology.

Perhaps epidemiological studies should focus mainly on patients with evident clinical disease according to the strict New York criteria—definite X-ray evidence of joint erosion and positive serological evidence of the presence of rheumatoid factors. The same criteria should probably also be used in all retrospective psychosomatic studies so that there can be no question about the diagnosis.

Distribution by Sex

It is generally believed that there are considerably more women than men with rheumatoid arthritis, and this belief has been borne out by many studies, though not all (Mikkelsen, 1966). Thus, in two large series the ratios found were 55:45 (Thompson et al., 1938) and 3:2 (Smith, 1932); but in other series the ratios were 5:2 (Mikkelsen et al., 1967), 3:1 (Gibberd, 1965), and 4:1 or higher (Cathcart and O'Sullivan, 1970). Probably, the earlier series relied mainly on hospitalized patients with a variety of other forms of chronic arthritis, or used clinical criteria only, which varied from series to series. Yet, even when "standard" clinical criteria were used, the female-to-male ratios varied widely, ranging from 0.5:1.0 (Behrend and Lawrence, 1965) to 13.0:1.0 (Shichikawa et al., 1966).

When X-ray evidence or tests for rheumatoid factors (SCAT and LFT or BFT) were used as diagnostic criteria, some equally startling discrepancies emerged in patients between the ages of 35 and 64. These discrepancies have been summarized by Kellgren (1968): in several series in which X-ray evidence alone was used, the female-to-male ratio ranged from 0.2:1.3. When the SCAT was used, the ratio ranged in various series from 0.3:2.8, and when the BFT or LFT was used, it ranged from 0.7:1.6.

Clearly, then, there seems to be no consistent trend; the female-to-male ratio depends, in part, on the diagnostic criteria used. On balance, the median ratio appears to be unity. Because women do not seem to be at greater risk than men, another possible clue to the etiology of the disease is false.

Age at Onset

Information about the age at onset of the disease may provide clues about its etiology and pathogenesis, but great variations exist from series to series as to the age of onset of rheumatoid arthritis. For a variety of reasons, many series exclude patients with juvenile rheumatoid arthritis. The peak incidence of onset has been between the ages of 20 and 40 in some series and between 40 and 50 in others (Empire Rheumatism Council, 1950; Short et al., 1957). However, the age distribution at onset may differ for men and women. Thus, in Short's series, the peak incidence in men occurred between the ages of 25 and 35, with a second peak between 45 and 55. In women, the peak incidence occurred between the ages of 50 and 60. In Gibberd's series (1965), on the other hand, the median age at onset was 43.6 in women, and 50 in men. There may also be an association between age of onset and marital status; Lewis-Faning (1950) found that the peak age at onset was earlier for single men and women than for married ones. And, finally, the disease may have an earlier onset in some countries than in others. In Nigeria, for example, the peak age at onset was between 20 and 40 (Greenwood, 1969a, c).

These incidence figures are based on hospitalized patients and records. In population surveys, the figures show that the point prevalence rises with age (Kellgren, 1966, 1968). But, according to Kellgren (1966), this rise is largely accounted for by mild cases occurring in women over 50 years of age, many of which are probably not seen in hospitals. X-ray evidence of joint erosions of the hands and feet occurs with about equally increasing prevalence as men and women become older. As noted earlier, tests for rheumatoid factors are also age-related, and become positive with increasing frequency in aging populations, especially in men over 65 (Kellgren, 1966, 1968). But this increase depends, in part, on which test is used.

It is tempting, of course, to try to relate the age of onset and the course of the disease to menopause in women. Unfortunately, the figures available are not sufficiently convincing to determine whether such an association occurs (Lewis-Faning, 1950; Short et al., 1957; Slacter, 1943).

Finally, it should be noted that efforts to accumulate definitive data regarding the age at onset of rheumatoid arthritis have been impeded by the fact that in some series, the peak ages at onset of osteoarthritis and rheumatoid arthritis have been about the same, especially for women, and the two diseases have been confused.

Ethnic Origin

In the series of hospitalized patients studied by Short et al. (1957) the incidence of rheumatoid arthritis in native-born American patients was greater than in the population at large. Short and his co-workers also found there were significantly more patients of both sexes of Scandinavian origin than would be expected by chance, and that the incidence of rheumatoid arthritis was very low in black persons. In contrast to these findings, a more recent U.S. survey of nonhospitalized persons, reported by Wolfe (1968), showed that the prevalence of rheumatoid arthritis was the same in blacks and whites without regard to sex, although Lichtman and his group (1967) subsequently found that the level of immunoglobulins (IgG) and the prevalence of rheumatoid factors in the blood of healthy black men and women was significantly higher than in white men, but not white women.

These findings cannot, of course, be translated into data on ethnic differences in the incidence of the disease. It cannot be assumed that the correlation of ethnic differences with differences in the levels of IgGs, and with the presence or absence of rheumatoid factors, is a causal one. Some authorities have ascribed these differences to genetic factors, and others to nutritional ones (Lichtman et al., 1967; Valkenburg, 1963). In any case, rheumatoid arthritis seems to occur with equal frequency in both black and white Americans, regardless of differences in IgG levels or in the presence or absence of rheumatoid factors. The disease has also been described in many different African countries, but no comparative studies have been made of its incidence and prevalence in black Africans and Americans (Cave et al., 1965; Greenwood, 1969a, b, c; Hall, 1965; Hijmans et al., 1964;

433

Shaper and Shaper, 1958). It may, run a different course in black Africans than in Americans; in Nigerians, at least, it appears to be less disabling (Greenwood, 1969a,c).

Socioeconomic Factors

Cobb et al. (1965) found that the male patients with rheumatoid arthritis in their series were less-well-educated than a control group, and that the great majority were manual workers. Similarly, Engel (1968) and Wolfe (1968) found that in the United States the clinical criteria of Ropes et al. (1958) and the BFT were more-frequently positive in subjects of poor education and low income (regardless of age) who were "nervous." According to Rimón (1969), rheumatoid arthritis is much more prevalent in the lower social classes in Finland.

The disease is more prevalent in the industrial north than in the rural south of England (Ball and Lawrence, 1961; Kellgren, 1966). According to Wolfe (1968), however, in the United States, prevalence rates are highest in those who live on farms, and in manual workers living either in a town or the country (Cobb et al., 1965). And Slacter (1943) found that 105 of the 288 patients in his series were engaged in domestic work. More of the patients in Lewis-Faning's series (1950) worked indoors than was customary for the population at large. Yet in the series studied by Short and his co-workers (1957) no relationship emerged between type of occupation and the onset or course of the disease.

On balance, therefore, one may conclude that the disease is more prevalent in the less-educated, unskilled, manual laborer for reasons that are poorly understood. It may be that such persons more-often injure, or at least use their extremities more, thus predisposing themselves to the disease.

Burch's finding (1968) that single and divorced patients with rheumatoid arthritis have a higher mortality rate than married patients does not parallel the incidence pattern reported earlier by Cobb et al. (1957). Specifically, the earlier authors had found an age- and sex-adjusted prevalence rate of 0.9 percent for single persons, 2.2 percent for married persons, and 3.6 percent for persons who were separated from a spouse by death or divorce. Two years later this report was amended: only male divorcees had a higher prevalence rate than married persons (King and Cobb, 1959). However, this later finding was not confirmed by Wolfe (1968).

On the other hand, the authors of three studies—Cobb et al. (1959), King and Cobb (1958), and Rimón (1969)—agree that the divorce rate in patients with rheumatoid arthritis is higher than in the population at large. In the series of 100 arthritic Finnish women studied by Rimón, the divorce rate was twice that of the Finnish population as a whole. Of the nondivorced patients in the series, 53 percent were married, 30 percent had never married, and 8 percent were widowed. (The age-adjusted rate for widowhood in this series was slightly lower than that in the general population.)

The data on socioeconomic factors in rheumatoid arthritis are often conflicting, and no definitive conclusion can be drawn from them. It is not possible to ascertain the reasons for these discrepancies. One may suspect that the patient populations reported in the various series are not comparable in regard to the diagnostic criteria used to select them. The inconclusive nature of the findings are regretable: were they conclusive we might be able to understand their meaning and the roles manual labor, climatic conditions, marital discord, or divorce play in this disease.

434

PSYCHOLOGICAL FACTORS

For many years, experienced clinicians have observed that rheumatoid arthritis may begin, or exacerbations may occur, in patients who find themselves in settings conducive to conscious worry, grief, or depression. Presumably, patients who are psychologically predisposed to this disease respond to events with these affects. What follows is a review of the nature of the events that produce these affects and the nature of the psychological predisposing factors that sensitize the future patient. Because no prospective studies have been done on subjects who are at risk for this disease, these predispositions have been arrived at retrospectively, after disease onset. They are based on self-descriptions and descriptions by others of the conflicts, defenses, behaviors, and the personal relationships of patients. The methodolgical problems inherent in such studies are especially severe and will be discussed first. The data that assigns to these patients a specific unconscious conflict about anger and rebellion expressed in a desire to dominate, control, or tyrannize others when they are adults will also be reviewed. The manner in which patients express their anger and rebellion has its own developmental history and is expressed differently during childhood, adolescence, and adulthood. By a conflict specific to rheumatoid arthritis patients, Alexander (1950) meant that the configuration of the conflict was different from the configuration seen in other "psychosomatic diseases." He did not mean that the configuration of the conflict was unique to these patients when compared to the general population. But he did believe that not everyone could develop this disease; only persons who harbored this conflict and were also physiologically predisposed to the disease would develop it when they were separated from the person whom they had previously dominated, controlled, or tyrannized.

In contrast, many others have described the control that many of these patients exert over the anger, bitterness, and resentment that are the heritage of unrequited dependency wishes in childhood. These reactions to frustration in childhood are general; they are not specific to these patients and not organized in any special configuration.

Methodological Issues

In the past 20 years three articles have been published—by King (1955), Moos (1964), and Scotch and Geiger (1962)—that deal with the methodological problems inherent in clinical studies of the role of sociological, psychological, and social variables in rheumatoid arthritis. Similar concerns could be expressed about clinical studies of rheumatoid arthritis at every level of investigation. Much of the clinical data reported in the literature to date is based on hospitalized patients, on chart records (which are notoriously poor sources of information), on studies of selected families, and on the assumption that rheumatoid arthritis is a disease of joints, so that disease onset is associated with the development of symptoms and signs of joint disease. In fact, however, there is impressive evidence that rheumatoid arthritis may be a systemic disease. Also no agreement has been reached about the status of Felty's or Sjögren's syndrome, psoriatic arthritis, and other disorders with regard to rheumatoid arthritis, so that some series include such patients and and others do not.

Thus, the task of selecting a homogeneous population for study poses a major problem not only for those who would address themselves to the psychological and social aspects of rheumatoid arthritis, but also for those who are concerned with the epidemiology and pathophysiology of this disease.

In addition to these core issues, five problems intrinsic to psychosomatic clinical research (but not unique to this aspect of clinical investigation) have been identified:

1. The problem of selecting control populations is emphasized in the three articles about methodology. The absence of control groups constitutes a serious methodological weakness in most psychiatrically oriented studies—and one that is rather surprising in light of Alexander's influence on psychosomatic research. Although they were not formally labeled as such, Alexander's studies on rheumatoid arthritis were implicitly comparative ones.

   The need for control groups is self-evident, and it is equally apparent that subjects and controls must be matched for age, sex, and other characteristics. But beyond these basic considerations, the criteria for selection of a comparison group may have to be determined by what one wishes to study. For example, there is evidence that, in terms of certain psychological test scores, patients with rheumatoid arthritis may differ more from each other than from healthy family members (Moos and Solomon, 1964a, 1965a) or from a hospital (control) population (Rimón, 1969). Again, if one wishes to control for the effects of pain on the psychological functioning of patients with rheumatoid arthritis, it is not enough to select a comparison group consisting of patients with another form of polyarthritis that is clearly distinct from rheumatoid arhritis, for the relationship of many of the other forms of painful polyarthritis to rheumatoid arthritis is by no means clear. But there is a more basic problem involved: how does one truly match subjects and controls on the severity of pain (Graham, 1972) or its duration and meaning to the patient?

2. Both King (1955) and Moos (1964) have pointed out that many psychosomatic clinical studies fail to provide sufficient information about the medical diagnostic criteria used to select patients for study; the medication prescribed for them; the presence or absence of rheumatoid factors; and the duration, severity, stage, and state of the disease (e.g., how many and which joints are involved and the degree of structural and functional impairment). It is, in addition, essential to know the age, socioeconomic status, intelligence, and educational background of patients and controls. Only in the last few years have investigators become aware of the need to incorporate these measures into their studies in order to eliminate sample bias.

3. Problems of experimenter bias and theoretical bias have been thoughtfully reviewed by Moos (1964): for example, the results obtained by the investigator who focuses on the feelings and motives of the patient, rather than the way in which these are expressed, transformed, or handled, will differ from the results reported by the investigator who places primary emphasis on the "effectiveness" of the patient's mode of expressing or handling his feelings and motives.

4. In many clinical psychiatric studies, inferences are made that could form the basis for validating studies by means of psychological tests. But the clinical observations are not verified, either because the tests are not sensitive enough to test the observations or the inferences from which they derive (King, 1955), or because

the tests attempt to quantify the unquantifiable. Although quantification and objectivity are much to be desired in such studies, a test like the MMPI only quantifies gross clinical categories or a very limited range of affects. The choice of the verifying test must be guided by the nature of the observation one wishes to verify and must, in addition, be sensitive enough to pick up the nuances in feelings, fantasy, or imagery of which human beings are capable.

5. Problems in the interpretation of data, which are often related to the use of appropriate control groups, emerge with particular clarity in the study published by the Empire Rheumatism Council (1950). Essentially, the Council found that "such mental stresses as may be engendered by the circumstances studied are likely to occur as frequently among non-sufferers as sufferers." Actually, the number of "circumstances" about which questions were asked was limited; questionnaires were used for this purpose, and no reliability checks were done. As many have pointed out, including the senior author of the Council's report, it is not the circumstance, per se, but its impact on and meaning for the patient that must be assessed. Nevertheless, despite its obvious conceptual and methodological flaws, this study is cited frequently in the literature in refutation of the role of psychological and social factors in rheumatoid arthritis.

Psychological Studies of Children with Rheumatoid Arthritis

The belief that juvenile rheumatoid arthritis is clinically distinct from the adult form is strongly held (Brewer et al., 1972; Bywaters, 1968; Calabro, 1966). Three distinct, clinical subforms of juvenile rheumatoid arthritis are now recognized (Brewer et al., 1972; Calabro et al., 1970). Because rheumatoid arthritis in children may be heterogeneous, the very few studies that have been done in the past may have to be repeated.

In fact, only one clinical study, by Blom and Nicholls (1953), has been reported in the past 20 years. (Another noteworthy study, by Thomas (1936), had been published 17 years earlier.) This study involved 28 hospitalized children (23 girls and 5 boys) who had been brought to the attention of a psychiatrist because of their depressive affect, as evidenced by their refusal to eat, to take medication, and to participate in physiotherapy. Thus, they represented a special group. In this series the illness had begun insidiously with vague symptoms: in 15 of the children the disease had its onset before the age of 6; in another 9 children it had begun between the ages of 10 and 12 years.

When seen in the hospital the children were all depressed, although three of them had previously been elated, only to become depressed, or had alternated between these moods. In addition to the behaviors described above, their depression was characterized by immobility, an apathetic expression, unresponsiveness, and a tendency to withdraw from others. When elated, one child, age 6, swore, spat at the hospital personnel, shouted, and spent much of her time making cutouts.

The children either could not or would not express their feelings and did not complain or make demands. They were neat, tidy, and self-contained. It was the authors' impression that all feelings and demands were perceived as dangerous, in part because they were associated with violent and destructive fantasies, often characterized by wishes to bite and devour or to be poisoned. The children's relationships to others (including their mothers) were profoundly ambivalent, but their ties to their mothers (in which wishes to receive

437

were predominant) were nevertheless very close. Their frustration tolerance was low. When frustration occurred, it was followed by the biting fanatasies. These impressions were confirmed by the author's observations of the nature and quality of the doctor-patient relationship as it evolved during the study.

The children's close, ambivalent ties to their mothers seemed to be related, in part, to the fact that the mothers were mistrustful of close relationships, fearing their dependency on others (including their children). Yet the children were very insistent on their demands for assistance from hospital personnel in managing the concrete details of their everyday lives. It is of interest that in one-third of the cases in this series, the mothers were themselves "deprived," or had lost important relatives, or had been separated from their husbands when the child was very young. Concomitantly, the authors found that these mothers were inordinately sensitive to loss and reacted to it with feelings of depression, resignation, fatalism, and stoicism, which made them unresponsive to the wishes of the child. In half of the cases studied, the child's disease was precipitated by a loss that occurred in the mother's life. And in about one-quarter of the cases, there was a recurrence of the arthritis when losses and separations occurred again or threatened the mother or the child.

All the mothers devoted themselves slavishly to their children, never complaining and never expressing their feelings. The child, in turn, developed an excessive dependence on his cold, self-sacrificing mother. The result was an intensely close relationship between the mother and this child who needed her. It differed from her relationship with her other children—in part, because very often this child was carried or born at a time when the mother had suffered a loss. Blom and Nicholls concluded from these observations that the children had become depressed during hospitalization in reaction to separation from their mothers.

The authors were also interested in the children's reactions to their disease and compared their findings in this regard to the findings obtained by Holder et al. (1953) in a similar study of children with rheumatic fever. Most of the children with rheumatic fever were anxious about being ill or felt guilty about something they thought they had done to cause the disease. In contrast, although the childen with rheumatoid arthritis were depressed about their hospitalization, they seemed fairly optimistic about their disease and free of guilt feelings.

Social and Psychological Precipitants of Adult Rheumatoid Arthritis

Descriptions of the nature of the life events that have been associated with the onset of rheumatoid arthritis, and figures on their frequency, have varied from series to series. In one of the most extensive (and controlled) series, Lewis-Faning (1950) studied 292 patients and the same number of control subjects by means of a questionnaire limited to eight categories of life events. The frequency of association with rheumatoid arthritis was:

Death in the family	14.4%
Illness or accident in the family	12.6%
Experience of an upsetting event	11.3%
Occasion to nurse a sick relative	9.2%
Period of unhappy family life	3.1%
Drop in family income	2.7%
Broken engagement	1.0%

438

He concluded that "mental stresses" occurred with equal frequency in patients and controls and stated that "any difference between the reaction of sufferers and non-sufferers to the stresses reside in some feature of the sufferer himself rather than in any difference of stress experience. . . . No evidence was obtained. . .that traumata or other events likely to be associated with mental stress were precipitating factors." He did not specify what the "features residing in the sufferer" were. The relative psychological impact and meaning of the event (King, 1955), conjoined with a biological predisposition to the disease, could account for the observation that one person fell ill and another did not when undergoing the same life experiences.

When patients were directly interviewed, there was an increase in the frequency of identifiable and meaningful life events that preceded, coincided, or were associated with the onset of joint manifestations. Such events were described by, respectively, 45 percent (Halliday, 1942), 62 percent (Cobb et al., 1939), and 100 percent (Shocket et al., 1969) of patients in studies published in the past 40 years.

It has been recognized for many years that there is an association between certain life events, the emotional response they occasion, and the onset of rheumatoid arthritis. The great clinician Sir William Osler wrote in 1892 that "the association of the disease with shock, worry and grief" was so frequent that it was not a chance one, and his statement has been confirmed in controlled studies (Cobb et al., 1939; Rimón, 1969) and in attempts to assess the meaning of an event to a patient and his psychological and behavioral responses to it. It is generally conceded that the life events that precede or coincide with the onset or the exacerbation of the disease run the gamut. However, the ones most frequently noted are: separation from a relative, or fear for an ill relative; bereavement by death, divorce, infidelity, separation, jilting, or job loss (Cecil, 1945; Cobb et al., 1939; Halliday, 1937b, 1941; Ludwig, 1952, 1954; Rimón, 1969; Shocket et al., 1969); disappointment and disillusionment by another person (Ludwig, 1952, 1954); and deprivation (or fear of it) as the result of financial loss or unemployment (Cecil, 1945; Cobb et al., 1939; Edstrom. 1952; Halliday, 1937b; Rimón, 1969). Interestingly enough, Ludwig (1952, 1954) described one patient who had annual recrudescences of arthritis on the anniversaries of the deaths of close relatives.

At times, the onset of the disease has not been clearcut but has occurred in concert with mounting perennial marital discord (Johnson et al., 1947; Rimón, 1969; Shocket et al., 1969), because of marked difficulties with other people at work (Cobb et al., 1959; Rimón, 1969), or when a patient was forced to submit sexually to someone (Alexander, 1950; French and Shapiro, 1949; Johnson et al., 1947; Rimón, 1969). Joint symptoms flared up and the patient became angry (Barchilon, 1963; Johnson et al., 1947), either because of an unwanted pregnancy or because the demands of caring for wanted or unwanted children had become intolerable (Rimón, 1969), or when the pressure of work or duties restricted personal freedom and caused feelings of resentment and rebellion (Cobb, 1959). Graham et al. (1962) reported that the "attitude" of "being tied down and struggling to get free" was specifically associated with flareups of arthritis.[*] They used this "attitude" as a diagnostic criterion to study in a controlled manner a number of patients with various diseases, and they found it had diagnostic validity.

---

[*] It is, of course, possible that this "attitude" describes in metaphor the perception of the physical restriction that the illness imposes upon the patient.

A very interesting and novel approach was taken by Meyerowitz et al. (1968). They studied eight sets of twins discordant for rheumatoid arthritis and observed that the twins in each pair differed in personality and behavoir. The affected twin had taken care of others, was disappointed by marriage or unhappily married, or had lost the emotional support of her parents. Each of these situations had made the arthritic twin feel restricted or imposed demands on her. She felt "entrapped" in them and limited in her choices, mobility, and activities.

From these studies, one may conclude that bereavement and separation form one class of events, and being overwhelmed, overpowered, or restricted form another. However, the matter is not so simple. A divorce was followed by clinical improvement (Shocket et al., 1969), presumably because the marriage had imposed an intolerable burden on the patient. Alexander et al. (1968) on the basis of their observations did not believe that the onset of the disease was caused by environmental demands that limited the future patient's freedom. Rather, they believed that disease onset was associated with the departure of someone whom the future patient had been able to dominate—a situation that is the opposite of that described by many others. The situations and psychological reactions associated with the onset of the disease have been observed to occur in concert with its exacerbations after a remission in its course (Barchilon, 1963; Cobb et al., 1939; Rimón, 1969).

However, the onset and course of rheumatoid arthritis is highly variable. It may begin suddenly or gradually, it may remit only to recur, or it may be remorselessly unremitting. Only Rimón (1969) has correlated the nature of the onset with the social setting and the patient's psychological reactions to it. On the basis of his study of 100 women, he concluded that in one group, environmental events were distinctly identifiable, the onset of the joint symptoms was sudden, and the symptoms of the disease were severe. The incidence of rheumatoid was low in the relatives of this group of patients. In a second group of patients the onset of the disease was insidious, the onset conditions could not be detected with certainty, and the disease was more prevalent in family members. However, this conclusion must be interpreted in the light of the fact that the reconstruction of past events in the lives of patients is more difficult when there is no abrupt or recent onset of symptoms. Rimón's second group of patients were also more likely to deny any perception of events and feelings and thus make their reliable retrieval difficult for the observer.

Rimón's study is, however, a noteworthy beginning. It may very well be that people with different kinds of psychological predispositions respond differently to different situations, depending on whether they come upon them abruptly or with a slowly rising crescendo. The women who, like a martyr, has dedicated herself to her children may suddenly be faced with their leaving home; another person who has long-suffered but adapted to mounting work pressures may finally find them intolerable.

Only future studies can find the answers to these speculations. In any case, there can be little doubt that in a proportion of patients the disease begins in a setting of bereavement and of separation from people with whom the patient had a rather specific relationship, which was colored either by a need to dominate or be dominated, or both.

It is of some interest then that Parkes (1964) found bereavement associated with complaints of musculoskeletal pains and many of the "prodromal" symptoms listed by Short et al. (1957). These, however, were not specifically ascribed to rheumatoid arthritis in Parkes' study. He observed an unselected group of widows, over and under the age of 65 years, for 2 years before and 1½ years after bereavement. The younger widows consulted the physician 240 percent more than previously for depression and insomnia, and significantly more for pains and aches referrable to the muscles and joints. Maddison and co-workers (1967, 1968) studied 375 widows and 199 married women up to 60 years of age in Boston, Massachusetts, and Sydney, Australia. Significant differences in responses to a health questionnaire were obtained: 21 percent of the American and 32 percent of the Australian widows complained of a decline in health, compared to 7.2 percent and 2.0 percent of the comparison group. The widows reliably complained more of headache, blurred vision, weight loss, anorexia or excessive eating, vomiting, indigestion, dyspnea, palpitations, frequent infection, chest pain, and generalized aches and pains.

Nature of the Reactions to the Social and Psychological Precipitants

In rheumatoid arthritis a wide variety of precipitating events have been described; these changes in the patient's life may disrupt his or her customary patterns of psychological adaptation, thus initiating the disease. These changes include the birth of a child, a miscarriage, a death in the family, changes in occupation and in marital adjustment, and disappointment. However, as Alexander (1950) and Rimón (1969) have pointed out, one must look for the meaning of these events to the patient. The meaning may be critical and individual. Alexander believed that in women patients, changes in a marriage, disappointment, or abandonment by a man increased their latent resentment and rebellion against men. When forced by events or experiences to accept a womanly (e.g., a mothering) status, against which she had secretly fought, the patient experienced angry resentment and nonacceptance of her new role. Resignation and hopelessness might follow such an experience. But other responses have also been documented: for example, fears of separation, resentment of superiors, or emotional "shock" following exposure to extreme danger (Cobb, 1959; Halliday, 1942). Outbursts of anger and jealous rage were observed by Barchilon (1963), Halliday (1942), and Rimón (1969) in their patients. However, the most-common and the best-studied responses have been depressive reactions at the time of onset of the disease or during its course.

The Relationship of Depression to the Precipitating Conditions, to Pain, and to the Course of the Illness

If bereavement plays a part in the onset of the disease in some patients, one might expect a priori a high incidence of grief or depressive reactions. As might also be expected, figures on the incidence of depressive feeling or mood states after disease onset vary widely from 2.2 percent (Gibberd, 1965) to 80 percent (Laine and Lehti, 1969). However, in reporting the lowest incidence, Gibberd did not specify by what criteria the mood states were ascertained, nor how carefully the inquiry was made. Depressive mood states have been identified in psychological test data of patients in both controlled and uncontrolled studies (Moos and Solomon, 1946a, 1965a; Nalven and O'Brien, 1968). In Ganz's (1972) controlled study, the prevalence of depressive symptomatology was 47 percent. In other studies the degree of depression has been described as moderate-to-mild (Ganz et al., 1972; Rimón, 1969; Shocket et al., 1969). Self-derogatory and self-accusatory trends have also been noted by Ludwig (1952, 1954), indicating that the depressive reactions were severe. Halliday (1942) noticed an air of

441

resignation about the depressive mood, which he believed was a response to the deformities of the disease. Ludwig (1952, 1954, 1967) also mentioned that in response to bereavement, rejection, and disillusionment, patients reacted with no perceptible grief reaction, but with depression and later with anger. There is some agreement that in view of the patients' difficulty in expressing anger, some of them become depressed and express guilt feelings, whereas other angry patients increase their motor activity when they are not helped (Barchilon, 1963; French and Shapiro, 1949) or when separation occurs.

It would of course be important to document that the depressive feeling or mood state antecedes disease onset. If it begins after the joint symptoms begin, it could be argued that the depressive mood state is the patient's response to pain or to having a chronic, recurrent, disabling disease (Hart, 1970). Thomas (1936) and Halliday (1937a), however, found that in 9 of 31 patients the depressive mood states had begun weeks or months prior to the physical disease. When the joint symptoms appeared, the depression was relieved (Kütemeyer, 1963).

Such a response probably occurs only in some patients, because it was not observed either by Mendelenyi and Marton (1960) or Rimón (1969). Some patients become depressed long after the start of the disease. Rimón (1969) found that 29 of the 100 women patients were depressed; 2 of the 29 had become so sometime during the course of the disease. Such a datum still does not tell us whether the depression was in response to the physical disease or to intercurrent life events. Three of Rimón's 29 depressed patients became less depressed during the course of the disease. Fully half of the patients who were depressed at the onset or during the course of the disease had had long-standing histories of psychiatric illnesses of various kinds, which were most-often depressive in nature. The rate of progression of the rheumatoid arthritis was slower and the degree of disability less in patients whose depressive mood improved after the onset of the illness: 7 of 10 women in whom the disease progressed very rapidly were overtly depressed.

In the light of these findings, it is of some interest that the physical disability improved when patients were treated with antidepressive medication, such as the monoamine oxidase inhibitors (Krammer, 1961; Scherbel and Harrison, 1959) and imiprimine (Scott, 1969). Scott noted that pain and stiffness were relieved and motor function improved. The effects were significantly greater than those brought about by a placebo. Wright et al. (1963) believed that the pathological process and physical disturbances in the disease were unchanged by nialamide, but that it improved the mood, brought about relief of symptoms, and decreased the need for steroid medication. Rowe (1969) and Shocket et al. (1969) reported that disabling deterioration of the disease could be prevented by the treatment of long-standing personality disturbance or a depressive mood, and Lowman et al. (1954) found that those patients who were more adaptable, able to rely on rehabilitative measures and on their physical, psychological, and social resources, were more hopeful, trusting, independent, and confident and could also be rehabilitated more easily. They had a better prognosis than those patients who felt hopeless and who made no attempt to care for themselves or be independent.

Moos and Solomon (1965c) studied two groups of women patients who were matched as far as possible for the stage and the duration of definite, or "classical," rheumatoid arthritis. The differences between the two groups consisted of a discrepancy between the functional incapacity and the "objective" signs of the disease. When MMPI test protocols were

442

independently and blindly sorted by two observers, those patients with the greater degree of functional incapacity were also more anxious, apathetic, depressed, and less likely to be motivated to recover. They were also socially more withdrawn, dependent, plaintive, and emotionally labile. In other words, they coped less well with their disease. In addition, these authors found (1964b) that those patients whose disease progressed more slowly scored higher on scales reflecting compliance, conscientiousness, perfectionism, denial of hostility, social responsibility and motives for social status, and strong moral principles. Furthermore, those patients whose disease was progressing more rapidly were unable to use previously successful "coping" mechanisms. They were more anxious and depressed than other patients; they were less compliant, compulsive, and able to control their anger; and they were more-socially isolated and, therefore, lonely.

Although the different reactions of these patients are not unique to rheumatoid arthritis but can be found in many diseases (Moos and Solomon, 1964b, 1965c), the results indicate that there are at least two groups of patients who demonstrate different interactions between the disease, their personal and emotional reactions to it, the incapacity, their response to treatment, and therefore their prognosis (Moos and Solomon, 1964b, c, 1965c; Solomon and Moos, 1965a). The interaction between their psychological symptoms and their disability seems to influence the course of the disease by determining how successfully they coped with their various distresses.

The question of the relationship of pain to depression has not been clarified by any of the foregoing. It is usually assumed that there is only one direction in which the equation can be written: pain causes depression. Basing his belief on common sense, Hart (1970) proclaimed that anyone with a chronic, recurrent, painful, or unremitting disease would be depressed, but quoted no data to support or refute his contention. And this belief has not been borne out by data: it does not explain, for example, why those patients who were the most-severely incapacitated or ill the longest were not all depressed. Ganz et al. (1972) found no relationship between the number of psychiatric symptoms and the duration of the disease, the age of the patient, or the medication he or she had received. Some patients responded to pain, care, or medication by a lifting of the depressive mood, and some did not. Others were indeed depressed by being physically ill or having pain and deformity (e.g., Nalven and O'Brien, 1964). However, much more-careful study must be done of the interactions of these factors and the specific personality of patients before this enigma is resolved. No simple relationship exists between pain, anger, guilt, or depression. Moldofsky and Chester (1970) and Moldofsky (1970) have reported on a prospective study in which they independently measured pain perception (by dolorimetry) and mood. They found two patterns of association between the two in two different groups of patients. In eight patients the onset of feelings of anxiety and anger preceded or coincided with the heightened perception of pain in the joints. The patients with this pattern also had a more benign form of the disease and a better prognosis. In another group of patients feelings of hopelessness alternated with a sense of confidence: increased joint pain coincided with confidence and optimism, and relief of pain with hopelessness and pessimism. The authors stated that neither age, sex, social status, medication, or the duration or stage of the disease had any bearing on these patterns in this two-year longitudinal study.

These studies are unique in pointing up the complex interactions of mood and feelings, pain and prognosis. Prognosis again seems to be related to depression, and the relationship

443

between personality and depression may be even more complex: the stoic, masochistic, or guilt-ridden patient may actually welcome "sweet" pain, while patients with other personal characteristics do not. Still other patients have been described as euphoric (Blom and Nicholls, 1953; Halliday, 1942), others as anxious, angry, and resentful rather than depressed (Cobb et al., 1965; Ludwig, 1949; Rimón, 1969; Shocket et al., 1969). Much has been made by some authors of the smouldering resentment that these patients harbor (Alexander, 1950; Cobb et al., 1969; Cobb, 1959; Moos and Solomon, 1965a, b). It may at times be expressed explosively and impulsively (Ludwig, 1954). Its existence, especially in women patients, has been observed and inferred clinically and confirmed in controlled studies by the use of psychological test instruments (Cobb, 1959; Cobb et al., 1969; Harburg et al., 1969; Mueller and Lefkovitz, 1956; Mueller et al., 1961; Rimón, 1969). It is a central, but by no means unique, feature of the prevailing emotional life of rheumatoid arthritis patients, who are also more-frequently apathetic, anxious, and depressed than their healthy siblings, as judged by MMPI test scores (Moos and Solomon, 1964a, 1965a, b).

Mueller and Lefkovitz (1956) have confirmed, by the use of the Rosenzweig picture-frustration test, that patients with rheumatoid arthrits are significantly less likely to express their resentments and hostility (Mueller et al., 1961). These patients are also more conventional in their behavior under stress, which seems to stem from a need to submit to parental authority.

But it has been difficult to obtain an accurate estimate of the respective incidence of the various emotional responses of these patients, either prior to or after the onset of the illness, because they do not easily express their feelings (Cobb, 1965; Cobb et al., 1965; King and Cobb, 1958, 1959; Ludwig, 1952; Moos, 1964; Mueller et al., 1961).

Defense Mechanisms

Many patients with rheumatoid arthritis either do not express their unpleasant feelings or complaints or limit and control them (Cobb, 1959, 1965; Cobb et al., 1965). They do so by a number of psychological defense mechanisms, among which denial, reaction formation, isolation, intellectualization, undoing, and avoidance can frequently be inferred. Feelings and perceptions are denied, according to Ludwig (1954) and Shocket et al. (1969). The patient's obsessive-compulsive traits allow the observer to infer isolation, ritualistic behavoir, reaction formation, and perhaps intellectualization. The patients tend to avoid relationships (including sexual ones) and appear to be shy and socially retiring. These observations and inferences have been confirmed by psychological tests (Moos and Solomon, 1964a, 1965a, b). In the first of their studies, Moos and Solomon showed that the patients scored significantly higher on denial of anger than their healthy female relatives.

In all of these studies it is assumed that the defense mechanisms are habitual and have been present before disease onset. From other studies the conclusion can be reached that the important parameter with regard to the initiation of the disease is not the nature of the defense mechanism, but rather its effectiveness in coping with certain life situations and the psychological threats and conflicts they engender.

444

Personality and Character Traits

Implicit in these studies is the fact that patients with rheumatoid arthritis respond in individual ways to changes and misadventures in their lives before or at the time of the onset of their disease, or to its pain, disability, and deformity. No one kind of person has rheumatoid arthritis. In fact, it is the current consensus that no one personality type characterizes all patients with rheumatoid arthritis. Rather, these patients have had certain personal problems and certain life experiences that may have sensitized them to later life events that were perceived as threatening. The emotional responses these life events elicit may or may not be successfully coped with, or defended against, coincidentally with the onset of the disease. At one time, of course, workers in this field held an opposing view about personality types. Halliday (1941, 1942), in particular, believed that a characteristic personality profile could be defined for patients with rheumatoid arthritis (Bayles, 1966). But Halliday also went on to say that some were hysterical, some were overscrupulous and obsessional, with a tendency to worry, and some suffered from phobias.

Halliday described the 14 female patients in his sample as emotionally calm, self-restricted, and detached, with marked compulsive traits. They seemed rather independent and self-sufficient. Self-restriction had begun early in life, and seemed to be a response to having to conform to strict and harsh parental discipline. As children, they had been shy and retiring. When they grew up, about half lived alone or with chronically ill relatives; some were domineering, but most were self-sacrificing and conscientious; and most led quiet lives and found it difficult to make friends. As a group, they were orderly, rigid, punctual, reliable, overly tidy, and compulsive about cleanliness. Eight of the 14 women in this sample had little interest in sex, or were frigid. In addition, Halliday noted that the patients seemed to have a marked tolerance for pain.

This personality profile of rheumatoid arthritis patients has been confirmed only in part; the traits defined by Halliday were elaborated on and clarified in subsequent studies —which, it should be noted, have dealt primarily with female patients. Thus, Johnson et al. (1947) emphasized the fact that, as little girls, the patients in their series had harbored a rebellious resentment against parental domination; this resentment found expression during childhood and adolescence in a tendency to engage in bodily activity, such as competitive sports and tomboyish play. With respect to character structure, Johnson and her co-workers agreed with Halliday: they classified their patients as hysterical or compulsive character types. Today most authorities agree that, in general, patients with rheumatoid arthritis epitomize a particular variant of the compulsive character type. They have been described as righteous, rigid, controlled, moralistic, dutiful, uncomplaining, confirming, reserved, shy, conscientious, or perfectionistic (Cobb et al., 1959, 1965; Moos, 1964; Moos and Solomon, 1964a, 1965a, b, 1966; Mueller et al., 1961), and hard-working (King and Cobb, 1958). But in addition they were masochistic—that is, long-suffering, self-sacrificing, and intrapunitive—and dependent in their relationships, for which they overcompensate with aggressiveness (Alexander, 1950; Halliday, 1942; Johnson et al., 1947; Ludwig, 1954; Shocket et al., 1969). The patients in some series have been described as benevolent tyrants; their masochistic need to serve other people exists in combination with their need to control and dominate them. And still other observers have depicted patients with rheumatoid arthritis as subservient and insecure, very sensitive to anger in others (Moos and Solomon, 1965a, b, 1966), or unsure of themselves (Mueller et al., 1961).

The validity of some of these findings has been questioned on the grounds that they may well be attributable to social and economic factors. It is likely that rheumatoid arthritis is more-commonly found in lower socioeconomic groups. Consequently, the observations reported above were based on women in these groups, most of whom had at least four children. Inasmuch as they lived on tight budgets, which contained no provision for extra help, one might expect to find these women to be described as "hard-working" and "self-sacrificing" (King and Cobb, 1958).

Other criticism has focused on the specific (compulsive) traits enumerated: the observation made by several authors that patients with rheumatoid arthritis are dependent in their relationships with others was not confirmed by MMPI test findings (Moos and Solomon, 1964a, 1965a, b), but seemed evident to clinical observers. Although some patients were said to be long-suffering, others had a low frustration tolerance (Ludwig, 1954).

Many authors have agreed with Halliday's observation, based on the small sample he studied, that patients with rheumatoid arthritis find it difficult to form friendships or establish "satisfactory" relationships (Booth, 1937; Ludwig, 1949; McLauglin et al., 1953). This may be due, in part, to their being very sensitive to the hostile feelings in others (Moos and Solomon, 1965a, b, 1966). However, this characteristic is not specific to patients with rheumatoid arthritis; it has also been observed in hypertensive patients (Thaler et al., 1957). Moreover, it is difficult to reconcile this finding with the reactions of children to separation from their parents, as noted by Blom and Nicholls (1953), and the similar adverse reactions of adults to the loss or separation of important persons in their lives, as observed by Ludwig (1949).

Conflict as a Predisposing Factor

The diversity of personality types that have been described for these patients may reflect various transformations of an unconscious conflict that, according to Alexander (1950) and Johnson et al. (1947), has a particular dynamic configuration. The same configuration may, of course, occur in persons who do not have rheumatoid arthritis because they are not immunologically or otherwise predisposed to the disease. Many workers in this field, however, do not believe that rheumatoid arthritis patients harbor a specific conflict that distinguishes them from patients with other psychosomatic diseases.

But this argument may be fruitless. Rheumatoid factors can be recovered from the serum of some, but not all, patients. In some others rheumatoid arthritis occurs with agammaglobulinemia. Therefore, several subforms of the disease may exist.

SPECIFIC CONFLICTS

The chief proponent of the conflict-specificity hypothesis was Alexander (1950). Yet, there is ample evidence that his basic propositions are still not fully understood. First, by "specificity" Alexander meant that the presence of a specific conflict distinguishes patients with rheumatoid arthritis, and especially women with the disease, from patients with other

446

psychosomatic diseases. But what needs to be emphasized, once again, is that Alexander does not imply that this conflict is unique to patients with rheumatoid arthritis; rather it assumes a specific configuration in this population. Second, Alexander does not contend that the unresolved conflict he describes could, in itself, "cause" rheumatoid arthritis. The psychological factors must interact with other (unspecified) predisposing factors of a physiological nature in order to produce the disease.

Based on clinical findings that derive primarily from studies of women, Alexander postulated that the core conflict in rheumatoid arthritis has its genesis in the restrictive and overprotective parental attitudes to which these patients were exposed in early childhood. The child rebels against the restrictions imposed by her domineering parent (usually the mother), but these children develop an excessive dependence on (and fear of) the punitive parent. Consequently, their rebellion must be repressed, for the overt expression of such impulses would endanger their dependent status. This inhibited rebellion gives rise, in turn, to hostile and aggressive impulses that are initially directed against the mother and must be similarly repressed lest the child lose her "anchor." In childhood and adolescence, tomboyish behavior (in girls), provides an outlet for the anger and rebellion that has been repressed. Later the situation becomes more complex. The rebellion against the mother's control is transferred to men, and this rebellion against being dominated by men commonly finds expression in a rejection of the feminine role. Concomitantly, these patients discharge their hostile aggression in sports, hard work, and by actively controlling their environment. They also learn to alleviate their guilt feelings by serving others. The disease has its onset when the patient can no longer discharge her hostility by dominating others or relieve her guilt by serving them. More precisely, when the patient's adaptive mode of expressing her hostile impulses by a combination of service and domination is disrupted, there is an increase in muscle tonus that in some way leads to arthritis.

The tendency for women who later develop rheumatoid arthritis to show tomboyish behavior and engage in outdoor activities and competitive sports in childhood and adolescence was also noted by Booth (1939); Cleveland and Fisher (1960); Cleveland et al. (1965); Cormier et al. (1957); Halliday (1942); McLauglin et al. (1953); Meyerowitz et al. (1968), and to a degree by Cobb (1959). The findings derived from these studies were based, in part, on patient reports. Cormier et al. (1957) noted, in particular, on the basis of such reports that these behaviors disappeared after adolescence. But the self-reported changes were confirmed by the patients' siblings.

On the other hand, Moos and Solomon (1965a, b) and Rimón (1969), using a variety of observational techniques, obtained descriptions that were the direct opposite of those made by Alexander. Rimón (1969) found that only 22 of the 100 women in this series were interested in sports. Nor was this interest confirmed by the direct observation, by Blom and Nicholls (1953), of hospitalized children of all ages, including preadolescent and adolescent. However, a subsequent study by Cleveland et al. (1965) of patients with juvenile rheumatoid arthritis, using psychological test findings, did uncover the increased interest in competitive sports and physical activity that Alexander had retrospectively found in his patients.

The research design of the validating study reported by Alexander and his co-workers in 1968, and the findings derived from this study, have been discussed in other chapters (see particularly the chapter on Graves' Disease). As was true of the other diseases, Alexander's formulations and hypotheses concerning patients with rheumatoid arthritis have been

447

modified and refined since 1950 on the basis of further clinical experience. Many, but not all, of these modifications have been incorporated into the preceding discussion.

Thus, Alexander et al. have stressed that their formulations were based mainly on studies of female patients. As children, these patients were controlled by their mothers, who punished them by restricting their physical activity, making them "stay put." They reacted to this restriction by engaging in physical activity more-commonly associated in our culture with boys. Later, when they became mothers, this rebellious attitude toward restriction was transmuted into restrictive attitudes toward their own children. Yet, although they were strict with their children, they were concerned about their well-being and did a great deal for them. Male patients with rheumatoid arthritis were exposed to the same controlling maternal attitudes, but they tended to identify with the restrictive mother.

Alexander and his co-workers suggested that patients with rheumatoid arthritis resembled those with essential hypertension, in the sense that both groups of patients had difficulty in handling their aggressive or hostile impulses. The arthritic patients sought to resolve these conflicts by exercising a "benevolent" tyranny over others and exerting self-control over their unacceptable impulses. The disease began when this solution failed. Thus, very often, the precipitating event was the loss of, or separation from, the person they had successfully restricted, dominated, controlled, and helped, or the growing assertiveness of a spouse or child.

Interestingly, although Alexander's original forumulations (1950) were derived from studies of female patients, in the validation study the initial "blind" diagnosis by nine psychoanalysts of 10 patients with rheumatoid arthritis was more accurate for men than for women. In fact, the rate of diagnostic accuracy initially was higher for the 10 patients with rheumatoid arthritis than for the remaining 75 patients with six other diseases. The probability of correctly diagnosing the patients with rheumatoid arthritis was statistically reliable. With further revision of the diagnostic criteria, the percentage figures for accurate diagnosis rose to 80 percent for the male and 53 percent for the female patients. When patients (especially women) with rheumatoid arthritis were misdiagnosed initially, the misdiagnosis was most-frequently hypertension, but there was also a tendency to misdiagnose rheumatoid arthritis as ulcerative colitis or peptic ulcer (especially in male patients); conversely, patients with neurodermatitis were often incorrectly diagnosed as suffering from rheumatoid arthritis.

On the whole, however, this study would seem to validate Alexander's revised formulations concerning the core conflict in rheumatoid arthritis in a small sample of patients —especially male patients with the disease. Nevertheless, certain key questions remain unanswered: if a specific conflict characterizes one psychosomatic disease, how can one explain the fact that another disease, such as peptic ulcer disease, may arise from the same conflict? Cobb and Hall (1965) found a statistically reliable clustering of rheumatoid arthritis, peptic ulcer, and tuberculosis, and a negative correlation between rheumatoid arthritis and myocardial infarction, in 244 men employed in a single industrial plant. It goes without saying, of course, that in such a study it is important to control for the fact that patients with rheumatoid arthritis take a number of medications that are known to increase the prevalence of peptic ulcer.

Cobb et al. (1965) sought to shed some light on this issue by comparing the social and psychological characteristics of patients with rheumatoid arthritis, hypertension, and duodenal ulcer, using a control series of hospitalized patients and healthy brothers and brothers-in-law. Data were obtained by the use of questionnaires. On various social variables, patients with rheumatoid arthritis tended more often to be manual workers, and their families were less-upwardly mobile than the other patient populations. They were also less inclined to change their habits, improve their educational or occupational status, or enhance their family and social relationships. In general, hospitalized controls had lower self-esteem than healthy controls, but hypertensive, arthritic, and hospitalized surgical patients ranked lowest on this variable. Only in two groups—those with arthritis and peptic ulcer—did a significant number of patients state that their mother had been the dominant figure in childhood, a finding that was confirmed by the patients' brothers. Despite this, the three patient groups (i.e., those with rheumatoid arthritis, hypertension, and peptic ulcer) felt that they resembled their fathers rather than their mothers. The arthritic, hypertensive, and surgical patients most-often described their childhood as unhappy, and complaints of unhappiness in adult life were expressed most frequently by hypertensive patients (and least frequently by patients with peptic ulcer and by healthy controls). About half of the patients with rheumatoid arthritis complained of unhappiness in childhood, but they and the healthy controls reported the fewest life crises, while the hypertensive patients were most likely to describe such crises. The authors also concluded from the data that patients with rheumatoid arthritis learn to hide their hurt feelings and do not voice their dissatisfaction.

The incidence of overt aggressiveness was especially low in hypertensive patients (10 percent) and highest in surgical patients (70 percent). Patients with duodenal ulcer and rheumatoid arthritis rated themselves about equally along this continuum (54 percent and 56 percent, respectively). According to observers, however, the patients with rheumatoid arthritis were least prone to angry-impulsive behavior (that is, they were the most controlled), and those with ulcer were most prone to such behavior. This study thus suggests that although patients with these three diseases have certain important psychosocial features in common, they differ in other respects. The question of why some patients suffer from more than one "psychosomatic" disease, either at the same time or in series, is not completely answered by these observations. In fact, the matter has never been satisfactorily settled. Several possibilities exist: (1) A patient may have an unconscious conflict to be fed or loved and be ashamed of it, while also harboring other conflicts about dependency and rebelliousness. The patient might, therefore, develop peptic ulcer disease and rheumatoid arthritis, if he had specific physiological predispositions for both diseases. (2) Although aspirin, indomethacin, and corticosteroid medications used to treat theumatoid arthritis are prone to cause peptic ulcer formation, they probably do so only in predisposed patients. (3) It is possible that some as-yet-unknown physiological factor in rheumatoid arthritis elevates gastrin levels, for example, which in turn cause the hypersecretion of hydrocholoric acid. A chain of physiological events is then set off which ends with peptic ulcer disease. Such a speculation would only hold if peptic ulcer disease followed the occurrence of rheumatoid arthritis and did not precede it.

NONSPECIFIC CONFLICTS

Many authors do not subscribe to Alexander's rather specific formulations about the core conflict in rheumatoid arthritis, but place the major burden on less-specific conflicts surrounding the contained hostility, resentment, and sexual conflicts of patients with this disease. The fact that women patients with rheumatoid arthritis find it difficult to express hostility, bitterness, and resentment has been noted by a number of workers (Cleveland and Fisher, 1954, 1960; Cobb, 1959; Cobb et al., 1965, 1969; Harburg et al., 1969; Johnson et al., 1947; McLaughlin et al., 1953; Moos, 1964; Rimón, 1969; Sanchez et al., 1959; Shocket et al., 1969), but because the resentment is conflictful, it is highly controlled. Male patients exercise greater control in this respect than female patients, who are more impulsive and are able to express their aggression more directly (Cobb and Kasl, 1966).

Some investigators believe that this hostility and resentment originate during the early years of life, that they arise in situations in which the child's dependency wishes are not met or are frustrated, and that they find expression initially in violent and destructive fantasies of an oral nature (Blom and Nicholls, 1953; Ludwig, 1954; Robinson, 1957; Shocket et al., 1969). Others believe that the arbitrary authority of the mother is the principal cause of this hostility (Harburg et al., 1969). In any event, the fears of expressing these hostile impulses lead to overcontrol (Cobb et al., 1965), emotional constriction, and, in time, to an inability to express feelings (Cobb, 1959; Cobb et al., 1965); to guilt (Cormier et al., 1957), and a concomitant lack of self-esteem (Cobb et al., 1965; Ludwig, 1949; Shocket et al., 1969); to a predisposition to depression (Cecil, 1945; Moos and Solomon, 1946a; Thomas, 1936); and to obsessive-compulsive behavior (Halliday, 1942; Johnson et al., 1947), or perfectionistic and self-sacrificing traits (Halliday, 1942; Johnson et al., 1947; Moos and Solomon, 1965a, b).

Rimón's study (1969) of female patients with rheumatoid arthritis has provided additional data on this patient population. Rimón's use of the Buss-Durkee Inventory enabled him to divide the patients in his sample into two groups. Those patients in whom disease onset was associated with precipitating events achieved approximately the same scores on the inventory as a control group of hospitalized women patients, with the exception that the patients with rheumatoid arthritis had lower scores on indirect aggression and guilt. On the other hand, those patients in whom disease onset could not be associated with any particular event, or in whom the association was doubtful, not only scored much lower than the two other groups on all verbal manifestations of irritability, anger, and hostility, but also scored lower on manifest guilt. Ideally, of course, these findings should be verified in another group. Nevertheless, Rimón postulates a relationship between physiological and psychological predisposing factors on the basis of these data: the disease has an acute onset, in a clearly identifiable setting, in patients who have few relatives with the disease, and whose inventory scores indicate that they are more likely to express their aggression directly. On the other hand, the disease begins slowly, with no readily discernible, clear-cut precipitating psychosocial events, in patients who have more relatives with the disease and whose ability to express their aggression is markedly inhibited, as is their conscious awareness of aggressive feelings.

The sexual behavior of patients with rheumatoid arthritis and their sexual identity and role may be an area of major conflict. Long-standing inhibitions of sexual behavior may be present (Booth, 1937; Halliday, 1942; Johnson et al., 1947; Thomas, 1936), that may be represented in dreams (French and Shapiro, 1949). Abstention from sexual intercourse and masturbation have been noted in male patients, and many of the women studied either had

450

no desire for intercourse or were unable to reach orgasm. Sexual adjustment was poor in about 50 percent of the patients studied by Lowman et al. (1954). Twenty-three percent of the patients in Rimón's series (1969) complained of frigidity, or were dissatisfied with their sex partner, or felt guilty about having intercourse, and another 30 percent complained that they had lost all interest in sex. Various explanations have been advanced for the conflicts that underlie these behaviors. As was mentioned earlier, women with rheumatoid arthritis frequently rebel against male domination and reject their feminine role. Not surprisingly, their resentment of men prevents them from achieving a satisfactory sexual adjustment (Johnson et al., 1947; Rowe, 1969). Rimón (1969) considered that a frequent and sufficient reason for the unsatisfactory sexual life of women with this disease was their depressed mood state. The burden of the sexual maladjustment in some men has been placed on their being "identified" with women (McLaughlin et al., 1953) and on conflicts about unconscious homosexuality (Geist, 1966). Many observers have blamed the poor sexual adjustment (Shocket et al., 1969) and the conflicts about sexual role on a hostile identification with the parent of the opposite sex (Booth, 1937; Johnson et al., 1947; Lowman et al., 1954; McLaughlin et al., 1953), or with several different family members of both sexes (Cobb et al., 1965; King and Cobb, 1959), which led to a confusion about their sexual role. In a later, verifying study, however, Harburg et al. (1969) could not confirm the previous findings in this area.

Other reasons for the lack of sexual satisfaction were uncovered by Cleveland and Fisher (1954), who inferred unconscious fantasy material from answers to the Rorschach test, TAT and Draw-a-Person test. In contrast to control patients with low back pain, men patients with rheumatoid arthritis conceived their bodies as rigid containers filled with fluid. The authors suggested on the basis of these results that inconsistent attitudes on the part of parents led to this conception about the body and to sexual role confusion in the men.

The Childhood Origin of the Conflict

Alexander (1950) and Johnson et al. (1947) ascribed the childhood origin of the conflict in arthritic women to the domineering and tyrannical attitudes of their mothers, which may have been the origin of the anger that the future patients directed at them (Alexander, 1950; Ludwig, 1949). The fathers have been described as gentle, compliant (Barchilon, 1963; Johnson et al., 1947), or unaffectionate (King and Cobb, 1959). Men patients added that their mothers were martyrs, efficient, hard-working, imbued with moral or religious principles (Cleveland and Fisher, 1954; Cobb et al., 1965). They described their fathers as being unpredictable and inconsistent. They emphasized the strict discipline, meanness, and unfairness in their families, characteristics that have also been reported by others (Cormier et al., 1957; Halliday, 1942; King and Cobb, 1959).[*] Women patients described their mothers in two ways. One group of women described their mothers (the descriptions were confirmed by their healthy siblings) as easy-going, implacable, serene, and helpful. The second group described their mothers as being cold, intolerant, impatient, rejecting, and strict, and their fathers as being strict. However, the siblings did not perceive their

---

[*] The descriptions in these studies are reminiscent of those for the families of patients with ulcerative colitis (Chapter 6) and for some of the mothers of patients with bronchial asthma (Chapter 3).

parents in the same way. They described their fathers either as irresponsible, intemperate, dominating, strict, unambitious, and brutal; or as lenient, affectionate, gentle, easy-going, tolerant, intelligent, good-natured, and kind, yet strict (Moos and Solomon, 1965a, b).

The study by Moos and Solomon did not investigate how the strictness of the parent manifested itself in the child, and whether it led to the rebelliousness, defiance, and resentment so often described in rheumatoid arthritis patients (Alexander, 1950; Barchilon, 1963; Blom and Nicholls, 1953; Cleveland and Fisher, 1954; Cobb, 1959; Cormier et al., 1957; Ludwig, 1954; Mueller et al., 1961), or to their emotional insecurity (Ludwig, 1949, 1954), or both. This insecurity has been ascribed to the parents' open rejection and lack of affection (King and Cobb, 1959), or to their overprotectiveness and extreme anxiety.

A clearer definition of these interrelationships was recently achieved by Harburg et al. (1969). Women with rheumatoid arthritis recalled their mothers as having exercised arbitrary authority. They reported more covert hostility toward their mothers than normal subjects did in the same circumstances. The depth of their resentment was proportional to the extent of their mothers' authoritarianism. The arthritic women who had been most resentful also thought less-well of themselves. Men patients did not remember that their mothers had exercised arbitrary control.

Childhood Deprivation as a Source of Later Conflict

Harburg's work, just reviewed, begins to account for the origins of the conflicts described in patients. In addition, other kinds of family relationships may play a role in originating these conflicts. In Rimón's series (1969) of 100 women, 37 came from broken homes and 25 of their parents or siblings had a history of psychiatric illnesses, consisting of alcoholism and the abuse of drugs. The prevalence of manifest psychopathology in the family was probably not excessive, although six patients did comment that the father's abuse of alcohol constituted a problem for them.

Severe emotional or physical deprivation (Blom and Nicholls, 1953), the death or divorce of parents, or separation of ill parents from their children has been reported (Blom and Nicholls, 1953; Cleveland and Fisher, 1954; Ludwig, 1949; Robb and Rose, 1965; Shocket et al., 1969) in up to 50 percent of several series of patients (Booth, 1937; Lowman et al., 1954; Rimón, 1969). King and Cobb (1959), however, found that the loss of a parent by death before the future patient was 12 years of age was recorded in less than one-half of their patients with mild arthritis, and that this loss was as frequent in those without the disease. Robb and Rose (1965) in a study done in New Zealand could not obtain evidence for the role of maternal deprivation in the disease.

Usually the loss of a parent occurred in the lives of patients before the age of 15. In Rimón's series in Finland, 16 of the 37 patients had lost their parents before the age of 5 years, 11 between 5 and 10 years, and 10 between 10 and 15 years. Eighteen of the patients lost their fathers and 14 their mothers by death. Two patients were illegitimate; divorce caused separation from one parent in two others; and one patient had been given up for adoption. Rimón could not confirm King's and Cobb's data. Although he conceded that the frequency of broken homes was about the same as in patients with various forms of psychopathology, it was twice as great as in the general population in Finland (Alanen et al., 1966).

452

Studies of Siblings

One might well ask why the siblings of patients are not also ill. Studies of patients with rheumatoid arthritis have at times used siblings as control subjects; for example, Cormier et al., (1957) found that siblings had been more reserved, conforming, shy, and quiet, and less athletic than the patients had once been. The patients were described by their siblings as having been active, athletic, and interested in sports in childhood. In adulthood, the patients, according to their siblings, had become punctual, tidy, perfectionistic, self-sacrificing, forgiving, and concerned with financial security. At times, they had outbursts of anger, which was considered to have been a residue of their childhood resentments and impulsive defiance. When an outburst of rage occurred, patients would be haunted by guilt and remorse and by a need for self-punishment. On the other hand, the siblings had grown up to develop poise and self-confidence and were less self-critical after being angry.

Moos and Solomon (1965a, b) compared patients and their siblings, using interview techniques, the MMPI, and specially constructed personality tests. Some of Cormier's descriptions of the traits of their adult patients were confirmed, but, in addition, the patients were described as being more perfectionistic, subservient, compliant, nervous, reserved, introverted, sensitive to another's anger, high-strung, anxious, and depressed. The siblings tended to like people and be comfortable with them. They were active, busy, hardworking, and productive people who enjoyed life. They were freer to express criticism of other people. The siblings were asked to describe the childhood personalities of their arthritic relatives, and these descriptions did not accord with Cormier's. The future arthritic was described as inferior, sickly, shy, worried, lazy, and inactive. In a later study carried out by Solomon and Moos (1965b), the women relatives of patients fell into two groups, which could be differentiated not only on the basis of the presence and absence of rheumatoid factors in their sera but also on the basis of the MMPI scores. The relatives of patients do not then constitute a homogeneous group, and may perceive their siblings differently. Or the childhood traits of patients may differ because there may be two or more different kinds of children who later develop arthritis.

The Marriages of Patients

The marriages of rheumatoid patients are often disturbed long before disease onset (Shocket et al., 1969), possibly because of their poor sexual adjustment. It has been said that the disease often begins in a setting of marital strife culminating in separation or divorce.

Moos and Solomon (1965b) had women patients and their healthy siblings describe their respective marriages. The siblings described theirs as happy and satisfactory. The patients described their husbands either in glowing hyperboles, or as being irresponsible, incapable of human understanding, alcoholic, mean, abusive, and physically violent. Thirteen of the 16 patients said they never had fights, even when the husband was described in these critical or adverse terms: long-suffering, martyr-like attitudes toward their husbands characterized these women. They expressed no resentment about the irresponsibility or brutality of their husbands. Although many ill women contained their bitter resentments about and anger at their husbands most of the time, they were also able

453

to express it impulsively and explosively on other occasions (Cobb et al., 1965; Cobb and Kasl, 1968). The men always contained their anger. The effect on the marriages of these two patterns of behavior was investigated. The marriages in which the women had arthritis were stormy; in contrast, when the husband had rheumatoid arthritis, the marriage was described as peaceful (Cobb and Kasl, 1968).

Other reasons for the stormy, unsatisfactory marriages of patients with rheumatoid arthritis have also been uncovered. King and Cobb (1958) first pointed out that there was a discrepancy between the income earned by men patients with rheumatoid arthritis and their level of education, whereas women patients were characterized by being discontented with their feminine role (1958). Patients of both sexes were, therefore, discontented (Cobb, 1959): the men were earning less than they should have been, and the women wished they were men. Cobb's description of his women patients in psychological terms equals Alexander's description in psychoanalytic terms. Alexander emphasized the tomboyish behavior of his patients, which suggested that they could not accept themselves as girls or women, and had identified themselves with their fathers or brothers (King and Cobb, 1959). Cobb also felt that the discontentment and envy in the women patients led to controlled hostility in them.

Cobb and his co-workers (1965) also reported on the families of his patients, emphasizing their social status. The families of 169 men and 155 women with rheumatoid arthritis were studied. The researchers found highly significant correlations between the status index of parents, the presence of anger, and the incidence of rheumatoid arthritis. The incongruent status index measured discrepancies between the reported occupation and education of the patient's father and the education of the mother. Incongruities occurred in both directions; usually the mother's social status was higher than the father's. When the discrepancy in social status between the parents was great, the degree of anger in women patients was higher, but in men it was lower. The daughters were also more likely to express their anger and irritation at their parents.

Psychopathology and Rheumatoid Arthritis

There is probably an increased incidence of psychosis (especially schizophrenic illness) in patients with ulcerative colitis. In rheumatoid arthritis, by contrast, the incidence of psychosis is lower than expected. Gregg (1939) found that the prevalence of rheumatoid arthritis in 15,196 psychotic patients was 0.13 percent, which is much lower than the prevalence of psychosis in the population at large. Not a single case of rheumatoid arthritis occurred in 3,000 autopsied psychotic patients. Nissen and Spencer (1936) did not diagnose rheumatoid arthritis once in 2,200 schizophrenic patients. Therefore, the conclusion seems warranted that schizophrenic patients are strangely immune to rheumatoid arthritis. Alternatively, hospitalization may have imparted some protection against its onset. Since that time, the lack of coincidence between schizophrenia and rheumatoid arthritis has been confirmed by a number of observers (King, 1955; Pilkington, 1956; Rothermilch and Philips, 1963; Trevathan and Tatum, 1954). But in Rimón's (1969) series of 100 women patients, 2 were said to be schizophrenic—an incidence of schizophrenia that is about the same as in the general population. Both patients had been schizophrenic for many years prior to the onset of rheumatoid arthritis. One patient had developed rheumatoid arthritis after discharge from a mental hospital. The other patient had become arthritic after her father's death and upon being moved to another hospital. Rimón described these patients as schizophrenic, but also wrote that they had "grave memory disturbances and pronounced dementia." In other words, they may also have been brain-damaged.

The relationship of psychosis to rheumatoid arthritis may be complicated (Cleveland and Fisher, 1954). Ludwig (1954) reported four psychotic patients with rheumatoid arthritis: in one an exacerbation of the arthritis was accompanied by hallucinations; in another, who had also developed a duodenal ulcer prior to the onset of rheumatoid arthritis, periodic depressions and episodes of panic with feelings of depersonalization and derealization occurred without the primary symptoms of schizophrenia. Ludwig considered the first patient to be psychotic and the second one schizophrenic. In a later report Ludwig (1967) wrote that patients with rheumatoid arthritis resembled "borderline" cases; he stressed their "weak," poorly integrated ego structure. By the use of projective tests a number os psychologists have diagnosed schizoid and other psychotic personality traits in patients with rheuamotid arthritis (Ellman and Mitchell, 1936; Geist, 1966; McLaughlin et al., 1953).

Care must be taken, however, that the psychotic symptomatology of patients is not the result either of brain damage caused by the disease or of treatment with drugs. Less has been written about the neuropathology of rheumatoid arthritis in the United States than in Europe (Hausmanova and Herman, 1957; Mitkow, 1959; Rimón, 1969; Tatibouet et al., 1961). Acute and chronic changes in the brain and organic brain syndromes have been described. Treatment with gold, antimalarial drugs, or cortisone and ACTH may produce profound behavioral and psychological disturbances, which may mimic many different psychotic syndromes (Bunim et al., 1955; Glaser, 1953; Goolker and Schein, 1953; Popert, 1966). Another important source of brain damage is SLE: many patients initially diagnosed as having rheumatoid arthritis have eventually turned out to have SLE, in which brain involvement has occurred in 25 to 50 percent of several series of patients (Clark and Bailey, 1956; Ganz et al., 1972; Gurland et al., 1972; Guze, 1967; O'Connor and Mosher, 1966; Stern and Robbins, 1960). The fact that 10 to 30 percent of the patients with SLE were said to have "functional" psychoses or neurotic symptoms indicated that the brain syndromes may have been overlooked. To date the best study on this topic has been reported by Ganz et al., (1972).

In summary, a review of the evidence on the psychological predisposing factors of patients with rheumatoid arthritis attests to the many methodological problems originally enumerated in the introduction to this book. Because of the flawed methods, it should enhance our knowledge if predictive studies were done, utilizing the fact that some persons with rheumatoid factors may go on to develop the disease. In addition, patient should be studied longitudinally, especially during remissions and exacerbations, so that the observer could sift out the enduring psychological characteristics of these patients from their psychological reactions to the pain, redness, deformity, and disability of joints.

It seems clear that a certain undetermined percentage of patients do go through the developmental sequence of submission, rebellion, tomboyish athleticism, and domination described by Johnson and Alexander. Their unconscious motives consist of violent, destructive fantasies of an oral-sadistic nature, directed particularly at a domineering,

455

controlling mother. As adults they are frequently righteous, moralistic, controlled, controlling, tyrannical, conscientious, guilt-ridden people who inhibit the expression of their feelings, especially the angry ones. They are long-suffering and often masochistic. These patients belong, more frequently than expected, to the lower socioeconomic groups and are frequently engaged in manual or other unskilled labor.

No consistent differences in conflicts has been found between twins discordant for arthritis (Meyerowitz et al., 1968), or in children with Still's disease (Cleveland et al., 1965). Some of the characteristic conflicts of patients with rheumatoid arthritis are shared with patients suffering from other psychosomatic diseases (Cleveland and Fisher, 1960; Engel, 1955; Halliday, 1942; Lidz, 1969; Mandelbrote and Wittkower, 1955; Moos and Solomon, 1964a). There are also unexplained differences in the psychological patterns of men and women with rheumatoid arthritis (Cobb et al., 1965; Johnson et al., 1947).

Another group of patients do not seem to fit the expectations of Alexander and his colleagues. This second group contains embittered, angry, resentful people who do not express either their angry or sexual feelings easily or at all. Their feelings are due to the frustration of dependency wishes, apparently occasioned at times by a parent's death or a divorce. Their dependency wishes have not been further specified, because the observations made on them had not used psychoanalytic techniques or had used only psychological tests. Many of these patients are unhappily married even before the onset of the disease.

The heterogenity of the psychological make-up either reflect differences in the techniques used to study patients in different series or may reflect a real heterogeneity caused by the fact that the disease is not a uniform one. But this lack of uniformity in patients also extends to its immunopathology, as not all patients seem to produce rheumatoid factors in their serum. And rheumatoid factors and complexes themselves may be chemically and immunologically heterogeneous.

Although the anatomical lesions in the joints of patients with rheumatoid arthritis may be similar, their appearance could mean that different predisposing factors may bring them about. The situation may resemble the one found in gout. Hyperuricemia predisposes most but not all patients with gout. Not all hyperuricemic subjects develop gouty arthritis. Some patients with gout have normal serum uric acid levels. The causes of hyperuricemia are heterogeneous; different enzymatic disturbances produce it. Why some but not all hyperuricemic subjects develop gouty arthritis is not known.

The Possible Mechanisms by which Psychological Responses to Precipitating Events Are Mediated

CONVERSION MECHANISMS

Two parts of Alexander's formulation about the psychological predisposition and the initiation of rheumatoid arthritis are in part correct. The third part of his formulation was that when the patient could no longer find an outlet for his or her need to dominate, the disease began. The need to dominate, tyrannize, or subjugate was an outlet for anger that, on frustration, was transformed into increased musculoskeletal tension. But in other patients Alexander (1950), Halliday (1941), and Johnson et al. (1947) noticed that the increase in muscle tonus was not due to an inhibition of aggressive impulses but was due to the "conversion" of specific, unconscious sexual impulses into increased muscle tonus. It is difficult to evaluate this second hypothesis. Generally speaking, diseases associated with structural change (such as rheumatoid arthritis), rather than being conversion symptoms, have not been considered the result of conversion "mechanisms": that is, they do not symbolize an unconscious fantasy that has been "converted" into a functional alteration. It is not possible from reading the protocols to determine the clinical characteristics of the patients in whom the arthritis was ascribed to conversion mechanisms. One cannot ascertain, for example, whether they suffered from rheumatoid arthritis or "psychogenic rheumatism" (Bayles, 1966; Halliday, 1937a), or whether the ongoing arthritis could have acquired symbolic meaning to the patient that was then believed to have antecedent (pathogenetic) significance (Halliday, 1937a, b). The problem of antecedence crops up repeatedly in the literature of psychosomatic medicine and constitutes a main methodological issue (Introduction). But additional problems occur in the interpretation of the symptoms of rheumatoid arthritis. Conversion symptoms are usually multiple. They may mimic the signs of peripheral neuropathy that has been described in this disease (Chamberlain and Bruckner, 1970). Without a careful examination the signs of the neuropathy could either be ascribed to the disease process or to a conversion hysterical one. In addition, physical diseases such as rheumatoid arthritis are often accompanied by conversion symptoms. However, the clinician may not conclude that because of the concomitance of these symptoms and signs that rheumatoid arthritis has a psychogenetic cause based on conversion mechanisms.

THE ROLE OF MUSCLE TENSION

The evidence reviewed strongly suggests that social and psychological factors play a role in the initiation of rheumatoid arthritis. The observed correlations between certain events in the lives of patients and the onset of the disease requires explanation, at least in those patients whose disease is not set off by infection. How can a disturbing event in the life of the patient be linked to the known pathological changes in the disease, such as the immunological process or physiological mechanisms? Once again, the answer must be that we do not know.

In an effort to provide an answer to this question, Alexander (1950) postulated that the inhibited aggressive motives and rebellious, protesting attitudes of his women patients were usually expressed in muscular activity. He observed that muscular stiffness and tenseness on awakening very often *preceded* attacks of joint pain produced when muscular activity was inhibited. (The symptom of stiffness on arising is one of the cardinal criteria used by rheumatologists to diagnose rheumatoid arthritis.) In other words, when the usual psychological adaption of increased motor (muscular) activity failed or was prevented, an increase in muscle tension and spasm led to stiffness and tenseness, culminating eventually in joint trauma and arthritis.

Barchilon (1963) psychoanalyzed a young woman who initially complained of a few fleeting arthritic pains in her wrists, neck, hips, and ankles. Three years later when she began treatment because of a fear of pregnancy, she had red, swollen wrists and finger joints. During the course of treatment Barchilon observed that the patient's hands and body were immobile, "lifeless and inert," during periods when her arthritis was dormant.

The immobility, therefore, could not be ascribed solely to pain, or to secondary changes in the joints. As a consequence of her immobility, the extensor tendons of her forearms became more visible, and her arms and legs became less powerful. The immobility and hypotonia of her arms were particularly noticeable when she was expressing her wishes to harm her mother, her guilt about wishing to do so, and her "paralyzing" fears of retribution. After such a confession, her everyday behavior would become physically more active. She would wash her car and clean her house. Such bursts of activity were followed by stiffness of the muscles and redness and swelling of the joints. Because of the periods of immobility, her muscles and joints were ill-prepared for such exertions. In summary, Barchilon interpreted the sequence of events as follows: the hostility to her mother was conscious, the hypotonia and immobility were "protecting" her against expressing it and caused musculoskeletal disuse, so that subsequent physical exertion produced symptoms of arthritis.

Further credence is added to Barchilon's thesis by the observation that immobility due to splinting or paralysis of an arthritic limb has improved the symptoms and signs of arthritis. The joints of a paralyzed, immobile limb were also protected against active rheumatoid arthritis that appeared elsewhere in the body.

Barchilon's formulations do not support Alexander's: whereas Alexander ascribed the onset of active arthritis to increased tension in muscles and their tendons surrounding a joint, Barchilon, on the basis of his observations of one patient, believed that exacerbations of the disease were preceded by a decrease of muscular tension. The conclusions of both workers are further complicated by the fact that a muscle disease is part of rheumatoid arthritis.

In addition, the rheumatoid process involves tendon sheaths and tendons, particularly at periarticular sites. Therefore, we cannot be certain whether the hypotonia, muscle atrophy, and immobility are primarily due to a rheumatoid or a psychological process, or whether the hypertonia that Alexander emphasized is not a response to pain. It seems clear, therefore, that much more data must be accumulated before we can be sure whether or how psychological factors bring about joint changes.

Alexander, in proposing a pathogenetic mechanism—the increased tension —attempted to explain the joint pathology in rheumatoid arthritis. Perhaps his attempt was a premature one, because no consensus has yet been reached as to the site in the joint or elsewhere where the disease begins.

Psychophysiological Studies: Relationship between Psychological Variables and Measurements of Muscle Tension in Patients and Controls

The hypothesis that psychological tension is translated into tension in muscles and tendons around joints is central to many past formulations about the initiation of rheumatoid arthritis. A number of studies have been designed to test this hypothesis by measuring muscle tension by means of electromyography (EMG). Morrison et al. (1947) found the EMG activity no different in patients with rheumatoid arthritis than in normal control subjects during voluntary motor activity. But they did observe that recurrent diphasic spike activity (possibly due to activity in single muscle units) occurred during involuntary motor activity (i.e., during relaxation) in one-half of the patients, and it was usually located in muscles near affected joints. In a case of unilateral joint involvement by

458

arthritis, diphasic spike activity was present in the muscles of an unaffected limb one week before its joints became inflamed. This observation suggested that this unusual form of activity might precede clinical evidence of arthritis. But other interpretations of the finding are possible; single-unit activity of this kind may reflect partial denervation, caused by the rheumatoid process affecting motoneurons first and joints later. Therefore, it is not conclusive that increases in muscle activity antecede joint disease and play a pathogenetic role; rather, both the abnormal EMG potentials and the joint inflammation may have been part of the same disease process.

Gottschalk et al. (1950) could find no difference in muscle potential between patients with rheumatoid arthritis and those with essential hypertension, either during voluntary movements or imaginary movements that subjects were instructed to make. However, patients with rheumatoid arthritis showed increased muscle tension when they overheard a (feigned) argument or listened to a story that had personal meaning for them. Patients with rheumatoid arthritis in psychoanalytic treatment had more muscle tension than a control group of psychiatric residents in treatment. Any conclusions from these studies must be drawn with care: experience has taught us that the intended psychological stimulus (for example, a feigned situation) does not necessarily produce its intended result; the critical variables may be the ongoing and specific relationship of the subject to the experimenter and the therapist. In Gottschalk's experiments, the responses of the patients with rheumatoid arthritis were not compared with controls on hearing the story and the feigned disagreement; therefore, one cannot be certain that the patients with rheumatoid arthritis responded differently from others. Had such differences been observed, one would still wonder whether the increased muscle tension in arthritic patients was not due to pain.

Southworth (1958) gave arthritic patients and patients with peptic ulcer a word-association test while measuring EMG activity in the frontalis and trapezius muscle. He found that arthritic patients had an increase in observable muscle tension in the frontalis muscle, while peptic ulcer patients had increased tension in the trapezius muscle; the tension tended to return to resting EMG levels more slowly in arthritic patients. These findings are difficult to interpret, however, because Malmo et al. (1950) and Sainsbury and Gibson (1954) had found that complaints of stiffness or soreness of particular muscle groups in subjects without arthritis were also reflected in an increase in muscle potentials under stress. Neither Gottschalk et al. nor Southwarth measured differences in tension between muscles near painful or painless sites, as subsequent investigators did. Moos and Engel (1962) compared potentials in muscle groups lying in areas of the body that had recently been painful with those that were free of pain. The study was carried out in patients with rheumatoid arthritis and with essential hypertension. The same muscle recording sites were used in both patient groups. During movement when the subject pressed a button, the same levels of muscle potentials were observed in all patients. But the patients with rheumatoid arthritis showed consistently higher EMG potentials in muscles near the site of joint pain; in other muscles no differences were found between subjects in the two groups. In addition, the EMG activity in patients with arthritis did not adapt over time when the patients were made to speak phrases that were personally meaningful to them.

In conclusion, the responses of arthritic patients were mainly evidenced in increased muscle tension near painful joints, whereas the responses of patients with hypertension (reflected in terms of a failure to show physiological adaptation) revealed themselves in the

459

persistence of an elevated blood pressure. These results mean that in different patient groups, psychological stimuli are reflected physiologically in different ways. The results bear only indirectly on the question of the initiation of rheumatoid arthritis. They partly support Alexander's hypothesis. However, the main finding is that pain heightens the responsivity and persistence of EMG activity, possibly by facilitation of the spinal motoneuronal pool.

The differences in physiological reactivity between patients with rheumatoid arthritis and others, as revealed by EMG changes, may, however, be related to some other variable. Williams and Krasnoff (1964) found that patients with well-defined "body boundaries" (a measure of a person's attitude to his body, as determined by responses to the Rorschach test) manifested significantly more EMG activity and a smaller increase in heart rate in response to "stressful" stimuli. The results of this study implied that the EMG activity was more related to body boundary than to a particular disease process. As patients with rheumatoid arthritis (and other people) have well-defined body boundaries (Cleveland and Fisher, 1954; Fisher and Cleveland, 1960), they would be expected to respond with increased muscle activity and galvanic skin responses (Fisher and Cleveland, 1960), as other people with this psychological characteristic do (Davis, 1960).

Interaction of Psychological and Immunological Factors in the Onset

There is a great deal of new evidence that rheumatoid arthritis is not merely a disease of the joints but a systemic disease. This evidence forces those investigating the onset conditions to account for the systemic disease, not just the local joint disorders. Furthermore, the disease may manifest itself only in rheumatoid nodules. Any hypothesis accounting only for the joint manifestations of the disease would be irrelevant to nodule formation; physical trauma or muscle tension may account for the local joint expression of the disease, but not for the disease itself.

Recognizing these conceptual issues, Solomon and Moos (1965b) compared the nonarthritic women relatives of patients (matched on a number of social and personal variables) on the basis of whether or not their sera contained rheumatoid factors. The authors caution that it is not possible from their study to tell whether the rheumatoid factors were the same as those found in the disease. Employing the MMPI, they reported that the relatives whose sera contained the factors scored significantly higher on inhibited aggression; on concern about the social desirability of their actions and about socioeconomic status; on compliance, shyness, conscientiousness and morality; and on the capacity for successful defense and adaptation. In some ways they resembled, and in others they did not resemble, patients with rheumatoid arthritis (Moos and Solomon, 1965a, b, 1966). But in contrast to patients with the disease, they were functioning well in their everyday lives. Interestingly enough, the relatives whose sera did not contain rheumatoid factors or contained them only in low titers scored high on those items that indicated obsessive compulsive traits and rituals; fears, anxiety, and guilt feelings; indecisiveness; self-critical attitudes; and bodily complaints; and they had a reduced capacity for successful "defense" against impulses. They complained of more psychiatric symptoms; they dissimulated, accepted themselves less, and felt alienated from others. They scored higher on dependency and inner-maladjustment scales. The study suggested that in order to develop rheumatoid arthritis, one must not only be able to develop rheumatoid factors but have certain psychological problems that one cannot contain or cope with.

Solomon (1969, 1970) proposed quite another mechanism. Based on work already reviewed in this chapter, he suggested that early life experience (Solomon and Moos, 1964; Solomon et al., 1968) and stress lowered a patient's resistance (Friedman et al., 1965; Soave, 1968) to a virus or depressed the immune response to the virus. If the immune response was depressed and excessive antigen formation ensued, antigen-antibody complexes would continue to circulate in the blood and be pathogenetic (Dixon et al., 1961). However, this model of the pathogenesis of rheumatoid arthrits has not been tested in humans; it was worked out experimentally in animals, and for experimental glomerulonephritis.

The work of Moos and Solomon is unique in taking into account modern information about the role of immune factors in the etiology and pathogenesis of rheumatoid arthritis. It implies that both the psychological and immunological predisposition are necessary in disease onset and that the disease occurs when the defenses that should enable the person to adapt to and deal with his problems break down.

The pathogenetic problem is, however, exacerbated by the fact that we still do not know just where in the body, or in the joint, the disease first manifests itself. Therefore, our ability to link psychological factors with the inital physiological disturbance in the disease is limited. When such links are finally forged, it will be possible to investigate the mechanisms that translate moods into pathogenetic mechanisms, which give rise to lesions. We might then ask how the antigenic properties of IgG are altered, and whether psychological factors could be mediated through autonomic outflow channels to produce vasoconstriction in the arterioles that supply the joints, cartilage, or synovial cells, altering their antigenic properties. Or, could altered mood states affect the likelihood of an infection? More investigation will be needed to verify or disprove any of these speculations.

PHYSIOLOGICAL FACTORS

A Review of Current Hypotheses

Many hypotheses and speculations about the factors that initiate rheumatoid arthritis have been proposed in the last two decades (Dressner, 1955; Ford, 1969; Hamerman, 1966, 1971a, 1975; Ziff, 1961; Zvaifler, 1965). One of the major impediments to deciding which hypothesis is correct is the observation that the joint symptoms may be anteceded by uveitis, scleritis, and a gamut of symptoms that are usually considered to lack specificity. These nonspecific, "prodromal" symptoms are considered by some to constitute the beginning of the disease (e.g., Cobb et al., 1939; Short et al., 1957). Other researchers time the onset of the disease by the start of the joint symptoms. If rheumatoid arthritis is a systemic disease, these so-called "prodromal" symptoms may constitute its first manifestations; yet the symptoms are sufficiently vague and nonspecific that they do not constitute adequate criteria for the diagnosis of the onset of rheumatoid arthritis. They could, for instance, herald the onset of other disease, such as psychogenic rheumatism (Bayles, 1966; Ellman and Shaw, 1950; Halliday, 1937a, b), fibrositis (Bayles, 1966), and depressive and anxiety reactions. Short et al. (1957) have commented upon this point and have called for

461

more intensive investigations. The problem of doing focused research into the initiating factors in this disease is also complicated by the fact that we really do not know in what part of the joint the pathogenetic process begins. Some authorities consider the primary lesion to occur in the synovial cells; others point to the cells or ground substance of the articular cartilage. It has been suggested by others that rheumatoid arthritis is a generalized disease that begins with disturbances either in the blood vessels or the lymphoreticular system.

In 1955, Dressner surveyed the many etiologic and pathogenetic hypotheses about rheumatoid arthritis and concluded that none had been proven. The hypotheses included infection at onset by viruses, streptococci and other bacteria; theories of focal sepsis, avitaminosis, endocrine dysfunction, disorders in carbohydrate metabolism and the metabolism of sulfur; and theories about disturbances of connective tissue metabolism or immune processes. At one time, rheumatoid arthritis was considered by some a "disease of adaptation," because experimental arthritis could be produced in adrenalectomized, unilaterally nephrectomized rats by the administration of 11-desoxycorticosterone. However, the joint lesions that resulted in animals did not have the appearance of the lesions in human rheumatoid arthritis.

Because the disease develops as if it were infectious—with fever, anorexia, weight loss, anemia, etc.—an infectious pathogenesis has retained its appeal. With the recent advances in virology, the possibility that viruses are the pathogenetic agents has again achieved prominence. A viral infection could set off a chain of events with immune processes later predominating to maintain the process. But the diesase is also characterized by autoimmune phenomena and by a profusion of B- and T- cells in the joints. There is at present no explanation for the role of the virus in eliciting either of these phenomena, although the field abounds with speculations to account for them. Specifically, we do not know what are the causes of the autoimmune phenomena, which are most evident in the presence of rheumatoid factors and antinuclear antibodies. Nor do we know how genetic factors play a role in the disease; they may determine the nature and severity of the response to an exogenous agent such as a virus (Ziff, 1961) or, alternatively, manifest themselves as mutations to produce autoantibodies (Burch, 1963, 1968; Rowell, 1967). At the present time, the most-fashionable pathogenetic hypotheses are that rheumatoid arthritis is either an infectious disease or is due to disturbances in immmune mechanisms. Despite the extraordinary achievements of immunology, virology, and cellular biolgy in the past 20 years, the initiating causes of this disease have not been identified.

Another unsolved mystery is in what sequence inflammation gives rise to immune responses in rheumatoid arthritis. Conversely, an immune process could give rise to an inflammatory response. Consesus has not been achieved on this crucial point.

Ziff (1965) stated that the synovial cells were not in themselves the target of the inflammatory process, but that nontheless, the synovial membrane contains rheumatoid complexes, fixes complement, and synthesizes rheumatoid factors, suggesting that it is the seat of an immunological process that produces inflammation. Zvaifler (1965) believes that the joint inflammation in rheumatoid arthritis is not necessarily the result of any specific initiating event. Rather, unspecified predisposing factors exist in the rheumatoid patient and a variety of insults are capable of initiating joint inflammation, which is perpetuated by immune processes. According to his opinion, the inflammation is primary and the immunological events occur secondarily in response to the inflammation in the predisposed person.

462

A possible genetic defect in the structure of collagen was suggested by Steven (1964). The genetic defect in collagen could incite an autoimmune process directed at the altered chemical compostion of collagen that would be recognized immunologically as a foreign constituent. Hamerman (1966, 1969), however, suggested that specific initiating factors exist and that the primary disturbance does not reside in synovial but in connective tissue cells—a hypothesis in agreement with one put forward by Kellgren (1952). Hamerman also suggested that the disease is initiated by bacteria whose cell walls and capsules contain carbohydrates and carbohydrate-peptides, which are taken up by connective tissue cells. Because the cells fail to metabolize them, they are incorporated into the carbohydrate-protein complexes of connective tissue. Being foreign substances, they give rise to immune responses (Hamerman and Sandson, 1970) and disorderly cell proliferation, and are insufficiently disposed of metabolically.

In 1970, Hamerman and Sandson also pointed out that four of the main components of connective tissue—hyaluranate, basement membrane, collagen, and cartilage protein-polysaccharides—had antigenic properties (Steffen, 1969) and that antibodies to one of these could crossreact with antigens contained in the other, thus producing an inflammatory response. Later, however, Hamermen (1971a) felt that this chain of events was initiated by a virus. The virus would be incorporated into connective tissue cells and alter their surface antigenic properties, thereby inciting antibody formation against them. A different sequence of events was suggested by Gardner (1971, 1972). He believed that the primary target at the start of the disease was the synovium, not collagen or connective tissue. He based his argument in part on the findings obtained in experimental adjuvant arthritis.

This brief review has attempted to highlight current thoughts about the initiating factors in rheumatoid arthritis. There is much accumulated evidence to suggest that psychosocial factors also play some role in the initiation of the disease. Although there are many serious methodological problems, the data speak for the role of these factors at the beginning of the disease and in its recurrences. However, the manner in which psychosocial factors interact with the putative infectious, and altered immunological processes, or some other pathogenetic sequence of events, remains unknown.

Therefore, to those interested in the psychosocial aspects of rheumatoid arthritis, the various hypotheses just outlined pose a major problem: it is not enough simply to say that psychosocial factors contribute some proportion of the initiating variance or contribute to the exacerbation of the disease. It is necessary to specify how they do so: do they, for example, contribute to the induction of a latent virus, or to the immunological response? Are they mediated by the neuroendocrine or the autonomic nervous system (e.g., to produce changes in blood flow about the joints) or by the neuromusclar system? In regard to the latter, it has been observed that active rheumatoid arthritis does not occur in joints of a paralyzed limb (Thompson and Bywaters, 1962), even if the joints of the other extremities are inflamed.

The Nature of the Initiating Event

The various categories of events that precede or correlate with the onset of rheumatoid arthritis vary widely in their incidence. Short et al. (1957) found that 50 percent of their series of 293 hospitalized patients recorded one or more precipitating events, which were distributed in the following manner:

mental and/or physical strain	27.3%
infection	16.7%
exposure to cold or dampness	10.6%
surgical operation	5.5%
trauma	5.1%
pregnancy	2.1%

The data were obtained by interview. "Strain" was defined as a period of unusual anxiety or physical exertion. Of those reporting strain, 60 percent ascribed it to their occupations, and 40 percent reported that a relative was ill or had died and this either had or had not caused additional strain at work. In other series, figures for strain have varied from 22 percent (Burt et al., 1938) to 48 percent (Patterson et al., 1943).

In their series, Short and his fellow authors described 4 of 186 women who had experienced the onset of arthritis within four weeks after childbirth. During pregnancy the onset or exacerbation of the disease is infrequent, but it may begin after a miscarriage or birth. For example, in Slacter's (1943) series the onset occurred in 25 percent of 107 patients within six months after parturition. There are many physiological changes during pregnancy, and we do not know which of them of them have an ameliorating effect on the course of rheumatoid arthritis. One of these changes consists of elevations of serum 17-OH corticosteroid levels. In some pregnant women mild jaundice may occur and may improve the symptoms or prevent the onset of rheumatoid arthritis in some as-yet-unknown manner (Hill and Holley, 1966). Both of these physiological changes of pregnancy could theoretically benefit the symptoms of the disease.

To summarize, we are at a loss to say very much about the mechanisms that bring about the pathological changes in joints and blood vessels and in other bodily systems. Nor do we know in what cellular system (e.g., synovial or cartilage cells) the initial pathological changes occur. The antecedent causes of the rheumatoid factors are also unknown. The role of viruses and other infectious agents in the inception of the disease remains mysterious. The fact that psychological factors or surgery correlate with the onset of the disease seems well-established, but the further mechanisms by which they do so are completely unknown.

Infection in the Initiation

Infectious disease precedes the onset of rheumatoid arthritis in 9.5 to 32 percent of patients in various series. In the series published by Short et al. (1957), the figure was 16.7 percent. The infection may be viral or bacterial, and frequently occurs in the upper respiratory tract. However, rheumatoid arthritis is not like the arthritis produced by the gonococcus or the tubercle bacillus. In many ways we have not progressed beyond Dresser's summary of the possible initiating factors in rheumatoid arthritis: it is not an acute infectious arthritis in the sense that gonococcal or staphylococcal arthritis is. Although many different bacteria have been isolated from the joints of patients with rheumatoid arthritis, their presence does not prove that they play a pathogenetic role. They may be contaminants of the culture medium, or they may reside in the joints as symbionts and not pathogens. Conventional methods of culturing the synovial fluid usually do not grow bacteria or viruses. Only when synovial cells are grown in tissue culture can a variety of organisms (corynebacteria, mycoplasmas and bacterial "L" forms) be recovered.

VIRUSES AS INITIATING AGENTS

In theory, there are a number of ways in which viruses may produce a disease: they may cause it directly in a susceptible individual; they may be incorporated into the cell nucleus and manifest themselves at a later time; or they may alter the antigenic properties of the cell membrane and stimulate the production of new antigens so that antibodies are formed against them.

There is no confirmed evidence that rheumatoid arthritis is initiated by the *direct* effect of viruses. It has been reported that viruses can be recovered from synovial cells or fluid (Warren et al., 1969a, b) and transferred to animals. Smith and Hamerman (1969), however, could not confirm this finding, and viruses have not been observed by electron microscopy in the synovial membranes of patients (Hamerman et al., 1969; Gardner, 1972).

Indirect evidence of viral infection can be obtained through the detection of increased antibody levels to a specific virus. After vaccination with rubella, concentrations of specific antibodies to the virus are increased in the bloodstream. Seventeen percent of a group of patients developed a polyarthritis after vaccination with rubella (Kilroy, 1970; Thompson et al., 1971). Although the relationship of rubella polyarthritis to rheumatoid arthritis has not yet been clarified (Kantor and Tanner, 1962), the onset of rheumatoid arthritis has been noted following rubella polyarthritis (Martenis et al., 1968). However, rheumatoid factors do not appear in the serum of patients with rubella polyarthritis (Bartfeld, 1969); and, conversely, antibody titers to rubella virus are normal in patients with rheumatoid arthritis (Kacaki et al., 1970). For that matter, antibody titers to herpes simplex virus, measles, and parainfluenza are not detectable in rheumatoid arthritis patients (Chandler et al., 1971; Phillips and Christian, 1970). However, Marin et al. (1969) detected significant antibody titers to adenovirus and enterovirus in the blood and the synovial fluid of patients with a variety of arthritic diseases, including rheumatoid arthritis. But the presence of antibodies in the body fluids of patients does not constitute proof that a prior viral infection initiated the disease; the infection may have been intercurrent, unrelated to, or permissive in the onset of the arthritis.

It is now recognized that viruses may enter a cell, be incorporated into its genetic apparatus, transform it (as in malignancy), or slowly preempt and alter its functions to produce disease. Such "slow" viruses may be detected by various means, but both Ford and Oh (1965) and Barnett et al. (1966) failed to do so with rheumatoid arthritis. However, Hamerman (1971a, b) cites indirect evidence for a viral pathogenesis. He states that synovial cells obtained from patients with rheumatoid arthritis show persistent functional changes when they are grown in tissue culture; for example, their histology, enzymatic activities, and secretory function are altered (Castor, 1971a, b; Hamerman et al., 1969). They are resistant in tissue culture to infection with rubella (Grayzel and Beck, 1970) and with Newcastle disease virus (Smith and Hamerman, 1969). Resistance to this second virus can be transferred from human rheumatoid synovial cells to rabbit synovial cells (Hamerman, 1971a, 1975). The resistance to infection manifested by these cells is not due to the production of the body's own antiviral agent, interferon (Grayzel and Beck, 1970). It may be the indirect manifestation of the presence of a virus in the cell; proof of its existence requires very special cellular biological techniques, of which cell-fusion experiments are one.

Such experiments consist of fusing a normal cell with another cell that presumably contains the virus. When a human rheumatoid synovial cell was fused with a normal synovial cell obtained from a rabbit, the rabbit cell became resistant to infection with rubella and Newcastle disease virus (Hamerman, 1971a, 1975). The results of these experiments suggest that rheumatoid synovial cells may harbor such a virus; they are not proof that either of these two viruses are the initiating agent of the disease.

Viruses may, therefore, play a pathogenetic role in rheumatoid arthritis, and in addition they may account for the disturbances in immune mechanisms in the disease. Specifically, the patients's own IgG acquires antigenic properties within the body, and in consequence antibodies are formed against the altered IgG. Hypothetically, the virus could share common antigenic properties with some cellular component of the joint (e.g., the synovial or cartilage cells), so that cross-reacting antibodies are formed, thereby giving rise to the disease (Ford, 1969). More specifically, the virus could alter the composition of the cell membranes and endow them with new antigenic properties that are no longer "recognized" as being native to that person, with the result that antibodies are formed against them. Other possibilities exist: the synthesis of IgG may be perverted or the structure of the IgG may be altered by interacting with the virus, with the result that it acquires antigenic properties. Finally, latent clones of immunologically competent cells, potentially capable of producing antibodies, may be "induced" by the virus to become active; these antibodies then react with antigens, of which they are not tolerant, to damage synovial or cartilage cells.

Perhaps the most relevant model of the action of a virus is provided by a disease produced in mice of the New Zealand "black" strain. This disease is characterized by the appearance of antinuclear factors, hemolytic anemia and renal lesions, which are important features of SLE in man. It is believed that this disease in mice is initiated by a virus (Mellors and Huang, 1967; Mellors et al., 1969). The virus is probably transmitted vertically from generation to generation. Antibodies are formed to antigens of the virus. The antigen-antibody complexes, which included complement, damage the cell membrane of red cells and the glomerulus of the kidney. The New Zealand black strain appears immunologically to be more reactive to viral antigens than other strains of mice.

However, no virus has as yet been identified in patients with SLE, and the pathogenesis of the disseminated lesions in this illness is unknown, although it is believed that antigen-antibody complexes play a mediating role. There are, of course, differences between rheumatoid arthritis and SLE. In SLE, the arthritis is caused by fibrin deposition on the synovial membrane; in rheumatoid arthritis, the renal lesions seen in SLE rarely occur (Gardner, 1972).

At the present time, it is impossible to decide between the alternative hypotheses that attempt to explain the altered immune mechanisms in rheumatoid arthritis. These alterations could come about either by the agency of a virus or through spontaneous mutations occurring in immunologically competent cells (Burnet, 1963).

466

"Diphtheroid" organisms have been isolated from the lymph nodes that drain rheumatoid arthritic joints (Alexander et al., 1968; Duthie et al., 1967; Stewart et al., 1969). They have also been isolated in patients with osteoarthritis, and may be contaminants of the culture medium (Hill et al., 1967).

The pathogenetic role of diphtheroids, as well as other bacteria, the mycoplasmas and listeria is not established, despite their isolation from patients and their growth in tissue culture. In fact, mycoplasmas do produce an inflammation of joints in a variety of animal species (Sharp, 1971). Nevertheless their pathogenetic role in human rheumatoid arthritis is both controversial and not reliably established (Barnett et al., 1966; Bartholomew, 1965; Christian, 1967; Dumonde, 1971; Ford and Oh, 1965; Fraser et al., 1971; Jansson et al., 1971; Pease, 1968, 1969; Williams, 1968; Williams and Bruckner, 1971; Williams et al., 1970).

Immunopathology

Rheumatoid factors are an important and common feature of the pathophysiology of rheumatoid arthritis. The SCAT was positive in 87 percent of 393 hospitalized patients and in 51 percent of 642 outpatients with rheumatoid arthritis (Kellgren and Ball, 1959). But the presence of rheumatoid factors is not confined to rheumatoid arthritis; they are present in the serum of patients with many kinds of infections and other diseases in which immunological disturbances or reactions occur (Bartfeld, 1960, 1969; Kellgren and Ball, 1959; Lawrence et al., 1971; Messner et al., 1968). Rheumatoid factors occur in infectious diseases due to viral, bacterial and parasitic agents (Lawrence et al., 1971); in pulmonary diseases such as asthma, pneumoconiosis, and especially idiopathic pulmonary fibrosis (Ward and Stalker 1965); in rheumatic fever; in hypergammoglobulinemia, macroglobulinemia, leukemia, hepatitis and hepatic cirrhosis, and tissue injury (Russell and Hutt, 1962); in Sjögren's syndrome (Bloch et al., 1965); and in patients receiving renal homografts (Bartfeld, 1960, 1969). Rheumatoid factors are also present in some patients with systemic lupus erythmatosus and periarteritis nodosa (Kellgren and Ball, 1959). They may also occur in schizophrenic and depressive psychoses (Fessel, 1962; Oreskes et al., 1968; Rosenblatt et al., 1968; Solomon et al., 1969). Rheumatoid factors were identifiable in the sera of from 0.6 to 1 percent or more of a population without disease (Bartfeld, 1960; Hill, 1969; Lawrence and Ball, 1958). Rheumatoid factors become more prevalent with age (Blumberg et al., 1961; Heimer et al., 1963; Kellgren, 1966, 1968; Lawrence and Ball, 1958; Litwin and Singer, 1965; Moskowitz et al., 1967) regardless of whether or not the population studied is ill. However, the presence of rheumatoid factors in sera is more prevalent in older people who have paralysis agitans, late-onset diabetes mellitus, and arteriosclerotic heart disease (Litwin and Singer, 1965). Whether the increasing prevalence of rheumatoid factors with age is due to the gradual accumulation of autoantibodies related to cellular changes and damage (Heimer et al., 1963), or whether it is due to past exposure to nonspecific antigens (Scotch and Geiger, 1962) or to infection awaits further investigation (Lawrence et al., 1971).

The development of rheumatoid factors in the course of infectious diseases (especially chronic infections) partly accounts for the belief that the pathogenesis of rhematoid arthritis is due to a virus or bacterium. Christian (1963) has also shown that the prolonged immunization of animals with bacteria (e.g., E. coli) produces antibodies with the properties of rheumatoid factors. One may conclude, therefore, that chronic infection can alter the structure of an immunoglobulin (IgG) so as to cause antibodies—the rheumatoid factors—to be formed against it. Rheumatoid factors may, therefore, play a role in the body's defenses against infection, or in the regulation of these defensive mechanisms. They also neutralize viruses and are involved in attracting leukocytes to the site of infection by fixing complement after they have reacted with antigen (Ashe et al., 1971; Notkins, 1971; Schmid et al., 1970; Stage and Mannik, 1972; Zvaifler and Schur, 1968).

THE ROLE OF AUTOANTIBODIES AND THE NATURE OF RHEUMATOID FACTORS

There is much evidence to suggest that the rheumatoid factors play an important role in rheumatoid arthritis, but the nature of that role remains uncertain. Some authorities postulate a pathogenetic role for these autoantibodies (Ziff, 1973) and others do not (Glynn and Holborow, 1965). Some claim a predisposing role for them in the disease (Vaughan, 1969).

Rheumatoid factors are antigammaglobulin autoantibodies (Glynn, 1968). The antigen responsible for their formation is the patient's own γ-globulin (IgG), which was first identified when it was shown that IgG from human serum inhibits the reaction of sensitized sheep red blood cells with rheumatoid serum. All subsequent tests for rheumatoid factors have been predicated on the assumption that rheumatoid serum contains antibodies to human IgG. The antibodies to IgG are not homogeneous (Heimer and Levin, 1964; Meltzer et al., 1966; Milgrom and Tönder, 1965); their heterogeneity has been demonstrated by their capacity to react with both human and animal immunoglobulins (Allen and Kunkel, 1964; Fudenberg and Kunkel, 1961). The usual human rheumatoid factor has a sedimentation constant of 19S (Svartz et al., 1958)—it is, therefore, a macroglobulin (IgM). Several other antibodies to IgG have been identified; some are an IgA and others an IgG (Bartfeld and Epstein, 1969; Christian, 1968). When the IgG antigen and the IgM antibody form a rheumatoid complex that is compounded of six molecules of the former and one molecule of the latter, with a sedimentation constant of 22S (Franklin et al., 1957). By the appropriate chemical methods the complex can be dissociated into its original components.

The process by which an immunoglobulin, the IgG, acquires antigenic properties has not been solved. Actually, only the Fc fragment of the IgG becomes antigenic, by virtue of being altered in conformation. In consequence, the immune system treats it as if it were a foreign antigen, and antibodies are formed against it (Edelman et al., 1958; Natvig et al., 1971).

The rheumatoid factors are produced in lymph nodes, synovial membranes, and subcutaneous rheumatoid nodules in rheumatoid arthritis (Bonomo et al., 1968; Mellors et al., 1961). Rheumatoid nodules may occur without any other lesion. Their location on flexor surfaces suggests that externally applied physical pressure or friction may play a role in their appearance. We have no ready explanation why rheumatoid factors are manufactured in the nodules and not in synovial cells in some patients, but not in others.

468

Any hypothesis about the initiation, recurrence, or maintenance of rheumatoid arthritis must account for the intense infiltration of synovial tissue by immunologically competent lymphocytes (B-cells) and plasma cells, and thymus derived lymphocytes (T-cells) (Julkunen, 1966), the increased concentrations of immunoglobulins and the presence of autoimmune antibodies in the blood. These antibodies, the rheumatoid factors, and the antinuclear antibodies react widely with, but probably do not by themselves damage, different tissues in the bodies of man and other animals.

But if these autoantibodies do not directly cause the tissue damage, what does? As has been mentioned, the rheumatoid factors are synthesized in synovial cells, lymph nodes and rheumatoid nodules (Mellors et al., 1961; Vazques and Dixon, 1957). In the early stages of the disease, only the IgG's (the antigen and its antibody) are found at these sites (Kaplan, 1963); later on in the disease, the IgG's, the IgA's, and IgM's (the antibodies) appear there (Kaplan and Vaughan, 1962; Ziff, 1973). Both forms of immunoglobulin are believed to be synthesized by B-lymphocytes in the synovium of patients with rheumatoid arthritis (Sliwinski and Zvaifler, 1970) in response to an unidentified stimulus to their production within the joint. In rheumatoid arthritis, synovial cells synthesize an excessive amount of IgG (Ziff, 1968) for reasons that still have not been clarified.

To summarize the present quandary about the source of the autoantibodies: It is not known whether they result from an infection (perhaps with a virus), an autoimmune process, or a disease process in which tissue injury releases antigens to which antibodies are formed. The fact that rheumatoid factors occur in healthy persons suggests that they indicate either a genetic tendency to hyperimmune reactivity or an exposure to a virus, perhaps a "slow" one.

Regardless of their origin, rheumatoid factors are thought to participate in producing the lesions of rheumatoid arthritis, despite the fact that they persist in patients whose arthritis has remitted. They are pathogenetic, it has been suggested, because they fix complement (Pekin and Zvaifler, 1964; Ruddy and Austen, 1970, 1975; Ziff, 1973, 1968; Zvaifler, 1969). One of the functions of complement is to attract polymorphonuclear cells to the site of antigen-antibody reactions (Vaughan et al., 1968b, 1969; Zvaifler, 1969). By fixing complement, rheumatoid factors would attract these cells to the joint (Ward, 1971). The cells, in turn, ingest the rheumatoid complexes and complement and release enzymes destructive to cartilage (Kinsella et al., 1970; Weisman and Spilber, 1968). The injurious agents are lysosomal enzymes. Lysosomes are cell organelles that contain a number of enzymes capable of breaking down many different kinds of large molecules, such as proteins and protein polysaccharide complexes that are contained in cartilage. Lysosomes and the enzymes they contain may play a role in the breakdown of articular cartilage in rheumatoid arthritis (Lack, 1969; Weissman and Spilberg, 1968; Weissman, 1965, 1971). Lysosomal hydrolases demonstrably digest the matrix of cartilage (Coombs and Fell, 1969; Lachmann et al., 1969). The content of a lysosomal enzyme, acid phosphatase, is increased in synovial cells of patients with rheumatoid arthritis (Hamerman et al., 1961; Jasani et al., 1969). But the data are not easily interpreted. In rheumatoid arthritis, the damage to joint cartilage is localized; if the enzymes were released into the joint space one would expect the damage to cartilage to be distributed generally. It is the consensus that lysosomal enzymes contribute to the pathophysiology of rheumatoid arthritis but not to its initiation, because their release depends on the prior formation of rheumatoid complexes.

The usual, clinical tests for rheumatoid factors only identify the IgM-rheumatoid factor and not the IgA- or IgG-rheumatoid factors. Therefore, it cannot be assumed that if the tests are negative the two latter rheumatoid factors are not present in serum (Panush et al., 1971; Torrigiani et al., 1969). In addition, rheumatoid factors can occur in synovial cells even if they are undetectable in serum. In fact, it seems to be true that the failure to detect them in serum does not preclude their role in the pathogenesis of the joint lesion. For example, IgG rheumatoid factors after complexing with IgG still bind complement in the same way as IgG-IgM complexes do (Kinsella et al., 1970; Lambert et al., 1975; Munthe et al., 1975; Natvig et al., 1975 Winchester, 1975).

RHEUMATOID FACTORS AND THE COURSE AND PROGNOSIS

Rheumatoid factors may, therefore, play a role in the pathogenesis of rheumatoid arthritis. They also play a role in its course and prognosis. Patients with strongly positive tests for rheumatoid factors tend to have the more severe, progressive, destructive form of the disease (Cats and Hazevoet, 1970; Franco and Schur, 1971). In patients who have negative tests for these factors (Dixon, 1961) the progress of the disease is either slower or does not occur at all.

Hill (1968) found that the SCAT was negative in 60 percent of his patients in whom the disease was not progressing (as indicated by X-ray evidence of the development of joint erosions), but it was negative in only 8 percent of the patients whose disease was progressing. In other words, Hill was able to establish a correlation between tests for rheumatoid factors and the course of the disease. The great majority of patients (92 percent) who suffered from a progressive form of the disease had a positive SCAT.

When the disease remits, rheumatoid factors tend to persist in the serum of patients. Therefore, one must conclude that rheumatoid factors alone cannot be pathogenetic, other factors—such as their complexing with the IgG antigen and being ingested by phagocytes may play a role (Hurd et al., 1970; Schur et al., 1975).

THE PATHOGENESIS OF RHEUMATOID ARTHRITIS IN IMMUNE DEFICIENCY DISEASE

One of the most potent arguments against the factors having a role in initiating rheumatoid arthritis is that the disease occurs in 33 percent of patients with hereditary agammaglobulinemia (Ford, 1969; Fundenberg, 1968, Gitlin et al., 1959; Good and Rotstein, 1960); or conditions in which IgA levels are depressed. For such patients rheumatoid factors are not detectable in the serum of either children or adults (Barnett etl., 1970).

Patients with hereditary agammaglobulinemia and arthritis still form rheumatoid nodules that contain lymphocytes and plasma cells. In those diseases in which the concentration of IgG or IgA in the blood is low (Cassidy et al., 1968), the synovial cells have been detected to produce small quantities of immunoglobulins that may be playing the same role in the pathogenesis of the disease as in the usual patients with rheumatoid arthritis who have elevated immunoglobulin levels (Claman and Merrill, 1966; Cockel et

470

al., 1971). In immunodeficient patients with arthritis, the synovial tissue can still fix complement (Munthe et al., 1975).

Patients with hereditary (X-linked) agammaglobulinemia are unusually prone to infections because of their inability to produce humoral antibodies. Rheumatoid arthritis is common in these patients because they are less able to control or combat the supposed infectious agent that incites the disease (Strober et al., 1972).

But the paradox that rheumatoid arthritis can occur with either elevated or depressed immunoglobulin levels has also been explained in another way: either an excess or an insufficiency of antigen or antibody leads to an imbalance between the two and results in the failure to clear the body of the antigen-antibody complexes, which are then deposited at various sites in the body (Christian, 1968; Dixon et al., 1959, 1961). Another reason for the imbalance may be that the disposition of antibodies (especially IgG and perhaps IgM) is accelerated in rheumatoid arthritis (Wochner, 1970). To summarize: In some people antibodies are formed poorly (possibly because of a genetic predisposition); in others an excess of antibody is formed. In either case the relationship of antigen to antibody is disturbed. In the first example, there is an excess of antigen; in the second, an excess of antibody. In either case, the disposition of antigen-antibody complexes is disrupted. This hypothesis would explain why some patients with rheumatoid arthritis are predisposed to react with excessive antibody production on antigenic challenge, while others develop the disease if they produce antibodies inadequately, for instance, those with agammaglobulinemia or hypogammaglobulinemia.

The Role of the Vascular Lesions

Vascular lesions, especially microvascular injury, are a significant feature of the morbid pathology of rheumatoid arthritis, even in its earliest phases (Radnai, 1953, 1969; Schumacher, 1975). Some authorities think they account for the widely disseminated pathological changes (Goldie, 1969; Kulka, 1959; Sokoloff, 1963, 1966). But because rheumatoid complexes, complement, and fibrin is deposited in the walls of blood vessels as a consequence of the inflammatory and immunopathological changes that occur in the disease, the vascular lesions generally are believed to be caused by these deposits and are not the primary disturbance leading to the arthritis, synovitis, or disease of the cartilage. IgM and IgG rheumatoid factors and complexes have now been identified in synovial fluid or tissue. They are also present in cartilage, ligaments and in the acute phase of the vascular lesions (Conn et al., 1972; Cooke et al., 1972, 1975; Weisman and Zvaifler, 1975).

Careful clinical observation (Schmid et al., 1961; Short et al., 1957) has suggested that vasomotor phenomena, dysesthesias, and paresthesias either precede the arthritis by many years, are a prominent feature of its "prodromal" phrase, or accompany (in 55 percent of patients) the onset of joint symptoms. Their occurrence may reflect changes in blood supply to the distal extremities or to peripheral nerves. But it is not possible to decide whether vascular disturbances antecede or follow the initiation of the disease when observations are made after its inception.

The Role of Other Autoantibodies

The presence of antinuclear factors in about 50 percent of patients with rheumatoid arthritis has not been explained so far (Condemi et al., 1965; Deicher and Frese, 1971;

471

Hijmans et al., 1961). Nor is it known why rheumatoid factors are prevalent in the relatives of patients with SLE. This link between these two diseases has remained unexplained. It has been suggested that the appearance of rheumatoid factors and antinuclear antibodies is an indication that the immune system is genetically predisposed to lose its tolerance of its own tissue components. This intolerance results in the development of antibodies both to normal antibody defenses (i.e., the IgG), thus forming rheumatoid factors, and to the various constituents of the nucleus of cells, producing antinuclear antibodies. Antinuclear antibodies and rheumatoid factors, according to this view, constitute "markers" of rheumatoid arthritis but play no initiating role in it. They identify an etiologic predisposition to this and certain other diseases, or they define their prognosis (Duthie et al., 1957).

Pearson (1966) considers the foregoing hypothesis unlikely, though not disproved. He argues that the rheumatoid factors and antinuclear antibodies are immunologically heterogeneous (Barnett et al., 1964, 1965; Heimer and Levin, 1964); therefore, a number of mutations in antibody production would have to take place. It seems more likely that a change in the conformation of several antigens accounts for the loss of tolerance and the heterogeneity of the antigen-antibody complexes that constitute the rheumatoid complexes.

Cellular Immune Mechanisms in the Initiation of Rheumatoid Arthritis

The unusually high incidence of rheumatoid arthritis in patients with absent or reduced IgG production has been used as a strong argument against an important pathogenetic role for either autoimmune or humorally mediated immune mechanisms. Some proponents of this thesis (Dumonde, 1971) believe that many of the lymphocytes present in the synovial tissue in this disease are of the T-cell line. Direct proof of this thesis has only recently been obtained. 70 to 85 percent of the lymphocytes in the synovium of each of eight patients were shown to be T-cells (Bach et al., 1975; van Boxel and Paget, 1975; Williams, 1975).

The recent demonstration that a predominant number of the lymphocytes in synovial tissue are of the T-cell line, suggests that cellular immunity also plays an important role in the pathological physiology of rheumatoid arthritis. Until direct proof of the presence of T-cells was obtained, there existed only indirect evidence for their presence in synovial tissue (Maini et al., 1970; Williams et al., 1970). Actually, the existence of T-cells in the joints does not in itself constitute proof that cellular immune mechanisms predominate in this disease. T-cells interact in complex ways to help or suppress the production of humoral antibodies by B-cells, in addition to being capable directly of injuring or killing cells.

The best evidence for a cellular immune pathogenesis for an arthritis has been obtained in animals. Dumonde and Glynn (1962) first injected human fibrin dissolved in Freund's adjuvant into rabbits. A subsequent, single, intra-articular injection of human fibrin or the rabbit's own fibrin elicited a delayed type of hypersensitivity (cellular immune) reaction in the injected joint, consisting of a periarticular infiltration with lymphocytes and plasma cells, which began to aggregate into nodules and granulomata. In addition to the cellular immune reaction, rabbits injected with human fibrin also had a humoral antibody response, while the cellular immune responses of those animals who were injected with their own fibrin resulted in the formation of granulomata but not in a lymphocyte reaction.

472

Dumonde (1971) reported that when chickens incapable of producing immunoglobulins were first immunized for delayed hypersensitivity, and then injected once in the ankle joint with an insoluble antigen, a chronic synovitis ensued, ending in a granulomatous arthritis. Dumonde (1971) and Pearson and Wood (1959, 1964) also reported that the passive transfer of delayed hypersensitivity could be accomplished by injecting an antigen and lymphocytes sensitized to the same antigen into the joint of guinea pigs. The sensitized lymphocytes seemed to act in the role of an adjuvant. Dumonde (1971) and Jennings (1971) believe that cell-mediated immune responses may play a role either in the inception, recrudescence, or maintance of rheumatoid arthritis, and they cite the foregoing evidence from their work to support their contention.

In summary, many facets of the pathogenesis of the inflammation of joints and of the vasculitis in rheumatoid arthritis remain unknown. We do not know what causes the IgG to assume antigenic properties, or whether rheumatoid factors and complexes antecede or are a consequence of the inflammation. The predominance of T-cells, and the minority of B-cells, in synovial tissue remains unexplained, but supports the concept that both a cellular and a humoral immunopathology occur in this disease. Early in the course of the disease, both the phagocytic cells and secretory cells of the synovial membrane are increased, and there is a progressive accretion of T- and B-cells. The nature of the stimulus to the increase in cells and to the presence of lymphocytes and plasma cells remains mysterious. The later destructive changes in the joints are probably brought about by catalytic enzymes released by the phagocytic cells, possibly in response to the products of antigen-antibody interactions or by rheumatoid complexes. The obliterative and necrotizing vascular lesions appear early and are probably also due to the deposition in blood vessels of these complexes.

The demonstration of rheumatoid factors in the sera of patients with rheumatoid arthritis opened an important era in our gradual understanding of the disease. Although much has been learned about their chemical structure, interactions with the antigen, and sites of origin, no definite conclusion has been reached about their role in the etiology and pathogenesis of the disease. They are present in the sera of the general population, in the healthy relatives of patients with rheumatoid arthritis and other diseases, and in patients with a considerable number of diseases that are not necessarily characterized by arthritis or vasculitis. Their absence from the sera in some patients with rheumatoid arthritis does not preclude their presence in synovial and other cells in the joints: in fact, this is the situation in the agammaglobulinemias and hypogammaglobulinemias that predispose with unusual frequency to rheumatoid arthritis. But, as we have also seen rheumatoid factors may appear after the onset of rheumatoid arthritis in some patients, and their presence has been correlated with the course and prognosis of the disease. In juvenile patients with rheumatoid arthritis and in many adult patients with the disease, rheumatoid factors are not as frequently recoverable from serum.

Much controversy surrounds the role of rheumatoid factors in bringing about the joint lesions. Most of the evidence does not support their direct pathogenetic role. Yet, as noted, rheumatoid factors are present in healthy persons, suggesting they are markers of an unusual immunological reactivity, and may constitute one of several risk factors in rheumatoid arthritis.

As was just mentioned, rheumatoid complexes are deposited in blood vessels in rheumatoid arthritis, probably to produce the vascular lesions. The best explanation is

473

that a two-way discrepancy between the amounts of antigen and rheumatoid factors may bring about the deposition of the complexes in the blood vessels of the joints and elsewhere in the body. Rheumatoid factors alone would not, therefore, account for the lesions, but an imbalance in their quantitative relationship to the antigen might.

The interaction of rheumatoid factors with the psychological and social variables described in this disease is as yet unknown. The rheumatoid factors might be used to select a population of subjects at risk in predictive studies. In addition, some aspect of formation, desposition, or interaction with antigen might be affected by the psychological state or the inciting social events of that state—but this is rank speculation.

IgM rheumatoid factors usually do not appear in the serum until after the onset of the disease (Sievers, 1965). However, 1.0 to 5.0 percent of the healthy population has rheumatoid factors in the serum. Positive tests for rheumatoid factors may be crucial to psychosomatic research in rheumatoid arthritis. In view of their presence in healthy individuals and the healthy relatives of patients, positive tests for rheumatoid factors may constitute an important criterion whereby a population at risk for the disease may be chosen (Ball and Lawrence, 1961; Lawrence, 1963). This contention is supported by figures provided by Lawrence and Ball (1958). About 20 to 25 percent of those persons in the population at large whose serum contains rheumatoid factors have symptoms and signs of rheumatoid arthritis. However, if those with the highest titers of rheumatoid factors were examined, in all likelihood the incidence of the disease would rise to 60 to 70 percent, although, as already emphasized, the critieria on which this diagnosis is based must be considered "shaky." Moreover, when 75 percent of those who had positive tests for rheumatoid factors were reexamined five years later, the incidence of rheumatoid arthritis was 36 percent—in contrast to the 8 percent incidence among those who had negative reactions on first examination (Lawrence, 1963). Briefly stated, the higher the titer, the greater was the likelihood that the individual would develop rheumatoid arthritis. One might conclude that there is a double predisposition to rheumatoid arthritis: one predisposition to form rheumatoid factors, and another to develop the disease. When these predispositions coincide, the probability that the disease will occur increases.

Good evidence exists, therefore, that persons with rheumatoid factors in the serum but no disease later develop rheumatoid arthritis. It is this group of persons, and an appropriate comparison group, who could be studied socially, psychologically, and physiologically, to confirm or refute many of the data reviewed in this chapter that has been gathered after the onset of the disease.

ANIMAL STUDIES: STRESS AND IMMUNE RESPONSES

Many of the so-called psychosomatic diseases can also be studied in animals. Animal models of these diseases have been used to demonstrate that: (1) there are no single or invariant etiological or pathogenetic factors in any disease. High blood pressure and gastric ulceration in animals can be brought about in many different ways and in many different species; (2) early social experiences may strongly influence the development of later disease; (3) early social experience, as well as genetic factors, can alter physiological functioning that leads to disease; (4) environmental stress can modify even those physiological changes that can largely be accounted for by genetic or other factors.

474

Human rheumatoid arthritis has a rich immunopathology. And arthritis in animals has been produced by viral, bacterial, and other foreign antigens (Christian, 1963; Dumonde, 1971; Gardner, 1960; Pearson, 1956, 1963, 1966; Phillips et al., 1966; Sharp, 1971). One form of animal arthritis is brought about by injecting rats with Freund's adjuvant that consists of killed tubercle bacillus, and emulsifying agent and mineral oil (Pearson, 1956). This adjuvant arthritis shares some features of human rheumatoid arthritis (Pearson and Wood, 1959). But it also differs from it (Glenn et al., 1965; Gryfe et al., 1971; Katz and Piliero, 1969; Pearson, 1966). Nonetheless, stress may alter the course of adjuvant arthritis.

In male rats, Amkraut et al. (1971) have reported, the stress of being housed in groups for one week before adjuvant arthritis was induced increased the intensity of the disease. The onset of the maximal intensity of the disease and the rate of recovery were also accelerated by prior stress. The group housing altered the course of the arthritis with or without overcrowding. The concentrations of corticosteroids in the plasma and serum fibrinogen and other proteins after the arthritis had set in were, however, the same in stressed rats as in other rats.

Ten to 20 percent of all patients with rheumatoid arthritis either show clinical evidence of amyloidosis or amyloid deposits in their organs at autopsy (Wolf, 1970). It is of some interest, therefore, as Ebbesen and Rask-Nielsen (1967) have reported, that when mice of the DBA/2, BALB/c, and CBA strains were grouped together according to sex, only male mice died an early death due to extensive and generalized amyloidosis. Fighting among the mice did not seem to be correlated with amyloid deposition. These findings have subsequently been confirmed and extended (Ebbesen, 1968): when male mice of the DBA/2 and BALB/c strains were grouped, they began at the age of 6 months to develop a syndrome of weight loss, a hunched posture, some alopecia, and bite marks on the back; and they died at an early age. Prior to this, at age 4 weeks, some of them had been treated with chlortetracycline and were thymectomized. Housing operated males together, or housing several male mice with a female mouse, was conducive to the development of the syndrome and hastened death. Unoperated mice of the CBA strain and female mice, regardless of strain, seldom fought each other or bit, and they remained healthy. Reserpine and castration protected the male animals of DBA/2 and BALB/c strains from the syndrome and from an early death due to amyloid disease. Castration decreased somewhat the survival time of CBA males. Whereas estrogen treatment only of BALB/c males caused an early death with testicular tumors, if they were castrated and given estrogen, they survived longer. Some DBA/2 males developed hypergammaglobulinemia. Ebbesen concluded that the cause of death was amyloidosis, that the exposure of males to males, and not their isolation from females, was the significant, stressful variable; that reserpine, in doses that tranquilized but did not inhibit androgen secretion, protected animals by diminishing the impact of the stress, and that bacterial infection played no part in the development of amyloid disease.

SUMMARY AND CONCLUSIONS

Any investigator of rheumatoid arthritis faces problems. Despite the great amount of data that has been accumulated about its pathophysiology at every level of biological organization, there is no satisfactory or coherent account of the etiology of this disease.

Throughout this chapter the problems inherent in the diagnosis of rheumatoid arthritis have been stressed in order to provide a guideline for the choice of patient populations for those interested in investigating the disease's psychosocial aspects. Much of what remains to be accomplished in this area has not yet even been attempted. Subjects must be chosen by clearly defined criteria, including the presence or absence of rheumatoid factors in their sera. A number of studies suggest that rheumatoid factors are probably necessary but not sufficient predisposing factors in rheumatoid arthritis. But their presence in serum does not necessarily mean that a person must develop either the systemic manifestations or the arthritis of the disease. They may, however, constitute markers of subjects at risk for the disease. Such subjects could be chosen for predictive studies. The purpose of such studies would be to verify the patient descriptions that have until now been obtained only after disease onset. A longitudinal approach in such studies would also allow the investigator to observe directly, not in in retrospect, the events in their lives that correlate with the onset of the arthritis.

The risk strategy could also be employed to discriminate between the great variety of biochemical and immunological changes that may antecede the disease process. For example, when and why in the course of a subject's life does the change in the antigenicity of the IgG occur, and, therefore, when do rheumatoid factors first appear in serum? In psychosocial studies on rheumatoid arthritis itself, patients with diseases such as Felty's and Sjögren's syndromes and SLE should probably be excluded. Subjects should be carefully matched by age, sex, and socioeconomic status. If comparative studies are done between SLE or these other syndromes and rheumatoid arthritis, the diagnostic critieria should be made explicit.

In summarizing the data on rheumatoid arthritis, one would have to conclude that there are multiple predispositions to this disease. It is the belief of some experts in the field that there is, at a minimum, a dual predisposition to rheumatoid arthritis: first, the capacity to form rheumatoid factors, and second, the capacity to develop the disease. But the exact nature of these capacities are not known. Since we still do not know the reasons for the development of rheumatoid factors, one would have to conclude that they may be indicators of frequently occurring and excessive immunological reactivity to unknown stimuli. Conversely, rheumatoid arthritis occurs with increased frequency in conjunction with diseases characterized by an impairment of immunological reactivity, such as X-linked agammaglobulinemia. Logically, therefore, one would conclude that either an excess or deficiency of the immune response places persons at risk for the disease. As in other diseases, such as gout, the same phenotypic expression—the disease process itself—may come about by different etiological mechanisms. The retrospective studies of the psychological characteristics of patients with rheumatoid arthritis that have been described in this chapter may, in part, account for some of the predisposition to develop the disease. These psychological characteristics seem to antedate the disease. A fair consensus about the characteristic conflicts of these patients has been arrived at by clinical observation and inference. However, psychological tests often do not verify observation and inference, because they may not elicit the same kind of data. To many readers this fact is a major source of discouragement and confusion: it appears to them that clinical observation has not been verified and should not be believed. It is true that the methodology of clinical observation could be improved. But it is more important, in using psychological tests, that the investigator first ascertain that his instrument is sensitive enough to elicit the kind of data that is appropriate to the hypothesis he is testing.

The retrospective clinical evidence suggests that rebellious, aggressive, tomboyish impulses, which in the patient's adolescence are expressed in speech and action, are later in life expressed in tyrannical and domineering behavior toward others, or are excessively controlled by various psychological defense mechanisms or by self-punitive actions, which often lead to suffering. Other (especially women) patients do not go through this development sequence and are angry, resentful, and embittered, but try not to express these feelings.

Only Rimón's study deals with the fact that patients do not constitute a homogeneous population, and that psychological factors may account for a different percentage of the predisposing and initiating variance and may also account for the different natural history of the disease in different populations. His study suggests that some patients with rheumatoid arthritis may have a greater biological (immunological?) predisposition than others, but that even for these patients, psychological factors play some role in the predisposition to and initiation of the disease. In patients with less of a biological predisposition, the relative psychological contribution to predisposition and initiation of the disease may be greater. However, this hypothesis requires further confirmation.

We also do not know enough about the factors that initiate rheumatoid arthritis. Trauma, surgery, infection and pregnancy certainly may do so. Bereavement and disappointments also do so. The disease may come on suddenly, especially in some patients, but its onset is usually gradual and is anteceded by a series of nonspecific complaints that could suggest other diseases. Therefore, in retrospective studies the exact dating of the onset of rheumatoid arthritis becomes hazardous and is fraught with the danger of unreliable correlations between life events and the inception of the disease.

Nonetheless, there is quite strong evidence that separation from another person, especially from someone who had previously been submissive to the patient, and felt trapped in the relationship, are common onset conditions. But once this has been said, we are at a loss to explain how such events and the psychological responses they occasion set in motion the series of physiological processes that conclude with the disease. In fact, we do not know where in the body the disease begins—in synovial or cartilage cells, in cartilage ground substance, or in the vascular tree. Any psychological hypothesis of pathogenesis that attempts to connect the emotional responses to separation with the process that starts the disease must await elucidation of the exact site at which that process begins. Nor as we have seen, do we know the nature of the pathogenetic agent. Recently, infection has once again achieved popularity in the role of the proximal pathogenetic agent. The infectious agent may be a virus which in some patients interacts with the multiple predisposing factors. But can bereavement or loss, grief or depression be accompanied by bodily changes which lead to virus induction? Or was Alexander right in stating that increased muscle tension somehow contributes to the joint lesion? We do not know. We suspect that muscular activity may worsen the joint lesion. Finally, this disease raises the question of whether psychological states such as depression may in some way interact with immunological processes in ways that at present are shrouded in mystery.

It is, of course, likely that these questions are irrelevant to the solution of the predisposition to and initiation of rheumatoid arthritis. There are so many gaps in our knowledge about the pathogenesis of the disease that we may not even know what the relevant questions are.

REFERENCES

Aho, K. 1961. A normal series for rheumatoid serology collected by random sampling. *Scand. J. Rheumatol.* 7:18.

Alanen, Y. O., Rekola, J. K., Stewen, A., Takala, K., and Tuovinen, M. 1966. The family in the pathogenesis of schizophenic and neurotic disorders. *Acta Psychiatr. Scand.* 42(Suppl.):189

Alexander, F. 1950. *Psychosomatic Medicine.* New York: Norton.

Alexander, F., French, T. M., and Pollock, G. H. 1968. *Psychosomatic Specificity: Experimental Study and Results.* Chicago: University of Chicago Press.

Alexander, W. R. M., Stewart, S. M., and Duthie, J. J. R. 1968. Etiological factors in rheumatoid arthritis. In *Rheumatic Diseases,* edited by J. J. R. Duthie and W. R. M. Alexander. Pfizer Medical Mongraphs No. 3. Edinburgh: Edinburgh University Press.

Allen, J. C., and Kunkel, H. G. 1964. Rheumatoid factors with hidden autospecificity. *Arthritis Rheum.* 1:725.

Amkraut, A. A., Solomon, G. F., and Kraemer, H. C. 1971. Stress, early experience and adjuvant-induced arthritis. *Psychosom. Med.* 33:203.

Ansell, B. M., and Lawrence, J. S. 1966. Fluoridation and the rheumatic diseases: a comparison of rheumatism in Watford and Leigh. *Ann. Rheum. Dis.* 25:67.

———, Bywaters, E. G. L., and Lawrence, J. S. 1962. A family study of Still's disease. *Ann. Rheum. Dis.* 21:243.

Ashe, W. K., Daniels, C. A., Scott, G. S., and Notkins, A. L. 1971. Interaction of rheumatoid factor with infectious herpes simplex virus—antibody complexes. *Science* 172:176.

Bach, J.-F., Dardenne, M., and Clot, J. 1975. Evaluation of serum thymic hormone and of circulating T cells in rheumatoid arthritis and in systemic lupus erythemotosus. *Rheumatology* 6:242.

Ball, J., and Lawrence, J. S. 1961. Epidemiology of the sheep cell agglutination test. *Ann. Rheum. Dis.* 20:235.

———, Bloch, K. J., Burch, T. A., Kellgren, J. H., Lawrence J. S., and Tsigalidou, V. 1962. Comparative studies of serologic tests for rheumatoid disease. *Arthritis Rheum.* 5:61.

Barchilon, J. 1963. Analysis of a woman with incipient rheumatoid arthrits. *Int. J. Psychoanal.* 44:163.

Barnett, E. V., Condemi, J. J., Leddy, J. P., and Vaughan, J. H. 1964. Gamma-2, gamma-1A and gamma-1M antinuclear factors in human sera. *J. Clin. Invest.* 43:1104.

———, North, A. F., Jr., Condemi, J. J., Jacox, R. F., and Vaughan, J. H. 1965. Antinuclear factors in systemic lupus erythematosus and rheumatoid arthritis. *Ann. Intern. Med.* 63:100.

———, Balduzzi, P., Vaughan, J. H., and Morgan, H. F. 1966. Search for infectious agents in rheumatoid arthritis. *Arthritis Rheum.* 9:720.

———, Winkelstein, A., and Weinberger, H. J. 1970. Agammaglogulinemia with polyarthritis and subcutaneous nodules. *Am. J. Med.* 48:40.

Barter, R. W. 1952. Familial incidence of rheumatoid arthritis and acute rheumatism in 100 rheumatoid arthritics. *Ann. Rheum. Dis.* 11:39.

Bartfeld, H. 1960. Incidence and significance of seropositive tests for rheumatoid factor in non-rheumatoid disease. *Ann. Intern. Med.* 52:1059.

——— 1969. Distribution of rheumatoid factor activity in nonrheumatoid states. *Ann. N.Y. Acad. Sci.* 168:30.

478

Bartholemew, L. E. 1965. Isolation and characterization of mycoplasmas (PPLO) from patients with rheumatoid arthritis, systemic lupus erythematosus and Reiter's syndrome. *Arthritis Rheum.* 8:376.

Bayles, T. B. 1966. Psychogenic factors in rheumatoid arthritis. In *Rheumatoid Arthritis*, 7th ed., edited by J. L. Hollander. Philadelphia: Lea & Febiger.

Beall, G., and Cobb, S. 1961. The frequency distribution of episodes of rheumatoid arthritis as shown by periodic examination. *J. Chronic Dis.* 14:291.

Behrend, T., and Lawrence, J. S. 1965. Epidemiologic studies in Germany. Proceedings of the XIth Congress of the International League Against Rheumatism. Amsterdam: Excerpta Medica.

Bennett, P. H., and Burch, T. A. 1967. New York symposioum on population studies in the rheumatoid diseases: new diagnostic criteria. *Bull. Rheum. Dis.* 17:453.

—— and —— 1968. Studies of rheumatoid arthritis. In *Population Studies of the Rheumatic Disease*, edited by P. H. Bennett and P. H. N. Wood. Amsterdam: Excerpta Medica.

Bevans, M., Nadell, J., De Martini, F., and Ragan, C. 1954. The systemic lesions of malignant rheumatoid arthritis. *Am. J. Med.* 16:197.

Bloch, K. J., Buchanan, W. W., Wohl, M. J., and Bunim, J. J. 1965. Sjögren's syndrome: a clinical, pathological and serological study of sixty-two cases. *Medicine* 44:187.

Blom, G. E., and Nicholls, G. 1953. Emotional factors in children with rheumatoid arthritis. *Am. J. Orthopsychiatry.* 24:588.

Blumberg, B. S., Bloch, K. J., Black, R. L., and Dotter, C. 1961. A study of the prevalence of arthritis in Alaskan Eskimos. *Arthritis Rheum.* 4:325.

Bonomo, L., Tursi, A., and Gillardi, U. 1968. Distribution of the anti-gamma globulin factors in the synovial membrane and other tissues in various diseases. *Ann. Rheum. Dis.* 27:122.

Booth, G. C. 1937. Personality and chronic arthritis. *J. Nerv. Ment. Dis.* 85:637.

—— 1939. The psychological approach in therapy of rheumatoid arthritis. *Rheumatism* 1:48.

Boynton, B. L., Leavitt, L. A., Schnur, R. R., Schnur, H. L., and Russell, M. A. 1953. Personality evaluation in rehabilitation of rheumatoid spondylitis. *Arch. Phys. Med. Rehabil.* 34:489.

Bremmer, J. M., Alexander, W. R. M., and Duthie, J. J. 1959. Familial incidence of rheumatoid arthritis. *Ann. Rheum. Dis.* 18:279.

Brewer Jr., E. J., Bass, J. C., Cassidy, J. T., Duran, B. S., Fink, C. W., Jacobs, J. C., Markowitz, M., Reynolds, W. E., Schaller, J., Stillman, J. S., and Wallace, S. L. 1972–3. Criteria for the classification of juvenile rheumatoid arthritis. *Bull. Rheum. Dis.* 23:712.

Buchanan, W. W. 1965. The relationship of Hashimoto's thyroiditis to rheumatoid arthritis. *Geriatrics.* 20:941.

——, Crooks, J., Alexander, W. D., Koutras, D. A., Wayne, E. J., and Gray, K. G. 1961. Association of Hashimoto's thyroiditis and rheumatoid arthritis. *Lancet.* i:245.

Bunim, J. J., Ziff, M., and McEwen, C. 1955. Evaluation of prolonged cortisone therapy in rheumatoid arthritis. *Am. J. Med.* 18:27.

Burch, P. R. J. 1963. Autoimmunity: some etiological aspects; inflammatory polyarthritis and rheumatoid arthritis. *Lancet.* i:1253.

—— 1968. Genetic aspects of rheumatic and arthritic diseases. In *Rheumatic Diseases*, edited by J. J. R. Duthie and W. R. M. Alexander. Edinburgh: Edinburgh University Press.

Burch, T. A. 1968. Mortality from rheumatoid arthritis in the United States 1959–1961. In *Population Studies of the Rheumatic Diseases*, edited by P. H. Bennett and P. H. N. Wood. Amsterdam: Excerpta Medica.

——, O'Brien, W. M., and Bunim, J. J. 1965. Family and genetic studies of rheumatoid arthritis and rheumatoid factor in Blackfeet Indians. In *Genetics and Epidemiology of Chronic Diseases*, edited by J. V. Neel, M. W. Shaw, and W. J. Shull. Washington: U.S. Department of Health, Education, and Welfare.

Burnet, F. M. 1963. *The Integrity of the Body*. Cambridge: Harvard University Press.

479

Burt, J. B., Gordon, R. G., and Brown, A. R. 1938. The autonomic nervous system in rheumatoid arthritis. In *A Survey of Chronic Rheumatic Diseases.* London: Oxford University Press.

Bywaters, E. G. L. 1968. Diagnostic criteria for Still's disease (Juvenile R. A.). In *Population Studies of the Rheumatic Diseases,* edited by P. H. Bennett and P. H. N. Wood. Amsterdam: Excerpta Medica.

Calabro, J. J. 1966. Juvenile rheumatoid arthritis. In *Rheumatoid Arthritis,* edited by J. L. Hollander. Philadelphia: Lea & Febiger.

———, Parrino, G. R., and Marchesano, J. M. 1970. Monarticular-onset juvenile rheumatoid arthritis. *Bull. Rheum. Dis.* 21:613.

Cassidy, J. T., Burt, A., Petty, R., and Sullivan, D. 1968. Selective IgA deficiency in connective tissue diseases. *N. Engl. J. Med.* 280:275.

Castor, C. W. 1971a. Connective tissue activation. II: Abnormalities of cultured rheumatoid synovial cells. *Arthritis Rheum.* 14:55.

——— 1971b. Abnormalities of connective tissue cells cultured from patients with rheumatoid arthritis. II: Defective regulation of hyaluronate and collagen formation. *J. Lab. Clin. Med.* 77:65.

Cathcart, E. S., and O'Sullivan, J. B. 1970. Rheumatoid arthritis in a New England town: A prevalence study in Sudbury, Massachusetts. *N. Engl. J. Med.* 282:421.

Cats, A., and Pit, A. A. 1969. Clinical significance of rheumatoid vasculitis and the incidence of digital vascular lesions. *Folia Med. Neerl.* 12:159.

———, and Hazevoet, H. M. 1970. Significance of positive tests for rheumatoid factor in the prognosis of rheumatoid arthritis. *Ann. Rheum. Dis.* 29:254.

Cave, L., Sankalé, M., Bobo, J., and Moulanier, M. 1965. Considerations about the radiological aspects of chronic rheumatism in black Africans. *Rheumatology.* 17:153.

Cecil, R. L. 1945. Environmental factors in the etiology of rheumatic conditions. *Med. Clin. North Am.* 29:566.

Chamberlain, M. A., and Bruckner, F. E. 1970. Rheumatoid neuropathy: clinical and electrophysiological features. *Ann. Rheum. Dis.* 29:609.

Chandler, R. W., Robinson, H., and Maso, A. T. 1971. Serologic investigations for evidence of infectious etiology in early rheumatoid arthritis. *Arthritis Rheum.* 14:154.

Cheng, C., and Persellin, R. H. 1971. Interference by C1g in slide latex tests for rheumatoid arthritis. *Ann. Intern. Med.* 75:683.

Christian, C. L. 1963. Rheumatoid factor properties of hyperimmune rabbit sera. *J. Exp. Med.* 18:827.

——— 1967. Editorial: Rheumatic diseases today. *Ann. Intern. Med.* 66:230.

——— 1968. Rheumatoid arthritis. In *Immunological Diseases,* 2nd ed., edited by M. Samter. Boston: Little, Brown.

Claman, H. N., and Merrill, D. A. 1966. Serum immunoglobulins in rheumatoid arthritis. *J. Lab. Clin. Med.* 67:850.

Clark, E. C., and Bailey, A. A. 1956. Neurologic and psychiatric signs associated with systemic lupus erythematosus. *J.A.M.A.* 160:455.

Cleveland, S. E., and Fisher, S. 1954. Behavior and unconscious fantasies of patients with rheumatoid arthritis. *Psychosom. Med.* 16:327.

——— and ——— 1960. A comparison of psychological characteristics and physiological reactivity in ulcer and rheumatoid arthritis groups I. *Psychom. Med.* 22:283.

———, Reitman, E. E., and Brewer, E. J., Jr. 1965. Psychological factors in juvenile rheumatoid arthritis. *Arthritis Rheum.* 8:1152.

Cobb, S. 1959. Contained hostility in rheumatoid arthritis. *Arthritis Rheum.* 2:419.

——— 1960. On the development of diagnostic criteria. *Arthritis Rheum.* 3:91.

480

———— 1965. Intrafamilial transmission of rheumatoid arthritis. In *Genetics and Epidemiology of Chronic Diseases*, edited by J. V. Neel, M. W. Shaw, and W. J. Schull. Washington, D.C.: U.S. Department of Health, Education, and Welfare.

———— and Hall, W. A. 1965. A newly identified cluster of diseases—rheumatoid arthritis, peptic ulcer, and tuberculosis. *J.A.M.A.* 193:1077.

———— and Kasl, S. V. 1966. The epidemiology of rheumatoid arthritis. *Am. J. Publ. Health.* 56:1657.

———— and ————. 1968. Epidemiologic contributions to the etiology of rheumatoid arthritis with special attention to psychological and social variables. In *Population Studies of the Rheumatic Diseases*, 3rd Internat. Symp., edited by P. H. Bennett and P. H. N. Wood. Amsterdam: Excerpta Medica.

———— and Lawrence, J. 1957. Towards a geography of rheumatoid arthritis. *Bull. Rheum. Dis.* 7:133.

————, Bauer, W., and Whiting, I. 1939. Environmental factors in rheumatoid arthritis. *J.A.M.A.* 113:668.

————, Schull, W. J., Harburg, E. 1969. The intrafamilial transmission of rheumatoid arthritis, I-VIII. *J. Chronic Dis.* 22:193.

————, Warren, J. E., Merchant, W. R., and Thompson, D. J. 1957. An estimate of the prevalence of rheumatoid arthritis. *J. Chronic Dis.* 5:636.

————, Miller, M., and Wieland, M. 1959. On the relationship between divorce and rheumatoid arthritis. *Arthritis Rheum.* 2:414.

————, Kasl, S. V., Chen, E., and Christenfeld, R. 1965. Some psychological and social characteristics of patients hospitalized for rheumatoid arthritis, hypertension and duodenal ulcer. *J. Chronic Dis.* 18:1259.

Cockel, R., Kendall, M. J., Becker, J. F., and Hawkinds, C. F. 1971. Serum biochemical values in rheumatoid disease. *Ann. Rheum. Dis.* 30:166.

Conn, D. L., McDuffie, F. C., and Dyck, P. J. 1972. Immunopathologic study of sural nerves in rheumatoid arthritis. *Arthritis Rheum.* 15:135.

Condemi, J. J., Barnett, E. V., Atwater, E. C., Jacox, R. F., Mongan, E. S., and Vaughan, J. H. 1965. The significance of antinuclear factors in rheumatoid arthritis. *Arthritis Rheum.* 8:1080.

Cooke, T. D., Hurd, E. R., Bienenstock, J., Jasin, H. E., and Ziff, M. 1972. The immunofluorescent identification of immunoglobulins and complement in rheumatoid arthritis collagenous tissue. *Arthritis Rheum.* 15:433.

Cooke, T. D. V., Richer, S., Hurd, E., and Jasin, H. E. 1975. Localization of antigen-antibody complexes in intraarticular collagenous tissues. *Ann. N.Y. Acad. Sci.* 256:10.

Coombs, R. R. A., and Fell, H. B. 1969. Lysosomes in tissue damage mediated by allergic reactions. In *Lysosomes in Biology and Pathology*, vol 2, edited by J. T. Dingle and H. B. Fell. Amsterdam: North Holland.

Cormier, B. M., Wittkower, E. D., Marcotte, V., and Forget, F. 1957. Psychological aspects of rheumatoid arthritis. *Can. Med. Assoc. J.* 77:533.

Davis, A. D. 1960. Some physiological correlates of Rorschach body image productions. *J. Abnorm. Psychol.* 60:432.

De Blécourt, J. J., Poleman, A., and De Blécourt-Meindersma, T. 1961. Hereditary factors in rheumatoid arthritis and ankylosing spondylitis. *Ann. Rheum. Dis.* 20:215.

De Graaff, R. 1959. Rheumatoid arthritis in the Netherlands: Its prevalence and social aspects. Proc. I.S.R.A. Symposium on the Social Aspects of Chronic Rheumatic Joint Affections especially Rheumatoid Arthritis. International Congress Series No. 23. Amsterdam: Excerpt Medica.

Deicher, H., and Frese, B. 1971. Correlation between presence of antinuclear serum factors and clinical profile in rheumatoid arthritis. In *Rheumatoid Arthritis,* edited by W. Muller, H.-G. Harwerth, and K. Fehr. New York: Academic.

Dequeker, J., Van Noyen, R., and Vandepitte, J. 1969. Age-related rheumatoid factors. Incidence and characteristics. *Ann. Rheum. Dis.* 28:431.

Dixon, A. St. J. 1960. "Rheumatoid Arthritis" with negative serological reaction. *Ann. Rheum. Dis.* 19:209.

———, Feldman, J., and Vasques, J., Immunology and pathogenesis of experimental serum sickness. In *Cellular and Humoral Aspects of Hypersensitivity States,* edited by S. H. Lawrence New York. Hoeber.

———, ———, and ——— 1961. Experimental glomerulonephritis. *J. Exp. Med.* 113:899.

Dressner, E. 1955. Aetiology and pathogenesis of rheumatoid arthritis. *Am. J. Med.* 18:74.

Dumonde, D. C. 1971. Rheumatoid arthritis as a disorder of cell-mediated immunity. In *Rheumatoid Arthritis,* edited by W. Müller, H.-G. Harwerth and K. Fehr. New York: Academic.

——— and Glynn, L. E. 1962. The production of arthritis in rabbits by an immunological reaction to fibrin. *Br. J. Exp. Pathol.* 43:373.

Duthie, J. J. R., Brown, P. E., Knox, J. D. E., and Thomson, M. 1975. Course and prognosis in rheumatoid arthritis. *Ann. Rheum. Dis.* 16:411.

———, Stewart, S. M., Alexander, W. R. M., and Dayhoff, R. E. 1967. Isolation of diphtheroid organism from rheumatoid synovial membrane and fluid. *Lancet.* i:142.

Ebbesen, P. 1968. Spontaneous amyloidosis in differently grouped and treated DBA/2, BALB/c and CBA mice and thymus fibrosis in estrogen-treated BALB/c males. *J. Exp. Med.* 127:387.

——— and Rask-Nielsen, R. 1967. Influence of sex segregated grouping and of innoculation with subcellular leukemic material on development of nonleukemic lesions in DBA/2, BALB/c and CBA mice. *J. Natl. Cancer Inst.* 39:917.

Edelman, G. M., Kunkel, H. G., and Franklin, E. C. 1958. Interaction of the rheumatoid factor with antigen-antibody complexes and aggravated gamma globlulin. *J. Exp. Med.* 108:105.

Edstrom, G. 1952. Rheumatoid arthritis and trauma. *Acta Med. Scand.* 142:11.

Ellman, P. and Mitchell, S. D. 1936. The psychological aspects of chronic rheumatic disease. In *Reports of Chronic Rheumatic Diseases,* vol. 2, edited by C. W. Buckley. New York: Macmillan.

——— and Shaw, D. 1950. The "chronic rheumatic" and his pains. Psychosomatic aspects of chronic nonarticular rheumatism. *Ann. Rheum. Dis.* 9:341.

Empire Rheumatism Council. 1950. A controlled investigation into the aetiology and clinical features of rheumatoid arthritis. *Br. Med. J.* 1:799.

Engel, A. 1968. National health examination survey: rheumatoid arthritis. Comments. *Population Studies of the Rheumatic Diseases,* edited by P. H. Bennett and P. H. N. Wood. Amsterdam: Excerpta Medica.

Engel, G. L. 1955. Studies of ulcerative colitis. III: The nature of the psychologic processes. *Am. J. Med.* 19:231.

Fessel, W. J. 1962. Blood proteins in functional psychoses. A review of the literature and unifying hypotheses. *Arch. Gen. Psychiatry.* 6:132.

Fisher, S., and Cleveland, S. E. 1960. A Comparison of psychological characteristics and physiological reactivity in ulcer and rheumatoid arthritis groups: II. Difference in physiological reactivity. *Psychom. Med.* 14:243.

Ford, D. K. 1969. Current views on the pathogenesis and etiology of rheumatoid arthritis. *Can. Med. Assoc. J.* 101:147.

——— and Oh, J. O. 1965. Use of "synovial" cell cultures in the search for virus in rheumatoid arthritis. *Arthritis Rheum.* 8:1047.

Franco, A. E., and Schur, P. H. 1971. Hypocomplementemia in rheumatoid arthritis. *Arthritis Rheum.* 14:231.

482

Franklin, E. C., Holman, H. R., Müller-Eberhard, H. J., and Kunkel, H. G. 1957. An unusual protein component of high molecular weight in the serum of certain patients with rheumatoid arthritis. *J. Exp. Med.* 105:435.

Fraser, K. B., Shirodaria, P. V., Haire, M., and Middleton, D. 1971. Mycoplasmas in cell cultures from rheumatoid synovial membranes. *J. Hyg.* (Camb.). 69:17.

French, T. M., and Shapiro, L. B. 1949. The use of dream analysis in psychosomatic research. *Psychom. Med.* 11:110.

Friedman, S. B., Ader, R., and Glasgow, L. A. 1965. Effects of psychological stress in adult mice inoculated with Coxsackie B viruses. *Psychom. Med.* 27:361.

Fudenberg, H. H. 1968. Are autoimmune diseases immunologic deficiency states? *Hosp. Prac.* 3:43.

―――― and Kunkel, H. G. 1961. Specificity of the reaction between rheumatoid factors and γ-globulin. *J. Exp. Med.* 114:257.

Ganz, V. H., Gurland, B. J., Deming, W. E., and Fisher, B. 1972. The study of the psychiatric symptoms of systemic lupus erythematosus. *Psychom. Med.* 34:207.

Gardner, D. L. 1960. The experimental production of arthritis: a review. *Ann. Rheum. Dis.* 1:297.

―――― 1971. Modern views on the nature of rheumatoid arthritis. *Orthopedics* (Oxford). 4:1.

―――― 1972. *The Pathology of Rheumatoid Arthritis.* London: Arnold.

Geist, H. 1966. *The Psychological Aspects of Rheumatoid Arthritis.* Springfield: Charles C Thomas.

Gibberd, F. B. 1965. A survey of four hundred and six cases of rheumatoid arthritis. *Acta Rheum. Scand.* 11:62.

Gitlin, D., Janeway, C. A., Apt, L., and Craig, J. M. 1959. Agammaglobulinemia. In *Cellular and Humoral Aspects of the Hypersensitive State*, edited by H. S. Lawrence. New York: Hoeber.

Glaser, G. H. 1953. Psychotic reactions induced by corticotrophin (ACTH) and cortisone. *Psychom. Med.* 15:280.

Glenn, E. M., Gray, J., and Kooyers, W. 1965. Chemical changes in adjuvant-induced polyarthritis of rats. *Am. J. Vet. Res.* 26:1195.

Glynn, L. E. 1968. Rheumatoid arthritis. In *Clinical Aspects of Immunology*, 2nd ed., edited by P. G. H. Gell and R. R. A. Coombs. Oxford: Blackwell.

―――― , and Holborow, E. J. 1965. *Autoimmunity and Disease.* Oxford. Blackwell.

Goldenberg, A., Singer, J. M., and Plotz, C. M. 1960. Hereditary factors in rheumatoid arthritis. *Arthritis Rheum.* 3:446.

Goldie, I. 1969. The synovial microvascular derangement in rheumatoid arthritis and osteo-arthritis. *Acta Orthop. Scand.* 40:751.

Good, R. A., and Rotstein, J. 1960. Rheumatoid arthritis and agammaglobulinemia. *Bull. Rheum. Dis.* 10:203.

Goolker, P., and Schein, J. 1953. Psychic effects of ACTH and cortisone. *Psychom. Med.* 15:589.

Gottschalk, L. A., Serota, H. M., and Shapiro, L. B. 1950. Psychophysiologic conflict and neuromuscular tension: I. Preliminary report on a method, as applied to rheumatoid arthritis. *Psychom. Med.* 12:315.

Graham, D. T. 1972. Psychosomatic medicine. In *Handbook of Psychophysiology*, edited by N. S. Greenfield and R. A. Sternbach. New York: Holt, Rinehart and Winston.

―――― , Lundy, R. M., Benjamin, L. S., Kabler, J. D., Lewis, W. C., Kunish, N. O., and Graham, F. K. 1962. Specific attitudes in initial interviews with patients having different "psychomatic diseases." *Psychom. Med.* 24:257.

Grayzel, A. I., and Beck, C. 1970. Rubella infection of synovial cells and the resistance of cells derived from patients with rheumatoid arthritis. *J. Exp. Med.* 131:367.

Greenwood, B. M. 1969a. Polyarthritis in Western Nigeria. I: Rheumatoid arthritis. *Ann. Rheum. Dis.* 28:488.

―――― 1969b. Polyarthritis in Western Nigeria. II: Still's disease. *Ann. Rheum. Dis.* 28:617.

483

—— 1969c. Acute tropical polyarthritis. *Quart. J. Med.* 38:295.

Gregg, D. 1939. The paucity of arthritis among psychotic patients. *Am. J. Psychiatry.* 95:853.

Gryfe, A., Sanders, P. M., and Gardner, D. L. 1971. The mast cell in early rat adjuvant arthritis. *Ann. Rheum. Dis.* 30:24.

Gurland, B. J., Ganz, V. H., Fleiss, J. L., and Zubin. J. 1972. The study of the psychiatric symptoms of systemic lupus erythematosus. *Psychom. Med.* 34:198.

Guze, S. B. 1967. The occurrence of psychiatric illness in systemic lupus erythematosus. *Am. J. Psychiatry.* 123:1562.

Habel, K. 1969. Antigens of virus-induced tumors. *Adv. Immunol.* 10:229.

Hall, L. 1966. Polyarthritis in Kenya. *East Afr. Med. J.* 43:161.

Halliday, J. L. 1937a. Psychological factors in rheumatism. A preliminary study. Part I. *Br. Med. J.* 1:213.

—— 1937b. Psychological factors in rheumatism. A preliminary study. Part II. *Br. Med. J.* 1:264.

—— 1941. The concept of psychosomatic rheumatism. *Ann. Intern. Med.* 15:666.

—— 1942. Psychological aspects of rheumatoid arthritis. *Proc. R. Soc. Med.* 35:455.

Hamerman, D. 1966. New thoughts on the pathogenesis of rheumatoid arthritis. *Am. J. Med.* 35:455.

—— 1969. Cartilage changes in the rheumatoid joint. *Clin. Orthop.* 64:91.

—— 1971a. Initiating factors in rheumatoid arthritis. In *Rheumatoid Arthritis,* edited by W. Müller, H.-G. Harwerth, and K. Fehr. New York: Academic.

—— 1971b. Disturbances of synthesis in the lining cells of the synovial membrane in rheumatoid arthritis. In *Rheumatoid Arthritis,* edited by W. Müller, H.-G. Harwerth, and K. Fehr. New York: Academic.

—— 1975. Evidence for an infectious etiology of rheumatoid arthritis. *Ann. N.Y. Acad. Sci.* 256:25.

—— and Sandson, J. 1970. Antigenicity of connective tissue components. *Mt. Sinai J. Med. N.Y.* 37:453.

——, Barland, P., and Janis, R. 1969. The structure and chemistry of the synovial membrane in health and disease. In *The Biological Basis of Medicine,* vol. 3, edited by E. E. Bittar and N. Bittar. New York: Academic.

——, Stephens, M., and Barland, P. 1961. Comparative histology and metabolism of synovial tissue in normal and arthritic joints. In *Inflammation and Diseases of Connective Tissue,* edited by L. C. Mills and J. H. Moyer. Philadelphia: Saunders.

Harburg, E., Kasl, S. V., Tabor, J., and Cobb, S. 1969. The intrafamilial transmission of rheumatoid arthritis. IV: Recalled parent-child relations by rheumatoid arthritics and controls. *J. Chronic Dis.* 22:223.

Hart, F. D. 1969. Extra-articular manifestations of rheumatoid arthritis. I. *Br. Med. J.* 3:131.

—— 1970. Rheumatoid arthritis: extra-articular manifestations. II. *Br. Med. J.* 2:747.

Harvald, B., and Hauge, M. 1965. Hereditary factors elucidated by twin studies. In *Genetics and Epidemiology of Chronic Diseases,* edited by J. V. Neel, M. W. Shaw and W. J. Schull. Washington, D.C.: U.S. Department of Health, Education, and Welfare.

Hausmanowa, I., and Herman, E. 1957. *Neurologische Syndrome bei Rheumatischen Erkrankungen.* Berlin: Springer.

Heimer, R., and Levin, E. M. 1964. Gamma 1A and gamma 2 rheumatoid factors. *Arthritis Rheum.* 7:738.

——, ——, and Rudd, E. 1963. Globulins resembling rheumatoid factor in serum of the aged. *Am. J. Med.* 35:175.

Hellgren, L. 1969. Rheumatoid arthritis in both marital partners. *Acta Rheum. Scand.* 15:135.

Hijmans, W., Doniach, D., Roitt, I. M., and Holborow, E. J. 1961. Serological overlap between lupus erythematosus, rheumatoid arthritis, and thyroid auto-immune disease. *Br. Med. J.* 2:209.

————, Valkenburg, H. A., Muller, A., and Gratama, S. 1964. Rheumatoid arthritis in Liberia with an assessment of serological findings. *Ann. Rheum. Dis.* 23:45.

Hill, A. G. S. 1968. Diagnostic and prognostic significance of the rheumatoid factor. In *Rheumatic Diseases*, edited by J. J. R. Duthie and W. R. M. Alexander. Pfizer Medical Monographs, No. 3. Edinburgh: Edinburgh University Press.

————, McCormick, J. N., Greenbury, G. L., Morris, C. J., and Keningale, J. 1967. Cultivation of micro-organisms from rheumatoid synovia. *Ann. Rheum. Dis.* 26:566.

Hill, S. R., Jr., and Holley, H. L. 1966. The ameliorating effect of pregnancy and jaundice on certain rheumatic diseases. In *Rheumatoid Arthritis*, 7th ed. edited by J. L. Hollander, Philadelphia: Lea & Febiger.

Hooper, B., Whittingham, S., Mathews, J. D., Mackay, I. R., and Curnow, D. H. 1972. Autoimmunity in rural community. *Clin. Exp. Immunol.* 12:79.

Hurd, E. R., Snyder, W. B., and Ziff, M. 1970. Choroidal nodules and retinal detachments in rheumatoid arthritis. Improvement with fall in immunoglobulin levels following prednisolone and cyclophosphamide therapy. *Am. J. Med.* 48:273.

————, LoSpalluto, J., and Ziff, M. 1970. Formation of leukocyte inclusions in normal polymorphonuclear cells incubated with synovial fluid. *Arthritis Rheum.* 13:724.

Jansson, E., Vainio, U., Snellman, O., and Tuuri, S. 1971. Search for mycoplasma in rheumatoid arthritis. *Ann. Rheum. Dis.* 30:413.

Jasani, M. K., Katori, M., and Lewis, G. P. 1969. Intracellular enzymes and kinin enzymes in synovial fluid in joints. *Ann. Rheum. Dis.* 28:497.

Jennings, J. F. 1971. Lymphocyte responsiveness in rheumatoid arthritis. *Lancet.* i:1239.

Johnson, A., Shapiro, L., and Alexander, F. 1947. Preliminary report on a psychosomatic study of rheumatoid arthritis. *Psychom. Med.* 9:295.

Julkunen, H. 1966. Synovial inflammatory cell reaction in chronic arthritis. *Acta Rheum. Scand.* 12:188.

Kacaki, J. N., Balduzzi, P. C., and Vaughan, J. H. 1970. A study of rubella hemagglutination inhibition antibodies in rheumatoid arthritis. *Clin. Exp. Immunol.* 6:885.

Kantor, T. G., and Tanner, M. 1962. Rubella arthritis and rheumatoid arthritis. *Arthritis Rheum.* 5:378.

Kaplan, M. H. 1963. Discussion: The site of formation of rheumatoid factor. *Arthritis Rheum.* 2:475.

———— and Vaughan, J. 1962. The site of formation of rheumatoid factor. In Conference on host response mechanisms in rheumatoid arthritis. *Arthritis and Rheumatism Foundation Conference Series.* 6:57.

Katz, L., and Piliero, S. J. 1969. A study of adjuvant-induced polyarthritis in the rate with special reference to associated immunological phenomena. *Ann. N.Y. Acad. Sci.* 147:515.

Kellgren, J. H. 1952. Some concepts of rheumatic disease. *Br. Med. J.* 1:1093.

———— 1956. Radiological signs of rheumatoid arthritis: a study of observer differences in the reading of hard films. *Ann. Rheum. Dis.* 15:55.

———— 1966. Epidemiology of rheumatoid arthritis. *Arthritis Rheum.* 9:658.

———— 1968. Epidemiology of rheumatoid arthritis. In *Rheumatic Diseases*, edited by J. J. R. Duthie and W. R. M. Alexander. Pfizer Medical Monographs, No. 3. Edinburgh: Edinburgh University Press.

———— and Ball, J. 1959. Clinical significance of the rheumatoid serum factor. *Br. Med. J.* I:523.

Kilroy, A. W., Schaffner, W., Fleet, W. F., Jr., Lefkowitz, L. B., Jr., Karzon, D. T., and Fenichel, G. M. 1970. Two syndromes following rubella immunization. *J.A.M.A.* 214:2287.

King, S. H. 1955. Rheumatoid arthritis: an evaluation of the literature. *J. Chronic Dis.* 2:287.

———— and Cobb, S. 1958. Psychosocial factors in the epidemiology of rheumatoid arthritis. *J. Chronic Dis.* 7:466.

485

———— and ———— 1959. Psychosocial studies of rheumatoid arthritis: parental factors compared in cases and controls. *Arthritis Rheum.* 2:322.

Kinsella, T. D., Baum, J., and Ziff, M. 1970. Studies of isolated synovial lining cells of rheumatoid and nonrheumatoid synovial membranes. *Arthritis Rheum.* 13:734.

Krammer, F. 1961. Die Bedeutung des Niamid in der Behandlung der Krankheiten des rheumatischen Formenkreises. *Wien. Med. Wochenschr.* 111:353.

Kulka, J. P. 1959. The pathogenesis of rheumatoid arthritis. *J. Chronic Dis.* 10:388.

Kütemeyer, W. 1963. *Die Krankheit in ihrer Menschlichkeit.* Göttingen: Springer.

Lachmann, P. J., Coombs, R. R. A., Fell, H. B., and Dingle, J. T. 1969. The breakdown of embryonic (chick) cartilage and bone cultivated in the presence of complement-sufficient antiserum: III. Immunological analysis. *Int. Arch. Allergy Appl. Immunol.* 36:469.

Lack, C. H. 1969. Lysosomes in relation to arthritis. In *Lysosomes in Biology and Pathology,* vol. 1, edited by J. T. Dingle and H. B Fell. Amsterdam: North-Holland.

Laine, V. A. I. 1962. Rheumatic complaints in an urban population in Finland. *Acta Rheum. Scand.* 8:81.

———— and Lehti, O. 1969. See R. Rimón (1969).

Lambert, P. H., Nydegger, U. E., Perrin, L. H., McCormick, J., Fehr, K., and Miescher, P. A. 1975. Complement activation in seropositive and seronegative rheumatoid arthritis. *Rheumatology.* 6:52.

Lawrence, J. S. 1961. Prevalence of rheumatoid arthritis. *Ann. Rheum. Dis.* 20:11.

———— 1963. Epidemiology of rheumatoid arthritis. *Arthritis Rheum.* 6:166.

———— 1967. Genetics of rheumatoid factor and rheumatoid arthritis. *Clin. Exp. Immunol.* 2:769.

———— 1970. Rheumatoid arthritis—nature or nurture? *Ann. Rheum. Dis.* 29:357.

———— and Ball, J. 1958. Genetic studies in rheumatoid arthritis. *Ann. Rheum. Dis.* 17:160.

———— and Bennett, P. H. 1960. Benign polyarthritis. *Ann. Rheum. Dis.* 19:20.

———— and Wood, P. H. N. 1968. Genetic influences on rheumatoid factor. In *Rheumatic Diseases,* edited by J. J. R. Duthie and W. R. M. Alexander. Pfizer Medical Monographs, No. 3. Edinburgh: Edinburgh University Press.

————, Bremmer, J. M., Ball, J. A., and Burch, T. A. 1966. Rheumatoid arthritis in a subtropical population. *Ann. Rheum. Dis.* 25:59.

————, Valkenburg, H. A., Tuxford, A. F., and Collard, P. J. 1971. Rheumatoid factor in the United Kingdom: II. Associations with certain infections. *Clin. Exp. Immunol.* 9:519.

Lewis-Faning, E. 1950. Report on an enquiry into the etiological factors associated with rheumatoid arthritis. *Ann. Rheum. Dis.* 9(Suppl.):94.

Lichtman, M. A., Vaughan, J. H., and Hames, C. G. 1967. The distribution of serum immunoglobulins, anti-γ-globulins ("rheumatoid factors") and antinuclear antibodies in white and Negro subjects in Evans County, Georgia. *Arthritis Rheum.* 10:204.

Lidz, T. 1969. Disruptions of defensive life patterns and psychosomatic disorders. *Johns Hopkins Med. J.* 125:233.

Litwin, S. D., and Singer, J. M. 1965. Studies of the incidence and significance of anti-gamma globulin factors in the aging. *Arthritis Rheum.* 8:538.

Lowman, E. W., Miller, S., Lee, P. R., Stein, H., King, R., and Heald, L. 1954. Psychological factors in rehabilitation of the chronic rheumatoid arthritic. *Ann. Rheum. Dis.* 13:312.

Ludwig, A. O. 1949. Emotional factors in rheumatoid arthritis: their bearing on the care and rehabilitation of the patient. *Physiotherapy Rev.* 29:339.

———— 1952. Psychogenic factors in rheumatoid arthritis. *Bull. Rheum. Dis.* 2:33.

———— 1954. Rheumatoid arthritis. In *Recent Developments in Psychosomatic Medicine,* edited by E. Wittkower and R. A. Cleghorn. Philadelphia: Lippincott.

486

——— 1967. Rheumatoid arthritis. In *Comprehensive Textbook of Psychiatry*, edited by A. M. Freedman and H. J. Kaplan. Baltimore: Williams & Wilkins.

Maddison, D. C., and Viola, A. 1968. The health of widows in the year following bereavement. *J. Psychosom. Res.* 12:297.

——— and Walker, W. L. 1967. Factors affecting the outcome of conjugal bereavement. *Br. J. Psychiatry.* 113:1057.

Maini, R. N., Stewart, S. M., and Dumonde, D. C. 1970. Peripheral leucocyte migration inhibited by diphtheroid organisms isolated from patients with rheumatoid arthritis. *Ann. Rheum. Dis.* 29:541.

Malmo, R., Shagass, C., and Davis, F. 1950. Symptom specificity and bodily reactions during psychiatric interview. *Psychom. Med.* 12:362.

Mandelbrote, B. M., and Wittkower, E. D. 1955. Emotional factors in Graves' disease. *Psychom. Med.* 17:109.

Mandema, E., Pollak, V. E., Kark, R. M., and Rezaian, J. 1961. Quantitative observations on antinuclear factors in systemic lupus erythematosus. *J. Lab. Clin. Med.* 58:337.

Marin, D., Stoia, I., Athanasiu, P., and Petrescu, A. 1969. Viral infections, factors with an allergic potential in the pathogenic complex of some chronic rheumatic diseases. *Rev. Roum. Inframicrobiol.* 6:277.

Martenis, T. W., Bland, J. H., and Phillips, C.A. 1968. Rheumatoid arthritis after rubella. *Arthritis Rheum.* 11:683.

Masiero, L., and Toso, M. 1961. Research on the familial presence of rheumatoid factor. *G. Clin. Med.* 42:1389.

McLaughlin, J. T., Zabarenko, R. N., Diana, P. H., and Quinn, B. 1953. Emotional reactions of rheumatoid arthritis to ACTH. *Psychom. Med.* 15:187.

Mellors, R. C., and Huang, C. Y. 1967. Immunopathology of NZB/BL mice: VI. Virus separable from spleen and pathogenic for Swiss mice. *J. Exp. Med.* 126:53.

———, Nowoslawski, A., Korngold, L., and Sengson, B. L. 1961. Rheumatoid factor and the pathogenesis of rheumatoid arthritis. *J. Exp. Med.* 113:475.

———, Aoki, T., and Huebner, R. J. 1969. Further implications of murine leukemia-like virus in the disorders of NZB mice. *J. Exp. Med.* 129:1045.

Meltzer, M., Franklin, E. C., Elias, K., McCluskey, R. T., and Cooper, N. 1966. Cryoglobulinemia—a clinical and laboratory study. II: Cryoglobulins with rheumatoid factor activity. *Am. J. Med.* 40:837.

Mendelenyi, M., and Marton, M. 1960. Persönlichkeitsuntersuchungen an Kranken mit primär chronischer Polyarthritis. *Z. Psychosom. Med. Psychonal.* 9:153.

Mendez-Bryan, R., Gonzáles-Alcover, R., and Roger, L. 1964. Rheumatoid arthritis: prevalence in a tropical area. *Arthritis Rheum.* 7:171.

Messner, R. P., Laxdal, T., Quie, P. G., and Williams, R. C., Jr. 1968. Rheumatoid factors in subacute bacterial endocarditis—bacterium, duration of disease or genetic predisposition. *Ann. Intern. Med.* 68:746.

Meyerowitz, S., Jacox, R. F., and Hess, D. W. 1968. Monozygotic twins discordant for rheumatoid arthritis: a genetic, clinical and psychological study of 8 sets. *Arthritis Rheum.* 11:1.

Miall, W. E. 1955. Rheumatoid arthritis in males: an epidemiological study of a Welsh mining community. *Ann. Rheum. Dis.* 14:150.

———, Ball, J. A., and Kellgren, J. H. 1958. Prevalence of rheumatoid arthritis in urban and rural population in South Wales. *Ann. Rheum. Dis.* 17:263.

Mikkelsen, W. M. 1966. The epidemiology of rheumatic diseases. In *Rheumatoid Arthritis*, 7th ed., edited by J. L. Hollander. Philadelphia: Lea & Febiger.

487

————, Dodge, H. J., Duff, I. F., and Kato, H. 1967. Estimates of the prevalence of rheumatic diseases in the population of Tecumseh, Michigan, 1959–1960. *J. Chronic Dis.* 20:351.

Milgrom, F., and Tönder, O. 1965. Multiplicity of rheumatoid factor. *Arthritis Rheum.* 8:203.

Mitkow, V. 1959. Neurologische und psychische Störungen beim Rheumatismus. *Folia Med.* (Plovdiv). 1:125.

Moesmann, G. 1959. Factors precipitating and predisposing to rheumatoid arthritis as illustrated by studies in monozygotic twins. *Acta Rheum. Scand.* 5:291.

Moldofsky, H. 1970. The significance of emotions in the course of rheumatoid arthritis. In *Modern Trends in Psychosomatic Medicine–2*, edited by O. W. Hill. New York: Appleton-Century-Crofts.

———— and Chester, W. J. 1970. Pain and mood patterns in patients with rheumatoid arthritis: a prospective study. *Psychom. Med.* 32:309.

Moos, R. H. 1964. Personality factors associated with rheumatoid arthritis: a review. *J. Chronic Dis.* 17:41.

———— and Engel, B. T. 1962. Psychophysiological reactions in hypertensive and arthritic patients. *J. Psychosom. Res.* 6:227.

———— and Solomon, G. F. 1964a. Minnesota Multiphasic Personality Inventory response patterns in patients with rheumatoid arthritis. *J. Psychosom. Res.* 8:17.

———— and ———— 1964b. Personality correlates of the rapidity of progression of rheumatoid arthritis. *Ann. Rheum. Dis.* 23:145.

———— and ———— 1964c. Personality correlates of rheumatoid arthritic patients' response to treatment. *Arthritis Rheum.* 7:331.

———— and ———— 1965a. Psychologic comparisons between women with rheumatoid arthritis and their non-arthritic sisters. 1. Personality test and interview rating data. *Psychom. Med.* 27:135.

———— and ———— 1965b. Psychologic comparisons between women with rheumatoid arthritis and their non-arthritic sisters. II. Content analysis of interviews. *Psychom. Med.* 27:150.

———— and ———— 1965c. Personality correlates of the degree of functional incapacity of patients with physical disease. *J. Chronic Dis.* 18:1019.

———— and ———— 1966. Social and personal factors in rheumatoid arthritis: pathogenic considerations. *Clin. Med.* 73:19.

Morrison, L., Short, C., Ludwig, A. O., and Schwab, R. 1947. The neuromuscular system in rheumatoid arthritis. Electromyographic and histologic observations. *Am. J. Med. Sci.* 214:33.

Moskowitz, R. W., Benedict, K. J., and Stauffer, R. 1967. Serum antibodies to gamma globulin: inter-relationships of aging, disease, and geography. *J. Chronic Dis.* 20:291.

Mueller, A. D., and Lefkovits, A. M. 1956. Personality structure and dynamics of patients with rheumatoid arthritis. *J. Clin. Psychol.* 12:143.

————, ————, Bryant, J. E., and Marshall, M. L. 1961. Some psychosocial factors in patients with rheumatoid arthritis. *Arthritis Rheum.* 4:275.

Munthe, E., Hoyeraal, H. M., Froland, S. S., Mellbye, O. J., Kass, E., and Natvig, J. B. 1975. Evidence for complement activation by the alternate pathway in the arthritis of hypogammaglobulinemic patients. *Rheumatology* 6:43.

Nalven, F. B., and O'Brien, J. F. 1964. Personality patterns of rheumatoid arthritic patients. *Arthritis Rheum.* 7:18.

———— and ———— 1968. On the use of the M.M.P.I. with rheumatoid arthritic patients. *J. Clin. Psychol.* 24:70.

Namba, T., and Grob, D. 1970. Familial concurrence of myasthenia gravis and rheumatoid arthritis. *Arch. Intern. Med.* 125:1056.

Natvig, J. B., Munthe, E., and Gaarder, P. I. 1971. Molecular specificity and possible biological significance of rheumatoid factors. In *Rheumatoid Arthritis,* edited by W. Müller, H.-G. Harwerth, and K. Fehr. New York: Academic.

————, ————, and Pahle, J. 1975. Evidence for intracellular complement-fixing complexes of IgG rheumatoid factor in rheumatoid plasma cells. *Rheumatology* 6:167.

Neri Serneri, G. G., and Bartoli, V. 1956. II: Researches on hereditary factors in primary chronic rheumatism. *Acta Genet. Med. Gemellol.* (Roma). 5:402.

Nissen, H. A., and Spencer, K. A. 1936. The psychogenic problem (endocrine and metabolic) in chronic arthritis. *N. Engl. J. Med.* 214:576.

Notkins, A. L. 1971. Infectious virus-antibody complexes: Interaction with anti-immunoglobulins, complement, and rheumatoid factor. *J. Exp. Med.* 134:41s.

O'Brien, W. M. 1967. The genetics of rheumatoid arthritis. *Clin. Exp. Immunol.* 2:785.

O'Connor, J. F. 1959. Psychoses associated with systemic lupus erythrmatosus. *Ann. Intern. Med.* 51:526.

———— and Mosher, D. M. 1966. Central nervous system involvement in systemic lupus erythematosus: a study of 150 cases. *Arch. Neurol.* 14:157.

Oreskes, I., Rosenblatt, S., Spiera, H., and Meadow, H. 1968. Rheumatoid factors in an acute psychiatric population. *Ann. Rheum. Dis.* 27:60.

Osler, W. 1892. *The Principles and Practice of Medicine.* New York: Appleton.

Panush, R. S., Bianco, N. E., and Schur, P. H. 1971. Serum and synovial fluid IgG, IgA and IgM antigammaglobulins in rheumatoid arthritis. *Arthritis Rheum.* 14:737.

————, ————, ————, Rocklin, R. E., David, J. R., and Stillman, J. S. 1972. Juvenile rheumatoid arthritis. Cellular hypersensitivity and selective IgA deficiency. *Clin. Exp. Immunol.* 10:103.

Parkes, C. W. 1964. Effects of bereavement on physical and mental health: a study of the medical records of widows. *Br. Med. J.* 2:274.

Patterson, R. M., Craig, J. B., Waggoner, R. W., and Freyberg, R. 1943. Studies on the relationship between emotional factors and rheumatoid arthritis. *Am. J. Psychiatry.* 99:775.

Pearson, C. M. 1956. Development of arthritis, periarthritis and periostitis in rats given adjuvant. *Proc. Soc. Exp. Biol. Med.* 91:95.

———— 1963. Experimental joint disease: observations on adjuvant-induced arthritis. *J. Chronic Dis.* 16:683.

———— 1966. Arthritis in animals. In *Arthritis and Allied Conditions,* 7th ed., edited by J. L. Hollander. Philadelphia: Lea & Febiger.

———— and Wood, F. D. 1959. Studies of polyarthritis and other lesions induced in rats by the injection of mycobacterial adjuvant. I. General clinical and pathological characteristics and some modifying factors. *Arthritis Rheum.* 2:440.

———— and ———— 1964. Passive transfer of adjuvant arthritis by lymph node or spleen cells. *J. Exp. Med.* 120:547.

Pease, P. E. 1968. Bacterial antigens in relation to rheumatic disease. In *Rheumatic Diseases,* edited by J. J. R. Duthie and W. R. M. Alexander. Pfizer Medical Monographs, No. 3. Edinburgh: Edinburgh University Press.

———— 1969. Bacterial L-forms in the blood and joint fluids of arthritic subjects. *Ann. Rheum. Dis.* 28:270.

Pekin, T. J., and Zvaifler, N. J. 1964. Hemolytic complement in synovial fluid. *J. Clin. Invest.* 43:1372.

Phillips, J. M., Kaklamanis, P., and Glynn, L. E. 1966. Experimental arthritis associated with auto-immunization to inflammatory exudates. *Ann. Rheum. Dis.* 25:165.

Phillips, P. E., and Christian, C. L. 1970. Myxovirus antibody increases in human connective tissue disease. *Science* 168:982.

Pilkington, T. L. 1956. The coincidence of rheumatoid arthritis and schizophrenia. *J. Nerv. Ment. Dis.* 124:604.

Popert, A. J. 1966. Gold and the antimalarius. In *Modern Trends in Rheumatology*, edited by A. G. S. Hill. London: Butterworth.

Radnai, B. 1953. Vascular changes in peripheral nerves and skeletal muscles in rheumatoid arthritis. *Acta Morphol. Acad. Sci. Hung.* 3:87.

——— 1969. Comparative morphology of small vessel lesions in rheumatoid arthritis and periarteritis nodosa. *Acta Morphol. Acad. Sci. Hung.* 17:69.

Rimón, R. 1969. A psychosomatic approach to rheumatoid arthritis. *Acta Rheum. Scand.* 13(Suppl.):1.

Robb, J. H., and Rose, N. S. 1965. Rheumatoid arthritis and maternal deprivation. A case study in the use of a social survey. *Br. J. Med. Psychol.* 38:147.

Robecchi, A., and Daneo, V. 1959. Research on the behavior, nature and meaning of the rheumatoid factor. *Acta Rheum. Scand.* 5:245.

Robinson, C. E. 1957. Emotional factors and rheumatoid arthritis. *Can. Med. Assoc. J.* 77:344.

Ropes, M. W., Bennett, G. A., Cobb, S., Jacox, R., and Jessar, R. A. 1958. 1958 Revision of diagnostic criteria for rheumatoid arthritis. *Bull. Rheum. Dis.* 9:175.

Rosen, F. S., and Janeway, C. A. 1966. The gammaglobulins. III. The antibody deficiency syndromes. *N. Engl. J. Med.* 275:709.

Rosenblatt, S., Oreskes, I., Meadow, H., and Spiera, H. 1968. The relationship between antigamma globulin activity and depression. *Am. J. Psychiatry.* 124:1640.

Rothermilch, N. O., and Philips, V. K. 1963. Rheumatoid arthritis in criminal and mentally ill populations. *Arthritis Rheum.* 6:639.

Rowe, A. J. 1969. Mental problems in rheumatoid arthritis. *Br. Med. J.* 4:806.

Rowell, N. R. 1967. Aetiology of certain connective tissue diseases. *Clin. Exp. Immunol.* 2:813.

Ruddy, S., and Austen, K. F. 1970. The complement system in rheumatoid synovitis. I. An analysis of complement component activities in rheumatoid synovial fluids. *Arthritis Rheum.* 13:713.

———, and ——— 1975. Activation of the complement and properidin systems in rheumatoid arthritis. *Ann. N.Y. Acad. Sci.* 256:96.

Russell, W. M., and Hutt, M. S. R. 1962. A rheumatoid-like factor in patients with tissue damage. *Ann. Rheum. Dis.* 21:279.

Sainsbury, P., and Gibson, J. 1954. Symptoms of anxiety and tension and the accompanying physiological changes in the muscular sytem. *J. Neurol. Neurosurg. Psychiatry.* 17:216.

Sanchez, V., Davanz, H., and Buvinic, M. 1959. Some psychiatric aspects of 50 cases of rheumatoid arthritis. *Arch. Argent. Reum.* 22:35.

Scherbel, A. L., and Harrison, J. W. 1959. The effect of iproniazid and other amine oxidase inhibitors in rheumatoid arthritis. *Ann. N.Y. Acad. Sci.* 80:820.

Schmid, F. R., and Slatis, H. 1962. Increased incidence of serum and clinical abnormalities in spouses of patients with rheumatoid arthritis. *Arthritis Rheum.* 5:319.

———, Cooper, N. S., Ziff, M., and McEwen, C. 1962. Arteritis in rheumatoid arthritis. *Am. J. Med.* 30:56.

Schull, W. J., and Cobb, S. 1969. The intrafamilial transmission of rheumatoid arthritis. III. The lack of support for a genetic hypothesis. *J. Chronic Dis.* 22:27.

———, Roitt, I. M., and Rocha, M. J. 1970. Complement fixation by a two component antibody system: Immunoglobulin G and immunoglobulin M antiglobulin (rheumatoid factor). *J. Exp. Med.* 132:673.

Schumacher, Jr., H. R. 1975. Synovial membrane and fluid morphologic alterations in early rheumatoid arthritis: Microvascular injury and virus-like particles. *Ann. N.Y. Acad. Sci.* 256:39.

490

Schur, P. H., and Austen, K. F. 1971–2. Complement in the Rheumatic Diseases. *Bull. Rheum. Dis.* 22:666.

————, Bianco, N. E., and Panush, R. S. 1975. Antigammaglobulins in normal individuals and in patients with adult and juvenile rheumatoid arthritis and osteoarthritis. *Rheumatology* 6:156.

Scotch, N. A., and Geiger, H. J. 1962. The epidemiology of rheumatoid arthritis: a review with special attention to social factors. *J. Chronic Dis.* 15:1037.

Scott, W. A., McD. 1969. The relief of pain with an anti-depressant in arthritis. *Practitioner* 202:802.

Shaper, A. G., and Shaper, L. 1958. Analysis of medical admissions to Mulago Hospital, 1957. *E. Afr. Med. J.* 35:647.

Sharp, J. T. 1971. Mycoplasmas and arthritis. *Arthritis Rheum.* 13:263.

————, Calkins, E., Cohen, A. S., Schubart, A. F., and Calabro, J. J. 1964. Observations on the clinical, chemical, and serological manifestations of rheumatoid arthritis, based on the course of 154 cases. *Medicine* 43:41.

Shickikawa, K., Mayeda, A., Komatsubara, Y., Yamamoto, T., Akabory, O., Hongo, I., Kosugi, T., Miyauchi, T., Orihara, M., and Akira, T. 1966. Rheumatic complaints in urban and rural populations in Osaka. *Ann. Rheum. Dis.* 25:25.

Shocket, B. R., Lisansky, E. T., Schubart, A. F., Fiocco, V., Kurland, S., and Pope, M. 1969. A medical-psychiatric study of patients with rheumatoid arthritis. *Psychosomatics* 10:271.

Short, C. L., Bauer, W., and Reynolds, W. E. 1957. *Rheumatoid Arthritis.* Cambridge: Harvard University Press.

Siegel, M., Lee, S. L., Widelock, D., Dwon, N. V., and Kravitz, H. 1965. A comparative family study of rheumatoid arthritis and systemic lupus erythematosus. *N. Engl. J. Med.* 273:893.

Sievers, K. 1965. The rheumatoid factor in definite rheumatoid arthritis. *Acta Rheumat. Scand.* 11:(Suppl. 9) 1.

Slacter, J. G. 1943. An analysis of 388 cases of rheumatoid arthritis. *Ann. Rheum. Dis.* 3:195.

Sledge, C. B., and Dingle, J. T. 1965. Activation of lysosomes by oxygen. *Nature* 205:140.

Sliwinski, A. J., and Zvaifler, N. H. 1970 *In vivo* synthesis of IgG by rheumatoid synovium. *J. Lab. Clin. Med.* 76:304.

Smith, C., and Hamerman, D. 1969. Significance of persistent differences between normal and rheumatoid synovial membrane cells in culture. *Arthritis Rheum.* 12:639.

Smith, M. 1932. A study of 102 cases of atrophic arthritis. I: Introduction; statistical data. *N. Engl. J. Med.* 206:103.

Soave, O. A. 1968. Reactivation of a rabies virus in the guinea pig due to the stress of crowding. *Am. J. Vet. Res.* 25:268.

Sokoloff, L. 1963. The pathophysiology of peripheral blood vessels in collagen diseases. In *Peripheral Blood Vessels,* edited by J. H. Orbison and D. E. Smith. Baltimore: Williams & Wilkins.

———— 1966. The pathology of rheumatoid arthritis and allied disorders. In *Arthritis and Allied Conditions,* 7th ed., edited by J. L. Hollander. Philadelphia: Lea & Febiger.

Solomon, G. F. 1969. Stress and antibody response in rats. *Arch. Allergol. Appl. Immunol.* 35:97.

———— 1970. Psychophysiological aspects of rheumatoid arthritis and auto-immune disease. In *Modern Trends in Psychosomatic Medicine–2,* edited by O. W. Hill. New York: Appleton-Century-Crofts.

———— and Moos, R. H. 1964. Emotions, immunity and disease: a speculative theoretical integration. *Arch. Gen. Psychiatry.* 11:657.

———— and ———— 1965a. Psychologic aspects of response to treatment in rheumatoid arthritis. *GP* 32:113.

———— and ———— 1965b. The relationship of personality to the presence of rheumatoid factor in asymptomatic relatives of patients with rheumatoid arthritis. *Psychom. Med.* 27:350.

————, Levine, S., and Kraft, J. 1968. Early experience and immunity. *Nature* 220:821.

————, Allansmith, M., McLellan, B., and Amkraut, A. 1969. Immunoglobulins in psychiatric patients. *Arch. Gen. Psychiatry*. 20:272.

Southworth, J. 1959. Muscular tension as a response to psychological stress in rheumatoid arthritis and peptic ulcer. *Genet. Psychol. Mongr.* 57:337.

Spector, W. G., and Heesom, N. 1969. The production of granulomata by antigen-antibody complexes. *J. Pathol.* 98:31.

Stage, D. E., and Mannik, M. 1972. Rheumatoid factors in rheumatoid arthritis. *Bull. Rheum. Dis.* 23:720.

Steffen, C. 1969. Tissue antibodies in rheumatoid arthritis and other connective tissues. *Ann. Immunol.* 1:47.

Stern, M., and Robbins, E. S. 1960. Psychoses in systemic lupus erythematosus. *Arch. Gen. Psychiatry*. 3:205.

Steven, F. S. 1964. Tryptic peptides obtained from gelatins derived from normal and rheumatoid arthritic collagens. *Ann. Rheum. Dis.* 23:405.

Stewart, S. M., Alexander, W. R. M., and Duthie, J. J. R. 1969. Isolation of diphtheroid bacilli from synovial membrane and fluid in rheumatoid arthritis. *Ann. Rheum. Dis.* 28:477.

Strober, W., Blaese, R. M., and Waldmann, T. A. 1971–2. Immunologic deficiency diseases. *Bull. Rheum. Dis.* 22:686.

Svartz, N., Carlson, L. A., Schlossman, K., and Ehrenberg, A. 1958. Isolation of the rheumatoid factor. *Acta Med. Scand.* 160:87.

Tatibouet, L., Duclos, G., and Weber, B. 1961. L'encéphalopathie rheumatismale. *Quest. Méd.* 14:707.

Thaler, M., Weiner, H., and Reiser, M. F. 1957. Exploration of the doctor-patient relationship through projective techniques: their use in psychosomatic illness. *Psychom. Med.* 19:228.

Thomas, G. W. 1936. Psychic factors in rheumatoid arthritis. *Am. J. Psychiatry*. 93:693.

Thompson, G. R., Ferreyra, A., and Brackett, R. G. 1971. Acute arthritis complicating rubella vaccination. *Arthritis Rheum.* 14:19.

Thompson, H. E., Wyatt, B. L., and Hicks, R. A. 1938. Chronic atrophic arthritis. *Ann. Intern. Med.* 11:1792.

Thompson, M. 1966. Non-articular features of rheumatoid disease. In *Modern Trends in Rheumatology*, edited by A. G. S. Hill. London: Butterworth.

———— and Bywaters, E. G. L. 1962. Unilateral rheumatoid arthritis following hemiplegia. *Ann. Rheum. Dis.* 21:370.

Thymann, G. 1957. Polyarthritis in twins. *Acta Gent. Stat. Med.* 7:148.

Torrigiani, G., Ansell, B. M., Chown, E. E. A., and Roitt, I. M. 1969. Raised IgG antiglobulin factors in Still's disease. *Ann. Rheum. Dis.* 28:424.

Trevathan, R. D., and Tatum, J. C. 1954. Rarity of concurrence of psychosis and rheumatoid arthritis in individual patients. *J. Nerv. Ment. Dis.* 120:85.

Turner-Warwick, M., and Doniach, D. 1965. Autoantibody studies in interstitial pulmonary fibrosis. *Br. Med. J.* 1:886.

Valkenburg, H. A. 1963. Rheumatoid factors in populations. In *Epidemiology of Chronic Rheumatism*, vol. 1, edited by J. H. Kellgren, M. R. Jeffrey, and J. Ball. Philadelphia: Davis.

van Boxel, J. A., and Paget, S. A. 1975. Predominantly T-cell infiltrate in rheumatoid synovial membranes. *N. Engl. J. Med.* 293:571.

Vaughan, J. H. 1969. Summary: Rheumatoid factors and their biological significance. *Ann. N.Y. Acad. Sci.* 168:204.

————, Barnett, E. V., Sobel, M. V., and Jacox, R. F. 1968a. Intracytoplasmic inclusions of immunoblobulins in rheumatoid arthritis and other diseases. *Arthritis Rheum.* 2:125.

492

————, Morgan, E. S., and Jacox, R. F. 1968b. Role of gamma globulin complexes in rheumatoid arthritis. *Trans. Assoc. Am. Physicians* 81:231.

————, Jacox, G. A., and Clark, R. 1969. Relation of rheumatoid factor to intracellular inclusions. *Ann. N.Y. Acad. Sci.* 168:111.

Vazquez, J. J., and Dixon, F. J. 1957. Immunhistochemical study of lesions in rheumatic fever, systemic lupus erythematosus and rheumatoid arthritis. *Lab. Invest.* 6:205.

Veenhof-Garman, A. M., Steiner, F. J. F., Westendorp-Boerma, F., DeBlécourt, J. J., and Valkenburg, H. A. 1968. The prevalence of rheumatoid arthritis and rheumatoid factor in relatives and spouses of seropositive and seronegative patients suffering from definite or classical rheumatoid arthritis. In *Population Studies of the Rheumatic Diseases*, edited by P. H. Bennett and P. H. N. Wood. Amsterdam: Excerpta Medica.

Waller, M. 1969. Methods of measurement of rheumatoid factor. *Ann. N.Y. Acad. Sci.* 168:5.

Ward, P. A. 1971. Complement-derived leukotactic factors in pathological fluids. *J. Exp. Med.* 134:109s.

Ward, R., and Stalker, R. 1965. Sheep cell agglutination test in chronic interstitial pulmonary fibrosis. *Ann. Rheum. Dis.* 24:246.

Warren, S. L., Marmor, L., Liebes, D. M., and Hollins, R. L. 1969a. An active agent from human rheumatoid arthritis which is transmissible in mice. *Arch. Intern. Med.* 124:629.

————, ————, Liebes, D. M., and Hollins, R. L. 1969b. Congenital transmission in mice of an active agent from rheumatoid arthritis. *Nature* 223:646.

Wasmuth, A. G., Veale, A. M. A., Palmer, D. G., and Highton, T. C. 1972. Prevalence of rheumatoid arthritis in families. *Ann. Rheum. Dis.* 31:85.

Weisman, M., and Zvaifler, N. 1975. Cryoglobulins in rheumatoid arthritis. *Rheumatology* 6:60.

Weissman, G. 1964. Lysosomes, autoimmune phenomena, and disease of connective tissue. *Lancet* ii:1373.

———— 1965. Lysosomes. *N. Engl. J. Med.* 273:1084,1143.

———— 1967. The role of lysosomes in inflammation and disease. *Ann. Rev. Med.* 18:97.

———— 1971. Lysosomes and the mediation of tissue injury in arthritis. In *Rheumatoid Arthritis*, edited by W. Müller, H.-G. Harwerth, and K. Fehr. New York: Academic.

———— and Spilberg, I. 1968. Breakdown of cartilage protein-polysaccharide by lysosomes. *Arthritis Rheum.* 2:162.

————, Dukor, P., and Zurier, R. B. 1971a. Effect of cyclic AMP on relase of lysosomal enzymes from phagocytes. *Nature (New Biol.)*. 231:131.

————, Zurier, R. B., Spieler, P. J., and Goldstein, I. M. 1971b. Mechanism of lysosomal enzyme relase from leukocytes exposed to immune complexes and other particles. *J. Exp. Med.* 134:149s.

Williams, M. H. 1968. Recovery of mycoplasma from rheumatoid synovial fluid. In *Rheumatic Diseases*, edited by J. J. R. Duthie and W. R. M. Alexander. Pfizer Medical Monographs, No. 3. Edinburgh: Edinburgh University Press.

———— and Bruckner, F. E. 1971. Immunological reactivity to mycoplasma fermentans in patients with rheumatoid arthritis. *Ann. Rheum. Dis.* 30:271.

————, Brostoff, J., and Roitt, I. M. 1970. Possible role of mycoplasma fermentans in pathogenesis of rheumatoid arthritis. *Lancet* ii:277.

Williams Jr., R. C. 1975. Blood and tissue distribution of lymphocytes in rheumatoid arthritis. *Rheumatology* 6:219.

Williams, R. L., and Krasnoff, A. G. 1964. Body image and physiological patterns in patients with peptic ulcer and rheumatoid arthritis. *Psychosom. Med.* 26:701.

Winchester, R. J. 1975. Characterization of IgG complexes in patients with rheumatoid arthritis. *Ann. N.Y. Acad. Sci.* 256:73.

Wochner, R. D. 1970. Hypercatabolism of normal IgG—an unexplained immunoglobulin abnormality in connective tissue diseases. *J. Clin. Invest.* 49:454.

Wolf, E. 1970. Amyloidosis in rheumatoid arthritis. *Harefuah* 78:549.

Wolf, J. K. 1962. Primary acquired agammaglobulinemia, with a family history of collagen disease and hematological disorders. *N. Engl. J. Med.* 266:473.

Wolfe, A. M. 1968. The epidemiology of rheumatoid arthritis: a review: I: Surveys. *Bull. Rheum. Dis.* 19:518.

Wright, V., Walker, W. C., and Wood, E. A. M. 1963. Nialamide as a "steroid sparing" agent in the treatment of rheumatoid arthritis. *Ann. Rheum. Dis.* 22:348.

Ziff, M. 1961. Editorial: Genetics, hypersensitivity and the connective diseases. *Am. J. Med.* 30:1.

——— 1965. Heberden Oration 1964: Some immunologic aspects of the connective tissue diseases. *Ann. Rheum. Dis.* 24:103.

——— 1968. Immunological aspects of rheumatoid arthritis. In *Rheumatic Diseases*, edited by J. J. R. Duthie and W. R. M. Alexander. Edinburgh: Edinburgh University Press.

——— 1973. Pathophysiology of rheumatoid arthritis. *Fed. Proc.* 32:131.

———, Schmid, F. R., Lewis, A. J., and Tanner, M. 1958. Familial occurrence of rheumatoid factor. *Arthritis Rheum.* 1:392.

Zvaifler, N. J. 1965. A speculation on the pathogenesis of joint inflammation in rheumatoid arthritis. *Arthritis Rheum.* 8:289.

——— 1969. Rheumatoid factor and the fixation of complement. *Ann. N.Y. Acad. Sci.* 168:146.

——— and Pekin, T. J. 1963. Complement components in synovial fluids. *Arthritis Rheum.* 6:308.

———, and Schur, P. H. 1968. Reactions of aggregated mecaptoethanol treated gamma globulin with rheumatoid arthritis—precipitin and complement fixation studies. *Arthritis Rheum.* 11:523.

494

6

ULCERATIVE COLITIS
with a Note
on Crohn's Disease

ULCERATIVE COLITIS

Ulcerative colitis and its close relative, regional enteritis, are two of the most mysterious and ominous diseases to which mankind is prey: mysterious because we do not know much more now than we did 20 years ago about the factors that predispose to these diseases or initiate them; ominous because patients with ulcerative colitis are unusually prone to chronic disability, have an unusually high incidence of carcinoma of the colon, and may also suffer a high incidence of serious mental illness. Regional enteritis can be remorseless. Even when a diseased section of the bowel is removed, the disease recurs elsewhere in about one-half of all patients.

Over the past two decades understanding of ulcerative colitis has been advanced principally in two areas: the natural history of the disease and the immunopathology. It has become clear that ulcerative colitis is not necessarily confined to the colon, and may be associated with disease in a number of other systems, such as the liver and the spine. Although psychological factors have long been implicated in the disease, there remains much controversy about the social and psychological components of these diseases. Patients with ulcerative colitis and regional enteritis are often very ill physically, and their psychological profile is almost always interlaced with their psychological reactions to such frightening symptoms as severe abdominal pain, rectal bleeding, weight loss, and severe diarrhea. Only Engel (1955), in his longitudinal studies, has sifted out the psychological antecedents of the disease from the psychological responses to it.

499

The discovery of antibodies in the serum to colonic tissue has engendered a major controversy about their origin and role in ulcerative colitis. Some authorities have proposed that antibodies to colonic tissue precede or precipitate the disease, others hold that such antibodies are formed after disease has damaged cells of the intestinal wall. One type of agent that might alter cell-wall constituents of the colonic epithelium, it has been suggested, is a latent virus. It has also been proposed that the antibodies are formed in response to exogenous antigens, for example common bacteria living in the colon; tertiary syphilis is one model for such a disease process.

Anticolon antibodies are reported to have been found in healthy relatives, especially female relatives, of patients with ulcerative colitis. If these recent reports are confirmed and such antibodies are present and are identical to those found in patients with the disease, the theory that antibodies are a predisposing condition will gain support. The discovery of such factors would also make possible the prospective studies needed to resolve controversies over the role of other predisposing factors including psychological and social factors. However, if the initiating factors of these diseases prove to be heterogeneous, and no progress is made in distinguishing which subsequent courses of the disease are attributable to the respective causes, research may be rendered all but impossible.

Our basic knowledge of intestinal physiology remains quite rudimentary, and our ability to create animal models of the disease is, so far, limited. Thus research is impeded by many factors, and the concepts reviewed in this chapter cannot provide a comprehensive picture of these two diseases.

BASIC METHODOLOGICAL PROBLEMS

Problems of Definition

Three major issues stand in the way of making any definitive statements about ulcerative colitis. The first is a methodogical issue: it is exemplified by the marked discrepancies to be found in the literature about every feature of the disease, including both its clinical characteristics—its symptoms, signs, course, or laboratory features—and its patient characteristics. Many published series are based on the retrospective use of hospital records, whose reliability cannot be ascertained. The second issue involves the difficulty of verifying the diagnosis even by sigmoidoscopy, X-ray, or the examination of biopsy specimens. The pathologist may have difficulty in ascertaining whether the lesion is characteristic of ulcerative colitis or some other disease, for example, granulomatous colitis (Farmer et al., 1968 a, b), in at least 10 percent of the specimens. Finally, what is now called ulcerative colitis may not represent a distinctive entity, but rather a group of diseases. Some forms of what is now called ulcerative colitis will no doubt be identified as separate diseases, just as other forms have been in the past. In the last decades, the infectious forms of colitis (produced, for example, by Entamebae, and by the the cholera, paratyphoid, and dysentery bacilli) have been differentiated from other inflammatory bowel diseases, such as ulcerative colitis. In the past 15 years, granulomatous colitis has also been distinguished from ulcerative colitis (Lockhart-Mummery and Morson, 1960, 1964).

Another interesting lesion of the colon has been recognized lately—since the advent of arterial surgery on the abdominal aorta (Smith and Szilagyi, 1960; Young et al., 1963). This lesion is segmental and often involves the splenic flexure and the descending colon. Ischemic changes in the colon, consisting of mucosal ulcers, submucosal hemorrhages, and eventually, gangrene, together with inflammatory changes in pericolic fat indenting the colon, have been produced experimentally in dogs and occur naturall, in man when temporary vascular occlusion of the arterial supply occurs (Boley et al., 1963; Engelhart and Jacobson, 1956; Marston et al., 1966; Young et al., 1963).

The clinical features of this form of acute segmental colitis in man consist either of rectal bleeding and abdominal pain acute in onset or of ileus. Histologically, the changes may be indistinguishable from ulcerative colitis (Kellock, 1957) and are very reminiscent of those described after experimental manipulation of the colonic blood supply in animals (such as lowering blood pressure in mesenteric arteries). In man these changes follow the demonstration of a vascular block by arteriography (Marston et al., 1966). Of even greater significance is that ischemia of the colon may occur without such a block, presumably due to a relative insufficiency of blood flow and supply (Deucher, 1963; Engelhart and Jacobson 1956; Marston, 1962, 1964), as, for instance, in shock. Because of its segmental distribution, this form of colitis may also be incorrectly diagnosed as granulomatous colitis (Meyer and Sleisenger, 1973).

However, a group of "idiopathic" inflammatory bowel diseases—nongranulomatous jejunoileitis, ileocolitis, and ulcerative colitis—remain to be distinguished from each other. The disagreement about their taxonomy is underscored by the fact that some authors also classify regional enteritis and granulomatous colitis (Crohn's disease of the ileum and of the colon, respectively) as inflammatory bowel diseases (Kirsner, 1970a). At present it is impossible to do more than distinguish these diseases according to their usual location in the bowel, although this approach may be misleading, because ulcerative "colitis" may involve the ileum, and Crohn's disease may occasionally be located at almost any other site in the gastrointestinal tract, including the colon (Truelove, 1971).

Despite attempts to differentiate neatly between ulcerative colitis and Crohn's disease, the matter is not so simple. Histologically, the lesion of ulcerative colitis is usually conceded to be confined to the mucosa of the colon and rectum, whereas Crohn's disease may involve all layers of the ileum and colon and is characterized by granulomata. However, the histopathology of the lesion in the same patient may show features of both diseases (Meyer, 1973). The granulomata of Crohn's disease may not necessarily be the principal or first lesion either; the lesion may initially be mucosal with enlargement of lymphoid follicles and lymphocytic infiltration (Morson, 1971). The systemic features of both ulcerative colitis and Crohn's disease are identical (Truelove, 1971) and the two diseases share many common immunopathological (Thayer et al., 1969) and psychological features (Engel, 1973). Meyer and Sleisenger (1973) have stated that in all probability 12 to 25 percent of patients clinically diagnosed as having ulcerative colitis in the past would prove to have granulomatous colitis on histopathological examination.

Another important histological discovery about ulcerative colitis has been made and verified: once the disease has developed, the mucosa remains permanently abnormal, whether symptoms are present or not (Dick and Grayson, 1961; Dick et al., 1966; Truelove and Richards, 1956). The mucosal biopsy was abnormal in 71 of 79 patients who had been free of symptoms for as long as 8 to 10 years. In 32 of 34 patients with symptoms, the biopsy was abnormal. Therefore, Dick et al., (1966) concluded that the presence or absence of histological abnormality bore no relationship to the duration of freedom from symptoms. The remarkable aspect of this is that renewal of the colonic mucosa occurs every 3 to 5 days; so the disease must be associated with some permanent alteration of the key cells at the base of the crypts, resulting in abnormal mucosa in most instances. Alternatively, it is possible that this alteration antecedes the initial onset of the disease and symptoms, though there is no evidence for this speculation.

Among experts, there is even disagreement whether ulcerative colitis is a homogeneous disease (de Dombal, 1971) or not (Burch et al., 1969; Evans and Acheson, 1965; Kirsner, 1970a, b). If it should turn out to be heterogeneous, we may not be dealing with the same predisposing or precipitating factors in every case—a hypothesis that would take some of the mystery out of the disease. Burch et al., (1969) argued that every series of patients consists of two populations—one younger and one older—under the single rubric of "ulcerative colitis." They found that relapse rates were lower in older patients, and that this lowering was not just a function of age, closer follow-up, or of the fact that they had seen the physician sooner after onset of symptoms. In addition, they cite as evidence the fact that age of onset of the disease shows a *bimodal distribution*—one peak occurs at 18 years and another at 50 years. They assert that early onset is associated with one genotype, and later onset with another. It is hard, however, to be certain about the empirical basis of their conclusion. Evans and Acheson (1965) have based their argument for heterogeneity partly on the finding that diarrhea was more common, and bleeding was less common, in patients over 55 years of age. The figures about the mode of onset of the disease that were published by Evans and Acheson (1965) are not borne out in other series. Also, the number of variables that affect relapse rates are large, and the bimodality of the distribution of the age of onset has not been substantiated by other investigators: it may, for instance, only apply to male patients (Jalan et al., 1971) or to female patients (Monk et al., 1967), or it may not occur at all (Bonnevie, 1967; Gjone and Myren, 1964). These studies exemplify the kind of inconsistencies in clinical data that vitiate attempts to arrive at generalizations and defy interpretaion.

The controversies about every phase of ulcerative colitis are, in all likelihood, because it is not homogeneous disease. Therefore, the behavioral scientist who clings to the notion that it is a uniform disease will, in all probability, include a variety of diseases in his ulcerative colitis patient sample. It is for this reason that the clinical investigator must carefully select his patient population and must specify painstakingly the criteria he has used. Every study should specify the exact symptomatology and duration of the disease, and the age, sex, and socioeconomic status of the patients, as well as their ethnic origin. The location and extent of the lesion in the colon should be verified by X-ray, proctoscopy, sigmoidoscopy, and biopsy. In addition, the associated symptoms and signs (e.g., ankylosing spondylitis, uveitis, skin lesions, etc.) and the presence or absence of autoantibodies in serum should be ascertained.

Problems of Diagnosis

Ulcerative colitis may begin at any age. It has been described in neonates, as early as the third day of life, or soon thereafter (Avery and Harkness, 1964; Beranbaum and Waldron, 1952; Enzer and Hijmans, 1963; Hart, 1946; Lagercrantz, 1949, 1955; Platt et al., 1960; Sundby and Auestad, 1967), and it may also begin in middle or old age. But

502

the most frequent age of onset is in the second and third decades of life. Four to 10 percent of all patients with the disease are under 10 years of age, and another 17 percent are in the second decade of life (Cullinan and McDougall, 1956; Jalan et al., 1971; Platt et al., 1960; Sloan et al., 1950). In childhood, boys and girls are equally afflicted (Hijmans and Enzer, 1962; Patterson et al., 1971). In the United States, the disease does not seem to occur often in black children (Hijmans and Enzer, 1962; Patterson et al., 1971; Reinhart, 1961).

The clinical features of ulcerative colitis in children are not much different from those in adults (Broberger and Lagercrantz, 1966; Helmholz, 1923; Hijmans and Enzer, 1962). The disease, by most accounts, begins with bloody diarrhea, abdominal pain, fever, and stools that contain pus, blood and mucus (Broberger and Lagercrantz, 1966; Hijmans and Enzer, 1962); the child may rapidly lose weight and physical strength (Almy and Lewis, 1963; Platt et al., 1960). Should the disease persist into adolescence, physical maturation and sexual development may be retarded (Davidson, 1964, 1967; Hollowach and Thurston, 1956; Lyons, 1956).

The course of the disease in childhood is highly variable for reasons not yet known. In 60 to 80 percent of all children, the disease runs an intermittent course, with repeated exacerbations interspersed with remissions of variable length (Largercrantz, 1949, 1955). There have been no long-term longitudinal psychological studies of children with ulcerative colitis that correlate the course of the disease with the behavior and mood of the child in the manner in which Engel (1955, 1956) studied adult patients with the disease. Such a study would naturally have to take into account the impact of the disease and its symptoms on the child, as well as the effect on the child of a delay in physical growth and sexual maturation.

Both in children (Broberger and Lagercrantz, 1966) and in adult patients the disease may begin in a fulminating manner or it may begin gradually. But no consensus has been reached as to what symptoms the disease begins with, either in children or in adults. In searching for psychological explanations for the symptoms of the disease, some authors have considered diarrhea as the first and main symptom, while others have correlated the psychological state of patients with bleeding as the first symptom.

Engel (1954a, b, 1955) found bleeding to be the first symptom in 69 percent of the 32 consecutive, adult patients in his series, comprising 9 men and 23 women. (The proportion of women is greater than in most series.) The age of onset of the disease was from 2 to 53 years. Bleeding was accompanied either by formed or constipated stools or by diarrhea. In 5 of 14 patients constipation rapidly changed to diarrhea, 7 did not develop diarrhea for months, and 4 had a brief period of constipation for which purgatives were taken or enemas used, following which diarrhea and bleeding ensued. Relapses were accompanied by bloody and formed stools in 13 of 17 patients.

The incidence of symptoms at onset in Engels's series is confirmed by Fullerton et al., (1962), who studied 47 patients, 45 men and 2 women (a preponderant proportion of men), all but three of whom were under 50 years of age. In 62 episodes of ulcerative colitis in this series, bleeding with normal stools or diarrhea occurred in 41 instances (67 percent). The symptoms at onset and at the time of recurrences were identical in this group of patients.

These figures for the symptom of onset are not borne out by Askevold (1964) or by Nefzeger and Acheson (1963), who found that diarrhea was the most frequent single

503

symptom (78.5 percent) and, in descending order of frequency, abdominal pain (70.5 percent), rectal bleeding (54.5 percent), weight loss (18 percent), tenesmus (16 percent), vomiting (14 percent), fever (11.2 percent), constipation (4.8 percent), and joint pain (2 percent) occurred.

However, the symptoms at onset (see Table 1) may vary according to the age of the patient: in patients of both sexes, uncomplicated bleeding was significantly more common in patients under 55 (33.7 percent) than in older patients (13 percent); the opposite trend was found for diarrhea (25 percent versus 41 percent, respectively). In Evans and Acheson's study, mucus-containing diarrhea and bleeding was the most common combination of presenting symptoms (41 percent and 46 percent) in both age groups (1965).

These divergent figures have been variously interpreted. Some believe the discrepancies are a function of the reliability of the observation, others consider them to be age-related, and still others think they indicate that ulcerative colitis is a heterogeneous disease (Burch et al., 1969).

Because one can never be sure about the antecedents (e.g., infection) of these symptoms, it is incumbent on the investigator to ascertain their true nature. Therefore, he may have to resort to stool cultures, X-rays, sigmoidoscopy and even biopsy before he can be certain that he is dealing with a patient with the syndrome of ulcerative colitis. Stool cultures may distinguish between infectious and ulcerative colitis. X-rays have a low interrater reliability according to Geffen et al., (1968): they concluded that the only X-ray criteria worth relying on were abnormal haustration on postevacuation films, decreased caliber, distensibility and length of the colon, the presence of longitudinal folds and ulceration on the filled film, decreased tone, and the presence of polyps. Thus, both verification of the diagnosis of the disease and determination of its stage by X-ray criteria are fraught with difficulties, a problem that investigators in the psychosomatic aspects of the disease would do well to bear in mind.

Furthermore, direct observation of the rectum or colon does not provide any specific diagnostic clues. Nor do biopsies, because the pathological changes in ulcerative colitis have not been diagnostically specific when examined by either light or electron microscopy (Gonzales-Licea and Yardley, 1966; Nagle and Kurtz, 1967); they closely resemble those seen during bacterial or parasitic infection of the colon. Furthermore, about 10 percent of 151 pathological specimens obtained by biopsy from patients with ulcerative colitis were indistinguishable from those from patients with granulomatous colitis (Farmer et al., 1968a, b).

Clearly, diagnostic reliability in ulcerative colitis is not easily attained, but it is essential if one wishes to exclude from a subject population patients who are suffering from a variety of other diseases of the large bowel.

One of the many perplexing features of ulcerative colitis is that the bowel symptoms are at times anteceded, accompanied, or followed by symptoms and lesions of a variety of other organ systems. Furthermore, some of these manifestations have been traced to autoimmune phenomena (e.g., autoimmune hepatitis) or disturbances in immune processes. This observation has raised the question of the role of autoimmunity or immunological disturbances as predisposing or initiating factors in ulcerative colitis.

The frequency of involvement of organ systems other than the colon has varied from series to series (Table 2). Combinations of organ systems may be affected: for example, in every case of erythema nodosum in patients with ulcerative colitis seen by Fernandez-

504

TABLE 1

Incidence of Onset Symptoms of Ulcerative Colitis Reported by Investigators

SYMPTOMS	CULLINAN (1956) N = 40	SPRIGGS (1943) N = 33	ENGEL (1954–5) N = 32	ACHESON AND NEFZEGER (1963)[a]	EVANS AND ACHESON (1965)	
					UNDER 55 YRS	OVER 55 YRS
	2–53 YRS OF AGE					
Diarrhea only (± pain)	27 (67%)	26 (78%)	6 (19%)	34%	25%	41%
Constipated stool only		1 (3%)	4 (12%)			
Formed stool only	11		0			
Formed stool with blood		3 (9%)	6 (19%)	6%	33%	13%
Constipatated stool with blood	24 (60%)	3 (9%)	10 (31%)			
Diarrhea with blood			6 (19%)	17%	41%	46%
Bleeding (± pain)				5%		
Diarrhea, bleeding and pain				38%		

[a] Definite diagnoses only (Army men).

TABLE 2

Incidence of Associated Diseases in Ulcerative Colitis Reported by Several Investigators

	EDWARDS AND TRUELOVE (1964) N = 624	HAMMER ET AL. (1968)* N = 97	
Arthritis (polyarthritis, rheumatoid arthritis, ankylosing spondylitis, sacroiliitis)	7.4%	12%	17%[a] (N = 555) (sacroiliitis)
Skin (erythema nodosum and multiforme, Pyodermia gangrenosum, Dermatitis etc.)	18.7%		
Eczema		23%	
Eye Lesions (conjunctivitis, uveitis, iritis, episcleritis, glaucoma)	7.5%		13%[b]
Hepatitis (cirrhosis, fat infiltration, cholangitis, hepatitis, pericholangitis, amyloidosis, abscesses, carcinoma)	7.4%		9.3%[c] (N = 420)

Renal Disease (pyelitis, pyelonephritis, glomerulitis, nephritis, calculi)	4.6%		70%[d] (nephritis)
Thrombosis and Embolus (thrombocytosis, vascular thrombosis, disseminated coagulation, thyroid disease)	8.0%		6%–9%[c]
Thyroid Disease		8% (4%)	
Oral Ulceration	8.2%		
Hay Fever		12%	
Asthma		5%	
Monilia	2.3%		
CNS (delirium, psychosis, neuropathy)	5.6%		

*Control groups: differences greater than chance.
[a] Fernandez-Herlihy (1959)
[b] Wright et al. (1965)
[c] Nugent and Rudolph (1966)
[d] Jensen et al. (1950)

Herlihy (1959) there was an associated arthralgia. The nature of this arthralgia, or arthritis, has not been specified. Bywaters and Ansell (1958) and Wright and Watkinson (1966) felt that (in many cases, at least) it was specific to ulcerative colitis, and distinct from rheumatoid arthritis, by virtue of its course and the absence of rheumatoid factors in the blood (Wright and Watkinson, 1959). Typically, this form of arthritis first affected a single joint, often a large one of the leg; later, other joints were involved. The arthritis consisted of an acute synovitis with effusion into the joint. Onset of the arthritis *preceded* the symptoms of the first attack, or a relapse of ulcerative colitis in a small but significant proportion of cases—5 to 6 percent in Edwards' and Truelove's series (1964a) and 11 percent in another (Wright and Watkinson, 1966). About one-third of the patients with this form of arthritis and ulcerative colitis also had ulcers in the mouth, and two-thirds had either erythema nodosum, pyoderma gangrenosum, or leg ulcers. Following colectomy, the arthritis did not recur—a datum suggesting that the coincidence was not due to chance.

Ankylosing spondylitis, another form of arthritis, also occurs with ulcerative colititis. The expected incidence of this disease in the general population is 0.05 percent (Hersh et al., 1950; West, 1949); in ulcerative colitis, its incidence varies from 1.1 to 6.4 percent (Acheson, 1960b; Fernandez-Herlihy, 1959; McBride et al., 1963; Wright and Watkinson, 1959, 1966). Men are affected twice as frequently as women. The spondylitis has preceded the colitis by several years in about one-third of the patients studied (Acheson, 1960b). Progression of spondylitis, unlike that of the specific arthritis, is not halted by colectomy.

An arthritis of the sacroiliac joints, which apparently differed from ankylosing spondylitis, was observed in 18 percent of a group of 234 patients with ulcerative colitis (Wright and Watkinson, 1966). In addition, 60 percent of those patients with sacroiliac disease had skin lesions; but they did not have uveitis or ulcers of the mouth.

Genuine rheumatoid arthritis has, of course, also been reported in a large series of patients with ulcerative colitis. Its incidence was 3 percent. It began before, or at the time of, the onset of the colitis, and it continued to progress after colectomy had been performed (Fernandez-Herlihy, 1959).

Skin lesions in ulcerative colitis occurred in 2 percent (Sloan et al., 1950) to 35 percent (Lindenberg, 1958) of all patients, more frequently in women. In Johnson's and Wilson's (1969) series, the figure was 4.8 percent. Erythema nodosum occurred in 8 of 20 patients and was associated with exacerbations of the disease. Pyoderma gangrenosum (7 patients) occurred at any time during the course of the disease; papillonecrotic lesions and ulcerating erythematous plaques were also observed. These authors had never seen the last named lesion except in association with either Crohn's disease or ulcerative colitis. Erythema multiforme, seen in only two patients, was attributed to medication in one case and to toxemia of pregnancy in another. Allergic vasculitis, purpura, subacute cellulitis, herpes zoster, and urticaria were other skin lesions that have been reported to coexist with ulcerative colitis (Edwards and Truelove, 1964a; Johnson and Wilson, 1969).

The eye lesions most commonly associated with ulcerative colitis are conjuctivitis and iritis, both of which preceded onset or relapse of the disease. The incidence of eye lesions in those suffering from ulcerative colitis is probably ten times that of the general population. In the series done by Wright and his co-workers' (1965), the incidence of uveitis

508

was 11.8 percent in 144 patients. It occurred in only 2 percent of a control population. Uveitis was commonly associated with ulcerative colitis and ankylosing spondylitis—an association which was unlikely to occur by chance alone.

The renal lesion most common in ulcerative colitis takes the form of a true nephritis. In Jensen's series (Jensen et al., 1950) it occurred in 70 percent of patients, but others have reported more modest figures. Some have found renal infection to be more common than true nephritis.

Hepatic lesions have been found to be much more common than was first assumed (Anthonisen et al., 1966; Wright and Watkinson (1966). Many of these lesions are asymptomatic and were discovered only at biopsy. Studies indicated that the predominant lesion was a pericholangitis (Mistilis and Goulston, 1965), often accompanied by an active hepatitis. When biopsies were performed, the observed incidence of changes in the liver was 40 percent (Anthonisen et al., 1966) or even 83 percent (de Dombal et al., 1966; Mistilis, 1965). In addition, autoimmune hepatitis has been linked to ulcerative colitis (Holdsworth et al., 1965). One of the many unexplained aspects of the numerous and diverse systemic correlates of ulcerative colitis is that the identical systemic manifestations occur in regional enteritis (Edwards and Truelove, 1964a).

I have emphasized the criteria used in the diagnosis of ulcerative colitis because the diagnosis is not an easy one to make. The very difficulty in reliably establishing its diagnosis probably accounts for many of the discrepant results that have been obtained in genetic studies or in investigations carried out by epidemiologists, medical sociologists and other behavioral scientists.

THE ROLE OF GENETIC FACTORS

Reports on the incidence of two or more cases of ulcerative colitis in the same family show a disheartening variability: they range from 0.6 percent in a series of 2,485 families (Brown and Scheifley, 1939) to 17 percent (Schlesinger and Platt, 1958) in another series. In 26 series totaling 10,905 patients, summarized by Sleight et al. (1971), the number of families containing more than a single affected member was 230, and the incidence of familial ulcerative colitis was 2.1 percent. But a higher figure (about 5 percent) has been more often quoted (Evans and Acheson, 1965; Goligher et al., 1968; Kirsner and Spencer, 1963; Singer et al., 1971). In some series, 5 to 15 percent of children with ulcerative colitis had relatives with a history of the same disease (Kirsner, 1961; Sherlock et al., 1963). In Jewish families, the incidence of ulcerative colitis in the families of probands may rise to 41 percent (Kirsner, 1970a; Singer et al., 1971).

In a study in which a matched comparison group was used, the incidence of ulcerative colitis in the family members of 152 probands was 5.7 percent, as against 0.7 percent in the comparison group (Binder et al., 1966). This figure accords with those reported by Cornes and Streher (1961), Kirsner and Palmer (1954b), and Sanford (1971). Therefore, it seems that, apart from local variations, the family incidence of ulcerative colitis is in fact about 5 to 6 percent.

Several members of the same family may suffer from ulcerative colitis. In reviewing the literature, Sanford (1971) found 292 families of patients that had more than one member with ulcerative colitis: in these 292 families there were 631 cases of the disease, an average of 2.16 per family. Both Davidson (1967) and Morris (1965) reported that eight members of one family were afflicted with the disease. Usually only one other member —sibling, collateral relative, parent, or child—share the disease (Almy and Sherlock, 1966; Bacon, 1958; Gelfand and Krone, 1970; McEwan-Alvarado and Bargen, 1967; Moltke, 1936). Ulcerative colitis has also been reported to occur in three consecutive generations (Morris, 1965; Wigley and McLaurin, 1962).

The mode of inheritance cannot easily be inferred from pedigree studies. Nor do such family studies per se prove a genetic factor in the disease. Many different variables besides genetic ones may account for the family aggregation of the disease. In fact, Almy and Sherlock (1966) reported ulcerative colitis occurring in a husband and wife who were not related by blood; this improbable occurrence is a strong argument for environmental factors, and against genetic factors. The data available from family studies has variously been interpreted as supporting a dominant mode of inheritance with incomplete penetrance (Sanford, 1971), or a polygenic mode (McConnell, 1965). And unfortunately, the mode of inheritance has not been clarified by studies on twins. The number of Mz and Dz twins with ulcerative colitis is too small to be conclusive. Concordance for ulcerative colitis has been reported in eight of ten Mz twin pairs (Lyons and Postlethwait, 1948; Moltke, 1936; Sanford, 1971; Sherlock et al., 1963; Sleight et al., 1971). In another study, two other Mz pairs were discordant for ulcerative colitis (Marie and Ledoux-Lebard, 1942), although one twin pair was concordant for liver disease. Of six Dz pairs of twins that have been studied, only two pairs were concordant for ulcerative colitis (Bacon, 1958; Binder et al., 1966; Finch and Hess, 1962; Kirsner and Spencer, 1963). In one family, a Mz pair of twin girls concordant for ulcerative colitis had a sister with ulcerative colitis (Sleight et al., 1971). Some of the studies in the older literature are difficult to evaluate, as modern methods for determining zygosity were not available.

Blood groups, Rh and other protein factors in blood are inherited characterisitics. Therefore, their association with a disease may indicate that heredity plays a prediposing role. In ulcerative colitis, the distribution of ABO blood groups is the same as in the general population (Atwell et al., 1965; Buchwalter et al., 1956; Jalan et al., 1971; Thayer and Bove, 1965; Winstone et al., 1960). However, both a low frequency of Rh negativity (Maur et al., 1964; Thayer and Bove, 1965) and a low frequency of homozygous CC rhesus antigens (Boyd et al., 1961) have been discovered in patients with ulcerative colitis.

In the search for hereditary factors in a disease one may also look for the association of that disease with other diseases that are known to be inherited: The incidence of ankylosing spondylitis was about four times as frequent in patients with ulcerative colitis as in a control series of patients (Jayson and Boucher, 1968; Sanford, 1971; Wright and Watkinson, 1965). The association of these two diseases is of interest, in light of the fact that ankylosing spondylitis is believed to be transmitted by an autosomal, dominant gene (Hersh et al., 1950). Its onset may precede or follow the onset of ulcerative colitis. It may, by itself, afflict one member of a family in which another member has ulcerative colitis (McBride et al., 1963).

In support of the contention that genetic and immunological factors play a role in ulcerative colitis are several reports that the relatives of patients with ulcerative colitis are

510

unusually prone to bronchial asthma, allergic rhinitis, urticaria, and atopic dermatitis (Hammer et al., 1968; Kirsner, 1970a; Lagercrantz et al., 1971). Although other studies (Binder et al., 1966) have not borne out this contention, the use of comparison groups in Hammer's studies did lend support to the thesis that diseases in which a certain class of immunoglobulins (IgE) play an etiological role are more frequent in the relatives of patients with ulcerative colitis.

Finally, rather conclusive evidence has been obtained that anticolon antibodies occur with a considerable incidence in the (women) members of the families of patients with ulcerative colitis. (This finding will be reported on more extensively in later sections of this chapter.)

EPIDEMIOLOGICAL STUDIES

Incidence and Prevalence

Only a minority of the studies done to date on the incidence and prevalence of ulcerative colitis come up to the exacting methodological standards for epidemiological studies promulgated by Pflanz (1971). In two studies that did approximate his criteria, the incidence figures were remarkably similar. The incidence in Oxfordshire, England (Evans and Acheson, 1965), and in Copenhagen County, Denmark (Bonnevie et al., 1968), is in the range of 5.8 to 6.7 per 100,000 for men, and 7.3 to 7.6 per 100,000 for women (Table 3). However, in the English study the incidence figures included cases of ulcerative proctitis as well as colitis. The incidence in Norway (Gjone and Myren, 1964) is one-third of that in England, but the incidence of the disease in that country seems to be increasing: over the 15-year period studied (1946–1960), the incidence rose from 0.85 to 2.1 per 100,000 of the population. In Denmark, the incidence seems to be on the increase as well.

The prevalence of ulcerative colitis is higher in England than in any other country for which figures are available. Prevalence in England is twice that of Denmark and 50 times that of Costa Rica, a country in which exact records are kept.

It is hard to know the true incidence and prevalence in the general population. There are "mild" forms of ulcerative colitis (Sparberg et al., 1966) that may not require hospital care. Fahrlander and Baerlocher (1971) estimated that in Switzerland, at least, only 50 percent of all patients with this disease were admitted to a hospital.

Geographic Distribution

Not too many years ago, ulcerative colitis was thought to be a disease of civilization (Bockus, 1964). Today the disease is generally conceded to have a worldwide distribution. Cases have been reported from all the corners of the earth (de Dombal, 1971; Weiner and Lewis, 1960), from developing countries as well as those that are technologically and economically advanced. Ulcerative colitis has been found in Bedouin Arabs (Salem and Shubair, 1967), in nomadic African tribesmen (Billinghurst and Welchman, 1966), as well as in Costa Rica (Miranda et al., 1969). However, Salem and Shubair

TABLE 3

Incidence and Prevalence of Ulcerative Colitis

Country	Year	Incidence[a]			Prevalence			Reference	Sources
		Men	Women	Both	Men	Women	Both		
Denmark	1940–61			1.6				Lindenberg and Aagard, 1964	
Uppsala, Sweden	1945–54			6				Samuelsson (see Norlen, 1970)	
Norway	1947–55			1.2				Ustvedt, 1958	Hospital discharges; records
Bristol, England							85.0	Houghton and Naish, 1958	
Oxfordshire, England	1951–60	4.5[b] – 1.1[c]	5.9[b] 1.1[c]	5.2[b] 1.1[c]	55.4 8.2	76.0 14.4	65.7 11.4	Evans and Acheson, 1965	Hospital, clinic, private patients
		5.8	7.3	6.5			79.9		
Northern Island, New Zealand	1954–58[c]			5.6			41.3	Wigley and McLaurin, 1962	Hospital discharge diagnoses
Norway	1956–60	2.0	2.1	2.1				Gjone and Myren, 1964	Hospital records[d]
Baltimore, Maryland	1960–63	3.9	5.2	4.6			42	Monk et al., 1967	Hospital records, biopsy, X-ray
Copenhagen County, Denmark	1961–67	6.7	7.6	7.3	38.6	49.3	44.1	Bonnevie et al., 1968	Case records, municipal registers, death certificates
Basel, Switzerland	1960–69			8.0				Fahrländer and Baerlocher, 1971	Private physicians, hospitals
Costa Rica	1960–69						1.6	Miranda et al., 1969	Private physicians, hospitals

[a] Per 100,000 population
[b] Ulcerative colitis
[c] Ulcerative proctitis
[d] All hospitals in Norway

(1967) have noted that relocation of Bedouin Arabs to the cities of the Arabian peninsula seems to be associated with an increase in various bowel diseases: 60 percent of those 140 patients in their sample who developed the irritable colon syndrome, and 8.5 percent of those with ulcerative colitis developed the diseases after relocation.

Distribution according to Sex

In several large series, the ratio of women to men with ulcerative colitis has ranged from a low of 0.6 to 1.0 to a high of 1.4 to 1.0. No fewer than six studies have shown a ratio of 1.4 to 1.0 (Edwards and Truelove, 1963; Fernandez-Herlihy, 1959; Jalan et al., 1971; Ustvedt, 1958; Watts et al., 1966b; Wigley and McLaurin, 1962). In addition to two studies showing ratios below 1 (Birnbaum et al., 1960; Watts et al., 1966b), the series of 2,000 patients reported by Sloan and co-workers (1950) yielded a ratio of 0.6 to 1.0.

Burch et al. (1969) have argued that ratios should be age-adjusted because there are two groups of patients: those under 60 with a modal age at onset of eighteen and those who are older and have experienced a later age of onset. In Sloan's series, the ratio of women to men in the younger group was 0.83 to 1.0 and in the older group was 0.5 to 1.0. In some of the other studies, in which women preponderated, age-adjusted ratios of women to men may be higher in the younger group than in the older (Watts et al., 1966a), about equal (Edwars and Truelove, 1963), or lower (McDougall, 1964). Thus, age-adjusted figures do not confer greater consistency on the data from these various studies.

Ethnic and Religious Factors

It is of particular interest to compare the incidence of ulcerative colitis among different ethnic groups living in the same geographic areas. In New Zealand, Maoris are said to be virtually unaffected by the disease (Wigley and McLaurin, 1962). In the United States, the ratio of black to white patients was 1 to 33 in one series (Kirsner, 1970a) and about equal in another (Acheson and Nefzeger, 1963). Yet in Monk's studies (Monk et al., 1967, 1969) three times as many whites were found to have the disease as blacks.

In the United States and England, Jews seem to be more commonly afflicted than those of other religious backgrounds (Acheson, 1960; Acheson and Nefzeger, 1963; Evans and Acheson, 1965; McKegney et al., 1970; Melrose, 1955; Monk et al., 1969; Nefzeger and Acheson, 1963; Paulley, 1950; Sloan et al., 1950; Weiner and Lewis, 1960). In several series, the percentage of Jews has varied from 9.4 percent (Sloan et al., 1950) to 42 percent (Kirsner, 1970a) or higher (Singer et al., 1971). Reports from several university hospitals in different cities have stressed the higher incidence of ulcerative colitis and regional enteritis among Jews (McKegney et al., 1970). The estimated risk for Jewish soldiers is two-to-four times higher than for non-Jews (Acheson, 1960a; Acheson and Nefzeger, 1963). Most incidence and prevalence figures are from hospitals, but Monk's series (Monk et al., 1967) confirms higher risk figures for the general Jewish population. Monk and her co-workers (1969) suggest that there may be a diagnostic bias at work in the tendency of physicians to diagnose ulcerative colitis more frequently in Jewish patients: Jews are more likely to contact their physicians when symptoms first occur and they are more frequently admitted to private rather than charitable hospitals (Weiner and Lewis, 1960).

In the U.S. Army series (Acheson and Nefzeger, 1963), there was no difference in incidence between native-born and foreign-born Jews. In Monk's study (Monk et al., 1969) there was no apparent relationship to the recency of their migration to the United States, and orthodoxy of belief seems to be an unimportant factor. In Jews immigrating to Israel, the incidence of hospitalized patients was shown to be greater in those coming from Europe and America than those from Asia and Africa (Birnbaum et al., 1960). However, the overall death rate in these patients is low and in Israel itself the incidence figures are not unusually high. In the United States, non-Jews with ulcerative colitis tend to have immigrated more recently than non-Jewish patients with other diseases and are more likely to have migrated from the British Isles and Empire countries than from any other countries (Monk et al., 1969).

Socioeconomic Factors

Although a number of studies have attempted to correlate the incidence of ulcerative colitis with socioeconomic variables, no uniform trend has been established. One group of studies has appeared to demonstrate that ulcerative colitis affects people with higher occupational status and higher educational backgrounds more than those with lower status and less education (Castelnuovo-Tedesco et al., 1970; Kirsner, 1970a; Monk et al., 1969). A well-controlled study from Denmark (Bonnevie, 1967) bears out the contention that ulcerative colitis patients seem to come from higher educational and socioeconomic levels; the Danish data are especially informative because access to medical care is provided to all Danish citizens without regard to socioeconomic status. Other series have not found a similar correlation (Acheson and Nefzeger, 1963; Mendeloff et al., 1966; Monk et al., 1969; Sloan et al., 1950); but even these negative studies have sometimes produced evidence of correlation with socioeconomic variables: e.g., status of father (Monk et al., 1969), military rank (Acheson and Nefzeger, 1963), or number of jobs held (Mendeloff et al., 1966; Monk et al., 1969; Singer et al., 1971).

Attempts have been made to demonstrate a difference between rural and urban populations. Again, various studies have yielded conflicting results (Acheson and Nefzeger, 1963; Gjone and Myren, 1964; Wigley and McLaurin, 1962).

All epidemiological studies reported to date have yielded conflicting results for reasons that are far from clear. Therefore, it cannot be ascertained why the incidence of ulcerative colitis seems to be increasing, or why Jews are particularly likely to have the disease.

Because studies using epidemiological methods are so contradictory it has not been possible to ascertain the role of environmental or sociocultural factors in predisposing to or initiating the disease.

THE ROLES OF PSYCHOLOGICAL AND PSYCHOPHYSIOLOGICAL FACTORS

Psychiatrists and psychologists have been studying patients with ulcerative colitis for almost 50 years. The descriptions of these patients at several levels of psychological organization have been quite consistent. However, most gastroenterologists, while acknowledging that these patients do have certain traits or patterns of personal relationships in common, do not accord them a major initiating role (e.g., Meyer, 1973). They quote psychiatric and psychological studies with negative findings that support their contention, rather than considering how psychological factors might predispose and initiate the disease in interaction with other predisposing factors. One of the studies that is frequently quoted to repudiate the notion that psychological and social factors may play an etiologic or pathogenetic role in ulcerative colitis was reported by Feldman et al. (1967). It is worth analyzing because it exemplifies many of the conceptual and methodological problems in this area. The authors studied 34 consecutive patients with ulcerative colitis over a two-year period. (Compared with other series, this one is somewhat biased toward younger patients.) These patients were compared with two other groups: (1) "a general population divided into normal and abnormal according to arbitrary criteria"; (2) 74 consecutive patients admitted to the gastroenterology service, exclusive of patients with regional enteritis and large-intestinal disease. Patients were interviewed so that they could be scored on a 65-point questionnaire "salient for personlity evaluation," which the authors never described. It is not clear from their report how, or if, its reliability and validity had been established. Interviews with each patient were also conducted for a minimum of 5 to 6 hours and an average of 10 to 12 hours. An attempt was made to quantitate each of the 65 variables in the questionnaire on a 5-point scale; a median score was considered normal. From the 65 points, T-scaled variables were derived from the questionnaire to show the degree of personality disorder: that is, whether a disorder was present or not; average or better "ego strength"; the presence or absence of emotional problems or conflicts, psychosis, impulse disorder, psychoneurosis or depression; evidence, or not, of "constructive handling of life's anxieties and problems"; no significant patterns of hypochondriasis or incapacity due to unexplained illness of any sort.

Of the 34 patients with ulcerative colitis, only 5 were judged by the authors to be abnormal in character. Yet 7 of the 34 patients had received psychotherapy of at least "several months duration." The 5 abnormal patients were classified as inadequate, infantile, passive, schizoid, depressive, or dependent. In addition, 8 patients were found to be passive-dependent, 5 passive-aggressive, 1 to be anxious, and 1 to be schizoid and psychopathic: the authors labeled these 15 subjects normal. When contrasted to the comparison group of patients with gastrointestinal disease, no apparent major differences emerge; it is stated that, if anything, the latter show more abnormal personality types, and fewer "precipitating circumstances after onset," and they seem to have been subject to more stress before onset or relapse.

This study is one of the few in which consecutive admissions to a hospital service were studied. However, it raises many questions of a methodological and conceptual nature. It is not clear whether the interviewer knew the medical diagnosis of his subject-patients prior to interview. Nowhere in the report were criteria for the establishment of character diagnoses set down. Despite laudable attempts in this study to quantitate normality, such quantitation is itself based on value judgments about inferences made from interview data. It is not possible for the reader of this report to assess why an inadequate or passive personality type is deemed more abnormal than a passive-dependent type. The data could well incline the reader to say that in fact only 15 of the 34 patients were normal, rather than 29—the number given in this report and quoted by others. Furthermore, the authors do not describe the personality traits and attitudes of those they considered normal.

The implication of this study is clear: if a person with ulcerative colitis is normal, his psychological make-up cannot contribute to the etiology or pathogenesis of the disease. The fact remains, however, that no one today considers that psychological factors *by themselves* are *the* cause of this or any other disease. They may account for a variable proportion of its etiological and pathogenetic variance, but they do not *by themselves* determine the particular disease, any more than the etiology of gout is determined by any one, exclusive biochemical defect. An exclusive psychological personality type, unconscious conflict, or type of relationship is not likely to be found for ulcerative colitis. What has emerged from most psychiatric studies is a picture of ulcerative colitis patients as people who may differ from each other in degree, but who demonstrate a spectrum of personal sensitivities and vulnerabilities that are brought to the fore in certain life settings or in the face of certain experiences. Other people may also find these experiences distressing but they do not fall ill if they are not biologically predisposed to ulcerative colitis.

Onset Conditions and the Nature of the Initiating Event

The precise timing of the onset of ulcerative colitis is not easy to determine. To begin with, many adult patients have had a long-standing history of bowel symptoms. Some have been chronically constipated; others have had a history of amebic or bacillary dysentery; still others have had nonbloody diarrhea, vomiting, abdominal cramps, or flatulence when they were distressed. Alternating symptoms of diarrhea and constipation may have occurred (Engel, 1954a, b; Fullerton et al., 1962; Jalan et al., 1971; Sloan et al., 1950). The frequency of such symptoms has not been established; it appears to vary widely from series to series, depending on the accuracy of history-taking and the recall capacity of the patient.

The usual method that has been used to time the onset of ulcerative colitis is to look for changes in bowel habits, whether sudden or gradual. However, this approach is fraught with difficulty if change is assessed from a fluctuating baseline, or, if diarrhea is anteceded, by days, weeks, or months, by the onset of constipation or rectal bleeding. In this second sequence, when there is antecedent constipation, the observer may have difficulty in deciding whether changes in the life of the patients should be correlated with the initial or subsequent changes in bowel habits as symptoms of onset.

Engel (1955) was able to time the onset of the disease with considerable accuracy in some patients; he found that their symptoms would follow a distressing experience by a matter of hours or of a day or two. In other patients the onset of symptoms was gradual, and began intermittently. In these latter instances, they were the culmination of cumulative psychological distress. The less-abrupt onset of the disease might begin with gradual changes in the lives and psychological state of his patients—such as the assumption of increased responsibility, the mounting pressure of demands or obligations on the patient, or the cumulative and various personal problems faced by an adolescent. In 26 of 30 patients such events antedated the disease; in one, it may have been insignificant, in two others (in which onset occurred in childhood) nothing could be remembered, and in a fourth no such event could be identified.

Two main categories of events that surround the onset of the disease have been identified. The first category is the rather general one of bereavement, or separation from a person on whom the future patient leans or depends. The second category can further be divided into three subgroups. These more specific events can only be understood in terms of the rather special psychological sensitivities of these patients, which are however not unique to them. Patients with ulcerative colitis regard every request as an intolerable demand to perform. They are reluctant to attempt carrying out the demand or fear failure in doing so. Other patients are particularly sensitive to humiliation or derogation.

A number of authors have emphasized that bereavements, disappointment in love, fear of loss of love, profound parental disapproval, and separation play a major role as onset conditions in the lives of ulcerative colitis patients (Arajärvi et al., 1961; Cobb, 1953; Crohn, 1963; Engel, 1955; Finch and Hess, 1962; Freyberger, 1970; Grace and Wolf, 1951; Groen, 1947; Hijmans and Enzer, 1962; Jackson, 1946; Jackson and Yalom, 1966; Karush and Daniels, 1953; Karush et al., 1968; Lindemann, 1945; McKegney et al., 1970; Masland, 1960; Prugh, 1951; Sifneos, 1964; Sperling, 1957; Wijsenbeek et al., 1968).

Lindemann (1945) found that bereavement anteceded the onset of the disease in 75 of the 87 patients in his series. Many patients have a long history of bereavement: McKegney et al. (1970) found that there was an unusual incidence of broken homes and parental deaths in the childhood histories of his patients. Many of the patients were not able to resolve their grief reactions to a prior bereavement. Engel (1955) reported that unresolved grief was a prominent feature in half of the 31 patients in his sample; in 10, the grief was due to the death of a close relative.

Various authors have obtained data on, or have inferred, the meanings such bereavements had for their patients. A disappointment in love or deprival of love may have humiliated the patient (Groen, 1947; Groen and Bastiaans, 1954; Groen and Van der Valk, 1956; Groen and Birnbaum, 1968), threatened to terminate a dependent relationship with its psychological rewards (Paulley, 1950; Grace and Wolf, 1951), and destroyed the patient's sense of personal security (Daniels, 1948). Dependency and personal security may also be threatened by one's having to grow up and become independent during adolescence.

Another category of precipitating events was related to the fear of failure. More precisely, the patient may have had the urge to give or accomplish something that he or she felt incapable of doing. The urge was then frustrated or inhibited, or the effort to accomplish it failed (Alexander, 1950), with the result that the patient was threatened with its reactivation after remission (De M'Uzan et al., 1958; Engel, 1955; Fullerton et ity, tasks, or pressures, developed the disease if what they were called upon to do was more than the resources they could summon to do them, especially if they felt they could get no help or support from others (Castelnuovo-Tedesco, 1962, 1966; Engel, 1955; Mohr et al., 1958; Mushatt, 1954; Rubin et al., 1963).

Closely linked to the fear of failure was a situation where the patient was in conflict between complying with the demands and wishes of someone on whom he depended and rebelling against them. The patient knew that his rebellion would fail, and he would continue to have to comply (Castelnuovo-Tedesco et al., 1970) or be punished for an outburst of rebellious or jealous rage (McDermott, 1966).

Grace and Graham (1952) and Graham et al. (1962) have identified another set of precipitating events. Specifically, the patient felt he had been injured or degraded by a particular person and wanted to be rid of that person. Whatever the cause, the feeling of degradation, and, at times, public humiliation, lowered the patient's tenous self-respect, and left him feeling humiliated, helpless, and defeated (Groen and Birbaum, 1968; Marder, 1967; Wijsenbeek et al., 1968).

The same types of life experiences that first initiated the disease have been associated with its reactivation after remission (De M'Uzan et al., 1958; Engel, 1955; Fullerton et al., 1962; Wittkower, 1938). In Wittkower's series, 70 percent of 40 patients had relapses, and 17 of these relapses were preceded by identifiable experiences that were analogous or identical with the initial, precipitating one, and caused the same kinds of affective responses.

The extreme sensitivity of some patients to brief separations from their physicians and other close persons, which produced symptom exacerbation, was documented by Engel (1955) and Freyberger (1970). Engel studied 30 relapses—defined as bleeding after a period of normal bowel activity of a month or more—in 10 patients. Twenty-four of these 30 episodes were associated with real, threatened, or symbolic separations, or with the anniversary of a separation. On these occasions, personal ties to another person on whom the patient depended were threatened or actually cut. The patient was then faced by the prospect of having to fend for himself. In the face of this threat, the patient felt helpless. In 6 other instances, relapses occurred in situations that enraged the patient but about which he felt powerless to do anything.

There are other categories of events with which disease onset has been associated. These include the strenuous use of laxatives, anorectal surgery, acute infectious diseases (not necessarily of the gastrointestinal tract), and pregnancy (Jalan et al., 1971; McKegney et al., 1970; Sloan et al., 1950). However, the meaning of these events to the patient were not assessed; therefore, they cannot be used to refute or support the importance of life experiences to the patient at the onset of the disease.

Attempts to assess the frequency with which meaningful life experiences occurred at the onset of the disease have resulted in widely divergent figures—from 2 percent to 90 percent or more (Lindemann, 1945; Sloan et al., 1950). There are several possible explanations for these discrepancies. On the one hand, low figures were obtained when chart records (which are notoriously unreliable) were used to collect large series of case records. The higher figures, on the other hand, were usually reported by psychiatrists. Sample bias may play a role when high figures are obtained, as most patients referred to psychiatrists are not consecutive patients seen in a clinic, private office, or in-patient service, but are selectively referred.

However, even when an unselected, consecutive series of patients was studied, the frequency of evident precipitating events was in the neighborhood of 85 percent. McKegney et al. (1970) interviewed 40 consecutive patients (21 with ulcerative colitis and 19 with regional enteritis) at the same hospital. The occurrence of a "well-defined and serious life crisis" during the six-month period prior to disease onset was verified in 86 percent of patients with ulcerative colitis and 68 percent of those with regional enteritis; the parental home was not intact at disease onset in 62 percent and 26 percent of patients, respectively. One parent had died before disease onset in 43 percent of the patients with ulcerative colitis.

One other conceptual problem requires discussion: the initiating experience does not have to be objectively gross or overwhelming. It can only be assessed in terms of the particular psychological sensitivities of the patient and his adaptive capacity for handling an experience that for him or her (not for others) may be overwhelming or portentously meaningful.

Therefore, the degree of "stress" cannot be assessed, in a quasiquantitative way, from the perspective of the observer, but only from the point of view of the patient. It is fallacious to try to develop "objective" indices of stress without taking into account the subject and his capacity for responding to specific stresses with idiosyncratic distress and a failure to cope, as exemplified by the oft-quoted study by Mendeloff and his co-workers (1970). They composed a life-stress score consisting of such items as whether the patient's parents had died before he was 16 years of age; socioeconomic mobility (defined as an inconsistency between the son's and father's jobs, or between the educational level attained by the father, son, or spouse and the jobs they held); differences in religious background between spouses; whether subjects were living alone, frequency of job changes, etc. The precipitating factors sought for in the interview comprised the following items: upper respiratory and other acute diseases, physical injury, increased job demands, loss of a job, financial pressures, family crisis, deaths of close friends or relatives, and a category of "events outstanding in the subject's memory." It is not clear from their report whether the reliability or validity of the stress index had been assessed before the study, nor is it clear why these particular "stresses" were chosen.

The study compared 102 subjects with the irritable colon syndrome, 227 subjects with "inflammatory bowel disease" (158 subjects with ulcerative colitis and 69 with regional enteritis), and 735 healthy subjects in the general population, who were not hospitalized. Comparisons were made on the basis of one lengthy interview by a lay interviewer. There were more Jewish subjects in both clinical groups than in the population sample. The non-Jewish subjects with the irritable colon syndrome had "stress scores" significantly higher than the scores attained by all patients with inflammatory bowel disease, and the non-Jewish women with the syndrome scored highest of all. Even Jewish women with the irritable colon syndrome had higher stress scores than subjects with inflammatory bowel diseases.

It is difficult to compare this study with any other, because of the unique categories of stress used. The authors conclude that "stress events are not important in the etiology of ulcerative colitis; or, at least, their effect is mediated by some other, possibly constitutional, factors in persons with the disease." But these factors were not measured. What was actually studied was data self-reported by Jews and non-Jews, with two kinds of bowel disease and by a control group; and the Jews in these three groups reported fewer "stressful events" (in Mendeloff's sense) than non-Jews.

In actuality, both child and adult patients with ulcerative colitis seem to be particularly (but not uniquely) incapable of adapting to certain life experiences (Engel, 1955; Finch and Hess, 1962). Prugh (1951) was able to show, in a qualitative way, that children with a fulminating onset were less able than children with slow onset to cope with the threatening life experience at the onset of the disease. Those children who had an insidious onset were also less dependent, less immature, and less guilt-ridden in response to angry feelings. He also correlated active coping behavior with the frequency of bowel movements. An increased frequency of bowel movements seemed to be correlated with mood and behavior. When the child was actively participating in play or work, the number of bowel movements was reduced; when he was inactive or anxious, depressed and preoccupied, the number was increased.

We have seen that many patients with ulcerative colitis have impaired adaptive capacities, strong persistent dependent attachments to important members of their families, and a great sensitivity to actual or imagined slights. They also have aspirations to comply with and please others but do not have a great capacity for perseverance at a task. These traits and relationships sensitize them to certain stressful life experiences, to which they respond by a deeply repressed rage and hostility at the departed, demanding, or disappointing person, and a feeling of being helpless to cope with the experience (Engel, 1955; Marder, 1967). Engel (1955, 1968) has outlined the subsequent feelings of giving up, helplessness, despair, and the sense of being overwhelmed. The patient's psychological responses impair his subsequent adaptation to the disease, his symptoms, and his environment.

The sense of helplessness, despair, sense of defeat, powerlessness, and being overwhelmed has been described by a number of observers before Engel and since (Groen, 1947; Groen and Bastiaans, 1954; Murray, 1930a, b; Mushatt, 1954; Sifneos, 1964). Some patients also become depressed (Karush and Daniels, 1953; De M'Uzan et al., 1958; Fullerton et al., 1962; Wijsenbeek et al., 1968), or have an exacerbation of unresolved sorrow or grief (Engel, 1955; Lindemann, 1945; Sperling, 1946). Others feel humiliated (Appel and Rosen, 1950; Grace et al., 1951). In some there is a fall in self-esteem (De M'Uzan et al., 1958). Feelings of being alone, bereft, deserted, unwanted, unworthy, (Engel, 1955) or hopeless are expressed (Karush and Daniels, 1953). The most common responses engendered were despair, hopelessness, helplessness, a sense of failure and defeat, and an inability to cope—when self-esteem fell, depression ensued.

Engel (1955, 1968, 1973), on the basis of his studies of patients with ulcerative colitis, has emphasized that these affects are facets of the "giving-up/given-up" complex—which he has recognized as the emotional setting for the inception of many diseases. Not everyone responds to loss in this manner—that is, with feelings of helplessness and hopelessness, low self-esteem, an incapacity for enjoyment, a disruption of the feeling of the continuity of the self in time, and a reactivation of memories of earlier periods of giving up. The giving-up/given-up complex described, in addition, a failure of adaptive capacity in psychological functioning, which is implicit in the patients' statements that they are not able to cope once they have been overcome by such feelings.

This response is not specific for ulcerative colitis: the specificity of the disease that ensues must be determined by a biological predisposition and by (unknown) brain, autonomic and hormonal correlates of the biological state of adaptive failure, which is expressed psychologically as the giving-up/given-up complex, and which sets in motion unknown pathogenetic mechanisms.

520

It is generally recognized that patients with ulcerative colitis may become psychotic during the initial and active phase of the disease (O'Connor et al., 1966). Or the disease may occur in a person who is already psychotic or has a history of psychosis. On occasion, ulcerative colitis may alternate with psychosis (Appel and Rosen 1950; Giovacchini, 1959; Grace and Wolf, 1951; Paneth, 1959; Swartz and Semrad, 1951), but this course of events appears to be the exception rather than the rule (Engel, 1955; O'Connor et al., 1966; Sullivan and Chandler, 1932; Wittkower, 1938).

The psychotic illness takes the form either of a psychotic depressive illness (De M'Uzan et al., 1958; Wijsenbeek et al., 1968) or a schizophrenic illness (McKegney et al., 1970). The incidence and prevalence of psychotic illness in ulcerative colitis patients has not been firmly established—once again the figures vary considerably. However, in the series of 624 patients gathered by Edwards and Truelove (1964a) "CNS complications," including delirium and psychosis, occurred in 5.6 percent. Using MMPI profiles, Fullerton et al.; (1962) found evidence of psychopathology equivalent to that found in a mixed hospitalized psychiatric population, amounting to 81 percent of his target population. Thirty-one of 47 patients were clinically depressed, with psychomotor retardation. Weinstock (1961) found the incidence of overt psychopathology to be 90 percent. In a selected group of 57 patients, 33 percent were adjudged to be schizophrenic (Daniels et al., 1962; Karush et al., 1968; O'Connor et al., 1964, 1966, 1970). The incidence of schizophrenia in this series may have been unusually high because these 57 patients were selected from a group of 104 patients referred to the psychiatrist for obvious psychopathology. The 104 patients had been selected, in turn, by the gastroenterologist out of a total of 900 patients. Notwithstanding this fact, one would still have to conclude that there is a considerable psychiatric morbidity in patients suffering from ulcerative colitis—a conclusion also reached by McKegney et al. (1970)—even when psychiatric illness is not induced by ACTH or corticosteroid medication, by dehydration, anemia, and other complications. Usually, the schizophrenic illness takes a paranoid form (Alexander, 1950; Appel and Rosen, 1950; Daniels, 1940; Engel, 1955; Fullerton et al., 1962; Karush and Daniels, 1953; Lindemann, 1945, 1950; Moses, 1954; O'Connor et al., 1966; Sperling, 1946; Wijsenbeek et al., 1968). In view of Engel's formulations, one would expect a priori that when psychotic illness occurs in these patients, it should take either a depressive form, or, at least, if it is schizophrenic the patient should also be depressed, hopeless, or helpless. In fact, Engel (1955) wrote that 2 of his 39 patients became so seriously depressed during a relapse of ulcerative colitis that they had to be treated with electroconvulsive therapy. Usually, however, a depressive reaction of clinical significance coincides with the onset of the disease, rather than antedating it (Cobb, 1953; Daniels, 1940; Engel, 1955; Lindemann, 1945, 1950; Tunis and Dorken, 1951). And Karush and his co-workers (1968) did find that the paranoid schizophrenic reaction was accompanied by a depressed mood: of the 30 patients they studied, 13 were only depressed, 10 had mixed paranoid and depressive reactions, and 7 were only paranoid.

These data have implications for treatment. Generally speaking, schizophrenic patients with ulcerative colitis do least well of all ulcerative colitis patients when treated psychotherapeutically (Daniels et al., 1962; Karush et al., 1968, 1969; O'Connor, 1970). That, perhaps, is why Chalke (1965) found that one-half of the patients he studied who were treated surgically were schizophrenic. Aylett (1960) reported that in two patients the schizophrenic reaction remitted following surgery, as did other various psychological symptoms.

It is, however, very difficult to interpret what would appear to be an increased incidence of schizophrenia in ulcerative colitis patients: a conservative estimate of the incidence of schizophrenia in these patients is 5 to 10 percent, which is about 5 times the incidence in the general population. This fact requires, but has resisted, explanation, except perhaps in psychological terms: patients prone to psychotic illness have lowered adaptive capacities and an impaired ability to handle their personal conflicts.

But the etiology of the psychoses is unknown, although it is increasingly apparent the genetic factors play an important etiologic role (Rosenthal, 1971). Should there really be such an increased coincidence of ulcerative colitis and psychosis, genetic factors common to both may exist. Identification of these factors would illuminate the etiology of both groups of diseases.

Other Psychological Responses to the Disease

It would seem self-evident that to have a chronic, debilitating, incurable, and, at times, dangerous disease, with ugly and frightening symptoms such as diarrhea, pain, rectal bleeding, and fever, would in itself be likely to cause psychological reactions (Aylett, 1960; Engel, 1952; Judd, 1966). In addition, the fluid and electrolyte imbalances that may occur during the acute phase of the disease may produce a delirious state and thereby impair the patient's adaptive, psychological capacities. This sequence might bring about regressive tendencies, which could be confounded with responses to life experiences, and the affective changes that have been described. Thus, the disease may make the patient feel helpless and dependent on others. Problems about incontinence and soiling may also be reactivated during the active phase of the disease. Fears of impending surgery, specifically the prospect of living with an ileostomy and its effects on human aspirations, may cause the patient to be apprehensive or hopeless about the future. In addition, this disease, like any other, focuses the patient's attention increasingly on himself.

On the other hand, it should not be forgotten that hospitalization frees the patient from having to contend with his family, his job, or whatever task he may have failed at; it puts him in a situation free from external, daily pressures. In some instances separation from the family has led to an improvement in the patient's symptoms (Lepore, 1965). This datum, of course, does not vitiate the observation of the effects of separation as a precipitating experience; but if life is intolerable in the family, escape from it may well ameliorate the patient's distress. Psychological responses to ileostomy or to diarrhea have also been described (Karush et al., 1968): in some patients the handling of the stoma was pleasurable and the pain of ileostomy a source of comfort; in others it is a cause for disgust. The patient's attention was focused on the stoma and its products, at the expense of personal relationships and other transactions with the real world (Engel, 1952). And for some patients the diarrhea begins to assume specific, personal meanings.

Clearly, it is not easy to separate antecedent from consequent psychological reactions in patients who already have ulcerative colitis. The only way of solving this problem unambiguously would be by studying a large population at risk *before* disease onset. This has not been done. In the meantime, the long-term study of patients during remission and active illness (Engel, 1952, 1954a, b, 1955, 1956, 1958g Karush et al., 1968; O'Connor, 1970; Sifneos, 1964) is the best method available.

Alternative Symptoms

We owe to Engel (1955, 1956) the interesting observation that during periods of remission from ulcerative colitis the patient may suffer from headaches. Although this symptom had been mentioned in the literature before (Chambers and Rosenbaum, 1953; Furmanski, 1952; Karush and Daniels, 1953; Sloan et al., 1950), no intensive study of its natural history or meaning had been carried out before Engel did so. Sloan et al., (1950) noted that 37 of 2,000 patients had a history of migraine; but they made no mention of other forms of headache. The incidence of headache in Engel's series (1956) was much higher: 20 of his 23 patients suffered from headaches. In ten patients the headache was migrainous. The headaches antedated the colitis (7 patients), or they occurred during periods when the bowel symptoms were quiescent. Only three of the 56 headache episodes coincided with periods of rectal bleeding. In other patients, headaches presaged the end of an attack of colitis. A somewhat lower frequency of headaches as alternative symptoms has been described since that time (Feldman et al., 1967; Fullerton et al., 1962; Wijsenbeek et al., 1968).

Engel correlated the behavior of his patients with the presence of headache. During 46 of 56 instances of headache, the patient was decisive, active, and aggressive, felt in control of a situation, related to others, and was actively dealing with and solving a problem, but he also manifested overt guilt, or derivatives of covert guilt feelings (Engel, 1955, 1956, 1958). When the patient felt hopeless, helpless, passive, and hapless, bleeding occurred, but the patient was free of headache (Engel, 1956, 1958). In some patients, the headache coincided with the anniversary of the solution of a significant personal problem. In one patient the headache was ascribed to an hysterical identification with her father, who had also suffered headaches (Engel, 1955).

The Personalities, Conflicts and Sensitivities of Patients with Ulcerative Colitis

CHILDREN

Some hospitalized children with ulcerative colitis have been described as perfectionistic, prim, proper, intellectualized, emotionless, punctilious, obedient, rigid, and obsessive. The boys appear to be "little old men." Other children (especially the girls) are manipulative; they play the hospital personnel off against each other and use their disease and its symptoms to gain their ends. When their wishes are not met, they are petulant and demanding.

There is agreement that most of these patients have serious problems in their relationship to their mother, including passivity, compliance, and a deep-seated desire to be taken care of by the mother. Either because of the danger to the relationship of outbursts of anger when their longings are frustrated, or because of the mother's continual interdictions against the expression of angry feelings or childish motivations—such as impulses to soil, eat, bite, or to display early sexual behaviors—the children inhibit the expression of these feelings. For whatever reason, either forced upon the child or motivated by longing or fear, the child's tie to the mother is intense, close, and reminiscent of early childhood (Arajärvi et al., 1961a, b; Arthur, 1963; Castelnuovo-Tedesco, 1962; Finch and Hess, 1962; Finch, 1964; McDermott, 1966; Mohr et al., 1958; Prugh, 1950, 1951; Sperling, 1949, 1955, 1960, 1969; Sundby and Auestad, 1967). Some children responded with jealous rage when they felt that more care or attention was lavished by their mothers on a sibling or another person. Other children became depressed during hospitalization (Prugh, 1951). In studies in which the effects of having a chronic illness and of being hospitalized were taken into account, these clinical observations were confirmed by psychological tests: Arajärvi et al. (1961a) administered the Rorschach test to 19 children with ulcerative colitis and 19 with rheumatic heart disease. They found that children with ulcerative colitis were not preoccupied with their illness to any greater extent than the children with heart disease. Significantly, children with ulcerative colitis abjured human contact. They perceived human relationships as impersonal and unrewarding. The children perceived themselves as passive and suffering. They were lonely, resigned, and withdrawn. They perceived their relationship to their mothers as if they were still physically connected to her. Passive wishes to be taken care of, and to receive from others, were frequently expressed. There was no desire to give to others. When verbal communication occurred between mother and child, it was in the form of a quarrel. Feelings were rarely expressed verbally; those feelings that were expressed were unpleasant. There was no joy in their lives. Strong but poorly formulated wishes to harm or hurt and feelings of hate were not expressed or were inadequately articulated.

Cognitive studies of these children have also been made: the children perceived their bodies as being faulty or defective, which might well be the consequence of the illness. Intellectually, they were of average intelligence. However, formal disturbances of their thought processes were unusually frequent in boys with ulcerative colitis (Arajärvi et al., 1961a; Finch and Hess, 1962; Wijsenbeek et al., 1968).

ADULT PATIENTS

Compulsive traits most frequently characterize patients with ulcerative colitis. However, other character traits have also been described, both before and after the onset of the disease. The compulsive traits of adult patients correspond with traits observed in some children with the disease. These compulsive traits include perfectionism, neatness, orderliness, conscientiousness, obstinacy, conformism, punctiliousness, and punctuality. The patients are often moralistic, humorless, timid, meticulous in speech and personal habits, with a tendency to worry and not to express angry or resentful feelings. They approach life intellectually and not emotionally (Bodman, 1935; Brown et al., 1938; Chambers and Rosenbaum, 1953; Craddock, 1953; Cushing, 1953; Daniels, 1942, 1948; De M'Uzan et al., 1958; Engel, 1955, 1973; Lepore, 1965; Mahoney et al., 1949; Malaguti, 1971; Murray, 1930a, b; Wijsenbeek et al., 1968; Wittkower, 1938). They do not develop a frank compulsive neurosis with compulsive thoughts and ritualistic actions, but they do tend to ruminate and worry. In Wittkower's series (1938), compulsive traits were present in 23 of 40 patients, and in Engel's series (1955) in 26 of 27. Engel also noted that these traits could change during the active disease: 23 of 25 patients became ingratiating, placating, and submissive, rather than directly demanding. The other two patients became more petulant, querulous, and openly demanding, presumably as a result of their reactions to the disease and to hospitalization. His observations extended previous descriptions of another group of patients, who were similarly described, but in addition were jealous and provocative, impatient, moody, easily provoked to tears, theatrical, argumentative, and exhibitionistic. Most of the patients who demonstrated these traits were women (Brown et al., 1938; Grace and Wolf, 1951; Groen, 1951; Mahoney et al., 1949; Paulley, 1950, 1956; Stewart, 1949; Wittkower, 1938). Wittkower (1938) described five of 40 patients who were shy, chronically depressed, and who were afraid of social contacts with other people, or of committing any kind of social transgression.

The literature on these patients also stresses that they were exquisitely attuned to any manifestation of rebuff or hostility. Their response would be to placate those who rebuffed them. Their feelings could also easily be hurt. Some acted in response to this sensitivity by nonchalance, haughtiness, aloofness, and excessive pride. Some were suspicious of the motives of other people, and, therefore, tended to avoid them (Bodman, 1935; Brown et al., 1938; Cushing, 1953; Daniels, 1940, 1943, 1948; Groen and Bastiaans, 1955; Grace and Wolf, 1951; Mahoney et al., 1949; Paulley, 1950, 1956; Wijsenbeek et al., 1968; Wittkower, 1938). In summary, although compulsive character traits were described most often, some patients demonstrated hysterical and paranoid character traits, which were present either before or during the active disease and its remission.

Adult patients with ulcerative colitis have often been described as being more intelligent than a representative sample of the population (Acheson and Nefzeger, 1963; Brown et al., 1938; Daniels, 1942; Fullerton et al., 1962; Groen, 1947; Heath, 1949; Kollar et al., 1964a; Krasner, 1953; Krasner and Kornreich, 1954; Mahoney et al., 1949; Schlesinger and Platt, 1958; Sullivan, 1936; Weiner and Lewis, 1960; Wijsenbeek et al., 1968). Findings on formal testing of patients bear out this impression. Twenty-seven male patients were tested by Krasner (1953), who found a mean IQ of 120 on the Wechsler-Bellevue Scale; this was significantly higher than male patients with peptic ulcer and a comparison group of hospitalized patients with other disorders matched for age.

Some ulcerative colitis patients make use of their intelligence and are successful. But most, despite their intelligence, lack ambition. They do not strive to achieve, either because their aspirations are low or they lack self-confidence. In some a serious depression interferes with their work. Finally, many writers have emphasized their unwillingness or impaired capacity to cope with and adapt to life changes and other forms of stress (De M'Uzan et al., 1958; Fullerton et al., 1962; Hecht, 1952; Krasner, 1953, Krasner and Kornreich, 1954; Mahoney et al., 1949; Poser and Lee, 1963; Schucman and Thetford, 1970; West, 1970; Wijsenbeek et al., 1968).

Intrapsychic conflict, as a predisposing and initiating factor in ulcerative colitis in adult patients, was emphasized in the period between Murray's first studies and the series of papers written by Engel 25 years later. Murray (1930a, b) had observed that while his women patients had conflicts about marriage, pregnancy, and abortion, his male patients had conflicts about leaving their mothers and marriage. Sperling (1946), on the basis of her observations, conceptualized her findings according to a Freudian model of the neuroses: the patient has an unconscious wish to rid himself of a mental representation of a hated person; this wish manifests itself in diarrhea.

On the basis of his studies, Alexander (1950) wrote that ulcerative colitis patients "closely resemble patients suffering from other forms of diarrhea." (This statement has often been overlooked in the literature.) In his view, the antecedent conflict was between the wish to carry out some obligation and the failure or unwillingness to do so, or the unpreparedness for, or the impossibility of, doing so. In women, he stated, this conflict usually took the form of a conflict about giving birth to a child and living up to maternal responsibilities. In men, there was a conflict between carrying out, or not, financial obligations. Alexander also inferred oral-dependent longings, whose frustration produced anxiety and guilt, for which restitution was attempted by the urge to accomplish and the wish to give. Several other observers have emphasized the oral nature of the patients' conflicts, created by the desire to take things by mouth, or to secure enough food, prestige, or success to meet the demands exacted by other people; others have described the demands for compliance of performance as anal derivatives (Castelnuovo-Tedesco, 1962, 1966; Cushing, 1953; Mushatt, 1954; Sperling, 1946, 1960; Szasz, 1950, 1951). Many of the formulations were explicit or implicit attempts to account for the diarrhea of the disease. But as Engel (1954a, b, 1955) pointed out bleeding is the more frequent harbinger, at least in his series of patients, and it cannot be accounted for strictly in psychological terms.

Many of these studies can be faulted because of the absence of a control group, and because the patient's disease was studied only after onset. The first objection—to the uncontrolled observation of patients—was met by Castelnuovo-Tedesco (1962, 1966). He compared 22 patients with peptic ulcer individually with 22 patients with ulcerative colitis (Castelnuovo-Tedesco et al., 1970), and concluded that the element of compliance to the perceived demands of others and rebellion against having to meet them was not a central conflict in the peptic ulcer patients but was in about one-third of those with ulcerative colitis. They were unable to care for themselves; they felt that they had to comply in order to be cared for and that any attempt to assert themselves or not to comply was feeble. The patients responded to their failure to rebel or assert themselves with a sense of helplessness, entrapment, frustrated resentment, and hopelessness. (We shall return to this theme again [emphasized by Engel, 1961, 1968] in reviewing the patients' responses to precipitating events; it unifies much of the controversy in the literature.)

The second main objection to previous studies was met by Alexander and his co-workers (1968), who carried out a "blind," validating, clinical study. Elaborating on their earlier formulation, they stated that "the central dynamic constellation . . . consists in losing hope that a task involving responsibility, effort and concentration can be accomplished. They are inclined to give up hope easily in the face of obstacles. Even though they may continue their external efforts towards achievement, they have already lost confidence, and work under internal compulsion." The observers also felt that the ambitions and expectations of the parents had pushed the children beyond their capacity to perform. But the children were not rewarded by the parents' love unless they complied and performed.

For five patients of each sex with ulcerative colitis, 44 percent of the initial predictions were correct, and 58 percent of the final ones—results that were significantly better than could be expected by chance. Interestingly enough, in this study, the disease with which ulcerative colitis was most frequently confused was peptic duodenal ulcer (see also Krasner, 1953).

Because of Engel (1955, 1958, 1961, 1973), there has been a shift in emphasis in the past 20 years in the study of patients with ulcerative colitis, from their intrapsychic conflict to their personal relationships. If the criterion of "adult" relationships is a charitable and enlightened interest in, concern for, and largely unambivalent love for others, then these patients fall far short of that ideal. They remain close to, and reliant on, parents or some substitute for them (such as a spouse). In that relationship they are motivated by the desire to receive (not to give) love, attention, affection, guidance, advice, or direction—and many of their traits can be seen in the light of this relationship and their hopes and expectations of it. Thus, compliance is mainly a matter of doing what someone else wishes in order not to offend. The patients are jealous if the parent loves or is attentive to another person. Their inability to give of themselves to others, except in primitve, childlike ways, makes them appear immature, as does their petulance and sulking when their unarticulated wishes are not fulfilled. Their relationships are a one-way street and thus they appear narcissistic to others. Yet their relationships may be endowed with unusually intense feeling—the patient may imagine the he or she cannot live apart or separate from the other person (Sperling, 1946). They are tied to that one person and thus may appear lonesome or unable to form friendships (Lindemann, 1945). They live vicariously through the figure to whom they are attached, or they are motivated by them (Engel, 1952, 1955). Yet, they are sensitive to, and often frustrated by, the person they lean on. In summary, ulcerative colitis patients are dependent upon only one person—at first their mother or father, later some parental substitute.

The vicissitudes of a dependent relationship are not hard to see in the lives of these patients. It is also clear that any frustration of their dependent longings causes a violent upsurge of angry feelings (De M'Uzan et al., 1958) and fantasies of destruction, which largely remain unexpressed, lest their expression endanger the vital relationship (Alexander, 1950; Bodman, 1935; Brown et al., 1938; Castelnuovo-Tedesco, 1962; Castelnuovo-Tedesco et al., 1970; Cushing, 1953; Daniels, 1942, 1948; Engel, 1955; Groen, 1951; Karush et al., 1968, 1969; Lindemann, 1945; Mahoney et al., 1949; Murray, 1930a, b; Mushatt, 1954; Sifneos, 1964; Sperling, 1946; Stewart, 1949; Sullivan, 1936; Wittkower, 1938).

This description of the personal relationships of these patients has important implications for their clinical management. Their pattern of relating is transferred to the physician, on whom they become inordinately dependent; or while, on the surface avoiding involvement they hanker after it. At times, when the patient is very ill, the doctor may be endowed with magical expectations. If the doctor tells the patient he cannot help, or he goes away, the patient may have a marked exacerbation of his symptoms (Engel, 1955; Freyberger, 1970; Poser and Lee, 1963).

527

Many patients marry with reluctance. When they do, their marital relationships and sexual lives, even before the onset of the disease, are a continuation of their relationships to their parents. The marital partner, or his or her parents, are often no more than a parent surrogate. Or the patient's mother or mother-in-law continues to live in the patient's home. The patient prefers to be held, cuddled, or stroked by the spouse than to have sexual intercourse. Patients show little interest in sexual relationships, which some of them consider to be dirty, unclean, or disgusting. Most women patients never, or only rarely, experience sexual pleasure. Many men patients are intermittently or frequently impotent. Some patients emphasize bodily cleanliness. It is not surprising then that the symptoms of the disease, the frequency of bowel movements, and the care of a colostomy, may be distasteful or disgusting to these patients (Chambers and Rosenbaum, 1953; De M'Uzan et al., 1958; Engel, 1955, 1973; Murray, 1930a, b; Sifneos, 1964).

The Origins of the Personalities and Conflicts of Patients with Ulcerative Colitis

THE MOTHER-CHILD RELATIONSHIP

The nature of the traits and personal relationships of patients with ulcerative colitis, including their relationships to the physician, can at present best be understood in ontogenetic terms, specifically in terms of the relationship of the patient to his or her mother. The description of that relationship, although not unique for these patients, is based not only on the perception of that relationship by the patient but also on the direct observation of mothers, on their psychological test profiles, and on the observation of the behaviors of mothers in their interactions with the family. Women patients tend to perceive the mothers differently than men patients (Arthur, 1963).

The conformity and perfectionism of children with ulcerative colitis has been in part ascribed to the restrictive and controlling attitudes of a mother who forbade her child's phase-specific impulses to bite, soil, and display sexual behavior. Particular restrictions were imposed by the mother on any display of anger and hostility in word or deed, so that the child ceased to express them. The mother dominated the child and kept it dependent on her. She was fearful (hence overprotective) lest harm befall the child in the world beyond the family (Arajärvi et al., 1961a, b; Broberger and Lagercrantz, 1966; Finch, 1964, Jackson and Yalom, 1966; Prugh, 1950, 1951; Sperling, 1946, 1969; Sundby and Auestad, 1967). Other mothers were overtly or covertly hostile to the child, or rejected it, or controlled it either by a protective overconcern or by acting the martyr (Castelnuovo-Tedesco, 1962; Mohr et al., 1958).

The hated mother was perceived by her young or adult daughter—or she actually was—either domineering, self-centered, controlling, and all-powerful, or inconsistent, strict, exacting, and judgmental, or cold, unaffectionate, and punitive. Some daughters felt that only by manipulating the mother could they obtain anything from her (Bodman, 1935; Daniels, 1948; Engel, 1952, 1955, 1973; Finch and Hess, 1962; Groen, 1951; Mahoney et al., 1949; Mohr et al., 1958; Rubin et al., 1963; Sifneos, 1964; Sperling, 1949, 1960; Wijsenbeek et al., 1968). Although the sons felt dominated by their mothers, they considered them to be concerned, and considerate about their well-being.

In any disagreement the daughters were inclined to fight with their mothers, while the sons preferred to give in to them (Engel, 1955, 1973).

As a group, the mothers were observed to be grim, joyless, unhappy, and pessimistic. They worried about their children; they were often ambitious for them, perfectionistic, and critical, but self-sacrificing. Eccentricity, religious and political fanaticism, quixotic attitudes, and self-righteousness characterized some of the mothers; they had little genuine capacity for affection, care, and love for their children. Other mothers were frankly paranoid, or chronically depressed. They did not wish their children well; in fact, some preferred them to be sick and dependent (Daniels, 1940, 1942, 1948; Engel, 1955, 1973; Sperling, 1946, 1955, 1960).

Curiously, the children, while complaining about their mothers, submitted to and complied with their wishes, willingly or not. They placated their mothers by being exquisitely attuned to their whims and wishes, in order to maintain their relationship with them. Their mothers' wishes were their command, as if they had coordinated their own behavior to every twist and turn of their mothers' behavior. Obedience and compliance were features of the sons' behavior. Children of both sexes felt this need to placate and comply; if they did not comply, the mother would withdraw her affection (Engel, 1955, 1973).

Although most of the descriptions are based on reports from patients, their assessments of their mothers are borne out by direct observation (Jackson and Yalom, 1966) and self-assessment by the mothers (Arajärvi et al., 1961a, b). The causal direction has been conventionally assumed to run from the mother to the child. It may do so, yet one wonders whether some of the behavior of the mother is not in response to the obstinacy, dependency, argumentativeness, and cantankerousness of her children, or to their over-passivity. Clearly much more investigation is required in this area. In addition it cannot be assumed that the origin of the patients' behaviors in interaction with their mothers was entirely the product of experience.

FATHERS OF PATIENTS

The fathers of child or adult patients with ulcerative colitis either described themselves, or were described by an observer, as being dissatisfied with their marriages or their jobs. They saw themselves as mere breadwinners. Usually they were discouraged, resigned, and lacking in ambition and self-esteem. They were passive and ineffectual. They did not help their wives in the care and rearing of their children (Finch and Hess, 1962; Jackson and Yalom, 1966; Mahoney et al., 1949; Mohr et al., 1958; Rubin et al., 1963). Women patients described their fathers as gentle, kind, and ineffectual. They were attached to their fathers, but some were critical of them for not protecting them against the mother's punitive, cold, and domineering ways (Engel, 1973; Groen and Bastiaans, 1954). Men patients described their fathers in quite another way: as coarse, intimidating, brutal, rude, and demanding. They complained that the fathers drank too much. The fathers placed an emphasis on their own or their son's manliness. They often threatened or abused their wives, so that their children became submissive to both parents. Some fathers were clinically paranoid (Castelnuovo-Tedesco, 1962; Engel, 1955, 1973; Groen and Bastiaäns, 1954; Krasner, 1953).

The Family Dynamics

A study of the interactions of family members was conducted by Jackson and Yalom (1966), who interviewed eight white, middle-class families of children, aged 7 to 17 years, with ulcerative colitis. The interviews were observed through a one-way screen and were also recorded on film and tape. The families were not additionally interviewed at home, nor is it clear from the report how these eight families were picked for study. The families were characterized by speaking quietly, with little expression of feeling, save embarrassment. They suppressed in themselves, and in each other, evidence of dissension, argument, and disagreement. They discouraged humorous expression. By precept and example, the parents failed to express tenderness and affection, and they restricted their children's friendships. They suppressed the expression of any (especially original) ideas and activities, and disapproved of the children being outgoing or creative. The parents and their children tended to placate, mollify, and subdue each other, especially in their expression of painful feelings about each other or disharmony within the family. The parents had few friends and acquaintances and were mainly involved with their children. The authors of this report concluded that these families showed a false solidarity, a "pseudomutuality," which has also been described in the families of schizophrenic children (Wynne et al., 1958).

Members of the families of patients may themselves either have, or be liable to, ulcerative colitis, and this introduces a variable that should be controlled in any investigations. Another important variable that must be controlled in such studies is the effect on family members of having a seriously and recurrently ill child in their midst. In addition, studies of mothers or families of children with ulcerative colitis should take into account that the disease may retard the physical and sexual development of the child. In families in which the father stresses the physical prowess and manliness of his son, a maturational lag of this kind may pose a special psychological demand on the boy.

The Siblings of Patients

Another approach to the study of patients with ulcerative colitis is to compare them with their siblings who do not have the disease. Until McMahon et al. (1973) did so systematically, the only account of siblings had been given by Jackson and Yalom (1966). They observed the siblings in interaction with their families and were surprised to find that their behavior was overtly disturbed. McMahon and co-workers compared 23 patient-sibling pairs. The patients were diagnosed as follows: 10 had ulcerative colitis, 7 granulomatous ileocolitis, 3 regional enteritis, 2 distal colitis, and 1 granulomatous colitis. The pairs were not exactly matched as to sex—48 percent of the patients and 30 percent of the siblings were male. The conclusions of this study, based on interviews and various psychological tests, were that the siblings had successfully broken away from their parents during adolescence to achieve independence and maturity, or they were in the process of doing so; the patients had not. In other important ways the patients confirmed many of the psychiatric impressions that have just been described. The siblings, on the other hand, were much less compliant and placating. The study also suggests that there are strong psychological similarities between patients with the various forms of ulcerative colitis and Crohn's disease.

530

Psychosomatic Theories of the Pathogenesis of Ulcerative Colitis

In this chapter many etiological and pathogenetic hypotheses have been reviewed and none have adequately been substantiated. Two facts about nonspecific ulcerative colitis seem, however, to emerge: the first is that once the disease has developed, and despite its partial or complete clinical remission, the mucosa of the colon remains permanently abnormal. The second fact, supported by a substantial body of accumulated experience, is that psychological responses to the disruption of a key personal relationship, to stern disapproval, or to the demand for the performance of a task that the patient feels he cannot carry out without someone's help, constitute the onset conditions of the disease and its relapses. The patient responds to these conditions by a failure of psychological adaptation. Regretfully, we have no idea by what intervening mechanisms this state of psychological decompensation is linked to the inception of, or in the case of relapse, the exaggeration or exacerbation of, the already existing, colonic mucosal pathology. The pathogenesis of ulcerative colitis is further confounded by the fact that there may be a combination of pathogenetic processes at work even if it proves to be a homogeneous disease, or, if ulcerative colitis should prove to be a heterogeneous disease, no single pathogenetic hypotheses would account for it.

A number of psychiatrists and psychoanalysts have linked their psychological observations and formulations with the onset symptoms of the disease. In particular, these formulations have either attempted to account for the onset of diarrhea or the onset of bleeding. Engel has also reviewed the possible mechanisms by which the psychological reaction might account for the bleeding.

The onset of diarrhea is the subject of the hypotheses of Alexander (1950, 1968), Szasz (1950, 1951), Grace et al. (1951), Groen (1947, 1951), and Groen and Van der Valk (1956). As Engel so cogently pointed out in his series of papers (1952, 1954a, b, 1955, 1956, 1958, 1961, 1968, 1969), not only does the disease, at least in the younger age groups, have a long antecedent history of constipation and other bowel symptoms, but bleeding is the most common initial symptom—a fact which had also impressed Sperling (1946). Engel (1952) felt that the bleeding, which constituted the "onset condition" in 68 percent of his series, was the result of vascular changes in the mucosa and submucosa. He based his hypotheses on both direct observation of the surgically exposed colon —which suggested that hyperemia was consistently observed, while motility changes were not—and on the previous work of Warren and Sommers (1949).

The authors of the various psychological formulations about the initiation of the disease may be divided into two groups: those who emphasize content and specific conflicts and seek to link these to putative physiological mechanisms that express the conflict, and those who place the burden on the affective reactions to life experiences. The latter conceptualize the affective change as one aspect of an organismic state that sets the disease into motion.

Alexander (1950) considered the conflict to be one between the reluctance to give up a prized possession, on the one hand, and the accomplishment that would result from doing so, on the other. The life situation that elicited this conflict was a demand for performance that the patient was unprepared to meet. This conflict was not dissimilar to one described by Castelnuovo-Tedesco (1962, 1966, 1970), who emphasized a battle between secret rebellion and compliance. Alexander speculated that this conflict caused diarrhea by activating parasympathetic pathways to the colon that enhance the passage of its fecal content. He also postulated that the protective mucosal barrier of the colon was lowered, and that mucosal digestion and bacterial invasion ensued. On the other hand, Szasz (1950, 1951) accounted for diarrhea (not only of ulcerative colitis) on the basis of conflicts about taking food into the mouth. When these impulses were inhibited by guilt, he suggested, the gastrocolic reflex was activated. The gastrocolic reflex, according to Szasz, was mediated by the autonomic nervous system. Wolf (1966), without mentioning Szasz, has, in fact, provided some observational evidence of physiological changes in the left side of the colon in ulcerative colitis consistent with those seen in the gastrocolic reflex. However, it may be that the mechanism of that reflex does not involve the parasympathetic nervous system but is mediated by the polypeptide, gastrin, which also controls the secretion of hydrochloric acid and pepsin in the stomach. Gastrin, in turn, is under the control of vagal discharge and the presence of food in the gastric antrum.

Sperling (1946, 1955, 1957, 1959, 1960, 1969) has emphasized the unconscious, conflictful fantasies that children and adults with ulcerative colitis had when the mother-child bond was broken. In psychoanalytic terms, she regards the disease as a "pregenital conversion symptom," the psychic mechanism of which consists of the "conversion" of specific unconscious (anxiety-provoking) impulses into a bodily process that alters the function or structure of an organ and which "symbolizes" the conflict. In her view, the unconscious and hateful impulse is to destroy and get rid of the mental image of the departed, devalued, dangerous mother, who is represented by blood and feces. Sperling also depicts other symptoms (such as anorexia, pain, vomiting) as symbolic expressions of wishes to devour, destroy, or expel the mother's image. As Engel (1954b) pointed out, Sperling tended to confound the meaning that the bodily symptoms of ulcerative colitis had for the patient after their inception with the pathogenetic conflict that anteceded the disease.

Grace et al. (1951) were inclined to formulate their findings not in terms of conflict, but in terms of a patient's psychophysiologic reaction to environmental demands to eject and rid himself of feces. They felt that several different kinds of persons might react to such demands with changes in colonic function if they were physiologically predisposed to react in this manner. They emphasized that feelings of inadequacy, anxiety, and resentment were important mediators of the hyperemia and hypermotility of the gut. Wolf (1966) agreed with these formulations and emphasized that neural and hormonal mediators of these physiological responses largely account for diarrhea.

Sullivan (1936), Sullivan and Chandler (1932), Daniels (1944), Groen (1947, 1951), Groen and Van der Valk (1956), and Prugh (1951) emphasized various emotional responses to distressing life experiences. Sullivan contended that "emotion" enhanced fecal flow and hypermotility, irritating the mucosa of the bowel. Daniels (1944) and Groen (1947) felt that interpersonal conflicts and humiliating experiences, which made the patient feel defeated, produced anxiety. These affects remained unexpressed, and were believed to produce prolonged spasm of the muscular wall of the colon, ischemia of the mucosa, and thus necrosis. Prugh (1951) emphasized the affect of anger when a child's security was threatened or lost.

Engel dismisses the emphasis on any particular unconscious conflict in ulcerative colitis patients but emphasizes their lifelong dependency and their response to the loss of a key relationship. Patients are not unique in their psychological make-up, rather what is unique is their biological predisposition to this disease or syndrome.

Engel's formulation also implies that persons predisposed to ulcerative colitis are less able to adapt to certain life experiences, perhaps because of earlier failures to do so. The limited psychological, adaptive capacity of patients with ulcerative colitis, as evidenced by the quality of their relationships with family members, has also been described by Karush and Daniels (1953) and by Mushatt (1954).

Engel (1954) described the organismic state of giving up and having given up, as presumably having its physiological concomitants, in the following manner:

> In my opinion, these data suggest that ulcerative colitis is a disorder involving primarily the mucosa and/or submucosa of the bowel, including at times the small bowel. Prominently implicated is the vascular system, so that hyperemia and hemorrhage are identifying features of the disease. The process characteristically does not involve all parts of the bowel with equal intensity and while the sigmoid is the area most commonly affected any part of the colon and ileum may be involved. The character of the bowel movements in any individual case is determined by the location, severity and extent of the colitic process. In other words, the bowel appears to be responding to local areas of surface irritation rather than as part of an integrated excretory act. The behavior of surgically bypassed bowel is also consistent with this.
>
> From both the clinical and pathologic points of view ulcerative colitis more closely resembles the dysenteries of bacterial origin than it does mucous colitis. Indeed some pathologists believe it difficult, if not impossible, to distinguish the early stages of ulcerative colitis and bacillary dysentery. While attempts to establish an infectious origin have proven unsuccessful, the similarity to disorders of such origin is of significance. It suggests that we are dealing with a process in which the bowel surface is responding as if to a noxious agent of microscopic or molecular size. This is in contrast to the response of the bowel as a whole to a bolus-sized agent, its usual excremental behavior. This conclusion is not essentially different from what has been generally suspected about ulcerative colitis since it was first described. Present knowledge does not permit any more precise identification than this. Included among the possible factors to be reckoned with are (1) reactions to known or unknown bacterial or viral agents and/or their products, (2) allergic phenomena, (3) Schartzman type reaction, (4) reactions of the type associated with the collagen disorders, (5) blood-borne chemical substances, (6) genetic or constitutional abnormalities of this level of tissue response or organization, especially as it involves the circulatory reaction, (7) metabolic or enzymic abnormalities.
>
> ENGEL, 1954

Thus Engel (1955) stated that these psychological responses were "frequent, perhaps necessary, but not sufficient conditions for the development of ulcerative colitis." He thereby refutes both a specificity hypothesis and a unitary "psychogenic" hypothesis. Engel (1955) also suggested that the ontogenesis of the psychological disturbance lies in a disturbed mother-child relationship. A review of the data, and of Jackson's and Yalom's (1966) study of families (though uncontrolled), would support this view.

However, it may very well be that the basis of the disturbance is even more complex: Engel spelled out this hypothesis in 1955. He stated that: (1) The mother of the future child has an unresolved involvement with her own mother (see also Mohr et al., 1958) which is transferred to the child. (2) The mother relates to the child conditionally—that is, as long as the child's behavior (including eating, bowel activity, and sexual non-behavior) does not arouse guilt and anxiety in her. (3) Among the behaviors controlled by the mother are the child's motor behaviors, including eating, defecating, and emotional behavior, which results in passivity, compliance, and arrests of "ego" and psychosexual development in the child. (4) The children have a defect in their capacity to relate to others (for reasons Engel was not fully able to specify), so that they never develop autonomy from other people, or an independent sense of self; this defect sensitizes them to separation. (5) The arrests of development at the oral, anal, and phallic levels stem from the failure of the children fully to separate and individuate themselves from their mothers.

Engel (1955) summarized his formulation (which he felt was tentative) as follows:

> In this formulation, then, ulcerative colitis develops in particular individuals under specific circumstances. The tissue reaction, which forms the basis of the colitis, develops only when other adaptive processes fail, and the significant object relationship is threatened or actually interrupted. The specific factors that go into the development of this relationship will help to determine the kinds of circumstances and the settings in which this takes place. Biologic and psychologic developmental factors will help to determine the bowel as the site of the tissue breakdown. As long as an object relationship is maintained, other pathologic processes may become manifest, but not colitis. Thus the pathologic character traits constitute means for maintaining the key relationship and satisfying needs within that framework. Other neurotic, psychotic or psychosomatic symptoms (e.g., headache) develop during conflict situations within the framework of this relationship, where the relationship is not seriously threatened.
>
> ENGEL, 1955

If the psychological responses to life events or changes precipitate ulcerative colitis in the predisposed person, it should be possible to develop animal models of the disease; to demonstrate pathological changes in the colon in response to experienced events, and to answer the question: what central neural and peripheral mechanisms mediate the organismic state described by Engel?

In regard to this question, our search for mediating mechanisms is seriously impeded by the fact that we know virtually nothing about the central regulation of colonic motor activity, about the regulation of blood flow to the colon by the nervous system, about the effect of neural regulatory influences on the release and activity of a whole series of chemical substances (e.g., kinins, the prostaglandins, substance P, "Darmstoff," the catecholamines, serotonin) known to affect colonic motility or blood flow, or about the influence of various hormones on colonic function. Potentially, experiences and their (unknown) neural correlates could be mediated by the autonomic nervous system, by the hypothalamic-pituitary-target-gland axis, or by immune mechanisms.

Psychophysiological Studies Relevant to Pathogenesis

The conventional wisdom holds that the emotions have a powerful influence on the functions of the intestine. Psychophysiological studies of the colon have had two aims in

534

mind: first, to document this obvious observation, and second, to study changes in colonic function in ulcerative colitis. But attempts to study the effect of emotions and thoughts on the function of the healthy or diseased colon are impeded by the limited techniques available and by difficulties in interpreting the results of such studies. However, the colon affected by ulcerative colitis does show altered and unusual patterns of movements, which may be due to the local disease process.

In view of the dearth of knowledge about the mechanisms involved in the inception of ulcerative colitis, the psychophysiologist is hard put to know which physiological variable to study. Specifically, should he measure the motility of the colon, its vascularity, the amount of lysozyme or mucus or what? The most exhaustive studies were carried out by Wolff and his co-workers (Grace et al., 1951; Wolf, 1966). They studied four patients with colostomies—two with and two without ulcerative colitis. Changes in the appearance of the colonic mucous membrane, the motility and contractile state of the exposed colon, and the secretion of lysozyme were observed. The contractile state is a measure of the baseline tension on which movements are superimposed; the movements could be observed and measured by means of pressure records obtained by a balloon placed within the colon. The colon affected by colitis sustained its contractions longer and in a more pronounced fashion. In all four subjects, responses to naturally occurring stimuli outside the laboratory, and to disturbing topics within the laboratory, produced hyperfunctioning of the colon, characterized by increased rhythmic contractions, intense and frequent waves in the cecum and ascending colon, and sustained contraction in the descending colon, with narrowing of the lumen, and hypersecretion of lysozyme. In two subjects petechial lesions began to appear on the mucosa, and in three the mucous membrane became more friable. Conflict situations that induced anger, hostility, resentment, anxiety, and apprehension were associated with increased movements, and later resulted in petechial lesions. Abject fear and dejection were associated with pallor, relaxation, and diminished contraction and secretion of the colon.

The correlation of hopelessness, self-reproach, feelings of inadequacy, or helplessness with a reduction in colonic tone and motility was also made by Almy and his co-workers (Almy, 1961a; Almy and Tulin, 1947; Almy et al., 1949a, b) in healthy subjects and in subjects with the irritable colon syndrome. However, Chin Kim and Barbero (1963), Connell (1961), Weeks (1946), and Wener and Polonsky (1950) observed the opposite colonic responses in concert with such feelings; although admittedly, the patient studied by Wener and Polonsky had a colostomy for ulcerative colitis. In a subsequent study of the same patient following vagotomy, the character of the colonic responses to emotional states was unchanged (Wener et al., 1952), a finding which suggested that the correlated changes were not mediated by the parasympathetic nervous system.

The pattern of colonic contractions has also been studied. In six patients with colostomies for ulcerative colitis, segmental, but not propulsive, contractions were correlated with the subjects' conscious or inferred anxiety about loss of love and support from parents, fears of retaliation by them, and a depressive affect (Karush et al., 1955). In a number of other studies, altered patterns of colonic movement have been observed in patients with ulcerative colitis, but these alterations appear to be a function of the symptoms (e.g., diarrhea) of the disease, and not the disease process.

In the first studies using balloon techniques for recording changes in intraluminal

535

pressure as a function of tension and movement, it was reported that in ulcerative colitis, the colon was the site of movements that were continuous and that increased without pause. Large waves were observed by Ganter and Statmüller (1924), and the intersegmental coordination of these waves was intact (Posey and Bargen, 1951). Spriggs et al. (1951) inserted balloons into the rectosigmoid colon of 10 patients with active rectocolitis. He found that, in this part of the gut at least, type II waves, usually associated with haustral movements, were less frequent than in the intact gut; instead he recorded type IV waves, which are believed to be due to propulsive, synchronous waves of long duration, and which are usually not observable in the normal colon. This altered wave pattern may, however, not be a characteristic feature of the disease; it was found in only 9 of 72 tracings in other studies (Almy, 1961a; Kern et al., 1951), and seems to occur only when severe diarrhea is present. Another form of contraction, a phasic one, was usually absent or reduced when diarrhea was present. Its absence could not be related to the severity or duration of the disease. Patients with no diarrhea but with evidence of active disease had a normal amount of colonic activity. Those in whom phasic activity was enhanced complained of constipation.

In view of the fact that patterns of colonic activity in the sigmoid colon are normal if ulcerative colitis is confined to the ascending colon, one must conclude that these findings tell us less about the pathogenesis of the disorder than about the mechanisms of symptom formation. It is recognized that similar changes are found in diarrhea and constipation regardless of their cause: hypomotility occurs with diarrhea, and hypermotility with constipation. The recording of a phasic wave depends not only on the contraction of the wall of the viscus but also on resistance to the escape of its contents. Thus, if colonic disease is extensive and haustration is lost there will be little or no resistance to flow (Connell, 1962; Ritchie et al., 1962).

Some cautionary remarks must also be made about the balloon technique itself. The balloon may itself evoke motor activity, and the balloon system may not veridically reflect the pressures within the lumen of the gut, since it is compressible and offers resistance to the contracting segment of the colon (Brody et al., 1940). The results depend upon the size of the balloon used: larger ones record a given pressure as higher than smaller ones do.

Therefore, other techniques have been developed. For instance, Davidson et al. (1956a, b) used open-ended tubes, not balloons, to study children with ulcerative colitis, but without diarrhea. They found that their motility patterns were essentially normal. Children with diarrhea but no ulcerative colitis, or when given a purgative, display pressure waves of high amplitude and long duration. These waves are probably the type IV waves recorded by the balloon technique. Chaudhary and Truelove (1961) also found that large pressure waves, recorded by means of open-ended tubes, were only present when adult patients with ulcerative colitis had bloody diarrhea. When mucosal inflammation unaccompanied by diarrhea was present, the records were flat.

Although the literature on this topic is confusing, certain tentative generalizations do seem possible. Studies of this kind must take into account the affects and the behavioral steady state of the patient. During sleep, for example, colonic motility is depressed; similar depression of motility occurs when the subject is awake, active or anxious (Chin Kim and Barbero, 1963; Connell, 1961). The baseline state of contraction of dilatation

536

and the speed of movements of the intestine must be considered (Chaudhary and Truelove, 1961; Connell, 1961) when evaluating change. The presence or absence of diarrhea also appears to be an important variable.

Two other important variables emerge from these studies: the relationship of the subject to the experimenter (Groen and Van der Valk, 1956), and whether the patient is thinking about or discussing topics that have deep personal meaning and are accompanied by appropriate feelings (Chaudhary and Truelove, 1961). The changes in motility seem to be correlated less with a particular feeling or mood (Deller and Wangel, 1965) than with how sincerely it is felt and how meaningful it is to the subject.

The Experimental Production of Colitis-like Lesions in Animals by Behavioral and Other Techniques

Porter et al. (1958) reported the production of chronic colitis in two monkeys, one of which also had a duodenal ulcer. One monkey had been subjected to conditioned avoidance procedures for eight days, and another had rewarded himself by stimulating various sites in the brain. The sites of implantation were the median forebrain bundle, the amygdala, the hippocampus, the septal region, the caudate nucleus, the anterior thalamic nuclei, the hypothalamus, and the mesencephalic reticular formation. Both animals had lost weight, having had diarrhea and melena for two weeks. The first had been in the experimental chair for 19 days, and the second for 52 days. No parasites were found in the stool. Cultures for bacteria were apparently not done. The colon showed punctate ulceration and hemorrhage, and the wall of the colon was thickened. In the first animal the entire colon was involved. In the other monkey only the rectosigmoid area showed lesions. Microscopically, the mucosa was disrupted; glandular degeneration, areas of erosion, and thickening of the submucosa were observed, and the muscularis was edematous. Lymphocytes infiltrated the mucosa and submucosa. Occasional thrombi were seen in blood vessels. Because multiple brain sites were stimulated in this experiment, it is impossible to infer which outflow circuits mediated brain stimulation, which circuits might have mediated the emotional influences of avoidance conditioning, or whether the stimuli activated autonomic or humoral mechanisms, or both (Truelove, 1966).

In a natural setting, monkeys are prone to infection by *Shigella*, which can produce no symptoms or colonic lesions. This bacterium can also cause either an acute infection with diarrhea or a prolonged and often intermittent bout of diarrhea. Chronic scarring, inflammation, and ulceration may occur in the colon of infected animals. Therefore, any report of colonic disease in monkeys must be evaluated in the light of their common infestation by *Shigella*. Stout and Snyder (1969) reported on a Siamang gibbon who had lost her mate six weeks before her own death. Her behavioral response to this loss was lethargy and a diminished food intake. Rectal and colonic ulcers were found on autopsy. Focal disruption of the mucosa with crypt abscesses were present. The lamina propria and mucosa was necrotic and contained plasma cells, lymphocytes, and polymorphonuclear leukocytes. The lesion spared the mucosa. Neither parasites nor bacteria were recovered or cultured. These authors also reported the deaths of three gibbons who had each been introduced into the cage of another animal of the opposite sex, who greeted the newcomer by becoming more active, and depriving him or her of food. The newcomers responded to this reception by developing bloody diarrhea, and all died within five days. Multiple focal, colonic ulcerations were observed. No amebae or parasites were recovered. Cultures for bacteria were not done, but none of the other monkeys in the colony had previously had diarrhea. It is possible that the dead monkeys may have harbored *Shigella,* which flared up during stress.

These observations have been used to support the idea that the "stress" of avoidance conditioning, of loss, and of changing the habitat of monkeys may produce lesions of the colon that have some of the characteristics of ulcerative colitis in man. But the fact remains that despite these scattered reports there have been few consistently successful attempts to reproduce the lesion of ulcerative colitis experimentally. The injection of adrenergic or cholinergic drugs (Lium, 1939; Moeller and Kirsner, 1954), the prolonged administration of histamine (Brasher et al., 1955) and its releasers, and of bacterial toxins (Lium, 1939), the oral and intra-arterial administration of the enzyme lysozyme (Prudden et al., 1950), various immunological procedures using dinitrochlorobenzene applied to the colons of guinea pigs and swine (Bicks and Rosenberg, 1964; Bicks et al., 1967) or antibodies against dog colon (Leveen et al., 1961), all have been used to produce experimental "colitis" in some form or other.

The meaning of these reactions for our understanding of human ulcerative colitis remains in doubt. Zweibaum et al. (1968) immunized rats with live E. coli in Freund's adjuvant and produced a hemorrhagic form of colitis that was remarkably reminiscent of human ulcerative colitis. In 1969, Marcus and Watt reported that a sulfated polysaccharide of high molecular weight, carrageenan, which was extracted from red seaweed and dissolved in drinking water, produced ulcerative disease of the colonic mucosa in rabbits, rats, mice, and guinea pigs on ingestion. Symptoms of diarrhea, and of visible or occult blood and mucus in the stool took about three weeks to develop (Watt and Marcus, 1971). Other high molecular weight sulfated products, not necessarily polysaccharides, produced similar lesions in rabbits (Marcus and Watt, 1971). Yet some of these products, including carrageenan, have been used in the treatment of peptic ulcer, or have been shown to prevent experimental gastric ulceration in animals (Bianchi and Cook, 1964). Human ulcerative colitis has not been reported after this treatment (Bonfils, 1970). In some cultures, red seaweed constitutes a part of the diet, but no increased incidence of ulcerative colitis has been reported. Thus, although the reports that sulfated products regularly produce a disease that bears some features reminiscent of the clinical and histopathological features of human ulcerative colitis is of interest, the mechanism by which the lesion is produced in these experiments is not known.

IMMUNOLOGICAL FACTORS

In the last fifteen years advances have been made in our understanding of the immunopathology of ulcerative colitis and Crohn's disease. This pathology consists of the presence of anticolon antibodies and other autoantibodies in the serum of about half the patients with these diseases, and that of their relatives. Not every investigator of the diseases has found these humoral antibodies. Those who have cannot agree about the role played by these autoantibodies in the disease. Some argue they play a predisposing role (because of their presence in the serum of healthy relatives); some maintain they are pathogenetic; still others state they either result from damage to the colonic mucosa, or they play no role at all because cellular immune mechanisms are pathogenetic.

If the predisposing role of autoantibodies were established, they could be used in predictive studies to confirm or refute the psychological formulations about the disease. If autoantibodies play a pathogenetic role a new set of scientific problems would be raised: how do psychological and immunological factors affect each other?; how do they interact?

In the meantime, much more work is required to establish the roles of humoral and cellular immune responses in this disease.

Immunopathology

In 1961, Truelove reported that ulcerative colitis remitted in some patients on a milk-free diet, only to relapse when they again drank milk. In the same year Taylor and Truelove (1961) reported an increased incidence and, at times, high titers of antibodies against lactalbumen, lactoglobulin, and casein in the sera of patients with ulcerative colitis. These findings have been verified by some investigators (Gray, 1961; Taylor, 1965) but not by others (Dudek et al., 1965; Sewell et al., 1963). The antibody titers of these components of milk did not correlate with any of the clinical features of the disease (Sewell et al., 1963). Antibodies to milk and its products have been demonstrated in normal persons, in those with celiac disease and idiopathic steatorrhea (Taylor, 1965b), and in children recovering from diarrhea (Gruskay and Cooke, 1955). Therefore, the tendency to form antibodies to milk proteins may be the result of the increased absorption of these proteins during and after gastrointestinal disease, rather than being an antecedent cause of ulcerative colitis.

However, in some infants and older children who probably did not have ulcerative colitis a syndrome of diarrhea, bleeding, and shock has been ascribed to the ingestion of milk. Two children passed bloody stools. In seven children, the histopathological picture of a biopsy specimen was one of mucosal destruction, infiltration with plasma cells, and crypt abscesses (Gryboski, 1967). In four children studied by Katz et al., (1968), antibodies to milk were present in the stool but not in the blood serum; they disappeared from the stool on withholding milk from the diet. Acheson and Truelove (1961) ascribed this syndrome to the fact that the children had been "prematurely" fed cow's milk—a conclusion that is not borne out by Lagercrantz's earlier studies (1949) on the age of weaning of infants with ulcerative colitis. In the meantime, the lactose in milk has been implicated as the agent which exacerbates the symptoms of inflammatory bowel disease (Chalfin and Holt, 1967; Fiddes and Baume, 1967).

A new era in the immunopathology of ulcerative colitis was ushered in when Broberger and Perlmann (1959) demonstrated that the sera of some patients with ulcerative colitis contained autoantibodies—specifically, antibodies to the glycoprotein fraction of human fetal colon (Perlmann et al., 1973). They demonstrated the presence of these antibodies in the sera of 20 of 30 children with ulcerative colitis, an incidence that was much higher than in the sera of a comparison group. Recently, Perlmann and his co-workers (1973) summarized their accumulated incidence figures: anticolon antibodies to colon antigen from germ-free rat colon was present in 10 percent of 193 healthy controls, 60 percent of

80 patients with ulcerative colitis, and 70 percent of 90 patients with Crohn's disease. (The antigen can be prepared in such a manner that it is not contaminated by antigens of bacterial origin.) Although the antigen has been located in colonic mucosa, it is also present in other tissues (Broberger and Perlmann, 1962; Hammerström et al., 1965). The circulating antibodies in patients with ulcerative colitis react with various components of human and animal colonic cells and their products: for example, with antigens present in the cytoplasm of colonic epithelium (Broberger and Perlmann, 1962; Harrison, 1965a; Klavins, 1963; Koffler et al., 1962; McGiven et al., 1967) and with colonic mucus, but also with small-intestinal epithelial cells, colonic cells of the human fetus, of the rabbit and rat, and with epithelial cells of the human stomach affected by gastritis (Harrison, 1965a).

Although Broberger and Perlmann's findings have been confirmed by some laboratories (Bregman and Kirsner, 1961; Polčak and Vokurka, 1960), other investigators have failed to do so (Bernier et al., 1961; Edgar, 1961; Gray et al., 1961; Kraft and Ardali, 1964; Talyor and Truelove, 1962). Wright and Truelove (1966b), however, found anticolon antibodies in 15.8 percent of a series of 273 patients with ulcerative colitis. In another series (Thayer et al., 1969) anticolon antibodies were found in the sera of 25 percent of patients with ulcerative colitis and in 30.5 percent of patients with regional enteritis (43 percent of the disease involved the colon). Lagercrantz et al., (1971) found the incidence among patients with ulcerative colitis to be higher for women (57 percent) than for men (35 percent). From the regional (intestinal) lymph nodes of patients with ulcerative colitis, Perlmann and Broberger (1960) have isolated antibodies that react with the antigen extracted from colonic tissue.

There are many possible sources of error in these studies: one is variation in the concentration of colonic antigen (Wright and Truelove, 1966b), another is that the source of the colonic antigen may depend on the blood group of the patient (Harrison, 1965a; Lagercrantz et al., 1966; McGiven et al., 1967). A part of the controversy in this area appears to be due to technical factors: nonspecific responses occurred when fluorescent techniques to label antibodies were used to stain sera (Holborow and Johnson, 1964; Kraft and Ardali, 1964); thus, colonic mucosal cells were stained by normal sera (McGiven et al., 1967). The specificity of the antibodies to colonic cells has also been questioned, in that they may be found in the sera of patients with carcinoma of the colon (Von Kleist and Burtin, 1966). Anticolon antibodies are also present in 10 percent of the sera of normal persons (McGiven et al., 1967; Perlmann et al., 1973) and in the relatives of patients with ulcerative colitis. Other autoantibodies, such as antinuclear antibodies, have been demonstrated in the sera of relatives of patients with ulcerative colitis.

Thayer and Spiro (1963) studied the incidence of thyroid autoantibodies, rheumatoid factors, lupus erythematosus (LE) cells, and antinuclear factors in the sera of 98 relatives of 34 patients with ulcerative colitis and 55 relatives of 27 patients with gastric carcinoma. Only in the case of antinuclear antibodies (that is, antibodies to components of the nucleus of cells, including deoxyribonucleic acid) was there a significantly increased incidence (23 percent versus 3 percent) in the sera of members of the families of patients with ulcerative colitis.

Antinuclear antibodies and antibodies against colonic tissue were also found, respec-

TABLE 4

Incidence of Autoantibodies in the Relatives of Patients with Ulcerative Colitis

	MALE RELATIVES			FEMALE RELATIVES		
	FATHER	OTHER [a]	TOTAL	MOTHER	OTHER [b]	TOTAL
Antinuclear antibodies	0/12	6/19	6/31	20/21	27/38	47/59
Anticolon antibodies	0/14	4/20	4/34	15/22	18/44	33/66

[a] Brothers, sons, and grandchildren
[b] Sisters, daughters, and grandchildren

tively, in the sera of 90 and 91 healthy family members of patients with ulcerative colitis: in women relatives they were seven times as frequent as in men (Polčak et al., 1967) (Table 4). Comparison groups of healthy subjects and patients with various unstated diseases were used. In a second and larger series (Polčak and Skalova, 1968), the presence of anticolon antibodies was most reliable in discriminating the relatives of patients from the relatives of healthy controls, although it is not clear whether the second series included patients from the first series. In any case, the incidence of both kinds of antibodies was significantly greater ($p < .001$) in relatives of ulcerative colitis patients than in two comparison groups, but the incidence figures for anticolon antibodies depended in part on the methods used to determine them (Polčak and Skalova, 1968). Nonetheless, in both series similar incidence figures were obtained. (In the case of the antinuclear antibodies, the incidence figures obtained by Polčak and his co-workers were about 2½ times those obtained by Thayer and Spiro.)

Interestingly enough, Polčak et al. (1967) also reported on a pair of presumably Mz girl twins discordant for ulcerative colitis, but concordant for the presence in serum of both types of antibodies. The antibodies were also present in the serum of their mother, but not their father.

Lagercrantz et al. (1971) confirmed these findings; in their series the incidence of anticolon antibodies was greater, and the titers higher, in the sera of the women relatives of patients with ulcerative colitis, but not in their male relatives. Additionally, the sera of the women relatives contained a higher incidence of antibodies to the E. coli 0 : 14 strain, but not to the 0 : 75 strain. The antigen extracted from fetal and adult colon shares a common antigenic property with a strain of the natural resident of the colon, E. coli 0 : 14. The sera of patients with ulcerative colitis and of their relatives contains antibodies against this specific, bacterial antigen (Perlmann et al., 1965), as does the sera of patients with regional enteritis (Lagercrantz et al., 1966; Thayer et al., 1969). The bacterial antigen has the characteristics of a lipopolysaccharide (Perlmann et al., 1965), and experimentally engenders antibodies in high titer (Whang and Neter, 1967).

E. coli 0 : 14 contains a second antigen that is heterogeneous (Whang and Neter, 1962); that is, it is present in other intestinal bacteria, such as Salmonellae and Shigellae (Cooke et al., 1968). This nonspecific antigen has been immunologically related to the first (the specific) antigen in E. coli 0 : 14 and hence to anticolon antigen. Therefore, antibodies stimulated by these two bacterial antigens might react with colonic tissue (Broberger, 1964; Perlmann et al., 1965, 1967).

Antibodies to E. coli O : 14 were recovered from the serum of 33 percent of patients with ulcerative colitis, and 39 percent of patients with Crohn's disease (Thayer et al., 1969). Anticolon antibodies and presumably the antibodies against E. coli O : 14 appear to be IgG antibodies (Broberger and Perlmann, 1962; Harrison, 1965a; Perlmann and Broberger, 1960), which are believed to be produced by microsomes in the regional colonic lymph nodes.

At present it is very difficult to ascribe to these antibodies a specific role in ulcerative colitis. They are not toxic to human colonic cells in tissue culture (Broberger and Perlmann, 1963). Although autoantibodies to intestinal (including colonic) epithelial cells have readily been produced in rabbits by the use of an antigen from rat gut in Freund's adjuvant (Holborow et al., 1963), by E. coli (Asherson and Holborow, 1966; Cooke, 1968), and by bacteria isolated from patients with ulcerative colitis (Cooke et al., 1968), these intestinal antibodies produced no colonic lesion in the host rabbit. The fact that the antibodies occur in patients without ulcerative colitis and Crohn's disease, and that there is no correlation between their presence or absence, or their titer in serum, and the extent and severity of the disease (Harrison, 1965a), throws serious doubt on their pathogenetic role.

Further potent arguments against these antibodies having a pathogenetic role include their presence in the sera of healthy relatives of patients with the two diseases, and the fact that both have been described in patients with agammaglobulinemia who are incapable of producing IgG's (Eggert et al., 1969; Sacrez et al., 1963). Hereditary, congenital, or acquired forms of agammaglobulinemia, with either IgG (Kirk and Freedman, 1967) or IgA (Bull and Tomasi, 1968) deficiency, have been described in patients with ulcerative colitis. The Swiss type of agammaglobulinemia has been related to ulcerative colitis, as well as to rheumatoid arthritis, and to the malabsorption syndrome in children (Sacrez et al., 1963). In a family in which a member had primary acquired agammaglobulinemia, a close relative had regional enteritis, and other relatives were deficient in immunoglobulins. (Wolf, 1962; Wolf et al., 1963).

It is hypothetically possible that the lesions in ulcerative colitis and regional enteritis have a vascular pathogenesis. A discrepancy between the *amounts* of antigen and antibody may lead to the formation of antigen-antibody complexes that are not cleared from the body and are laid down in the arterioles of the ileum or colon. This sequence of events has also been suggested in the pathogenesis of glomerulonephritis, SLE, and rheumatoid arthritis.

Thus, there are potent arguments against ascribing a pathogenetic role to these anticolon autoantibodies. Some authorities believe that their presence is merely a secondary phenomenon, reflecting a response to damage of the intestinal epithelium (Thayer et al., 1969). But it might then be asked why persons with no disease manifest them in serum. And their presence in the sera of relatives of patients remains unexplained; if their presence there is confirmed, it would suggest that the predisposition to form anticolon autoantibodies constitutes a risk factor both for ulcerative colitis and Crohn's disease, or, at least, for some patients with these diseases. If this speculation is confirmed, it should be possible to identify persons who are healthy but at risk and study their psychological makeup prior to the onset of these diseases.

542

Immunoglobulins

Anticolon antibodies belong to the IgG fraction of serum gammaglobulins, although they may additionally be found in the IgM and IgA fractions (Perlmann et al., 1965, 1973). Conversely, both ulcerative colitis and regional enteritis have, as has been mentioned, been described in states of gammaglobulin deficiency, although blood levels of both IgG and IgM are usually within the normal range in these diseases.

Because the production of IgA occurs mainly in the lymphoid cells of the intestine and appears in intestinal secretions (Crabbe, 1969; Crabbe and Heremans, 1969; Gelzayd et al., 1967; Jeffries, 1965; Tomasi, 1968), attention has been directed to this gammaglobulin. At birth, neither the blood serum nor the secretions of the gut of the infant contain IgA. Probably as the result of contact with exogenous antigens, IgA appears initially in the serum, and later in the secretions of the gut. Interestingly enough, these two IgA's differ in molecular weight and chemical composition (Tomasi, 1968), and the secretory IgA of the gut may have antibacterial (Adinolfi et al., 1966) and antiviral properties (Tokumaru, 1966). In ulcerative colitis, serum levels of IgA, IgM, and IgG are usually normal, although slight elevations of IgA may occur (Gelfand and Krone, 1970). In a study of 23 patients with ulcerative colitis, secretory IgA was detectable in five—an incidence in excess of that found in control subjects (Thompson et al., 1969). Secretory IgA is also abnormally distributed in the extracellular space of the colonic mucosa of ulcerative colitis patients (Gelzayd et al., 1968).

One-time measurements of gammaglobulin levels may not be as revealing as longitudinal studies of levels during the course of the disease. Furthermore, autoantibodies may not necessarily be found in any of the gammaglobulin fractions. Burch and his co-workers (1969) have put forward the interesting thesis that the autoantibody is likely to be found in the α_2-globulin fraction of the serum, synthesized by mast cells. They base their hypothesis on the following line of evidence: de Dombal (1967b) studied the IgG levels of 32 hospitalized patients and 72 outpatients with ulcerative colitis; he found 14 patients whose serum IgG levels were in the normal range during the disease but rose with its remission. In patients who had had to have surgery, the initial mean levels were somewhat lower. The levels continued to fall as the disease progressed. He also found that α_2-globulin levels were raised during active phases of ulcerative colitis (Bicks et al., 1959; Brooke et al., 1961; Soergel and Ingelfinger, 1961), and the levels never fall in patients with recurrences of the disease; in fact, the increased levels persisted until the next attack. Patients without further recurrences during a period of three months of observation manifested low or normal α_2-globulin levels.

de Dombal (1967a) also discovered that α_2-globulin levels were higher, at operation, in the inferior mesenteric vein than in the artery in ten patients with ulcerative colitis (but not in nine patients with carcinoma of the colon); conversely, IgG levels were greater in the mesenteric artery than vein. He believed that these changes reflected production or release of the α_2-globulin and destruction or fixation of the IgG in the colon. The changed levels of the α_2-globulin were not due to hemoconcentration, but may reflect the effects of secondary inflammation (Heim and Lane, 1964) in ulcerative colitis. The chemical isolation and identification of this α_2-globulin and the demonstration of its capability to produce lesions in the colon has not as yet been reported.

The elevation of serum α_2-globulin has been confirmed by Dearing et al. (1969), who

543

also found a correlation between its level and the severity of the disease. These findings seem to bear more upon the course and prognosis of the disease than on its pathogenesis. There is no proof that the α_2-globulins are autoantibodies capable of initiating ulcerative colitis (Burch et al., 1968).

Cellular Immunity

Although humoral anticolon antibodies in the sera of patients with ulcerative colitis are not toxic to colon cells in tissue culture, the white blood cells (presumably lymphocytes) of such patients are cytotoxic to colon cells (Broberger and Perlmann, 1963; Watson et al., 1966). This finding suggests that the disease is initiated by cellular rather than humoral immune processes. However, white blood cells from patients with Crohn's disease are also cytotoxic (Shorter et al., 1968, 1969a, b), but only to colonic, not to ileal cells (Shorter et al., 1969a); a result which casts doubt on the role of cellular immunity in producing the ileal lesion.

The cytotoxicity of lymphocytes taken from patients is apparently not conferred by some substance in the serum, but by some factor within the lymphocyte, because extracts of lymphocytes were similarly cytotoxic (Watson et al., 1966). The extracts alter the permeability of colonic cells. The skin of patients with ulcerative colitis responded with a cellular immune response to the injection of the patient's own white cells (Watson et al., 1965). The rectal mucosa of patients (but not healthy persons) responded with gross and microscopic lesions to the same injection (Fink et al., 1967), but with a short latency period that was not characteristic of a cellular immune reaction. The cytotoxicity of the lymphocytes disappears after colectomy, but not during the clinical remission of ulcerative colitis, and it can be inhibited in vitro by antilymphocyte and antithymus antiserum (Shorter et al., 1968, 1969b).

The obvious question that these studies raise is what stimulus causes the lymphocytes to become cytotoxic. So far, several strains of E. coli 0 : 14, normal human colon extracts, and germ-free rat feces have been used to try and render lymphocytes cytotoxic, all to no avail (Hinz et al., 1967; Stefani and Fink, 1967a). Another strain of E. coli, 0 : 119 : B14, may, however, have such an effect (Stefani and Fink, 1967b). Another possibility is that—inasmuch as the chemical nature of the substance responsible for the cytotoxic effect is unknown—the cytotoxic effect may be nonspecific (Holm and Perlmann, 1967; Ruddle and Waksman, 1967) and may not be caused by specific tissue antigens.

It has also been argued that the granulomata of Crohn's disease are an expression of a cellular immune response, and, therefore, that cellular immunity plays a role in the pathogenesis, at least of this particular lesion. However, there is also strong evidence that cellular immune responses are depressed in Crohn's disease (Bendixen, 1969; Parent et al., 1971; Sachar et al., 1973; Verrier Jones et al., 1969); this effect, however, is not specific to this disease alone, and the explanation for it is unknown.

Effects of Immunosuppressive Drugs

One of the major advances in the treatment of ulcerative colitis has come from the use of drugs with immunosuppressive action. Their efficacy derives from their interruption of

544

the immunological process at some point. A drug such as azathioprine suppresses the increases of lymphoid cells that occur in response to an antigen. The corticosteroids have, of course, a multiplicity of actions, in that they are anti-inflammatory and also interfere with the interaction of antigen and antibody on or about the cell surface. Other drugs that are employed seem to be both anti-viral and immunosuppressive.

The therapeutic efficacies of 6-mercaptopurine (Bean, 1966a, b), the related drug azathioprine (Arden Jones, 1969; Mackay et al., 1966; Theodor et al., 1968), and corticosteroids (Sparberg and Kirsner, 1965; Spencer and Kirsner, 1962) have been demonstrated. Less-favorable results have been obtained with antilymphocyte serum (Krisner, 1970a).

Inasmuch as these drugs all have actions additional to immunosuppression, the demonstration of their efficacy cannot be taken as proving that immunological factors are etiological or pathogenetical in ulcerative colitis or in Crohn's disease.

THE ROLE OF INFECTION IN THE INITIATION OF ULCERATIVE COLITIS

All attempts to culture or to identify, by various forms of microscopy, the viruses, bacteria, or fungi in patients with ulcerative colitis have proven fruitless (Bacon, 1958; Weinstein, 1961). The disease cannot be transmitted to animals, or to unrelated members of the same household. Nonetheless, the microscopic appearance of the affected bowel closely resembles other forms of inflammation of the mucosa and tissue reactions associated with known bacterial and parasitic pathogens.

Although the hypothesis has been put forward that bacterial infection plays no role in the pathogenesis of ulcerative colitis, the following data should give the skeptic some pause. Felson (1936) reported that after a proven outbreak of bacillary dysentary in Jersey City, 10 percent of those afflicted subsequently developed ulcerative colitis, and 2.5 percent, Crohn's disease. Such data do not necessarily prove that a bacterial infection may directly *cause* these diseases. It may mean that (1) damage to the epithelium brings about permanent changes in the intestinal mucosa or a self-perpetuating autoimmune process in the predisposed person; (2) bacterial antigens produce antibodies that react with antigens in the colonic epithelium; (3) damage by bacteria opens the colonic tissue to the entry of dietary antigens that produce antibodies—either a hypersensitive state is produced, or the antigen-antibody complexes are themselves antigenic; (4) damage leads to the entry of nonpathogenic intestinal flora that then become antigenic through one of several possible mechanisms.

Another possible reason why a bacterial pathogen has not been identified in ulcerative colitis is that the pathogen may have undergone lysogeny. It is now known that bacteriophages may be lysogenic to bacteria in the body. Lysogeny may account for the failure to recover a pathogenetic bacterium in this disease.

Moreover, and as was mentioned earlier, the incidence of carcinoma of the colon is higher in patients who have had ulcerative colitis than in the general population (Goldgraber et al., 1958, 1959; Goldgraber and Kirsner, 1964). Patients with early and long-standing ulcerative colitis are more likely later to develop carcinoma of the colon (Kirsner, 1970a, b). Infection by a virus could hypothetically account for pathogenesis of

545

ulcerative colitis and the carcinoma of the colon. A virus could also produce the immunopathology of ulcerative colitis. It may be present in cells and gradually alter their metabolism in such a way that the chemical composition of parts of the cell membrane is changed. This "foreign" lipoprotein of the cell membrane is then responded to by antibody formation. In many ways, this hypothesis unifies the role of a virus in the pathogenesis of ulcerative colitis with the autoimmune factors. What remains to be discovered is why the latent virus becomes activated, if indeed a latent virus is the initiating agent of the disease.

Ulcerative colitis has also been described as a late sequela of amebic dysentery (Sloan et al., 1950). In fact, nonspecific ulcerative colitis may be indistinguishable from ulcerative postdysenteric colitis on clinical, sigmoidoscopic, and radiographic findings. However, in ulcerative postdysenteric colitis, remissions and relapses are not usual, and the systemic complications and carcinoma of the colon that are characteristic of the nonspecific form of ulcerative colitis have not been observed (Powell and Wilmot, 1966). It follows that any patient who has a clear-cut past history of Entameba histolytica infection should probably not be included in any series of patients with nonspecific ulcerative colitis.

SUMMARY AND CONCLUSIONS

Ulcerative colitis is an inflammatory disease, predominantly of the mucosa of the rectum and the left side of the colon. It may, however, affect any and all parts of the colon, and, at times, especially following surgery, involve the mucosa of the ileum. It has been described in infants, even during the first week of life, and in adults, often after the age of 50 years. It may begin in a fulminating manner or insidiously. It shortens the lives of patients. Its most dreaded complication is carcinoma of the colon, which has a cumulative probability of occurring in 45 percent of patients surviving 30 years after disease onset. It is preceded by or associated with diseases in many different organ systems, including the eye, mouth, liver, spine, and large joints. The incidence of the disease is considerably higher than the incidence in families in which no member has the disease. Curiously enough, the relatives of patients with Crohn's disease are equally likely to develop ulcerative colitis as regional enteritis, but not vice versa.

Although patients with ulcerative colitis appear to share features with those who have Crohn's disease, this similarity must be regarded with some skepticism: in the last 15 years, it has been recognized that, in some instances, Crohn's disease may be located exclusively in the colon (Lockhart-Mummery and Morson, 1960, 1964). Therefore, the common features that the patients share may be, in part, a function of a mislabeling of the disease. Although Crohn's disease of the colon (granulomatous colitis) can usually be distinguished on clinical, radiological, and histopathological grounds, a number of authorities have pointed out that the histopathological lesions of both forms of colitis may exist side by side in the colon. One would have to conclude that all studies (social, psychological, immunological, epidemiological) done before 1960, based on the concept that nonspecific ulcerative colitis was a homogeneous disease, have erroneously included conditions and groups of patients no longer entitled to such a designation. It is, perhaps, this reason alone that accounts for the similarities noted between many features of nonspecific ulcerative colitis and Crohn's disease.

546

The immunopathology of these two disorders is also very similar: the sera of 60 percent and 70 percent of patients with ulcerative colitis and Crohn's disease, respectively, contain anticolon antibodies; 40 percent of the healthy women relatives of patients with both disease's also have elevated titers (Perlmann et al., 1973). This finding suggests that these autoimmune anticolon antibodies are not pathogenetic of the lesion of ulcerative colitis, nor are they the *result* of the lesion. Patients with long-standing colonic lesions, with carcinoma of the colon, or with amebic dysentery do not have a greater incidence of anticolon antibodies than can be found in the general population. Thus, chronic tissue lesions cannot be solely responsible for the enhanced incidence of anticolon antibodies. Nor is the titer changed following colectomy for ulcerative colitis (Di Belgiojoso and Ciba, 1968; Lagercrantz et al., 1966). The anticolon antibodies cross-react with an antigen found in strains of the common intestinal bacterium, E. coli, and it has been suggested that stimulation by cross-reacting bacterial antigens, present in small amounts in the human intestine, may give rise to the antibodies. These in turn would react with the colonic antigen present in the mucus and mucosal cells of the colonic crypts in persons genetically predisposed to forming the antibodies.

However, anticolon antibodies are not toxic to colon cells in tissue culture (Broberger and Perlmann, 1963). Therefore, much research interest has now been directed at cellular immune responses in ulcerative colitis, and also to the mediators of these responses, the thymus cells (T-cells) both alone and in interaction with the mediators of humoral immune responses, the B-cells. This promising line of research is supported by the finding that lymphocytes (presumably T-cells) from patients with ulcerative colitis are toxic to colon cells in tissue culture (Perlmann and Broberger, 1963; Shorter et al., 1969a, b). Although all of these data are of great interest, it is still too early to decipher their meaning. Suffice it to say that the instigator for anticolon antibody formation has not been identified.

Another important series of facts that seems to be emerging is the recognition that the mucosal lesion in ulcerative colitis persists for many years after disease onset, whether or not the patient has symptoms (Dick et al., 1966; Truelove and Richards, 1956). The persistence of the histological change remains unexplained; for instance, we do not know what produces remissions or relapses despite the persistent mucosal lesion. It is possible that the lesion may be present early in life, which would account for the occurrence of the disease in infants. It might also explain how social and psychological factors could interact with this persisting lesion to produce exacerbations or remissions.

In any case, the accumulated evidence is that psychological factors do account for an unidentified proportion of the etiological and pathogenetical variance. Many of the studies, as mentioned, were done before 1960; many others, both supporting and refuting the roles of the factors, are flawed by serious problems in design. However, those persons who have been studied show similar conflicts and personal relationships, although these may be expressed in different traits. Most patients attempt, by compliance and placating attitudes, to maintain a close relationship to their mothers or to surrogates. They cannot separate themselves from or give to this person, and when they are forced to give up the relationship or give of themselves, they cannot adapt to the change. They feel helpless, desperate, and hopeless. They give up striving, and a disproportionate number become psychotic. This sequence of psychological events has been outlined by Engel (1952, 1955, 1956, 1961, 1973); interestingly enough many of the same traits, relationships,

547

and sensitivities to certain life events have been described in patients with Crohn's disease (McKegney et al., 1970; Whybrow et al., 1968).

But we have no idea through what mechanisms this "complex" of giving up may initiate, exacerbate, or produce relapses. Our knowledge of gastrointestinal physiology is rudimentary and its elucidation is further impeded by the absence of an adequate animal model for ulcerative colitis.

Except for the advances in the immunopathology of ulcerative colitis, and the identification and discernment of acute segmental colitis due to vascular occlusion or deficiency of granulomatous colitis and of postinfectious colitis, little progress has been made in our understanding of this disease since Engel reviewed its etiology and pathogenesis in the 1950s. No evidence has supported its infectious etiology. Some of the data reviewed in this chapter support the idea that genetic factors play a role in its etiology: the higher incidence in Jews than non-Jews and in white persons than black persons in the United States is suggestive; the increased incidence among members of patients' families, as compared to families of a comparison group without ulcerative colitis, is also suggestive of genetic factors, as is the association of ulcerative colitis with ankylosing spondylitis, in which a genetic transmission has been established. However, these statements about the disproportionate numbers of Jews and relatives liable to ulcerative colitis can also be applied to Crohn's disease.

The immunopathology of ulcerative colitis is not fully worked out. Nonetheless, the apparently increased incidence of anticolon antibodies in the female relatives of patients with both ulcerative colitis and Crohn's disease should allow one to identify persons who may be at risk for the disease. Studies employing a risk strategy would permit the comparison and contrasting of persons who, despite being at risk, may differ in their social and psychological characteristics. One might then identify how those who do develop the disease differ from those who do not. Additional evidence about the role of social and psychological factors could be obtained by a careful analysis of how such factors affect the course of the disease both in patients known to have a persistent mucosal abnormality and those who do not have such an abnormality during periods in which they are symptom-free. It would then be possible to study them when symptoms recur. In those who do not have a persistent abnormality the disease might have a different course.

One of the most perplexing aspects of ulcerative colitis is the status of the association with anticolon antibodies, which are also found in such diverse diseases as pernicious anemia, carcinoma of the colon, and collagen diseases (Meyer, 1973), although not with a greater incidence than in the healthy population. Also, the anticolon antibodies are not toxic to human fetal colon cells in tissue culture. Their pathogenetic role is, therefore, discounted by many immunologists.

Psychosomatic research in this area is, however, burdened by many problems that also beset investigators at other levels of organization. All studies are not careful enough in ascertaining the diagnosis—undoubtedly many patients and series have included patients with granulomatous colitis or other diseases of the colon. It is not certain from published reports whether patients had a mild, moderate, or severe form of the disease, and what their sigmoidoscopies, biopsy, or X-ray findings were. Finally, investigators in this area (except for Engel) have not made sufficiently explicit their contention that social and psychological factors *by themselves* do not account for the predisposition or onset of the disease(s) now called ulcerative colitis.

548

A NOTE ON CROHN'S DISEASE
(Regional Enteritis and Granulomatous Colitis)

BASIC METHODOLOGICAL PROBLEMS

Much effort continues to be expended by gastroenterologists and pathologists in differentiating Crohn's disease from ulcerative colitis on clinical, radiological, and histopathological grounds. This effort is even more difficult since it is recognized today that Crohn's disease frequently involves the colon (including the rectum) either with or without involvement of the ileum, in which case it is now called granulomatous colitis in the United States (Korelitz, 1967; Lockhart-Mummery and Morson, 1960, 1964; McGovern and Goulston, 1968). Granulomatous colitis can also frequently be distinguished on clinical, radiological, and histopathological grounds from ulcerative colitis, but in many instances an admixture of the two conditions, based on histology, has been found. On other levels, Crohn's disease of the ileum and colon shares many demographic, ethnic, social, immunopathological, and psychosocial features with ulcerative colitis for reasons which remain unknown.

The distinctive feature of Crohn's disease is that it is a chronic inflammatory disease of the small and large bowel, not caused by any specific pathogen, such as the tubercle bacillus. The lesion, which is usually discontinuous in the gut, is described most frequently as granulomatous in nature, with inflammation extending through the entire thickness of the gut wall. In the last few years, a number of pathologists have considered the granulomata as a late, or secondary, characteristic of the disease and as a response to an initial mucosal ulceration and inflammatory process of the submucosa (Allen, 1971; Amman and Bockus, 1971; Kent et al., 1970). In fact, some authorities consider the mucosal lesion in Crohn's disease to be secondary to a primary arteriolar and lymphatic lesion in the gut (Mendeloff, 1972; Morson, 1968), of which the pathogenesis is not understood.

Because granulomatous colitis has been distinguished from ulcerative colitis only since 1960, reports in the literature published before that date must be viewed with caution for they undoubtedly contain a mixed population of patients with some diagnosed as having ulcerative colitis when actually they were suffering from granulomatous colitis.

In addition, it may very well be true that Crohn's disease is not a disease entity with a common etiology and pathogenesis. It is possible that, like ulcerative colitis, it is a term for a heterogeneous group of diseases, which share certain features in common but have a different etiology and pathogenesis (Meyer and Sleisenger, 1973).

Problems of Diagnosis

Crohn's disease may first be diagnosed at any time of life. It has been described in newborns, children, and in the elderly (Crispin and Tempany, 1967; Cuthbertson and

Hughes, 1969; Donaldson, 1973). Its symptoms at onset may be very variable, and long delays in arriving at a diagnosis have been reported (Dyer and Dawson, 1970; Law, 1969). The patient may have an acute attack of pain in the lower-right quadrant of the abdomen, with fever and perhaps diarrhea. Examination elicits pain, tenderness, and a local mass. At operation, the disease is located in the terminal ileum. Or there may be recurrent bouts of (colicky) abdominal pain with or without diarrhea (which is often watery). The disease may begin with the symptoms and signs of ileitis. In other patients, intermittent pain and diarrhea are associated with weight loss, fever, and anemia (Lennard-Jones et al., 1968). It may begin as an episode of bloody diarrhea with or without fever, or as fever of unknown origin. Anemia may be the only finding; the anemia may be due to iron, vitamin B12, or folic acid deficiencies, either singly or combined. Hypoproteinemia with edema may be the presenting signs and symptoms. The disease may be anteceded by symptoms of any of its systemic complications. A child having the disease may fail to grow physically and to achieve sexual maturation. When anorexia, weight loss, and amenorrhea are prominent symptoms, it may be misdiagnosed as anorexia nervosa (Truelove, 1971).

In order to achieve diagnostic accuracy in choosing a population to study, certain clinical features of Crohn's disease (especially of the colon) can be used to distinguish it from ulcerative colitis: rectal bleeding with or without diarrhea and involvement of the rectum are more common in ulcerative than in granulomatous colitis. In fact, exclusive involvement of the rectum is rarely, if ever, seen in granulomatous colitis. Although ulcerative colitis may occasionally (5 percent of patients) extend to the mucosa and submucosa of the ileum, the association of transmural ileal and colonic disease in Crohn's disease occurs in 75 to 80 percent of all patients (Fahrländer and Baerlocher, 1971; Meyer and Sleisenger, 1973). However, anal or perianal involvement (consisting of perianal swelling, ulceration and infection, narrowing, and fissure or fistula formation) is much more commonly associated with Crohn's disease involving either the small or large bowel or both. On X-ray, areas of involvement and narrowing of the large bowel, which are interspersed with normal bowel, and strictures of the involved bowel, may be diagnostic or at least occur twice as frequently in granulomatous colitis than in ulcerative colitis. Biopsy specimens of the colon showing noncaseating granulomata and involvement of all layers of the gut wall are distinctive but not exclusive features in granulomatous colitis. When deep ulcers of the colon are seen on sigmoidoscopy, they are more likely to be due to granulomatous colitis, although they are also seen in ulcerative colitis (Meyer and Sleisenger, 1973). In general, the barium enema is more useful in the diagnosis of granulomatous colitis, whereas sigmoidoscopy and biopsy are the best aids in the diagnosis of ulcerative colitis. The two diseases may on occasion occur together in the same person, with ulcerative colitis confined to the colon and Crohn's disease to the ileum (Crohn and Yarnis, 1958; Edwards and Truelove, 1964a; Hammer et al., 1968).

Any and all the systemic complications and associated lesions that have been described in patients with ulcerative colitis also occur in Crohn's disease. These include conjunctivitis, iritis, uveitis, ulcers of the mouth, erythema nodosum, pyoderma gangrenosum, ankylosing spondylitis, migratory monoarthritis or polyarthritis, and liver and renal disease. Hammer et al. (1968), in a controlled study, reported a significantly higher incidence of eczema, polyarthritis, and hay fever in patients with regional enteritis. In 39 patients with regional enteritis, 15 had other diseases—arthritis (7 patients), thyrotoxicosis (2 patients), hypothyroidism (1 patient), or peptic ulcer (1 patient)—which preceded, were associated with, or developed after, the onset of regional enteritis.

In a number of these associated lesions, genetic (e.g., in ankylosing spondylitis) or immunological processes (in the eye and skin lesions) have been implicated. As a result, there has been an exhaustive search for genetic and immunopathological factors in Crohn's disease.

THE ROLE OF GENETIC FACTORS

A genetic susceptibility to Crohn's disease has been sought in family and twin studies. Of course, a genetic susceptibility cannot by itself explain the purported increase in the incidence and prevalence of the disease in the past few decades. Nor can a genetic susceptibility adequately be determined by the established family aggregation of the disorder.

From 2½ to 11 percent of patients with Crohn's disease have a family history either of Crohn's disease or ulcerative colitis. These diseases occur most frequently in one other sibling or a parent, and less frequently in several siblings or collateral relatives (Almy and Sherlock, 1966; Crohn and Yarnis, 1958; Kirsner and Spencer, 1963; Sherlock et al., 1963). This distribution of the disease suggests a polygenic form of inheritance.

Unfortunately, only a few twins with Crohn's disease have been reported. Of six pairs of monozygotic (Mz) twins, five were concordant for Crohn's disease; two pairs of dizygotic (Dz) twins were discordant for the disease (Hislop and Grant, 1970; Morris, 1965; Sherlock et al., 1963).

One of the least explained findings in Crohn's disease is that the relatives of patients with the disease are almost as likely to have ulcerative colitis as Crohn's disease, whereas the relatives of patients with ulcerative colitis are five to six times more likely to suffer from that disease than Crohn's disease (Crohn, 1949; Hammer et al., 1968; Houghton and Naish, 1958; Kirsner and Spencer, 1963).

These findings suggest an association of ulcerative colitis with regional enteritis in families, but the meaning of the association has remained unclear. The correlation could be clarified if exact figures for the incidence and prevalence of both diseases were known in a population, and if systematic studies of the incidence of each disease in the relatives of patients with the disease were compared with the incidence in the relatives of a control population. To date, only crude estimates can be made of the incidence or regional enteritis in the relatives of patients: these estimates run from ¼ to 1 percent in first-degree relatives. Since the incidence of regional enteritis in a general population is only about 1/10 as great (Table 5), the probablility of acquiring regional enteritis if one has a first-degree relative with the disease is greater by a factor of 10 than if one has no such relative. One of the other unexplained aspects of the family aggregation of regional enteritis is that members of different generations have been reported to develop the disease at or about the same point in their lives (Steigmann and Shapiro, 1961).

The studies published to date indicate that although genetic factors play an etiologic role, the mode of inheritance and the nature of the inherited defect remain unknown.

551

TABLE 5

Incidence and Prevalence of Regional Enteritis

COUNTRY	YEAR	INCIDENCE[a]				REFERENCE	SOURCES
		MEN	WOMEN	BOTH			
Bristol, England,	1958				14		
Oxfordshire, England	1951–60	0.8	0.8	0.8	9.0	Evans and Acheson (1965)	Hospitalized, clinic, private patients
Norway	1956–63	0.26	0.25	0.26		Gjone et al. (1966)	Acute and chronic cases; hospitalized patients, X-ray, 90% operated
	1964–69	1.0	0.8	0.9		Myren (1971)	
Uppsala and Västmanland, Sweden	1956–61	1.8	1.8	1.8	27.0	Norlén et al. (1970)	Chronic cases; hospitalized patients, diagnostic X-rays all hospitals 90% with pathologic confirmation
	1962–68	3.4	2.8	3.1		Krause (1971)	
Baltimore, Maryland	1960–63	2.5	1.2	1.8		Monk et al. (1967)	Hospital incidence, biopsy, X-ray, etc.
Northeast Scotland	1956–61	1.4	1.9	1.6		Kyle and Blair (1965)	Acute cases included
	1962–68	1.6	3.0	2.3		Smith (1971)	
Switzerland	1960–69	1.8	1.4	1.6		Fahrländer and Baerlocher (1971)	Chronic cases; hospitalized, private practitioners

[a] Per 100,000 population

EPIDEMIOLOGICAL FACTORS

Incidence and Prevalence

The incidence of regional enteritis is 2½ to 6 times less than that of ulcerative colitis (Evans and Acheson, 1965; Fahrländer and Baerlocher, 1971; Monk et al., 1967). There is considerable geographic variation in the incidence and prevalence figures for regional enteritis, as shown in Table 5. Both the lowest and the highest figures occur in Scandinavian countries (Gjone et al., 1966; Krause, 1971; Norlen et al., 1970). The reason for this discrepancy is unknown.

It seems probable that the incidence of regional enteritis is increasing in Scandinavia, Switzerland, and Scotland (Fahrländer and Baerlocher, 1971; Krause, 1971; Myren, 1971; Smith, 1971). The fact that the same investigators were at work in the Scandinavian and the Swiss series suggests that results from the two studies are truly comparable, but there are uncertainties about the definition of the disease in those various series. An acute, nonrecurring form of regional enteritis seems to be more common in Japan than elsewhere (Yamase et al., 1967).

One study indicates that there is a marked rural-urban difference in incidence (Smith, 1971); other studies fail to demonstrate such a difference (Acheson, 1965; Krause, 1971).

Ethnic and Religious Factors

The incidence of regional enteritis in Jewish men, 7 per 100,000 of the population, is 3.5 to 9 times greater than in men of other religious backgrounds (Monk et al., 1967). In various populations with the diagnosis of regional enteritis, the proportion of Jews has ranged from 33 to 42 percent (Acheson, 1960; McKegney et al., 1970; Rubie et al., 1957; Singer et al., 1971). In American hospital populations, the highest prevalence rates occur among Jewish men (Monk et al., 1967), but may be three times as high in Jewish women as in women of other faiths. Similarly, in Sweden the mortality from regional enteritis is greatest in Jews (Brahme, quoted by Krause, 1971), but this pattern seems not to hold in Norway, where *no* case of regional enteritis was described in the Jewish population (of 750 people) over an eight-year period (Gjone et al., 1966). In black Americans, the disease is rare (Mendeloff et al., 1966; Monk et al., 1967; Whybrow et al., 1968).

Effects of Socioeconomic Variables

In the series of Mendeloff et al. (1966) and Monk et al. (1969), it was found that regional enteritis was more likely to occur in white persons living in the northeastern part of the United States, rather than in the border or southern states. Their forebears were more likely to be recent immigrants; they and their fathers (Monk et al., 1969) belonged to somewhat higher socioeconomic groups, or, in the Army, were more-frequently officers (Acheson and Nefzeger, 1963); and they had attained higher educational levels. They were likely to be single and had made more job changes. They were also likely to have lost a father before the age of 15. (Almost all of this, it will be noted, duplicates findings quoted with regard to ulcerative colitis.)

THE ROLES OF PSYCHOLOGICAL AND SOCIAL FACTORS

The roles of psychological and social factors in the etiology and pathogenesis of Crohn's disease are not accorded much status by authors of textbooks of internal medicine or gastroenterology. At the same time, they frequently write that no one knows *the cause*. In view of the fact that there is no single cause of most diseases this statement reflects a narrow perspective on the etiology and pathogenesis of disease. Criticism has been directed at the retrospective and "anecdotal" nature of psychological and social studies of this disease. Since it is not known who is at risk for the disease, studies of every kind (e.g., radiological and histopathological) are equally retrospective. Further criticism has been directed at these studies because they seem to point to remarkable similarities between the psychological and social characteristics of patients with Crohn's disease and patients with ulcerative colitis. This finding could mean one of several things: (1) Either the correct diagnosis was not made, or, as in other areas of clinical investigation, not enough care was taken in discriminating between the two diseases. (2) Our observational and psychological test techniques are too crude to make fine discriminations. (3) Patients with these diseases share many common psychological and social characteristics; they respond to similar environmental conditions or experiences; and the diseases have a quantitatively related genetic basis. A larger concentration of relevant genes or a more complete genotype could account for Crohn's disease; fewer relevant genes might account for ulcerative colitis. This would explain some of the reports that ulcerative colitis is almost as likely to occur as Crohn's disease in the relatives of patients suffering from the latter (McConnell, 1971). (4) The phenotypic expression consists of some unspecified disturbance of the gastrointestinal tract, which may occur at any age, and which affects the personality development of both groups of patients in a similar manner.

The common psychological characteristics of patients with the two diseases are either known from clinical experience (Engel, 1973) or from a comparative study carried out by McKegney and his co-workers (1970) who studied a total of 123 cases—83 retrospectively and 40 consecutively. In the first phase, the method used was a review of the charts of hospitalized patients. In the second phase of the study, 40 patients were interviewed, and had the Cornell Medical Index (CMI) administered to them. Of these 40 patients, 21 had ulcerative colitis (in 9 the process was confined to the rectosigmoid juncture), 19 had Crohn's disease (in 5 it was confined to the ileum, 3 had ileocolitis, 11 had granulomatous colitis). The only statistically significant difference among the group of patients in the first phase of the study was that patients with ulcerative colitis were more likely to have lost a parent before the onset of the disease.

In both groups of patients there was a high frequency of identifiable initiating events before disease onset, which will be described below. These events occurred in 82 percent of the patients with ulcerative colitis and in 68 percent of those with Crohn's disease. The incidence in both groups of an overt psychopathology was 38 percent and 47 percent respectively, which was confirmed by independent measures of emotional disturbance on the CMI. In both diseases there was a positive correlation between the severity of the physical disease and the degree of emotional disturbance; and the more emotionally disturbed the patient the greater was the duration of the disease.

These patients also have character traits in common with patients with ulcerative colitis—some patients with both diseases had a compulsive character structure, and others a paranoid one. In their relationships to other people they were either dependent, confirming and placating, and timid in their expression of anger, or excessively demanding, excitable, and seductive (Cohn et al., 1970; Ford et al., 1969; McKegney et al., 1970; Paulley, 1948; Riemer, 1960; Sperling, 1960; Stewart, 1949). The mothers of these patients have been described in terms that are remarkably similar to those used to depict the mothers of ulcerative colitis patients—they were demanding women who dominated their household; if they expressed affection to their child they did so on condition that he or she comply and achieve. They frequently blamed the child for wrongdoing. Some mothers or fathers were coldly unaffectionate all the time (Cohn et al., 1970; Ford et al., 1969).

The relationship of distressing experiences to the onset of regional eneritis has been affirmed by many observers (Grace, 1954; McKegney et al., 1970; Mersereau, 1963; Paulley, 1948, 1971; Sperling, 1960; Stewart, 1949; Whybrow et al., 1968) and denied by others (Blackburn et al., 1939; Crocket, 1952; Crohn et al., 1956; Kraft and Ardali, 1964; Monk et al., 1970). These experiences, when described, most frequently took the form of a loss of a close relative, a loss of self-respect, a struggle to complete a demand or task, or an inability to find or difficulty in finding a solution for a significant personal problem. Pregnancy or retirement have also been described as settings in which the symptoms began (Cohn et al., 1970; Ford et al., 1969; Grace, 1954; McKegney et al., 1970; Whybrow et al., 1968).

The responses to these life events have been studied with much less care in patients with Crohn's disease than in patients with ulcerative colitis. Psychopathology, as mentioned, was overt and frequent, but often antedated the onset of the symptoms. In Whybrow's study, 24 patients (62.5 percent) were adjudged to have identifiable psychiatric symptoms or illnesses (such as schizophrenia); in 8 of these the symptoms preceded the onset of Crohn's disease by years. In addition, in 5 of 21 patients who were receiving steroid medication there was a probable correlation between mood disturbance and the medication. In 10 patients the psychiatric problems were so severe as to require psychiatric intervention. The most frequent symptoms were anxiety (18 percent) and depression (38 percent). There was a relationship between the incidence of depression, the length of the illness, and the administration of steroids. The regressive, demanding behavior seen in 41 percent of the group was a function of the chronic disease and the effects of hospitalization (Whybrow et al., 1968). The frequent occurrence of depression, helplessness, or hopelessness, and an inability to cope has also been observed or found on psychological testing of patients (Cohn et al., 1970; Ford et al., 1969).

Some authors do not accept the thesis that regional enteritis is initiated by stressful life events, but do concede that exacerbations of symptoms—diarrhea, in particular—are related to such events. Ford et al. (1969), Paulley (1948, 1949, 1971), Stewart (1949), and Whybrow et al. (1968) have published such correlations. Whybrow et al. (1968) found that psychological distress and exacerbations of the disease coincided in 25 of 39

555

patients. The most frequent symptom of exacerbation was an increase in bowel movements. The stressful events most frequently encountered were moving away from home, school examinations, pregnancy, marital discord, and increased work responsibility. When these events were recurrent, they coincided with repeated exacerbations. The patients responded by becoming anxious or depressed, but it is not clear whether these affects were in response to the life events' or to the increase in diarrhea signifying a worsening of the disease.

Although a fairly consistent picture of psychological and social factors is presented by these studies, the medical literature emphasizes those studies that have turned up negative findings. One often-quoted study of this sort was done by Feldman et al. (1967). The interviewer knew the patients' diagnosis and the hypotheses tested; the conclusions of the study were that, despite a six-to-nine year duration of Crohn's disease, the patients were "supernormal." This study was carried out in 19 moderately or severely ill patients with Crohn's disease, with the same methods and same conclusions as in the study on patients with ulcerative colitis. Two comparison groups were used. Patients and comparison subjects were classified as normal or not. Of the 19 patients, 17 were rated as more normal than the comparison group; the remaining 2 were a "compulsive and somewhat impulsive" man and an "impulsive, somewhat eccentric, adventurous" woman. Of the normal group, 8 were regarded as "normal passive personality types" and 9 as "normal aggressive types." No precipitating "stresses" to the disease were uncovered; in 2 instances "stress" preceded relapses of the disease. No "separation anxiety" was uncovered. In 6 patients, psychological conflict was manifest, but was not considered "extreme." Four patients were moderately depressed, presumably about the severity of their disease. Many of the other factors that McKegney et al. (1970) and Whybrow et al. (1968) had controlled for were not considered in this study.

SUMMARY AND CONCLUSIONS

No satisfactory conclusion can be drawn from this welter of conflicting data about Crohn's disease. To those interested in the psychosomatic aspects of Crohn's disease, a clear-cut message emerges. Every patient so-classified should have his diagnosis rigorously confirmed. Patients who suffer only from granulomatous colitis should be compared with those in whom Crohn's disease involves only the ileum, or the ileum and the colon. There is good evidence to suggest that the course and prognosis of the ileocolitis and the colitis of Crohn's disease are different. However, the investigator must recognize that granulomatous colitis cannot easily be differentiated from ulcerative colitis without histopathological verification (Meyer and Sleisenger, 1973).

Nonetheless, the behavioral scientist has much to contribute to a further understanding of this disease. Rigorous epidemiological studies are called for. There should be an effort to identify those factors in the society, culture, or subculture that may have contributed to an increase in the incidence and prevalence of the disease, if indeed this increase is verified. Concordance and discordance in twins should be studied along with their family structures. Siblings who are healthy should be compared with their diseased brothers and sisters. The prevalence of anticolon antibodies might be employed as a variable to identify persons as risk in families in which some members suffer from the disease. Exacerbations and remissions of the disease should be carefully studied in a longitudinal manner by psychological techniques; the highly variable course of the disease might be explained by data provided by such studies.

Since American Jews seem to be particularly prone to the disease, there should be combined studies of population genetics and of the cultural variables that might account for this tendency. The increased occurrence of the diseases associated with Crohn's disease also calls for genetic studies that might explain the heritability of an immune predisposition to the disorder, which is known to exist but has not yet been identified (Hammer et al., 1968).

Finally, knowledge of Crohn's disease would be enhanced by the development of an animal model. The cocker spaniel can "spontaneously" develop a chronic inflammation of the terminal ileum and colon characterized by a lymphangitis, mesenteric thickening, and lymph-node involvement, intermittently present in the gut. Boxer dogs develop a granulomatous colitis without ulceration or the formation of fistulae (Rappaport et al., 1951; Strande et al., 1954), but it is not known why.

Although many studies carried out by psychiatrists and other behavioral scientists have been seriously criticized from many different quarters, the main criticism leveled against them should be the failure to identify clearly their subject population. The diagnosis of Crohn's disease is not easy, and the disease should be clearly differentiated for the present from ulcerative colitis, nongranulomatous ulcerative jejunoileitis (Jeffries et al., 1968), lymphoma of the small intestine, fungal and tubercular infections of the small intestine, and the bowel disease of the colon produced by ischemia, which may produce segmental distortion of the colon.

REFERENCES

Ulcerative Colitis

Acheson, E. D. 1960a. The distribution of ulcerative colitis and regional enteritis in United States veterans, with particular reference to the Jewish religion. Gut 1:291.

———— 1960b. An association between ulcerative colitis, regional enteritis and ankylosing spondylitis. Q J. Med. 29:489.

———— and Nefzeger, M. D. 1963. Ulcerative colitis in the United States Army in 1944. Gastroenterology 44:7.

———— and Truelove, S. C. 1961. Early weaning in the etiology of ulcerative colitis. Br. Med. J. 2:929.

Adinolfi, M., Glynn, A. A., Lindsay, M., and Nulne, C. M. 1966. Serological properties of gamma A antibodies to E. coli present in human colostrum. J. Immunol. 97:248.

Alexander, F. 1950. Psychosomatic Medicine. New York: Norton.

————, French, T. M., and Pollock, G. H. 1968. Psychosomatic Specificity. Chicago: University of Chicago Press.

Almy, T. P. 1961a. Observations on the pathologic physiology of ulcerative colitis. Gastroenterology 40:299.

———— 1961b. Ulcerative colitis. Gastroenterology 41:391.

———— and Lewis, C. M. 1963. Ulcerative colitis: report of progress based on the recent literature. Gastroenterology 45:515.

———— and Sherlock, P. 1966. Genetic aspects of ulcerative colitis and regional enteritis. *Gastroenterology* 51:757.

———— and Tulin, M. 1947. Alterations in colonic function in man under stress: I. Experimental production of changes simulating the "irritable colon." *Gastroenterology* 8:616.

————, Kern, F., and Tulin, M. 1949a. Alterations in colonic function in man under stress: II. Experimental production of sigmoid spasm in healthy persons. *Gastroenterology* 12:425.

————, Hinkle, L. E., Jr., Berle, B., and Kern, F., Jr. 1949b. Alterations in colonic function in man under stress: III. Experimental production of sigmoid spasm in patients with spastic constipation. *Gastroenterology* 12:437.

Anthonisen, P., Christoffersen, P., Riis, P., Schourup, K., and Schwartz, M. 1966. Liver function and histology in patients with non-specific hemorrhagic proctocolitis (hemorrhagic proctitis and ulcerative colitis). *Ugeskr. Laeger.* 128:471.

Appel, J., and Rosen, S. 1950. Psychotic factors in psychosomatic illness. *Psychosom. Med.* 12:236.

Arajärvi, T., Pentti, R., and Aukee, M. 1961a. Ulcerative colitis in children: I. Psychological study. *Ann. Clin. Res.* 7:1.

————, ————, and ————. 1961b. Ulcerative colitis in children: II. A clinical, psychological, and social follow-up study. *Ann. Clin. Res.* 7:259.

Arden Jones, R. 1961. Immunosuppressive therapy in ulcerative colitis. *Proc. R. Soc. Med.* 62:499.

Arthur, B. 1963. Role perceptions of children with ulcerative colitis. *Arch. Gen. Psychiatry* 8:537.

Asherson, G. L., and Holborow, E. J. 1966. Autoantibody production in rabbits. VII. Autoantibodies to gut produced by the injection of bacteria. *Immunology* 10:161.

Askevold, F. 1964. Studies in ulcerative colitis. *J. Psychosom. Res.* 8:89.

Atwell, J. D., Duthie, H. L., and Goligher, J. C. 1965. The outcome of Crohn's disease. *Br. J. Surg.* 52:966.

Avery, G. B., and Harkness, M. 1964. Bloody diarrhea in the newborn infant of a mother with ulcerative colitis. *Pediatrics* 34:875.

Aylett, S. 1960. Diffuse ulcerative colitis and its treatment by ileo-rectal anastomosis. *Ann. R. Coll. Surg. Engl.* 27:260.

Bacon, H. E. 1958. *Ulcerative Colitis.* Philadelphia: Lippincott.

Bean, R. H. D. 1966a. Treatment of ulcerative colitis with antimetabolites. *Br. Med. J.* 1:1081.

———— 1966b. Dangers of immunosuppressive drugs in ulcerative colitis. *Br. Med. J.* 2:361.

Bendixen, G. 1969. Cellular hypersensitivity to components of intestinal mucosa in ulcerative colitis and Crohn's disease. *Gut* 10:631.

Beranbaum, S. L., and Waldron, R. 1951. Chronic ulcerative colitis: case report in a newborn infant. *Pediatrics* 9:773.

Bernier, J., Lambling, A., and Terris, G. 1961. Les iléites allergiques expérimentales par auto-anticorps. *Acta Gastroenterol. Belg.* 24:7.

Bianchi, R. G., and Cook, D. L. 1964. Antipeptic and antiulcerogenic properties of a synthetic sulfated polysaccharide (SN-263). *Gastroenterology* 47:409.

Bicks, R. O., and Rosenberg, E. W. 1964. A chronic delayed hypersensitivity reaction in the guinea pig colon. *Gastroenterology* 46:543.

————, Kirsner, J. B., and Palmer, W. L. 1959. Serum proteins in ulcerative colitis. I. Electrophoretic patterns in active disease. *Gastroenterology* 37:256.

————, Azar, M. M., Rosenberg, E. W., Dunham, W. G., and Luther, J. 1967. Delayed hypersensitivity reactions in the intestinal tract. I. Studies of 2,4-dinitrochlorobenzene-caused guinea pig and swine colon lesions. *Gastroenterology* 53:422.

Billinghurst, J. R., and Welchman, J. M. 1966. Idiopathic ulcerative colitis in the African: a report of four cases. *Br. Med. J.* 1:211.

Binder, J. H., Spiro, H. M., and Thayer, W. R., Jr. 1966. Delayed hypersensitivity in regional enteritis and ulcerative colitis. *Am. J. Dig. Dis.* 11:572.

Birnbaum, D., Groen, J. J., and Kallner, G. 1960. Ulcerative colitis among the ethnic groups in Israel. *Arch. Intern. Med.* 105:843.

Bockus, H. L. 1964. *Gastroenterology.* Philadelphia: Saunders.

Bodman, F. 1935. The psychologic background of colitis. *Am. J. Med. Sci.* 190:535.

Boley, S. T., Schwartz, S., Lash, J., and Sternhill, V. 1963. Reversible vascular occlusion of the colon. *Surg. Gynecol. Obstet.* 116:53.

Bonfils, S. 1970. Carrageenan and the human gut. *Lancet* ii:414.

Bonnevie, O. 1967. A socioeconomic study of patients with ulcerative colitis. *Scand. J. Gastroenterol.* 2:129.

————, Riis, P., and Anthonisen, P. 1968. An epidemiologic study of ulcerative colitis in Copenhagen County. *Scand. J. Gastroenterol.* 3:432.

Boyd, W. C., Heisler, M., and Orowan, E. 1961. Correlation between ulcerative colitis and Rh blood groups. *Nature,* 190:1123.

Brasher, P. H., Landov, J. H., Rigler, S. P., and Dragstedt, L. R. 1955. Gastric, duodenal, and colonic ulcerations induced by histamine. *Arch. Surg.* 71:299.

Bregman, E., and Kirsner, J. P. 1961. Some properties of colon antibodies in ulcerative colitis. *Fed. Proc.* 20:13.

Broberger, O. 1964. Immunologic studies in ulcerative colitis. *Gastroenterology* 47:229.

———— and Lagercrantz, R. 1966. Ulcerative colitis in childhood and adolescence. *Adv. Pediatr.* 14:9.

———— and Perlmann, P. 1959. Autoantibodies in human ulcerative colitis. *J. Exp. Med.* 110:657.

———— and ———— 1962. Demonstration of an epithelial antigen in colon by means of fluorescent antibodies from children with ulcerative colitis. *J. Exp. Med.* 115:13.

———— and ———— 1963. *In vitro* studies of ulcerative colitis. I. Reactions of patients' serum with human fetal colon cells in tissue cultures. *J. Exp. Med.* 117:705.

Brody, D. A., Werle, J. M., Meschan, I., and Quigley, J. P. 1940. Intralumen pressures of the digestive tract, especially the pyloric region. *Am. J. Physiol.* 130:791.

Brooke, B. N., Dykes, P. W., and Walker, F. C. 1961. A study of liver disorder in ulcerative colitis. *Postgrad. Med. J.* 37:245.

Brown, P. W., and Scheifley, C. H. 1939. Chronic regional enteritis occurring in three siblings. *Am. J. Dig. Dis.* 6:257.

Brown, W. T., Preu, P. W., and Sullivan, A. 1938. Ulcerative colitis and the personality. *Am. J. Psychiatry* 95:407.

Buckwalter, J. A., Wohlwend, E. B., Colter, D. C., Tidrick, R. T., and Knowler, L. A. 1956. ABO blood groups and disease. *J.A.M.A.* 162:1210.

Bull, D. M., and Tomasi, T. B. 1968. Deficiency of immunoglubulin A in intestinal disease. *Gastroenterology* 54:313.

Burch, P. R. J., Rowell, N. R., and Burwell, R. G. 1968. Schizophrenia: autoimmune or autoaggressive? *Br. Med. J.* 2:50.

————, de Dombal, F. T., and Watkinson, G. 1969. Etiology of ulcerative colitis. II. A new hypothesis. *Gut* 10:277.

Bywaters, E. G. L., and Ansell, B. M. 1959. Arthritis associated with ulcerative colitis. *Ann. Rheum. Dis.* 17:169.

Castelnuovo-Tedesco, P. 1962. Ulcerative colitis in an adolescent boy subjected to a homosexual assault. *Psychosom. Med.* 24:148.

———— 1966. Psychiatric observations on attacks of gout in a patient with ulcerative colitis. *Psychosom. Med.* 28:781.

559

————, Schwertfeger, H. D., and Hanowsky, D. S. 1970. Psychological characteristics of patients with ulcerative colitis and patients with peptic ulcer: a comparison. *Psychiatry Med.* 1:59.

Chalfin, D., and Holt, P. 1967. Lactase deficiency in ulcerative colitis, regional enteritis and viral hepatitis. *Am. J. Dig. Dis.* 12:81.

Chalke, F. C. R. 1965. Effect of psychotherapy for psychosomatic disorders. *Psychosomatics* 6:125.

Chambers, W. W., and Rosenbaum, M. 1953. Ulcerative colitis. *Psychosom. Med.* 15:523.

Chaudhary, N. A., and Truelove, S. C. 1961. Human colonic motility: a comparative study of normal subjects, patients with ulcerative colitis, and patients with the irritable colon syndrome. Part II. The effect of prostigmine. Part III. Effects of emotions. *Gastroenterology* 40:1.

Chin Kim, I., and Barbero, G. J. 1963. The pattern of rectosigmoid motility in children. *Gastroenterology* 45:57.

Cobb, S. 1953. Clinic on psychosomatic problems: anaclitic treatment in a patient with ulcerative colitis. *Am. J. Med.* 14:731.

Connell, A. M. 1961. The motility of the pelvic colon. Part I: Motility in normals and in patients with asymptomatic duodenal ulcer. *Gut* 2:175.

———— 1962. The motility of the pelvic colon. Part II: Paradoxical motility in diarrhea and constipation. *Gut* 3:342.

Cooke, E. M. 1968. Properties of strain of *Escherichia coli* isolated from the feces of patients with ulcerative colitis, patients with acute diarrhea and normal persons. *J. Pathol. Bact.* 95:101.

————, Filipe, M. I., and Dawson, I. M. P. 1968. The production of colonic autoantibodies in rabbits by immunization with *Escherichia coli*. *J. Pathol. Bact.* 96:125.

Cornes, J. S., and Streher, M. 1961. Primary Crohn's disease of the colon and rectum. *Gut* 2:189.

Crabbe, P. A. 1969. The distribution of immunoglobulin-containing cells along the human gastrointestinal tract. *Gastroenterology* 51:305.

———— and Heremans, J. F. 1969. The significance of local IgA in the physiology of the intestinal mucosa. *Neth. J. Med.* 12:100.

Craddock, C. G. 1953. Chronic ulcerative colitis: effect of a specific psychotherapeutic measure. *Psychosom. Med.* 15:513.

Crohn, B. B. 1963. Psychosomatic factors in ulcerative colitis in children. *N.Y. State J. Med.* 63:1456.

Cullinan, E. R., and McDougall, J. P. 1956. The natural history of ulcerative colitis. *Gastroenterologia* 86:582.

Cushing, M. M. 1953. The psychoanalytic treatment of a man suffering with ulcerative colitis. *J. Am. Psychoanal. Assoc.* 1:510.

Daniels, G. E. 1940. Therapy of a case of ulcerative colitis, associated with hysterical depression. *Psychosom. Med.* 2:276.

———— 1942. Psychiatric aspects of ulcerative colitis. *N. Engl. J. Med.* 226:187.

———— 1944. Nonspecific ulcerative colitis as a psychosomatic disease. *Med. Clin. North Am.* 28:593.

———— 1948. Psychiatric factors in ulcerative colitis. *Gastroenterology* 10:59.

————, O'Connor, J. F., Karush, A., Moses, L., Flood, C. A., and Lepore, M. 1962. Three decades in the observation and treatment of ulcerative colitis. *Psychosom. Med.* 24:85.

Davidson, M. 1964. Management of ulcerative colitis in children. *Am. J. Surg.* 107:452.

————, Sleisenger, M. H., Steinberg, H., and Almy, T. P. 1956a. Studies of distal colonic motility in children. Part I: Non-propulsive patterns in normal children. *Pediatrics* 17:807.

————, ————, ———— and ———— 1956b. Studies of distal colonic motility in children. II: Propulsive activity in normal states. *Pediatrics* 17:820.

Dearing, W. H., McGuckin, W. F., and Elveback, L. R. 1969. Serum α_1-glycoprotein in chronic ulcerative colitis. *Gastroenterology* 56:295.

560

de Dombal, F. T. 1967a. Serum proteins in ulcerative colitis: electrophoretic patterns in the inferior mesenteric artery and vein. *Gut* 8:482.

———— 1967b. The prognostic value of the serum proteins in ulcerative colitis. *Br. J. Surg.* 54:857.

———— 1971. Ulcerative colitis: Epidemiology and aetiology, course and prognosis. *Br. Med. J.* 1:649.

————, Goldie, W., Watts, J. McK., and Goligher, J. C. 1966. Hepatic histological changes in ulcerative colitis. A series of 58 consecutive operative liver biopsies. *Scand. J. Gastroenterol.* 1:220.

Deller, D. J., and Wangel, G. 1965. Intestinal motility in man. I. A study combining the use of intraluminal pressure recording and cineradiography. *Gastroenterology* 48:45.

De M'Uzan, M., Bonfils, S., and Lambling, N. 1958. Étude psychosomatique de 18 cas de rectocôlite hémorrhagique. *Sem. Hôp. Paris.* 34:922.

Deucher, F. 1963. Causes and origins of ulcerative colitis. *Wien. Med. Wochenschr.* 113:745.

De Belgiojoso, B., and Ciba, A. M. 1968. Fundamental characteristics of anti-colon antibodies in the serum of a patient with ulcerative colitis. *Acta Gastroenterol. Belg.* 31:483.

Dick, A. P., and Grayson, M. J. 1961. Ulcerative colitis: A follow-up investigation with mucosal biopsy studies. *Br. Med. J.* 1:160.

————, Holt, L. P., and Dalton, E. R. 1966. Persistence of mucosal abnormality in ulcerative colitis. *Gut* 7:355.

Dudek, B., Spiro, H. M., and Thayer, W. R. 1965. A study of ulcerative colitis and circulating antibodies to milk proteins. *Gastroenterology* 49:544.

Edgar, W. M. 1961. Specific antibody against gastrointestinal mucosa. *Lancet* ii:109.

Edwards, F. C., and Truelove, S. C. 1963. The course and prognosis of ulcerative colitis. I. and II. *Gut* 4:299.

———— and ———— 1964a. The course and prognosis of ulcerative colitis. III. Complications. *Gut* 5:1.

———— and ———— 1964b. The course and prognosis of ulcerative colitis. IV. Carcinoma of the colon. *Gut* 5:15.

Eggert, R. C., Wilson, I. D., and Good, R. A. 1969. Agammaglobulinemia and regional enteritis. *Ann. Intern. Med.* 71:581.

Engel, G. L. 1952. Psychological aspects of the management of patients with ulcerative colitis. *N.Y. State J. Med.* 52:2255.

———— 1954a. Studies of ulcerative colitis: I. Clinical data bearing on the nature of the somatic processes. *Psychosom. Med.* 16:496.

———— 1954b. Studies of ulcerative colitis. II. The nature of the somatic processes and the adequacy of psychosomatic hypotheses. *Am. J. Med.* 16:416.

———— 1955. Studies of ulcerative colitis. III. The nature of the psychologic processes. *Am. J. Med.* 19:231.

———— 1956. Studies of ulcerative colitis. IV. The significance of headaches. *Psychosom. Med.* 18:334.

———— 1958. Studies of ulcerative colitis. V. Psychological aspects and their implications for treatment. *Am. J. Dig. Dis.* 3:315.

———— 1961. Biologic and psychologic features of the ulcerative colitis patient. *Gastroenterology* 40:313.

———— 1968. A life setting conducive to illness. The giving-up—given-up complex. *Ann. Intern. Med.* 69:293.

———— 1969. (Comment) *Gastroenterology* 57:262.

———— 1973. Ulcerative colitis. In *Emotional Factors in Gastrointestinal Illness*, edited by A. E. Lindner. Amsterdam: Excerpta Medica.

Engelhart, J. E., and Jacobson, G. 1956. Infarction of the colon, demonstrated by barium enema. *Radiology* 67:573.

Enzer, N. B., and Hijmans, J. C. 1963. Ulcerative colitis beginning in infancy: report of 5 cases. *J. Pediatr.* 63:437.

Evans, J. G., and Acheson, E. D. 1965. An epidemiological study of ulcerative colitis and regional enteritis in the Oxford area. *Gut* 6:311.

Fahrländer, H., and Baerlocher, C. 1971. Clinical features and epidemiological data in the Basel Area. In *Regional Enteritis*, edited by A. Engel and T. Larsson. Stockholm: Nordiska.

Farman, J., Betancourt, E., and Kilpatrick, Z. M. 1968. The radiology of ischemic proctitis. *Radiology* 91:302.

Farmer, R. G., Deodhar, S. D., and Michener, W. M. 1968a. Immunologic aspects of ulcerative colitis and regional enteritis of the colon. *Gastroenterology* 54:1232.

———, Hawk, W. A., and Turnbull, R. B., Jr. 1968b. Regional enteritis of the colon: a clinical and pathologic comparison with ulcerative colitis. *Am. J. Dig. Dis.* 13:501.

Feldman, F., Cantor, D., Soll, S., and Bachrach, W. 1967. Psychiatric study of a consecutive series of 34 patients with ulcerative colitis. *Br. Med. J.* 3:14.

Felsen, J. 1936. Relationship of bacillary dysentery to distal ileitis, chronic ulcerative colitis and non-specific intestinal granuloma. *Ann. Intern. Med.* 10:645.

Fernandez-Herlihy, J. S. 1959. The articular manifestations of chronic ulcerative colitis: an analysis of 555 patients. *N. Engl. J. Med.* 261:259.

Fiddes, P., and Baume, P. 1967. Disaccharidase deficiency in regional enteritis. *Aust. N.Z. J. Med.* 16:339.

Finch, S. M. 1964. The treatment of children with ulcerative colitis. *Am. J. Orthopsychiatry* 34:142.

——— and Hess, J. H. 1962. Ulcerative colitis in children. *Am. J. Psychiatry* 118:819.

Fink, W., Donnelly, W. J., and Jablokow, V. R. 1967. Rectal reaction to injected ulcerative colitis leukocytes and plasma. *Gut* 8:20.

Freyberger, H. 1970. The doctor-patient relationship in ulcerative colitis. *Psychother. Psychosom.* 18:80.

Fullerton, D. T., Kollar, E. J., and Caldwell, A. B. 1962. A clinical study of ulcerative colitis. *J.A.M.A.* 181:463.

Furmanski, A. R. 1952. Dynamic concepts of migraine. *Arch. Neurol. Psychiatry* 67:23.

Ganter, G., and Statmüller, K. 1924. Studien am menschlichen Darm. III. Mitteilung. Über die normale Dickdarmbewegung des Menschen und ihre Beeinflussung durch Pharmaka. *Z. Ges. Exp. Med.* 42:143.

Geffen, N., Darnborough, A., de Dombal, F. T., Watkinson, G., and Goligher, J. C. 1968. Radiological signs of ulcerative colitis: Assessment of their reliability by means of observer variation studies. *Gut* 9:150.

Gelfand, M. D., and Krone, C. L. 1970. Inflammatory bowel disease in family: observations related to pathogenesis. *Ann. Intern. Med.* 72:903.

———, ———, and Kirsner, J. B. 1968a. Distribution of immunoglobulins in human rectal mucosa. I. Normal control subjects. *Gastroenterology* 54:334.

———, ———, Fitch, F. W., and Kirsner, J. B. 1968b. Distribution of immunoglobulins in human rectal mucosa. II. Ulcerative colitis and abnormal mucosal controls. *Gastroenterology* 54:341.

Gelzayd, E. A., Kraft, S. C., and Fitch, F. W. 1967. Immunoglobulin A: Localization in rectal mucosal epithelial cells. *Science* 157:930.

———, ———, ———, and Kirsner, J. 1968. Distribution of immunoglobulins in human rectal mucosa: II. Ulcerative colitis and abnormal mucosal control subjects. *Gastroenterology* 54:341.

Giovacchini, P. L. 1959. The ego and the psychosomatic state. *Psychosom. Med.* 21:106.

Gjone, E., and Myren, J. 1964. Ulcerative colitis in Norway. *Nord. Med.* 71:143.

Goldgraber, M. B., Humphreys, E. M., Kirsner, J. B., and Palmer, W. L. 1958. Carcinoma and ulcerative colitis—a clinical-pathologic study. I. Cancer deaths. II. Statistical analysis. *Gastroenterology* 34:839.

——, ——, ——, and —— 1959. Carcinoma and ulcerative colitis—a clinical-pathologic study. III. Survivors. *Gastroenterology* 36:613.

——, and Kirsner, J. B. 1964. Carcinoma of the colon in ulcerative colitis. *Cancer* 17:657.

Goligher, J. C., de Dombal, F. T., Watts, J. M., and Watkinson, G. 1968. *Ulcerative Colitis.* London: Ballière, Tindall, and Cassell.

Gonzales-Licea, A., and Yardley, J. H. 1966. Nature of the tissue reaction in ulcerative colitis. Light and electron microscopic findings. *Gastroenterology* 51:825.

Grace, W. J., and Graham, D. T. 1952. Relationship of specific attitudes and emotions to certain bodily diseases. *Psychosom. Med.* 14:243.

—— and Wolf, A. G. 1951. Treatment of ulcerative colitis. *J.A.M.A.* 146:981.

——, Wolf, S., and Wolff, H. G. 1951. *The Human Colon: An experimental study based on direct observation of four fistulous subjects.* New York: Hoeber.

Graham, D. T., Lundy, R. M., Benjamin, L. S., Kabler, J. D., Lewis, W. C., Kunish, N. O., and Graham, F. K. 1962. Specific attitudes in initial interviews with patients having different "psychosomatic diseases." *Psychosom. Med.* 24:257.

Gray, J. 1961. Antibodies to cow's milk in ulcerative colitis. *Br. Med. J.* 2:1265.

Gray, J. G., Walker, F. C., and Thompson, D. 1961. Autoimmunity in ulcerative colitis. *Lancet* ii:51.

Groen, J. 1947. Psychogenesis and psychotherapy of ulcerative colitis. *Psychosom. Med.* 9:151.

—— 1951. Emotional factors in the etiology of internal disease. *Mt. Sinai J. Med. N.Y.* 18:71.

—— and Bastiaans, J. 1954. Studies on ulcerative colitis. In *Modern Trends in Psychosomatic Medicine,* edited by D. O'Neill. New York: Hoeber.

—— and Birnbaum, D. 1968. Conservative (supportive) treatment of severe ulcerative colitis. *Isr. J. Med. Sci.* 4:130.

—— and Van der Valk, J. M. 1956. Psychosomatic aspects of ulcerative colitis. *Gastroenterologia* (Basel) 86:591.

Gruskay, F. L., and Cooke, R. E. 1955. The gastrointestinal absorption of unaltered protein in normal infants and in infants recovering from diarrhoea. *Pediatrics* 16:763.

Gryboski, J. D. 1967. Gastrointestinal milk allergy in infants. *Pediatrics* 40:354.

Hammarström, S., Lagercrantz, R., Perlmann, P., and Gustafsson, B. E. 1965. Immunological studies in ulcerative colitis. II. 'Colon' antigen and human blood group H and H-like antigens in germ free rats. *J. Exp. Med.* 122:1075.

Hammer, B., Ashurst, P., and Naish, J. 1968. Diseases associated with ulcerative colitis and Crohn's disease. *Gut* 9:17.

Harrison, W. J. 1965a. Autoantibodies against intestinal and gastric mucous cells in ulcerative colitis. *Lancet* i:1346.

—— 1965b. Thyroid, gastric (parietal-cell) and nuclear antibodies in ulcerative colitis. *Lancet* i:1350.

Hart, J. A. 1946. Ulcerative colitis with perforation in the newborn. *Tex. Med.* 42:286.

Heath, F. K. 1949. Ulcerative colitis. *Am. J. Med.* 6:481.

Hecht, I. 1952. The difference in goal striving behavior between peptic ulcer and ulcerative colitis patients as evaluated by psychological techniques. *J. Clin. Psychol.* 8:262.

Heim, W. G., and Lane, P. H. 1964. Appearance of slow alpha-2-globulin during the inflammatory response of the rat. *Nature* 203:1077.

Helmholz, H. F. 1923. Chronic ulcerative colitis in children. *Amer. J. Dis. Child.* 26:418.

Hersh, A. H., Stecher, R. M., Solomon, M., Walter, M., and Wolpaw, R. 1950. Heredity in ankylosing spondylitis. *Am. J. Hum. Genet.* 2:391.

Hijmans, J. C., and Enzer, N. B. 1962. Ulcerative colitis in childhood: study of 43 cases. *Pediatrics* 29:389.

Hinz, C. F., Perlmann, P., and Hammerström, S. 1967. Reactivity in vitro of lymphocytes from patients with ulcerative colitis. *J. Lab. Clin. Med.* 70:752.

Holborow, E. J., Asherson, G. L., and Wigley, R. D. 1963. Autoantibody production in rabbits. VI: The production of autoantibodies against rabbit, gastric, ileal and colonic mucosa. *Immunology* 6:551.

Holdsworth, C. F., Hall, E. W., Dawson, A. M., and Sherlock, S. 1965. Ulcerative colitis in chronic liver disease. *Q. J. Med.* 34:211.

Hollowach, J., and Thurston, D. L. 1956. Chronic ulcerative colitis in childhood. *J. Pediatr.* 48:279.

Holm, G., and Perlmann, P. 1967. Cytotoxic potential of stimulated human lymphocytes. *J. Exp. Med.* 125:721.

Jackson, D. D. 1946. The psychosomatic factors in ulcerative colitis. A case report. *Psychosom. Med.* 8:278.

——— and Yalom, I. 1966. Family research on the problem of ulcerative colitis. *Arch. Gen. Psychiatry* 15:410.

Jalan, K. N., Prescott, R. J., Sircus, W., Card, W. I., McManus, J. P. A., Falconer, C. W. A., Small, W. P., Smith, A. N., and Bruce, J. 1971. Ulcerative colitis: a clinical study of 399 patients. *J. R. Coll. Surg. Edinb.* 16:338.

Jayson, M. I. V., and Boucher, I. A. D. 1968. Ulcerative colitis with ankylosing spondylitis. *Ann. Rheum. Dis.* 27:219.

Jeffries, G. H. 1965. Immunofluorescent studies in adult celiac disease. *J. Clin. Invest.* 44:475.

Jensen, E. J., Baggenstoss, A. H., and Bargen, J. A. 1950. Renal lesions associated with chronic ulcerative colitis. *Am. J. Med. Sci.* 219:281.

Johnson, M. H., and Wilson, H. T. H. 1969. Skin lesions in ulcerative colitis. *Gut* 10:255.

Judd, S. E. 1966. Surgical progress in the management of chronic ulcerative colitis. *Surgery* 60:783.

Karush, A., and Daniels, G. E. 1953. Ulcerative colitis: the psychoanalysis of two cases. *Psychosom. Med.* 15:140.

———, Hiatt, R. B., and Daniels, G. E. 1955. Psychophysiological correlations in ulcerative colitis. *Psychosom. Med.* 17:36.

———, Daniels, G. E., O'Connor, J. F., and Stern, L. O. 1968. The response to psychotherapy in chronic ulcerative colitis. I. Pretreatment factors. *Psychosom. Med.* 30:255.

———, ———, ———, and ——— 1969. The response to psychotherapy in chronic ulcerative colitis. II. Factors arising from the therapeutic situation. *Psychosom. Med.* 31:201.

Katz, J., Spiro, H. M., and Herskovic, T. 1968. Milk-precipitating substances in the stool in gastrointestinal milk sensitivity. *N. Engl. J. Med.* 278:1191.

Kellock, T. D. 1957. Acute segmental ulcerative colitis. *Lancet* ii:660.

Kern, F., Jr., Almy, T. P., Abbot, F. K., and Bogdonoff, M. 1951. The motility of the distal colon in ulcerative colitis. *Gastroenterology* 19:492.

Kirk, B. W., and Freedman, S. O. 1967. Hypogammaglobulinemia, thymoma and ulcerative colitis. *Can. Med. Assoc. J.* 96:1272.

Kirsner, J. B. 1961. Reflections on aspects of ulcerative colitis. *Am. J. Dig. Dis.* 6:914.

——— 1970a. Ulcerative colitis, 1970—recent developments. *Scand. J. Gastroenterol.* 5(Suppl. 6):63.

564

————— 1970b. Ulcerative colitis: "Puzzles within puzzles." *N. Engl. J. Med.* 282:625.

————— and Palmer, W. L. 1954a. Clinical course of non-specific ulcerative colitis. *J.A.M.A.* 155:341.

————— and ————— 1954b. Ulcerative colitis—considerations of its etiology and treatment. *J.A.M.A.* 155:341.

————— and Spencer, J. 1963. Family occurrences of ulcerative colitis, regional enteritis and ileocolitis. *Ann. Intern. Med.* 59:133.

Klavins, J. V. 1963. Cytoplasm of colonic mucosal cells as site of antigen in ulcerative colitis. *J.A.M.A.* 183:547.

Koffler, D., Garlock, J., and Rothman, W. 1962. Immunocytochemical reactions of serum from ulcerative colitis patients. *Proc. Soc. Exp. Biol. Med.* 109:358.

Kollar, E. J., Caldwell, A. B., and Fullerton, D. T. 1964a. Clinical notes: Intelligence testing in ulcerative colitis. *Am. J. Psychiatry* 120:1002.

Kraft, S. C., Rimpila, J. J., Fitch, F. W., and Kirsner, J. B. 1964. Immunofluorescent studies of ulcerative colitis colon: specificity and non-specificity. *Gastroenterology* 46:747.

—————, —————, —————, and ————— 1966. Immuno-histochemical studies of the colon in ulcerative colitis. *Arch. Pathol.* 82:369.

Krasner, L. 1953. Personality differences between patients classified as psychosomatic and non-psychosomatic. *J. Abnorm. Psychol.* 48:190.

————— and Kornreich, M. 1954. Psychosomatic illness and projective tests: The Rorschach test. *J. Proj. Tech.* 18:355.

Lagercrantz, R. 1949. Ulcerative colitis in children. *Acta Pediat.* Supplement 75.

————— 1955. Follow-up investigation of children with ulcerative colitis, with special reference to indications for surgical therapy. *Acta Paediatr.* 44:302.

—————, Hammerström, S., Perlmann, P., and Gustafsson, B. E. 1966. Immunological studies in ulcerative colitis. III. Incidence of antibodies to colon-antigen in ulcerative colitis and other gastro-intestinal diseases. *Clin. Exp. Immunol.* 1:263.

—————, Perlmann, P., and Hammerström, S. 1971. Immunological studies in ulcerative colitis. V. Family studies. *Gastroenterology* 60:381.

Lepore, J. T. 1965. The importance of emotional disturbances in chronic ulcerative colitis. *J.A.M.A.* 191:819.

Leveen, H. H., Falk, G., and Schatman, B. 1961. Experimental ulcerative colitis produced by anticolon sera. *Ann. Surg.* 154:275.

Lindemann, E. 1945. Psychiatric problems in conservative treatment of ulcerative colitis. *Arch. Neurol. Psychiatry* 53:322.

————— 1950. Modifications in the course of ulcerative colitis in relationship to changes in life situations and reaction patterns. *Res. Publ. Assoc. Res. Nerv. Ment. Dis.* 29:706.

Lindenberg, J. 1958. Ulcerative colitis. Treatment and prognosis studied in 161 cases. *Acta Chir. Scand.* Suppl. 236, 56.

Lium, R. 1939. Etiology of ulcerative colitis. Part II. Effect of induced muscular spasm on colonic explants in dogs, with comment on relation of muscular spasm to ulcerative colitis. *Arch. Intern. Med.* 63:210.

Lockhart-Mummery, H. E., and Morson, B. C. 1960. Crohn's disease (regional enteritis) of the large intestine and its distinction from ulcerative colitis. *Gut* 1:87.

————— and ————— 1964. Crohn's disease of the large intestine. *Gut* 5:493.

Lyons, A. S. 1956. Ulcerative colitis in childhood. *Pediatr. Clin. North Am.* 3:153.

Lyons, C. R., and Postlewait, R. W. 1948. Chronic ulcerative colitis in twins. *Gastroenterology* 10:544.

Mackay, I. R., Wall, A. J., and Goldstein, G. 1966. Response to azathioprine in ulcerative colitis. *Am. J. Dig. Dis.* 11:536.

Mahoney, V. P., Bockus, H. L., Ingram, M., Hundley, J. W., and Yaskin, J. C. 1949. Studies in ulcerative colitis. I. A study of the personality in relation to ulcerative colitis. *Gastroenterology* 13:547.

Malaguti, P. 1971. La colite ulcerosa ad interferenza psicogena. *Minerva Gastroenterol.* 17:6.

Marcus, R., and Watt, J. 1969. Seaweeds and ulcerative colitis in laboratory animals. *Lancet* ii:489.

———, and ———. 1971. Experimental ulceration of the colon induced by non-algal sulphated products. *Gut* 12:868.

Marder, L. 1967. Symposium: Psychiatric aspects of ulcerative colitis. *South. Med. J.* 60:1281.

Marie, J., and Ledoux-Lebard, G. 1942. Rectôlite hemorragique chez un enfant. Caractère familial de l'affection. *Arch. Mal. Appar. Dig.* 31:76.

Marston, A. 1962. The bowel in shock. *Lancet* ii:365.

——— 1964. Patterns of intestinal ischemia. *Ann. R. Coll. Surg. Engl.* 35:151.

———, Pheils, M. T., Thomas, M. L., and Morson, B. C. 1966. Ischaemic colitis. *Gut* 7:1.

Masland, R. P. 1960. Ulcerative colitis. *Pediatr. Clin. North Am.* 7:197.

Maur, M., Toranzo, J. C., and Marcelo, F. A. 1964. ABO and Rh blood groups in colonic disease. *Semana Med.* (Buenos Aires) 124:634.

McBride, T. A., King, M. J., Baikie, A. G., Crean, G. P., and Sircus, W. 1963. Ankylosing spondylitis and chronic inflammatory disease of the intestines. *Br. Med. J.* 2:483.

McConnell, R. B. 1965. Genetics and gastroenterology. In *Recent Advances in Gastroenterology*, edited by J. Badenoch and B. N. Brooke. Boston: Little, Brown.

McDermott, J. F., Jr. 1966. Children with ulcerative colitis: Their own perception of the disease. *Psychosomatics* 7:163.

McDougall, I. P. M. 1964. The cancer risk in ulcerative colitis. *Lancet* ii:655.

McEwan-Alvarado, G., and Bargen, J. A. 1967. Chronic ulcerative colitis in mother and daughter. *Tex. Med.* 63:60.

McGiven, A. R., Ghose, T., and Nairin, R. C. 1967a. Autoantibodies in ulcerative colitis. *Br. Med. J.* 2:19.

———, Datta, S. P., and Nairin, R. C. 1967b. Human serum antibodies against rat colon mucosa. *Nature* 214:288.

McKegney, F. P., Gordon, R. O., and Levine, S. M. 1970. A psychosomatic comparison of patients with ulcerative colitis and Crohn's disease. *Psychosom. Med.* 32:153.

McMahon, A. W., Schmitt, P., Patterson, J. F., and Rothman, E. 1973. Personality differences between inflammatory bowel disease patients and their healthy siblings. *Psychosom. Med.* 35:91.

Melrose, A. G. 1955. The geographical incidence of chronic ulcerative colitis in Britain. *Gastroenterology* 29:1055.

Mendeloff, A. I., Monk, M., Siegel, C. I., and Lilienfeld, A. 1966. Some epidemiological features of ulcerative colitis and regional enteritis. *Gastroenterology* 51:748.

———, ———, ———, and ——— 1970. Illness experience and life stresses in patients with irritable colon and with ulcerative colitis. *N. Engl. J. Med.* 282:14.

Meyer, J. H. 1973. Ulcerative colitis. In *Gastrointestinal Disease*, edited by M. H. Sleisinger and J. S. Fordtran. Philadelphia: Saunders.

Miranda, M., Salas, J., Umana, R. A. Jiménex, G., and Acosta, A. 1969. Non-specific ulcerative colitis in Costa Rica. *Gastroenterology* 56:310.

Mistilis, S. P. 1965. Pericholangitis and ulcerative colitis. I. Pathology, etiology and pathogenesis. *Ann. Intern. Med.* 63:1.

——— and Goulston, S. 1965. Liver disease in ulcerative colitis. In *Recent Advances in Gastroenterology*, edited by J. Badenoch and B. N. Brooke. Boston: Little, Brown.

Moeller, H. C., and Kirsner, J. B. 1954. The effect of drug-induced hypermotility on the gastrointestinal tract of dogs. *Gastroenterology* 26:303.

Mohr, G. J., Josselyn, I. M., Spurlock, J., and Barron, S. H. 1958. Studies in ulcerative colitis in children. *Am. J. Psychiatry* 114:1067.

Moltke, O. 1936. Familial occurrences of ulcerative colitis. *Acta Med. Scand.* Suppl. 77:426.

Monk, M., Mendeloff, A. I., Siegel, C. I., and Lilienfeld, A. 1967. An epidemiological study of ulcerative colitis and regional enteritis among adults in Baltimore. I. Hospital incidence and prevalence, 1960 to 1963. *Gastroenterology* 53:198.

———, ———, ———, and ——— 1969. An epidemiological study of ulcerative colitis and regional enteritis among adults in Baltimore. II. Social and demographic factors. *Gastroenterology* 56:847.

Morris, P. J. 1965. Familial ulcerative colitis. *Gut* 6:176.

Morson, B. G. 1971. Histopathology. In *Regional Enteritis,* edited by A. Engel and T. Larsson. Stockholm: Nordiska.

Moses, L. 1954. The colon: its normal and abnormal physiology and therapeutics. *Ann. N.Y. Acad. Sci.* 58:405.

Murray, C. D. 1930a. Psychogenic factors in the etiology of ulcerative colitis and bloody diarrhoea. *Am. J. Med. Sci.* 180:239.

——— 1930b. A brief psychological analysis of a patient with ulcerative colitis. *J. Nerv. Ment. Dis.* 72:617.

Mushatt, C. 1954. Psychological aspects of non-specific ulcerative colitis. In *Recent Developments in Psychosomatic Medicine,* edited by E. D. Wittkower and R. A. Cleghorn. Philadelphia: Lippincott.

Nagle, G. J., and Kurtz, S. M. 1967. Electron microscopy of the human rectal mucosa, a comparison of idiopathic ulcerative colitis with inflammation of known etiologies. *Am. J. Dig. Dis.* 12:541.

Nefzeger, D., and Acheson, E. D. 1963. Ulcerative colitis in the United States Army in 1944: Follow-up with particular reference to mortality in cases and controls. *Gut* 4:183.

O'Connor, J. F. 1970. A comprehensive approach to the treatment of ulcerative colitis. In *Modern Trends in Psychosomatic Medicine,* vol. 2, edited by O. W. Hill. New York: Appleton-Century-Crofts.

———, Daniels, G., Flood, C., Karush, A., Moses, L., and Stern, L. O. 1964. An evaluation of the effectiveness of psychotherapy in the treatment of ulcerative colitis. *Ann. Intern. Med.* 60:587.

———, ———, Karush, A., Flood, C., and Stern, L. O. 1966. Prognostic implications of psychiatric diagnosis in ulcerative colitis. *Psychosom. Med.* 28:375.

Paneth, H. 1959. Some observations on the relation of psychotic states to psychosomatic disorders. *Psychosom. Med.* 21:106.

Parent, K., Barrett, J., and Wilson, I. D. 1971. Investigation of the pathogenic mechanisms in regional enteritis with in vitro lymphocyte cultures. *Gastroenterology* 61:431.

Patterson, M., Castiglioni, L., and Sampson, L. 1971. Chronic ulcerative colitis beginning in children and teenagers. A review of 43 patients. *Am. J. Dig. Dis.* 16:289.

Paulley, J. W. 1950. Ulcerative colitis; study of 173 cases. *Gastroenterology* 16:566.

——— 1956. Psychotherapy in ulcerative colitis. *Lancet* ii:215.

Perlmann, P., and Broberger, O. 1960. Autoantibodies against antigen derived from the colon in the microsomes of regional colonic lymph glands in human ulcerative colitis. *Nature,* 188:749.

——— and ——— 1963. In vitro studies of ulcerative colitis. 2. Cytotoxic action of white blood cells from patients on human fetal colon cells. *J. Exp. Med.* 117:717.

———, Hammerström, S., Lagercrantz, R., and Gustafsson, B. E. 1965. Antigen from colon of germfree rats and antibodies in human ulcerative colitis. *Ann. N.Y. Acad. Sci.* 124:377.

————, ————, ————, and Campbell, D. 1967. Autoantibodies to colon in rats and human ulcerative colitis: cross reactivity with E. coli 0:14 antigen. Proc. Soc. Exp. Biol. Med. 125:975.

————, ————, and ———— 1973. Immunological features of idiopathic ulcerative colitis and Crohn's Disease. Rendic. Gastroenterol. 5:17.

Pflanz, M. 1971. Epidemiological and sociocultural factors in the etiology of duodenal ulcer. Adv. Psychosom. Med. 6:121.

Platt, T. W., Schlesinger, B. E., and Benson, P. F. 1960. Ulcerative colitis in childhood. Q. J. Med. 29:257.

Polčak, J., and Skalova, M. 1968. Immunologic manifestations of healthy consanguineous relatives of patients suffering from ulcerative colitis. Am. J. Proctol. 19:197.

———— and Vokurka, V. 1960. Autoimmune reactions in the course of ulcerative colitis. Am. J. Dig. Dis. 5:395.

————, ————, and Skalova, M. 1967. Immunological phenomena in families with ulcerative colitis. Gastroenterologia 107:164.

Porter, R. W., Brady, J. V., Conrad, D., Mason, J. W., Galambos, R., and Rioch, D. McK. 1958. Some experimental observations on gastrointestinal lesions in behaviorally conditioned monkeys. Psychosom. Med. 20:379.

Poser, E. G., and Lee, S. G. 1963. Thematic content associated with two gastrointestinal disorders. Gastroenterology 25:162.

Posey, L. E., and Bargen, J. A. 1951. Observations of normal and abnormal human intestinal function. Am. J. Med. Sci. 221:10.

Powell, S. J., and Wilmot, A. J. 1966. Ulcerative post-dysenteric colitis. Gut 7:438.

Prudden, J. F., Lane, N., and Meyer, K. 1950. The effect of orally and intra-arterially administered lysozyme on the canine gastrointestinal tract. Am. J. Med. Sci. 219:291.

Prugh, D. G. 1950. Variations in attitudes, behavior and feeling states as exhibited in the play of children during modifications in the course of ulcerative colitis. Res. Publ. Assoc. Res. Nerv. Ment. Dis. 29:692.

———— 1951. The influence of emotional factors on the clinical course of ulcerative colitis in children. Gastroenterology 18:339.

Reinhart, J. B. 1961. Ulcerative colitis in Negro children. Am. J. Dis. Child. 101:401.

Ritchie, J. A. G., Ardran, M., and Truelove, S. C. 1962. Motor activity of the sigmoid colon of humans. A combined study by intraluminal pressure recording and cineradiography. Gastroenterology 43:642.

Rosenthal, D. 1971. Genetics of Psychopathology. New York: McGraw-Hill.

Rubin, J., Payson, H., and Pilot, M. 1963. Psychosomatic case conference. Psychiatr. Q. 37:25.

Ruddle, N. H., and Waksman, B. H. 1967. Cytotoxic effect of lymphocyte-antigen interaction in delayed hypersensitivity. Science 157:1060.

Sachar, D. B., Taub, R. N., Brown, S. M., Present, D. H., Korelitz, B. I., and Janowitz, H. D. 1973. Impaired lymphocyte responsiveness in inflammatory bowel disease. Gastroenterology 64:203.

Sacrez, R., Willard, D., Beauvais, P., and Korn, R. 1963. Étude des troubles digestifs et réspiratoires dans un cas de lymphocytophtisie du nourisson. Arch. F. Pédiatr. 20:401.

Salem, S. N., and Shubair, K. S. 1967. Non-specific ulcerative colitis in Bedouin Arabs. Lancet i:473.

Sanford, G. E. 1971. Genetic implications in ulcerative colitis. Am. Surg. 37:512.

Schlesinger, B., and Platt, J. 1958. Ulcerative colitis in childhood and a follow-up study. Proc. R. Soc. Med. 51:733.

Schucman, H., and Thetford, W. N. 1970. A comparison of personality traits in ulcerative colitis and migraine patients. J. Abnorm. Psychol. 76:443.

Sewell, P., Cooke, W. T., Cox, E. V., and Meynell, M. J. 1963. Milk intolerance in gastrointestinal disorders. *Lancet* ii:1132.

Sherlock, P., Bell, B. M., Steinberg, H., and Almy, T. P. 1963. Familial occurrence of regional enteritis and ulcerative colitis. *Gastroenterology* 45:413.

Shorter, R. G., Spencer, R. J., Huizenga, K. A., and Hallenbeck, G. A. 1968. Inhibition of *in vitro* cytotoxicity of lymphocytes from patients with ulcerative colitis and granulomatous colitis for allogeneic colon epithelial cells using horse anti-human thymus serum. *Gastroenterology* 54:227.

————, Cardoza, M., Spencer, R. J., and Huizenga, K. A. 1969a. Further studies of *in vitro* cytotoxicity of lymphocytes from patients with ulcerative and granulomatous colitis for allogeneic colonic epithelial cells, including the effects of colectomy. *Gastroenterology* 56:304.

————, ————, Huizenga, K. A., Re Mine, S. G., and Spencer, R. J. 1969b. Further studies of *in vitro* cytotoxicity of lymphocytes for colonic epithelial cells. *Gastroenterology* 57:30.

Sifneos, P. E. 1964. *Ascent from Chaos.* Cambridge: Harvard University Press.

Singer, H. C., Anderson, J. G. D., Frischer, H., and Kirsner, J. B. 1971. Familial aspects of inflammatory bowel disease. *Gastroenterology* 61:423.

Sleight, D. R., Galpin, J. E., and Condon, R. E. 1971. Ulcerative colitis in female monozygotic twins and a female sibling. *Gastroenterology* 61:507.

Sloan, W. P., Jr., Bargen, J. A., and Gage, R. P. 1950. Life histories of patients with chronic ulcerative colitis; a review of 2,000 cases. *Gastroenterology* 16:25.

Smith, R. F., and Szilagyi, D. E. 1960. Ischemia of the colon as a complication in the surgery of the abdominal aorta. *Arch. Surg.* 80:806.

Soergel, K. H., and Ingelfinger, F. J. 1961. Proteins in serum and rectal mucus of patients with ulcerative colitis. *Gastroenterology* 40:37.

Sparberg, M., and Kirsner, J. B. 1965. Corticosteroid therapy of ulcerative colitis: Status after 15 years. *Curr. Ther. Res.* 7:324.

————, Fennessy, J., and Kirsner, J. B. 1966. Ulcerative proctitis and mild ulcerative colitis: a study of 220 patients. *Medicine* (Baltimore) 45:391.

Spencer, J., and Kirsner, J. B. 1962. Experience with short- and long-term courses of local adrenal steroid therapy for ulcerative colitis. *Gastroenterology* 42:669.

Sperling, M. 1946. Psychoanalytic study of ulcerative colitis in children. *Psychoanal. Q.* 15:302.

———— 1949. The role of the mother in psychosomatic disorders in children. *Psychosom. Med.* 11:377.

———— 1955. Psychosis and psychosomatic illness. *Int. J. Psychoanal.* 36:320.

———— 1957. The psychoanalytic treatment of ulcerative colitis. *Int. J. Psychoanal.* 38:341.

———— 1959. Psychiatric aspects of ulcerative colitis. *N.Y. State J. Med.* 59:3801.

———— 1960. Unconscious phantasy life and object relationships in ulcerative colitis. *Int. J. Psychoanal.* 41:450.

———— 1969. Ulcerative colitis in children. *J. Am. Acad. Child. Psychiatry* 8:336.

Spriggs, E. A., Code, C. F., Bargen, J. A., Curtis, R., and Hightower, N. 1951. Motility of the pelvic colon and rectum of normal persons and patients with ulcerative colitis. *Gastroenterology* 19:480.

Stefani, S., and Finnk, S. 1967a. The ulcerative colitis lymphocyte: Reaction to *E. coli* 0:14 and colon antigens. *Scand. J. Gastroenterol.* 2:333.

———— and ———— 1967b. Effect of *E. coli* antigens, tuberculin and phytohemagglutinin upon ulcerative colitis lymphocytes. *Gut* 8:249.

Stewart, W. A. 1949. Ulcerative colitis. *Am. J. Med.* 6:486.

Stout, C., and Snyder, R. L. 1969. Ulcerative colitis-like lesion in Siamang gibbons. *Gastroenterology* 57:256.

Sullivan, A. J. 1936. Psychogenic factors in ulcerative colitis. *Am. J. Dig. Dis.* 2:651.

———— and Chandler, A. C. 1932. Ulcerative colitis of psychogenic origin: a report of 6 cases. *Yale J. Biol. Med.* 4:779.

Sundby, H. S., and Auestad, A. 1967. Ulcerative colitis in children. *Acta Psychol. Scand.* 43:410.

Swartz, S., and Semrad, E. 1951. Psychosomatic disorders and psychosis. *Psychosom. Med.* 13:314.

Szasz, T. 1950. Physiological and psychodynamic mechanisms in constipation and diarrhoea. *Psychosom. Med.* 13:112.

———— 1951. Oral mechanisms in constipation and diarrhea. *Int. J. Psychoanal.* 32:196.

Taylor, K. B. 1965. Immune mechanisms in gastroenterology. In *Recent Advances in Gastroenterology*, edited by J. Badenoch and B. N. Brooke. Boston: Little, Brown.

———— and Truelove, S. C. 1961. Circulating antibodies to milk proteins in ulcerative colitis. *Br. Med. J.* 2:924.

———— and ———— 1962. Immunological reactions in gastrointestinal disease: A review. *Gut* 3:277.

Thayer, W. R., Jr., and Bove, J. R. 1965. Blood groups and ulcerative colitis. *Gastroenterology* 48:326.

————, and Spiro, H. M. 1963. Protein abnormalities in ulcerative colitis patients and their families. *Gastroenterology* 44:444.

————, Brown, M., Sangree, M. H., Katz, J., and Hersh, T. 1969. *Escherichia coli* 0:14 and colon hemagglutinating antibodies in inflammatory bowel disease. *Gastroenterology* 57:311.

Theodor, E., Gilon, E., and Waks, U. 1968. Treatment of ulcerative colitis with azathioprine. *Br. Med. J.* 2:741.

Thompson, R. A., Asquith, P., and Cooke, W. T. 1969. Secretory IgA in the serum. *Lancet* ii:517.

Tokumaru, T. 1966. A possible role of gamma A immunoglobulin in herpes simplex virus infection in man. *J. Immunol.* 97:248.

Tomasi, T. B., Jr. 1968. Human immunoglobulin A. *N. Engl. J. Med.* 279:1327.

Truelove, S. C. 1961. Ulcerative colitis provoked by milk. *Br. Med. J.* 1:154.

———— 1966. Movements of the large intestine. *Physiol. Rev.* 46:457.

———— 1971a. Medical management. *Br. Med. J.* 1:651.

————. 1971b. Course and prognosis. In *Regional Enteritis*, edited by A. Engel and T. Larsson. Stockholm: Nordiska.

———— and Richards, W. C. D. 1956. Biopsy studies in ulcerative colitis. *Br. Med. J.* 1:1315.

Tunis, M. M., and Dorken, J., Jr. 1951. A case of reactive depression suffering from ulcerative colitis: serial psychological investigation. *Psychiat. Q.* 25(Suppl. 1):22.

Ustvedt, H. J. 1958. Ulcerative colitis: a study of cases discharged from Norwegian hospitals. In *Recent Studies in Epidemiology*, edited by J. Pemberton and H. Willard. Oxford: Blackwell.

Verrier Jones, J., Housley, P., Ashurst, C., and Hawkins, F. 1969. Development of delayed hypersensitivity to dinitrochlorobenzene in patients with Crohn's Disease. *Gut* 10:52.

Von Kleist, S., and Burtin, P. 1966. On the specificity of autoantibodies present in colon carcinoma patients. *Immunology* 10:507.

Warren, S., and Sommers, S. 1949. Pathogenesis of ulcerative colitis. *Am. J. Pathol.* 25:657.

Watson, D. W., Styler, H. J., and Bolt, R. J. 1965. The autologous leukocyte skin test in patients with ulcerative colitis. *Gastroenterology* 49:649.

————, Quigley, A., and Bolt, R. J. 1966. Effect of lymphocytes from patients with ulcerative colitis on human adult colon epithelial cells. *Gastroenterology* 51:985.

Watt, J., and Marcus, R. 1971. Carrageenan-induced ulceration of the large intestine in the guinea pig. *Gut* 12:164.

Watts, J. McK., de Dombal, F. T., Watkinson, G., and Goligher, J. C. 1966a. Early course of ulcerative colitis. *Gut* 7:16.

————, ————, ————, and ———— 1966b. Long-term prognosis of ulcerative colitis. *Br. Med. J.* 1:1447.

Webb, R. L., Jr. 1965. The occurrences of ulcerative colitis in twin males. *Gastroenterology* 50:323.

Weeks, D. M. 1946. Observations of small and large bowel motility in man. *Gastroenterology* 6:185.

Weiner, H. A., and Lewis, C. M. 1960. Some notes on the epidemiology of non-specific ulcerative colitis: an apparent increase in incidence in Jews. *Am. J. Dig. Dis.* 5:406.

Weinstein, L. 1961. Bacteriologic aspects of ulcerative colitis. *Gastroenterology* 40:323.

Weinstock, H. I. 1961. Hospital psychotherapy in severe ulcerative colitis. *Arch. Gen. Psychiatry* 4:509.

Wener, J., and Polonsky, A. 1950. The reaction of the human colon to naturally occurring and experimentally induced emotional states. Observations through a transverse colostomy on a patient with ulcerative colitis. *Gastroenterology* 15:84.

————, Morton, H. S., and Polonsky, A. 1952. The effect of vagotomy on colonic function; observations through a transverse colostomy in a patient with ulcerative colitis. *Gastroenterology* 22:250.

West, H. F. 1949. The etiology of ankylosing spondylitis. *Ann. Rheum. Dis.* 8:143.

West, K. L. 1970. MMPI correlates of ulcerative colitis. *J. Clin. Psychol.* 26:214.

Whang, H., and Neter, E. 1962. Immunological studies of a heterogenetic enterobacterial antigen (Kunin). *J. Bacteriol.* 84:1245.

———— and ———— 1967. Further studies on effect of endotoxin on antibody response of rabbits to common antigen of enterobacteriaciae. *J. Immunol.* 98:948.

Whybrow, P. C., Kane, F. J., Jr., and Lipton, M. A. 1968. Regional ileitis and psychiatric disorder. *Psychosom. Med.* 30:209.

Wigley, R. D., and McLaurin, B. P. 1962. A study of ulcerative colitis in New Zealand showing a low incidence in Maoris. *Br. Med. J.* 2:228.

Wijsenbeek, H., Maoz, B., Nitzan, I., and Gill, R. 1968. Ulcerative colitis: Psychiatric and psychological study of 22 patients. *Psychiatr. Neurol. Neurochir.* 71:409.

Winstone, N. E., Henderson, A. J., and Brooke, B. N. 1960. Blood-groups and secretor status in ulcerative colitis. *Lancet* ii:64.

Wittkower, E. 1938. Ulcerative colitis: Personality studies. *Br. Med. J.* 2:1356.

Wolf, J. K. 1962. Primary acquired agammaglobulinemia, with a family history of collagen disease and hematological disorder. *N. Engl. J. Med.* 266:473.

————, Gokcen, M., and Good, R. A. 1963. Heredo-familial disease of the mesenchymal tissues: clinical and laboratory study of one family. *J. Lab. Clin. Med.* 61:230.

Wolf, S. 1966. The central nervous system regulation of the colon. *Gastroenterology* 51:810.

Wright, R. and Truelove, S. C. 1966a. Circulating and tissue eosinophils in ulcerative colitis. *Am. J. Dig. Dis.* 11:831.

———— and ———— 1966b. Autoimmune reactions in ulcerative colitis. *Gut* 7:32.

————, Lumsden, K., Luntz, M. H., Sevel, D., and Truelove, S. C. 1965. Abnormalities of the sacro-iliac joints and uveitis in ulcerative colitis. *Q. J. Med.* 34:229.

Wright, V., and Watkinson, G. 1959. The arthritis of ulcerative colitis. *Medicine* 38:243.

———— and ———— 1965. Sacro-iliitis and ulcerative colitis. *Br. Med. J.* 2:675.

———— and ———— 1966. Articular complications of ulcerative colitis. *Am. J. Proctol.* 17:107.

Wynne, L. C., Rychoff, I., Day, J., and Hersh, S. H. 1958. Pseudomutuality in the family relations of schizophrenics. *Psychiatry* 21:205.

Young, J. R., Humphries, A. W., DeWolfe, V. G., and Lefevre, F. A. 1963. Complications of abdominal aortic surgery. II. Intestinal ischemia. *Arch. Surg.* 86:51.

Zweibaum, A., Morard, J. C., and Halpern, B. 1968. Réalisation d'une côlite ulcéro-hémorragique expérimentale par immunisation bactérieene. *Pathol. Biol.* (Paris) 16:813.

Crohn's Disease

Acheson, E. D. 1960. The distribution of ulcerative colitis and regional enteritis in United States veterans, with particular reference to the Jewish religion. *Gut* 1:291.

———— 1965. Epidemiology of ulcerative colitis and regional enteritis. In *Recent Advances in Gastroenterology,* edited by J. Badenoch and B. N. Brooke. London: Churchill.

———— and Nefzeger, M. D. 1963. Ulcerative colitis in the United States Army in 1944. *Gastroenterology* 44:7.

Allen, A. C. 1971. A unified concept of the vascular pathogenesis of enterocolitis of varied etiology. *Am. J. Gastroenterol.* 55:347.

Almy, T. P., and Sherlock, P. 1966. Genetic aspects of ulcerative colitis and regional enteritis. *Gastroenterology* 51:757.

Amman, R. W., and Bockus, H. L. 1961. Pathogenesis of regional enteritis. *Arch. Intern. Med.* 107:504.

Blackburn, G., Hadfield, G., and Hunt, A. H. 1939. Regional Ileitis. *St. Barth. Hosp. Rep.* 72:181.

Cohn, E. M., Lederman, I. I., and Shore, E. 1970. Regional enteritis and its relation to emotional disorders. *Am. J. Gastroenterol.* 54:378.

Crispin, A. R., and Tempany, E. 1967. Crohn's disease of the jejunum in children. *Arch. Dis. Child.* 42:631.

Crocket, R. W. 1952. Psychiatric findings in Crohn's disease. *Lancet* i:946.

Crohn, B. B. 1949. *Regional Ileitis.* London: Staples.

———— and Yarnis, H. 1958. *Regional Ileitis.* New York: Grune Stratton.

————, ————, and Korelitz, B. I. 1956. Regional ileitis complicating pregnancy. *Gastroenterology* 31:615.

Cuthbertson, A. M., and Hughes, E. S. R. 1969. A comparative study of ulcerative colitis and Crohn's disease in Cleveland, Ohio and in Melbourne. *Gut* 10:952.

Donaldson, R. M., Jr. 1973. Regional enteritis. In *Gastrointestinal Disease,* edited by M. H. Sleisenger and J. S. Fordtran. Philadelphia: Saunders.

Dyer, N. H., and Dawson, A. M. 1970. Diagnosis of Crohn's disease. A continuing source of error. *Br. Med. J.* 1:735.

Edwards, F. C., and Truelove, S. C. 1964. The course and prognosis of ulcerative colitis. III. Complications. *Gut* 5:1.

Engel, G. L. 1973. Ulcerative colitis. In *Emotional Factors in Gastrointestinal Illness,* edited by A. E. Lindner. Amsterdam: Excerpta Medica.

Evans, J. G., and Acheson, E. D. 1965. An epidemiological study of ulcerative colitis and regional enteritis in the Oxford area. *Gut* 6:311.

Fahrländer, H., and Baerlocher, C. 1971. Clinical features and epidemiological data in the Basle Area. In *Regional Enteritis,* edited by A. Engel and T. Larsson. Stockholm: Nordiska.

Feldman, F., Cantor, D., Soll, S., and Bachrach, W. 1967. Psychiatric study of a consecutive series of 19 patients with regional ileitis. *Br. Med. J.* 4:711.

Ford, C. V., Glober, G. A., and Castelnuovo-Tedesco, P. 1969. A psychiatric study of patients with regional enteritis. *J.A.M.A.* 208:311.

Gjone, E., Orning, O. M., and Myren, J. 1966. Crohn's disease in Norway, 1956–1963. *Gut* 7:372.

Grace, W. J. 1954. Life stress and regional ileitis. *Gastroenterology* 23:542.

Hammer, B., Ashurst, P., and Naish, J. 1968. Diseases associated with ulcerative colitis and Crohn's disease. *Gut* 9:17.

Hislop, I. G., and Grant, A. K. 1970. Genetic tendency in Crohn's disease. *Gut* 10:994.

Houghton, E. A. W., and Naish, J. M. 1958. Familial ulcerative colitis and ileitis. *Gastroenterologia* (Basel) 89:65.

Jeffries, G. H., Steinberg, H., and Sleisenger, M. H. 1968. Chronic ulcerative nongranulomatous jejunitis. *Am. J. Med.* 44:47.

Kent, T. H., Ammon, R. K., and Denbesten, L. 1970. Differentiation of ulcerative colitis and Crohn's disease of the colon. *Arch. Pathol.* 89:20.

Kirsner, J. B., and Spencer, J. 1963. Family occurrences of ulcerative colitis, regional enteritis and ileocolitis. *Ann. Intern. Med.* 59:133.

Korelitz, B. I. 1967. Clinical course, late results and pathological nature of inflammatory disease of the colon initially sparing the rectum. *Gut* 8:281.

Kraft, I. A., and Ardali, C. 1964. A psychiatric study of children with the diagnosis of regional ileitis. *South. Med. J.* 57:799.

Krause, U. 1971. Epidemiology in Sweden. In *Regional Enteritis*, edited by A. Engel and T. Larsson. Stockholm: Nordiska.

Kyle, J., and Blair, D. W. 1965. Epidemiology of regional enteritis in North-east Scotland. *Brit. J. Surg.* 52:215.

Law, D. H. 1969. Regional enteritis. *Gastroenterology* 56:1086.

Lennard-Jones, J. E., Lockhart-Mummery, H. E., and Morson, B. C. 1968. Clinical and pathological differentiation of Crohn's disease and proctocolitis. *Gastroenterology* 54:1162.

Lockhart-Mummery, H. E., and Morson, B. C. 1960. Crohn's disease (regional enteritis) of the large intestine and its distinction from ulcerative colitis. *Gut* 1:87.

———— and ———— 1964. Crohn's disease of the large intestine. *Gut* 5:493.

McConnell, R. B. 1971. Genetic factors in Crohn's disease. In *Regional Enteritis*, edited by A. Engel and T. Larsson. Stockholm: Nordiska.

McGovern, V. J., and Goulston, S. J. M. 1968. Crohn's disease of the colon. *Gut* 9:164.

McKegney, F. P., Gordon, R. O., and Levine, S. M. 1970. A psychosomatic comparison of patients with ulcerative colitis and Crohn's disease. *Psychosom. Med.* 32:153.

Mendeloff, A. I. 1972. Crohn's disease: Progress confounded. *Ann. Intern. Med.* 76:138.

————, Monk, M., Siegel, C. I., and Lilienfeld, A. 1966. Some epidemiological features of ulcerative colitis and regional enteritis. A preliminary report. *Gastroenterology* 51:748.

Mersereau, S. 1963. Regional ileitis in depressed patients. *Am. J. Psychiatry* 119:1099.

Meyer, J. H., and Sleisenger, M. H. 1973. Granulomatous disease of the colon. In *Gastrointestinal Disease*, edited by M. H. Sleisenger and J. S. Fordtran. Philadelphia: Saunders.

Monk, M., Mendeloff, A. I., Siegel, C. I., and Lilienfeld, A. 1967. An epidemiological study of ulcerative colitis and regional enteritis among adults in Baltimore. I. Hospital incidence and prevalence, 1960 to 1963. *Gastroenterology* 53:198.

————, ————, ————, and ———— 1969. An epidemiological study of ulcerative colitis and regional enteritis among adults in Baltimore. II. Social and demographic factors. *Gastroenterology* 56:847.

————, ————, ————, and ———— 1970. An epidemiological study of ulcerative colitis and regional enteritis among adults in Baltimore. III. Psychological and possible stress precipitating factors. *J. Chronic. Dis.* 22:565.

Morris, P. J. 1965. Familial ulcerative colitis. *Gut* 6:176.

Morson, B. C. 1968. Histopathology of Crohn's disease. *Proc. R. Soc. Med.* 61:79.

Myren, J. 1971. Discussion in *Regional Enteritis*, edited by A. Engel and T. Larsson. Stockholm: Nordiska.

Norlén, B. J., Krause, U., and Bergman, L. 1970. An epidemiological study of Crohn's disease. *Scand. J. Gastroenterol.* 5:385.

573

Paulley, J. W. 1948. Regional ileitis. *Lancet* i:923.

———— 1949. Chronic diarrhea. *Proc. R. Soc. Med.* 42:241.

———— 1971. Crohn's disease. *Psychother. Psychosom.* 19:111.

Rappaport, H., Burgoyne, F., and Smetana, H. 1951. The pathology of regional enteritis. *Military Surg.* 109:463.

Riemer, M. D. 1960. Ileitis-underlying aggressive conflicts. *N. Y. State J. Med.* 60:552.

Ruble, P. E., Meyers, S. G., and Ashley, L. B. 1957. Regional enteritis. *Harper Hosp. Bull.* 15:142.

Sherlock, P., Bell, B., Steinberg, H., and Almy, T. 1963. Familial occurrence of regional enteritis and ulcerative colitis. *Gastroenterology* 45:413.

Singer, H. C., Anderson, J. G. D., Frischer, H., and Kirsner, J. B. 1971. Familial aspects of inflammatory bowel disease. *Gastroenterology* 61:423.

Smith, T. 1971. Discussion in *Regional Enteritis*, edited by A. Engel and T. Larsson. Stockholm: Nordiska.

Sperling, M. 1960. The psychoanalytic treatment of regional ileitis. *Int. J. Psychoanal.* 41:612.

Steigmann, F., and Shapiro, S. 1961. Familial regional enteritis. *Gastroenterology* 40:215.

Stewart, W. A. 1949. Psychosomatic aspects of regional ileitis. *N.Y. State J. Med.* 49:2820.

Strande, A., Sommers, S. C., and Petrak, M. 1954. Regional enterocolitis in cocker spaniel dogs. *Arch. Pathol.* 57:357.

Truelove, S. C. 1971. Course and prognosis. In *Regional Enteritis*, edited by A. Engel and T. Larsson. Stockholm: Nordiska.

Whybrow, P. C., Kane, F. J., Jr., and Lipton, M. A. 1968. Regional ileitis and psychiatric disorder. *Psychosom. Med.* 30:209.

Yamase, K., Masuda, K., Shimada, S., and Yamada, Y. 1967. Regional enteritis in Japan: A review of 548 cases. *Int. Surg.* 47:497.

7

PSYCHOBIOLOGICAL CONTRIBUTIONS TO HUMAN DISEASE

THE PREDISPOSITION TO DISEASE

We have no complete explanation of all the causes of any disease. Most medical explanations of disease are functional in nature. For example, they tell us about the relationship of a low cardiac output to pulmonary edema, but they do not tell us why at a particular point in time the heart failed. In other words, most explanations of the symptoms and signs of a disease (and the functional disturbances that they express) do not explain its antecedents. But the disadvantage of historical explanation is that it is descriptive and not predictive—the variety of animal or plant species can, in part, be explained by genetic mutation, but the theory does not predict when a new mutation will occur. A complete theory of disease would allow us to predict who is at risk for a particular disease and when and in what circumstances the predisposed person is likely to develop it. A complete theory of disease would need to be functional, historical, and predictive.

The contribution of psychosomatic research to medicine has been to provide historical as well as functional explanations of certain diseases. The contributors have concentrated on the historical nature of the psychological predisposition. But they tended at first to overemphasize the role of the psychological predisposition in the etiology of disease. It remained for Alexander (1950) to redress the balance and point out that the conflicts* that

---

* The conflicts that Alexander described had their historical roots in childhood. The explanation that psychological conflict plays a role in the inception of disease is a functional one.

correlated with a disease made up only a part of the predisposing variance. Significantly, he also stated, in 1950, that there were additional (possibly genetically determined) physiological and biochemical predisposing factors which, in conjunction with the specific conflict, were the necessary if not sufficient conditions anteceding the disease.

Alexander did not specify the nature of the biochemical and physiological factors that predisposed to the diseases that he had studied. It remained for Mirsky (1957) to specify one of these. He suggested that because of genetic variation, serum levels of the enzyme-precursor pepsinogen might be higher in some members of a population than in others. Those with the highest levels of serum pepsinogen might be at risk for the development of peptic duodenal ulcer if they were also psychologically predisposed (by virtue of unconscious conflict) to the disease, and also were exposed to a setting that activated the conflict. Mirsky was proposing both an historical and a predictive explanation of peptic duodenal ulcer. Its predictive nature was shown to be correct (Weiner et al., 1957; Yessler et al., 1959).

Since that time it has become clear that Alexander was correct in general. In order for a disease to occur, multiple predispositions must be present. But when a person is predisposed to a disease, it does not mean that he is fated to fall ill with it.

It is now possible to specify many of the predisposing factors for each of the diseases reviewed in this book. In addition to psychological conflicts, the predisposing factors to duodenal ulcer may in some patients consist of elevated levels of serum pepsinogen, an increased parietal cell mass in the stomach, increased rates of gastric acid secretion, and a disturbance in the regulatory relationship between gastrin and hydrochloric acid. But not all patients with duodenal ulcer have high resting rates of gastric acid secretion. And the disturbance in regulation and increase in parietal cell mass has only been proven for some patients with the disease.

Disturbances in the regulation of the bronchiolar musculature, producing a bronchoconstrictor tendency, are the necessary predisposing factors in bronchial asthma. But a person must also be psychologically predisposed to bronchial asthma. And, at least in the extrinsic form of the disease, he or she must have the capacity to form IgE antibodies. The capacity to form these antibodies does not inevitably lead to asthma. They must also be fixed by cells in the bronchial wall.

We know less about the multiple predispositions to essential hypertension, ulcerative colitis, rheumatoid arthritis, and Graves' disease, despite the fact that a great deal is known about the pathophysiology in all but ulcerative colitis. Therefore, we have an almost complete functional explanation of these diseases. Much still needs to be learned about the historical origins of the physiological disturbances that characterize these diseases.

The fact that anticolon antibodies are found in the serum of the healthy relatives of patients with ulcerative colitis and regional enteritis is tantalizing evidence that their presence predisposes to the diseases. Rheumatoid factors also occur with an increased incidence in the family members of patients with rheumatoid arthritis. The presence of rheumatoid factors in the blood of many suggests that a considerable number of persons have a tendency and excessive capacity to form them, but only some develop rheumatoid arthritis; others develop only rheumatoid nodules, and still others either systemic lupus erythematosus (SLE) or no disease at all. The inability to produce IgG antibodies, rather than an excessive capacity, also constitutes a risk factor for rheumatoid arthritis. The excessive capacity to form a number of antibodies—the long-acting thyroid stimulator (LATS) and its protector, antithyroglobulin, thyroid antimicrosomal and antinuclear antibodies—characterizes Graves' disease, and may predispose to it.

Being predisposed to a disease does not necessarily mean that one will get it. A comprehensive theory of disease should also explain why many predisposed persons remain healthy. One reason is that additional factors, such as psychological maturity and health, may play a role in maintaining physical health in some undisclosed manner. Another reason might be that single predisposing factors are never etiologically sufficient. They must be combined with one or several additional predisposing factors.

This statement is best exemplified by gout—a disease that has not been discussed in this book. Most, but not all, patients with gout have elevated serum uric acid (SUA) levels. Only a small proportion of those with elevated SUA levels develop gout. Yet, the obese son of a gouty father almost inevitably develops gout, if he—the son—also has elevated SUA levels (Katz et al., 1973). Such an observation, however, provides no clues that might resolve several further questions. We still do not know why such a predisposed person develops gout at a particular time in his life and not another, or why recurrences occur at particular moments. Nor do we know why gout is much more frequent in men—in whom it has its onset only after puberty. Women usually only develop gout after the menopause; but with the introduction and use of oral contraceptives, the incidence of gout seems to be increasing in younger women.

Clearly, some additional mechanisms must be identified before we have a better understanding of this disease. One point of departure is that the elevated levels of serum uric acid are probably the product of a variety of different mechanisms: either active secretion of urate by the distal kidney tubules is impaired, excessive purine biosynthesis (whose causes are in turn heterogeneous) occurs, or the biosynthetic and renal variations may be combined. These variations are under genetic control (Kelley et al., 1967); whether the same genes account both for the obesity and for the variations of enzyme levels that lead to excessive purine biosynthesis remains unknown.

A variety of enzymatic defects produce elevated levels of SUA. These enzymatic defects take different forms. In some instances, enzyme levels are low; in other instances, the chemical structure of enzyme is abnormal. Different genes are responsible for these different enzymatic defects (Kelley et al., 1967). An historical explanation of a disease must include an account of how a predisposition, such as elevated SUA levels, comes about. The answer in this example seems to be that predispositions may come about in different ways.

Indeed that has been the tentative conclusion of the review carried out in this book. Some believe that the tendency to bronchoconstriction in bronchial asthma is innate; some believe it is due to early life experience. Alexander (1950) thought that increased gastric acid secretion was the product of long-standing wishes to be fed that caused continuous vagal discharge. Some believe that chronic gastric hypersecretion is the result of an inherited increase in the parietal cell mass. There are other possible answers: Mirsky (1958) postulated that increased pepsinogen and pepsin production in the stomach might somehow alter the mother-child relationship and cause the predisposing psychological conflict to a disease, such as peptic duodenal ulcer. Answers to the question of the origins of all the predisposing factors in these diseases are urgently needed.

The recognition and specification of multiple factors that predispose to "psychosomatic" (and other) diseases is a major step forward. Once identified, the predisposing factors make a partial predictive explanation of a disease possible. The explanation is only partial, because we have also learned that the same factors may predispose for different diseases —for example, IgE antibodies predispose to allergic rhinitis, atopic eczema, and bronchial asthma. And different factors may predispose to the same disease. Therefore, a full explanation of the "choice" of a disease is only partly answered by our present knowledge of its predispositions.

The Problem of the Choice of a Disease

If these assertions and speculations about the nature of psychobiological predispositions are borne out, it would have to be assumed that in any population there is a pool of persons at risk for a certain disease, and to whom the risk has been imparted by the presence of a specific combination of the several predisposing factors. It would be the particular constellation of predisposing factors that specify the disease. Although we do not yet know why antibodies are fixed in one person by the skin and in another by the nasal or bronchial mucosa, this approach assumes that, for example, a child with a predisposition to form reaginic antibodies may either develop atopic dermatitis, allergic rhinitis, or bronchial asthma. According to this view, the child will develop bronchial asthma only when there is an (additional) predisposition to bronchoconstriction, and if the reaginic antibodies are fixed in the tissue of the lung. In such a child, the tendency to form these antibodies, to fix them in the mucosa of the lung, and to develop bronchoconstriction form some of the predisposition to asthmatic illness. They are "givens." Additional factors (such as exposure to an allergen and/or specific psychological events) determine when the asthmatic attack will occur.

Alexander was clearly correct in asserting that it is not the specific psychological conflict *alone* that specifies the "choice of illness," but that a combination of factors account for the fact that one person and not another may develop a particular disease. Thus, a child may be psychologically predisposed, but physiologically and immunologically not predisposed, to bronchial asthma. On the other hand, the child who is not psychologically predisposed to bronchial asthma, even if he does have the immunological and physiological predisposition, may not develop the disease.

The question of how much of the overall predisposing variance is accounted for by each of the predispositions to bronchial asthma has been illuminated by the work of Leigh, Rees, Block and co-workers (Chapter 3). According to their observations, the contributions of the individual factors to the predisposing variance may differ from person to person, and in different age groups of people at risk. Substance has been added to these formulations by our present understanding of other diseases. Elevated levels of serum pepsinogen occur in persons who do not develop peptic ulcer, while antinuclear antibodies are present in the serum of persons who do not have SLE, and who may never develop it. Until a sound epidemiology of autoantibodies and many other substances in blood has been developed, many of the questions about predisposition and disease itself will remain unanswered.

Perhaps the manner in which Alexander enunciated his multiple factor hypothesis can help us to understand why combinations of these diseases may occur. Diseases do cluster —for example, peptic ulcer and rheumatoid arthritis commonly occur in the same person.

582

Although this fact has been used to refute Alexander's initial hypothesis that specific psychological conflicts correlate with specific diseases, such a clustering of diseases could equally well mean that both conflicts are present in the one person; one conflict is activated at one time, the other at a different time.

An alternative hypothesis would be that a person may carry within him multiple psychological predispositions—a predisposition, for example, to rheumatoid arthritis by virtue of his capacities to form rheumatoid factors, to have an increased parietal cell mass, and to form greater quantities of hydrochloric acid, gastrin and pepsin (or a particular pepsinogen isoenzyme), or for the relationship between these variables to be altered. Is there any evidence for such a postulation? Gastrin levels are increased in patients with rheumatoid arthritis and may become elevated with the experimental production of adjuvant arthritis in the rat. We have seen that patients with rheumatoid arthritis not only form rheumatoid factors but also antinuclear antibodies, and that patients with Graves' disease, thyroiditis, and primary adult hypothyroidism and myxedema are characterized by the tendency to form antithyroglobulin antibodies. Although we cannot explain them at present, such correlations should ultimately help us understand why several diseases occur in the same person. Yet, patients with Graves' disease may also form antibodies against gastric parietal cells without developing atrophic gastritis, and patients with primary myxedema form antibodies against adrenocortical cell components without suffering from adrenocortical insufficiency.

It is significant to note that in the last two examples, a change in normal function is not always expressed as disease. The presence of specific antibodies against the cellular components of an organ may not be reflected in altered function (such as lowered gastric secretion or adrenocortical insufficiency), or structure (gastritis or adrenocortical atrophy). This principle is well illustrated in molecular disease, in which a structural change in an enzyme may exist without its being expressed as disease. Of equal interest is that a disease is expressed, in part, in response to a quantitative factor: the complete absence of an enzyme is expressed in one way; the relative deficiency of the same enzyme is reflected in another manner, or not at all.

An elucidation of these phenomena would, perhaps, clarify what has always been assumed, if not proven—that the incidence and prevalence of some diseases varies in different historical periods. This observation has suggested that the pool of predisposed persons in a specific population may be quite stable, but that changing environmental conditions may alter the frequency with which the predispositions are expressed. In any theory of disease, changing environmental conditions must, of course, be taken into account: changes in nutrition, social, political, economic, familial, and historical conditions may prove stressful to some persons but not to others. The rate at which such changes occur may also be critical to some, with the form of their disease varying according to the nature of their correlated predispositions.

In any stable pool of predisposed persons, therefore, the rate and character of change in the human and physical environment may elicit some diseases in fewer or more members of the pool at any given time. Cross-cultural comparisons may additionally disclose that the number of predisposed persons in two cultures may be different. The potentiating effect of stressful environmental change on predisposed individuals has been, in part, extrapolated from the data on the study (Chapter 1) of young men in the U.S. Army who were at risk for peptic ulcer. Of the 63 subjects, 9 were either found to have ulcers or to later develop ulcers over a period of 8 to 16 weeks. Only one other man developed an ulcer during the subjects' remaining two-year service in the Army.

This observation neither refutes nor denies Alexander's "specificity" hypothesis in regard to understanding why a person develops a series of diseases. Within this framework, it becomes vital to consider the significance of factors of aging, particularly for the serial development of disease. A predisposition may be present, but it only takes expression in clinical form after a particular period of time has passed. Genetic factors, for example, are believed to play a role in schizophrenia, gout, and diabetes mellitus, yet the peak incidence of these diseases is many years after birth. In gout, serum uric acid levels do not begin to diverge until puberty. The onset of primary anorexia nervosa is said most often to occur before puberty in boys and at or about menarche in girls. With rheumatoid arthritis the incidence of the disease peaks at the age of 45 to 50, when the incidence of the presence of rheumatoid factors in serum also rises sharply.

The choice of a disease is, therefore, partially determined by several predisposing factors. Being predisposed to a disease does not mean that the disease will inevitably develop. But no disease will develop if the person is not predisposed to it. The fluctuating incidence of some diseases suggests that in every population there are more persons predisposed to disease than develop it. As environmental conditions change, a greater or lesser number of persons develop the disease. The same exogenous source—such as a drug—of the disease does not inevitably produce the same morbid condition; it may produce different diseases in different persons. The specific disease produced by the drug depends on the person's predispositions to it.

Predisposing Factors May Be Age-dependent

Unfortunately, we do not know enough yet about developmental physiology to draw firm conclusions about the age-dependent and age-related aspects of physiological processes. There is, however, provocative evidence indicating that a number of basic immunological and physiological mechanisms may alter during maturation and with aging. Some immunoglobulins produced in the young appear to be highly specific to an antigen; they possess little or no capacity to cross-react with other antigens. With maturation and aging, changes occur in the synthesis—and, thus, the structure—of these immunoglobulins, resulting in a diminution of the tendency to react only with specific antigens. With aging, the capacity of these immunoglobulins to react with several, albeit related, antigens is widened. As a result, broad-spectrum antibodies are produced and a range of cross-reactions with several chemically similar antigens may take place. It is possible that such alterations occur both in the systems mediating humoral antibodies and in the recognition system mediated by cellular immunity.

Age-dependent changes in the regulation of heart rate (Hofer and Reiser, 1969), the regulation of renal function, and related maturational patterns of the circadian output of pituitary hormones—such as luteinizing (LH) and follicle stimulating hormones (FSH)—have also been described (Boyar et al., 1972). Age-inappropriate patterns of LH secretion in women with primary anorexia nervosa have now been observed during both late adolescence and early adulthood (Boyar et al., 1974). Although we do not as yet know

584

whether the immature pattern of LH secretion is an antecedent or consequent condition of this disease, the finding emphasizes the need to study the relationship of personality development to physiological development in much greater detail. It also underlines the prospect that disease may involve, on both the psychological and physiological levels, limitations in the capacity to adapt to specific situational events—not only at different ages, but as a result of lags in the maturation of regulatory mechanisms involved in adaptation.

The contributions of the various predisposing factors, then, may vary with the age of the person, possibly because a particular predisposing factor (such as autoimmune antibody) has not yet been formed, or because a maturational lag in important physiological regulatory mechanisms and psychological adaptive capacities has resulted in an alteration in the ability to adapt.

Do Psychosocial Factors Alone Predispose to Disease?

For some time, there has been dissatisfaction with the term "psychosomatic," since it has inevitably implied that the predisposition to, and the initiation of, disease is exclusively "psychogenic." It is a position that can no longer be maintained; but despite the contrary observations and arguments of Alexander, Engel, and Mirsky the concept lingers on. In keeping with their injunctions, it can be asserted quite categorically that the adumbration of social and psychological factors per se is not adequate to explain the predisposing and initiating variances involved in the diseases reviewed in this book, and, perhaps many other diseases.

Alexander did not believe that specific conflictful configurations provided a complete explanation of the etiology and pathogenesis of the diseases with which they were correlated. He stated quite explicitly that these conflicts could occur in persons who never suffered from the disease, and postulated that *additional* "local or somatic" factors—whose relative impact might vary for different individuals—had to be assumed to act in concert with the psychological elements.

Addressing himself to the problem of the "choice" of illness, Alexander generalized that, given the activation of specific psychological conflicts, there must be predisposing bodily factors that would determine the disease. Once activated, the conflicts and the emotions they generated—particularly anger, anxiety, and depression—were mediated by autonomic and endocrine mechanisms that served to initiate the disease. Alexander's view of this process, though a general rather than fully realized statement, is borne out by the material reviewed throughout this volume.

If the concept of multiple, rather than of exclusively psychosocial, predisposing factors is valid, we must identify the relative contributions of each element in the overall dynamic constellation of these predispositions. In any event, since it is now overwhelmingly apparent that psychological and social factors alone do not determine the choice of an illness, the concept of "psychogenicity" can be discarded once and for all. As the thrust of all previous comments indicates, this does not mean that psychosocial factors play no part in the predisposition to disease. The task is to make more-fruitful inquiries as to their nature and their relative contributions in the overall psychobiology of disease.

585

Are There Specific or Nonspecific Psychological Predispositions?

One of the concepts central to the early development of "psychosomatic medicine" has been that specific unconscious conflicts and the emotions they engender are correlated with a specific disease. Derived from Alexander and his colleagues, this view has—either implicitly or explicitly—been a "logical" assumption of many people working in the field. The problem that this view presents, both conceptually and in terms of investigative studies, is remarkably simple: when a person is studied after disease onset, one cannot state irrefutably that certain conflicts—whether observed or inferred—existed in that person prior to falling ill. For this reason alone, it has now become essential that investigators add substance to their formulations by the study of groups prior to disease onset—that is, by testing the predisposition hypothesis in the manner outlined.

Another requirement for future studies is an inevitable conclusion drawn from a review of the literature in the field. The argument as to whether or not there are specific psychological conflicts or attitudes in those predisposed to a disease cannot be resolved if two or more groups of investigators use different methods and instruments, each with different reliabilities and varying capacities to provide the required data. A third "given" for future work—essential to any progress in our understanding of psychobiological disease—is careful selection, control, and evaluation of comparative groups and populations under study.

In all fairness to Alexander and his collaborators, it should be noted that, although they formulated and explicated the hypothesis that specific unconscious conflicts and behaviors could be correlated with specific diseases, they eschewed the concept that specific types of personalities were prone to particular diseases. Alexander described additional and common psychological characteristics such as hostile impulses and fantasies, anxiety, dependent longings, and low self-esteem in patients with these diseases. But he contended that these common characteristics were arranged in different psychological configurations in different diseases. Alexander asserted that specific onset conditions would sensitize and activate the conflicts in vulnerable individuals. These conditions, Alexander implied, were specific to the person experiencing them, and the latent conflict sensitized that person to perceive and interpret the social conditions or settings in terms of his individual predisposition.

The reason for this statement is simple. As our psychological understanding of people has evolved, it has become clear that each personality is a final common pathway of many factors. There is no one unconscious conflict that is expressed in a particular kind of personality type. Conversely, different conflicts may be expressed in the same type of personality (this point was extensively discussed the chapter on bronchial asthma).

Alexander's specificity hypothesis—inductively arrived at—tentatively described the conflicts in patients having one and not another of these diseases. He was carrying out comparative studies. He did not say that the specific conflict observable in one disease was unique to Mankind. He simply stated that it was specific to that disease, but would not explain the occurrence of the disease unless other predisposing factors were also taken into account.

Support for the proposition that there is typically no single and central predisposing conflict is provided by the studies of Engel on ulcerative colitis (1955), Knapp and Nemetz (1960) on bronchial asthma, and Weisman (1956) and de M'Uzan and Bonfils (1961) on peptic duodenal ulcer. Each study concluded that there were several conflicts in individual patients, or across patient groups.

As a possible fruitful future refinement of the concept that multiple specific conflicts are predisposing, there now exists a large body of observed data indicating that patients with the seven diseases reviewed in this volume are more psychologically alike than they are different. This data suggests that for these patients, dependency plays a dominant role in their relationships to others. Unfortunately, in much of this work, "dependent" relationships are not defined further in terms of their quality. Two persons may be dependent in their relationship to other persons, but still have different unconscious conflicts. The nonspecific nature of personal relationships does not itself contradict Alexander's contention that specific unconscious conflicts can be identified in patients who are dependent.

A broader and more generalized view of the psychosocial framework of illness onset has been enunciated by Engel (1965) and Schmale (1958). Their central thesis is that personal loss and bereavement are the general setting in which many diseases (in addition to those reviewed in this book) are initiated. According to Engel, the psychologically predisposed person—especially one who is dependent—responds to loss and bereavement by perceiving and interpreting it as a threat to personal security, and by feelings of helplessness and hopelessness, so that he gives up altogether. In effect, an adaptive psychological failure occurs. Presumably, this adaptive failure has physiological concomitants that antecede disease onset in the predisposed person.

Both Alexander and Engel assume that it is not the precipitating event per se that is of central importance, but rather its meaning for the person and the responses it generates. However, their different interpretations of the essential character of the precipitating "event" or process are difficult to reconcile. Alexander believed that the specific psychological conflict sensitized the patient to respond to specific life experiences. The life experience was colored and made particularly poignant by the conflict. The conflict, in turn, gave special meaning to the life experience. The conflict was activated by the experience ("the repressed returned"), and was accompanied by strong feelings. He implied that the activated conflict did not disrupt other areas of the patient's psychological functioning and, therefore, his adaptation. Engel's concept is much more wide-ranging. Helplessness and hopelessness color all one's attitudes and future prospects. If a person feels helpless, he cannot cope with anything. If there is no hope, future prospects are bleak. Engel's formulation suggests also that it is not the conflict as such that specifies the vulnerability to disease, but variations in adaptive psychological capacities.

These contradictory views are not easily reconciled on the basis of the available evidence. Engel's observations and formulations appear to be valid for some patients with certain diseases, but not for others. They are supported by his observations on patients with ulcerative colitis, and by some of the studies on rheumatoid arthritis, peptic duodenal ulcer, and a subgroup of patients with bronchial asthma. On the other hand, Knapp and his associates (1970) observed that in some patients with bronchial asthma, helplessness and hopelessness were not antecedents and correlates of the asthmatic attack, but that attacks were preceded by a biphasic cycle of excitement and anxiety and followed by depression. Engel's general conclusion that diseases began in a nonspecific setting is also not borne out by Weisman's observations (1956). Weisman has described that several different kinds of settings in addition to bereavement may antecede recurrences of peptic ulcer. Weisman

587

was also able to correlate the settings in which recurrences began with the psychological conflicts of his patients: different settings correlated with different conflicts.

The evidence suggests that specific conflicts, as described by Alexander, occur in about one-half of the patients with these diseases (Alexander et al., 1968). These conflicts sensitize them to rather specific life experiences that act as the initiating event for disease onset. If one studies the personal relationships of these patients, rather than their conflicts, another initiating event comes to the fore—bereavement. But bereavement is not usually the exclusive event, although it is in some patients. In other patients, there was no single conflict and no single event. In them, different conflicts are activated by different life events and experiences.

These conflicting observations and views have usually been ascribed to the unreliability of clinical observation or to the lack of sensitivity of psychological tests used to verify clinical psychiatric observations.

But there may be another explanation: each of the diseases reviewed in this volume is, in all likelihood, heterogeneous in character. Therefore, the different psychiatric observations and formulations may be correct for one subgroup and not another. It follows that all future studies must rigorously define, probably in physiological terms, the subgroup of the disease. The heterogeneity of disease probably accounts for the results of these predictive studies carried out by Alexander and his associates (1968). As noted earlier, despite the fact that this research group's identification of diseases by means of specific psychological criteria was more accurate than could be anticipated on the basis of chance results, they never achieved a diagnostic accuracy greater than 60 percent for any one disease. One reason for this result may well be that representatives from two or more subgroups of a disease were included. Therefore, an acute awareness of the potential importance of the heterogeneity of a disease may not only account for inconsistent data obtained in the past—either by means of observation or by psychological tests—but should also serve to increase the validity of data obtained in the future. To obtain such reliable data, comparison groups must be clearly evaluated, defined, and utilized in the manner in which Moos and Solomon designed their study of patients with rheumatoid arthritis (1966). Granting, of course, that it is often difficult to ascertain whether a patient has a toxic diffuse or multinodular goiter, low- or high-renin hypertension, or one of a number of probably different forms of peptic ulcer, every effort would be made to define research populations along these lines.

The issue of specific or nonspecific psychological predisposition can be summarized by suggesting that, in some areas of psychological functioning, certain specific conflicts and attitudes may obtain only in a subgroup of patients with particular diseases. Other areas of psychological functioning, such as the character of relationships, cannot yet be distinguished in terms of any special quality. If, in addition, these diseases are in fact heterogenous, there may also be heterogeneity in psychological factors; the psychological conflicts and personal relationships may differ in patients suffering from different forms of the same disease.

HOW DO THE PREDISPOSING FACTORS TO DISEASE COME ABOUT?

The observations and other data reviewed throughout this book suggest that there are multiple predispositions to these seven diseases. One of these predispositions is psychological: many of the patients have been sensitized to bereavement, others are sensitized within themselves to more-specific life events by reason of their long-standing conflicts. In adults, the sensitivity to bereavement may come about because they may have lost a parent or another relative earlier in life. But an actual loss may not have previously occurred in their lives. Dependent people react adversely to actual or threatened bereavement because it mobilizes feelings of anger towards or rage at the person upon whom they are no longer able to lean. They also feel that without another's support they cannot cope—they feel helpless. The mobilization of anger or rage may produce conflict because it threatens their relationship with those upon whom they did, or do, depend.

Other patients harbor more-specific conflicts. Some patients with rheumatoid arthritis wish to dominate their husbands or children. The wish to dominate is frustrated when the dominated child leaves for college or gets married. Some bronchial asthmatic patient who hopes to be engulfed or protected develops an asthmatic attack when his hopes are dashed.

Therefore, one might ask, how did this sensitivity to bereavement or to these conflicts come about? In most instances we do not have the answer to this question. Nor do we have the answer to questions about the ontogenesis of the physiological predispositions to these diseases. Until these questions are answered, a comprehensive theory of disease still eludes us.

Among the specific questions that must be answered are: what factors during personality development account for the persistence of psychological conflicts originating in childhood? Why are predisposed persons so vulnerable to bereavement? Why are the personal relationships of these patients so frequently of a dependent nature? Why do these patients have such a low tolerance of frustration and of changes in their life situations? Can a bodily process alter personality development? Does genetic variation in enzyme production in the brain alter the mother-child relationship and other childhood experiences and, therefore, development? Does early experience alter physiological functioning in the body and brain? Or can genetic variation or early childhood experience alter brain function in the same directions: for example, by changing levels of important biosynthetic or degradative enzymes or their products, thereby affecting later behavior? How does the same life experience affect bodily and psychological functioning at different age periods?

Many behavioral scientists believe that fundamental conflicts arise in childhood either because of the child's failure to master them and the associated feelings or because of actual life experiences within the family that sensitize the child. The source of the conflict is either the attitude of one or both parents or derives from specific family relationships that exist during the most-formative years in the child's development.

At this point, there is not sufficient, substantive data to lend firm support to either of these hypotheses. The information that is available is sparse and not convincing. For example, the family relationships of, and parental attitudes toward, the future victim of ulcerative colitis are not specific to this disease. They resemble the relationships described for families with schizophrenic children. The mothers of children with bronchial asthma are not uniformly or uniquely overprotective in their attitudes toward their offspring. Four different kinds of attitudes have been described; presumably, each of these parental attitudes promotes an arrested psychological development in the child. One can never be certain that a parental attitude is not a product of the child's disease. A child having an asthmatic attack is a frightening and disturbing spectacle. The protective or restrictive parental attitude may be a "reasonable" response to the child's own attitudes or behaviors.

In any case, the broadest area of agreement concerning the origin of psychological predispositions is that either a failure to master conflictful motivations in childhood or actual experiences within the family are the source of conflicts persisting in later life.

An alternative hypothesis is based on the assumption that early life experiences may alter or "condition" bodily function. For example, it has been proposed that aspects of early mother-child relationships that cause undue crying, with its associated effects on cardiopulmonary function and the circulation, may condition the child either to the asthmatic attacks (Stein, 1962) or to essential hypertension (Reiser, 1970). Still another hypothesis put forward first by Alexander (1950) and later by Mirsky (1958) proposed that physiological variations might alter personality development. Alexander's postulation, which he utilized to account for the predisposing psychological characteristics of patients with hyperthyroidism, was extensively reviewed in Chapter 4. Mirsky suggested a similar hypothesis; that genetic variations in the secretory capacity of the stomach might alter the mother-child relationship during the period of nursing, by changing patterns of hunger by altering the capacity for satiety, or in some other undefined manner, resulting in the child's chronic sense of unsatisfied longing for food and care. None of these hypotheses has ever been put to an empirical test.

Even in the absence of studies designed specifically to validate the individual hypotheses, there is provocative data that provides some support for each. There is evidence that experience does alter brain function in animals, both on the neuronal and chemical level. Altered function serves to determine behavioral reaction tendencies or the processing of subsequent experiences. Experience may also alter bodily function, which, in turn, may affect brain function and, therefore, the processing of subsequent experiences. Finally, there is data indicating that genetic endowment or variations may interact with experience to alter brain or bodily functioning.

The Effects of Experience on Behavior and Neuronal Function

A number of experiments, including one series of major significance, have clearly demonstrated the generalized role of early experience in the development of the nervous system and the functions that it subserves. If young mammals are reared in an environment that provides only limited sensory (visual, tactual, kinesthetic) stimuli for an extended period of time and are then exposed to an increase in such stimuli, they show a syndrome of perceptual deficiencies, hyperexcitability, paroxysmal fear, susceptibility to convulsions, and optic nystagmus (Riesen, 1961).

The neuronal and behavioral consequences of varying and altering visual inputs have been demonstrated in impressive detail by Wiesel and Hubel (1963a, b, 1965a, b). They experimentally closed one eye of kittens 10 days old or younger for a three-month period, thus depriving them of visual form and diffuse-light stimulation, while presumably altering the way they experienced the environment. The investigators then studied the effect of this procedure on the morphology of cells and neuronal unit activity in the visual system and found that profound changes had occurred in the cells of layers of the lateral geniculate body receiving input from the closed eyes. More precisely, these changes consisted of a reduction in size and an increase in the pallor of cells and of their nuclei. However, no such changes could be seen in the retina, superior colliculi, or visual cortex (Wiesel and Hubel,

1963b), and, despite these morphological alterations, there was remarkably little change in the electrophysiology of geniculate neurons. The physiologic changes that did occur consisted of a tendency to respond more-slowly to retinal illumination and to respond to illumination of larger patches of the retina than usual.

Morphological changes in the lateral geniculate also occurred if one eye of the kittens was closed for one to four months after they had reached 2 months of age. But closing the eye of an adult cat did not cause any atrophic changes. In other words, the possibility that monocular deprivation will produce behavioral blindness, morphological changes in the lateral geniculate body, and disruption of innately determined structures seems to be greatest when such deprivation occurs very early in life. The effect of monocular deprivation then, is to disrupt a system present and capable of functioning at birth. Visual experience usually interacts with an innate structure. When the cat is deprived of such experience, the structure becomes defective by the morphological and physiological criteria cited above.

According to Wiesel and Hubel the effect of deprivation of patterned light stimulation in cats depends not only on the age of the animal but also on the period of deprivation. Interestingly, they found that the receptive field organization of the retina, the interaction of the visual system of input from both eyes, and the functional architecture of the visual cortex were not only present at birth but on the whole remained present for at least 19 days after birth, despite the absence of patterned visual stimulation (Hubel and Wiesel, 1963). However, at some point two to three months after the nineteenth day of monocular deprivation, there was a marked functional disruption of the connections that were present at birth between the lateral geniculate body and the visual cortex. Blindness occurred in the deprived eye only. Either very few cortical neurons could be driven by stimulation of the deprived retina and those that were responded abnormally (Wiesel and Hubel, 1963a), or the cortical neurons remained spontaneously active but were not affected by stimulation (Wiesel and Hubel, 1963b). Recovery of function over a period of 3 to 15 months, after the eye had been closed for 3 months, was severely limited (Wiesel and Hubel, 1965b).

It would seem reasonable to assume from the foregoing that depriving both eyes of visual input for equal periods of time would lead to a complete lack of response of visual cortical units to retinal stimulation. Surprisingly, Wiesel and Hubel (1965a) found that this was not so. Despite the expected shrinkage of geniculate neurons and blindness, only 41 percent of the cortical neurons responded abnormally. That is, they responded to non-specific rather than specific visual stimuli, and some were abnormally responsive to stimulation of both eyes. There was also an abnormal tendency of units to fatigue.

The authors concluded from these findings that the blindness of the monocularly deprived kittens must have different antecedents. Even more significantly, they found that it was difficult to reconcile the results of the two procedures at the neuronal level. Only one conclusion emerged clearly: the functional integrity of the visual system depends not only on input but on the interaction of inputs from both eyes.

Hubel and Wiesel have suggested that the different ways in which the visual world is experienced have different neuronal consequences, and their study of the neuronal effects of producing a squint in kittens 8 to 10 days old attests to the validity of this contention. Within 3 to 12 months after one medial rectus muscle had been cut, the kittens showed abnormal neuronal patterns, although these patterns varied. Spontaneous cortical activity

591

was normal, but evoked activity was not. For example, most units were driven by only one eye; and, in contrast to the normal state, one cortical region was under the stimulus dominance of one eye, only to give way to an adjacent region dominated by the other. According to Hubel and Wiesel, the results produced by these experiments cannot be ascribed to the fact that both eyes were open at the same time; rather, they can be attributed to an abnormal relationship between signals in the two afferent pathways (Hubel and Wiesel, 1965).

Hubel and Wiesel also studied the behavioral effects of visual deprivation on a kitten. After one of the kitten's eyes had been closed for three months and then opened, vision was gradually and partially restored. When the "good" eye was then covered, the kitten sometimes followed large moving objects with its previously sutured eye, but when the kitten was free to roam, it would often bump into objects, especially small ones. Closing the "good" eye after opening the previously sutured one affected the animal's social standing as well: it lost its dominant position in a group of cats (Wiesel and Hubel, 1965b). When both eyes were closed the animal would still move about, and seemed to be able to familiarize itself with the objects in its home room. However, if one eye was opened after 3½ months of lid closure, the kitten could not, or would not, utilize visual clues (Wiesel and Hubel, 1965a). It has been speculated that these behavioral and social effects on the kitten result from its altered visual perception of the environment, a conclusion clearly based on inference. We cannot know what the kitten experiences with any degree of certainty. We do know, however, that the kitten's behavior is altered in several spheres.

The work of Hubel and Wiesel has justifiably been hailed as having significant implications for our understanding of normal neuronal functioning and the impact of experience on its development—a central issue in all of developmental biology, and in physiology, psychoanalysis, and psychosomatic medicine. In this context, recapitulation of the main conclusions of Hubel and Wiesel should be useful.

1. There is little correlation between the morphological changes that occur in the lateral geniculate body after the closure of one eye and the neuronal unit activity recorded from it.
2. Altering experiences of the visual world in different ways has different neuronal consequences.
3. At birth, the visual system exhibits normal neuronal characteristics despite the absence of previous patterned visual stimulation. In the absence of further visual experience, attrition in these structures occurs. It appears, from this observation, that it is the interaction of such structures with experience that leads to normal functioning as development proceeds. (It should be noted that this conclusion supports the epigenetic concept in developmental psychology.)
4. A majority of cortical neurons respond to nonspecific, rather than specific, stimuli when both eyes are deprived of visual input. This finding suggests that at neuronal level, at least, total deprivation of visual input leads to less-differentiated functioning, either as a result of dedifferentiation or as a result of a failure of differentiation. In any event, permanent neuronal consequences ensue.

Most other models of the effects of experience have concerned themselves with alterations of neuronal or neural functioning at the synaptic level (Kandel and Spencer, 1968).

Here, changes occur because the postsynaptic membrane has been altered or because of a growth of synaptic connections with experience. That experience alters neuronal functioning appears to be incontrovertible, but the manner in which this happens is still unknown. It is a topic of active scientific debate in any discussion of how early experience may alter brain function. As noted, the work of Hubel and Wiesel indicates that at birth, cortical neurons already exist that selectively respond to certain configurations of a visual stimulus. Conflicting data recently accumulated by Pettigrew and his co-workers (1973) suggest that visual cortical neurons are, instead, equipotential at birth and that their responsivity to the configurations of a stimulus are determined by experience. Additional studies reinforce the idea that sensory stimulation early in life may also produce effects at other levels of neural organization. Sensory input to the brain, such as handling, may alter brain maturation. Conversely, social isolation or lack of sensory stimulation may impair levels of neurotransmitter substances in the brain. In 1933, Langworthy observed that visual stimulation accelerates myelinization in the optic tracts of premature and term infants. Other workers (Feitelberg and Lampl, 1935; Serota and Gerard, 1938) have shown that flashing a light in a cat's eye will increase the blood flow, temperature, and metabolism, specifically in the occipital cortex, lateral geniculate body, and optic and olfactory cortex (Richter, 1952). Dehydration, a stimulus to antidiuretic hormone (ADH) secretion, has been shown to cause a large increase in the ribonucleic acid (Edstrom et al., 1961) and acetylcholinesterase contents (Pepler and Pearse, 1957) of the supraoptic and paraventricular nuclei of young rabbits.

Hubel and Wiesel had focused their investigation on the interaction of visual experience with genetically and maturationally determined neural structures. There is initial evidence from two other groups indicating that it may be necessary to take other factors into account as well. A study of the light-regulated synthesis of melatonin in the pineal gland of the adult rat showed that it could be subserved by an extraretinal pathway until the rat was 27 days old; thereafter, a retinal pathway was necessary (Zweig et al., 1966). And Amassian et al. (1971) have shown that a subcortical pathway subserves the contact-placing reaction in the cat, but that this pathway becomes nonfunctional after about 30 days, at which point this motor behavior is controlled by a double circuit. One circuit is routed via the ventroposterior nucleus of the thalamus to the cortical sensorimotor area; the other is routed via the ventrolateral nucleus of the thalamus to the same cortical area (Amassian et al., 1972a). One fundamental conclusion that may be drawn from this group of studies is that different brain circuits can subserve the same behaviors and functions at different ages. Clearly, then, a neurophysiological analysis of a behavior and its ontogenesis must take into account the age of the animal. In all likelihood this is true of investigations on the level of brain chemistry as well.

Maturational changes in neurotransmitter levels have been observed in experimental animals. These changes may, in turn, depend on the relative availability of the appropriate substrate in the diet. It may be that prior experience interacts with the maturation of the chemical apparatus of the brain, in some as yet unknown manner. According to this view, the same experience at one point early in life may alter brain function in a different manner than at another point—depending on the maturation of certain (transmitter or other) substances in the brain, which are themselves the product of the availability of substrate and a genetic program that unfolds with advancing age. Examples of such a maturational program include: (1) the rat's capacity to excrete norepinephrine and its metabolites, which develops with increasing efficiency only after the eleventh day of life (Glowinski et al., 1964) and (2) the rapid rise of endogeneous levels of brain norepinephrine in the second week of the rat's life, so that by 12 days the levels are only slightly lower than at 24 days and in adulthood, but are quite markedly influenced by external factors such as nutrition (Shoemaker and Wurtman, 1971).

At present, the available evidence suggests that permanent changes either in behavior or physiological function that are regulated by the brain can only be accomplished during sensitive, developmental periods. We know little about what such periods represent in terms of the specific functions of the brain. The study of the interaction of experience with the biochemical and physiological maturation of the brain is a major and largely unexplored area of neurobiology.

The Effects of Experience on Brain Chemistry

Early social experiences, as well as the nutrition of the infant animal, appear to affect not only brain enzyme levels and turnover rates, but levels of many different amino acids and biogenic amines as well. These levels are, in turn, functionally related to different behaviors, such as the emotional responsivity of an animal, its aggressiveness, or its dominant behavior. Levels of the enzymes tyrosine hydroxylase, phenylethanolamine N-methyl transferase (PNMT), acetyl cholinesterase, and cholinesterase are low in animals reared in social isolation. Levels of serotonin, 5-hydroxyindole acetic acid, dopamine, norepinephrine, aspartic acid, glutamic acid, glutamine, and γ-aminobutyric acid are also affected by the environments in which animals are raised. The critical environmental variable appears to be the mean level of stimulation that the environment provides.

Welch and Welch (1969) have pointed out that, although changes in biogenic amine levels and turnover rates may occur as the result of socially isolating an animal, and, in turn, may be related in a functional way to the behavioral changes that ensue, there is no reason as yet for assuming that amine levels bear a direct relationship to any specific behavior.

The result of certain early experiences that modify enzyme and substrate levels and turnover rates may later be manifested when the animal is challenged by some stressful experience. Welch and Welch (1968) have shown that restraint stress can cause a greater elevation of brain norepinephrine and serotonin in mice that had previously spent eight to twelve weeks in isolation than in littermates housed in groups. The elevation of brain amines occurs despite the fact that the isolated mice have a slower baseline turnover of brain biogenic amines than those housed in groups.

Restraint, both alone and in combination with exposure to cold, also seems to affect other brain amines. Histamine levels in the hypothalamus and cerebral cortex of rats are depleted significantly in the first two hours during these "stresses." Apparently, there is an initial and marked enhancement of synthesis, but it cannot keep pace with the rate of release and destruction of the amine, leading to the depletion of levels (Taylor and Snyder, 1971).

This work on the effect of early experience on behavior and brain chemistry has several important implications: that previous experience affects behavioral response tendencies is demonstrated by the observation that isolated mice are more hyperexcitable behaviorally

594

than group-housed controls. The finding of different turnover rates and greater elevations following immobilization clearly indicates that previous experience may lead to individual differences in brain amine levels as well as behavior and to different responses to later restraint stress.

The Effects of Prior Experience on Body Function

The possibility that early experience can "condition" bodily function, in addition to affecting neural function and behavior, is derived from the number of inferences drawn from observations of humans and animals. Some of the most illuminating studies on animals have been carried out by Henry and his co-workers (1967, 1971a), who found that a variety of previous experiences determined an animal's response to the stress of social confrontation with members of its own species (Chapter 2). Mixing male mice from different boxes or confining them in small boxes, exposing mice to a cat for many months, and producing territorial conflict resulted in sustained elevations of systolic blood pressure, arteriosclerosis, and an interstitial nephritis. Male mice exhibited higher levels of systolic blood pressure. Female mice that had been previously isolated failed to reproduce. Castration of or administration of reserpine to stressed male mice resulted in minimal changes in blood pressure. An animal's previous social experience of living together with its kind attenuated the effects on blood pressure of experimentally induced aggregation and territorial conflict. On the other hand, isolation of animals from each other, after weaning and to maturity, exacerbated the effects of crowding on blood pressure levels.

Recently, both Axelrod and colleagues (1970) and Henry and colleagues (1971b) reported that socially isolated mice showed a decreased activity of tyrosine hydroxylase and phenylethanolamine N-methyl transferase activity in the adrenal gland in the baseline state. When these animals were later crowded together, the activity of these enzymes was increased significantly more than in mice already accustomed to crowding. The activity of the same enzymes and of monoamine oxidase (MOA) and the levels of norepinephrine and epinephrine in the adrenal gland were more elevated in animals who were in constant contact with each other than in animals who were normally housed but not previously isolated. In other words, amine and enzyme levels in the adrenal glands of socially isolated animals were lower than in animals housed together, but a marked reactive "overshooting" in activity occurred under stress.

These studies indicate that psychophysiological responses to "stress" are determined by prior experience; in this case, by the social conditions of early life. There also is evidence that other classes of experience occurring in utero and early life have effects on important physiological systems. Milković and Milković (1959a) have shown that adrenalectomy of a mother rat prior to parturition, or unilateral ligation of the Fallopian tube prior to conception (1959b), results in an offspring with the capacity to display an adrenal response to severe "stress" as early as one or two days after birth. The work done by Thoman and her co-workers (1970) suggests that changes in adrenocortical activity during both prenatal and early postnatal life can affect subsequent patterns of neuroendocrine response in the adult organism. In these studies, the newborn rat pups of mothers adrenalectomized prior to conception had hypertrophied adrenal glands and higher plasma corticosterone levels than the offspring of normal mothers. As adults, these two groups of rats showed different responses to stress; the offspring of adrenalectomized mothers responded to stress with significantly higher hormonal levels than did the offspring of normal mothers. Thoman's view is that these differences are almost exclusively due to the prenatal events mediated by their effects on the mother, since switching the litters of adrenalectomized and nonadrenalectomized mother rats had no effect on the differences in adrenal function in the offspring, despite the fact that adrenalectomized mothers lactated less. Thus, the effects of the maternal adrenalectomy on the offspring must have occurred in utero.

Other information has been accumulated about the effects of postnatal events on the adrenocortical response to stress. Levine and co-workers (1958) showed that rats handled as infants had a more marked adrenocortical response when exposed to cold in adulthood than did unmanipulated littermates. Rats that were handled as infants also showed a greater adrenocortical response when exposed to a brief electric shock in adulthood (Levine, 1962). A significantly greater and more-sustained increase in plasma corticoids was also observed in handled animals, in comparison with unhandled control animals, despite the fact that the resting plasma levels of corticoids were the same for both groups and that the weights of the adrenal glands in both groups did not differ. When less-drastic stresses were used, neonatally handled rats had a less-marked adrenocortical response than control animals that had not been gentled. When exposed to an open-field trial for three minutes in adulthood, the handled rats showed some increase in plasma corticoids but significantly less than the control animals (Levine and Mullins, 1968). To explain these seemingly inconsistent findings, Levine postulated that one of the major consequences of handling young rats "is to endow the organism with the capacity to make finer discriminations concerning relevant aspects of the environment. The animal then is able to make responses more appropriate to the demands of the environment including appropriate responses to stress."

Just how these experiences permanently alter the function of the adrenal cortex so that the adult shows a greater repertoire of adrenal responses is unknown. There does appear to be a general acceleration of maturation as a result of early handling (Levine, 1962): body hair, the opening of the eyes, and the beginning of adequate locomotion appear from one to four days earlier in a stimulated animal. It is also likely that the onset of puberty is hastened and the myelinization of tracts in the central nervous system (CNS) accelerates as a result of handling. Early handling of rats alters the responsivity of the pituitary-adrenocortical axis (Denenberg et al., 1967; Levine, 1968). When rats are handled in the first two days of life, an increase in circulating corticoids occur. Further elevations are seen when animals are stressed on the third day of life, when animals were once considered to be unresponsive to stress. Ader (1969) has demonstrated that early handling or exposure to shock accelerates the maturation of the 24-hour adrenocortical rhythm. The characteristic 24-hour adrenocortical rhythm was observed to develop at least five days earlier in rats who had been stimulated either by shock or by handling.

Several groups of investigators have suggested (Schapiro et al., 1962; Smelik, 1963; Yates and Urquhart, 1962) that the control of the endocrine system in the adult is partially accomplished by a feedback mechanism, or "hormonostat." This mechanism, they assert, constantly "monitors" levels of plasma corticoids, compares these levels with a controlling "set point," and adjusts ACTH secretion according to the plasma level. The crucial feature of this postulated regulatory system requires that the "set point" not be fixed, but rather that it vary according to the metabolic demands placed upon the organism. Since the sensitivity of such a regulatory mechanism could be brought about by a number of variables, one of which is stressful early experience during a "sensitive" period of development, it is possible that early experiences allow for more graded and versatile responses. This assumption may explain why stimulated (handled) rats show a moderate increase in steroid output when placed in an open-field situation, and a large and rapid increase when subjected to electroshock. Unstimulated animals tend to react hormonally in a more stereotyped way, with large increases in hormone levels in response to change, because of a more limited "hormonostatic" repertoire. Nevertheless, handling an infant rat reduces both emotional and adrenocortical reactivity (Ader and Grota, 1973).

When handled animals are later challenged by various forms of "stresses," some investigators have found an increased adrenocortical reactivity and others have not. Handling does appear to protect animals from gastric erosion and to delay the growth of transplanted tumors. Although it decreases resistance to transplanted leukemia, handling does not affect the response to the latent virus that produces murine leukemia in the AKR strain of mice. On the basis of these data, Ader and Grota (1973) have concluded that the specific manner in which neonatally handled rodents differ from nonstimulated animals depends on the nature of the subsequent stimulus applied to them as adults.

The results of these studies do not explain the exact mechanism whereby emotional and adrenocortical reactivity are altered by neonatal handling. Ader and Grota (1973) noted that after handling, the emotional and hormonal reactivity of rodents during a later test situation varied independently of each other. This observation may mean that neonatal handling independently affects the brain and the response of the adrenal gland. Only future work will elucidate whether prior experience (1) affects both brain and behavior, simultaneously but independently; or (2) affects bodily structure and function through the agency of the brain; or (3) affects bodily function, which, in turn, alters neural functioning.

In the meantime we have also learned from animal experiments about the effects of social experience on immune responses and responses to infectious agents. Immune responses are clearly inplicated in the diseases reviewed in this book and in other diseases not reviewed. Some types of hereditary immunoglobulin deficiency are implicated in the predisposition to rheumatoid arthritis. We are just beginning to learn that varying early experiences may influence immune responses. Friedman et al. (1965) have shown that the effects of early experience on immunity vary with the challenging agent, with the time during the host's life that the challenge occurs, and with the genetic strain of the animal. These investigators exposed groups of mice to periodic, paired light and shock, periodic light and aperiodic shock, and periodic light without shock. They found that the animals subjected to the first of these conditions were very likely to develop an infection on exposure to Coxsackie B-2 virus, as compared with the other groups and with matched controls. The strain of mice used is ordinarily highly resistant to this virus. Yet exposure to Coxsackie B-1 virus (a strain to which these animals are usually highly susceptible) resulted in no significant difference in morbidity or mortality between groups. Inoculating stressed mice with *Plasmodium berghei* resulted in a decreased susceptibility and mortality.

Ader and Friedman (1965) have demonstrated similar variations in response in mice implanted with Walker sarcoma. The mice were either handled or given a three-minute period of electric shock before weaning. When they were 45 days old, they were injected with a standard dose of Walker sarcoma. Animals that had been handled throughout the preweaning period showed a retarded rate of tumor growth. The mortality rate was higher for those animals handled only in the first week of life; there was no difference in mortality between animals handled later in the preweaning period and unhandled controls. Mice that received electric shocks in the first week of life had a higher mortality than other groups, but animals shocked throughout the preweaning period or during the third week only had a lower death rate than other groups of mice, including unshocked control animals. Thus, the effects of early experiences on resistance to Walker sarcoma depended upon the nature of the experience and the time during early life when it occurred.

The Effects of Body Functioning on the Brain and Behavior

So far we have seen that prior experience may affect both brain and body function; it may, therefore, influence the subsequent processing of experience and behavioral response tendencies. On the other hand, Mirsky (1957) has suggested that body functioning can influence or alter the mother-child relationship in a manner that affects subsequent behavior, character, and personal relationships. Although, as has been mentioned, no empirical verification of this sequence has been made, other examples of this conceptual scheme have been developed. A variant of this scheme is that experience may alter bodily functioning, which, in turn, alters brain function and behavior.

An example of the first of these alternatives is the influence of the gonadal hormones on brain and behavior during sensitive periods of development. The gonadal hormones determine sexual and reproductive behavior and the gonadotropic function of the pituitary gland of the adult animal (Levine and Mullins, 1966). Harris (1964) and Young (1961) have hypothesized that the sexually undifferentiated brain is "organized" by gonadal hormones during fetal and early neonatal life. Subsequently, several investigators have shown (Barraclough, 1961; Harris and Levine, 1965; Young et al., 1964) that the presence of androgens in small amounts during the first five days of life in female rats alters the regular cycle of gonadotropin release to an aperiodic sequence. In the absence of any gonadal hormones, the gonadotropins are secreted cyclically; thus, the absence of androgens in the male rat in the first 48 hours of life results in the cyclic elaboration of gonadotropins. In addition, the neonatal castration of a male rat drastically alters his sexual behavior. When injected with low doses of estrogens and progesterone as an adult, he exhibits the complete repertoire of female sexual behavior (Young et al., 1964). Castration of adult males and similar treatment with estrogen and progesterone does not yield such results.

It is apparent from these data that during a "critical" period in early development, androgens acting on the brain are responsible for the acyclic secretion of gonadotropins. They determine male sexual behavior in much the same way as they affect the development of male sexual morphology. Sex hormones in early life play a major part in structuring sexual behavior, morphology, and physiology. It is also possible, as Levine (1970) has pointed out, that the adrenal corticosteroids may have a profound effect upon the organization of the brain and may influence a number of functions that are associated with neuroendocrine regulation of ACTH. These effects may occur at different ages in different

598

species. The main effect of the sex hormones on behavior and gonadotropin release may occur before birth in the monkey and after birth in the rat.

The Role of Genetic Factors in Predisposition

Animal studies have concerned themselves mainly with the influence of prior experience on behavior and physiological functioning later in life. Individual differences in "emotionality" and corticosteroid output have been ascribed to differences in prior experience (Ader and Grota, 1973). In man, however, Hamburg (1967) observed that individual differences in 17-hydroxycorticosteroid excretion were consistent over months and through several "stressful" episodes. He ascribed these individual differences to genetic factors having no apparent correlation with early experiential ones.

Genetic factors seem to play a predisposing role in each of the diseases reviewed in this book. But the relative weight of genetic endowment in predisposition to each disease is uncertain. Obviously, in some forms of hyperthyroidism—such as in thyroid binding globulin (TBG) deficiency—genetic factors may be predominant. The same is probably true for the propensity in some of these diseases to produce an excess or a deficiency of antibodies. Our inability to assess the role of genetic factors in the etiology of psychological predispositions is largely a function of limited information. A priori, we may conclude either that genetic factors play no role in the ontogenesis of the psychological factors identified, that they may influence or arrest psychological development, or that they exert their effects through variations in bodily function that influence psychological development—for example, by distorting the mother-child relationship. There is, of course, another possibility; as we have seen, social isolation may lower brain levels of the biosynthetic enzymes of putative transmitter substances and produce idiosyncratic response tendencies in specified social situations (Welch and Welch, 1965, 1968). It seems likely that these individual responses have functional biochemical correlates. It also seems reasonable to believe that genetic variation may produce similar or the same low levels of these biosynthetic enzymes. Consequently, the rate of synthesis of the putative neurotransmitters would be slowed to produce the same idiosyncratic response tendencies to test situations as social isolation does. Therefore, one could postulate that the behavioral phenotype may be the product of experience, of genetic variation or of the two in interaction.

These observations are, of course, only intended to suggest a possible focus for speculation and investigation—not as a specification, in any sense, of the role of genetic factors in predisposing to certain diseases. Genes may express themselves quantitatively, qualitatively, not at all, or only in interaction with environmental factors. For example, deficiency of the enzyme glucose-6-phosphate dehydrogenase is expressed in a variety of ways. Eighteen different genetically determined varieties of the deficiency have now been identified (Harris, 1968). It is likely that each separate form of the deficiency is the product of a distinctive change in the structure of the protein, possibly due to the substitution of a single aminoacid for the usual one at a single position in the polypeptide chains that form the enzyme. In part, the manifestations of the defect are a product of the level of abnormal enzyme in red blood cells. One variant expresses itself only when the person is exposed to certain drugs, another when he is exposed to fava beans. In some variants a chronic hemolytic anema occurs "spontaneously," in still other forms no clinical expression of the enzyme variation occurs. The genetic variation, in this instance, expresses itself in a qualitative change in enzyme structure, which may or may not manifest itself.

Quantitative genetic factors also play a role by lowering the amount or level of an enzyme or by causing its absence. In other cases, the enzyme may be chemically unstable or its rate of synthesis may be slowed. For example, in the Lesch-Nyhan syndrome, an abnormal gene on the X-chromosome is apparently responsible for a virtual absence of the enzyme hypoxanthine guanine phosphoribosyl transferase. (The deficiency of this enzyme has also been found in some patients with gout.) Not only may enzyme levels in such patients be markedly reduced, but at least two forms of structural alteration of the enzyme itself are known. It is also worth noting that various structural alterations of this enzyme may express themselves in the same phenotype—i.e., as gout —but the virtual *absence* of the enzyme results in the Lesch-Nyhan syndrome, which is a very different diseae from gout (Harris, 1968). The Lesch-Nyhan syndrome is one of a series of diseases in which genes alter brain function, resulting in changes in behavior and the capacity to learn. As in many other genetic-metabolic diseases (the aminoacidurias, phenylketonuria, etc.) genetic defects help to limit learning, the processing and retention of experience, and, therefore, personality development. It is possible that, in some undisclosed manner, genes express themselves by limiting a man's capacity for psychological adaptation—a limitation that is so characteristic of patients at the onset of psychosomatic diseases. But it is the contention here that the same poorly adapted phenotype may result either from prior experience or from genetic expression in interaction with life experience. To further complicate the matter, different forms of genetic variation may have the same phenotypic expression. In gout, purine biosynthesis is excessive, or uric acid secretion by the distal renal tubules is defective, or both defects are present, all leading to elevated serum uric acid and to gouty arthritis in some persons. However, genetic variation may not be expressed phenotypically at all, for reasons that are still not understood. Only a small proportion of persons with elevated levels of serum uric acid or pepsinogen develop clinical gout or peptic duodenal ulcer, respectively. Genetic variation may also account for the increased capacity to form pepsinogen in the stomach, or for the occurrence of a unique pepsinogen isoenzyme. Excessive pepsinogen production may, on the other hand, merely be due to a quantitative phenomenon—in that it may stem from an increased size of the parietal cell mass, the origin of which is still unknown.

In summary, the body of information reviewed in this section links early or prior experience to alterations in behavior, brain, and bodily function. The "thrust" of this information supports the assumption that early experience is responsible for the arrests in personality development seen in patients predisposed to, or suffering from, psychosomatic disease. We do not know enough about the genetics of behavior to determine whether these arrests are a function of genetic influences. Obviously, the absence of specific enzymes may alter the disposition of important metabolites so as to impair brain function and development, as exemplified by phenylketonuria and the various aminoacidurias. One can hypothesize, then, that genetic variation may alter the rate of synthesis of brain enzymes and, thereby, personality development.

In addition, the prominence of immune factors—which are also under genetic control—in psychosomatic diseases suggests that these factors may also influence personal-

600

ity development. Antibodies are known to be produced in or to enter the brain. Therefore, antibody production in the brain might influence personality development. Conversely, early experiences may alter antibody production either in the brain or elsewhere in the body. Nutritional deprivation of children is one form of early experience that may alter antibody production. The inadequate nutrition of children occurs during wartime, is widespread in economically underprivileged populations, or results from parental neglect. Although I am not aware of any data indicating that an antibody-production effect occurs, the work of Ebbesen, reviewed in Chapter 5, suggests that genetic strain differences, varying prior experience, and stress seem to interact in the production of amyloid deposition. (Amyloid is composed of the light chains of immunoglobulins).

We may conclude, without additional information, that prior experience does alter brain levels of the enzymes involved in the synthesis of acetylcholine, norepinephrine, epinephrine, serotonin, and various amino acids. Hormone levels, and perhaps the circadian rhythms of polypeptide hormone secretion, are also influenced by early experience. Later stress responses are, in part, determined by the initial enzyme level. Thus, if enzyme levels are high or low in the adrenal medulla as the result of genetic variation, different physiological responses to stress may occur. A third variable that should be considered is that enzyme levels are not only determined by early experience and genetic variation, but are also affected by the availability of their substrates and are under the control of other hormones. The level of the enzyme PNMT, for example, is in part controlled by ACTH, secretion of which is itself influenced by "stress."

We have as yet no reliable or adequate explanation for the psychological predispositions to the seven diseases. Many, perhaps all, patients appear to suffer from arrests at early stages of personality development, which sensitize them to loss and bereavement, to frustration, to various kinds of demands upon them, and to the domination of others. Why should this be so? We do not know.

These arrests are genuine, because they manifest themselves before the onset of the disease. They are, therefore, not only the result of the patients' reactions to the disease and its treatment. Although fear and anxiety due to the uncertainty of diseases outcome, pain, and prospective surgery may retrogressively produce less-mature behavior and personal relationships, most of the clinical evidence suggests that none of the patients with these diseases have achieved psychological maturity. In the studies where this issue has been directly addressed (as in Engel's work on ulcerative colitis and in the predictive studies reviewed in this book), a retrogressive shift in personality organization and in personal relationships was only partly attributable to psychological responses to the disease. The fact that such retrogressive shifts occur (they are called "regressive" in psychoanalytic terminology) implies that there have been arrests of personality development. In such cases, personality functioning is age-inappropriate and, in many areas, much less capable of adapting to the tasks and complexities that face an adult. That these arrests at an earlier level of personality organization occur in concert with disease onset (Grinker, 1953; Schur, 1953) tells us something about the character of brain function.

Adaptability, stability, and continuity of behavior and psychological functioning characterizes mature adults. By comparison, the behavior of children is variable. Their psychological development does not proceed smoothly, but rather in regressive and progressive fits and starts. During their development, discontinuities in psychological

601

functioning and behavior occur. The adaptability of the child, especially when very young, is limited partly because the psychological functions that make adaptation possible either have not developed or are in the process of developing. The psychological characteristics of children, and of adults who show arrests of psychological development, would suggest that their brain—as the organ of mind and behavior—is more plastic. Therefore, their behavior and psychological functioning is less stable and may undergo a reversion to earlier modes.

The ease with which retrogression in personality organization occurs under perceived stress is, perhaps, a function of increased plasticity of the brain. The nature and origins of such plasticity in neurobiological terms are, however, unknown. There is some evidence that at least one behavior is subserved by one set of neural circuits at one age, and a different set of circuits at another age. When this second set of circuits was surgically disrupted in adult animals, the behavior was not abolished, but occurred with a much lower probability. In terms of some of its characteristics (such as the latency of onset), the disrupted behavior was more like the behavior seen in a very young animal. Therefore, it is not unlikely that following the destruction of the circuits that subserve the behavior in the adult, the circuits that had subserved the behavior in early life once again became activated (Amassian et al., 1971, 1972a and b). The results of these experiments suggest one possible explanation for neural plasticity.

In summary, the arrests in psychological development—the excessive dependency—of patients with these diseases have usually either been attributed to the persistence of psychological conflict, or to the attitudes of mothers that induce conflict in the child or keep him in dependent bondage. The data suggest that other factors may also play a role. But our ignorance of developmental neurobiology and psychobiology prevents us from coming to a decision as to which model of maturation and development is the correct one to explain these arrests. There is plenty of evidence that experiences early in life alter brain and body function. Altered brain function, in turn, alters later behavioral responses when an animal is challenged. These observations do not account for arrested development. They only described changed response tendencies. On the other hand, genetic variation could explain the developmental arrest. In fact, a number of genetically determined variations do just that—most-probably by impairing the capacity to learn. These gross disturbances of development are, however, not the kind seen in persons with these diseases, who can learn, but develop no adaptive or interpersonal competence. Later, faced with change, loss, or personally significant experiences, they collapse psychologically because they cannot adapt.

Be that as it may, the intent has been to review alternative models of the manner in which genetic variation and experience might interact to predispose to the diseases discussed in this book.

THE NATURE OF THE PREDISPOSING FACTORS TO DISEASE

Even if a validated concept of multiple predispositions to a disease were ultimately to provide an answer to the problem of the choice of that disease, the answer might well prove to be unsatisfactory on a number of scores. It would almost certainly not be a parsimonious concept. It would not tell us why persons with the same set of predispositions fall ill, while others remain healthy. And it would not accord an appropriately dynamic role to predispositions in the "physiological economy" of the organism.

By the physiological economy of the organism is meant that overall process by which every integrated physiological function—the circulation, the output of hormones, the respiration, or gastric secretion—is regulated in a complex manner to maintain equilibrium conditions. These functions are carried out by specialized cells and the organs they constitute. Organs in turn belong to integrated systems. Cells are internally regulated ("self-regulation"), and also externally regulated by a large variety of hormones, ions, transmitter substances, nutrients, and antibodies. Some cells are externally regulated by only some of these substances; they have specific receptors for only these substances, and not for others. Other cells are regulated by most or all of these substances, because their surface membranes contain a larger number of specific receptors.

Two major classes of regulatory processes are known—self-regulatory and external regulatory ones. The self-regulatory processes, which enable the cell to regulate its own function include: (1) "feedback inhibition," in which the initial or final enzymes in a biosynthetic pathway, consisting of several enzymatic steps, may be repressed by an excess of the end-product of the pathway; (2) several initial enzymes in a common biosynthetic pathway that act in conjunction to catalyze some of the same chemical reactions, but are subject to feedback regulation by different end-products; and (3) self-regulation, as in protein synthesis, achieved via the rate at which the *initial* step in the synthesis of the protein chain occurs, and not by the rate of enzyme synthesis.

Although other forms of molecular autoregulatory activity (Mandell, 1973) have been carefully conceptualized, they do not fit any of these three models. Each organ also regulates its own activities: the denervated heart beats regularly, albeit slowly; the kidney regulates its own functions and also controls blood pressure by virtue of its capacity to form hypertensive and antihypertensive substances.

In addition to these self-regulatory processes, the activity of cells and organs is subject to regulation by inputs from the autonomic nervous system, by the supply of substrate, by various hormones, and by immune substances. Enzymes, for example, are not continuously being formed, but are normally only induced in the presence of specific substrates, hormones, or transmitter substances. We know that hormones such as epinephrine, acting upon specific receptors at the cell membrane, activate the cyclic-AMP system and depress the cyclic-GMP system to induce enzyme formation. Ultimately, the level of hormones, of epinephrine, and nutritional intake, i.e., substrate, are under the control of the brain.

Presumably, autoregulatory and regulatory processes are in continual interaction to maintain health or produce illness. Figure 1 of Chapter 2 details some of the multiple variables involved in the autoregulation and regulation of blood pressure. A similar kind of flow chart can illustrate the multifactor control of gastric secretion, bronchial patency, respiration, or thyroid function. It would show, in the case of thyroid function, that the activity of the peripheral thyroid hormones is not only dependent on iodine input and available protein to synthesize thyroglobulin, but that the effective amounts of the hormones depend on the binding protein levels and the rates of their disposition. The autoregulation of thyroid function is well understood and is remarkably stable, but thyroid function is also under the control of TSH and of the rate of disposal of the free thyroid hormones in the blood, which in turn regulate TRH and TSH release.

Another instance of interaction is the patency of the bronchi and bronchioles, which is ultimately regulated by a balance between parasympathetic and α- and β-adrenergic activity. In gout, serum uric acid levels are determined by the rates of biosynthesis of purines and of their disposition, including the disposition of their products, such as uric acid. For gastric function, local autoregulation is achieved through gastrin, which appears to be incited by vagal and sympathetic neural input. Gastrin enhances hydrochloric acid production and release, which in turn serves to inhibit gastrin production.

In a number of instances, then, regulation of the function of organs is controlled by neuronal and hormonal input—under the ultimate control of the brain—and by immunological agents (antibodies). The immune system stands, in the present view, in an intermediate position between the self-regulatory function of an organ and its superordinate regulation by the brain. In the immediate form of hypersensitivity that characterizes bronchial asthma, the interaction of an allergen with its IgE antibody releases a number of substances from mast cells and basophiles that are capable of producing bronchoconstriction. Therefore, the products of this form of immune response can regulate the patency of bronchioles in the lung. In turn, anaphylaxis, another type of the immediate form of hypersensitivity, can be modified by hypothalamic and brain-stem lesions. Whether other forms of human immune processes are regulated by the CNS remains a moot question. There is some evidence that the immediate type of humorally mediated hypersensitivity is influenced by the brain in a manner that still must be determined. Whether delayed forms of humorally mediated immune responses or cell-mediated immune responses are controlled in this manner is equally uncertain. It is, of course, possible that the action of the nervous system may not be direct, but that hormones and transmitter substances may potentiate, compete, or interfere with the products of immune responses at effector cells.

Cells are regulated by a large variety of substances that interact with, modify, potentiate, or inhibit each other's actions. These interactions occur at the surface of the cell, and their effects are transmitted to the interior of the cell by the adenylate cyclase—cyclic-AMP, and guanosylate cyclase—cyclic GMP systems (Watson et al., 1973). For example, it is believed that the LATS may act on cyclic-AMP, as do the corticosteroids and catecholamines, to promote the entrance of iodine into thyroid cells (McKenzie, 1968). Other workers have demonstrated that adrenalectomy (Char and Kelley, 1962) and the administration of thyroid hormone (Long and Shewell, 1955) enhance antibody formation. That the nervous system may regulate immune processes was suggested in a study in which avoidance-conditioning influenced immunological responses (Marsh et al., 1963; Rasmussen et al., 1957). Evidence also indicates that midbrain (Freedman and Fenichel, 1958) and hypothalamic (tuberal) lesions (Szentivanyi and Filipp, 1958) can protect guinea pigs against anaphylactic shock. Anterior hypothalamic lesions have been found to lower circulating antibodies to the same antigen in guinea pigs and to make them less-sensitive to toxic doses of histamine (Schiavi et al., 1966), possibly by modifying the physiological reactivity of the bronchiolar tree to the constrictive effects of histamine.

If, in fact, such interrelationships of the brain and immune processes do operate in man, they must all still be elucidated in detail. It is a scientific question that has barely been addressed, and the answers may have profound implications for psychosomatic research and theory.

It is also evident that the variability of some physiological functions, or levels of hormones, is considerably greater than was once believed, because increasingly efficient and sensitive techniques for the continuous monitoring of a function or the level of a hormone have become available. In consequence, there has been a shift in emphasis in the past decades from the study of the equilibrium conditions of an organ and its functions to a study of the ongoing processes that are responsible for the maintenance and regulation of the equilibrium conditions.

An ongoing process, when continually monitored, is dynamic over the very short term, over the longer term, or not at all. There is a discontinuous, i.e., quantal, release of transmitter substance at the neuromuscular junction. Circadian secretory patterns for human growth hormone (hGH) and cortisol have also been described. Sleep and wakefulness, even some enzyme levels, change rhythmically during a 24-hour period. Some of the polypeptide hormones of the pituitary gland, such as ACTH, are not only secreted in pulses over the very short term and show several secretory episodes in a 24-hour period, but in the adult show a circadian rhythm with peak secretory rates just before awakening. Altered psychological states correlate with increases both in the number of episodes and baseline levels.

In addition, the secretory levels and rhythmic patterns for some pituitary hormones are age-dependent. In the case of LH there is a definite maturational sequence. Only in childhood and in adulthood are the levels steady over a 24-hour period, and even here, the level is maintained by repeated, brief pulses.

If our attention is now primarily directed toward an understanding of these ongoing and fluctuating processes, the concept of a relatively "ideal" homeostatic equilibrium that must be preserved to maintain health is no longer as useful. One building block in a newly conceptualized view of equilibrium conditions is the observation by Richards (1970) and Selye (1973) that the very complex processes that underlie the maintenance of the circulation or the bodily responses to injury, bacteria, antigens, or toxins, may respond excessively in one direction or the other or may be inadequate. For example, antibody formation may result in anaphylactic or allergic reactions, and phagocytosis or fibrosis may protect a bacterium from further destruction or clearance from the body. The effects of some drugs impair the body's capacity for immune and inflammatory responses to viruses, bacteria, or yeasts. A failure of immunoglobulin formation may seriously predispose a person to infection, to malignancies, and to rheumatoid arthritis. Absolute or relative deficiencies of enzyme formation may, as was previously noted, manifest themselves only in the presence of drugs or dietary substances, and then in different ways.

Under Selye's hypothesis, excessive ongoing responses create a wholly new set of equilibrium conditions. I should like to suggest, however, that excessive responses and the creation of new equilibrium conditions are probably predetermined by virtue of a preexisting bias introduced into the autoregulatory mechanisms of an organ, or through the superordinate regulatory mechanisms that regulate and control that organ. Thus, the response to an antigenic stimulus may take the form of excessive antibody formation, or none at all; or the response to a drug may lead to excessive induction of a degradative enzyme, or none at all.

The presence and process of bias in regulatory systems may be identified at a physiological level (e.g., for all the variables controlling and regulating blood pressure) or at a biochemical level (e.g., the steps in the biosynthesis or degradation of epinephrine, or the biosynthesis of thyroid hormones). In order to develop a more-comprehensive understanding of these events, one must know not only levels of the substrate for, and products of, enzyme synthesis and the rates at which they are formed, but also each step in the complex self-regulatory processes that are entailed.

It has been noted, for example, that an enzyme may be inhibited by the end product in its pathway, which ultimately determines its level and rate of formation. Bias may be introduced into this mechanism if end-product inhibition of enzyme formation does not occur, so that the new enzyme continues to be produced. In the presence of a constant supply of aminoacids, this endless production would distort or preempt the supply, to the detriment of the formation of other enzymes. Regulation of enzyme synthesis may also be biased due to the absence of a "regulator" gene that forms a "repressor" (Jacob and Monod, 1961); in such an instance, enzymes are continually formed in the absence of substrate. Disturbances in the interaction of the "repressor" and the gene area (the operator, which regulates enzyme synthesis), due to structural alterations (e.g., the length) of the gene, may also lead to enzyme formation in the absence of substrate.

At the molecular level, such biases may alter the function of cells and their relationship to other cells. One can also conclude that the same end-result may be produced in several different ways: continuous enzyme formation, for example, may be occasioned by three different mechanisms. Therefore, different mechanisms may bring about the same functional disturbance.

In this view, then, the predisposing factors to some diseases we have reviewed may take the form of biases, in one direction or another, of important ongoing self-regulatory or regulatory processes. Bias may be introduced into these regulatory systems by a genetic variation, such as a mutation. The mutation may be expressed by the absence of an enzyme, by a variation in the structure of an enzyme, or by variations in the amount of an enzyme produced, possibly because the rate of biosynthesis of this enzyme can vary.

What consequences ensue when enzyme levels are low? We have learned that in the presence of low levels of an enzyme, sudden marked increases in enzyme levels may occur in response to social stimulation, and this, in turn, suddenly and markedly elevates the levels of biosynthetic products. The consequences that such sudden increases have for a regulatory system, or for behavior, have not yet been fully explicated. In any case, such sudden changes in response to stimulation would tend to alter equilibrium conditions.

The bias is easier to specify in some of these diseases than others. In the case of bronchial asthma, the bias may take the form of an inherent tendency to bronchoconstriction in response to a variety of stimuli (Szentivanyi, 1968). In addition to the products released by antigen-antibody reactions, a number of stimuli enhance this bias to promote an attack, whereas a variety of agents can abort it. Epinephrine, aminophylline, and sodium cromoglycate act at different points in the series of steps that lead to an attack of bronchial asthma.

In rheumatoid arthritis, the predisposition seems to take the form either of excessive or inadequate immunoglobulin formation. In the case of excessive formation, the immunoglobulins form complexes with other immunoglobulins (IgG-IgG, IgG-IgA, IgG-IgM complexes). Either an excess or a deficiency of IgG formation seems to lead to a failure of antigen-antibody clearance from the body, with the result that the complexes are deposited in tissues and in blood vessels. In this example, the *relationships* between the amounts of antibody formed in response to the antigen are altered. Here, either excessive or inadequate antibody formation relative to the antigen may predispose to the disease. In either case, the tendency to form inadequate or excessive antibody seems to be genetically determined and may entail a defect in the genetic control of antibody formation, or in some other mechanism, such as the cyclic-AMP system (Kemp and Duquesnoy, 1973; Kemp et al., 1973).

The "direction" of a predisposing bias need not necessarily be expressed as an excessive or deficient response. In some instances, rather, the predisposition may take the form of a disturbance in the *relationship* between regulatory substances whose absolute values are normal. The predisposition to some forms of peptic duodenal ulcer may consist of disturbances in the reciprocal relationship of gastrin to hydrochloric acid, in addition to an increased secretory capacity of the stomach. One indication supporting the prospective validity of this view is that in the presence of high levels of acid, gastrin levels are typically normal rather than depressed. Similarly, in some forms of essential hypertension it is the relationship of renin and angiotensin to aldosterone that is altered. In the presence of low levels of renin, aldosterone levels may be unexpectedly normal (instead of low), possibly due to a heightened "sensitivity" of some aspect (e.g., the receptor sites) of adrenocortical cells to angiotensin II. On the other hand, it is possible that the disposition of aldosterone has been altered. These examples should emphasize that if we only measure absolute values of regulatory substances in the body, we may mistakenly be led to conclude that no alteration has occurred. In dynamic regulatory systems, it is essential that turnover and production rates are measured.

Thus, in four of the diseases reviewed in this book the relationship between regulatory or autoregulatory systems is altered. Such biases, I would suggest, are one form of predisposition to these diseases. Similar biases may occur in the other diseases. In Graves' disease, it would appear that the bias can take the form of the presence of the LATS and its protector, which preempt the external regulation of the thyroid gland. Other aspects of bias in this disease may be reflected in the form of increased disposition of T_3 and T_4*. In the case of ulcerative colitis we are less-able to specify the nature of the predisposition, except to note that there appears to be a predisposition to form anticolon antibodies in some patients with this disease (Perlmann et al., 1973).

The amount of bias introduced into the regulatory or autoregulatory mechanism may be a crucial element in the predisposition to disease. The predisposition to gout, marked by the presence of excessive serum uric acid levels, seem to be a quantitative alteration. Here, the bias is expressed in the form of increased purine biosynthesis, decreased renal clearance of uric acid, or both.

To propose that predisposing biases exist in regulatory systems does not, of course, necessarily implicate them as immediate antecedent causes of disease. Conditions resulting from such a bias may be present without frank clinical signs of disease. Excessive pepsin and hydrochloric acid secretion are present during periods of remission from peptic ulcer; the tendency to bronchoconstriction is present between attacks of bronchial asthma; the presence of the LATS can, at times, outlast Graves' disease by many years. A primary task in future studies is to determine whether these altered relationships—e.g., between gastrin and hydrochloric acid in peptic duodenal ulcer, and between renin and aldosterone —antecede the respective diseases or are only present during remission.

---

* The presence and action of antithyroglobulin and antimicrosomal antibodies in Graves' disease pose further questions as to how the thyroid gland's regulatory systems may be biased.

Self-regulatory systems in cells and organs, and regulatory systems external to them, may be biased in one direction or another. The bias is either present during remission of a disease or before it occurs. The biases in these systems may arise through different mechanisms. One may suppose that they arise because of genetic variation. For example, the receptor for angiotensin II at adrenocortical cells may either be insensitive or unusually sensitive because of genetic variation. In the first instance, greater than the usual amounts of angiotensin II may elicit normal, or less than the normal amounts of aldosterone. In the second, very small amounts of angiotensin II will cause the secretion of normal or more than the usual amounts of aldosterone.

Genetic variation may not be the only cause of bias in regulatory systems. Repeated exposure of a receptor may lower its threshold to a stimulus: the sensitivity to histamine of bronchiolar musculature increases during repeated attacks of bronchial asthma.

Within the context of these comments on the role of bias, all seven diseases might be described as diseases of regulation, rather than diseases of homeostasis as they have been called in the past (e.g., Shapiro, 1973). Certainly, the concept of homeostasis has required substantial qualification. It now seems likely that health is not a product of the mainte-nance of equilibrium conditions—constant levels of enzymes, hormones, and behaviors—but is a result of patterned, dynamic processes that are constantly changing over both the short and long term. It may be that a disruption in the rhythm of these processes, or a lag in their maturation, may produce disease.

If biases are present in regulatory systems, the stressful factors that initiate disease need not be awesome or unusual. Admittedly, many persons exposed to extreme conditions, such as a terrifying explosion, develop high blood pressure. But the elevated blood pressure may last only two months, and then the blood pressure returns to normal levels.

In the past, much controversy has been engendered by the concept of "stress." For a time during the development of the concept, "stress" was considered to be a quantitative phenomenon. Then it became evident that stress did not have to be overwhelming for disease to occur. The stressed person could not cope with the stress and became distressed. The person's reaction to the perceived stress became the critical variable in the equation. In some, this formulation may indeed be correct. Many, but not all, persons who become ill become helpless and hopeless after the stress of bereavement, in the manner that Engel and his colleagues have described. Some seem essentially untouched by their (supposedly stressful) experiences, as Nemiah and Sifneos have noted (1970). They seem no different than many others exposed to the everyday vicissitudes of life.

Perhaps one may understand their lack of distress in the framework of the hypothesis expounded in this section. If these people differ by virtue of some bias in a particular physiological system, the everday vicissitudes of life—a job change, a promotion, a child going to college, or a family argument—may tip the balance from health to disease. The life situation is neither intolerable nor excessively distressful but the physiological changes that accompany it tip the scale toward disease, because they interact with a biased physiological system. Had no bias been present, no disease would have occurred. One may, therefore, conclude that neither the particular quality nor the quantity of a life event determines whether disease will occur—but the physiological predisposition to it does.

Intrinsic to every hypothesis that social and psychological factors play a role in predispos-ing to a disease is the belief that these psychological and social factors act in some manner through the brain and its outflow systems. The brain, in turn, regulates superordinately every organ and its functions. This does not mean, as theorists in psychosomatic medicine have assumed, that social and psychological events are directly translated into hormonal, autonomic, or neuromuscular outputs. It is entirely possible that the initiation of the disease may be brought about in other ways. (see pp. 622–636, this Chapter).

This is not to imply that the physiological concomitants of a perceived threat and of adaptive failure on the psychological side do not occur. However, we have always proceeded on the belief that it is the emotional consequences of threat and loss that are directly translated into bodily changes.

THE HETEROGENEITY OF PREDISPOSING FACTORS TO DISEASE AND THE HETEROGENEITY OF DISEASE

A particular disease is not necessarily the result of the same etiological and pathogenetic mechanisms. Some patients with gout have normal levels of SUA. Elevations of SUA do not inevitably cause gout. Elevations of SUA are produced by several different mechanisms. The pathogenetic mechanisms responsible for acute gouty arthritis in patients with normal or elevated SUA levels are unknown. The list of the heterogeneity of the etiology and pathogenesis of many diseases is long. Therefore, and in all likelihood, each of the diseases in this book is heterogeneous in character. Even if a single mechanism, or a consistent series of mechanisms, could be identified as the primary antecedent factor in any one of these diseases (Moos and Solomon, 1966), our ignorance about the pathogenetic patterns would make it extremely difficult to establish a correlation between the psychological response and the physiological manifestation. Further, if different pathogenetic mechanisms can produce the same or similar anatomical and functional changes, the achievement of such a correlation is virtually impossible. There is good reason to believe that an anatomical lesion such as a duodenal ulcer or a functional increase in systolic blood pressure may be brought about by a variety of pathogenetic mechanisms (Brunner et al., 1972).

Duodenal ulceration occurs in a variety of clinical situations that do not share a common pathogenetic mechanism. In the Zollinger-Ellinson syndrome, gastrin levels are usually, but not always, increased. Increases in gastrin levels may also occur in rheumatoid arthritis and in patients with burns or brain lesions. But elevations of gastrin levels do not occur with carcinoid tumors of the stomach, and they have not been shown to occur with drugs that produce duodenal ulceration. A drug, like aspirin, inhibits the synthesis of mucin—the protective layer. To further complicate the picture, not everyone who has a brain lesion, terminal illness, who has been burned, or who takes aspirin develops a duodenal ulcer.

The "choice" of disease is determined by the person's predisposition to it. Not everyone who takes reserpine becomes depressed. Taking the oral contraceptive pill may lead to weight gain in some, to hypertension in others, and to thromboembolic disease in still others. Predisposition interacts with pathogenesis. And pathogenesis is not invariant in a particular disease. Elevated blood pressure levels can be produced by pheochromocytomas, aldosterinomas, reninomas, coarctation of the aorta, elevated intracranial pressure, and perhaps by psychosocial factors.

Psychosocial, allergic, and infectious factors as well as irritation of the nose, nasal sinuses, and exercise can all incite attacks of bronchial asthma, if the predisposition to bronchoconstriction is present. The LATS and possibly other immunoglobulins seem to play a pathogenetic role in most, but not all, cases of Graves' disease. Psychological factors also seem to precipitate the onset on Graves' disease. But our knowledge about the manner in which they do so remains rudimentary.

One must, therefore, conclude that no one pathogenetic mechanism invariably produces a disease. In fact, a combination of mechanisms may account for the onset of a disease. This statement is exemplified by the case of peptic ulcer. Menguy (1964) and State (1971) have suggested that there are four major variables which, either singly or in combination, might produce an ulcer: the parietal cell mass, the vagal input to the stomach, the blood supply to the stomach, and the mucous-defense. These variables appear to exert their influence by a variety of means, and our knowledge of the processes involved is still quite scant. As noted previously, an increased parietal cell mass can express itself by an expanded capacity for pepsin and hydrochloric acid production, which may, in turn, be mediated by the vagus nerve and by gastrin levels. Little as yet is known about how the blood supply of the stomach is regulated by sympathetic and vagal means. Mucosal ischemia alone will not produce an ulcer, but it is possible that ischemia in combination with high output-levels of pepsin and acid may do so.

The diagnosis of a peptic duodenal ulcer is not often made in infants and children. Little is known about its pathogenesis in children. Immediately after birth, high levels of hydrochloric acid secretion are found in the stomach and are believed to play a role in peptic ulcer disease in infants. Later in childhood, the levels of gastric acid fall. Little, in addition, is known about the pathogenetic factors in childhood peptic ulcer disease (Ackerman, 1975). Gastric ulcer in rats can be produced by a variety of methods (Ader, 1971). The earliest age that rats, prematurely weaned at 15 days, develop gastric ulcers is at 22 days. When adult, these rats are more resistant to gastric ulcer formation than rats normally weaned at 21 days (Ackerman et al., 1975). The meaning of these results seems to be that different mechanisms are responsible for gastric ulcer formation in rats at different times in their lives, and that premature weaning makes rats more susceptible to gastric ulcers at one age and more resistant to them when they are older.

In other diseases, the situation is even more perplexing. There are formidable gaps in our knowledge, which, even with a coherent hypothesis concerning predisposition, make it extremely difficult to speculate about pathogenetic mechanisms. This is true even in a case such as Graves' disease, where much is now known about normal thyroid autoregulation and its control by the hypothalamic-pituitary axis, as well as about the fundamental pathophysiology of the disease. The problem is even more confounding in ulcerative colitis, where neither the immediate pathogenetic factors nor the mechanisms that control them are known. We do not know—indeed, we cannot even guess—the location of the initial lesion, and our knowledge of all the hormonal, autonomic, and vascular influences that affect the colon is still rudimentary.

It is not unlikely that both ulcerative colitis and rheumatoid arthritis are systemic diseases. If, then, the focus of psychobiological conceptualization and investigation is on a *local* manifestation—on, say a lesion in the colon or in the joint—it will fail to provide us with a comprehensive understanding of the more-general process. Thus, our present

610

ignorance about the nature and initiation of disease is a major obstacle in the development of testable hypotheses that link psychosocial factors to the pathogenesis of these diseases.

THE INITIATION OF DISEASE

There are currently three major psychosomatic theories of the initiation of disease—the specific conflict theory, the situational theory, and the stress theory—associated respectively with the names of Alexander, Engel, and Selye. None of these theories is completely satisfactory. Alexander implied that emotional states were translated into a physiological response in a linear manner, but he did not say specifically how this translation was to be mediated, or why a particular emotional state was "channeled" into one physiological response and not another. The chain of events that begins with an experience and ends with a lesion is largely unknown. A fundamental problem is that we cannot now explain how the perceived event and the psychological responses that it occasions are transformed by the brain into physiological events mediated by the release of tropic hormones from the pituitary, by the autonomic nervous system, by the neuromuscular apparatus, and possibly by immunological events. Alexander assumed that the pathogenetic mechanism in each disease is always the same. In the light of our present knowledge this assumption is probably incorrect. Different pathogenetic mechanisms may bring about the same disease or the same anatomical lesion.

We do not know how emotions bring about bodily changes. The local physiological changes in the stomach and duodenum that cause the formation of a duodenal ulcer are also largely unknown. We do not know whether rheumatoid arthritis is a systemic disease or one that begins in synovial or cartilage cells, ground substance, or blood vessels. If, for example, a slow virus that has infected synovial cells is primarily involved, our attention would have to be directed to brain-regulated processes that promote virus induction. On the other hand, if the rheumatoid process begins in blood vessels, assuming that this is not a secondary aspect indicating the presence of latent slow virus, we would look for disturbances in the regulation and function of blood vessels.

In both Engel's and Alexander's models, events that produce a critical emotional response are described as "stressful" situations. Selye conceived of stress as directly straining the organism. His concept of stress has undergone modification through the work of Hamburg and Adams (1967), Katz and his associates (1970a and b), Lazarus (1966), Mason (1968, 1971) and Wolff (1953). Selye believed that stress invariably and directly produces physiological and anatomical changes by straining the adaptive *physiological* capacities of his animals. The revised version of his concept is that in man the same event is stressful to some and not to others. The event must be *perceived* as stressful; it must acquire meaning to the person. To some the meaning of the perceived event is distressful and is accompanied by physiological changes when the distress is not coped with. To others, the meaning of the event is banal and causes no distress. A third group copes with the distress, psychological adaptation to the event occurs, and no physiological changes occur. The observation that the responses to stressful life events and situations are highly individual and may or may not be accompanied by physiological changes has also been extended to stresses that are usually considered to be physical. Mason (1968, 1971) believes that the

611

effect of exposing an animal to heat, cold, and painful electric shock cannot be understood unless the emotional responses to these thermal or physical stimuli are also taken into account. He believes that the stimuli first produced an emotional response, which is then translated into physiological change. Because the emotional responses of animals are individual and variable, the physiological responses are also.

Before we have a comprehensive psychogiological theory of disease, much more information is needed about the psychobiology of bereavement, "stress," conflict, and, above all, of emotion. In the following sections, some aspects of the psychobiology of each of these four areas is reviewed, and the gaps in our current knowledge are indicated.

Toward a Psychobiology of Bereavement

Engel's view is that many diseases begin in a setting of bereavement. This experience, he postulated, produces a state of adaptive failure characterized psychologically by hopelessness, helplessness, and a giving-up/having-given-up complex conditioned by prior life experiences.

The most characteristic feature of this response is the sense of "psychological impotence"—a feeling that one is unable to cope with any task. The response is complex and manifested by (1) feelings of helplessness and hopelessness, (2) low self-esteem, (3) an inability to enjoy the company of other people, one's work, hobbies, etc., (4) a disruption of the sense of continuity of one's personal, past, present, and future, and (5) a reactivation of memories of earlier periods of "giving-up." Engel believes that this state of mind could last for varying periods of time, that it is commonplace for people to experience it several times during a lifetime, and that disease tends to occur in situations in which prompt resolution was impossible and periods of "struggling" alternated with periods of "giving-up."

The loss of another person does not need to be real for helplessness or hopelessness to occur. The loss may be threatened, assumed, or imagined. Prior experiences sensitize many persons to loss. Dependent or self-centered people are particularly sensitive to real losses, or they interpret every change in their relationships to others as a loss. Because children are also especially sensitive to real or threatened losses, the assumption has been made that from birth on, strong bonds of attachment are formed between the child and others. Such bonds of attachment have also been studied in other mammals, and their importance for the well-being of the organism is dramatically demonstrated when these bonds of attachment are broken, permanently or briefly (Harlow, 1961; Himwich et al., 1968; Hinde and Spencer-Booth, 1971; Hofer, 1971, 1975; Kaufman and Rosenblum, 1969; Mason et al., 1968). The breaking of the bond between human beings may have one of several consequences. The usual response to the experience is grief, which is gradually dispelled by the process of mourning. Another person may, however, react with depression or suicide, with helplessness or hopelessness, sometimes even with elation or schizophrenia; or an attempt to "drown" the grief or depression in alcohol or other mood-changing drugs. The psychological complex described by Engel is probably the most-extreme form of response to bereavement. The variety of psychological responses are the result of differing response methods of coping or not coping with bereavement.

612

Psychological defenses and other "coping" mechanisms in man have been viewed as mediators between the perception of an event—such as a loss—and its interpretation as a threat. It seems likely that these mechanisms were involved in Engel's studies, where, although the five manifestations of the "giving-up/given-up" complex were experienced singly or in combination by many people in response to stressful experiences throughout their lifetime, most dealt with them without giving up.

One of the ways of coping with stressful everyday (or even extreme) situations is to seek for information that can be used to overcome them (Hamburg and Adams, 1967). Stressful events can span the range from separation of children from their parents to the threat of war, or war itself. Other stressful common experiences include illness, the birth of siblings, going to school, puberty, marriage, pregnancy, the birth of children, and migration. Hamburg and Adams noted that most of the relevant psychiatric literature has emphasized the utilization of "defenses" to avoid the impact, or minimize the mental pain, of such stressful experiences. But these experiences need not be stressful and disrupt psychological functioning, because some persons are successful in coping with them. Successful adaptive methods of coping with stressful experiences lead to new psychological "skills" in coping with stress (Chodoff et al., 1964; Friedman et al., 1963; Hamburg et al., 1953a, b). In one such study of victims of severe burns received in combat, Hamburg and his co-workers (1953a, b) noted that the patients tended, at first, to deny or minimize the nature and extent of the injury and its probable consequences, but that they were gradually able to accept injury and the possibility of their rehabilitation. After some periods of discouragement and depression, the subjects came to terms with the realities of their situation, their prospects for recovery, and the limitations that might be imposed on their future lives. When permanent disability resulted, the group noted, the "coping" process was aided by a sense of belonging to a "special" group. An opportunity to discuss personal concerns about the injury and its consequences with a physician occasionally resulted in dramatic improvement of mood in several of the patients. In an effort to relieve their own distress and difficulty, some patients were ultimately able to accept certain facts and to make use of them in a way that they had previously avoided. Thus, the seeking and utilizing of information provided by another person may be useful to some patients as a means of coping with injury.

A similar conclusion was reached by Wolff et al. (1964) in a study of parents of children dying of leukemia. After an initial period of shock, disbelief, and depression when first being told about their children's disease, these parents gradually came to accept it by discussing it. Their sense of guilty responsibility for the disease was dispelled by a frank discussion of its nature, by information about treatment, and, finally, by advice and sympathy about the anticipated loss of their child. A variety of (successful) methods of coping, even with the impending tragedy of a child's death, are available to most human beings.

The remainder, who are not so fortunate, become ill in various ways or die. Following a real bereavement, morbidity and mortality are increased. The mortality among widowers 55 years old or older in the first six months after the death of their spouse was 40 percent greater than in married men who had suffered no such loss (Young et al., 1963). The mortality of younger men and women who had recently lost a spouse is also higher than

613

expected (Kraus and Lilienfeld, 1959). The loss of a spouse does not necessarily lead to death, but it increases the risk of mental illnesses serious enough to require hospitalization (Adamson and Schmale, 1965; Parkes, 1964).

Bereavement that is not coped with and that produces the "giving-up/given-up" complex has been estimated to precede many different diseases. Engel (1968) has stated that the complex is associated with disease onset in 70 to 80 percent of all patients. Bereavement plays a role in most, if not all, patients with the diseases discussed in this book. Real or threatened loss has been cited by many authors as a factor contributing to the initiation of other diseases not discussed in this volume: cancer (Bahnson, 1969; Kissen, 1967; LeShan, 1966), tuberculosis (Day, 1951), diabetes mellitus (Hinkle and Wolf, 1952), lymphomas and leukemias (Greene, 1954), juvenile diabetes mellitus (Stein and Charles, 1971), and the onset of congestive heart failure (Perlman, 1971).

A variety of other diseases in patients hospitalized in a general medical ward has started in a setting of loss and bereavement that had occurred one week or one month before onset (Schmale, 1958). Depressive moods, the attitude of giving up, and the loss of all hope adversely affects the successful outcome of surgical operations (Kimball, 1969). Postoperative complications and operative mortality are increased in patients who have lost all hope before undergoing cardiac surgery (Kennedy and Bakst, 1966).

The cause of a comprehensive psychobiology of disease would be furthered immeasurably were we to know the physiological mechanisms that produce an increased mortality and morbidity, and enhance the risks of surgery, in hopeless, depressed, and helpless patients, or those who have given up. We do know that bereaved persons may cope psychologically with their loss, and when they do certain correlated physiological (hormonal) responses are minimal. When they do not cope, hormone levels increase and their 24-hour rhythms may be altered. Most of the behavioral biology of depressive states and psychological disorganization has been elucidated through the study of adreno-cortical and -medullary hormones in psychiatric patients. In the work by Sachar et al. (1963) with acute schizophrenic patients there was a statistically reliable correlation between acute states of panic and disruption of most psychological functions, and elevated urinary levels of 17-hydroxycorticoids (17-OHCS), epinephrine, and norepinephrine. Peak values occurred during the acute state of emotional turmoil at the onset of the psychosis. With the appearance of an elaborate and well-formed delusional system, hormone levels returned to normal for a period of time only to rise again when the patient was confronted with the reasons for his breakdown (such as bereavement). During the recovery phase, urinary levels of 17-OHCS, epinephrine, and norepinephrine returned to normal. The *apparent* agitation and misery also serves, in the same way, to protect the depressed patient from the pain of realizing his loss and mourning (Bunney, 1965). Sachar (1969) and his group also found a correlation (1967), in a study of acutely depressed women in an inpatient setting, between urinary 17-OCHS levels and observed patient behavior. They postulated that if depressive symptoms actually protected a patient against the realization of loss, confronting her with the loss should provoke psychological "disequilibrium" and result in a rise in the excretion level of 17-OHCS. And this, indeed, was what they observed. Later, using more sophisticated techniques, Sachar and his colleagues (1970) concluded that ". . . adrenocortical activity in depressed patients is primarily related to dimensions of emotional arousal and psychotic disorganization rather than to depressive illness *per se*" or, for that matter, to schizophrenia.

This conclusion implies that the emotional consequences of loss—the "giving-up/given-up" complex—may result form a failure of psychological "coping" mechanisms, leading to the psychological reactions described, and to physiological changes, including, perhaps, physical disease. A perceived threat or "stress" results in the increased secretion of ACTH and cortisol. These hormones are known to have wide-ranging effects on a variety of systems and functions (electrolyte balance, glucose and fat metabolism, nitrogen excretion, the induction of the biosynthetic enzyme of epinephrine, stabilization of the membrane of cell organelles, immune mechanisms, the suppression of prostaglandin release, and the electrical excitability of the brain). Their release in concert with states of grief, depression, and an inability to cope with them may possibly be related to the onset of disease.

The relationship of various ways of coping with real or actual loss has not only been studied in psychotic patients. The same correlations between the effectiveness of coping and urinary levels of 17-OHCS have been obtained by studying the parents of leukemic children (Friedman et al., 1963; Hofer et al., 1972a, b; Wolff et al., 1964). At each stage of the child's illness, 17-OHCS levels could reliably be predicted from the parents' ability to cope with the impending or actual death of their child. The criteria for predicting these levels were the "integrity" of inferred psychological "defenses" (such as repression, denial, isolation, and identification), and the extent of emotional arousal (especially of unpleasant feelings). The characteristic differences between individual parents were studied with the hypotheses that the more-effectively the person defended against impending loss, the lower the mean 17-OHCS urinary excretion rate would be. In 23 of 31 instances, predictions of the levels of 17-OHCS excretion were made from the psychological data; the results supported the hypothesis that the more "effective" the defenses, the lower the mean 17-OHCS excretion level. One of the implications of this study, then, is that the baseline level of an individual's 17-OHCS excretion level may reflect the general effectiveness of psychological defenses.

Hofer et al. (1972a, b), continued to study these parents after their children had died. They found that the threat of bereavement may have different psychological and hormonal consequences than the actuality of loss. Many of the parents who originally had high levels, later (one to two years after their children had died) had low 17-OHCS excretion levels, and vice versa. Once again the psychoendocrine correlations were valid: most of those who later had high levels openly expressed grief, sadness, distress, or guilt, while six of nine parents with low excretion levels had overcome their grief, or were bland and impersonal, overcontrolled emotionally, or jovial.

Persons can not only overcome grief, but they may become accustomed to and cope with wartime danger; in one group, studied after the adaptation to danger had been made, urinary levels of 17-OHCS were low. During the training period, when no psychological adaptations to danger had been made, the levels were high (Bourne et al., 1967).

Variations in urinary excretion levels of 17-OHCS probably reflect changes in the production and secretion rates of the corticosteroids by the adrenal gland. It has become possible to measure the production rates of one of them, cortisol. This measure was used to show that cortisol production rates covary with dejection or despair and the effectiveness of coping with the threat of anticipated breast biopsy. In a group of women awaiting breast biopsy for a suspected tumor, those who showed the greatest emotional distress, or experienced unpleasant feelings such as fear, dejection, despair, or apprehension, tended to have relatively elevated hydrocortisone production rates, while those who were more hopeful about the outcome of surgery showed relatively low rates (Katz et al., 1970a, b).

Other types of loss have been correlated with changes in body biochemistry, even though the mechanisms involved are still unknown. Kasl and his colleagues (1968) reported a longitudinal study of changes in SUA and cholesterol levels in men who were losing their jobs. The subjects were 56 married men, 35 to 60 years of age, who had held "blue collar" jobs for a minimum period of three years, and who were about to lose them because of a permanent plant shutdown. They were seen by Public Health nurses approximately three months before they lost their jobs and then 1, 4, 8, 12, and 24 months after. On each visit, blood and urine specimens were collected, and the blood pressure, pulse rate, height, and weight were measured. A structured interview schedule was administered for the purpose of collecting various social, psychological, and health data. Thirty-four control subjects who came from plants that were continuing to operate were also studied in terms of the same parameters. The principal findings in this study were: (1) Anticipation of plant shutdown was associated with elevated SUA and normal cholesterol levels; (2) SUA levels rapidly dropped to premorbid levels if new employment was quickly found; otherwise, they tended to remain elevated until reemployment; (3) the more "stressful" the man found the period of anticipated job loss, the greater was the change in SUA level; (4) those men who did not wait for their jobs to be terminated, but resigned in order to seek new jobs, had high stable SUA levels; (5) cholesterol levels did not rise while the loss of a job was anticipated but rose during the period of unemployment, returning to previous levels only after a new job was found; and (6) members of the control group showed no significant fluctuations either in serum uric acid or cholesterol levels during the period of study.

The psychological and physiological effects of loss have usually been studied after it has occurred. A verification of the effects of loss ideally requires prospective studies in which human beings are experimentally separated from each other. Since such human studies would be unethical, they have been tested instead in mammals by several groups of investigators. In these animals, experience of separation induced profound, immediate behavioral consequences, including marked motor activity, pitiful crying, sleep disruption that gradually progresses to immobility, and very characteristic species-specific postures (Bronfenbrenner, 1968; Harlow, 1961; Hinde and Spencer-Booth, 1971; Kaufman and Rosenblum, 1969).

Analysis of the effects of separation in 14 day-old rats has revealed that the processes governing these behavioral changes are different from those at work on physiological and respiratory systems (Hofer, 1971, 1975; Hofer and Weiner, 1971a, b). Absence of the mother induces in infant rats a progressive increase in locomotor, self-grooming, and "emotional" behavior (defecation-urination), with an onset time of four to eight hours. Infusions of milk over 24 hours have no significant effect on these behavioral changes, but provision of a nonlactating foster mother prevents them. Here, the behavioral interaction with the mother appears to be the major element, and further studies have suggested that

616

deprivation of tactile and olfactory sensory stimulation is critical, while thermal, visual, auditory, and vestibular systems are far less-likely to have an influence.

Separating young rats from their mothers also has demonstrable physiological effects (Hofer, 1971, 1975; Hofer and Weiner, 1971a, b, 1975), the full range of which has not as yet been elucidated. Different facets of the separation experience affect different systems. The physical presence of the mother reverses some of the behavioral manifestations produced by separation. The milk she provides maintains the infant rat's normal heart rate. Other studies have made it clear that the immediate effects of separation are different in different genera, and even different species of mammals (Kaufman and Rosenblum, 1969).

Other animal studies have described the long-range impact of separation on behavior. Baby animals were taken away from their mothers at birth and "artificially" reared. The results indicate that, over the long term, every major aspect of adult behavior—social, reproductive, maternal, and aggressive—was affected (Harlow, 1961; Mason et al., 1968).

The information provided through both animal and human studies indicates that: separation and bereavement usually, but not invariably, produce changes in behavior and physiological function. Not everyone is affected in the same way by bereavement. Some grieve. Others become helpless and hopeless. Some become physically, and others emotionally, ill. Those who change have been sensitized to actual, threatened, or imaginary loss or bereavement by prior experience with loss. They are also less capable of dealing with current losses. Those who do not change are either not threatened by separation and bereavement or are able to cope with them by the usual process of grief and mourning. Other bereaved people find surrogates—to replace the lost person—who sustain them in their loss. The capacity to adapt in a way that reduces "stresses" or bereavement allows the bereaved to "integrate" these experiences in a healthy way. The threat of bereavement may produce different behavioral and physiological consequences than the actuality of loss. The long-term effects of separating young animals from their mothers at birth are general and profound. They may differ from the acute, short-term effects of separating young animals some time after birth.

Bereavement in human beings is associated with increased morbidity and with physiological changes. The specific disease a person gets is determined by multiple predisposing factors. But we do not know how the physiological changes accompanying bereavement interact with predisposing factors. Nor do we know whether the relationship between the physiological, behavioral, and psychological changes is a causal one. The symptoms and signs of a disease may begin or recur at certain times of the year, and at specific times of the day or night. An understanding of these phenomena will have to be included in a full explanation of a disease. Attacks of bronchial asthma occur in some patients only at night, for reasons that are not understood. We do know, however, that during the first part of the night the pulsatile production of glucocorticoids is very low, and then as morning approaches it markedly increasees. In addition, during REM periods, autonomically mediated functions are highly variable. Therefore, in order to understand the onset or recurrence of a disease, one has to take into account the time of day. Because a number of hormones, enzymes, and other physiological systems show circadian variations, the time when a symptom occurs may be of critical importance (Curtis, 1972). We also know that the circadian rhythms of sleep and of cortisol production may be disrupted during depressive mood states (Sachar et al., 1970). Some circadian rhythms also undergo maturational changes with age (Boyar et al., 1972) and may revert to age-inappropriate patterns during a disease (Boyar et al., 1974). Variations or disruptions of circadian patterns may help us to understand why a disease manifests itself at a particular time during the day and not at another time, or at a particular age of the patient and not at another age.

A Psychobiology of Stress—Physiological Patterns

Although a great deal of attention has been devoted in this book to bereavement as a framework for human disease onset, there are, of course, other "stresses"—many of them already detailed in earlier chapters—which act as the setting in which disease may begin. The physiological concomitants of other types of "stress" have been studied in animals in great detail, often with unexpected implications for our understanding of the broad range of bodily changes that ensue.

The observation that a broad range of physiological changes occur in stressed animals and humans fails to support the idea that specific emotional responses co-relate with specific physiological changes—an assumption that Alexander (1950) made in his formulations about the pathogenetic mechanisms of the psychosomatic diseases. Each feeling or mood does not have its specific physiological correlates. Neither anger nor fear are accompanied by specific or discrete physiological changes. The physiological changes that have been correlated with emotional states may also be produced by cognitive tasks such as mental arithmetic (see Chapter 2), or by avoidance conditioning of man and animals.

In a shock-avoidance study with monkeys, Mason (1968) demonstrated the probable existence of neural and neuroendocrine mechanisms that regulate the orderly and sequential release of hormones. When the monkeys Mason studied were actively engaged in avoiding shock over a 72-hour period, some hormone levels increased rapidly during and following the avoidance session; the levels of other hormones declined; levels of still other hormones remained altered long after the session had been terminated. For example, urinary 17-OHCS and epinephrine levels rose during the session. After the session, 17-OHCS levels declined slowly, but there was a rapid fall in epinephrine levels. Norepinephrine levels in urine rose during the session, continued to rise after it had ended, and remained elevated for at least six days thereafter. Thyroid responses rose slowly during the session and fell slowly after the session. Insulin levels rose only after the session had been over for a period of time, after having shown a slight dip during and immediately following its termination. The production of male and female sex hormones and the volume of urine excreted tended to be depressed during the session and for at least one day after the experimental procedure had been concluded.

Although the monkeys in Mason's study showed some individual variations in production levels and response patterns, the results suggest that avoidance conditioning causes an organized pattern of hormonal release. But these findings do not tell us what regulates such release, or what specific aspect of the experimental situation sets the regulatory devices into motion. As enumerated by Mason, the experience included such elements as sleep deprivation, the muscular activity entailed in lever pressing, the visual stimulus of the warning light, tactile and proprioceptive feedback when the lever was manipulated, the mild pain of electric shock when the lever was not pressed, and the novelty of the experimental situation. However, Mason has cogently refuted the argument that any one of these variables might have induced stress to any significant degree. Rather, he believes that the prepotent stressful factor in the avoidance conditioning experience was the emotional disturbance that the avoidance behavior evoked. In short, he contends that the monkey's emotional response to this experience was in itself the critical intervening variable in the experimental situation, which, in turn, implies that it was the animal's emotional response that triggered the complex pattern of hormonal release.

In all probability, the patterns of hormonal release that Mason studied were determined in part by hypothalamic and adrenal transducer cells. But we have yet to determine by what circuits and mechanisms these cells were linked to the monkey's emotional response. Once we have answered this question, we will have solved the problem of the transduction of experience by the brain.

Additional data about the integrated patterns of hormone release come from another series of investigations (von Euler, 1971). Axelrod (1971a, b) and his co-workers (Axelrod et al., 1970; Mueller et al., 1970; Weinshilboum and Axelrod, 1970) have demonstrated that the patterns can be analyzed into separate components. For example, the biosynthesis of catecholamines in the adrenal gland is under the control of several different mechanisms. ACTH exerts long-term hormonal control over three of the enzymes involved in the biosynthesis of these catecholamines, and both short- and long-term neural control and regulation of the same enzymes exists.

The existence of separate mechanisms is also implicit in Mason's work. The novel experience for a monkey of sitting in a chair prior to the avoidance session produced immediate effects on 17-OHCS hormone levels that were not unlike those produced by the experimental procedure. When the avoidance procedures were repeated at weekly intervals, there was a gradual decrease in hormone levels with each successive session, and finally there was a suppression of 17-OHCS levels.

Organized patterns also emerge when cardiovascular responses to psychological tasks are measured and when more than one physiological measure is taken (see Chapter 2). Using mental arithmetic performed under duress as the psychological stimulus, Brod (1960, 1970) and his co-workers (1959, 1962) produced increases in blood pressure, cardiac output, muscle blood flow and splanchnic vasoconstriction in both normotensive and hypertensive human subjects. However, they noted in hypertensive subjects a tendency toward greater renal vasoconstriction and less vasodilatation in muscle. In addition, the hypertensive subjects differed from the comparison group in that hemodynamic changes and elevations of blood pressure persisted for a longer period after the psychological stimulus had ceased.

The pattern that Brod and his group (1959, 1962, 1970) demonstrated is probably under the control of the sympathetic vasodilator system (Uvnäs, 1960). One of the main relay stations of this system is located in the perifornical hypothalamus. According to Abrahams and his co-workers (1960), brief stimulation of this area in cats produced both cardiovascular and behavioral responses that consisted of sympathetic vasodilatation in muscle, increased heart rate, vasoconstriction in the vascular beds (other than muscle), and an increased secretion of catecholamines. This pattern is analogous, if not homologous, to that which Brod described in man. Of even greater interest in this context is the successful effort by Folkow and Rubenstein (1966) to produce sustained hypertension in rats by mild and intermittent stimulation of this locus in the brain over a period of several months.

In 1967 and 1968, Rahe, Arthur and their co-workers reported a study in which SUA and cholesterol levels were measured three times weekly in 32 men undergoing training in a Navy underwater demolition team. These exercises are considered to be among the most "rigorous . . . and stressful" training experiences in military life. The subjects were picked randomly from a class and observed until they had either successfully completed the course or had withdrawn from it. The behavioral data were obtained by means of clinical interviews and a psychological questionnaire prepared by Holmes and Rahe.

The investigators found statistically significant ($p < .025$) elevations in mean SUA level on mornings when the subjects were eagerly preparing to take on new, challenging, and often physically complicated activities. A significant fall in mean SUA levels occurred on days of prolonged, tedious, and unpleasant physical activity, or when the schedule was unusually light. These fluctuations were more dramatic in the group of 20 men who successfully completed the course than in the 12 who did not. In general, SUA levels were higher and cholesterol levels lower in those who completed the course with the greatest success. Serum cholesterol levels generally tended to fluctuate inversely with SUA levels. Illustrative of this pattern were the changes that occurred during the first week of training when the men were most-enthusiastic, -alert, and -generally confident of their ability to cope with the task at hand; at this time, group mean SUA levels were at their highest (7.78 mg percent) and serum cholesterol levels near their lowest values. By the time the training course was almost completed, the enthusiasm of the participants had waned considerably as the task had become routine but physically overwhelming; during this second period, SUA levels fell to relatively low levels (mean is 5.46 mg percent), while cholesterol levels reached their peak.

The authors concluded that the SUA levels had become elevated in response to dire conditions. However, while training for underwater demolition is undoubtedly "stressful" for any situation to be genuinely distressing to an individual, it must be perceived as a threat (Hamburg and Adams, 1967; Katz et al., 1970b). For someone who viewed successful completion of the Navy course as a personal challenge, this situation might indeed represent a potential threat. However, the authors presented relatively little information as to the precise emotional impact of this experience on the different individuals in the study and did not discuss this point in relationship to individual differences in fluctuations of SUA levels.

In their second report on the same study, Rahe et al. (1968) suggested that an analysis of serum cortisol levels might reveal further interesting relationships between SUA, cholesterol, and cortisol under "stressful" conditions. Rubin and his co-workers (1969, 1970) found that while their subjects tended to run chronically elevated serum cortisol levels during the period of training, further significant but transient elevations of serum cortisol also occurred during periods when the men were *anxiously* (rather than eagerly) anticipating training situations that promised to be particularly demanding. Since, for many subjects, situations that were likely to evoke anxious anticipation alternated with those associated with eager optimism about completing the task, SUA and cortisol levels were frequently out of phase with each other; i.e., one would be falling while the other was rising, or vice versa. The reciprocal relationship between SUA and cortisol may be relevant to the pathogenesis of gout—a topic about which we still know very little. If SUA levels rise when cortisol levels fall, after periods of anxious anticipation, the stage may be set for a bout of gouty arthritis. Corticosteroids have also been shown to have, in addition to their anti-inflammatory action, the capacity to increase uric acid excretion by the kidneys (Hellman et al., 1948). Thus, a precipitous decline in relatively elevated serum cortisol level could conceivably result in a rebound elevation (via decreased renal clearance) in SUA levels, and might then be associated with an attack of acute gouty arthritis. A sudden decline in cortisol levels may precipitate acute gouty arthritis or asymptomatic hyperuricemic subjects following the termination of a course of therapy with ACTH (Hellman, 1949).

Our understanding of patterned physiological change has been inhibited by the frequent tendency among experimenters to limit their investigations of physiological changes induced by psychological stimuli to the study of a single dependent variable over a brief period of time. It is important to investigate as many of the behavioral and physiological responses to a specific psychological experience as is consistent with a sound research design, for only then can we get a complete picture of the pattern of physiological change evoked by psychological experience. The data obtained from multivariable studies can then, it is hoped, be correlated with validated physiological findings obtained by other means. A useful focus of investigation, for example, is the known patterns of physiological change produced by the stimulation of discrete brain sites. When stimulation at relevant sites is carried out, it becomes more apparent that the brain is capable of regulating a pattern of physiological change that is mediated by autonomic and hormonal outputs.

Not only does the brain control integrated patterns of physiological and behavioral change—it can also regulate discrete physiological change with exquisite precision (Miller, 1969; DiCara, 1971). In the curarized rat, heart rate, systolic blood pressure (independent of heart rate), peripheral vasomotor responses, gastrointestinal motility, and urine formation can be specifically modified in an expected direction by instrumental learning. Only the rewarded response changes, and the learned response is specific to the type of response rewarded and is not limited to general patterns of autonomic discharge. Attempts to verify these results have failed. Therefore, their potential therapeutic importance and scientific significance remains uncertain. They suggest, nonetheless, that discrete bodily responses may be generated under certain conditions by the brain.

The Effects of Temporal Factors on Psychophysiological Relationships and Their Underlying Mechanisms

Work with both animal and human subjects has made it evident that in any effort to understand psychophysiological correlations at least four key variables must be taken into account. They are the timing and duration of the experience or experimental manipulation, and the prior experience and age of the person or animal. As noted earlier, Mason found that repeated sessions of avoidance conditioning produced a marked attenuation and, ultimately, a suppression of 17-OHCS levels in monkeys. From work on human subjects we know that, while unexpected or novel situations and the anticipation of a stressful task can elicit marked physiologic change, repeated exposure to stress produces an adaptation or habituation. Other studies indicate that early experiences modify later behavioral as well as physiological response tendencies and adaptations to stress. These data imply that changes occurring in the brain as a consequence of early experiences permanently alter the manner in which later experience is transduced. It appears likely that

621

the specificity and individuation that characterize human behavior can only be understood, at least in part, within this framework.

It is now known that acute stresses, such as novel experiences and preparation to take action evoke anticipatory (Burstein and Russ, 1965; Fenz and Epstein, 1967; Mason, 1968; Moncrief et al., 1953; Price et al., 1957; Sabshin et al., 1957; Schwartz and Higgins, 1971; Weiner et al., 1962) and reactive responses (Moncrief et al., 1953; Price et al., 1957; Weiner et al., 1962), which are associated with increases in systolic blood pressure, heart rate, and catecholamine and steroid excretion (Carlson et al., 1967; Von Euler, 1971). In all likelihood such physiologic responses are mediated neuronally by an increase in the firing of sympathetic neurons. When an increase in sympathetic nerve activity occurs, the mechanism underlying the increase in catecholamine production, especially norepinephrine secretion (Von Euler, 1971), appears to be due to a sharp increase in norepinephrine synthesis from tyrosine (Alousi and Weiner, 1966; Bygdeman and Von Euler, 1958; Roth et al., 1966; Sedvall and Kopin, 1967) but not from dopa. No increase in tyrosine hydroxylase (TH) activity occurs, however, from which we can assume that no new enzyme is formed or that, if one is, its formation is inhibited by norepinephrine (Alousi and Weiner, 1966).

The absence of change in the TH content of tissue during acute experiences of stimulation stands in marked contrast to the changes produced by sustained experiences or sympathetic nerve activity. Thoenen et al. (1969a, b) and Mueller et al. (1969a) have shown that a reflex increase in sympathetic nerve activity over a period of several days produces a marked increase in TH activity of the adrenal gland, in the superior cervical ganglion of the rat, and the brainstem of the rabbit. The activity of phenylethanolamine-N-methyl transferase (PNMT) increases as well (Thoenen et al., 1970a). Moreover, by means of a number of experimental procedures, Thoenen and his co-workers (1969a, b, 1970a) have demonstrated that the changes in content of these enzymes in the adrenal gland and in the superior cervical ganglion are not only neuronally mediated, but also dependent on the formation of new protein (Mueller et al., 1969b). In other words, the increase in TH activity is transsynaptically induced.

This neuronally mediated increase in PNMT activity is also under the control of ACTH (Mueller et al., 1970). It depends on new protein (enzyme) synthesis and occurs after hypophysectomy and the experimental administration of ACTH. The two other biosynthetic enzymes, TH and dopamine-β-hydroxylase, are similarly controlled, albeit to a much-lesser degree (Axelrod, 1971a).

The exemplary studies by Henry and his co-workers (1971a, b) attest to the fact that such changes in enzyme activity during sustained neuronal activity are not limited to the laboratory setting. Chronic stressful experience produces marked changes in the biosynthetic enzymes for norepinephrine in addition to correlated changes in blood pressure and renal pathology.

The use of restraint has proved extremely effective in producing gastric ulcers in animals and has elucidated some of the mechanisms by which this particular experience leads to the formation of a gastric ulcer (Bonfils et al., 1957; Brodie and Hanson, 1960). Many of the experimental parameters, specifically the genetic and experiential factors that promote or prevent the development of gastric ulcers in animals, have been identified (Ader, 1971). One finding in Ader's studies (1964, 1967) lends crucial support to the assumption that response to an experience depends largely on the behavioral state of the organism.

622

Specifically, Ader found that the rats he studied were much more likely to develop gastric ulcers when they were immobilized during the peak rather than the trough of the behavioral activity cycle—a compelling indication that experience interacts with the organism's behavioral state and its neuronal correlates.

Restraint-immobilization also produces potent effects on the levels of the biogenic amines in body fluids and in the brain. Kvetnansky and Mikulaj (1970) found that immobilizing rats for a single 90-minute session produced an increase in the excretion level of norepinephrine and epinephrine, associated with a depletion of adrenal epinephrine (but not adrenal norepinephrine) level, which persisted for 24 hours after the experimental procedure had been terminated. When there was a resumption of the immobilization procedure, no change could be detected in adrenal epinephrine level, but the level of norepinephrine increased, and the increase noted previously in the excretion of epinephrine in the urine persisted. These results suggest that the adrenal medulla adapts to repeated restraint immobilization that causes the release of epinephrine by increasing the production of its precursor, norepinephrine. This adaptation to stressful experience appears to be due to a sympathetically mediated, *neuronally* dependent elevation of TH and PNMT in the adrenal medulla (Kvetnansky et al., 1970a). When immobilization was discontinued, TH levels diminished with a half-life of about three days. Following the termination of each immobilization session, there was a latency period of approximately six hours before TH and PNMT levels became elevated, and they continued to rise in the next seven days of immobilization. But after six weeks of daily immobilization, no further increases occurred.

The long-term increases in catecholamine levels in the adrenal medulla produced by immobilization not only are neuronally dependent but *also* are under the control of the pituitary gland—specifically, of ACTH. In the study just cited, there was a greater depletion of adrenal epinephrine levels during restraint as a result of hypophysectomy performed on some rats. Levels of adrenal TH and PNMT fell in the hypophysectomized rats. On repeated immobilization, TH (but not PNMT) levels did rise in the hypophysectomized rats; however, they never reached the levels attained by the animals that were not hypophysectomized. The rise in TH levels in the rats who had been operated on was largely neuronally dependent, while the rise in PNMT and an additional rise in TH levels was due almost entirely to the fact that ACTH had been administered to hypophysectomized rats prior to their exposure to stress (Kvetnansky et al., 1970b).

On the other hand, serum dopamine-β-hydroxylase (DBH), which transforms dopamine into norepinephrine, increased after rats had been immobilized for a single 30-minute session and continued to increase when they were immobilized daily for a week. The source of this increase was not the adrenal gland but sympathetic nerve endings (Weinshilboum et al., 1971). Immobilization for a 3-hour period also significantly accelerated the disappearance of radioactive norepinephrine from heart and kidney (Rubeson, 1969).

Levine and Senay (1970) found that when rats were restrained in a cold climate, intragastric pH fell and the rats developed gastric ulcers. The administration of an antacid prevented ulcer formation under these conditions. However, the antacid did not prevent the stress-induced increase in the activity of histidine decarboxylase in the stomach. The increased activity of this enzyme has been positively correlated with incidence and severity of ulcers, although antacid protects the stomach from increased acid content. (The main

623

regulator of normal acid secretion in the stomach of rats is histamine. An increase in the activity of histidine decarboxylase increases the production of histamine and consequently of hydrochloric acid.)

The question of how immobilization is centrally translated into neuronally and hormonally dependent peripheral changes remains unanswered. Restraint has been shown to cause a greater elevation of *brain* norepinephrine and serotonin in mice who had previously spent 8 to 12 weeks in isolation, as compared to their littermates who had been housed in groups (Welch and Welch, 1968). Moreover, this elevation of brain amines occurred despite the fact that the isolated mice had a slower baseline turnover of brain biogenic amines than those mice who had been housed with others. One can draw several important inferences from this work. It was evident from their behavior that the isolated mice were more hyperexcitable than the housed controls. Clearly, previous experience—in this case, isolation—had affected behavioral response tendencies. The finding that immobilization produced different turnover rates and greater elevations of brain norepinephrine and serotonin in the isolated mice than in the control group clearly indicates that previous experience may lead to individual differences in brain biogenic amine metabolism as well as in behavior.

Restraint and exposure to cold, either singly or in combination, also affect other brain amines. In the first two hours of restraint and cold-exposure, a significant depletion of histamine levels in the hypothalamus and cerebral cortex of rats occurs. Apparently, there is an initial and marked enhancement of synthesis but it cannot keep pace with the rate of release and destruction of the amine, and histamine levels are eventually depleted (Taylor and Snyder, 1971).

Our discussion so far has focused primarily on the "output side" of the effects of experience. The emphasis in the discussion has been on the regulation of the peripheral and physiological effects of experience. Less consideration has been given to the question of input—to the identification of the critical intervening variable in the restraint situation, how this variable is perceived, and how that perception is translated by the brain into peripheral changes in function. Although some work has been done on the changes in brain biogenic amines that are produced by stress, we know very little as yet about the effects of experience on the brain. An important prospect here is that once permanent changes in neuronal activity are produced, the interaction of input with the steady-state activity of neurons is altered, resulting in a different type of interaction than previously occurred. It is not unlikely that the immediate effects of experience, which can be very acute, derive primarily from changes in neuronal activity in the brain from a steady-state level. Neurons are capable of rapid axonal transmission and have brief synaptic delays; they are capable of mediating very rapid changes. On the other hand, the long-term changes that have been observed are more likely to have been mediated by neuro-chemical and hormonal means.

TOWARD AN UNDERSTANDING OF THE TRANSDUCTION OF EXPERIENCE BY THE BRAIN

Psychosomatic medicine has been criticized for its failure to provide concrete evidence to document the assumption that perceived social experiences or psychological conflicts and induced emotions can be translated (transduced) into physiological changes leading to

624

disease. A comprehensive understanding of the extremely complex processes by which the translation of the psychological (the nonmaterial) into the physiological (the material) eludes us still. The failure to answer this particular question has, historically, both conceptual and empirical roots. It is a matter that philosophers have debated for centuries, and which neurobiologists have only recently begun to address. At this juncture, only the barest outlines of a comprehensive theory are beginning to emerge. The following section indicates the kinds of data that must be obtained and integrated before any meaningful progress can be made toward formulating an answer.

The Problem of Transduction

We do not understand how emotions are translated by efferent neural pathways into physiological changes in the body. And we do not know how afferent neuronal activity, carried in sensory pathways, acquires psychological meaning and produces emotional responses. The translation from the neural to the psychological must occur twice, and involves a transduction from one form of activity or process to another.

Delbrück (1970) has described transduction as the central problem of neurobiology. Transduction, he asserted, entails more than the entrainment of nerve impulses at a peripheral receptor, as when a photon falling on the vertebrate retina gives rise to impulses in the optic nerve through the mediation of chemical pigments (Wald, 1968). (How the pigment excites the optic nerve terminals in the retina is still not understood.) Visual receptors act as "analyzers": three different retinal cone pigments respond to different wavelengths of light, and therefore to different colors. The pigment contained in retinal rods is responsive to yet another wavelength. Sounds are also analyzed according to their wavelengths in the organ of Corti, and the olfactory mucosa may separate different odorants according to the different migration rates of their constitutent molecules (Mozell and Jagodowicz, 1973).

Once past the receptor and specific sensory pathways, the information carried as spike-trains—which measure the intensities of stimuli or the time derivatives of these intensities—are themselves transformed at each relay nucleus (Amassian et al., 1964). The dynamic changes that occur in the first relay nucleus depend on its current state (Viernstein and Grossman, 1961).

Nerve impulses or spikes are quantal phenomena: impulses do not vary with stimulus intensity once the stimulus exceeds threshold. Further, the impulses lack specificity—they are propagated in all axons, regardless of origin, by the same mechanism, but with different rates of transmission and with different timing. Further, the number of axons entrained may vary according to the intensity of the stimulus. Yet, on the input side, we are accustomed to believe that man responds to structured aspects of his environment—that is, to "wholes" or Gestalten. Even in this process, however, man usually abstracts and selects one whole from others—one configuration from the ground in which it is embedded. He responds to one configuration at a particular time and to a different configuration at another; both the structure and the context of the perceptual field are of crucial import.

We will begin to understand the transduction process better when we can relate the rate and timing of axonal transmission, and the number of axons entrained to the perception of structures. A major thread of continuity in man's view of "perception"—from the "natural philosophy" of the past to the psychology and biophysics of today—is that all we know of the external world and the objects and events in it, natural and human, is their structure. Although the sound waves generated by a musical instrument and the light reflected from a painting are physically different from the nerve impulses in the auditory or optic nerve, the relationship between the sound waves and light waves is largely preserved in the nervous system. The brain conserves the intensity, timing, persistence, and duration and the ratios between the frequencies of simultaneous sounds and their sequences and harmonics. A change in musical key or in the illumination of a picture still allows us to recognize the tune or the theme of the picture and even the artist who composed or painted it.

Although modifications of spike-trains may occur at relay nuclei, the essential structural relationships between the components of complex stimuli are preserved. Beyond this observation, we can say little about the processes that ultimately enable us to "recognize" a tune or picture, or about how they may acquire meaning for us. Presumably, there is an interaction of sensory input with memory stores, which allows us to identify the structure of the input.

But even if we did know how the nervous system preserves a structure and assigns meaning to it, we would still not know how to relate such a perception and the emotional response it elicits to the output via autonomic, humoral, and neuromuscular channels. Implicit in this statement is the conviction that the perceived event and the emotional response it occasions give rise in a causal, linear manner to physiological responses that are controlled by the brain. In its simplest form, this belief is expressed in the statement that fear and joy, for example, "cause" an increased heart rate.

Once again, the form in which the belief is stated may be a barrier to the resolution of the inherent and underlying issue. I would like to suggest two other possibilities: (1) this causal link between psychological events and physiological changes may be infinitely more complex than we now suspect, or (2) this assumed causal link may not exist at all; concurrent events are not necessarily causally related. We cling to the assumption that there is a causal link between these events despite our inability to accumulate sufficient empirical data to show that psychological response and physiological change are consistently correlated in man. Moreover, we have rationalized our failure to accumulate such data on the grounds that there are individual variations in response, or, more precisely, in individual methods of coping with experience, and that these structure the physiological response in some manner. Indeed, such individual types of coping responses can be identified. But this does not mean that the range and specificity of responses are the only reason for low correlation between psychological and physiological responses.

Three Classical Models of Transduction

One of the major reasons for our failure to solve the central problem of transduction is that we have had only one hypothesis in psychobiology to guide us. This hypothesis is a linear one. It states that psychological distress is directly translated into physiological changes. A variant of this hypothesis is that physiological changes, mediated by visceral afferents, can be consciously experienced. But we do not know how impulses arriving over sympathetic or vagal afferent pathways can be perceived or acquire conscious meanings. We are faced by the insuperable problem of how nerve impulses, changes in enzyme levels, or turnover rates of transmitter substances (putative or actual) can "produce" ideas, thoughts, images, feelings, and moods, or vice versa!

626

A familiar approach to transduction—the traditional linear model employed by most psychobiologists—is represented in Figure 1. Here, the social event of situation is perceived (1), acquires emotional meaning and produces a physiological response and (2) may influence the social transaction. The emotional impact of the event may interact with inferred defense mechanisms that, if effective, modify and temper the physiological responses (3) which may themselves be perceived (4) or affect the social event (5)—for example, the child in an asthmatic attack may elicit a solicitous (or other) response from a parent, nurse, or a group of its peers.

A modification of this model states that correlated psychological and physiological responses appear to be so different because each is the product of the different "techniques" whereby we study them. The mental experience—the thought, mental image, or feeling—is the *inner* aspect of the subject's response to the event as he perceives it. The neural and bodily events are the *outer*, and often measurable, aspects of his response to the event. The connection between the mental and the neural and bodily processes cannot be established by simple cross-identity. The difference between these processes (e.g., extension in space and time in the case of bodily events and nonextension in the case of mental ones) lies in the way they are presented and made accessible to us (Descartes, 1911). They must, therefore, be studied by different techniques. We may legitimately study the heart rate physiologically during the solution of a difficult mathematical problem. The solution of the problem may be exquisitely correlated in time with an increase in heart rate. But we cannot assume that the task of finding the solution "causes" the increased heart rate. Concurrent events may not be causally related. The may, for example, be the product of some third unmeasured or unidentified variable.

The third and classical model of transduction is based on the view that despite the coextensiveness of the psychological and physiological, the two belong to wholly unrelated realms. Although we may study the physiology and psychology of an ill person together, they really have nothing to do with each other and proceed independently. In this view,

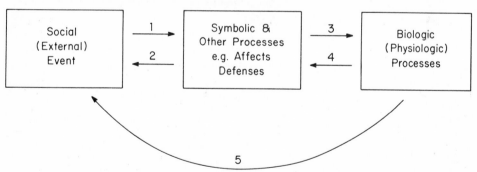

FIGURE 1 **The Transactional Model** In this model the social (external) event or stimulus produces psychological experiences and responses (1) which may, in turn, modify the social transaction or event (2). The psychological process directly causes the physiological one (3) which may, in turn, (as e.g., in a delirium), modify the psychological process (4). The process (3) by which psychological processes are transduced into physiological ones are usually not specified, or are unknown. The manifest physiological process may influence the social one (5), either by positive or negative feedback (e.g., an asthmatic attack in a child may influence another person or a group). Modified from Knapp, 1971.

627

a bereavement may produce grief, but the physiological changes involved in weeping, or in rheumatoid arthritis, are independent of the experience of loss. With this model, in effect, the physiological cannot occur in any manner truly accessible to our understanding.

An External Loop Model of Transduction

We do not understand how nerve impulses can achieve psychological representation in the form of thoughts, memories, and feelings. And we have no concept to help us explain how feelings bring about physiological changes in the body. Therefore, we do not understand how a situation can be perceived as threatening or frightening and then be transduced into physiological discharge through the outflow channels of the brain. In a similar vein, the concept that a chronic unconscious conflict can produce tonic vagal discharge to increase gastric acid secretion is unproven and unproveable. Because these conceptual and empirical problems have not been solved, we do not understand the mechanisms by which changes in psychological state initiate disease.

Perhaps, the mystery of the "leap from the mind to the body" (Deutsch, 1959) is not so deep after all, if we were to assume that the gaps between brain and body do not have to be bridged directly. The gap could be narrowed a little if we could prove that the threatened or bereaved person behaves differently than he did before the threat or loss. It is not the emotional states but the changes in behavior—for example, not eating, insomnia, drinking alcohol, and taking medication—that become the immediate antecedents of the disease. It is, of course, true that we do not know how the mind or brain regulates actions and behavior, but we do know that drinking alcohol or taking aspirin may incite exacerbations of peptic duodenal ulcer. In fact, Weisman (1956) observed that in some patients with peptic duodenal ulcer, various emotional and psychological reactions led to the drinking of alcohol. Similarly, Katz and his co-workers (1973) observed that in 60 percent of their subjects attacks of gout followed situations in which predisposed patients felt that they had to "prove" themselves in their jobs, which led to excessive eating and use of alcohol. Patients with hypertension seem to prefer diets high in salt if given a choice (see Chapter 2). These examples suggest that, for at least some predisposed persons, the psychological responses to "threatening" situations or to bereavement are mediated through changes in diet, in eating, and in drinking behavior. The examples suggest a different model of transduction than the ones traditionally used in the field of psychosomatic medicine. In this model, the patient's actions or behavior are an "external loop." A variant of the external loop model may also provide insight into some aspects of primary anorexia nervosa. About one-third to one-half (or more) of all cases of this disease begin with amenorrhea. Recent evidence indicates that the amenorrhea and the disease is correlated with immature (age-inappropriate) secretory patterns of pituitary LH and FSH (Boyar et al., 1974). It is not known, however, whether these immature secretory patterns antecede the disease, or why they occur at all. In any event, the amenorrhea *antecedes* the remorseless dieting in some patients with anorexia nervosa. The frequently described oral-impregnation fantasies, rather than being the antecedents of the disease, may be the consequences of amenorrhea. The amenorrhea is misinterpreted by the patient as a pregnancy. The patient incorrectly attributes the cause of the pregnancy to conflictful fantasies of oral impregnation, which in turn leads to her not eating.

628

The two variants of the "external loop" model can be represented in the following manner:

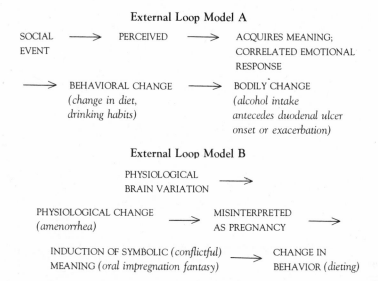

External Loop Model A

SOCIAL $\longrightarrow$ PERCEIVED $\longrightarrow$ ACQUIRES MEANING;
EVENT   CORRELATED EMOTIONAL
                                        RESPONSE

$\longrightarrow$ BEHAVIORAL CHANGE $\longrightarrow$ BODILY CHANGE
         (change in diet,   *(alcohol intake*
         drinking habits)   *antecedes duodenal ulcer*
                                                 onset or exacerbation)

External Loop Model B

PHYSIOLOGICAL $\longrightarrow$
BRAIN VARIATION

PHYSIOLOGICAL CHANGE $\longrightarrow$ MISINTERPRETED $\longrightarrow$
(amenorrhea)   AS PREGNANCY

INDUCTION OF SYMBOLIC *(conflictful)* $\longrightarrow$ CHANGE IN
MEANING *(oral impregnation fantasy)*   BEHAVIOR *(dieting)*

Clearly, model B is not the only explanatory schema for anorexia nervosa. It might not apply, for example, to those instances where amenorrhea is a late manifestation of the disease that begins with not eating and weight loss. One conception of this form of "primary" anorexia nervosa is that it is not initially a disturbance of eating but a failure to recognize enteroreceptive hunger signals, and the inability to discriminate these from other bodily sensations and feelings. Either the sensation of hunger or its meaning has never been learned (Bruch, 1973), or the development of this failure to discriminate is associated with early experiences during the feeding of the infant. In addition, a child with true anorexia nervosa is typically found to be very compliant and well-behaved and, at the onset of puberty, does not eat because of a fear of growing fat or growing-up.

Yet there is one striking fact that this account does not consider: true anorexia nervosa occurs about ten times as frequently in girls as boys. When it occurs in boys, it often precedes puberty; in girls, it follows puberty. This incidence suggests a protective role for male sex hormones and an initiating role for female hormones. During puberty (the age at which the incidence of some forms of anorexia nervosa is highest) a reorganization of hypothalamic function and the hypothalamic-pituitary axis occurs. In normal adolescence, there may also be bouts of asceticism and self-denial during which all gratification, including eating, is suppressed, followed by bouts of self-indulgence. Patients with anorexia nervosa are even more-remorseless in not eating, yet they often also gorge themselves with food and then vomit. The behavioral, psychological, and physiological events in anorexia nervosa can be seen as a by-product of the aberrant reorganization of hypothalamic function during adolescence, as manifested by tonic inhibition of eating behavior, increased motor activity, and failure of adult patterns of LH and FSH release to occur (although other pituitary hormones such as TSH and possibly hGH may be normally produced and released). The antecedents of this disturbance may be life experience that

629

alter hypothalamic function—specifically, levels of neurotransmitter synthesis, release, re-uptake, or degradation. In this view, early experiences alter bodily function and the psychology of the child. The burden of the inception of the disease is placed, then, not only on conflictful fantasies, but on a complex interplay of experience, physiology, and psychology in which the conflictful fantasy may in some patients be a response to, and not the cause of, the amenorrhea.

Collateral Models of Transduction

Alexander's concept that the emotional response to the precipitating event in psychosomatic diseases was transduced into physiological changes was a modification of Freud's ideas about the production of the symptoms and signs of conversion hysteria—a (sexual) conflict was converted into somatic symptoms and signs that symbolically expressed the conflict. Alexander believed that in psychosomatic diseases, the emotional response to the conflict was expressed in physiological changes that produced anatomical lesions.

Alexander may still be correct in some instances, but the evidence suggests that he was not completely right in all cases. The conflict may be the psychological response to a physical change in the body. And the onset or exacerbation of a psychosomatic disease may be brought on by the patient's ill-advised actions.

Alexander also assumed that the perceived threat brought about the conflict and its emotional response that, in turn, generated the physiological response. He never considered two possibilities: (1) that the perception of an event could be mediated by one brain system. At the same time, *but separately*, the percept could bring about physiological changes by another system of pathways in the brain; (2) that the threatening event or situation did not have to be perceived as a whole but could be analyzed by the mind (brain) into separate components. As a result of this analysis, one component acquires threatening psychological meaning and another component results in physiological changes.

Research on subliminal perception has proved indirect evidence to support this second possibility (Block and Reiser, 1962; Reiser and Block, 1962). Direct evidence is much more-difficult to obtain in intact human beings, but some recent experiments support the idea that different aspects of an event are responded to separately. These experiments were designed to carry out a precise analysis of the specific constellation of stimuli or events that impinge on the organism to structure its behavioral and physiological state. In such experiments we need to know precisely what it is about restraint-immobilization, crowding, or separation that is "stressful" to animals. During restraint or crowding, is it the continuous sensory input from skin when the animal is closely confined, does it sleep, is it awake, or what is the sensory input from muscle-tendon receptors when it fights or struggles? Or is it the absence of the mother, or the deprivation of food or water, or a fall in body temperature that produces the effect of separation? Further, we must know whether each variable is equally capable of producing behavioral and physiological results. And, if so, are these effects mediated by the same or by different circuits in the brain? Is it possible that one aspect of the "stressful" configuration produces the behavioral effect, and another aspect the physiologic one? Three series of experiments have substantially advanced our understanding of the transduction process. In doing so, they have provided us with new

630

models that contribute to—if not make necessary—a change in our traditional view of some aspects of the mind-body relationship.

In the past, most studies of the effects on young animals of separation from their mother have been based on the assumption that the removal of the mother was a holistic psychological experience for her offspring that could not be broken down into its components (Bronfenbrenner, 1968; Harlow, 1961; Hinde and Spencer-Booth, 1971; Kaufman and Rosenblum, 1969; Mason et al., 1968). Therefore, no attempt was made in these experiments to determine the separate effects on the infant of the deprivation of nutritional, olfactory, tactile, auditory, visual, or thermal stimuli. In the absence of such an analysis it is impossible to determine whether deprivation of these simpler forms of stimulation could produce, or at least contribute to, the observed sequelae of separation. Because prematurely separated young animals eat less and lose weight, their food intake may well be the most critical uncontrolled variable in these experiments. Hofer (1971, 1975), by a careful analysis of the various aspects of the separation experience, has showed that the presence of a mother unable to nurse her offspring because her nipples were ligated did not restore to normal rates a 40 percent drop in heart and respiratory rates that had occurred during the first 12 to 16 hours following separation (Hofer and Weiner, 1971a, b). But artificially feeding the separated young rats restored the rates to their usual levels. Hofer had identified the absence of the mother's milk as the critical variable that produced the cardiovascular and respiratory effects in infant rats. The milk seems to act by a neural mechanism involving the upper gastrointestinal tract on the afferent side, the CNS at the cervical spinal level or higher, and the sympathetic (β-adrenergic) cardioaccelerator pathway on the efferent side (Hofer and Weiner, 1975). The afferent arc in the loop that mediates the nutritional effects on the heart remains unknown. If this arc were known, we would have a clue as to what brain sites transduce the nutritional effects to produce increased heart rates on feeding. The obvious next step, as Hofer has pointed out (1971), would be to investigate how milk sustains heart and respiratory rates; in other words, we could identify the afferent neural pathways and then the substances in milk that sustain these rates by acting on the brain. In order to specify how milk acts on the brain we might ask: does the absence of milk produce changes in important neurochemical mediators in the brain (Himwich et al., 1968)? This question is not as far-fetched as it might seem, when one considers the known long-term effects of lowered protein intake on dopamine, norepinephrine, and TH in the perinatal period (Shoemaker and Wurtman, 1971). What still remains to be done is to determine the short-term effects on brain amines of nutritional deprivation following separation. Twenty-four hour infusions of milk to separated infant rats prevented cardiac and respiratory changes from taking place, but had no significant effect on behavior changes (Hofer and Weiner, 1971b). On the other hand, provision of a nonlactating foster mother prevented the behavioral effects that were manifested by separated and nutritionally deprived baby rats. After separation from their mother, the babies behave more actively and had a greater tendency to rear up on their hind legs. When studied in groups of four, the rats show more self-grooming, increased defecaton and urination, and a decreased tendency to enter active sleep (Hofer, 1975). These results suggest that the cardiorespiratory changes that occurred in separated baby rats were due to the absence of milk, while the behavioral changes (apart from the lowered probability of entering REM sleep) were due to the physical absence of the mother. The point is that

631

certain aspects of separation affect a physiological system, while others affect the behavioral system. Having specified which aspects of the organismic response to experience affect which system, analysis of the physiological mechanisms that mediate the behavioral, cardiovascular or sleep effects can proceed.

Hofer's analysis supports the idea that the baby rat, at least, responds to different aspects of the separation experience in separate ways. it does not respond *in toto* to the absence of the mother. The behavioral consequences, mediated by brain do not serially "cause" the drop in heart and respiratory rates. The changes occur in parallel. The pup abstracts elements of the whole separation experience and responds to each individually. These findings support the more general idea that the brain has the capacity to abstract elements of a situation and respond specifically to each of them. And, indeed, there is considerable empirical work—best exemplified by studies of the visual system—to substantiate this assertion (Hubel, 1959, 1960; Hubel and Wiesel, 1959, 1960, 1962, 1964, 1968). The application of this more-general concept to a complex event such as separation leads us to speculate whether the separation leads to bodily changes not solely because of the absence of the mother, but because her physical presence may "control" the pup's behavior, her bodily warmth may maintain its temperature, her milk may regulate its heart rate, and her smell may cause its attachment to her. The mother's absence when the pup is prematurely weaned may immediately lead to its not eating for 2 to 3 days, and may later make it prone to gastric ulceration on not feeding, possibly because its body temperature falls (Ackerman et al., 1975). Yet other behaviors, such as nonnutritional sucking, may be unaffected by separation (Hofer, 1975). These data suggest that some behaviors are directly under the control of the presence of the mother, others are independent of her presence and are autoregulatory, and other bodily functions (heart rate regulation) are under the control of a third variable—milk.

Once a psychobiological analysis such as Hofer's has been made, and the critical variables producing specific but different effects have been isolated, we have the elements necessary for a concrete investigation of whether the brain can actively abstract and respond to each of the set of variables. And if it is true that the brain is capable of abstracting certain aspects of a whole, one might further hypothesize that early experiences bias the brain to respond to analogous or homologous aspects of experience later in time, specifically, by abstracting the analogue or homologue from the later constellation of events.

An analysis such as Hofer's also raises another fundamental question about the nature of transduction. Once a specific aspect of a complex situation has been correlated with a specific physiological effect, does the brain transduce this intervening variable by one or by several circuits? Or, to rephrase the question, is it possible that even a single (simple) stimulus may produce different effects by different, that is, collateral, pathways? One process in which the entire transduction of input and the resulting physiological changes are known provides a clear-cut answer to this question. I refer to the process by which light affects the functioning of the pineal gland. Fiske et al. (1960) have shown that the weight of the pineal gland decreases when rats are continuously exposed to light, and that female rats remain in continuous vaginal estrus under such lighting conditions (Browman, 1937; Fiske et al., 1960). These findings, plus the observation that extracts of the pineal gland of cattle inhibit estrus, led Wurtman et al. (1963a) to conclude that melatonin from the pineal gland reduces the incidence of estrus in the rat. We are further indebted to Axelrod

632

and his group for working out the biosynthetic pathway from tryptophan to melatonin:

$$\text{TRYPTOPHAN} \xrightarrow{\textit{tryptophanhydroxylase}} \text{5-HYDROXYTRYPTOPHAN} \xrightarrow[\textit{decarboxylase}]{\textit{aromatic amino-acid}}$$

$$\text{SEROTONIN} \xrightarrow[\textit{transferase}]{\textit{N-acetyl}} \text{N-ACETYLSEROTONIN} \xrightarrow{\textit{HIOMT}} \text{MELATONIN}$$

More specifically, Wurtman et al. (1963b) found that levels of hydroxy-indole-O-methyltransferase (HIOMT) in the pineal gland were elevated when rats were kept in the dark and reduced when they were exposed to continuous light. These fluctuations could explain how light inhibits the synthesis and release of melatonin and continuous light produces persistent estrus.

If we were to adhere to the hypothetic psychophysiological model that is traditionally used, we would say that it is the *experience* of light that regulates the release of melatonin (Figure 1). But this is not what happens. Axelrod and his associates have worked out the rather complex and indirect pathway from the retina to the pineal gland and the manner in which the biosynthetic machinery of the gland is influenced (Moore et al., 1967). In the mammal (Figure 2), nerve impulses stimulated by light pass through the retina to the inferior accessory optic tract, to the preganglionic sympathetic fibers of the spinal cord, and then to the superior cervical ganglion, from which postganglionic fibers pass upward to the parenchymal cells of the pineal gland, whose terminals release norepinephrine (Axelrod et al., 1969; Axelrod, 1971b).

Obviously, light also stimulates the retina to entrain impulses that pass via the classic visual pathways to the visual cortex to produce the *experience* of light. It needs to be emphasized, however, that this experience is subserved by quite separate mechanisms from those that influence pineal functioning.

The elucidation of the separate pathways over which light effects the function of the pineal gland and causes the light to be experienced does not explain why continuous illumination produces continuous vaginal estrus in female rats and reduces levels of the enzyme HIOMT. Under conditions of alternating light and dark, a circadian rhythm in levels of serotonin (Owman, 1965) and norepinephrine occurs in the pineal gland. In order to understand the rhythm the role of norepinephrine must be known. The release of norepinephrine in the pineal gland influences the formation of melatonin from tryptophan by inducing the enzyme N-acetyltransferase (Klein and Weller, 1970), which converts serotonin into N-acetylserotonin. The content of serotonin is highest during the day under normal lighting conditions, and lowest at 11:00 P.M. (Quay, 1963). This rhythm is endogenous (Snyder et al., 1965), and although its driving oscillator is unknown, it can be entrained by light, when day and night are reversed experimentally (Snyder et al., 1967). On the other hand, norepinephrine content, which reaches its highest levels at night, is not controlled by an endogenous oscillator but is under the direct environmental control of light. Thus, its high nocturnal content corresponds to the high nocturnal content of HIOMT and, therefore, of melatonin synthesis.

Of particular interest is the fact that the oscillator for serotonin is not operative until the rat is 6 days old. This underscores the importance of the second variable, the animal's age at

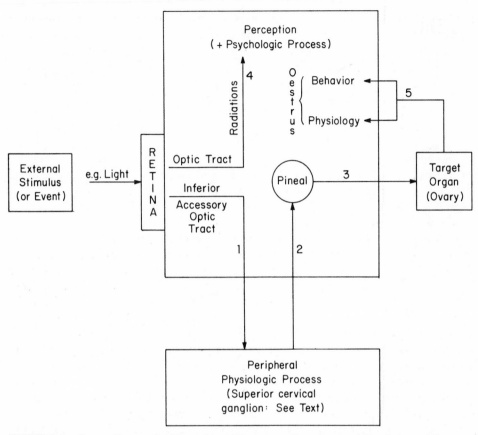

FIGURE 2 Concomitance of a Physiological Process and an Assumed Psychological Process, Presumably Not Causally Related. The model portrayed is based on the regulation of estrus in the rat by melatonin whose synthesis is controlled (reduced) by light. Light falling on the retina sets off a train of neural impulses which: (1) Pass via the inferior accessory optic tract ⟶ medial forebrain bundle ⟶ medial terminal nucleus of the accessory optic system ⟶ preganglionic fibers in the spinal cord ⟶ superior cervical ganglion. (2) From the superior cervical ganglion impulses pass to the parenchymal cells of the pineal gland to release noradrenaline which increases melatonin synthesis. (3) Melatonin is released to suppress estrus, presumably by its action on the ovary. (4) The experience of light is presumably mediated by the classical visual pathways. (5) Presumably the decrease of estrogens effects behavior by its impact on brain circuits, while also regulating the release of tropic pituitary hormones. For references, see text.

the time an experience occurs. In young rats not yet 27 days old, light travels via an extraretinal pathway to affect the serotonin level in the pineal gland (Axelrod, 1971; Zwieg et al., 1966); once rats have reached the age of 27 days, this earlier pathway is no longer operative and is apparently replaced by the one illustrated in Figure 2.

The principle illustrated by Axelrod's work is not unique to the pineal gland. When the stimulus for a behavior has been clearly identified, and the behavior has been carefully analyzed, one finds that even the components of the *behavior*, although they appear to form an interrelated whole, are actually separate and distinct and, as such, require individual analysis. These separate components may be subserved by different neural pathways. One example is the contact-placing reaction produced by a light touch on the dorsum of a cat's paw. Careful analysis of this behavior discloses that the bending of hairs entrains impulses that travel by at least two routes. As illustrated in Figure 3, the early components of the biceps response as shown on an electromyogram (EMG) and the first phase of the placing

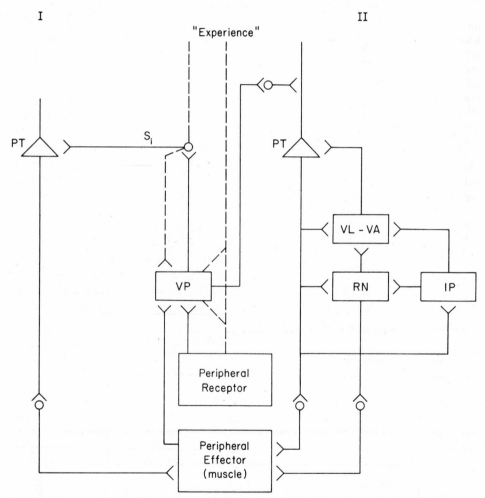

FIGURE 3   Some of the Brain Circuits Responsible for the Contact Placing Reaction in the Cat.   The two (I and II) known pathways and circuits which subserve a very simple behavior (contact placing) in the cat. The heavy lines denote known circuits, the broken lines putative ones. At each level (e.g., IP, VL-VA and PT) the information is processed differently. Note that there are at least two circuits subserving different aspects of the behavior. *Legend:* PT = pyramidal tract neuron; S 1 = somatosensory cortex; IP = nucleus interpositus of cerebellum; RN = red nucleus; VL-VA = ventrolateral and ventroanterior nucleus of thalamus; VP = ventroposterior nucleus of thalamus. After Amassian, Weiner, Rosenblum (1972a).

movement are activated by the ventroposterior nucleus (VP) of the thalamus. Later components are probably activated by a complex circuit that passes through the VP, sensorimotor cortex, pyramidal tract, red nucleus, interpositus nucleus of the cerebellum, the ventrolateral-ventroanterior nucleus of the thalamus, and, once again, through the sensorimotor cortex (Amassian et al., 1972a, b). What is more, these circuits are not fixed. A lesion in one circuit may cause the behavior to disappear for a time, only to return when, presumably, another circuit has taken over the function of the destroyed circuit.

In summary, we may conclude from the available evidence that even a simple behavior produced by a very simple stimulus is the product of separate components that are regulated by different neural circuits. It would appear that the critical element in the production of a behavior is the timing of the output of the various components by the different circuits—in the case of the contact-placing reaction, the sequential and orderly activation of different muscles of the forelimb long after the stimulus that initiated the behavior has ceased.

Axelrod's work on the pineal gland, which gives a complete picture of the manner and mechanism by which an environmental influence on an organism is transduced into a highly relevant physiological chain of events, appears to have broad implications for the mind-brain-body problem. It suggests that a specified input (light) may have physiological and psychological effects, which, though correlated and concomitant, are not causally related. In fact, the input to the receptor travels quite different neural routes to produce a complex phenomenon (the experience of light) and other behavioral and physiological effects (a reduction in the synthesis and release of melatonin, and estrus).

As pointed out earlier, those who subscribe to the traditional model of psychophysiological relationships would contend, in this instance, that it is the experience of light that regulates the release of melatonin. For the assumption that mental experiences initiate physiological events is, of course, a fundamental precept of psychosomatic medicine. In light of Axelrod's findings, however, one must question the accuracy of this view of the supremacy of the mental over the physiological.

Data accumulated from other sources also serve to raise questions about the prepotency of mental experiences. Specifically, there are three known instances in which strict isomorphism exists between neural and behavioral events:

1. There is a linear correspondence between neuronal activity and muscular activity in the case of the spinal cord motoneuron and the skeletal muscle that it innervates.

2. An increase or reduction of an adequate stimulus gives rise to a homologous change in the discharge frequency of the axon leading away from a receptor. In neural coordinates, the frequency profile in a population of peripheral axons maps the contour, spatial position, and intensity of a stationary stimulus. The transform from receptor to the axonal population is isomorphic.

3. When a stimulus is applied to the brain rather than to the receptors, the strength-rate functions for electrically elicited overt behaviors are isomorphic with those that obtain for neurons. Kestenbaum et al. (1970) have shown that in the rat the mean percentage of lever-pressing responses to avoid aversive brain stimulation correlates with the known properties of neurons and axons—latent addition, the absolute refractory period, and temporal summation decay.

As noted earlier, the application of Axelrod's findings is not limited to the functioning of the pineal gland. On the other hand, it is impossible to say how many instances of the model actually occur in nature. Clearly, however, Axelrod's work refutes the traditional, linear, theoretical model of mind-body interaction that we have accepted virtually without reservation and that has been the basis for research in psychobiology until now. Thus, at the very least, Axelrod's work raises the possibility that other models can be utilized in the future.

In essence, then, we can no longer automatically assume that psychosocial events and external stimuli alter bodily function in health and disease solely by their impact on the mind. Recent studies have suggested alternative models of mind-body interaction by which the brain transduces experience to produce changes in behavior and bodily function. This transduction may occur via collateral neural pathways. Through this process, psychological and physiological events might occur simultaneously. They may be correlated, but cannot be considered to "cause" each other.

An Internal Loop Model of Transduction

A sixth model of transduction has been proposed by Reiser (1975). Under this model, the inability to cope with the threat of a perceived "stress" and the reactivation of an unconscious conflict are associated with emotional arousal and a spectrum of autonomic and hormonal responses that in turn affect brain function and psychological responses. For example, cognitive processes (Pollin and Goldin, 1961) and a susceptibility to anxiety (Levitt et al., 1963) are influenced by the infusion of hydrocortisone (Weiner et al., 1963) or epinephrine; cognition may also be affected by peripheral autonomic changes (Callaway and Thompson, 1953). Glucocorticoids may affect catecholamine (Maas and Mednieks, 1971) and indoleamine (Azmitia and McEwen, 1969; Green and Curzon, 1968) levels in the brain and induce changes in patterns of neuronal discharge. Various dosage levels of prednisone can markedly reduce the percentage of REM sleep (Gillin et al., 1972).

Reiser suggests that these physiological changes acting upon the brain are reflected in altered psychological functioning, which is expressed in ever more-primitive ways of perceiving and thinking, evaluating danger, and coping with the threat and the unconscious conflict. In Reiser's postulated cycle of events, a series of more-vigorous bodily changes would result next. As these bodily changes continue, the changes in circulating hormones would make the function of the brain more plastic—inactive brain circuits would be brought into play and "make connection with appropriate efferent fibers to the viscera" to produce altered function. The psychological expression of the activation of these pathways would be manifested in altered states of consciousness, whereas the physiological expression would be the activation of new outflow pathways that alter visceral function, which would also interact with predispositions to disease.

Reiser also postulated that once the outflow channels (autonomic, humoral, and neuromuscular) were activated they would alter visceral function and would interact with the predisposing factors of the particular disease. The initiating psychoneuroendocrine sequence that he outlined is not specific for each disease (in contrast to Alexander's hypotheses), but the predisposition to a particular disease is.

The internal loop of this model is Step I in Figure 4. The model has much to recommend it, since it subsumes in an orderly way many relevant phenomena, such as the exacerbations of certain diseases during sleep, and the involvement of rhythmic processes, such as

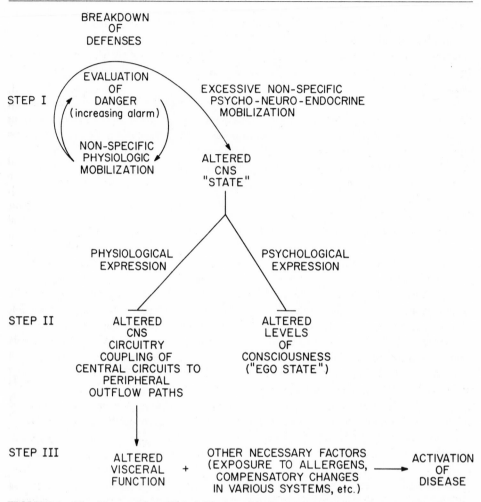

FIGURE 4   The "Internal Loop" Model Proposed by Reiser (1975). From *American Handbook of Psychiatry*, vol. IV. Copyright 1975 by Basic Books. Reprinted by permission.

circadian cycles in the pathogenesis of disease. However, the internal loop model does not explain how an alarm response occasions physiological mobilization or how altered brain physiology is expressed psychologically. As with the traditional psychosomatic model, the problem of translating these two categories of events into each other remains unsolved. All six models that have been discussed in this section attempt to bridge the gap between environmental events, mental processes, brain mechanisms, physiological mechanisms, and disease. Their value is heuristic. Alternative ways of organizing data may provide us with the insights needed ultimately to develop an accurate overview that bridges the gap between mind, brain, and body in health and disease—a gap that remains a crucial factor in biology and medicine.

638

FACTORS THAT SUSTAIN OR AMELIORATE DISEASE

Each of the diseases reviewed in this book has an unpredictably variable natural history. Some cases remit unexpectedly, or fluctuate inconsistently, others progress inexorably toward disability and death. We still do not know how to account for the variable course of these diseases. Psychosocial factors may play several different roles. As we have seen, childhood bronchial asthma may remit rapidly when the child is removed from his home. The onset of the accelerated ("malignant") phase of hypertensive disease has been correlated with life situations and events (as well as raised levels of serum renin) that are similar if not identical with those in and with which the disease is first detected (Chapter 2).

The psychological responses to chronic disease and disability may help to sustain them. Some patients refuse to take prescribed medication because they do not provide relief or they cause unpleasant side-effects. Chronic disease is frequently accompanied by depression and helplessness. The helpless patient refuses to participate in his treatment. The hopeless patient sees no point in it. The uncertainty about the outcome of the disease or the sudden onset of disease may be frightening to some who are chronically ill, while others become resigned or may even openly or covertly welcome their invalidism (Engel, 1967; Ruesch et al., 1947; Wiener, 1952). How these various reactions influence the course of the disease is still largely unknown. Nor do we know how each of these various psychological responses interacts with the pathophysiology of a disease or the chronic changes —whether in the joints, the bronchioles, or the colon—that have already taken place.

In all retrospective studies, the more-general reactions to a disease must be clearly separated from the more-specific responses with which disease onset is associated, and from the specific meanings that are engendered by the disease and that may play a role in sustaining it (Garma, 1960). In the future, it would be fruitful to separate out those multiple variables at the various levels of biological organization that predispose to, initiate, and sustain disease. For instance, we now know that following the first attack of some diseases changes in the function of organs persist. The disposition to form IgE antibodies and to respond with bronchoconstriction continues despite the absence of clinical asthma. Permanent changes in the colonic mucosa without clinical symptoms often persist after remission from the first attack of ulcerative colitis. Persistent changes in many aspects of thyroid function may follow Graves' disease even though the patient is in clinical remission. The elevated basal secretion of pepsin and hydrochloric acid in the stomach continues during the quiescent phase of duodenal ulcer in some patients. Therefore, one may conclude that these apparently permanent changes in function are, in part, responsible for exacerbations of each disease. And they interact with recurring failures in psychological adaptation to cause renewed bouts of the disease.

Secondary and permanent changes in cells, tissues, and organs occur as the result of the disturbances in physiology. These changes sustain the disease. Long-standing high blood pressure predisposes to damage to arterioles and arteries. If the renal artery is damaged and narrowed, high blood pressure may be increased or be sustained. Damage to cerebral arteries may impair the psychological adaptation of the hypertensive patient. The increased peripheral resistance in essential hypertension is enhanced by secondary swelling of the arteriolar wall. Spasm or narrowing by scars or spasm of the pyloric portion of the duodenum in duodenal ulcer may slow gastric emptying time and expose the duodenum and stomach to high concentrations of gastric acid. These and other secondary changes in these diseases help to sustain them and prevent remission or cure.

SUMMARY AND CONCLUSIONS

Psychosomatic medicine has often been defined as merely an "approach" to disease and to the care of patients. Actually, its contribution is more substantial: its aim has always been to contribute to a comprehensive account of the etiology and pathogenesis of disease. Social, familial, and psychological factors need to be incorporated into any comprehensive theory of disease.

Twenty-five years ago, physicians were preoccupied with the mechanisms of a disease after its onset. Today, physicians are increasingly aware of the fact that they are faced with a sudden increase in the incidence of diabetes mellitus and cancer that has attained epidemic proportions. They cannot explain why cancer of the lung, once rare in women, is becoming more and more frequent and that cancer of the stomach in men is becoming much less common. The prevalence of essential hypertension is much greater in black than in white Americans, for undisclosed reasons. Facts of this kind have directed the attention of physicians to environmental factors in the etiology and pathogenesis of disease. Social, economic, nutritional, political, industrial, and ecological factors constitute some of these environmental factors. As physicians have become aware of the role of environmental factors in disease, they have also become increasingly receptive to some of the concepts that have guided investigations in psychosomatic medicine.

This book has attempted to review and update the data and concepts of psychosomatic medicine. It has tried to do justice to the data of a variety of fields and to make available in one place the information from a number of relevant disciplines that may contribute to a comprehensive theory of disease. In particular, the book has attempted to make available to behavioral scientists some of the latest data of the physiology, biochemistry, and immunology of several chronic and common diseases, in the hope that a knowledge of these predisposing factors might be used to verify the psychological observations that have been made after the onset of the disease by means of predictive studies.

This book has tried to point out the gaps in our knowledge, so that future investigators might fill them in. In particular, it has stressed the multiplicity of predisposing factors in each disease. The question has been raised why those who are predisposed to a disease do not fall ill. What maintains health? Perhaps an answer to this question would enable us to prevent disease.

We also need to know much more about the relationship of age to disease onset. A comprehensive developmental biology that is integrated with developmental psychology and neurobiology is needed to answer the question of the age-dependent nature of these and many other diseases.

We have no real idea about the origins of the predisposing factors to disease—whether they are genetic, environmental, or both in origin. We also know rather little about the origin of the psychological factors in these diseases. For this reason, a number of different alternative theories about the role of genes and the environment in development have been explored.

The same predisposing factors of a disease can come about by a variety of ways. In fact, most diseases are heterogeneous in origin. Conversely, the same disease can have different predispositions. The heterogeneous form that a disease takes has confounded psychosomatic research. Therefore, a great deal more taxonomic information about disease is needed. But the fact that every disease reviewed in this book is probably heterogeneous in the sense just-mentioned should warn future investigators of the danger of generalizing from one population of patients.

The gaps in our knowledge that make a comprehensive theory of disease premature have been emphasized in this book. We know much more about the predisposition of one disease than we do of another. In some diseases the inciting factors are known, but the predisposing ones are not. And in a disease like essential hypertension, our knowledge of its pathophysiology is elegant, but our knowledge about its predisposition is rudimentary.

We need to know more about how psychological threat, distress and bereavement initiate disease. A true and inclusive psychophysiology of these states is impeded by that most insuperable and indissoluble of scientific and philosophical problems—the problem of mind, brain, and body. An attempt has been made in this book to suggest several alternative hypotheses that need to be tested in order to arrive at an understanding of how emotions interact with predisposition to bring about disease. The help of neurobiologists in the solution of this problem is devoutly to be sought.

The implicit message in this book is that a comprehensive theory of disease will require the best endeavors of representatives of many different fields, who in the past have been shut off from each other. In this way, we may gradually and eventually close the gap between mind, brain, and body and in so doing help our fellow men and women who become ill.

REFERENCES

Abrahams, V. C., Hilton, S. M., and Zbrozyna, A. 1960. Active muscle vasodilatation produced by stimulation of the brainstem: its significance in the defense reaction. *J. Physiol.* (London) 154:491.

Ackerman, S. H. 1975. Editorial: Restraint ulceration as an experimental disease model. *Psychosom. Med.* 37:4.

———, Hofer, M. A., and Weiner, H. 1975. Age at maternal separation and gastric erosion susceptibility in the rat. *Psychosom. Med.* 37:180.

Adamson, J. D., and Schmale, A. H., Jr. 1965. Object loss, giving up and the onset of psychiatric disease. *Psychosom. Med.* 27:557.

Ader, R. 1964. Gastric erosions in the rat: Effects of immobilization at different points in the activity cycle. *Science* 145:406.

——— 1967. Behavioral and physiological rhythms and the development of gastric erosions in the rat. *Psychosom. Med.* 29:345.

——— 1969. Early experiences accelerate maturation of the 24-hour adreno-cortical rhythm. *Science* 163:1225.

——— 1971. Experimentally induced gastric lesions: results and implications of studies in animals. *Adv. Psychosom. Med.* 6:1.

———— and Friedman, S. B. 1965. Differential early experiences and susceptibility to transplanted tumor in the rat. *J. Comp. Physiol. Psychol.* 59:361.

———— and Grota, L. J. 1973. Adrenocortical mediation of the effects of early life experiences. In *Progress in Brain Research*, vol. 39, *Drug Effects on Neuroendocrine Regulation*, edited by E. Zimmerman, W. H. Gispen, B. H. Marks, and D. De Wied. Amsterdam: Elsevier.

Alexander, F. 1950. *Psychosomatic Medicine*. New York: Norton.

————, French, T., and Pollock, G. H. 1968. *Psychosomatic Specificity*. Chicago: University of Chicago Press.

Alousi, A., and Weiner, N. 1966. The regulation of norepinephrine synthesis in sympathetic nerves: effect of nerve stimulation, cocaine, and catecholamine-releasing agents. *Proc. Natl. Acad. Sci. U.S.A.* 56:1491.

Amassian, V. E., Macy, J., Jr., Waller, H. J., Leader, H. S., and Swift, M. 1964. Transformation of afferent activity at the cuneate nucleus. *Proc. Int. Union Physiol. Sci.* 3:235.

————, Ross, R., and Donat, J. 1971. Development of contact placing and thalamocortical organization in kittens. *Fed. Proc.* 30:434.

————, Weiner, H., and Rosenblum, M. 1972a. Neural systems subserving the tactile placing reaction: a model for the study of higher level control of movement. *Brain Res.* 40:171.

————, Ross, R., Wertenbaker, C., and Weiner, H. 1972b. Cerebellothalamocortical interrelations in contact placing and other movements in cats. In *Corticothalamic Projections and Sensorimotor Activities*, edited by T. L. Frigyesi, E. Rinvik, and M. D. Yahr. New York: Raven.

Axelrod, J. 1971a. Brain monoamines: biosynthesis and fate. *Neurosci. Res. Program. Bull.* 9:188.

———— 1971b. Noradrenaline: fate and control of its biosynthesis. *Science* 173:598.

————, Shein, H. M., and Wurtman, R. J. 1969. Stimulation of C^{14}-melatonin synthesis from C^{14}-tryptophan by noradrenaline in rat pineal in organ culture. *Proc. Natl. Acad. Sci. U.S.A.* 62:544.

————, Mueller, R. A., Henry, J. P., and Stephens, P. M. 1970. Changes in enzymes involved in the biosynthesis and metabolism of noradrenaline and adrenaline after psychosocial stimulation. *Nature* 225:1059.

Azmitia, E. C., Jr., and McEwen, B. S. 1969. Corticosterone regulation of tryptophan hydroxylase in midbrain of the rat. *Science* 166:1274.

Bahnson, C. B. 1969. Psychophysiological complimentarity in malignancies: past work and future vistas. *Ann. N.Y. Acad. Sci.* 164:319.

Barraclough, C. A. 1961. Production of anovulatory, sterile rats by single injection of testosterone proprionate. *Endocrinolgy* 68:62.

Bliss, E. L., Migeon, C. J., Branch, C. H. H., and Samuels, L. T. 1956. Reaction of the adrenal cortex to emotional stress. *Psychosom. Med.* 18:56.

Block, J. D., and Reiser, M. F. 1962. Discrimination and recognition of weak stimuli. I. Psychological and physiological relationships. *Arch. Gen. Psychiatry* 6:25.

Bonfils, S., Liefooghe, G., Rossi, G., and Lambling, A. 1957. L'ulcère de constrainte du rat blanc. *C. R. Soc. Biol.* (Paris) 151:1149.

Bourne, P. G., Rose, R. M., and Mason, J. W. 1967. Urinary 17-OHCS levels: data on seven helicopter ambulance medics in combat. *Arch. Gen. Psychiatry.* 17:104.

Boyar, R. M., Finkelstein, J., Roffwarg, H., Kapen, S., Weitzman, E. D., and Hellman, L. 1972. Synchronization of augmented luteinizing hormone secretion with sleep during puberty. *N. Engl. J. Med.* 287:582.

————, Katz., J., Finkelstein, J. W., Kapen, S., Weiner, H., Weitzman, E. D., and Hellman, L. 1974. Anorexia nervosa: immaturity of the 24-hour luteinizing hormone secretory pattern. *N. Engl. J. Med.* 291:861.

Brod, J. 1960. Essential hypertension—hemodynamic observations with bearing on its pathogenesis. *Lancet* ii:773.

642

———— 1970. Hemodynamics and emotional stress. *Bibl. Psychiat.* 144:13.

————, Fencl, V., Hejl, Z., and Jirka, J. 1959. Circulatory changes underlying blood pressure elevation during acute emotional stress (mental arithmetic) in normotensive and hypertensive subjects. *Clin. Sci.* 18:269.

————, ————, ————, ————, and Ulrych, M. 1962. General and regional hemodynamic pattern underlying essential hypertension. *Clin. Sci.* 23:339.

Brodie, D. A., and Hanson, H. M. 1960. A study of the factors involved in the production of gastric ulcers by the restraint technique. *Gastroenterology* 38:353.

Bronfenbrenner, U. 1968. Early deprivation in mammals: A cross species analysis. In *Early Experience and Behavior*, edited by G. Newton. Springfield, Ill.: Charles C Thomas.

Browman, L. B. 1937. Light in its relation to activity and estrous rhythm in the albino rat. *J. Exp. Zool.* 75:375.

Bruch, H. 1973. *Eating Disorders—Obesity, Anorexia Nervosa and the Person Within.* New York: Basic Books.

Brunner, H. R., Laragh, J. H., Baer, L., Newton, M. A., Goodwin, F. T., Krakoff, L. R., Bard, R. H., and Bühler, F. R. 1972. Essential hypertension: renin and aldosterone, heart attack and stroke. *N. Engl. J. Med.* 286:441.

Bunney, W. E. 1965. A psychoendocrine study of severe psychotic depressive crises. *Am. J. Psychiatry* 122:72.

Burstein, B., and Russ, J. J. 1965. Preoperative psychological state and corticosteroid levels of surgical patients. *Psychosom. Med.* 27:309.

Bygdeman, S., and Von Euler, U. S. 1958. Resynthesis of catechol hormones in the cat's adrenal medulla. *Acta Physiol. Scand.* 44:375.

Callaway, E., and Thompson, S. V. 1953. Sympathetic activity and perception. *Psychosom. Med.* 15:433.

Carlson, L. A., Levi, L., and Orö, L. 1967. Plasma lipids and urinary excretion of catecholamines during acute emotional stress in man and their modification by nicotinic acid. *Forsvars Med.* 3:129.

Char, D. F. B., and Kelley, V. C. 1962. Serum antibody and protein studies following adrenalectomy in rabbits. *Proc. Soc. Exp. Biol. Med.* 109:599.

Chodoff, P., Friedman, S. B., and Hamburg, D. A. 1964. Stress, defenses and coping behavior: observations in parents of children with malignant disease. *Am. J. Psychiatry.* 120:743.

Curtis, G. C. 1972. Psychosomatics and chronobiology: possible implications of neuroendocrine rhythms. *Psychosom. Med.* 34:235.

Day, G. 1951. The psychosomatic approach to pulmonary tuberculosis. *Lancet* 260:1025.

Delbrück, M. 1970. A physicist's renewed look at biology: twenty years later. *Science* 168:1312.

de M'Uzan, M., and Bonfils, S. 1961. Étude et classification des aspects psychosomatiques de l'ulcère gastro-duodénal en milieu hospitalier. *Rev. Fr. Clin. Biol.* 6:46.

Denenberg, V. H., Brumaghin, J. T., Haltmeyer, G. C., and Zarrow, M. X. 1967. Increased adrenocortical activity in the neonatal rat following handling. *Endocrinology* 81:1047.

Descartes, R. 1911. The Discourse on Method. In *The Philosophical Works of Descartes*, edited by E. S. Haldane and G. T. R. Ross. Cambridge: Cambridge University Press.

Deutsch, F. 1959. *On the Mysterious Leap from the Mind to the Body.* London: International Universities Press.

DiCara, L. 1971. Plasticity in the autonomic nervous system: instrumental learning of glandular and visceral responses. In *The Neurosciences: Second Study Program*, edited by F. O. Schmitt. New York: Rockefeller University Press.

Edstrom, J. E., Eichner, D., and Schor, N. 1961. Quantitative ribonucleic acid measurements in functional studies of nucleus supraopticus. In *Regional Neurochemistry*, edited by S. S. Kety and J. Elkes. New York: Pergamon.

Engel, G. L. 1955. Studies of ulcerative colitis. III. The nature of the psychologic processes. *Am. J. Med.* 19:231.

—— 1967. *Psychological Development in Health and Disease.* Philadelphia: Saunders.

—— 1968. A life setting conducive to illness: The giving-up, given-up complex. *Arch. Intern. Med.* 69:293.

Feitelberg, S., and Lampl, H. 1935. Warmertonung der Grosshirnrinde bei Erregung und ruhe Bzw. *Arch. Exp. Pathol. Pharmakol.* 177:725.

Fenz, W. D., and Epstein, S. 1967. Gradients of physiological arousal in parachutists as a function of an approaching jump. *Psychosom. Med.* 29:33.

Fiske, V. M., Bryant, G. K., and Putnam, J. 1960. Effect of light on the weight of the pineal in the rat. *Endocrinology* 66:489.

Folkow, B., and Rubinstein, E. H. 1966. Cardiovascular effects of acute and chronic stimulation of the hypothalamic defense area in the rat. *Acta Physiol. Scand.* 68:48.

Freedman, D. X., and Fenichel, G. 1958. Effect of midbrain lesions in experimental allergy. *Arch. Neurol. Psychiatry* 79:164.

Friedman, S. B., Mason, J. W., and Hamburg, D. A. 1963. Urinary 17-hydroxycorticosteroid levels in parents of children with neoplastic disease: A study of chronic psychological stress. *Psychosom. Med.* 25:364.

——, Ader, R., and Glasgow, L. A. 1965. Effects of psychological stress in adult mice inoculated with Coxsackie B viruses. *Psychosom. Med.* 27:361.

Garma, A. 1960. The unconscious images in the genesis of peptic ulcer. *Int. J. Psychoanal.* 41:444.

Gillin, J. C., Jacobs, L. S., Fram, D. H., and Snyder, F. 1972. Acute effect of a glucocorticoid on normal human sleep. *Nature* 237:398.

Glowinski, J., Axelrod, J., Kopin, I. J., and Wurtman, R. J. 1964. Physiological disposition of H₃-norepinephrine in the developing rat. *J. Pharmacol. Exp. Ther.* 146:48.

Green, A. R., and Curzon, G. 1968. Decrease of 5-hydroxytryptamine in the brain provoked by hydrocortisone and its prevention by allopurinol. *Nature* 220:1095.

Greene, W. A., Jr., 1954. Psychological factors and reticuloendothelial disease. I. Preliminary observations on a group of males with lymphomas and leukemias. *Psychosom. Med.* 16:220.

Grinker, R. R. 1953. *Psychosomatic Research.* New York: Norton.

Hamburg, D. A. 1962. Plasma urinary corticosteroid levels in naturally occurring psychological stress. *Res. Publ. Assoc. Res. Nerv. Ment. Dis.* 40:406.

—— 1967. Genetics of adrenocortical hormone metabolism in relation to psychological stress. In *Behavior-Genetic Analysis,* edited by J. Hirsch. New York: McGraw-Hill.

—— and Adams, J. E. 1967. A perspective on coping behavior. *Arch. Gen. Psychiatry* 17:277.

——, Artz, C. P., Reiss, E., Amspacher, W. H., and Chambers, R. E. 1953a. Clinical importance of emotional problems in the care of patients with burns. *N. Engl. J. Med.* 248:355.

——, Hamburg, B., and DeCoza, S. 1953b. Adaptive problems and mechanisms in severely burned patients. *Psychiatry* 16:1.

Harlow, H. F. 1961. The development of affectional patterns in infant monkeys. In *Determinants of Infant Behavior,* edited by B. M. Foss. London: Methuen.

Harris, G. W. 1964. Sex hormones, brain development and brain function. *Endocrinology* 75:627.

—— and Levine, S. 1965. Sexual differentiation of the brain and its experimental control. *J. Physiol.* (London) 181:379.

Harris, H. 1968. Molecular basis of hereditary disease. *Br. Med. J.* 2:135.

Hellman, L. 1949. Production of acute gouty arthritis by adrenocorticotropin. *Science* 109:280.

——, Weston, R. E., Escher, D. J. W., and Leiter, L. 1948. The effect of adrenocorticotropin on renal hemodynamics and uric acid clearance. *Fed. Proc.* 7:52.

Henry, J. P., Meehan, J. P., and Stephens, P. M. 1967. The use of psychosocial stimuli to induce prolonged systolic hypertension in mice. *Psychosom. Med.* 29:408.

644

————, Ely, D. L., and Stephens, P. M. 1971a. Role of the autonomic system in social adaptation and stress. *Proc. Int. Union Physiol. Sci.* 8:50.

————, Stephens, P. M., Axelrod, J., and Mueller, R. A. 1971b. Effect of psychosocial stimulation on the enzymes involved in the biosynthesis and metabolism of noradrenaline and adrenaline. *Psychosom. Med.* 33:227.

Himwich, W., Davis, J. M., and Agraval, H. C. 1968. Effects of early weaning on some free amino acids and acetylcholinesterase activity of rat brain. In *Recent Advances in Biological Psychiatry*, edited by J. Wortis. New York: Plenum.

Hinde, R. A., and Spencer-Booth, Y. 1971. Effects of brief separations from mother on rhesus monkeys. *Science* 173:111.

Hinkle, L. E., and Wolf, S. 1952. A summary of experimental evidence relating life stress to diabetes mellitus. *Mt. Sinai J. Med. N.Y.* 19:537.

Hofer, M. A. 1971. Regulation of cardiac rate by nutritional factor in young rats. *Science* 172:1039.

———— 1975. Studies on how early maternal separation produces behavioral change in young rats. *Psychosom. Med.* 37:245.

———— and Reiser, M. F. 1969. The development of cardiac rate regulation in preweaning rats. *Psychosom. Med.* 31:372.

———— and Weiner, H. 1971a. The development and mechanisms of cardiorespiratory responses to maternal deprivation in rat pups. *Psychosom. Med.* 33:353.

———— and ———— 1971b. Physiological and behavioral regulation by nutritional intake during early development of the laboratory rat. *Psychosom. Med.* 33:468.

———— and ———— 1975. Physiological mechanisms for cardiac control by nutritional intake after maternal separation in the young rat. *Psychosom. Med.* 37:8.

————, Wolff, C. T., Friedman, S. B., and Mason, J. W. 1972a. A psychoendocrine study of bereavement. I. 17-hydroxycorticosteroid excretion rates of parents following death of their children from leukemia. *Psychosom. Med.* 34:481.

————, ————, ————, and ———— 1972b. A psychoendocrine study of bereavement. II. Observations on the process of mourning in relation to adrenocortical function. *Psychosom. Med.* 34:492.

Hubel, D. H. 1959. Single unit activity in striate cortex of unrestrained cats. *J. Physiol.* (London) 147:226.

———— 1960. Single unit activity in lateral geniculate body and optic tract of unrestrained cats. *J. Physiol.* (London) 150:91.

———— and Wiesel, T. N. 1959. Receptive fields of single neurons in the cat's striate cortex. *J. Physiol.* (London) 148:574.

———— and ———— 1960. Receptive fields of optic nerve fibers in the spider monkey. *J. Physiol.* (London) 154:572.

———— and ———— 1962. Receptive fields, binocular interaction and functional architecture in the cat's visual cortex. *J. Physiol.* (London) 160:106.

———— and ———— 1963. Receptive fields of cells in striate cortex of very young, visually inexperienced kittens. *J. Neurophysiol.* 26:994.

———— and ———— 1964. Responses of monkey geniculate cells to monochromic and white spots of light. *Physiologist* 7:162.

———— and ———— 1965. Binocular interaction in striate cortex of kittens reared with artifical squint. *J. Neurophysiol.* 28:1041.

———— and ———— 1968. The functional architecture of the striate cortex. In *Physiological and Biochemical Aspects of Nervous Integration*, edited by F. D. Carlson. Englewood Cliffs, N.J.: Prentice Hall.

Jacob, F., and Monod, J. 1961. Genetic regulatory mechanisms in the synthesis of proteins. *J. Mol. Biol.* 3:318.

Kandel, E. R., and Spencer, W. A. 1968. Cellular neurophysiological approaches in the study of learning. *Physiol. Rev.* 48:65.

Kasl, S. V., Cobb, S., and Brooks, G. W. 1968. Changes in serum uric acid and cholesterol levels in men undergoing job loss. *J.A.M.A.* 206:1500.

Katz, J. L., and Weiner, H. 1972. Psychosomatic considerations in hyperuricemia and gout. *Psychosom. Med.* 34:165.

——, Ackman, P., Rothwax, Y., Sachar, E. J., Weiner, H., Hellman, L., and Gallagher, T. F. 1970a. Psychoendocrine aspects of cancer of the breast. *Psychosom. Med.* 32:1.

——, Weiner, H., Gallagher, T. F., and Hellman, L. 1970b. Stress, distress and ego defenses. *Arch. Gen. Psychiatry* 23:131.

——, ——, Gutman, A., and Yu, T.-F. 1973. Hyperuricemia, gout and the executive suite. *J.A.M.A.* 224:1251.

Kaufman, I. C., and Rosenblum, L. 1969. Effects of separation from mother on the emotional behavior of infant monkeys. *Ann. N.Y. Acad. Sci.* 159:681.

Kelley, W. N., Rosenbloom, F. M., Henderson, J. F., and Seegmiller, J. E. 1967. A specific enzyme defect in gout associated with overproduction of uric acid. *Proc. Nat. Acad. Sci. U.S.A.* 57:1735.

Kemp, R. G., and Duquesnoy, R. J. 1973. Thymus adenylate cyclase activity during murine leukemogenesis. *Science* 183:218.

——, Huang, Y.-C., and Duquesnoy, R. J. 1973. Decreased epinephrine response of adenylate cyclase activity of lymphoid cells from immunodeficient pituitary dwarf mice. *J. Immunol.* 111:1855.

Kennedy, J. A., and Bakst, H. 1966. The influence of emotions on the outcome of cardiac surgery: A predictive study. *Bull. N.Y. Acad. Med.* 42:811.

Kestenbaum, R. S., Deutsch, J. A., and Coons, E. E. 1970. Behavioral measurement of neural post-stimulation excitability cycle: pain cells in the brain of the rat. *Science* 167:393.

Kimball, C. 1969. A predictive study of adjustment to cardiac surgery. *J. Thorac. Cardiovasc. Surg.* 58:891.

Kissen, D. M. 1967. Psychological factors, personality, and lung cancer in men aged 55–64. *Br. J. Med. Psychol.* 40:29.

Klein, D. C., and Weller, J. 1970. Serotonin N-acetyl transferase activity is stimulated by norepinephrine and dibutyryl cyclic adenosine monophosphate. *Fed. Proc.* 29:615.

Knapp, P. H. 1971. Revolution, relevance and psychosomatic medicine: where the light is not. *Psychosom. Med.* 33:363.

—— and Nemetz, S. J. 1960. Acute bronchial asthma—concomitant depression with excitement and varied antecedent patterns in 406 attacks. *Psychosom. Med.* 22:42.

——, Mushatt, C., Nemetz, J. S., Constantine, H., and Friedman, S. 1970. The context of reported asthma during psychoanalysis. *Psychosom. Med.* 32:167.

Kraus, A. S., and Lilienfeld, A. M. 1959. Some epidemiological aspects of the high mortality in a young widowed group. *J. Chronic Dis.* 10:207.

Kvetnansky, R., and Mikulaj, L. 1970. Adrenal and urinary catecholamines in rats during adaptation to repeated immobilization stress. *Endocrinology* 87:738.

——, Weise, V. K., and Kopin, I. J. 1970a. Elevation of adrenal tyrosine hydroxylase and phenylethanolamine-N-methyl transferase by repeated immobilization of rats. *Endocrinology* 87:744.

——, Gewirtz, G. P., Weise, V. K., and Kopin, I. J. 1970b. Effect of hypophysectomy on immobilization-induced elevation of tyrosine hydroxylase and phenylethanolamine-N-methyl transferase in the rat adrenal. *Endocrinology* 87:1323.

646

Langworthy, O. R. 1933. Development of behavioral patterns and myelinization of the central nervous system in the human fetus and infant. *Carnegie Inst. Contrib. Embryol.* 24:1.

Lazarus, R. S. 1966. *Psychological Stress and the Coping Process.* New York: McGraw-Hill.

LeShan, L. I. 1966. An emotional life history pattern associated with neoplastic disease. *Ann. N.Y. Acad. Sci.* 125:780.

Levine, S. 1962. The psychophysiological effects of infantile stimulation. In *Roots of Behavior,* edited by E. Bliss. New York: Harper & Row.

—— 1968. Influence of infantile stimulation on the response to stress during preweaning development. *Dev. Psychobiol.* 1:67.

—— 1970. The pituitary-adrenal system and the developing brain. In *Progress in Brain Research,* vol. 32, edited by D. DeWied and J. A. W. M. Weignen. Amsterdam: Elsevier.

—— and Mullins, R. F., Jr. 1966. Hormonal influences on brain organization in infant rats. *Science* 152:1585.

—— and —— 1968. Hormones in infancy. In *Early Experience and Behavior,* edited by G. Newton and S. Levine. Springfield: Charles C Thomas.

—— and Senay, E. C. 1970. Studies on the role of acid in the pathogenesis of experimental stress ulcers. *Psychosom. Med.* 32:61.

——, Alpert, M., and Lewis, G. W. 1958. Differential maturation of an adrenal response to cold stress in rats manipulated in infancy. *J. Comp. Physiol. Psychol.* 51:774.

Levitt, E. E., Persky, H., Brady, J. P., and Fitzgerald, J. A. 1963. The effect of hydrocortisone infusion in hypnotically induced anxiety. *Psychosom. Med.* 25:158.

Löfving, B. 1961. Cardiovascular adjustments induced from the rostral cingulate gyrus with special reference to sympathoinhibitory mechanisms. *Acta Physiol. Scand.* 53(Suppl. 184):1.

Long, D. A., and Shewell, J. 1955. The influence of the thyroid gland on the production of antitoxin in the guinea pig. *Br. J. Exp. Pathol.* 36:351.

Luparello, T. J., Stein, M., and Park, C. D. 1964. Effect of hypothalamic lesions on rat anaphylaxis. *Am. J. Physiol.* 207:911.

Maas, J. W., and Mednieks, M. 1971. Hydrocortisone-mediated increase of norepinephrine uptake by brain slices. *Science* 171:178.

Mandell, A. J. 1973. Neurobiological barriers to euphoria. *Am. Sci.* 61:565.

Marsh, J. T., Lavender, J. F., Chang, S.-S., and Rasmussen, A. F. 1963. Poliomyelitis in monkeys: decreased susceptibility after avoidance stress. *Science* 140:1414.

Mason, J. W. 1968. Organization of psychoendocrine mechanisms. *Psychosom. Med.* 30:565.

—— 1971. A re-evaluation of the concept of "non-specificity" in stress theory. *J. Psychiatr. Res.* 8:323.

Mason, W. A., Davenport, R. K., Jr., and Menzel, E. W., Jr. 1968. Early experiences and the social development of rhesus monkeys and chimpanzees. In *Early Experience and Behavior,* edited by G. Newton and S. Levine. Springfield: Charles C Thomas.

McKenzie, J. M. 1968. Humoral factors in the pathogenesis of Graves' disease. *Physiol. Rev.* 48:252.

Melzack, R. 1969. The role of early experience on emotional arousal. *Ann. N.Y. Acad. Sci.* 159:721.

Menguy, R. 1964. Current concepts of the etiology of duodenal ulcer. *Am. J. Dig. Dis.* 9:199.

Milković, K., and Milković, S. 1959a. The influence of adrenalectomy of pregnant rats on the reactiveness of the pituitary-adrenal system of newborn animals. *Arch. Int. Physiol. Biochim.* 67:24.

—— and —— 1959b. Reactiveness of the pituitary-adrenal system of newborn animals. *Endokrinologie* 37:301.

Miller, N. E. 1969. Learning of visceral and glandular responses. *Science* 163:434.

Mirsky, I. A. 1957. The psychosomatic approach to the etiology of clinical disorders. *Psychosom. Med.* 19:424.

647

—— 1958. Physiologic, psychologic and social determinants in the etiology of duodenal ulcer. *Am. J. Dig. Dis.* 3:285.

Moncrief, J. A., Weichselbaum, T. E., and Elman, R. 1953. Changes in adrenocortical steroid concentration of peripheral plasma following surgery. *Surg. Forum* 4:469.

Moore, R. Y., Heller, A., Wurtman, R. J., and Axelrod, J. 1967. Visual pathway mediating pineal response to environmental light. *Science* 155:220.

Moos, R. H., and Solomon, G. F. 1966. Social and personal factors in rheumatoid arthritis: pathogenetic considerations. *Clin. Med.* 73:19.

Mozell, M. M., and Jagodowicz, M. 1973. Chromatographic separation of odorants by the nose: retention times measured across in vivo olfactory mucosa. *Science* 181:1247.

Mueller, R. A., Thoenen, H., and Axelrod, J. 1969a. Increase in tyrosine hydroxylase activity after reserpine administration. *J. Pharmacol. Exp. Ther.* 169:74.

——, ——, and —— 1969b. Inhibition of transsynaptically increased tyrosine hydroxylase activity by cycloheximide and actinomycin D. *Mol. Pharmacol.* 5:463.

——, ——, and —— 1970. Effect of pituitary and ACTH on the maintenance of basal tyrosine hydroxylase activity in the rat adrenal gland. *Endocrinology* 86:751.

Nemiah, J. C., and Sifneos, P. E. 1970. Affect and fantasy in patients with psychosomatic disorders. In *Modern Trends in Psychosomatic Medicine*, vol. 2, edited by O. W. Hill. London: Butterworth.

Owman, C. H. 1965. Localization of neuronal and parenchymal monoamines under normal and experimental conditions in the mammalian pineal gland. *Prog. Brain Res.* 10:423.

Parkes, C. M. 1964. Recent bereavement as a cause of mental illness. *Br. J. Psychiatry* 110:198.

Pepler, W. J., and Pearse, A. G. E. 1957. The histochemistry of the esterase of rat brain with special reference to those of the hypothalamic nuclei. *J. Neurochem.* 1:193.

Perlman, L. V., Ferguson, S., Bergum, K., Isenberg, E. L., and Hammarsten, J. F. 1971. Precipitation of congestive heart failure: social and emotional factors. *Ann. Intern. Med.* 75:1.

Perlmann, P., Hammarström, S., and Lagercrantz, R. 1973. Immunological features of idiopathic ulcerative colitis and Crohn's disease. *Rendic. Gastroenterol.* 5:17.

Pettigrew, J., Olson, C., and Barlow, H. B. 1973. Kitten visual cortex: short-term, stimulus-induced changes in connectivity. *Science* 180:1202.

Pollin, W., and Goldin, S. 1961. The physiological effects of intravenously administered epinephrine and its metabolism in normal and schizophrenic men. II. *J. Psychiatr. Res.* 1:50.

Price, D. B., Thaler, M., and Mason, J. W. 1957. Preoperative emotional states and adrenal cortical activity: studies on cardiac and pulmonary surgery patients. *Arch. Neurol. Psychiatry* 77:646.

Quay, W. B. 1963. Circadian rhythm in rat pineal serotonin and its modification by estrus cycle and photoperiod. *Gen. Comp. Endocrinol.* 3:473.

Rahe, R. H., and Arthur, R. J. 1967. Stressful underwater demolition training: serum urate and cholesterol variability. *J.A.M.A.* 202:1052.

——, Rubin, R. T., Arthur, R. J., and Clark, B. R. 1968. Serum uric acid and cholesterol variability: a comprehensive view of underwater demolition team training. *J.A.M.A.* 206:2875.

Rasmussen, A. F., Marsh, J. T., and Brill, N. Q. 1957. Increased susceptibility to herpes simplex in mice subjected to avoidance-learning stress or restraint. *Proc. Soc. Exp. Biol. Med.* 96:183.

Reiser, M. F., and Block, J. D. 1962. Discrimination and recognition of weak stimuli. II. A possible autonomic feedback mechanism. *Arch. Gen. Psychiatry* 6:37.

Reiser, M. F. 1970. Theoretical considerations of the role of psychological factors in pathogenesis and etiology of essential hypertension. *Bibl. Psychiatr.* 144:117.

—— 1975. Changing theoretical concepts in psychosomatic medicine. In *American Handbook of Psychiatry*, vol. 4, edited by M. F. Reiser. New York: Basic Books.

Richards, D. W. 1970. Homeostasis: its dislocations and perturbations. In *Medical Priesthoods and Other Essays*. Hartford: Connecticut Printers.

Richter, D. 1952. Brain metabolism and cerebral function. *Biochem. Soc. Symp.* 8:62.

648

Riesen, A. H. 1961. Excessive arousal effects of stimulation after early sensory deprivation. In *Sensory Deprivation*, edited by P. Solomon. Cambridge: Harvard University Press.

Roth, R. H., Stjärne, L., and Von Euler, U. S. 1966. Acceleration of noradrenaline biosynthesis by nerve stimulation. *Life Sci.* 5:1071.

Rubeson, A. 1969. Alterations in noradrenaline turnover in the peripheral sympathetic neurons induced by stress. *J. Pharm. Pharmacol.* 21:878.

Rubin, R. T., Rahe, R. H., Arthur, R. J., and Clark, B. R. 1969. Adrenal cortical activity changes during underwater demolition team training. *Psychosom. Med.* 31:553.

———, ———, Clark, B. R., and Arthur, R. J. 1970. Serum uric acid, cholesterol, and cortisol levels: interrelationships in normal men under stress. *Arch. Intern. Med.* 125:815.

Ruesch, J., Christiansen, C., Patterson, L. C., Dewees, S., and Jacobson, A. 1947. Psychological invalidism in thyroidectomized patients. *Psychosom. Med.* 9:77.

Sabshin, M., Hamburg, D. A., and Grinker, R. R. 1957. Significance of pre-experimental studies in the psychosomatic laboratory. *Arch. Neurol. Psychiatry* 78:207.

Sachar, E. J. 1969. Psychological homeostasis and endocrine function. In *Psychochemical Strategies in Man: Methods, Strategy and Theory*, edited by A. Mandell and M. Mandell. New York: Academic Press.

———, Mason, J. W., Kollmer, H., and Artiss, K. 1963. Psychoendocrine aspects of acute schizophrenic reactions. *Psychosom. Med.* 25:510.

———, Mackenzie, J. M., Binstock, W. A., and Mack, J. E. 1967. Corticosteroid responses to psychotherapy of depressions. I. Elevations during confrontation of loss. *Arch. Gen. Psychiatry* 16:461.

———, Hellman, L., Fukushima, D. K., and Gallagher, T. F. 1970. Cortisol production in depressive illness: a clinical and biochemical clarification. *Arch. Gen. Psychiatry* 23:289.

Samloff, I. M. 1969. Multiple molecular forms of pepsinogen and their distribution in gastric and duodenal mucosa. *Clin. Res.* 17:310.

——— and Townes, P. L. 1969. Heterogeneity and genetic polymorphism of human pepsinogen. *Gastroenterology* 56:1194.

——— and ——— 1970. Pepsinogens: genetic polymorphism in man. *Science* 168:144.

Schapiro, S., Geller, E., and Eiduson, S. 1962. Corticoid response to stress in the steroid-inhibited rat. *Proc. Soc. Exp. Biol. Med.* 109:935.

Schiavi, R. C. 1966. Effect of hypothalamic lesions on histamine toxicity in the guinea pig. *Am. J. Physiol.* 211:1269.

Schmale, A. H., Jr., 1958. Relation of separation and depression to disease. I. A report on a hospitalized medical population. *Psychosom. Med.* 20:259.

Schur, M. 1955. Comments on the metapsychology of somatization. *Psa. Study Ch.* 10:119.

Schwartz, G. E., and Higgins, J. D. 1971. Cardiac activity preparatory to overt and covert behavior. *Science* 173:1144.

Sedvall, G. C., and Kopin, I. J. 1967. Acceleration of norepinephrine synthesis in the rat submaxillary gland in vivo during sympathetic nerve stimulation. *Life Sci.* 6:45.

Selye, H. 1950. *Stress.* Montreal: Acta.

——— 1973. Homeostasis and heterostasis. *Perspect. Biol. Med.* 16:441.

Serota, H. M., and Gerard, R. W. 1938. Localized thermal changes in the cat's brain. *J. Neurophysiol.* 1:115.

Shapiro, A. P. 1973. Essential hypertension—Why idiopathic? *Am. J. Med.* 54:1.

Shoemaker, W. J., and Wurtman, R. J. 1971. Perinatal undernutrition: accumulation of catecholamines in rat brain. *Science* 171:1017.

Smelik, P. G. 1963. Relation between the blood level of corticoids and their inhibiting effect on the hypophyseal stress response. *Proc. Soc. Exp. Biol. Med.* 113:616.

Snyder, S. H., Zweig, M., Axelrod, J., and Fischer, J. F. 1965. Control of the circadian rhythm in serotonin content of the rat pineal gland. *Proc. Nat. Acad. Sci. U.S.A.* 53:301.

————, ————, and ———— 1967. Circadian rhythm in the serotonin content of the rat pineal gland: regulating factors. *J. Pharmacol. Exp. Ther.* 158:206.

State, D. 1971. Peptic ulceration: physiologic considerations. *Adv. Psychosom. Med.* 6:104.

Stein, M. 1962. Etiology and mechanisms in the development of asthma. In *Psychosomatic Medicine,* edited by J. H. Nodine and J. H. Moyer. Philadelphia: Lea & Febiger.

Stein, S., and Charles, E. 1971. Emotional factors in juvenile diabetes mellitus: A study of early life experiences of adolescent diabetics. *Am. J. Psychiatry* 128:700.

Szentivanyi, A. 1968. Beta adrenergic theory of atopic abnormality in bronchial asthma. *J. Allergy* 42:203.

————, and Filipp, G. 1958. Anaphylaxis and the nervous system. *J. Allergy* 16:143.

Taylor, K. M., and Snyder, S. H. 1971. Brain histamine: rapid apparent turnover altered by restraint and cold stress. *Science* 172:1037.

Taylor, W. H. 1970. Pepsins of patients with peptic ulcer. *Nature* 227:76.

Thoenen, H., Mueller, R. A., and Axelrod, J. 1969a. Increased tyrosine hydroxylase activity after drug-induced alteration of sympathetic transmission. *Nature* 221:1264.

————, ————, and ———— 1969b. Transsynaptic induction of adrenal tyrosine hydroxylase. *J. Pharmacol. Exp. Ther.* 169:249.

————, ————, and ———— 1970a. Neuronally dependent induction of adrenal phenylethanolamine N-methyltransferase by hydroxydopamine. *Biochem. Pharmacol.* 19:669.

————, ————, and ———— 1970b. Phase difference in the induction of tyrosine hydroxylase in cell body and nerve terminals of sympathetic neurones. *Proc. Natl. Acad. Sci. U.S.A.* 65:58.

Thoman, E. B., Sproul, M., Seeler, B., and Levine, S. 1970. Influence of adrenalectomy in female rats on reproductive processes including effects on the fetus and offspring. *J. Endocrinol.* 46:297.

Uvnäs, B. 1960. Central cardiovascular control. In *Handbook of Physiology: Neurophysiology,* vol. 2. Washington: American Physiological Society.

Viernstein, L. J., and Grossman, R. G. 1961. Neural discharge patterns in the transmission of sensory information. In *Information Theory,* edited by C. Cherry. London: Butterworth.

von Euler, U. S. 1971. Adrenergic neurotransmitter functions. *Science* 173:202.

Wald, G. 1968. Molecular basis of visual excitation. *Science* 162:230.

Watson, J., Epstein, R., and Cohn, M. 1973. Cyclic nucleotides as intracellular mediators of the expression of antigen-sensitive cells. *Nature* 246:405.

Weiner, H., Thaler, M., Reiser, M. F., and Mirsky, I. A. 1957. Etiology of duodenal ulcer. I. Relation of specific psychological characteristics to rate of gastric secretion (serum pepsinogen). *Psychosom. Med.* 19:1.

————, Singer, M. T., and Reiser, M. F. 1962. Cardiovascular responses and their psychological correlates: a study in healthy young adults and patients with peptic ulcer and hypertension. *Psychosom. Med.* 24:477.

Weiner, S., Dorman, D., Persky, H., Stack, T. W., Martin, J., and Levitt, E. E. 1963. Effects on anxiety of increasing the plasma hydrocortisone level. *Psychosom. Med.* 25:69.

Weinshilboum, R. M., and Axelrod, J. 1970. Dopamine-β-hydroxylase activity in human blood. *Pharmacologist* 12:214.

————, Kvetnansky, R., Axelrod, J., and Kopin, I. J. 1971. Elevation of serum dopamine-β-hydroxylase activity with forced immobilization. *Nature* [New Biol.] 230:287.

Weisman, A. 1956. A study of the psychodynamics of duodenal ulcer exacerbations with special reference to treatment and the problem of specificity. *Psychosom. Med.* 18:2.

Welch, B. L., and Welch, A. S. 1965. Effect of grouping on the level of brain norepinephrine in white Swiss mice. *Life Sci.* 4:1011.

——— and ——— 1968. Differential activation by restraint stress of a mechanism to conserve brain catecholamines and serotonin in mice differing in excitability. *Nature* 218:575.

——— and ——— 1969. Agression and the biogenic amines. In *Biology of Aggressive Behavior*, edited by S. Garattini and E. B. Siggs. Amsterdam: Excerpta Medica.

Wiener, D. N. 1952. Personality characteristics of various disability groups. *Genet. Psychol. Monogr.* 45:175.

Wiesel, T. N., and Hubel, D. H. 1963a. Effects of visual deprivation on morphology and physiology of cells in the cat's lateral geniculate body. *J. Neurophysiol.* 26:978.

——— and ——— 1963b. Single-cell responses in striate cortex of kittens deprived of vision in one eye. *J. Neurophysiol.* 26:1003.

——— and ——— 1965a. Comparison of the effects of unilateral and bilateral eye closure on cortical unit responses in kittens. *J. Neurophysiol.* 28:1029.

——— and ——— 1965b. Extent of recovery from the effects of visual deprivation in kittens. *J. Neurophysiol.* 28:1060.

Wolff, C., Friedman, S. B., Hofer, M. A., and Mason, J. W. 1964. Relationship between psychological defenses and mean urinary 17-hydroxycorticosteroid excretion rates: I. A predictive study of parents of fatally ill children. *Psychosom. Med.* 26:576.

Wolff, H. G. 1953. *Stress and Disease.* Springfield, Ill.: Charles C Thomas.

Wurtman, R. J., Axelrod, J., and Chu, E. W. 1963a. Melatonin, a pineal substance: effect on rat ovary. *Science* 141:277.

———, ———, and Phillips, L. S. 1963b. Melatonin synthesis in the pineal gland: control by light. *Science* 142:1071.

Yates, F. E., and Urquhart, J. 1962. Control of plasma concentrations of adrenocortical hormones. *Physiol. Rev.* 42:359.

Yessler, P. G., Reiser, M. F., and Rioch, D. McK. 1959. Etiology of duodenal ulcer II. Serum pepsinogen and peptic ulcer in inductees. *J.A.M.A.* 169:451.

Young, M., Benjamin, B., and Wallis, C. 1963. The mortality of widowers. *Lancet* ii:454.

Young, W. C. 1961. The hormones and mating behavior. In *Sex and Internal Secretions*, vol. 2, edited by W. C. Young. Baltimore: Williams & Wilkins.

———, Goy, R. W., and Phoenix, C. H. 1964. Hormones and sexual behavior. *Science* 143:212.

Zweig, M., Snyder, H. M., and Axelrod, J. 1966. Evidence for a non-retinal pathway of light to the pineal gland of newborn rats. *Proc. Natl. Acad. Sci. U.S.A.* 56:515.

Index

Numbers in italic type refer to tables in the text.

A

ABH ANTIGEN, and peptic ulcer disease, 39–40

ACETYLCHOLINE
and bronchial asthma, 290–91, 296
and pepsinogen secretion, 71

ACHLORHYDRIA, 73

ACIDOSIS, and bronchial asthma, 224

ACID PHOSPHATASE, and rheumatoid arthritis, 469

ACTH (ADRENOCORTICOTROPIC HORMONE)
and aldosterone secretion, 166
and bronchial asthma, 244
in Graves' disease, 362–63, 364
and 18-hydroxy-desoxycorticosterone, 170
and peptic ulcer disease, 68
and rheumatoid arthritis, 455

ADAPTATION
failure of in diseases, 4
and nervous system, 5
and physiological changes, 3

ADDISON'S DISEASE, and thyrotoxicosis, 324–25

ADENOSINE MONOPHOSPHATE (CYCLIC)
and bronchial asthma, 290–92
and Graves' disease, 371–72
and neurotransmitters, 5–6

ADH. *See* ANTIDIURETIC HORMONE (ADH).

ADRENOCORTICAL DISEASE, and high blood pressure, 165

ADRENOCORTICAL HORMONES, and gastric secretion, 67–69

AGAMMAGLOBULINEMIA
and rheumatoid arthritis, 424, 426, 468, 470–71, 476
and ulcerative colitis, 542

AGE
and blood pressure, 117–18
and bronchial asthma, 227, 237–38
and disease predisposition, 584–85
and rheumatoid arthritis, 432–33

AGGRESSION, and hypertension, 140–43

ALCOHOL
and essential hypertension, 123
and gastric secretion, 63
and peptic ulcer disease, 43, 53–54

ALDOSTERONE
and blood pressure, 165–68
and 18-hydroxy-desoxycorticosterone, 170
and hypertension, 110
and glucocorticoids, 168–170
and sodium retention, 146, 157

ALEXANDER, F., 7–9, 11–13, 16, 47, 84–85
and bronchial asthma, 244–50
and disease predisposition, 579–582, 585, 586, 611
and Graves' disease, 343, 344, 350, 380–82
and hypertension, 126

ALEXANDER, F. (cont'd)
  and peptic ulcer disease, 36–37, 42–43,
    45–47
  and rheumatoid arthritis, 420, 435, 441,
    446–48
  and ulcerative colitis, 517, 526, 531
ALLERGY
  in animal models, 282–84
  and bronchial asthma, 224, 253,
    254–58, 255, 276, 285–86, 293–95
  and genetic factors, 229–34
  and histamine, 286–289
  neural mechanisms of, 291–93
L-AMINO ACID DECARBOXYLASE, and
    hypertension, 145
AMINOTRANSFERASE
    FRUCTOSE-6-PHOSPHATE, and
    salicylates, 55
ANAPHYLAXIS, 5, 6
ANEMIA
  and pepsinogen levels, 72
  and rheumatoid arthritis, 462
ANGER
  and blood pressure, 131–32, 135
  and bronchial asthma, 227, 243, 249,
    253–54, 279, 297–98
  and Crohn's disease, 555
  and gastric secretion, 56, 57, 59, 60
  and hypertension, 112–13, 119–20,
    124–33, 141
  and rheumatoid arthritis, 444, 447–51,
    455–56
  and salt intake, 123
  and ulcerative colitis, 520, 524, 532, 535
ANGIOTENSIN
  and aldosterone, 165–67
  and essential hypertension, 154–59
ANKYLOSING SPONDYLITIS, and ulcerative
    colitis, 510
ANOREXIA
  and Crohn's disease, 550
  and rheumatoid arthritis, 462
ANTACIDS, and duodenal ulcers, 35
ANTICHOLINERGIC AGENTS, and duodenal
    ulcer, 335
ANTIDIURETIC HORMONE (ADH), and

essential hypertension, 163–65
ANTIGASTRIC PARIETAL CELL ANTIBODIES,
    and Graves' disease, 329
ANTIMALARIAL DRUGS, and rheumatoid
    arthritis, 455
ANTIMICROSOMAL ANTIBODIES, and
    Graves' disease, 324, 328–30, 374–75
ANTITHYROGLOBULIN, and Graves's
    disease, 324, 328–30
ANXIETY
  and alcohol use, 53–54
  and bronchial asthma, 227, 242, 249,
    252, 253–54, 266, 272, 279, 297–98
  and essential hypertension, 124–30,
    131–34, 137
  and gastric secretion, 59, 60
  and Graves' disease, 339, 342–43
  and peptic ulcer disease, 46
  and perforation, 53
  and rheumatoid arthritis, 435, 439, 443
  and ulcerative colitis, 520, 532, 535
APPETITE, and gastric secretion, 59, 63
ARTHRITIS, RHEUMATOID, 12, 419–78
  animal studies of, 474–75
  autoantibodies and, 468–72
  definition of, 419–21
  depression and, 440–44
  diagnostic criteria for, 428–29, 476
  epidemiological factors in, 426–34
  ethnic origins and, 433–34
  genetic factors in, 421–26
  immunology and, 421, 460–63, 467–74
  incidence of, 419, 429–33
  initiation of, 463–67, 469
  juvenile form of, 420
  marriages of patients and, 453–54
  muscle tension and, 457–58
  physiological factors of, 461–74
  psychological factors of, 419–20, 435–61
  psychophysiological factors of, 457–61
  sexual inhibitions and, 450–51, 456–57
  socioeconomic factors in, 426–34
  and ulcerative colitis, 508
ARTERY DISEASE, 111
ASPIRIN
  and bronchial asthma, 294

and mucoprotein inhibition, 84
and peptic ulcer disease, 34
ASTHMA, BRONCHIAL, 223–89
  allergens and, 276–77, 293–94
  age and, 237–38
  animal models for, 282–84
  community structure and, 4
  definition of, 224
  drug action and, 18
  epidemiology of, 234–39
  genetic factors and, 229–34
  hypnosis and, 277–78, 280
  immunology and, 224–25, 284–93
  intelligence and, 239
  mortality of patients, 275
  neural mechanisms of, 291–93
  odors and, 258–61
  psychological factors in, 239–75
  psychophysiological factors in, 275–84
  relaxation training and, 278–79
  sex and, 238
  sleep and, 279
  socioeconomic factors in, 238
  stress and, 279–82
ATROPINE, in bronchial asthma studies,
    277
ATROPINE SULPHATE, and lesion
    formation, 80
AUTOANTIBODIES, 17
  in Graves' disease, 374–77
  in rheumatoid arthritis, 462–63, 468–72
  in ulcerative colitis, 539–43, 541, 547
AUTONOMIC NERVOUS SYSTEM, 5
  and bronchial asthma, 281–82
  and cell regulation, 24
AUTOREGULATORY MECHANISMS,
    602–609
AVOIDANCE BEHAVIOR, 12–13
AZATHIOPRINE, and ulcerative colitis, 545

B

BACTERIA, and rheumatoid arthritis,
    465–66
BEREAVEMENT, 3
  and changes in cell chemistry, 5

and disease predisposition, 25, 589
and essential hypertension, 124
and Graves' disease, 333–34, 341, 358
and initiation of disease, 612–18
and rheumatoid arthritis, 439–41
and ulcerative colitis, 517
BIOFEEDBACK, and blood pressure, 136
BLEEDING
  gastrointestinal, and salicylates, 55
  rectal, and ulcerative colitis, 503–4, 523
BLOOD, and coronary artery disease, 6
BLOOD FLOW
  and gastric secretion, 63, 69
  and hypertension, 133–34
  in mucus under stress, 59
BLOOD GROUP
  and peptic ulcer disease, 39–41
  and ulcer classification, 35
  and ulcerative colitis, 510
BLOOD PRESSURE
  adrenocortical disease and, 165
  age and, 118
  aldosterone and, 166–68
  angiotensin and, 158–59
  conditioning studies and, 135–48
  coronary disease and, 127
  corticoids and, 168–70
  dopamine β-hydroxylase level, 131, 140,
    142, 145, 147, 170
  genetic factors and, 113–16, 143–47
  hypertension and, 111, 113
  kidney and, 153–59
  oral contraceptives and, 115
  pain and, 130–31, 134
  personality and, 125–28
  prostaglandins and, 159
  psychophysiological factors in, 120–37
  regulation of, 24
  renin and, 154–59
  salt and, 118–19, 122–23
  socioeconomic factors in, 118–120
  stress and, 112, 114, 119–120, 121, 135,
    137
BODY BUILD, as marker for peptic ulcer
    disease, 40
BODY IMAGE, as research tool, 49

BRADYKININ, in bronchial asthma, 289, 291

BRAIN
and anaphylaxis, 5, 293
and antidiuretic hormone, 164–65
and blood pressure, 145–47, 176, 177–82
and cell regulation, 24
chemistry and environment, 594–95
and disease predisposition, 590–95, 598–99
and essential hypertension, 140–43
and immunological responses, 17
peptic ulcer disease and, 85
physiological processes and, 5
rheumatoid arthritis and, 455
transduction and, 624–38
ulcerative colitis and, 520

BRONCHOCONSTRICTION, and asthma, 225, 229, 276–77, 294–98

C

CALCITONIN, effect on hydrochloric acid secretion, 64–65
CARBACHOL, and peptic ulcer disease, 77
CARBENOXOLONE, and gastric ulcer, 35
CARBOHYDRATE, intolerance to, 110
CARCINOID SYNDROME, 14
CARDIOVASCULAR SYSTEM, and essential hypertension, 149–53

CALCIUM
and hypertension, 151–52
and peptic ulcer disease, 70

CATECHOLAMINES
and bronchial asthma, 290, 296
and essential hypertension, 170–73, 179
and gastrin secretion, 69, 81
and Graves' disease, 359–61
and stress, 131, 146

CENTRAL NERVOUS SYSTEM
and blood pressure control, 173–82
and essential hypertension, 173–82
effect on stomach physiology, 65–66

CHILDREN

bronchial asthma and, 227, 235, 236, 237–38, 241–43, 245–47, 252–58, 261–74
essential hypertension and, 126–27, 129–30
Graves' disease, 326, 335, 339
rheumatoid arthritis and, 437–38, 451–53
ulcerative colitis and, 503, 519–20, 523–24, 526–27, 533–34

CHLOROTHIAZIDE, and salt, 160

CIRCADIAN RHYTHM, 24
and gastric secretion in ulcer disease, 61

CIRCULATION, and essential hypertension, 149–53

COLITIS, ULCERATIVE, 15, 499–548
animal models in, 537–38
arthritis and, 508
definition of, 500–508, 505, 546
diagnosis of, 502–508, 536
diseases associated with, 506–507
epidemiology of, 511–14
eye lesions and, 508–509
genetic factors in, 509–11
immunological factors in, 538–545, 547
incidence of, 511, 512
infection and, 545–46
initiation of, 516–22
personality and, 523–28
psychological factors and, 514–34, 547–48
psychophysiological factors and, 533–36
psychosis, 521–22
physiology of, 533
socioeconomic factors in, 514

COMMUNITY STRUCTURE, affect on diseases, 3–4

COMPULSION, and ulcerative colitis, 524

CONDITIONING
cardiovascular response, 135–48
gastric secretion, 78–80

CONFLICT
and alcohol use, 53–54
and peptic ulcer disease, 52–53, 79–80

CONN'S SYNDROME, 110, 165

656

NUCLEOTIDES, CYCLIC, and bronchial asthma, 290–91

O

OBESITY, and high blood pressure, 119
ODOR, and bronchial asthma, 258–61
ORAL DEPENDENCY, and peptic ulcer disease, 37
OXYTOCIN, and guanosine monophosphate, 6

P

PAF, in bronchial asthma, 289
PAIN
  in Crohn's disease, 550
  and depression, 443–45
  and high blood pressure, 130–31, 134
  and ulcerative colitis, 522
PANTOTHENIC ACID, and peptic ulcer disease, 54
PARASYMPATHETIC NERVOUS SYSTEM, and bronchial asthma, 277
PARATHYROID
  adenoma, 325
  hormone, 70
PEPSIN
  neural mediation of, 65
  regulation of, 71–72
  and stress, 59
  and ulcerative colitis, 532
  and ulcer types, 34–35
  and vagal discharge, 66
PEPSINOGEN
  and alcohol, 54
  and gastric erosions, 77–78
  and peptic ulcer disease, 40, 49–52
  populational distribution of, 52
  regulation of, 49, 63, 71–72
  types of, 72
PERFORATION, ULCER, 53
PERIPHERAL RESISTANCE, and essential hypertension, 149–53

PERSONALITY, 6
  of arthritic patients, 437–38, 445–46, 451–53
  of asthmatics' parents, 256–7, 262–69
  of asthmatic patients, 241–47
  classification problems and, 48
  and coronary disease, 127
  and disease predisposition, 6–10, 584
  and essential hypertension, 124–30
  of Graves' disease patients, 340–44, 351
  and peptic ulcer disease, 42–45
  and ulcerative colitis, 523–30
PH, effect on gastrin release, 64
PHENYLBUTAZONE, and peptic ulcer disease, 67
PHENYLETHANOLAMINE N-METHYLATRANSFERASE, and essential hypertension, 141
PHENYLTHIOCARBAMIDE (PTC), as marker for peptic ulcer disease, 41
PHEOCHROMOCYTOMA, and thyrotoxicosis, 325
PHOSPHODIESTERASE, and bronchial asthma, 290
PINEAL GLAND, and aldosterone secretion, 166
PITUITARY
  and Graves' disease, 351
  and hypertension, 144
  and thyroid gland regulation, 323, 324, 362
POLYOSTATIC FIBROUS DYSPLASIA, and thyrotoxicosis, 325
POTASSIUM
  and aldosterone, 165–66
  and 18-hydroxy-desoxycorticosterone, 170
  and peptic ulcer disease, 69
PREGNANCY
  and Crohn's disease, 555
  and Graves' disease, 337–38, 346
PROGESTERONE, and salt intake, 169
PROSTAGLANDINS
  and blood pressure, 159
  and bronchial asthma, 289–91, 294, 296

and corticoids, 168
and peptic ulcer disease, 70
PSYCHOANALYSIS, 41–42
use in peptic ulcer disease, 47
predictive value of, 46–47
PSYCHOLOGICAL FACTORS
in bronchial asthma, 225–75, 226,
297–298
in Crohn's disease, 554–56
and disease predisposition, 586–96
in Graves' disease, 324, 334–56, 380–82
in rheumatoid arthritis, 419–20, 435–61,
475
in ulcerative colitis, 514–34
PSYCHOPHYSIOLOGICAL FACTORS, 2–3
in bronchial asthma, 275–84
in disease predisposition, 595–99
in essential hypertension, 120–37
of gastric functioning, 57–60
in peptic ulcer disease, 56–60
in rheumatoid arthritis, 457–61
in ulcerative colitis, 534–36
PSYCHOSIS
and bronchial asthma, 274–75
and rheumatoid arthritis, 454–56
and ulcerative colitis, 521
PSYCHOSOCIAL FACTORS, in peptic ulcer
disease, 41–56
PYELONEPHRITIS, and high blood pressure,
118
PYLORIC GLANDS, 63
PYODERMA GANGRENOSUM, and ulcerative
colitis, 508

R

RADIOIODINE, in Graves' disease research,
347–49, 354–55
RAPID EYE MOVEMENT (REM), and gastric
secretion, 60
REJECTION, and essential hypertension, 121
RELAXATION TRAINING, and bronchial
asthma, 278–79
REM. See RAPID EYE MOVEMENT (REM).

RENIN
and blood pressure, 167
and 18-hydroxy-desoxycorticosterone,
170
and hypertension, 110, 112, 113, 116,
144, 154–57
RESENTMENT
and gastric secretion, 56
and peptic ulcer, 53
RESERPINE
and blood pressure, 171
and thyrotropin, 365
RHINITIS, and IgE antibodies, 285, 295

S

SALICYLATES, and peptic ulcer disease, 55,
67
SALT
and aldosterone levels, 146
and blood pressure, 114, 116, 118–19,
122–23, 143, 146–48
and desoxycorticosterone, 169
and peripheral resistance, 151–52
and water metabolism, 159–65
SARCOIDOSIS, and peptic ulcer disease, 70
SCAT. See SHEEP CELL AGGLUTINATION
TEST (SCAT).
SCHIZOPHRENIA
and Graves' disease, 341
and social isolation, 2
and ulcerative colitis, 521–22
SECRETIN, 64
SEROTONIN
and bronchial asthma, 289–90
and gastric erosion, 80–81
and hypertension, 141–42, 146
and peptic ulcer disease, 70
SEX
and bronchial asthma, 238, 250–51
differentials in Graves' disease, 326
effect on ulcer type, 34
hormones and peptic ulcer, 44, 70
hormones and peptic ulcer, 44, 70

research on, 16
and stress, 353–57
THYROID STIMULATING HORMONE (TSH), 12, 17
in animal models, 364–67
in Graves' disease, 323, 324, 332, 348, 352, 357–60, 362, 371–79, 382, 384–88
hypothalmic regulation of, 367–70
in pregnancy, 337
and stress, 353
THYROTOXICOSIS
animal models for, 363–67
autoantibodies and, 374–75
and diet, 334
in Graves' disease, 324–25, 328, 346–48
incidence of, 331–33
and long acting thyroid stimulator, 378–80
and pregnancy, 337–38
psychological factors in, 346–53, 380–82
TRANSDUCTION, EXPERIENCE, 624–38
TRAUMA, PHYSICAL, and gastric ulcer, 34
TRIGLYCERIDE, and coronary artery disease, 6
TRIIODOTHYRONINE (T3)
in Graves' disease, 323, 324, 325, 333–34, 336–37, 345–46, 351, 359, 376, 378, 383–88
hypothalmic regulation and, 367–70
and infection, 338
and stress, 353–54
TUMOR, CARCINOID
and histamine, 75–76
of stomach, 35
TYROSINE HYDROXYLASE, and hypertension, 141

U

ULCER DISEASE, PEPTIC, 9, 33–85
and acid secretion, 59, 63–64
and alcohol, 18–19, 53–54
and community structure, 4

definition of, 34–37
epidemiology of, 37–39
genetic factors in, 39–41
hormone mediation of, 67–70
methodological problems and, 14, 16, 35–36, 41–42
and gastric secretion, 59–60
psychological studies of, 42–52, 82–85
psychophysiological factors in, 56–60
psychosocial factors in, 41–56
and vagus nerve, 65–67

V

VAGUS NERVE
and aldosterone secretion, 166
in bronchial asthma, 291–92
and gastric secretion, 56, 63, 65–67
in peptic ulcer disease, 85
and ulcerative colitis, 532
VASOCONSTRICTION
in conditioning studies, 135–36
and hypertension, 150–53
and pain, 131
VASOPRESSIN
and Graves' disease, 361–62
and peptic ulcer disease, 70
VIRUS, and rheumatoid arthritis, 465–66
VOLUNTARY NERVOUS SYSTEM, and cell regulation, 24

X

X-RAY
and peptic ulcer disease, 36, 37, 50
and rheumatoid arthritis, 421, 423, 427, 429, 432
and ulcerative colitis, 504

Z

ZOLLINGER-ELLISON SYNDROME, 14, 35
and gastrin secretion, 70, 71, 73, 74